Microsoft® PUBLISHER 2010

COMPREHENSIVE

Microsoft® PUBLISHER 2010

COMPREHENSIVE

Gary B. Shelly

Joy L. Starks

COURSE TECHNOLOGY
CENGAGE Learning

SHELLY
CASHMAN
SERIES®

Australia • Brazil • Japan • Korea • Mexico • Singapore • Spain • United Kingdom • United States

COURSE TECHNOLOGY
CENGAGE Learning

Microsoft® Publisher 2010: Comprehensive
Gary B. Shelly, Joy L. Starks

Vice President, Publisher: Nicole Pinard

Executive Editor: Kathleen McMahon

Product Manager: Jon Farnham

Associate Product Manager: Aimee Poirier

Editorial Assistant: Lauren Brody

Director of Marketing: Cheryl Costantini

Marketing Manager: Tristen Kendall

Marketing Coordinator: Stacey Leasca

Print Buyer: Julio Esperas

Director of Production: Patty Stephan

Content Project Manager: Jennifer Feltri

Development Editor: Lyn Markowicz

Copyeditor: Foxxe Editorial

Proofreader: Kathy Orrino

Indexer: Rich Carlson

QA Manuscript Reviewers: Chris Scriver, Teresa Storch, Serge Palladino, Susan Pedicini, Susan Whalen, Danielle Shaw

Art Director: Marissa Falco

Cover Designer: Lisa Kuhn, Curio Press, LLC

Cover Photo: Tom Kates Photography

Text Design: Joel Sadagursky

Compositor: PreMediaGlobal

Library of Congress Control Number: 2010939930

International Edition:
ISBN-13: 978-0-538-74619-9
ISBN-10: 0-538-74619-x

Cengage Learning International Offices

Asia
www.cengageasia.com
tel: (65) 6410 1200

Australia/New Zealand
www.cengage.com.au
tel: (61) 3 9685 4111

Brazil
www.cengage.com.br
tel: (55) 11 3665 9900

India
www.cengage.co.in
tel: (91) 11 4364 1111

Latin America
www.cengage.com.mx
tel: (52) 55 1500 6000

UK/Europe/Middle East/Africa
www.cengage.co.uk
tel: (44) 0 1264 332 424

Represented in Canada by
Nelson Education, Ltd.
tel: (416) 752 9100 / (800) 668 0671
www.nelson.com

Cengage Learning is a leading provider of customized learning solutions with office locations around the globe, including Singapore, the United Kingdom, Australia, Mexico, Brazil, and Japan. Locate your local office at: **www.cengage.com/global**

For product information: **www.cengage.com/international**
Visit your local office: **www.cengage.com/global**
Visit our corporate Web site: **www.cengage.com**

We dedicate this book to the memory of James S. Quasney (1940 – 2009), who for 18 years co-authored numerous books with Tom Cashman and Gary Shelly and provided extraordinary leadership to the Shelly Cashman Series editorial team. As series editor, Jim skillfully coordinated, organized, and managed the many aspects of our editorial development processes and provided unending direction, guidance, inspiration, support, and advice to the Shelly Cashman Series authors and support team members. He was a trusted, dependable, loyal, and well-respected leader, mentor, and friend. We are forever grateful to Jim for his faithful devotion to our team and eternal contributions to our series.

The Shelly Cashman Series Team

Printed in the United States of America
1 2 3 4 5 6 7 14 13 12 11

Microsoft PUBLISHER 2010
COMPREHENSIVE

Contents

Preface   xii

Microsoft Office 2010 and Windows 7

Office 2010 and Windows 7: Essential Concepts and Skills

Objectives	**OFF 1**
Office 2010 and Windows 7	**OFF 2**
Overview	OFF 2
Introduction to the Windows 7 Operating System	**OFF 2**
Using a Mouse	OFF 2
Scrolling	OFF 4
Shortcut Keys	OFF 4
Starting Windows 7	OFF 5
To Log On to the Computer	OFF 6
The Windows 7 Desktop	OFF 7
Introduction to Microsoft Office 2010	**OFF 7**
Microsoft Office 2010 Programs	OFF 8
Microsoft Office 2010 Suites	OFF 8
Starting and Using a Program	**OFF 9**
Publisher	OFF 9
To Start a Program Using the Start Menu	OFF 10
To Maximize a Window	OFF 12
The Publisher Window, Ribbon, and Elements Common to Office Programs	OFF 12
To Display a Different Tab on the Ribbon	OFF 16
To Minimize, Display, and Restore the Ribbon	OFF 16
To Display and Use a Shortcut Menu	OFF 17
To Customize the Quick Access Toolbar	OFF 18
To Enter Text in a Blank Publication	OFF 19
Saving and Organizing Files	**OFF 19**
Organizing Files and Folders	OFF 20
To Create a Folder	OFF 20
Folder Windows	OFF 22
To Create a Folder within a Folder	OFF 23
To Expand a Folder, Scroll through Folder Contents, and Collapse a Folder	OFF 23
To Switch from One Program to Another	OFF 24
To Save a File in a Folder	OFF 25
Navigating in Dialog Boxes	OFF 27
To Minimize and Restore a Window	OFF 27

Screen Resolution	**OFF 29**
To Change the Screen Resolution	OFF 30
To Quit a Program with One Publication Open	OFF 31
Additional Common Features of Office Programs	**OFF 32**
To Start a Program Using the Search Box	OFF 32
To Open an Existing File from the Backstage View	OFF 33
To Create a New Publication from the Backstage View	OFF 35
To Close a File Using the Backstage View	OFF 36
To Open a Recent Office File Using the Backstage View	OFF 36
To Create a New Blank Document from Windows Explorer	OFF 37
To Start a Program from Windows Explorer and Open a File	OFF 38
To Save an Existing Publication with the Same File Name	OFF 39
Moving, Renaming, and Deleting Files	**OFF 40**
To Rename a File	OFF 40
To Move a File	OFF 41
To Delete a File	OFF 42
Microsoft Office and Windows Help	**OFF 42**
To Open the Help Window in an Office Program	OFF 43
Moving and Resizing Windows	OFF 43
To Move a Window by Dragging	OFF 43
To Resize a Window by Dragging	OFF 44
Using Office Help	OFF 45
To Obtain Help Using the 'Type words to search for' Text Box	OFF 45
To Obtain Help Using the Help Links	OFF 47
To Obtain Help Using the Help Table of Contents	OFF 48
Obtaining Help while Working in an Office Program	OFF 49
Using Windows Help and Support	OFF 49
To Start Windows Help and Support	OFF 49
Chapter Summary	**OFF 50**
Learn It Online	**OFF 51**
Apply Your Knowledge	**OFF 52**
Extend Your Knowledge	**OFF 52**
Make It Right	**OFF 53**
In the Lab	**OFF 54**
Cases and Places	**OFF 56**

Microsoft **Publisher 2010**

CHAPTER ONE
Creating a Flyer

Objectives	PUB 1
Introduction	PUB 2
Project — Flyer Publication	PUB 2
Overview	PUB 4
Creating a Flyer	**PUB 5**
The New Template Gallery	PUB 6
To Select a Template	PUB 7
Customizing Templates	PUB 9
To Choose Publication Options	PUB 9
To Hide the Page Navigation Pane	PUB 13
Selecting Objects and Zooming	**PUB 14**
To Display Boundaries	PUB 15
To Select	PUB 15
To Zoom	PUB 16
Selecting and Entering Text	**PUB 16**
Text Boxes	PUB 17
To Replace Placeholder Text	PUB 17
To Replace Other Text	PUB 18
Bulleted Lists	PUB 19
To Enter Bulleted Text	PUB 20
To Enter Tear-Off Text	PUB 22
Formatting Fonts	**PUB 23**
To Increase the Font Size	PUB 24
Autofitting Text	PUB 24
To Autofit Text	PUB 25
Deleting Objects	**PUB 26**
To Delete Objects	PUB 26
Using Graphics	**PUB 27**
To Insert a Photograph into a	
Picture Placeholder	PUB 28
Picture Styles	PUB 30
To Apply a Picture Style	PUB 31
Building Blocks	PUB 32
To Use the Building Block Library	PUB 32
Moving, Resizing, and Aligning Objects	**PUB 34**
To Move an Object	PUB 34
To Resize an Object	PUB 35
To Align an Object	PUB 35
To Change the Font Color	PUB 36
Changing Publication Properties	**PUB 38**
To Change Publication Properties	PUB 38
Printing a Publication	**PUB 40**
To Print a Publication	PUB 41
Starting Publisher and Opening	
a Publication	**PUB 43**
Changing a Publication	**PUB 43**
To Draw a Text Box	PUB 44
To Center Text	PUB 45
Checking Spelling	**PUB 46**
To Check Spelling as You Type	PUB 47
Creating a Web Page from a Publication	**PUB 47**
To Save a Print Publication as a	
Web Publication	PUB 48
To Preview the Web Publication in	
a Browser	PUB 50

Chapter Summary	PUB 51
Learn It Online	PUB 52
Apply Your Knowledge	PUB 52
Extend Your Knowledge	PUB 54
Make It Right	PUB 56
In the Lab	PUB 58
Cases and Places	PUB 63

CHAPTER TWO
Publishing a Trifold Brochure

Objectives	PUB 65
Introduction	PUB 66
Project — Spring Break Brochure	PUB 66
Overview	PUB 66
The Brochure Medium	**PUB 68**
Creating a Trifold Brochure	**PUB 70**
Making Choices about Brochure Options	PUB 70
To Search for a Template	PUB 70
To Choose Brochure Options	PUB 71
Copying and Pasting	**PUB 74**
Paste Options	PUB 75
To Copy and Paste	PUB 75
Typing Paragraphs of Text	**PUB 78**
To Display Formatting Marks	PUB 79
To Wordwrap Text as You Type	PUB 79
Formatting Characters	**PUB 81**
To Italicize Text	PUB 81
To Underline a Word	PUB 82
To Bold Text	PUB 83
Stylistic Sets and Alternates	PUB 83
To Display Text in a Stylistic Set	PUB 84
To Create a Drop Cap	PUB 84
Ligatures	PUB 85
To Enable a Ligature	PUB 86
Font Effects	PUB 88
To Apply a Font Effect	PUB 89
To Use the Format Painter Button	PUB 91
Clip Art	**PUB 94**
To Replace a Graphic Using the Clip Art Task Pane	PUB 94
To Resize the Graphic	PUB 97
To Insert a New Graphic Using the Clip	
Art Task Pane	PUB 98
To Insert a New Graphic on Page 2	PUB 101
Captions	**PUB 102**
To Edit Captions	PUB 103
To Use the Caption Gallery	PUB 104
Checking the Publication	**PUB 106**
To Check the Spelling of the	
Entire Publication	PUB 107
To Run the Design Checker	PUB 108
Previewing and Printing	**PUB 109**
To Preview Multiple Pages	
before Printing	PUB 110
To Print a Publication with Settings	PUB 111
To Print on Both Sides	PUB 112
Printing Considerations	**PUB 113**
Paper Considerations	PUB 113
Color Considerations	PUB 114
To Choose a Color Model	PUB 115

Packaging the Publication for the
    Printing Service **PUB 116**
    To Use the Pack and Go Wizard PUB 116
    Using PostScript Files PUB 118
Chapter Summary **PUB 119**
Learn It Online **PUB 119**
Apply Your Knowledge **PUB 120**
Extend Your Knowledge **PUB 122**
Make It Right **PUB 123**
In the Lab **PUB 125**
Cases and Places **PUB 132**

CHAPTER THREE

Designing a Newsletter

Objectives **PUB 133**
Introduction **PUB 134**
Project — Newsletter **PUB 134**
    Overview PUB 136
    Benefits and Advantages of Newsletters PUB 137
    Newsletter Design Choices PUB 138
    To Set Page Options PUB 140
    Changing the Number of Pages in a Newsletter PUB 143
Editing the Masthead **PUB 143**
    To Edit the Masthead PUB 143
Newsletter Text **PUB 145**
    Replacing Placeholder Text Using an Imported File PUB 146
    To Edit the Lead Story Headline PUB 147
    To Import a Text File PUB 147
    To Continue a Story across Pages PUB 149
    To Manually Continue the Story across Pages PUB 151
    To Format with Continued Notices PUB 152
Customizing the Ribbon **PUB 157**
    To Customize the Publisher Ribbon PUB 157
Editing Stories in Microsoft Word **PUB 159**
    To Edit a Story Using Word PUB 159
    To Format while Editing in Microsoft Word PUB 161
    To Quit Word and Return to Publisher PUB 161
    To Edit the Back Page Story PUB 164
Using Graphics in a Newsletter **PUB 166**
    To Replace a Graphic Using the Shortcut Menu PUB 166
    To Select Adjacent Objects by Dragging PUB 171
Page Parts **PUB 172**
    To Edit a Sidebar PUB 173
    To Insert a Pull Quote PUB 175
    To Insert Text in a Pull Quote PUB 177
    To Duplicate a Graphic PUB 180
    To Flip a Graphic PUB 181
Advertisements **PUB 181**
    To Insert and Format a Coupon PUB 182
Revising a Newsletter **PUB 184**
    Moving Text PUB 185
    To Drag and Drop Text PUB 185
    Hyphenation PUB 187
    To Check Hyphenation PUB 187
Creating a Template **PUB 189**
    Saving the Template and Setting
        File Properties PUB 189
    To Create a Template with Property Changes PUB 189
Chapter Summary **PUB 191**
Learn It Online **PUB 192**
Apply Your Knowledge **PUB 192**

Extend Your Knowledge **PUB 194**
Make It Right **PUB 195**
In the Lab **PUB 195**
Cases and Places **PUB 198**

CHAPTER FOUR

Creating a Custom Publication from Scratch

Objectives **PUB 201**
Introduction **PUB 202**
Project — Newspaper Advertisement **PUB 202**
    Overview PUB 203
Creating a Custom-Sized Publication **PUB 204**
    To Select a Blank Publication PUB 205
    To Create a Custom Page Size PUB 206
Custom Color Schemes **PUB 208**
    To Create a New Color Scheme PUB 209
Custom Font Schemes **PUB 210**
    To Create a New Font Scheme PUB 211
Editing Graphics **PUB 213**
    Rotating and Flipping Objects PUB 214
    To Flip a Picture PUB 214
    Cropping Graphics PUB 215
    To Crop a Graphic PUB 216
    To Edit Wrap Points PUB 217
    To Recolor a Graphic PUB 220
    Grouping Objects PUB 222
    To Select Multiple Objects PUB 223
    To Group Selected Objects PUB 223
    To Save a Graphic as a Picture PUB 224
Shapes **PUB 225**
    To Insert a Shape PUB 225
    Shape Fills PUB 226
    To Create a Gradient Fill Effect PUB 227
    To Select a Color for the Shape Outline PUB 230
    To Change the Shape Outline PUB 232
    To Fill a Shape with a Picture PUB 233
    To Add to the Building Block Library PUB 234
Font Styles **PUB 236**
    To Apply a Style PUB 236
Columns **PUB 238**
    To Turn on Boundaries PUB 239
    To Set Columns PUB 240
    To Change Line Spacing PUB 241
WordArt **PUB 242**
    To Insert a WordArt Object PUB 243
    To Add Shadow Effects PUB 245
    To Close a Publication without
        Quitting Publisher PUB 247
Using Customized Sizes, Schemes, and Building Blocks **PUB 247**
    To Open a Customized Blank Page PUB 248
    To Apply Customized Color and Font Schemes PUB 249
    To Insert a Customized Building Block PUB 250
Deleting Customizations **PUB 251**
    To Delete Content from the Building Block Library PUB 251
    To Delete the Customized Color Scheme PUB 252
    To Delete the Customized Font Scheme PUB 253
    To Delete the Customized Blank Page PUB 254
Chapter Summary **PUB 255**
Learn It Online **PUB 256**
Apply Your Knowledge **PUB 256**

Extend Your Knowledge **PUB 258**
Make It Right **PUB 259**
In the Lab **PUB 260**
Cases and Places **PUB 264**

CHAPTER FIVE
Using Business Information Sets
Objectives **PUB 265**
Introduction **PUB 266**
Project — Business Cards and Stationery **PUB 266**
    Overview PUB 267
Creating Letterhead **PUB 269**
    To Create a Letterhead Template PUB 269
Creating a Business Information Set **PUB 270**
    To Create a Business Information Set PUB 271
    To Insert a Business Information Field PUB 275
Using the Measurement Toolbar **PUB 276**
    To Display the Measurement Toolbar PUB 276
    To Position Objects Using
        the Measurement Toolbar PUB 277
Creating a New Style **PUB 278**
    To Sample a Font Color PUB 279
    To Create a New Style PUB 280
    To Apply the New Style PUB 281
Customizing the Letterhead for Interactivity **PUB 282**
    Using an Automatic Date PUB 283
    To Create a Formatted Text Box PUB 283
    To Insert an Automatic Date PUB 284
    Read-Only Files PUB 286
    To Set the Read-Only Attribute PUB 286
    Using the Custom Letterhead Template PUB 287
    To Open a Publication from
        the Recent Documents List PUB 287
    To Type a Letter PUB 289
    To Save the Letter PUB 289
Envelopes **PUB 292**
    To Create an Envelope PUB 292
    To Address the Envelope PUB 294
    To Choose Settings and Print the Envelope PUB 295
Business Cards **PUB 297**
    To Print the Business Cards PUB 300
Creating Portable Files **PUB 303**
    To Publish in a Portable Format PUB 303
Embedding Fonts **PUB 305**
    To Embed Fonts PUB 306
    To Delete the Business Information Set PUB 307
Chapter Summary **PUB 309**
Learn It Online **PUB 309**
Apply Your Knowledge **PUB 310**
Extend Your Knowledge **PUB 312**
Make It Right **PUB 314**
In the Lab **PUB 315**
Cases and Places **PUB 320**

CHAPTER SIX
Working with Publisher Tables
Objectives **PUB 321**
Introduction **PUB 322**
Project — Schedule, Calendar, and Business Table **PUB 322**
    Overview PUB 324

Creating Reusable Parts **PUB 325**
    Creating a Business Information Set PUB 325
    To Change the Shape of a WordArt Object PUB 328
    To Change the Shape Outline PUB 329
    To Change the Page Orientation PUB 330
    To Snap an Object to the Margin Guide PUB 332
    To Align Relative to Margin Guides PUB 332
Using Tables **PUB 334**
    To Insert an Empty Table PUB 334
    To Enter Data in a Table PUB 336
    To Delete a Column PUB 337
    To Insert a Row PUB 338
    To Apply a Table Format PUB 339
    Selecting Table Contents PUB 340
    To Select a Row PUB 341
    To Merge Cells PUB 342
    To Align Data in Cells PUB 344
    To Change Column Width PUB 346
    To Resize the Table PUB 346
    To Create a Cell Diagonal PUB 348
    Deleting Table Data PUB 350
Calendars **PUB 352**
    To Create a 12-Month Calendar PUB 352
    Customizing the Calendar PUB 355
    Borders PUB 358
    To Add Borders to a Table PUB 359
Using Excel Tables **PUB 361**
    To Create an Embedded Table PUB 364
    To Format an Embedded Table PUB 366
    To Sum in an Embedded Table PUB 367
Chapter Summary **PUB 372**
Learn It Online **PUB 372**
Apply Your Knowledge **PUB 373**
Extend Your Knowledge **PUB 374**
Make It Right **PUB 376**
In the Lab **PUB 378**
Cases and Places **PUB 382**

CHAPTER SEVEN
Advanced Formatting and Merging Publications with Data
Objectives **PUB 383**
Introduction **PUB 384**
Project — Merging Form Letters and Ticket Numbers **PUB 384**
    Overview PUB 386
Watermarks and Master Pages **PUB 388**
    To View the Master Page PUB 388
Graphic Adjustments **PUB 389**
    To Recolor the Picture PUB 392
    To Compress the Picture PUB 393
    To Close the Master Page PUB 394
    To Insert Letterhead Information PUB 395
Spacing between Characters **PUB 396**
    To Track Characters PUB 397
    To Kern Character Pairs PUB 398
Working with Tabs and the Ruler **PUB 399**
    To Set a Tab Stop PUB 401
    To Enter Tabbed Text PUB 401
Merging Data into Publications **PUB 403**
    Creating a Data Source PUB 404
    To Use the Mail Merge Wizard PUB 404

To Customize Data Source Columns   PUB 406
Entering Data in the Data Source   PUB 409
To Enter Data in the Data Source File   PUB 409
To Create New Entries in the Data Source   PUB 410
To Save the Data Source   PUB 411
Inserting Field Codes   PUB 412
To Insert Grouped Field Codes   PUB 413
To Insert Individual Field Codes   PUB 415
To Create the Merged Publication   PUB 417
Managing Merged Publications   PUB 417
To Preview the Form Letters   PUB 418
Creating Tickets   **PUB 419**
The Mailings Tab   PUB 421
To Select Recipients   PUB 421
To Filter Data   PUB 423
To Insert Merge Field Codes   PUB 425
To Preview Results   PUB 427
To Print a Page of Tickets   PUB 427
Chapter Summary   **PUB 430**
Learn It Online   **PUB 431**
Apply Your Knowledge   **PUB 431**
Extend Your Knowledge   **PUB 434**
Make It Right   **PUB 435**
In the Lab   **PUB 436**
Cases and Places   **PUB 440**

CHAPTER EIGHT
Generating Data-Driven Catalogs
Objectives   **PUB 441**
Introduction   **PUB 442**
Project — Textbook Catalog   **PUB 442**
Overview   PUB 443
Catalogs   **PUB 444**
To Create a Two-Page Spread   PUB 445
Alternating Master Pages   **PUB 446**
Backgrounds   PUB 446
To Add a Background to a Master Page   PUB 446
Headers and Footers   PUB 448
To Insert a Header   PUB 448
To Duplicate the Master Page   PUB 450
To Insert Alternating Footers   PUB 450
To AutoCorrect as You Type   PUB 452
To Use the AutoCorrect Options Button   PUB 453
To Create an AutoCorrect Entry   PUB 454
The AutoCorrect Dialog Box   PUB 456
To Apply Master Pages   PUB 456
Creating the Main Publication   **PUB 459**
To Use an AutoCorrect Entry   PUB 462
Generating the Catalog Merge   **PUB 465**
Catalog Pages   **PUB 467**
To Create Catalog Pages   PUB 467
To Select the Data Source   PUB 469
The Catalog Tools Format Tab   PUB 470
To Insert a Picture Field   PUB 471
To Insert Text Fields   PUB 472
To Find Entries   PUB 474
To Preview the Merge   PUB 476
The Graphics Manager   **PUB 477**
To Work with the Graphics Manager   PUB 477
Translating Text   **PUB 480**
To Translate Text and Insert   PUB 482

Merging Catalogs   **PUB 485**
To Merge to a Printer   PUB 485
Chapter Summary   **PUB 488**
Learn It Online   **PUB 488**
Apply Your Knowledge   **PUB 489**
Extend Your Knowledge   **PUB 491**
Make It Right   **PUB 493**
In the Lab   **PUB 495**
Cases and Places   **PUB 502**

CHAPTER NINE
Sharing and Distributing Publications
Objectives   **PUB 503**
Introduction   **PUB 504**
Project — Distributed Publications   **PUB 504**
Overview   PUB 506
E-Mail Templates   **PUB 507**
To Change the E-Mail Message Page Size   PUB 508
To Set the E-Mail Background   PUB 510
To Create a Callout   PUB 515
Symbols and Special Characters   **PUB 517**
To Insert a Symbol from the Symbol Dialog Box   PUB 517
To Insert a Special Character Using the
        Symbol Dialog Box   PUB 519
To Insert a Symbol from the Insert Symbol Gallery   PUB 520
Research Task Pane   **PUB 522**
To Use the Research Task Pane   PUB 522
To Create a Cited Definition   PUB 524
Creating Hyperlinks and Hot Spots   **PUB 525**
Editing the Hyperlink   PUB 525
To Insert a Hyperlink   PUB 525
To Insert a Hot Spot   PUB 525
To Insert a Mailto Hyperlink   PUB 526
Design Issues in E-Mail   PUB 527
To Choose Design Checker Options   PUB 528
Sending an E-Mail Message Using Publisher   **PUB 530**
To Preview an E-Mail Message   PUB 531
To Send an E-Mail Message Using Publisher   PUB 532
Sending Print Publications as E-Mail Messages   PUB 533
Postcards   **PUB 534**
To Send a Postcard as an Attachment   PUB 535
Greeting Cards   **PUB 536**
To Insert a Border   PUB 538
To Print a Folded Publication   PUB 543
Chapter Summary   **PUB 545**
Learn It Online   **PUB 545**
Apply Your Knowledge   **PUB 546**
Extend Your Knowledge   **PUB 547**
Make It Right   **PUB 549**
In the Lab   **PUB 551**
Cases and Places   **PUB 554**

CHAPTER TEN
Editing Large-Scale Publications
Objectives   **PUB 555**
Introduction   **PUB 556**
Project — Creating a Conference Agenda   **PUB 556**
Overview   PUB 557
Designing the Layout   **PUB 559**
To Create Sections   PUB 560

Pagination **PUB 562**
To Insert Page Numbers Using the Ribbon PUB 562
To Specify a Starting Page Number PUB 563
To Specify a Starting Page Number Using the
Shortcut Menu PUB 565
To Remove Page Numbering from
Specific Pages PUB 567
BorderArt and Backgrounds **PUB 568**
To Create BorderArt PUB 570
To Create a Shade Background PUB 574
To Collapse Sections PUB 578
Cell and Text Box Margins **PUB 579**
To Change Cell Margins PUB 581
To Change the Text Direction PUB 585
Ruler Guide Patterns **PUB 586**
To Select a Guide Pattern PUB 586
To Link Text Boxes Using the Ribbon PUB 588
To Duplicate a Page PUB 590
To Merge Sections PUB 591
Find and Replace **PUB 594**
To Use the Find Command PUB 594
To Find Whole Words Only PUB 596
To Use the Replace Command PUB 597
Thesaurus **PUB 598**
To Use the Thesaurus PUB 599
Research Task Pane Options PUB 600
Page Breaks **PUB 601**
To View a Two-Page Spread PUB 601
To Insert a Page Break PUB 602
Updating the Table of Contents PUB 606
Navigating through a Large-Scale Publication **PUB 607**
To Use the Go To Page Command PUB 608
To Create a Bookmark PUB 609
To Use Bookmarks to Create Hyperlinks PUB 611
To Test a Hyperlink PUB 612
To Navigate with Bookmarks in a PDF File PUB 614
Chapter Summary **PUB 616**
Learn It Online **PUB 616**
Apply Your Knowledge **PUB 617**
Extend Your Knowledge **PUB 619**
Make It Right **PUB 621**
In the Lab **PUB 622**
Cases and Places **PUB 626**

CHAPTER ELEVEN
Creating an Interactive Web Site
Objectives **PUB 627**
Introduction **PUB 628**
Project — Creating an interactive Web Site **PUB 629**
Overview PUB 630
Creating a Business Information Set PUB 632
Editing the Home Page **PUB 632**
To Create a Web Masthead PUB 633
Navigation Bars **PUB 636**
To Insert a Navigation Bar PUB 636

To Add Secondary Pages to a Web Site PUB 637
To Edit the Navigation Bar Properties PUB 639
Web Graphics **PUB 643**
Animated Graphics PUB 644
To Preview an Animated Graphic PUB 644
Alternative Text PUB 646
To Add Alternative Text PUB 646
Setting Web Page Options **PUB 647**
To Edit Web Page Options PUB 647
To Insert a Background Sound PUB 648
Editing a Calendar Web page **PUB 649**
Editing a Contact Us Web page **PUB 652**
Form Controls **PUB 653**
Labels PUB 654
To Create Text Boxes for Labels PUB 655
Textbox Form Controls PUB 657
To Insert Textbox Form Controls PUB 658
To Edit Textbox Form Control Properties PUB 659
To Insert a Text Area Form Control PUB 660
To Edit Text Area Form Control Properties PUB 661
Checkbox Form Controls PUB 662
To Insert Checkbox Form Controls PUB 662
To Edit Checkbox Form Control Properties PUB 663
To Insert Option Button Form Controls PUB 664
To Edit Option Button Form Control Properties PUB 665
To Insert a List Box Form Control PUB 667
To Edit List Box Form Control Properties PUB 667
To Insert Submit Form Controls PUB 669
To Edit Form Properties PUB 671
Web Hot Spots **PUB 672**
To Insert a Web Hot Spot PUB 672
HTML Code Fragments **PUB 672**
Creating a Scrolling Marquee PUB 673
To Insert an HTML Code Fragment PUB 673
To Preview and Test a Web Site PUB 674
Visual Basic for Applications **PUB 678**
To Display the Developer Tab PUB 678
Using the Visual Basic Editor PUB 679
To Open the VBA Code Window PUB 680
Entering Code Statements and Comments PUB 680
To Program a BeforeClose Event PUB 681
Security Levels **PUB 682**
Setting Security Levels in Publisher PUB 682
To Set a Security Level in Publisher PUB 683
Completing the Web Site **PUB 683**
Checking for Spelling and Design Errors PUB 683
Testing the Web Site PUB 685
Testing the Macro and Quitting Publisher PUB 685
To Test the Macro and Quit Publisher PUB 686
Chapter Summary **PUB 686**
Learn It Online **PUB 687**
Apply Your Knowledge **PUB 687**
Extend Your Knowledge **PUB 689**
Make It Right **PUB 690**
In the Lab **PUB 691**
Cases and Places **PUB 696**

Appendices

APPENDIX A
Project Planning Guidelines
Using Project Planning Guidelines   **APP 1**
   Determine the Project's Purpose   APP 1
   Analyze Your Audience   APP 1
   Gather Possible Content   APP 2
   Determine What Content to Present
      to Your Audience   APP 2
Summary   **APP 2**

APPENDIX B
Publishing Office 2010 Web Pages Online
   Using an Office Program to Publish Office 2010
      Web Pages   APP 3

Index   **IND 1**

Quick Reference Summary   **QR 1**

Preface

The Shelly Cashman Series® offers the finest textbooks in computer education. We are proud that since Mircosoft Office 4.3, our series of Microsoft Office textbooks have been the most widely used books in education. With each new edition of our Office books, we make significant improvements based on the software and comments made by instructors and students. For this Microsoft Publisher 2010 text, the Shelly Cashman Series development team carefully reviewed our pedagogy and analyzed its effectiveness in teaching today's Office student. Students today read less, but need to retain more. They need not only to be able to perform skills, but to retain those skills and know how to apply them to different settings. Today's students need to be continually engaged and challenged to retain what they're learning.

With this Microsoft Publisher 2010 text, we continue our commitment to focusing on the user and how they learn best.

Objectives of This Textbook

Microsoft Publisher 2010: Comprehensive is intended for a ten- to fifteen-week period in a course that teaches Publisher 2010 as the primary component. No experience with a computer is assumed, and no mathematics beyond the high school freshman level is required. The objectives of this book are:

- To offer a comprehensive presentation of Microsoft Publisher 2010

- To expose students to practical examples of the computer as a useful tool

- To acquaint students with the proper procedures to create publications suitable for coursework, professional purposes, and personal use

- To help students discover the underlying functionality of Publisher 2010 so they can become more productive

- To develop an exercise-oriented approach that allows learning by doing

New to this Edition

Microsoft Publisher 2010: Comprehensive offers a number of new features and approaches, which improve student understanding, retention, transference, and skill in using Publisher 2010. The following enhancements will enrich the learning experience:

- Office 2010 and Windows 7: Essential Concepts and Skills chapter presents basic Office 2010 and Windows 7 skills.

- Streamlined first chapter allows the ability to cover more advanced skills earlier.

- Chapter topic redistribution offers concise chapters that ensure complete skill coverage.

- New pedagogical elements enrich material creating an accessible and user-friendly approach.

  - Break Points, a new boxed element, identify logical stopping points and give students instructions regarding what they should do before taking a break.

  - Within step instructions, Tab | Group Identifiers, such as (Home tab | Bold button), help students more easily locate elements in the groups and on the tabs on the Ribbon.

  - Modified step-by-step instructions tell the student what to do and provide the generic reason why they are completing a specific task, which helps students easily transfer given skills to different settings.

The Shelly Cashman Approach

A Proven Pedagogy with an Emphasis on Project Planning

Each chapter presents a practical problem to be solved, within a project planning framework. The project orientation is strengthened by the use of Plan Ahead boxes, which encourage critical thinking about how to proceed at various points in the project. Step-by-step instructions with supporting screens guide students through the steps. Instructional steps are supported by the Q&A, Experimental Step, and BTW features.

A Visually Engaging Book that Maintains Student Interest

The step-by-step tasks, with supporting figures, provide a rich visual experience for the student. Call-outs on the screens that present both explanatory and navigational information provide students with information they need when they need to know it.

Supporting Reference Materials (Appendices and Quick Reference)

The appendices provide additional information about the Application at hand and include such topics as project planning guidelines and certification. With the Quick Reference, students can quickly look up information about a single task, such as keyboard shortcuts, and find page references of where in the book the task is illustrated.

Integration of the World Wide Web

The World Wide Web is integrated into the Publisher 2010 learning experience by (1) BTW annotations; (2) BTW, Q&A, and Quick Reference Summary Web pages; and (3) the Learn It Online section for each chapter.

End-of-Chapter Student Activities

Extensive end-of-chapter activities provide a variety of reinforcement opportunities for students where they can apply and expand their skills.

Instructor Resources

The Instructor Resources include both teaching and testing aids and can be accessed via CD-ROM or at login.cengage.com.

Instructor's Manual Includes lecture notes summarizing the chapter sections, figures and boxed elements found in every chapter, teacher tips, classroom activities, lab activities, and quick quizzes in Microsoft Word files.

Syllabus Easily customizable sample syllabi that cover policies, assignments, exams, and other course information.

Figure Files Illustrations for every figure in the textbook in electronic form.

PowerPoint Presentations A multimedia lecture presentation system that provides slides for each chapter. Presentations are based on chapter objectives.

Solutions to Exercises Includes solutions for all end-of-chapter and chapter reinforcement exercises.

Test Bank & Test Engine Test Banks include 112 questions for every chapter, featuring objective-based and critical thinking question types, and including page number references and figure references, when appropriate. Also included is the test engine, ExamView, the ultimate tool for your objective-based testing needs.

Data Files for Students Includes all the files that are required by students to complete the exercises.

Additional Activities for Students Consists of Chapter Reinforcement Exercises, which are true/false, multiple-choice, and short answer questions that help students gain confidence in the material learned.

> **Book Resources**
>
> 🔒 **Additional Faculty Files**
> 🔒 **Blackboard Testbank**
> 🔒 **Data Files**
> 🔒 **Instructor's Manual**
> 🔒 **Lecture Success System**
> 🔒 **PowerPoint Presentations**
> 🔒 **Solutions to Exercises**
> 🔒 **Syllabus**
> 🔒 **Test Bank and Test Engine**
> 🔒 **WebCT Testbank**
> **Chapter Reinforcement Exercises**
> **Student Downloads**

Content for Online Learning

Course Technology has partnered with the leading distance learning solution providers and class-management platforms today. To access this material, instructors will visit our password-protected instructor resources available at login.cengage.com. Instructor resources include the following: additional case projects, sample syllabi, PowerPoint presentations per chapter, and more. For additional information or for an instructor user name and password, please contact your sales representative. For students to access this material, they must have purchased a WebTutor PIN-code specific to this title and your campus platform. The resources for students may include (based on instructor preferences), but are not limited to: topic review, review questions, and practice tests.

CourseNotes

Course Technology's CourseNotes are six-panel quick reference cards that reinforce the most important and widely used features of a software application in a visual and user-friendly format. CourseNotes serve as a great reference tool during and after the student completes the course. CourseNotes are available for software applications such as Microsoft Office 2010, Word 2010, Excel 2010, Access 2010, PowerPoint 2010, and Windows 7. Topic-based CourseNotes are available for Best Practices in Social Networking, Hot Topics in Technology, and Web 2.0. Visit www.cengagebrain.com to learn more!

A Guided Tour

Add excitement and interactivity to your classroom with "*A Guided Tour*" product line. Play one of the brief mini-movies to spice up your lecture and spark classroom discussion. Or, assign a movie for homework and ask students to complete the correlated assignment that accompanies each topic. "*A Guided Tour*" product line takes the prep work out of providing your students with information about new technologies and applications and helps keep students engaged with content relevant to their lives; all in under an hour!

  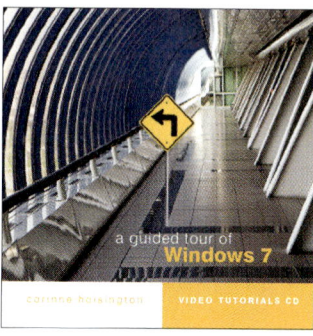

About Our Covers

The Shelly Cashman Series is continually updating our approach and content to reflect the way today's students learn and experience new technology. This focus on student success is reflected on our covers, which feature real students from the University of Rhode Island using the Shelly Cashman Series in their courses, and reflect the varied ages and backgrounds of the students learning with our books. When you use the Shelly Cashman Series, you can be assured that you are learning computer skills using the most effective courseware available.

Textbook Walk-Through

The Shelly Cashman Series Pedagogy: Project-Based — Step-by-Step — Variety of Assessments

Plan Ahead boxes prepare students to create successful projects by encouraging them to think strategically about what they are trying to accomplish before they begin working.

Step-by-Step instructions now provide a context beyond the point-and-click. Each step provides information on why students are performing each task, or what will occur as a result.

Navigational callouts in red show students where to click.

Explanatory callouts summarize what is happening on screen.

Overview

As you read this chapter, you will learn how to create the flyer shown in Figure 1–1 on the previous page by performing these general tasks:

- Choose a template and select schemes and components.
- Replace placeholder text in the publication.
- Replace the template graphic.
- Delete unused objects.
- Insert an attention getter.
- Save the publication.
- Print the publication.
- Close and then reopen the publication.
- Draw a text box.
- Check the spelling as you type.
- Convert the publication to a Web flyer.

Plan Ahead

General Project Guidelines

When you create a Publisher publication, the actions you perform and decisions you make will affect the appearance and characteristics of the finished publication. As you create a flyer, such as the one shown in Figure 1–1, you should follow these general guidelines:

1. **Select template options.** The choice of an appropriate template, font, and color scheme is determined by the flyer's purpose and intended audience.

2. **Choose words for the text.** Follow the *less is more* principle. The less text, the more likely the flyer will be read. Use as few words as possible to make a point.

3. **Identify how to format various objects in the flyer.** The overall appearance of a publication significantly affects its capability to communicate clearly. Examples of how you can format or modify the appearance of text include changing its shape, size, color, and position on the page. Formatting a graphic might include editing its borders, shadows, style, size, and location.

4. **Find the appropriate graphic.** An eye-catching graphic should convey the flyer's overall message. It might show a product, service, result, or benefit, or it might convey a message visually that is not expressed easily with words.

5. **Determine the best method for distributing the document.** Documents can be distributed on paper or electronically.

6. **Decide if the flyer will work as a Web publication.** The flyer should grab the attention of visitors to the Web site and draw them into reading the flyer.

When necessary, more specific details concerning the above guidelines are presented at appropriate points in the chapter. The chapter also will identify the actions performed and decisions made regarding these guidelines during the creation of the flyer shown in Figure 1–1.

For an introduction to Office 2010 and instruction about how to perform basic tasks in Office 2010 programs, read the Office 2010 and Windows 7 chapter at the beginning of this book, where you can learn how to start a program, use the Ribbon, save a file, open a file, quit a program, use Help, and much more.

To Start Publisher

If you are using a computer to step through the project in this chapter and you want your screens to match the figures in this book, you should change your screen's resolution to 1024 × 768. For information about how to change a computer's resolution, refer to the Office 2010 and Windows 7 chapter at the beginning of this book.

The following steps, which assume Windows 7 is running, start Publisher based on a typical installation. You may need to ask your instructor how to start Publisher for your

To Select a Template

The following steps select a template from the New template gallery.

1
- Drag the scroll box down to show additional folders in the gallery.
- Point to the Flyers folder to highlight it (Figure 1–3).

Q&A Why does my gallery of folders look different?

Someone may have downloaded additional templates on your computer. Or, your resolution may be different. Thus, the size and number of displayed folders may vary.

Note: To screen element reference instruction and comma uses red b these scre

More Templates — More Templates area

Flyers folder

Advertisements   Award Certificates   Banners   Business Forms

Flyers   Gift Certificates   Import Word   Invitation Cards

mouse pointer appears as a hand

Resumes   More

Figure 1–3

2
- Click the Flyers folder in the More Templates area to display the templates and folders of additional templates (Figure 1–4).

Experiment
- Scroll through the available templates and click various flyers in the gallery. Watch the preview change in the top-right portion of the Backstage view.

Q&A Could I use the Apartment for Rent Marketing flyer?

You could, but it does not have the same template features as the one in this chapter.

Microsoft Publisher

Home   Insert   Page Design   Mailings   Review   View

Available Templates

Installed and Online Templates   Search for template

Home ▶ Flyers

preview of template

Arrows

scroll box

Event
Arrows   Bounce   Brocade   All Event

Marketing
Arrows   Bounce   Brocade   All Marketing

Customize
Color scheme:
(default template colors)
Font scheme:

Flyer template thumbnails and folders are organized by purpose

Real estate   Real estate area

Options
Include mailing address
Include graphic
Tear-offs:
None

Create

Figure 1–4

Textbook Walk-Through

Q&A boxes offer questions students may have when working through the steps and provide additional information about what they are doing right where they need it.

Experiment Steps within our step-by-step instructions, encourage students to explore, experiment, and take advantage of the features of the Publisher 2010 user interface. These steps are not necessary to complete the projects, but are designed to increase the confidence with the software and build problem-solving skills.

To Hide the Page Navigation Pane

The **Page Navigation pane** (Figure 1–13) displays all of the current pages in the publication as thumbnails in a panel on the left side of the workspace. Because the flyer contains only one page, you will hide the Page Navigation pane using the Page Number button on the status bar. The following step hides the Page Navigation pane.

1
- Click the Page Number button on the status bar to close the Page Navigation pane (Figure 1–14).

Q&A I do not see the Page Navigation pane. What did I do wrong?

It may be that someone has closed the Page Navigation pane already. The Page Number button opens and closes the Page Navigation pane. Click it again to view the Page Navigation pane.

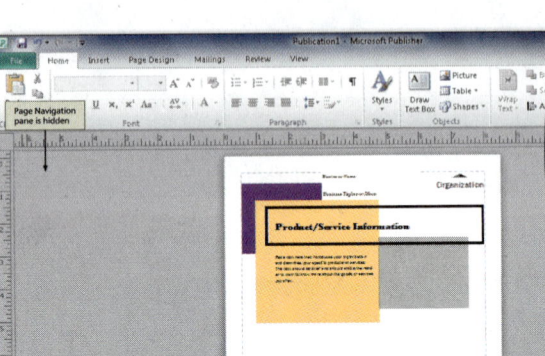

Figure 1–14

Other Ways
1. Click Page Navigation check box (View tab | Show group)

...ects, text, pictures, ...blication. Those

...ck box on the

To Apply a Picture Style

The following steps apply a picture style to the photograph in the flyer.

1
- Click the photograph to select it.
- Click Picture Tools Format on the Ribbon to display the Picture Tools Format tab.
- Click the More button (Picture Tools Format tab | Picture Styles group) to display the Picture Styles gallery.
- Point to Picture Style 4 in the Picture Styles gallery to display a live preview of that style (Figure 1–44).

 Experiment
- Point to various picture styles in the Picture Styles gallery and watch the format of the picture change in the publication window.

Figure 1–44

2
- Click Picture Style 4 in the Picture Styles gallery to apply the selected style to the picture.
- Click outside the picture to deselect it (Figure 1–45).

 Q&A Should I be concerned that the picture overlaps the tear-offs slightly?

No. Tear-offs commonly are scored vertically, so the photograph will not be affected.

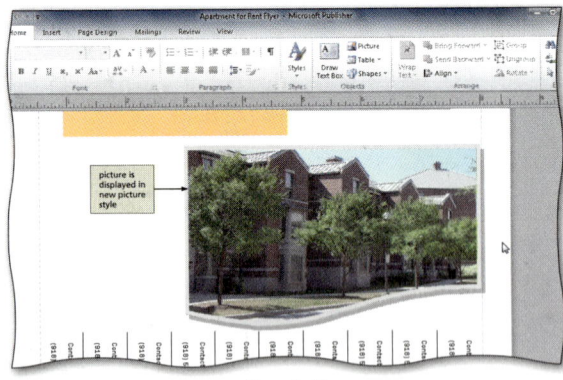

Figure 1–45

Break Points identify logical breaks in the chapter if students need to stop before completing the project.

Break Point: If you wish to take a break, this is a good place to do so. To resume at a later time, continue following the steps from this location forward.

Starting Publisher and Opening a Publication

Once you have created and saved a publication, you may need to retrieve it from your

To Quit Publisher

The following steps quit Publisher.

1 If you have one Publisher document open, click the Close button on the right side of the title bar to close the document and quit Publisher; or if you have multiple Publisher documents open, click File on the Ribbon to open the Backstage view and then click Exit on the Publisher tab to close all open documents and quit Publisher.

2 If a Microsoft Publisher dialog box appears, click the Don't Save button to discard any changes made to the document since the last save.

BTW

Quick Reference
For a table that lists how to complete the tasks covered in this book using the mouse, Ribbon, shortcut menu, and keyboard, see the Quick Reference Summary at the back of this book, or visit the Publisher 2010 Quick Reference Web page (scsite.com/pub2010/qr).

Chapter Summary A concluding paragraph, followed by a listing of the tasks completed within a chapter together with the pages on which the step-by-step, screen-by-screen explanations appear.

Chapter Summary

In this chapter, you have learned how to choose a publication template, set font and color schemes, enter text in a publication, delete objects from a publication, insert a photograph and building block, print a publication, and save a print publication as a Web publication. The items listed below include all the new Publisher skills you have learned in this chapter.

1. Start Publisher (PUB 4)
2. Select a Template (PUB 7)
3. Choose Publication Options (PUB 9)
18. Use the Building Block Library (PUB 32)
19. Move an Object (PUB 34)
20. Resize an Object (PUB 35)
21. Align an Object (PUB 35)
22. Change the Font Color (PUB 36)
23. Change Publication Properties (PUB 38)
24. Save an Existing Publication with the Same File Name (PUB 40)
25. Print a Publication (PUB 41)
26. Quit Publisher (PUB 42)
27. Open a Publication from Publisher (PUB 43)
28. Draw a Text Box (PUB 44)
29. Center Text (PUB 45)
30. Check Spelling as You Type (PUB 47)
31. Save a Print Publication as a Web Publication (PUB 48)
32. Preview the Web Publication in a Browser (PUB 50)

STUDENT ASSIGNMENTS

Learn It Online

Test your knowledge of chapter content and key terms.

Instructions: To complete the Learn It Online exercises, start your browser, click the Address bar, and then enter the Web address **scsite.com/pub2010/learn**. When the Office 2010 Learn It Online page is displayed, click the link for the exercise you want to complete and then read the instructions.

Chapter Reinforcement TF, MC, and SA
A series of true/false, multiple choice, and short answer questions that test your knowledge of the chapter content.

Flash Cards
An interactive learning environment where you identify chapter key terms associated with displayed definitions.

Practice Test
A series of multiple choice questions that test your knowledge of chapter content and key terms.

Who Wants To Be a Computer Genius?
An interactive game that challenges your knowledge of chapter content in the style of a television quiz show.

Wheel of Terms
An interactive game that challenges your knowledge of chapter key terms in the style of the television show *Wheel of Fortune*.

Crossword Puzzle Challenge
A crossword puzzle that challenges your knowledge of key terms presented in the chapter.

Apply Your Knowledge

Reinforce the skills and apply the concepts you learned in this chapter.

Revising Text and Graphics in a Publication
Instructions: Start Publisher. Open the publication, Apply 3-1 Math Class Newsletter Draft, from the Data Files for Students. See the inside back cover of this book for instructions on downloading the Data Files for Students, or contact your instructor for more information about accessing the required files.

The publication you open is a two-page newsletter. You are to revise the publication as follows: enter the date in the masthead, import stories, use continued notices, insert a pull quote with text, insert a pattern, resize a graphic and flip it, and check the publication for errors. The revised publication is shown in Figure 3–82.

Perform the following tasks:

1. Enter the current date in the masthead.
2. Select the Lead Story Headline text and then type **A Note from Mr. Miller** as the new headline.
3. Click the lead story to select it. Click the Insert File button (Insert tab | Text group) and then navigate to the Data Files for Students. Insert the file named, Apply 3-1 Miller Note. When prompted, continue the story to the back page, at the bottom.
4. Delete the two empty text boxes for the back page story.
5. Right-click the remaining text box and then click Format Text Box on the shortcut menu. When the Format Text Box dialog box is displayed, click the Text Box tab, and then click the Include "Continued from page…" check box to select it. Click the OK button to close the Format Text Box dialog box.
6. Select the Back Page Story headline, and then type **… from Mr. Miller** as the new headline text.

Learn It Online Every chapter features a Learn It Online section that is comprised of six exercises. These exercises include True/False, Multiple Choice, Short Answer, Flash Cards, Practice Test, and Learning Games.

Apply Your Knowledge This exercise usually requires students to open and manipulate a file from the Data Files that parallels the activities learned in the chapter. To obtain a copy of the Data Files for Students, follow the instructions on the inside back cover of this text.

Textbook Walk-Through

STUDENT ASSIGNMENTS

Extend Your Knowledge

Extend the skills you learned in this chapter and experiment with new skills. You may need to use Help to complete the assignment.

Working with Linked Text Boxes and Microsoft Word

Instructions: Start Publisher. Open the publication, Extend 3-1 Go Green Newsletter Draft, from the Data Files for Students. See the inside back cover of this book for instructions on downloading the Data Files for Students, or contact your instructor for more information about accessing the required files.

You will edit a newsletter to import stories, edit stories in Microsoft Word, unlink connected text boxes, and insert graphics.

Perform the following tasks:

1. Replace all graphics with graphics related to green technology and recycling.
2. Edit the lead story in Microsoft Word. Use bullets and indents to highlight the main topics. Use Microsoft Word Help to research the Increase Indent button (Word Ribbon | Home tab | Paragraph Group).
3. Return to Publisher and format the story with continued notices. (*Hint:* Use the next and previous arrow buttons to find the rest of the story.) Adjust the graphic to make the story wrap more neatly. Create an appropriate headline for the second part of the story on page 2.
4. Replace the caption with the words **Is your recycle bin full?** as the new text.
5. Use Publisher Help to research the Linking group on the Text Box Tools tab. Unlink the third column of the secondary story.
6. On page 2, in the empty text box at the top, insert the file

Figure 3–83

Extend Your Knowledge

projects at the end of each chapter allow students to extend and expand on the skills learned within the chapter. Students use critical thinking to experiment with new skills to complete each project.

STUDENT ASSIGNMENTS

Publisher Chapter 3

Make It Right

Analyze a publication and correct all errors and/or improve the design.

Fixing Overflow Errors

Instructions: Start Publisher. Open the publication, Make It Right 3-1 National Corps Newsletter, from the Data Files for Students. See the inside back cover of this book for instructions on downloading the Data Files for Students, or contact your instructor for more information about accessing the required files.

The publication is a newsletter that has stories in overflow, as shown in Figure 3–84. You are to link the overflow to text boxes on page 2, check the document for other errors, and hyphenate the stories.

Perform the following steps:

1. Run the Design Checker and find the first overflow error. Click the Text in Overflow button and link the story to a text box on page 2. Add continued notices. Hyphenate the story.
2. Find the next overflow error and continue that story to a different text box on page 2. Add continued notices. Edit the Back Page Story Headline to match the story. Hyphenate the story.
3. Fix any other design errors.
4. Check the spelling of the publication.
5. Change the publication properties as specified by your instructor.
6. Save the revised publication and then submit it in the format specified by your instructor.

Figure 3–84

Make It Right projects call on students to analyze a file, discover errors in it, and fix them using the skills they learned in the chapter.

In the Lab

Design and/or create a publication using the guidelines, concepts, and skills presented in this chapter. Labs are listed in order of increasing difficulty.

Lab 1: Creating a Newsletter Template

Problem: As a marketing intern with the Department of Natural Resources (DNR), you have been asked to create a template for a newsletter about white-water rafting in the state. The DNR wants a four-page newsletter, with space for several articles, a masthead, pictures with captions, and a sign-up form. If your supervisor approves your template, she will send you stories and pictures at a later date. She reminds you

Continued >

In the Lab

Lab 2: Newsletter Analysis

Problem: Use a copy of a newsletter that you regularly receive, or obtain one from a friend, company, or school. Using the principles in this chapter, analyze the newsletter.

Instructions: Start Publisher. Open the publication, Lab 3-2 Newsletter Analysis Table, from the Data Files for Students. See the inside back cover of this book for instructions on downloading the Data Files for Students, or contact your instructor for more information about accessing the required files. Use the skills you learned in editing sidebars to fill in each of the empty cells in the table as it applies to your selected newsletter. The topics to look for are listed below:

- Purpose
- Audience
- Paper
- Distribution
- Font and color scheme

- Consistency
- Alignment
- Repeated elements
- Continued notices and ease of navigation
- Sidebars, pull quotes, patterns, etc.

Print the publication and attach a copy of the newsletter. Turn in both to your instructor.

In the Lab

Lab 3: Creating a Masthead

Problem: You and your friends belong to a role-playing game club. To spread the word and attract new members, you are thinking of creating a Web site with news and articles about the club. You have decided to use building block items to design a masthead and save it as a Web page. You prepare the masthead shown in Figure 3–86.

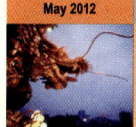

Volume 1, Issue 1
May 2012

ROLE-PLAYING GA

When Dragons

Figure 3–86

Instructions: Start Publisher and choose the Blank 8.5 × 11" template. C▮ (Page Design tab | Schemes group). Using the Building Blocks group on ▮ bar from Borders and Accents. Insert the Fall heading from Page Parts. Se▮ replace it with a clip art image related to the term, dragon. Edit the text to▮ the publication on a USB flash drive, using Lab 3-3 Game Club Masthead▮ techniques from Chapter 1 on pages PUB 48 through PUB 49, use the Pu▮ Save & Send tab in the Backstage view to save the masthead as a Single Fi▮

In the Lab Three all new in-depth assignments per chapter require students to utilize the chapter concepts and techniques to solve problems on a computer.

Cases & Places exercises call on students to create open-ended projects that reflect academic, personal, and business settings.

Cases and Places

Apply your creative thinking and problem solving skills to design and implement a solution.

Note: To complete these assignments, you may be required to use the Data Files for Students. See the inside back cover of this book for instructions on downloading the Data Files for Students, or contact your instructor for information about accessing the required files.

1: Design and Create an Advising Sign

Academic

You are a student worker in the Computer Information Technology Department. You have been asked to create a sign that displays advising hours for the upcoming registration period. Using the Business Hours template in the Signs folder in the Backstage view, create a sign that lists advising hours. Change the headline to Advising Hours. Change the times to: Monday and Wednesday from 8:00 a.m. to 5:00 p.m.; Tuesday and Thursday from 12:00 p.m. to 8:00 p.m.; and Friday from 8:00 a.m. to 3:30 p.m. The advising office is closed on Saturdays and Sundays. In the lower text box, list the office number, ET 220, and the telephone number, 555-HELP. Change the publication properties, as specified by your instructor.

2: Design and Create a Reunion Flyer

Personal

Your high school has asked you to create a flyer for the upcoming 10-year class reunion. Use the concepts and techniques presented in this chapter to create the flyer with information from your high school. Use the Apartment to Rent template with the Orchid color scheme and the Industrial font scheme. Autofit the headline. Delete any unnecessary objects. Include your e-mail and telephone number in the contact information tear-offs. Use the following bulleted list for details about the reunion:

- Wear your letter jacket!
- Show your school spirit!
- High School Gym, 7:00 p.m.!
- RSVP to Jesse by 05/07/12!

Insert a formatted attention getter with the words, Dress is casual. Insert a picture of your high school, if you have one. Change the publication properties, as specified by your instructor.

3: Design and Create a Business Announcement

Professional

Your Internet service provider (ISP) maintains an electronic bulletin board where customers may post one-page business announcements. Create an advertising flyer for the place you work, or where you want to work. You may use one of Publisher's Flyer templates or choose a blank template and design the flyer using Building Blocks. Replace all text and graphics. Use font colors and font sizes to attract attention. Instead of tear-offs, draw a text box that includes the company's Web page address and telephone number. Correct any spelling errors. Change the publication properties, as specified by your instructor. Assign publication properties and include keywords that will produce many hits during Web searches. Save the flyer as a single page Web publication.

Microsoft® PUBLISHER 2010

COMPREHENSIVE

Office 2010 and Windows 7: Essential Concepts and Skills

Objectives

You will have mastered the material in this chapter when you can:

- Perform basic mouse operations
- Start Windows and log on to the computer
- Identify the objects on the Windows 7 desktop
- Identify the programs in and versions of Microsoft Office
- Start a program
- Identify the components of the Microsoft Office Ribbon

- Create folders
- Save files
- Change screen resolution
- Perform basic tasks in Microsoft Office programs
- Manage files
- Use Microsoft Office Help and Windows Help

Office 2010 and Windows 7: Essential Concepts and Skills

Office 2010 and Windows 7

This introductory chapter uses Publisher 2010 to cover features and functions common to Office 2010 programs, as well as the basics of Windows 7.

Overview

As you read this chapter, you will learn how to perform basic tasks in Windows and Publisher by performing these general activities:

- Start programs using Windows.
- Use features in Publisher that are common across Office programs.
- Organize files and folders.
- Change screen resolution.
- Quit programs.

Introduction to the Windows 7 Operating System

Windows 7 is the newest version of Microsoft Windows, which is the most popular and widely used operating system. An **operating system** is a computer program (set of computer instructions) that coordinates all the activities of computer hardware such as memory, storage devices, and printers, and provides the capability for you to communicate with the computer.

The Windows 7 operating system simplifies the process of working with documents and programs by organizing the manner in which you interact with the computer. Windows 7 is used to run **application software**, which consists of programs designed to make users more productive and/or assist them with personal tasks, such as word processing.

Windows 7 has two interface variations, Windows 7 Basic and Windows 7 Aero. Computers with up to 1 GB of RAM display the Windows 7 Basic interface (Figure 1a). Computers with more than 1 GB of RAM also can display the Windows Aero interface (Figure 1b), which provides an enhanced visual appearance. The Windows 7 Professional, Windows 7 Enterprise, Windows 7 Home Premium, and Windows 7 Ultimate editions have the capability to use Windows Aero.

Using a Mouse

Windows users work with a mouse that has at least two buttons. For a right-handed user, the left button usually is the primary mouse button, and the right mouse button is the secondary mouse button. Left-handed people, however, can reverse the function of these buttons.

(a) Windows 7 Basic interface

(b) Windows 7 Aero interface

Figure 1

Table 1 explains how to perform a variety of mouse operations. Some programs also use keys in combination with the mouse to perform certain actions. For example, when you hold down the CTRL key while rolling the mouse wheel, text on the screen becomes larger or smaller based on the direction you roll the wheel. The function of the mouse buttons and the wheel varies depending on the program.

Table 1 Mouse Operations		
Operation	**Mouse Action**	**Example***
Point	Move the mouse until the pointer on the desktop is positioned on the item of choice.	Position the pointer on the screen.
Click	Press and release the primary mouse button, which usually is the left mouse button.	Select or deselect items on the screen or start a program or program feature.
Right-click	Press and release the secondary mouse button, which usually is the right mouse button.	Display a shortcut menu.
Double-click	Quickly press and release the left mouse button twice without moving the mouse.	Start a program or program feature.
Triple-click	Quickly press and release the left mouse button three times without moving the mouse.	Select a paragraph.
Drag	Point to an item, hold down the left mouse button, move the item to the desired location on the screen, and then release the left mouse button.	Move an object from one location to another or draw pictures.
Right-drag	Point to an item, hold down the right mouse button, move the item to the desired location on the screen, and then release the right mouse button.	Display a shortcut menu after moving an object from one location to another.
Rotate wheel	Roll the wheel forward or backward.	Scroll vertically (up and down).
Free-spin wheel	Whirl the wheel forward or backward so that it spins freely on its own.	Scroll through many pages in seconds.
Press wheel	Press the wheel button while moving the mouse.	Scroll continuously.
Tilt wheel	Press the wheel toward the right or left.	Scroll horizontally (left and right).
Press thumb button	Press the button on the side of the mouse with your thumb.	Move forward or backward through Web pages and/or control media, games, etc.

*Note: the examples presented in this column are discussed as they are demonstrated in this chapter.

Scrolling

A **scroll bar** is a horizontal or vertical bar that appears when the contents of an area may not be visible completely on the screen (Figure 2). A scroll bar contains **scroll arrows** and a **scroll box** that enable you to view areas that currently cannot be seen. Clicking the up and down scroll arrows moves the screen content up or down one line. You also can click above or below the scroll box to move up or down a section, or drag the scroll box up or down to move up or down to move to a specific location.

Shortcut Keys

In many cases, you can use the keyboard instead of the mouse to accomplish a task. To perform tasks using the keyboard, you press one or more keyboard keys, sometimes identified as

Figure 2

a **shortcut key** or **keyboard shortcut**. Some shortcut keys consist of a single key, such as the F1 key. For example, to obtain help about Windows 7, you can press the F1 key. Other shortcut keys consist of multiple keys, in which case a plus sign separates the key names, such as CTRL+ESC. This notation means to press and hold down the first key listed, press one or more additional keys, and then release all keys. For example, to display the Start menu, press CTRL+ESC, that is, hold down the CTRL key, press the ESC key, and then release both keys.

Starting Windows 7

It is not unusual for multiple people to use the same computer in a work, educational, recreational, or home setting. Windows 7 enables each user to establish a **user account**, which identifies to Windows 7 the resources, such as programs and storage locations, a user can access when working with a computer.

Each user account has a user name and may have a password and an icon, as well. A **user name** is a unique combination of letters or numbers that identifies a specific user to Windows 7. A **password** is a private combination of letters, numbers, and special characters associated with the user name that allows access to a user's account resources. A **user icon** is a picture associated with a user name.

When you turn on a computer, an introductory screen consisting of the Windows logo and copyright messages is displayed. The Windows logo is animated and glows as the Windows 7 operating system is loaded. After the Windows logo appears, depending on your computer's settings, you may or may not be required to log on to the computer. **Logging on** to a computer opens your user account and makes the computer available for use. If you are required to log on to the computer, the **Welcome screen** is displayed, which shows the user names of users on the computer (Figure 3). Clicking the user name or picture begins the process of logging on to the computer.

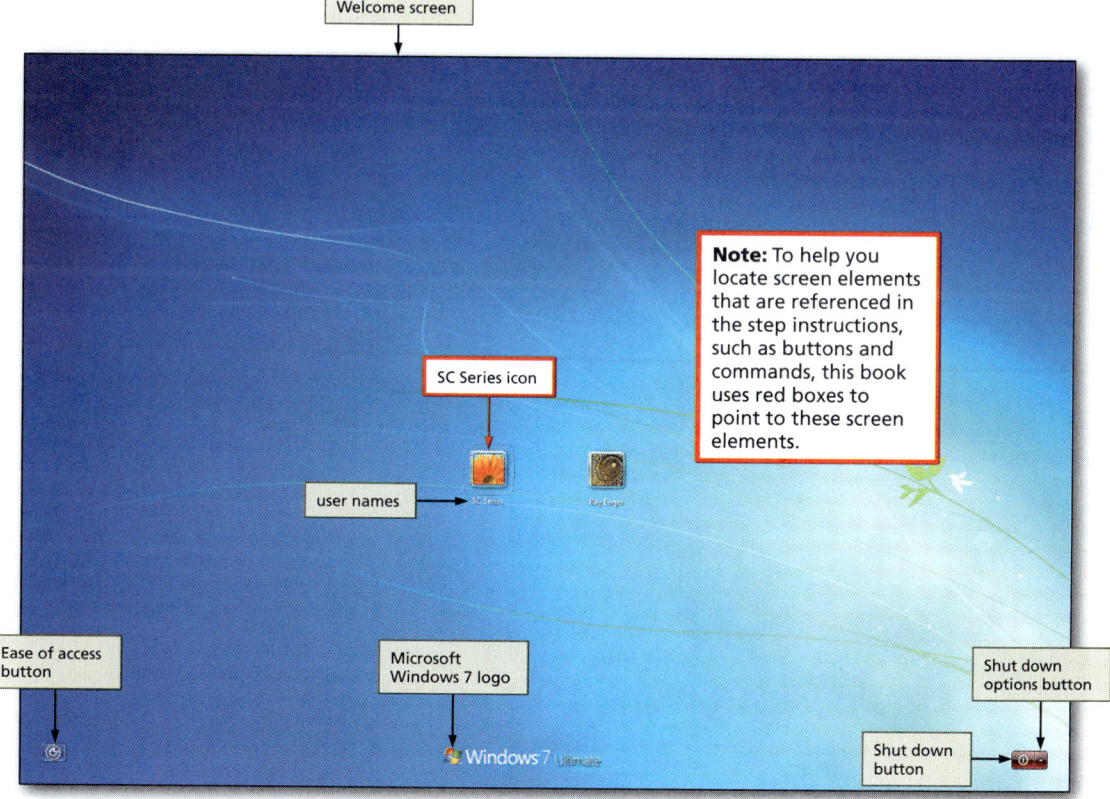

Figure 3

At the bottom of the Welcome screen is the 'Ease of access' button, Windows 7 logo, a Shut down button, and a 'Shut down options' button. The following list identifies the functions of the buttons and commands that typically appear on the Welcome screen:

- Clicking the 'Ease of access' button displays the Ease of Access Center, which provides tools to optimize your computer to accommodate the needs of the mobility, hearing, and vision impaired users.
- Clicking the Shut down button shuts down Windows 7 and the computer.
- Clicking the 'Shut down options' button, located to the right of the Shut down button, displays a menu containing commands that perform actions such as restarting the computer, placing the computer in a low-powered state, and shutting down the computer. The commands available on your computer may differ.
  - The **Restart command** closes open programs, shuts down Windows 7, and then restarts Windows 7 and displays the Welcome screen.
  - The **Sleep command** waits for Windows 7 to save your work and then turns off the computer fans and hard disk. To wake the computer from the Sleep state, press the power button or lift a notebook computer's cover, and log on to the computer.
  - The **Shut down command** shuts down and turns off the computer.

To Log On to the Computer

After starting Windows 7, you might need to log on to the computer. The following steps log on to the computer based on a typical installation. You may need to ask your instructor how to log on to your computer. This set of steps uses SC Series as the user name. The list of user names on your computer will be different.

- Click the user icon (SC Series, in this case) on the Welcome screen (shown in Figure 3 on the previous page); depending on settings, this either will display a password text box (Figure 4) or will log on to the computer and display the Windows 7 desktop.

Why do I not see a user icon?

Your computer may require you to type a user name instead of clicking an icon.

What is a text box?

A text box is a rectangular box in which you type text.

Figure 4

Why does my screen not show a password text box?

Your account does not require a password.

2

- If Windows 7 displays a password text box, type your password in the text box and then click the arrow button to log on to the computer and display the Windows 7 desktop (Figure 5).

Q&A

Why does my desktop look different from the one in Figure 5?

The Windows 7 desktop is customizable, and your school or employer may have modified the desktop to meet its needs. Also, your screen resolution, which affects the size of the elements on the screen, may differ from the screen resolution used in this book. Later in this chapter, you learn how to change screen resolution.

Figure 5

The Windows 7 Desktop

The Windows 7 desktop (Figure 5) and the objects on the desktop emulate a work area in an office. Think of the Windows desktop as an electronic version of the top of your desk. You can perform tasks such as placing objects on the desktop, moving the objects around the desktop, and removing items from the desktop.

When you start a program in Windows 7, it appears on the desktop. Some icons also may be displayed on the desktop. For instance, the icon for the **Recycle Bin**, the location of files that have been deleted, appears on the desktop by default. A **file** is a named unit of storage. Files can contain text, images, audio, and video. You can customize your desktop so that icons representing programs and files you use often appear on your desktop.

Introduction to Microsoft Office 2010

Microsoft Office 2010 is the newest version of Microsoft Office, offering features that provide users with better functionality and easier ways to work with the various files they create. These features include enhanced design tools, such as improved picture formatting tools and new themes, shared notebooks for working in groups, mobile versions of Office programs, broadcast presentation for the Web, and a digital notebook for managing and sharing multimedia information.

Microsoft Office 2010 Programs

Microsoft Office 2010 includes a wide variety of programs such as Word, PowerPoint, Excel, Access, Outlook, Publisher, OneNote, InfoPath, SharePoint Workspace, Communicator, and Web Apps:

- **Microsoft Word 2010**, or Word, is a full-featured word processing program that allows you to create professional-looking documents and revise them easily.
- **Microsoft PowerPoint 2010**, or PowerPoint, is a complete presentation program that allows you to produce professional-looking presentations.
- **Microsoft Excel 2010**, or Excel, is a powerful spreadsheet program that allows you to organize data, complete calculations, make decisions, graph data, develop professional-looking reports, publish organized data to the Web, and access real-time data from Web sites.
- **Microsoft Access 2010**, or Access, is a database management system that allows you to create a database; add, change, and delete data in the database; ask questions concerning the data in the database; and create forms and reports using the data in the database.
- **Microsoft Outlook 2010**, or Outlook, is a communications and scheduling program that allows you to manage e-mail accounts, calendars, contacts, and access to other Internet content.
- **Microsoft Publisher 2010**, or Publisher, is a desktop publishing program that helps you create professional-quality publications and marketing materials that can be shared easily.
- **Microsoft OneNote 2010**, or OneNote, is a note taking program that allows you to store and share information in notebooks with other people.
- **Microsoft InfoPath 2010**, or InfoPath, is a form development program that helps you create forms for use on the Web and gather data from these forms.
- **Microsoft SharePoint Workspace 2010**, or SharePoint, is collaboration software that allows you to access and revise files stored on your computer from other locations.
- **Microsoft Communicator** is communications software that allows you to use different modes of communications such as instant messaging, video conferencing, and sharing files and programs.
- **Microsoft Web Apps** is a Web application that allows you to edit and share files on the Web using the familiar Office interface.

Microsoft Office 2010 Suites

A **suite** is a collection of individual programs available together as a unit. Microsoft offers a variety of Office suites. Table 2 lists the Office 2010 suites and their components.

Programs in a suite, such as Microsoft Office, typically use a similar interface and share features. In addition, Microsoft Office programs use **common dialog boxes** for performing actions such as opening and saving files. Once you are comfortable working with these elements and this interface and performing tasks in one program, the similarity can help you apply the knowledge and skills you have learned to another Office program(s). For example, the process for saving a file in Publisher is the same in PowerPoint, Excel, and the other Office programs. While briefly showing how to use Publisher, this chapter illustrates some of the common functions across the Office programs and also identifies the characteristics unique to Publisher.

Table 2 Microsoft Office 2010 Suites	Microsoft Office Professional Plus 2010	Microsoft Office Professional 2010	Microsoft Office Home and Business 2010	Microsoft Office Standard 2010	Microsoft Office Home and Student 2010
Microsoft Word 2010	✔	✔	✔	✔	✔
Microsoft PowerPoint 2010	✔	✔	✔	✔	✔
Microsoft Excel 2010	✔	✔	✔	✔	✔
Microsoft Access 2010	✔	✔	✘	✘	✘
Microsoft Outlook 2010	✔	✔	✔	✔	✘
Microsoft Publisher 2010	✔	✔	✘	✔	✘
Microsoft OneNote 2010	✔	✔	✔	✔	✔
Microsoft InfoPath 2010	✔	✘	✘	✘	✘
Microsoft SharePoint Workspace 2010	✔	✘	✘	✘	✘
Microsoft Communicator	✔	✘	✘	✘	✘

Starting and Using a Program

To use a program, such as Publisher, you must instruct the operating system to start the program. Windows 7 provides many different ways to start a program, one of which is presented in this section (other ways to start a program are presented throughout this chapter). After starting a program, you can use it to perform a variety of tasks. The following pages use Publisher to discuss some elements of the Office interface and to perform tasks that are common to other Office programs.

Publisher

Publisher is a full-featured desktop publishing program that allows you to create professional-looking publications and revise them easily. A publication is a printed or electronic medium that people use to communicate with others. With Publisher, you can develop many types of personal and business publications, including flyers, letters, brochures, catalogs, reports, fax cover sheets, mailing labels, and newsletters. Publisher also provides tools that enable you to create Web pages and save these Web pages directly on a Web server.

Publisher has many features designed to simplify the production of publications and add visual appeal. Using Publisher, you easily can change the shape, size, and color of text and graphics. You also can include borders, shading, tables, images, pictures, charts, and Web addresses in publications.

While you are typing, Publisher performs many tasks automatically. For example, Publisher detects and corrects design errors and spelling errors in several languages. Publisher's thesaurus allows you to add variety and precision to your writing. Publisher also can format text, such as headings, lists, fractions, borders, and Web addresses, as you type.

To Start a Program Using the Start Menu

Across the bottom of the Windows 7 desktop is the taskbar. The taskbar contains the **Start button**, which you use to access programs, files, folders, and settings on a computer. A **folder** is a named location on a storage medium that usually contains related files. The taskbar also displays a button for each program currently running on a computer.

Clicking the Start button displays the Start menu. The **Start menu** allows you to access programs, folders, and files on the computer and contains commands that allow you to start programs, store and search for files, customize the computer, and obtain help about thousands of topics. A **menu** is a list of related items, including folders, programs, and commands. Each **command** on a menu performs a specific action, such as saving a file or obtaining help.

The following steps, which assume Windows 7 is running, use the Start menu to start the Microsoft Publisher 2010 program based on a typical installation. You may need to ask your instructor how to start Publisher for your computer. Although the steps illustrate starting the Publisher program, the steps to start any program are similar.

1
- Click the Start button on the Windows 7 taskbar to display the Start menu (Figure 6).

Q&A
Why does my Start menu look different?

It may look different depending on your computer's configuration. The Start menu may be customized for several reasons, such as usage requirements or security restrictions.

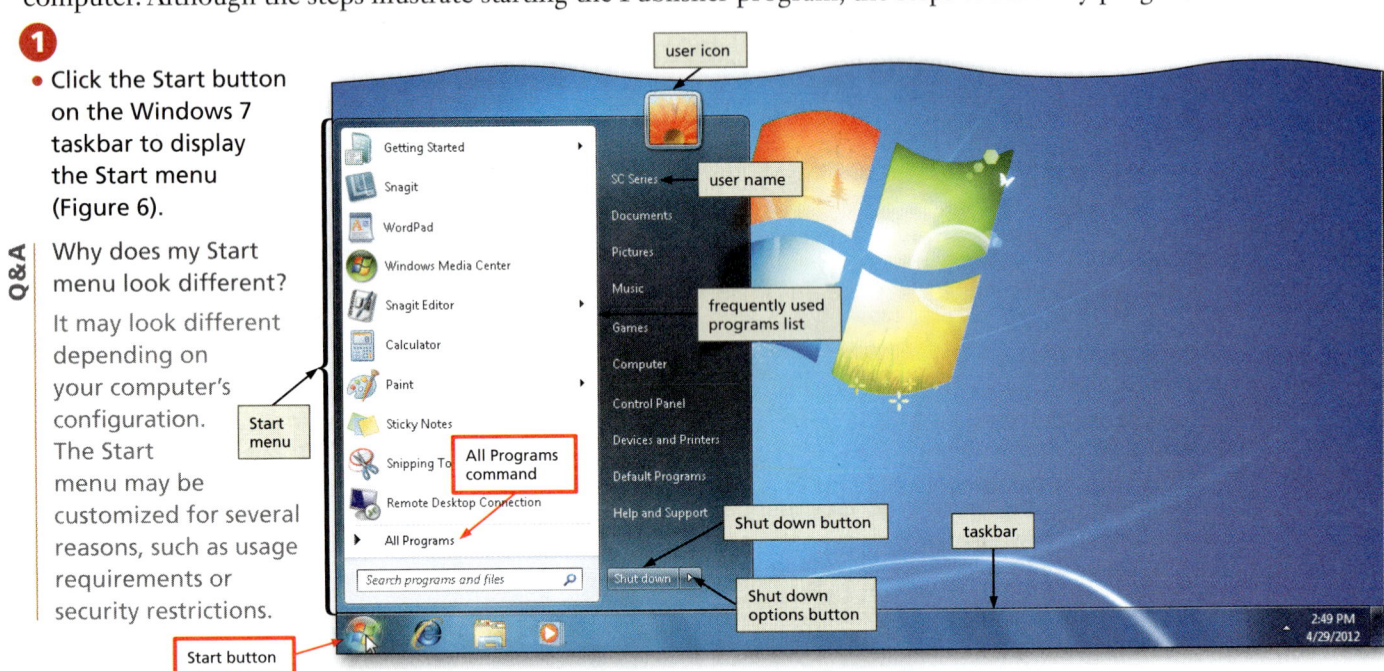

Figure 6

2
- Click All Programs at the bottom of the left pane on the Start menu to display the All Programs list (Figure 7).

Q&A
What is a pane?

A **pane** is an area of a window that displays related content. For example, the left pane on the Start menu contains a list of frequently used programs, as well as the All Programs command.

Q&A
Why might my All Programs list look different?

Most likely, the programs installed on your computer will differ from those shown in Figure 7. Your All Programs list will show the programs that are installed on your computer.

Figure 7

3

- If the program you wish to start is located in a folder, click or scroll to and then click the folder (Microsoft Office, in this case) in the All Programs list to display a list of the folder's contents (Figure 8).

Q&A Why is the Microsoft Office folder on my computer?

During installation of Microsoft Office 2010, the Microsoft Office folder was added to the All Programs list.

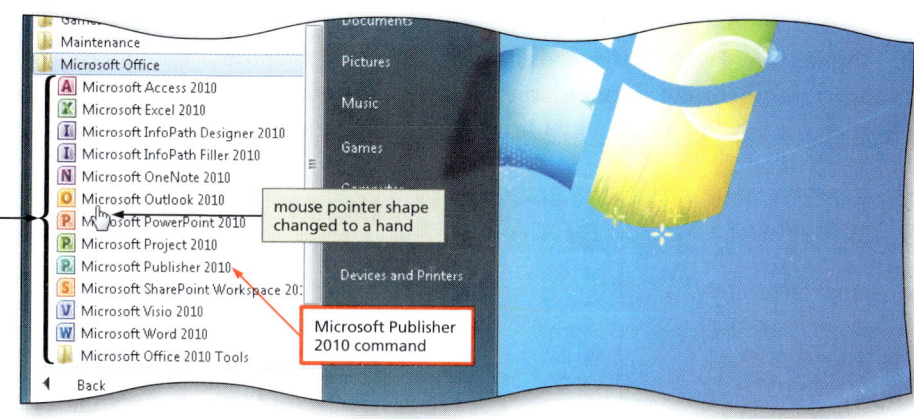

Figure 8

4

- Click, or scroll to and then click, the program name (Microsoft Publisher 2010, in this case) in the list to start the selected program (Figure 9).

Q&A What happens when you start a program?

Many programs initially display a blank document in a program window; others provide a means for you to create a blank document. A **window** is a rectangular area that displays data and information. The top of a window has a **title bar**, which is a horizontal space that contains the window's name.

Figure 9

Q&A Why is my program window a different size?

The Publisher window shown in Figure 9 is not maximized. Your Publisher window already may be maximized. The steps on the next page maximize a window.

Other Ways

1. Double-click program icon on desktop, if one is present

2. Click program name in left pane of Start menu, if present

3. Display Start menu, type program name in search box, click program name

4. Double-click file created using program you want to start

To Maximize a Window

Sometimes content is not visible completely in a window. One method of displaying the entire contents of a window is to **maximize** it, or enlarge the window so that it fills the entire screen. The following step maximizes the Publisher window; however, any Office program's window can be maximized using this step.

- If the program window is not maximized already, click the Maximize button (shown in Figure 9 on the previous page) next to the Close button on the window's title bar (the Publisher window title bar, in this case) to maximize the window (Figure 10).

Q&A What happened to the Maximize button?

It changed to a Restore Down button, which you can use to return a window to its size and location before you maximized it.

Q&A How do I know whether a window is maximized?

A window is maximized if it fills the entire display area and the Restore Down button is displayed on the title bar.

Figure 10

Other Ways

1. Double-click title bar
2. Drag title bar to top of screen

The Publisher Window, Ribbon, and Elements Common to Office Programs

The Publisher window consists of a variety of components to make your work more efficient and publications more professional. These include the publication window, Ribbon, Mini toolbar, shortcut menus, and Quick Access Toolbar. Most of these components are common to other Microsoft Office 2010 programs; others are unique to Publisher.

You view a portion of a publication on the screen through a **publication window** (Figure 11). The default (preset) view is **Single Page view**, which shows the publication on a mock sheet of paper in the publication window.

Scroll Bars   You use a scroll bar to display different portions of a publication in the publication window. At the right edge of the publication window is a vertical scroll bar. If a publication is too wide to fit in the publication window, a horizontal scroll bar also appears at the bottom of the publication window. On a scroll bar, the position of the scroll box reflects the location of the portion of the publication that is displayed in the publication window.

Figure 11

Status Bar   The **status bar,** located at the bottom of the publication window above the Windows 7 taskbar, presents information about the publication, the progress of current tasks, and the status of certain commands and keys; it also provides controls for viewing the publication. As you type text or perform certain tasks, various indicators and buttons may appear on the status bar.

The left side of the status bar in Figure 11 shows the current page followed by the total number of pages on the Page Number button. To the right of the Page Number button are the Object Position and Object Size buttons. The right side of the status bar includes buttons and controls you can use to change the view of a publication, adjust the size of the displayed publication, and show the whole page.

Page Navigation Pane   The Page Navigation pane, located on the left side of the publication window, displays all of the current pages in the publication as thumbnails, or small images. Clicking the Page Number button on the status bar displays or hides the Page Navigation pane.

Ribbon The Ribbon, located near the top of the window below the title bar, is the control center in Publisher and other Office programs (Figure 12). The Ribbon provides easy, central access to the tasks you perform while creating a publication. The Ribbon consists of tabs, groups, and commands. Each **tab** contains a collection of groups, and each **group** contains related functions. When you start an Office program, such as Publisher, it initially displays several main tabs, also called default tabs. All Office programs have a **Home tab**, which contains the more frequently used commands.

In addition to the main tabs, Office programs display **tool tabs**, also called contextual tabs (Figure 13), when you perform certain tasks or work with objects such as pictures or tables. If you insert a picture in a Publisher publication, for example, the Picture Tools tab and its related subordinate Format tab appear, collectively referred to as the Picture Tools Format tab. When you are finished working with the picture, the Picture Tools Format tab disappears from the Ribbon. Publisher and other Office programs determine when tool tabs should appear and disappear based on tasks you perform. Some tool tabs, such as the Table Tools tab, have more than one related subordinate tab.

Items on the Ribbon include buttons, boxes (text boxes, check boxes, etc.), and galleries (Figure 12). A **gallery** is a set of choices, often graphical, arranged in a grid or in a list. You can scroll through choices in an in-Ribbon gallery by clicking the gallery's scroll arrows. Or, you can click a gallery's More button to view more gallery options on the screen at a time.

Figure 12

Some buttons and boxes have arrows that, when clicked, also display a gallery; others always cause a gallery to be displayed when clicked. Most galleries support **live preview**, which is a feature that allows you to point to a gallery choice and see its effect in the publication — without actually selecting the choice (Figure 13).

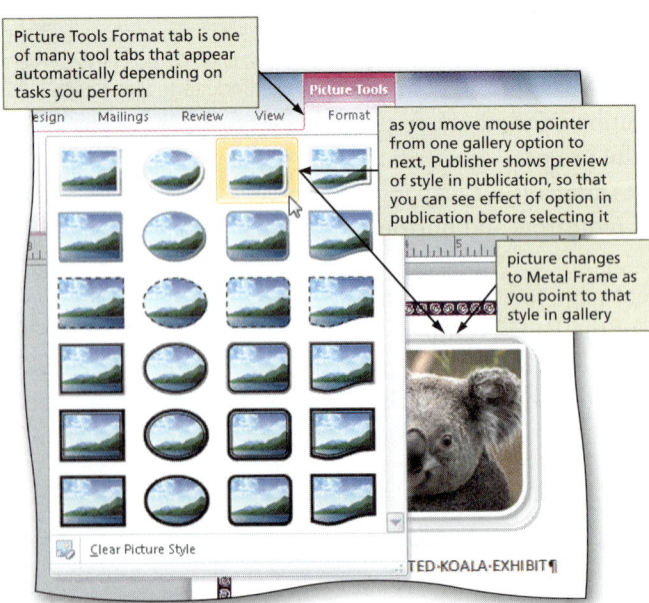

Figure 13

Some commands on the Ribbon display an image to help you remember their function. When you point to a command on the Ribbon, all or part of the command glows in shades of yellow and orange, and an Enhanced ScreenTip appears on the screen. An **Enhanced ScreenTip** is an on-screen note that provides the name of the command, available keyboard shortcut(s), a description of the command, and sometimes instructions for how to obtain help about the command (Figure 14). Enhanced ScreenTips are more detailed than a typical ScreenTip, which usually displays only the name of the command.

Some groups on the Ribbon have a small arrow in the lower-right corner, called a **Dialog Box Launcher**, that when clicked, displays a dialog box or a task pane with additional options for the group (Figure 15). When presented with a dialog box, you make selections and must close the dialog box before returning to the publication. A **task pane**, in contrast to a dialog box, is a window that can remain open and visible while you work in the publication.

Figure 14

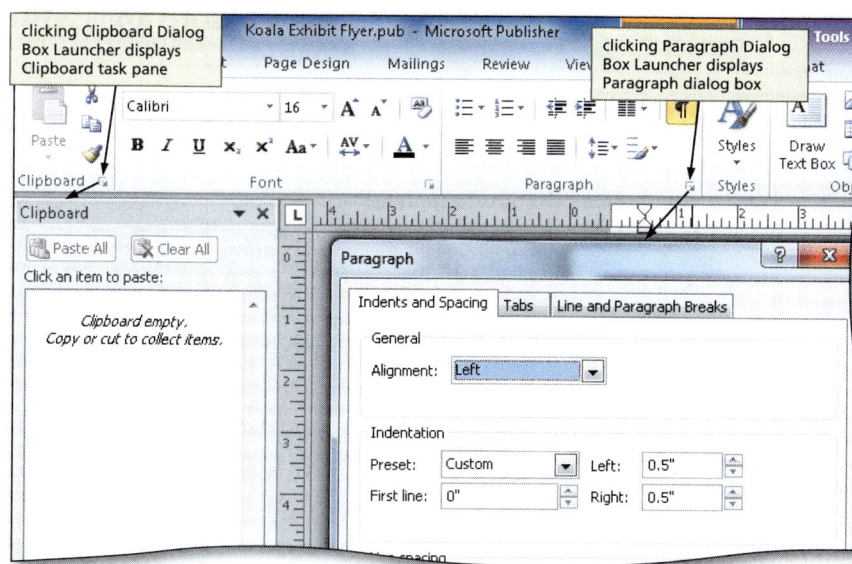

Figure 15

Mini Toolbar   The **Mini toolbar**, which appears automatically based on tasks you perform, contains commands related to changing the appearance of text in a publication. All commands on the Mini toolbar also exist on the Ribbon. The purpose of the Mini toolbar is to minimize mouse movement.

When the Mini toolbar appears, it initially is transparent (Figure 16a). If you do not use the transparent Mini toolbar, it disappears from the screen. To use the Mini toolbar, move the mouse pointer into the toolbar, which causes the Mini toolbar to change from a transparent to bright appearance (Figure 16b). If you right-click an item in the publication window, Publisher displays both the Mini toolbar and a shortcut menu, which is discussed in a later section in this chapter.

(a) transparent Mini toolbar

(b) bright Mini toolbar

Figure 16

Quick Access Toolbar   The **Quick Access Toolbar**, located initially (by default) above the Ribbon at the left edge of the title bar, provides convenient, one-click access to frequently used commands (Figure 14). The commands on the Quick Access Toolbar always are available, regardless of the task you are performing. The Quick Access Toolbar is discussed in more depth later in the chapter.

KeyTips   If you prefer using the keyboard instead of the mouse, you can press the ALT key on the keyboard to display **KeyTips**, or keyboard code icons, for certain commands

Figure 17

(Figure 17). To select a command using the keyboard, press the letter or number displayed in the KeyTip, which may cause additional KeyTips related to the selected command to appear. To remove KeyTips from the screen, press the ALT key or the ESC key until all KeyTips disappear, or click the mouse anywhere in the program window.

To Display a Different Tab on the Ribbon

When you start Publisher, the Ribbon displays seven main tabs: File, Home, Insert, Page Design, Mailings, Review, and View. The tab currently displayed is called the **active tab**.

The following step displays the Insert tab, that is, makes it the active tab.

- Click Insert on the Ribbon to display the Insert tab (Figure 18).

🔍 **Experiment**

- Click the other tabs on the Ribbon to view their contents. When you are finished, click the Insert tab to redisplay the Insert tab.

Figure 18

Q&A If I am working in a different Office program, such as PowerPoint or Access, how do I display a different tab on the Ribbon?

Follow this same procedure; that is, click the desired tab on the Ribbon.

To Minimize, Display, and Restore the Ribbon

To display more of a publication or other item in the window of an Office program, some users prefer to minimize the Ribbon, which hides the groups on the Ribbon and displays only the main tabs. Each time you start an Office program, such as Publisher, the Ribbon appears the same way it did the last time you used that Office program. The chapters in this book, however, begin with the Ribbon appearing as it did at the initial installation of Publisher.

The following steps minimize, display, and restore the Ribbon in Publisher.

- Click the Minimize the Ribbon button on the Ribbon (shown in Figure 18) to minimize the Ribbon (Figure 19).

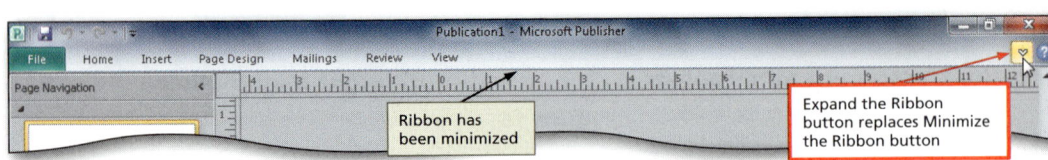

Figure 19

Q&A What happened to the groups on the Ribbon?

When you minimize the Ribbon, the groups disappear so that the Ribbon does not take up as much space on the screen.

Q&A What happened to the Minimize the Ribbon button?

The Expand the Ribbon button replaces the Minimize the Ribbon button when the Ribbon is minimized.

2

- Click Home on the Ribbon to display the Home tab (Figure 20).

Q&A

Why would I click the Home tab?

If you want to use a command on a minimized Ribbon, click the main tab to display the groups for that tab. After you select a command on the Ribbon, the groups will be hidden once again. If you decide not to use a command on the Ribbon, you can hide the groups by clicking the same main tab or clicking in the program window.

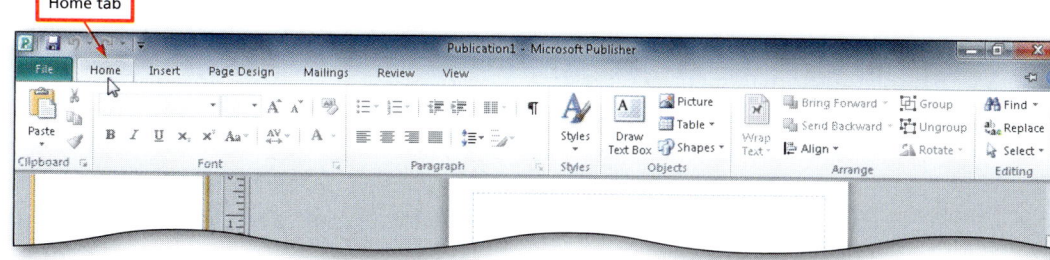

Figure 20

3

- Click Home on the Ribbon to hide the groups again (shown in Figure 19).

- Click the Expand the Ribbon button on the Ribbon (shown in Figure 19) to restore the Ribbon.

Other Ways

1. Double-click Home on the Ribbon
2. Press CTRL+F1

To Display and Use a Shortcut Menu

When you right-click certain areas of the Publisher and other program windows, a shortcut menu will appear. A **shortcut menu** is a list of frequently used commands that relate to the right-clicked object. When you right-click a scroll bar, for example, a shortcut menu appears with commands related to the scroll bar. When you right-click the Quick Access Toolbar, a shortcut menu appears with commands related to the Quick Access Toolbar. You can use shortcut menus to access common commands quickly. The following steps use a shortcut menu to move the Quick Access Toolbar, which by default is located on the title bar.

1

- Right-click the Quick Access Toolbar to display a shortcut menu that presents a list of commands related to the Quick Access Toolbar (Figure 21).

Figure 21

2

- Click Show Quick Access Toolbar Below the Ribbon on the shortcut menu to display the Quick Access Toolbar below the Ribbon (Figure 22).

Figure 22

3

• Right-click the Quick Access Toolbar to display a shortcut menu (Figure 23).

4

• Click Show Quick Access Toolbar Above the Ribbon on the shortcut menu to return the Quick Access Toolbar to its original position (shown in Figure 21 on the previous page).

Figure 23

To Customize the Quick Access Toolbar

The Quick Access Toolbar provides easy access to some of the more frequently used commands in Office programs. By default, the Quick Access Toolbar contains buttons for the Save, Undo, and Redo commands. You can customize the Quick Access Toolbar by changing its location in the window, as shown in the previous steps, and by adding more buttons to reflect commands you would like to access easily. The following steps add the Quick Print button to the Quick Access Toolbar in the Publisher window.

1

• Click the Customize Quick Access Toolbar button to display the Customize Quick Access Toolbar menu (Figure 24).

Q&A Which commands are listed on the Customize Quick Access Toolbar menu?

It lists commands that commonly are added to the Quick Access Toolbar.

Q&A What do the check marks next to some commands signify?

Check marks appear next to commands that already are on the Quick Access Toolbar. When you add a button to the Quick Access Toolbar, a check mark will be displayed next to its command name.

Figure 24

2

• Click Quick Print on the Customize Quick Access Toolbar menu to add the Quick Print button to the Quick Access Toolbar (Figure 25).

Q&A How would I remove a button from the Quick Access Toolbar?

You would right-click the button you wish to remove and then click Remove from Quick Access Toolbar on the shortcut menu. If you want your screens to match the screens in the remaining chapters in this book, you would remove the Quick Print button from the Quick Access Toolbar.

Figure 25

To Enter Text in a Blank Publication

When you displayed other tabs on the Ribbon (Figure 18 on page OFF 16), Publisher started a blank publication for you rather than opening a template from the New template gallery. The following steps type the first line of text, which creates a text box in Publisher.

- Press the F9 key on the keyboard to zoom to 100% magnification. Type **SEE THE RENOVATED KOALA EXHIBIT** as the text (Figure 26).

Q&A What is the blinking vertical bar to the right of the text?

The insertion point. It indicates where text, graphics, and other items will be inserted in the publication. As you type, the insertion point moves to the right, and when you reach the end of a line, it moves downward to the beginning of the next line.

Q&A What if I make an error while typing?

You can press the BACKSPACE key until you have deleted the text in error and then retype the text correctly.

Figure 26

- Press the ENTER key to move the insertion point to the beginning of the next line (Figure 27).

Q&A Why did blank space appear between the entered text and the insertion point?

Each time you press the ENTER key, Publisher creates a new paragraph and inserts blank space between the two paragraphs.

Figure 27

Saving and Organizing Files

While you are creating a publication, the computer stores it in memory. When you save a publication, the computer places it on a storage medium such as a hard disk, USB flash drive, or optical disc. A saved publication is referred to as a file. A **file name** is the name assigned to a file when it is saved. It is important to save a publication frequently for the following reasons:

- The publication in memory might be lost if the computer is turned off or you lose electrical power while a program is running.
- If you run out of time before completing a project, you may finish it at a future time without starting over.

When saving files, you should organize them so that you easily can find them later. Windows 7 provides tools to help you organize files.

Organizing Files and Folders

A file contains data. This data can range from a research paper to an accounting spreadsheet to an electronic math quiz. You should organize and store these files in folders to avoid misplacing a file and to help you find a file quickly.

If you are a freshman taking an introductory computer class (CIS 101, for example), you may want to design a series of folders for the different subjects covered in the class. To accomplish this, you can arrange the folders in a hierarchy for the class, as shown in Figure 28.

REMOVABLE (E:)

CIS 101

Word   PowerPoint   Excel   Access   Outlook   Publisher   OneNote

Figure 28

The hierarchy contains three levels. The first level contains the storage device, in this case a USB flash drive. Windows 7 identifies the storage device with a letter, and, in some cases, a name. In Figure 28, the USB flash drive is identified as REMOVABLE (E:). The second level contains the class folder (CIS 101, in this case), and the third level contains seven folders, one each for a different Office program that will be covered in the class (Word, PowerPoint, Excel, Access, Outlook, Publisher, and OneNote).

When the hierarchy in Figure 28 is created, the USB flash drive is said to contain the CIS 101 folder, and the CIS 101 folder is said to contain the separate Office folders (i.e., Word, PowerPoint, Excel, etc.). In addition, this hierarchy easily can be expanded to include folders from other classes taken during additional semesters.

The vertical and horizontal lines in Figure 28 form a pathway that allows you to navigate to a drive or folder on a computer or network. A **path** consists of a drive letter (preceded by a drive name when necessary) and colon, to identify the storage device, and one or more folder names. Each drive or folder in the hierarchy has a corresponding path.

Table 3 shows examples of paths and their corresponding drives and folders.

Table 3 Paths and Corresponding Drives and Folders	
Path	**Drive and Folder**
Computer ▶ REMOVABLE (E:)	Drive E (REMOVABLE (E:))
Computer ▶ REMOVABLE (E:) ▶ CIS 101	CIS 101 folder on drive E
Computer ▶ REMOVABLE (E:) ▶ CIS 101 ▶ Publisher	Publisher folder in CIS 101 folder on drive E

The following pages illustrate the steps to organize folders for a class and save a file in a folder:

1. Create a folder identifying your class.
2. Create a Publisher folder in the folder identifying your class.
3. Save a file in the Publisher folder.
4. Verify the location of the saved file.

To Create a Folder

When you create a folder, such as the CIS 101 folder shown in Figure 28, you must name the folder. A folder name should describe the folder and its contents. A folder name can contain spaces and any uppercase or lowercase characters, except a backslash (\), slash (/), colon (:), asterisk (*), question mark (?), quotation marks ("), less than symbol (<), greater than symbol (>), or vertical bar (|). Folder names cannot be CON, AUX, COM1, COM2, COM3, COM4, LPT1, LPT2, LPT3, PRN, or NUL. The same rules for naming folders also apply to naming files.

To store files and folders on a USB flash drive, you must connect the USB flash drive to an available USB port on a computer. The following steps create your class folder (CIS 101, in this case) on a USB flash drive.

1

- Connect the USB flash drive to an available USB port on the computer to open the AutoPlay window (Figure 29). (You may need to click the Windows Explorer program button on the taskbar to make the AutoPlay window visible.)

Q&A Why does the AutoPlay window not open?

Some computers are not configured to open an AutoPlay window. Instead, they might display the contents of the USB flash drive automatically, or you might need to access contents of the USB flash drive using the Computer window. To use the Computer window to display the USB flash drive's contents, click the Start button, click Computer on the Start menu, click the icon representing the USB flash drive in the navigation pane, and then proceed to Step 3 on the next page.

Q&A Why does the AutoPlay window look different from the one in Figure 29?

The AutoPlay window that opens on your computer might display different options. The type of USB flash drive, its contents, and the next available drive letter on your computer all will determine which options are displayed in the AutoPlay window.

Figure 29

2

- Click the 'Open folder to view files' link in the AutoPlay window to open the USB flash drive window (Figure 30).

Q&A Why does Figure 30 show REMOVABLE (E:) for the USB flash drive?

REMOVABLE is the name of the USB flash drive used to illustrate these steps. The (E:) refers to the drive letter assigned by Windows 7 to the USB flash drive. The name and drive letter of your USB flash drive probably will be different.

Figure 30

3

- Click the New folder button (Figure 30 on the previous page) on the toolbar to display a new folder icon with the name, New folder, selected in a text box.

- Type CIS 101 (or your class code) in the text box to name the folder.

- Press the ENTER key to create a folder identifying your class on the selected drive (Figure 31). If the CIS 101 folder does not appear in the navigation pane, double-click REMOVABLE (E:) in the navigation pane to display the folder just added.

Q&A What happens when I press the ENTER key?

The class folder (CIS 101, in this case) is displayed in the File list, which contains the folder name, date modified, type, and size.

Figure 31

Q&A Why is the folder icon displayed differently on my computer?

Windows might be configured to display contents differently on your computer.

Folder Windows

The USB flash drive window (shown in Figure 31) is called a folder window. Recall that a folder is a specific named location on a storage medium that contains related files. Most users rely on **folder windows** for finding, viewing, and managing information on their computer. Folder windows have common design elements, including the following (Figure 31).

- The **Address bar** provides quick navigation options. The arrows on the Address bar allow you to visit different locations on the computer.
- The buttons to the left of the Address bar allow you to navigate the contents of the left pane and view recent pages. Other buttons allow you to specify the size of the window.
- The **Previous Locations button** saves the locations you have visited and displays the locations when clicked.
- The **Refresh button** on the right side of the Address bar refreshes the contents of the right pane of the folder window.
- The **search box** to the right of the Address bar contains the dimmed word, Search. You can type a term in the search box for a list of files, folders, shortcuts, and elements containing that term within the location you are searching. A **shortcut** is an icon on the desktop that provides a user with immediate access to a program or file.
- The **Command bar** contains five buttons used to accomplish various tasks on the computer related to organizing and managing the contents of the open window.
- The **navigation pane** on the left contains the Favorites area, Libraries area, Computer area, and Network area.

• The **Favorites area** contains links to your favorite locations. By default, this list contains only links to your Desktop, Downloads, and Recent Places.
• The **Libraries area** shows links to files and folders that have been included in a library.

A **library** helps you manage multiple folders and files stored in various locations on a computer. It does not store the files and folders; rather, it displays links to them so that you can access them quickly. For example, you can save pictures from a digital camera in any folder on any storage location on a computer. Normally, this would make organizing the different folders difficult; however, if you add the folders to a library, you can access all the pictures from one location regardless of where they are stored.

To Create a Folder within a Folder

With the class folder created, you can create folders that will store the files you create using Publisher. The following steps create a Publisher folder in the CIS 101 folder (or the folder identifying your class).

• Double-click the icon or folder name for the CIS 101 folder (or the folder identifying your class) in the File list to open the folder (Figure 32).

Figure 32

• Click the New folder button on the toolbar to display a new folder icon and text box for the folder.

• Type `Publisher` in the text box to name the folder.

• Press the ENTER key to create the folder (Figure 33).

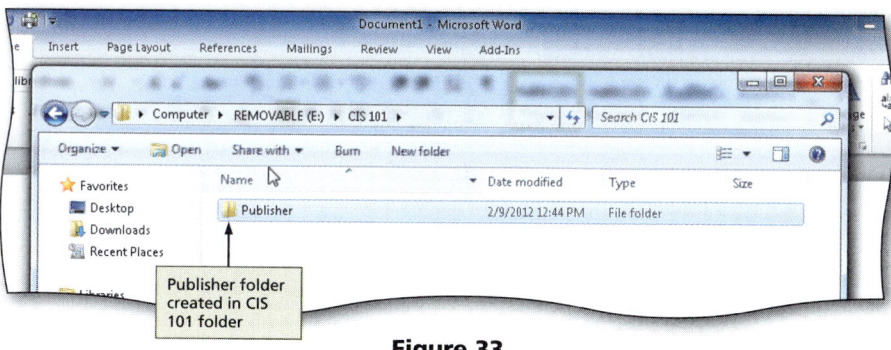

Figure 33

To Expand a Folder, Scroll through Folder Contents, and Collapse a Folder

Folder windows display the hierarchy of items and the contents of drives and folders in the right pane. You might want to expand a drive in the navigation pane to view its contents, scroll through its contents, and collapse it when you are finished viewing its contents. When a folder is expanded, it lists all the folders it contains. By contrast, a collapsed folder does not list the folders it contains. The steps on the next page expand, scroll through, and then collapse the folder identifying your class (CIS 101, in this case).

1

- Double-click the folder identifying your class (CIS 101, in this case) in the navigation pane, which expands the folder to display its contents and displays a black arrow to the left of the folder icon (Figure 34).

Q&A

Why is the Publisher folder indented below the CIS 101 folder in the navigation pane?

It shows that the folder is contained within the CIS 101 folder.

Q&A

Why did a scroll bar appear in the navigation pane?

When all contents cannot fit in a window or pane, a scroll bar appears. As described earlier, you can view areas currently not visible by (1) clicking the scroll arrows, (2) clicking above or below the scroll bar, and (3) dragging the scroll box.

Figure 34

Experiment

- Click the down scroll arrow on the vertical scroll bar to display additional content at the bottom of the navigation pane.

- Click the scroll bar above the scroll box to move the scroll box to the top of the navigation pane.

- Drag the scroll box down the scroll bar until the scroll box is halfway down the scroll bar.

2

- Double-click the folder identifying your class (CIS 101, in this case) in the navigation pane to collapse the folder (Figure 35).

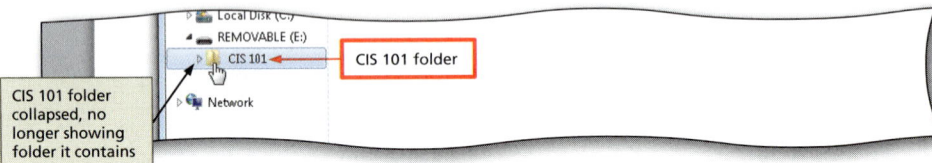

Figure 35

Other Ways
1. Point in navigation pane to display arrows, click white arrow to expand or click black arrow to collapse 　　2. Select folder to expand or collapse using arrow keys, press RIGHT ARROW to expand; press LEFT ARROW to collapse

To Switch from One Program to Another

The next step is to save the Publisher file containing the headline you typed earlier. Publisher, however, currently is not the active window. You can use the program button on the taskbar and live preview to switch to Publisher and then save the publication in the Publisher publication window.

If Windows Aero is active on your computer, Windows displays a live preview window whenever you move your mouse on a button or click a button on the taskbar. If Aero is not supported or enabled on your computer, you will see a window title instead of a live preview. These steps use the Publisher program; however, the steps are the same for any active Office program currently displayed as a program button on the taskbar.

The next steps switch to the Publisher window.

1

- Point to the Publisher program button on the taskbar to see a live preview of the open publication(s) or the window title(s) of the open publication(s), depending on your computer's configuration (Figure 36).

2

- Click the program button or the live preview to make the program associated with the program button the active window (shown in Figure 27 on page OFF 19).

Q&A

What if multiple publications are open in a program?

If Aero is enabled on your computer, click the desired live preview. If Aero is not supported or not enabled, click the window title.

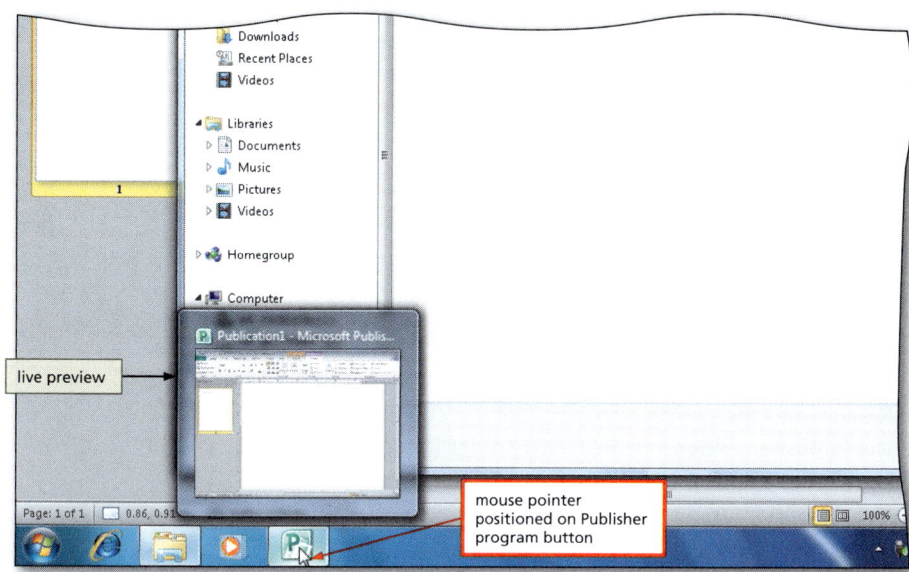

Figure 36

To Save a File in a Folder

Now that you have created the Publisher folder for storing files, you can save the Publisher publication in that folder. The following steps save a file on a USB flash drive in the Publisher folder contained in your class folder (CIS 101, in this case) using the file name, Koala Exhibit.

1

- With a USB flash drive connected to one of the computer's USB ports, click the Save button on the Quick Access Toolbar to display the Save As dialog box (Figure 37).

Q&A

Why does a file name already appear in the File name text box?

Publisher automatically suggests a file name the first time you save a publication. The file name normally contains the word, Publication, followed by a number indicating how many publications you have opened during the current session. Because the suggested file name is selected, you do not need to delete it; as soon as you begin typing, the new file name replaces the selected text.

Figure 37

● Type **Koala Exhibit** in the File name text box (Save As dialog box) to change the file name. Do not press the ENTER key after typing the file name because you do not want to close the dialog box at this time (Figure 38).

Q&A What characters can I use in a file name?

The only invalid characters are the backslash (\), slash (/), colon (:), asterisk (*), question mark (?), quotation mark ("), less than symbol (<), greater than symbol (>), and vertical bar (|).

● Navigate to the desired save location (in this case, the Publisher folder in the CIS 101 folder [or your class folder] on the USB flash drive) by performing the tasks in Steps 3a – 3c.

3a

● If the navigation pane is not displayed in the dialog box, click the Browse Folders button to expand the dialog box.

● If Computer is not displayed in the navigation pane, drag the navigation pane scroll bar until Computer appears.

● If Computer is not expanded in the navigation pane, double-click Computer to display a list of available storage devices in the navigation pane.

● If necessary, scroll through the dialog box until your USB flash drive appears in the list of available storage devices in the navigation pane (Figure 39).

3b

● If your USB flash drive is not expanded, double-click the USB flash drive in the list of available storage devices in the navigation pane to select that drive as the new save location and display its contents in the right pane.

3c

● If your class folder (CIS 101, in this case) is not expanded, double-click the CIS 101 folder to select the folder and display its contents in the right pane.

Q&A What if I do not want to save in a folder?

Although storing files in folders is an effective technique for organizing files, some users prefer not to store files in folders. If you prefer not to save this file in a folder, skip all instructions in Step 3c and proceed to Step 4.

● Click the Publisher folder to select the folder and display its contents in the right pane (Figure 40).

Figure 38

Figure 39

Figure 40

4

- Click the Save button (Save As dialog box) to save the publication in the selected folder on the selected drive with the entered file name (Figure 41).

Q&A

How do I know that the file is saved?

While an Office program such as Publisher is saving a file, it briefly displays a message on the status bar indicating the amount of the file saved. In addition, the USB flash drive may have a light that flashes during the save process.

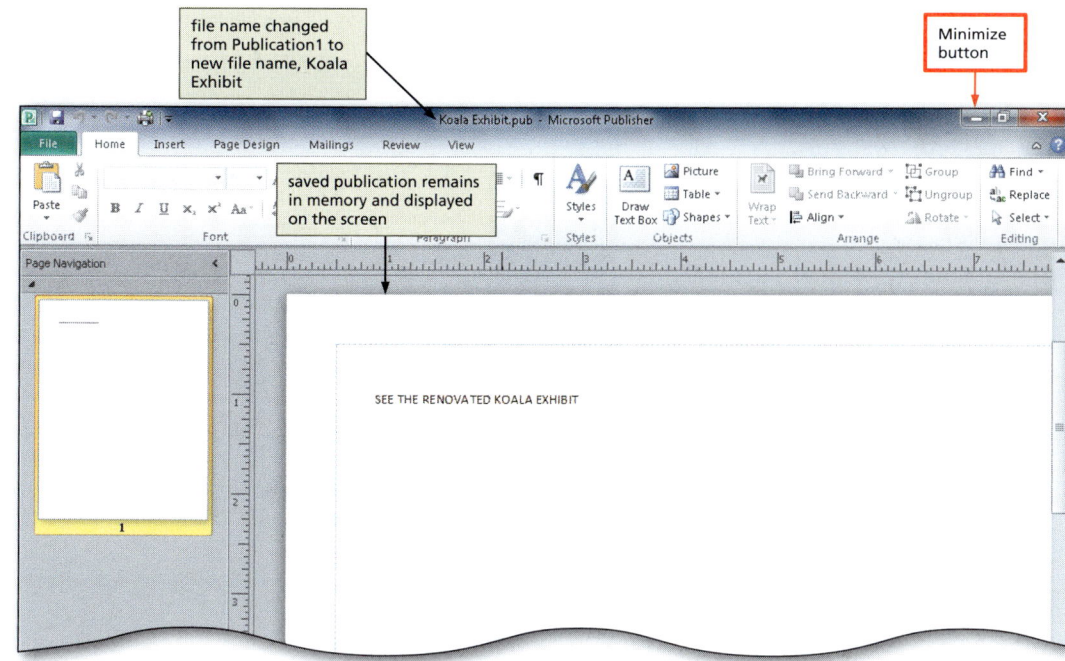

Figure 41

Other Ways	
1. Click File on Ribbon, click Save, type file name, navigate to desired save location, click Save button	2. Press CTRL+S or press SHIFT+F12, type file name, navigate to desired save location, click Save button

Navigating in Dialog Boxes

Navigating is the process of finding a location on a storage device. While saving the Koala Exhibit file, for example, Steps 3a – 3c in the previous set of steps navigated to the Publisher folder located in the CIS 101 folder. When performing certain functions in Windows programs, such as saving a file, opening a file, or inserting a picture in an existing publication, you most likely will have to navigate to the location where you want to save the file or to the folder containing the file you want to open or insert. Most dialog boxes in Windows programs requiring navigation follow a similar procedure; that is, the way you navigate to a folder in one dialog box, such as the Save As dialog box, is similar to how you might navigate in another dialog box, such as the Open dialog box. If you chose to navigate to a specific location in a dialog box, you would follow the instructions in Steps 3a – 3c on page OFF 26.

BTW

File Type
Depending on your Windows 7 settings, the file type .pub may be displayed immediately to the right of the file name after you save the file. The file type .pub is a Publisher 2010 publication.

To Minimize and Restore a Window

Before continuing, you can verify that the Publisher file was saved properly. To do this, you will minimize the Publisher window and then open the USB flash drive window so that you can verify the file is stored on the USB flash drive. A **minimized window** is an open window hidden from view but that can be displayed quickly by clicking the window's program button on the taskbar.

In the following example, Publisher is used to illustrate minimizing and restoring windows; however, you would follow the same steps regardless of the Office program you are using.

The steps on the next page minimize the Publisher window, verify that the file is saved, and then restore the minimized window.

1

- Click the Minimize button on the program's title bar (shown in Figure 41 on the previous page) to minimize the window (Figure 42).

Q&A

Is the minimized window still available?

The minimized window, Publisher in this case, remains available but no longer is the active window. It is minimized as a program button on the taskbar.

- If necessary, click the Windows Explorer program button on the taskbar to open the USB flash drive window.

Figure 42

2

- Double-click the Publisher folder to select the folder and display its contents (Figure 43).

Q&A

Why does the Windows Explorer button on the taskbar change?

The button changes to reflect the status of the folder window (in this case, the USB flash drive window). A selected button indicates that the folder window is active on the screen. When the button is not selected, the window is open but not active.

3

- After viewing the contents of the selected folder, click the Publisher program button on the taskbar to restore the minimized window (as shown in Figure 41 on the previous page).

Other Ways

1. Right-click title bar, click Minimize on shortcut menu, click taskbar button in taskbar button area
2. Press WINDOWS+M, press WINDOWS+SHIFT+M

Figure 43

Screen Resolution

Screen resolution indicates the number of pixels (dots) that the computer uses to display the letters, numbers, graphics, and background you see on the screen. When you increase the screen resolution, Windows displays more information on the screen, but the information decreases in size. The reverse also is true: as you decrease the screen resolution, Windows displays less information on the screen, but the information increases in size.

Screen resolution usually is stated as the product of two numbers, such as 1024 × 768 (pronounced "ten twenty-four by seven sixty-eight"). A 1024 × 768 screen resolution results in a display of 1,024 distinct pixels on each of 768 lines, or about 786,432 pixels. Changing the screen resolution affects how the Ribbon appears in Office programs. Figure 44, for example, shows the Publisher Ribbon at screen resolutions of 1024 × 768 and 1280 × 800. All of the same commands are available regardless of screen resolution. Publisher, however, makes changes to the groups and the buttons within the groups to accommodate the various screen resolutions. The result is that certain commands may need to be accessed differently depending on the resolution chosen. A command that is visible on the Ribbon and available by clicking a button at one resolution may not be visible and may need to be accessed using its Dialog Box Launcher at a different resolution.

Comparing the two Ribbons in Figure 44, notice the changes in content and layout of the groups and galleries. In some cases, the content of a group is the same in each resolution, but the layout of the group differs. For example, the same gallery and buttons appear in the Schemes groups in the two resolutions, but the layouts differ. In other cases, the content and layout are the same across the resolution, but the level of detail differs with the resolution. In the Page Setup group, when the resolution increases to 1280 × 800, the buttons in the group appear in a row. At the lower resolution, they are grouped in a column.

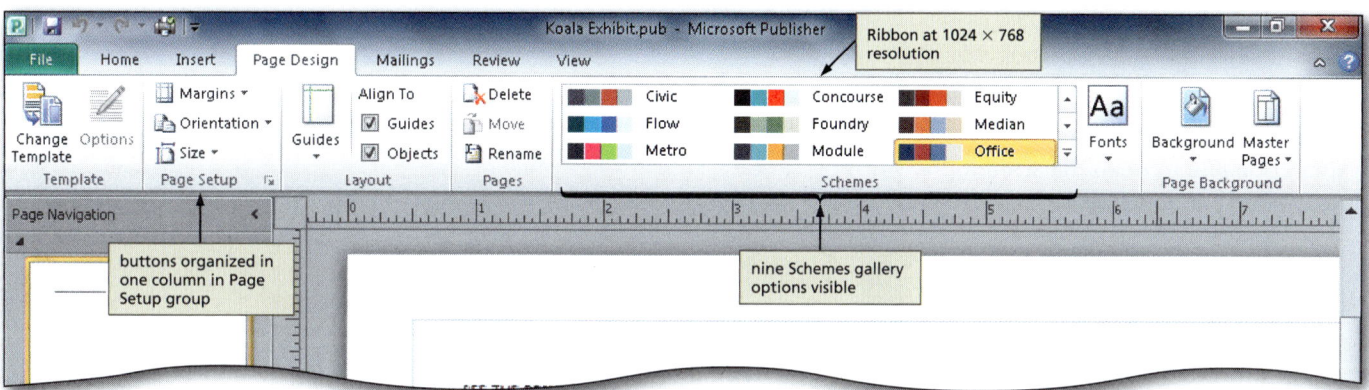

(a) Ribbon at Resolution of 1024 x 768

(b) Ribbon at Resolution of 1280 x 800

Figure 44

To Change the Screen Resolution

If you are using a computer to step through the chapters in this book and you want your screen to match the figures, you may need to change your screen's resolution. The figures in this book use a screen resolution of 1024 × 768. The following steps change the screen resolution to 1024 × 768. Your computer already may be set to 1024 × 768 or some other resolution. Keep in mind that many computer labs prevent users from changing the screen resolution; in that case, read the following steps for illustration purposes.

- Click the Show desktop button on the taskbar to display the Windows 7 desktop.

- Right-click an empty area on the Windows 7 desktop to display a shortcut menu that displays a list of commands related to the desktop (Figure 45).

Q&A

Why does my shortcut menu display different commands?

Depending on your computer's hardware and configuration, different commands might appear on the shortcut menu.

Figure 45

- Click Screen resolution on the shortcut menu to open the Screen Resolution window (Figure 46).

Figure 46

3

- Click the Resolution button in the Screen Resolution window to display the resolution slider.

Q&A

What is a slider?

A **slider** is an object that allows users to choose from multiple predetermined options. In most cases, these options represent some type of numeric value. In most cases, one end of the slider (usually the left or bottom) represents the lowest of available values, and the opposite end (usually the right or top) represents the highest available value.

4

- If necessary, drag the resolution slider until the desired screen resolution (in this case, 1024 × 768) is selected (Figure 47).

Q&A

What if my computer does not support the 1024 × 768 resolution?

Some computers do not support the 1024 × 768 resolution. In this case, select a resolution that is close to the 1024 × 768 resolution.

Figure 47

5

- Click an empty area of the Screen Resolution window to close the resolution slider.

- Click the OK button to change the screen resolution and display the Display Settings dialog box (Figure 48).

- Click the Keep changes button (Display Settings dialog box) to accept the new screen resolution.

Q&A

Why does a message display stating that the image quality can be improved?

Some computer monitors are designed to display contents better at a certain screen resolution, sometimes referred to as an optimal resolution.

Figure 48

To Quit a Program with One Publication Open

When you quit an Office program, such as Publisher, if you have made changes to a file since the last time the file was saved, the Office program displays a dialog box asking if you want to save the changes you made to the file before it closes the program window. The dialog box contains three buttons with these resulting actions: the Save button saves the changes and then quits the Office program, the Don't Save button quits the Office program without saving changes, and the Cancel button closes the dialog box and redisplays the file without saving the changes.

If no changes have been made to an open publication since the last time the file was saved, the Office program will close the window without displaying a dialog box.

The following steps quit Publisher. You would follow similar steps in other Office programs.

- If necessary, click the Publisher program button on the taskbar to display the Publisher window on the desktop.

- Point to the Close button on the right side of the program's title bar, Publisher in this case (Figure 49).

Figure 49

- Click the Close button to close the publication and quit Publisher.

Q&A What if I have more than one publication open in Publisher?

You would click the Close button for each open publication. When you click the last open publication's Close button, Publisher also quits. As an alternative, you could click File on the Ribbon to open the Backstage view and then click Exit in the Backstage view to close all open publications and quit Publisher.

Q&A What is the Backstage view?

The **Backstage view** contains a set of commands that enable you to manage publications and data about the publications. The Backstage view is discussed in more depth later in this chapter.

> **Other Ways**
>
> 1. Right-click the Office program button on Windows 7 taskbar, click Close window or 'Close all windows' on shortcut menu
> 2. Press ALT+F4

- If a Microsoft Publisher dialog box appears, click the Save button to save any changes made to the publication since the last save.

Break Point: If you wish to take a break, this is a good place to do so. To resume at a later time, continue to follow the steps from this location forward.

Additional Common Features of Office Programs

The previous section used Publisher to illustrate common features of Office and some basic elements unique to Publisher. The following sections continue to use Publisher to present additional common features of Office.

In the following pages, you will learn how to do the following:

1. Start an Office program (Publisher) using the search box.
2. Open a publication in an Office program (Publisher).
3. Close the publication.
4. Reopen the publication just closed.
5. Create a blank Office document from Windows Explorer and then open the file.
6. Save a document with a new file name.

To Start a Program Using the Search Box

The next steps, which assume Windows 7 is running, use the search box to start Publisher based on a typical installation; however, you would follow similar steps to start any program. You may need to ask your instructor how to start programs for your computer.

- Click the Start button on the Windows 7 taskbar to display the Start menu.

- Type **Microsoft Publisher** as the search text in the 'Search programs and files' text box and watch the search results appear on the Start menu (Figure 50).

Q&A

Do I need to type the complete program name or correct capitalization?

No, just enough of it for the program name to appear on the Start menu. For example, you may be able to type Publisher or publisher, instead of Microsoft Publisher.

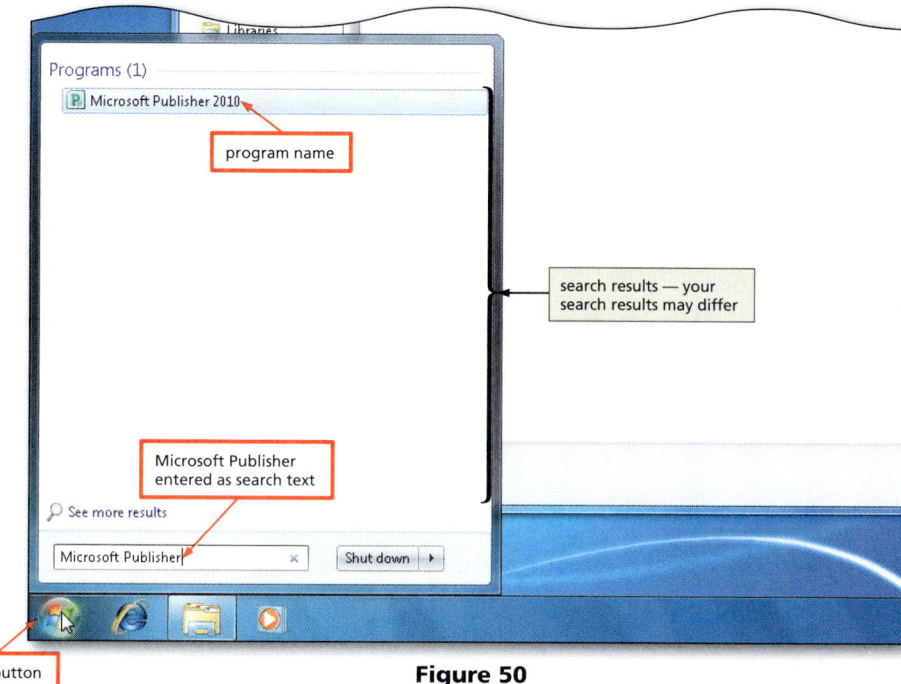

program name

search results — your search results may differ

Microsoft Publisher entered as search text

Start button

Figure 50

Restore Down button replaces Maximize button

- Click the program name, Microsoft Publisher 2010 in this case, in the search results on the Start menu to start Publisher and display the New template gallery in the Publisher window.

- If the program window is not maximized, click the Maximize button on its title bar to maximize the window (Figure 51).

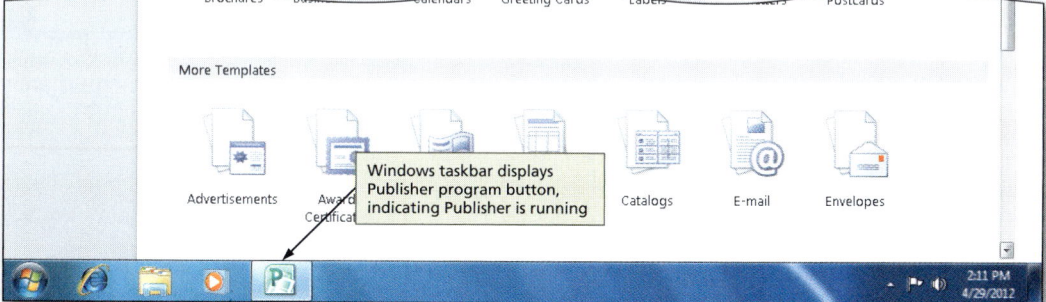

Windows taskbar displays Publisher program button, indicating Publisher is running

Figure 51

To Open an Existing File from the Backstage View

As discussed earlier, the Backstage view provides data about publications and contains a set of commands that assist you with managing publications. From the Backstage view in Publisher, for example, you can create, open, print, and save publications. You also can share documents, manage versions, set permissions, and modify publication properties.

Assume you wish to continue working on an existing file, that is, a file you previously saved. The following steps use the Backstage view to open a saved file, specifically the Koala Exhibit file, from the USB flash drive.

1

- With your USB flash drive connected to one of the computer's USB ports, if necessary, click File on the Ribbon to open the Backstage view (Figure 52).

Q&A What is the purpose of the File tab?

The File tab is used to display the Backstage view for each Office program.

Figure 52

2

- Click Open in the Backstage view to display the Open Publication dialog box (Figure 53).

3

- Navigate to the location of the file to be opened (in this case, the USB flash drive, then to the CIS 101 folder [or your class folder], and then to the Publisher folder). For detailed steps about navigating, see Steps 3a – 3c on page OFF 26.

Q&A What if I did not save my file in a folder?

If you did not save your file in a folder, the file you wish to open should be displayed in the Open dialog box before navigating to any folders.

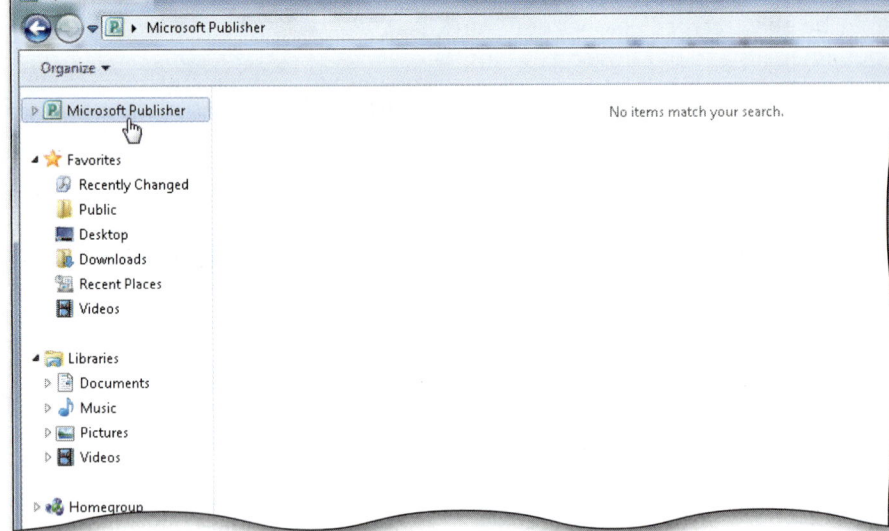

Figure 53

4

- Click the file to be opened, Koala Exhibit in this case, to select the file (Figure 54).

5

- Click the Open button (Open dialog box) to open the selected file and display the opened file in the current program window (shown in Figure 41 on page OFF 27).

Other Ways

1. Click File on the Ribbon, click Recent in Backstage view, double-click file
2. Press CTRL+O
3. Navigate to file in Windows Explorer, double-click file

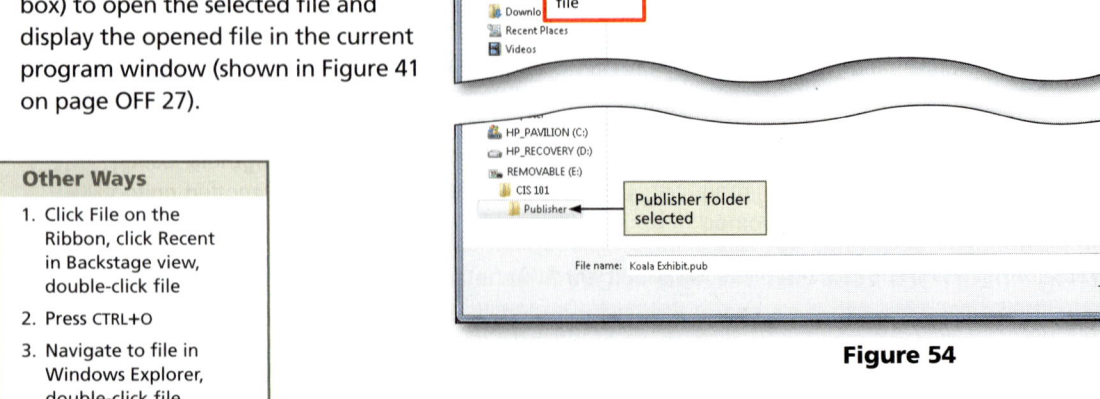

Figure 54

To Create a New Publication from the Backstage View

You can create multiple publications at the same time in an Office program, such as Publisher. The following steps create a file, a blank publication in this case, from the Backstage view.

1
- Click File on the Ribbon to open the Backstage view.

- Click the New tab in the Backstage view to display the New template gallery (Figure 55).

Q&A

Can I create publications through the Backstage view in other Office programs?

Yes. If the Office program has a New tab in the Backstage view, the New gallery displays various options for creating a new file.

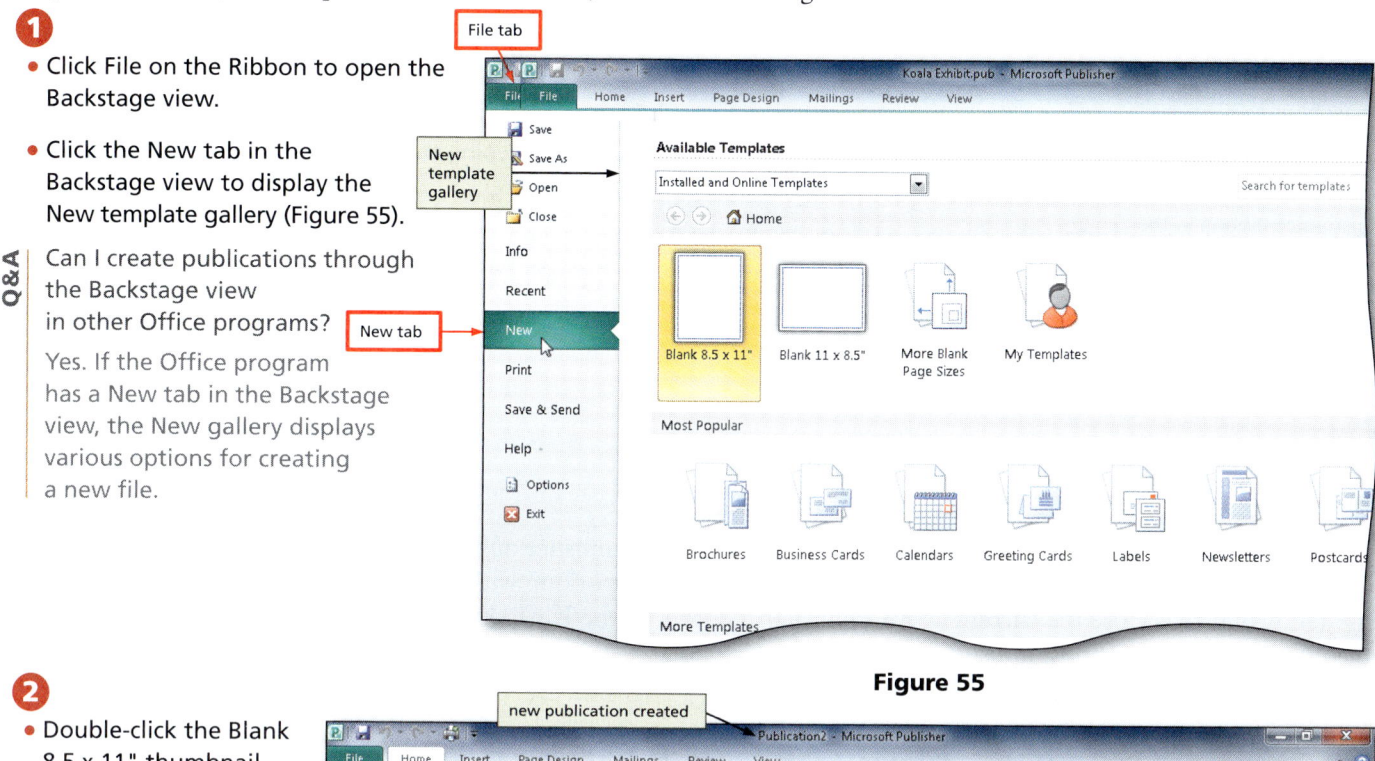

Figure 55

2
- Double-click the Blank 8.5 x 11" thumbnail to create a new publication (Figure 56).

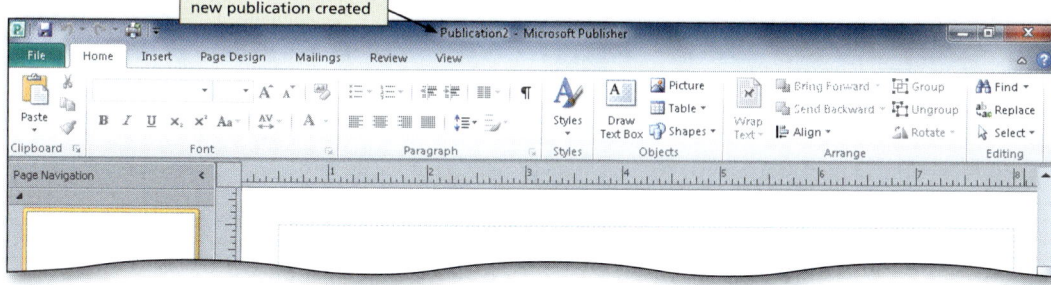

Figure 56

Other Ways
1. Press CTRL+N

To Enter Text in a Publication

The next Publisher publication identifies the names of the Koala Exhibit sponsors. The following step enters text in a publication.

1
Type **List of Current Sponsors for the Koala Exhibit** and then press the ENTER key to move the insertion point to the beginning of the next line (Figure 57).

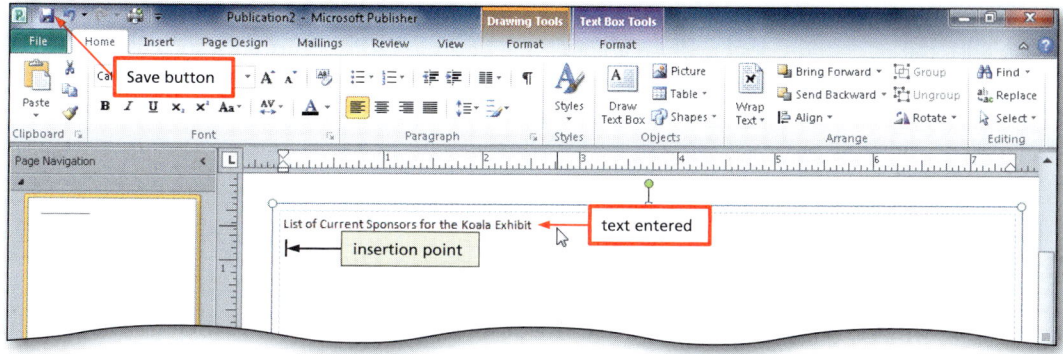

Figure 57

BTW

Customizing the Ribbon
In addition to customizing the Quick Access Toolbar, you can add items to and remove items from the Ribbon. To customize the Ribbon, click File on the Ribbon to open the Backstage view, click Options in the Backstage view, and then click Customize Ribbon in the left pane of the Options dialog box. More information about customizing the Ribbon is presented in a later chapter.

To Save a File in a Folder

The following steps save the second publication in the Publisher folder in the class folder (CIS 101, in this case) on a USB flash drive using the file name, Koala Exhibit Sponsors.

1 With a USB flash drive connected to one of the computer's USB ports, click the Save button on the Quick Access Toolbar to display the Save As dialog box.

2 If necessary, type **Koala Exhibit Sponsors** in the File name text box to change the file name. Do not press the ENTER key after typing the file name because you do not want to close the dialog box at this time.

3 If necessary, navigate to the desired save location (in this case, the Publisher folder in the CIS 101 folder [or your class folder] on the USB flash drive).

4 Click the Save button (Save As dialog box) to save the publication in the selected folder on the selected drive with the entered file name.

To Close a File Using the Backstage View

Sometimes, you may want to close an Office file, such as a Publisher publication, entirely and start over with a new file. You also may want to close a file when you are finished working with it so that you can begin a new file. The following steps close the current active Publisher file (that is, the Koala Exhibit Sponsors publication) without quitting the active program (Publisher in this case).

- Click File on the Ribbon to open the Backstage view (Figure 58).

- Click Close in the Backstage view to close the open file (Koala Exhibit Sponsors, in this case) without quitting the active program.

Q&A

What if Publisher displays a dialog box about saving?

Click the Save button if you want to save the changes, click the Don't Save button if you want to ignore the changes since the last time you saved, and click the Cancel button if you do not want to close the publication.

Figure 58

Q&A

Can I use the Backstage view to close an open file in other Office programs, such as PowerPoint and Excel?

Yes.

To Open a Recent File Using the Backstage View

You sometimes need to open a file that you recently modified. You may have more changes to make such as adding more content or correcting errors. The Backstage view allows you to access recent files easily. The next steps reopen the Koala Exhibit Sponsors file just closed.

1

- Click File on the Ribbon to open the Backstage view.

- Click the Recent tab in the Backstage view to display the Recent gallery (Figure 59).

2

- Click the desired file name in the Recent gallery, Koala Exhibit Sponsors in this case, to open the file (shown in Figure 57 on page OFF 35).

Q&A

Can I use the Backstage view to open a recent file in other Office programs, such as PowerPoint and Excel?

Yes, as long as the file name appears in the list of recent files in the Recent gallery.

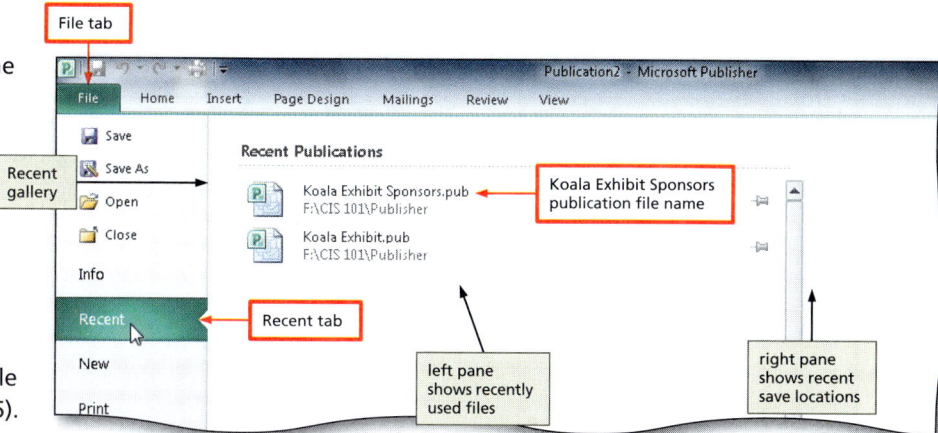

Figure 59

Other Ways	
1. Click Start button, point to program name, click file name on submenu	2. Click File on Ribbon, click Open in Backstage view, navigate to file (Open dialog box), click Open button

To Create a New Blank Document from Windows Explorer

Windows Explorer provides a means to create a blank Office document without ever starting an Office program. The following steps use Windows Explorer to create a blank Publisher document.

1

- Click the Windows Explorer program button on the taskbar to make the folder window the active window in Windows Explorer.

- If necessary, navigate to the desired location for the new file (in this case, the Publisher folder in the CIS 101 folder [or your class folder] on the USB flash drive).

- With the Publisher folder selected, right-click an open area in the right pane to display a shortcut menu.

- Point to New on the shortcut menu to display the New submenu (Figure 60).

Figure 60

- Click Microsoft Office Publisher Document on the New submenu to display an icon and text box for a new file in the current folder window (Figure 61).

Figure 61

- Type **Koala Exhibit Volunteers** in the text box and then press the ENTER key to assign a name to the new file in the current folder (Figure 62).

Figure 62

To Start a Program from Windows Explorer and Open a File

Previously, you learned how to start an Office program (Publisher) using the Start menu and the search box. Another way to start an Office program is to open an existing file from Windows Explorer, which causes the program in which the file was created to start and then open the selected file. The following steps, which assume Windows 7 is running, use Windows Explorer to start Publisher based on a typical installation. You may need to ask your instructor how to start Publisher for your computer.

- If necessary, display the file to open in the folder window in Windows Explorer (shown in Figure 62).

- Right-click the file icon or file name (Koala Exhibit Volunteers, in this case) to display a shortcut menu (Figure 63).

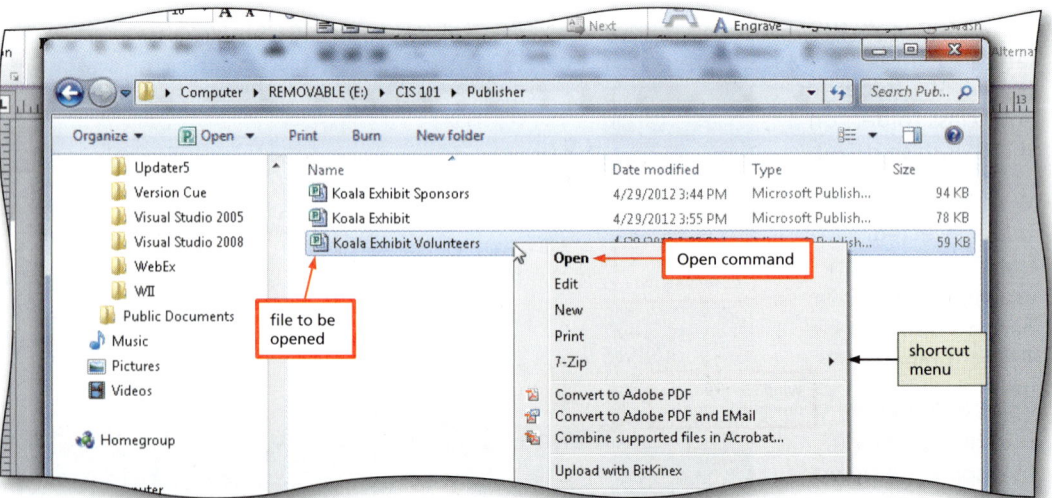

Figure 63

2

- Click Open on the shortcut menu to open the selected file in the program used to create the file, Microsoft Publisher in this case (Figure 64).

- If the program window is not maximized, click the Maximize button on the title bar to maximize the window.

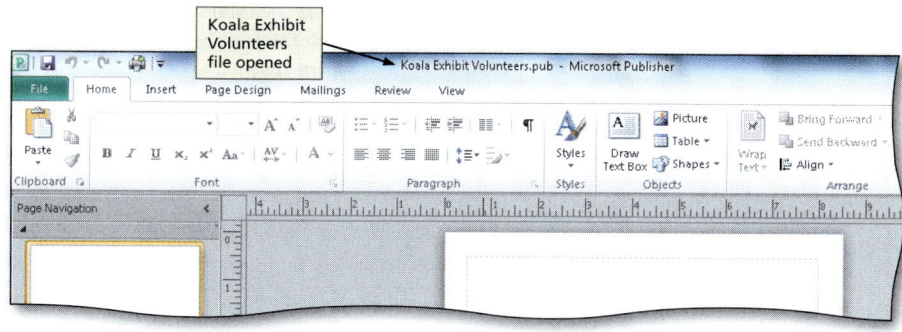

Figure 64

To Enter Text in a Publication

The next step is to enter text in this blank Publisher document. The following step enters a line of text.

1 Type **Koala Exhibit Staff and Volunteers** and then press the ENTER key to move the insertion point to the beginning of the next line (shown in Figure 65).

To Save an Existing Publication with the Same File Name

Saving frequently cannot be overemphasized. You have made modifications to the file (publication) since you created it. Thus, you should save again. Similarly, you should continue saving files frequently so that you do not lose your changes since the time you last saved the file. You can use the same file name, such as Koala Exhibit Volunteers, to save the changes made to the publication. The following step saves a file again.

1

- Click the Save button on the Quick Access Toolbar to overwrite the previously saved file (Koala Exhibit Volunteers, in this case) on the USB flash drive (Figure 65).

Q&A

Why did the Save As dialog box not appear?

Office programs, including Publisher, overwrite the publication using the setting specified the first time you saved the publication.

Figure 65

Other Ways

1. Press CTRL+S or press SHIFT+F12

To Use Save As to Change the Name of a File

You might want to save a file with a different name and even to a different location. For example, you might start a homework assignment with a data file and then save it with a final file name for submitting to your instructor, saving it to a location designated by your instructor. The following steps save a file with a different file name.

1 With your USB flash drive connected to one of the computer's USB ports, click File on the Ribbon to open the Backstage view.

2 Click Save As in the Backstage view to display the Save As dialog box.

3 Type **Koala Exhibit Staff and Volunteers** in the File name text box (Save As dialog box) to change the file name. Do not press the ENTER key after typing the file name because you do not want to close the dialog box at this time.

4 If necessary, navigate to the desired save location (the Publisher folder in the CIS 101 folder [or your class folder] on the USB flash drive, in this case).

5 Click the Save button (Save As dialog box) to save the file in the selected folder on the selected drive with the new file name.

To Quit an Office Program

BTW

Multiple Open Files
If the program button on the taskbar displays as a tiered stack, you have multiple files open in the program.

You are finished using Publisher. The following steps quit Publisher. You would use similar steps to quit other office programs.

1 Because you have multiple Publisher publications open, click File on the Ribbon to open the Backstage view and then click Exit in the Backstage view to close the publication.

2 If a dialog box appears, click the Save button to save any changes made to the file since the last save. Repeat for each open publication.

Moving, Renaming, and Deleting Files

Earlier in this chapter, you learned how to organize files in folders, which is part of a process known as **file management**. The following sections cover additional file management topics including renaming, moving, and deleting files.

To Rename a File

In some circumstances, you may want to change the name of, or rename, a file or a folder. For example, you may want to distinguish a file in one folder or drive from a copy of a similar file, or you may decide to rename a file to better identify its contents. The Publisher folder shown in Figure 66 contains the Publisher publication. Koala Exhibit. The following steps change the name of the Koala Exhibit file in the Publisher folder to Koala Exhibit Flyer.

1

• If necessary, click the Windows Explorer program button on the taskbar to display the folder window in Windows Explorer.

• If necessary, navigate to the location of the file to be renamed (in this case, the Publisher folder in the CIS 101 [or your class folder] folder on the USB flash drive) to display the file(s) it contains in the right pane.

• Right-click the Koala Exhibit icon or file name in the right pane to select the Koala Exhibit file and display a shortcut menu that presents a list of commands related to files (Figure 66).

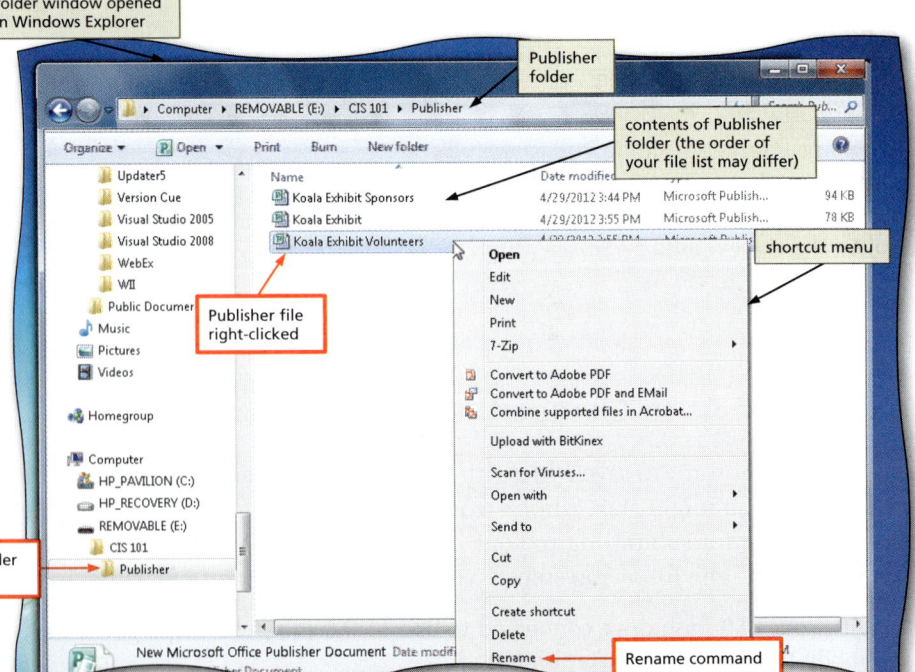

Figure 66

2

- Click Rename on the shortcut menu to place the current file name in a text box.

- Type **Koala Exhibit Flyer** in the text box and then press the ENTER key (Figure 67).

Q&A Are any risks involved in renaming files that are located on a hard disk?

If you inadvertently rename a file that is associated with certain programs, the programs may not be able to find the file and, therefore, may not execute properly. Always use caution when renaming files.

Q&A Can I rename a file when it is open?

No, a file must be closed to change the file name.

Figure 67

Other Ways

1. Select file, press F2, type new file name, press ENTER

To Move a File

At some time, you may want to move a file from one folder, called the source folder, to another, called the destination. When you move a file, it no longer appears in the original folder. If the destination and the source folders are on the same disk drive, you can move a file by dragging it. If the folders are on different disk drives, then you will need to right-drag the file. The following step moves the Koala Exhibit Volunteers file from the Publisher folder to the CIS 101 folder.

1

- In Windows Explorer, if necessary, navigate to the location of the file to be moved (in this case, the Publisher folder in the CIS 101 folder [or your class folder] on the USB flash drive).

- If necessary, click the Publisher folder in the navigation pane to display the files it contains in the right pane.

- Drag the Koala Exhibit Volunteers file in the right pane to the CIS 101 folder in the navigation pane and notice the ScreenTip as you drag the mouse (Figure 68).

Figure 68

Other Ways

1. Right-click file, drag file to destination folder, click Move here
2. Right-click file to move, click Cut on shortcut menu, right-click destination
   folder, click Paste on shortcut menu
3. Select file to move, press CTRL+X, select destination folder, press CTRL+V

To Delete a File

A final task you may want to perform is to delete a file. Exercise extreme caution when deleting a file or files. When you delete a file from a hard disk, the deleted file is stored in the Recycle Bin where you can recover it until you empty the Recycle Bin. If you delete a file from removable media, such as a USB flash drive, the file is deleted permanently. The next steps delete the Koala Exhibit Volunteers file from the CIS 101 folder.

 1

- In Windows Explorer, navigate to the location of the file to be deleted (in this case, the CIS 101 folder [or your class folder] on the USB flash drive).

- If necessary, click the CIS 101 folder in the navigation pane to display the files it contains in the right pane.

- Right-click the Koala Exhibit Volunteers icon or file name in the right pane to select the file and display a shortcut menu (Figure 69).

Figure 69

 2

- Click Delete on the shortcut menu to display the Delete File dialog box (Figure 70).

- Click the Yes button (Delete File dialog box) to delete the selected file.

Q&A

Can I use this same technique to delete a folder?

Yes. Right-click the folder and then click Delete on the shortcut menu. When you delete a folder, all of the files and folders contained in the folder you are deleting, together with any files and folders on lower hierarchical levels, are deleted as well.

Figure 70

Other Ways

1. Select icon, press DELETE

Microsoft Office and Windows Help

At any time while you are using one of the Microsoft Office 2010 programs, such as Publisher, you can use Office Help to display information about all topics associated with the program. This section illustrates the use of Publisher Help. Help in other Office 2010 programs operates in a similar fashion.

In Office 2010, Help is presented in a window that has Web-browser-style navigation buttons. Each Office 2010 program has its own Help home page, which is the starting Help page that is displayed in the Help window. If your computer is connected to the Internet, the contents of the Help page reflect both the local help files installed on the computer and material from Microsoft's Web site.

To Open the Help Window in an Office Program

The following step opens the Publisher Help window. The step to open a Help window in other Office programs is similar.

- Start Publisher.

- Click the Microsoft Publisher Help button near the upper-right corner of the Backstage view to open the Publisher Help window. Click the Home button (Figure 71).

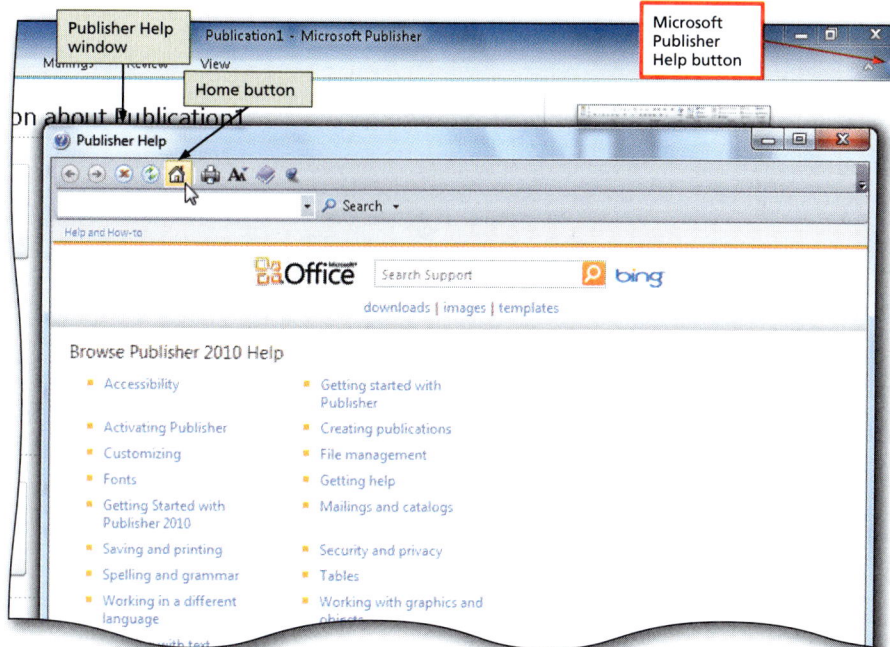

Figure 71

Other Ways
1. Press F1

Moving and Resizing Windows

Up to this point, this chapter has used minimized and maximized windows. At times, however, it is useful, or even necessary, to have more than one window open and visible on the screen at the same time. You can resize and move these open windows so that you can view different areas of and elements in the window. In the case of the Help window, for example, it could be covering objects in the Publisher window that you need to see.

To Move a Window by Dragging

You can move any open window that is not maximized to another location on the desktop by dragging the title bar of the window. The step on the next page drags the Publisher Help window to the top left of the desktop.

1

● Drag the window title bar (the Publisher Help window title bar, in this case) so that the window moves to the top left of the desktop, as shown in Figure 72.

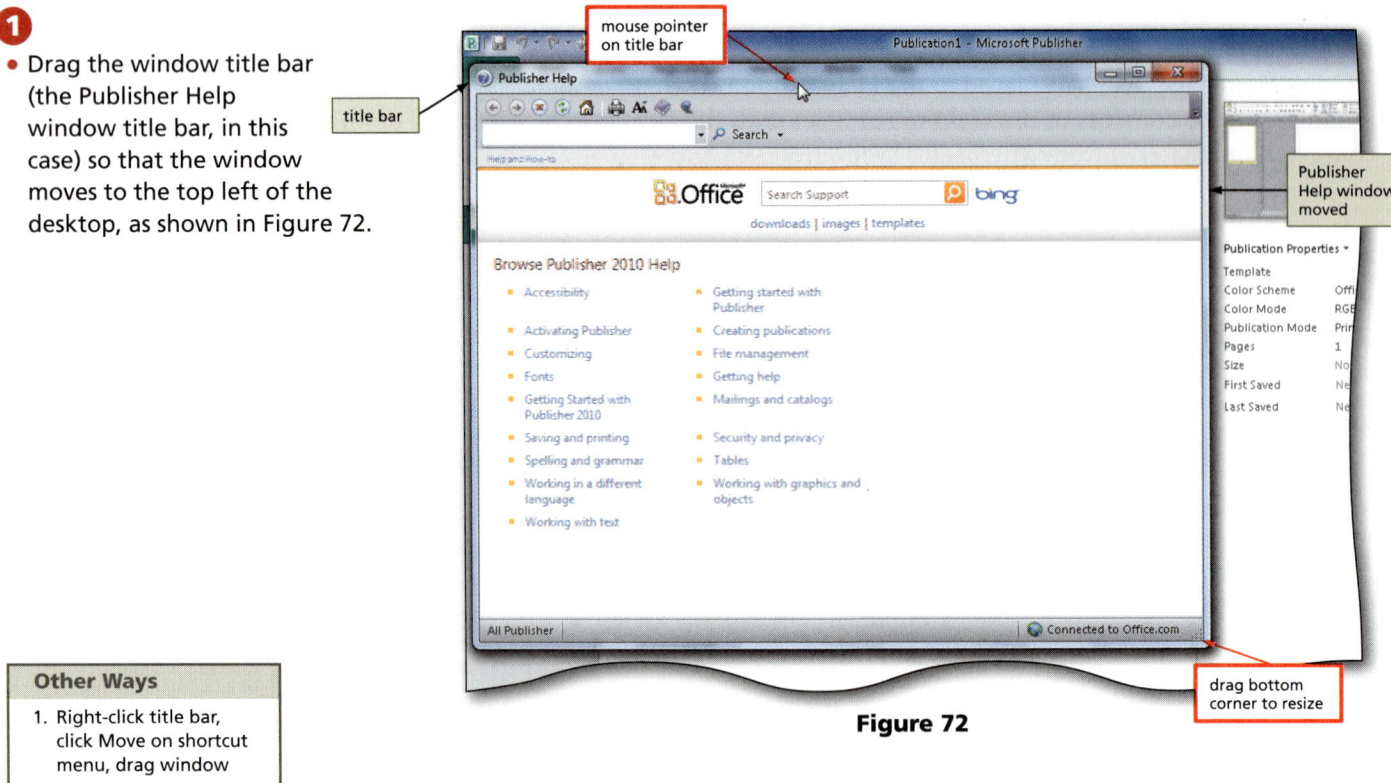

Figure 72

Other Ways

1. Right-click title bar, click Move on shortcut menu, drag window

To Resize a Window by Dragging

Sometimes, information is not visible completely in a window. A method used to change the size of the window is to drag the window borders. The following step changes the size of the Publisher Help window by dragging its borders.

1

● Point to the lower-right corner of the window (the Publisher Help window, in this case) until the mouse pointer changes to a two-headed arrow.

● Drag the bottom border downward to display more of the active window (Figure 73).

Q&A Can I drag other borders on the window to enlarge or shrink the window?

Yes, you can drag the left, right, and top borders and any window corner to resize a window.

Q&A Will Windows 7 remember the new size of the window after I close it?

Yes. When you reopen the window, Windows 7 will display it at the same size it was when you closed it.

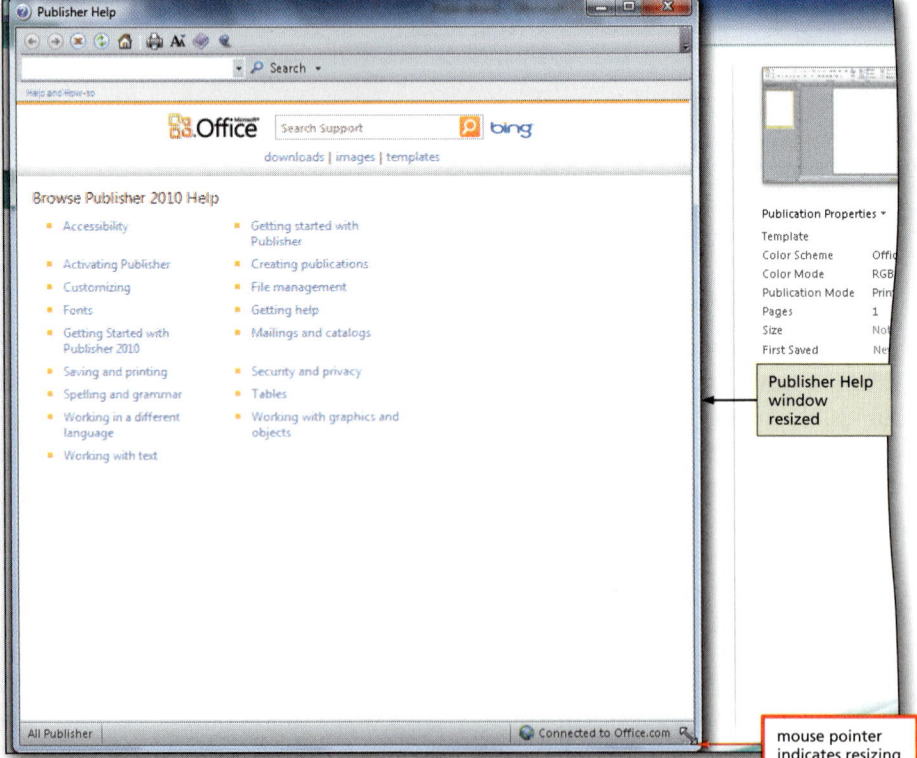

Figure 73

Using Office Help

Once an Office program's Help window is open, several methods exist for navigating Help. You can search for help by using any of the three following methods from the Help window:

1. Enter search text in the 'Type words to search for' text box.
2. Click the links in the Help window.
3. Use the Table of Contents.

To Obtain Help Using the 'Type words to search for' Text Box

Assume for the following example that you want to know more about the Backstage view. The following steps use the 'Type words to search for' text box to obtain useful information about the Backstage view by entering the word, Backstage, as search text.

1

- Type **Backstage** in the 'Type words to search for' text box at the top of the Publisher Help window to enter the search text.

- Click the Search button arrow to display the Search menu (Figure 74).

- If it is not selected already, click All Publisher on the Search menu, so that Help performs the most complete search of the current program (Publisher, in this case). If All Publisher already is selected, click the Search button arrow again to close the Search menu.

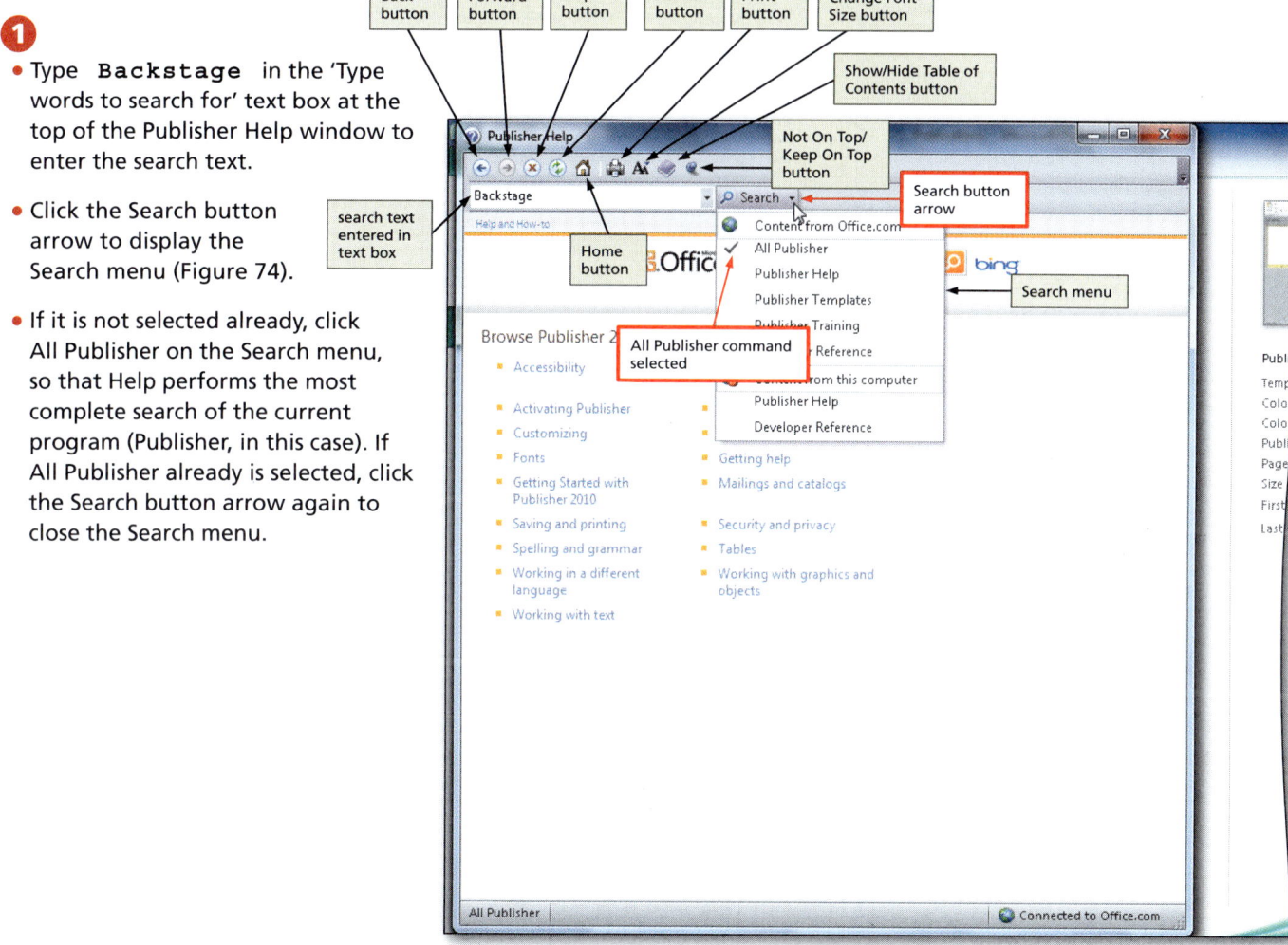

Figure 74

Why select All Publisher on the Search menu?

Selecting All Publisher on the Search menu ensures that Publisher Help will search all possible sources for information about your search term. It will produce the most complete search results.

2

● Click the Search button to display the search results (Figure 75).

Q&A Why do my search results differ?

If you do not have an Internet connection, your results will reflect only the content of the Help files on your computer. When searching for help online, results also can change as material is added, deleted, and updated on the online Help Web pages maintained by Microsoft.

Q&A Why were my search results not very helpful?

When initiating a search, be sure to check the spelling of the search text; also, keep your search specific, with fewer than seven words, to return the most accurate results.

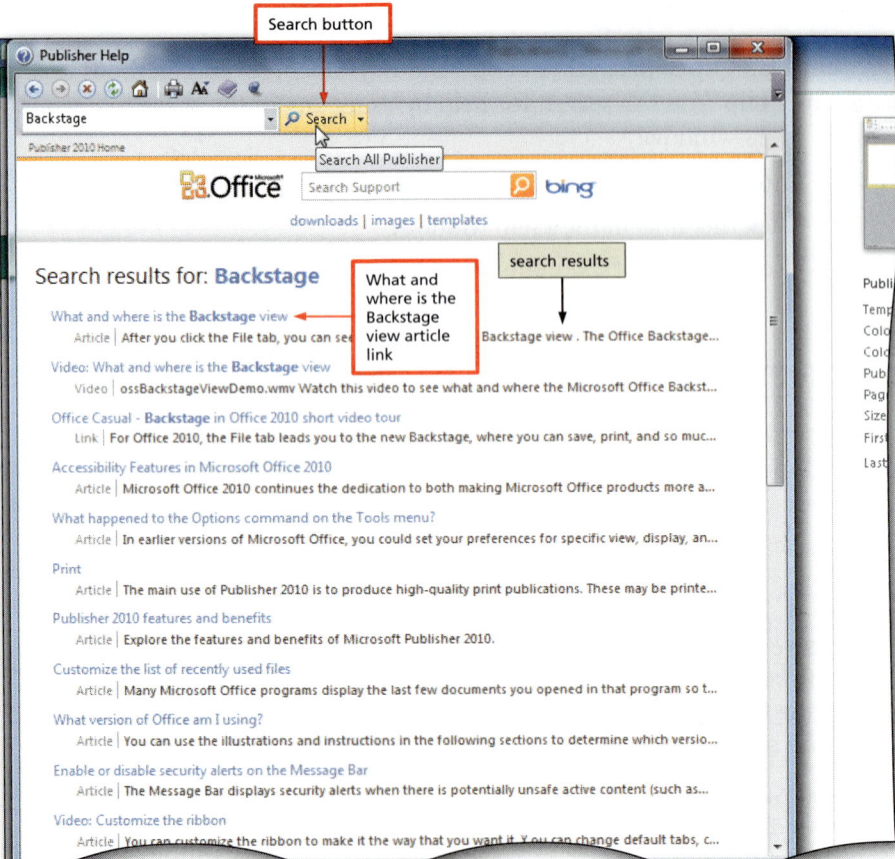

Figure 75

3

● Click the What and where is the Backstage view link to open the Help document associated with the selected topic (Figure 76).

Figure 76

4

- Click the Home button on the toolbar to clear the search results and redisplay the Help home page (Figure 77).

Figure 77

To Obtain Help Using the Help Links

If your topic of interest is listed in the Browse area of the Help window, you can click the link to begin browsing the Help categories instead of entering search text. You browse Help just as you would browse a Web site. If you know which category contains your Help information, you may wish to use these links. The following step finds the Fonts Help information using the category links from the Publisher Help home page.

1

- Click the see all link to display additional Help topics.

- Click the Fonts link to display the Fonts page (Figure 78).

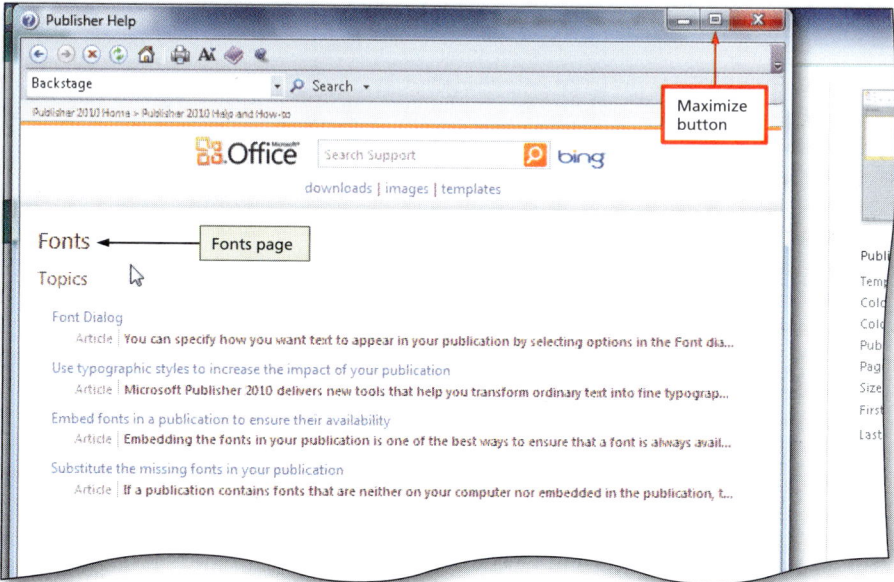

Figure 78

To Obtain Help Using the Help Table of Contents

A third way to find Help in Office programs is through the Help Table of Contents. You can browse through the Table of Contents to display information about a particular topic or to familiarize yourself with an Office program. The following steps access the Help information about themes by browsing through the Table of Contents.

- Click the Home button on the toolbar to display the Help home page.

- Click the Show Table of Contents button on the toolbar to display the Table of Contents pane on the left side of the Help window. If necessary, click the Maximize button on the Help title bar to maximize the window (Figure 79).

Q&A

Why does the appearance of the Show Table of Contents button change?

When the Table of Contents is displayed in the Help window, the Hide Table of Contents button replaces the Show Table of Contents button.

Figure 79

- Click the Creating publications link in the Table of Contents pane to view a list of Help subtopics.

- Click the Building Blocks link in the Table of Contents pane to view the selected Help document in the right pane (Figure 80).

- After reviewing the page, click the Close button to quit Help.

- Click Publisher's Close button to quit Publisher.

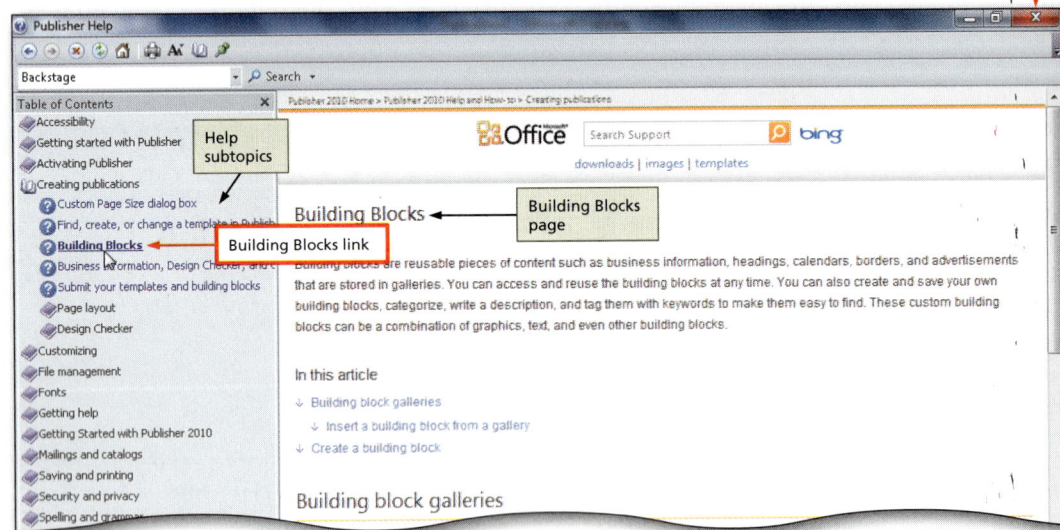

Figure 80

Q&A

How do I remove the Table of Contents pane when I am finished with it?

The Show Table of Contents button acts as a toggle. When the Table of Contents pane is visible, the button changes to Hide Table of Contents. Clicking it hides the Table of Contents pane and changes the button to Show Table of Contents.

Obtaining Help while Working in an Office Program

Help in Office programs, such as Publisher, provides you with the ability to obtain help directly, without the need to open the Help window and initiate a search. For example, you may be unsure about how a particular command works, or you may be presented with a dialog box that you are not sure how to use.

Figure 81 shows one option for obtaining help while working in Publisher. If you want to learn more about a command, point to the command button and wait for the Enhanced ScreenTip to appear. If the Help icon appears in the Enhanced ScreenTip, press the F1 key while pointing to the command to open the Help window associated with that command.

Figure 82 shows a dialog box that contains a Help button. Pressing the F1 key while the dialog box is displayed opens a Help window. The Help window contains help about that dialog box, if available. If no help file is available for that particular dialog box, then the main Help window opens.

Figure 81

Using Windows Help and Support

One of the more powerful Windows 7 features is Windows Help and Support. **Windows Help and Support** is available when using Windows 7 or when using any Microsoft program running under Windows 7. This feature is designed to assist you in using Windows 7 or the various programs. Table 4 describes the content found in the Help and Support Center. The same methods used for searching Microsoft Office Help can be used in Windows Help and Support. The difference is that Windows Help and Support displays help for Windows 7, instead of for Microsoft Office.

Figure 82

Table 4 Windows Help and Support Center Content Areas	
Area	**Function**
Find an answer quickly	This area contains instructions about how to do a quick search using the search box.
Not sure where to start?	This area displays three topics to help guide a user: How to get started with your computer, Learn about Windows Basics, and Browse Help topics. Clicking one of the options navigates to corresponding Help and Support pages.
More on the Windows Website	This area contains links to online content from the Windows Web site. Clicking the links navigates to the corresponding Web pages on the Web site.

To Start Windows Help and Support

The steps on the next page start Windows Help and Support and display the Windows Help and Support window, containing links to more information about Windows 7.

- Click the Start button on the taskbar to display the Start menu (Figure 83).

Q&A Why are the programs that are displayed on the Start menu different?

Windows adds the programs you have used recently to the left pane on the Start menu. You have started Publisher while performing the steps in this chapter, so that program now is displayed on the Start menu.

Figure 83

- Click Help and Support on the Start menu to open the Windows Help and Support window (Figure 84).

- After reviewing the Windows Help and Support window, click the Close button to quit Windows Help and Support.

Other Ways

1. Press CTRL+ESC, press RIGHT ARROW, press UP ARROW, press ENTER
2. Press WINDOWS+F1

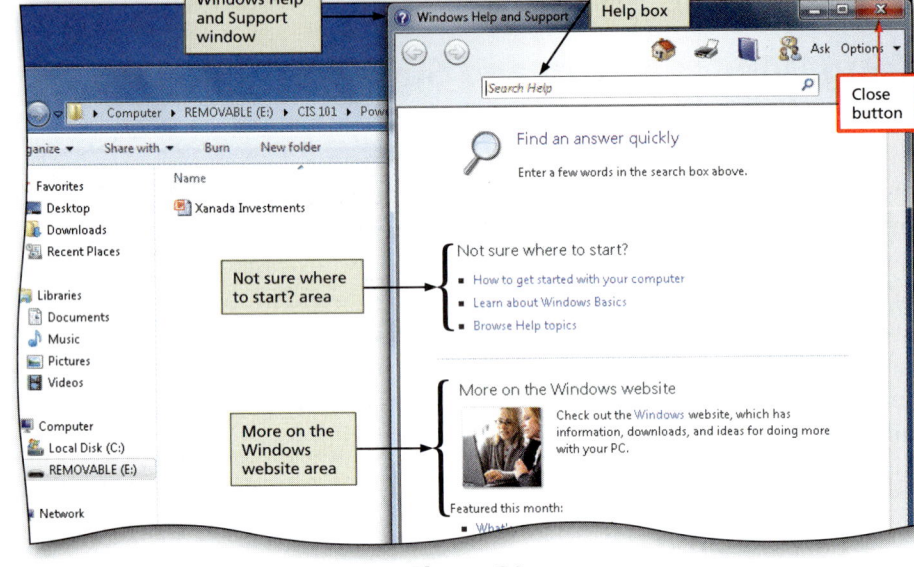

Figure 84

Chapter Summary

In this chapter, you learned about the Windows 7 interface. You started Windows 7, were introduced to the components of the desktop, and learned several mouse operations. You opened, closed, moved, resized, minimized, maximized, and scrolled a window. You used folder windows to expand and collapse drives and folders, display drive and folder contents, create folders, and rename and then delete a file.

You also learned some basic features of Microsoft Publisher 2010. As part of this learning process, you discovered the common elements that exist among Microsoft Office programs.

Microsoft Office Help was demonstrated using Publisher, and you learned how to use the Publisher Help window. You were introduced to the Windows 7 Help and Support Center and learned how to use it to obtain more information about Windows 7.

The items listed below include all of the new Windows 7 and Publisher 2010 skills you have learned in this chapter.

1. Log On to the Computer (OFF 6)
2. Start a Program Using the Start Menu (OFF 10)
3. Maximize a Window (OFF 12)
4. Display a Different Tab on the Ribbon (OFF 16)
5. Minimize, Display, and Restore the Ribbon (OFF 16)
6. Display and Use a Shortcut Menu (OFF 17)
7. Customize the Quick Access Toolbar (OFF 18)
8. Enter Text in a Blank Publication (OFF 19)
9. Create a Folder (OFF 20)
10. Create a Folder within a Folder (OFF 23)
11. Expand a Folder, Scroll through Folder Contents, and Collapse a Folder (OFF 23)
12. Switch from One Program to Another (OFF 24)
13. Save a File in a Folder (OFF 25)
14. Minimize and Restore a Window (OFF 27)
15. Change the Screen Resolution (OFF 30)
16. Quit a Program with One Publication Open (OFF 31)
17. Start a Program Using the Search Box (OFF 32)
18. Open an Existing file from the Backstage View (OFF 33)
19. Create a New Publication from the Backstage View (OFF 35)
20. Close a File Using the Backstage View (OFF 36)
21. Open a Recent File Using the Backstage View (OFF 36)
22. Create a New Blank Document from Windows Explorer (OFF 37)
23. Start a Program from Windows Explorer and Open a File (OFF 38)
24. Save an Existing Publication with the Same File Name (OFF 39)
25. Rename a File (OFF 40)
26. Move a File (OFF 41)
27. Delete a File (OFF 42)
28. Open the Help Window in an Office Program (OFF 43)
29. Move a Window by Dragging (OFF 43)
30. Resize a Window by Dragging (OFF 44)
31. Obtain Help Using the 'Type words to search for' Text Box (OFF 45)
32. Obtain Help Using the Help Links (OFF 47)
33. Obtain Help Using the Help Table of Contents (OFF 48)
34. Start Windows Help and Support (OFF 49)

Learn It Online

Test your knowledge of chapter content and key terms.

Instructions: To complete the Learn It Online exercises, start your browser, click the Address bar, and then enter the Web address `scsite.com/pub2010/learn`. When the Office 2010 Learn It Online page is displayed, click the link for the exercise you want to complete and then read the instructions.

Chapter Reinforcement TF, MC, and SA

A series of true/false, multiple choice, and short answer questions that test your knowledge of the chapter content.

Flash Cards

An interactive learning environment where you identify chapter key terms associated with displayed definitions.

Practice Test

A series of multiple choice questions that test your knowledge of chapter content and key terms.

Who Wants To Be a Computer Genius?

An interactive game that challenges your knowledge of chapter content in the style of a television quiz show.

Wheel of Terms

An interactive game that challenges your knowledge of chapter key terms in the style of the television show *Wheel of Fortune*.

Crossword Puzzle Challenge

A crossword puzzle that challenges your knowledge of key terms presented in the chapter.

Apply Your Knowledge

Reinforce the skills and apply the concepts you learned in this chapter.

Creating a Folder and a Publication

Instructions: You will create a Publisher folder and then create a Publisher publication and save it in the folder.

Perform the following tasks:

1. Connect a USB flash drive to an available USB port and then open the USB flash drive window.

2. Click the New folder button on the toolbar to display a new folder icon and text box for the folder name.

3. Type **Publisher** in the text box to name the folder. Press the ENTER key to create the folder on the USB flash drive.

4. Start Publisher and click the Home tab.

5. Enter the text shown in Figure 85.

6. Click the Save button on the Quick Access Toolbar. Navigate to the Publisher folder on the USB flash drive and then save the publication using the file name, Apply 1 Class List.

7. If your Quick Access Toolbar does not show the Quick Print button, add the Quick Print button to the Quick Access Toolbar. Print the publication using the Quick Print button on the Quick Access Toolbar. When you are finished printing, remove the Quick Print button from the Quick Access Toolbar.

8. Submit the printout to your instructor.

9. Quit Publisher.

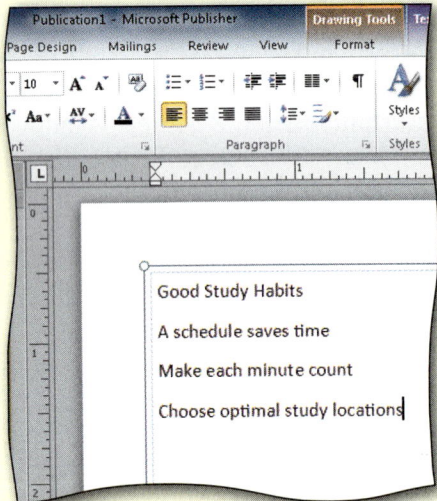

Figure 85

Extend Your Knowledge

Extend the skills you learned in this chapter and experiment with new skills. You will use Help to complete the assignment.

Using Help

Instructions: Use Publisher Help to perform the following tasks.

Perform the following tasks:

1. Start Publisher.

2. Click the Microsoft Publisher Help button to open the Publisher Help window (Figure 86).

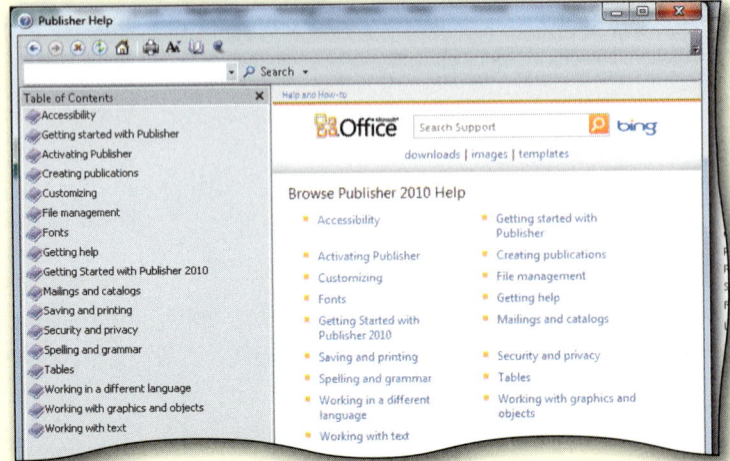

Figure 86

3. Search Publisher Help to answer the following questions.

   a. What are three features new to Publisher 2010?

   b. What type of training courses are available through Help?

   c. What are the steps to add a new group to the Ribbon?

   d. What are Building Blocks?

   e. What are publication properties?

   f. What is a template?

   g. How do you print a publication?

   h. What type of graphics can you insert in a publication?

   i. What is cropping?

   j. What is the purpose of the Page Navigation pane?

4. Submit the answers from your searches in the format specified by your instructor.

5. Quit Publisher.

Make It Right

Analyze a file structure and correct all errors and/or improve the design.

Organizing Vacation Photos

Note: To complete this assignment, you will be required to use the Data Files for Students. See the inside back cover of this book for instructions on downloading the Data Files for Students, or contact your instructor for information about accessing the required files.

Instructions: Traditionally, you have stored photos from past vacations together in one folder. The photos are becoming difficult to manage, and you now want to store them in appropriate folders. You will create the folder structure shown in Figure 87. You then will move the photos to the folders so that they will be organized properly.

1. Connect a USB flash drive to an available USB port to open the USB flash drive window.

2. Create the hierarchical folder structure shown in Figure 87.

3. Move one photo to each folder in the folder structure you created in Step 2. The five photos are available on the Data Files for Students.

4. Submit your work in the format specified by your instructor.

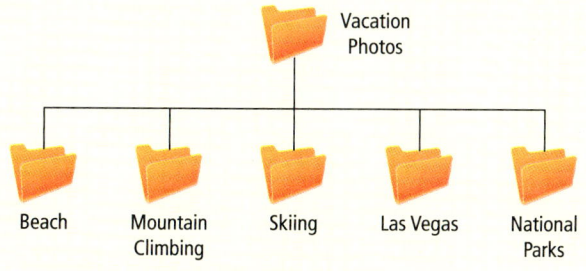

Figure 87

In the Lab

Use the guidelines, concepts, and skills presented in this chapter to increase your knowledge of Windows 7 and Publisher 2010. Labs are listed in order of increasing difficulty.

Lab 1: Using Windows Help and Support

Problem: You have a few questions about using Windows 7 and would like to answer these questions using Windows Help and Support.

Instructions: Use Windows Help and Support to perform the following tasks:

1. Display the Start menu and then click Help and Support to start Windows Help and Support.

2. Use the Help and Support Content page to answer the following questions.

   a. How do you reduce computer screen flicker?

   b. Which dialog box do you use to change the appearance of the mouse pointer?

   c. How do you minimize all windows?

   d. What is a VPN?

3. Use the Search Help text box in Windows Help and Support to answer the following questions.

   a. How can you minimize all open windows on the desktop?

   b. How do you start a program using the Run command?

   c. What are the steps to add a toolbar to the taskbar?

   d. What wizard do you use to remove unwanted desktop icons?

4. The tools to solve a problem while using Windows 7 are called **troubleshooters**. Use Windows Help and Support to find the list of troubleshooters (Figure 88), and answer the following questions.

   a. What problems does the HomeGroup troubleshooter allow you to resolve?

   b. List five Windows 7 troubleshooters that are not listed in Figure 88.

5. Use Windows Help and Support to obtain information about software licensing and product activation, and answer the following questions.

   a. What is genuine Windows?

   b. What is activation?

   c. What steps are required to activate Windows?

   d. What steps are required to read the Microsoft Software License Terms?

   e. Can you legally make a second copy of Windows 7 for use at home, work, or on a mobile computer or device?

   f. What is registration?

6. Close the Windows Help and Support window.

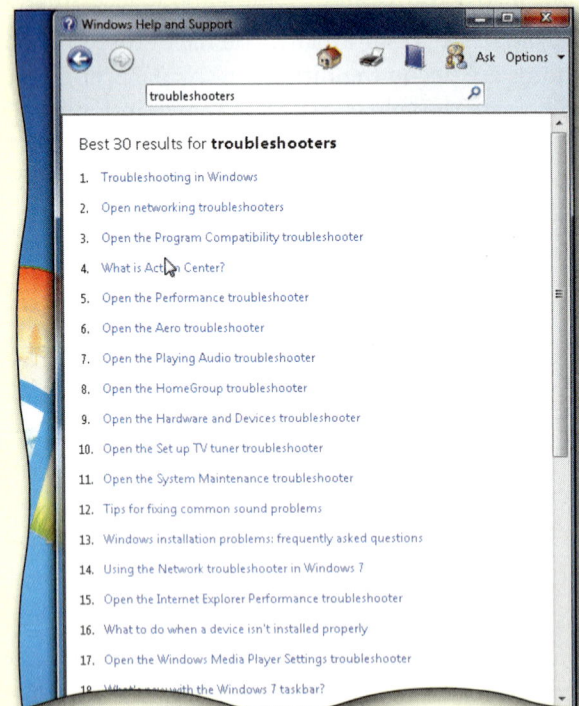

Figure 88

In the Lab

Lab 2: Creating Folders for a Pet Supply Store

Problem: Your friend works for Pete's Pet Supplies. He would like to organize his files in relation to the types of pets available in the store. He has five main categories: dogs, cats, fish, birds, and exotic. You are to create a folder structure similar to Figure 89.

Instructions: Perform the following tasks:

1. Connect a USB flash drive to an available USB port and then open the USB flash drive window.

2. Create the main folder for Pete's Pet Supplies.

3. Navigate to the Pete's Pet Supplies folder.

4. Within the Pete's Pet Supplies folder, create a folder for each of the following: Dogs, Cats, Fish, Birds, and Exotic.

5. Within the Exotic folder, create two additional folders, one for Primates and the second for Reptiles.

6. Submit the assignment in the format specified by your instructor.

Figure 89

In the Lab

Lab 3: Creating Publisher Publications and Saving Them in Appropriate Folders

Problem: You are taking a class that requires you to complete three Publisher chapters. You will save the work completed in each chapter in a different folder (Figure 90).

Instructions: Create the folders shown in Figure 90. Then, using Publisher, create three small files to save in each folder.

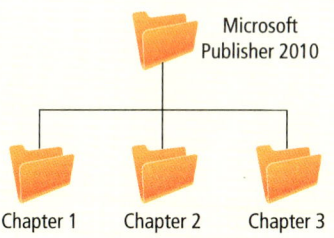

Figure 90

1. Connect a USB flash drive to an available USB port and then open the USB flash drive window.

2. Create the folder structure shown in Figure 90.

3. Navigate to the Chapter 1 folder.

4. Create a Publisher publication containing the text, My Chapter 1 Publisher Publication, and then save it in the Chapter 1 folder using the file name, Publisher Chapter 1 Publication.

5. Navigate to the Chapter 2 folder.

6. Create another Publisher publication containing the text, My Chapter 2 Publisher Publication, and then save it in the Chapter 2 folder using the file name, Publisher Chapter 2 Publication.

7. Navigate to the Chapter 3 folder.

8. Create another Publisher publication containing the text, My Chapter 3 Publisher Publication, and then save it in the Chapter 3 folder using the file name, Publisher Chapter 3 Publication.

9. Quit Publisher.

10. Submit the assignment in the format specified by your instructor.

Cases and Places

Apply your creative thinking and problem solving skills to design and implement a solution.

Note: To complete these assignments, you may be required to use the Data Files for Students. See the inside back cover of this book for instructions on downloading the Data Files for Students, or contact your instructor for information about accessing the required files.

1: Creating Beginning Files for Classes

Academic

You are taking the following classes: Introduction to Engineering, Beginning Psychology, Introduction to Biology, and Accounting. Create folders for each of the classes. Use the following folder names: Engineering, Psychology, Biology, and Accounting, when creating the folder structure. In the Engineering folder, use Publisher to create a publication with the name of the class and the class meeting location and time (MW 10:30 – 11:45, Room 317). In the Psychology folder, use Publisher to create a publication containing the text, Behavioral Observations. In the Biology folder, use Publisher to create a publication with the title Research in the Biology folder. In the Accounting folder, create a Publisher publication with the text, Tax Information. Use the concepts and techniques presented in this chapter to create the folders and files.

2: Using Help

Personal

Your parents enjoy working and playing games on their home computers. Your mother uses a notebook computer downstairs, and your father uses a desktop computer upstairs. They expressed interest in sharing files between their computers and sharing a single printer, so you offered to research various home networking options. Start Windows Help and Support, and search Help using the keywords, home networking. Use the link for installing a printer on a home network. Start Publisher, click the Home tab, and then type the main steps for installing a printer. Use the link for setting up a HomeGroup and then type the main steps for creating a HomeGroup in the Publisher publication. Use the concepts and techniques presented in this chapter to use Help and create the Publisher publication.

3: Creating Folders

Professional

Your boss at the bookstore where you work part-time has asked for help with organizing her files. After looking through the files, you decided upon a file structure for her to use, including the following folders: books, magazines, tapes, DVDs, and general merchandise. Within the books folder, create folders for hardback and paperback books. Within magazines, create folders for special issues and periodicals. In the tapes folder, create folders for celebrity and major release. In the DVDs folder, create a folder for book to DVD. In the general merchandise folder, create folders for novelties, posters, and games. Use the concepts and techniques presented in this chapter to create the folders.

1 | Creating a Flyer

Objectives

You will have mastered the material in this chapter when you can:

- Choose Publisher template options
- Describe the Publisher window
- Select objects and zoom
- Replace Publisher template text
- Create a bulleted list and synchronize objects
- Format fonts and autofit
- Delete objects
- Insert and format a photo

- Insert and format a building block
- Move, resize, and align objects
- Change publication properties
- Print a publication
- Open and modify a publication
- Check spelling as you type
- Save a print publication as a Web publication

1 | Creating a Flyer

Introduction

To publicize an event, advertise a sale or service, promote a business, or convey a message to the community, you may want to create a **flyer** and post it in a public location. These single-page publications printed on various sizes of paper announce personal items for sale or rent (car, boat, apartment); garage or block sales; services being offered (housecleaning, lessons, carpooling); membership, sponsorship, or donation requests (club, religious organization, charity); and other messages. Flyers are an inexpensive means of reaching the community, yet many go unnoticed because they are designed poorly. A good flyer, or any publication, must deliver a message in the clearest, most attractive and effective way possible. You must clarify your purpose and know your target audience. You need to gather ideas and plan for the printing. Finally, you must edit, proofread, and then publish your flyer. Flyers must stand out to be noticed.

Flyers also can be posted on the Web. Electronic bulletin boards, social networking Web sites, and online auction Web sites are good places to reach people with flyers, advertising everything from a bake sale to a part-time job.

To illustrate the features of Publisher, this book presents a series of projects that create publications similar to those you will encounter in academic and business environments.

Project Planning Guidelines

> The process of developing a publication that communicates specific information requires careful analysis and planning. As a starting point, establish why the publication is needed. Once you establish the purpose, analyze the intended audience and its unique needs. Then, gather information about the topic and decide what to include in the publication. Define a plan for printing, including printer, color, paper, and number of copies. Finally, determine the publication design, layout, and style that will be most successful at delivering the message. After editing and proofreading, your publication is ready to print or upload to the Web. Details of these guidelines are provided in Appendix A. In addition, each project in this book provides practical applications of these planning considerations.

Project — Flyer Publication

The project in this chapter uses Publisher and a flyer template to create the flyer shown in Figure 1–1. This colorful flyer advertises an apartment for rent, close to campus. The **headline** clearly identifies the purpose of the flyer, using large, bold letters. Below that, a contrasting font is used for the bulleted list. The name of the rental agency and a tagline appear above the headline. The photo of the apartment is formatted to be eye-catching and entices people to stop and look at the flyer. An attention getter, positioned in proximity to the bulleted items, highlights an important selling point of the apartment. The tear-offs, aligned at the bottom of the flyer, include the e-mail address and telephone number of the apartment contact. Finally, the font and color schemes make the text in the attention getter stand out.

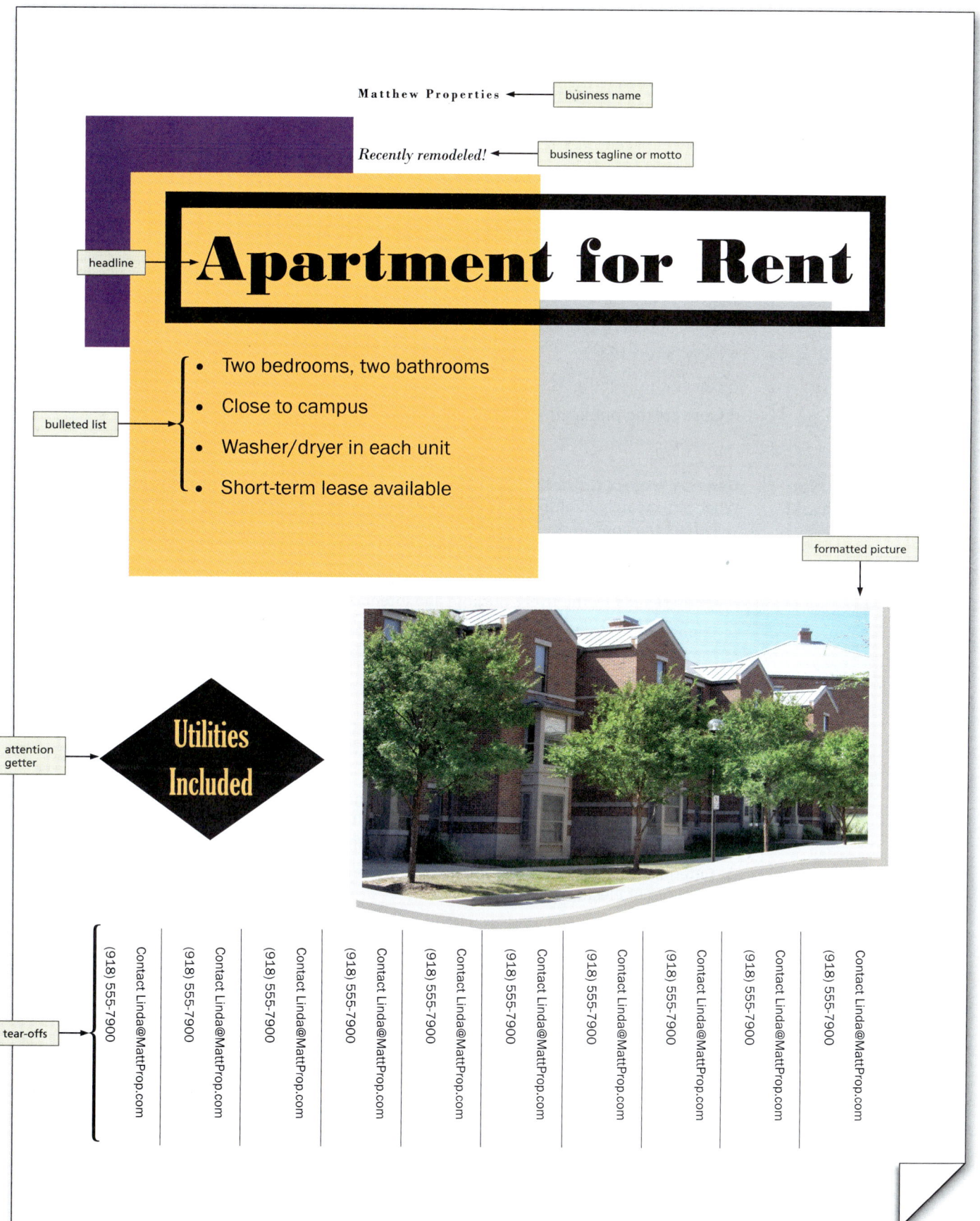

Figure 1–1

Overview

As you read this chapter, you will learn how to create the flyer shown in Figure 1–1 on the previous page by performing these general tasks:

- Choose a template and select schemes and components.
- Replace placeholder text in the publication.
- Replace the template graphic.
- Delete unused objects.
- Insert an attention getter.
- Save the publication.
- Print the publication.
- Close and then reopen the publication.
- Draw a text box.
- Check the spelling as you type.
- Convert the publication to a Web flyer.

Plan Ahead

> **General Project Guidelines**
>
> When you create a Publisher publication, the actions you perform and decisions you make will affect the appearance and characteristics of the finished publication. As you create a flyer, such as the one shown in Figure 1–1, you should follow these general guidelines:
>
> 1. **Select template options.** The choice of an appropriate template, font, and color scheme is determined by the flyer's purpose and intended audience.
>
> 2. **Choose words for the text.** Follow the *less is more* principle. The less text, the more likely the flyer will be read. Use as few words as possible to make a point.
>
> 3. **Identify how to format various objects in the flyer.** The overall appearance of a publication significantly affects its capability to communicate clearly. Examples of how you can format or modify the appearance of text include changing its shape, size, color, and position on the page. Formatting a graphic might include editing its borders, shadows, style, size, and location.
>
> 4. **Find the appropriate graphic.** An eye-catching graphic should convey the flyer's overall message. It might show a product, service, result, or benefit, or it might convey a message visually that is not expressed easily with words.
>
> 5. **Determine the best method for distributing the document.** Documents can be distributed on paper or electronically.
>
> 6. **Decide if the flyer will work as a Web publication.** The flyer should grab the attention of visitors to the Web site and draw them into reading the flyer.
>
> When necessary, more specific details concerning the above guidelines are presented at appropriate points in the chapter. The chapter also will identify the actions performed and decisions made regarding these guidelines during the creation of the flyer shown in Figure 1–1.

For an introduction to Office 2010 and instruction about how to perform basic tasks in Office 2010 programs, read the Office 2010 and Windows 7 chapter at the beginning of this book, where you can learn how to start a program, use the Ribbon, save a file, open a file, quit a program, use Help, and much more.

To Start Publisher

If you are using a computer to step through the project in this chapter and you want your screens to match the figures in this book, you should change your screen's resolution to 1024×768. For information about how to change a computer's resolution, refer to the Office 2010 and Windows 7 chapter at the beginning of this book.

The following steps, which assume Windows 7 is running, start Publisher based on a typical installation. You may need to ask your instructor how to start Publisher for your computer. For a detailed example of the procedure summarized below, refer to the Office 2010 and Windows 7 chapter.

1 Click the Start button on the Windows 7 taskbar to display the Start menu.

2 Type **Microsoft Publisher** as the search text in the 'Search programs and files' text box and watch the search results appear on the Start menu.

3 Click Microsoft Publisher 2010 in the search results on the Start menu to start Publisher and display the Backstage view.

4 If the Publisher window is not maximized, click the Maximize button next to the Close button on the Publisher title bar to maximize the window.

BTW
The Ribbon and Screen Resolution
Publisher may change how the groups and buttons within the groups appear on the Ribbon, depending on the computer's screen resolution. Thus, your Ribbon may look different from the ones in this book if you are using a screen resolution other than 1024 × 768.

Creating a Flyer

Publisher provides many ways to begin the process of creating and editing a publication. You can:

- Create a new publication from a design template.
- Create a new publication or a Web page from scratch.
- Create a new publication based on an existing one.
- Open an existing publication.

Choosing the appropriate method depends upon your experience with desktop publishing and on how you have used Publisher in the past.

Because many people find that composing and designing from scratch is a difficult process, Publisher provides templates to assist in publication preparation. Publisher has hundreds of templates for creating professionally designed and unique publications. A **template** is a tool that helps you through the design process by offering you publication options and changing your publication accordingly. A template is similar to a blueprint you can use over and over, filling in the blanks, replacing prewritten text as necessary, and changing the art to fit your needs. In this first project, as you are beginning to learn about the features of Publisher, a series of steps is presented to create a publication using a design template.

BTW
Starting Publisher
When you first start Publisher, the Backstage view usually is open. If it is not, click the File tab on the Ribbon, and then, when the Backstage view opens, click Options. When the Publisher Options dialog box is displayed, click General on the left side of the dialog box and then click to display the check mark in the Show the New template gallery when starting Publisher check box.

Plan Ahead

Select template options.
Publisher organizes flyer templates by purpose. A good flyer must deliver a message in the clearest, most attractive, and most effective way possible. The purpose is to communicate a single concept, notion, or product in a quick, easy-to-read format. The intended audience may be a wide, nonspecific audience, such as those who walk by a community bulletin board, or the audience may be a more narrowly defined, specialized audience, such as those who visit an auction Web site.

You must make four primary choices:

- **Template** – Choose a template that suits the purpose, with headline and graphic placement that attracts your audience. Choose a style that has meaning for the topic.
- **Font Scheme** – Choose a font scheme that gives your flyer a consistent professional appearance and characterizes your subject. Make intentional decisions about the font style and type. Avoid common reading fonts such as Arial, Times New Roman, and Helvetica that are used in other kinds of print publications. Flyers are more effective with stronger or unusual font schemes.

(continued)

BTW
BTWs
For a complete list of the BTWs found in the margins of this book, visit the Publisher 2010 BTW Web page (scsite.com/pub2010/btw).

Plan Ahead

(continued)

- **Color Scheme** – Choose a color scheme that is consistent with your company, client, or purpose. Do you need color or black and white? Think about the plan for printing and the number of copies, in order to select a manageable color scheme. Remember that you can add more visual interest and contrast by bolding the color of text in the scheme; however, keep in mind that too many colors can detract from the flyer and make it difficult to read.

- **Other Options** – Decide if you need a graphic or tear-offs. Will the publication need to be mailed? Might any specific information be difficult for your audience to remember? What kind of tear-off makes sense for your topic and message?

The New Template Gallery

In the Backstage view, Publisher displays the New tab and the New template gallery organized by publication types (Figure 1–2).

Figure 1–2

The New template gallery contains templates and folders of templates organized by publication type. Templates are displayed in the gallery as **thumbnails**, or small images. When you click a folder, it opens and displays thumbnails and other folders organized by category (for example, Marketing). It also displays a preview of the selected template, along with customization options (Figure 1–4).

To Select a Template

The following steps select a template from the New template gallery.

 1

- Drag the scroll box down to show additional folders in the gallery.

- Point to Flyers to highlight it (Figure 1–3).

Q&A

Why does my gallery of folders look different?

Someone may have downloaded additional templates on your computer. Or, your resolution may be different. Thus, the size and number of displayed thumbnails may vary.

Figure 1–3

 2

- Click Flyers in the More Templates area to display the templates and folders of additional templates (Figure 1–4).

 Experiment

- Scroll through the available templates and click various flyers in the gallery. Watch the preview change in the top-right portion of the Backstage view.

Q&A

Could I use the Apartment for Rent Marketing flyer?

You could, but it does not have the same template features as the one in this chapter.

Figure 1–4

3

- If necessary, scroll down to locate the Real estate area and then click the All Real estate folder to display the thumbnails (Figure 1–5).

Q&A

Can I go back and choose a different category of templates?

Yes, you can click the File tab in the upper-left corner of the gallery, or you can click Home or Flyers to move back to those previous locations.

BTW

Q&As
For a complete list of the Q&As found in many of the step-by-step sequences in this book, visit the Publisher 2010 Q&A Web page (scsite.com/pub2010/qa).

Figure 1–5

4

- Scroll down in the gallery to the More Built-in Templates area. Locate the Blocks thumbnail, below the Informational heading.

- Click the Blocks thumbnail to select it and to show the template preview (Figure 1–6).

Q&A

What else can I do in the New template gallery?

When you click the Installed and Office Online Templates box arrow, you can limit the display to templates installed on your computer or only those online. If you know the name of the template you want, you can type its name in the Search for templates box.

Figure 1–6

Other Ways

1. On New tab in Backstage view, type template name in Search for templates box

Customizing Templates

Once you choose a template, you should make choices about the color scheme, font schemes, and other components of the publication. A **color scheme** is a defined set of colors that complement each other when used in the same publication. Each Publisher color scheme provides four complementary colors. A **font scheme** is a defined set of fonts associated with a publication. A **font**, or typeface, defines the appearance and shape of the letters, numbers, and special characters. A font scheme contains one font for headings and another font for body text and captions. Font schemes make it easy to change all the fonts in a publication to give it a new look. Other customization options allow you to choose to include business information, a mailing address, a graphic, or tear-offs.

To Choose Publication Options

The following steps choose publication options. As you choose customization options, the preview in the upper-right portion of the Backstage view will reflect your choices.

1

- Click the Color scheme box arrow in the Customize area to display the Color scheme gallery (Figure 1–7).

Q&A

What are the individual colors used for in each scheme?

By default, the text will be black and the background will be white in each color scheme. Publisher uses the first and second scheme colors for major color accents within a publication. The third and fourth colors are used for shading and secondary accents.

Figure 1–7

2

- Scroll as necessary and then click the Crocus color scheme to select the color scheme (Figure 1–8).

 Experiment

- Click various color schemes and watch the changes in all of the thumbnails. When you finish experimenting, click the Crocus color scheme.

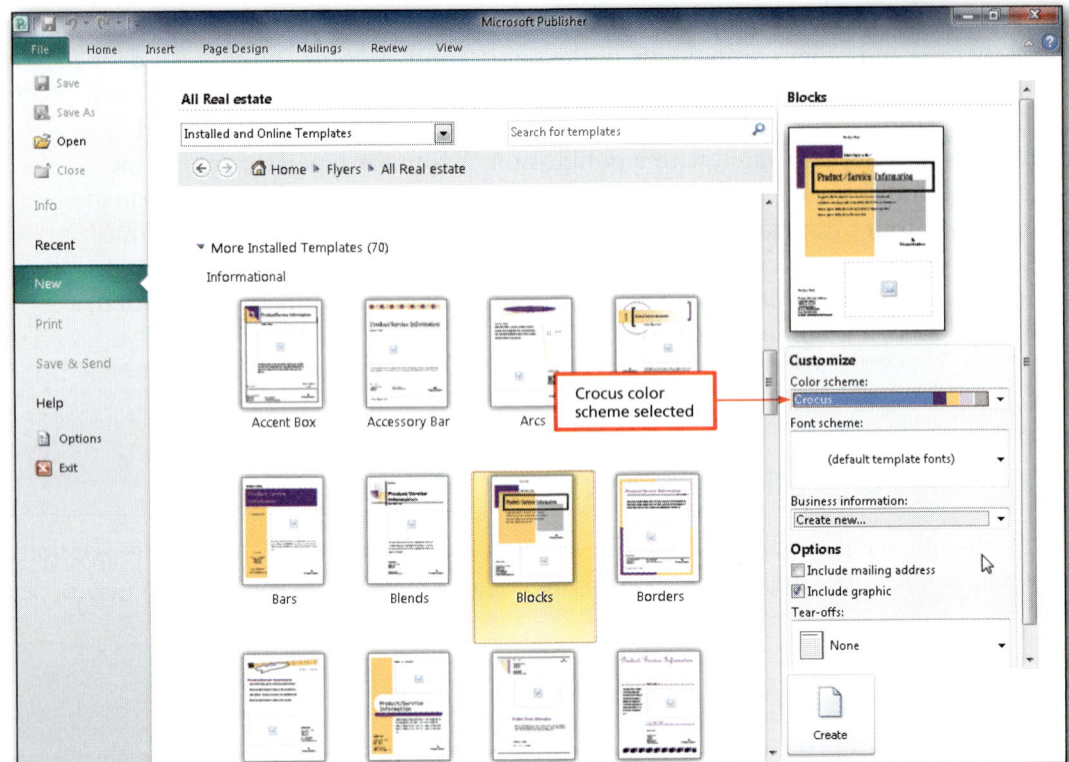

Figure 1–8

3

- Click the Font scheme box arrow in the Customize area to display the Font scheme gallery (Figure 1–9).

Q&A

What are the three items listed in each scheme?

The first line is the generic name of the scheme. Below that, both a major font and a minor font are specified. Generally, a major font is used for titles and headings, and a minor font is used for body text.

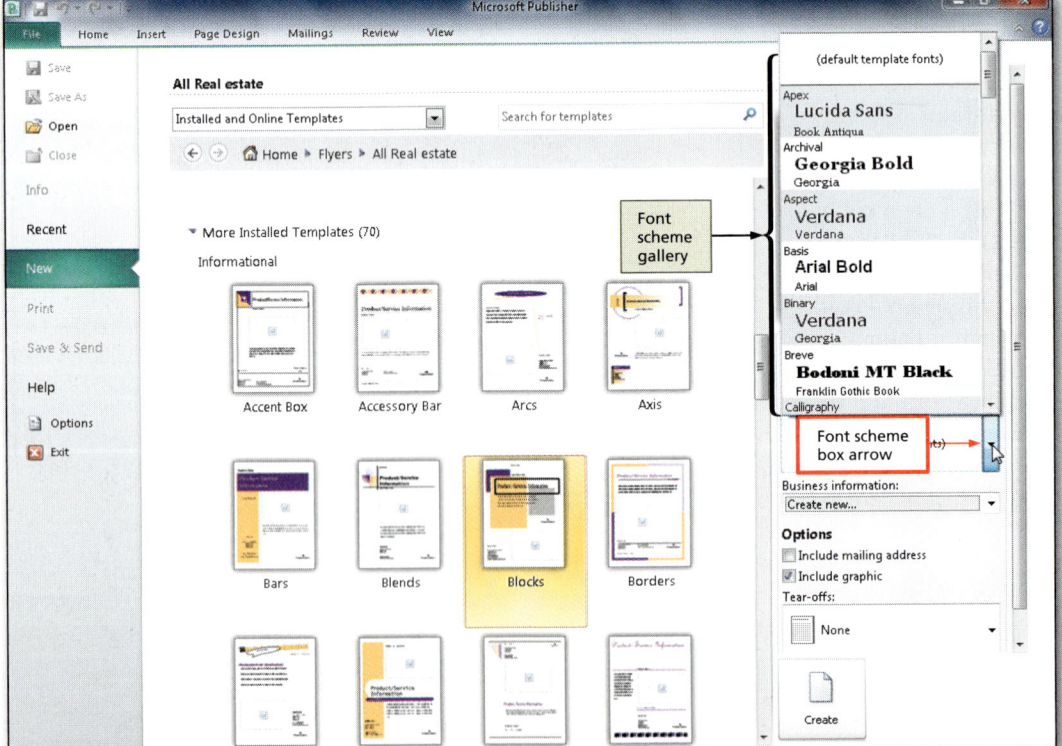

Figure 1–9

4

• Scroll as necessary in the list, and then click Breve to select the font scheme (Figure 1–10).

Q&A How are the font schemes organized?

The schemes are first organized by group, such as Built-In or Built-In Classic, and within the group they are alphabetized by name.

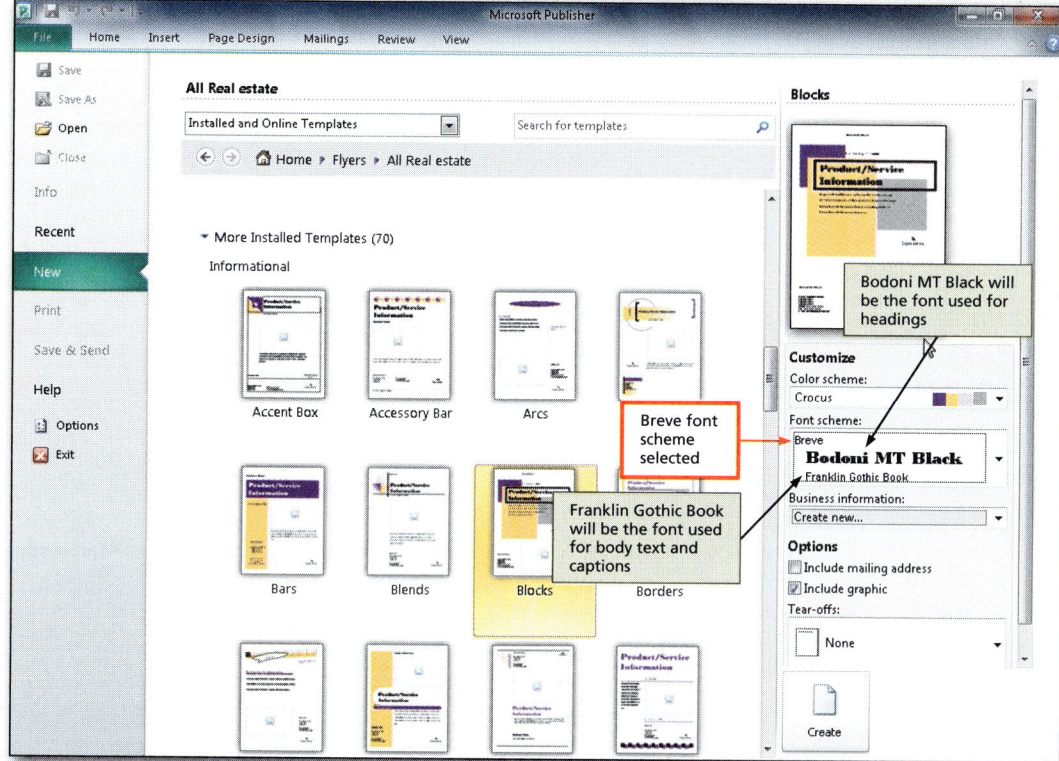

Figure 1–10

5

• Click the Tear-offs box arrow in the Options area to display the Tear-offs gallery (Figure 1–11).

Q&A What are the other kinds of tear-offs?

You can choose to display tear-offs for coupons, order forms, response forms, and sign-up forms.

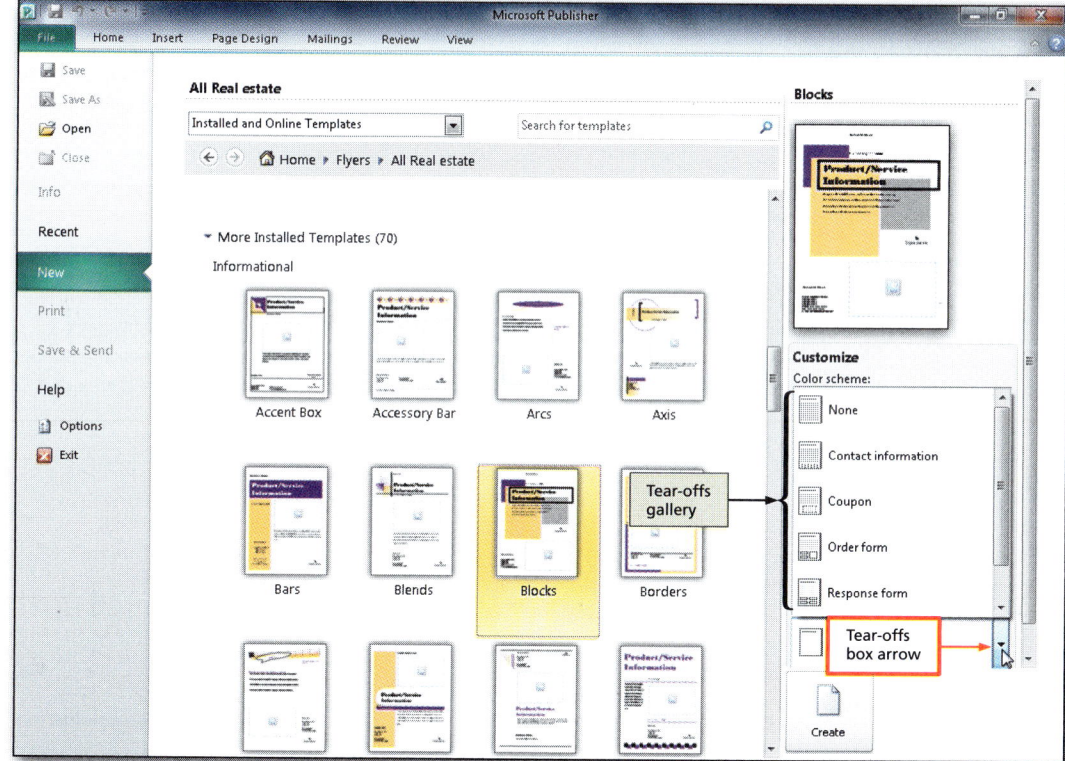

Figure 1–11

6

● Click Contact information in the list to select tear-offs that will display contact information (Figure 1–12).

Q&A Should I change the check boxes in the Options area?

No, the flyer you created in this chapter uses the default settings of no mailing address, but includes a graphic.

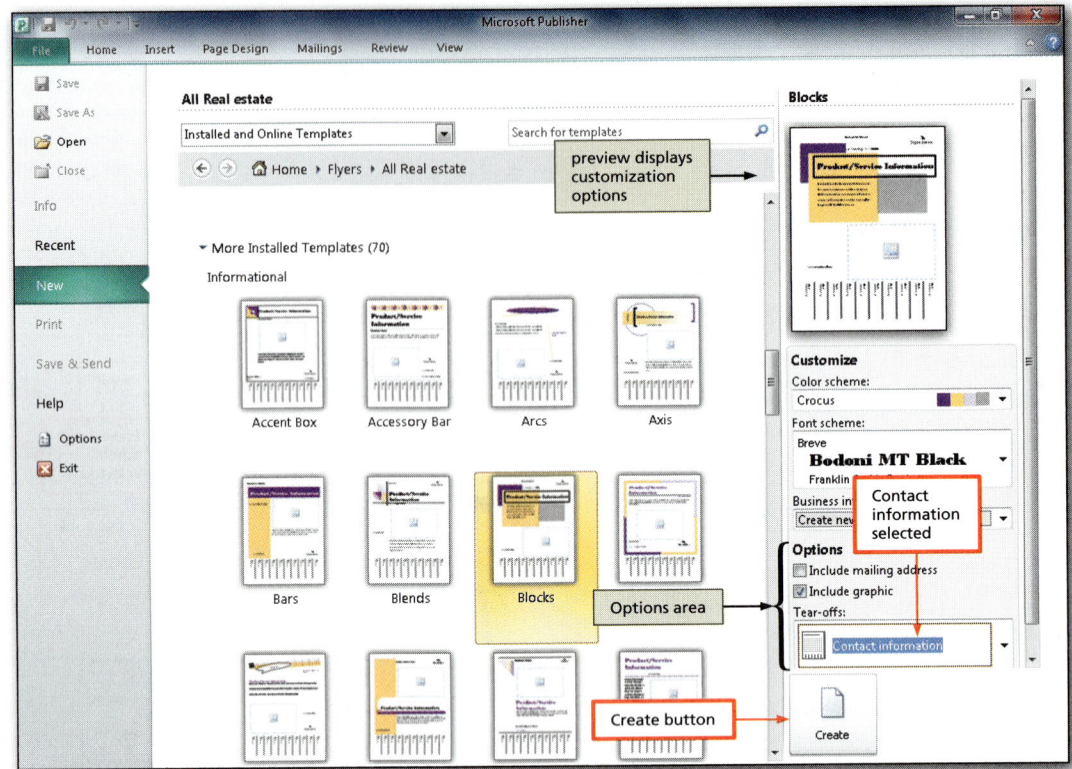

Figure 1–12

7

● Click the Create button to create the publication using the selected template and options (Figure 1–13).

Q&A Is there a way to go back if you change your mind?

You can click File on the Ribbon and start a new publication, or you can make changes to the template, font scheme, color scheme, and other options using the Ribbon, as you will see in this and subsequent chapters.

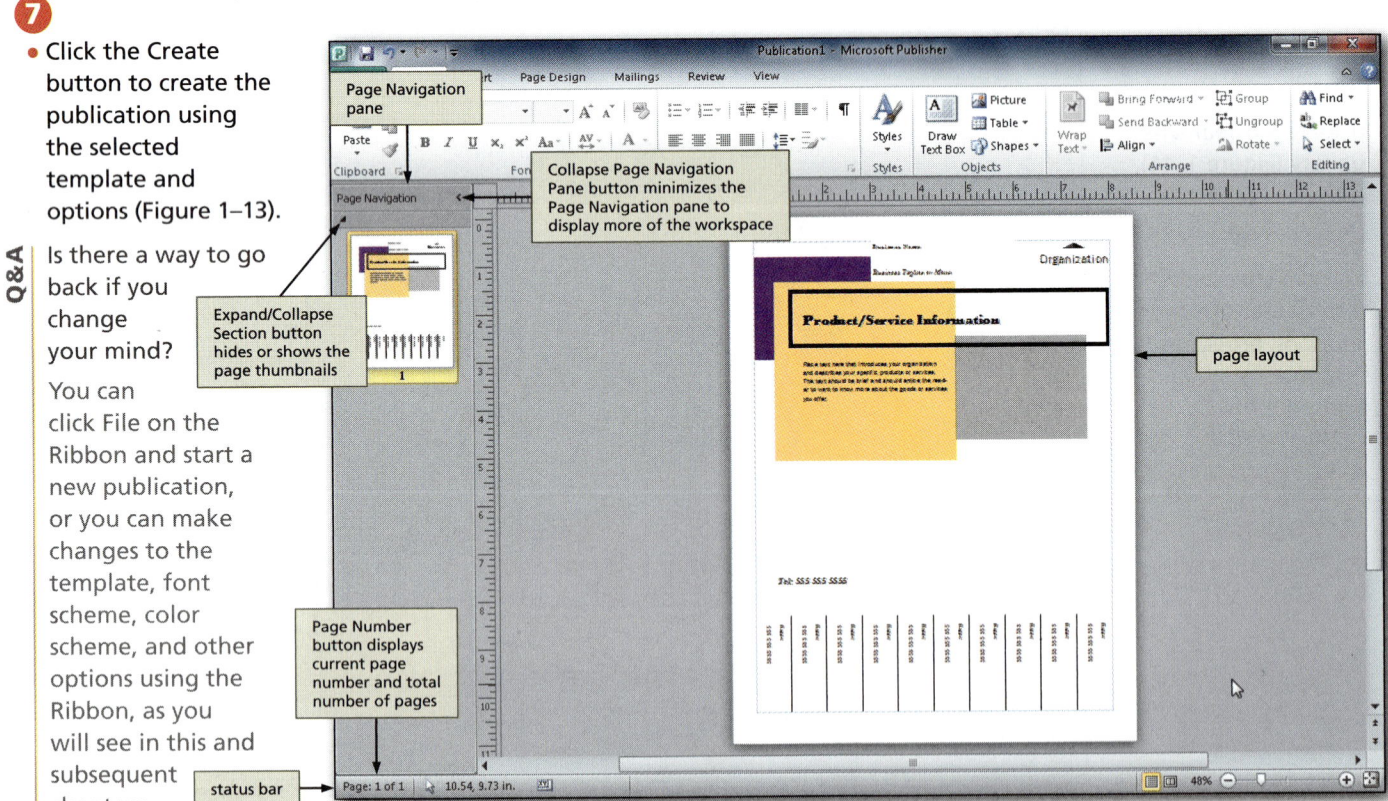

Figure 1–13

To Hide the Page Navigation Pane

The **Page Navigation pane** (Figure 1–13) displays all of the current pages in the publication as thumbnails in a panel on the left side of the workspace. Because the flyer contains only one page, you will hide the Page Navigation pane using the Page Number button on the status bar. The following step hides the Page Navigation pane.

1

• Click the Page Number button on the status bar to close the Page Navigation pane (Figure 1–14).

Q&A

I do not see the Page Navigation pane. What did I do wrong?

It may be that someone has closed the Page Navigation pane already. The Page Number button opens and closes the Page Navigation pane. Click it again to view the Page Navigation pane.

Figure 1–14

BTW

Other Guides
Additional ruler, grid, and baseline guides can be added to assist you in organizing objects, text, pictures, and other components into columns and rows, and to give a consistent look to your publication. Those guides will be discussed as they are used in subsequent chapters.

BTW

The Publisher Workspace
If the rulers or margin guides do not appear in the workspace, click the appropriate check box on the View tab in the Show group.

Selecting Objects and Zooming

When you **select** an object in Publisher, the object displays a dark blue box with sizing handles and a rotation handle. Selected objects can be magnified, moved, edited, resized, and rotated, among other actions.

Objects such as photos, clip art, and shapes are easy to select. You simply click them. With other objects such as text boxes, logos, and placeholders, you first must point to them – to display their boundaries – and then click the boundary. Clicking or selecting text does not necessarily select the text box object that holds the text; rather, it may select the text itself. Clicking the boundary is the best way to select a text box object.

Once selected, the size of the object might be small and, therefore, difficult to edit. Publisher provides several ways to **zoom**, or change the magnification of an object, to facilitate viewing and editing.

Table 1–1 shows several zoom methods.

Table 1–1 Zoom Methods		
Tool	**Method**	**Result**
function key	To zoom in on an object, press the f9 key on the keyboard.	Selected object appears centered in the workspace at 100% magnification.
Zoom slider	To change the magnification of the entire page, drag the Zoom slider on the status bar.	Objects appear at selected magnification.
Zoom Out button Zoom In button	To decrease or increase the magnification, click the Zoom Out or Zoom In button on the status bar.	Page layout appears 10% smaller or larger with each click.
Zoom Level button	To display the Zoom dialog box, click the Zoom level button on the status bar, and then select the desired magnification. Click the OK button.	Page layout appears at selected magnification.
shortcut menu	To zoom in on an object, right-click the object. Point to Zoom on the shortcut menu. Click the desired magnification.	Object appears at selected magnification.
Ribbon	To use the Ribbon, click the View tab. In the Zoom group, click the desired button or the Zoom box arrow. Click the desired magnification.	Page layout appears at selected magnification.
mouse wheel	Press and hold the CTRL key and then move the mouse wheel down or up.	Pay layout appears 20% smaller or larger.
Page Width button	To zoom to page width, click the Page Width button (View tab | Zoom group); or right-click the object, point to Zoom, and then click Page Width.	Page layout expands to fill the workspace horizontally.
Whole Page button	To zoom to whole page, click the Whole Page button (View tab | Zoom group); or right-click the object, point to Zoom, and then click Whole Page.	Page layout is magnified as much as possible in the workspace.
Selected Objects button	To zoom to objects, click the Selected Objects button (View tab | Zoom group); or right-click the object, point to Zoom, and then click Objects.	Selected object appears centered in the workspace at 100% magnification.

To Display Boundaries

Pointing to objects on the page layout causes the boundary to appear as a gray dotted line. The following step points to the picture placeholder, just above the tear-offs, to show where it is located.

1

- Point to the area above the tear-offs, on the right side of the page layout, to display the placeholder boundary and the placeholder icon (Figure 1–15).

Q&A Can I turn on the boundary so that I can see it without pointing to it?

Yes. Click the Boundaries check box (View tab | Show group), which will display the boundaries on all objects.

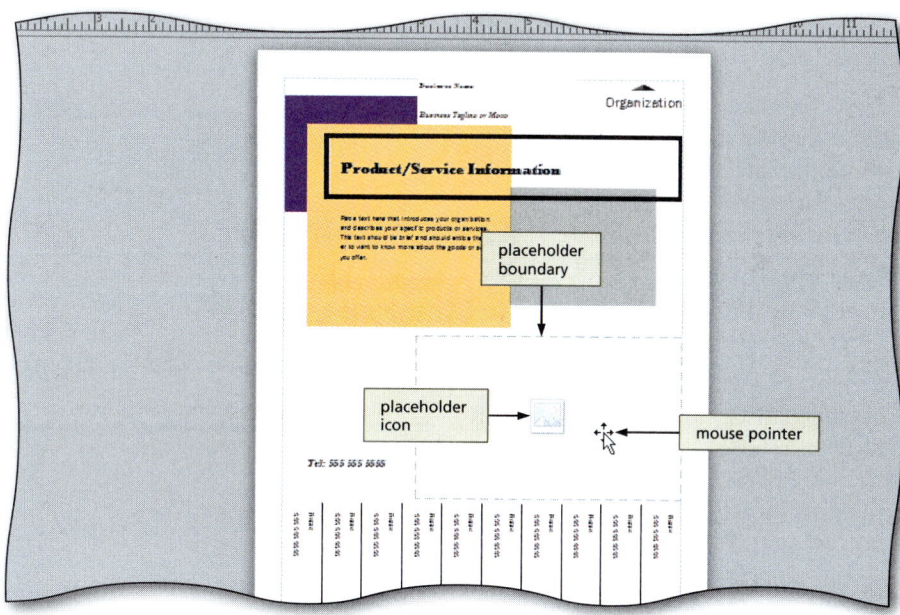

Figure 1–15

Other Ways

1. Click Boundaries check box (View tab | Show group)

To Select

The following step selects the box that surrounds the headline in the flyer by clicking it.

1

- Point to the black box around the headline and then click it to select the object (Figure 1–16).

Q&A What is the dark blue line around the box?

Publisher displays a blue selection border around selected objects. Selection borders typically display sizing handles and a green rotation handle.

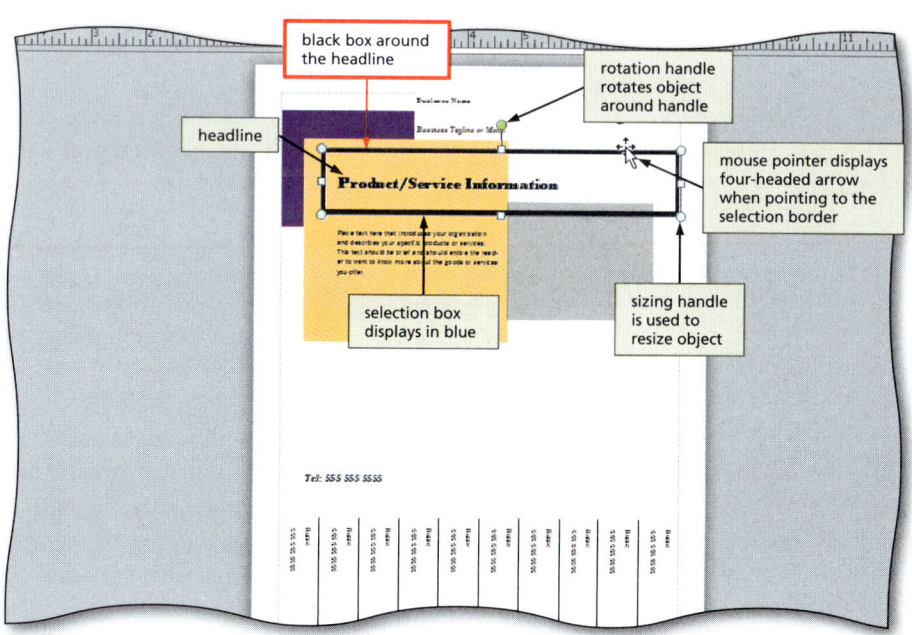

Other Ways

1. With no object selected, press TAB until desired object is selected

Figure 1–16

To Zoom

Editing small areas of text is easier if you use zooming techniques to enlarge the view of the publication. When you view an entire printed page, 8½-by-11 inches, the magnification is approximately 45%, which makes reading small text difficult. You press the F9 key to enlarge selected objects to 100% magnification. Pressing the F9 key a second time returns the layout to its previous magnification. The following step zooms in on the selected item.

- Press the F9 key on the keyboard to zoom the selected object to 100% (Figure 1–17).

Q&A

What is the best way to zoom to 100%?

If an object on the page is selected, pressing the F9 key toggles between a zoom of 100% and the previous zoom percentage. You also can choose 100% by clicking the Zoom box arrow (View tab | Zoom group) and then clicking 100% in the list.

Figure 1–17

Other Ways

1. Right-click publication, point to Zoom, click magnification
2. Click Zoom box arrow (View tab | Zoom group), click magnification
3. Drag Zoom slider on status bar

Selecting and Entering Text

The first step in editing a publication template is to replace its text by typing on the keyboard. In a later section of this chapter, you will learn how to **format**, or change the appearance of, the entered text.

Plan Ahead

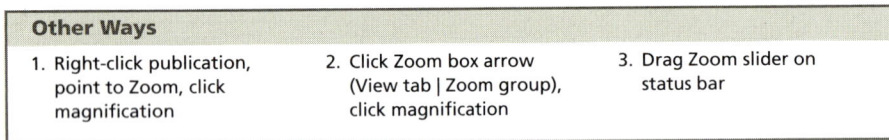

Choose the words for the text.

The text in a flyer usually is organized into several areas: headline, body copy, bulleted lists, business name, informational text boxes, taglines, attention getter, and tear-offs. Not all templates contain all of the text areas.

- The headline is the largest text on the flyer. It conveys the product or service being offered, such as a car for sale or personal lessons, or the benefit that will be gained, such as a convenience, better performance, greater security, higher earnings, or more comfort.

- The body copy and bulleted list contain descriptive text below the headline to highlight the key points of the message in as few words as possible. It should be easy to read and follow. While emphasizing the positive, the text must be realistic, truthful, and believable.

- Sometimes supplied by a database or information set, the business name, tagline, and informational text boxes need to be accurate and easy to read.

(continued)

(continued)

- The tear-offs must contain just enough information to contact the flyer's creator or to turn around requested information.

- Attention getter text should include information about a special offer, sale, price, or Web page.

Plan
Ahead

Text Boxes

Most of Publisher's templates come with text already inserted into text boxes. A **text box** is an object in a publication designed to hold text in a specific shape, size, and style. Text boxes also can be drawn on the page using the Draw Text Box button (Home tab | Objects group). Text boxes can be formatted using the Ribbon, the Mini toolbar, or the shortcut menu. A text box has changeable properties. A **property** is an attribute or characteristic of an object. Within text boxes, you can **edit**, or make changes to, many properties such as font, spacing, alignment, line/border style, fill color, and margins, among others.

To Replace Placeholder Text

Publisher templates use two types of text in template text boxes. You select **placeholder text**, such as that in the flyer headline, with a single click, allowing you to begin typing immediately. Other text, such as the business name, address, or tagline, is selected by dragging through the text, by double-clicking specific words, or by pressing CTRL+A to select all of the text in the text box. Then, you simply type to replace the text.

The following steps select and replace placeholder text in the headline.

1
- Click the headline placeholder text to select it (Figure 1–18).

Q&A What are the extra tabs on the Ribbon?

Those **tool tabs** or contextual tabs appear when you use a text box and a graphic. You will use tool tabs later in this chapter and in subsequent chapters.

Q&A Why does my template list a different business name?

The person who installed Microsoft Publisher 2010 on your computer or network may have set or customized the field.

Figure 1–18

2

- Type `Apartment for Rent` to replace the text (Figure 1–19).

Q&A

What if I make an error while typing?

Common word processing techniques work in Publisher text boxes. For example, you can press the BACKSPACE key until you have deleted the text in error and then retype the text correctly.

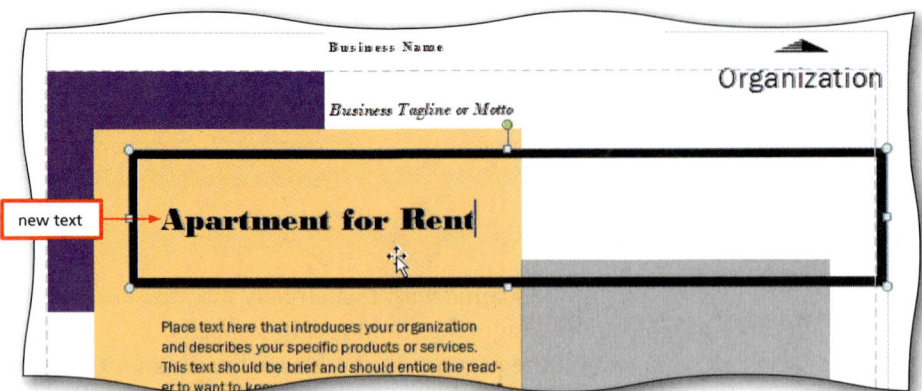

Figure 1–19

To Replace Other Text

The following steps replace the **default**, or preset, text in other template text boxes by selecting all of the text and then typing the new text.

1

- Click the text in the Business Name text box to position the insertion point inside the text box (Figure 1–20).

Q&A

Why is my default text different?

Text in the Business Name text box might be filled in from data entered into the software by another user. The text still can be edited.

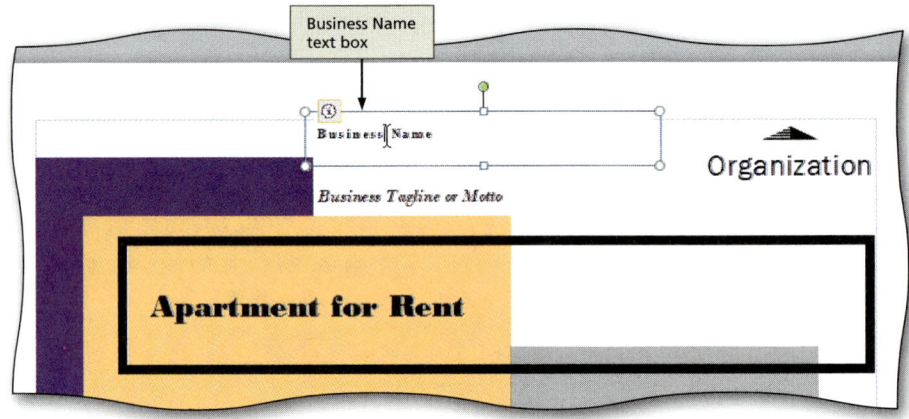

Figure 1–20

2

- Press CTRL+A to select all of the text in the text box (Figure 1–21).

Q&A

What is the button that displays the letter i?

It is a smart tag button. If you click it, Publisher offers to fill in the text for you with various options. A **smart tag button** appears when you point to certain text boxes that are part of the business information set or when you click a logo.

Figure 1–21

3

• Type **Matthew Properties** to replace the text (Figure 1–22).

Should I press the DELETE key before typing?

It is not necessary to press the DELETE key; the text you type deletes the selected text automatically.

Figure 1–22

4

• Click the text in the Business Tagline or Motto text box to position the insertion point inside the text box.

• Press CTRL+A to select all of the text in the text box.

• Type **Recently remodeled!** to replace the text (Figure 1–23).

Figure 1–23

Other Ways

1. Select text box, click Select button (Home tab | Editing group), click Select All Text in Text Box, type new text

2. Select text box, drag through text to select it, type new text

Bulleted Lists

A **bulleted list** is a series of lines, each beginning with a bullet character. To turn bullets on or off, you click the Bullets button (Home tab | Paragraph group) on the Ribbon (Figure 1–24). The Paragraph group includes buttons and boxes to help you format lines of text, including line spacing, alignment, columns, bullets, and numbering.

Figure 1–24

As you learned in the Office 2010 and Windows 7 chapter, the Ribbon is the control center in Publisher. The Ribbon provides easy, central access to the tasks you perform while creating a publication. The Ribbon consists of tabs, groups, and commands. Each tab contains a collection of groups, and each group contains related commands. When you start Publisher, the Ribbon displays seven main tabs: File, Home, Insert, Page Design, Mailings, Review, and View. Other tool tabs appear when they are used.

To Enter Bulleted Text

When you click the Bullets button (Home tab | Paragraph group), Publisher displays the **Bullet Styles gallery**, which is a clickable list of thumbnails and commands that show different bullet styles. A **gallery** is a set of choices, often graphical, arranged in a grid or in a list. You can scroll through choices in a gallery by clicking the gallery's scroll arrows. Some buttons and boxes have arrows that, when clicked, also display a gallery. Most galleries support **live preview**, which is a feature that allows you to point to a gallery choice and see its effect in the publication, without actually selecting the choice.

The following steps create a bulleted list by formatting and replacing the placeholder text in the text box below the headline.

- In the text box below the headline, click the placeholder text to select it.

- Click the Bullets button (Home tab | Paragraph group) to display the Bullet Styles gallery (Figure 1–25).

Figure 1–25

Q&A

Could I choose other bullet characters that do not appear in the gallery?

Yes. You may click the Bullets and Numbering command at the bottom of the Bullet Styles gallery to select other bullet characters.

2

• Click Large Bullets in the gallery to choose the bullet character (Figure 1–26).

Why does my Bullet Styles gallery look different?

It could be that someone has changed the bullet styles in your gallery. Choose a bullet style similar to the one shown in Figure 1–26.

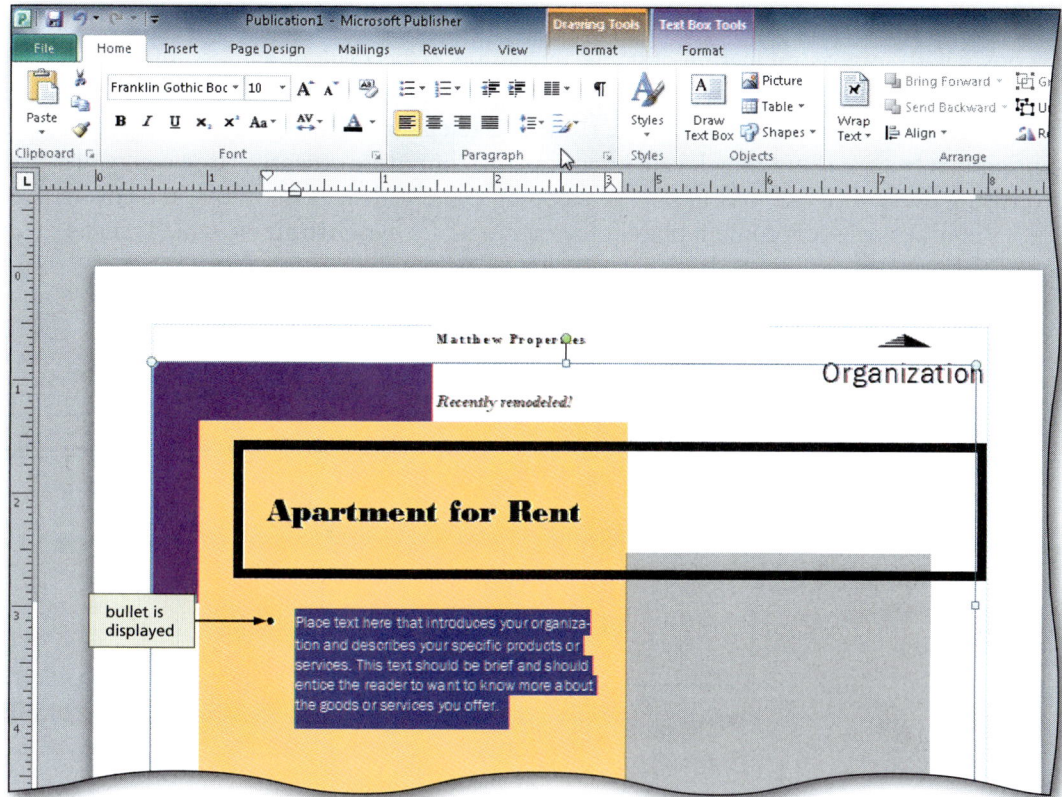

Figure 1–26

3

• Type **Two bedrooms, two bathrooms** and then press the ENTER key.

• Type **Close to campus** and then press the ENTER key.

• Type **Washer/dryer in each unit** and then press the ENTER key.

• Type **Short-term lease available** to complete the bulleted list (Figure 1–27).

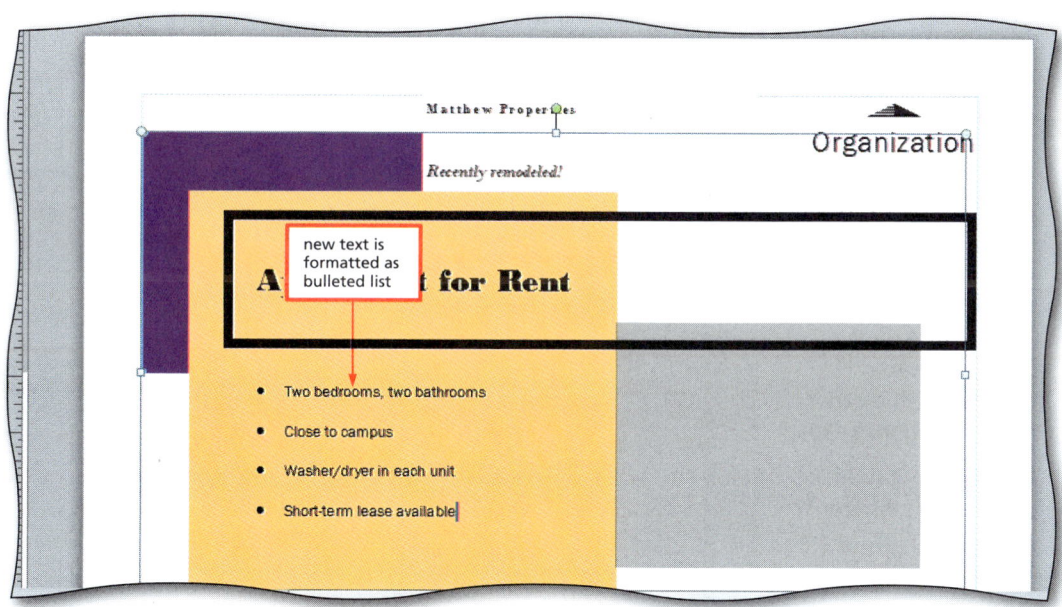

Figure 1–27

Other Ways
1. Click Bullets button on Mini toolbar, type text

To Enter Tear-Off Text

Across the lower portion of the flyer are contact information tear-offs. **Tear-offs** are small, ready-to-be scored text boxes with some combination of name, telephone, fax, e-mail, or address information. Designed for customer use, tear-offs typically are perforated so that a person walking by can tear off a tab to keep, rather than having to stop, find a pen and paper, and write down the name and telephone number. Traditionally, small businesses or individuals wanting to advertise something locally used tear-offs, but more recently, large companies have begun mass-producing advertising flyers with tear-offs to post at shopping centers, display in offices, and advertise on college campuses.

Publisher tear-offs contain placeholder text and are **synchronized**, which means that when you finish editing one of the tear-off text boxes, the others change to match it automatically.

The following steps edit the tear-off text boxes.

1
- Drag the vertical scroll box down to display the lower portion of the flyer.

- Click the text in one of the tear-off text boxes to select it (Figure 1–28).

Figure 1–28

2
- Type `Contact Linda@MattProp .com` and then press the ENTER key.

- Type `(918) 555-7900` to complete the tear-off (Figure 1–29).

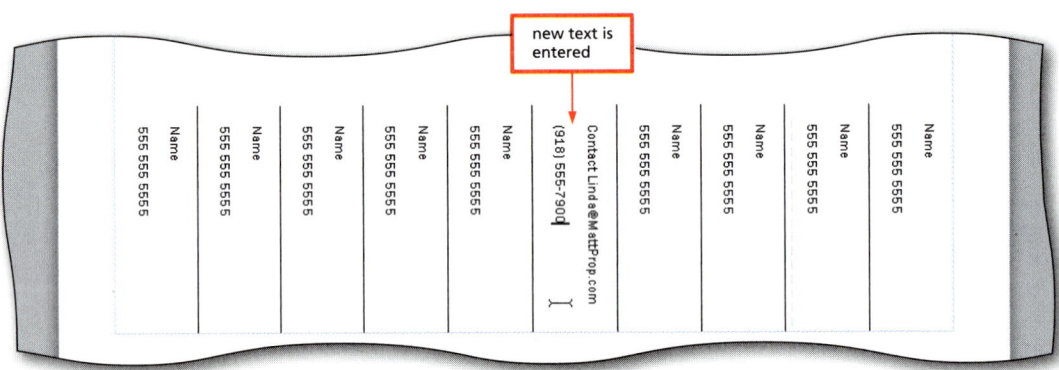

Figure 1–29

3
- Click outside of the text box to synchronize the other tear-offs (Figure 1–30).

What if I want to make each tear-off different?

Typically, all of the tear-offs are the same, but you can undo synchronization by clicking the Undo button on the Quick Access Toolbar and then typing the text for other tear-offs.

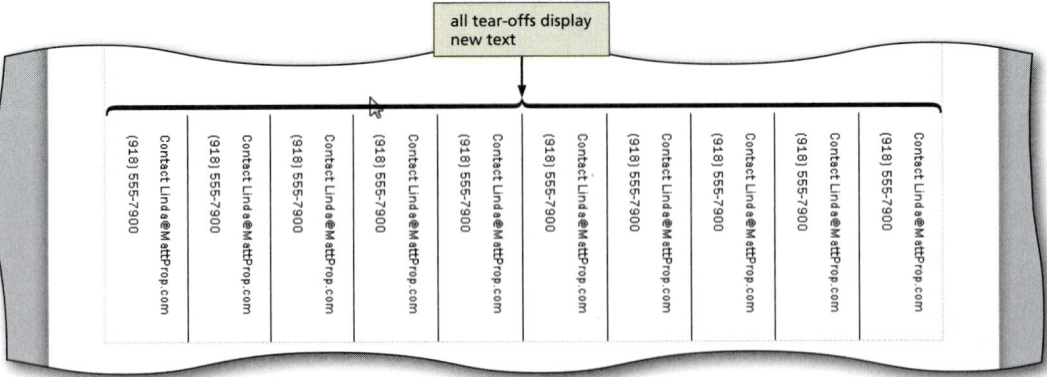

Figure 1–30

Formatting Fonts

Publisher provides many ways to modify the appearance, or **format**, of selected text. Some formatting options include editing the font, paragraph, alignment, typography, copy fitting, and special effects. The more common formatting commands are shown in the Font group on the Home tab of the Ribbon (Figure 1–31). These include the ability to change the font size, color, and style. You will learn more about each of the formatting options in the Font group as you use them.

Figure 1–31

Many of these formatting tools also appear on a Mini toolbar when you point to text. Recall that the Mini toolbar, which appears automatically based on the tasks you perform, contains commands related to changing the appearance of text or graphics in a publication. The purpose of the Mini toolbar is to minimize mouse movement.

A third way to format text involves using the shortcut menu, which appears when you right-click an object. The shortcut menu is a list of frequently used commands that relate to the right-clicked object. When you right-click some items, Publisher displays both the Mini toolbar and a shortcut menu.

Identify how to format various objects in the flyer.
By formatting the text and other objects in a publication, you can improve its overall appearance. For a flyer, consider the following formatting suggestions.

- Increase the font size of characters. Flyers usually are posted on a bulletin board or in a window. Thus, the font size should be as large as possible so that passersby can read the flyer easily. To give the headline more impact, its font size should be larger than the font size of the text in the body copy.

- Use fonts that are easy to read. The font schemes suggest using only two different fonts in a flyer, for example, one for the headline and the other for all other text. Too many fonts can make the flyer visually confusing.

- Overall placement of objects should be done with purpose. Objects usually should be aligned with the margin or with other objects on the page. Objects similar in nature, such as text boxes that contain information about the company, should be kept in close proximity to one another.

- Delete objects that are unnecessary or ones that detract from the purpose of the flyer. Not every flyer needs every template object. Determine which ones emphasize your purpose and design, or which ones provide information — delete the rest.

Plan Ahead

To Increase the Font Size

The following steps use the Increase Font Size button to enlarge the bulleted text so that it is easier to read.

- Scroll up to display the bulleted list.

- Click the text and then press CTRL+A to select all of the text in the bulleted list.

- Click the Increase Font Size button (Home tab | Font group) three times to enlarge the text (Figure 1–32).

Q&A

Are there other ways to increase the font size?

Yes. In later chapters, you will learn how to use the Font Size box arrow (Home tab | Font group), and later in this chapter, you will use autofitting to increase the font size.

Figure 1–32

 Experiment

- Click the Decrease Font Size button (Home tab | Font group) to watch the font grow smaller. Then, click the Increase Font Size button again, until the text fills the text box.

Other Ways

1. Select text, click Font Size box arrow (Home tab | Font group), click larger font size

Autofitting Text

Sometimes the replacement text that you enter into a template does not fit the same way as the original template text — there might be too much text to fit, or too little text to fill the box. In those cases, you may want to **autofit** or **copy fit** the text, to adjust the way the text fits into the text box. Publisher autofitting choices are listed in Table 1–2.

Table 1–2 Autofitting Choices

Type of Autofitting	Result
Best Fit	Shrinks or expands text to fit in the text box, even when the text box is resized
Shrink Text On Overflow	Reduces the point size of text until there is no text in overflow
Grow Text Box to Fit	Enlarges text box to fit all of the text at its current size
Do Not Autofit	Text appears at its current size

To Autofit Text

The following steps use the shortcut menu to autofit the text in the headline. Each of the autofit commands appears on the shortcut menu related to the text.

1

- Right-click the headline text to display the shortcut menu and Mini toolbar (Figure 1–33).

Q&A Do I have to select all of the text in a text box in order to autofit it?

No. Because all of the text in the text box is included automatically in autofitting, you do not need to select the text in order to autofit it.

Q&A Why do I have different buttons on my shortcut menu?

Someone may have copied objects that are still in the Office clipboard, or they may have chosen different settings on your computer. Autofitting will not be affected.

Figure 1–33

2

- Click Best Fit to autofit the text in the text box (Figure 1–34).

Q&A Could I have used the Increase Font Size button (Home tab | Font group) to make the headline larger?

Yes, but you would have had to estimate how big to make the text. Autofitting is different from using the Increase Font Size button. With autofitting, the text is increased, or decreased, to fit the given size of the text box automatically, even if the text box is resized.

Figure 1–34

Other Ways	
1. Click Format Text Box Dialog Box Launcher (Text Box Tools Format tab | Text group), click	Text Box tab, click Best Fit option button, click OK button (Format Text Box dialog box)

Deleting Objects

Templates may display objects in the page layout that you do not wish to use. In those cases, or when you change your mind about including an inserted object, you must delete objects.

To Delete Objects

In order to delete an object, it must be selected. The following steps delete the organizational logo and telephone text box. Recall that pointing to an object displays its boundary.

1
- Point to the organization logo to display the boundary and then click the boundary to select the object. Do not select the text (Figure 1–35).

Q&A What if I want to delete just part of the logo?

The template logo, in this case, is a small picture and the word Organization grouped together. To delete one or the other, select the logo first, and then click only the part of the object you wish to delete. Press the DELETE key to delete that part of the grouped object.

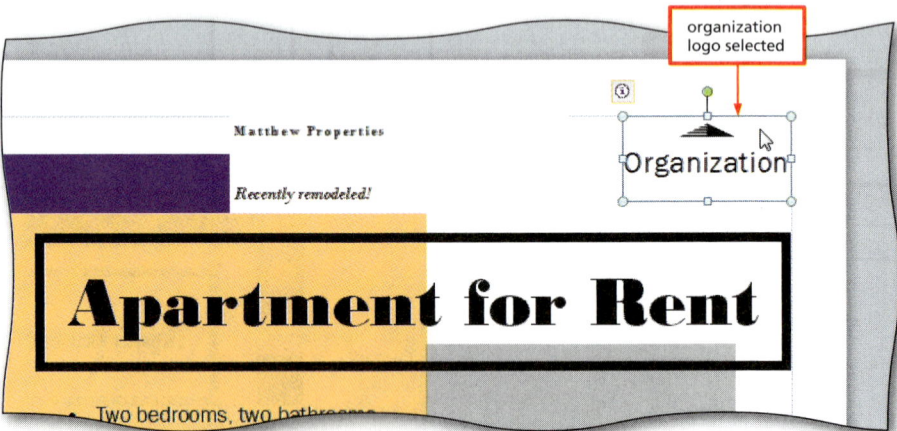

Figure 1–35

2
- Press the DELETE key to delete the selected object (Figure 1–36).

Q&A Why did only the text disappear?

You may have selected the boundary of the text box, instead of the boundary of the entire logo. Select the remaining object and press the DELETE key.

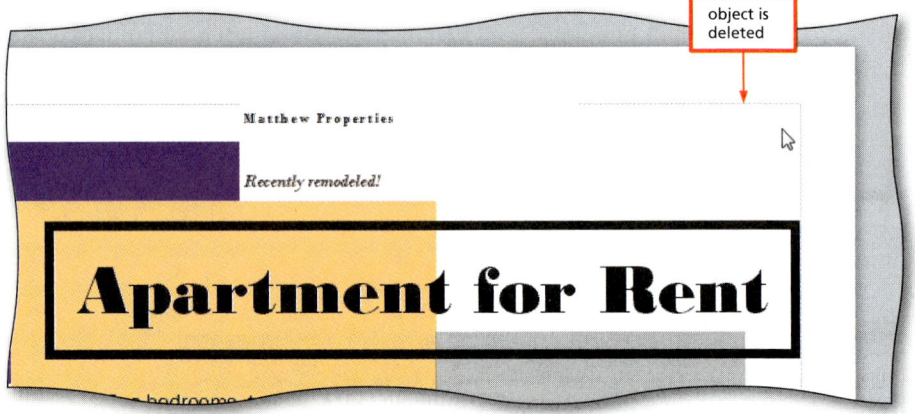

Figure 1–36

3
- Scroll down as necessary and then point to the border of the telephone text box. Click the border to select the telephone text box. Do not select the text (Figure 1–37).

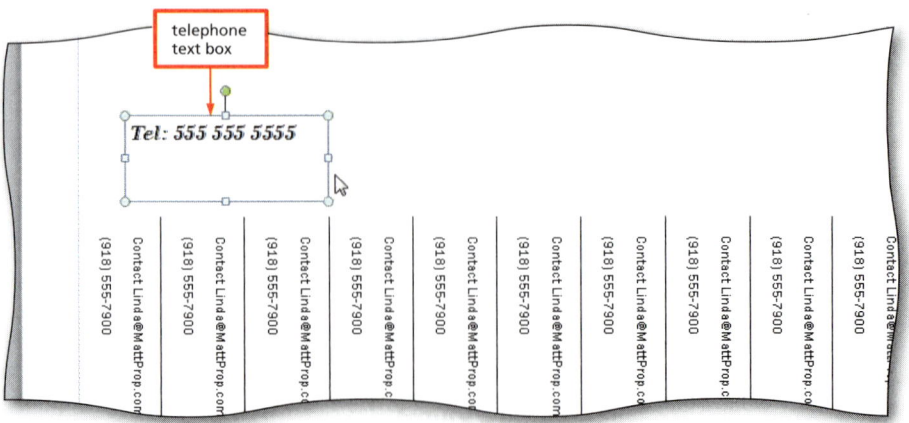

Figure 1–37

4
- Press the DELETE key to delete the object (Figure 1–38).

Q&A

What if I delete an object by accident?

Press CTRL+Z to undo the most recent step, or click the Undo button on the Quick Access Toolbar. The object will reappear in the original location.

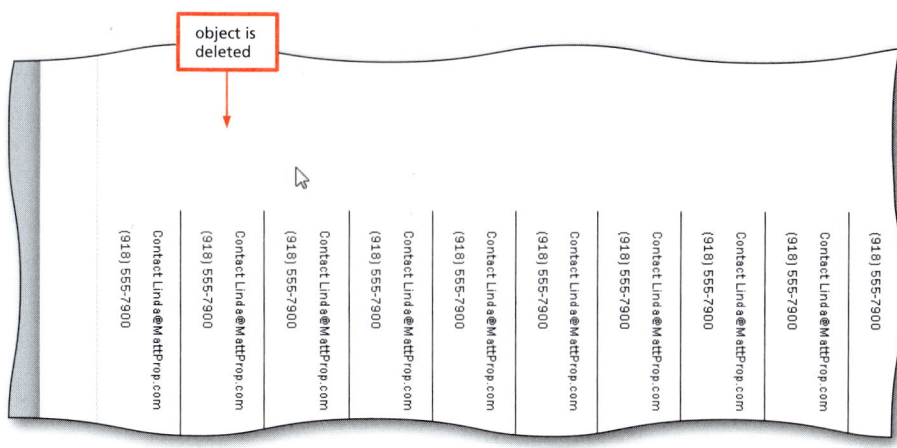

Figure 1–38

Other Ways
1. Right-click object, click Delete Object on shortcut menu
2. Select object, press BACKSPACE key

To Save a Publication

You have performed many tasks while creating this flyer and do not want to risk losing work completed thus far. Accordingly, you should save the publication.

The following steps assume you already have created folders for storing your files, for example, a CIS 101 folder (for your class) that contains a Publisher folder (for your assignments). Thus, these steps save the document in the Publisher folder in the CIS 101 folder on a USB flash drive using the file name, Apartment for Rent Flyer. For a detailed example of the procedure summarized below, refer to the Office 2010 and Windows 7 chapter at the beginning of this book.

BTW

Saving
It is important to save a publication frequently. The publication in memory will be lost if the computer is turned off or if you lose electrical power while Publisher is open. If you run out of time before completing your project, you can save the publication and then finish it at a future time without starting over.

1 With a USB flash drive connected to one of the computer's USB ports, click the Save button on the Quick Access Toolbar to display the Save As dialog box.

2 Type **Apartment For Rent Flyer** in the File name text box to change the file name. Do not press the ENTER key after typing the file name because you do not want to close the dialog box at this time.

3 Navigate to the desired save location (in this case, the Publisher folder in the CIS 101 folder [or your class folder] on the USB flash drive).

4 Click the Save button (Save As dialog box) to save the document in the selected folder on the selected drive with the entered file name.

Break Point: If you wish to take a break, this is a good place to do so. You can quit Publisher now. To resume at a later time, start Publisher, open the file called Apartment for Rent Flyer, and continue following the steps from this location forward.

Using Graphics

Files containing graphical images, also called **graphics**, are available from a variety of sources. Publisher includes a series of predefined graphics, such as drawings, photographs, sounds, videos, and other media files, called clips. A **clip** is a single media file, including art, sound, or animation, that you can insert and use in print publications, Web publications, and other Microsoft Office documents. **Picture** is a generic term for photographs and clip art. Other kinds of graphics include building blocks, attention getters, logos, sidebars, and accents, among others.

<table>
<tr><td>**Plan Ahead**</td><td>**Find the appropriate graphical image.**
To be used in a Publisher publication, a graphical image must be stored digitally in a file. Files containing graphical images are available from a variety of sources:

• You can insert a graphic or photo stored on one of your computer's storage devices.

• Publisher includes a collection of predefined graphical images or clip art that you can insert in a publication.

• Microsoft has free digital images on the Web for use in a publication. Other Web sites also have images available, some of which are free, while others require a fee.

• You can take a photo with a digital camera and download it, which is the process of copying the digital photo from the camera to your computer.

• With a scanner, you can convert a printed photo, drawing, or diagram to a digital file.</td></tr>
</table>

BTW

New Features
This latest version of Publisher has many new features, including the Ribbon, to make you more productive. With new predefined templates and graphical elements designed to help you prepare publications, Publisher 2010 also includes building blocks; charting and diagramming tools; visual panning, cropping, and zooming; the Backstage view; and a print preview mode.

Appropriate images not only should refer to the context of the publication, but also should represent the reality of that context. If you are trying to sell something specific or describe a particular person or place, use a photograph. If you are describing a service or general object, you can use clip art. For example, if you are trying to sell a used car, try to use a real photograph of the car. If you are describing cars in general, you can use clip art.

If you receive a graphic from a source other than yourself, do not use the file until you are certain it does not contain a virus. A **virus** is a computer program that can damage files and programs on your computer. Use an antivirus program to verify that any files you use are virus free.

To Insert a Photograph into a Picture Placeholder

Recall that a placeholder reserves space on the page layout but is not displayed until you point to it or insert something in it. The following steps replace the picture placeholder in the Flyer template with a photograph. The photograph, which was taken with a digital camera, is available in the Data Files for Students. See the inside back cover of this book for instructions on downloading the Data Files for Students, or contact your instructor for information about accessing the required files.

• Insert the USB flash drive that contains the Data Files for Students into one of the computer's USB ports.

• Scroll as necessary to point to the area above the tear-offs to display the boundary of the picture placeholder and then point to the placeholder icon (Figure 1–39).

Q&A

Why does no ScreenTip appear for the picture placeholder?

By default, ScreenTips do not appear on objects in the workspace. You can turn on ScreenTips for those objects by doing the following: open the Backstage view, click Options, click Advanced, and then click the Show ScreenTips on objects check box.

Figure 1–39

2

• Click the placeholder icon to display the Insert Picture dialog box.

• Navigate to the Data Files for Students location. Double-click the Publisher folder. Double-click the Chapter 01 folder. For a detailed example of this procedure, refer to Steps 3a – 3c in the To Save a File in a Folder section in the Office 2010 and Windows 7 chapter at the beginning of this book (Figure 1–40).

Figure 1–40

3

• Double-click the Apartment Building file to insert the photograph into the picture placeholder (Figure 1–41).

Figure 1–41

4
- Click outside the photograph to display the photograph without a boundary (Figure 1–42).

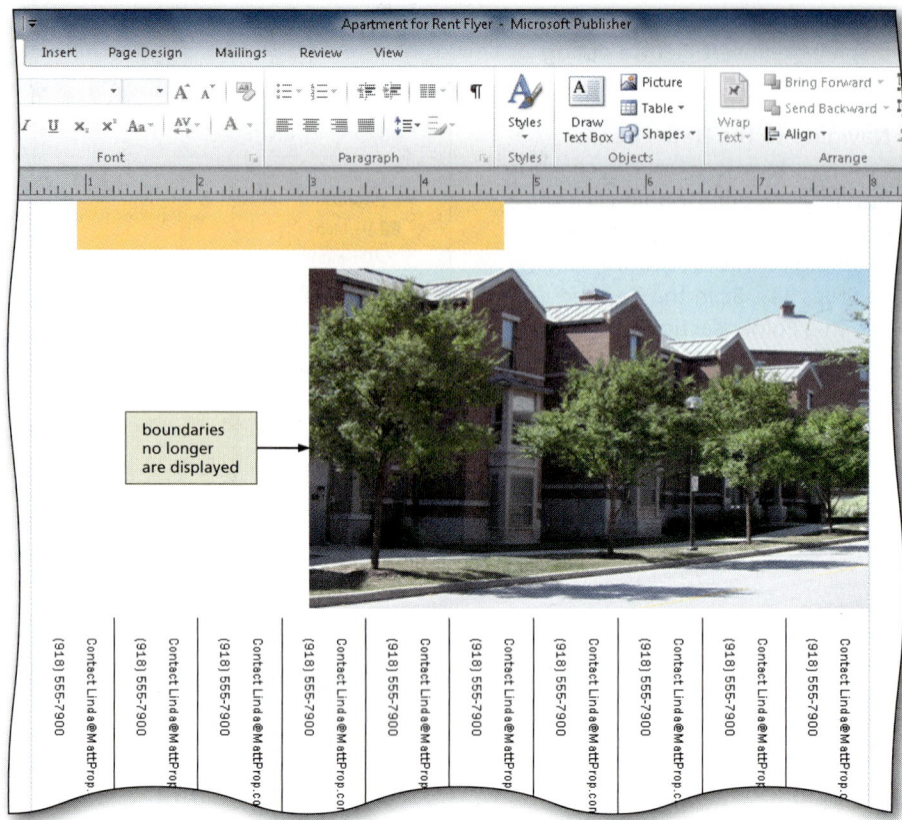

Figure 1–42

Other Ways

1. Right-click placeholder, point to Change Picture on shortcut menu, click Change Picture

Picture Styles

Picture styles allow you easily to change the basic rectangle format to a more visually appealing style. Publisher provides a gallery of 24 picture styles, which include a variety of shapes, borders, and scallops. The flyer in this chapter uses a picture style with a border and a scalloped bottom edge. Using the Picture Tools Format tab on the Ribbon, you also can set picture borders, shapes, and captions (Figure 1–43).

Figure 1–43

To Apply a Picture Style

The following steps apply a picture style to the photograph in the flyer.

1

- Click the photograph to select it.

- Click Picture Tools Format on the Ribbon to display the Picture Tools Format tab.

- Click the More button (Picture Tools Format tab | Picture Styles group) to display the Picture Styles gallery.

- Point to Picture Style 4 in the Picture Styles gallery to display a live preview of that style (Figure 1–44).

 Experiment

- Point to various picture styles in the Picture Styles gallery and watch the format of the picture change in the publication window.

Figure 1–44

2

- Click Picture Style 4 in the Picture Styles gallery to apply the selected style to the picture.

- Click outside the picture to deselect it (Figure 1–45).

 Should I be concerned that the picture overlaps the tear-offs slightly?

No. Tear-offs commonly are scored vertically, so the photograph will not be affected.

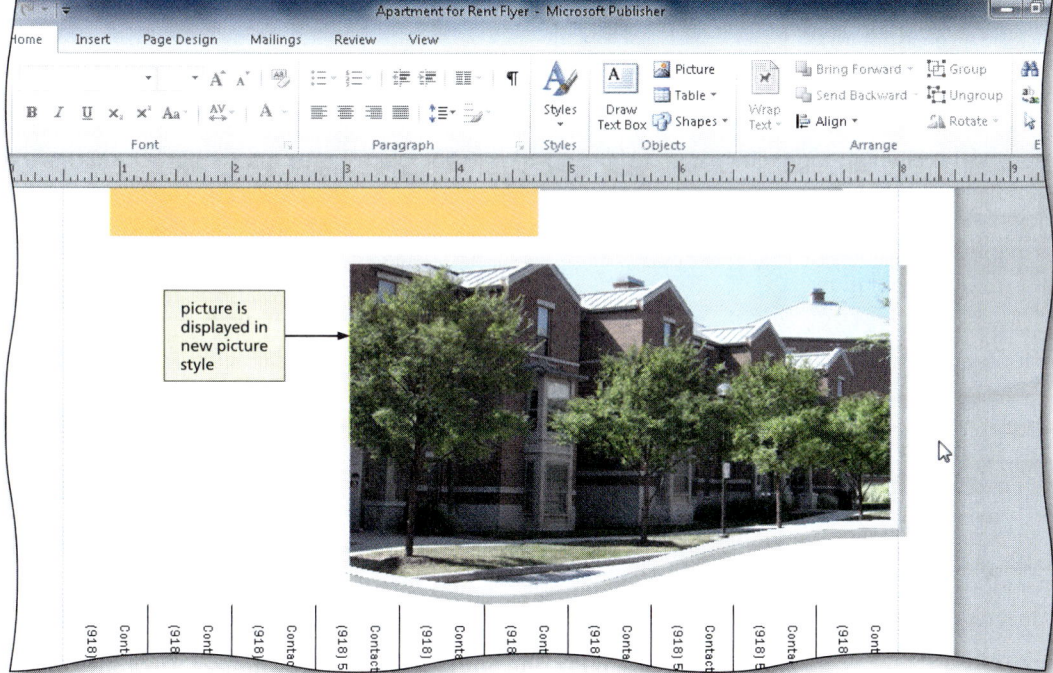

Figure 1–45

Building Blocks

A **building block** is a graphical or text element that you can insert in a publication. Building blocks include advertisement items, business information components, calendars, design accents, and page parts. The **Building Block Library** displays a wide variety of building block components and navigation tools.

Building blocks are located in a group on the Insert tab, along with other objects that you can insert into publications (Figure 1–46). One category in the Advertising building blocks consists of attention getters. An **attention getter** is an eye-catching graphic that draws attention to a location on the page. Attention getters may contain graphics, text boxes, geometric designs, and colors intended to add interest to your publication.

Figure 1–46

To Use the Building Block Library

The following steps use the Building Block Library to insert an attention getter in the publication.

1
- Click Insert on the Ribbon to display the Insert tab.

- Click the Show Building Block Library Dialog Box Launcher (Insert tab | Building Blocks group) to open the Building Block Library window (Figure 1–47).

Q&A

How can I navigate through the Building Block Library?

You can click a folder to view the building blocks inside. Remember that the folders are opened with a single click. The Forward and Back buttons, as well as the previous location links, assist you in moving through the building blocks.

Figure 1–47

2
● Click the
Advertisements
folder to open it, and
then scroll down to
display the Attention
Getters area
(Figure 1–48).

Q&A

Is the Diamond
attention getter a
graphic?

Yes. It is actually a
shape and a text box
grouped together.

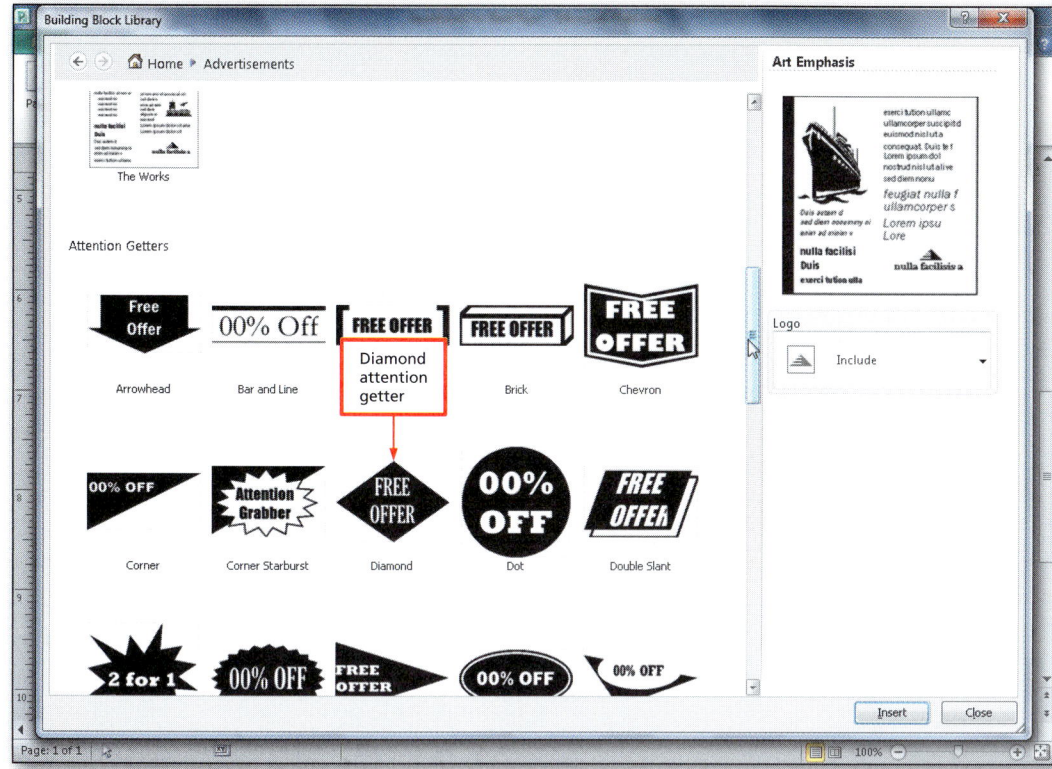

Figure 1–48

3
● Double click the
Diamond attention
getter to insert it
into the publication
(Figure 1–49).

Q&A

Why was the
attention getter
placed right in front
of the picture?

Publisher inserts
building blocks in
the center of the
current view of the
page layout. The
placement of your
attention getter
may differ.

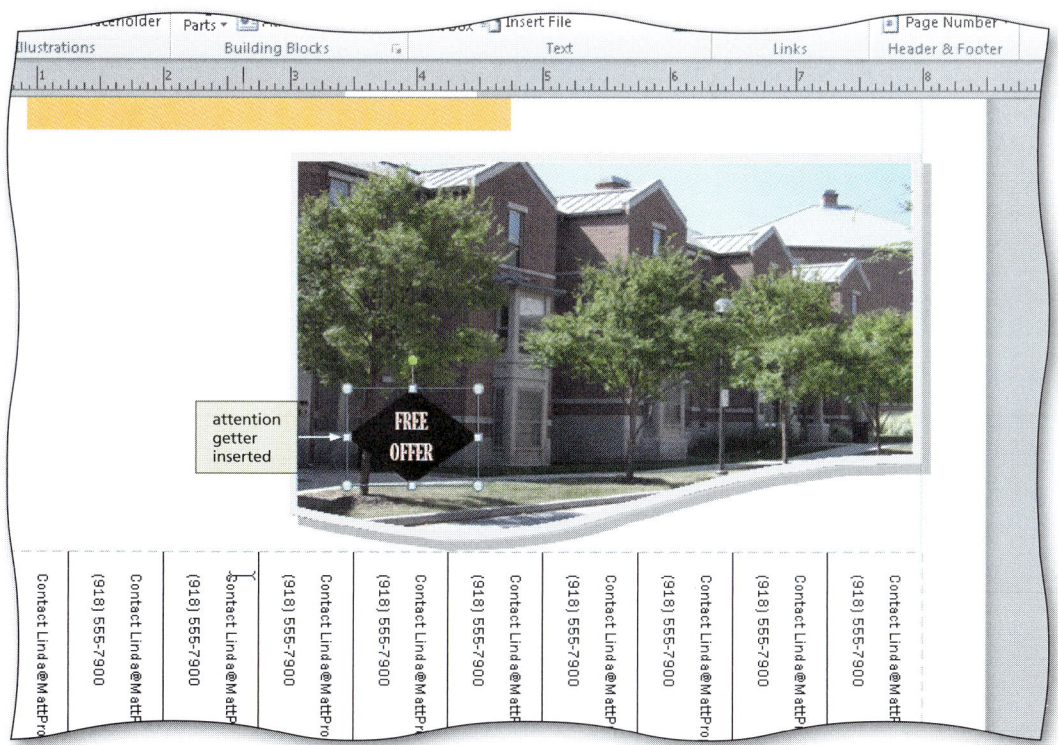

Figure 1–49

Moving, Resizing, and Aligning Objects

Many times, even when using a template, you will want to move objects around on the page layout, or you may want to change the size of objects as you did with the size of text. To **move** an object, you first point to its boundary; then, when the mouse pointer changes to a double two-headed arrow, you drag the object to the new location or to the scratch area. The **scratch area** is the gray area that appears outside the publication page. If you press and hold the SHIFT key while dragging, the object moves in a straight line. Pressing the CTRL key while dragging creates a copy of the object. As you move an object, Publisher displays **visual layout guides** to help you place the object and align it to other objects on the page layout. When you **align** an object to another object, their edges or center points line up, either vertically or horizontally. The visual layout guides are displayed as pink lines that move from object to object as you drag. Visual layout guides appear when you align the left, right, top, bottom, or middle of objects.

Sometimes pictures and graphics are not the right size. In that case, you need to resize or scale the object. To **resize** any object in Publisher, select the object, and then drag a handle. A **handle** is one of several small shapes displayed around an object when the object is selected. To resize by dragging, position the mouse pointer over one of the handles and then drag the mouse. Pressing the CTRL key while dragging keeps the center of the graphic in the same place while resizing. Pressing the SHIFT key while dragging maintains the graphic's proportions while resizing. Finally, pressing the SHIFT and CTRL keys while dragging maintains the proportions and keeps the center in the same place.

To Move an Object

The following step moves the attention getter from its current location to a location left of the photograph.

1

- With the attention getter still selected, drag the boundary of the attention getter to a location left of the photograph (Figure 1–50).

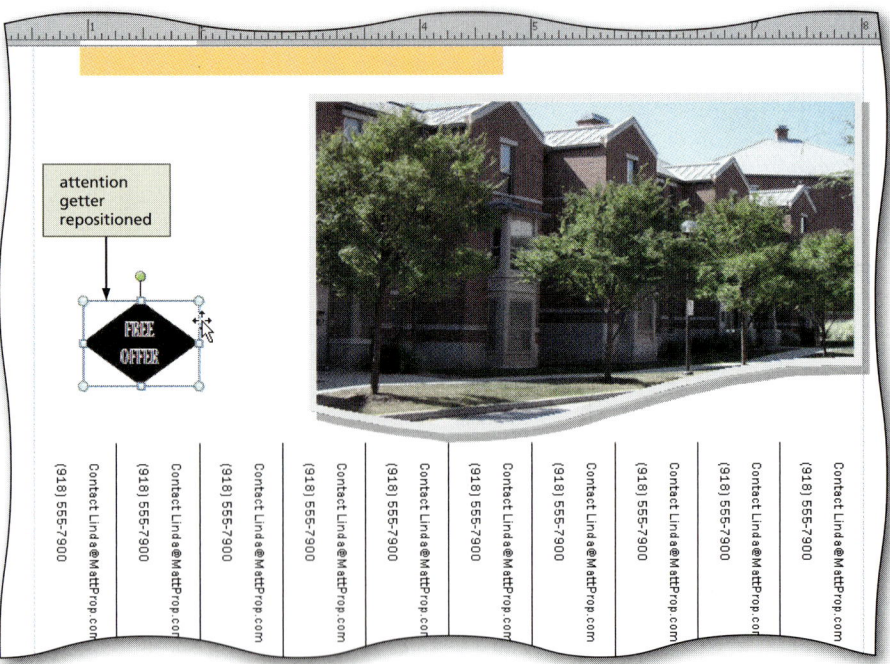

attention getter repositioned

FREE OFFER

Figure 1–50

To Resize an Object

The next step resizes the attention getter and makes it slightly larger, so that it fills the space to the left of the photograph.

1

• With the attention getter still selected, SHIFT+CTRL+drag a corner sizing handle outward to resize the object to a larger size (Figure 1–51).

 Q&A

Do I have to hold the SHIFT and the CTRL keys while dragging?

Yes, because doing so resizes the object while maintaining the proportions and keeping the center in the same place.

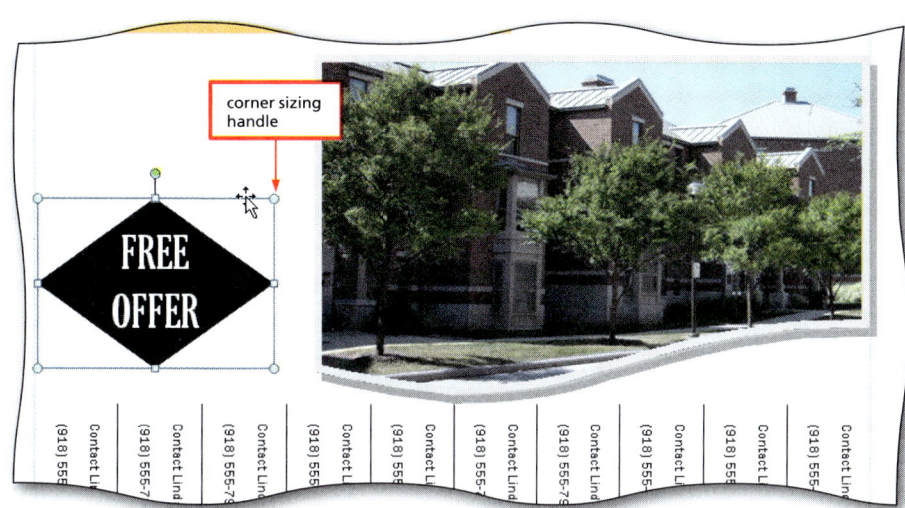

Figure 1–51

Other Ways

1. Click Object Size box on status bar, enter dimensions in Width and Height boxes, click Close button

To Align an Object

The following steps align the horizontal center of the attention getter with the horizontal center of the photograph.

 1

• With the attention getter still selected, drag the boundary of the object until a pink visual layout guide appears in the middle of the photograph (Figure 1–52).

2

• Release the mouse button to position the attention getter.

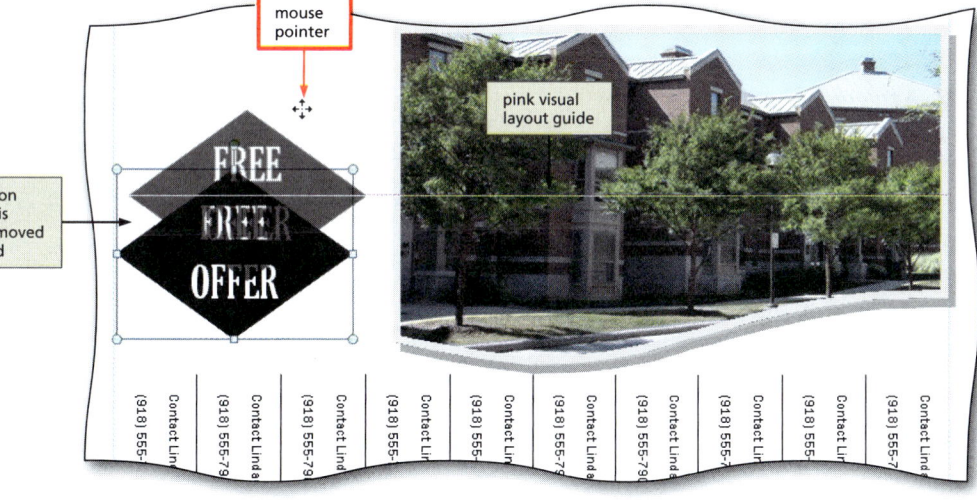

Figure 1–52

Other Ways

1. Click first object, shift+click second object, click Align button (Drawing Tools Format tab | Arrange Group), click desired alignment

To Edit the Attention Getter Text

The following steps edit the attention getter text.

1 Click the text in the attention getter to select it.

2 Type `Utilities Included` to replace the default text (Figure 1–53).

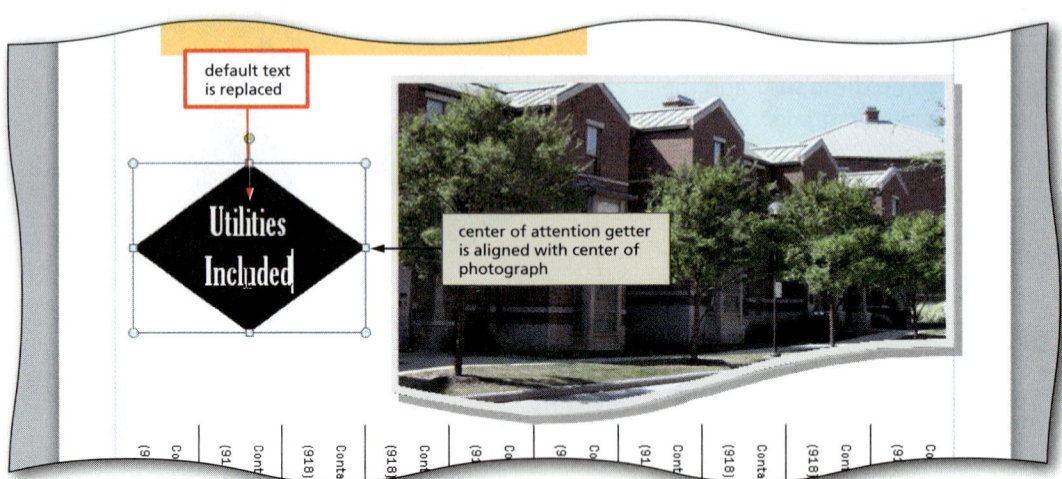

Figure 1–53

To Change the Font Color

The following steps use the Mini toolbar to change the color of the attention getter's text by changing the font color.

1

- Select the text in the attention getter.

- Move the mouse pointer over the text until the Mini toolbar begins to appear (Figure 1–54).

Q&A
I cannot get the Mini toolbar to appear. Am I doing something wrong?

It takes a bit of practice to find the spot that triggers the Mini toolbar. Remember that the Mini toolbar first appears in a transparent manner and then gets darker as you move the mouse pointer toward it. If you cannot see it, right-click the text, and then point to the Mini toolbar above the shortcut menu.

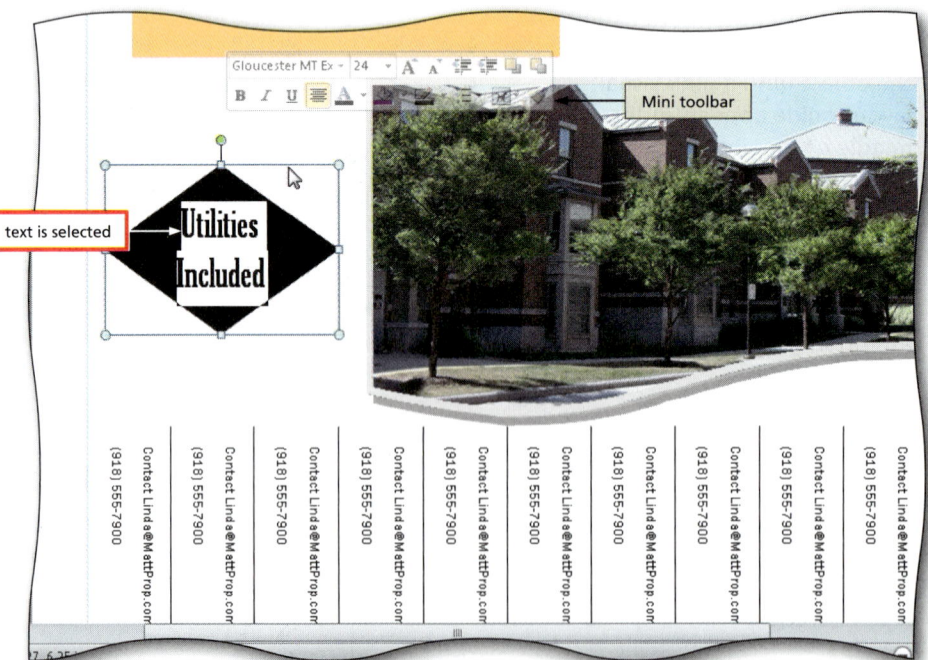

Figure 1–54

2

- Click the Font Color button arrow on the Mini toolbar to display the Font Color gallery.

- Point to Accent 2 (RGB (255, 204, 102)) that is displayed as gold in the first row in the Font Color gallery (Figure 1–55).

Q&A What is the first row of colors?

Those colors are the Crocus color scheme colors that you chose at the beginning of the chapter.

Experiment

- Move the mouse pointer over several colors in various parts of the gallery and watch the live preview change the color of the text in the attention getter.

Figure 1–55

3

- Click Accent 2 (RGB (255, 204, 102)) to change the color of the text.

- Click away from the attention getter to deselect it (Figure 1–56).

Q&A What do the numbers in the color name signify?

Those are the intensity values of red, green, and blue that define the gold color.

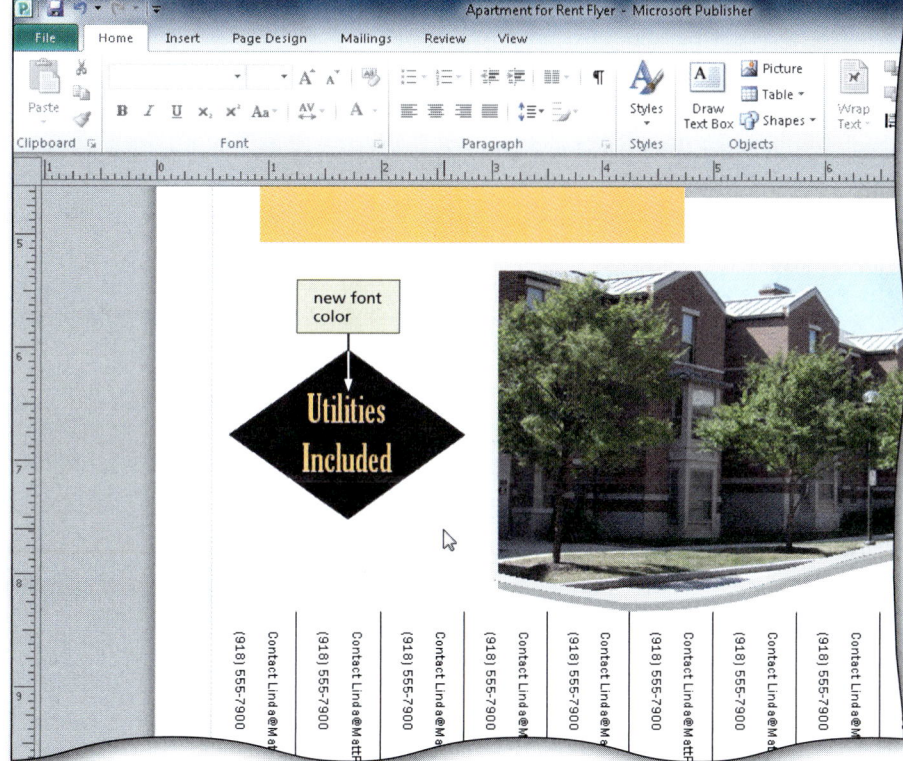

Figure 1–56

Other Ways

1. Click Font Color button arrow (Home tab | Font group), click desired color

Changing Publication Properties

BTW

Other Uses for Publication Properties
You or your instructor can insert comments about the publication in the Comments text box in the Properties dialog box. In the Custom sheet, you can assign other properties, such as editor, department, language, or publisher, and then enter text, date, yes/no, or a numeric value to these custom properties. For example, your instructor can grade your publication, typing his or her name in the Checked by category, and then assign a letter or numeric grade in the Project or Disposition category.

Publisher helps you organize and identify your files by using **publication properties**, which are the details about a file. Publication properties, also known as **metadata**, can include information such as the project author, title, subject, and keywords. A **keyword** is a word or phrase that further describes the publication. For example, a class name or publication topic can describe the file's purpose or content.

Publication properties are valuable for a variety of reasons:

- Users can save time locating a particular file because they can view a publication's properties without opening the publication.
- By creating consistent properties for files having similar content, users can better organize their publications.
- Some organizations require Publisher users to add publication properties so that other employees can view details about these files.

Two different types of publication properties exist in Publisher. **Advanced properties** are associated with all Microsoft Office publications and include author, title, subject, and keywords, among others. Advance properties are edited in the Backstage view. **Automatically updated properties** include template, color scheme, file system properties (such as the date you create or change a file), and statistics (such as the file size). Automatically updated properties are changed by editing the publication.

To Change Publication Properties

You can view and change publication properties at any time while you are creating a publication. Before saving the flyer again, you want to add your name and course information as publication properties. The following steps change publication properties.

1
- Click File on the Ribbon to open the Backstage view.
- If necessary, click the Info tab in the Backstage view to display the Info gallery.
- Click the Publication Properties button in the right pane of the Info gallery to display the Publication Properties menu (Figure 1–57).

Q&A

How do I close the Backstage view?

Click File on the Ribbon or click the preview of the document in the Info gallery to return to the publication window.

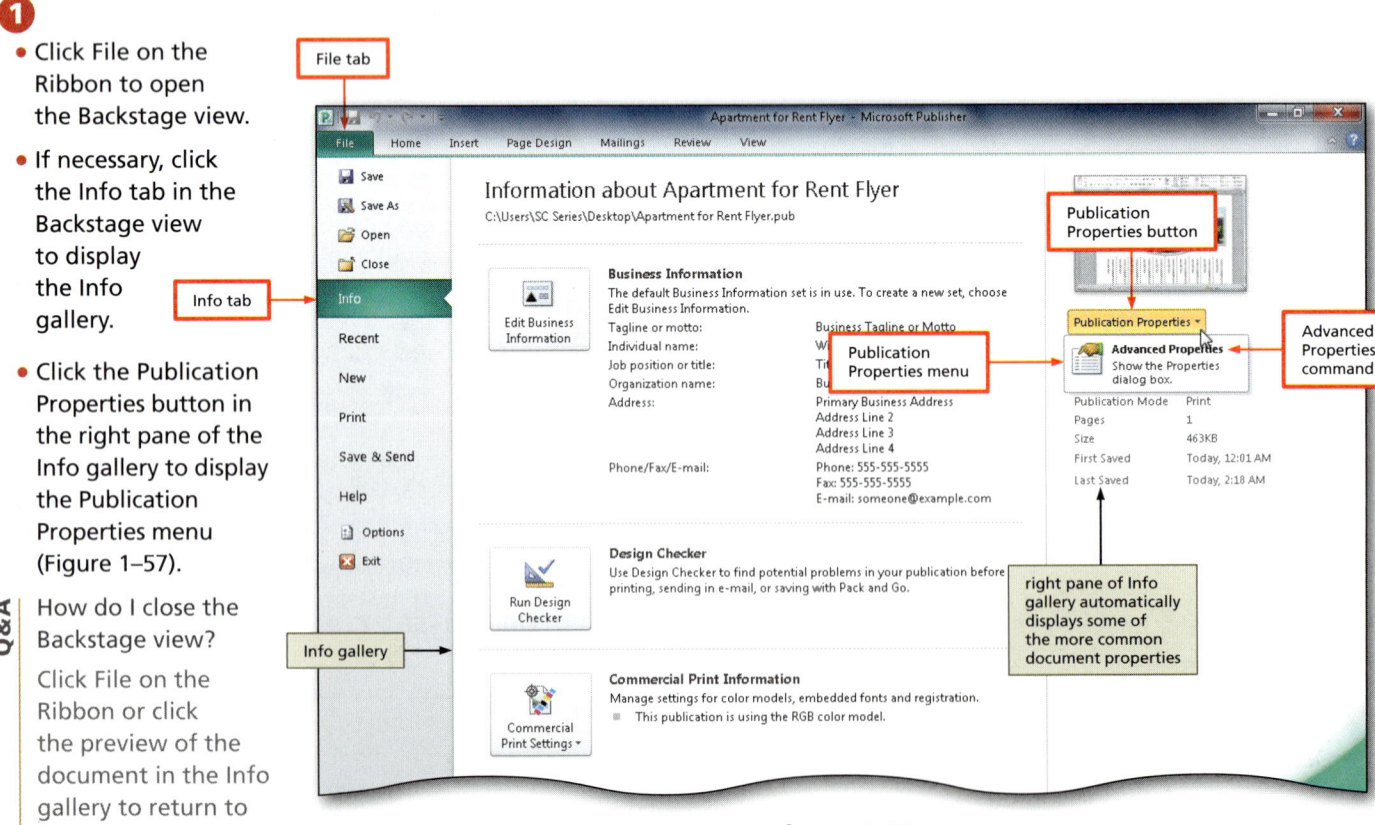

Figure 1–57

2

- Click Advanced Properties to display the Properties dialog box.

- If necessary, click the Summary tab, and then delete any text that is displayed in the text boxes (Figure 1–58).

Q&A Why were some of the publication properties in my Properties dialog box already filled in?

The person who installed Microsoft Publisher 2010 on your computer or network may have set or customized the properties.

Figure 1–58

3

- Click the Title text box and then type **Apartment For Rent Flyer** as the title.

- Click the Subject text box and then type your course and section as the Subject property.

- Click the Author text box and then type your name as the Author property.

- Click the Keywords text box and then type **apartment, rental, campus** as the keywords (Figure 1–59).

Q&A What types of publication properties does Publisher collect automatically?

Publisher records details such as time spent editing a publication, the number of times a publication has been revised, and the fonts and themes used in a publication.

Figure 1–59

4

- Click the OK button (Properties dialog box) so that the dialog box no longer is displayed.

- Click the File tab to return to the publication.

To Save an Existing Publication with the Same File Name

You have made several modifications to the publication since you last saved it. Thus, you should save it again. The following step saves the publication again. For an example of the step listed below, refer to the Office 2010 and Windows 7 chapter at the beginning of this book.

 Click the Save button on the Quick Access Toolbar to overwrite the previously saved file.

Printing a Publication

After creating a publication, you may want to print it. Printing a publication enables you to distribute the publication to others in a form that can be read or viewed but typically not edited. It is a good practice to save a publication before printing it, in the event you experience difficulties printing.

Plan Ahead

Determine the best method for distributing the publication.
The traditional method of distributing a publication uses a printer to produce a hard copy. A **hardcopy** or **printout** is information that exists on a physical medium such as paper. For users that can receive fax publications, you can elect to print a hard copy on a remote fax machine. Hard copies can be useful for the following reasons:

• Many people prefer proofreading a hard copy of a publication rather than viewing it on the screen to check for errors and readability.

• Hard copies can serve as reference material if your storage medium is lost or becomes corrupted and you need to recreate the publication.

    Instead of distributing a hard copy of a publication, users can choose to distribute the publication as an electronic image that mirrors the original publication's appearance. The electronic image of the publication can be e-mailed, posted on a Web site, or copied to a portable storage medium such as a USB flash drive. Two popular electronic image formats, sometimes called fixed formats, are PDF by Adobe Systems and XPS by Microsoft. In Word, you can create electronic image files through the Print tab in the Backstage view, the Save & Send tab in the Backstage view, and the Save As dialog box. Electronic images of publications, such as PDF and XPS, can be useful for the following reasons:

• Users can view electronic images of publications without the software that created the original publication (e.g., Word). Specifically, to view a PDF file, you use a program called Acrobat Reader, which can be downloaded free from Adobe's Web site. Similarly, to view an XPS file, you use a program called an XPS Viewer, which is included in the latest versions of Windows and Internet Explorer.

• Sending electronic publications saves paper and printer supplies. Society encourages users to contribute to **green computing**, which involves reducing the environmental waste generated when using a computer.

To Print a Publication

With the completed publication saved, you may want to print it. The following steps print the contents of the saved Apartment For Rent Flyer publication.

1

- If necessary, click File on the Ribbon to open the Backstage view.

- Click the Print tab in the Backstage view to display the Print gallery (Figure 1–60).

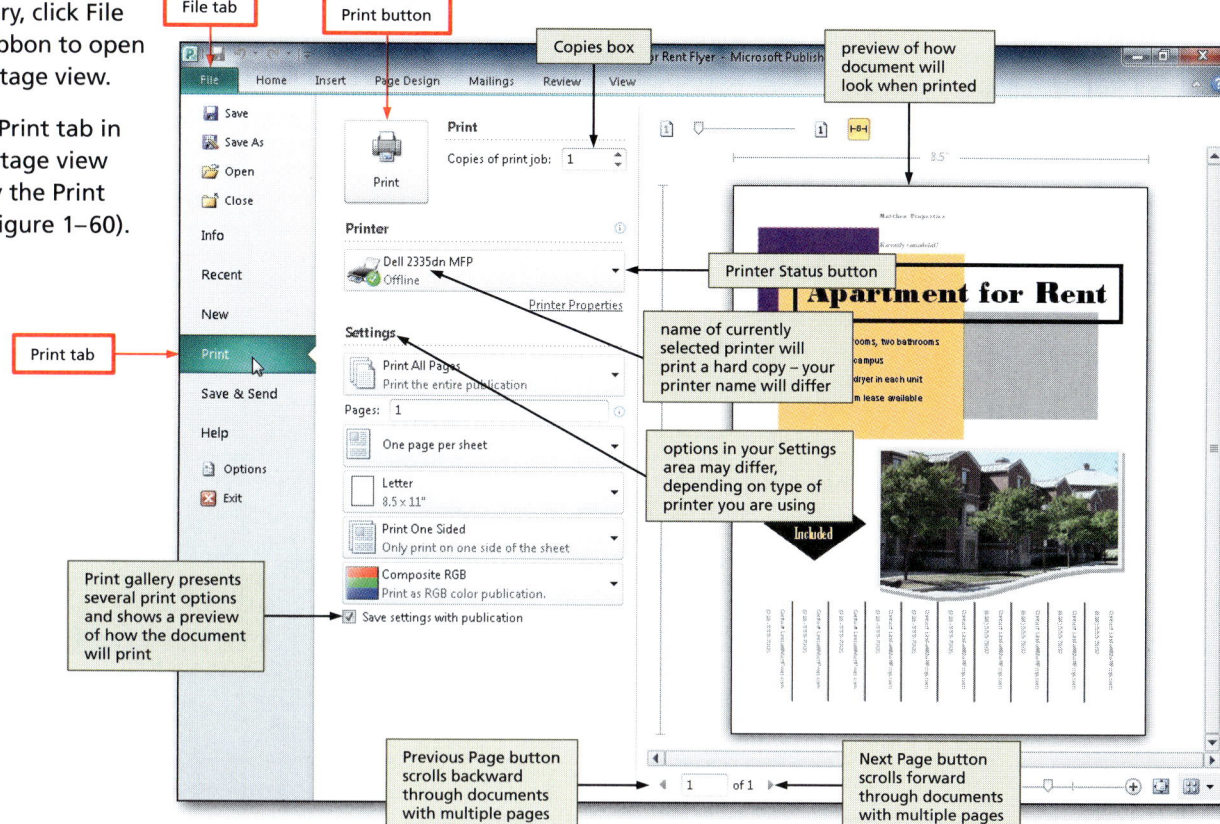

Figure 1–60

2

- Verify that the printer name that appears on the Printer Status button will print a hard copy of the document. If necessary, click the Printer Status button to display a list of available printer options and then click the desired printer to change the currently selected printer.

Q&A If my publication is multiple pages, how do I preview pages beyond the first page?

Click the Next Page button in the Print gallery to scroll forward through pages in the publication; similarly, click the Previous Page button to scroll through previous pages.

Q&A What if I decide not to print the publication at this time?

Click File on the Ribbon to close the Backstage view and return to the publication window.

3

- Click the Print button in the Print gallery to print the publication.

- When the printer stops, retrieve the printed publication (Figure 1–61).

Q&A How can I print multiple copies of my publication?

Click File on the Ribbon, click the Print tab in the Backstage view increase the number in the Number of Copies box in the Print gallery, and then click the Print button.

Q&A Do I have to wait until my publication is complete to print it?

No, you can follow these steps to print a publication at any time while you are creating it.

Q&A What if I want to print an electronic image of a document instead of a hard copy?

You would click the Printer Status button in the Print gallery and then select the desired electronic image option such as a Microsoft XPS Document Writer, which would create an XPS file.

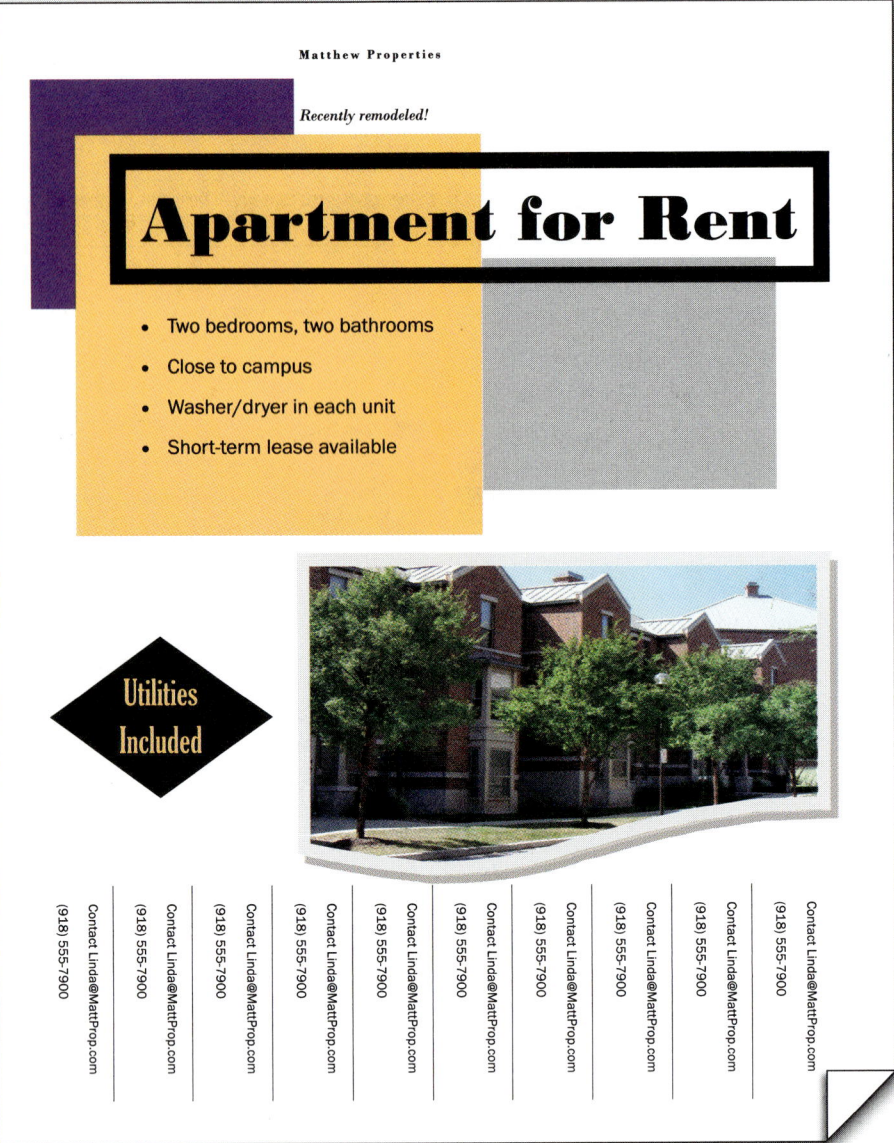

Figure 1–61

Other Ways

1. Press CTRL+P, click Print button

To Quit Publisher

This project now is complete. The following steps quit Publisher. For a detailed example of the procedure summarized below, refer to the Office 2010 and Windows 7 chapter at the beginning of this book.

1 If you have one Publisher document open, click the Close button on the right side of the title bar to close the document and quit Publisher; or if you have multiple Publisher documents open, click File on the Ribbon to open the Backstage view and then click Exit in the Backstage view to close all open documents and quit Publisher.

2 If a Microsoft Publisher dialog box appears, click the Save button to save any changes made to the document since the last save.

Break Point: If you wish to take a break, this is a good place to do so. To resume at a later time, continue following the steps from this location forward.

Starting Publisher and Opening a Publication

Once you have created and saved a publication, you may need to retrieve it from your storage medium. For example, you might want to revise the publication or reprint it. Opening a publication requires that Publisher be running on your computer.

To Start Publisher

The following steps start Publisher. For a detailed example of the procedure summarized below, refer to the Office 2010 and Windows 7 chapter at the beginning of this book.

1 Click the Start button on the Windows 7 taskbar to display the Start menu.

2 Type `Microsoft Publisher` as the search text in the 'Search programs and files' text box and watch the search results appear on the Start menu.

3 Click Microsoft Publisher 2010 in the search results on the Start menu to start Publisher and display the Backstage view.

4 If the Publisher window is not maximized, click the Maximize button next to the Close button on its title bar to maximize the window.

To Open a Publication from Publisher

Earlier in this chapter you saved your project on a USB flash drive using the file name, Apartment For Rent Flyer. The following steps open the Apartment For Rent Flyer file from the Publisher folder in the CIS 101 folder on the USB flash drive. For a detailed example of the procedure summarized below, refer to the Office 2010 and Windows 7 chapter at the beginning of this book.

1 With your USB flash drive connected to one of the computer's USB ports, click File on the Ribbon to open the Backstage view.

2 Click Open in the Backstage view to display the Open dialog box.

3 Navigate to the location of the file to be opened (in this case, the USB flash drive, then to the CIS 101 folder [or your class folder], and then to the Publisher folder).

4 Click Apartment for Rent Flyer to select the file to be opened.

5 Click the Open button (Open dialog box) to open the selected file and display the opened publication in the Publisher window.

Changing a Publication

After creating a publication, you often will find that you must make changes to it. Changes can be required because the publication contains an error or because of new circumstances. The types of changes made to publications normally fall into one of the three following categories: deletions, additions, or modifications.

Deletions Sometimes deletions are necessary in a publication because objects are incorrect or no longer are needed. For example, the Apartment For Rent Flyer no longer will need the tear-offs if you place it on a Web site. In that case, you would delete them from the page layout.

Additions Additional text, objects, or formatting may be required in the publication. For example, you would like to insert a text box in the advertising flyer that will be displayed when the flyer is published to the Web.

Modifications If you make modifications to text or graphics, normal techniques of inserting, deleting, editing, and formatting apply. Publisher provides several methods for detecting problems in a publication and making modifications, including spell checking and design checking.

To Delete the Tear-Offs

If this flyer is displayed on a campus Web site for student ads, the tear-offs are unnecessary and should be deleted. The following step deletes the tear-offs using the shortcut menu.

1 Right-click any one of the tear-offs to display the shortcut menu and then click Delete Object to delete the tear-offs (Figure 1–62).

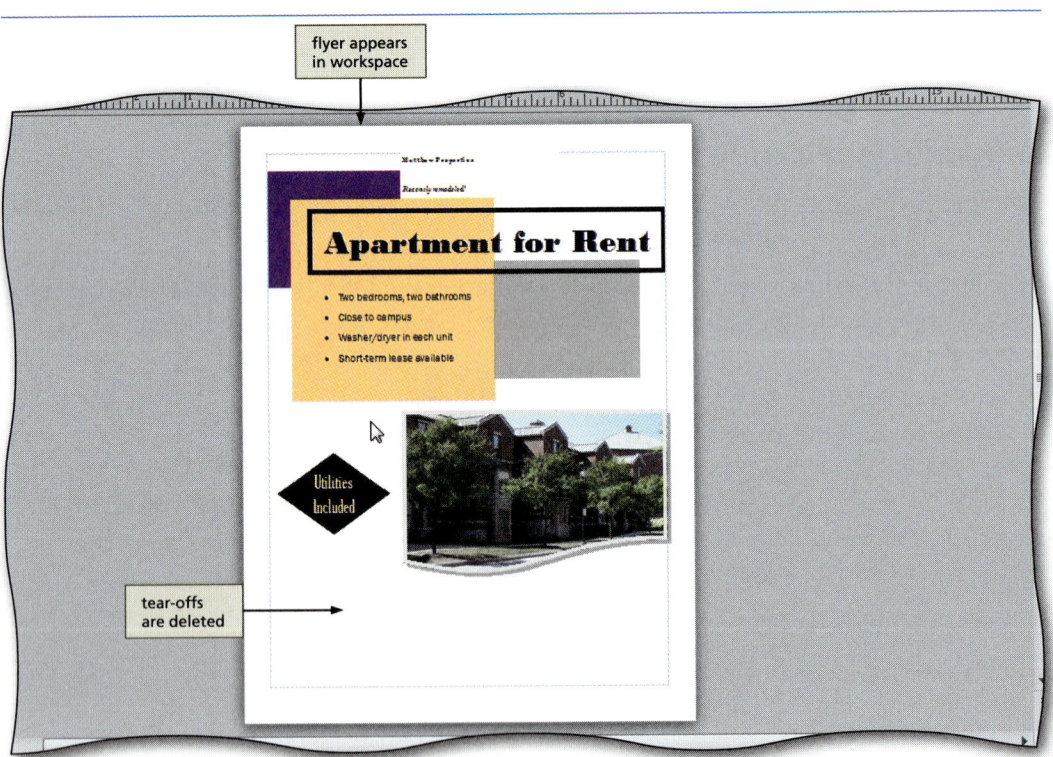

Figure 1–62

To Draw a Text Box

The next step in modifying the flyer is to create a new text box in preparation for creating a Web version of the publication. The Insert tab on the Ribbon contains many different kinds of objects that you can insert into publications. Once the text box is created, you can type in it just as you did with those supplied by the template.

The following step creates a new text box in the lower portion of the flyer.

1

- Click the Draw Text Box button (Home tab | Objects group) to select it.

- Position the mouse pointer in the upper-left corner of the empty area and then drag downward and to the right, forming a rectangle, to create a new text box that fills the area vacated by the tear-offs (Figure 1–63).

Q&A

Why did my text box move slightly when I released the mouse button?

When an object is close to a guide, Publisher will **snap**, or automatically align, the object to that guide.

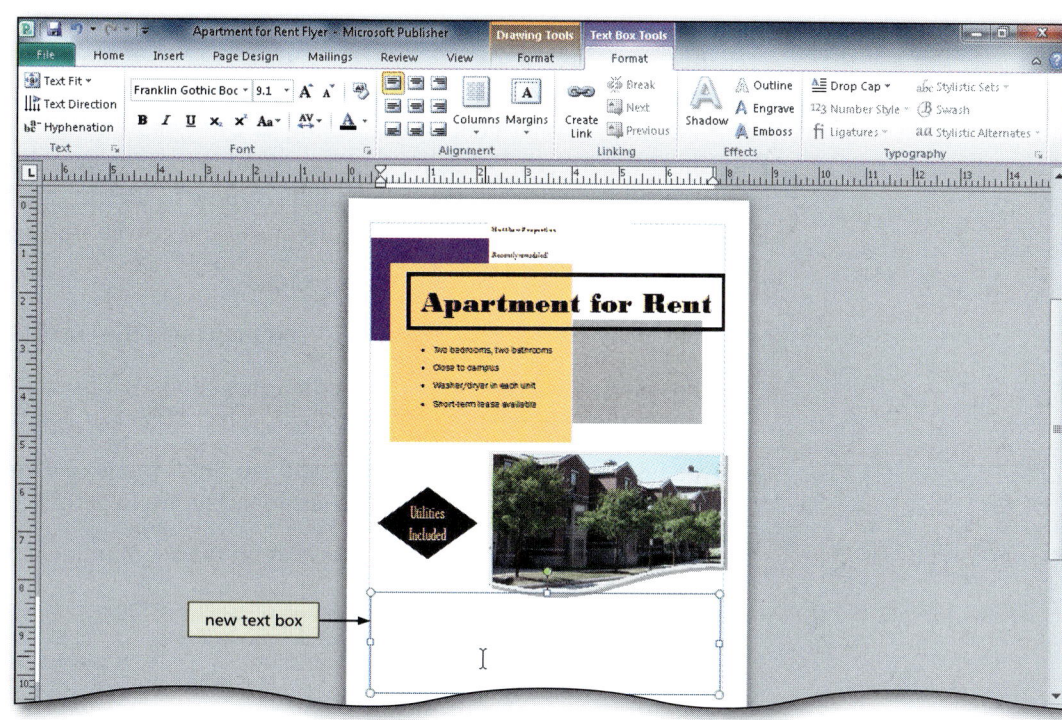

Figure 1–63

To Center Text

The default alignment for text is left aligned. You want the text in the new text box to be **centered**, that is, positioned horizontally between the left and right boundaries of the text box. The following step centers the insertion point in the text box.

1

- Click Home on the Ribbon to display the Home tab.

- With the insertion point in the text box, click the Center button (Home tab | Paragraph group) to center the insertion point (Figure 1–64).

Figure 1–64

Other Ways

1. Press CTRL+E

To Enter Text and Autofit

As you enter text in the following steps, you will purposefully misspell the word, information. Publisher checks for spelling as you type. The word, informtin, is not in Publisher's dictionary. Publisher flags potential errors in the publication with a red wavy underline. Later in the project, you will learn how to use the spell checking features of Publisher to make the red, wavy line disappear and correct the error.

1 Press the F9 key to zoom the object to 100%.

2 Type **For more informtin,** and then press the ENTER key.

3 Type **e-mail Linda@MattProp.com** and then press the ENTER key. If Publisher changes the first letter to an uppercase E, select the letter and type a lowercase e.

4 Type **or call (918) 555-7900** to finish the text. If Publisher changes the first letter to an uppercase O, select the letter and type a lowercase o.

5 Right-click the text and then click Best Fit on the shortcut menu to autofit the text (Figure 1–65).

Figure 1–65

Checking Spelling

As you type text in a publication, Publisher checks your typing for possible spelling errors. As mentioned earlier, Publisher **flags** the potential error in the publication window with a red wavy underline. A red wavy underline means the flagged text is not in Publisher's dictionary (because it is a proper name or misspelled). Although you can check the entire publication for spelling errors at once, you also can check these flagged errors as they appear on the screen.

To display a list of corrections for flagged text, right-click the flagged text. Publisher displays a list of suggested spelling corrections on the shortcut menu. A flagged word, however, is not necessarily misspelled. For example, many names, abbreviations, and specialized terms are not in Publisher's main dictionary. In these cases, you instruct Publisher to ignore the flagged word. As you type, Publisher also detects duplicate words while checking for spelling errors. For example, if your publication contains the phrase, to the the store, Publisher places a red wavy underline below the second occurrence of the word, the.

To Check Spelling as You Type

The following steps direct Publisher to replace a misspelled word with the correct one.

1
- Right-click the word, informtin, to display a shortcut menu that includes a list of suggested spelling corrections for the flagged word (Figure 1–66).

Q&A What if Publisher does not flag my spelling errors with wavy underlines?

To verify that the 'Check spelling as you type' features are enabled, open the Backstage view click Options on the Publisher tab, and then click Proofing. When the Publisher Options dialog box is displayed, ensure the 'Check spelling as you type' check box contains a check mark and the 'Hide spelling errors' check box does not contain a check mark. Click the Cancel or OK button to return to the publication.

Figure 1–66

2
- Click information on the shortcut menu to replace the flagged word (Figure 1–67).

What if, when I right-click the misspelled word, my desired correction is not in the list on the shortcut menu?

You can retype the correct word, or you can click the Spelling button (Home tab | Editing group) to display the Spelling dialog box.

Figure 1–67

Creating a Web Page from a Publication

You can create two types of publications with Microsoft Publisher: print publications and Web publications. A **Web publication** is one suitable for publishing to the Web, containing certain objects, formatting options, hyperlinks, and other features specific to Web pages. You can create a Web publication from scratch, or you can save the print publication as a Web publication.

<table>
<tr><td>**Plan
Ahead**</td><td>**Decide if the flyer will work as a Web publication.**
Will the publication be accessible and practical on the Web? Is the target audience common Web users? If so, determine whether an e-mail, Web page, or Web site would be the most efficient means of communication. How will readers find the Web page? When converting to a Web publication, determine which objects will work effectively on the Web and which ones will not, and then modify the publication as necessary.</td></tr>
</table>

To Save a Print Publication as a Web Publication

The Share tab in the Backstage view includes a group of commands that allow you to distribute publications as e-mail, to save publications in different file types, or to package publications for sending to other users. In the following steps, you will share the publication by publishing it to the Web. **Publishing HTML** or **publishing to the Web** is the process of making Web pages available to others, for example, on the World Wide Web or on a company's intranet. Files intended for use on the Web, however, need a different format. A **Hypertext Markup Language (HTML)** file is a file capable of being stored and transferred electronically on a file server in order to be displayed on the Web. For more information on publishing to the Web, and on using Web folders and servers, see Appendix B.

The following steps save the publication as a Web flyer by publishing it as **MHTML** (Mime Hypertext Markup Language), a small single-file file format that does not create a supporting folder of resources. The MHTML file can be published to and downloaded from the Internet quickly.

1

- With a USB flash drive connected to one of the computer's USB ports, click File on the Ribbon to open the Backstage view.

- Click the Save & Send tab to display the gallery.

- Click the Publish HTML button to display its options (Figure 1–68).

Figure 1–68

• Click the Web Page (HTML) button to display the other options for publishing HTML (Figure 1–69).

Figure 1–69

• Click Single File Web Page (MHTML) to select it.

• Click the Publish HTML button to display the Save As dialog box.

• Navigate to your USB flash drive storage location.

• Type **Apartment for Rent Web Flyer** in the File name text box. Do not press the ENTER key after typing the file name (Figure 1–70).

• Click the Save button in the Save As dialog box to save the publication on the USB flash drive with the file name, Apartment for Rent Web Flyer.

Other Ways

1. Click Save As in Backstage view, enter file name, click 'Save as type' box arrow, click Single File Web Page (*.mht;*. mhtml), click Save button (Save As dialog box)

Figure 1–70

To Preview the Web Publication in a Browser

To preview the Web publication you must open it in a Web browser. The following steps navigate to your storage device and then double-click the Web page file to open it. For more information on folder navigation, refer to the Office 2010 and Windows 7 chapter at the beginning of this book.

1

• Click the Start button on the Windows 7 taskbar to display the Start menu and then click Computer to open the Computer folder window (Figure 1–71).

• Navigate to your storage location (in this case, the Chapter 01 folder in the Publisher folder in the CIS 101 folder [or your class folder] on the USB flash drive). For a detailed example of this procedure, refer to Steps 3a – 3c in the To Save a File in a Folder section in the Office 2010 and Windows 7 chapter at the beginning of this book.

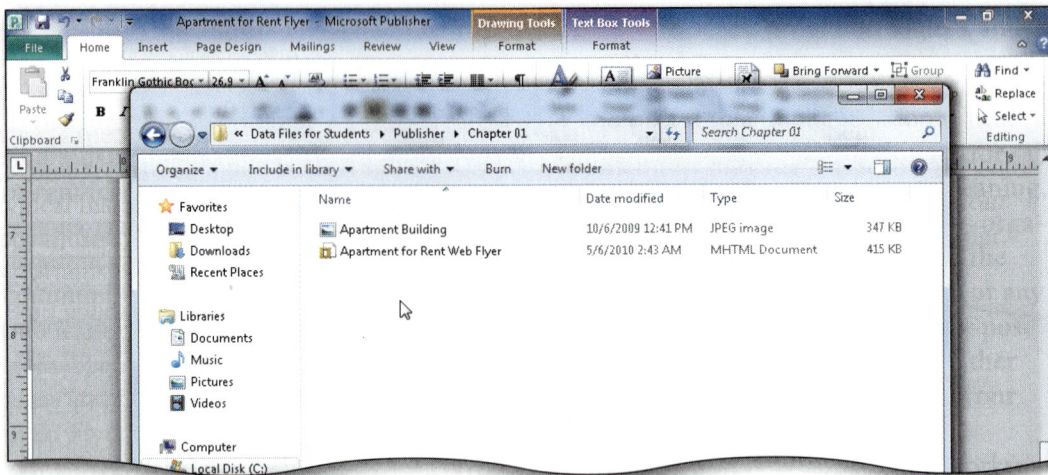

Figure 1–71

2

• Double-click the Apartment for Rent Web flyer.mht file to open it in your browser.

• If necessary, maximize the window when the browser window opens (Figure 1–72).

Q&A Why does my display look different?

Each brand and version of Web browser software displays information in a slightly different manner. Additionally, your browser settings, such as text size and zoom level, may differ.

Q&A I cannot see all of my Web page. What should I do?

Your browser may have a Change zoom level button arrow that you can click to display a list of magnifications. Click a smaller magnification percentage or click the Zoom out command if available.

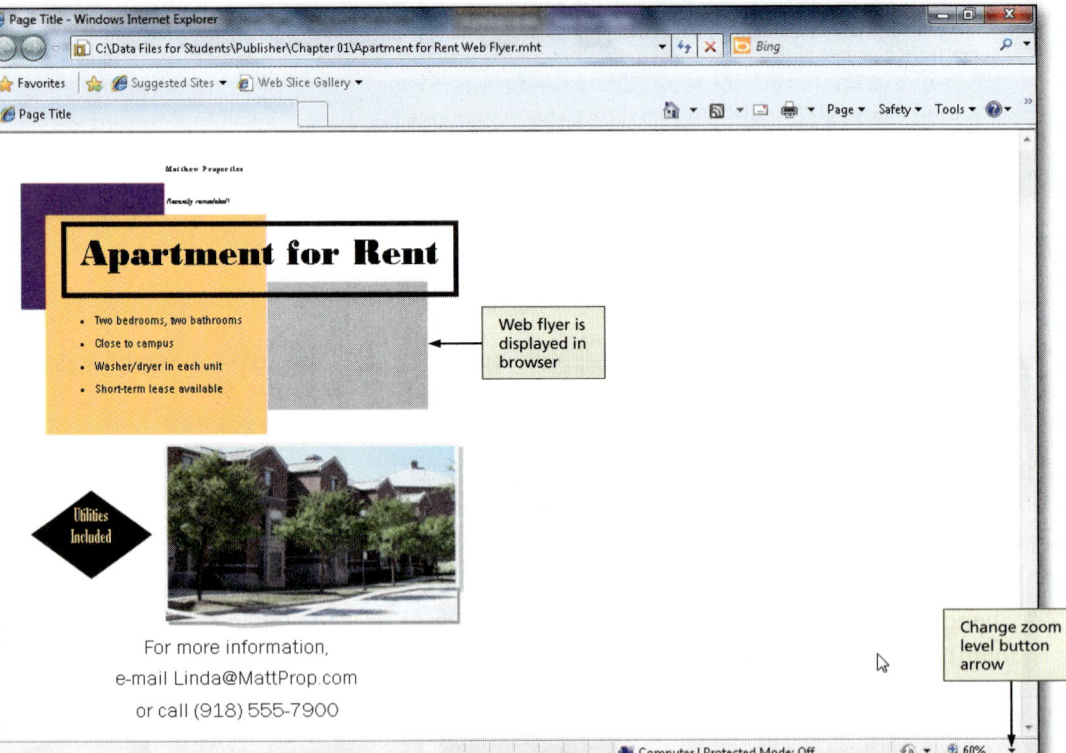

Figure 1–72

3
- Click the Close button on the browser window's title bar.
- Click the Close button on the open folder window title bar.

To Quit Publisher

The following steps quit Publisher.

1 If you have one Publisher document open, click the Close button on the right side of the title bar to close the document and quit Publisher; or if you have multiple Publisher documents open, click File on the Ribbon to open the Backstage view and then click Exit on the Publisher tab to close all open documents and quit Publisher.

2 If a Microsoft Publisher dialog box appears, click the Don't Save button to discard any changes made to the document since the last save.

BTW

Quick Reference
For a table that lists how to complete the tasks covered in this book using the mouse, Ribbon, shortcut menu, and keyboard, see the Quick Reference Summary at the back of this book, or visit the Publisher 2010 Quick Reference Web page (scsite.com/pub2010/qr).

Chapter Summary

In this chapter, you have learned how to choose a publication template, set font and color schemes, enter text in a publication, delete objects from a publication, insert a photograph and building block, print a publication, and save a print publication as a Web publication. The items listed below include all the new Publisher skills you have learned in this chapter.

1. Start Publisher (PUB 4)
2. Select a Template (PUB 7)
3. Choose Publication Options (PUB 9)
4. Hide the Page Navigation Pane (PUB 13)
5. Display Boundaries (PUB 15)
6. Select (PUB 15)
7. Zoom (PUB 16)
8. Replace Placeholder Text (PUB 17)
9. Replace Other Text (PUB 18)
10. Enter Bulleted Text (PUB 20)
11. Enter Tear-Off Text (PUB 22)
12. Increase the Font Size (PUB 24)
13. Autofit Text (PUB 25)
14. Delete Objects (PUB 26)
15. Save a Publication (PUB 27)
16. Insert a Photograph into a Picture Placeholder (PUB 28)
17. Apply a Picture Style (PUB 31)
18. Use the Building Block Library (PUB 32)
19. Move an Object (PUB 34)
20. Resize an Object (PUB 35)
21. Align an Object (PUB 35)
22. Change the Font Color (PUB 36)
23. Change Publication Properties (PUB 38)
24. Save an Existing Publication with the Same File Name (PUB 40)
25. Print a Publication (PUB 41)
26. Quit Publisher (PUB 42)
27. Open a Publication from Publisher (PUB 43)
28. Draw a Text Box (PUB 44)
29. Center Text (PUB 45)
30. Check Spelling as You Type (PUB 47)
31. Save a Print Publication as a Web Publication (PUB 48)
32. Preview the Web Publication in a Browser (PUB 50)

Learn It Online

Test your knowledge of chapter content and key terms.

Instructions: To complete the Learn It Online exercises, start your browser, click the Address bar, and then enter the Web address **scsite.com/pub2010/learn**. When the Office 2010 Learn It Online page is displayed, click the link for the exercise you want to complete and then read the instructions.

Chapter Reinforcement TF, MC, and SA
A series of true/false, multiple choice, and short answer questions that test your knowledge of the chapter content.

Flash Cards
An interactive learning environment where you identify chapter key terms associated with displayed definitions.

Practice Test
A series of multiple choice questions that test your knowledge of chapter content and key terms.

Who Wants To Be a Computer Genius?
An interactive game that challenges your knowledge of chapter content in the style of a television quiz show.

Wheel of Terms
An interactive game that challenges your knowledge of chapter key terms in the style of the television show *Wheel of Fortune*.

Crossword Puzzle Challenge
A crossword puzzle that challenges your knowledge of key terms presented in the chapter.

Apply Your Knowledge

Reinforce the skills and apply the concepts you learned in this chapter.

Modifying Text and Formatting a Publication
Instructions: Start Publisher. Open the publication, Apply 1-1 Mountain Bike For Sale Unformatted, from the Data Files for Students. See the inside back cover of this book for instructions on downloading the Data Files for Students, or contact your instructor for more information about accessing the required files.

The publication you open is a flyer in which you replace text, delete objects, insert and format a building block. You then will save the print publication as a Web publication (Figure 1–73).

For Sale

Mountain Bike

⇒ Great Condition
⇒ New Tires
⇒ Light, Aluminum Frame
⇒ New Chain

Perfect for any terrain!

$300.00

Call Steve:

555-2354

Figure 1–73

Continued >

STUDENT ASSIGNMENTS

Perform the following tasks:

1. Use the Save As command in the Backstage view to save the file on your storage device with the file name, Apply 1-1 Mountain Bike For Sale Flyer.

2. Autofit the headline text.

3. Edit the text in the bulleted list so it reads as shown in Figure 1–73 on the previous page. Increase the font size of the bulleted text and subheading. Select the text and then select an arrow bullet style from the Bullet Styles gallery.

4. Insert a photograph in the picture placeholder. Use the file named, Mountain Bike, from the Data Files for Students.

5. Delete the tear-offs and the text box above them with the name and telephone number. Draw a large text box in the lower portion of the flyer. Enter the text **Call Steve:** and then press the ENTER key. Type **555-2354** and then center and autofit the text.

6. Insert a building block attention getter similar to the one in Figure 1–73 on the previous page. *Hint:* Attention getters are in the Advertisements folder in the Building Block Library dialog box. Resize the attention getter as necessary.

7. Select the text in the attention getter and then type **Perfect for any terrain!** to replace it. Change the font color using the Mini toolbar. Choose the Accent 2 scheme color.

8. Change the publication properties, as specified by your instructor. Include searchable keywords.

9. Save the publication again.

10. Save the publication as a Web publication, using the Share command in the Backstage view. When asked for a file name, type **Apply 1-1 Mountain Bike For Sale Web Flyer** to replace the default text.

11. Preview the Web publication using a browser.

12. Submit the revised publications, as specified by your instructor.

Extend Your Knowledge

Extend the skills you learned in this chapter and experiment with new skills. You may need to use Help to complete the assignment.

Modifying Text and Graphics Formats

Instructions: Start Publisher. You will create the flyer shown in Figure 1–74.

Figure 1–74

Continued >

Perform the following tasks:

1. Use Help to learn about picture shapes, shadows, and rotating objects.

2. Using the New tab in the Backstage view, select the Sports Event Flyer. *Hint:* Navigate through the Flyers folder, the All Event folder, and then scroll down to the Other area to locate the template. Use the Wildflower color scheme and the Foundry Font scheme. Choose to include no tear-offs.

3. When the template is displayed, if the Page Navigation pane appears, click the Page Number button on the status bar to hide it.

4. Replace all template text using Figure 1–74 on the previous page as a guide. For the bulleted list, after choosing a bullet style and typing the bullets, select all of the text in the list and then click the Increase Font Size button (Home tab | Font group) three times.

5. Delete the 'Describe your location' text box, the organization logo, and the default graphic.

6. Click the Picture Placeholder button (Insert tab | Illustrations group). Move the placeholder to a location in the lower-left portion of the flyer. Resize the placeholder to approximately three inches square. Use the size notation on the status bar as a guide.

7. Click the placeholder icon. When Publisher displays the Insert Picture dialog box, navigate to the Data Files for Students and then insert the Playing Cards photograph from the Chapter 01 folder. Once the photo is inserted, drag the left and right cropping handles to the edge of the picture placeholder.

8. With the photograph selected, click the Picture Border button (Picture Tools Format tab | Picture Styles group), and then click the Accent 1 Red scheme color. Click the Picture Shape button (Picture Tools Format tab | Picture Styles group), and then click the Trapezoid shape in the first row. Use Help to learn how to choose a Shadow effect. *Hint:* You may want to use the Shadow Effect button (Picture Tools Format tab | Shadow Effects group) and choose a style and color from the gallery.

9. With the photograph still selected, rotate the photograph by dragging the green rotation handle slightly to the left, as shown in Figure 1–74 on the previous page.

10. Change the publication properties, as specified by your instructor. Save the revised publication and then submit it in the format specified by your instructor.

Make It Right

Analyze a publication and correct all errors and/or improve the design.

Correcting Replacement Text and Grammar Errors

Instructions: Start Publisher. Open the publication, Make It Right 1-1 Comedy Club Flyer, from the Data Files for Students. See the inside back cover of this book for instructions on downloading the Data Files for Students, or contact your instructor for more information about accessing the required files.

The publication is a flyer that contains template text boxes that have yet to be replaced, an organization logo that needs to be deleted, text that is too small for a flyer, and spelling errors, as shown in Figure 1–75. You are to replace the placeholder text in the Date and Time text boxes. Use the current date, and insert a time of 8:00 p.m. Autofit the text in the lower-left portion of the flyer so that it is easier to read. Delete the organization logo in the lower-right corner of the publication. Finally, where Publisher displays the red wavy underlines, you are to correct each spelling error by right-clicking the flagged text and then clicking the appropriate correction on the shortcut menu.

Change the publication properties, as specified by your instructor. Save the revised publication and then submit it in the format specified by your instructor.

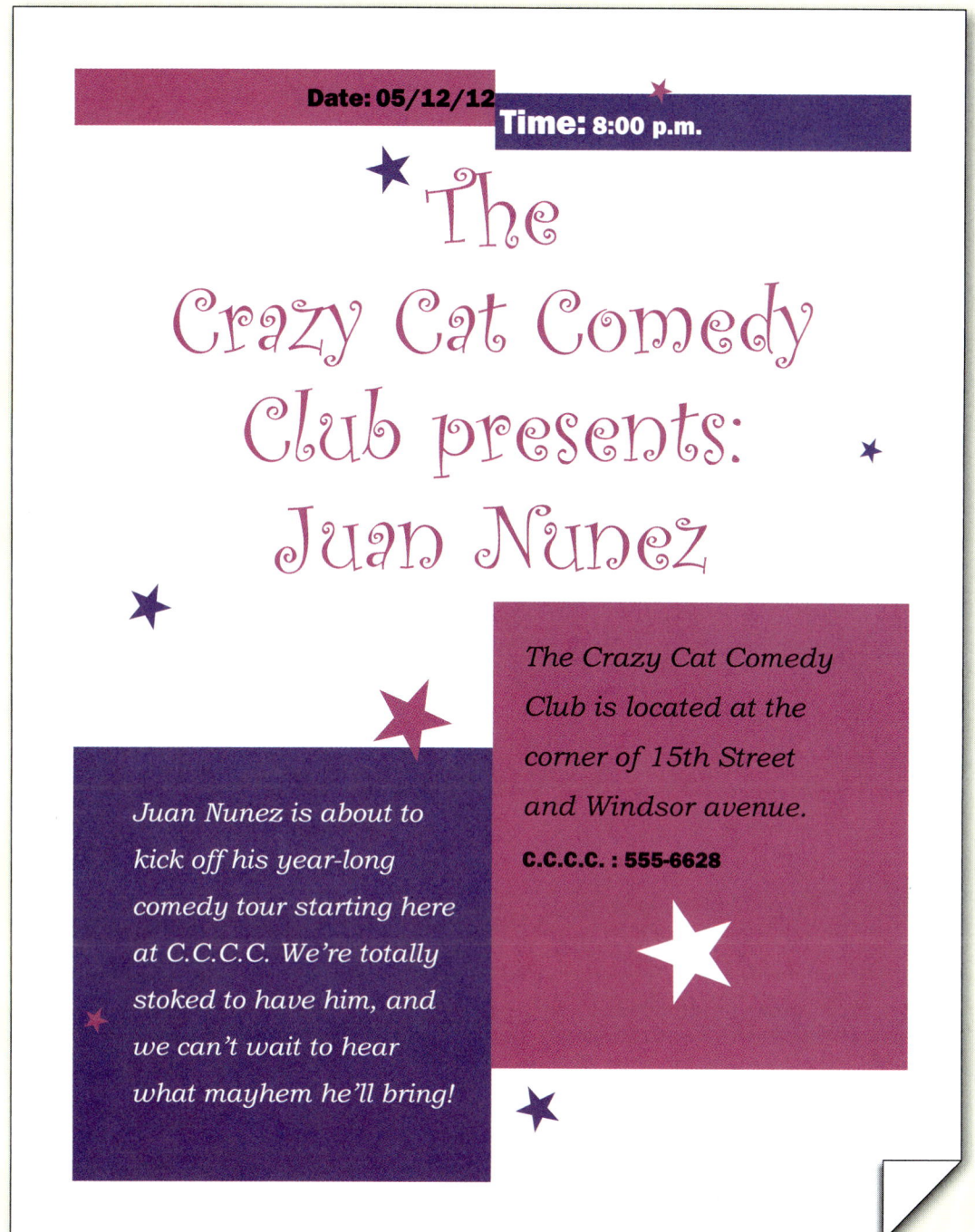

Figure 1–75

In the Lab

Design and/or create a publication using the guidelines, concepts, and skills presented in this chapter. Labs are listed in order of increasing difficulty.

Lab 1: Creating a Flyer with a Picture

Problem: You work part-time for the Alumni Association at the local college. Your supervisor has asked you to prepare a flyer that advertises the homecoming barbeque. You prepare the flyer shown in Figure 1–76.

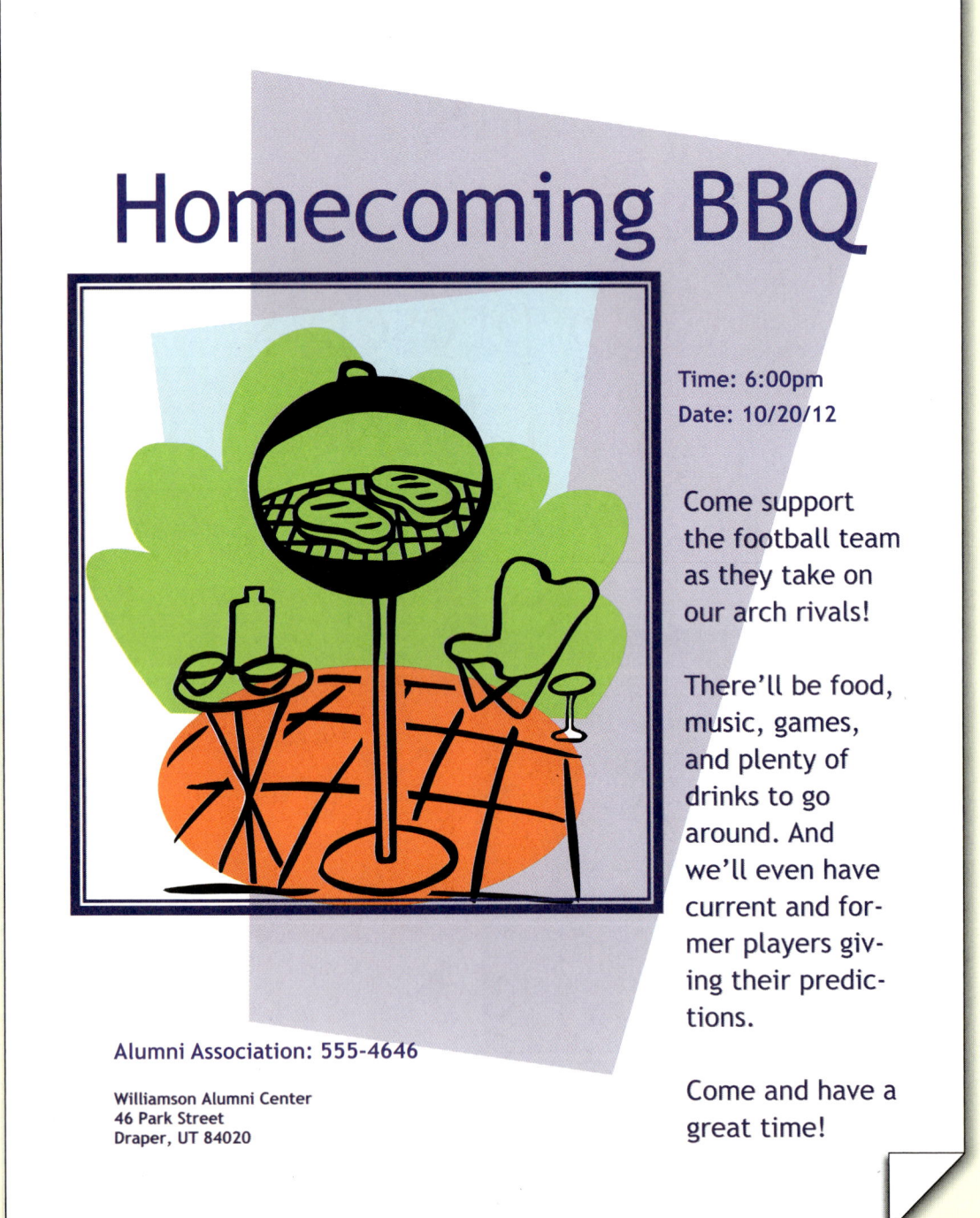

Figure 1–76

Instructions: Perform the following tasks:

1. Start Publisher.

2. In the Backstage view, click the Flyers folder in the New template gallery, and then click the All Event folder. Choose the BBQ flyer template, the Dark Blue color scheme, and the Archival font scheme. Do not include tear-offs.

3. Create the publication and, if necessary, close the Page Navigation pane.

4. Select the headline text and then type **Homecoming BBQ** to replace the headline text.

5. Select the graphic. Display the Picture Tools Format tab on the Ribbon. Click the More button (Picture Tools Format tab | Picture Styles group), and then choose Picture Style 17.

6. One at a time, move the Time, Date, and description text boxes to the right so that they do not overlap the border of the picture. *Hint:* As you move the text boxes, align their left edges using the pink visual layout guides.

7. Select only the description text box. Drag the right center sizing handle to the left until the text box boundary aligns with the margin guide. That way, the text box still fits within the margins.

8. Edit the template text in those boxes to match Figure 1–76. Autofit the text in the description text box.

9. Save the publication on a USB flash drive using the file name, Lab 1–1 Homecoming BBQ Flyer.

10. Zoom to the lower-left portion of the flyer.

11. Select the text in the contact text box. Type **Alumni Association: 555-4646** to replace the text.

12. Select the text in the 'Describe your location' text box. Type the following to replace the text, pressing the ENTER key at the end of each line:
Williamson Alumni Center
46 Park Street
Draper, UT 84020

13. Zoom out to display the entire flyer in the workspace.

14. Right-click any flagged words and correct the spelling. Change the publication properties, as specified by your instructor.

15. Save the publication again, and submit it in the format specified by your instructor.

In the Lab

Lab 2: Creating a Bake Sale Sign

Problem: The DPT club on campus is sponsoring a bake sale. The proceeds will be donated to the local soup kitchen. You have been asked to create a simple sign that advertises the bake sale. The club has taken a picture of a brownie for you to use as a graphic. The completed flyer is shown in Figure 1–77.

Figure 1–77

Instructions: Perform the following tasks:

1. Start Publisher. When the Backstage view is open, click the Signs folder and then click the Garage Sale #3 template. Select the Solstice color scheme and the Fusion font scheme, and then click the Create button.

2. If necessary, close the Page Navigation pane.

3. Click the headline text and type **Bake Sale** to replace the text.

4. Select the other template text and replace it using the text in Figure 1–77.

5. To create another shape and text box:

    a. Select the circular shape around the Date text box by clicking it.

    b. SHIFT+click to select the Date text box itself.

    c. CTRL+drag the two selected objects to a location in the lower-left portion of the template, creating a copy.

    d. Select the text in the copy and replace it using the text in Figure 1–77.

6. Correct any spelling errors. If necessary, autofit the text.

7. Click the Insert Picture from File button (Insert tab | Illustrations group) and insert the photo of the brownie from the Data Files for Students. Resize the photo as necessary and move it to the upper-right corner of the flyer.

8. Change the publication properties as specified by your instructor.

9. Save the flyer with the name, Lab 1-2 Bake Sale Sign.

10. Submit the publication in the format specified by your instructor.

In the Lab

Lab 3: Creating a Gift Certificate

Problem: You are a desktop publishing intern at the Write Store, a unique gift shop located close to school. Your supervisor has asked you to create a gift certificate for customers to purchase. You prepare the gift certificate shown in Figure 1–78.

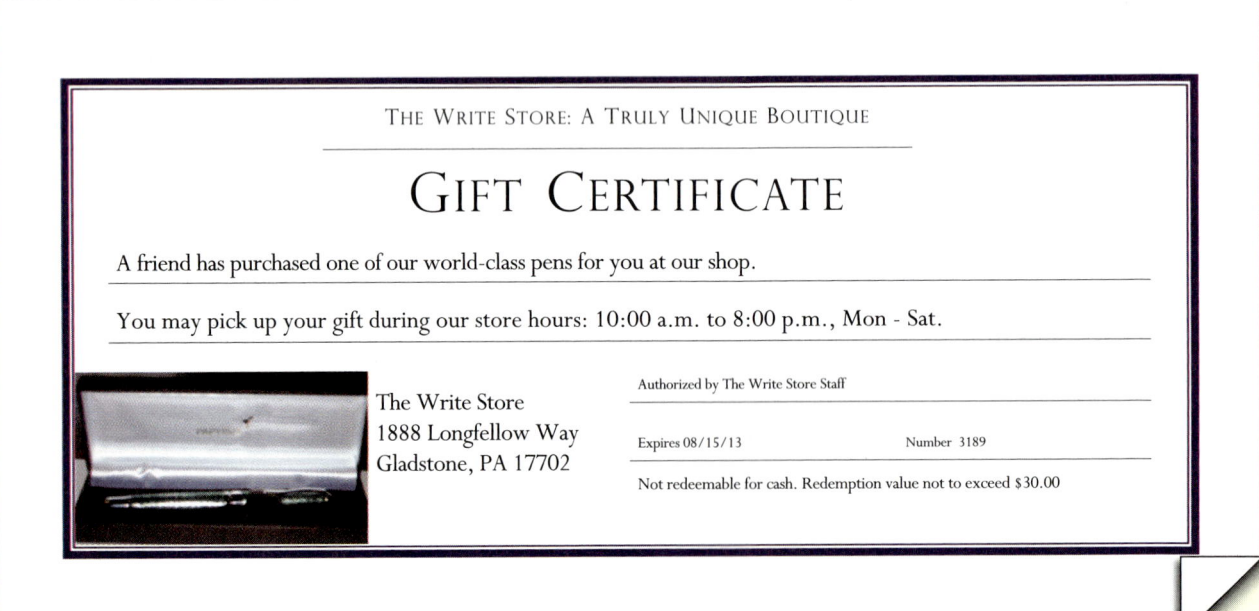

THE WRITE STORE: A TRULY UNIQUE BOUTIQUE

GIFT CERTIFICATE

A friend has purchased one of our world-class pens for you at our shop.

You may pick up your gift during our store hours: 10:00 a.m. to 8:00 p.m., Mon - Sat.

The Write Store
1888 Longfellow Way
Gladstone, PA 17702

Authorized by The Write Store Staff

Expires 08/15/13   Number 3189

Not redeemable for cash. Redemption value not to exceed $30.00

Figure 1–78

Instructions: Start Publisher. Select Gift Certificates in the New template gallery and then choose the Refined template. Choose the Black & White color scheme and the Etched font scheme. Replace all the text boxes, using the text shown in Figure 1–78. Delete the logo. Use a picture placeholder and insert the Pen photo from the Data Files for Students. See the inside back cover of this book for instructions on downloading the Data Files for Students, or contact your instructor for more information about accessing the required files. Correct any spelling errors and change the publication properties, as specified by your instructor. Save the publication using the file name, Lab 1-3 Gift Certificate. Submit the publication in the format specified by your instructor.

Cases and Places

Apply your creative thinking and problem solving skills to design and implement a solution.

Note: To complete these assignments, you may be required to use the Data Files for Students. See the inside back cover of this book for instructions on downloading the Data Files for Students, or contact your instructor for information about accessing the required files.

1: Design and Create an Advising Sign

Academic

You are a student worker in the Computer Information Technology Department. You have been asked to create a sign that displays advising hours for the upcoming registration period. Using the Business Hours template in the Signs folder in the Backstage view, create a sign that lists advising hours. Change the headline to Advising Hours. Change the times to: Monday and Wednesday from 8:00 a.m. to 5:00 p.m.; Tuesday and Thursday from 12:00 p.m. to 8:00 p.m.; and Friday from 8:00 a.m. to 3:30 p.m. The advising office is closed on Saturdays and Sundays. In the lower text box, list the office number, ET 220, and the telephone number, 555-HELP. Change the publication properties, as specified by your instructor.

2: Design and Create a Reunion Flyer

Personal

Your high school has asked you to create a flyer for the upcoming 10-year class reunion. Use the concepts and techniques presented in this chapter to create the flyer with information from your high school. Use the Apartment to Rent template with the Orchid color scheme and the Industrial font scheme. Autofit the headline. Delete any unnecessary objects. Include your e-mail and telephone number in the contact information tear-offs. Use the following bulleted list for details about the reunion:

- Wear your letter jacket!
- Show your school spirit!
- High School Gym, 7:00 p.m.!
- RSVP to Jesse by 05/07/12!

Insert a formatted attention getter with the words, Dress is casual. Insert a picture of your high school, if you have one. Change the publication properties, as specified by your instructor.

3: Design and Create a Business Announcement

Professional

Your Internet service provider (ISP) maintains an electronic bulletin board where customers may post one-page business announcements. Create an advertising flyer for the place you work, or where you want to work. You may use one of Publisher's Flyer templates or choose a blank template and design the flyer using Building Blocks. Replace all text and graphics. Use font colors and font sizes to attract attention. Instead of tear-offs, draw a text box that includes the company's Web page address and telephone number. Correct any spelling errors. Change the publication properties, as specified by your instructor. Assign publication properties and include keywords that will produce many hits during Web searches. Save the flyer as a single page Web publication.

2 | Publishing a Trifold Brochure

Objectives

You will have mastered the material in this chapter when you can:

- Discuss advantages of the brochure medium
- Choose brochure options
- Copy and paste with paste options
- Wordwrap text
- Format characters with italic, underline, bold, and drop cap
- Use stylistic sets, alternates, and ligatures
- Apply a font effect

- Copy formatting with the Format Painter
- Insert clip art
- Edit captions and caption styles
- Check the spelling of the entire publication
- Run the Design Checker
- Choose appropriate printing services, paper, and color libraries
- Package a publication for a printing service

2 | Publishing a Trifold Brochure

Introduction

Whether you want to advertise a service, event, or product, or merely want to inform the public about a current topic of interest, brochures are a popular type of promotional publication. A brochure, or pamphlet, usually is a high-quality publication with lots of color and graphics, created for advertising purposes. Businesses that may not be able to reach potential clientele effectively through traditional advertising media, such as newspapers and radio, can create a long-lasting advertisement with a well-designed brochure.

Brochures come in all shapes and sizes. Colleges and universities produce brochures about their programs. The travel industry uses brochures to entice tourists. In addition, service industries and manufacturers display their products using this visual, hands-on medium.

Project — Spring Break Brochure

The project in this chapter shows you how to build the two-page, trifold brochure shown in Figure 2–1. The brochure informs students about a spring break travel company that specializes in Florida vacations. Each side of the brochure has three panels. Page 1 contains the front and back panels, as well as the inside fold. Page 2 contains a three-panel display that, when opened completely, provides the reader with more details about the company and a response form.

On page 1, the front panel contains shapes, text boxes, and a graphic designed to draw the reader's attention and inform the reader of the intent of the brochure. The back panel, which is displayed in the middle of page 1, contains the name of the company, the address, and telephone numbers. The inside fold, on the left, contains an article about the details of the location.

The three inside panels on page 2 contain more information about the vacations and a form the reader may use to request more information.

Overview

As you read this chapter, you will learn how to create the brochure shown in Figure 2–1 by performing these general tasks:

- Select a brochure template and specify the layout options.
- Edit and format the template text.
- Use typography tools to apply stylistic formatting.
- Insert clip art with captions.
- Proofread the brochure with spell checking and the Design Checker.
- Prepare the brochure for commercial printing.

Figure 2–1

General Project Guidelines

When you create a Publisher brochure, the actions you perform and decisions you make will affect the appearance and characteristics of the finished publication. As you create a brochure, such as the project shown in Figure 2–1 on the previous page, you should follow these general guidelines:

1. **Decide on the purpose, shelf life, and layout.** Spend time brainstorming ideas for the brochure. Think about why you want to create one. Decide on the purpose of the brochure. Is it to inform the public, sell a product, attract customers, or advertise an event? Adjust your template, fonts, colors, and graphics to match that purpose. Brochures commonly have a wider audience than flyers. They need to last longer. Carefully consider whether to add dated material or prices. Create a timeline of effectiveness and plan to have the brochure ready far in advance. Decide how many panels your brochure should have, and how often you are going to produce it. If you are working for someone, draw a storyboard and get it approved before you begin. Think about alignment of objects, proximity of similar data, contrast, and repetition.

2. **Create the brochure.** Gather all the information, such as stories, graphics, logos, colors, shapes, style information, and watermarks. Use a template until you are more experienced in designing brochures. Save copies or versions along the way. If you have to create objects from scratch, have someone else evaluate your work and give you constructive feedback. If you are using forms in your brochure, verify the manner in which the viewer will return the form. Check and double-check all prices, addresses, and phone numbers.

3. **Proofread and check the publication.** If possible, proofread the brochure with a fresh set of eyes, that is, at least one to two days after completing the first draft. Insert repeated elements and special objects, such as watermarks and logos, which need to be placed around, or behind, other objects. Look at text wrapping on every graphic. Ask someone else to proofread the brochure and give you suggestions for improvements. Revise as necessary and then use the spelling and design checking features of the software.

4. **Plan for printing.** Consult with commercial printers ahead of time. Brochures are more effective on heavier paper, with strong colors and a glossy feel. Choose a paper that is going to last. Discuss commercial printing color modes and fonts. Check to make sure the commercial printer can accept Microsoft Publisher 2010 files. Designing an effective brochure involves a great deal of planning. A good brochure, or any publication, must deliver a message in the clearest, most attractive, and most effective way possible.

When necessary, more specific details concerning the above guidelines are presented at appropriate points in the chapter. The chapter also will identify the actions performed and decisions made regarding these guidelines during the creation of the brochure shown in Figure 2–1 on the previous page.

The Brochure Medium

Professionals commonly print brochures on special paper to provide long-lasting documents and to enhance the graphics. The brochure medium intentionally is tactile. Brochures are meant to be touched, carried home, passed along, and looked at, again and again. Newspapers and fliers usually have short-term readership, on paper that readers throw away or recycle. Brochures, on the other hand, frequently use a heavier stock of paper so that they can stand better in a display rack.

The content of a brochure needs to last longer, too. On occasion, the intent of a brochure is to educate, such as a brochure on health issues in a doctor's office. More commonly, though, the intent is to market a product or sell a service. Prices and dated materials that are subject to frequent change affect the usable life of a brochure.

Typically, brochures use a great deal of color, and they include actual photographs instead of drawings or graphic images. Photographs give a sense of realism to a publication and show actual people, places, or objects, whereas images or drawings are more appropriate for conveying concepts or ideas.

Brochures, designed to be in circulation for longer periods as a type of advertising, ordinarily are published in greater quantities and on more expensive paper than other single-page publications and are, therefore, more costly. The cost, however, is less prohibitive when the brochure is produced **in-house** using desktop publishing, rather than by an outside service. The cost per copy is lower when producing brochures in mass quantities. Table 2–1 lists some benefits and advantages of using the brochure medium.

Table 2–1 Benefits and Advantages of Using the Brochure Medium	
EXPOSURE	An attention getter in displays
	A take-along document encouraging second looks
	A long-lasting publication due to paper and content
	An easily distributed publication — mass mailings, advertising sites
INFORMATION	An in-depth look at a product or service
	An opportunity to inform in a nonrestrictive environment
	An opportunity for focused feedback using tear-offs and forms
AUDIENCE	Interested clientele and retailers
COMMUNICATION	An effective medium to highlight products and services
	A source of free information to build credibility
	An easier means to disseminate information than a magazine

For an introduction to Windows 7 and instruction about how to perform basic Windows 7 tasks, read the Office 2010 and Windows 7 chapter at the beginning of this book, where you can learn how to resize windows, change screen resolution, create folders, move and rename files, use Windows Help, and much more.

Plan Ahead

Decide on the purpose, shelf life, and layout.

- The first impression of a company is created by its brochure. Thus, it is important that your brochure appropriately reflect the essence of the business, item, or event. Determine the shelf life of your brochure and its purpose.

- Choose your template, font, colors, panels, and forms. Choose a template that matches the feeling of your topics. Use colors and fonts already in use in graphics provided by the company, school, or event organizers.

To Start Publisher

The following steps, which assume Windows 7 is running, start Publisher based on a typical installation. You may need to ask your instructor how to start Publisher for your computer. For a detailed example of the procedure summarized below, refer to the Office 2010 and Windows 7 chapter.

1 Click the Start button on the Windows 7 taskbar to display the Start menu.

2 Type `Microsoft Publisher` as the search text in the 'Search programs and files' text box and watch the search results appear on the Start menu.

3 Click Microsoft Publisher 2010 in the search results on the Start menu to start Publisher and display the Backstage view and the New template gallery.

4 If the Publisher window is not maximized, click the Maximize button next to the Close button on its title bar to maximize the window.

For an introduction to Office 2010 and instruction about how to perform basic tasks in Office 2010 programs, read the Office 2010 and Windows 7 chapter at the beginning of this book, where you can learn how to start a program, use the Ribbon, save a file, open a file, quit a program, use Help, and much more.

BTW

How Brochures Differ
Each brochure template produces two pages of graphics, business information text boxes, and story boxes. Differences among templates include the look and feel of the front panel, the location and style of the shapes and graphics, the design of any panel dividers, and the specific kind of decorations unique to each publication set.

BTW

BTWs
For a complete list of the BTWs found in the margins of this book, visit the Publisher 2010 BTW Web page (scsite.com/pub2010/btw).

Creating a Trifold Brochure

Publisher-supplied templates use proven design strategies and combinations of objects, which are placed to attract attention and disseminate information effectively. The options for brochures differ from those for other publications in that they allow you to choose from page sizes, special kinds of forms, and panel/page layout options.

> **Plan Ahead**
>
> **Create the brochure.**
> Gather all the information and objects. Once you make a few changes, save a copy as the rough draft version. As you add new objects, verify the accuracy of all your information. Get a second opinion on anything created from scratch.

Making Choices about Brochure Options

For the Spring Break brochure, you will use an informational brochure template, named Layers, making changes to its color scheme, font scheme, page size, and forms. **Page size** refers to the number of panels in the brochure. Form options, which are displayed on page 2 of the brochure, include None, Order form, Response form, and Sign-up form. The Order form displays fields for the description of items ordered as well as types of payment information, including blank fields for entering items, quantities, and prices. The Response form displays check box choices, fields for comments, blanks for up to four multiple-choice questions, and a comment section. The Sign-up form displays check box choices, fields for time and price, and payment information. All three forms are detachable to use as turnaround documents.

To Search for a Template

The following steps use the 'Search for templates' box to search for the desired template by name.

1

- Click the Brochures folder to display brochure templates and other folders (Figure 2–2).

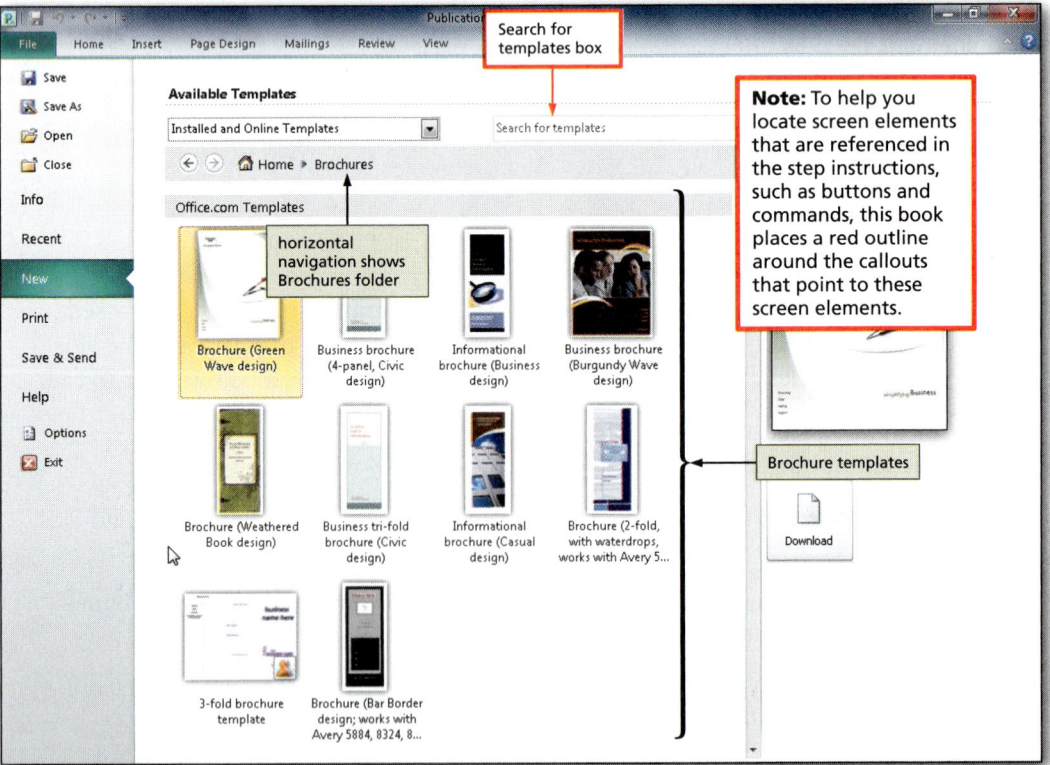

Figure 2–2

2

- Click the 'Search for templates' box.

- Type **Layers** as the search text and then press the ENTER key to search for the template.

- After a few moments, if necessary, click the Layers template in the Informational area to choose the template (Figure 2–3).

Q&A Why does my preview look different?

Your preview may contain a color scheme or font scheme from a previous publication. Figure 2–3 uses the default settings.

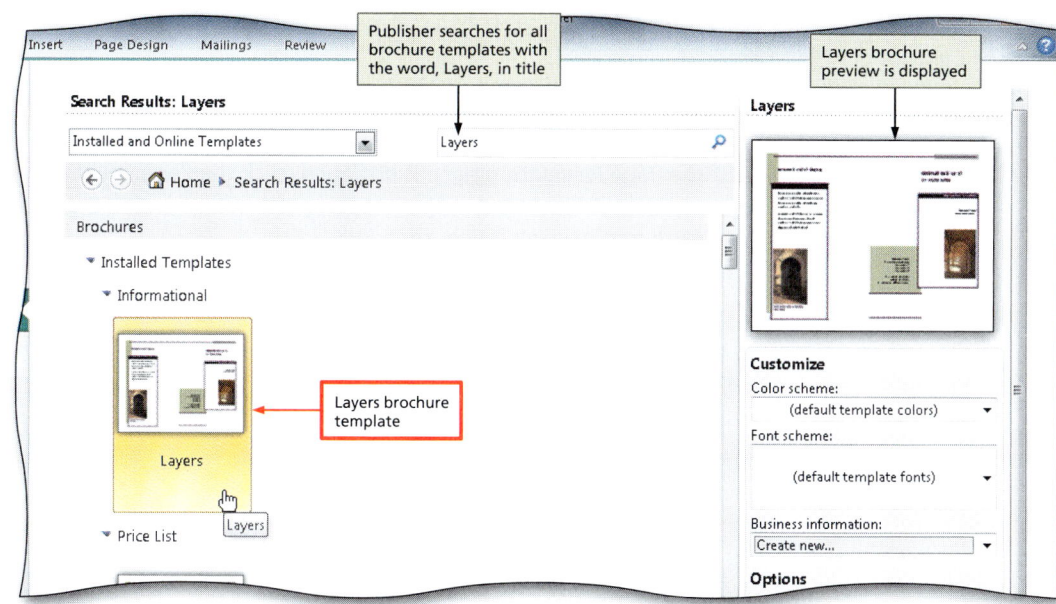

Figure 2–3

To Choose Brochure Options

The following steps choose brochure options.

1

- Click the Color scheme box arrow and then click Lagoon to choose the color scheme.

- Click the Font scheme box arrow and then click Metro to choose the font scheme.

- Do not click the Business information box arrow because it is not used in this publication.

- Click the Page size box arrow in the Options area and then, if necessary, click 3-panel to choose the number of panels.

- If necessary, click to remove the check mark in the 'Include customer address' check box.

- If necessary, scroll down and then click the Form box arrow in the Options area. Click Response form to choose the type of form (Figure 2–4).

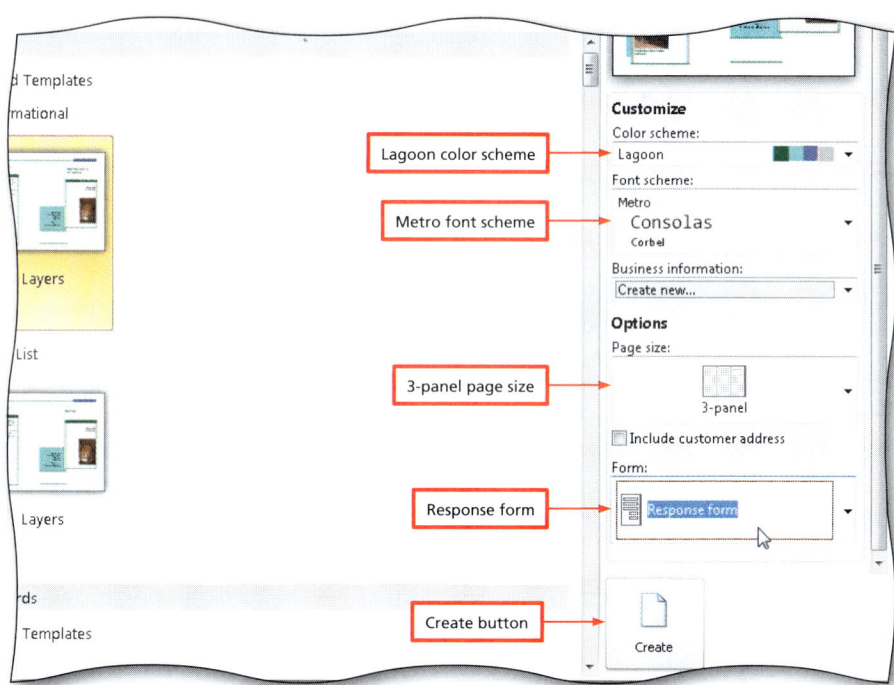

Figure 2–4

2

- Click the Create button in the lower-right corner of the window to create the publication based on the template settings.

BTW

Q&As
For a complete list of the Q&As found in many of the step-by-step sequences in this book, visit the Publisher 2010 Q&A Web page (scsite .com/pub2010/qa).

BTW

The Ribbon and Screen Resolution
Publisher may change how the groups and buttons within the groups appear on the Ribbon, depending on the computer's screen resolution. Thus, your Ribbon may look different from the ones in this book if you are using a screen resolution other than 1024 × 768.

BTW

Brochure Page Size
In addition to the intent and content of the brochure, you must consider the shape and size of the page when designing a brochure. Publisher can incorporate a variety of paper sizes; the most common are 8 ½ × 11 inches and 11 × 17 inches. You also can design smaller brochures, such as those used as liner notes for CD jewel cases or inserts for videotapes.

BTW

Automatic Saving
Publisher can save your publication at regular intervals for you. In the Backstage view, click Options and then click Save (Publisher Options dialog box). Make sure the 'Save AutoRecover information every' check box contains a check mark. In the Minutes box, specify how often you want Publisher to save files. Do not use AutoRecover as a substitute for regularly saving your work.

To Open the Page Navigation Pane

The following step opens the Page Navigation pane to view both pages of the brochure.

1 If the Page Navigation pane is not open, click the Page Number button on the status bar to open it. If the Page Navigation pane is minimized, click the Expand Page Navigation Pane button to maximize it (Figure 2–5).

Figure 2–5

To Save a Publication

You have performed many tasks while creating this publication and do not want to risk losing work completed thus far. Accordingly, you should save the publication. The following steps assume you already have created folders for storing your files, for example, a CIS 101 folder (for your class) that contains a Publisher folder (for your assignments). Thus, these steps save the document in the Publisher folder in the CIS 101 folder on a USB flash drive using the file name, Spring Break Brochure. For a detailed example of the procedure summarized below, refer to the Office 2010 and Windows 7 chapter at the beginning of this book.

1 With a USB flash drive connected to one of the computer's USB ports, click the Save button on the Quick Access Toolbar to display the Save As dialog box.

2 Type **Spring Break Brochure** in the File name text box to change the file name. Do not press the ENTER key after typing the file name because you do not want to close the dialog box at this time.

3 Navigate to the desired save location (in this case, the Publisher folder in the CIS 101 folder [or your class folder] on the USB flash drive).

4 Click the Save button (Save As dialog box) to save the document in the selected folder on the selected drive with the entered file name.

To Edit Text Boxes on the Front Panel

Recall that replacing text involves selecting the current text and replacing it with new, appropriate text. The following steps select and then replace text in the right panel on page 1.

1 In the right panel of page 1, select the text, Product/Service Information. Click the Zoom In button on the status bar several times to facilitate editing. Type `Spring Break` and then press the ENTER key. Type `2012` to replace the text.

2 Right-click the text to display the shortcut menu and then click Best Fit to autofit the text.

3 Below the heading, select the text Business Tagline or Motto, and then type `Starfish Vacations` to replace the text (Figure 2–6).

Figure 2–6

To Delete Objects

You will not use some of the objects in the brochure. The following steps delete the unused objects.

1 Point to the Business Name text box in the right panel and then click the border to select the text box. Press the DELETE key to delete the object.

2 Point to the telephone number text box and then click the border to select the text box. Press the DELETE key to delete the object.

3 Click the Show Whole Page button on the status bar to display the entire page. Select the organization logo by clicking its border. Press the DELETE key to delete the object (Figure 2–7 on the next page).

BTW

Brochure Features
Many brochures incorporate newspaper features, such as columns and a masthead, and add eye appeal with logos, sidebars, shapes, and graphics. Small brochures typically have folded panels. Larger brochures resemble small magazines, with multiple pages and stapled bindings.

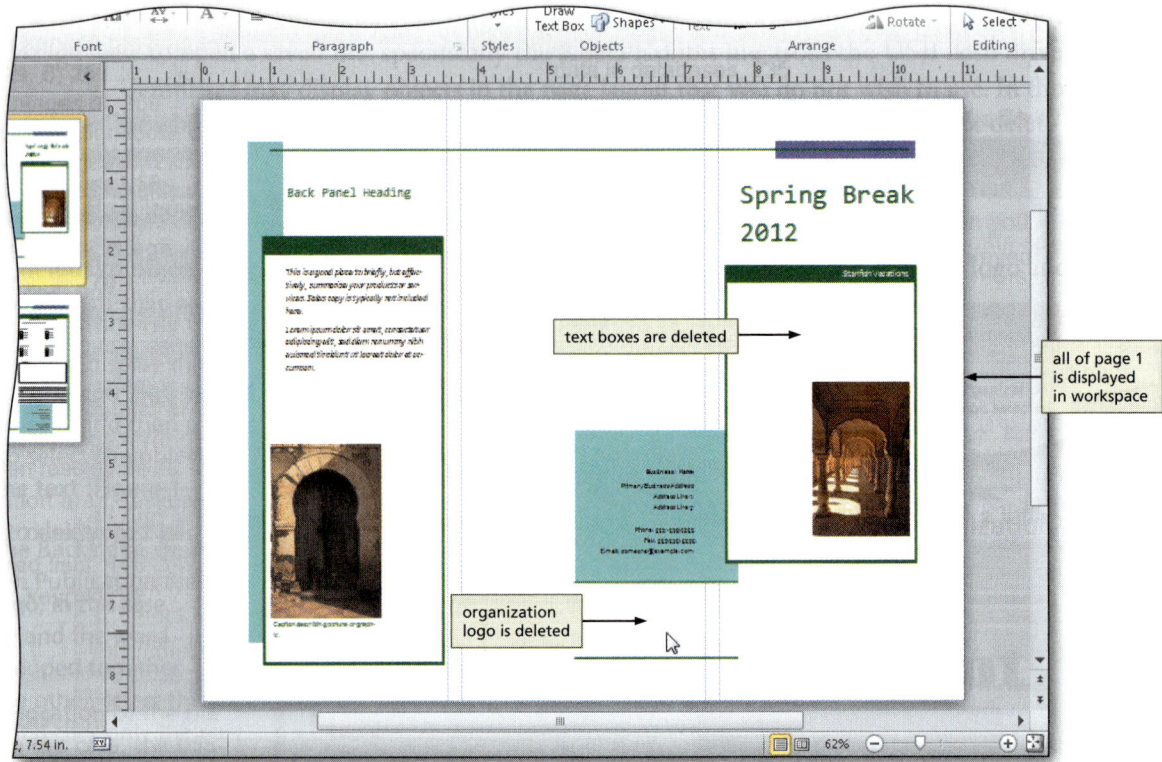

Figure 2–7

Copying and Pasting

The next step in editing the Brochure is to replace text on the center panel of page 1, which will be displayed on the back of the folded brochure. One way to enter this information in the brochure is to type it. Recall, however, that you already typed Starfish Vacations on the right panel. Thus, a timesaving alternative would be to copy and paste the text. The copy and cut functions transfer text or objects to the Windows Clipboard and to the Office Clipboard. A clipboard is a temporary storage area for text or objects copied or cut from a publication. The Windows Clipboard holds the most recent items copied or cut. The Office Clipboard, which you will learn about in a future chapter, holds the 24 most recently copied or cut items. When you copy text, it remains in the publication and is copied to the Clipboard. When you cut text, however, it is placed on the Clipboard, but removed from the publication. Table 2–2 displays various methods for copying, cutting, pasting, and deleting selected text.

Table 2–2 Copy, Cut, Paste, and Delete Methods				
Method	**Copy**	**Cut**	**Paste**	**Delete**
shortcut menu	Right-click to display the shortcut menu and then click Copy	Right-click to display the shortcut menu and then click Cut	Right-click to display the shortcut menu and then click Paste	Right-click to display the shortcut menu and then click Delete Text
Ribbon	Click the Copy button (Home tab | Clipboard group)	Click the Cut button (Home tab | Clipboard group)	Click the Paste button (Home tab | Clipboard group)	Click the Cut button (Home tab | Clipboard group)
keyboard	Press CTRL+C	Press CTRL+X	Press CTRL+V	Press the DELETE key or BACKSPACE key

Paste Options

When you are ready to paste, Publisher displays paste options. **Paste options** are small thumbnails representing format choices that appear in a small gallery on the shortcut menu. They also appear when you click the Paste button (Home tab | Clipboard group) or when you click the Paste Options button after you paste.

Depending on the content of the Clipboard, you may see different thumbnails with advanced options for pasting. For example, the Keep Source Formatting option pastes the copied content *as is* without any formatting changes. The Merge Formatting option mixes the source and destination font styles. The Keep Text Only option pastes the copied text as plain unformatted text and removes any styles or hyperlinks.

BTW

Moving Text
If you want to use the mouse to move text from one location to another, you can select the text and then drag it to the new location. Publisher will display a small rectangle attached to the mouse pointer as you position the mouse in the new location. Moving text or objects also can be accomplished by cutting and then pasting.

To Copy and Paste

The following steps copy text from the right panel of the brochure and then paste it to the center panel. You will use the Keep Text Only paste option. The text box is synchronized, so the business name also will appear on page 2 of the brochure.

- Zoom in on the right panel of page 1.

- Select the text, Starfish Vacations, by dragging through it.

- Right-click to display the shortcut menu (Figure 2–8).

Figure 2–8

Q&A

Why does my shortcut menu already display paste options?

Someone may have copied or cut something to the Clipboard on your machine. It will not affect your current steps.

2

- Click Copy on the shortcut menu to copy the selection to the Clipboard.

- Scroll to the lower portion of the center panel. Zoom to 200%.

- Select the text, Business Name, in the center panel of page 1.

- Right-click to display the shortcut menu (Figure 2–9).

Q&A

Why does my Business Name text box display different words?

The person who set up your installation may have supplied a default name for Publisher Business Name text boxes.

⚲ Experiment

- Point to each of the Paste Options thumbnails to view the ScreenTip and the live preview.

Figure 2–9

3

- Click the Keep Text Only button to paste only the text and not the formatting into the destination location (Figure 2–10).

4

- Right-click the text and then click Best Fit on the shortcut menu to autofit the text.

Figure 2–10

Other Ways

1. Click Copy button (Home tab | Clipboard group), click Paste button (Home tab | Clipboard group), click desired Paste Option button

2. Press CTRL+C, press CTRL+V, click desired Paste Option button

To Create a New Text Box and Paste Text

The following steps create a new text box in the center panel and then paste the copied text.

1 Scroll and zoom as necessary to display the upper portion of the center panel.

2 Click the Draw Text Box button (Home Tab | Objects group).

3 Drag in the center panel to create a text box, approximately 2.5 inches square. Watch the status bar as you drag to estimate the size.

4 With the new text box selected, right-click to display the shortcut menu and the Paste Options gallery. Click the Keep Text Only button to paste the text, Starfish Vacations, from the Clipboard to the text box.

5 Right-click the text and then click Best Fit on the shortcut menu to autofit the text (Figure 2–11).

Figure 2–11

To Replace Text in the Center Panel

The following steps replace the text in the address and contact information text boxes in the center panel. The text boxes are synchronized, so the address and contact information also will appear on page 2 of the brochure. Ignore any wavy lines as you type the text. You will check the spelling later in the chapter.

1 Scroll to the lower portion of the center panel and then zoom as necessary to select all of the text in the Primary Business Address text box.

2 Type P. O. Box 350 and then press the ENTER key.

3 Type `Lykins, FL 32301` to complete the address.

4 Autofit the text.

5 Select the text in the contact information text box.

6 Type `Phone Toll-Free 866-555-6837` and then press the ENTER key.

7 Type `Fax: 850-555-6838` and then press the ENTER key.

8 Type `E-mail: info@starfishvacations.com` to complete the entry.

9 Press CTRL+A to select all of the text. Right-click the selection and then click Best Fit on the shortcut menu to autofit the text (Figure 2–12).

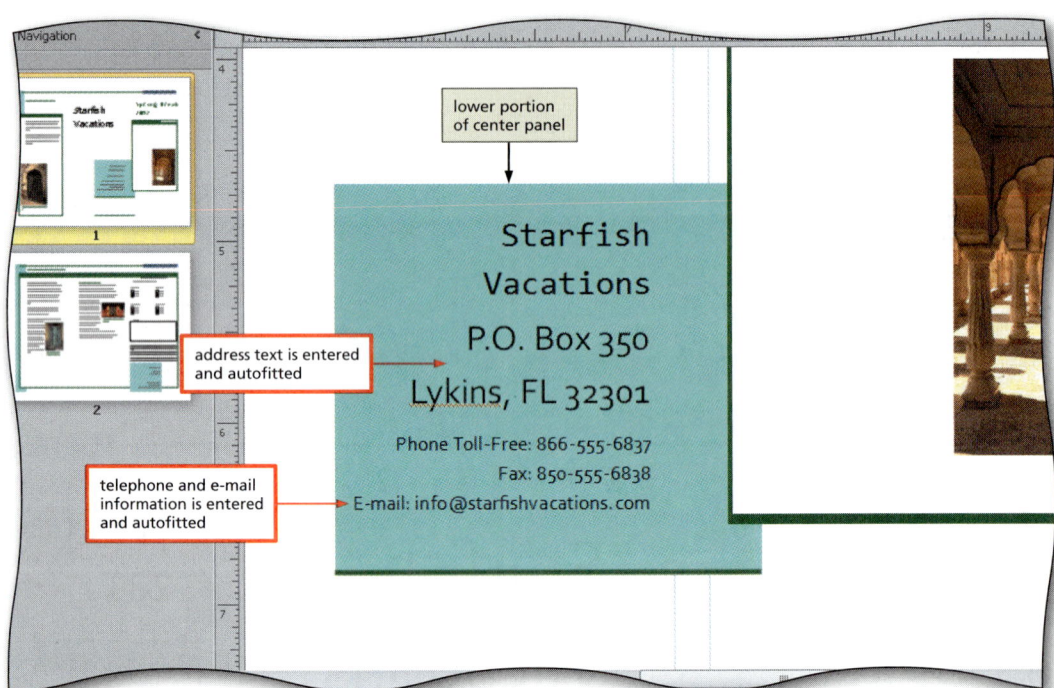

Figure 2–12

Typing Paragraphs of Text

When you type paragraphs of text, you will use Publisher's wordwrap feature. Wordwrap allows you to type words in a text box continually without pressing the ENTER key at the end of each line. When the insertion point reaches the right margin of a text box, Publisher automatically positions the insertion point at the beginning of the next line. As you type, if a word extends beyond the right margin, Publisher also automatically positions that word on the next line along with the insertion point.

Publisher creates a new paragraph or hard return each time you press the ENTER key. Thus, as you type text in a text box, do not press the ENTER key when the insertion point reaches the right margin. Instead, press the ENTER key only in these circumstances:

- To insert blank lines in a text box
- To begin a new paragraph
- To terminate a short line of text and advance to the next line
- To respond to questions or prompts in Publisher dialog boxes, panes, and other on-screen objects

To view where in a publication you pressed the ENTER key or SPACEBAR, you may find it helpful to display formatting marks. A **formatting mark**, sometimes called a non-printing character, is a special character that Publisher displays on the screen, but is not visible on a printed publication. For example, the paragraph mark (¶) is a formatting mark that indicates where you pressed the ENTER key. A raised dot (·) appears where you pressed the spacebar. An end of field marker (¤) is displayed to indicate the end of text in a text box. Other formatting marks are discussed as they appear on the screen.

To Display Formatting Marks

Depending on settings made during previous Publisher sessions, your Publisher screen already may display formatting marks (Figure 2–13). The following step displays formatting marks, if they do not show already on the screen.

1

• If it is not selected already, click the Special Characters button (Home tab | Paragraph group) to display formatting marks (Figure 2–13).

Q&A

What if I do not want formatting marks to show on the screen?

If you feel the formatting marks clutter the screen, you can hide them by clicking the Special Characters button again. The publication windows presented in the rest of this chapter show the formatting marks.

Figure 2–13

Other Ways
1. Press CTRL+SHIFT+Y

To Wordwrap Text as You Type

The step on the next page wordwraps as you type text in the left panel.

1

- Scroll to the upper-left portion of the publication to display the left panel.

- Select the text in the text box below the title.

- Type, without pressing the ENTER key, **Our oceanfront locations are the capital cities of spring break in the U.S.! With miles and miles of white sand beaches surrounded by the turquoise waters of the Gulf of Mexico, it's no wonder that Florida attracts so many students for their spring break vacations.** and notice that Publisher wraps the text when you get close to the right edge of the text box (Figure 2–14).

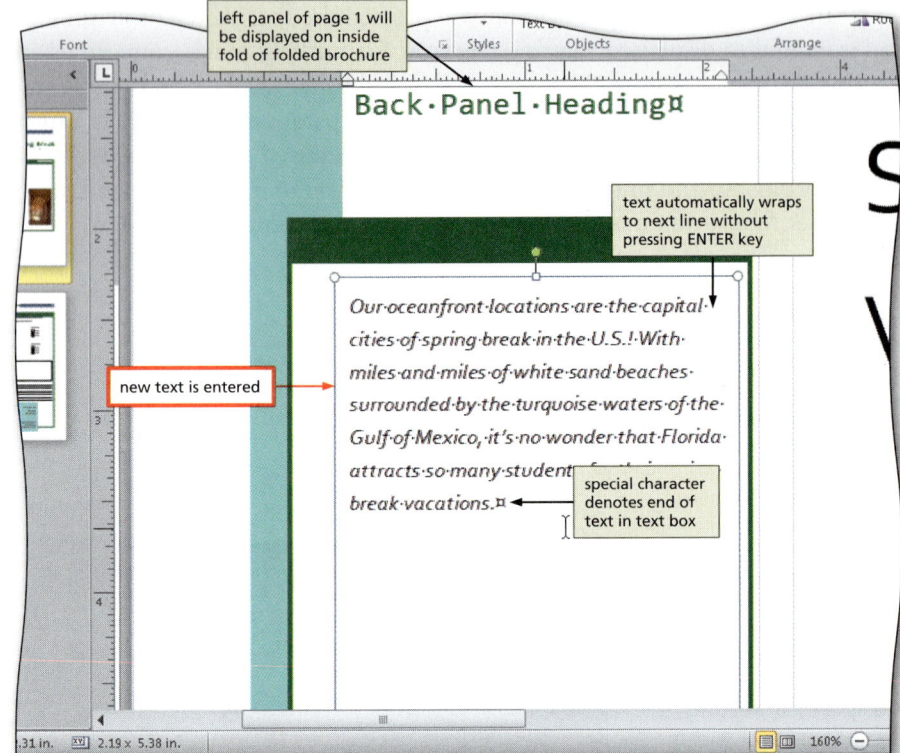

Figure 2–14

Q&A Why does my publication wrap on different words?

Differences in wordwrap relate to your printer. It is possible that the same publication could wordwrap differently if printed on different printers.

To Replace the Title

The following steps replace the default text in the title of the left panel.

1 Select the text in the title of the left panel.

2 Type **Leisure Time** to replace the text (Figure 2–15).

Figure 2–15

Formatting Characters

Character formatting is the process of changing the way characters appear on the screen and in print. Characters include letters, numbers, punctuation marks, symbols, and other typographical elements. You use character formatting to emphasize certain words and improve the readability of a document. For example, you can italicize, underline, or bold characters. Many of the character formatting options appear in the Font group on the Home tab. Other font effects, such as embossing, superscripting, or subscripting, are available in the dialog box that is displayed when you click the Font Dialog Box Launcher. Although you can format characters before you type, many Publisher users enter text first and then format the existing text.

In Publisher, typography refers to specialized effects and fonts including drop caps, number styles, and glyphs. A glyph is a special stroke that appears in text that is not part of the normal font set. Diacritical marks, such as the umlaut or cedilla, use glyphs. Ligatures, stylistic sets, swashes, and stylistic alternates, as well as some alphabetic characters that are not part of the English language also are created using glyphs.

BTW

Character Typography
Typography also includes scaling, tracking, and kerning of characters. You will learn about these spacing options in a future chapter.

To Italicize Text

To emphasize the title of the left panel, you will apply italic formatting in the brochure. Italicized text has a slanted appearance. To italicize multiple words, you must select them. If you want to italicize only one word, the word does not have to be selected. Simply click anywhere in the word and then apply the desired format. The following step selects the title and then italicizes it.

- Select the title text, Leisure Time.

- Click the Italic button (Home tab | Font group) to italicize the selected text (Figure 2–16).

Q&A

How would I remove an italic format?

You would click the Italic button a second time, or you could click the Undo button on the Quick Access Toolbar, immediately after clicking the Italic button.

Q&A

How can I tell what formatting has been applied to text?

The selected buttons and boxes on the Home tab show the formatting characteristics of the location of the insertion point.

Figure 2–16

Other Ways
1. Click Italic button on Mini toolbar
2. Right-click selected text, point to Change Text on shortcut menu, click Font, click Italic in Font style list (Font dialog box), click OK button
3. Click Font Dialog Box Launcher, click Italic in Font style list (Font dialog box), click OK button
4. Press CTRL+I

To Underline a Word

As with bold text, an **underline** emphasizes or draws attention to specific text. Underlined text prints with an underscore (_) below each character. In the left panel of the brochure, the word, Florida, is emphasized with an underline.

As with the italic format, if you want to underline a single word, you do not need to select the word. Simply position the insertion point somewhere in the word and apply the desired format. The following step formats a word with an underline.

1
- In the story in the left panel, click somewhere in the word, Florida.

- Click the Underline button (Home tab | Font group) to underline the word containing the insertion point (Figure 2–17).

Figure 2–17

How would I remove an underline?

You would click the Underline button a second time, or you could click the Undo button on the Quick Access Toolbar, immediately after clicking the Underline button.

Q&A Are other types of underlines available?

In addition to the basic solid underline shown in Figure 2–17, Publisher has many decorative underlines, such as double underlines, dotted underlines, and wavy underlines. You can access the decorative underlines in the Font dialog box using the Underline box arrow.

Other Ways
1. Right-click text, point to Change Text on shortcut menu, click Font, click Underline box arrow (Font dialog box), click desired underline style, click OK button
2. Click Font Dialog Box Launcher, click Font, click Underline box arrow (Font dialog box), click desired underline style, click OK button
3. Press CTRL+U

BTW

Serif Fonts
Serif fonts are considered Oldstyle when they display a slanted serif. Fonts are considered Modern when they use horizontal serifs.

To Bold Text

Bold characters appear somewhat thicker and darker than those that are not bold. As with italic and underline formatting, to bold multiple words, you must select them. If you want to bold only one word, the word does not have to be selected. Simply click anywhere in the word and then apply the bold format. The following step formats the brochure title as bold.

1

- Scroll to display the brochure title. Select the text, Spring Break 2012, by dragging through the text.

- Click the Bold button (Home tab | Font group) to format the selected text in bold (Figure 2–18).

Q&A

How would I remove a bold format?

You would click the Bold button a second time, or you could click the Undo button on the Quick Access Toolbar immediately after clicking the Bold button.

Figure 2–18

Other Ways

1. Click Bold button on Mini toolbar
2. Right-click selected text, point to Change text on shortcut menu, click Font, click Bold in Font style list (Font dialog box), click OK button
3. Click Font Dialog Box Launcher, click Bold in Font style list (Font dialog box), click OK button
4. Press CTRL+B

BTW

OpenType Fonts
Stylistic sets are more common in OpenType fonts. An **OpenType** font is a cross-platform, scalable font format with a wider range of characters than TrueType or PostScript fonts. If your printer can support them, OpenType fonts display a small computer icon or an uppercase O next to the font name when you click the Font box arrow (Format tab | Font group).

Stylistic Sets and Alternates

A stylistic set is an organized set of alternate letters and glyphs, allowing you to change what the font looks like. Besides its regular display, almost every font has three common stylistic sets: bold, italic, and the combination of bold and italic. The letters are displayed in the same font but use a heavier or slanted glyph. Another example with which you may be familiar is a font family that has both serif and sans serif stylistic sets. A serif is small line, flourish, or embellishment that crosses the strokes of letters in some fonts. A sans serif, or without flourish, set has no extra embellishment at the end of characters. Other stylistic sets include alternates for characters such as e, j, g, or y.

In Publisher, you also can choose a stylistic alternate set, which creates a random pattern from among the various stylistic sets available for the current font.

BTW

Stylistic Alternate Sets
If you use a script font that looks like cursive writing, a stylistic alternate can simulate handwriting by using a set of randomly chosen glyphs with slight differences in appearance.

To Display Text in a Stylistic Set

The following steps display a stylistic set for the title of the brochure.

- If necessary, select the text in the brochure title again.

- Click Text Box Tools Format on the Ribbon to display the Text Box Tools Format tab.

- Click the Stylistic Sets button (Text Box Tools Format tab | Typography group) to display the Stylistic Sets gallery. Scroll down in the gallery to see the changes (Figure 2–19).

Experiment

- Point to each stylistic alternate set and watch the live preview in the text box.

Figure 2–19

- Click the third set from the bottom of the gallery to apply the stylistic set to the selected text (Figure 2–20).

Q&A

Do all fonts have fancy stylistic sets?

No, usually only OpenType or scalable fonts contain stylistic sets other than bold and italic.

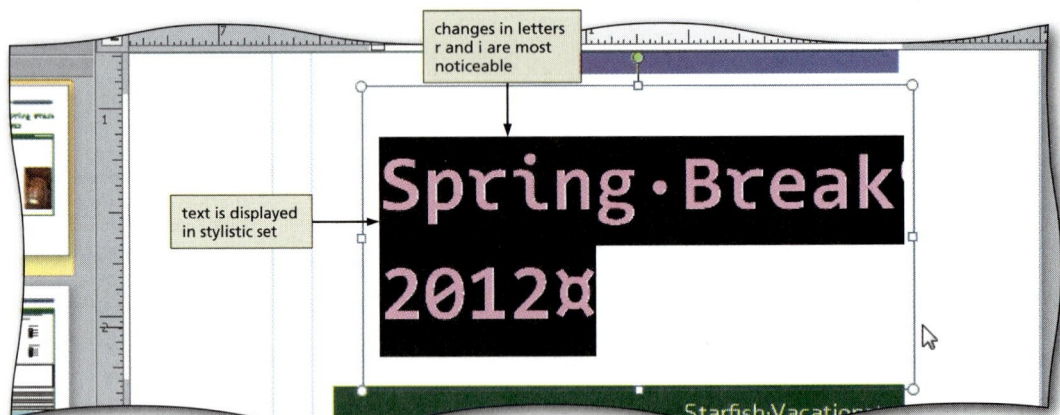

Figure 2–20

To Create a Drop Cap

A dropped capital letter, or **drop cap**, is a decorative large initial capital letter extending below the other letters in the line. If the text wraps to more than one line, the paragraph typically wraps around the dropped capital letter.

The following steps create a dropped capital letter S to begin the words Starfish Vacations in the center panel.

1

- Scroll to the upper portion of the center panel and then click to the left of the letter S in Starfish.

- Click the Drop Cap button (Text Box Tools Format tab | Typography Group) to display the Drop Cap gallery (Figure 2–21).

 Experiment

- Point to each of the Available drop caps to view the different default styles.

Figure 2–21

 2

- Click the Drop Cap Style 7 preview to select it (Figure 2–22).

Q&A Can I format more than just the first letter to be a drop cap?

Yes, you can format up to 15 contiguous letters and spaces as drop caps at the beginning of each paragraph.

Q&A Will this drop cap look inconsistent with the other fonts on the page?

After you fold the brochure, the drop cap will appear on the back of the brochure and will not detract from or interact with any other font.

Figure 2–22

BTW

Drop Caps
Microsoft's collection of clip art, accessed through the Clip Art task pane, includes stylized letters that can be used as drop caps. Simply type the desired letter in the Search for text box and then click the Go button. The selected graphic can serve as the drop cap for a line of text, which is placed close to a text box that contains the rest of the text.

Ligatures

Ligatures are two or more characters combined into a single character in order to create more readable or attractive text, especially in larger font sizes. The most common ligature is a combination of the letter f, followed by the letter i. Because the glyph of the f and the dot of the i may overlap slightly in some fonts, an awkward bulge may appear on the f as it runs into the dot of the i. The fi ligature creates a cleaner line. Figure 2–23 on the next page shows the fi combination, first without the ligature and then with the ligature.

BTW

Ligatures
When a program automatically changes a typed fraction, for example, 1/2 to ½, it is creating a ligature for you. The 1/2 requires three spaces, whereas the ½ requires only one.

dot of letter i runs into overhang on letter f

combining letters into ligature makes them easier to read

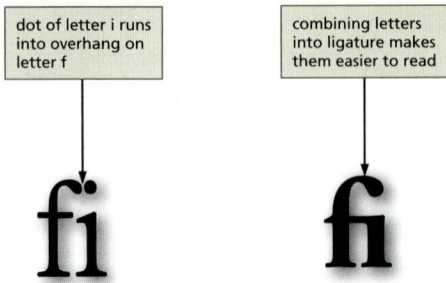

Figure 2–23

To Enable a Ligature

The following steps change the letters fi in the word, Starfish, to a ligature.

 1

- Scroll to the upper portion of the center panel and then select the letters, fi.

- Click the Ligatures button (Text Box Tools Format tab | Typography group) to display the Ligatures gallery (Figure 2–24).

Q&A

Are there other ligatures?

The standard ligatures are fi, ffi, and fl; however, in some font families, Publisher offers discretionary ligatures that you may create, including all of the ascending letters that might follow the letter, f, as well as ligatures such as ki, th, or ae.

Figure 2–24

 2

- If necessary, click Standard Only to enable the ligature (Figure 2–25).

Experiment

- If your ligatures already were enabled, click No Ligatures to view the difference. Then, click Standard Only to enable the ligature again.

Figure 2–25

Other Ways
1. Click Symbol button (Insert tab | Text group), click More Symbols in gallery,	click fi ligature, click Insert button

To Switch to Page 2 and View the Whole Page

The following steps switch to page 2 in the brochure and display the entire page.

1 Click Page 2 in the Page Navigation pane to move to page 2.

2 Click View on the Ribbon to display the View tab.

3 Click the Whole Page button (View tab | Zoom Group) to display the entire page (Figure 2–26).

BTW

Swashes
A **swash** is an exaggerated serif or glyph that typically runs into the space above or below the next letter. Some swashes can cause an unattractive appearance when used with adjacent descending letters such as g, j, or y; however, when used correctly, a swash produces a flowing, linear appearance that adds interest to the font.

Figure 2–26

To Enter Text on Page 2

The following steps enter text for page 2 of the brochure.

1 Click the text, Main Inside Heading, to select it.

2 Type `Starfish Spring Break Vacations` to replace the text.

3 If necessary, select the text in the Business Name text box in the lower-right portion of the page, and then type `Starfish Vacations` to replace the text (Figure 2–27 on the next page).

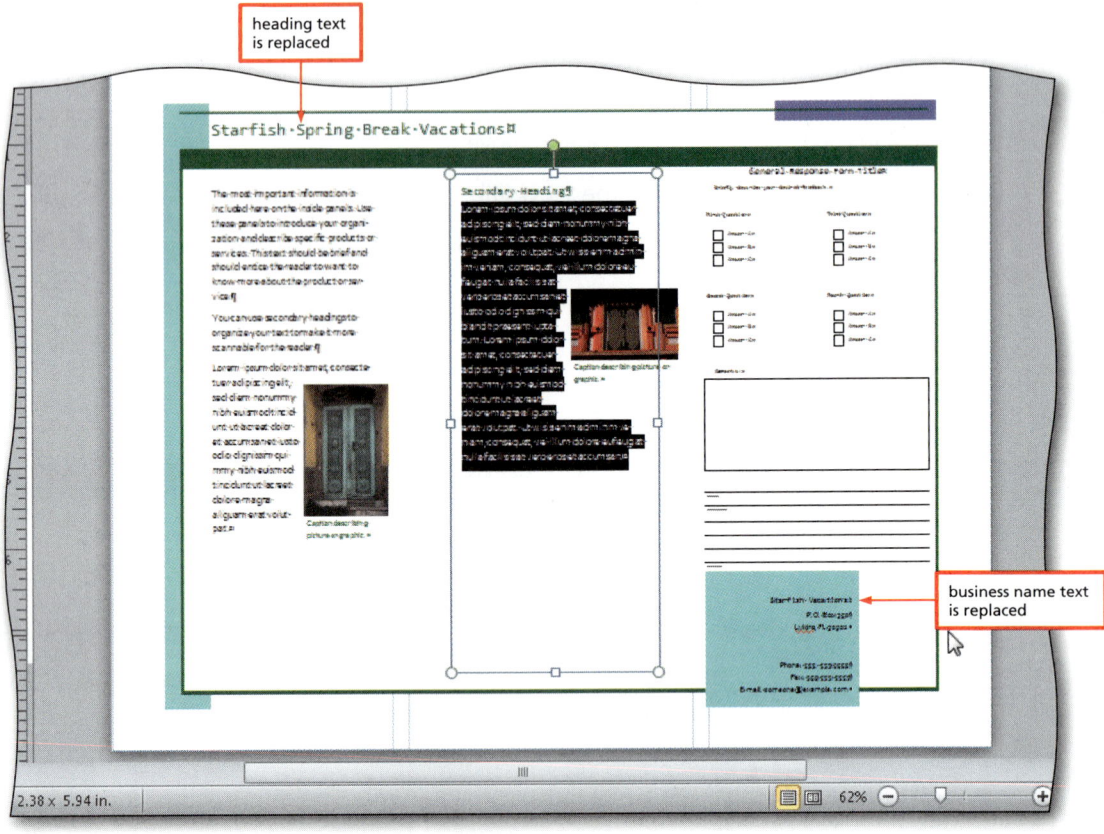

Figure 2–27

BTW

Superscripts and Subscripts
Two special font effects are superscript and subscript. A superscript is a character that appears slightly higher than other text on a line, such as that used in footnotes (reference[1]). A subscript is text that is slightly lower than other text on a line, such as that used in scientific formulas (H_2O).

Font Effects

Another way to format fonts is to use an effect. An **effect** is a special font option to add distinction to your text, including such ornamentation as outlining, embossing, and shadows.

Table 2–3 lists the font effects available in Publisher. The specific appearances of the font effects are printer- and screen-dependent.

Table 2–3 Font Effects	
Font Effect	**Description**
All caps	Formats lowercase letters as capitals. All caps formatting does not affect numbers, punctuation, nonalphabetic characters, or uppercase letters.
Emboss	The selected text appears to be raised off the page in relief.
Engrave	The selected text appears to be imprinted or pressed into the page.
Outline	Displays the inner and outer borders of each character.
Shadow	Adds a shadow beneath and to the right of the selected text.
Small caps	Formats selected lowercase text as capital letters and reduces their size. Small caps formatting does not affect numbers, punctuation, nonalphabetic characters, or uppercase letters.
Strikethrough	Adds a horizontal strikethrough line to each character.
Subscript	Lowers the selected text below the baseline.
Superscript	Raises the selected text above the baseline.

To Apply a Font Effect

The following steps apply the outline effect to the main inside heading of the brochure.

1

- Select the text, Starfish Spring Break Vacations in the heading.

- Click Home on the Ribbon to display the Home tab.

- Click the Font Dialog Box Launcher (Home tab | Font group) to display the Font dialog box.

- Click Outline in the Effects area to display the preview (Figure 2–28).

Figure 2–28

2

- Click the OK button to close the dialog box and apply the font effect.

- Click the text to deselect it and view the effect (Figure 2–29).

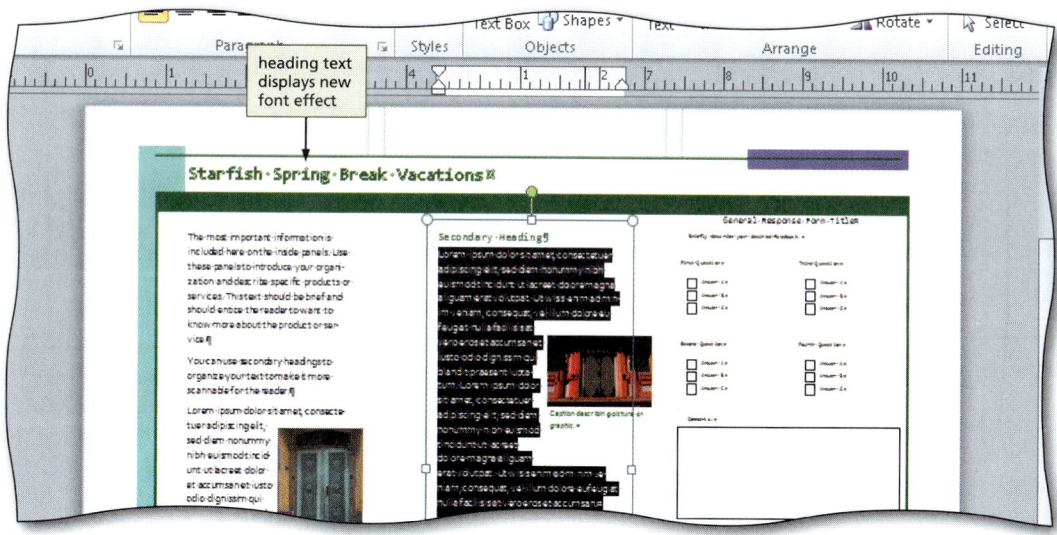

Figure 2–29

Other Ways
1. Press CTRL+SHIFT+F, click desired font effect check box (Font dialog box), click OK button	2. Right-click selected text, point to Change Text on shortcut menu, click Font, click desired Font effect (Font dialog box), click OK button

To Enter Text in the Left Panel on Page 2

The following steps enter text in the story in the left panel on page 2.

1 Click the text of the story in the left panel and then zoom to facilitate editing.

2 Type the following sentences: **At Starfish Vacations, your wonderful spring break experience is our #1 priority. We have designed our packages to maximize fun, food, and fantastic weather!**

3 Press the ENTER key and then type: **Whether it's tanning on the beach, experiencing the nightlife on the strip, or participating in the many sports and activities, you will find plenty of things to do that match your spring break style.**

4 Press the ENTER key and then type: **Our customers say it best: "The snorkeling and kayaking were great! We stayed at a four-star resort. We are so glad that we chose Starfish. It was highly recommended by the student travel bureau."** (Figure 2–30).

Figure 2–30

To Increase the Font Size

The following steps select all of the text in the story and then increase the font size.

1 Press CTRL+A to select all of the text in the left panel story.

2 Click the Increase Font Size button (Home tab | Font group) to increase the font size.

To Enter Text in the Center Panel on Page 2

The following steps enter text in the heading and story in the center panel on page 2.

1 Click the heading text of the story in the center panel.

2 Type `Keep in Touch` to replace the text.

3 Select the story in the center panel.

4 Type the following sentences: `All of our hotels offer free Wi-Fi that extends to the water's edge. It's easy to keep in touch with friends and family, update your Facebook page, or Twitter from the beach.` to complete the text (Figure 2–31).

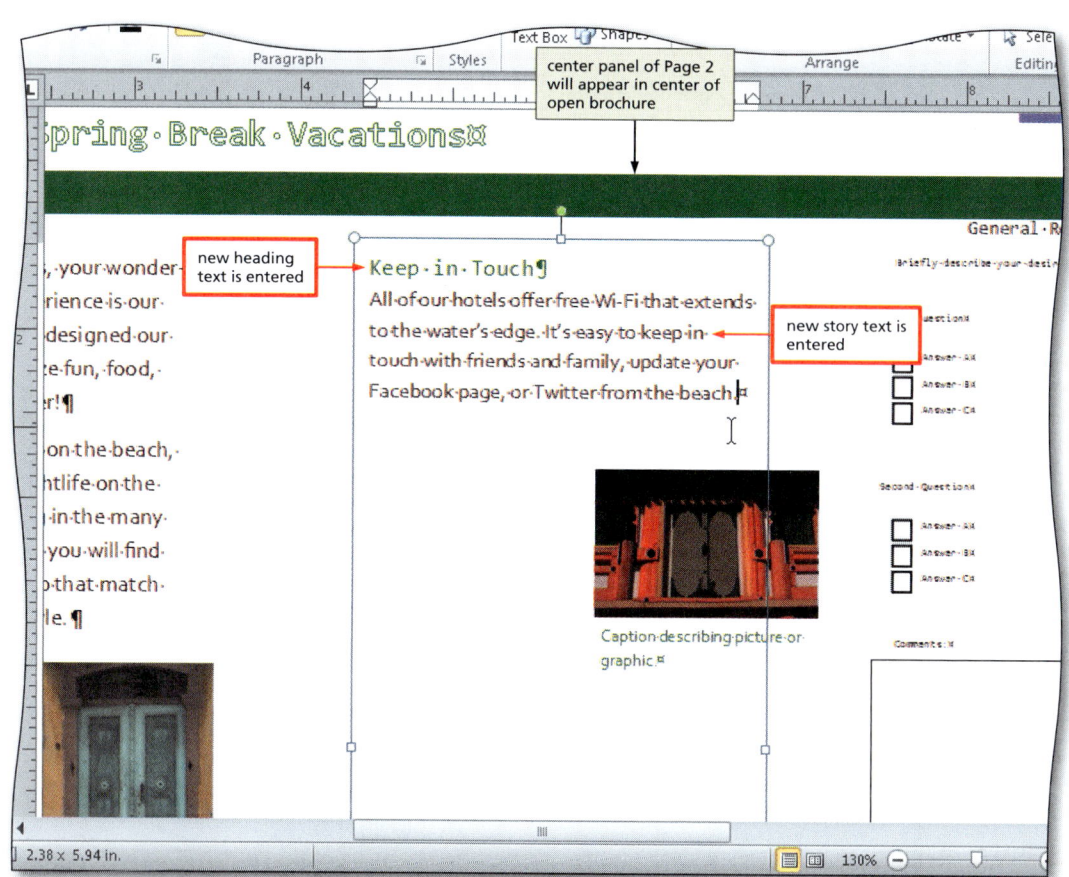

Figure 2–31

To Use the Format Painter Button

Another way to apply specific formatting is to copy the formatting from existing text or objects using the Format Painter button (Home tab | Clipboard group). When using the Format Painter with text, click anywhere in the source text, click the Format Painter button, and then drag through the destination text. The steps on the following page copy the formatting from the left panel story to the center panel story.

1

- Scroll as necessary to click the text in the left panel story.

- Click the Format Painter button (Home Tab | Clipboard group) to copy the formatting.

- Move the mouse pointer into the workspace (Figure 2–32).

Q&A Why does the mouse pointer display a paintbrush?

The mouse pointer changes when a format has been copied. Once you apply the format by clicking somewhere else, the paintbrush will disappear.

Figure 2–32

 2

- Drag through the text in the story in the center panel to apply the formatting (Figure 2–33).

Q&A Can I use the Format Painter button to apply the copied formatting to multiple locations?

To apply formatting to multiple locations, double-click the Format Painter button so that it stays on. When you finish, click the Format Painter button again to turn it off.

Q&A Can I use the Format Painter button on objects other than text?

Yes. You can copy applied formatting of a graphic, WordArt, shapes, fills, or any object from the Building Blocks gallery. If you can change the style or set formatting options, you can copy them from one object to another.

Figure 2–33

Other Ways

1. Select source text, click Format Painter button — on Mini toolbar, click destination text

To Edit the Sign-Up Form

To complete the text editing on page 2, the following steps edit the response form. Each check box and its text are grouped together. You can select a **grouped object** with a single click. Individual objects within the group, such as the check box itself, are selected with a second click. Template text in a grouped object usually can be selected with a single click. You will learn more about creating forms and check boxes in a later chapter.

1 Scroll to the right panel of page 2 and then zoom in on the response form.

2 Click the Zoom In button on the status bar several times to zoom to 250%.

3 Replace the title, directions, and subheadings as shown in Figure 2–34. One at a time, click each text box and then type the text from Figure 2–34 to replace the default text.

Figure 2–34

To Delete Objects on Page 2

The following steps delete the picture and its grouped caption from the left panel of page 2.

1 Scroll to the left panel and then zoom out to 100%.

2 Click the grouped picture and caption object to select it.

3 Press the DELETE key to delete the object (Figure 2–35 on the next page).

BTW

Using Forms
Each form contains blanks for the name and address of prospective customers or clients. The company not only verifies the marketing power of its brochure, it also is able to create a customer database with the information.

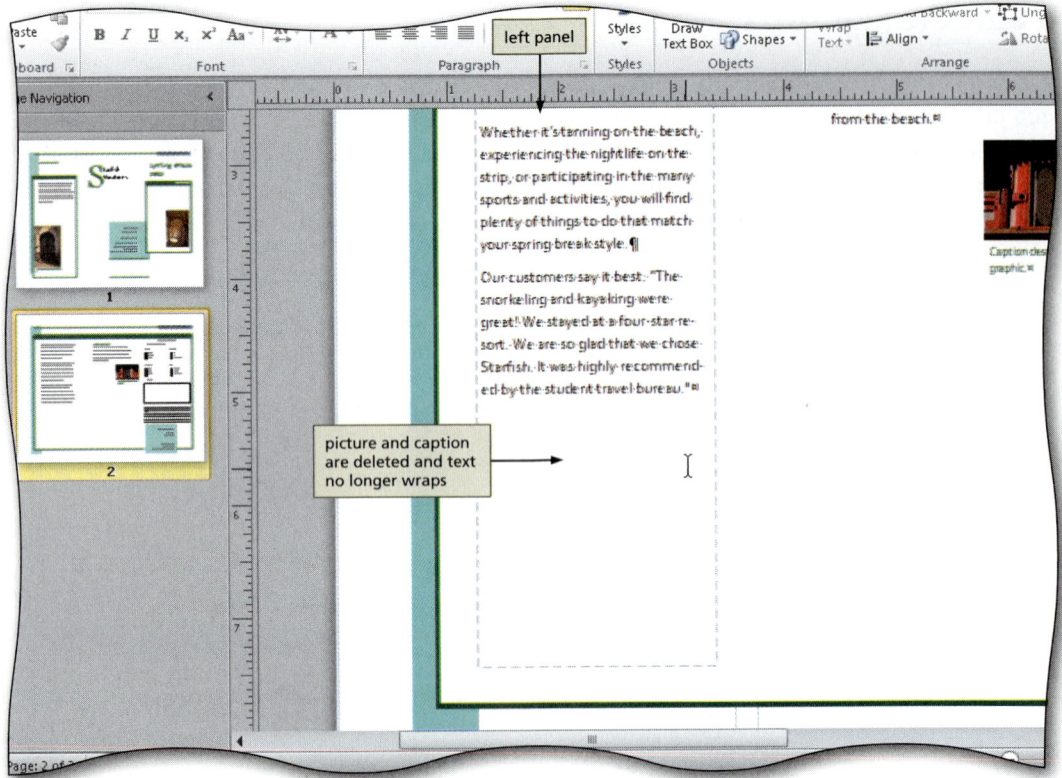

Figure 2–35

To Save the Publication Again

You have made several modifications to the text in the brochure since you last saved it. Thus, you should save it again. The following step saves the publication again. For an example of the step listed below, refer to the Office 2010 and Windows 7 chapter at the beginning of this book.

 With a USB flash drive connected to one of the computer's USB ports, click the Save button on the Quick Access Toolbar to overwrite the previously saved file.

Break Point: If you wish to take a break, this is a good place to do so. You can quit Publisher now. To resume at a later time, start Publisher, open the file called Spring Break Brochure, and continue following the steps from this location forward.

Clip Art

In Chapter 1, you inserted a digital photo taken with a digital camera in a publication. In this project, you insert **clip art**, which is a predefined graphic. You can search for graphics and clip art by descriptive keywords, file name, or file format, or from the clip collection. In the Microsoft Office programs, clip art is located in the Clip Organizer, which contains a collection of clip art, photographs, sounds, and videos.

To Replace a Graphic Using the Clip Art Task Pane

Because this brochure is advertising a location with services, it is more appropriate to choose a graphic related to the beach than the picture supplied by the template, as a graphic should enhance the message of the publication. The following steps retrieve an appropriate graphic, using the Clip Art task pane to replace the supplied graphic.

BTW

Clip Art Sources
In addition to the clip art images included in the Clip Art task pane previews, other sources for clip art include retailers specializing in computer software, the Internet, bulletin board systems, and online information systems. A bulletin board system is a computer service that allows users to communicate with each other and share files. Microsoft has created a page on its Web site where you can add new clips to the Clip gallery.

1

- Go to page 1 and scroll as necessary to display the right panel.

- Click the graphic to select it.

- Click Insert on the Ribbon to display the Insert tab.

- Click the Clip Art button (Insert tab | Illustrations group) to display the Clip Art task pane (Figure 2–36).

Q&A Do I have to select the picture first?

To replace the current graphic, yes. Otherwise, the clip art is inserted in the middle of the workspace.

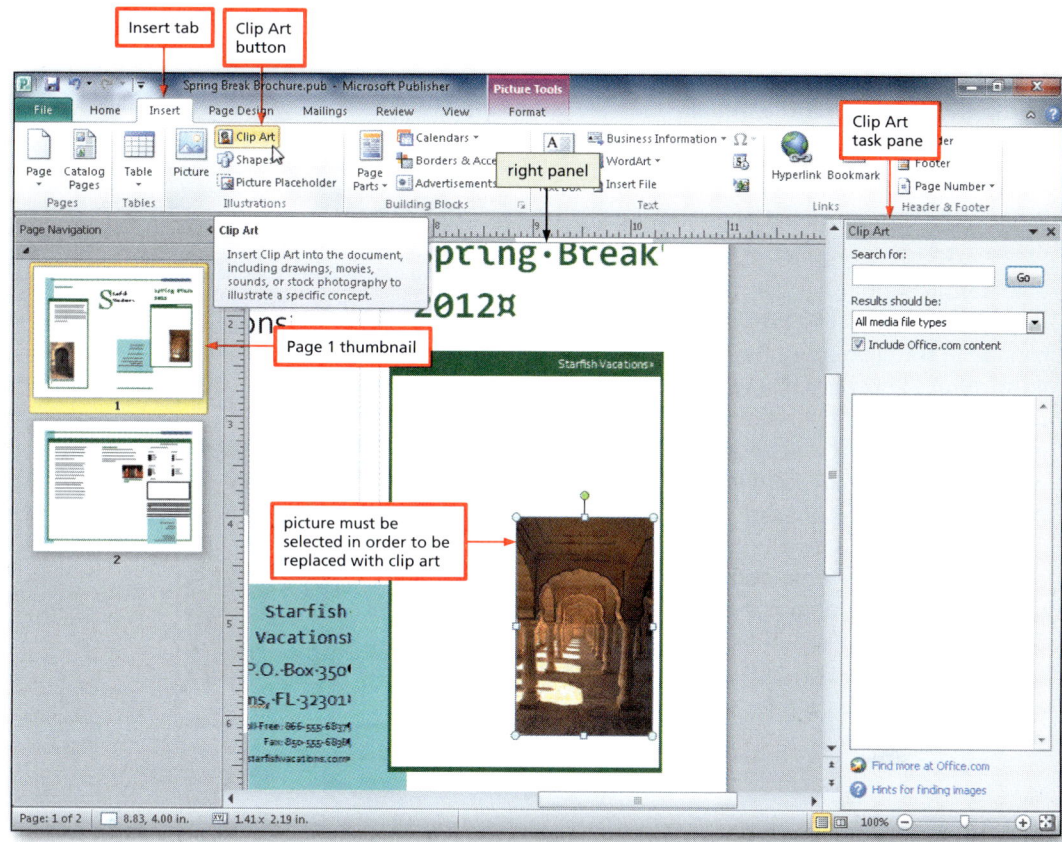

Figure 2–36

2

- In the Clip Art task pane, if the Search for text box contains text, drag through the text to select it.

- If necessary, click the Include Office .com content check box to select it.

- Type **beach** in the Search for text box to enter a searchable keyword (Figure 2–37).

Q&A What if I am not connected to the Web?

If you are not connected to the Web, the Include Office.com content check box will not be checked. Your search then would be limited to the clip art installed locally on your computer.

Q&A What if I want to use a photo from a file?

If you want to use a photo stored on another medium, close the Clip Art task pane and then right-click the graphic. Point to Change Picture on the shortcut menu and then click Change Picture. Browse to the location of the photo, as you did in Chapter 1. Click the Insert button (Insert Picture dialog box).

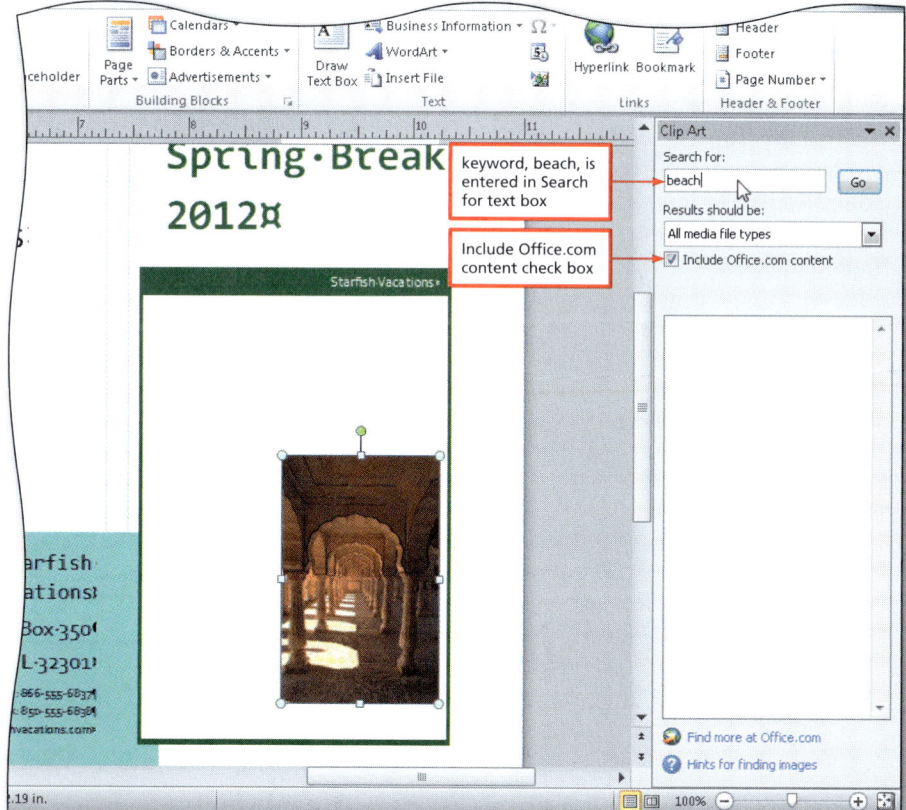

Figure 2–37

3

- Click the 'Results should be' box arrow and ensure that the 'All media types' check box displays a check mark (Figure 2–38).

Q&A What is the difference between the media types?

The 'Results should be' box arrow displays four types of media to include in the search results: Illustrations, Photographs, Video, and Audio Illustrations includes all images that are not real photos, without animation or sound. **Photographs** are pictures of real objects. **Video** includes all clips that contain any kind of animation or action. **Audio clips** do not display a graphic, but play a sound if the speakers are turned on. Video and audio clips are used for Web publications.

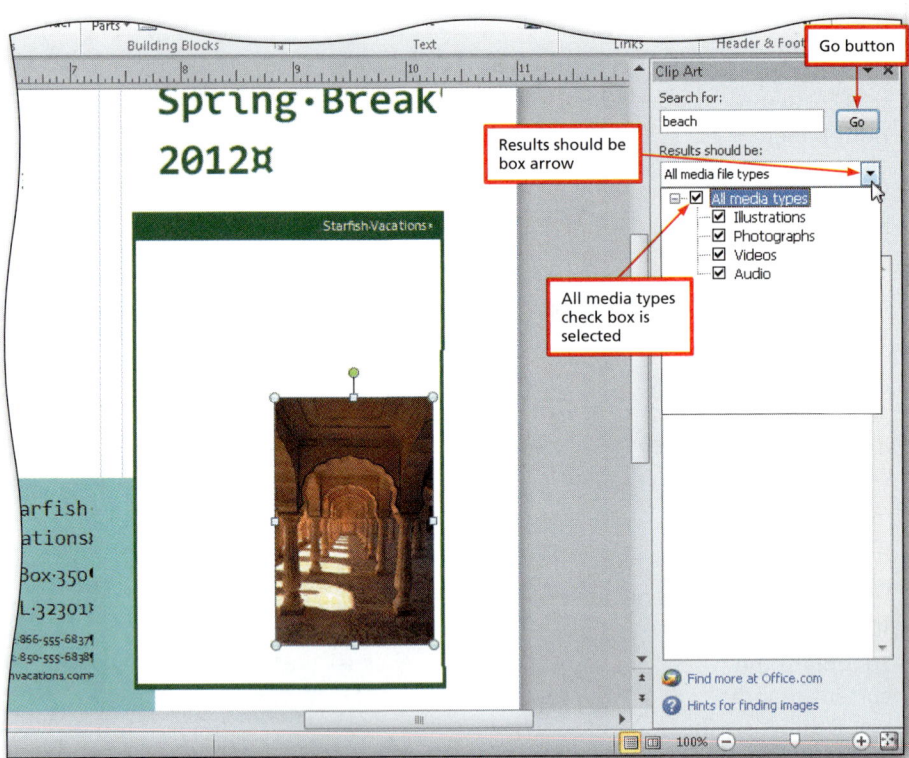

Figure 2–38

4

- Click the Go button to begin the search for clip art (Figure 2–39).

Q&A What are the links at the bottom of the Clip Art task pane?

The first link starts a Web browser and displays content from Office .com. The second link offers tips from the Publisher Help system on finding images.

Figure 2–39

5

- When the previews are displayed, click the down scroll arrow until the preview of the beach and starfish is displayed.

- Click the preview shown in Figure 2–40 or another photo from your clip art collection to replace the current graphic.

Q&A

What are the black handles that are displayed around the photo?

Recall from Chapter 1 that Publisher automatically displays cropping handles that allow you to crop the photo, if necessary.

6

- Click outside the graphic to hide the cropping handles.

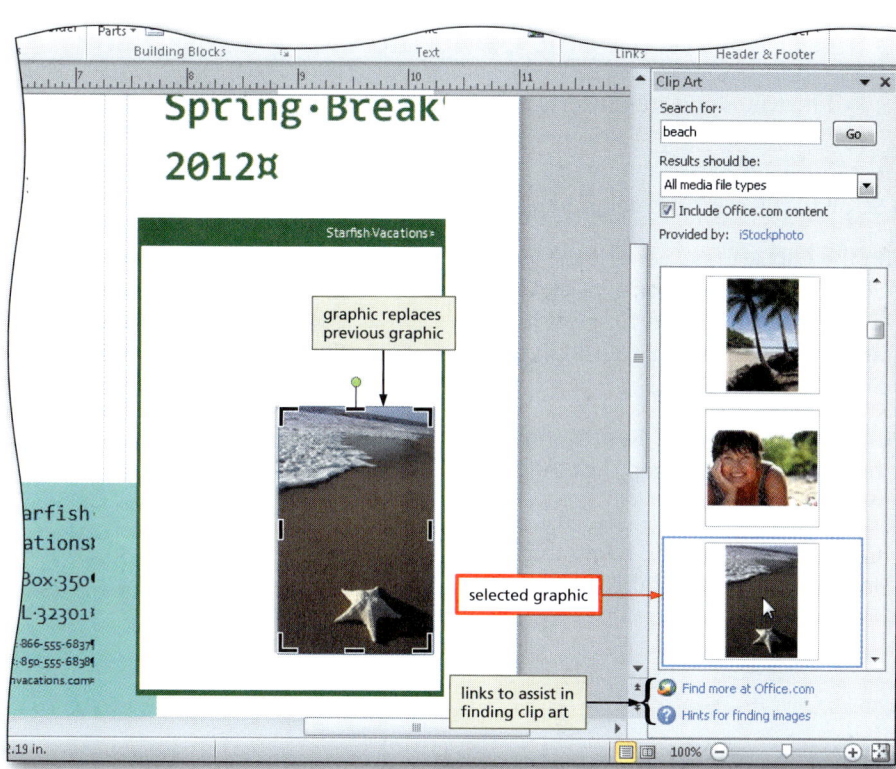

Figure 2–40

To Resize the Graphic

The following steps resize the graphic to make it larger. Your screen may differ. Recall that visual layout guides appear as pink lines as you resize or move objects.

1

- Click the graphic once to select it.

- SHIFT+drag the upper-left sizing handle until the vertical visual layout guide appears. If you do not see a vertical visual layout guide, resize the graphic to be approximately 2.94 inches tall as shown on the status bar (Figure 2–41).

- Release the mouse button and then click outside the graphic to deselect it.

Figure 2–41

To Insert a New Graphic Using the Clip Art Task Pane

The following step inserts a new graphic to use in the center panel of page 1.

1

- Scroll to the center panel of page 1.

- In the Clip Art task pane, if the Search for text box contains text, drag through the text to select it and then type **starfish** in the Search for text box.

- If necessary, click the 'Results should be' box arrow and then click 'All media types'.

- Click the Go button to begin the search for clip art (Figure 2–42).

Figure 2–42

2

- If necessary, when the previews are displayed, click the down scroll arrow until the preview of the starfish is displayed.

- Click the preview shown in Figure 2–43 or another one from your clip art collection to insert the graphic.

Figure 2–43

To Resize and Reposition the Graphic

The following steps resize and reposition the graphic in the middle panel.

1 SHIFT+drag a corner sizing handle to resize the graphic to approximately 1.85 inches square.

2 Drag the border of the graphic to move it to a location that does not overlap any text in the publication, but aligns with the lower text boxes as shown in Figure 2–44.

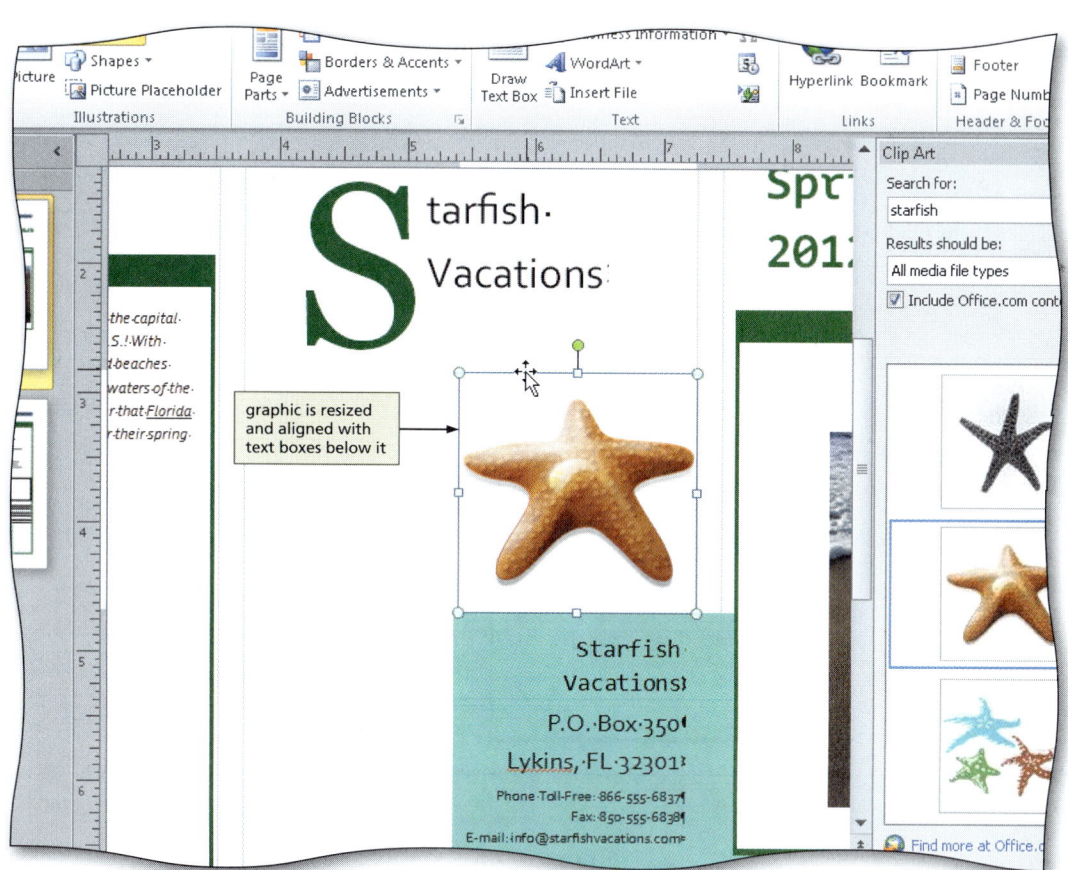

Figure 2–44

To Replace the Graphic in the Left Panel of Page 1

The following steps replace the graphic in the left panel.

1 Zoom and scroll as necessary to display the left panel.

2 Click the grouped graphic in the left panel and then click the photo a second time to select only the photo.

3 Using the Clip Art task pane, enter `volleyball nets` in the Search for text box.

4 If necessary, click the Include Office.com content check box to select it.

5 If necessary, click the 'Results should be' box arrow and then click 'All file types'.

6 Click the Go button to search for clip art related to the keyword, volleyball.

7 When the clips are displayed, scroll to find a graphic similar to the one shown in Figure 2–45.

8 Click the graphic to insert the picture into the brochure (Figure 2–45).

Figure 2–45

To Replace the Graphics in the Center Panel of Page 2

The following steps replace the graphic in the center panel of page 2.

1 Go to page 2 and select the graphic only in the center panel.

2 Type **beach laptop** in the Clip Art task pane Search for box. Verify that the search will include all locations and all media types.

3 Click the Go button and then scroll as necessary to display the photo shown in Figure 2–46 or a similar photo.

4 Click the photo to insert it (Figure 2–46).

5 Click outside the graphic to deselect it.

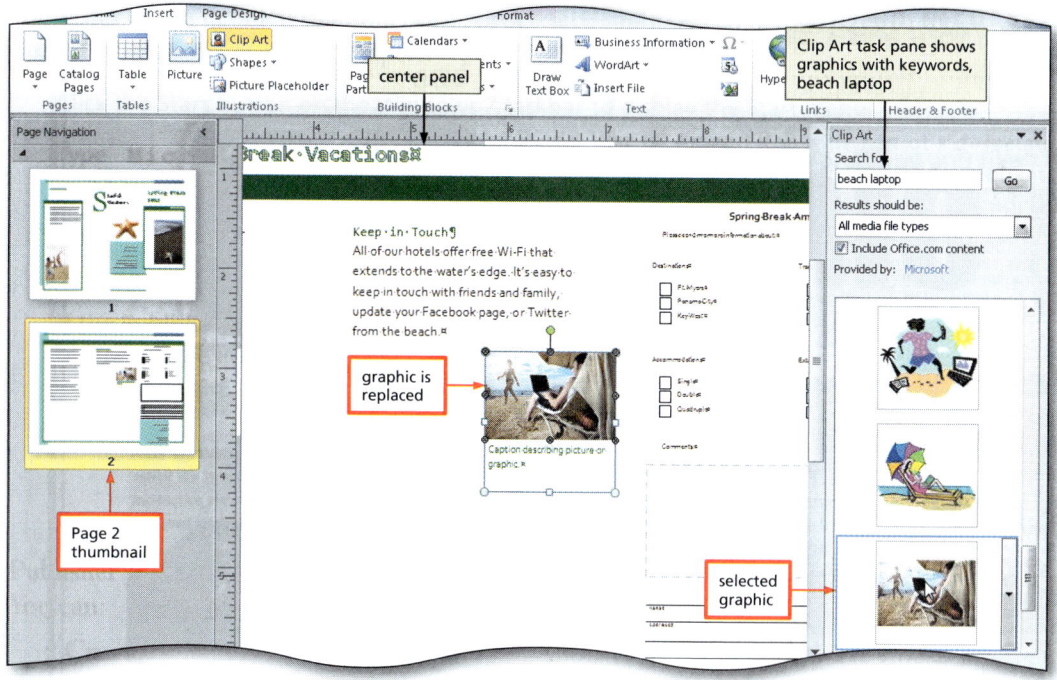

Figure 2–46

To Insert a New Graphic on Page 2

The following step inserts a new graphic on page 2 of the brochure.

1

- If necessary, scroll to display the lower portion of the center panel.

- In the Clip Art task pane, type **sunset** in the Search for box. Verify that the search will include all locations and all media types.

- Click the Go button and then scroll as necessary to display the photo shown in Figure 2–47 or a similar photo.

- Click the photo to insert it (Figure 2–47).

Q&A Could I have used a picture placeholder for this clip art?

You could have clicked the Picture Placeholder button (Insert tab | Illustrations group) first to create a sized boundary; however, the picture placeholder creates an icon to open the Insert Picture dialog box, rather than the Clip Art task pane.

Figure 2–47

To Resize and Reposition the Photo

The following steps resize and reposition the graphic.

1 With the sunset photo still selected, SHIFT+drag a corner handle until the photo fits the space in the middle panel.

2 If necessary, drag the photo to the bottom of the center panel, as shown in Figure 2–48.

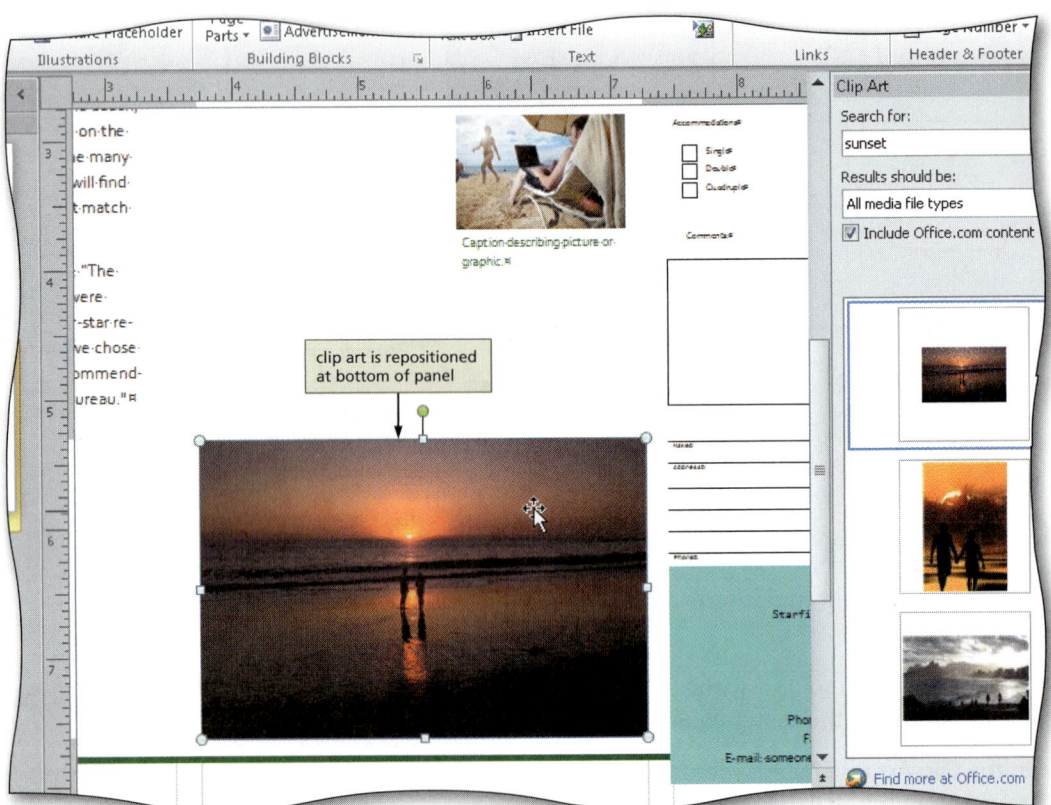

Figure 2–48

To Close the Clip Art Task Pane

You are finished inserting clip art in the brochure. The following step closes the Clip Art task pane.

1 Click the Close button on the Clip Art task pane title bar to close the task pane.

Captions

A **caption** is explanatory or identification text or a title that accompanies a graphic, figure, or photo. A caption can be as simple as a figure number, as you see in the figures of this book; or, a caption can identify people, places, objects, or actions occurring in the graphic. In Publisher templates, some captions already exist near a graphic. In those cases, the caption is a text box grouped with a graphic. If a graphic or photo does not have a caption, you can add one using the Caption gallery.

To Edit Captions

The following steps edit the text in the caption on page 1.

1

• Go to page 1 of the brochure and scroll to the left panel. Zoom as necessary to display the photo and its caption.

• Click the caption text below the photo to select it (Figure 2–49).

Figure 2–49

2

• Type `Have fun on the beach with your friends!` to replace the text (Figure 2–50).

Q&A

Can you delete a caption?

Yes, but be sure to delete the text box as well as the text. If the caption is part of a group, click once to select the group, then point to the border of the text box and click to select it. Finally, press the DELETE key to delete the caption text box.

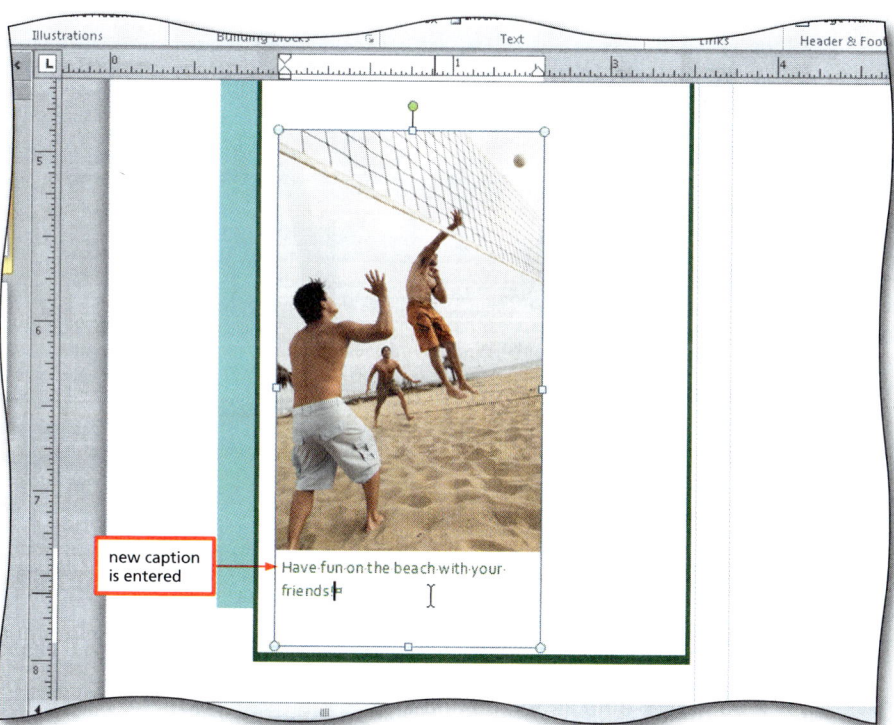

Figure 2–50

To Edit the Caption on Page 2

The following steps edit the caption under the photo in the middle panel on page 2.

1 Go to page 2 of the brochure and select the caption text in the center panel. Zoom as necessary.

2 Type `Follow Starfish Vacations on Twitter.` to replace the caption (Figure 2–51).

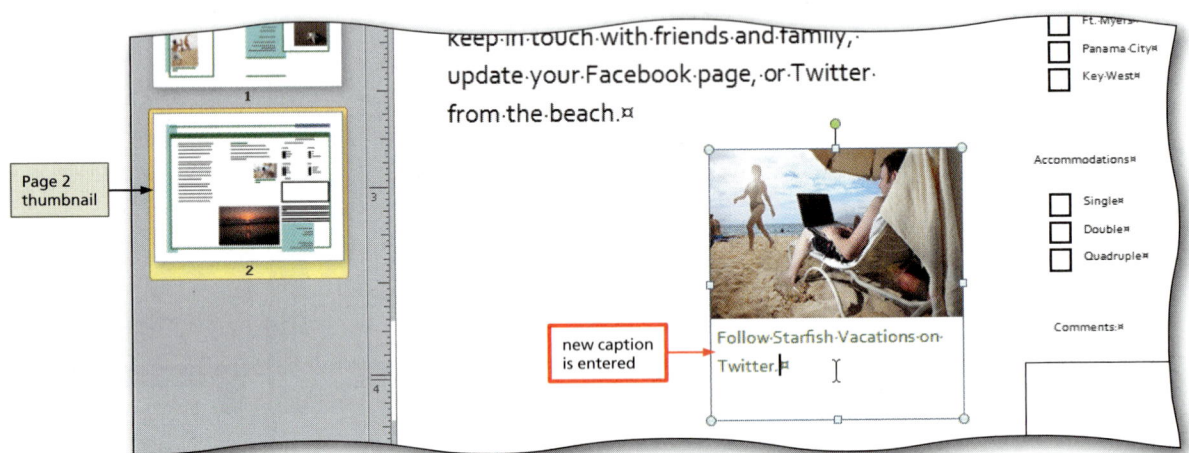

Figure 2–51

To Use the Caption Gallery

The following steps apply a new, decorative caption to an existing photo using the Caption gallery.

1

- Select the newly added photo in the lower portion of the center panel.

- Click Picture Tools Format on the Ribbon to display the Picture Tools Format tab.

- Click the Caption button (Picture Tools Format tab | Picture Styles group) to display its gallery (Figure 2–52).

🔍 **Experiment**

- Point to each of the thumbnails in the Caption gallery and watch how the graphic and caption change.

Figure 2–52

2

- Scroll as necessary to display the Overlay area.

- In the third row, first column of the Overlay area, click Band – Layout 1 to apply the caption style to the picture (Figure 2–53).

Figure 2–53

To Edit the Text and Font Size of the Caption

The following steps edit the caption and increase the font size.

1 Click the default caption text to select it and then type `Panama City at dusk.` to replace the text.

2 Press CTRL+A to select all of the text and then click the Increase Font Size button three times to enlarge the text in the caption (Figure 2–54).

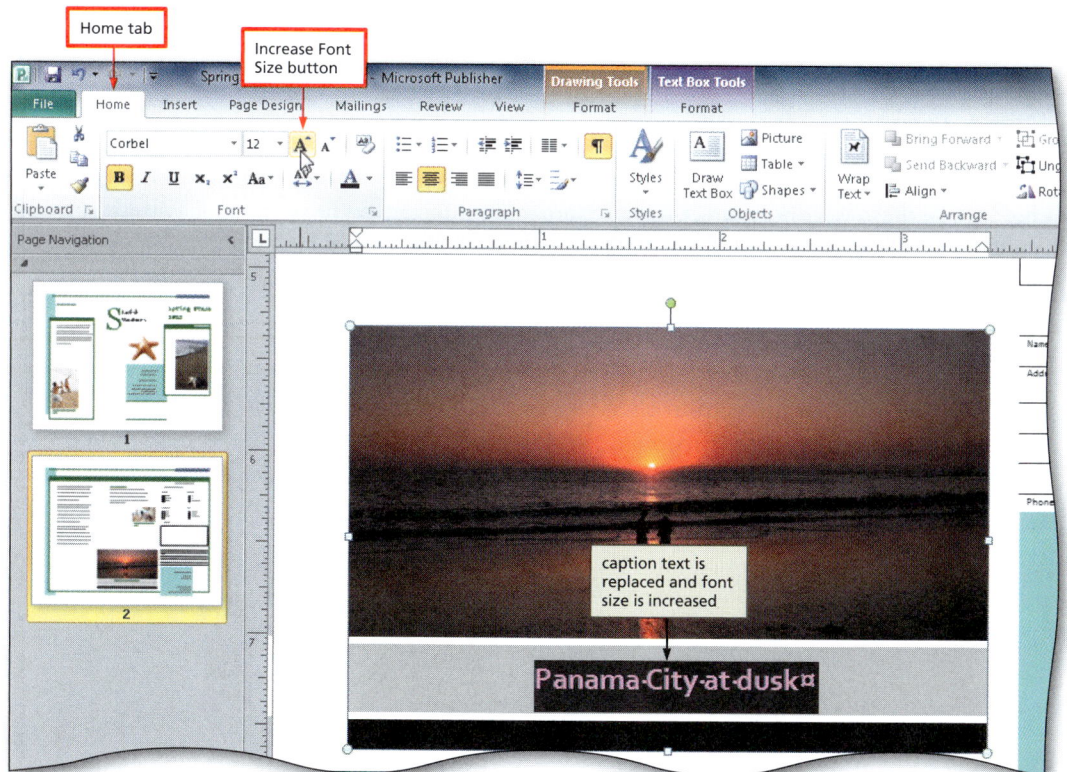

Figure 2–54

Checking the Publication

Recall that you checked a publication for spelling errors as you typed in Chapter 1. A wavy line indicated a word that was not in Publisher's dictionary. You then used the shortcut menu to choose the correct word. Additionally, Publisher can check the entire publication once you have finished editing it. Publisher's Review tab (Figure 2–55) contains proofing and language commands to help check the document for errors, research terms or concepts, change words using a thesaurus, translate text, or set the languge. The Spelling button (Review tab | Proofing group) starts the process of checking your entire publication for spelling errors. The spelling checker moves from text box to text box and offers suggestions for words it does not find in its dictionary. Publisher does not look for grammatical errors. You will learn more about other features on the Review tab in later chapters.

Figure 2–55

Plan Ahead

Plan for printing.
Make a firm decision that quality matters and consult with several commercial printers ahead of time. Get prices, color modes, number of copies, paper, and folding options in writing before you finish your brochure. Brochures are more effective on heavier paper, with strong colors and a glossy feel. Together with the commercial printer, select a paper that is going to last. Check to make sure the commercial printer can accept Microsoft Publisher 2010 files.

A second kind of publication check is called the Design Checker. The Design Checker finds potential design problems in the publication, such as objects hidden behind other objects, text that does not fit in its text box, or a picture that is scaled disproportionately. As with the spelling check, you can choose to correct or ignore each design problem.

To Check the Spelling of the Entire Publication

The following steps check the entire publication for spelling errors.

1

- Click Review on the Ribbon to display the Review tab.

- Click the Spelling button (Review tab | Proofing group) to begin the spelling check in the current location, which, in this case, is inside the caption text box (Figure 2–56).

Q&A Can I check spelling of just a section of a publication?

Yes, select the text before starting the spelling check.

Figure 2–56

2

- Click the Yes button to tell Publisher to check the rest of the publication (Figure 2–57).

Q&A What if the proper noun is spelled correctly?

If the flagged word is spelled correctly, click the Ignore button to ignore the flag, or click the Ignore All button if the word occurs more than once.

Figure 2–57

3
- With the word, Lykens, selected in the Change to box, click the Change All button in the Change Spelling dialog box to change the flagged word, Lykins, to the selected suggestion, Lykens, both here and on the other page (Figure 2–58).

- If Publisher flags any other words, choose the correct spelling in the Suggestions list box and then continue the spelling check until the next error is identified or the end of the publication is reached.

- Click the OK button to close the dialog box.

Figure 2–58

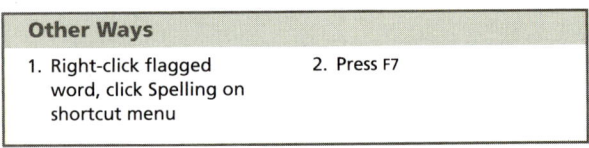

Other Ways	
1. Right-click flagged word, click Spelling on shortcut menu	2. Press F7

To Run the Design Checker

The following steps run the Design Checker to troubleshoot and identify potential design problems in the publication.

1
- Click File on the Ribbon to open the Backstage view and, by default, select the Info tab (Figure 2–59).

Q&A
Will the Design Checker fix the problems automatically?

In some cases, you will have the option of choosing an automatic fix for the issue; in other cases, you will have to fix the problem manually.

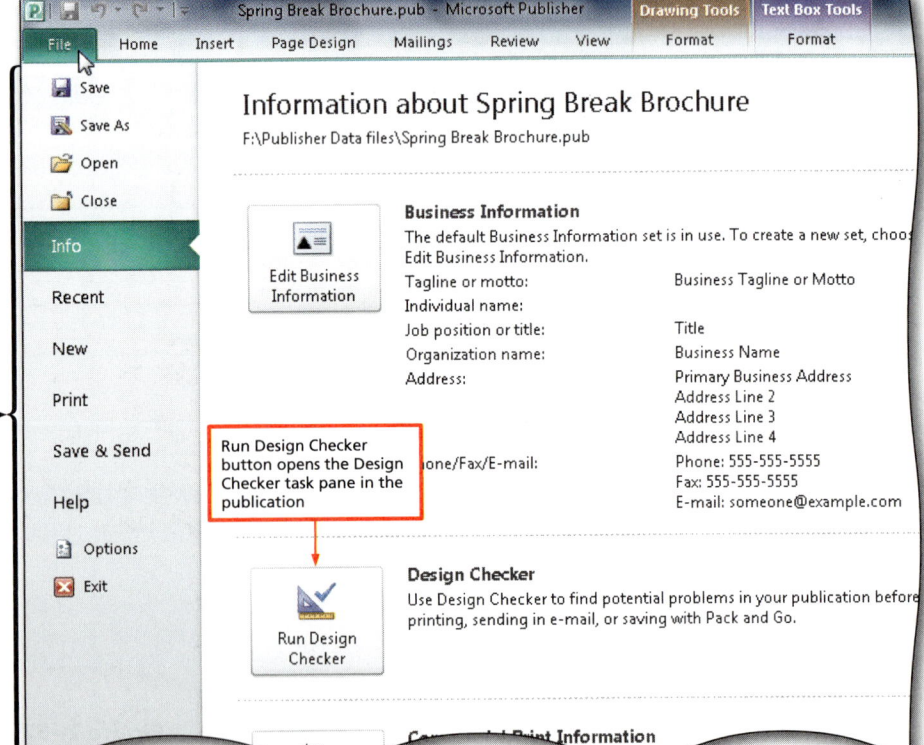

Figure 2–59

2

• Click the Run Design Checker button in the Info gallery to display the Design Checker task pane (Figure 2–60).

Q&A

What are the links at the bottom of the Design Checker task pane?

You can click the Design Checker Options link to specify the order in which the Design Checker checks the pages of your publication, or to specify which kinds of design issues to include. The second link offers tips from the Publisher Help system on running the Design Checker.

Q&A

What are the listed design problems?

A small amount of space appears between the margin of the page and the closest object to the margin. This is intentional and was part of the template, but the Design Checker notes the problem, for your information only. If this is not fixed, print quality will not be affected.

Figure 2–60

3

• If you have problems other than margin spacing, point to the problem in the 'Select an item to fix' box. When a button appears on the right side of the problem, click the button and then click the given Fix command.

4

• Click the Close Design Checker button to close the Design Checker and return to the publication.

To Save the Publication after Checking It

You have made several modifications to the document since you last saved it. Thus, you should save it again. The following step saves the document again. For an example of the step listed below, refer to the Office 2010 and Windows 7 chapter at the beginning of this book.

1 Click the Save button on the Quick Access Toolbar to overwrite the previously saved file.

BTW

Printer Memory
Some printers do not have enough memory to print a wide variety of images and color. In these cases, the printer prints up to a certain point on a page and then stops — resulting in only the top portion of the publication printing. Check with your instructor to see if your printer has enough memory to work with colors.

Previewing and Printing

When you work with multi-page publications, it is a good idea to preview each page before printing. Additionally, if you decide to print on special paper, or print on both sides of the paper, you must adjust certain settings in the Print gallery in the Backstage view.

To Preview Multiple Pages before Printing

The first step in getting the publication ready for outside printing is to examine what the printed copy will look like from your desktop. The following steps preview both pages of the brochure before printing.

1

- If necessary, go to page 1.

- Click File on the Ribbon to open the Backstage view.

- Click the Print tab to display the Print gallery (Figure 2–61).

Q&A What are the rulers in the Print gallery?

Publisher displays rulers at the top and left of the print preview to help you verify the size of the printed page. You can turn off the ruler display by clicking the Ruler button at the top of the right pane.

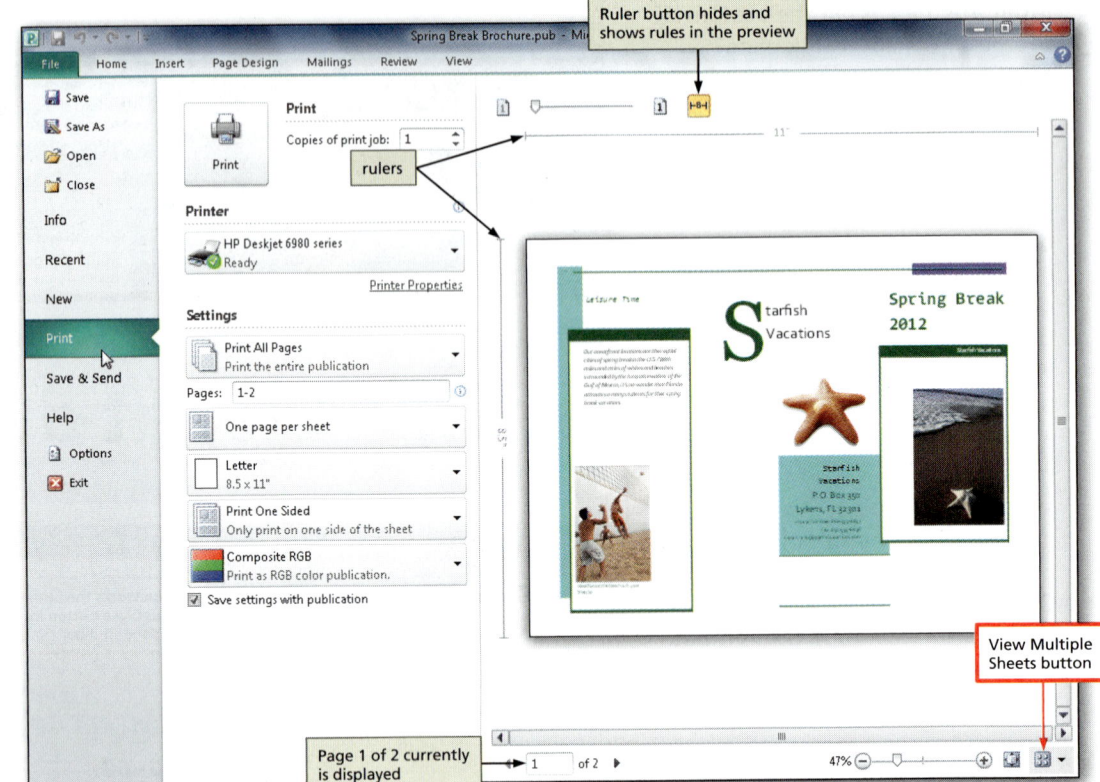

Figure 2–61

2

- Click the View Multiple Sheets button to display the preview grid options (Figure 2–62).

Q&A If the brochure has only two pages, why do all of those preview grids exist?

Publisher allows for more pages in every kind of publication, should you decide to add them. If you click a button in the grid for more than two pages — either horizontally or vertically — the size of the preview is reduced.

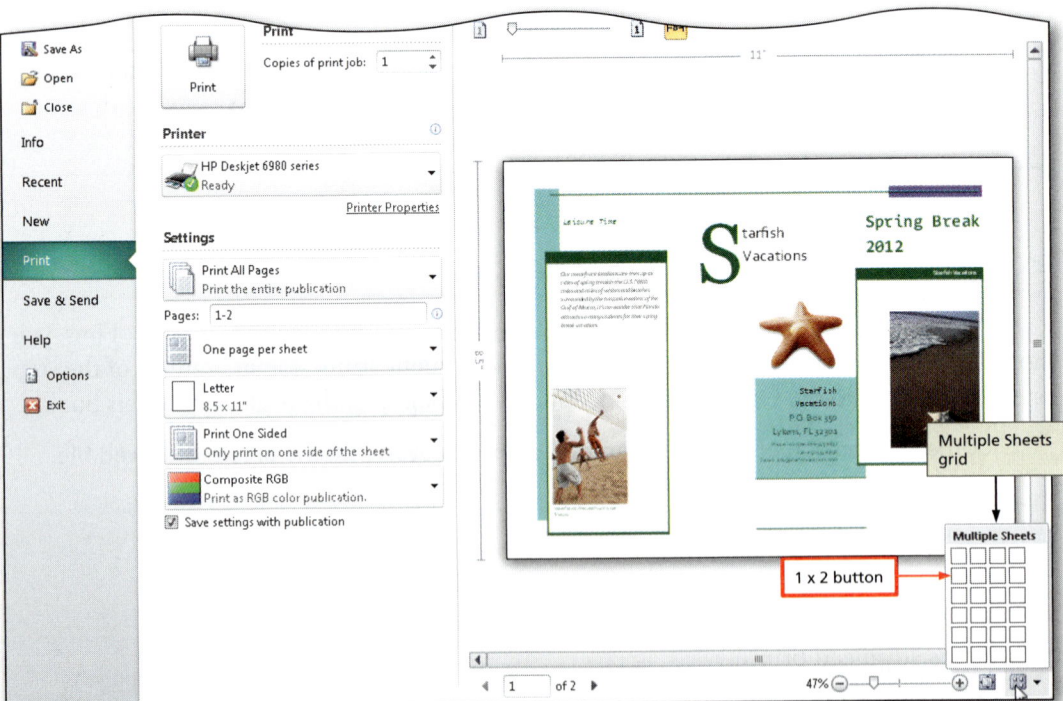

Figure 2–62

3

- Click the 2 × 1 button to display the pages above one another (Figure 2–63).

Q&A

Is that the best way to preview the brochure?

Viewing two full pages with intensive graphics and text may give you a good overview of the publication; however, do not substitute the preview for checking the publication for errors by reading the content carefully and running the spell and design checking tools.

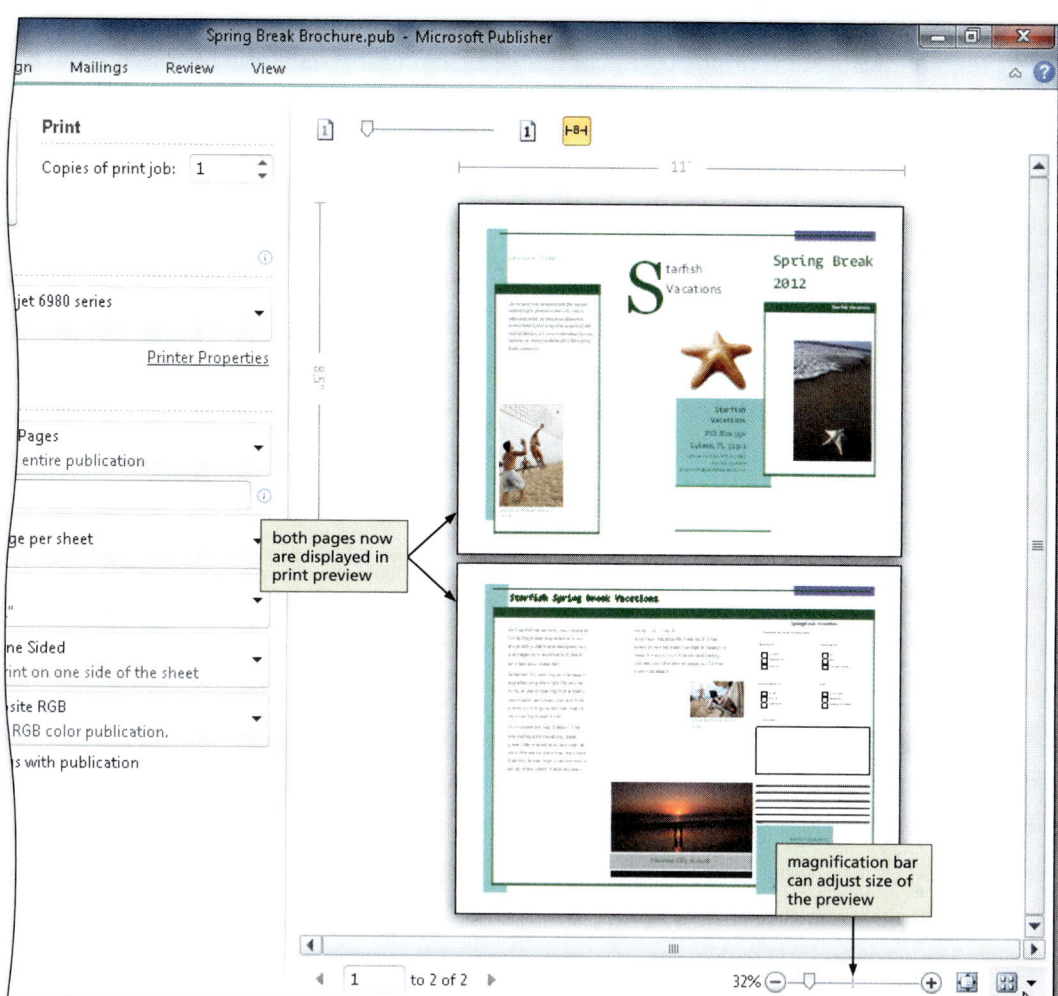

both pages now are displayed in print preview

magnification bar can adjust size of the preview

Figure 2–63

To Print a Publication with Settings

The following steps print the brochure on a high grade of paper to obtain a professional look, and print on both sides of the paper. A heavier stock paper helps the brochure to stand up better in display racks, although any paper will suffice. Brochure paper is a special paper with creases that create a professional-looking fold, and with a paper finish that works well with color and graphics.

TO PRINT ON SPECIAL PAPER

If you have special paper, you would perform the following steps to choose that special paper before printing. See your instructor for assistance in choosing the correct option associated with your printer.

1. Open the Backstage view and then click the Print tab.
2. Click the Printer Properties link at the bottom of the middle pane to display your printer's advanced printing dialog box.
3. Find the paper or quality setting and then choose your paper.
4. Click the OK button in that dialog box to return to the Backstage view.

BTW

Conserving Ink and Toner
If you want to conserve ink or toner, you can instruct Publisher to print draft quality documents by clicking File on the Ribbon to open the Backstage view, clicking Print in the Backstage view to display the Print gallery, clicking the Printer Properties link, and then choosing a draft quality. Then, use the Backstage view to print the document as usual.

To Print on Both Sides

The following steps print the brochure on both sides. If your printer does not have that capability, follow your printer's specifications to print one side of the paper, turn it over, and then print the reverse side.

1

- If necessary, click the Print tab in the Backstage view to display the Print gallery.

- Click the Print One Sided button to display the list of options (Figure 2–64).

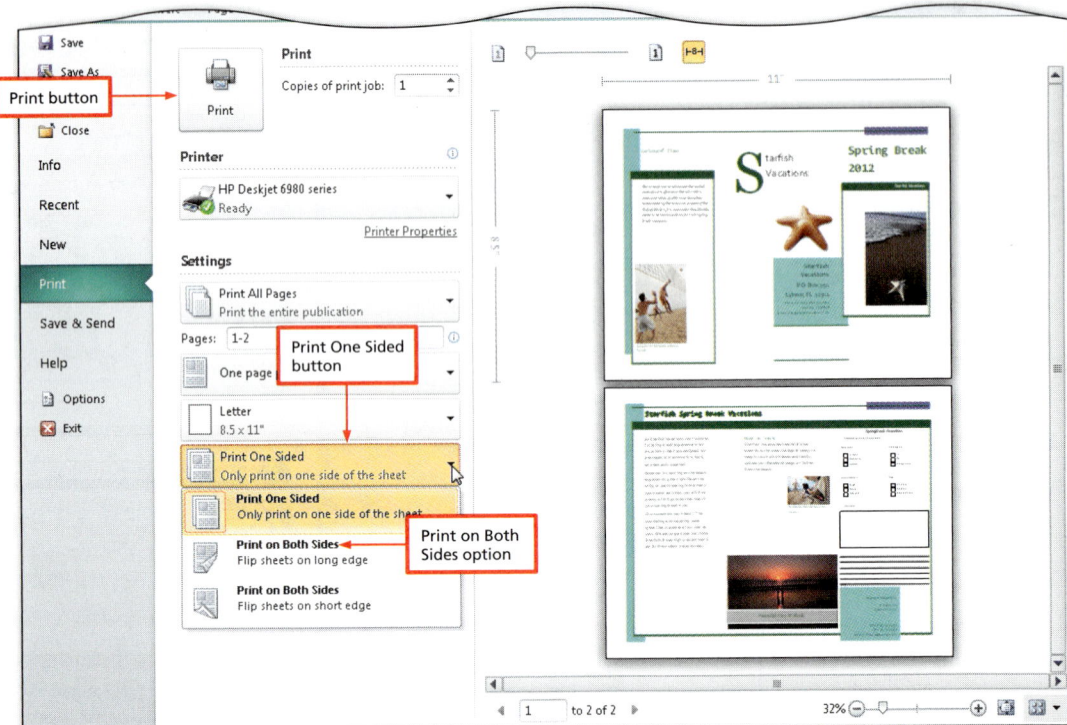

Figure 2–64

2

- If your list displays a Print On Both Sides (Flip Sheets on long edge) option, click it to select automatic printing of both sides.

- If your list displays a Manual 2 Sided Print (Flip Sheets on long edge) option, click it to select manual printing.

- Click the Print button to print the brochure.

- When the printer stops, retrieve the printed publication (Figure 2–65).

Figure 2–65

Other Ways

1. Press CTRL+P, chose settings, click Print button

Printing Considerations

When they need mass quantities of publications, businesses generally outsource, or submit their publications to an outside printer, for duplicating. You must make special considerations when preparing a publication for outside printing.

If you start a publication from scratch, it is best to set up the publication for the type of printing you want before you place objects on the page. Otherwise, you may be forced to make design changes at the last minute. You also may set up an existing publication for a printing service. In order to provide you with experience in setting up a publication for outside printing, this project guides you through the preparation steps — even if you are submitting this publication only to your instructor.

Printing options, such as whether to use a copy shop or commercial printer, have advantages and limitations. You may have to make some trade-offs before deciding on the best printing option. Table 2–4 shows some of the questions you can ask yourself about printing.

Table 2–4 Picking a Printing Option			
Consideration	**Questions to Ask**	**Desktop Option**	**Professional Options**
Color	Is the quality of photographs and color a high priority?	Low to medium quality	High quality
Convenience	Do I want the easy way?	Very convenient and familiar	Time needed to explore different methods, unfamiliarity
Cost	How much do I want to pay?	Printer supplies and personal time	High-resolution color/high quality is expensive; the more you print, the less expensive the per-copy price
Quality	How formal is the purpose of my publication?	Local event; narrow, personal audience	Business, marketing, professional services
Quantity	How many copies do I need?	1 to 10 copies	10 to 500 copies: use a copy shop; 500+ copies: use a commercial printer
Turnaround	How soon do I need it?	Immediate	Rush outside printing is probably an extra cost

BTW

Plan for Printing
Make a firm decision that quality matters and consult with several commercial printers ahead of time. Get prices, color modes, copies, paper, and folding options in writing before you finish your brochure. Brochures are more effective on heavier paper, with strong colors and glossy feels. Together with the commercial printer, select a paper that is going to last. Check to make sure the commercial printer can accept Microsoft Publisher 2010 files.

BTW

T-Shirts
You can use Publisher to create T-shirt designs with pictures, logos, words, or any other Publisher objects. First, purchase thermal T-shirt transfer paper that is widely available for most printers. Then, create your design in Publisher. If your design is a picture, clip art, or WordArt, flip it horizontally. If your design includes text, cut it from the text box, insert it into a WordArt object, and then flip it horizontally.

Paper Considerations

Professional brochures are printed on a high grade of paper to enhance the graphics and provide a longer lasting document. Grades of paper are based on weight. Desktop printers commonly use 20-lb. bond paper, which means they use a lightweight paper intended for writing and printing. A commercial printer might use 60-lb. glossy or linen paper.

The finishing options and their costs are important considerations that may take additional time to explore. Glossy paper is a coated paper, produced using a heat process with clay and titanium. Linen paper, with its mild texture or grain, can support high-quality graphics without the shine and slick feel of glossy paper. Users sometimes pick a special stock of paper, such as cover stock, card stock, or text stock. This textbook is printed on 45-lb., blade-coated paper. Blade-coated paper is coated and then skimmed and smoothed to create the pages you see here.

BTW

CMYK Colors
When Process Colors are selected, Publisher converts all colors in text, graphics, and other objects to CMYK values and then creates four plates, regardless of the color scheme originally used to create the publication. Some RGB colors, including some of Publisher's standard colors, cannot be matched exactly to a CMYK color. After setting up for process-color printing, be sure to evaluate the publication for color changes. If a color does not match the color you want, you will have to include the new color library when you pack the publication.

BTW

Spot Colors
If you choose black plus one spot color in a publication, Publisher converts all colors except for black to tints of the selected spot color. If you choose black plus two spot colors, Publisher changes only exact matches of the second spot color to 100 percent of the second spot color. All other colors in the publication, other than black, are changed to tints of the first spot color. You then can apply tints of the second spot color to objects in the publication manually.

BTW

Embedding Font Sets
To embed the fonts for a commercial printing service, click the Commercial Print Settings button in the Backstage view and then click Manage Embedded Fonts. Select the 'Embed TrueType fonts when saving publication' check box (Fonts dialog box).

These paper and finishing options may seem burdensome, but they are becoming conveniently available to desktop publishers. Local office supply stores have shelf after shelf of special computer paper specifically designed for laser and ink-jet printers. Some of the paper you can purchase has been prescored for special folding.

Color Considerations

When printing colors, desktop printers commonly use a color scheme called RGB. RGB stands for the three colors — red, green, and blue — that are combined to produce the colors used in your publication. Professional printers, on the other hand, can print your publication using color scheme processes, or libraries. These processes include black and white, spot color, and process color.

In black-and-white printing, the printer uses only one color of ink (usually black, but you can choose a different color). You can add accent colors to your publication by using different shades of gray or by printing on colored paper. Your publication can have the same range of subtleties as a black-and-white photograph.

A spot color is used to accent a black-and-white publication. Newspapers, for example, may print their masthead in a bright, eye-catching color on page 1 but print the rest of the publication in black and white. In Publisher, you may apply up to two spot colors with a color-matching system called Pantone. Spot-color printing uses semitransparent, premixed inks typically chosen from standard color-matching guides, such as Pantone. Choosing colors from a color-matching library helps ensure high-quality results, because printing professionals who license the libraries agree to maintain the specifications, control, and quality.

In a spot-color publication, each spot color is separated to its own plate and printed on an offset printing press. The use of spot colors has become more creative in the last few years. Printing services use spot colors of metallic or fluorescent inks, as well as screen tints, to provide color variations without increasing the number of color separations and the cost. If your publication includes a logo with one or two colors, or if you want to use color to emphasize line art or text, then consider using spot-color printing.

With process-color printing, your publication can include color photographs and any color or combination of colors. One of the process-color libraries, called CMYK, or four-color printing, is named for the four semitransparent process inks — cyan, magenta, yellow, and black. CMYK process-color printing can reproduce a full range of colors on a printed page. The CMYK color model defines color as it is absorbed by and reflected on a printed page, rather than in its liquid state.

Process-color printing is the most expensive proposition; black-and-white printing is the cheapest. Using color increases the cost and time it takes to process the publication. When using either the spot-color or process-color method, the printer first must output the publication to film on an image setter, which recreates the publication on film or photographic paper. The film then is used to create color printing plates. Each printing plate transfers one of the colors in the publication onto paper in an offset process. Publisher can print a preview of these individual sheets showing how the colors will separate before you take your publication to the printer.

A new printing technology called digital printing uses toner instead of ink to reproduce a full range of colors. Digital printing does not require separate printing plates. Although not yet widely available, digital printing promises to become cheaper than offset printing without sacrificing any quality.

Publisher supports all three kinds of printing and provides the tools commercial printing services need to print the publication. You should ask your printing service which color-matching system it uses.

To Choose a Color Model

After making the decisions about printing services, paper, and color, you must prepare the brochure for outside printing. The following steps assign a color model from the commercial printing tools.

1
- Click File on the Ribbon to open the Backstage view and, by default, select the Info tab.

- Click the Commercial Print Settings button in the center pane of the Info gallery to display the options for commercial printing tools (Figure 2–66).

Figure 2–66

2
- Click Choose Color Model to display the Color Model dialog box.

- Click Process colors (CMYK) to select it (Figure 2–67).

3
- Click the OK button in the Microsoft Publisher dialog box.

- Click the OK button in the Color Model dialog box.

Figure 2–67

Packaging the Publication for the Printing Service

The publication file can be packaged for the printing service in two ways. The first way is to give the printing service the Publisher file in Publisher format using the Pack and Go Wizard. The second way is to save the file in a format called Encapsulated PostScript. Both of these methods are discussed in the following sections.

To Use the Pack and Go Wizard

The Pack and Go Wizard guides you through the steps to collect and pack all the files the printing service needs and then compress the files. Publisher checks for and embeds the TrueType fonts used in the publication, in case the printing service does not have those fonts available. The following steps use the Pack and Go Wizard to ready the publication for submission to a commercial printing service.

1
- With a USB flash drive connected to one of the computer's USB ports, open the Backstage view, if necessary.
- Click the Save & Send tab in the Backstage view to display the Share gallery.
- In the Pack and Go area, click the Save for a Commercial Printer button (Figure 2–68).

Q&A Should I save my file first?

You do not have to save it again; however, if you use a storage device other than the one on which you previously saved the brochure, save it again on the new medium before beginning the process.

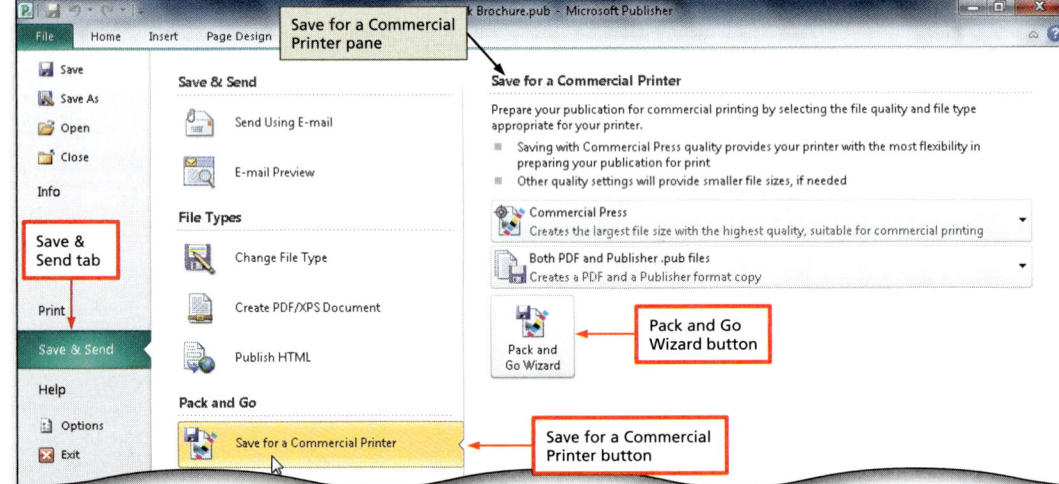

Figure 2–68

2
- Click the Pack and Go Wizard button to begin the Pack and Go wizard (Figure 2–69).

Q&A What does the Save for Another Computer button do?

It performs the same collection process as the Pack and Go wizard, but it allows you to choose whether or not to embed fonts and include any linked graphics.

Figure 2–69

3

- Click the Browse button, navigate to your USB flash drive, and then click the OK button to specify the location (Figure 2–70).

Q&A What if I run out of room on my storage device?

Graphic files and fonts require a great deal of disk space, but should fit on most USB flash drives. If your USB flash drive is full, have another storage device ready. Publisher will prompt you to insert it.

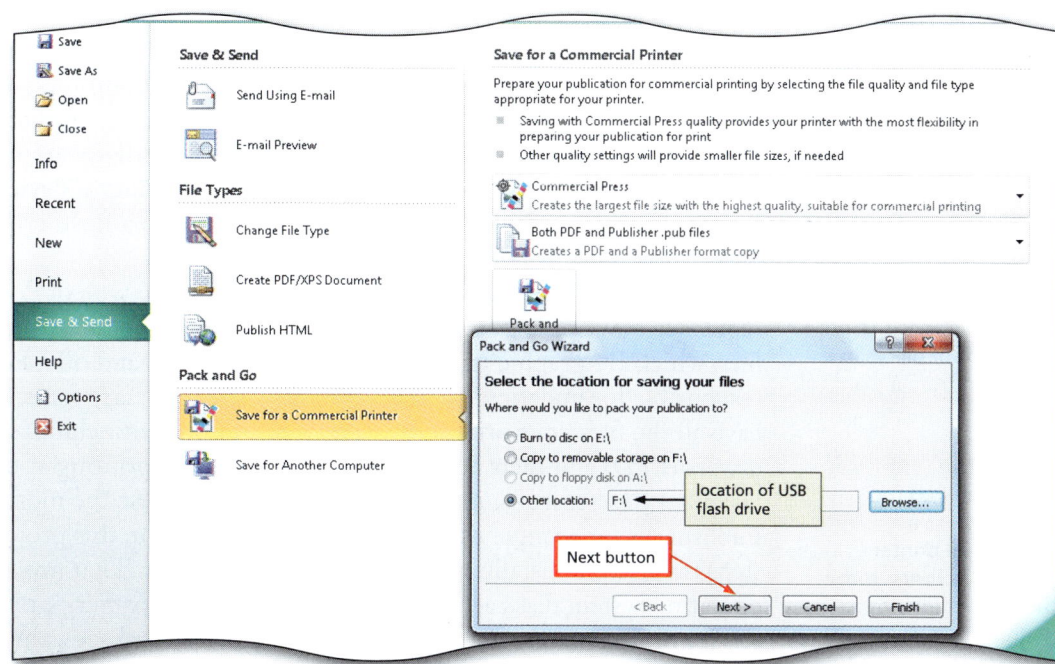

Figure 2–70

4

- Click the Next button to display the embedded fonts and save the file.

- When the final dialog box is displayed, remove the check mark in the 'Print a composite proof' box (Figure 2–71).

Q&A Publisher displayed a Pack and Go font embedding error message. Did I do something wrong?

Probably not. You may not own rights to the fonts on your computer, if you are connected to a network printer. Click the OK button to continue with the Pack and Go wizard.

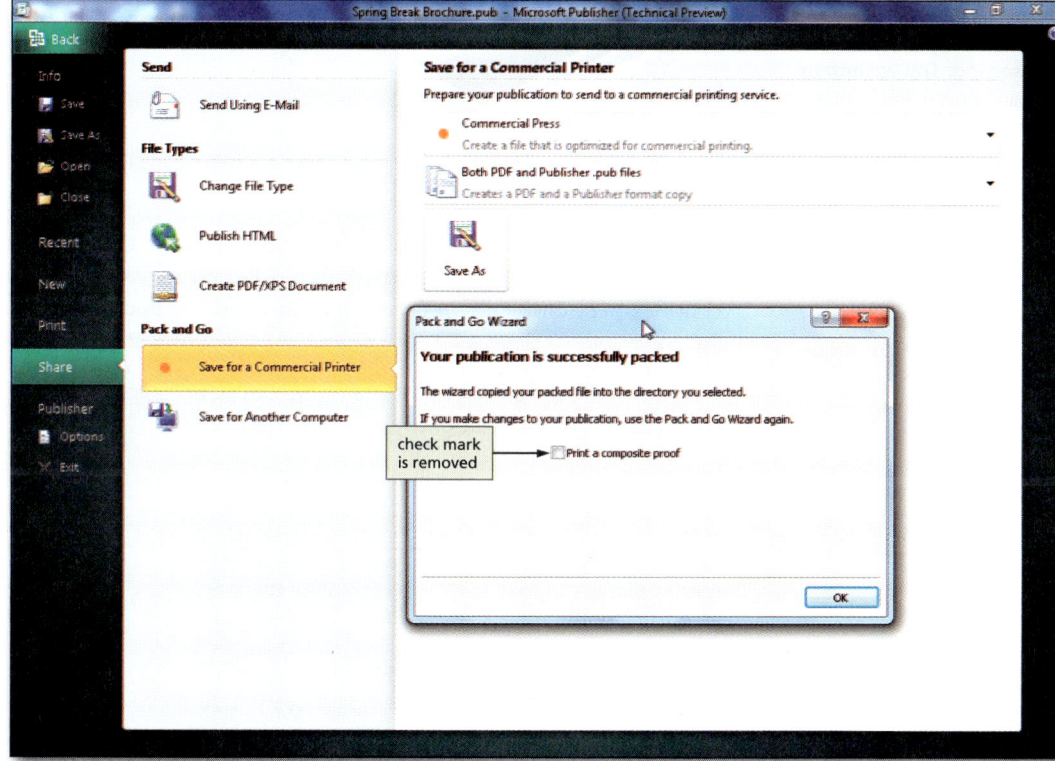

Figure 2–71

5

- Click the OK button to close the Pack and Go Wizard dialog box.

Using PostScript Files

If your printing service does not accept Publisher files, you can hand off, or submit, your files in PostScript format. PostScript is a page definition language that describes the document to be printed in language that the printer can understand. The PostScript printer driver includes a page definition language translator to interpret the instructions and print the document on a printer or a PostScript output device, such as an image setter. Because you cannot open or make changes directly to a PostScript file, everything in the publication must be complete before you save it.

Nearly all printing services can work with some type of PostScript file, either regular PostScript files, known as PostScript dumps, or Encapsulated PostScript (EPS) files, which are graphic pictures of each page. If you hand off a PostScript file, you are responsible for updating graphics, including the necessary fonts, and ensuring that you have all the files your printing service needs. Publisher includes several PostScript printer drivers (PPD) and their description files to facilitate printing at the publisher. You must install a PPD before saving in PostScript form. Because the most common installation of Publisher is for a single user in a desktop environment, this project does not provide the steps involved in installing a PostScript printer driver. That process would require original operating system disks and advanced knowledge of PostScript printers. Ask your printing service representative for the correct printer driver, and see your Windows documentation for information about installing it. Then use the Save As dialog box to save the publication in PostScript format.

Another question to ask your printing service is whether it performs the prepress tasks or a preflight check. You may be responsible for color corrections, separations, setting the printing options, and other printing tasks.

To Quit Publisher

The following steps quit Publisher.

1 If you have one Publisher publication open, click the Close button on the right side of the title bar to close the publication and quit Publisher; or if you have multiple Publisher publications open, Click File on the Ribbon to open the Backstage view and then click Exit on the Publisher tab to close all open publications and quit Publisher.

2 If a Microsoft Office Publisher dialog box appears, click the Save button to save any changes made to the publication since the last save.

Chapter Summary

In this chapter, you were introduced to the brochure medium. You learned how to create custom color schemes, apply font effects, and change paragraph formatting. You learned about the use of photographs versus images, and how to insert clip art. After entering new text and deleting unwanted objects, you created a logo using a formatted shape and autofitted text. You also learned about design and printing considerations, such as overlapping, separations, color libraries, paper types, and costs. In anticipation of taking the brochure to a professional publisher, you previewed and printed your publication and then used the Pack and Go Wizard to create the necessary files. The items listed below include all the new Publisher skills you have learned in this chapter.

1. Search for a Template (PUB 70)
2. Choose Brochure Options (PUB 71)
3. Edit Text Boxes on the Front Panel (PUB 73)
4. Copy and Paste (PUB 75)
5. Display Formatting Marks (PUB 79)
6. Wordwrap Text as You Type (PUB 79)
7. Italicize Text (PUB 81)
8. Underline a Word (PUB 82)
9. Bold Text (PUB 83)
10. Display Text in a Stylistic Set (PUB 84)
11. Create a Drop Cap (PUB 84)
12. Enable a Ligature (PUB 86)
13. Apply a Font Effect (PUB 89)
14. Use the Format Painter Button (PUB 91)
15. Edit the Sign-Up Form (PUB 93)
16. Replace a Graphic Using the Clip Art Task Pane (PUB 94)
17. Resize the Graphic (PUB 97)
18. Insert a New Graphic Using the Clip Art Task Pane (PUB 98)
19. Edit Captions (PUB 103)
20. Use the Caption Gallery (PUB 104)
21. Check the Spelling of the Entire Publication (PUB 107)
22. Run the Design Checker (PUB 108)
23. Preview Multiple Pages before Printing (PUB 110)
24. Print on Special Paper (PUB 111)
25. Print on Both Sides (PUB 112)
26. Choose a Color Model (PUB 115)
27. Use the Pack and Go Wizard (PUB 116)

Learn It Online

Test your knowledge of chapter content and key terms.

Instructions: To complete the Learn It Online exercises, start your browser, click the Address bar, and then enter the Web address **scsite.com/pub2010/learn**. When the Publisher 2010 Learn It Online page is displayed, click the link for the exercise you want to complete and then read the instructions.

Chapter Reinforcement TF, MC, and SA
A series of true/false, multiple choice, and short answer questions that test your knowledge of the chapter content.

Flash Cards
An interactive learning environment where you identify chapter key terms associated with displayed definitions.

Practice Test
A series of multiple choice questions that test your knowledge of chapter content and key terms.

Who Wants To Be a Computer Genius?
An interactive game that challenges your knowledge of chapter content in the style of a television quiz show.

Wheel of Terms
An interactive game that challenges your knowledge of chapter key terms in the style of the television show *Wheel of Fortune*.

Crossword Puzzle Challenge
A crossword puzzle that challenges your knowledge of key terms presented in the chapter.

Apply Your Knowledge

Reinforce the skills and apply the concepts you learned in this chapter.

Revising Text and Graphics in a Publication

Instructions: Start Publisher. Open the publication, Apply 2–1 Sandwich Shop Menu, from the Data Files for Students. See the inside back cover of this book for instructions on downloading the Data Files for Students, or contact your instructor for more information about accessing the required files.

You are to revise the two-page menu as follows: enter new text and text boxes, use stylistic sets and ligatures, replace graphics, create decorative captions, delete objects, and check the publication for errors. Finally, you will pack the publication for a commercial printing service. The revised publication is shown in Figure 2–72.

Perform the following tasks:

1. Open the Page Navigation pane and display special characters in the Publisher workspace.

2. On page 1, make the following text changes, scrolling and zooming as necessary:

   a. In the right panel, Select the Business Tagline or Motto text and then type `The World's Sandwich Shop` to replace the text.

   b. Select the description text box below the word, Menu, in the right panel. Type `We offer the world's most` and then press the ENTER key. Then type `traditional sandwiches –` and then press the ENTER key. Finally, type `everything around the globe` to complete the text. *Hint:* If Publisher capitalizes the first letter of each line, highlight the letter and type a lowercase letter to replace it. Autofit the text.

   c. Select the Business Name text in the right panel and then type `Un Croque Monsieur` to replace it. Select the new text and copy it to the Clipboard. Autofit the text. With the text still selected, click Text Box Tools Format on the Ribbon to display the Text Box Tools Format tab. Click the Stylistic Sets button (Text Box Tools Format tab | Typography group) and choose a set.

   d. Scroll to the lower portion of the left panel and draw a text box just above the decorative border. Make the text box the same width as the text box below the graphic, using the visual layout guides. Click inside the text box to position the insertion point. Right-click to display the shortcut menu, and then, in the Paste Options gallery, click the Keep Text Only preview. After the text is pasted, type: `is owned and operated by Jacques Reneau.` to enter the rest of the sentence. Autofit the text.

   e. Return to the right panel and click inside the title, Un Croque Monsieur, again. Click the Format Painter (Home tab | Clipboard group) and then paste the formatting to the word, MENU, below the graphic. Resize the Menu text box as necessary.

3. Go to page 2 and make the following text changes, scrolling and zooming as necessary:

   a. For each of the food category headings, click to the left of the first letter. Go to the Text Box Tools Format tab on the Ribbon. Click the Drop Cap button (Text Box Tools Format tab | Typography group). Choose the Drop Cap Style 6 style.

   b. Scroll to the upper portion of the center panel. Scroll to 400% magnification. Highlight the letters fi in the menu offering for tuna fish salad. Click the Ligatures button (Text Box Tools Format tab | Typography group) and enable ligatures.

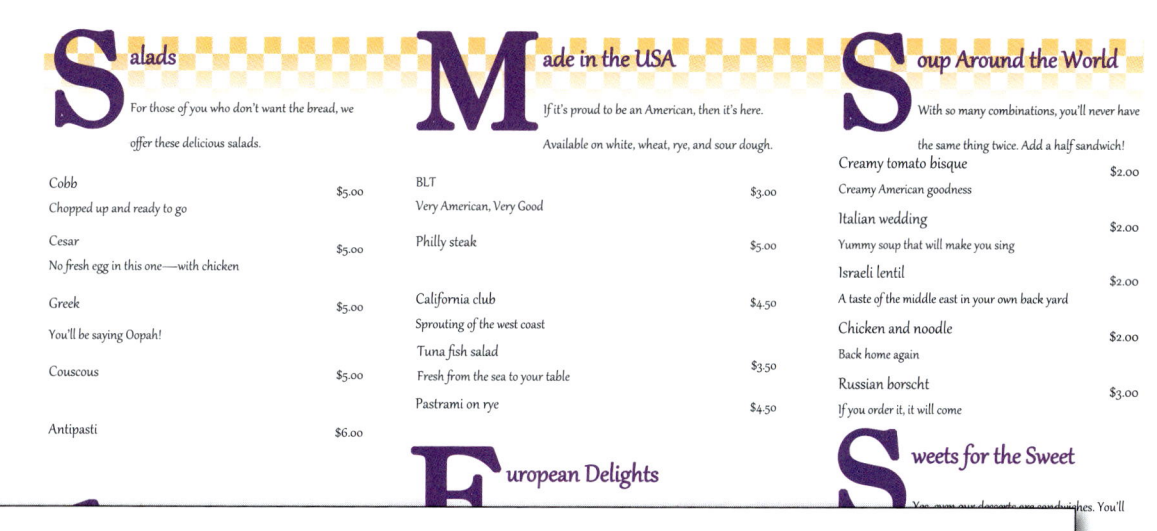

Salads

For those of you who don't want the bread, we offer these delicious salads.

Cobb	$5.00
Chopped up and ready to go	
Cesar	$5.00
No fresh egg in this one—with chicken	
Greek	$5.00
You'll be saying Oopah!	
Couscous	$5.00
Antipasti	$6.00

Made in the USA

If it's proud to be an American, then it's here. Available on white, wheat, rye, and sour dough.

BLT	$3.00
Very American, Very Good	
Philly steak	$5.00
California club	$4.50
Sprouting of the west coast	
Tuna fish salad	$3.50
Fresh from the sea to your table	
Pastrami on rye	$4.50
If you order it, it will come	

Soup Around the World

With so many combinations, you'll never have the same thing twice. Add a half sandwich!

Creamy tomato bisque	$2.00
Creamy American goodness	
Italian wedding	$2.00
Yummy soup that will make you sing	
Israeli lentil	$2.00
A taste of the middle east in your own back yard	
Chicken and noodle	$2.00
Back home again	
Russian borscht	$3.00

European Delights

Sweets for the Sweet

	3.50 for two
	3.50 for two
	$3.00
	$2.50
	$2.00

We also do catering. Let the world's best sandwiches come to you.

Call us for your next event.

We accept Visa, MasterCard,

Un Croque Monsieur is owned and operated by Jacques Reneau.

Hours

Monday-Friday 11:00a.m.-10:00p.m.

Saturday 12:00p.m.-11:p.m.

Sunday 11:00a.m.-7:00p.m.

1000 Gruyère Lane

Florence, S. C. 29501

Phone: 843-555-1886

Fax: 843-555-1719

Email: info@uncroquemonsieur

Gruyère & Pine

The World's Sandwich Shop!

Un Croque Monsieur

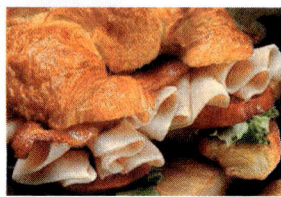

MENU

We offer the world's most traditional sandwiches —

Figure 2–72

Continued >

Apply Your Knowledge *continued*

4. Use the Clip Art task pane to replace each of the graphics on page 1, by selecting the graphic and then clicking the Clip Art button (Insert tab | Illustrations group). Use keywords such as sandwich and food to locate clip art images similar to the ones in Figure 2–72.

5. Click the Map to select it. Click the Caption button (Picture Tools Format tab | Picture Styles group) to add a decorative caption to the map. Choose the Band – Layout 1 style.

6. Check spelling and run the Design Checker. Correct errors if necessary. Choose to ignore foreign words and names.

7. Click File and then click Save As. Use the file name, Apply 2–1 Sandwich Shop Menu Modified.

8. In the Backstage view, click the Commercial Printing Setting button, and then click Choose Color Model. When the Color Printing dialog box is displayed, click Process colors (CMYK). When Publisher displays an information dialog box, click the OK button; then, click the OK button in the Color Printing dialog box.

9. In the Backstage view, click the Save & Send tab. Click Save for a Commercial Printer and then click the Save As button to start the Pack and Go wizard. Browse to your USB drive and then click the Next button to create the compressed files. When the wizard completes the packing process, if necessary, click the 'Print a composite proof' check box to display its check mark. The composite will print on two pages.

Extend Your Knowledge

Extend the skills you learned in this chapter and experiment with new skills. You may need to use Help to complete the assignment.

Working with Typography and Building Blocks

Instructions: Start Publisher. Open the publication, Extend 2–1 Retreat Brochure, from the Data Files for Students. See the inside back cover of this book for instructions on downloading the Data Files for Students, or contact your instructor for more information about accessing the required files.

You will enhance the look of the brochure and include a sign-up form for the corporation to fill in with times and prices.

Perform the following tasks:
1. Use Help to learn about 4-panel paper sizes, picture borders, and building blocks.

2. Select the title text in the second panel on page 1, which is the front of the brochure. Apply a stylistic set.

3. Select the graphic in the same panel and add a strong black border.

4. Select the graphic in the first panel on the left. To add a thick blue border, click the Picture Border button (Picture Tools Format tab | Pictures Styles group) and then click Sample Line Color, as shown in Figure 2–73 on the next page. Click a blue color in the graphic to sample the color and add it to the color palette. Then, add a thick blue border to the graphic.

5. Add a building block on page 2 in the far right panel. Search for a Narrow Sign-up form.

6. Change the picture border on page 2 in the first panel. Use the same color of blue that you used on page 1, but use a patterned border.

7. Change the document properties, including keywords, as specified by your instructor. Save the revised publication with a new file name and then submit it in the format specified by your instructor.

Figure 2–73

Make It Right

Analyze a publication and correct all errors and/or improve the design.

Fixing a Theater Program

Instructions: Start Publisher. Open the publication, Make It Right 2–1 Theatre Program, from the Data Files for Students. See the inside back cover of this book for instructions on downloading the Data Files for Students, or contact your instructor for more information about accessing the required files.

The document is a two-page, two-panel program that contains spelling errors, design errors, autofitting errors, misalignments, and missing text boxes, as shown in Figure 2–74. You are to correct each spelling error by clicking the Spelling button (Review tab | Proofing group) and fix each error as it appears. Run the Design Checker in the Backstage view and look for errors (Figure 2–74). Fix the object overlap on page 2 in the lower portion of the right panel, by dragging the line down below the text and aligning it with the other objects in the panel. Also on page 2, use the Format Painter to copy the formatting of the first act to the second and third. Add a text box on page 1, in the right panel, with the date and time of the play on March 22, 23, and 24, 2012, at 7:00 p.m.

Change the document properties, including keywords, as specified by your instructor. Save the revised document with a new file name and then submit it in the format specified by your instructor.

Continued >

STUDENT ASSIGNMENTS

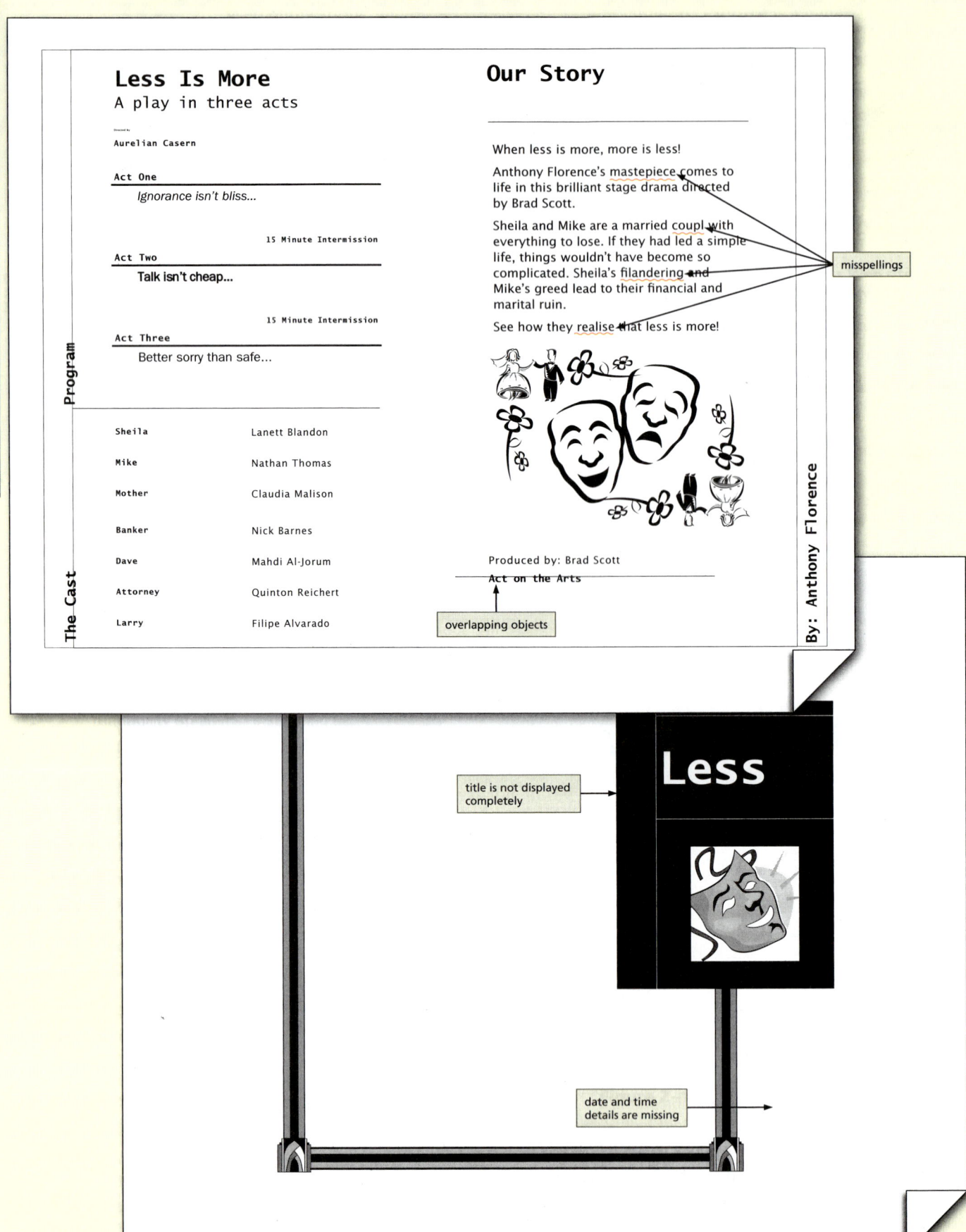

Less Is More
A play in three acts

Directed by
Aurelian Casern

Act One

Ignorance isn't bliss...

15 Minute Intermission

Act Two

Talk isn't cheap...

15 Minute Intermission

Act Three

Better sorry than safe...

Program

The Cast

Sheila	Lanett Blandon
Mike	Nathan Thomas
Mother	Claudia Malison
Banker	Nick Barnes
Dave	Mahdi Al-Jorum
Attorney	Quinton Reichert
Larry	Filipe Alvarado

Our Story

When less is more, more is less!

Anthony Florence's mastepiece comes to life in this brilliant stage drama directed by Brad Scott.

Sheila and Mike are a married coupl with everything to lose. If they had led a simple life, things wouldn't have become so complicated. Sheila's filandering and Mike's greed lead to their financial and marital ruin.

See how they realise that less is more!

Produced by: Brad Scott
Act on the Arts

By: Anthony Florence

misspellings

overlapping objects

title is not displayed completely

Less

date and time details are missing

Figure 2–74

In the Lab

Lab 1: Creating a Brochure with a Response Form

Problem: A wind farm in central Kansas has opened a new visitors' center, complete with production displays and a video about how wind farms work. They offer seasonal tours to tourists, school groups, and corporate investors. They would like you to create an informational brochure that they can use to advertise the wind farm and its renewable energy features. The wind farm publication should be a trifold brochure with graphics and information about the business. On the inside of the brochure, the manager would like a turnaround response form for visitors who want more information.

Instructions: Start Publisher and perform the following tasks to create the brochure shown in Figure 2–75. The front cover photograph, which was taken with a digital camera, is available in the Data Files for Students. See the inside back cover of this book for instructions on downloading the Data Files for Students, or contact your instructor for information about accessing the required files.

Figure 2–75

Continued >

In the Lab *continued*

1. Search for the Brocade Informational Brochure. Choose the Foundry color scheme, the Offset Font scheme, and a 3-panel brochure with a response form. Click the Create button.

2. Click the Save button on the Quick Access Toolbar and then save the publication on your USB flash drive with the name, Lab 2–1 Wind Farm Brochure.

3. Click the Page Number button on the status bar to open the Page Navigation pane. Click the Special Characters button (Home tab | Paragraph group) to display the special characters.

4. To edit the text boxes:

   a. Edit the text frames on page 1 with the information from Table 2–5. As you enter text, press the ENTER key at the end of paragraphs and after short lines, like those in the title and address. Remember that some text boxes synchronize to other text boxes. Zoom and scroll as necessary.

Table 2–5 Text for Page 1		
Location	**Text Box**	**Text**
Right panel	Business Name	Old Dutch Wind Farms
	Business Tagline or Motto	Sponsored by the Colby County Convention and Visitors Bureau
	Product/Service Information	Wind Farms: The Future of Clean Energy
	Telephone number	Tel: 913-555-0707
Center panel	Primary Business Address	425 County Road Z Leon, KS 66850
	Telephone, Fax and E-mail	Phone: 913-555-0707 Fax: 913-555-0808 E-mail: info@olddutchwf.biz
Left panel	Back Panel Heading	Get Up Close and Personal with Our Windmills
	story	Come take a tour!
		We are open from 10 a.m. to 6 p.m., Tuesday through Saturday, from May through September. We are closed on Mondays.
		Tours leave on the hour from the Visitor Center located adjacent to the wind farm. Tours are free and last 50 minutes. A donation is requested.
		Don't forget to walk through the interactive exhibits in our Visitor Center and watch our 20-minute video about windmill construction and renewable, clean energy.
		Pack your lunch and enjoy our shady picnic area!
	caption	Visitor Center

   b. Autofit the Business Name text box that now displays the words, Old Dutch Wind Farms. Autofit the story in the left panel.

   c. Go to page 2. Edit the text frames on page 2 with the information from Table 2–6. Autofit the story text boxes as necessary.

Table 2–6 Text for Page 2

Location	Text Box	Text
Left panel	Main Inside Heading	Go Green for Clean Energy
	story	Everyone has a responsibility to keep our planet clean, so we here at Old Dutch Wind Farms are doing our part.
		We started as wheat farmers here in Kansas. When we were approved by the Department of Energy to install these windmills on our property, we jumped at the chance.
		That was in 2007, and now we've become one of the main wind farmers in the state. We harvest and monitor over 10 Gigawatt-hours a year. That's a lot of energy! In the future, we hope to install more windmills and increase our output by 15%. More clean energy for our state!
	caption	Did you know that not all windmills are the same size?
Center panel	Secondary Heading	Good for You. Good for the Earth.
	story	Clean air energy benefits everyone and everything! Wind power is a renewable resource. We'll never run out. It's constant. And there are no emissions on our wind farm. We keep the air that we use clean. Wind farms are also green in the financial sense. After the cost of installation, we're making money. Whether you lease your land to a corporation or invest yourself, the rewards are major.
	Secondary Heading	What You'll See on the Tour:
	story	We start at the Visitor Center, where you will see a film that reviews the progress of windmill power through the ages, including local construction. Next, you will enter a mockup of the base of a modern windmill and see its inner workings. Finally, our guide will take you to the wind farm where you will stand at the base of a working windmill. You will see the inner workings of the windmill through a glass door. After your tour, you are free to visit our authentic Dutch windmill at the Visitor Center.
	caption	Authentic Dutch windmill

d. Edit the Response Form in the right panel of page 2, making the text changes indicated in Figure 2–76.

Figure 2–76

Continued >

In the Lab *continued*

5. To edit the graphics:

   a. Go to page 1. Delete the logo in the center panel.

   b. With the USB flash drive that contains the Data Files for Students inserted into one of the computer's USB ports, right-click the graphic in the front panel to display the shortcut menu. Click Change picture to open the Insert Picture dialog box. Navigate to the Chapter 02 folder and insert the Windmill picture.

   c. Click Picture Tools Format on the Ribbon to display the Picture Tools Format tab. Click the More button (Picture Tools Format tab | Picture Styles group) and click the Picture Style 7 preview.

   d. Scroll to the lower portion of the center panel. Click Insert on the Ribbon to display the Insert tab. Click the Picture button (Insert tab | Illustrations group) and then navigate to the Chapter 02 folder and insert the Wooden Shoes photo.

   e. Select the graphic in the left panel. Do not select the caption. Click the Clip Art button (Insert tab | Illustrations group) and then search for a picture related to the keyword house or farm. Choose a graphic similar to the one in Figure 2–75 on page PUB 125. *Hint:* The template graphic is in portrait mode, or taller than wider. If you select a landscape graphic, you may lose some of the right and left edges of the photo.

   f. Click the border of the graphic and caption grouped object. Click Picture Tools Format on the Ribbon to display the Picture Tools Format tab. Click the Caption button (Picture Tools Format tab | Picture Styles group) and click the Offset – Layout 1 preview.

   g. Go to page 2. Replace both graphics with Clip Art. Search for the word, windmill.

6. Check the spelling of the entire brochure. Open the Backstage view and run the Design Checker. Fix any problems.

7. Save the brochure again. See your instructor for ways to submit this assignment.

In the Lab

Lab 2: Creating a Price List Brochure

Problem: You have just received an internship with the Chamber of Commerce. One of their members, the Association of Dogs and Dog Lovers (ADDL) would like a new brochure to advertise and present a price list of membership fees and services.

Instructions: Start Publisher and perform the following tasks to create the brochure shown in Figure 2–77. The front cover photograph, which was taken with a digital camera, is available in the Data Files for Students. See the inside back cover of this book for instructions on downloading the Data Files for Students, or contact your instructor for information about accessing the required files.

1. Select the Perforation Price List Brochure template. Choose the Office color scheme, the Civic Font scheme, and a 3-panel brochure. Click the Create button.

2. Click the Save button on the Quick Access Toolbar and then save the publication on your USB flash drive with the name, Lab 2–2 Animal Brochure.

3. Edit the text frames on page 1 with the information from Table 2–7.

Figure 2–77

Table 2–7 Text for Page 1		
Location	**Text Box**	**Text**
Right panel	Business Name	ADDL-USA
	Product/Service Information	Membership for the Association of Dogs and Dog Lovers USA
	Telephone number	Tel: 575-555-1111
Center panel	Primary Business Address	5450 Agape Street Lovington, NM 88260
	Telephone, Fax and E-mail	Phone: 575-555-1111 Fax: 575-555-2222 E-mail: max@addl.dog.org
Left panel	Back Panel Heading	Contact us with your dog questions:
	story	Training tips Agility tips Registration Experts in your area Grooming Food And much more!
	caption	Vet tech services

Continued >

In the Lab *continued*

4. To format the story, select all of the text in the left panel story. Click the Left Align button (Home Tab | Paragraph group). Click the Bullets button (Home Tab | Paragraph group) and choose a diamond-shaped bullet.

5. Edit the text frames on page 2 with the information from Table 2–8.

Table 2–8 Text for Page 2

Location	Text Box	Text	
Left panel	Main Inside Heading	Your Local ADDL	
	story	Whether you're a person who wants a dog or a person who's had a dog for years, the ADDL is for you! We are an association of dog enthusiasts who work to prevent cruelty, educate people on owning a dog, and advocate on behalf of our furry canine companions. We also post adoptions on our Web site, so if you're looking for an addition to your family, our reputable adoption database is the place to start.	
		Membership includes our magazine, The World's Gone to the Dogs!, regional breeder information, regional and national competitions, as well as much more. We hope you'll become a member and show your love for man's best friend.	
Center panel	heading	Services and Fees:	
	price list	Grooming	$30.00
		Show-Grade Grooming	$40.00
		Puppy Obedience Classes (8 weeks)	$100.00
		Teach Old Dogs New Tricks (8 weeks)	$100.00
		Competitive Scenting Classes (6 weeks)	$75.00
		Before the Puppy Arrives	$30.00
		Daily Kennel Rates (5-40 pounds)	$30.00
		Daily Kennel Rates (41+ pounds)	$35.00
Right panel	price list	Vet Tech Hotline (1 year)	$100.00
		Yearly Membership (corporate or society)	$150.00
		Yearly Membership (human)	$45.00
		Yearly Membership (canine)	FREE

6. To edit the graphics:

   a. On page 1, replace the right panel picture with the Man and Dog picture from the Data Files for Students. Delete the organizational logo and insert a new clip art image of a dog. Add a picture style. Select the photo in the left panel and replace it with a graphic similar to the one in Figure 2–77 on the previous page.

   b. On page 2, replace the graphic with a photo or clip art image of your choosing.

7. Check the spelling of the entire brochure. Open the Backstage view and run the Design Checker. Fix any problems.

8. Save the brochure again. See your instructor for ways to submit this assignment.

In the Lab

Lab 3: Creating an Informational Hospital Brochure

Problem: The Eliza Wiley Children's Hospital in Chino Hills, California, is designing a brochure to make medical procedures less frightening for children. They have asked you to design a rough draft of a full-color trifold brochure on glossy paper that includes pictures of a CT scanner, cartoons, or cute graphics similar to the one shown in Figure 2–78. This hospital wants to mail the brochure, so it is important that the back panel have enough room for a mailing label. Note that your finished product is only a design sample; if the hospital likes the sample, they will submit text for the other text boxes.

Figure 2–78

Cases and Places

Apply your creative thinking and problem-solving skills to design and implement a solution.

Note: To complete these assignments, you may be required to use the Data Files for Students. See the inside back cover of this book for instructions on downloading the Data Files for Students, or contact your instructor for information about accessing the required files.

1: Design and Create an International Research Brochure

Academic

Your ancient Greek archeology professor is sponsoring a trip to Greece to work on an archeological dig. Your professor would like you to create a brochure to distribute to your fellow students to increase interest in and generate funding for the trip. Create a three-panel brochure. Replace each of the graphics with clip art, using the keywords, Greece and archeology. Sample text is located in the Data Files for Students. Use the concepts and techniques presented in this chapter to create this brochure. Submit your assignment in the format specified by your instructor.

2: Design and Create a CD/DVD Liner

Personal

Use the CD/DVD Booklet Template to create a CD liner for your favorite musical artist or group. A sample graphic and list of titles are included in the Data Files for Students. Replace all template text with appropriate information. Click the Page button (Insert tab | Pages group) to insert a new page. Draw a large text box in the right panel, and create a bulleted list of songs or performances. Insert a graphic in the left panel and apply a caption style. Use at least one of the following: drop cap, ligature, stylistic set, swash, or stylistic alternate. Use the concepts and techniques presented in this chapter to create this CD/DVD liner. Submit your assignment in the format specified by your instructor.

3: Design and Create an Event Brochure

Professional

You have recently joined Success America, Incorporated, as the new in-house desktop publisher. You are to design a trifold event brochure for their April 2012 training event in Orlando, Florida. The theme will be Every American Can! Featured speakers will include former U.S. Senator Charles Maxwell, television news anchor Leslie Jane Benedict, and prominent businessperson Anita Montgomery. Your employer wants to mail the brochures to potential attendees. Create a rough draft using an event brochure that includes a sign-up form with the customer's address, e-mail address, and telephone number. Sample text is included in the Data Files for Students. Use the concepts and techniques presented in this chapter to create this brochure. Submit your assignment in the format specified by your instructor.

3 Designing a Newsletter

Objectives

You will have mastered the material in this chapter when you can:

- Describe the advantages of using a newsletter medium and identify the steps in its design process

- Edit a newsletter template and navigate pages

- Set page options

- Edit a masthead

- Import text files

- Continue a story across pages and insert continued notices

- Customize the Ribbon

- Use Publisher's Edit Story in Microsoft Word feature

- Select adjacent objects by dragging

- Insert Page Parts

- Edit sidebars and pull quotes

- Insert and edit coupons and patterns

- Duplicate a graphic and flip it

- Drag and drop text

- Hyphenate stories

- Create a template with property changes

3 | Designing a Newsletter

Introduction

Desktop publishing is becoming an increasingly popular way for businesses of all sizes to produce their printed publications. The desktop aspects of design and production make it easy and inexpensive to produce high-quality publications in a short time. **Desktop publishing** (DTP) implies performing all publishing tasks from a desk, including the planning, designing, writing, and layout, as well as printing, collating, and distributing. With a personal computer and a software program, such as Publisher, you can create a professional publication from your computer without the cost and time of using a professional printer.

Project — Newsletter

Newsletters are a popular way for offices, businesses, schools, and other organizations to distribute information to their clientele. A **newsletter** usually is a double-sided multipage publication with newspaper features, such as columns and a masthead, and the added eye appeal of sidebars, pictures, and other graphics.

Newsletters have several advantages over other publication media. Typically, they are cheaper to produce than brochures. Brochures, designed to be in circulation longer as a type of advertising, are published in greater quantities and on more expensive paper than newsletters, making brochures more costly. Newsletters also differ from brochures in that newsletters commonly have a shorter shelf life, making newsletters a perfect forum for dated information. Newsletters are narrower and more focused in scope than newspapers; their eye appeal is more distinctive. Many companies distribute newsletters to interested audiences; however, newsletters also are becoming an integral part of many marketing plans to widen audiences because they offer a legitimate medium by which to communicate services, successes, and issues.

The project in this chapter uses a Publisher newsletter template to produce New Ways of Banking, the newsletter shown in Figure 3–1. This monthly publication informs the community about Micah National Bank. The bank's four-page newsletter contains a masthead, headings, stories, sidebars, pull quotes, a coupon, and graphics.

A monthly newsletter of the
Micah National Bank

East: 10 Main Street
West: 7905 W. Dixon
Downtown: 10 Main Street
Micah, OR 97360

Phone: 1-800-555-8642
Fax: 971-555-8643
E-mail: info@mnb.com

We're on the Web!
www.mnb.com

Micah National Bank is a locally owned and operated bank offering a wide variety of financial services. Personal products include free cash back checking, free debit card, no-fee ATM, CDs, IRAs, money market accounts, lines of credit, mortgages, and home equity loans. The bank also offers a multitude of business products including merchant services, remote deposit capture, cash management, courier service, and more.

Micah National Bank focuses on the delivery of exceptional service to customers who desire a high standard of personalized service. In doing this, the bank's goal is to distinguish itself within the market. Individual consumers and small- to medium-sized businesses are the target client base.

Micah National Bank employs a team of bankers with more than 50 years of combined experience, providing consistent and exceptional service.

Page 2 · Volume 1, Issue 1

Banking 101

(Continued from page 1)

At Banking 101, you will learn what things go into creating your credit score,

when obtaining credit, and ways to keep your budget-challenged spouse in the loop!

focuses on sound financial literacy.

Your children will learn how a savings account grows,

New Ways of Banking · Page 3

Employee of the Month

Kelly Robertson, a teller at the east branch of Micah National Bank, has been recognized as the Employee of the Month.

MNB President Stephen Kramer cited Kelly's attitude as playing a huge part in her selection. "Kelly approaches every ... knowledge of MNB ... years after earning ... University School

... "I was really surprised," she said. "This is a great ... in. Every day, I look forward to my job. I love to help ... receives a one-time bonus, lunch with the bank president

Kelly Roberts works at the east branch.

...s in Open!

... floor. The lower level has meeting rooms and plenty ...

... ers to the public. We're pleased that our growth has ... ions for this area," said MNB President, Stephen ... ce to share this success with community leaders and ...

... saying "With our new architectural design and a cozy, ... perience will never be the same!"

A monthly newsletter of the Micah National Bank

Volume 7 Issue 4

April 16, 2012

New Ways of Banking

Current Rates:

Savings	.17%
Money Market	1.06%
5-year IRA	2.96%
90-day CD	1.25%
1-year CD	1.34%
3-year CD	1.88%
5-year CD	2.96%

"We're proud to have MNB as a member of our community."

Chamber of Commerce

Banking Hours

- 9-5 Monday—Thursday
- 9-7 Friday
- 9-2 Saturday

Our New Location is Open!

Micah National Bank opened its newest location at 7905 W. Dixon on April 5th. Bank employees, community officials, and many customers were on hand for the ribbon cutting ceremony. Mayor Glenda Allen cut the ribbon to open the new branch in a ceremony that included refreshments, entertainment, and prizes. Rob Jenson won a $50 savings certificate by being the first customer through the new, state-of-the-art banking drive-up.

The new branch will service the west side of the city with all of the banking services you've come to expect at our downtown location.

The Chamber of Commerce president, Jamal Aldine, congratulated Micah National Bank on its expansion. "We're proud to have MNB as a member of our community. The 'green' design of the building and its setting complement the neighborhood."

Come visit our new west branch at 7905 W. Dixon

Local architects, Bertrand and Sons, designed the new 6,000 sq. ft. building. Arbor Construction, a local firm who specializes in reducing the overall impact of construction on human health and the natural environment provided the construction. The lobby

(Continued on page 3)

Banking 101

Confused about saving plans? Need to set a budget? Are you planning for retirement?

Come get the answers to these and other questions at our monthly Banking 101

class. The two-hour class, held at 10:00 a.m. on the first Saturday of each month, will help you figure out the best way to borrow, spend, and save for the future. To protect your finan-

cial health you must educate and prepare yourself for all kinds of money-related issues.

(Continued on ...)

Figure 3–1

Overview

As you read this chapter, you will learn how to create the brochure shown in Figure 3–1 on the previous page by performing these general tasks:

- Select a template with font and color schemes, and specify the page layout.
- Type articles from scratch and import other articles from files.
- Use continued notices and connect stories across pages.
- Import graphics from files and clip art.
- Create sidebars, pull quotes, coupons, and patterns.
- Save the newsletter and create a template.

Plan Ahead

General Project Guidelines

When you create a Publisher newsletter, the actions you perform and decisions you make will affect the appearance and characteristics of the finished publication. Designing an effective newsletter involves a great deal of planning. A good newsletter, or any publication, must deliver a message in the clearest, most attractive, and most effective way possible. As you create a newsletter, such as the one shown in Figure 3–1, you should follow these general guidelines:

1. **Decide on the purpose and audience.** Spend time brainstorming ideas for the newsletter. Think about why you want to create one. Decide on one purpose, and adjust your plans to match that purpose. Decide if the audience is composed of local, interested clientele, patrons, employees, prospective customers, or family members. Keep in mind the age of your readers and their backgrounds, including both present and future readers.

2. **Plan for the layout and printing.** Decide how many pages your newsletter should have and how often you are going to produce it. Base your decisions on regular content that will continue into future newsletters. Choose the paper size and determine how columns, a masthead, and graphics will affect your layout. A consistent look and feel with simple, eye-catching graphics normally is the best choice for the design set. Plan to include one graphic with each story. Because newsletters usually are mass-produced, collated, and stapled, you should make a plan for printing and decide if you are going to publish it in-house or externally. Choose a paper that is going to last until the next newsletter.

3. **Research the topic as it relates to your purpose, and gather data.** Gather credible, relevant information in the form of articles, pictures, dates, figures, tables, and discussion threads. Plan far enough ahead so that you have time to take pictures or gather graphics for each story — even if you end up not using them. Stay organized. Keep folders of information. Store pictures and stories together.

4. **Create the first draft.** Create a layout and masthead. Receive approval if necessary. Follow any guidelines or required publication styles. Provide references for all sources of information. Import stories and graphics as necessary. Determine the best layout for eye appeal and reliable dissemination of content.

5. **Proofread and revise the newsletter.** If possible, proofread the paper with a fresh set of eyes,that is, at least one to two days after completing the first draft. Proofreading involves reading the newsletter with the intent of identifying errors (spelling, grammar, continued notices, etc.) and looking for ways to improve it (purposeful graphics, catchy headlines, sidebars, pull quotes, etc.). Try reading the newsletter aloud, which helps to identify unclear or awkward wording. Ask someone else to proofread the paper and give you suggestions for improvements. Revise as necessary and then use the spelling and design checking features of the software.

When necessary, more specific details concerning the above guidelines are presented at appropriate points in the chapter. The chapter also will identify the actions performed and decisions made regarding these guidelines during the creation of the newsletter shown in Figure 3–1.

Benefits and Advantages of Newsletters

Table 3–1 lists some benefits and advantages of using the newsletter medium.

Table 3–1 Benefits and Advantages of Using a Newsletter	
Purpose	**Benefits and Advantages**
Exposure	An easily distributed publication via office mail, by bulk mail, or electronically A pass-along publication for other interested parties A coffee-table reading item in reception areas
Education	An opportunity to inform in a nonrestrictive environment A directed education forum for clientele Increased, focused feedback — unavailable in most advertising
Contacts	A form of legitimized contact A source of free information to build credibility An easier way to expand a contact database than other marketing tools
Communication	An effective medium to highlight the inner workings of a company A way to create a discussion forum A method to disseminate more information than a brochure
Cost	An easily designed medium using desktop publishing software An inexpensive method of mass production A reusable design using a newsletter template

The Publisher newsletter templates include a four-page layout with stories, graphics, sidebars, and other elements typical of newsletters using a rich collection of intuitive design, layout, typography, and graphic tools. Because Publisher takes care of many of the design issues, using a template to begin a newsletter gives you the advantage of proven layouts with fewer chances of publication errors.

For an introduction to Windows 7 and instruction about how to perform basic Windows 7 tasks, read the Office 2010 and Windows 7 chapter at the beginning of this book, where you can learn how to resize windows, change screen resolution, create folders, move and rename files, use Windows Help, and much more.

Plan Ahead

Decide on the purpose and audience.
As you consult with all parties involved in the decision to create a newsletter, make sure you have a clear purpose. Remember that newsletters both communicate and educate. Ask yourself why you want to create a newsletter in the first place.

- **Decide on the audience.** As you decide on your audience, ask yourself these questions:
  - Who will be reading the articles?
  - What are the demographics of this population? That is, what are their characteristics, such as gender, age, educational background, and heritage?
  - Why do you want those people to read your newsletter?
- **Finally, choose your general topic.** As you make your final decisions on the topic, consider the following:
  - Will the newsletter be about the company in general, or about only one aspect of the company?
  - Will the newsletter cover a narrow topic or be more of a general information newsletter?
  - Use the phrase, "I want to tell <audience> about <topic> because <purpose>."

After starting Publisher, the following pages choose a template and select font and color schemes.

To Start Publisher

The following steps, which assume Windows 7 is running, start Publisher based on a typical installation. You may need to ask your instructor how to start Publisher for your computer. For a detailed example of the procedure summarized below, refer to the Office 2010 and Windows 7 chapter.

1 Click the Start button on the Windows 7 taskbar to display the Start menu.

2 Type **Microsoft Publisher** as the search text in the 'Search programs and files' text box, and watch the search results appear on the Start menu.

3 Click Microsoft Publisher 2010 in the search results on the Start menu to start Publisher and open the Backstage view.

4 If the Publisher window is not maximized, click the Maximize button next to the Close button on its title bar to maximize the window.

For an introduction to Office 2010 and instruction about how to perform basic tasks in Office 2010 programs, read the Office 2010 and Windows 7 chapter at the beginning of this book, where you can learn how to start a program, use the Ribbon, save a file, open a file, quit a program, use Help, and much more.

Newsletter Design Choices

Publisher's many design-planning features include more than 100 different newsletter templates from which you may choose, each with its own set of design, color, font, and layout schemes. Each newsletter template produces four pages of stories, graphics, and other objects in the same way. The difference is the location and style of the shapes and graphics, as well as the specific kind of decorations unique to each publication set. A **publication set** is a predefined group of shapes, designed in patterns to create a template style. A publication set is constant across publication types; for example, the Bars newsletter template has the same shapes and style of objects as does the Bars brochure template. A publication set helps in branding a company across publication types.

Plan Ahead

> **Plan for the layout and printing.**
> Choosing a layout and printing options before you even write the articles is a daunting but extremely important task. The kind of printing process and paper you will be using will affect the cost and, therefore, the length of the newsletter. Depending on what you can afford to produce and distribute, the layout may need more or fewer articles, graphics, columns, and sidebars. Decide on a consistent theme with repeated elements on each page. Make informed decisions about the kind of alignment you plan to use with the masthead, graphics, and text. Decide what kinds of features in the newsletter should be close to each other.

To Choose a Newsletter Template and Options

The following steps choose a newsletter template and make design choices.

1 In the New template gallery, click Newsletters in the Most Popular area to display the newsletter templates.

2 Scroll as necessary and then click the Bars template to select it.

3 In the Customize area, click the Color scheme box arrow and then click the Peach color scheme.

4 Click the Font scheme box arrow and then click the Civic font scheme (Figure 3–2).

5 Click the Create button in the lower-right corner of the window to create the publication based on the template settings.

Figure 3–2

To Open the Page Navigation Pane and Minimize It

The following steps open the Page Navigation pane and minimize it.

① If the Page Navigation pane is not open, click the Page Number button on the status bar to open the Page Navigation pane.

② If the Page Navigation pane is maximized, click the Collapse Page Navigation Pane button to minimize it.

To Display Formatting Marks

As discussed in Chapter 2, it is helpful to display formatting marks, which indicate where in the publication you pressed the ENTER key, SPACEBAR, and other keys. The following step displays formatting marks.

① If the Special Characters button (Home tab | Paragraph group) is not selected already, click it to display formatting marks on the screen.

BTW

The Ribbon and Screen Resolution
Publisher may change how the groups and buttons within the groups appear on the Ribbon, depending on the computer's screen resolution. Thus, your Ribbon may look different from the ones in this book if you are using a screen resolution other than 1024 × 768.

To Set Page Options

Publisher newsletters can display one, two, or three columns of story text, or mix the format. The following steps select the mixed format for page 1 and page 3.

1

- Display the Page Design tab.

- Click the Options button (Page Design tab | Template group) to display the Page Content dialog box.

- Click the Columns box arrow to display the choices (Figure 3–3).

Q&A

Does the column choice affect the objects down the left side of the newsletter page?

No, the number of columns that you choose will be displayed in the stories or articles only, and the choice affects only the current page.

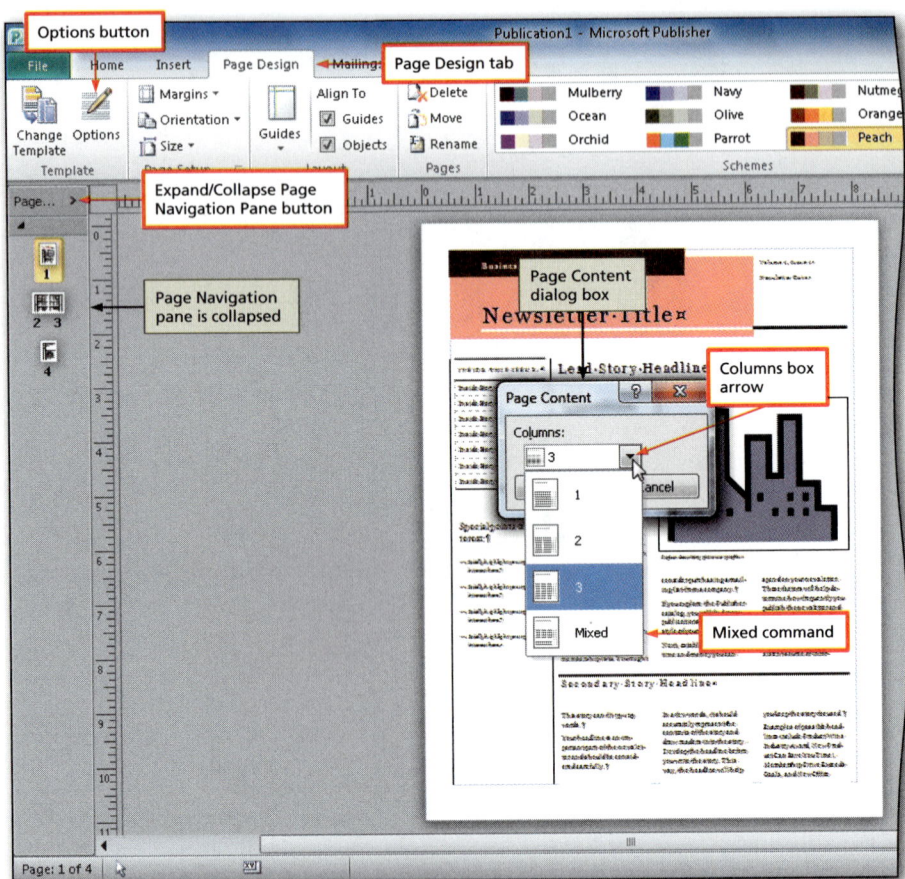

Figure 3–3

2

- Click Mixed to choose a mixed number of columns for the stories on page 1 (Figure 3–4).

Figure 3–4

3

- Click the OK button (Page Content dialog box) to change the options for the page (Figure 3–5).

Q&A

Is one choice better than another?

No, it is a personal or customer preference. Longer stories may need to be continued at different places, depending upon how many columns of text you have. The more columns you have, the more white space is created on the page.

lead story displays two columns

secondary story displays three columns

Figure 3–5

4

- Click Page 2 and Page 3 in the Page Navigation pane to display the pages in the workspace.

- Click the Options button (Page Design tab | Template group) to display the Page Content dialog box.

- Click the 'Select a page to modify' box arrow to display its list (Figure 3–6).

Q&A

What is the 'Content for page' list?

The 'Content for page' list is a list of other objects, including calendars and forms, that you might want to use in your newsletter.

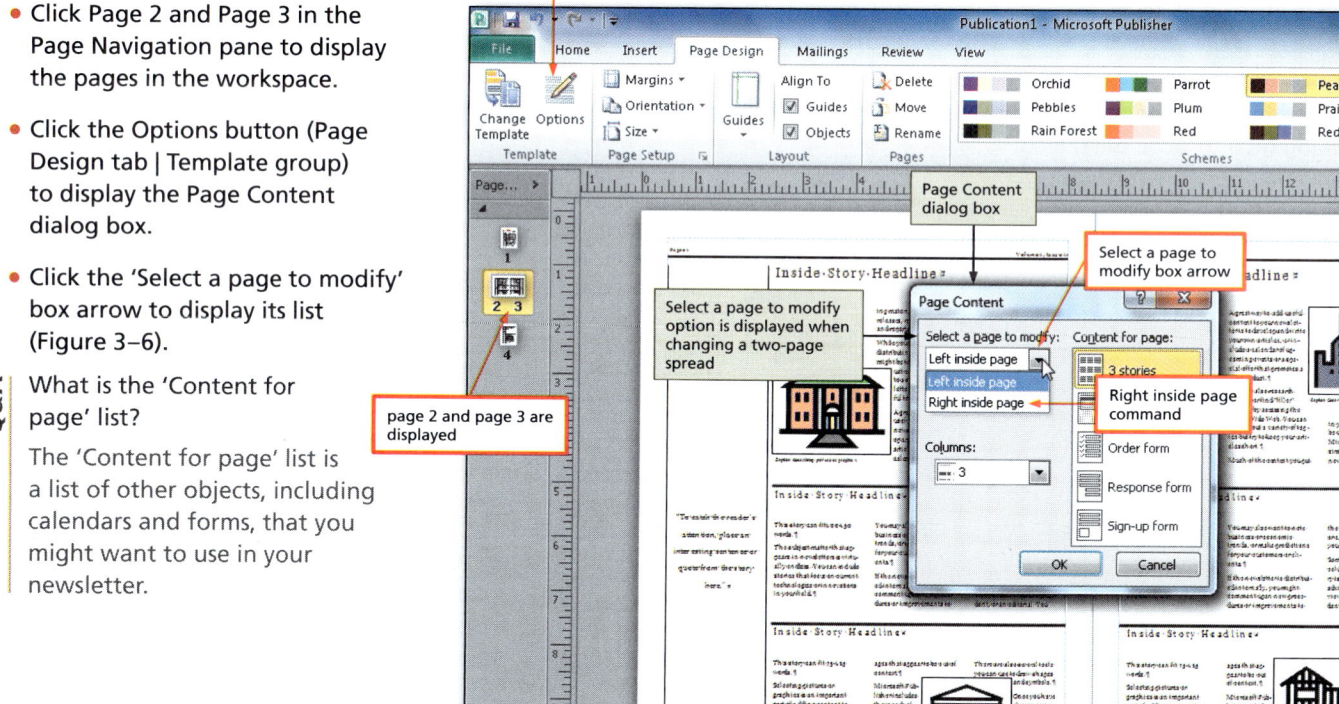

Options button

Page Content dialog box

Select a page to modify box arrow

Select a page to modify option is displayed when changing a two-page spread

Right inside page command

page 2 and page 3 are displayed

Figure 3–6

5

- Click 'Right inside page' in the list to adjust the columns on page 3.

- Click the Columns box arrow to display its list (Figure 3–7).

Q&A

What if I want to change the number of pages in my newsletter?

To change the number of pages, you can right-click a page thumbnail in the Page Navigation pane and then choose Insert Page or Delete Page on the shortcut menu.

Figure 3–7

6

- Click 1 in the list to choose a single column for the stories on page 3 (Figure 3–8).

Q&A

Can I move pages around in my newsletter?

Yes, you can right-click a page thumbnail in the Page Navigation pane and then choose Move on the shortcut menu. Publisher will display a dialog box, allowing you to specify which page to move and the new location.

Figure 3–8

7

- Click the OK button (Page Content dialog box) to close the dialog box and apply the settings (Figure 3–9).

Figure 3–9

Changing the Number of Pages in a Newsletter

Not all newsletters are four pages long. Some will have more or fewer pages. The following sections describe how to add or delete pages from a newsletter template.

To Delete Pages from a Newsletter

If you were designing a newsletter with only two pages, it would be best to delete pages 2 and 3 because page 4 already is formatted to be a back page in most templates. Pages 2 and 3 have inside page numbers and graphics. You would perform the following steps to delete pages 2 and 3.

1. Right-click the Page 2 and Page 3 icon in the Page Navigation pane to display the shortcut menu.

2. Click Delete to delete pages 2 and 3. When Publisher displays the Delete Page dialog box for confirmation, click Both pages and then click the OK button.

To Add Pages to a Newsletter

If you wanted to add extra pages to a newsletter, you would perform the following steps.

1. Right-click the Page 2 and Page 3 icon in the Page Navigation pane to display the shortcut menu.

2. Click Insert Page to insert a new page. Follow the directions in the dialog box to insert either a left-hand or right-hand page, or both.

BTW

Inserting Pages
Inserting pages in a newsletter is just as easy as deleting them. The Page button (Insert tab | Pages group) provides the option of inserting a left-hand page or right-hand page. It also offers choices in the types of objects to display on the page. When you choose to insert or delete when working on the first or last page, Publisher will warn you of pagination problems and will display a confirmation button.

Editing the Masthead

Most newsletters and brochures contain a masthead similar to those used in newspapers. A **masthead** is a box or section printed in each issue that lists information, such as the name, publisher, location, volume, and date. The Publisher-designed masthead, included in the Bars newsletter publication set, contains several text boxes and color-filled shapes that create an attractive, eye-catching graphic to complement the set. You need to edit the text boxes, however, to convey appropriate messages.

BTW

Q&As
For a complete list of the Q&As found in many of the step-by-step sequences in this book, visit the Publisher 2010 Q&A Web page (scsite.com/pub2010/qa).

To Edit the Masthead

The following steps edit text in the masthead.

- Click Page 1 in the Page Navigation pane to change the display to page 1.

- Click the text, Newsletter Title, to select it.

- Press the F9 key to view the masthead at 100% magnification.

- Type `New Ways of Banking` to replace the text (Figure 3–10).

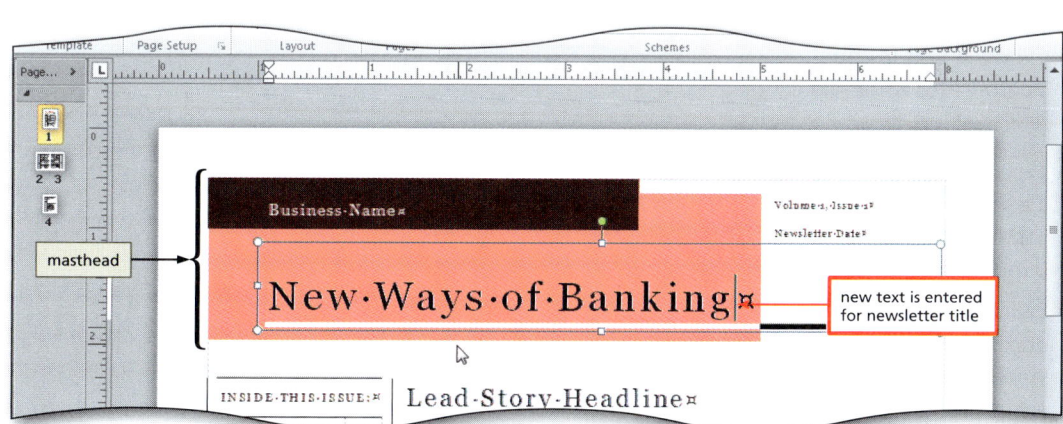

Figure 3–10

Why does my font look different?

Publisher replaces the selected text using the font from the design set. Because fonts sometimes are printer-dependent, your font may differ from the one shown.

2

- Click the placeholder text in the Business Name text box, and then press CTRL+A to select all of the text (Figure 3–11).

Q&A What is the button with the i on it?

The button is a **smart tag** notation. Clicking the smart tag button allows you to change information in the business information set. Certain template text boxes hold business information, taglines, and address data. Each of these special text boxes will display this kind of smart tag notation.

Figure 3–11

3

- Type **A monthly newsletter of the Micah National Bank** to replace the text (Figure 3–12).

Q&A What if my text does not fit in the box?

Template text boxes for business information components, headlines, and other special boxes use autofitting techniques. Publisher should decrease the font size for longer text as you type. If it does not, someone has turned off the autofitting option; right-click the text and then click Best Fit on the shortcut menu to autofit the text.

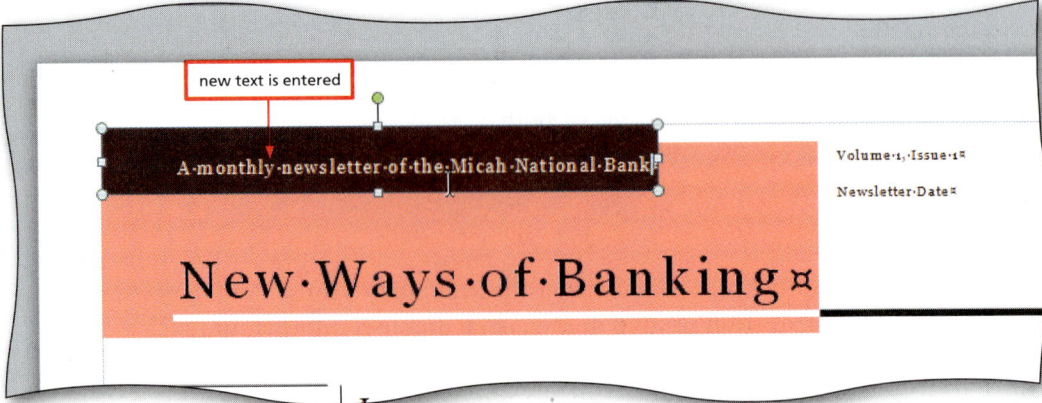

Figure 3–12

4

- Click the text in the Volume and Issue text box to select it.

- Type **Volume 7 Issue 4** to replace the text (Figure 3–13).

Q&A What do the volume and issue numbers stand for?

Publications typically use volume numbers to indicate the number of years the publication has been in existence. The issue number indicates its sequence. Volume numbers and issue numbers do not necessarily correlate to the calendar year and months. Schools, for example, sometimes start in the fall with Volume 1, Issue 1.

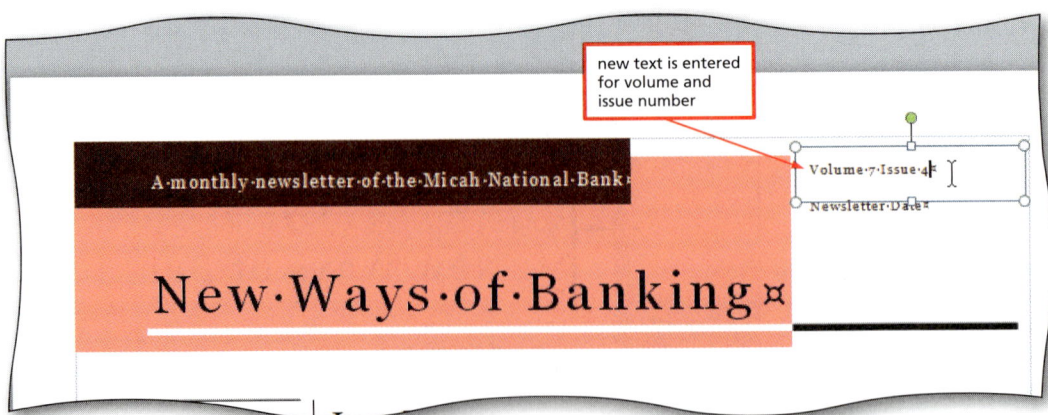

Figure 3–13

5
- Click the text in the Newsletter Date text box to select it.

- Type **April 16, 2012** to replace the text (Figure 3–14).

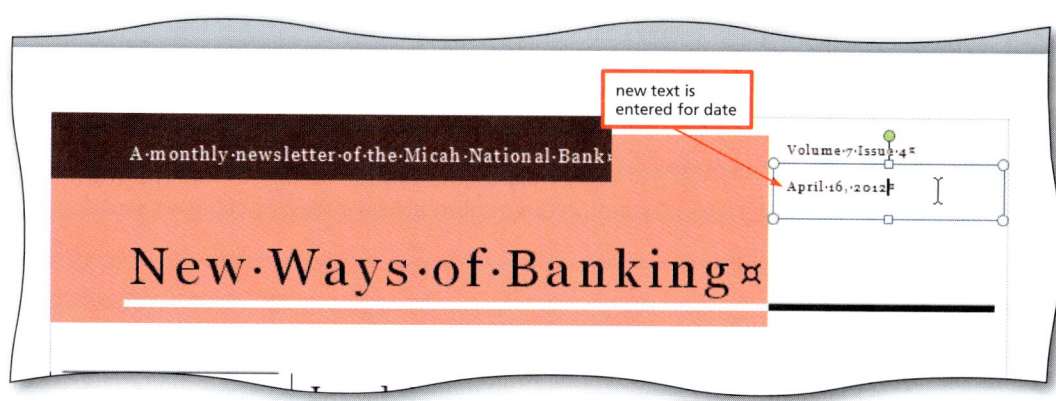

Figure 3–14

To Save a Publication

The following steps save the publication on a USB flash drive using the file name, Bank Newsletter. For a detailed example of the procedure summarized below, refer to the Office 2010 and Windows 7 chapter at the beginning of this book.

1 With a USB flash drive connected to one of the computer's USB ports, click the Save button on the Quick Access Toolbar to display the Save As dialog box.

2 Type **Bank Newsletter** in the File name text box to change the file name. Do not press the ENTER key after typing the file name because you do not want to close the dialog box at this time.

3 Navigate to the desired save location (in this case, the Publisher folder in the CIS 101 folder [or your class folder] on the USB flash drive).

4 Click the Save button (Save As dialog box) to save the document in the selected folder on the selected drive with the entered file name.

Newsletter Text

Newsletter content may be submitted to you in various ways. Story authors may submit their text in e-mail or as attachments. Others may post a Microsoft Word document or a graphic on the company common storage drive. Still other authors may handwrite their stories or record them on a recording device. In those cases, you will have to type the story yourself.

Publisher allows users to import text and graphics from many sources, from a variety of different programs, and in many different file formats. Publisher uses the term, **importing**, to describe inserting text or objects from any other source into the Publisher workspace. Publisher uses the term, **story**, when referring to text that is contained within a single text box or a chain of linked text boxes. Each newsletter template provides **linked text boxes**, or text boxes whose text flows from one to another. In the templates, two or three text boxes may be linked automatically; however, if a story is too long to fit in the linked text boxes, Publisher will offer to link even more text boxes for easy reading.

Plan Ahead

> **Research the topic as it relates to your purpose, and gather data.**
>
> - **Researching the topic.** If you have to write a story from scratch, gather your data, do your research, and have an informed reader go over your content. The same principles of audience, purpose, and topic apply to individual stories, just as they did for the newsletter as a whole. Evaluate your sources for authority, timeliness, and accuracy. Be especially wary of information obtained from the Web. Any person, company, or organization can publish a Web page on the Internet. Ask yourself these questions about the source:
>
>   - Authority: Does a reputable institution or group support the source? Is the information presented without bias? Are the author's credentials listed and verifiable?
>
>   - Timeliness: Is the information up to date? Are the dates of sources listed? What is the last date that the information was revised or updated?
>
>   - Accuracy: Is the information free of errors? Is it verifiable? Are the sources clearly identified?
>
> - **Gather the data.** Identify the sources for your text and graphics. Notify all writers of important dates, and allow time for gathering the data. Make a list for each story: include the author's name, the approximate length of the story, the electronic format, and associated graphics. Ask the author for suggestions for headlines. Consult with colleagues about other graphics, features, sidebars, and the masthead.
>
> - **Acknowledge all sources of information; do not plagiarize.** Not only is plagiarism unethical, it also is considered an academic crime that can have severe consequences, such as failing a course or being expelled from school.
>
>   When you summarize, paraphrase (rewrite information in your own words), present facts, give statistics, quote exact words, or show a map, chart, or other graphical image, you must acknowledge the source. Information that commonly is known or accessible to the audience constitutes common knowledge and does not need to be acknowledged. If, however, you question whether certain information is common knowledge, you should document it — just to be safe.

BTW

Importing Text
Importing the articles instead of typing them saves time, reduces the possibility of introducing new errors, and adds the convenience of using word processing. Publisher accepts most file formats from popular word processing programs and text editors.

Replacing Placeholder Text Using an Imported File

Publisher suggests that 175 to 225 words will fit in the space allocated for the lead story. The story is displayed in a two-column text box format that **connects**, or wraps, the running text from one text box to the next. Publisher links text boxes and displays arrow buttons to navigate to the next and previous text boxes.

This edition of New Ways of Banking contains several stories, some of which have been typed previously and stored using Microsoft Word. The stories, stored on the Data Files for Students, are ready to be used in the newsletter. The final story you will type yourself. Each story will include a **headline**, which is a short phrase printed at the top of a story, usually in a bigger font than the story. A headline summarizes the story that follows it.

To Edit the Lead Story Headline

The following step edits the Lead Story Headline placeholder text.

1

• Click the text, Lead Story Headline, to select it.

• Type `Our New Location Is Open!` to replace the text (Figure 3–15).

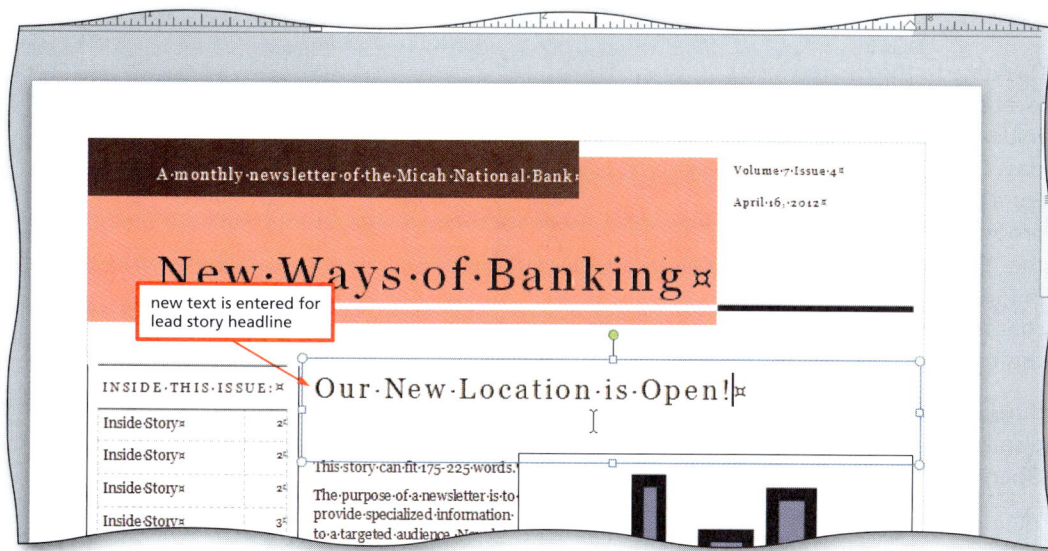

Figure 3–15

To Import a Text File

The following steps import a text file to replace the Publisher-supplied default text. The text file is included in the Data Files for Students. See the inside back cover of this book for instructions on downloading the Data Files for Students, or contact your instructor for more information about accessing the required files. Because the story is too long to fit in the space provided, you will connect the story to other text boxes, later in the chapter.

1

• Scroll down to display the story below the headline.

• Click the text in the story (Figure 3–16).

🔍 **Experiment**

• Scroll as necessary to read the story in order to learn about design suggestions related to newsletter publications.

Figure 3–16

- Display the Insert tab.

- Click the Insert File button (Insert tab | Text group) to display the Insert Text dialog box.

- Navigate to the desired insert location (in this case, the Publisher folder in the CIS 101 folder [or your class folder] on the USB flash drive). For a detailed example of this procedure, refer to Steps 3a–3c in the To Save a File in a Folder section in the Office 2010 and Windows 7 chapter at the beginning of this book.

- If necessary, scroll in the list to display the Micah National Bank Opens Its Doors file (Figure 3–17).

Q&A What kinds of text files can Publisher import?

Publisher can import files from most popular applications. If you click the All Text Files button, you can see a list of all of the file types and extensions.

Figure 3–17

- Double-click the file, Micah National Bank Opens Its Doors, to insert the text into the newsletter and to display the Microsoft Publisher dialog box (Figure 3–18).

- Do not close the dialog box or click any of the buttons.

Q&A Did Publisher insert the text from the Word file on page 1?

Yes, but the story was too long to fit in the two columns on page 1; that is why the dialog box was displayed. In the next steps, you will tell Publisher how to use the rest of the text.

Figure 3–18

Other Ways

1. Right-click article, point to Change Text, click Text File, select File, click OK button

To Continue a Story across Pages

Continuing a story across columns or pages is one of the functions that Publisher helps you to perform. If the story contains more text than will fit in the default text box, Publisher displays a message to warn you. You then have the option to allow Publisher to connect or **autoflow** the text to another available text box, or to flow the text yourself, manually. The following steps continue the story from page 1 to page 3, using Publisher dialog boxes.

1

- In the Microsoft Publisher dialog box, click the No button to move to the next story (Figure 3–19).

Q&A Did anything change in my publication?

Publisher moved from the first story on page 2 to the second story, as noted by the text box selection shown below the dialog box.

Figure 3–19

2

- As Publisher moves from story to story, click the No button three more times. Publisher will stop at the second story on page 3, as shown in Figure 3–20.

Q&A What do the three buttons do?

If you click the Yes button, Publisher will insert the rest of the text in the currently selected text box. If you click the No button, Publisher will move to the next story and ask again. If you click the Cancel button, you will have to autoflow the text manually.

Figure 3–20

3

● Click the Yes button to continue the story in the selected text box (Figure 3–21).

Q&A

What if I have no more spare text boxes in which to flow?

Publisher will ask if you want to create new text boxes. If you answer yes, Publisher will automatically create a new page with new text boxes.

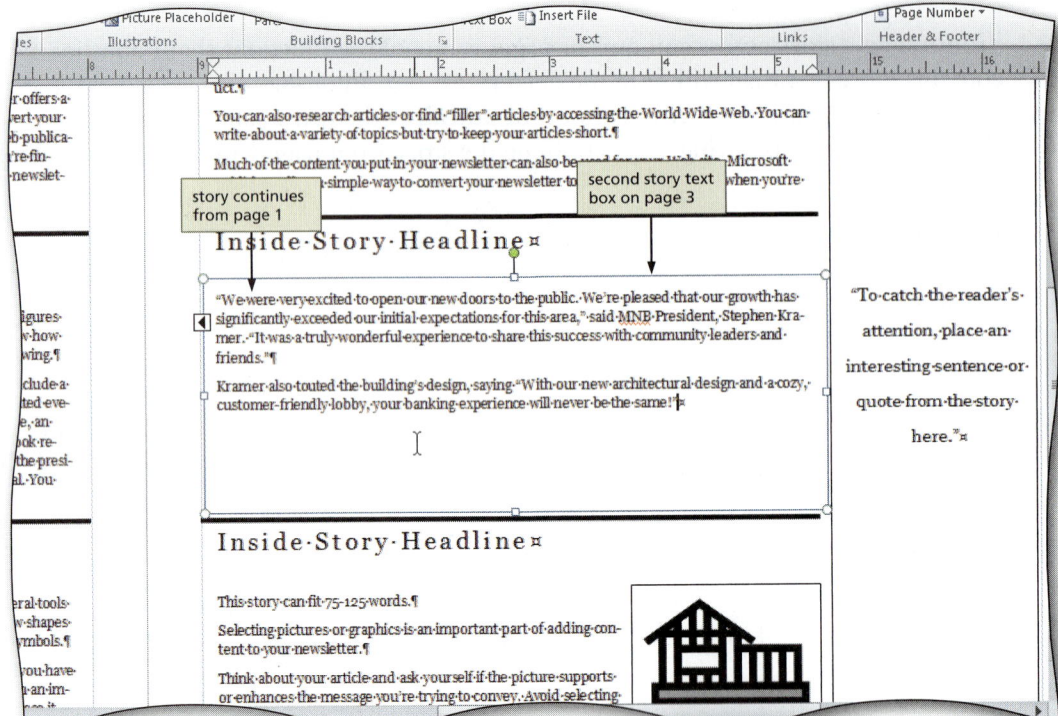

Figure 3–21

To Edit the Secondary Story Headline

The following steps edit the Secondary Story Headline placeholder text.

1 Click Page 1 in the Page Navigation pane to move to page 1.

2 Click the text, Secondary Story Headline, to select it.

3 Type **Banking 101** to replace the text.

BTW

Text in Overflow
The overflow area is an invisible storage location within a publication that holds extra text, similar to a clipboard. The overflow area is not electricity-dependent; rather, its contents are saved with the publication. You can move text out of overflow and back into a publication by one of several means: flowing text into a new text box, autofitting text, enlarging the text box, changing the text size, changing the margins within the text box, or deleting some of the text in the text box.

To Insert Another Text File

The following steps insert a secondary story from a text file.

1 Click the secondary story text on page 1 to select it.

2 Click the Insert File button (Insert tab | Text group) to display the Insert Text dialog box.

3 If necessary, navigate to the Data Files for Students and the Chapter 03 folder.

4 Double-click the file named, Banking 101, to insert the text file.

5 When Publisher displays the Microsoft Publisher dialog box, click the Cancel button to cancel the autoflow.

To Manually Continue the Story across Pages

When a story does not fit in a text box, Publisher displays a **Text in Overflow** button to indicate additional text exists that is not currently displayed. The following steps continue the secondary story on page 1 by manually connecting the text boxes, using the Text in Overflow button.

1

- Scroll to the lower-right corner of page 1.

- If necessary, click the third column in the Banking 101 story.

- Click the Text in Overflow button to display the pitcher mouse pointer (Figure 3–22).

Q&A What is the button with the left-pointing arrow?

The arrow buttons allow you to move to the previous or next column within the same story.

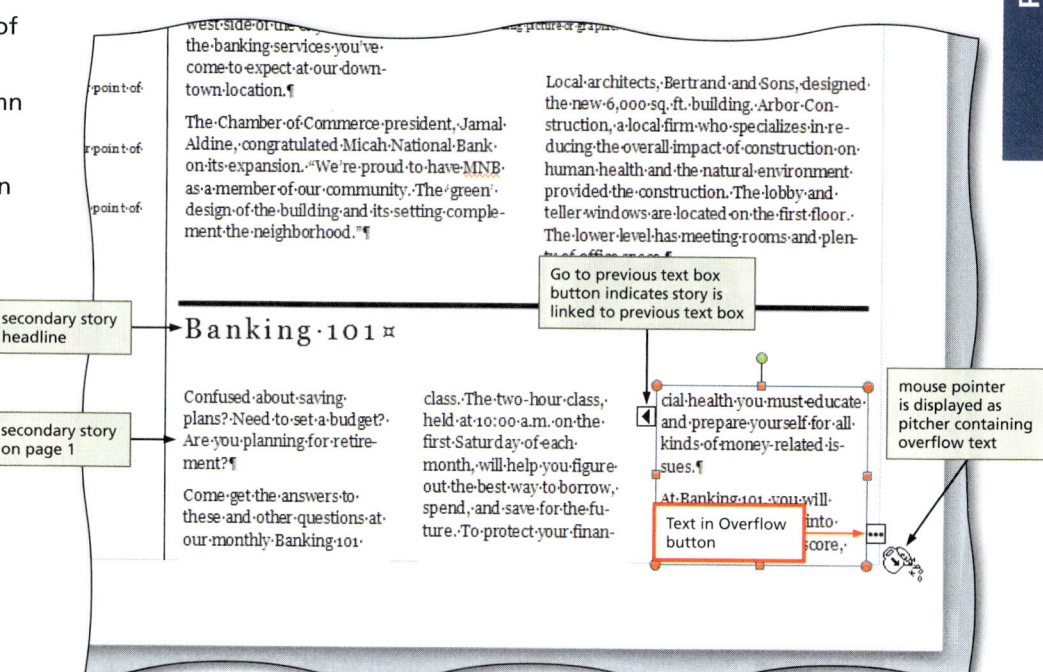

Figure 3–22

2

- Click Page 2 and Page 3 in the Page Navigation pane to display the pages.

- Zoom and scroll as necessary to display the first story on page 2.

- With the pitcher mouse pointer, click the text in the first story to continue the story (Figure 3–23).

Q&A My text wraps at different places. Did I do something wrong?

Your story may wrap differently depending upon your printer's capability of reproducing the font.

Q&A What if I change my mind and want to continue to a different text box?

You can click the Undo button on the Quick Access toolbar, or you can click the last column of the story on page 1 and then click the Break button (Text Box Tools Format tab | Linking Group). You then can click the Text in Overflow button again.

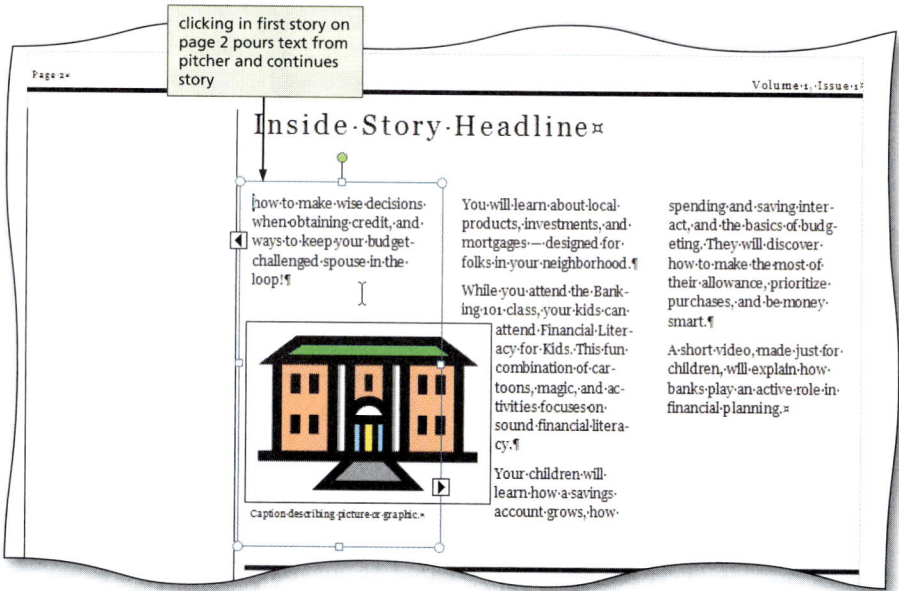

Figure 3–23

Other Ways

1. Right-click text, click Create Link, navigate to next text box, click text

2. Click text, click Create Link button (Text Box Tools Format tab | Linking group), navigate to next text box, click text

To Format with Continued Notices

In stories that flow from one page to another, it is a good practice to add **continued notices**, or **jump lines**, to guide readers through the story. The following steps format the last box on page 1 with a continued on notice. Then, on page 3, the first text box in the rest of the story is formatted with a continued from notice.

1

- Navigate to page 1.

- Right-click the second column of text in the lead story to display the shortcut menu (Figure 3–24).

Q&A Will Publisher ask me what page number to use?

The placement of the notices and the page numbering are automatic.

Figure 3–24

2

- Click Format Text Box to display the Format Text Box dialog box.

- Click the Text Box tab to display its settings.

- Click to display a check mark in the Include "Continued on page ..." check box (Figure 3–25).

Q&A What do I do if my dialog box is covering up the text box?

The setting changes will take place when you click the OK button. If you want to see both the dialog box and the text box, you can drag the title bar of the dialog box to the left, as shown in Figure 3–25.

Figure 3–25

3

• Click the OK button (Format Text Box dialog box) to insert the continued notice (Figure 3–26).

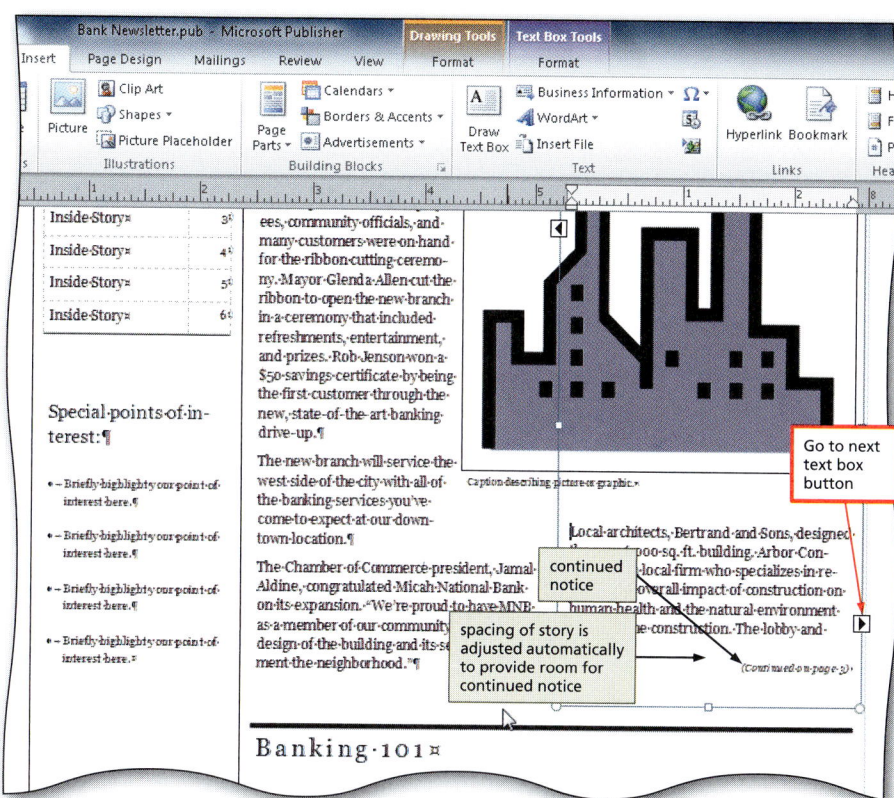

Figure 3–26

4

• Click the 'Go to next text box' button to navigate to the second story on page 3, where the story flows.

• Right-click the text in the center story on page 3 to display the shortcut menu.

• Click Format Text Box on the shortcut menu to display the Format Text Box dialog box.

• Click the Text Box tab to display its settings.

• Click to display a check mark in the Include "Continued from page …" check box (Figure 3–27).

Figure 3–27

5

- Click the OK button (Format Text Box dialog box) to insert the continued from notice (Figure 3–28).

Experiment

- Use the arrow buttons to move between the linked text boxes on pages 1 and 3. Examine the jump lines with the supplied page numbers.

Figure 3–28

Other Ways

1. Select text box, click Format Text Box Dialog Box Launcher (Text Box Tools Format tab | Text group), click Text Box tab (Format Text Box dialog box), click desired continued notice check box, click OK button

---

To Format the Secondary Story with Continued Notices

The following steps format the secondary story with continued notices.

1 If necessary, navigate to page 1 and the secondary story.

2 Right-click the third column of text in the second story on page 1 to display the shortcut menu and then click Format Text Box to display the Format Text Box dialog box.

3 Click the Text Box tab to display its settings and then click to display a check mark in the Include "Continued on page …" check box.

4 Click the OK button (Format Text Box dialog box) to insert the continued notice.

5 Click the 'Go to next text box' button to jump to the rest of the story on page 2.

6 Right-click the first column of text in the rest of the story on page 2 to display the shortcut menu and then click Format Text Box on the shortcut menu to display the Format Text Box dialog box.

7 Click the Text Box tab to display its settings and then click to display a check mark in the Include "Continued from page …" check box.

8 Click the OK button (Format Text Box dialog box) to insert the continued notice (Figure 3–29).

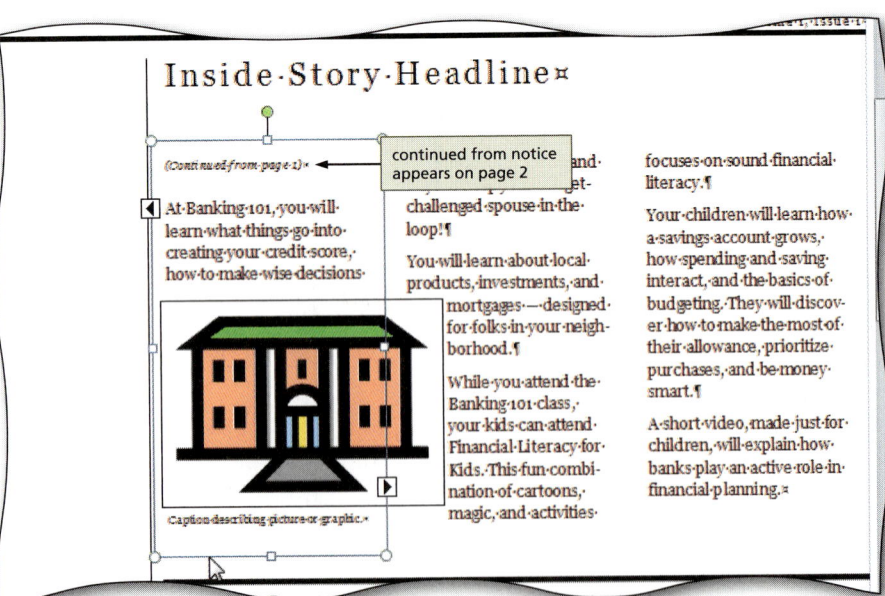

Figure 3–29

To Edit the Headlines for the Continued Stories

The following steps edit the inside headlines for the continued stories.

1 Navigate to the first story on page 2.

2 Click the headline text to select it and then type `Banking 101` to replace the text.

3 Navigate to the second story on page 3.

4 Click the headline text to select it and then type `Our New Location Is Open!` to replace the text.

Edit a Headline and Import a Text File on Page 2

The following steps edit the headline and import the text for the second story on page 2.

1 Scroll to display the middle portion of page 2 and then click the Inside Story Headline placeholder text to select it.

2 Type `MNB New Cash Back Checking` to replace the selected headline.

3 Click the text in the inside story text box to select it.

4 Click the Insert File button (Insert tab | Text group) to display the Insert Text dialog box.

5 If necessary, navigate to the Data Files for Students and the Chapter 03 folder.

6 Double-click the file named, Cash Back Checking, to insert the text file (Figure 3–30).

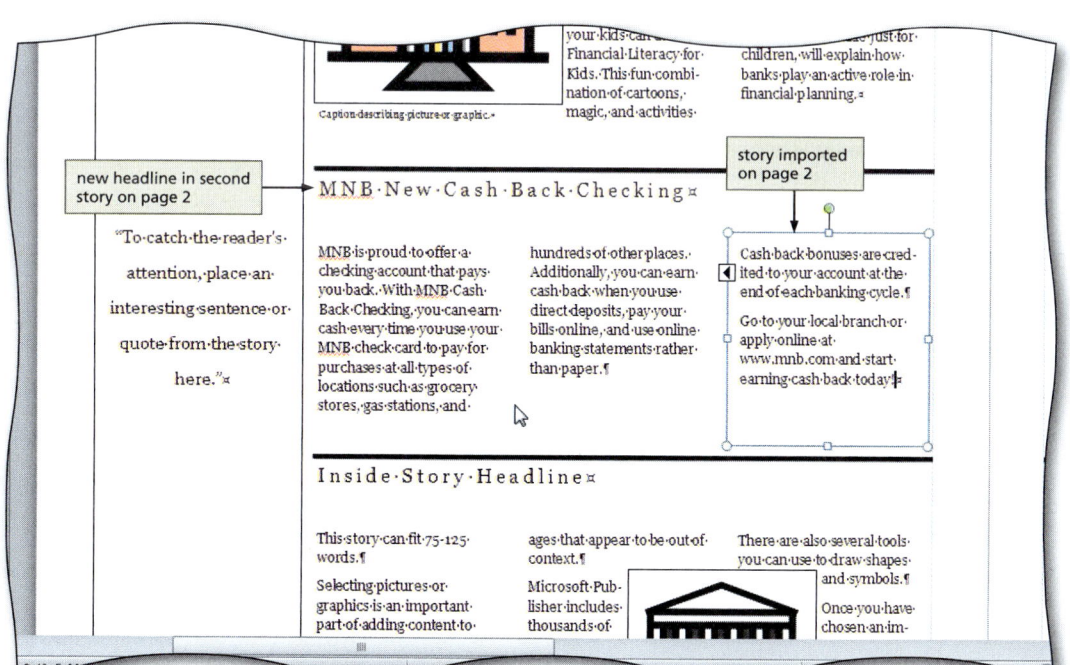

Figure 3–30

Edit a Headline and Import a Text File on Page 3

The following steps edit the headline and import the text for the first story on page 3.

1 Scroll to display the upper portion of page 3 and then click the Inside Story Headline placeholder text to select it.

2 Type **Employee of the Month** to replace the selected headline.

3 Click the text in the inside story text box to select it.

4 Click the Insert File button (Insert tab | Text group) to display the Insert Text dialog box.

5 If necessary, navigate to the Data Files for Students and the Chapter 03 folder.

6 Double-click the file named, Employee of the Month, to insert the text file (Figure 3–31).

Figure 3–31

Customizing the Ribbon

It is easy to **customize**, or personalize, the ribbon the way that you want it. Customizing allows you to:

- Create custom groups and custom tabs to contain frequently used commands
- Rearrange or rename buttons, groups, and tabs to fit your work style
- Rename or remove buttons and boxes from an existing tab and group
- Add new buttons to a custom group

When you add new buttons to the Ribbon, you may choose from a list that includes commands that you may use elsewhere in Publisher such as those on shortcut menus, from the Backstage view, or those that are not on the Ribbon by default. Or, you can create a new button that executes a command or set of commands that you record. (You will create this type of button in a later chapter.) In this chapter, you will create a custom group on the Review tab and add a command that is not currently on the Ribbon. The command will display as a button in the new custom group.

You can customize the Ribbon in all Microsoft Office applications, but the customizations are application-specific. The changes you make to the Publisher Ribbon will not change the Ribbon in any other Office program. When you no longer need the customization, it can be removed; or, the entire Ribbon can be reset to its default settings, removing all customizations.

> If your computer already displays the Edit Story in Microsoft Word button (Review tab | New group), you can skip these steps and proceed to page PUB 159.

To Customize the Publisher Ribbon

The following steps create a custom group on the Review tab and then add an Edit Story in Microsoft Word button to the new group on the Publisher Ribbon.

1

- Click File on the Ribbon to open the Backstage view and then click the Options command to display the Publisher Options dialog box.

- Click the Customize Ribbon button to display the Customize the Ribbon gallery.

- Click the 'Choose commands from' box arrow to view the list of commands (Figure 3–32).

Figure 3–32

2

- Click Commands Not in the Ribbon to display the list.

- Click Edit Story in Microsoft Word to select the command.

- Click Review in the list of Main Tabs to choose the tab group for the new button.

- Click the New Group button to create a new group.

- Click the Add button to add the Edit Story in Microsoft Word command to the new group (Figure 3–33).

Figure 3–33

3

- Click the OK button (Publisher Options dialog box) to close the dialog box and create the custom group.

- Click Review on the Ribbon to display the Review tab and its new group and button (Figure 3–34).

Q&A

Why was the Review tab chosen for the new custom group?

The Review tab has empty space to hold custom groups. The other tabs are full. Adding a custom group to one of the other tabs would compress the existing groups, which might make it more difficult to locate buttons and boxes.

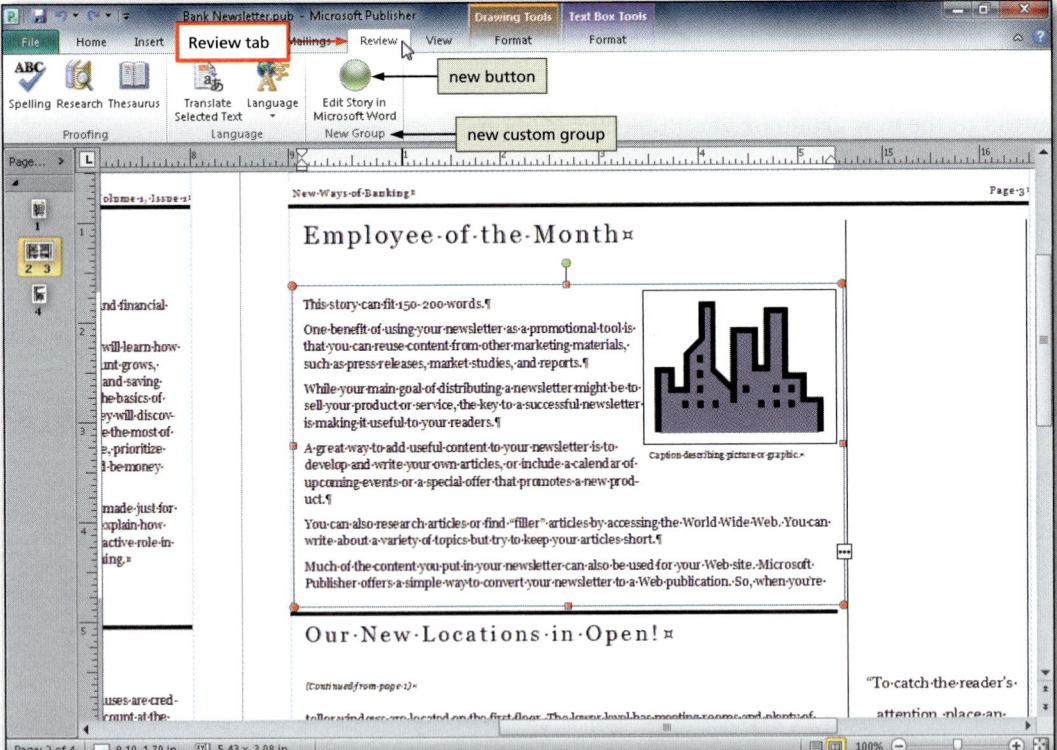

Figure 3–34

Other Ways

1. Right-click Ribbon, click Customize the Ribbon, choose or create groups, add commands, click OK button

Editing Stories in Microsoft Word

You have seen that you can edit text directly in Microsoft Publisher or import text from a previously stored file. A third way to edit text is to use Microsoft Word as your editor. Publisher provides an interactive link between the two applications.

If you need to edit only a few words, it is faster to continue using Publisher. If you need to edit a longer story or one that has not been previously stored, it sometimes is easier to edit the story in Word. Many users are accustomed to working in Word and want to take advantage of available Word features, such as grammar checking and revision tracking. It sometimes is easier to drag and drop paragraphs in a Word window than to perform the same task in a Publisher window, especially when it involves moving across pages in a larger Publisher publication.

Occasionally, if you have many applications running, such as virus protection and other memory-taxing programs, Publisher may warn you that you are low on computer memory. In that case, close the other applications and try editing the story in Word again.

While you are working on a story in Word, you cannot edit the corresponding text box in Publisher. Editing your stories in Word allows you to manipulate the text using the full capabilities of a wordprocessing program.

BTW

BTWs
For a complete list of the BTWs found in the margins of this book, visit the Publisher 2010 BTW Web page (scsite.com/pub/2010/btw).

To Edit a Story Using Word

The following steps use Microsoft Word in conjunction with Publisher to create the text on the back page of the newsletter. Microsoft Word version 6.0 or later must be installed on your computer for this procedure to work.

1

- Navigate to page 4.

- Scroll to display the text box in the upper portion of page 4.

- Select the placeholder text.

- If necessary, display the Review tab (Figure 3–35).

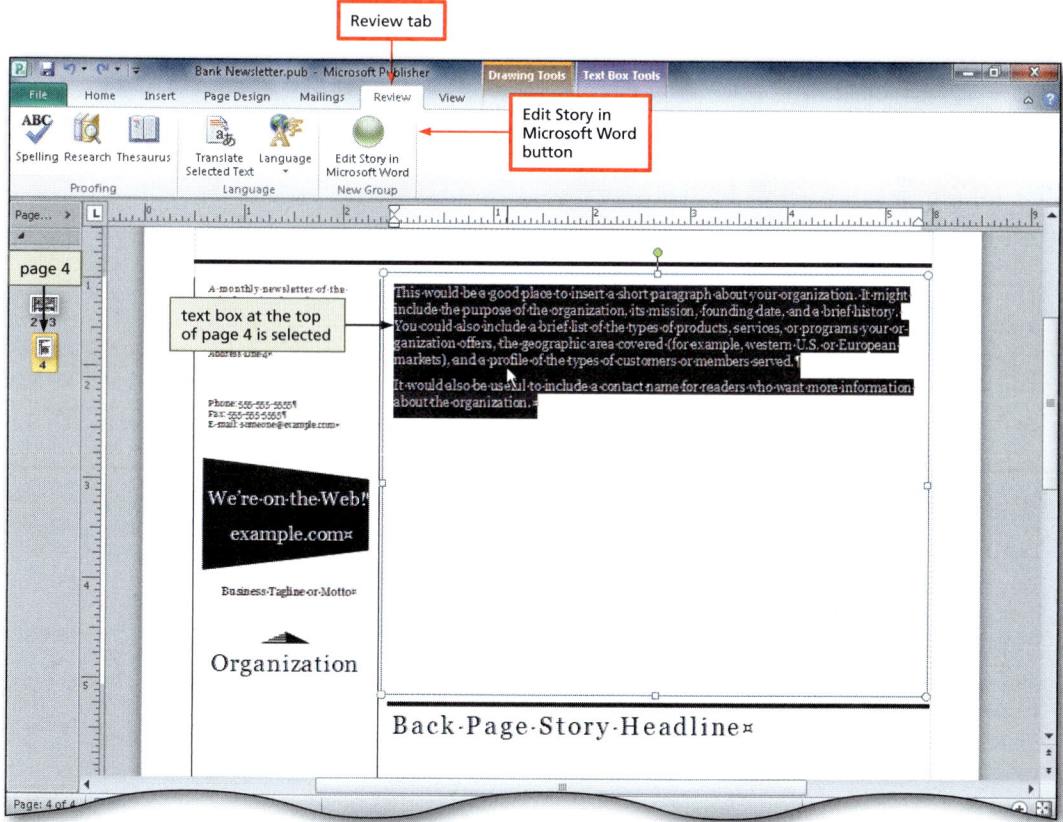

Figure 3–35

2

• Click the Edit Story in Microsoft Word button (Review tab | New Group) to start the Microsoft Word program.

• If necessary, maximize the Word window. Press CTRL+A to select all of the text. Type `Micah National Bank is a locally owned and operated bank offering a wide variety of financial services. Personal products include free, cash back checking, free debit card, no-fee ATM, CDs, IRAs, money market accounts, lines of credit, mortgages, and home equity loans. The bank also offers a multitude of business products including merchant services, remote deposit capture, cash management, courier service, and more.` to enter the text (Figure 3–36).

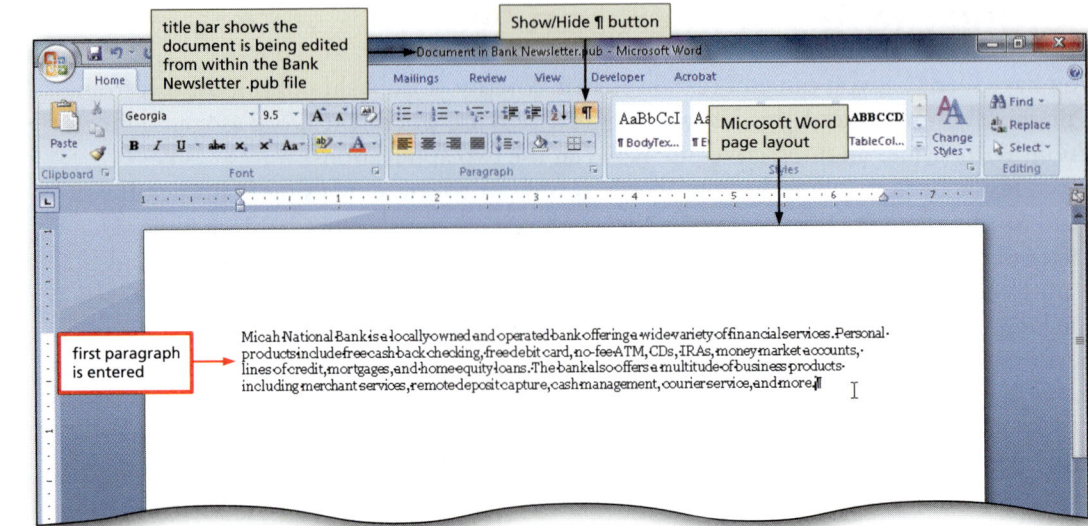

Figure 3–36

Q&A

Why are my formatting marks not showing in Microsoft Word?

It is possible that someone has turned off formatting marks. Click the Show/Hide ¶ button (Home tab | Paragraph group) to turn them on and off.

3

• Press the ENTER key to begin a new paragraph. Type `Micah National Bank focuses on the delivery of exceptional service to customers who desire a high standard of personalized service. In doing this, the bank's goal is to distinguish itself within the market. Individual consumers and small- to medium-sized businesses are the target client base.` to enter the text.

Figure 3–37

• Press the ENTER key to begin a new paragraph. Type `Micah National Bank employs a team of bankers with more than 50 years of combined experience, providing consistent and exceptional service.` to finish the text (Figure 3–37).

To Format while Editing in Microsoft Word

The following step selects multiple sections of nonadjacent text and formats them using Microsoft Word.

1

- Drag to select the first three words of the first paragraph, Micah National Bank.

- CTRL+drag to select the same words in the second paragraph.

- CTRL+drag to select the same words in the third paragraph.

- Click the Bold button (Home tab | Font group) on the Word Ribbon (Figure 3–38).

Q&A Could I do that formatting in Publisher?

You could bold the text, but you cannot select nonadjacent text in Publisher.

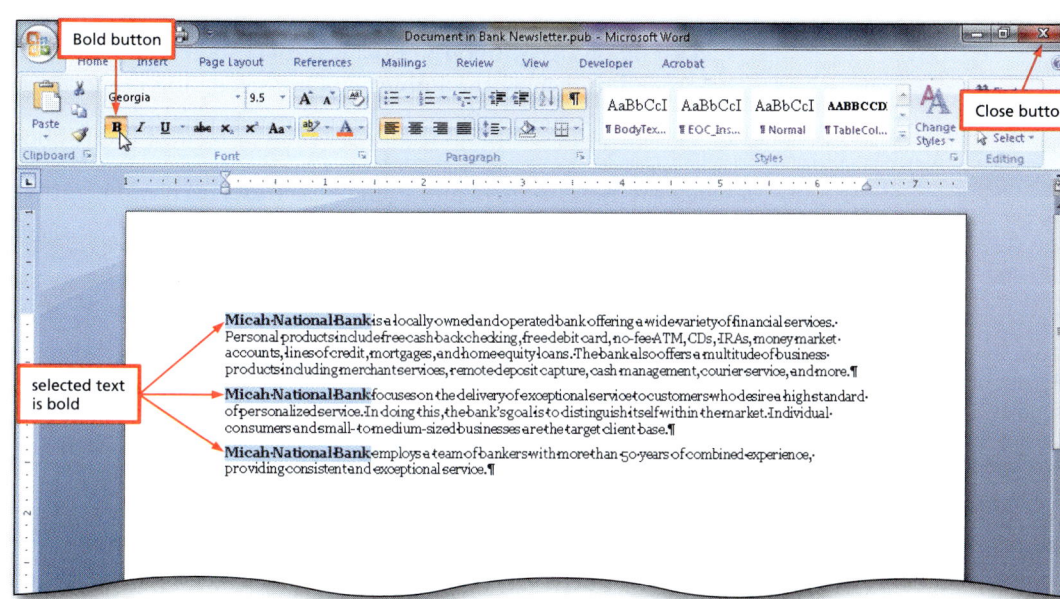

Figure 3–38

To Quit Word and Return to Publisher

The following step quits Word and returns to Publisher.

1

- Click the Close button on the title bar of the Document in Bank Newsletter – Microsoft Word window to quit Word (Figure 3–39).

Q&A Why do I see only gray lines instead of the text?

Starting Microsoft Word from within Microsoft Publisher is a drain on your computer's memory and on the refresh rate of your screen. Try navigating to page 1 and then back to page 4 to refresh the screen.

- Right-click the text to display the shortcut menu and then click Best Fit to autofit the text.

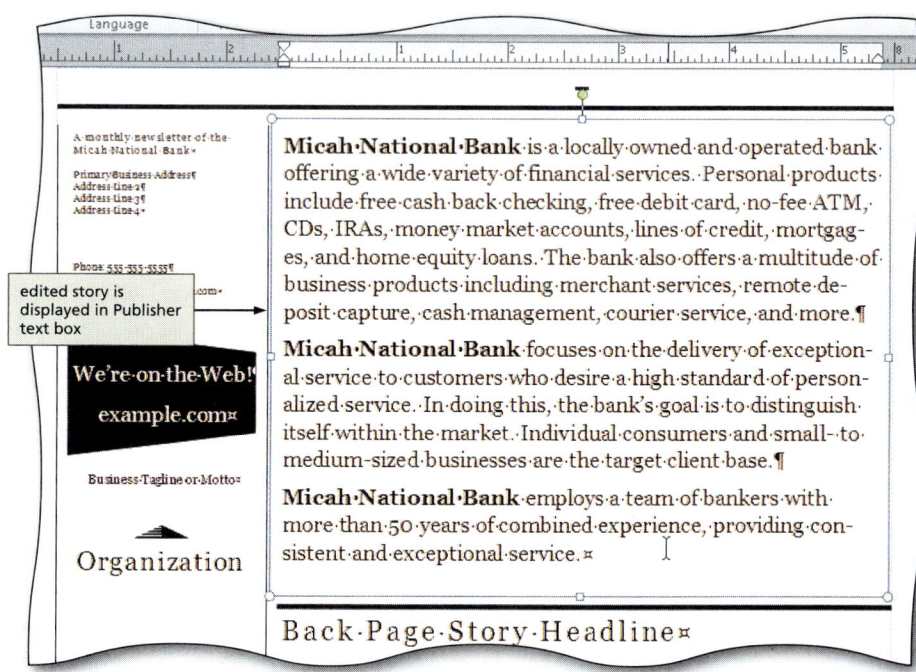

Figure 3–39

TO REMOVE ALL RIBBON CUSTOMIZATION

If you are working in a lab environment, you should remove all Ribbon customization after you finish the exercises at the end of the chapter. If you wanted to remove all Ribbon customization, you would perform the following steps.

1. Click File on the Ribbon to open the Backstage view and then click the Options command to display the Publisher Options dialog box.

2. Click Customize Ribbon to display the Customize the Ribbon gallery.

3. Click the Reset button and then click 'Reset all customizations' in the list.

4. Click the OK button (Publisher Options dialog box) to close the dialog box.

BTW

Zooming
Recall that the F9 key toggles between the current page view and 100% magnification, or actual size. **Toggle** means the same key will alternate views, or turn a feature on and off. Editing text is easier if you view the text at 100% magnification or even larger.

To Edit Other Objects on Page 4

The following steps delete the logo and edit other text boxes on page 2. Table 3–2 lists text for the other objects on page 4.

Table 3–2	
Location	**Text**
Primary Business Address	East: 4320 Samoan Road West: 7905 W. Dixon Downtown: 10 Main Street Micah, OR 97360
Phone, Fax, E-mail text box	Phone: 1-800-555-8642 Fax: 971-555-8643 E-mail: info@mnb.com
Attention getter	We're on the Web! www.mnb.com
Business Tagline or Motto	<delete>
Organization logo	<delete>
Back Page Story Headline	Online Banking
Back page story	With online banking you can: Get your balance 24/7 Transfer money Pay bills online Set up direct deposit Open new accounts Use auto-transactions For more details visit www.mnb.com or call us at 1-800-555-8642.

1 In the upper-left portion of page 4, click the text in the Primary Business Address text box. Press CTRL+A to select all of the text. Enter the text from the first row of Table 3–2.

2 Select the text in the Phone, Fax, E-mail text box, and then enter the text from the second row of Table 3–2.

3 Select the text in the attention getter, and then enter the text from the third row of Table 3–2.

4 Select the organization logo and delete it.

5 Select the business tagline or motto placeholder and delete it.

6 Zoom out to display the entire page.

7 Select the graphic and its caption in the back page story and delete it (Figure 3–40).

BTW

Whole Page View
The Show Whole Page button on the right side of the Publisher status bar displays the entire page. Page editing techniques, such as moving graphics, inserting new objects, and aligning objects, are performed more easily in Whole Page view. You also may choose different magnifications and views by clicking the Zoom box arrow (View tab | Zoom group).

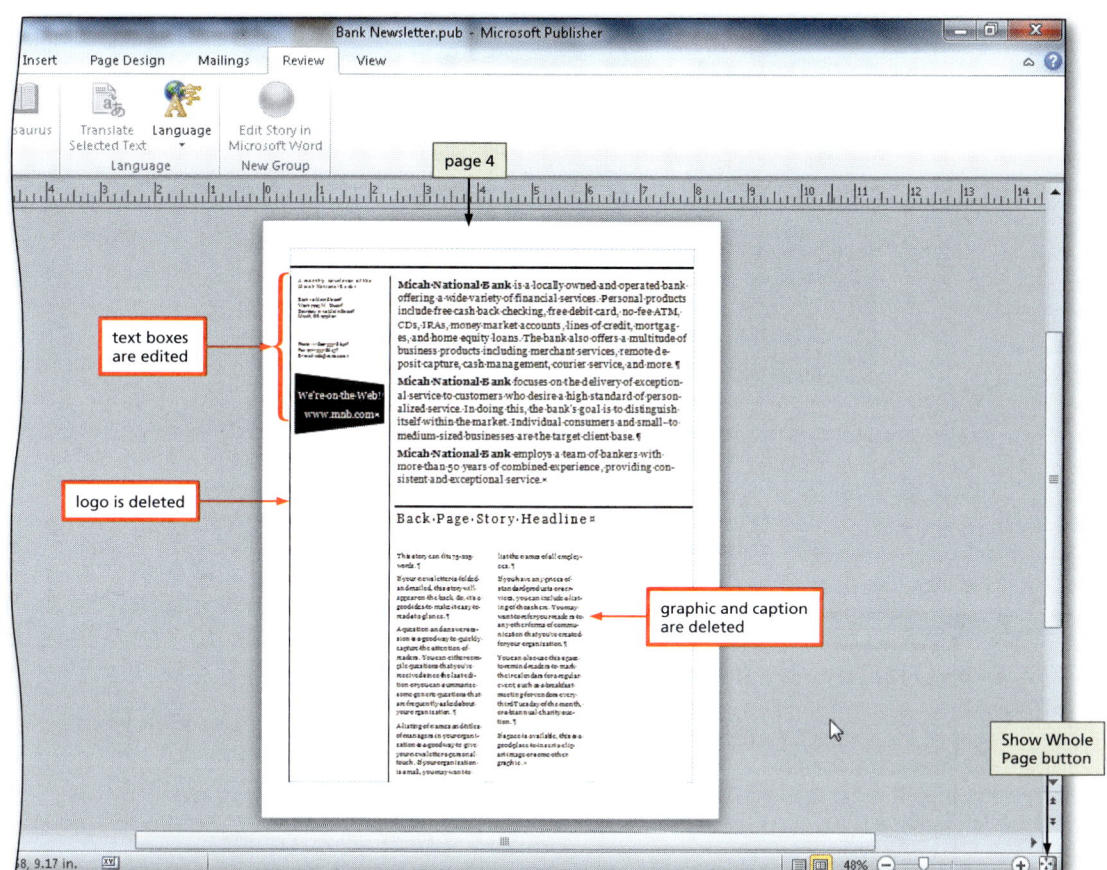

Figure 3–40

To Edit the Back Page Story

The following steps edit the back page story by inserting new text, deleting the second column, and widening the first column.

1

- Select the Back Page Story Headline.

- Zoom to 120%.

- Type **Online Banking** to replace the text.

- Select the story below the headline (Figure 3–41).

Figure 3–41

2

- Type the new text from the last row of Table 3–1, pressing the ENTER key at the end of each line (Figure 3–42).

Q&A

The text is very small on the screen. Should I increase the font size?

No, press the F9 key or use the zoom tools on the status bar to increase the magnification.

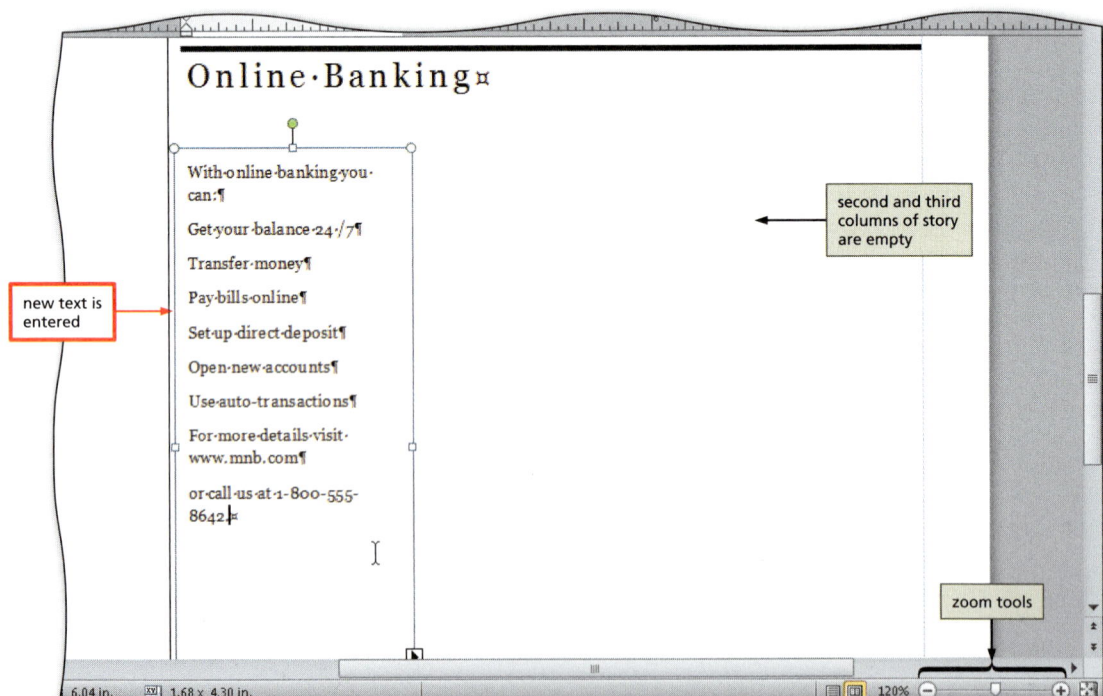

Figure 3–42

3

- Point to the empty second column of the story. When the boundary appears, click it and then press the DELETE key.

- Point to the empty third column of the story. When the boundary appears, click it and then press the DELETE key.

- Click the first column text box and then drag the right-middle sizing handle to the right until it measures approximately 2.8 inches wide, as noted on the status bar (Figure 3–43).

Figure 3–43

4

- Display the Home tab.

- Select all of the text and change the font size to 14.

- Select the first line of text. Press CTRL+B to bold the text.

- Select the next six lines of text. Click the Bullets button (Home tab | Paragraph group) and choose an asterisk (*) bullet from the list of styles.

- Select the last three lines of text. Press CTRL+E to center the text.

- Click outside the selected text to view the formatting (Figure 3–44).

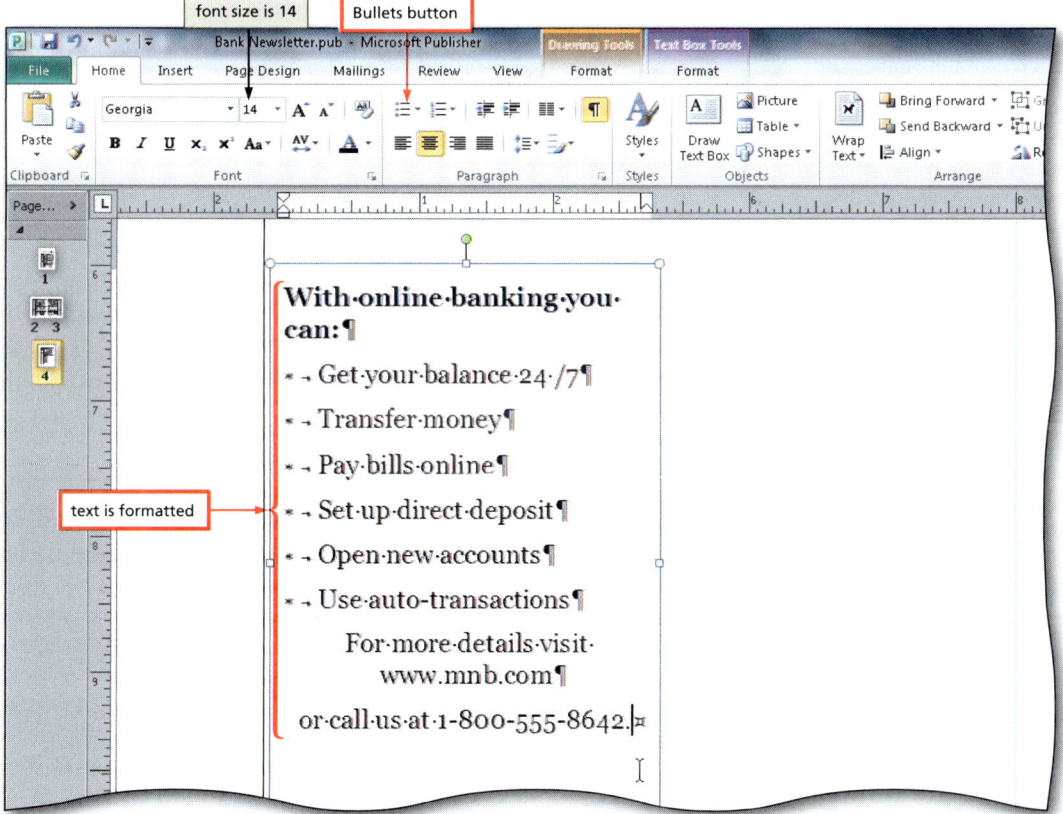

Figure 3–44

To Save the Publication Again

The following step saves the publication again.

1 Click the Save button on the Quick Access Toolbar to overwrite the previously saved file.

Break Point: If you wish to take a break, this is a good place to do so. You can quit Publisher now. To resume at a later time, start Publisher, open the file named Bank Newsletter, and continue following the steps from this location forward.

BTW

Accessing Headers and Footers
You can access the header and footer areas by clicking the Insert Header or Footer buttons (Insert tab | Header & Footer group). Publisher opens a special layout with a text box at the top and bottom that you can use to add additional information. The Header & Footer group (Insert tab) helps you insert the page number, date, and time, and allows you to navigate between the header and footer.

Using Graphics in a Newsletter

Most graphic designers employ an easy technique for deciding how many graphics are too many. They hold the publication at arm's length and glance at it. Then, closing their eyes, they count the number of things they remember. Remembering more than five graphics indicates too many; fewer than two indicates too few. Without question, graphics can make or break a publication. The world has come to expect them. Used correctly, graphics enhance the text, attract the eye, and brighten the look of the publication.

You can use Publisher's clip art images in any publication you create, including newsletters. Publisher also accepts graphics and pictures created by other programs, as well as scanned photographs and digital photos. You can import and replace graphics in publications in the same way that you imported stories and replaced template text. Once inserted, graphics can be resized and moved to appropriate locations. In newsletters, you should use photographs for true-to-life representations, such as pictures of employees and products. Drawings, on the other hand, can explain, instruct, entertain, or represent images for which you have no picture. The careful use of graphics can add flair and distinction to your publication.

Plan Ahead

> **Create the first draft.**
> As you insert graphics and arrange stories, follow any guidelines from the authors or from the company for which you are creating the newsletter. Together, determine the best layout for eye appeal and reliable dissemination of content. Make any required changes. Print a copy and mark the places where sidebars and pull quotes would make sense. Verify that all photographs have captions.

The following sections import graphics from the Data Files for Students, edit the captions and sidebar text, delete a sidebar (but not the graphic behind it), and insert a pull quote.

To Replace a Graphic Using the Shortcut Menu

The following steps replace a graphic with one from the Data Files for Students. See the inside back cover of this book for instructions on downloading the Data Files for Students, or contact your instructor for more information about accessing the required files.

1

- Navigate to page 1.

- Scroll and zoom as necessary to display the graphic in the lead story.

- Click the graphic once to select the combined graphic and picture. Click the graphic again to select only the picture.

- Right-click the graphic to display the shortcut menu and then point to Change Picture to display its submenu (Figure 3–45).

Q&A What is the toolbar that appeared on the screen?

When a picture is selected, Publisher displays a Mini toolbar in case you want to make changes to the picture.

Figure 3–45

2

- Click Change Picture on the submenu to display the Insert Picture dialog box.

- Navigate to the desired insert location (in this case, the Chapter 03 folder in the Publisher folder in the Data Files for Students. For a detailed example of this procedure, refer to Steps 3a – 3c in the To Save a File in a Folder section in the Office 2010 and Windows 7 chapter at the beginning of this book. (Figure 3 – 46).

Q&A What do the other choices on the Change Picture submenu do?

As shown in Figure 3–45, the Remove Picture command deletes the picture but retains the picture placeholder. The Reset Picture command removes any previous cropping or resizing.

Figure 3–46

3

- To insert the picture, double-click the file named, Bank.

- Click outside the picture to view the insertion. (Figure 3–47).

Q&A

What if I choose a bigger or smaller picture?

Because you are replacing the graphic, rather than inserting a picture, Publisher resizes and crops the picture to fit the space. The picture automatically is scaled in proportion.

Figure 3–47

To Edit the Caption

The following steps edit the caption for the new picture on page 1.

1 Select the text in the caption.

2 Type `Come visit our new west branch at 7905 W. Dixon` to replace the selected placeholder text (Figure 3–48).

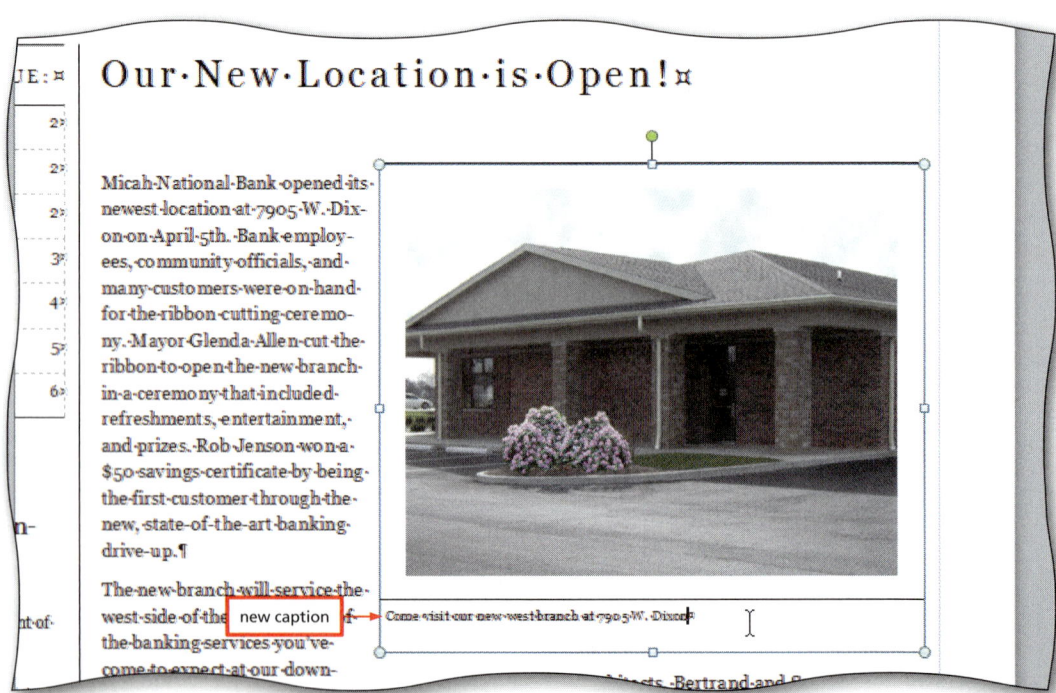

Figure 3–48

To Replace a Graphic with Clip Art

The following steps replace the graphic in the first story on page 2 using the Clip Art task pane.

1 Navigate to page 2.

2 Click the grouped picture and caption in the first story. Click the picture again to select only the picture.

3 Display the Insert tab on the Ribbon.

4 Click the Clip Art button (Insert tab | Illustrations group) to open the Clip Art task pane.

5 If necessary, select any text that appears in the Search for box and delete it. Type `coins` in the Search for box.

6 If necessary, click the 'Results should be' box arrow and then click 'All media types' in the list.

7 Click to display a check mark in the Include Office.com content check box.

8 Click the Go button to search for clips related to the search term, coins.

9 Scroll as necessary in the Clip Art task pane and then click a picture similar to the one in Figure 3–49 to replace the graphic.

Figure 3–49

BTW

Resizing Clip Art
Clip art graphics are not all the same size. Some clip art images appear in **portrait orientation**, which means they are taller than they are wide. The opposite graphic orientation is **landscape orientation**. Clip art graphics are proportional, which means the height and width have been set in relation to each other, so as not to distort the picture. If you resize a graphic, be sure to hold down the SHIFT key while dragging a corner handle. SHIFT+dragging maintains the graphic's proportions.

BTW

Wrapping Text
Text automatically wraps around graphics in newsletter templates. When you change graphics, your choice may alter both the way the columns look and where the columns break. Experiment with repositioning the picture in small increments to make the columns symmetrical.

To Edit the Caption on Page 2

The following steps replace the caption below the first story picture on page 2.

1 Select the text in the caption below the coins.

2 Type `Your savings can really pile up!` to change the caption.

To Replace the Graphic and Caption on Page 3

The following steps replace the graphic in the first story on page 3 using the Clip Art task pane.

1 Navigate to page 3.

2 Click the grouped picture and caption in the first story. Click the picture again to select only the picture.

3 Select any text that appears in the Search for box (Clip Art task pane) and delete it. Type `businesswoman` in the Search for box.

4 If necessary, click the 'Results should be' box arrow and then click 'All media types' in the list. If necessary, click to display a check mark in the Include Office.com content check box.

5 Click the Go button to search for clips related to the search term, businesswoman.

6 Scroll as necessary in the Clip Art task pane and then click a picture similar to the one in Figure 3–50 to replace the graphic.

7 Select the text in the caption below the picture.

8 Type `Kelly Robertson works at the east branch.` to change the caption.

9 Click the Close button in the Clip Art task pane.

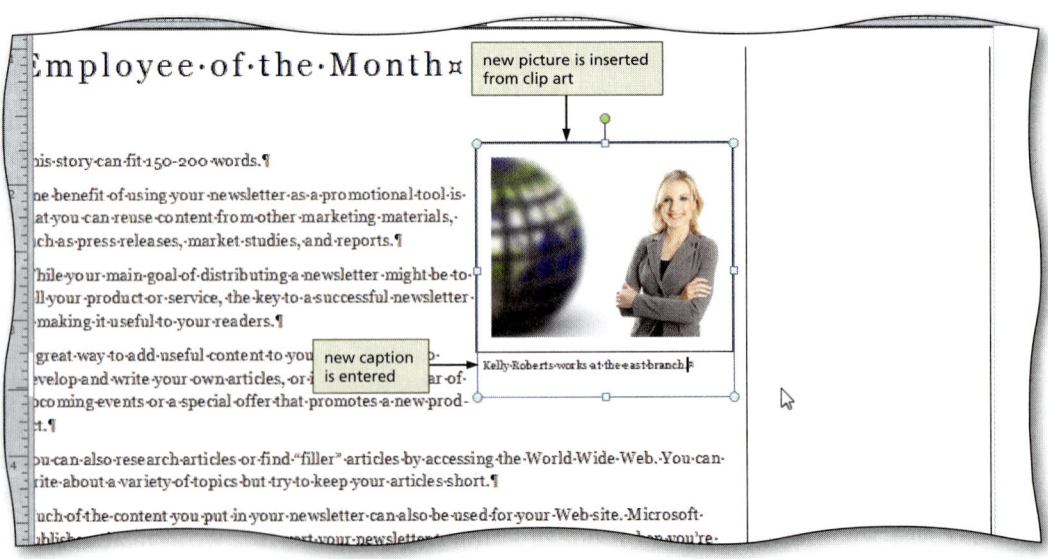

Figure 3–50

To Select Adjacent Objects by Dragging

Recall from a previous chapter that you used SHIFT+click to select more than one object. In Publisher, when you want to select multiple items that are adjacent, you can use the mouse to drag around all of the objects, automatically selecting them. The following steps select adjacent objects by dragging around them. You then will delete the selected objects.

1

- Zoom out to display the entire two-page spread of pages 2 and 3.

- Starting at a location above and to the left of the horizontal black line and third story on page 2, drag down and to the right to include the line, headline, story, picture, and caption at the bottom of page 2 (Figure 3–51).

2

- Press the DELETE key to delete the selected objects.

headline, text boxes, graphic, and caption are selected

Figure 3–51

Other Ways

1. SHIFT+click each of the adjacent objects, press CTRL+X

To Select and Delete More Objects

The following steps delete the article and associated graphics at the bottom of page 3.

1 Starting at a location above and to the left of the black line and third story on page 3, drag down and to the right to include the line, headline, story, picture, and caption at the bottom of page 3.

2 Press the DELETE key to delete the selected objects.

3 Delete the text box and text in the left margin of page 2.

4 Delete the text box and text in the right margin of page 3 (Figure 3 – 52).

Figure 3–52

Left and Right Pages
In printing and publishing, the left-hand page of a two-page spread is called **verso**. The right-hand page is called **recto**. Typically, the first page of a book or chapter is a recto page; thus, all recto pages will have odd page numbers and all verso pages will have even page numbers.

Page Parts

Publisher newsletter templates include margin elements and layout features to make the newsletter more attractive and add interest to the page. These objects, called **Page Parts** in Publisher, include sidebars, tables of contents, pull quotes, and other small, building block objects. A **sidebar**, or **breakout**, is a small piece of text, set off with a box or graphic, and placed beside an article. It contains text that is not vital for understanding the main text, but usually adds interest or additional information. Tables of contents, art boxes, and bulleted points of interest are examples of sidebars. A newsletter **table of contents**, or margin table, usually is a narrow, short list that is used to refer readers to specific pages or to present listed or numeric items in the margin area. A **pull quote, or pullout,** is an excerpt from the main article used to highlight the ideas or to attract readers. Pull quotes, like sidebars, can be set off with a box or graphic.

To Edit a Sidebar

The Bars newsletter template includes two sidebars on page 1. The first one is a sidebar table. Some newsletters use a sidebar table as an index to locate articles in longer newsletters; they also are used to break up a long text page and attract readers to inside pages. Other newsletters use sidebar tables to display numerical data and lists. In the New Ways of Banking newsletter, the sidebar is used to display current banking rates. The following steps edit the sidebar.

1

- Navigate to page 1.

- Locate the Inside this Issue sidebar, and zoom in to 150% magnification.

- Click the text, INSIDE THIS ISSUE, to select it (Figure 3–53).

Q&A

Is the heading part of the table?

No, the heading is a text box grouped with subsequent rows, which comprise a table. You will learn more about tables in a future chapter.

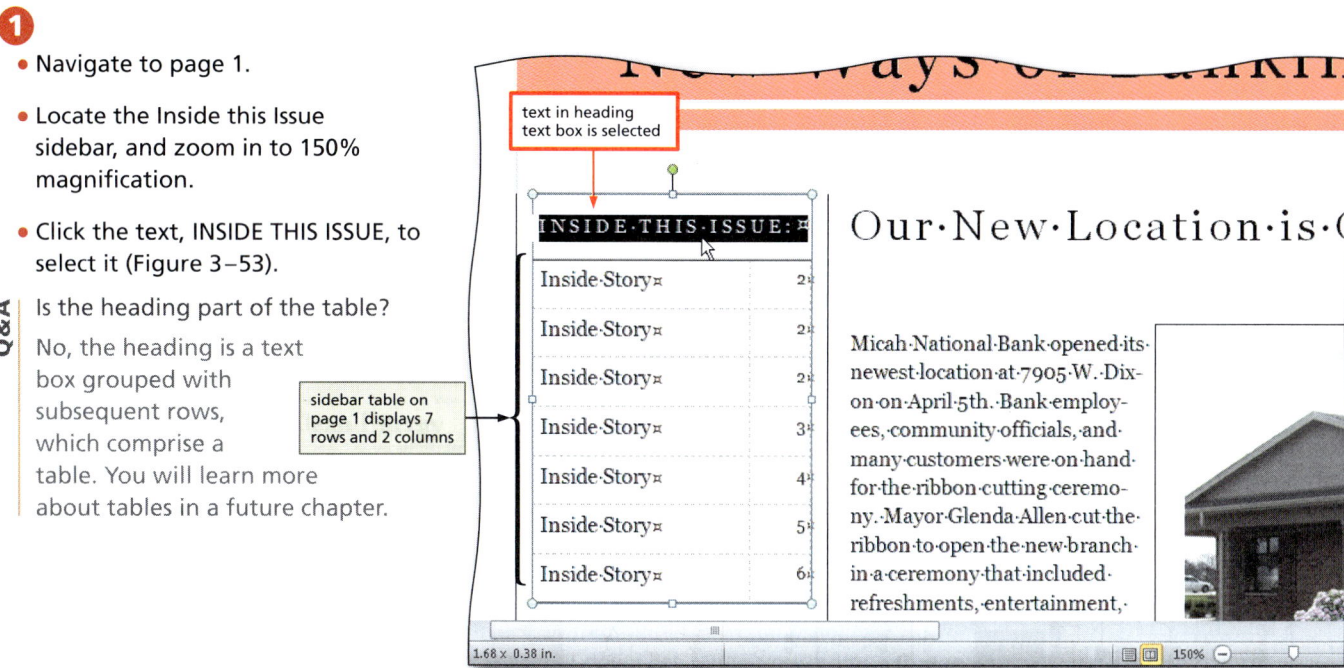

Figure 3–53

2

- Type **Current Rates:** to replace the text.

- Click the text, Inside Story, in the first row to select it (Figure 3–54).

Q&A

What are the dotted gray lines in the table?

Publisher displays dotted gray lines to indicate the size of each cell in the table. They do not print.

Figure 3–54

3

- Type `Savings` to replace the text.

- Press the TAB key to move to the next cell in the table (Figure 3–55).

Q&A

Could I click the next cell instead of using the TAB key?

You could click the cell, but you then would need to select the page number and type to replace it. Pressing the TAB key both advances to and then selects the data in the next cell.

Figure 3–55

4

- Complete the table with the data shown in Figure 3–56. Use the TAB key to move from cell to cell.

Figure 3–56

To Edit the Second Sidebar and Reposition It

The second sidebar is a bulleted list of special points of interest. The following steps edit that bulleted list.

1 Scroll down on page 1 to display the second sidebar.

2 Click the text in the sidebar, Special points of interest, to select it.

3 Type **Banking Hours** to replace the text.

4 Select the bulleted list.

5 Type **9-5 Monday – Thursday** and then press the ENTER key.

6 Type **9-7 Friday** and then press the ENTER key.

7 Type **9-2 Saturday** to complete the list.

8 Scroll to display the area below the sidebar. To move the sidebar, drag the border of the sidebar down until it snaps to the lower margin guide (Figure 3–57).

Figure 3–57

To Insert a Pull Quote

People often make reading decisions based on the size of the story. Using a pull quote brings a small portion of the text to their attention and invites them to read more. Pull quotes are especially useful for breaking the monotony of long columns of text and adding visual interest.

The steps on the next page insert a pull quote using Page Parts. You will use function keys to copy and paste the quote from the lead story.

1

- Scroll up on page 1 to display the empty spot between the two sidebars and the first column of the lead story.

- Click the Page Parts button (Insert tab | Building Blocks group) to display the gallery (Figure 3–58).

How are pull quotes and sidebars used?

Pull quotes and sidebars are good multiple-entry devices, offering readers many ways to digest information.

Figure 3–58

2

- Click the Pure pull quote to insert it into the newsletter (Figure 3–59).

How do I know which one to choose?

The previews are displayed in alphabetical order in the Pull Quotes area, and a ScreenTip displays the preview's name when you point to it. Some of the pull quotes match a specific design set, while others are merely decorative. You should choose one that complements your publication and makes the quote stand out.

Figure 3–59

3

- Drag the border of the pull quote to a location where it snaps to the black line at the left margin.

- Drag the middle-right sizing handle to the left, so that the pull quote fits within the two black lines for the margin elements.

- If necessary, drag the border of the pull quote so it appears centered between the other two sidebars (Figure 3–60).

Q&A

When I drag, text moves instead of the pull quote. What did I do wrong?

When you want to move an object, you must drag it by its border — the gray dotted line surrounding the object. If your text moved, you dragged the text rather than the entire object. Press CTRL+Z to undo the move, and try again, dragging the border.

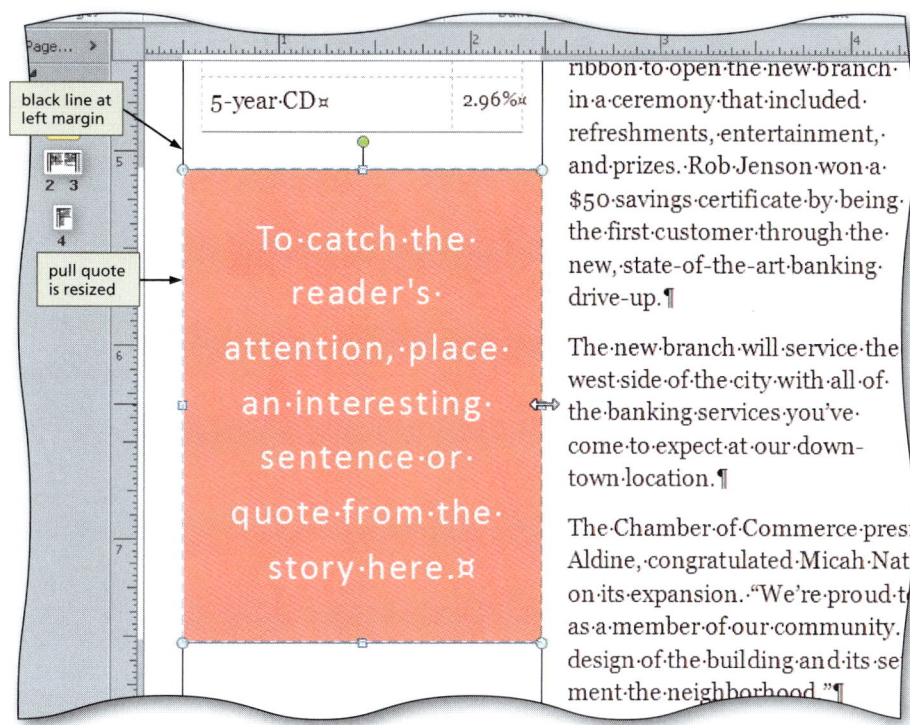

Figure 3–60

To Insert Text in a Pull Quote

The following steps use a quote from the story to replace the default text in the pull quote.

1

- In the first column of the lead story, select the second sentence in the last paragraph by dragging through it. Include the quotation mark at the beginning of the sentence and the period at the end of the sentence (Figure 3–61).

Q&A

Other than dragging, how can I select the sentence?

You can click at the beginning of the sentence and then SHIFT+click at the end of the sentence.

Figure 3–61

2

- Press CTRL+C to copy the sentence to the Clipboard.

- Right-click the default text in the pull quote to display the shortcut menu (Figure 3–62).

🔎 **Experiment**

- Point to each of the Paste Option buttons to watch the text change in the pull quote.

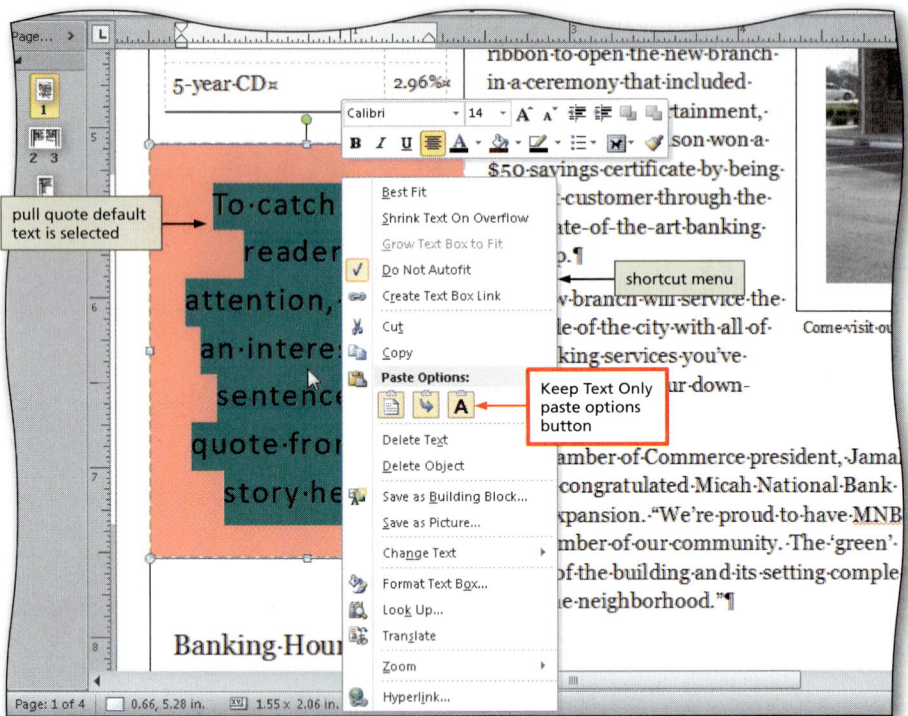

Figure 3–62

3

- Click the Keep Text Only paste option button to paste the text from the Clipboard.

- If necessary, press the BACKSPACE key to delete the space after the period.

- Type a closing quotation mark (″), press the ENTER key, and then type **Chamber of Commerce** to complete the citation (Figure 3–63).

Q&A

How should I choose the text for the pull quote?

Layout specialists say pull quotes should summarize the intended message in one or two sentences.

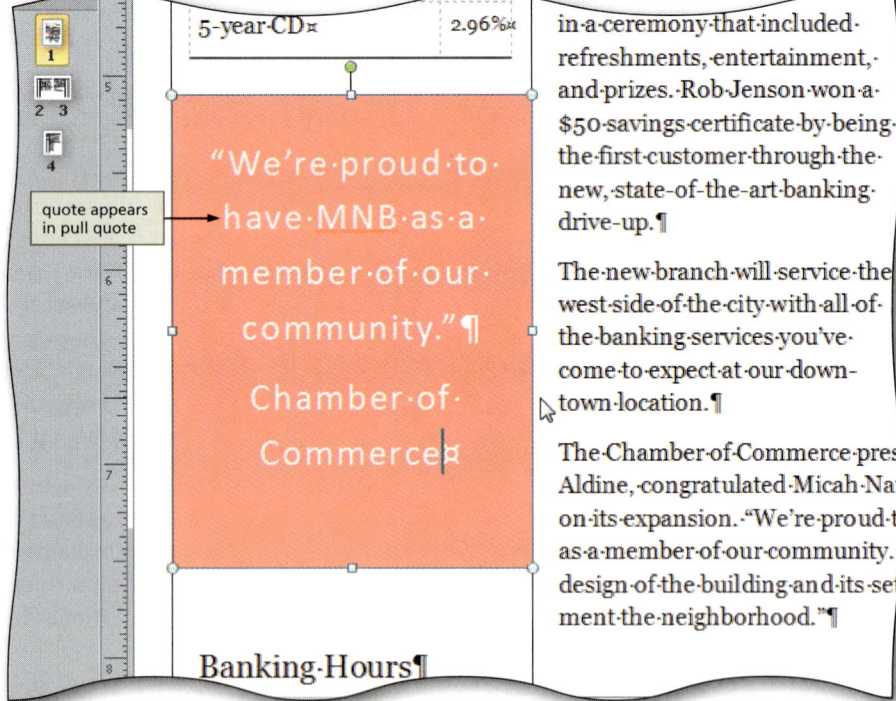

Figure 3–63

Other Ways

1. Click Building Blocks Dialog Box Launcher (Insert tab | Building Blocks group), click Page

Parts folder, click desired pull quote, edit pull quote text

To Insert and Edit Another Page Part

The following steps insert and edit another Page Part for the lower-left portion of page 3.

1 Navigate to page 3 and scroll to the lower portion.

2 Click the Page Parts button (Insert tab | Building Blocks group) to display the gallery and then click the Convention (Layout 1) sidebar.

3 Drag the border of the sidebar to move the sidebar to the lower-left corner of page 3.

4 Edit the text as shown in Figure 3–64.

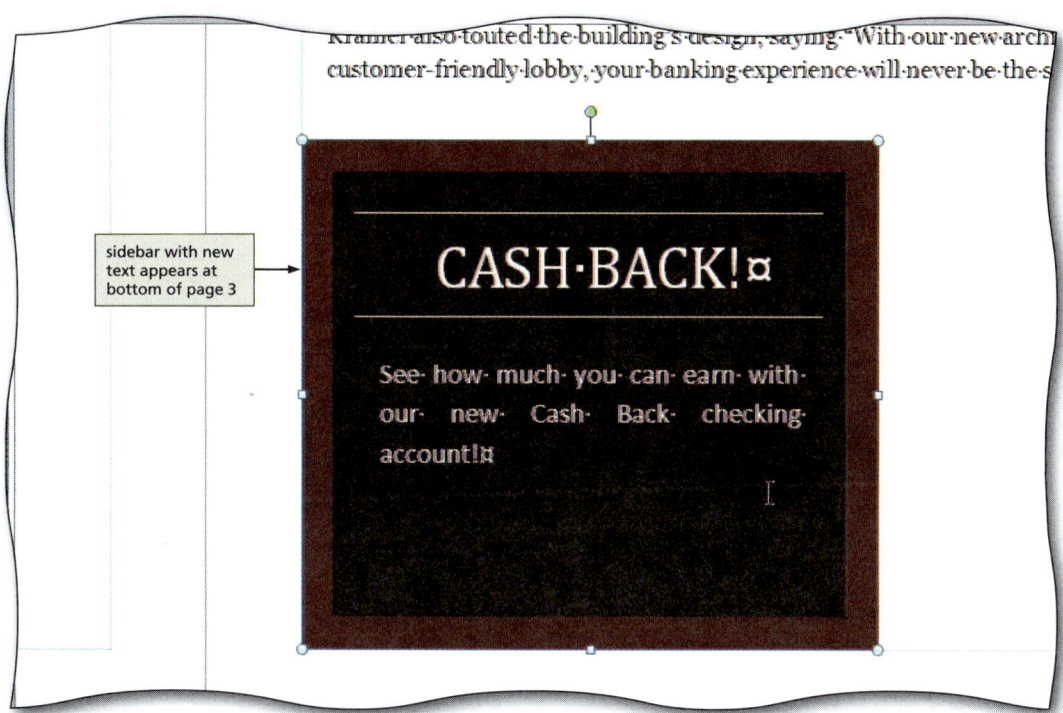

sidebar with new text appears at bottom of page 3

Kramer also touted the building's design, saying, "With our new arch customer-friendly lobby, your banking experience will never be the s

CASH·BACK!¤

See how much you can earn with our new Cash Back checking account!¤

Figure 3–64

To Insert a Pattern

The following steps insert another building block called a pattern. A **pattern** is a decorative shape that is designed to fit with the current color scheme and template.

1 Zoom out to display pages 2 and 3 in the workspace.

2 Click the Building Blocks Dialog Box Launcher (Insert tab | Building Blocks group) to display the gallery.

3 Click the Borders and Accents folder to open it. Scroll to the lower portion of the gallery to display the Patterns area.

4 Click the Tri-shape graphic to select it, and then click the Insert button to insert the graphic in the publication.

5 Drag the border of the graphic to move it to the upper-right corner of page 3, just below the page number.

6 SHIFT+drag the lower-left sizing handle until the graphic fills the margin element between the two black lines (Figure 3–65).

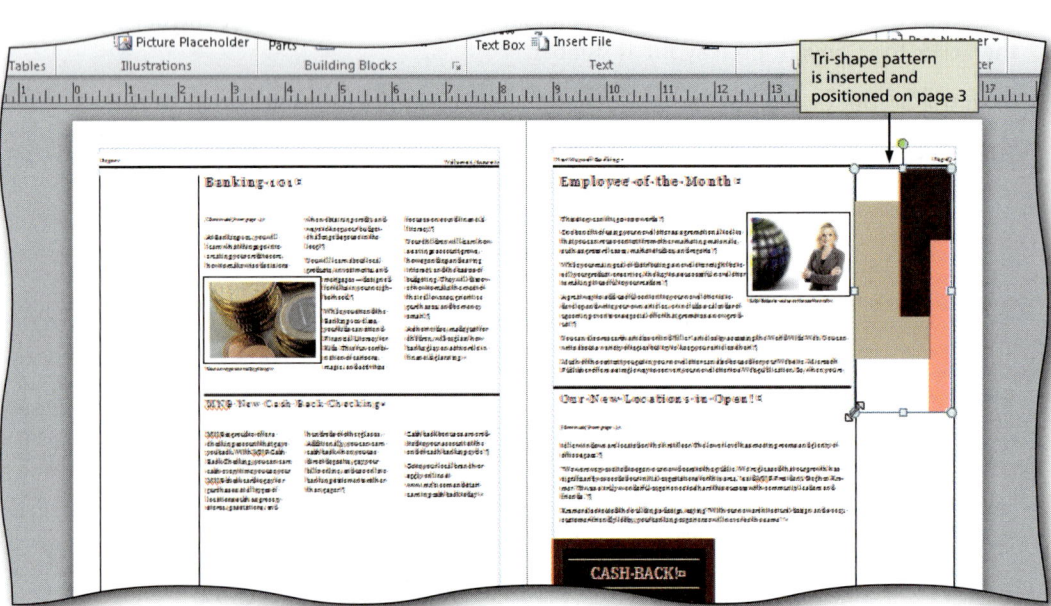

Figure 3–65

To Duplicate a Graphic

When you **duplicate** a graphic, you use a shortcut method, such as CTRL+drag, or CTRL+SHIFT+drag, to create a copy, rather than the traditional copy-and-paste method. A duplicate does not use the Clipboard. The following step duplicates the Tri-shape graphic.

1
- CTRL+SHIFT+drag the Tri-shape graphic from the upper-right corner of page 3 to the upper-left corner of page 2 (Figure 3–66).

Q&A

Why do I need to press the CTRL and the SHIFT keys while dragging?

The CTRL key creates the duplicate copy, and the SHIFT key keeps the graphic in line with its source as you drag it.

Figure 3–66

To Flip a Graphic

When you **flip** a graphic, you invert it horizontally or vertically. The following steps invert the duplicate Tri-shape graphic horizontally.

1

- With the Tri-shape graphic on page 2 still selected, click Drawing Tools Format on the Ribbon to display the Drawing Tools Format tab.

- Click the Rotate button (Drawing Tools Format tab | Arrange group) to display the gallery (Figure 3–67).

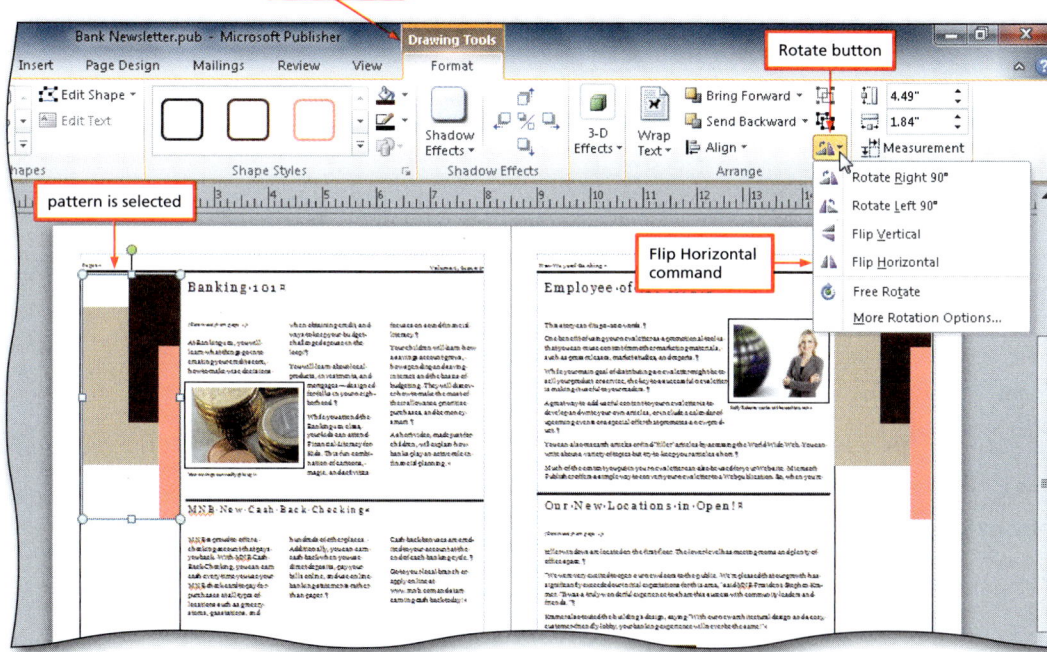

Figure 3–67

2

- Click Flip Horizontal to flip the selected graphic horizontally (Figure 3–68).

Q&A Should you always flip margin art such as this pattern?

Flipping the graphic, or even flipping the order of the chapter name and page number as is done in this book, balances a two-page spread and provides a visual outer border.

Figure 3–68

Advertisements

Publisher **advertisements** include a group of promotional templates and objects used to market a product or service, including ads that might be placed in newspapers, attention getters, and coupons. Advertisements can be stand-alone publications or inserted as building block items in larger publications. On page 2 of the newsletter, the bank will offer a coupon. A **coupon** is a promotional device used to market a product or service. Customers exchange coupons for discounts when purchasing a product. Some coupons offer rebates or free items to attract customers. Coupons are often widely distributed as small printed documents through mail, magazines, newspapers, and newsletters. More recently, however, they are distributed as electronic tags collected through preferred customer cards via the Internet and mobile devices such as cell phones.

To Insert and Format a Coupon

The following steps insert a coupon on page 2 of the newsletter.

1

- Zoom to 80% magnification.

- Navigate to the lower portion of page 2 in the newsletter.

- If necessary, display the Insert tab.

- Click the Advertisements button (Insert tab | Building Blocks group) to display the gallery (Figure 3–69).

Q&A

Why does my gallery look different?

Your Advertisements gallery may have an area of recently used items. If necessary, scroll down in the gallery to display the Coupons area.

Figure 3–69

2

- If necessary, scroll to the Coupons area, and then click the Tilted Box coupon to insert it in the newsletter.

- Drag the border of the inserted coupon to move it to a location that snaps to the bottom margin guide and the black horizontal line, as shown in Figure 3–70.

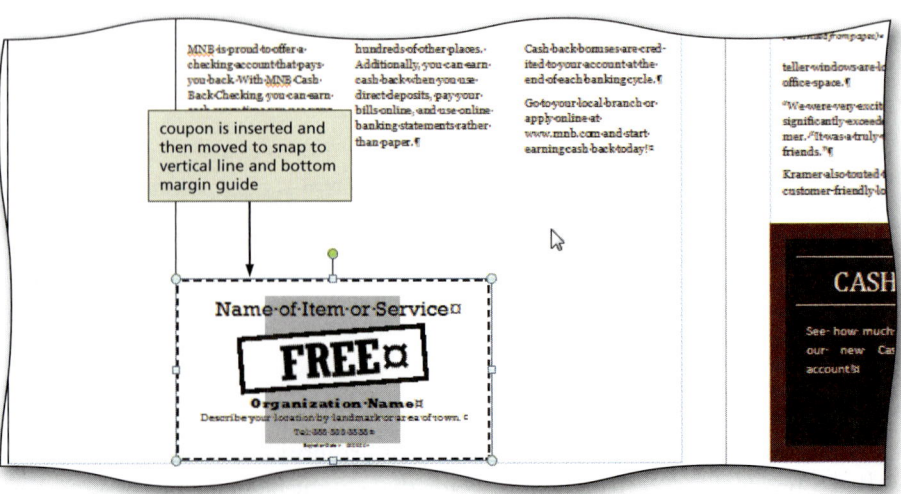

Figure 3–70

3

- SHIFT+drag the upper-right sizing handle to the right margin guide to resize the coupon (Figure 3–71).

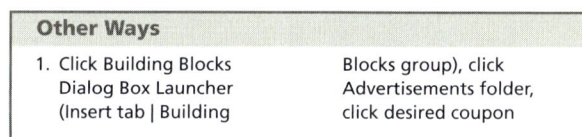

Figure 3–71

Other Ways	
1. Click Building Blocks Dialog Box Launcher (Insert tab | Building	Blocks group), click Advertisements folder, click desired coupon

To Edit the Coupon

The following steps edit the text boxes in the coupon.

1 Zoom to 150% magnification.

2 Replace the Name of Item or Service text with the words `Savings Piggy Bank` as the new text.

3 Replace the Organization Name text with the words `For children ages 0-12` as the new text.

4 Replace the 'Describe your location by landmark or area of town' text with the words `When you open an Education Savings Account` as the new text.

5 Zoom as necessary to delete the text in the telephone and expiration date text boxes. The end of text formatting marks will remain (Figure 3–72).

Figure 3–72

To Insert Other Clip Art

The following steps insert other graphics on the other pages of the newsletter.

1 Navigate to page 4. Use the Clip Art task pane to search for a picture related to the term, computing. Insert a picture of your choice in the lower-right corner of the page. Resize the picture as necessary to fit the empty space beside the bulleted list.

2 Navigate to page 2. Use the Clip Art task pane to search for a picture of a bank. Insert a picture of a piggy bank in the lower-left corner of page 2.

3 Navigate to page 3. Use the Clip Art task pane to search for a picture of a calculator. Insert the picture in the lower-right corner of page 3. The picture will cover part of the vertical black line (Figure 3–73).

4 Close the Clip Art task pane.

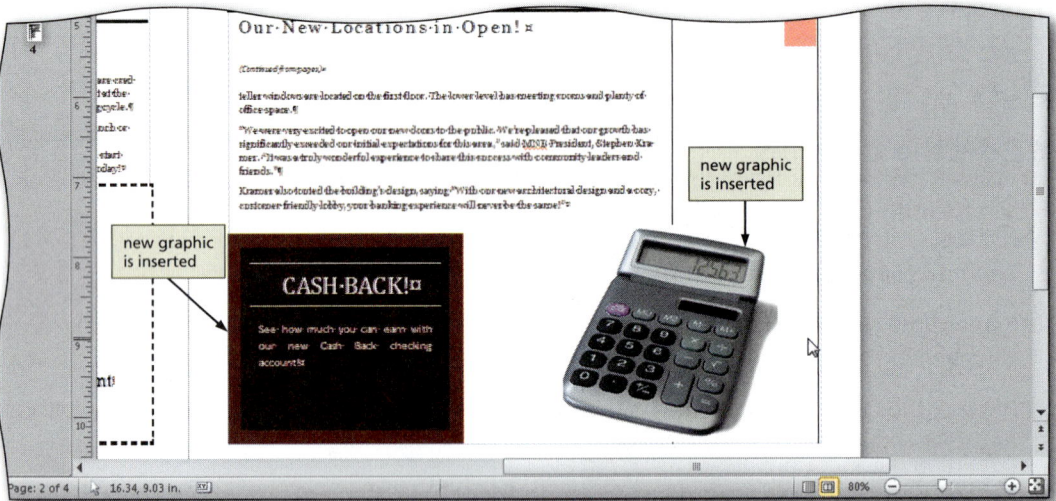

Figure 3–73

To Save the Publication before Revising

It is a good idea to save the newsletter before going back and revising it. The following step saves the publication again.

1 Click the Save button on the Quick Access Toolbar to save the file again, with the same file name and in the same location.

Break Point: If you wish to take a break, this is a good place to do so. You can quit Publisher now. To resume at a later time, start Publisher, open the file named Bank Newsletter, and continue following the steps from this location forward.

Revising a Newsletter

As discussed in Chapter 1, once you complete a publication, you may find it necessary to make changes to it. Before submitting a newsletter to a customer or printing service, you should proofread it. While **proofreading**, you look for grammatical errors and spelling errors. You want to be sure the layout, graphics, and stories make sense. If you find errors, you must correct, make changes to, or edit the newsletter. Other readers, perhaps customers or editors, may want to proofread your publication and make changes, such as moving text. You also should check how Publisher has hyphenated your stories.

Plan Ahead

> **Proofread and revise the newsletter.**
> As you proofread the newsletter, look for ways to improve it. Check all grammar, spelling, and punctuation. Be sure the text is logical and transitions are smooth. Where necessary, add text, delete text, reword text, and move text to different locations. Ask yourself these questions:
>
> - Does the title suggest the topic?
> - Does the first line of the story entice the reader to continue?
> - Is the purpose of the newsletter clear?
> - Are all sources acknowledged?

The final phase of the design process is a synthesis involving proofreading, editing, and publishing. Publisher offers several methods to check for errors in your newsletter. None of these methods is a replacement for careful reading and proofreading.

Moving Text

If you decide to move text, such as words, characters, sentences, or paragraphs, you first select the text to be moved and then use drag-and-drop editing or the cut-and-paste technique to move the selected text. With **drag-and-drop editing**, you drag the selected item to the new location and then insert, or *drop*, it there. Moving text in this manner does not transfer data to the Clipboard; nor does it cause Publisher to display the Paste Options button. Any format changes to the text must be made manually.

When moving text between pages, use the cut-and-paste method. When moving text a long distance or between programs, open the Office Clipboard task pane by clicking the Clipboard Dialog Box Launcher (Home tab | Clipboard group), then cut and paste. When moving text a short distance, the drag-and-drop technique is more efficient. Thus, the steps on the following pages demonstrate drag-and-drop editing.

To Drag and Drop Text

The editor of the newsletter has decided that two paragraphs on page 3 should be inverted so that the story will read better. The following steps move paragraphs by dragging and dropping.

1
- Navigate to page 3 of the newsletter and scroll to the first story.
- Zoom to Whole Page.
- Triple-click to select the second paragraph (Figure 3–74).

Q&A Could I drag to select the sentence?

Yes; however, it is more efficient to triple-click, which automatically selects the entire paragraph and the paragraph mark at the end of it.

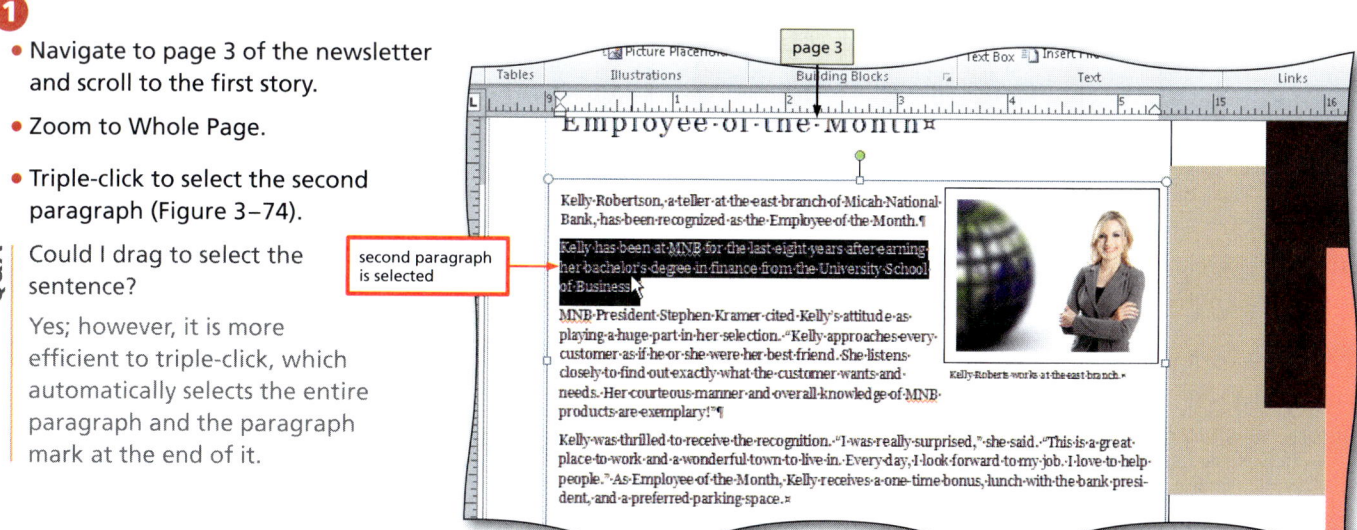

Figure 3–74

2

- Drag the selection to the beginning of the fourth paragraph. Do not release the mouse button (Figure 3–75).

Q&A My drag is not working. What did I do wrong?

It may be that someone has turned off drag-and-drop editing. Click File on the Ribbon to open the Backstage view. Click the Options tab and then click Advanced. Click to display a check mark in the 'Allow text to be dragged and dropped' check box.

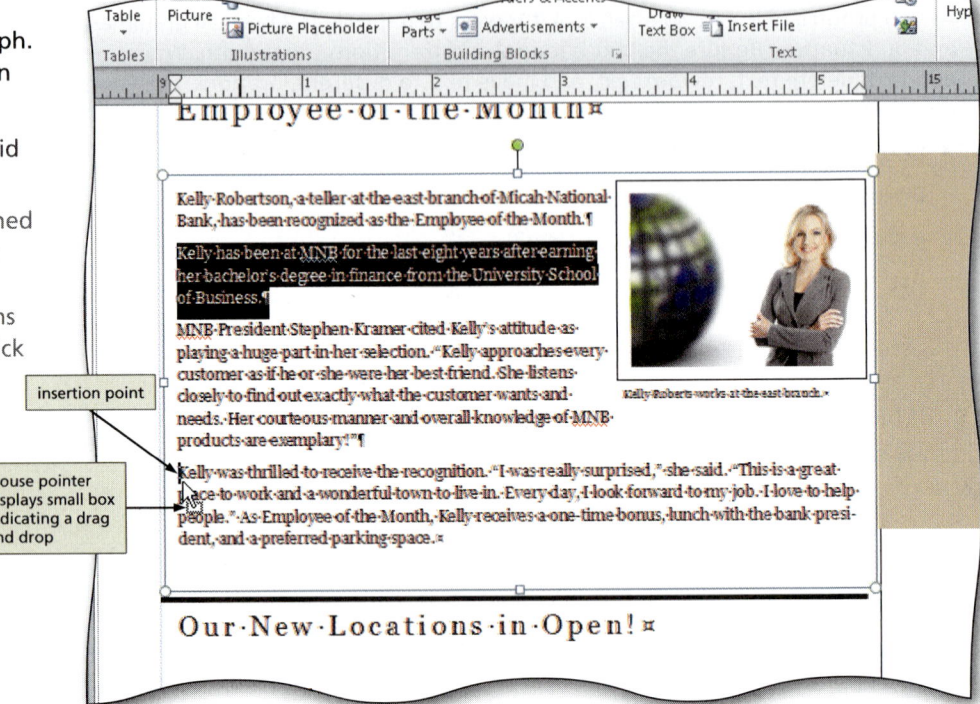

insertion point

mouse pointer displays small box indicating a drag and drop

Figure 3–75

3

- Release the mouse button to move the selected text to the location of the mouse pointer.

- Click the workspace to deselect the text (Figure 3–76).

Q&A What if I accidentally drag text to the wrong location?

Click the Undo button on the Quick Access Toolbar, or press CTRL+Z and try again.

Q&A Can I use drag-and-drop editing to move any selected item?

Yes, you can select words, sentences, phrases, and graphics and then use drag-and-drop editing to move them.

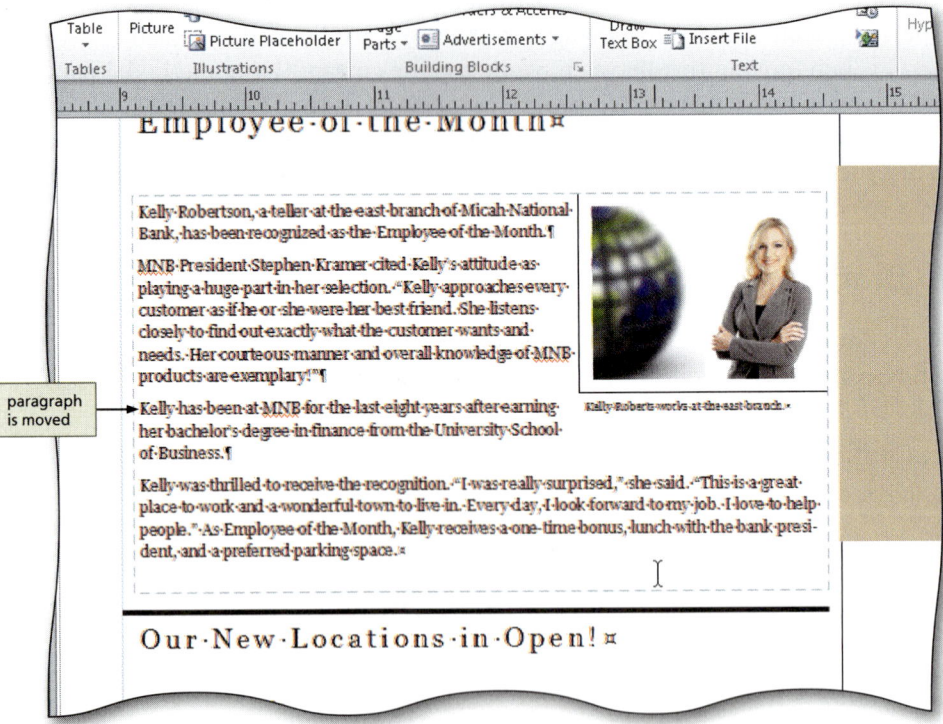

paragraph is moved

Figure 3–76

Other Ways

1. Select item, click Cut button (Home tab | Clipboard group), click where text is to be pasted, click Paste button (Home tab | Clipboard group)

2. Right-click selected item, click Cut on shortcut menu, right-click where text is to be pasted, click Paste Option button on shortcut menu

3. Select item, press CTRL+X, position insertion point where text is to be pasted, press CTRL+V

Hyphenation

Hyphenation refers to splitting a word that would otherwise extend beyond the right margin. Because Publisher bases hyphenation on words in its dictionary, it is a good idea to review the hyphenation. Publisher's hyphenation feature allows you to automatically or manually hyphenate the text, insert optional or **nonbreaking hyphens**, and set the maximum amount of space allowed between a word and the right margin without hyphenating the word. When you use automatic hyphenation, Publisher automatically inserts hyphens where they are needed. When you use manual hyphenation, Publisher searches for the text to hyphenate and asks you whether you want to insert the hyphens in the text. Some rules for hyphenation include:

- Hyphenate at standard syllable breaks.
- Hyphenate words that are already hyphenated at the hyphen location.
- Avoid hyphenating two lines in a row.
- Avoid hyphenating a line across text boxes or pages.
- Avoid hyphenations that leave only two letters at the beginning of the second line, when possible.

To Check Hyphenation

The following steps hyphenate the stories using Publisher's automatic hyphenation.

1

- Navigate to page 1 and click in the first column of the lead story.

- Click Text Box Tools Format on the Ribbon to display the Text Box Tools Format tab.

- Click the Hyphenation button (Text Box Tools Format tab | Text group) to display the Hyphenation dialog box.

- Click to remove the check mark in the 'Automatically hyphenate this story' check box (Figure 3–77).

Q&A

What is the hyphenation zone?

The **hyphenation zone** is the maximum amount of space Publisher allows between a word and the right margin without hyphenating the word. To reduce the number of hyphens, increase the hyphenation zone. To reduce the ragged edge of the right margin, decrease the hyphenation zone.

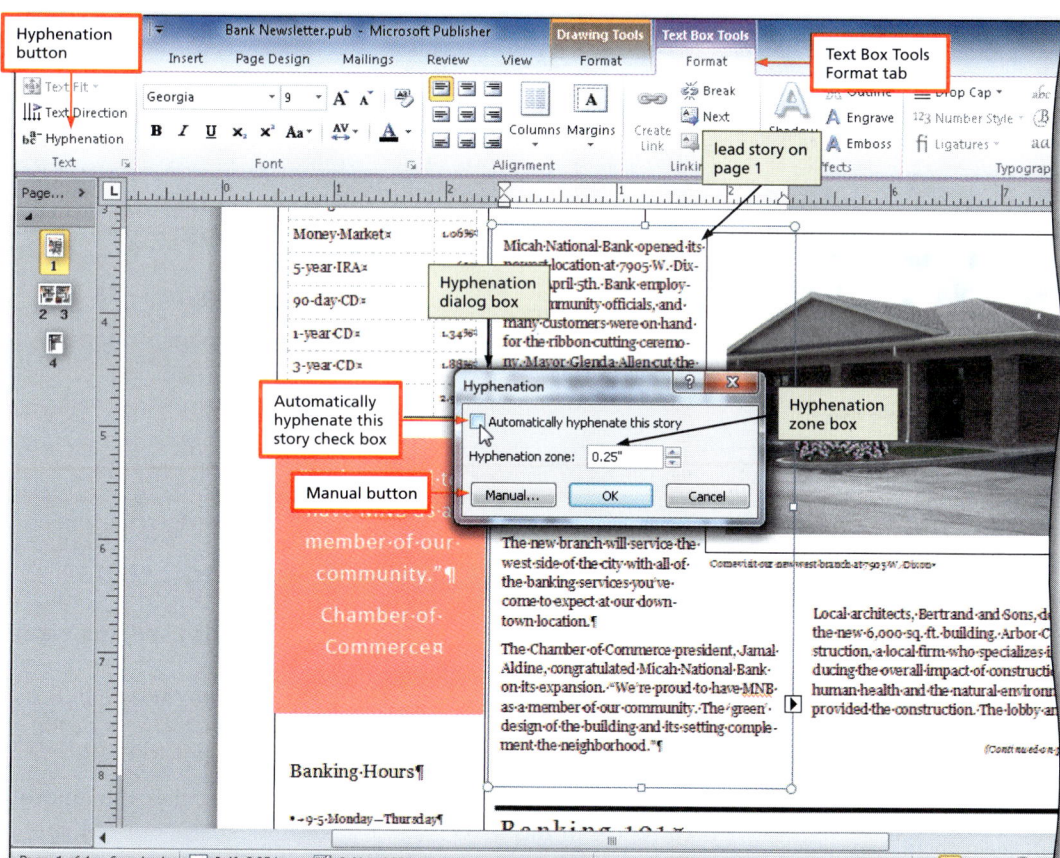

Figure 3–77

2

- Click the Manual button to hyphenate the story manually (Figure 3–78).

Figure 3–78

3

- When Publisher offers to hyphenate the street name, Dixon, click the No button because two letters would be left on the second line (Figure 3–79).

Q&A

Why is the text already hyphenated?

The default value is automatic hyphenation. Publisher hyphenates after standard syllables.

4

- As Publisher moves through the story, click the Yes or No button using the hyphenation rules listed previously.

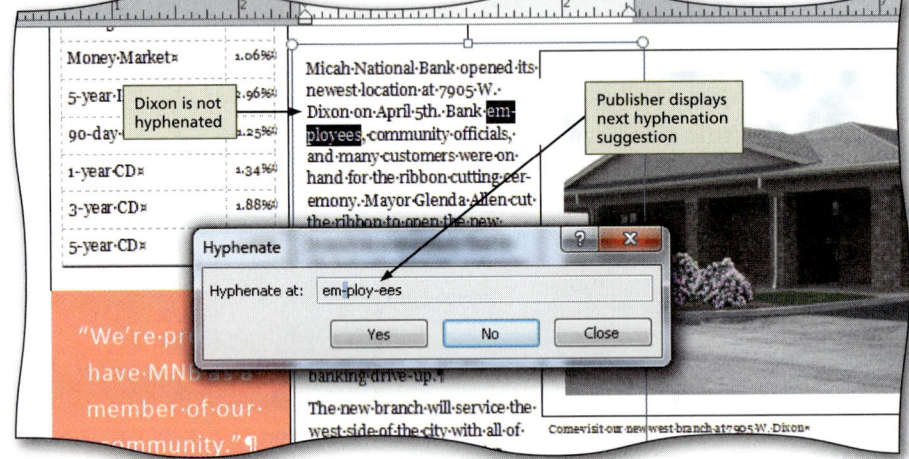

Figure 3–79

- When Publisher finishes highlighting the lead story and its continuation on page 3, manually hyphenate the other stories in the newsletter.

Other Ways
1. Press CTRL+SHIFT+H, click OK button

To Check the Newsletter for Spelling Errors

BTW

Spelling
Even if text is checked for spelling before it is imported, Publisher flags words, phrases, and punctuation not found in its dictionary. The process is worth the time it takes, but again, there is no substitute for proofreading the text yourself.

The following steps check the newsletter for spelling errors.

1 Click Review on the Ribbon to display the Review tab.

2 Click the Spelling button (Review tab | Proofing group) to start the spell checking process.

3 If Publisher flags, MNB, the initials of the bank, click the Ignore All button to ignore all occurrences of this text.

4 Click the Ignore button if Publisher flags any personal nouns or titles that are spelled correctly. If you have other errors, choose the appropriate measure to fix or ignore them.

5 Click the OK button in the Microsoft Publisher dialog box when the spelling check is complete.

To Check the Newsletter for Design Errors

In the following steps, Publisher checks for design errors throughout the newsletter.

1 Click File on the Ribbon to open the Backstage view. If necessary, click the Info tab.

2 Click the Run Design Checker button.

3 If the Design Checker finds errors, choose to fix or ignore them as necessary. When the Design Checker terminates, close the Design Checker task pane.

To Save the Revised Publication

The following step saves the publication again.

1 Click the Save button on the Quick Access Toolbar to save the file again with the same name, and in the same location.

Creating a Template

Newsletters typically retain their masthead, color scheme, font scheme, and other graphics from issue to issue. In a first issue, you must make design choices and implement them to make sure the newsletter is displayed correctly, which takes time and reviewing. You do not have to do all of that for subsequent issues. Once the decisions have been made and the publication has been distributed, you can reuse the same publication as a template.

Publisher saves templates in the My Templates folder for easy access from the Backstage view. When you open a saved template, a new publication is created from the template, so that users do not overwrite the template file. In lab situations, you should not save a personal template in the My Templates folder. You should save it on your own storage device and change the system properties to prevent overwriting, as shown in the next set of steps.

Saving the Template and Setting File Properties

Recall that in Chapter 1, you set file properties using the Properties command from the File menu. Two specific properties can be set at the time you save a publication or template. The author and tag properties can be entered into any of the Save As dialog boxes, which can save you several steps. A tag is a custom file property used to help you find and organize files. Although many properties are associated with files, tags often are the most useful because you can add words or phrases that make the files easier to find. Adding or changing properties of a file when you save it eliminates the need to find the file and apply properties afterward. Later, to find a file containing a tag, you can type tag words into the Search box of any Windows 7 folder.

To Create a Template with Property Changes

The steps on the next page create a template with property changes and save it on a USB flash drive. It is not recommended to save templates on lab computers or computers belonging to other people.

BTW

Storing Templates
On a business computer, for an organization that routinely uses templates, you should save templates in the default location. Templates stored in the default location (within the program data in a folder named, Templates) are displayed in the catalog when you click the My Templates button. Templates, however, can be stored in several places: on a personal computer, on a Web server, or on a common drive for use by multiple employees or students.

BTW

Tags
Tags are one of many file properties to help you find and organize the files. In addition to tags, other properties include the Date Modified, Author, and Subject. They become the keywords in the Properties dialog box. Unlike some predefined properties, tags can be anything you choose, such as "Brochures," "Vacation," or even "My Stuff."

1

- With a USB flash drive connected to one of the computer's USB ports, click File on the Ribbon to open the Backstage view.

- Click the Save As command to display the Save As dialog box.

- Type **Bank Newsletter Template** to change the name of the publication. Do not press the ENTER key.

- Click the 'Save as type' box arrow to display the list of file types (Figure 3–80).

🔎 **Experiment**

- Scroll through the many types of file formats available for publications.

Figure 3–80

2

- Click Publisher Template (*.pub) to choose to save the publication as a template.

- Navigate to your USB flash drive.

- If your name does not appear next to the word, Authors, in the lower portion of the dialog box, double-click the text and then type your name to replace the text.

- Click the Tags box and then type **monthly newsletter** to add the tag words (Figure 3–81). The current text in the Tags text box will disappear as you start to type.

Q&A What does the Change button do?

If you plan to create many templates, you can organize them into categories. Clicking the Change button displays a dialog box that allows you to create or navigate to categories of templates.

Figure 3–81

3

- Click the Save button to save the template.

To Print the Newsletter

If you have access to a printer that can accept 17 × 11.5 inch paper, you can print double-sided and then fold the paper to create the newsletter. If you want to print double-sided on 8.5 × 11 inch paper, the newsletter will print on the back and front of two pages that you then can staple. For a detailed example of the procedure summarized below, refer to pages 110 through 112 in Chapter 2.

The following steps print the newsletter.

1 Ready the printer according to the printer instructions. Click File on the Ribbon to open the Backstage view.

2 Click the Print tab in the Backstage view to display the Print gallery.

3 Make any necessary changes to the print settings for your paper size and duplex printing.

4 Click the Print button in the Print gallery to print the document.

5 When the printer stops, retrieve the printed document, as shown in Figure 3–1 on page PUB 135.

BTW

Quick Reference
For a table that lists how to complete the tasks covered in this book using the mouse, Ribbon, shortcut menu, and keyboard, see the Quick Reference Summary at the back of this book, or visit the Publisher 2010 Quick Reference Web page (scsite.com/pub2010/qr).

To Quit Publisher

This project is complete. The following steps quit Publisher.

1 To quit Publisher, click the Close button on the right side of the title bar.

2 If a Microsoft Publisher dialog box is displayed, click the Don't Save button so that any changes you have made are not saved.

Chapter Summary

In this chapter, you learned how to select template options for a newsletter, edit the masthead and sidebars, import stories, insert continued notices across pages, and create original stories using the Edit in Microsoft Word command. You inserted a pull quote, coupon, and pattern. In revising the newsletter, you used drag-and-drop editing techniques, hyphenated the stories, checked the spelling, and ran the Design Checker. The items listed below include all the new Publisher skills you have learned in this chapter.

1. Set Page Options (PUB 140)
2. Delete Pages from a Newsletter (PUB 143)
3. Add Pages to a Newsletter (PUB 143)
4. Edit the Masthead (PUB 143)
5. To Edit the Lead Story Headline (PUB 147)
6. Import a Text File (PUB 147)
7. Continue a Story across Pages (PUB 149)
8. Manually Continue the Story across Pages (PUB 151)
9. Format with Continued Notices (PUB 152)
10. Customize the Publisher Ribbon (PUB 157)
11. Edit a Story Using Word (PUB 159)
12. Format while Editing in Microsoft Word (PUB 161)
13. Quit Word and Return to Publisher (PUB 161)
14. Edit the Back Page Story (PUB 164)
15. Replace a Graphic Using the Shortcut Menu (PUB 166)
16. Select Adjacent Objects by Dragging (PUB 171)
17. Edit a Sidebar (PUB 173)
18. Insert a Pull Quote (PUB 175)
19. Insert Text in a Pull Quote (PUB 177)
20. Duplicate a Graphic (PUB 180)
21. Flip a Graphic (PUB 181)
22. Insert and Format a Coupon (PUB 182)
23. Drag and Drop Text (PUB 185)
24. Check Hyphenation (PUB 187)
25. Create a Template with Property Changes (PUB 189)

Learn It Online

Test your knowledge of chapter content and key terms.

Instructions: To complete the Learn It Online exercises, start your browser, click the Address bar, and then enter **scsite.com/pub2010/learn** as the Web address. When the Office 2010 Learn It Online page is displayed, click the link for the exercise you want to complete and then read the instructions.

Chapter Reinforcement TF, MC, and SA
A series of true/false, multiple choice, and short answer questions that test your knowledge of the chapter content.

Flash Cards
An interactive learning environment where you identify chapter key terms associated with displayed definitions.

Practice Test
A series of multiple choice questions that test your knowledge of chapter content and key terms.

Who Wants To Be a Computer Genius?
An interactive game that challenges your knowledge of chapter content in the style of a television quiz show.

Wheel of Terms
An interactive game that challenges your knowledge of chapter key terms in the style of the television show *Wheel of Fortune*.

Crossword Puzzle Challenge
A crossword puzzle that challenges your knowledge of key terms presented in the chapter.

Apply Your Knowledge

Reinforce the skills and apply the concepts you learned in this chapter.

Revising Text and Graphics in a Publication
Instructions: Start Publisher. Open the publication, Apply 3-1 Math Class Newsletter Draft, from the Data Files for Students. See the inside back cover of this book for instructions on downloading the Data Files for Students, or contact your instructor for more information about accessing the required files.

The publication you open is a two-page newsletter. You are to revise the publication as follows: enter the date in the masthead, import stories, use continued notices, insert a pull quote with text, insert a pattern, resize a graphic and flip it, and check the publication for errors. The revised publication is shown in Figure 3–82.

Perform the following tasks:
1. Enter the current date in the masthead.
2. Select the Lead Story Headline text and then type **A Note from Mr. Miller** as the new headline.
3. Click the lead story to select it. Click the Insert File button (Insert tab | Text group) and then navigate to the Data Files for Students. Insert the file named, Apply 3-1 Miller Note. When prompted, continue the story to the back page, at the bottom.
4. Delete the two empty text boxes for the back page story.
5. Right-click the remaining text box and then click Format Text Box on the shortcut menu. When the Format Text Box dialog box is displayed, click the Text Box tab, and then click the Include "Continued from page…" check box to select it. Click the OK button to close the Format Text Box dialog box.
6. Select the Back Page Story headline, and then type … **from Mr. Miller** as the new headline text.

7. Navigate to page 1 and right-click the third column of the lead story. Click Format Text Box on the shortcut menu. When the Format Text Box dialog box is displayed, click the Text Box tab, and then click the Include "Continued on page . . . " check box to select it.

8. For the secondary story, insert the file named Apply 3-1 Testing.

9. Type **Statewide Technology and Testing** to replace the title.

10. On page 2, for the story at the top of the page, import the file named Apply 3-1 Contact Information.

11. Use the Clip Art task pane and the search term, math, to find a picture related to math and insert it in the middle of page 2. Position the inserted graphic as shown in Figure 3–82.

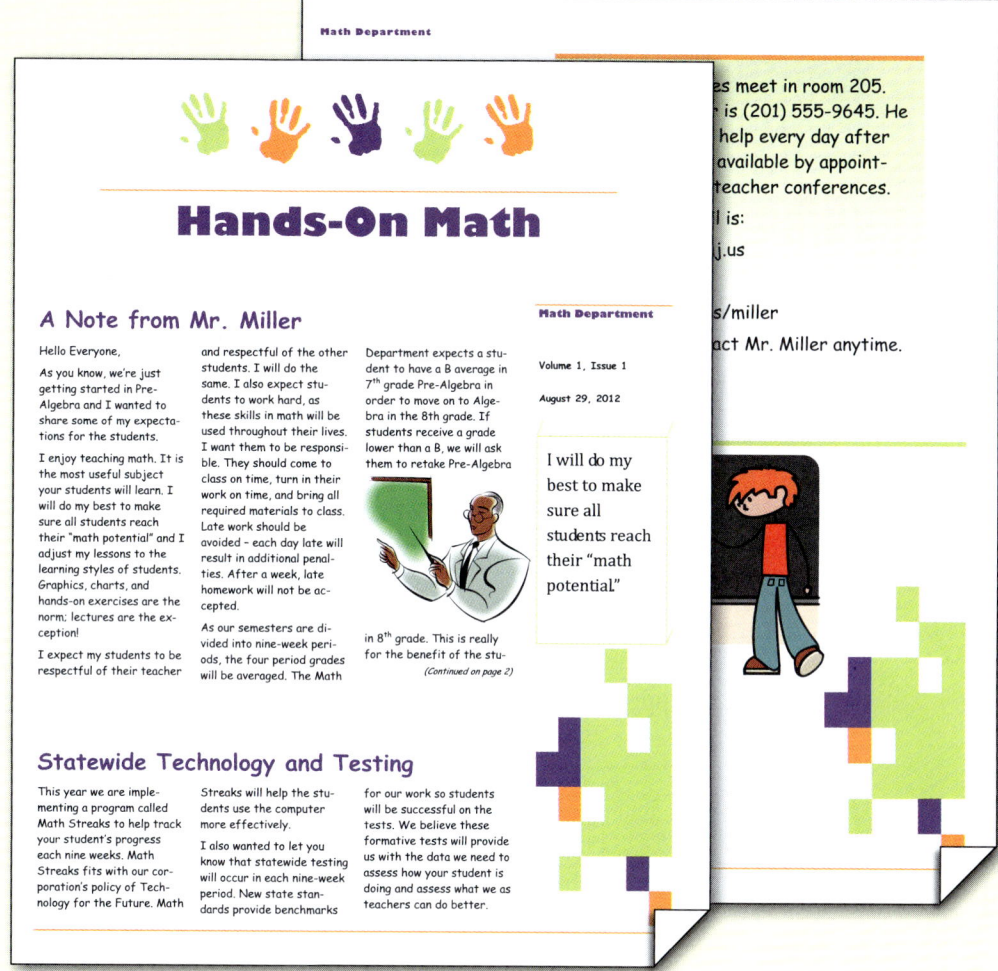

Figure 3–82

12. On page 1, delete the Special Points of Interest sidebar. Click the Page Parts button (Insert tab | Building Blocks group). Insert the Geometric pull quote from Page Parts, and position it as shown in Figure 3–82. Copy the phrase from the second paragraph of the lead story, I will do my best to make sure all students reach their "math potential", to replace the default text in the pull quote. Insert a period before the closing quotation mark.

13. Delete the Inside this Issue sidebar. Insert the Pixel Pattern pattern in its place. Resize the graphic to fill the area by dragging corner sizing handles.

14. Duplicate the pattern by CTRL+dragging the pattern's border into the workspace, to the right of the page layout. Navigate to page 2. Drag the duplicate from the workspace to a location in the lower-right corner of page 2.

15. Return to page 1. Click the lead story text, and then click the Hyphenation button (Text Box Tools tab | Text group). Hyphenate the story.

16. Run the publication through the Design Checker and check the spelling. Fix any errors you find. Choose to ignore names of people and businesses.

17. Change the publication properties as specified by your instructor.

18. Save the publication using the file name, Apply 3-1 Math Class Newsletter Modified.

19. Print the publication using duplex printing.

Extend Your Knowledge

Extend the skills you learned in this chapter and experiment with new skills. You may need to use Help to complete the assignment.

Working with Linked Text Boxes and Microsoft Word

Instructions: Start Publisher. Open the publication, Extend 3-1 Go Green Newsletter Draft, from the Data Files for Students. See the inside back cover of this book for instructions on downloading the Data Files for Students, or contact your instructor for more information about accessing the required files.

You will edit a newsletter to import stories, edit stories in Microsoft Word, unlink connected text boxes, and insert graphics (Figure 3–83).

Perform the following tasks:

1. Replace all graphics with graphics related to green technology and recycling.

2. Edit the lead story in Microsoft Word. Use bullets and indents to highlight the main topics. Use Microsoft Word Help to research the Increase Indent button (Word Ribbon | Home tab | Paragraph Group).

3. Return to Publisher and format the story with continued notices. (*Hint:* Use the next and previous arrow buttons to find the rest of the story.) Adjust the graphic to make the story wrap more neatly. Create an appropriate headline for the second part of the story on page 2.

4. Replace the caption with the words **Is your recycle bin full?** as the new text.

5. Use Publisher Help to research the Linking group on the Text Box Tools tab. Unlink the third column of the secondary story.

6. On page 2, in the empty text box at the top, insert the file named, Extend 3-1 Values.

7. Using drag-and-drop editing, invert the second and third paragraph.

8. Make other appropriate changes to the publication, such as inserting a graphic with a caption from the building blocks or searching for appropriate clip art using the Clip Art task pane.

9. Use the spelling and design checking features of Publisher.

10. Remove all Ribbon customization from the Ribbon, following the steps at the top of page PUB 162.

11. Save the newsletter with the file name, Extend 3-1 Go Green Newsletter Modified, and print the newsletter.

Figure 3–83

Make It Right

Analyze a publication and correct all errors and/or improve the design.

Fixing Overflow Errors

Instructions: Start Publisher. Open the publication, Make It Right 3-1 National Corps Newsletter, from the Data Files for Students. See the inside back cover of this book for instructions on downloading the Data Files for Students, or contact your instructor for more information about accessing the required files.

The publication is a newsletter that has stories in overflow, as shown in Figure 3–84. You are to link the overflow to text boxes on page 2, check the document for other errors, and hyphenate the stories.

Perform the following steps:

1. Run the Design Checker and find the first overflow error. Click the Text in Overflow button and link the story to a text box on page 2. Add continued notices. Hyphenate the story.

2. Find the next overflow error and continue that story to a different text box on page 2. Add continued notices. Edit the Back Page Story Headline to match the story. Hyphenate the story.

3. Fix any other design errors.

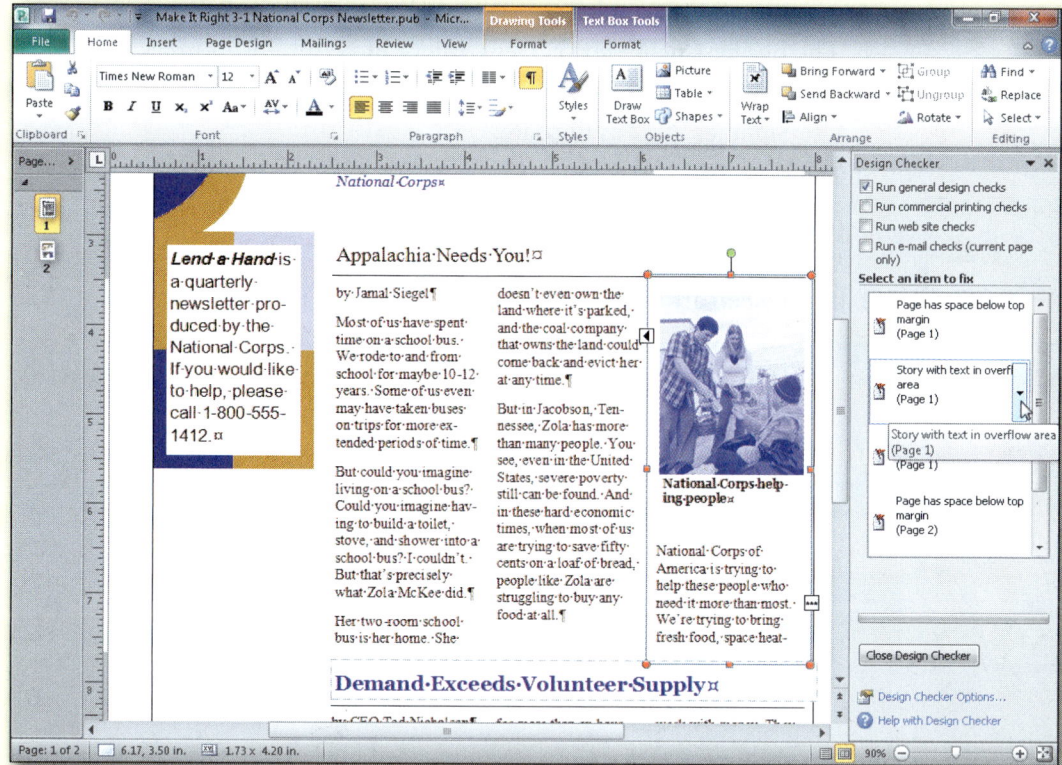

Figure 3–84

4. Check the spelling of the publication.
5. Change the publication properties as specified by your instructor.
6. Save the revised publication and then submit it in the format specified by your instructor.

In the Lab

Design and/or create a publication using the guidelines, concepts, and skills presented in this chapter. Labs are listed in order of increasing difficulty.

Lab 1: Creating a Newsletter Template

Problem: As a marketing intern with the Department of Natural Resources (DNR), you have been asked to create a template for a newsletter about white-water rafting in the state. The DNR wants a four-page newsletter, with space for several articles, a masthead, pictures with captions, and a sign-up form. If your supervisor approves your template, she will send you stories and pictures at a later date. She reminds you

Continued >

In the Lab *continued*

that this newsletter will be mailed, so you should leave sufficient space on the back for mailing information. You prepare a newsletter template similar to the one whose masthead is shown in Figure 3–85.

Perform the following tasks:

1. Start Publisher. Select the Waves newsletter template. Choose the Aqua color scheme and the Apex font scheme.

2. On page 1, click the Options button (Page Design tab | Template group). In the Page Options dialog box, choose the Mixed format. Change each of the inside pages to a Mixed format. On page 3, the right inside page, use the Page Options dialog box to insert a sign-up form. Do not change the page options on page 4.

3. Return to page 1 and edit the following:

   a. The title of the newsletter is White-Water Rafting.

   b. The business name text is Department of Natural Resources.

   c. Use Volume X and Issue X as the text in the template boxes, which will be replaced each month. Use Summer 2012 as the date.

   d. Delete the Special Points of Interest sidebar.

   e. Move the Inside this Issue sidebar to the bottom of the page. Edit the page number cells to reflect only four pages of articles.

   f. Insert a clip art image related to rafting.

4. On pages 2 and 3, replace the graphics with clip art related to water, rafting, and parks — even though you will be sent new pictures at a later time. Delete the organization logo.

5. On page 4, drag through all of the adjacent objects at the bottom of the page to select them. Press the DELETE key to delete the selected objects.

6. Run the Design Checker to fix any errors that may have occurred from your editing.

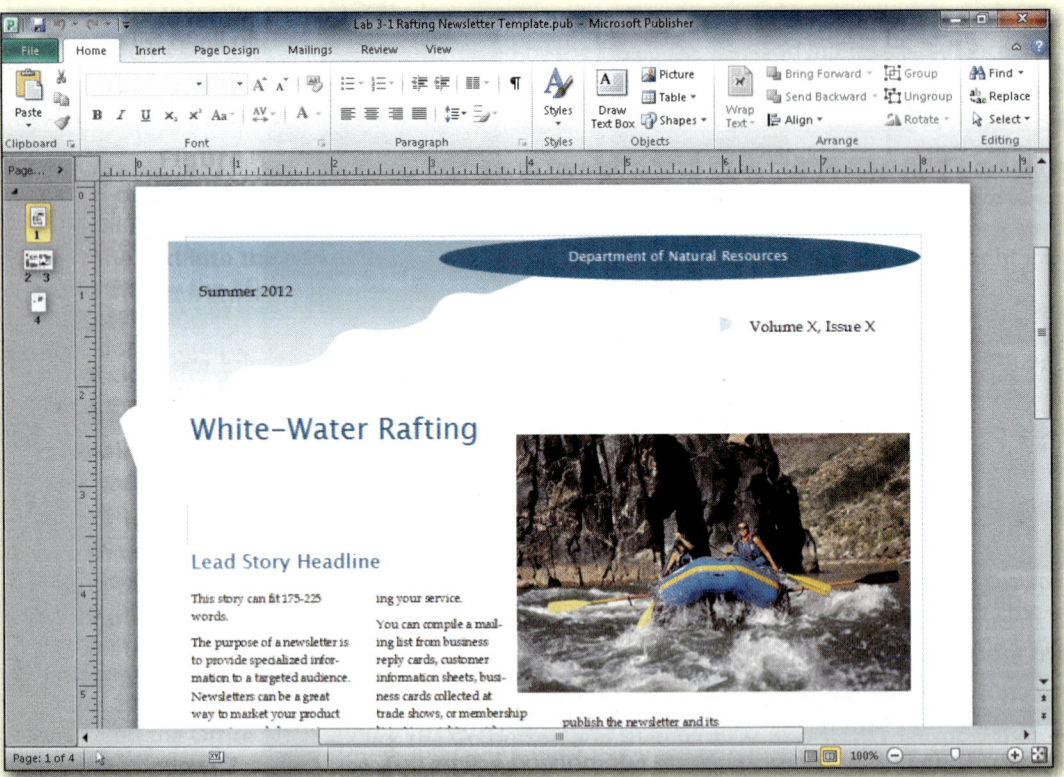

Figure 3–85

7. Change the publication properties as specified by your instructor.

8. Save the publication on a USB flash drive, using Lab 3-1 Rafting Newsletter Template as the file name. E-mail the newsletter as an attachment to your instructor.

In the Lab

Lab 2: Newsletter Analysis

Problem: Use a copy of a newsletter that you regularly receive, or obtain one from a friend, company, or school. Using the principles in this chapter, analyze the newsletter.

Instructions: Start Publisher. Open the publication, Lab 3-2 Newsletter Analysis Table, from the Data Files for Students. See the inside back cover of this book for instructions on downloading the Data Files for Students, or contact your instructor for more information about accessing the required files. Use the skills you learned in editing sidebars to fill in each of the empty cells in the table as it applies to your selected newsletter. The topics to look for are listed below:

- Purpose
- Audience
- Paper
- Distribution
- Font and color scheme

- Consistency
- Alignment
- Repeated elements
- Continued notices and ease of navigation
- Sidebars, pull quotes, patterns, etc.

Print the publication and attach a copy of the newsletter. Turn in both to your instructor.

In the Lab

Lab 3: Creating a Masthead

Problem: You and your friends belong to a role-playing game club. To spread the word and attract new members, you are thinking of creating a Web site with news and articles about the club. You have decided to use building block items to design a masthead and save it as a Web page. You prepare the masthead shown in Figure 3–86.

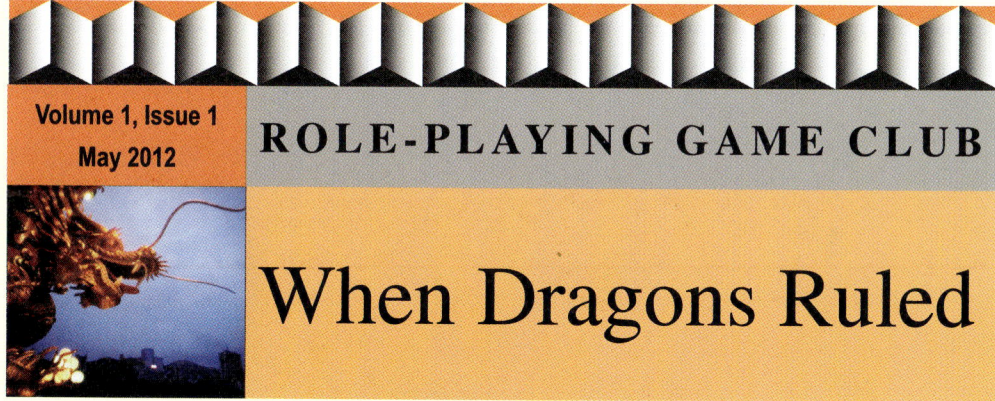

Figure 3–86

Instructions: Start Publisher and choose the Blank 8.5 × 11" template. Choose the Aspect Color Scheme (Page Design tab | Schemes group). Using the Building Blocks group on the Insert tab, insert a Bellows bar from Borders and Accents. Insert the Fall heading from Page Parts. Select the graphic only, and then replace it with a clip art image related to the term, dragon. Edit the text to match Figure 3–86. Save the publication on a USB flash drive, using Lab 3-3 Game Club Masthead as the file name. Using the techniques from Chapter 1 on pages PUB 48 through PUB 49, use the Publish HTML command on the Save & Send tab in the Backstage view to save the masthead as a Single File Web Page (MHTML).

Cases and Places

Apply your creative thinking and problem-solving skills to design and implement a solution.

Note: To complete these assignments, you may be required to use the Data Files for Students. See the inside back cover of this book for instructions on downloading the Data Files for Students, or contact your instructor for information about accessing the required files.

1: Create a Band Booster Quarterly Newsletter

Academic

A two-page newsletter will be sent to band students, parents, and other interested parties. Use the Rhythm template, the Concourse color scheme, and the Literary font scheme. The name of the newsletter is *High Notes*. Use Austin Meadows High School as the business name. For the lead story, import the file named, Case 3-1 Spring Fling. For the secondary story, include the headline, Band Member of the Month, and leave the default text, because the story will be completed at a later time. For the back page story, import the file named, Case 3-1 Auditions, and then change the headline. Include a sidebar with upcoming performances: Spring Concert May 17, Drumming Up Business May 24, and Graduation June 2. Use another sidebar to display reminders: Turn in your marching uniform, Pay your cleaning fee, and Sign out summer instruments. Use appropriate clip art. Save the newsletter as a template for the band boosters to use in the future. For extra credit on this assignment, create a list of instructions for template users.

2: Create a Restaurant Review Newsletter

Personal

You are a member of a restaurant and food review club. Because you have a background in desktop publishing, you prepare the monthly two-page newsletter for club members. Your assignment is to design the newsletter and develop the next issue. The newsletter should have a feature article and some announcements for club members. Your feature article could discuss/review a restaurant, a deli, an online or local grocery store, a recipe, or any other aspect of food or food service. Use the Internet, visit a restaurant, interview restaurant or grocery store patrons, prepare a dish using a new recipe, and so on, to obtain information for the article and announcements. The feature article should be continued on page 2. Enhance the newsletter with color and font schemes, graphics, sidebars, and pull quotes.

3: Create an Organization Newsletter

Professional

Use the Blends Newsletter template, the Wildflower color scheme, and the Capital font scheme to create a two-page newsletter for the local food pantry. For the newsletter title, use The Pantry Shelf, and place today's date in the masthead. Import the Case 3-3 Award file for the lead story, and change the title. For the secondary story, import the file named, Case 3-3 Counseling Center, and then change the headline. For the back page story, import the file named Case 3-3 Thanksgiving, and then change the headline. Replace all placeholder text with the text from Table 3–3. On page 1, create a sidebar and pull quote with the text from Table 3–3. Delete pages 2 and 3. On the back page, create an attention getter with the text from Table 3–3. Replace the graphics with suitable pictures using the Clip Art task pane.

Table 3–3	
Location	**Text**

Page 1 sidebar	Dates to Remember
	• Shop and Share
	  Fund-Raiser/Food Mart
	  November 9
	• Food Drop Off
	  Pie Baking Day
	  November 17
	• Thanksgiving baskets
	  November 19-22

Page 1 pull quote	"2012 Guardian Award Presented to Antoine Beal For his dedication and faithful service to the Community Pantry and the people it serves."
Business Tagline or Motto	The Community Pantry is open to people of all nationalities, races, and creeds.
Business Name	The Community Pantry
Address	1248 Howard Avenue Snow Hill, IL 61998
Phone, Fax, and E-mail	Telephone: 312-555-9876 Hours: Monday through Saturday, 8:00 a.m. to 8:00 p.m.
Attention Getter	Charitable donations totaled $70,000 last month. Thank you!

4 Creating a Custom Publication from Scratch

Objectives

You will have mastered the material in this chapter when you can:

- Create a custom publication size
- Create a color scheme
- Create a font scheme
- Rotate and flip objects
- Crop a graphic and edit the wrap points
- Recolor a graphic
- Select and group multiple objects
- Save an edited graphic as a picture
- Insert a shape

- Format an object with a gradient fill, differentiating among text, patterns, pictures, tints, and shades
- Fill a shape with a picture, and edit the shape outline, weight, and color
- Add to and delete from the Building Block Library
- Apply styles
- Create columns within a text box
- Close a publication without quitting Publisher
- Delete custom sizes and schemes

4 | Creating a Custom Publication from Scratch

Introduction

Customizing publications, tailored to a specific organization with font schemes, color schemes, page dimensions, and margins, allows desktop publishers to be more creative and provide made-to-order publications for their clients. The process of developing a publication that communicates a company brand and specific requirements requires careful analysis and planning. Coordinating design choices with the customer and gathering required information will determine the design and style that will be most successful in delivering the company's message. Whether you are creating a publication from scratch or using a template, many settings and preferences can be customized and saved. Once saved, the settings can be reused, which results in increased productivity.

Project — Newspaper Advertisement

Newspaper advertising is one of the more popular advertising media for small businesses, allowing the companies to focus on a specific customer base at a lower cost than other media. Newspaper ads especially are useful for selling to a general market, because nearly all segments of the population have access to newspapers. Even though newspapers are no longer the exclusive source of news that they once were, the print and Web versions of newspapers reach a large audience. Customized, eye-appealing advertisements with catchy graphics become a good source of leads for a small business.

To illustrate some of the customizable features of Microsoft Publisher, this project presents a series of steps to create a 1/8-page newspaper advertisement for a small computer repair business. A customized color scheme with black text and blue and red secondary colors represents the company colors. A customized font scheme will include the OCR A Std Font for headings and a secondary font of Garamond for body text.

The graphic in the upper-left corner combines two pieces of clip art and then uses the combined image to fill a graphical shape, repeating the color scheme.

With a gradient in the background, information at the top of the advertisement provides the company's name, address, telephone and fax numbers, and Web site address. A two-column bulleted list presents the services. Finally, a WordArt object with a reflective shadow announces free estimates at the bottom of the page, as shown in Figure 4–1.

Figure 4–1

Overview

As you read this chapter, you will learn how to create the publication shown in Figure 4–1 by performing these general tasks:

- Select a new blank publication size and specify the page layout.
- Create custom color and font schemes.
- Edit, arrange, group, and save graphics as pictures.
- Insert and format shapes using fill effects.
- Customize the Building Block Library.
- Apply styles.
- Create columned text boxes.
- Use WordArt to create decorative text.

**Plan
Ahead**

General Project Guidelines

When creating a Publisher publication from scratch, the actions you perform and decisions you make will affect the appearance and characteristics of the finished publication. As you create publications, such as the project shown in Figure 4–1 on the previous page, you should follow these general guidelines:

1. **Decide on the purpose, schemes, and paper size.** Define the purpose of the publication. Does it fill a need for the customer? Decide if a template would be a better choice than starting from scratch. Design color and font schemes that are suitable for the customer. Research publications that are similar to the one you have decided to create from scratch. Choose a size that is compatible with others used in the industry.

2. **Choose a layout and elements.** Carefully consider the necessary elements and their placement. Choose margins and a paper size that will help standardize the publication. Decide whether to add dated material or prices. Think about alignment of elements and proximity of similar data. Create appropriate contrast or repetition when using fonts and colors.

3. **Create the publication.** Gather all the necessary components, such as information about the business, text, and graphics. Check and double-check all business information. Make decisions about formatting such as headings, formatted text, columns, and decorative text. Proofread, revise, and add the final touches. Revise as necessary and then use the spelling, grammar, and design checking features of the software.

When necessary, more specific details concerning the above guidelines are presented at appropriate points in the chapter. The chapter also will identify the actions performed and decisions made regarding these guidelines during the creation of the edited photo shown in Figure 4–1 on the previous page.

To Start Publisher

The following steps, which assume Windows 7 is running, start Publisher based on a typical installation. You may need to ask your instructor how to start Publisher for your computer. For a detailed example of the procedure summarized below, refer to the Office 2010 and Windows 7 chapter.

1 Click the Start button on the Windows 7 taskbar to display the Start menu.

2 Type `Microsoft Publisher` as the search text in the 'Search programs and files' text box, and watch the search results appear on the Start menu.

3 Click Microsoft Publisher 2010 in the search results on the Start menu to start Publisher and open the Backstage view.

4 If the Publisher window is not maximized, click the Maximize button next to the Close button on its title bar to maximize the window.

Creating a Custom-Sized Publication

Newspapers are available in many sizes, as are their advertisements. **Broadsheet** is a term used to describe a familiar newspaper format that is approximately 22 inches long and at least 11 inches wide when folded into a newspaper page, although other sizes are common. Broadsheet usually has .5-inch margins, 6 1.5-inch columns, and anywhere from .125- to .25-inch **gutters**, which are the spaces between columns. Most newspapers offer advertising space that is measured using a representation of the number of columns multiplied by the number of vertical inches. In the broadsheet format, a 1/8-page advertisement would be 3 columns wide (approximately 5.25 inches) by 5 inches tall with 1/8-inch (or .125-inch) margins.

> **Decide on the purpose, schemes, and paper size.** Discuss the purpose of the publication with others who have a vested interest. Choose a font scheme and color scheme to match the customer's logo or company colors. Define which pieces of business information you plan to use. Does the proposed publication fulfill the need? If you are working from scratch, look at similar publication templates. Choose margins and a paper size that will help standardize the publication with others used in the industry.

Plan
Ahead

To Select a Blank Publication

When you first start Publisher, the New template gallery displays a list of templates and blank publications. Most users select a publication template and then begin editing. It is not always the case, however, that a template will fit every situation. Sometimes you want to think through a publication while manipulating objects on a blank page, trying different shapes, colors, graphics, and effects. Other times you may have specific goals for a publication, such as size or orientation, that do not match any of the templates. For these cases, Publisher provides **blank publications** with no preset objects or design, allowing you to start from scratch.

The following step selects an 8.5 × 11" blank print publication.

1
- Click the Blank 8.5 × 11" thumbnail in the New template gallery to create a blank publication in the Publisher window (Figure 4–2).

Figure 4–2

To Collapse the Page Navigation Pane

Because the advertisement you are creating is a single page, collapsing the Page Navigation pane will give you more room in the Publisher workspace. The following step collapses the Page Navigation pane.

1 Click the Page Number button (Figure 4–2 on page PUB 205) on the status bar to collapse the Page Navigation pane.

To Create a Custom Page Size

The following steps create a new, custom page size based on the requirements of a 1/8-page advertisement using broadsheet sizes. Publisher and other Office applications use the term **page setup** to refer to the process of changing the margins, orientation, and size, among other settings.

1
- Display the Page Design tab.

- Click the Page Size button (Page Design tab | Page Setup group) to display the list of standard page sizes and options for other sizes (Figure 4–3).

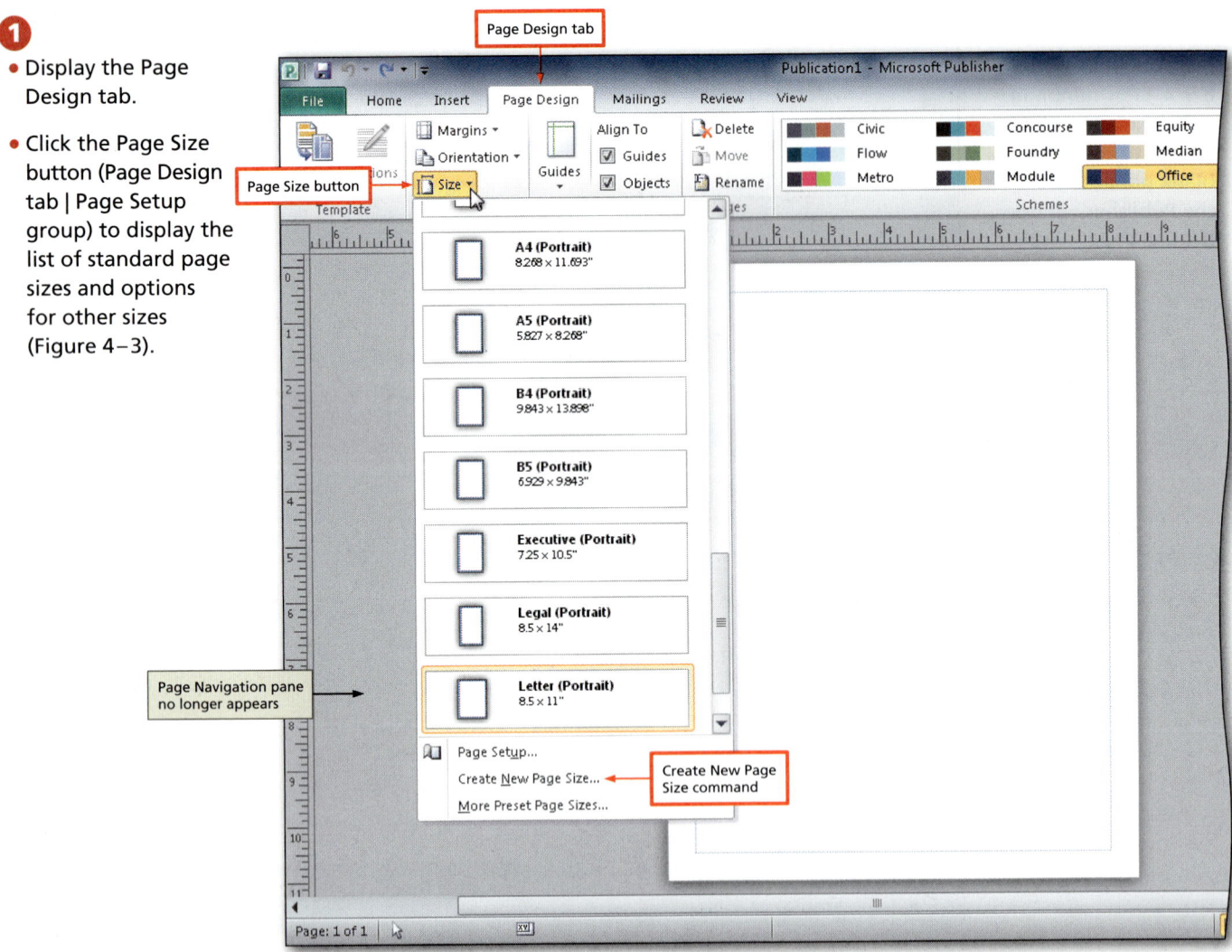

Figure 4–3

2

• Click Create New Page Size at the bottom of the list to display the Create New Page Size dialog box.

• In the Name text box, type **1/8 Page Advertisement** (Create New Page Size dialog box) to name the custom size.

• Click the Layout type box arrow to display the list of layouts (Figure 4–4).

How does the Create New Page Size command differ from the Page Setup command?

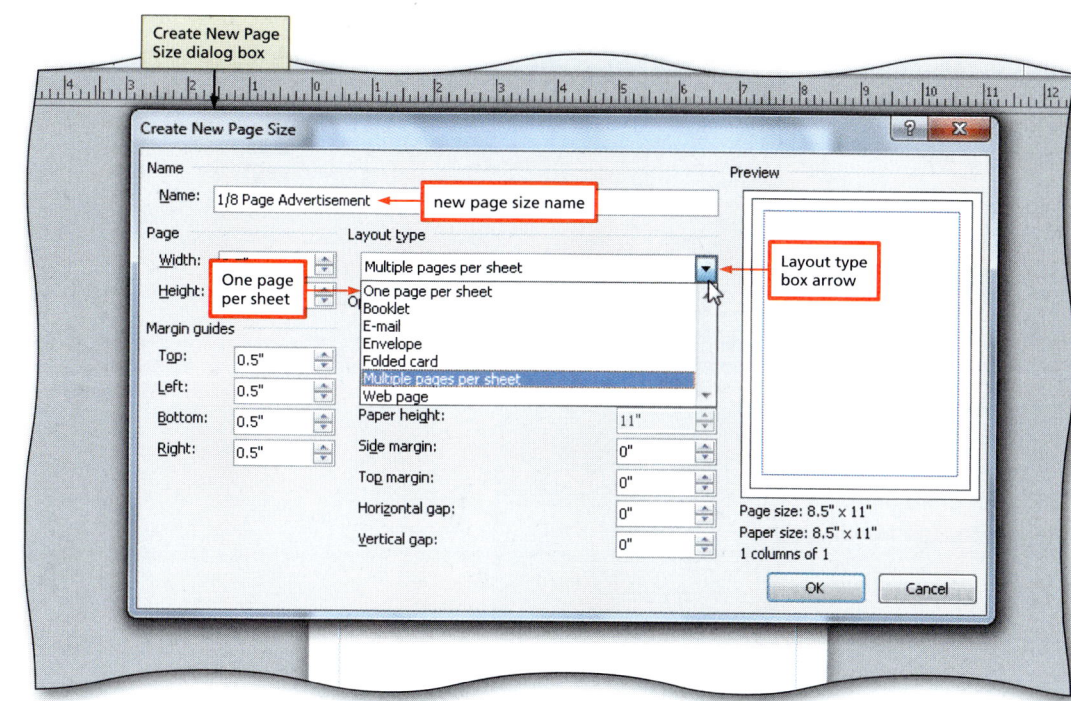

Figure 4–4

When you create a new page size, a new thumbnail will appear in the New template gallery every time you start Publisher, which allows you to reuse the page size for other publications. Page Setup affects only the current publication.

3

• Click 'One page per sheet' to display the settings associated with single publications on a sheet of paper.

• Select the text in the Width box and then type **5.5** to set the width for the advertisement.

• Select the text in the Height box and then type **5** to set the height for the advertisement.

• One at a time, select the text in each of the four Margin guide boxes and type **.125** to create a 1/8-inch margin on each side of the advertisement (Figure 4–5).

Is there any easier way to replace the text in consecutive boxes?

In most dialog boxes, you can press the TAB key, which will move the insertion point to the next box and select the text at the same time.

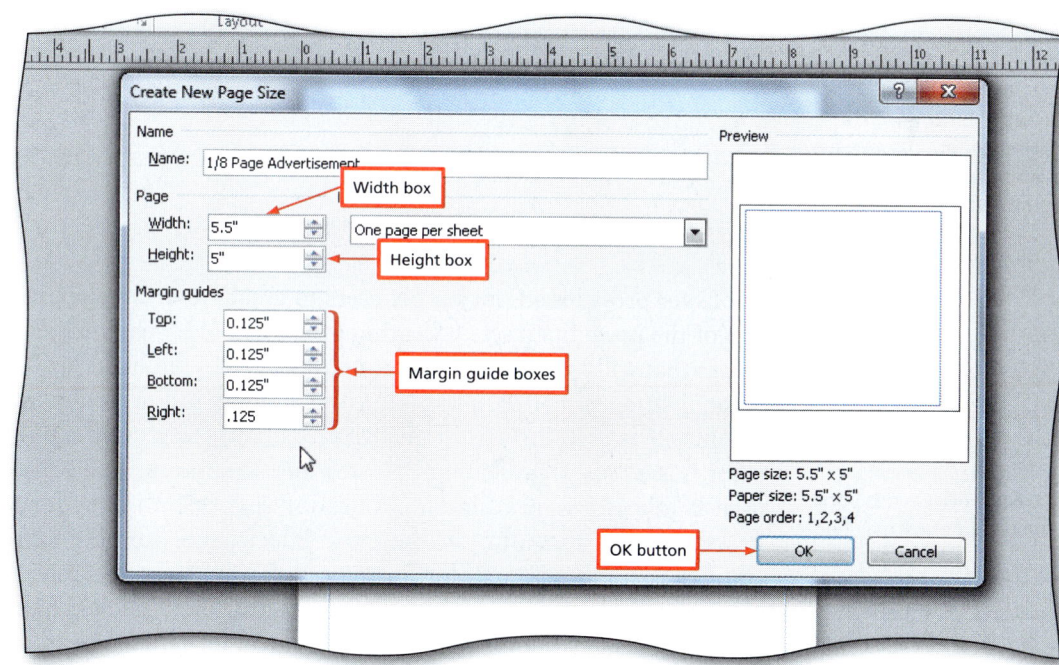

Figure 4–5

4

- Click the OK button to save the page layout, size, and margins (Figure 4–6).

Q&A

Where will the custom layout be saved?

The layout will appear in the New template gallery when you first start Publisher, or when you click New in the Backstage view. To view custom sizes, click the More Blank Page Sizes thumbnail.

Figure 4–6

Custom Color Schemes

Publisher provides an option for users to create their own color schemes rather than using one of the predefined sets. Creating a custom color scheme means choosing your own colors that will be applied to text and objects in a publication. You may choose one main color, five accent colors, a hyperlink color, and a followed hyperlink color. The main color commonly is used for text in major eye-catching areas of the publication. The first accent color is used for graphical lines, boxes, and separators. The second accent color typically is used as fill color in prominent publication shapes. Subsequent accent colors may be used in several ways, including shading, text effects, and alternate font color. The hyperlink color is used as the font color for hyperlink text. After clicking a hyperlink, its color changes to show users which path, or trail, they have clicked previously.

Once a custom color scheme is created, its name appears at the top of the Color scheme list and gallery. The chosen colors also will appear in the galleries related to shapes, fills, and outlines.

To Create a New Color Scheme

The advertisement will use accent colors of blue and red, as well as a black main color for text. The following steps create a custom color scheme.

1
- Click the More button (Page Design tab | Schemes group) to display the Colors Scheme gallery (Figure 4–7).

Q&A What is the default color scheme?

Typical installations use Office as the default color scheme.

Figure 4–7

2
- Click Create New Color Scheme in the Color Scheme gallery to display the Create New Color Scheme dialog box.

- Type **Computer First Aid** in the Color scheme name text box (Create New Color Scheme dialog box) to name the color scheme with the same name as the company (Figure 4–8).

Q&A What if I do not enter a name for the modified color scheme?

Publisher assigns a name that begins with the letters, Custom, followed by a number (i.e., Custom 8).

Figure 4–8

3

- In the Scheme colors area, click the second New box arrow, which corresponds to the Accent 1 color to display a gallery of color choices (Figure 4–9).

Q&A

What colors are displayed when you click the New box arrow?

Publisher presents 40 of the common printing colors for desktop printers in a small gallery or palette. You can click the More Colors command in the gallery to display the Colors dialog box, where you can choose other colors, create your own colors by entering color numbers, or choose a publishing color system, such as **Pantone**, a popular color system for professional printing.

Figure 4–9

4

- Click Dark Teal to select the Accent 1 color.

- Click the Accent 2, New box arrow and then click Red to select the Accent 2 color (Figure 4–10).

Q&A

Can I delete a color scheme once I create it?

Yes. To delete a color scheme, first display the list of color schemes, and then right-click the custom color scheme. Click Delete Scheme on the shortcut menu.

5

- Click the Save button to save the new color scheme.

Q&A

Where is the new color scheme stored?

Each color scheme that you create will appear at the top of the gallery, alphabetized by name (shown in Figure 4–11).

Figure 4–10

Custom Font Schemes

Publisher provides an option for users to create their own font schemes rather than using one of the predefined sets. Creating a **custom font scheme** means choosing your own fonts to use in a publication. You may choose one heading font and one body font. Choosing complementary fonts takes practice. In general, either the heading font and body font should match exactly but perhaps appear in different sizes; or, the two fonts should contrast with each other dramatically in features such as size, type ornamentation, and direction. **Type ornamentation** refers to serif, structure, form, or style.

Custom font schemes contain a name that will appear in the font scheme list. The chosen fonts also will appear in the Styles list. The body font will be the default font for new text boxes.

To Create a New Font Scheme

Because the company involves a highly technical service, a customized font scheme will include the OCR A Std font that simulates the kind of font read by optical character recognition (OCR) devices. A secondary font of Garamond provides a nice font contrast with the OCR A Std font used in the headings. Garamond is a TrueType font with serifs, which is easily legible in print publications. **TrueType** refers to scalable fonts that produce high-quality characters on both computer screens and printers.

The following steps create a custom font scheme.

1
- Click the Scheme Fonts button (Page Design tab | Schemes group) to display the Scheme Fonts gallery (Figure 4–11).

Q&A

What is the default font scheme?

Typical installations use Office 1 as the default font scheme.

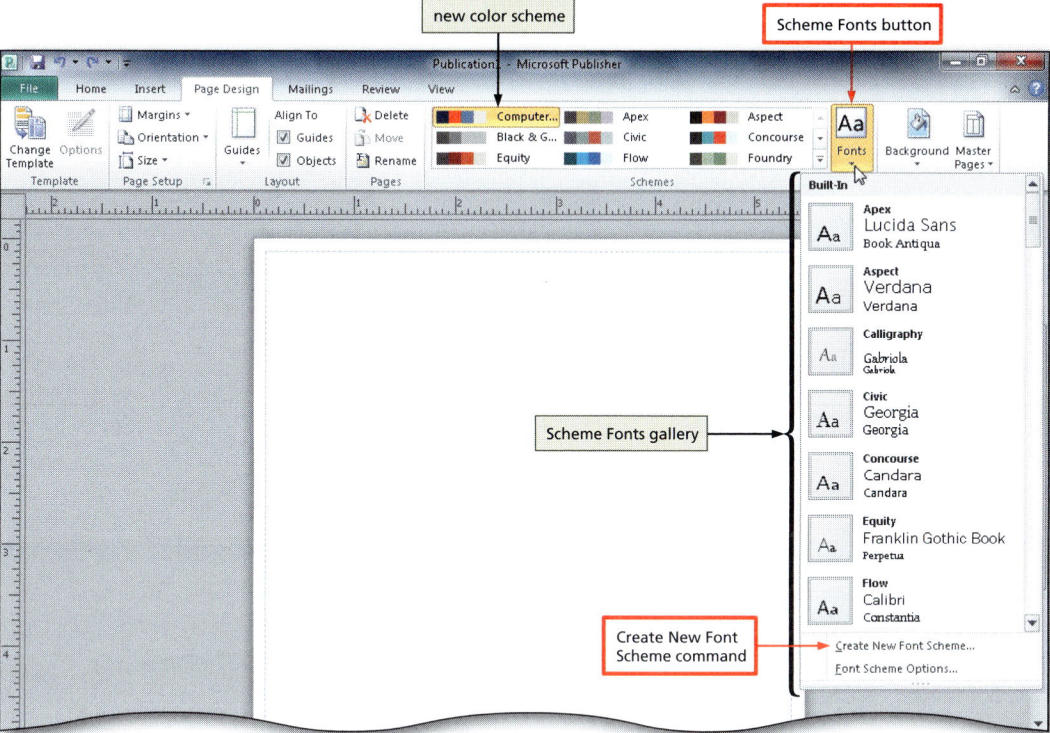

Figure 4–11

2
- Click Create New Font Scheme in the Scheme Fonts gallery to display the Create New Font Scheme dialog box.

- Type **Computer First Aid** in the 'Font scheme name' text box (Create New Font Scheme dialog box) to name the font scheme with the same name as the company (Figure 4–12).

Figure 4–12

3

- Click the Heading font box arrow to display the list of fonts (Figure 4–13).

 Experiment

- Click different fonts in the Heading font list and watch the text in the Sample box change (Create New Font Scheme dialog box).

Figure 4–13

4

- Scroll as necessary and then click the OCR A Std font or a similar font to select it.

- Click the Body font box arrow and then click Garamond to select the body font (Figure 4–14).

Q&A Can I delete a font scheme once I create it?

Yes. To delete a font scheme, display the list of font schemes and right-click the custom font scheme. Click Delete Scheme on the shortcut menu. You also can rename or duplicate the scheme.

Figure 4–14

5

- Click the Save button to save the new font scheme.

Q&A Where is the new font scheme stored?

Each font scheme that you create will appear at the top of the Font Scheme gallery, alphabetized by name.

Plan Ahead   **Choose a layout and elements.** Work with the customer to create the necessary elements. Consider the graphics carefully. Do not use copyrighted materials. If you create objects from scratch or edit graphics, have the customer approve the graphics before proceeding with the publication. Remember that dated material and prices will shorten the shelf life of the publication.

As you place items on the page, place similar items together; for example, the address and telephone number should be in close proximity.

Editing Graphics

Recall that you have inserted graphics or pictures into publications by choosing them from the Clip Art task pane and by importing them from a file. Graphics add value and visual flair to publications; however, to create a unique publication for a business, it is good to enhance and customize the graphic through editing. Many times customers are bored by stock graphics and clip art because of their overuse. A well-edited graphic not only contributes to the uniqueness of the publication; it also adds a personal touch. Publications with edited graphics do not look rigid or computer-generated. The graphic for the Computer First Aid company is a picture of a sickly face on a monitor, inside a red cross shape. First, you will insert a picture, crop it, flip it, and then group it with a recolored and scaled clip art illustration. Finally, you will save the graphic and place it inside a cross shape, with an outline color from the color scheme.

BTW

Scaling
The term, **scaling**, when it applies to graphics, means changing the vertical or horizontal size of the graphic by a percentage. Scaling can create interesting graphic effects. Caricature drawings and intentionally distorted photographs routinely use scaling. When used for resizing, scaling is appropriate to make a graphic fit in tight places.

To Insert a Picture

The following steps insert a picture into the publication. The picture is available on the Data Files for Students. See the inside back cover of this book for instructions on downloading the Data Files for Students, or contact your instructor for information about accessing the required files.

1 Insert the USB flash drive that contains the Data Files for Students into one of the computers' USB ports.

2 Display the Insert tab.

3 Click the Insert Picture from File button (Insert tab | Illustrations group) to display the Insert Picture dialog box.

4 Navigate to your USB storage location or the location of the Data Files for Students on your system.

5 Double-click the folder labeled Chapter 04 to display the files in the folder.

6 Double-click the Computer System file to insert the picture into the publication (Figure 4–15).

Computer System picture

Figure 4–15

Contrast and Brightness
You can increase the contrast or brightness of a graphic. **Contrast** is the saturation or intensity of the color — the higher the contrast percentage, the more intense the color. **Brightness** is the amount of black or white added to the color — the higher the brightness percentage, the more white is added.

Rotating and Flipping Objects

When you **rotate** an object in Publisher, you turn it so that the top of the object faces a different direction. For example, a picture of a person could be rotated to look like that person was standing on his or her head. Each selected object in Publisher displays a green rotation handle used to rotate the object freely. To rotate in 15-degree increments, hold down the SHIFT key while dragging the rotation handle. To rotate an object on its base, hold down the CTRL key and drag the green rotation handle — the object will rotate in a circle by pivoting around the handle. You can enter other rotation percentages in the Format dialog box that appears when you click the Format AutoShape: Size button (Picture Tools Format tab | Size group).

Publisher also allows you to **flip** objects. For example, a picture of a person facing left could be flipped horizontally so that it would appear that the person is facing right.

To Flip a Picture

The following steps flip the picture horizontally.

1

- If necessary, display the Picture Tools Format tab.

- With the picture still selected, click the Rotate button (Picture Tools Format tab | Arrange group) to display the Rotate gallery (Figure 4–16).

Experiment

- Point to each rotation and flip option and watch how the graphic changes in the page layout.

Figure 4–16

2

• Click Flip Horizontal in the Rotate gallery to flip the picture horizontally (Figure 4–17).

Q&A

What does Free Rotate mean?

The Free Rotate command places green rotation handles on each of the four corners of a selected object. As you drag a rotation handle, the graphic rotates while keeping the center of the graphic in the same place on the page. Pressing the CTRL key while you rotate a corner handle keeps the opposite corner in the same place on the page and rotates around it.

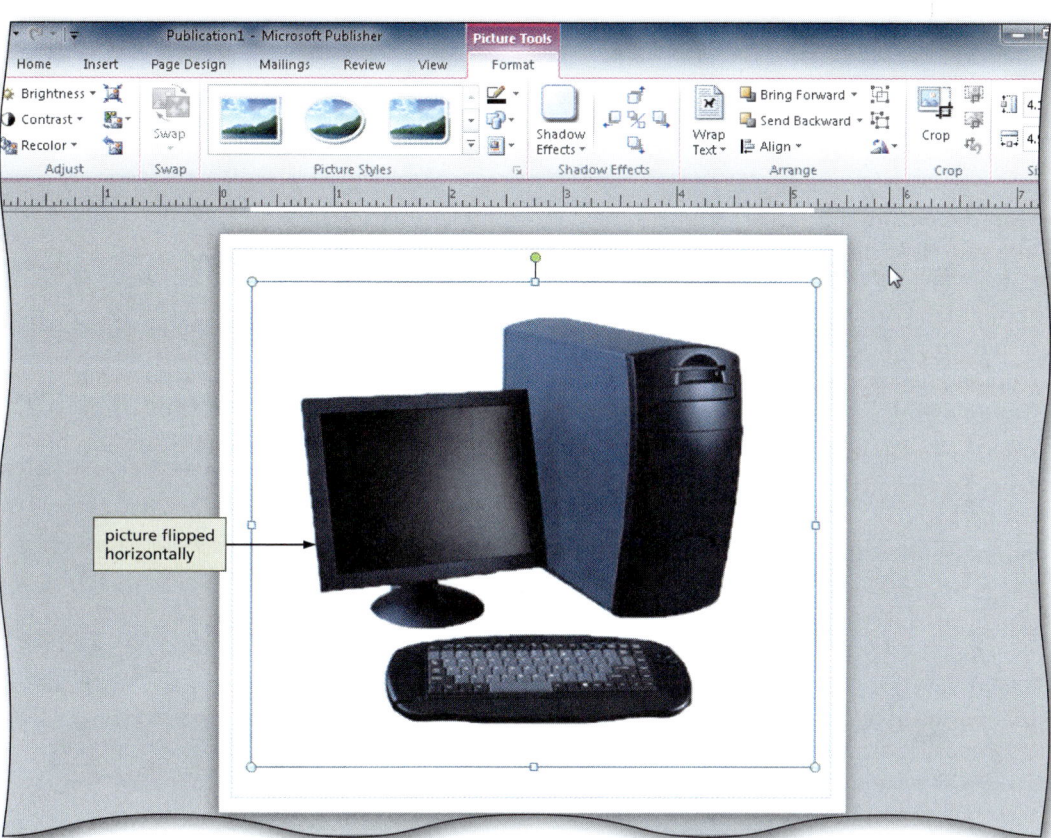

picture flipped horizontally

Figure 4–17

Other Ways

1. Select object, drag rotation handle	rotation percentage on Measurement toolbar	menu, click Size tab (Format Picture dialog box), enter rotation percentage
2. Click Object Position button on status bar, enter	3. Right-click graphic, click Format Picture on shortcut	

Cropping Graphics

If a graphic is too large to fit in the space you designated for it, or if you want to display only a portion of a graphic, Publisher allows you to **crop**, or trim, the vertical or horizontal edges. People crop graphics to focus attention on a particular area and remove background clutter. Other Crop tools include Fit, Fill, and Clear Crop (Figure 4–18). If your picture is larger or smaller than the picture area, clicking the Fit button (Picture Tools Format tab | Crop group) will let you resize the picture while maintaining the original aspect ratio. To fill a picture area while maintaining the original aspect ratio you can use the Fill button. Finally, if you change your mind, you can undo the crop, fit, or fill by clicking the Clear Crop button.

BTW

Cropping vs. Resizing
Cropping is different from resizing. Both techniques reduce the overall size of the graphic display; however, with cropping you eliminate part of the graphic from the display while maintaining the size of the objects in the picture. With resizing, the entire graphic becomes smaller or larger. For additional editing possibilities, you can resize a cropped graphic or crop a resized graphic. If you want to undo a cropping effect, you can click the Reset Picture button (Picture Tools Format tab | Adjust group).

Figure 4–18

To Crop a Graphic

The computer system picture has a keyboard and system unit that are not needed in the final display. The following steps crop the graphic.

• With the picture still selected, click the Crop button (Picture Tools Format tab | Arrange group) to display the cropping handles (Figure 4–19).

Q&A How do you use the other commands in the list?

The Fit command places the entire, original graphic within the cropping handle dimensions, even if that means creating a disproportional image. The Fill command places the original graphic within the cropping handles maintaining proportions, which sometimes means a slight cropping occurs if the cropping handle dimensions are not the same shape as the original. The Clear Crop command resets the graphic to its original size and dimension with no cropping. The commands become enabled after an initial crop.

Figure 4–19

• Drag the lower-center cropping handle upward to crop out the keyboard (Figure 4–20).

Experiment

• Drag the side and corner crop handles back and forth at different magnifications to see how much Publisher crops from the graphic.

Q&A How do you use the other commands in the list?

The Fit command places the entire, original graphic within the cropping handle dimensions, even if that means creating a disproportional image. The Fill command places the original graphic within the cropping handles maintaining proportions, which sometimes means a slight cropping occurs if the cropping handle dimensions are not the same shape as the original. The Clear Crop command resets the graphic to its original size and dimension with no cropping. The commands become enabled after an initial crop.

Figure 4–20

● Drag the upper-right cropping handle toward the center to crop out as much of the system unit as possible, without cropping any of the monitor (Figure 4–21).

Q&A

Why did the mouse pointer change?

When the cropping button is selected, the cropping mouse pointer appears as a pushpin.

● Click the Crop button (Picture Tools Format tab | Arrange group) to hide the cropping handles.

Other Ways

1. Right-click graphic, click Crop button on Mini toolbar, drag handles

2. Right-click graphic, click Format Picture, click Picture tab (Format Picture dialog box), enter Crop from measurements

Figure 4–21

To Edit Wrap Points

Cropping removes portions of graphics in rectangular segments. Because of this, sometimes a crop does not crop out all of the fine details or slanted items that you wish to remove from the graphic. In those cases, you can remove nonrectangular areas by using wrap points. **Wrap points** are square black handles along a red, dashed outline that can be dragged to create irregular shapes. Wrap points also are used to change how text wraps around a graphic. The following steps edit the wrap points to crop to a nonrectangular area.

● Click the Wrap Text button (Picture Tools Format tab | Arrange group) to display the text wrapping options (Figure 4–22).

Q&A

How do you use the other commands in the list?

The other Wrap Text commands allow you to wrap text around pictures in a variety of ways depending on your needs. You will learn more about wrapping text around pictures in a later chapter.

Figure 4–22

2

- Click Edit Wrap Points to display the red, dashed lines and wrap points (Figure 4–23).

Q&A

Do all pictures display wrap points around the edges of the objects?

Pictures that have a white fill in the background display wrap points only at the four corners. Pictures with a transparent background display many wrap points around the outer edges of the objects in the picture.

Experiment

- Drag a wrap point in and out to watch how the red dotted line changes.

Figure 4–23

3

- Click the red line at a location near the lower-right corner of the monitor and then drag the line until it touches the corner of the monitor (Figure 4–24).

What if I make a mistake?

If you drag too far or to an incorrect position, you can fix the problem by dragging the wrapping point to a new location — even farther away from the graphic, if you like. To delete a wrapping point, CTRL+click the wrapping point.

Figure 4–24

4
- Drag the upper-right wrap point to the upper right corner of the monitor to outline the slant of the monitor (Figure 4–25).

 How do I insert and delete extra wrap points?

Clicking or dragging the red line creates wrap points. You can CTRL+click a wrap point to delete it.

corner wrap point

Figure 4–25

5
- Drag any other wrap points as necessary to hide the system unit and remove most of the white space, so that only the monitor remains (Figure 4–26).

 Why do I need to remove the white space if it does not appear when the document is printed?

Later in the chapter, if you have extra white space, the graphic will not be centered when this graphic is placed inside a shape.

6
- Click outside of the graphic to deselect it.

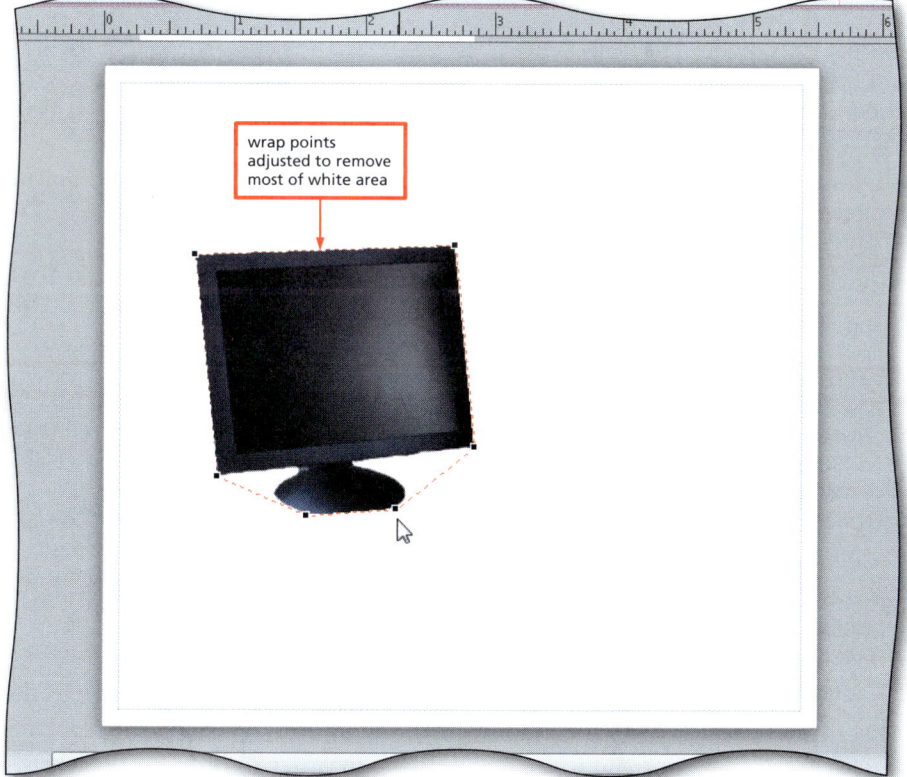

wrap points adjusted to remove most of white area

Figure 4–26

Photo Editing
Although Publisher provides some photo editing capabilities that allow you to crop a picture to rectangular and irregular shapes, it is not a photo-editing program. You cannot crop a shape, WordArt object, or an animated graphic or movie. To crop an animated GIF, use an animated GIF editing program and then insert the file again.

To Insert Another Graphic

The following steps insert another graphic into the publication. The graphic is available on the Data Files for Students. See the inside back cover of this book for instructions on downloading the Data Files for Students, or contact your instructor for information about accessing the required files.

1 Insert the USB flash drive that contains the Data Files for Students into one of the computers' USB ports.

2 Display the Insert tab.

3 Click the Insert Picture from File button (Insert tab | Illustrations group) to display the Insert Picture dialog box.

4 If necessary, navigate to your USB storage location or the location of the Data Files for Students on your computer.

5 If necessary, double-click the folder labeled Chapter 04 to display the files in the folder.

6 Double-click the Face file to insert the graphic into the publication (Figure 4–27).

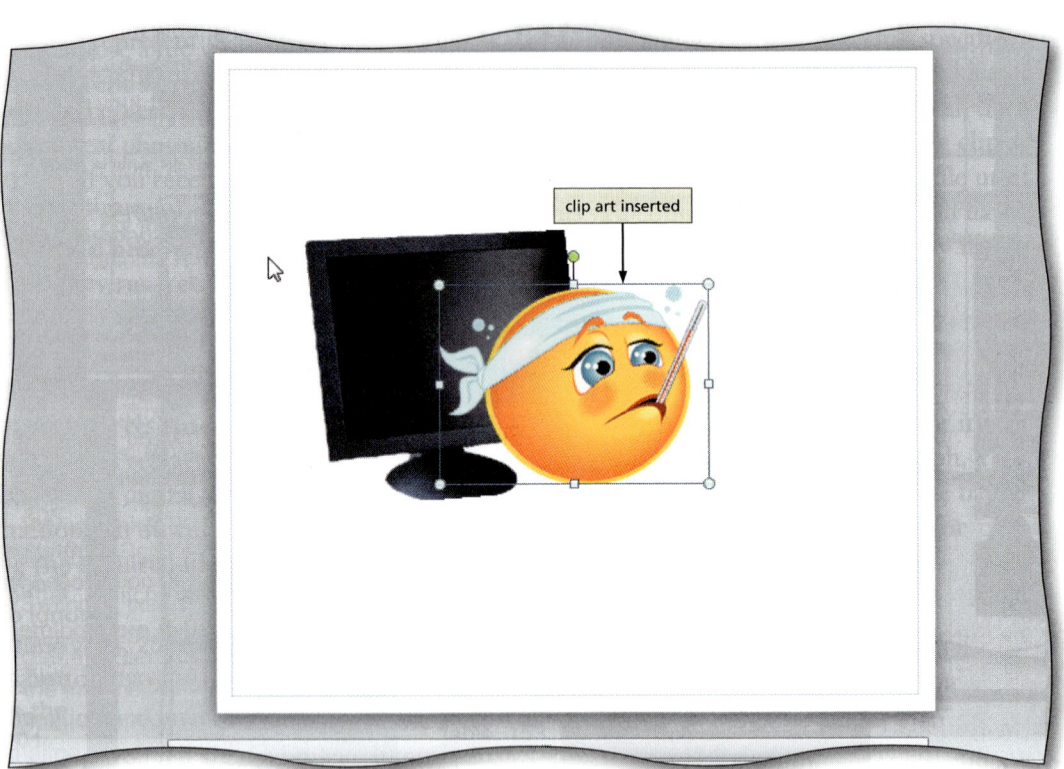

clip art inserted

Figure 4–27

Recoloring
Most pictures imported into Publisher can be recolored. This procedure does not apply to pictures that are in Encapsulated PostScript (EPS) format, however. EPS graphics are designed to print to PostScript-compatible printers and cannot be recolored.

To Recolor a Graphic

When you **recolor** a graphic, you make a large-scale color change to the entire graphic. When chosen, the color applies to all parts of the graphic, with the option of leaving the black parts black. It is an easy way to convert a color graphic to a black and white line drawing in order to print more clearly. The reverse also is true; if you have a black and white graphic, you can convert it to a tint or shade of any one color.

The following steps recolor the clip art of the face.

1

- If necessary, display the Picture Tools Format tab.

- Click the Recolor button (Picture Tools Format tab | Adjust group) to display the Recolor gallery (Figure 4–28).

🔍 **Experiment**

- Point to each of the color modes and variations and watch how the graphic changes.

Figure 4–28

2

- Click More Variations to display the Recolor Picture dialog box.

- Click the Color box arrow (Recolor Picture dialog box) to display the color gallery (Figure 4–29).

Q&A

What does the More Colors command do?

The More Colors command displays the same Colors dialog box, as it did when you chose a color for the color scheme, allowing you to choose colors based on a color number, palette, or coloring system.

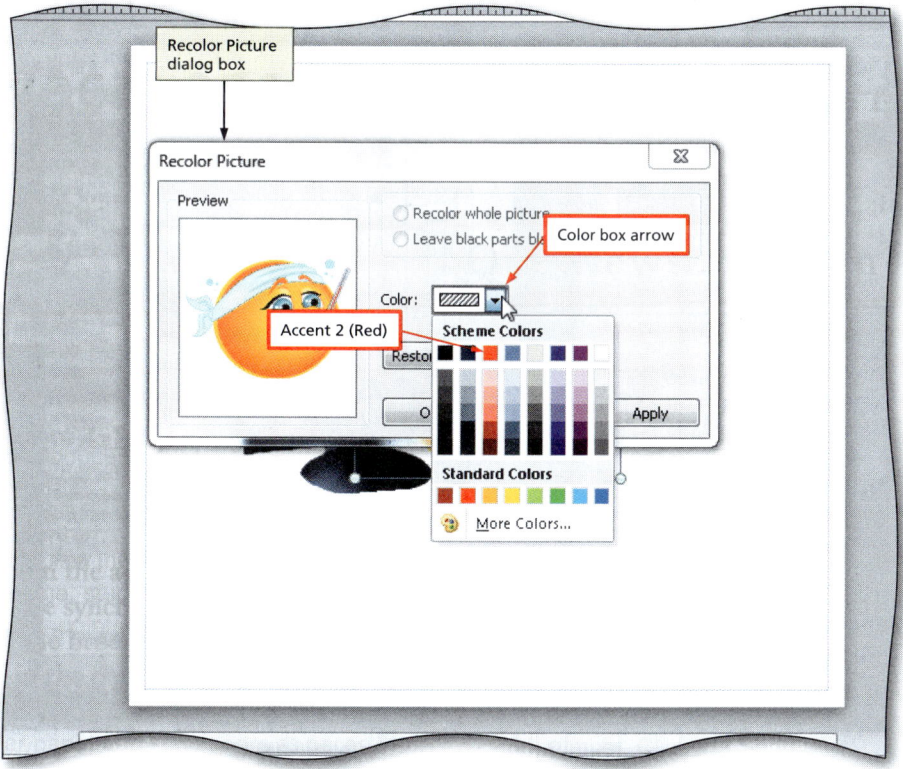

Figure 4–29

3

- Click Accent 2 (Red) to select it.

- Click the 'Leave black parts black' option button to select it (Figure 4–30).

Q&A

Do I have to choose a scheme color?

No, you do not have to choose a scheme color, but using scheme colors provides consistency in your publication.

4

- Click the OK button to close the Recolor Picture dialog box.

Figure 4–30

Other Ways

1. Right-click graphic, click Format Picture on shortcut menu, click Picture tab (Format Picture dialog box), click Recolor button, choose settings, click OK button (Recolor Picture dialog box), click OK button (Format Picture dialog box)

To Move and Resize the Graphic

The following steps move the graphic.

1 Drag the face graphic to a location in front of the monitor.

2 SHIFT+drag a corner sizing handle to resize the graphic proportionally and make it fit within the monitor screen (Figure 4–31).

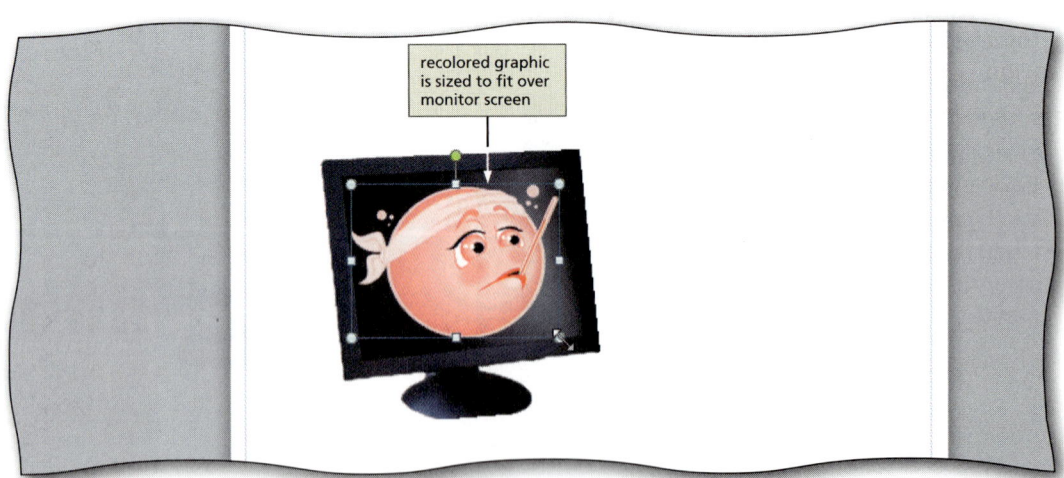

Figure 4–31

Grouping Objects

When multiple objects are selected, you can **group** them, which means they stay together for purposes such as cutting, pasting, moving, and formatting. When you **ungroup** objects, they can be selected and manipulated individually.

To Select Multiple Objects

The following step selects multiple objects.

- If necessary, click the face graphic to select it.

- SHIFT+click the monitor graphic, outside the boundaries of the other clip art to add it to the selection (Figure 4–32).

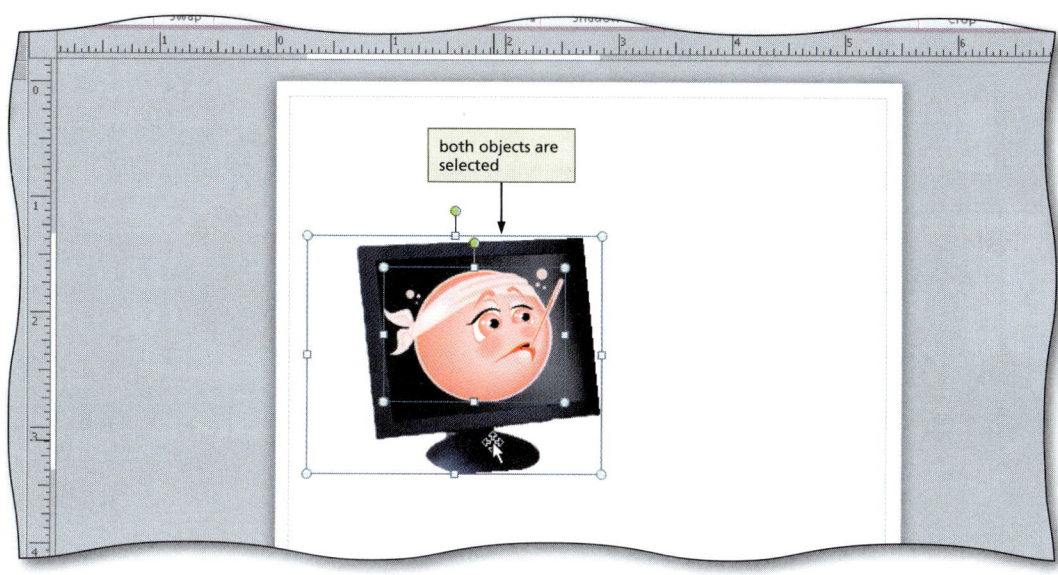

Figure 4–32

To Group Selected Objects

The following step groups the selected objects.

- Click the Group button (Picture Tools Format tab | Arrange group) to group the selected objects (Figure 4–33).

Figure 4–33

To Save a Graphic as a Picture

Because a graphic that you edit in Publisher is stored only in the publication in which you use it, it is a good idea to save the graphic independently. That way you can use it in other publications and in other formatting and editing situations. The following steps save the graphic with the file name, Computer Face.

1

- With a USB flash drive connected to one of the computer's USB ports, right-click the grouped graphic to display the shortcut menu (Figure 4–34).

Figure 4–34

2

- Click Save as Picture to display the Save As dialog box.

- Type **Computer Face** in the File name text box to change the file name. Do not press the ENTER key.

- Navigate to your USB flash drive (Figure 4–35).

Q&A

What is the PNG Portable Network Graphics Format?

PNG is the default format for saving graphics from within Publisher publications. **PNG** is a graphic file format supported by most Web browsers. PNG files are compressed bitmap files that support variable transparency of images and brightness on different computers. You can save the graphic in other formats by clicking the 'Save as type' box arrow (Save As dialog box) and then choosing a format in the list.

3

- Click the Save button (Save As dialog box) to save the graphic on the USB flash drive with the file name, Computer Face.

Figure 4–35

To Delete the Graphic

Now that you have saved the graphic, and because you will use the graphic in a different way later in the project, the following steps delete the graphic from the publication layout for the time being.

1 If necessary, select the graphic.

2 Press the DELETE key to delete the graphic.

Shapes

Publisher has more than 150 shapes that you can use to create logos, graphics, banners, illustrations, and other ornamental objects. Shapes, also called AutoShapes, exist separately from clip art shapes and first appear with a simple border, filled with no color. You can apply fill effects, line/border styles, shadows, 3-D styles, and other special effects to shapes.

To Insert a Shape

The following steps insert a rectangle shape in the advertisement.

1

- Display the Insert tab.

- Click the Shapes button (Insert tab | Illustrations group) to display the Shapes gallery (Figure 4–36).

Q&A

Why is my gallery different?

Publisher displays the most recently used shapes at the top of the gallery. The recently used shapes on your computer will differ.

Figure 4–36

2

- Click the Rectangle button in the Basic Shapes category to select it.

- Move the mouse pointer into the publication and then drag from the upper-left corner, at the margin, to the lower-right corner to create a rectangle that fills the entire advertisement (Figure 4–37).

Q&A

How would I create a perfect square?

SHIFT+dragging maintains the proportions of any shape. If you SHIFT+drag the rectangle shape, it will create a square; to create a circle, you can SHIFT+drag an oval.

rectangle shape fills area within margins

Figure 4–37

Shape Fills

In Publisher, you can **fill**, or paint, the inside of any object with a color or with an effect. **Shape fills** include fill colors, gradients, textures, patterns, pictures, and tints/shades. You can apply fills to text boxes, shapes, and even WordArt objects in Publisher. Shape fills add subtle contrast and create an illusion of texture and depth.

A **gradient** is a gradual progression of colors and shades, usually from one color to another color, or from one shade to another shade of the same color. Gradient fills create a sense of movement to draw attention and add dimension to a publication, with patterns ranging from stars and swirls to arrows and three-dimensional abstractions.

A **texture fill** is a combination of color and patterns without gradual shading. Publisher provides 24 different textures from which you may choose.

Patterns include variations of repeating designs such as lines, stripes, checks, and bricks. Publisher uses the base color and a second color to create the pattern. When publications are destined for commercial printing, patterns usually are more expensive than tints and shades, because they increase the time it takes to image the file to film.

A **picture fill** is a special effect that inserts clip art or your own graphic to create a unique and personal shape. A picture fill gives the appearance of a picture, cropped to a specific shape, such as a star or circle.

A **tint** is a color created from a base color mixed with a percentage of white. A **shade**, on the other hand, is a mixture of a base color and black. You use tints and shades to create a more sophisticated color scheme. Tints and shades are applied in 10-percent increments. For example, the first tint of red is nine parts red and one part white. Therefore, Publisher displays ten tints and ten shades of each basic color on the Tints sheet in the Fill Effects dialog box.

In the advertisement, you will use a gradient-filled rectangle shape as a background; later, you will add a cross shape with an inserted picture and border.

To Create a Gradient Fill Effect

The following steps fill the rectangle with a gradient fill effect.

1
- If necessary, display the Drawing Tools Format tab.

- With the rectangle still selected, click the Shape Fill button arrow (Drawing Tools Format tab | Shape Styles group) to display the Shape Fill gallery.

- Point to Gradient in the Shape Fill gallery to display the Gradient gallery (Figure 4–38).

 Experiment
- Point to various preset gradients and watch how the fill in the rectangle changes.

Figure 4–38

2
- Click the More Gradients command to display the Fill Effects dialog box.

- If necessary, click the Gradient tab (Fill Effects dialog box) (Figure 4–39).

 Experiment
- In the Colors area, click One color to view the previews of single-color gradients from dark to light of the same color. Click Preset and then click the Preset colors box arrow, choosing different predefined gradients, such as Horizon, Calm Water, and Rainbow.

Figure 4–39

- In the Colors area, click Two colors.

- Click the Color 1 box arrow to display its list (Figure 4–40).

Q&A

What is the purpose of the Transparency sliders?

When you choose one color for your gradient, the Transparency sliders allow you to specify what percentage of **transparency**, or opacity, for the beginning and end of the gradient. A 100% transparency appears white. A 0% transparency displays the chosen color.

Figure 4–40

- Click the Accent 1 (Dark Teal), Lighter 80% color to select it.

- Click the Color 2 box arrow and then click Accent 5 (White) to select the second color (Figure 4–41).

Experiment

- In the Shading styles area, click each of the style option buttons one at a time. Look at the variant previews.

Figure 4–41

5

- In the Shading styles area, click From center to select a star pattern.

- In the Variants area, click the right variant to select a gradient with blue edges and a white center (Figure 4–42).

Figure 4–42

6

- Click the OK button to apply the gradient (Figure 4–43).

 Q&A

What other elements can I fill with effects?

You can fill text boxes, master pages, Web page backgrounds, tables, pictures, and WordArt with gradients, texture, patterns, pictures, or tints/shades.

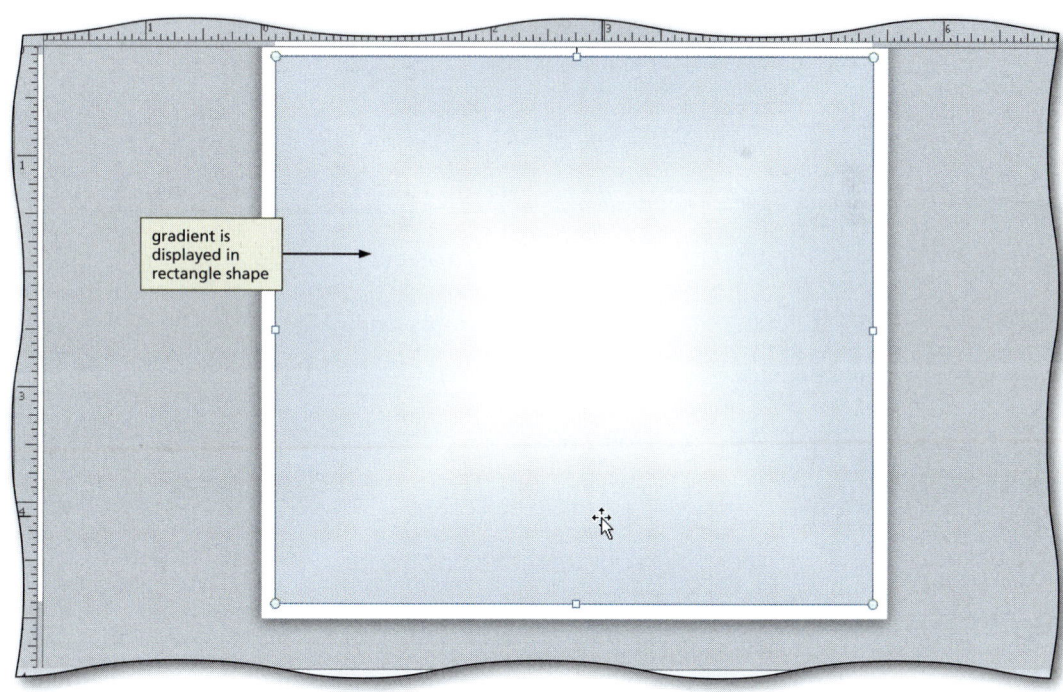

Figure 4–43

Other Ways

1. Click Format Shape Dialog Box Launcher (Drawing Tools Format tab | Shape Styles group), click Colors and Lines tab (Format AutoShape dialog box), click Fill Effects button, choose settings, click OK button

2. Right-click rectangle, click Format AutoShape on shortcut menu, click Colors and Lines tab (Format AutoShape dialog box), click Fill Effects button, choose settings, click OK button

BTW

Trapping

When a publication is printed by a professional printer using spot colors or process colors, Publisher creates a **trap**, or small overlap, where the colors of the shape meet the color of the printed page. The amount of overlap varies between printers. If the printed page is white, trapping is not a problem; however, if a background object or color is on the page around the shape, the colors will trap depending on the kind of separations you print. The borders around a shape filled with color will trap to the fill color, if necessary.

To Insert and Position Another Shape

The following steps insert and position a cross shape in the publication.

1 Display the Insert tab.

2 Click the Shapes button (Insert tab | Illustrations group) to display the list of shapes.

3 Click the Cross button in the Basic Shapes area to select it.

4 Move the mouse pointer into the publication and then SHIFT+drag to create a cross, approximately 1-inch square.

5 Drag the cross to a location in the upper-left corner of the publication (Figure 4–44).

Figure 4–44

To Select a Color for the Shape Outline

Shape outline refers to the color, weight, style, and/or pattern of the outline around the current shape. It does not change the shape of the chosen graphic itself. The following steps choose a color for the outline of the graphic.

1

- Display the Drawing Tools Format tab.

- With the graphic still selected, click the Shape Outline button arrow (Drawing Tools Format tab | Shape Styles group) to display the Shape Outline gallery (Figure 4–45).

Q&A Can I create an object with no border at all?

Yes. Select the object, click the Shape Outline button arrow, and then place a check mark in the No Outline check box.

Figure 4–45

2

- Click Accent 2 (Red) to add a red border to the shape (Figure 4–46).

Q&A How do you use the Sample Line color command?

When you click the Sample Line color command, Publisher allows you to select the color from anywhere in the page layout by clicking the desired color. The color is added to the color palette and you then can apply the new color to a font, line, or fill. When sampling a color, the mouse pointer displays an eyedropper as if it were picking up or suctioning the color from the display.

Figure 4–46

Other Ways

1. Click Format Shape Dialog Box Launcher (Drawing Tools Format tab | Shape Styles group), click Colors and Lines tab (Format AutoShape dialog box), click Color box arrow, click color

2. Right-click shape, click Format AutoShape on shortcut menu, click Colors and Lines tab (Format AutoShape dialog box), click Color box arrow, click color

To Change the Shape Outline

The following steps edit the shape outline to display a weight of 3 points. A **point** is a physical measurement that is approximately equal to 1/72nd of an inch. A point is not always the same as a pixel. A **pixel**, short for picture element, is a single resolution unit on the display. A point is the same as a pixel only if your monitor's resolution is set to 72 pixels per inch.

- With the graphic still selected, click the Shape Outline button arrow (Drawing Tools Format tab | Shape Styles group) to display the Shape Outline gallery.

- Point to Weight in the Shape Outline gallery to display the Weight gallery (Figure 4–47).

Figure 4–47

- Click 3 pt in the Weight gallery (Figure 4–48).

Figure 4–48

Other Ways

1. Right-click graphic, click Format AutoShape on shortcut menu, click Colors and Lines tab (Format AutoShape dialog box), click Style box arrow, choose setting, click OK button

To Fill a Shape with a Picture

The following steps fill the cross shape with the previously saved picture.

- Insert your USB flash drive into one of the computers' USB ports.

- With the shape still selected, click the Shape Fill button arrow (Drawing Tools Format tab | Shape Styles group) to display the Shape Fill gallery and then click Picture to display the Select Picture dialog box.

- Navigate to your USB flash drive, and then select the Computer Face file (Figure 4–49).

Figure 4–49

- Click the Insert button (Select Picture dialog box) to insert the picture (Figure 4–50).

Figure 4–50

Other Ways

1. Right-click graphic, click Format AutoShape on shortcut menu, click Colors and Lines tab (Format AutoShape dialog box), click Fill Effects button, choose settings, click OK button

To Add to the Building Block Library

Recall from Chapter 1 that you inserted objects from the Building Block Library into your publication. The following steps add content to the Building Block Library for future use.

1

- Right-click the red cross graphic to display the shortcut menu (Figure 4–51).

Q&A

What is the difference between saving as a picture and saving to the Building Block Library?

Saving as a picture saves a copy on your storage device, which may be unavailable to other users. Saving to the Building Block Library keeps a copy within Publisher, for all users of the computer.

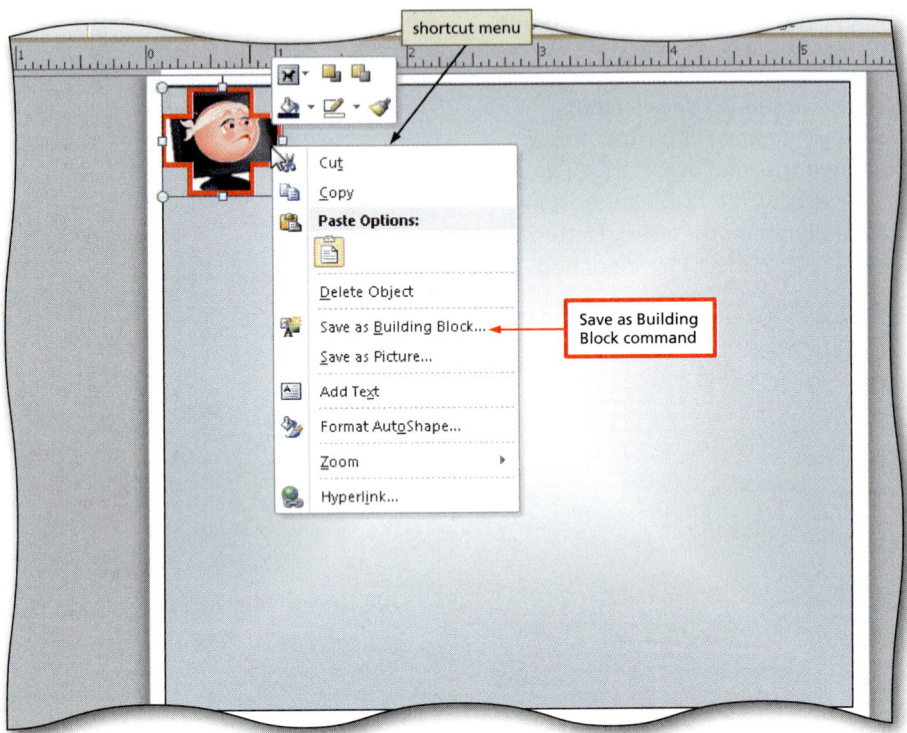

Figure 4–51

2

- Click Save as Building Block to display the Create New Building Block dialog box.

- Type **Computer First Aid Graphic** to replace the text in the Title text box.

- Press the TAB key to move to the Description box and then type **red cross with picture of a monitor and a sickly face** to insert a description (Figure 4–52).

Experiment

- Click the Gallery box arrow to view the different galleries. Click the Category box arrow to view the available categories.

Figure 4–52

3
- Click the Keywords text box and then type `cross, monitor, face` to enter keywords (Figure 4–53).

4
- Click the OK button to close the Create New Building Block dialog box.

Figure 4–53

Other Ways

1. Click Page Parts button (Insert tab | Building Blocks group), click Add Selection to Page Parts Gallery, enter information, click OK button (Create New Building Block dialog box)

To Save the Advertisement

You have made many edits to the publication; it is time to save it to your storage device. The following steps save the advertisement with the file name Computer First Aid Advertisement.

1 With a USB flash drive connected to one of the computer's USB ports, click the Save button on the Quick Access Toolbar to display the Save As dialog box.

2 Type `Computer First Aid Advertisement` in the File name text box to change the file name. Do not press the ENTER key after typing the file name because you do not want to close the dialog box at this time.

3 Navigate to the desired save location (in this case, the Publisher folder in the CIS 101 folder [or your class folder] on the USB flash drive).

4 Click the Save button (Save As dialog box) to save the document on the selected drive with the entered file name.

BTW

Building Block Categories
In the Create New Building Block dialog box, you cannot change the Gallery list, but you can enter a new category and save your graphic to that new category. Once you click the OK button, the new category will appear each time you access the Building Block Library.

Break Point: If you wish to take a break, this is a good place to do so. You can quit Publisher now. To resume at a later time, start Publisher, open the file called Computer First Aid Advertisement, and continue following the steps from this location forward.

Font Styles

Each of the font schemes contains numerous styles. In Publisher, a **style** is a combination of formatting characteristics, such as font size, effects, and formatting. When you select or create a font scheme, Publisher creates styles for titles, headings, accent text, body text, lists, bullets, and normal text using the fonts from the current font scheme.

Plan Ahead

> **Create the publication.** Make decisions about formatting such as headings, formatted text, columns, and decorative text. Proofread, revise, and add the final touches. Revise as necessary and then use the spelling, grammar, and design checking features of the software.

To Draw a Text Box

The following steps draw a text box at the top of the advertisement that will contain the heading with an applied font style.

1. If necessary, click outside the graphic to deselect it.

2. Display the Home tab.

3. Click the Draw Text Box button (Home tab | Objects group) to select it.

4. Drag in the publication to draw a text box approximately 3.5 inches wide and .5 inches tall, to the right of the graphic, as shown in Figure 4–54.

BTW

The Ribbon and Text Boxes
As soon as you draw a text box using the Draw Text Box button on the Home tab, the Ribbon changes to display the Text Box Tools Format tab.

Figure 4–54

To Apply a Style

When you apply a style, all of the formatting instructions in that style are applied at one time. To apply a style to new text, you either can select the style from the Style list and then type the text, or you can type the text first, select it, and then apply the style.

The following steps apply a style generated from the Computer First Aid font scheme that you created earlier in the chapter.

1

- If necessary, display the Home tab.

- Click the Styles button (Home tab | Styles group) to display the Styles gallery.

- Scroll, if necessary, to display the Heading 1 style in the Styles gallery (Figure 4–55).

 Experiment

- Scroll in the Styles gallery to view the various font sizes, alignments, and formatting.

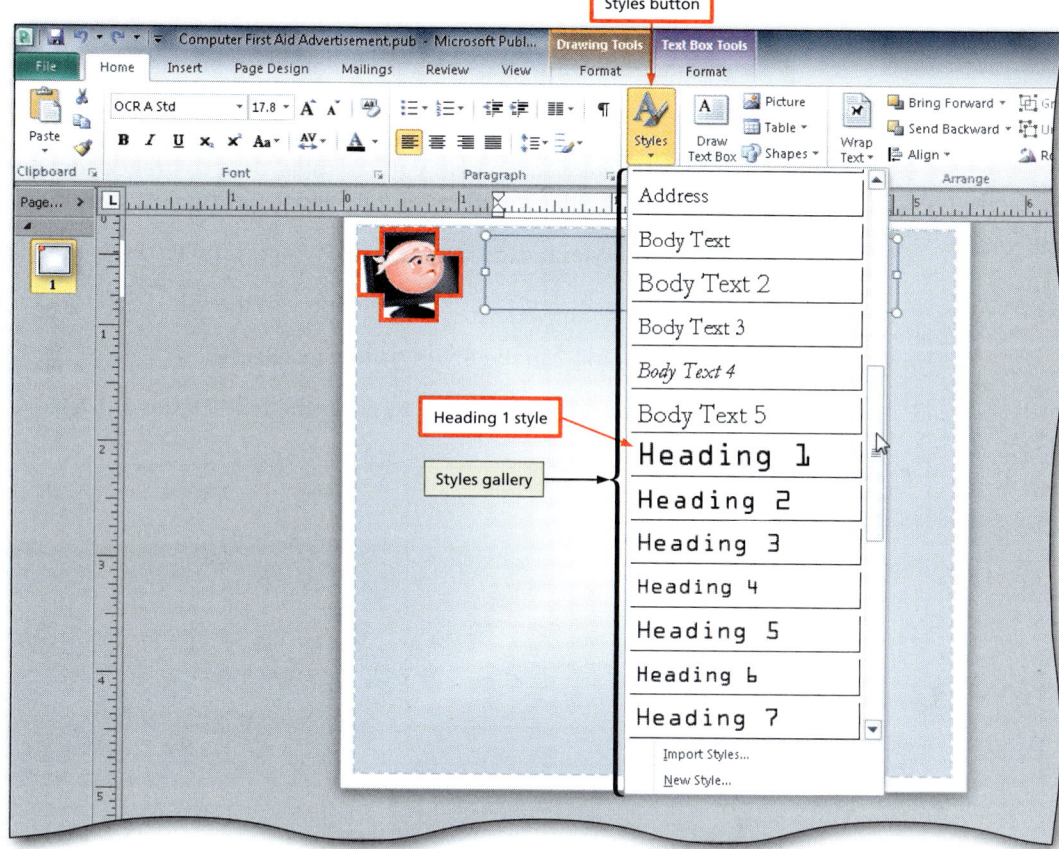

Figure 4–55

2

- Click Heading 1 to select it.

- Type **Computer First Aid** to enter the text (Figure 4–56).

Q&A

Can I add other styles?

Yes. The New Style command at the bottom of the Styles gallery displays the New Styles dialog box. In a later chapter, you will learn how to create, edit, and import styles.

Figure 4–56

To Create More Heading Text

The following steps create a second text box using the Heading 2 style.

1 Click the Draw Text Box button (Home tab | Objects group) to select it.

2 Approximately 1 inch below the graphic, drag to draw a text box approximately 2.25 inches wide and .5 inches tall, aligned at the left margin.

3 Click the Styles button (Home tab | Styles group) to display the Styles gallery.

4 Scroll, if necessary, to display Heading 2 in the list.

5 Click Heading 2 in the Styles gallery to select it.

6 Type `Our Services:` to enter the text (Figure 4–57).

Figure 4–57

Columns

When you first create a text box in Publisher, it has one column, but you can divide it into multiple columns to make the text easier to read, to create lists, or to keep similar items together. Unlike Microsoft Word, you do not have to use section breaks or specialized controls to create columns; however, as you are typing, if you want to change to a different number of columns, you must create a new text box. Publisher's columns automatically include 1/16-inch margins and gutters.

A second way to create columns is to use linked text boxes as you did in Chapter 3 and the newsletter. For long stories, linked text boxes work better; for columned lists, a single text box provides more formatting options.

Recall from Chapter 1 that Publisher displays a boundary around objects when you point to them. When working with columns, text box margins, and gutters, it is a good idea to see the boundary, even when you are not pointing to it. A check box on the View tab on the Ribbon allows you to turn on boundaries that appear all the time.

To Create a Text Box

The following steps create a text box for the contact information in the advertisement.

1 Click the Draw Text Box button (Home tab | Objects group) to select it.

2 Drag to draw a text box below the Heading 1 text box, approximately 3.53 inches wide and .75 inches tall (Figure 4–58).

Figure 4–58

To Turn on Boundaries

The following step turns on boundaries that will display in the text box.

1

• Display the View tab.

• Click the Boundaries check box (View tab | Show group) to display boundaries in the text box.

• If your text boxes overlap significantly, drag their boundaries to rearrange them (Figure 4–59).

Q&A

Will boundaries now appear in all publications?

No, boundaries appear only in saved publications in which the Boundaries check box is selected (View tab | Show group).

Figure 4–59

To Set Columns

The following steps choose a two-column format for the contact information text box.

- Display the Home tab.

- Click the Columns button (Home tab | Paragraph group) to display the Columns gallery (Figure 4–60).

Experiment

- Point to each of the column formats in the Columns gallery and watch the text box to see how it changes.

Figure 4–60

- Click Two Columns in the Columns gallery to select the format for the text box (Figure 4–61).

Q&A

What does the More Columns command do?

The More Columns command displays the Columns dialog box, where you can specify the number of columns you want to use and the spacing.

Figure 4–61

Other Ways

1. Right-click text box, click Format Text box on shortcut menu, click Text Box tab (Format Text Box dialog box) click Columns button, enter column settings (Columns dialog box), click OK button

To Change Line Spacing

Line spacing is the amount of space from the bottom of one line of text to the bottom of the next line, which determines the amount of vertical space between lines of text in a paragraph. By default, the Normal style is single-spaced, but because Publisher accommodates the largest font in any given line, plus a small amount of extra space, the actual line spacing value is 1.19. The following steps change the line spacing to 1.0.

- Click the Line Spacing button (Home tab | Paragraph group) to display the Line Spacing gallery (Figure 4–62).

2
- Click 1.0 in the Line Spacing gallery to select single spacing.

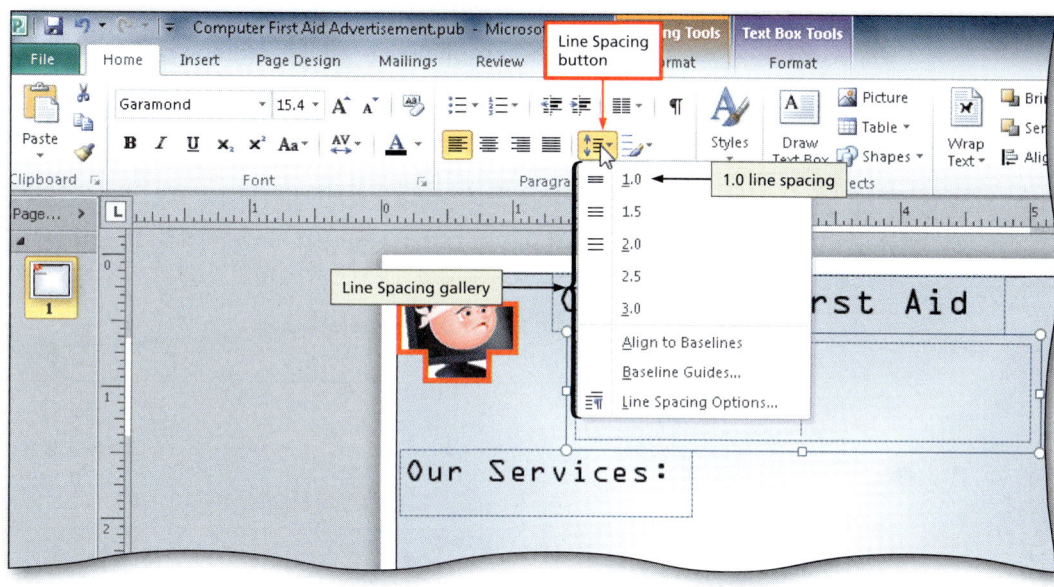

Other Ways

1. Click Paragraph Dialog Box Launcher (Home tab | Paragraph group), enter new setting in Between lines box (Paragraph dialog box), click OK button

Figure 4–62

To Set the Font Size and Enter Text

The following steps set the font size and enter text in the contact information text box.

1 Click the Font Size box arrow (Home tab | Font group) and then click 10 to set the font size.

2 Enter the contact information from Figure 4–63, pressing the ENTER key at the end of each line.

Figure 4–63

To Create Another Columned Text Box

The following steps create another text box for the bulleted list of services in the advertisement.

1 Click the Draw Text Box button (Home tab | Objects group) to select it.

2 Drag to draw a text box just below the Heading 2 text box, from the left margin to the right margin, approximately 2.2 inches tall.

3 Click the Columns button (Home tab | Paragraph group) to display the Columns gallery and then click Two Columns in the Columns gallery to select the format for the text box.

4 Click the Bullets button (Home tab | Paragraph group) to display the Bullet Styles gallery.

5 Click Large Bullets in the Bullet Styles gallery to create a bulleted list.

6 Enter the list of services from Figure 4–64, pressing the ENTER key at the end of each line, except the last.

7 Click outside the text box to deselect it.

Figure 4–64

WordArt

WordArt is a gallery of text styles that works with Publisher to create fancy text effects. A WordArt object actually is a graphic, not text. Publication designers typically use WordArt to create eye-catching headlines, banners, or watermark images.

To Insert a WordArt Object

The following steps add a WordArt object at the bottom of the advertisement. While a formatted text box with font effects might create a similar effect, using WordArt increases the number of special effect possibilities and options.

1

- Display the Insert tab.

- Click the WordArt button (Insert tab | Text group) to display the WordArt gallery (Figure 4–65).

Figure 4–65

2

- Click the Gradient Fill – Red, Outline - Red preview in the WordArt gallery to select it.

- Type **Call for Free Estimates** (Edit WordArt Text dialog box) to enter the text (Figure 4–66).

Figure 4–66

3

- Click the Size box arrow to display the font sizes (Figure 4–67).

Q&A

Can I change the font?

Yes, if you click the Font box arrow, you will see all of the available fonts that WordArt can reproduce.

Figure 4–67

4

- Click 24 to choose a 24-point font size.

- Click the OK button to close the dialog box and insert the WordArt graphic.

- Drag the WordArt graphic to the lower portion of the advertisement, and align it with the left margin (Figure 4–68).

Figure 4–68

To Add Shadow Effects

The following steps add a reflection shadow to the WordArt graphic.

1

- Click WordArt Tools Format on the Ribbon to display the WordArt Tools Format tab.

- With the WordArt object still selected, click the Shadow Effects button (Word Art Tools Format tab | Shadow Effects group) to display the Shadow Effects gallery (Figure 4–69).

Experiment

- Point to each effect in the gallery to display a preview of the effect in the publication.

Figure 4–69

2

- Click Shadow Style 9 in the Shadow Effects gallery to add the shadow to the graphic (Figure 4–70).

- Drag the right-center sizing handle to make the WordArt objects fill the area between the left and right margins.

- Reposition as necessary so that the WordArt object does not overlap into the margins.

Q&A

What does the Shadow Color command do?

The Shadow Color command displays a gallery of scheme colors and shades to change the color of the shadow.

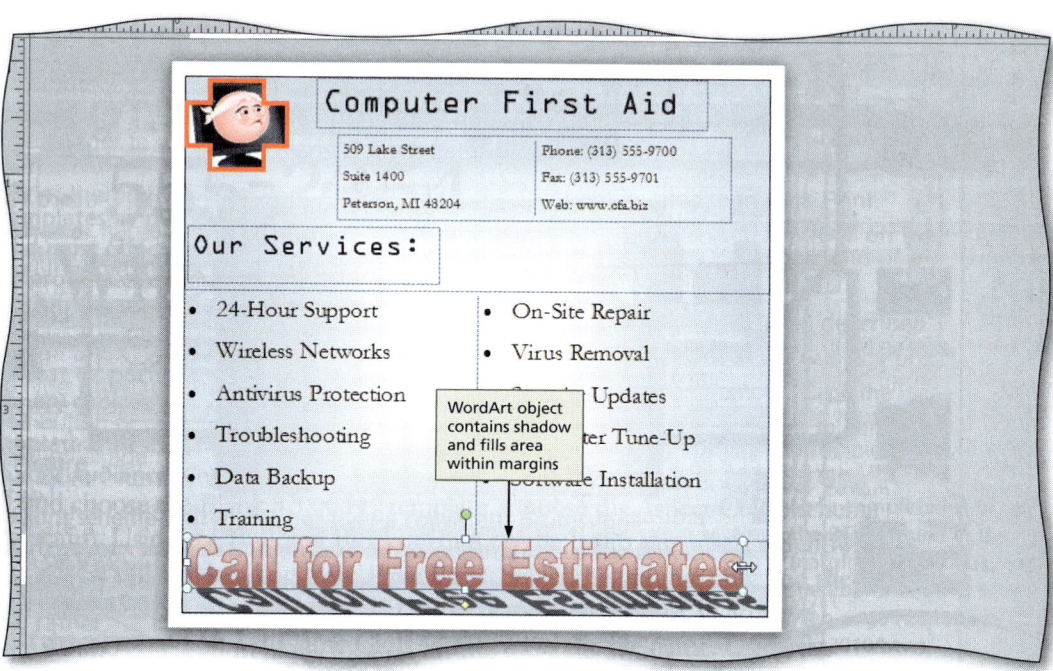

Figure 4–70

To Check the Publication for Errors

The following steps check the publication for errors.

1 Press the F7 key to begin checking the publication for spelling errors. If Publisher flags any words, fix or ignore them as appropriate.

2 When Publisher displays a dialog box asking if you want to check the entire document, click the Yes button.

3 When the spell checking is complete, click the OK button.

4 Click File on the Ribbon to open the Backstage view and, by default, select the Info tab.

5 Click the Run Design Checker button.

6 When Publisher displays the Design Checker task pane, ignore any messages about transparency or picture resolution.

7 If the Design Checker identifies any other errors, fix them as necessary.

8 Close the Design Checker task pane.

To Save an Existing Publication with the Same File Name

You are finished editing the advertisement. Thus, you should save it again. The following step saves the publication again.

1 Click the Save button on the Quick Access Toolbar to overwrite the previously saved file.

To Print the Advertisement

The following steps print a hard copy of the advertisement.

1 Click File on the Ribbon to open the Backstage view and then click the Print tab in the Backstage view to display the Print gallery.

2 Verify the printer name in the Printer box will print a hard copy of the document. If necessary, click the Printer status button to display a list of available printer options and then click the desired printer to change the currently selected printer.

3 Click the Print button in the Print gallery to print the advertisement on the currently selected printer (shown in Figure 4–1 on page PUB 203).

To Close a Publication without Quitting Publisher

The following steps close the advertisement without quitting Publisher.

 1
- Click File on the Ribbon to open the Backstage view (Figure 4–71).

 2
- If necessary, click Close to close the publication without quitting Publisher and to return to the New template gallery.

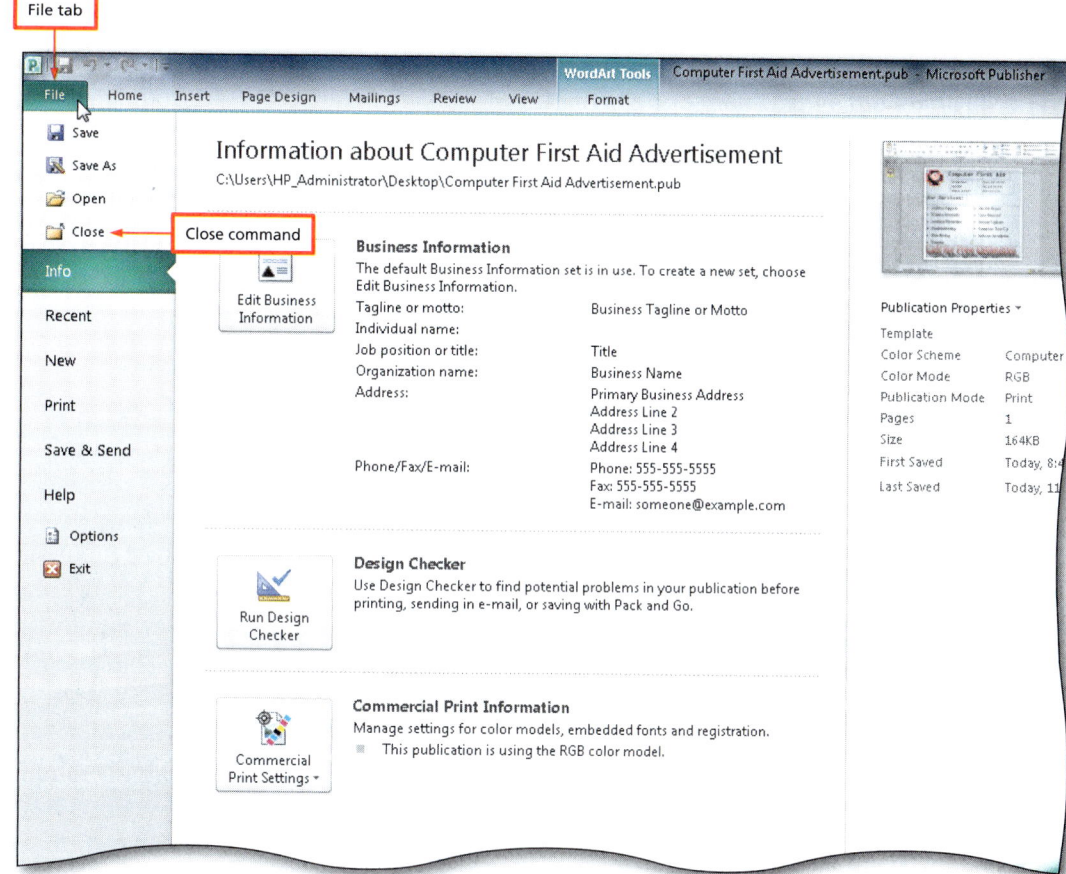

Figure 4–71

Other Ways
1. Press CTRL+F4

Break Point: If you wish to take a break, this is a good place to do so. You can quit Publisher now. To resume at a later time, start Publisher and continue following the steps from this location forward.

Using Customized Sizes, Schemes, and Building Blocks

Earlier in this chapter, you created a custom blank page for 1/8-page newspaper advertisements, a customized font scheme, a customized color scheme, and a graphic that you stored as a building block. These customizations are meant to be used again. They also can be deleted if you no longer need them.

In the following sections, you will open and access the customizations as if you were going to create a second advertisement for the same company. You then will delete them.

To Open a Customized Blank Page

The following steps open a customized blank page.

1
- With Publisher running, if necessary, click File on the Ribbon to open the Backstage view.

- Click New to display the New template gallery (Figure 4–72).

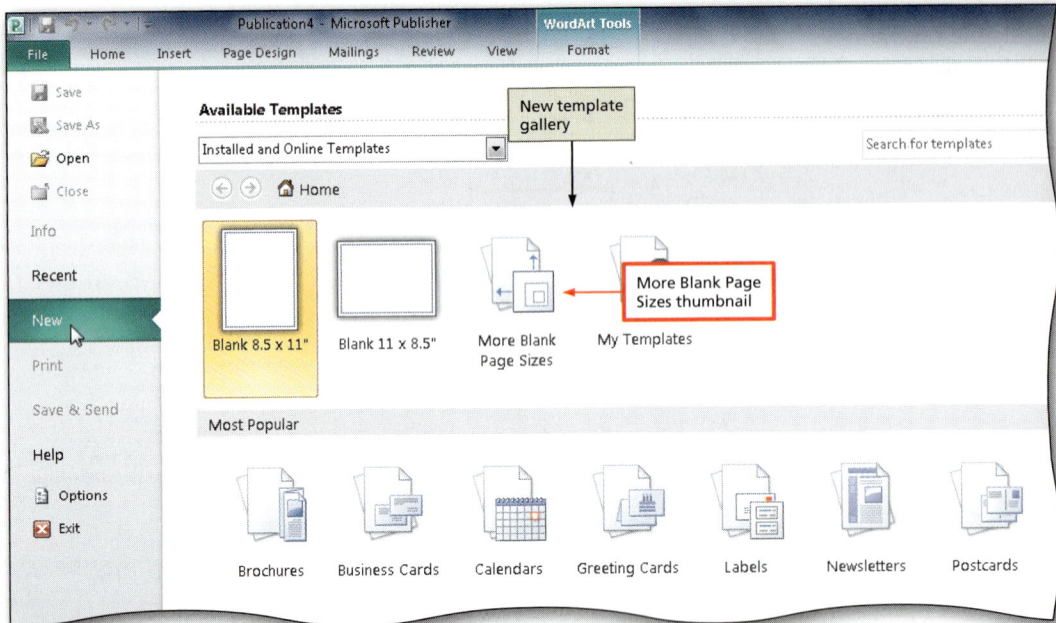

Figure 4–72

2
- Click the More Blank Page Sizes thumbnail to view the Standard and Custom page sizes.

- Scroll as necessary and click the 1/8 Page Advertisement thumbnail to select it (Figure 4–73).

Figure 4–73

To Apply Customized Color and Font Schemes

The following steps apply customized color and font schemes.

1
● Click the Color scheme box arrow to display the custom and standard color schemes (Figure 4–74).

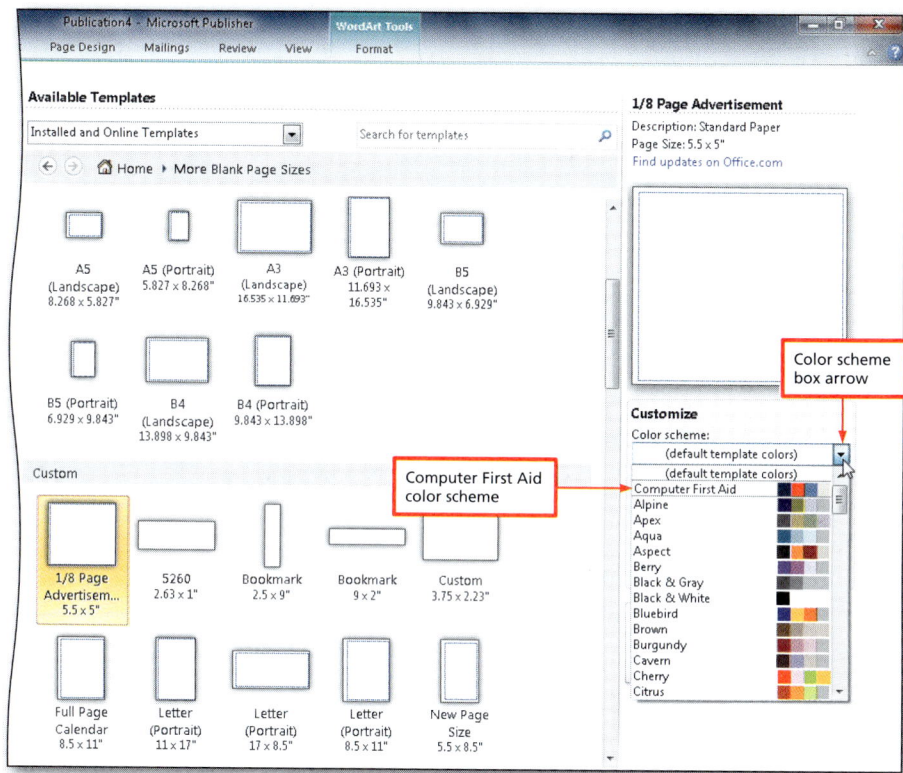

Figure 4–74

2
● Click the Computer First Aid color scheme to select it.

● Click the Font scheme box arrow to display the custom and standard font schemes and then click the Computer First Aid font scheme to select it (Figure 4–75).

3
● Click the Create button to create the publication.

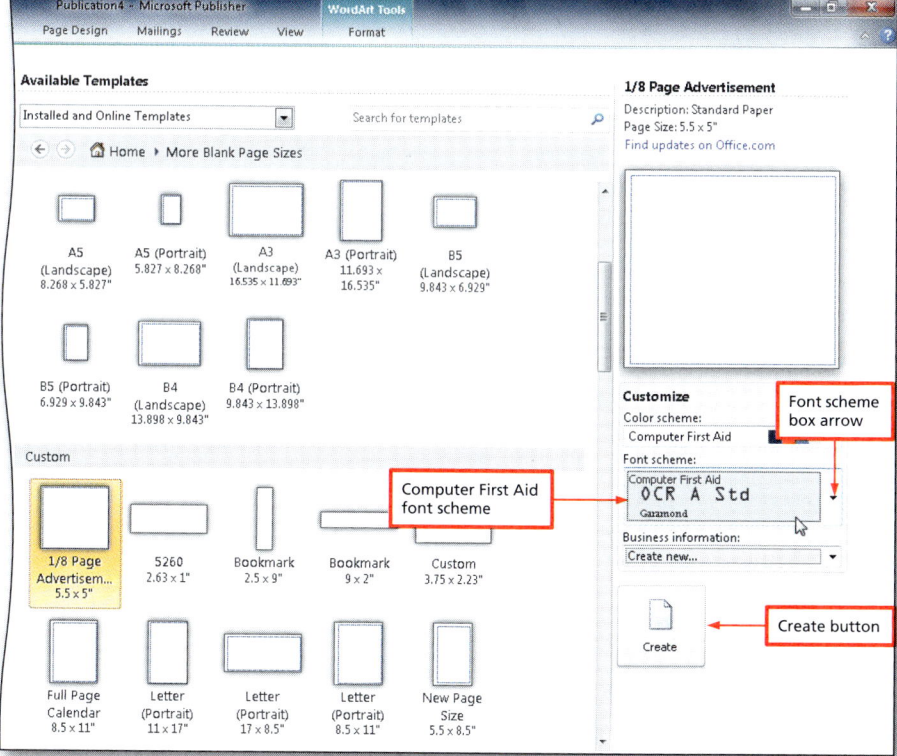

Figure 4–75

To Insert a Customized Building Block

The following steps insert the customized building block into the blank publication.

1

• Display the Insert tab.

• Click the Page Parts button (Insert tab | Building Blocks group) to display the Page Parts gallery (Figure 4–76).

Q&A Why is the graphic displayed twice?

It is displayed in the Recently Used section because you just added it to the General section.

Figure 4–76

2

• Click the Computer First Aid Graphic in the General area in the Page Parts gallery to insert it in the publication (Figure 4–77).

Q&A What is the button that appears below the graphic?

The button is a Format Options button. When you click it, you can choose to change the graphic's color to the current color scheme of the publication.

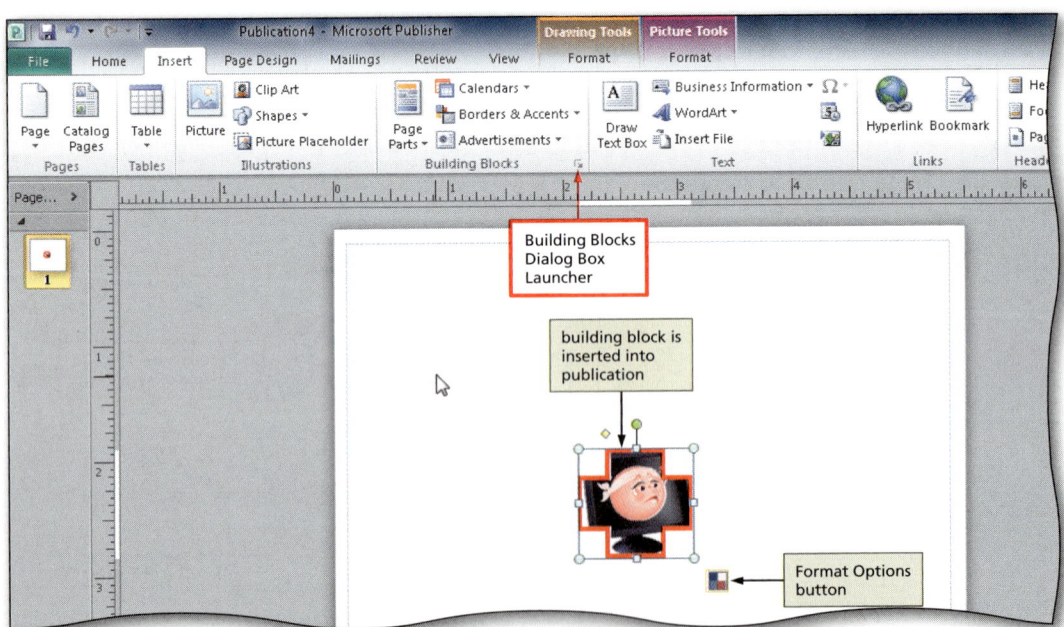

Figure 4–77

Deleting Customizations

In laboratory environments, where many students work on the same computers throughout the day, it is a good idea to delete content you have created that is stored on the computer. You also might want to delete customization and content for companies with which you no longer do business.

To Delete Content from the Building Block Library

The following steps delete the red cross graphic from the Building Block Library. Deleting it from the library does not delete the graphics from saved publications.

• Click the Show Building Block Library Dialog Box Launcher (Insert tab | Building Blocks group) to display the Building Block Library dialog box.

• Click the Page Parts folder (Building Block Library dialog box) to open it.

• Right-click the Computer First Aid graphic to display its shortcut menu (Figure 4–78).

Experiment

• Click Edit Properties on the shortcut menu and view the Edit Building Block Properties dialog box and its fields of information that Publisher saves. When finished, click the OK button to close the dialog box, and then right-click again to display the graphic's shortcut menu.

Figure 4–78

• Click Delete on the shortcut menu to delete the graphic (Figure 4–79).

• When Publisher displays a dialog box asking if you want to delete the building block permanently, click the Yes button.

• Click the Close button (Building Block Library dialog box) to close the dialog box.

Figure 4–79

To Delete the Customized Color Scheme

The following steps delete the Computer First Aid color scheme from the Publisher list of color schemes. Deleting the color scheme does not change the colors in previously created publications.

- Click Page Design on the Ribbon to display the Page Design tab.

- Click the More button (Page Design tab | Schemes group) to display the Color Scheme gallery.

- Right-click the Computer First Aid color scheme in the Color Scheme gallery to display the shortcut menu (Figure 4–80).

Figure 4–80

Q&A

How does the Add Gallery to Quick Access Toolbar command work?

Recall that the Quick Access Toolbar appears above the Ribbon on the Publisher title bar. It contains buttons for commonly used commands and settings, and it is customizable. Clicking the command will add a button on the right side of the toolbar, that when clicked, will set your color scheme automatically.

2

- Click Delete Scheme on the shortcut menu to delete the color scheme.

- When Publisher displays a dialog box asking if you want to delete the color scheme permanently, click the Yes button.

To Delete the Customized Font Scheme

The following steps delete the Computer First Aid font scheme from the list of font schemes. Deleting the font scheme does not change the fonts in previously created publications.

1

- Click the Scheme Fonts button (Page Design tab | Schemes group) to display the Scheme Fonts gallery.

- Right-click the Computer First Aid font scheme in the Scheme Fonts gallery to display the shortcut menu (Figure 4–81).

Figure 4–81

Q&A How does the Update Scheme from Publication Styles command work?

If you change the font in some of your text boxes and like it better than the original one in the font scheme, you can click the command to change the font scheme permanently.

2

- Click Delete Scheme on the shortcut menu to delete the font scheme.

- When Publisher displays a dialog box asking if you want to delete the building block permanently, click the Yes button.

To Delete the Customized Blank Page

The following steps delete the customized blank page size named 1/8 Page Advertisement. Deleting the page size does not change the size of previously created publications.

1

● Click the Page Size button (Page Design tab | Page Setup group) to display the Page Size gallery (Figure 4–82).

Figure 4–82

2

● Right-click the 1/8 Page Advertisement to display the shortcut menu (Figure 4–83).

3

● Click Delete on the shortcut menu to delete the page size.

● When Publisher displays a dialog box asking if you want to delete the size permanently, click the Yes button.

Figure 4–83

To Quit Publisher

The following steps quit Publisher without saving the current publication.

1 Click the Close button on the Publisher title bar.

2 If Publisher displays a dialog box, asking if you want to save the document, click the Don't Save button.

Chapter Summary

In this chapter, you learned how to customize Publisher with page sizes, content, color schemes and font schemes. First, you created a custom blank page size for a newspaper advertisement that would cover 1/8 of the page. You created an original graphic by cropping, editing wrapping points, flipping, grouping, and inserting it in a shape. Next, you added the graphic to the Building Block Library and used it to create an advertisement. You created text boxes with columns and inserted a WordArt object with a reflective shadow. Finally, you deleted the customized objects. The items listed below include all the new Publisher skills you have learned in this chapter.

1. Select a Blank Publication (PUB 205)
2. Create a Custom Page Size (PUB 206)
3. Create a New Color Scheme (PUB 209)
4. Create a New Font Scheme (PUB 211)
5. Flip a Picture (PUB 214)
6. Crop a Graphic (PUB 216)
7. Edit Wrap Points (PUB 217)
8. Recolor a Graphic (PUB 220)
9. Select Multiple Objects (PUB 223)
10. Group Selected Objects (PUB 223)
11. Save a Graphic as a Picture (PUB 224)
12. Insert a Shape (PUB 225)
13. Create a Gradient Fill Effect (PUB 227)
14. Select a Color for the Shape Outline (PUB 230)
15. Change the Shape Outline (PUB 232)
16. Fill a Shape with a Picture (PUB 233)
17. Add to the Building Block Library (PUB 234)
18. Apply a Style (PUB 236)
19. Turn on Boundaries (PUB 239)
20. Set Columns (PUB 240)
21. Change Line Spacing (PUB 241)
22. Insert a WordArt Object (PUB 243)
23. Add Shadow Effects (PUB 245)
24. Close a Publication without Quitting Publisher (PUB 247)
25. Open a Customized Blank Page (PUB 248)
26. Apply Customized Color and Font Schemes (PUB 249)
27. Insert a Customized Building Block (PUB 250)
28. Delete Content from the Building Block Library (PUB 251)
29. Delete the Customized Color Scheme (PUB 252)
30. Delete the Customized Font Scheme (PUB 253)
31. Delete the Customized Blank Page (PUB 254)

Learn It Online

Test your knowledge of chapter content and key terms.

Instructions: To complete the Learn It Online exercises, start your browser, click the Address bar, and then enter the Web address `scsite.com/pub2010/learn`. When the Publisher 2010 Learn It Online page is displayed, click the link for the exercise you want to complete and then read the instructions.

Chapter Reinforcement TF, MC, and SA

A series of true/false, multiple choice, and short answer questions that test your knowledge of the chapter content.

Flash Cards

An interactive learning environment where you identify chapter key terms associated with displayed definitions.

Practice Test

A series of multiple choice questions that test your knowledge of chapter content and key terms.

Who Wants To Be a Computer Genius?

An interactive game that challenges your knowledge of chapter content in the style of a television quiz show.

Wheel of Terms

An interactive game that challenges your knowledge of chapter key terms in the style of the television show *Wheel of Fortune*.

Crossword Puzzle Challenge

A crossword puzzle that challenges your knowledge of key terms presented in the chapter.

Apply Your Knowledge

Reinforce the skills and apply the concepts you learned in this chapter.

Formatting a Flyer

Instructions: Start Publisher. Open the publication, Apply 4-1 Dog Grooming Flyer, from the Data Files for Students. See the inside back cover of this book for instructions on downloading the Data Files for Students, or contact your instructor for more information about accessing the required files.

The publication you open contains unformatted text boxes in which you modify the style and columns, and apply a gradient. The resulting publication is shown in Figure 4–84.

Perform the following tasks:

1. Apply the Heading 7 style to the first text box by clicking the text and then applying the style.
2. Apply the Heading 7 style to the third text box by clicking the text and then applying the style.
3. Apply two columns to the second text box by clicking the text and then applying the columns. Resize the text box so that the two columns are even.
4. Apply two columns to the fourth text box by clicking the text and then applying the columns. Resize the text box so that the two columns are even.
5. Open the Clip Art task pane. Search for a clip related to the keyword, dog. Click a picture of a dog, similar to the one shown in Figure 4–84 to add it to the publication.
6. Right-click the picture to display its shortcut menu and then click Save as Picture on the shortcut menu. Navigate to your USB flash drive and then save the picture with the file name, Dog. Once the picture is saved, delete the picture from the publication.
7. Display the Shape gallery and choose the Bevel shape in the Basic Shapes category.
8. Drag in the publication to create a bevel shape, approximately 2.5 inches square. Position the shape to the right of the second and third text boxes.

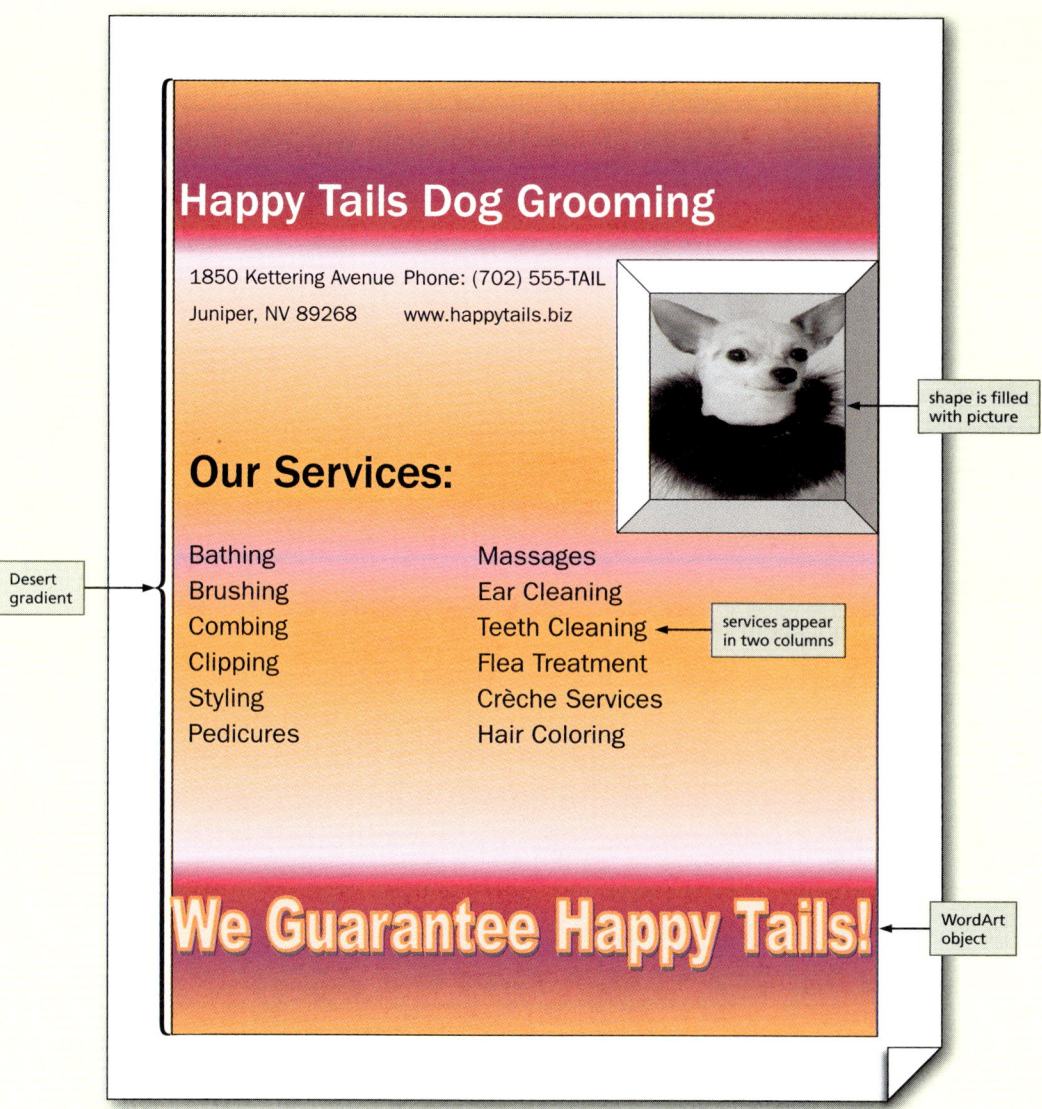

Figure 4–84

9. Resize the text boxes as necessary to fit in the publication next to the shape.

10. Use the Shape Fill gallery to fill the shape with the picture of the dog.

11. Click the large rectangle shape to select it. Click the Shape Fill button (Drawing Tools Format tab | Shape Styles group) and then point to Gradient to display the Gradient gallery. Click More Gradients to display the Fill Effects dialog box. If necessary, click the Gradient tab (Fill Effects dialog box). In the Colors area, click Preset. Click the Preset colors box arrow and then click Desert. Choose a horizontal shading style and use the fourth variant. *Hint:* if the gradient appears in front of the text, click the Send Backward button (Drawing Tools Format tab | Arrange group), until all of the text is in front.

12. Select the text in the first text box and then change the font color to white.

13. Insert a WordArt object using the Fill – Light Orange, Outline – Orange style. Type `We Guarantee Happy Tails!` as the WordArt text. Position the WordArt as shown in Figure 4–84.

14. Click File on the Ribbon and then click Save As. Save the document using the file name, Apply 4-1 Dog Grooming Flyer Formatted.

15. Submit the revised publication as specified by your instructor.

Extend Your Knowledge

Extend the skills you learned in this chapter and experiment with new skills. You may need to use Help to complete the assignment.

Editing Graphics

Instructions: Start Publisher. Open the publication, Extend 4-1 Tiger Graphic, from the Data Files for Students. See the inside back cover of this book for instructions on downloading the Data Files for Students, or contact your instructor for more information about accessing the required files.

Figure 4–85

You will edit the graphic so that it appears as shown in Figure 4–85.

Perform the following tasks:

1. Use Help to learn more about recoloring graphics and changing shadow settings.

2. Zoom to 100%. Click the graphic to select it. Click the Recolor button (Picture Tools Format tab | Adjust group) to display the Recolor gallery. Click More Variations to display the Recolor Picture dialog box. Click the Color box arrow (Recolor Picture dialog box) and choose a dark orange color.

3. Crop the tiger so that only its head remains.

4. Resize the graphic to approximately 2 inches by 1.75 inches.

5. Edit wrapping points as necessary to remove the background. Keep as much of the whiskers as possible.

6. Flip the tiger so that it faces the other way.

7. Use the Save as Picture command to save the tiger graphic as a PNG file on your USB drive, with the name Tiger Face.

8. Delete the tiger graphic from the publication.

9. Draw a Hexagon shape, approximately 4 inches square.

10. With the Hexagon shape selected, click the Shape Fill button (Drawing Tools Format tab | Shape Styles group) and then click Picture to display the Select Picture dialog box. Navigate to your USB flash drive and then select the tiger face file.

11. Click the Shape Outline button (Drawing Tools Format tab | Shape Styles group) and then click Sample Line Color to display the eyedropper mouse pointer. Click the darkest orange color in the picture.

12. Right-click the graphic to display the shortcut menu and then click Format AutoShape to display the Format AutoShape dialog box. If necessary, click the Colors and Lines tab (Format AutoShape dialog box). Click the Style box arrow and then click the 6 pt, multiline style.

13. Click the Shadow Effects button (Drawing Tools Format tab | Shadow Effects group) to display the Shadow Effects gallery. Click Shadow Style 2 in the gallery.

14. Change the publication properties, as specified by your instructor. Save the revised publication and then submit it in the format specified by your instructor.

Make It Right

Analyze a document and correct all errors and/or improve the design.

Editing Cropping and Wrap Points

Instructions: Start Publisher. Open the publication, Make It Right 4-1 Garden Postcard, from the Data Files for Students. See the inside back cover of this book for instructions on downloading the Data Files for Students, or contact your instructor for more information about accessing the required files.

You decide to improve the postcard by changing the cropping and wrap points of the graphic and right-justifying the text.

Perform the following tasks:

1. Select the graphic.

2. Click the Crop button (Picture Tools Format tab | Size group) to view how the picture was cropped (Figure 4–86).

Figure 4–86

3. Drag the left cropping handle to display more of the water can. *Hint:* you will need to drag into the workspace, outside of the page layout.

4. Click the Crop button (Picture Tools Format tab | Size group) again to hide the cropping handles. Drag the graphic to align it with the left margin of the page layout.

Continued >

Make It Right *continued*

5. Click the Wrap Text button (Picture Tools Format tab | Arrange group) and then click Edit Wrap Points. On the slanted, right side of the graphic, CTRL+click the red dotted line to create a new wrap point approximately 1.5 inches from the top. Drag the new wrap point to the top margin creating a shape with three straight sides and one slanted side.

6. Select the text in the text box. Press CTRL+R to right-justify the text.

7. Change the publication properties, as specified by your instructor. Save the revised publication and then submit it in the format specified by your instructor.

In the Lab

Design and/or create a document using the guidelines, concepts, and skills presented in this chapter. Labs are listed in order of increasing difficulty.

Lab 1: Creating a Bookmark

Problem: The town of Anton, Nebraska wants you to create a promotional bookmark to raise awareness about fire safety. You decide to create a custom page size and use graphics to promote October as fire safety month (Figure 4–87).

October is Fire Safety Month

Let's keep Anton safe!

Figure 4–87

Instructions: Perform the following tasks:

1. Start Publisher with a blank publication.

2. Click the Page Size button (Page Design tab | Page Setup group) and then click Create New Page Size in the Page Size gallery.

3. Name the new page size Bookmark. Click the Layout type box arrow (Create New Page Size dialog box) and then click 'One page per sheet'. Use a width of 9 inches and a height of 2 inches. Enter 0 in each of the Margin guide boxes, as the bookmark will have no margin. Click the OK button to return to the publication.

4. Use the Shape gallery to choose a Rectangle shape and drag a rectangle that fills the entire bookmark.

5. Click the Shape Fill button arrow (Drawing Tools Format tab | Shape Styles group) and then point to Gradient to display the Gradient gallery. Click More Gradients at the bottom of the Gradient gallery. Click Preset in the Colors area (Fill Effects dialog box) and then click the Preset colors box arrow. Choose the preset gradient named Fire. Choose the Diagonal up shading style and the lower-right variant. Click the OK button to close the dialog box.

6. Click the Clip Art button (Insert tab | Illustrations group) to display the Clip Art task pane. Search for a picture of a fire extinguisher similar to the one in Figure 4–87. Resize the graphic and place it on the right side of the bookmark.

7. Use the Clip Art task pane to search for a picture of a firefighter's helmet. The clip art has a fire hose around the helmet. Crop as much of the hose as possible, and then edit the wrap points to remove the rest of the hose. Resize the graphic and place it on the left side of the bookmark, as shown in Figure 4–87.

8. Between the two graphics, draw a text box in the upper half of the bookmark. Click the Styles button (Home tab | Styles group) to display the Styles gallery. Choose the Heading 1 style in the Styles gallery and then type `October is Fire Safety Month` to enter the text in the text box. Press CTRL+E to center the text.

9. Between the two graphics, draw a text box in the lower half of the bookmark. Click the Styles button (Home tab | Styles group) to display the Styles gallery. Choose the Heading 2 style in the Styles gallery and then type `Let's keep Anton safe!` to enter the text in the second text box. Press CTRL+E to center the text.

10. Save the publication on a USB flash drive using the file name, Lab 4-1 Fire Safety Bookmark, and then print a copy using landscape orientation.

In the Lab

Lab 2: Recoloring and Using Wrap Points

Problem: You work part-time for the state music teachers' association. You have to prepare several publications related to the upcoming marching band season and the field band competitions. They want an old-fashioned look for their graphic. You decide that storing it as a building block would save you a lot of time. The final version of the graphic is shown in Figure 4–88.

Figure 4–88

Continued >

STUDENT ASSIGNMENTS

In the Lab *continued*

Instructions: Perform the following tasks:

1. Start Publisher.

2. Choose the Blank 8.5 × 11" thumbnail to create a blank publication.

3. Click the Clip Art button (Insert tab | Illustrations group) to display the Clip Art task pane. Click the 'Results should be' box arrow and select only Illustrations. Search for clips related to the keyword, bands.

4. Choose a picture similar to the one in the background of Figure 4–88 on the previous page. *Hint:* the clip art will appear in full color.

5. With the picture selected, click the Recolor button (Picture Tools Format tab | Adjust group) and then choose the Sepia format in the Recolor gallery.

6. One at a time, add each graphic using the Clip Art task pane. Search for terms such as trumpet, drum, and flute. For each graphic, crop as necessary and edit the wrap points to show only the instrument. Recolor each one using the Sepia format.

7. Drag the graphics on top of one another to resemble Figure 4–88.

8. Click the bands picture to select it. *Hint:* click the edge of the bands picture to select only it.

9. Click the Picture Border button (Picture Tools Format tab | Picture Styles group) and then click Sample Line Color to display the eyedropper mouse pointer. Click the darkest brown color in the graphic. Click the Picture Border button (Picture Tools Format tab | Picture Styles group) again and then click the brown color that was added to the gallery. Finally, click the Picture Border button (Picture Tools Format tab | Picture Styles group) again, point to Weight, and then click 6pt in the Weight gallery.

10. Press CTRL+A to select all of the graphics. Click the Group button (Picture Tools Format tab | Arrange group) to group the graphics.

11. Right-click the graphic, and then click Save as Building Block. Name the building block, Band Graphic. Include a description and keywords.

12. Save the publication with the file name, Lab 4-2 Band Graphic. Print the graphic on a color printer if possible.

13. Submit the publication or building block in the format specified by your instructor. If you are using a lab computer, delete the graphic from the Building Block Library after submission.

In the Lab

Lab 3: Experimenting with Fills

Problem: You have decided to investigate the different gradient fills among the tints, shades, patterns, and textures available in Publisher 2010. You create a blank publication sampler for future reference.

Instructions: Perform the following tasks:

1. Start Publisher.
2. Create a blank publication, 8.5 by 11 inches, portrait orientation, with 1-inch margins.
3. Turn on boundaries.
4. Draw a Rectangle shape, approximately 2 inches square. Copy the rectangle and then deselect it. Paste a new rectangle and drag it to a location to the right of the first rectangle. Paste 13 more times to create a total of 15 rectangles, 3 across and 5 down.
5. One at a time, select each rectangle. Use the Shape Fill button arrow (Drawing Tools Format tab | Shape Styles group) to fill each rectangle as follows:
   - Fill one rectangle with a solid color, no border.
   - Fill one rectangle with a different solid color and a 3 pt black border.
   - Fill one rectangle with a one-color gradient, using a From center shading style.
   - Fill one rectangle with a two-color gradient, using a Diagonal down shading style.
   - Fill one rectangle with a texture from the Texture gallery, using a dashed border style.
   - Fill one rectangle with a dark texture from the Texture gallery, using a contrasting border color.
   - Fill one rectangle with a black and white striped pattern.
   - Fill one rectangle with a different pattern, using colors other than black and white.
   - Fill one rectangle with a picture and no border.
   - Fill one rectangle with a picture and flip it vertically.
   - Fill one rectangle with a tint of 20% (do not use black or white).
   - Fill one rectangle with a shade of 60% (do not use black or white).
   - Fill one rectangle with a fill of your choice, and add a shadow.
   - Fill one rectangle with a fill of your choice, and add a 3-D Style.
   - Fill one rectangle with a solid color and Border Art.
6. Change the publication properties, as specified by your instructor.
7. Save the publication on a USB flash drive, using the file name, Lab 4-3 Fill Sampler. Submit the publication in the format specified by your instructor.

Cases and Places

Apply your creative thinking and problem solving skills to design and implement a solution.

Note: To complete these assignments, you may be required to use the Data Files for Students. See the inside back cover of this book for instructions on downloading the Data Files for Students, or contact your instructor for information about accessing the required files.

1: Create a Custom Building Block

Academic

The American Sign Language Club has a chapter at your school. They would like to create a building block that includes the signs for A, S, and L. They plan to use the building block in several ways, including on their correspondence, Web site, and flyers. Open a blank publication. Use the Clip Art task pane to look for graphics related to sign language. One at a time, insert the signs for A, S, and L into the publication. Select the three graphics and group. Add a 3-point black border around the grouping. Save the publication that shows the grouped graphic. Add the group to the Building Block Library. Remember to include a description and searchable keywords. If you create the building block on a lab computer, remember to delete it after submitting the assignment to your instructor.

2: Create a Personal Brand

Personal

You would like to create graphics and documents for social media and tracking Web sites that display your own special flair and style. You also would like to use the fonts and colors in your e-portfolio. Create a custom color scheme using black as the text color and your favorite two colors as Accent 1 and Accent 2. Also change the color of the hyperlink. Save the color scheme, using your name as the new scheme name. Look through the fonts available on your computer. Pick out a strong bold font for headings and then choose a body font that contrasts it in type ornamentation. Create a custom font scheme with those two fonts. Save the font scheme using your name as the new scheme name. Create a simple document to demonstrate the fonts and colors. If you create the schemes on a school computer, remember to delete them after submitting the assignment to your instructor.

3: Create a Banner

Professional

A local farmer's market has asked you to create a banner. They would like a wave shape that fills the banner, with a gradient fill to serve as a background for the words, The Merry Market. Create a blank page publication size of approximately 17 inches wide and 8.5 inches tall. Insert a Wave shape and resize it to fill the banner. Use a one color gradient any shade of green. Use a large text box and style for the company name, placed in front of the wave shape. Insert a text box in the lower-left corner of the banner that displays the address and telephone number: 1350 Ridgeway Avenue, Blue Dust, MO 64319, (816) 555-3770.

5 | Using Business Information Sets

Objectives

You will have mastered the material in this chapter when you can:

- Design a letterhead
- Create a business information set
- Insert business information fields into a publication
- Use the Measurement toolbar to position and scale objects
- Create and apply a new text style
- Insert an automatically updated date and time

- Apply the read-only attribute to a publication
- Add user-friendly features to an interactive publication
- Create an envelope
- Change printer page settings
- Create and print business cards
- Publish a portable PDF/XPS file
- Embed fonts in a publication

5 | Using Business Information Sets

Introduction

Incorporating personal information unique to a business, organization, or individual user expands the possibilities for using Publisher as a complete application product for small businesses. Business information sets, which include pieces of information such as a name, an address, a motto, or even a logo, can be inserted automatically and consistently across all publications. Publisher allows you to insert, delete, and save multiple business information sets and apply them independently.

Business information sets are just one way that people expand Publisher's capabilities. Some users create large text boxes and use Publisher like a word processor. Others create a table and perform mathematical and statistical operations or embed charts as they would with a spreadsheet. Still others create a database and use Publisher for mass mailings, billings, and customer accounts. Publisher's capabilities make it an efficient tool in small business offices — without the cost and learning curve of some of the high-end dedicated application software.

Project — Business Cards and Stationery

Storing permanent information about a business facilitates the customization of publications such as business cards and stationery. A **business information set** is a group of customized information fields about an individual or an organization that can be used to generate information text boxes across publications. Many of the Publisher templates automatically create business information text boxes to incorporate data from the business information set. Publications created from scratch also can integrate a business information set by including one or more pieces in the publication. For example, you can save your name, address, and telephone number in the business information set. Whenever you need that information, you can insert it in a publication without retyping it.

To illustrate some of the business features of Microsoft Publisher, this project presents a series of steps to create a business information set. You will use the business information set in a letterhead, envelope, and business card. You also will create a portable file for easy viewing, and embed fonts in the Publisher file for editing on a different computer. The project creates publications for a business named Pool Haven, as shown in Figure 5–1.

Figure 5–1

Overview

As you read through this chapter, you will learn how to create the publications shown in Figure 5–1 by performing these general tasks:

- Design and compose a letterhead.
- Create a business information set.
- Create and apply a style.
- Type a letter with an automatic date.
- Create an envelope and business card.
- Publish a PDF/XPS file and embed fonts.

Plan
Ahead

General Project Guidelines

When you create a Publisher publication from scratch, the actions you perform and decisions you make will affect the appearance and characteristics of the finished publication. As you create publications, such as the project shown in Figure 5–1 on the previous page, you should follow these general guidelines:

1. **Design the letterhead.** Whether you use a template or start from scratch, organize your tasks starting with a consultation with the customer. Agree on the color scheme, font scheme, and style for stationery. Decide what pieces of information need to be included and how much white space is needed. Discuss a plan for printing.

2. **Employ reusable business information sets.** When you are creating more than one publication for a given company, or plan to create more publications for it in the future, you can save time by creating a business information set. Check and double-check all data from the customer.

3. **Apply styles.** Use a matching or complementary color when creating a new text style. Choose settings such as font, font size, and special formatting. Save the style with a user-friendly name.

4. **Make interactive publications user-friendly.** Help the user by using an automatic date and/or time in the publication. Position text boxes or other items edited by the user in front of other objects for easy editing. Apply read-only settings to publications that will serve as a template so that they cannot be changed accidentally.

5. **Create files in portable formats.** Depending on its use, you might have to distribute your publication in a variety of formats. Portability is an important consideration. After designing a file in Publisher, use software tools to convert it to the PDF or XPS format, or embed the fonts so that users can view and edit them.

To Start Publisher

The following steps, which assume Windows 7 is running, start Publisher based on a typical installation. You may need to ask your instructor how to start Publisher for your computer. For a detailed example of the procedure summarized below, refer to the Office 2010 and Windows 7 chapter.

1. Click the Start button on the Windows 7 taskbar to display the Start menu.

2. Type **Microsoft Publisher** as the search text in the 'Search programs and files' text box, and watch the search results appear on the Start menu.

3. Click Microsoft Publisher 2010 in the search results on the Start menu to start Publisher and open the Backstage view.

4. If the Publisher window is not maximized, click the Maximize button next to the Close button on its title bar to maximize the window.

Plan
Ahead

Design the letterhead.

Work with the customer to design a letterhead that matches the color and font schemes of the company, if any. Decide on placement of vital information, page size, and white space. Discuss a plan for printing. Will the customer send the letterhead out for commercial printing or print copies themselves? Will users want to type directly on the Publisher letterhead? Define user-friendly features such as an automatic date and easy-to-use text box for typing letters.

Creating Letterhead

In many businesses, **letterhead** is preprinted stationery with important facts about the company and blank space to contain the text of the correspondence. Letterhead, typically used for official business communication, is an easy way to convey company information to the reader and quickly establish a formal and legitimate mode of correspondence. The company information may be displayed in a variety of places — across the top, down the side, or split between the top and bottom of the page. Although most business letterhead is 8½ × 11 inches, other sizes are becoming more popular, especially with small agencies and not-for-profit organizations.

Generally, it is cost effective for companies to outsource the printing of their letterhead. Designing the letterhead in-house and then sending the file to a commercial printer saves design consultation time, customization, and money. Black-and-white or spot-color letterhead is more common and less expensive than composite or process color. Businesses sometimes opt to not purchase preprinted letterhead because of its expense, color, or limited quantity required. In those cases, companies design their own letterhead and save it in a file. In some cases, businesses print multiple copies of their blank letterhead and then, using application software, they prepare documents to print on the letterhead paper.

To Create a Letterhead Template

The following steps create a letterhead template and apply color and font schemes.

1

- In the New template gallery, scroll as necessary to click Letterhead in the More Templates area.

- Scroll to the More Installed Templates area and click the Batik letterhead.

- Click the Color scheme box arrow and then click Sapphire in the Color scheme list.

- Click the Font scheme box arrow and then click Galley in the Font scheme list.

- If necessary, click the Include logo check box to select it (Figure 5–2).

Figure 5–2

2

• Click the Create button to display the letterhead page (Figure 5–3).

3

• If necessary, click the Collapse Page Navigation Pane button to collapse the Page Navigation pane.

Figure 5–3

Plan Ahead

> **Employ reusable business information sets.**
> Obtain business information from the customer. Check and double-check it for accuracy. Decide whether to use a logo in the business information set, and obtain necessary permissions and graphics. Save the business information set using the name of the company. If you are in a laboratory setting, delete the information set after you use it.

Creating a Business Information Set

Business information sets store data about a company. This data then is used in publications whenever you need it or when a Publisher template incorporates it. For example, rather than typing the name of the company multiple times, you can insert the data from a field in the business information set. A **field** is a specific component in the set, such as an individual's name, job position or title, organization name, address, telephone and fax number, e-mail address, tagline, or logo. When inserting a field, Publisher places a text box in your publication and supplies the text.

Publisher allows you to create and save as many different business information sets as you want. If you have more than one set saved, you can choose the set you need from a list. The sets are stored within the Publisher application files on your computer. When you create a new publication, the business information set used most recently populates the new publication. When Publisher first is installed, the business information is generic, with words such as Title and Business Name. In a laboratory situation, the business information set may be populated with information about your school, which was provided when Microsoft Office 2010 was installed.

If you edit a text box within a publication that contains personal information, you change the set for that publication only, unless you choose to update the set. To affect changes for all future publications, you edit the business information set itself. You can edit the stored business information set at any time — before, during, or after performing other publication tasks.

Many types of publications use logos to identify and distinguish the page. A **logo** is a recognizable symbol that identifies a person, business, or organization. A logo may be composed of a name, a picture, or a combination of symbols, text, and graphics. The Building Block Library contains many logo styles from which you may choose, or you can create a logo from a picture, from a file, or from scratch. Although Publisher's logo styles are generic, commercial logos typically are copyrighted. Consult with a legal representative before you commercially use materials bearing clip art, logos, designs, words, or other symbols that could violate third-party rights, including trademarks.

Table 5–1 displays the data for each of the fields in the business information set that you will create in this project.

BTW

Business Information Sets
Using different business information sets allows you to maintain alternate information about your business; a second or related business, such as a major supplier or home business; an outside organization for which you maintain information, such as scouting or sports; and your personal home or family information.

Table 5–1 Data for Business Information Fields

Fields	Data
Individual name	Max Richards
Job or position or title	Manager
Organization name	Pool Haven
Address	1750 Quincy Street Springfield, SC 31692
Phone, fax, and e-mail	Phone: 803-555-2795 Fax: 803-555-2796 E-mail: info@poolhaven.biz
Tagline or motto	Great Quality. Reasonable Prices.
Business Information set name	Pool Haven
Logo	Pool Logo.png on Data Files for Students

To Create a Business Information Set

The steps on the next page create a business information set for Pool Haven and apply it to the current publication. You will enter data for each field. The logo is available on the Data Files for Students. See the inside back cover of this book for instructions on downloading the Data Files for Students, or contact your instructor for information about accessing the required files.

1

- Display the Insert tab.

- Click the Business Information button (Insert tab | Text group) to display the list of business information fields and commands (Figure 5–4).

Q&A Why does my screen look different?

If you have business information sets saved on your computer, your list may contain data in each field.

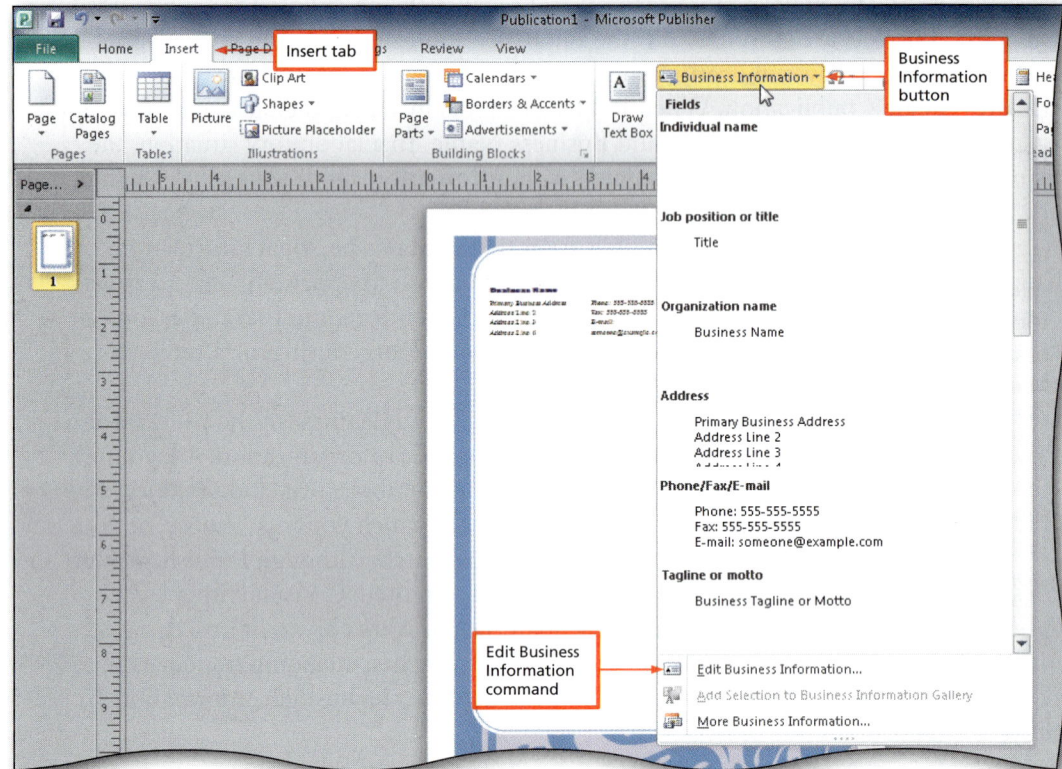

Figure 5–4

2

- Click Edit Business Information to display the Create New Business Information Set dialog box (Figure 5–5).

Q&A Publisher displayed the Business Information dialog box. What should I do?

Click the New button to display the Create New Business Information Set dialog box.

Figure 5–5

Q&A Why does the Individual name text box already have a name in it?

The person or company that installed Publisher may have supplied data for the business information set. You will replace the data in the next step.

Q&A How do you use the other commands in the list (shown in Figure 5–4)?

The Add Selection to Business Information Gallery command allows you to add selected text and graphics as a Publisher building block. The More Business Information command opens the Building Block Library from which you can add objects to your publication.

3

- Enter the data from Table 5–1 on page PUB 271, pressing the TAB key to advance from one field to the next (Figure 5–6).

How do I delete data once it is inserted in a field?

In the Create New Business Information Set dialog box, you can select the text in the field and then press the DELETE key. To remove a business information field while editing a publication, you simply delete the text box from the publication itself; however, this does not delete it permanently from the set. You can remove entire business information sets once they are stored; you will see how to do this later in this chapter.

Figure 5–6

4

- Click the Change button (Create New Business Information Set dialog box) to display the Insert Picture dialog box.

- Navigate to the location of the Data Files for Students on your computer.

- Double-click the folder labeled Chapter 05 to display the picture files in the folder (Figure 5–7).

Figure 5–7

5

- Double-click the file named Pool Logo (Insert Picture dialog box) to insert the logo (Figure 5–8).

Figure 5–8

6

- Click the Save button (Create New Business Information Set dialog box) to save the business information set and display the Business Information dialog box (Figure 5–9).

Q&A

Does saving the business information set also save the publication?

No, you are saving a separate, internal data file that contains only the data in the fields and the logo.

Figure 5–9

7

- Click the Update Publication button (Business Information dialog box).

- Zoom to 100% to see the business information fields (Figure 5–10).

Figure 5–10

Other Ways

1. In publication, click smart tag button, click Edit Business Information, enter data, click Update Publication button (Business Information dialog box)

Previous Business Information Set

If other people have used the computer you are working on, it is possible that other business information sets appear in your list. If you need to delete a business information set, click the 'Select a business information set' box arrow (Figure 5–9), select the set, and then click the Delete button (Business Information dialog box).

TO APPLY A BUSINESS INFORMATION SET IN THE NEW TEMPLATE GALLERY

If you wanted to choose an information set while working with a template in the New template gallery, you would perform the following tasks.

1. Click to select the desired template.

2. In the Customize area on the right side of the New template gallery, click the Business Information box arrow to display the available business information sets.

3. Click the business information set you wish to use.

TO CHANGE THE BUSINESS INFORMATION SET OF AN EXISTING PUBLICATION

If you wanted to apply a different business information set to a publication, you would perform the following tasks.

1. Open a publication.
2. Display the Insert tab.
3. Click the Business Information button (Insert tab | Text group) to display the list of business information fields and commands.
4. Click Edit Business Information to open the Business Information dialog box.
5. Click the 'Select a Business Information set' box arrow to display the available business information sets.
6. Click the business information set you wish to use.

To Insert a Business Information Field

When you insert an individual field, Publisher places either a text box with the information in the center of the screen with a preset font and font size, or a picture box with the logo. You then may move the field and format the text as necessary. Applied formatting affects the current publication only. The following steps insert a field, in this case the tagline or motto, from the business information set into the current publication.

1

• If necessary, click the scratch area so that no objects are selected in the page layout.

• Scroll to the lower portion of the page layout.

• Click the Business Information button (Insert tab | Text group) to display the list of new business information fields and commands (Figure 5–11).

Figure 5–11

2

- Click the Tagline or motto field to insert it into the publication (Figure 5–12).

Q&A

All of the words do not display in the text box. Should I fix that?

No, you will fix it in the next set of steps.

Figure 5–12

Other Ways

1. Click Building Blocks Dialog Box Launcher, click Business Information folder (Building Block Library dialog box), select Object, click Insert button

Using the Measurement Toolbar

To place and scale objects precisely, rather than estimating by dragging and resizing, you use the **Measurement toolbar** to enter the exact values for the horizontal position, vertical position, width, and height of the object. The Measurement toolbar not only sets the location and size of an object but also sets the angle of rotation. If the object is text, the Measurement toolbar offers additional character spacing or typesetting options. The Measurement toolbar is a floating toolbar with nine text boxes. Entries can be typed in each box or set by clicking the appropriate arrows. Table 5–2 lists the first five boxes on the Measurement toolbar, which edit the position, size, and rotation of an object.

Table 5–2 Position, Size, and Rotation Boxes on the Measurement Toolbar

Display	Box Name	Specifies	Preset Unit of Measurement
x	Horizontal Position	Horizontal distance from the left edge of the page to the upper-left corner of the object	Inches
y	Vertical Position	Vertical distance from the top of the page to the upper-left corner of the object	Inches
▥	Width	Width of object	Inches
▥	Height	Height of object	Inches
⊿	Rotation	Rotate the object counterclockwise from the original orientation	Degrees

To Display the Measurement Toolbar

The following step displays the Measurement toolbar.

- Display the Drawing Tools Format tab.

- Click the Measurement button (Drawing Tools Format tab | Size group) to display the Measurement toolbar (Figure 5–13).

My Measurement toolbar covers up my text. How can I move it?

Drag the toolbar's title bar to move the floating toolbar.

Figure 5–13

To Position Objects Using the Measurement Toolbar

Using the Measurement toolbar, you can resize and position the tagline or motto field at the bottom of the page. The customer also has asked that the Pool Haven logo appear more prominently in the letterhead. The following steps position and scale the objects precisely using the Measurement toolbar.

- On the Measurement toolbar, select the text in the Horizontal Position box and then type 1 to replace it. Press the TAB key to advance to the next box.

- Type 8.85 in the Vertical Position box and then press the TAB key.

- Type 6.2 in the Width box and then press the TAB key.

- Type .6 in the Height box and then press the ENTER key (Figure 5–14).

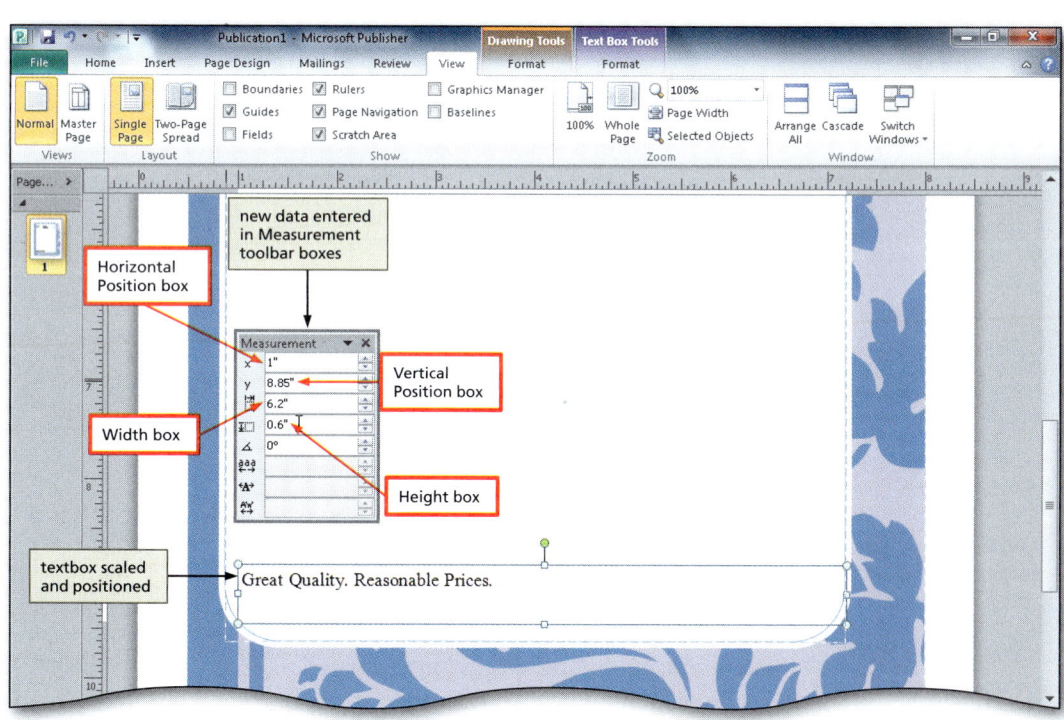

Figure 5–14

Should I change the value in the Rotation box?

No. A zero value is appropriate for an object that should appear straight up and down.

2

- Scroll as necessary and click the logo to select it.

- Select the text in the Horizontal Position box and then type `4.71` to replace it. Press the TAB key to advance to the next box.

- Type `.5` in the Vertical Position box and then press the TAB key.

- Type `2.5` in the Width box and then press the TAB key.

- Type `2` in the Height box and then press the ENTER key (Figure 5–15).

Figure 5–15

3

- Click the Close button on the Measurement toolbar to close it.

Other Ways

1. Right-click object, click Format on shortcut menu, click Size tab (Format dialog box), enter measurements

Plan Ahead

Apply styles.

When creating a new text style, consult with the customer about company colors and/or font schemes. Sample colors from the company logo to make sure the colors match. Keep in mind reusability when assigning font formats. Remind the customer of possible formatting features such as shadow, engrave, emboss, and others. Save the style with the name of the company. If you are creating multiple styles, include the type of data in the style name, such as My Company Footnote Style.

BTW

AutoFit Text
Some Publisher template and business information set text boxes, such as titles, mastheads, and taglines, are preset to Shrink Text On Overflow. You can change the autofitting settings by right-clicking the text box and choosing the style on the shortcut menu.

Creating a New Style

Publisher allows you to create a new text and formatting style from scratch or one based on a current style or text selection. Recall that a style is a named group of formatting characteristics, including font, font size, font color, character spacing, bullets, and shadows, among other attributes. The default style in Publisher is called the **Normal style**, which includes the body font from the current font scheme in a black font color with left-justified alignment. The default settings for line and paragraph settings are determined by the style used; however, in general, the default line spacing for text boxes is dependent on the template and the font scheme, because Publisher accommodates the largest character of the font family and adds an additional amount of space for the text box margin. The line spacing varies between 1.0 and 1.2 spaces. The default spacing between paragraphs varies between 6 and 9 points (or 1/12-inch and 1/8-inch).

Creating a new style is a good idea when you want to change those defaults or you have multiple text passages that must be formatted identically and the desired attributes are not saved as a current style. For the customer in this chapter, you will create a new style named Pool Haven that will contain a 20-point blue font with a shadow. You will apply the style to both the name of the company and the tagline.

To Sample a Font Color

The first step in creating a new style will be to choose a font color. For consistency, you will sample the dark blue color in the logo. When you **sample** a color, the mouse pointer changes to an eyedropper; then, any color that you click in the publication is added to all color galleries, just below the color scheme palette. The following steps sample the font color.

1

- Triple-click the text, Pool Haven, to select it.

- Display the Text Box Tools Format tab.

- Click the Font Color button arrow (Text Box Tools Format tab | Font group) to display the Font Color gallery (Figure 5–16).

Q&A

Does it make any difference whether I use the Font Color button on the Home tab or on the Text Box Tools Format tab?

You may use either one. Typically, when you select text, Publisher automatically displays the Text Box Tools Format tab, so that button would be quicker to use.

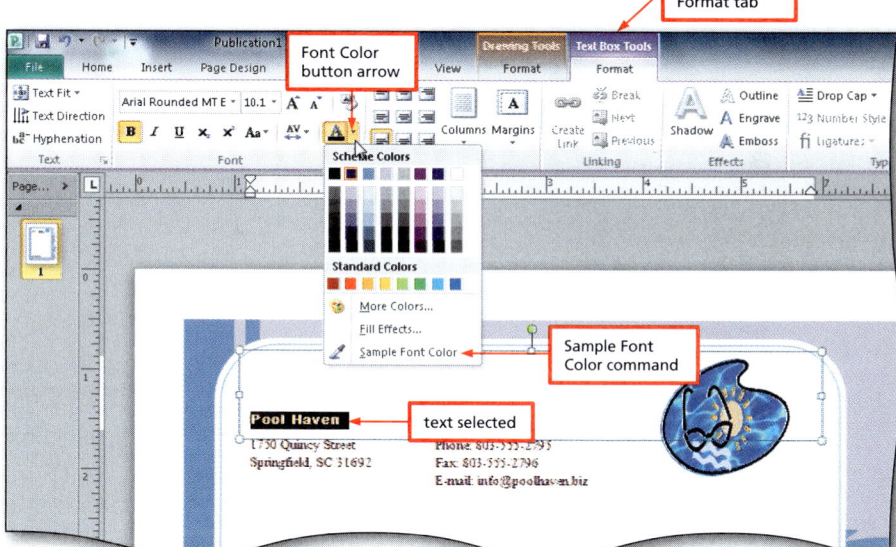

Figure 5–16

2

- Click Sample Font Color in the Font Color gallery to display the eyedropper mouse pointer.

- Click the darkest blue color in the logo to apply the color to the selected text (Figure 5–17).

Figure 5–17

To Create a New Style

The following steps display the New Style Dialog box to create a new style based on the current selection.

1

• Display the Home tab.

• Click the Styles button (Home tab | Styles group) to display the Styles gallery (Figure 5–18).

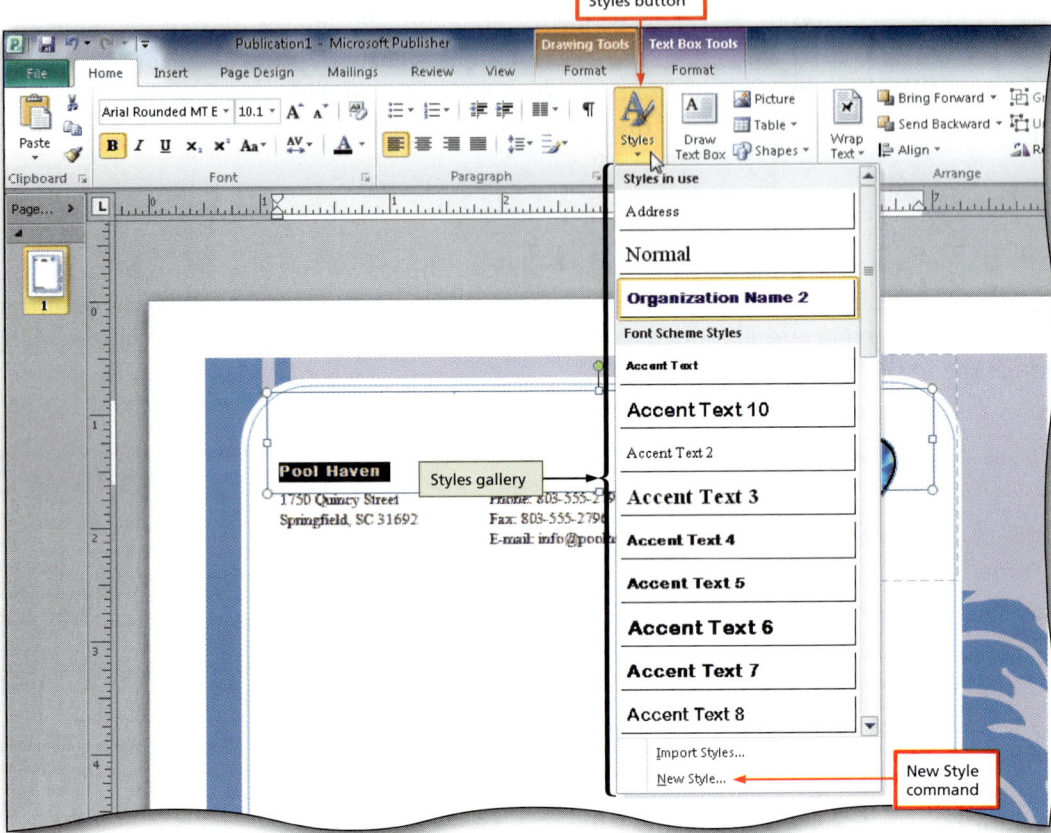

Figure 5–18

2

• Click New Style to display the New Style dialog box.

• In the 'Enter new style name' text box, type **Pool Haven** to name the style (Figure 5–19).

Q&A

Why did the name also appear in the 'Style for the following paragraph' box?

Publisher assumes you will want to use the same style for subsequent paragraphs. If you want to change that setting, you can click the 'Style for the following paragraph' box arrow (New Style dialog box), and then click a different style.

Figure 5–19

3

- Click the Font button (New Style dialog box) to display the Font dialog box.

- Enter 20 in the Size box (Font dialog box) to set the font size.

- Click the Shadow check box in the Effects area to select it (Figure 5–20).

4

- Click the OK button (Font dialog box) to close the Font dialog box.

- Click the OK button (New Style dialog box) to close the New Style dialog box.

Figure 5–20

To Apply the New Style

The following steps apply the new style to text in the publication.

1

- With the Pool Haven text still selected, click the Styles button (Home tab | Styles group) to display the Styles gallery.

- Scroll to display the Pool Haven style (Figure 5–21).

Figure 5–21

2

- Click the Pool Haven style to apply it to the text.

- Click outside the selection to view the change more easily (Figure 5–22).

Q&A Will I be able to use this style in a different publication?

Publisher attaches new styles only to the publication in which they are created; however, you can import styles from one publication to another. The process copies all of the styles, not just the new ones.

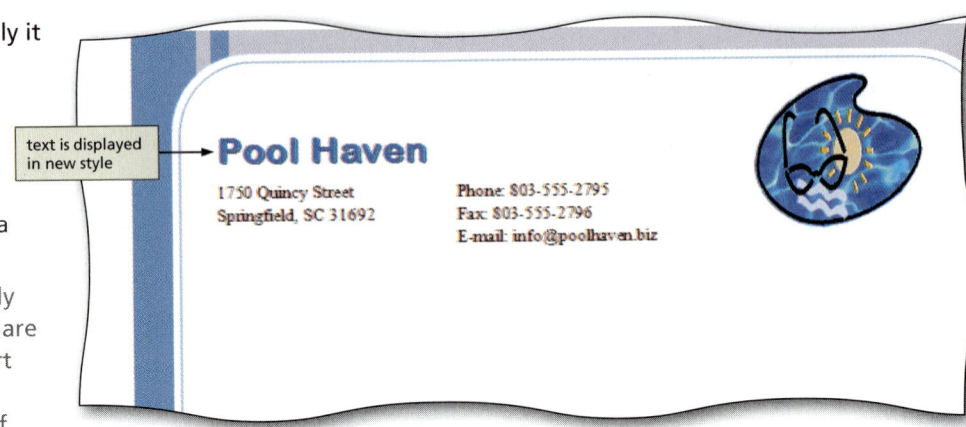

Figure 5–22

3

- Scroll in the workspace to display the lower portion of the letterhead.

- Triple-click the text in the tagline or motto text box to select it.

- Click the Styles button (Home tab | Styles group) to display the Styles gallery and then click the Pool Haven style to apply it to the selected text.

- Click outside the selection to view the new formatting (Figure 5–23).

Q&A Could I use the Format Painter to copy the formatting attributes?

Yes, you can edit the formatting either way.

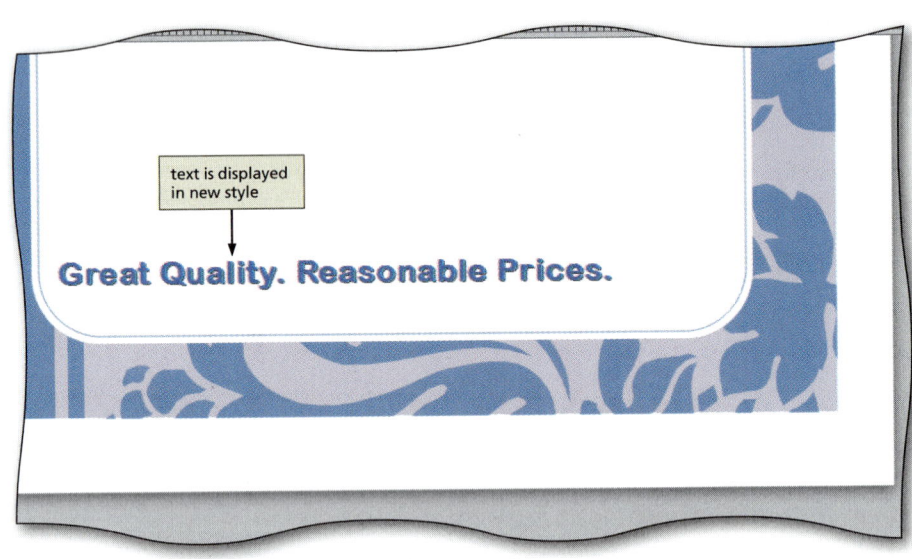

Figure 5–23

Plan Ahead

BTW

VBA
VBA or Visual Basic for Applications allows designers to write code in Publisher to customize the user experience further. For example, if you want to remind users to save the file with a different name, you can include message box code. You also can place the insertion point, select objects, and create buttons — all of which display when the user opens the publication.

> **Make interactive publications user-friendly.**
> When you are creating a custom template that users will interact with on a regular basis, include a date and time that will update automatically. Add extra lines and position the insertion point to help draw the user's eyes to where text or data should be entered. Create typing areas that are obvious and in the foreground. Apply read-only settings to publications that will serve as custom templates.

Customizing the Letterhead for Interactivity

When creating publications that are designed to be edited by others or publications with which users must interact, it is important to make the publication as user-friendly as possible. Prepare the publication with the novice user in mind. Always place the interactive components in the front, or on top, of other objects in the publication. Use updateable fields when possible, and insert blank lines or tabs to help users know where to type. In a later chapter, you also will learn how to create customized code to turn on and off certain Publisher features and create dialog box reminders for the user.

Using an Automatic Date

Publisher and other Microsoft Office applications can access your computer's stored date and time. You then can retrieve the current date and/or time and display it in a variety of formats. Additionally, you can choose to update the date and time automatically each time the file is accessed, or keep a static date and time.

To Create a Formatted Text Box

To make the letterhead more functional for the company, you will insert a large text box in which users can type their text. The following steps create a text box and set the font and font size.

1

- If it is not selected already, click the Special Characters button (Home tab | Paragraph group) to display formatting marks.

- Click the Show Whole Page button on the status bar and then click the scratch area so no object is selected.

- Click the Draw Text Box button (Home tab | Objects group) to select it.

- Drag to create a large rectangle that fills the white area in the center of the letterhead. As you drag the mouse pointer, you will see a pink visual layout guide that will help you align the text box (Figure 5–24).

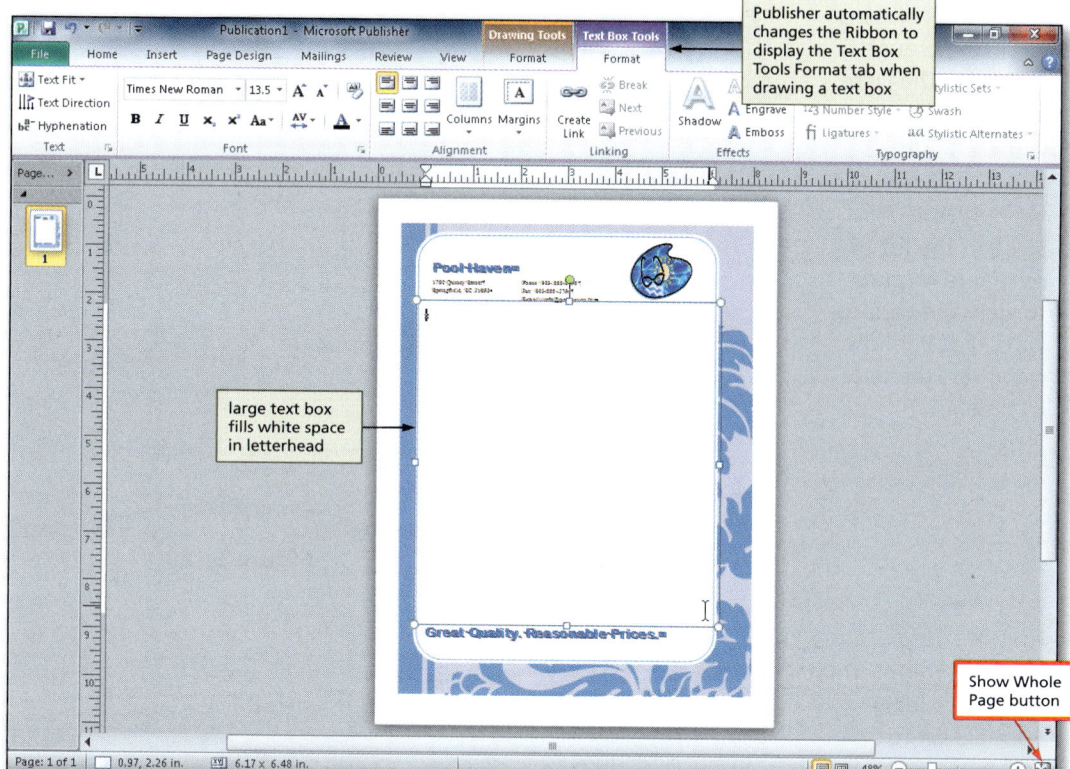

Figure 5–24

2

- Press the F9 key to zoom the text box to 100%.

- If necessary, click the Font box arrow (Text Box Tools Format tab | font group) and then click Times New Roman in the Font gallery.

- If necessary, click the Font Size box arrow (Text Box Tools Format tab | Font group) and then click 12 in the Font Size gallery (Figure 5–25).

Why am I setting the font before I type?

It is easier to set it before typing than to select all of the text later and then set the font.

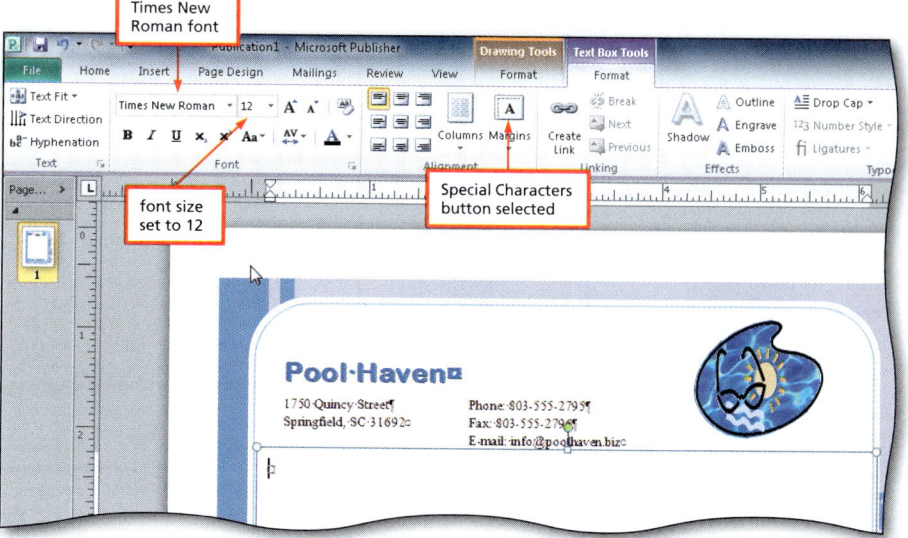

Figure 5–25

To Insert an Automatic Date

The date appears at the top of most business letters. The following steps insert a date that will be current whenever the user opens the letterhead to prepare a new letter.

1

• With the insertion point positioned in the new text box, display the Insert tab.

• Click the Date & Time button (Insert tab | Text group) to display the Date and Time dialog box (Figure 5–26).

Experiment

• Scroll in the list of Available formats to view the various ways that Publisher can insert the date or time.

Figure 5–26

2

• Click the third format in the Available Formats list to select it.

• Click the Update automatically check box so that it contains a check mark (Figure 5–27).

Q&A

What does the Default button do?

When you click the Default button, the current settings for date and time are chosen automatically every time you insert the date or time.

Figure 5–27

3

- Click the OK button (Date and Time dialog box) to close the dialog box.

- Press the ENTER key twice to create a blank line after the date (Figure 5–28).

Q&A Why is my date different?

Checking the Update automatically check box causes Publisher to access your computer's system date. The publication will display your current date.

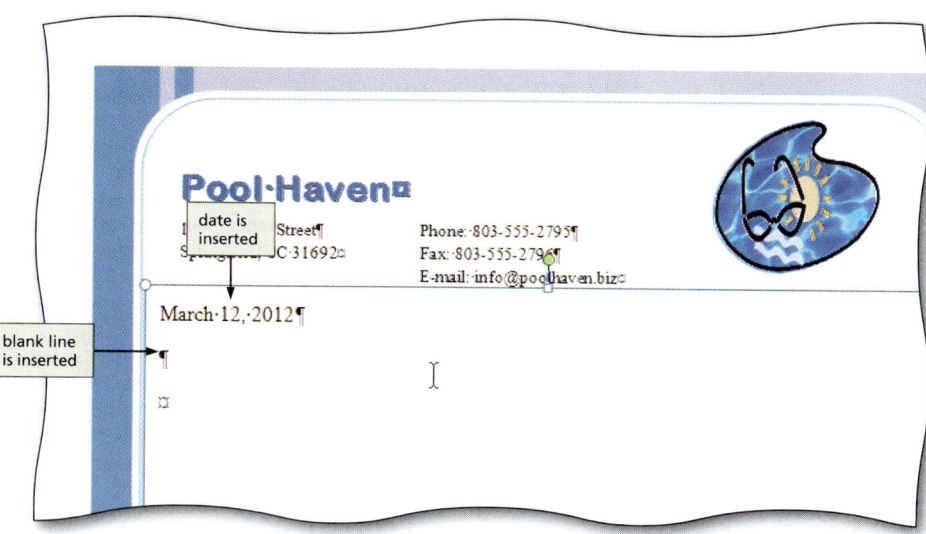

Figure 5–28

To Save the Letterhead

You have performed many tasks while creating this letterhead and do not want to risk losing work completed thus far. Accordingly, you should save the document.

The following steps assume you already have created folders for storing your files, for example, a CIS 101 folder (for your class) that contains a Publisher folder (for your assignments). Thus, these steps save the document in the Publisher folder in the CIS 101 folder on a USB flash drive using the file name, Pool Haven Letterhead. For a detailed example of the procedure summarized below, refer to the Office 2010 and Windows 7 chapter at the beginning of this book.

1 With a USB flash drive connected to one of the computer's USB ports, click the Save button on the Quick Access Toolbar to display the Save As dialog box.

2 Type **Pool Haven Letterhead** in the File name text box to change the file name. Do not press the ENTER key after typing the file name because you do not want to close the dialog box at this time.

3 Navigate to the desired save location (in this case, the Publisher folder in the CIS 101 folder [or your class folder] on the USB flash drive).

4 Click the Save button (Save As dialog box) to save the publication on the selected drive with the entered file name.

To Close a Publication without Quitting Publisher

The following step closes the letterhead without quitting Publisher.

1 Click the File tab to open the Backstage view and then click the Close command to close the publication without quitting Publisher and to return to the New template gallery.

Read-Only Files

Once a generic letterhead is created, it is a good idea to change the file's attribute to read-only. With a read-only file you can open and access the file normally, but you cannot make permanent changes to it. That way, users will be forced to save the publication with a new file name, keeping the original letterhead intact and unchanged for the next user.

While you can view system properties in Publisher 2010, you cannot change the read-only attribute. Setting the read-only attribute is a function of the operating system.

To Set the Read-Only Attribute

The following steps set the read-only attribute for the Pool Haven Letterhead file, using Windows 7.

- Click the Start button on the Windows 7 taskbar to display the Start menu.

- Type **Pool Haven Letterhead** as the search text in the 'Search programs and files' text box and watch the search results appear on the Start menu (Figure 5–29).

Q&A My search produced no results. What should I do?

Your file should be the most recent and appear at the top of the list, provided you saved the publication recently. If your file is not displayed, click the 'See more results' button and then navigate to your storage location.

Figure 5–29

②

- Right-click Pool Haven Letterhead in the search results on the Start menu to display the shortcut menu (Figure 5–30).

Q&A What is the difference between applying a read-only attribute and creating a Publisher template?

Publisher templates do not prevent users from saving the template with the same name, which would destroy the default settings and user text box features. The read-only attribute keeps the file unchanged and the same for every user.

Q&A Why is my shortcut menu different?

You may have different programs installed on your computer that affect the shortcut menu.

Figure 5–30

- Click Properties on the shortcut menu to display the Pool Haven Letterhead.pub Properties dialog box.

- If necessary, click the General tab (Pool Haven Letterhead.pub Properties dialog box) to display its settings.

- Verify that the file is the one you previously saved on your storage device by looking at the Location information.

- Click to place a check mark in the Read-only check box in the Attributes area (Figure 5–31).

- Click the OK button (Pool Haven Letterhead.pub Properties dialog box) to close the dialog box and apply the read-only attribute.

Figure 5–31

Other Ways
1. Click Start button, click Computer, navigate to file, right-click file, click Properties on shortcut menu, click General tab (Properties dialog box), click Read-only check box, click OK button

To Return to Publisher

1. Click the Publisher program button on the Windows 7 taskbar to return to Publisher and the New template gallery.

Break Point: If you wish to take a break, this is a good place to do so. You can quit Publisher now. To resume at a later time, start Publisher and continue following the steps from this location forward.

Using the Custom Letterhead Template

In this project, employees will open the letterhead file in Publisher, type the text of their letter, and then save the finished product with a new file name — thus preserving the original letterhead file.

To Open a Publication from the Recent Documents List

Just like the Windows 7 Start menu, Publisher maintains a list of the last few publications that have been opened or saved on your computer. The **Recent Documents list** allows you to click the name of the publication to open it, without browsing to the location. The steps on the next page open the Pool Haven Letterhead from the Recent Documents list.

BTW

Using Read-Only Files
Read-only files can be deleted and moved, but Windows will prompt you with a special dialog box asking you to confirm that you want to move or delete the read-only file.

1

- Click Recent to display the Recent Documents list (Figure 5–32).

Q&A What does the Quickly access this number of Recent Documents check box do?

When you place a check mark in that check box and then enter a number in the box to the right, the number you enter determines how many recent publication file names appear on the File tab, just below the Close button. They also appear in the Recent Documents list.

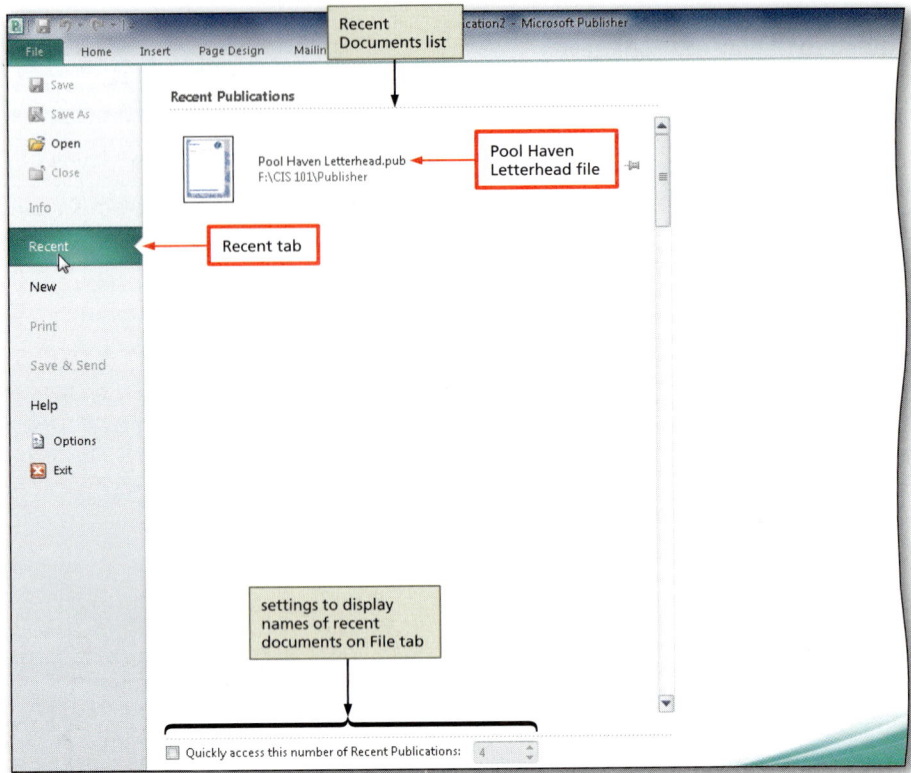

Figure 5–32

2

- Click Pool Haven Letterhead in the Recent Documents list to open the file (Figure 5–33).

Q&A Can I change the total number of publications listed in the Recent Documents list?

Yes. To do so, click the File tab to open the Backstage view. Click the Options button, click Advanced, and then change the number in the Show this number of Recent Documents box in the Display area.

Figure 5–33

To Type a Letter

Because you earlier created a text box with the automatic date and a blank line, users can simply click in the appropriate area to begin typing their letter. The following steps enter the text of a letter.

1
- Click the center of the letterhead to place the insertion point in the main text box.

- Zoom to 100% (Figure 5–34).

Q&A

Is there a way to position the insertion point automatically for the user?

Yes. In a later chapter, you will learn how to write a macro event to help the user further with data entry.

Figure 5–34

2
- Type the letter as shown in Figure 5–35, using the default line and paragraph spacing. Press the ENTER key only to complete a paragraph or to insert a blank line.

Q&A

Could I copy and paste text in a custom template?

Yes, you can perform any of the text editing techniques and use the Ribbon as much as you want.

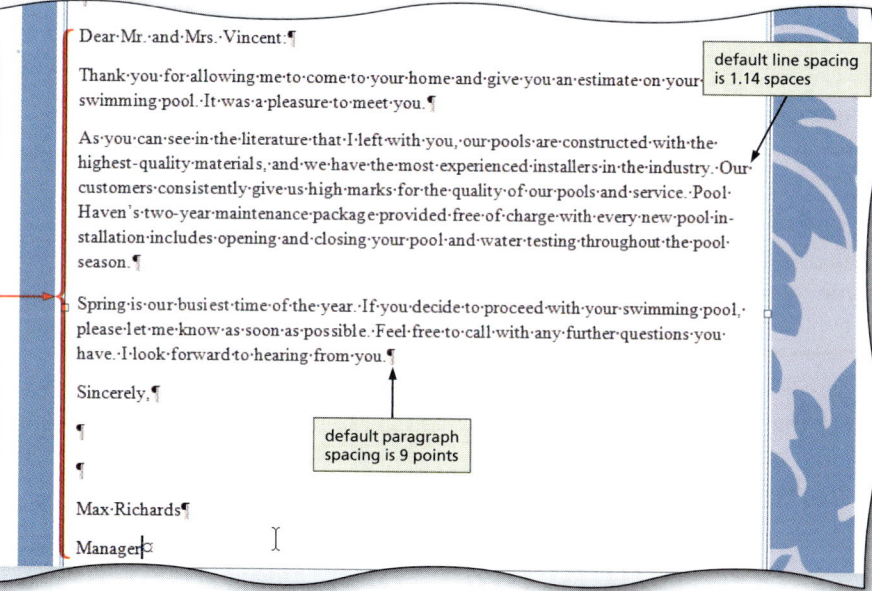

Figure 5–35

To Save the Letter

To illustrate the read-only properties of the letter, you will try to save the publication in the same location with the same name file name, Pool Haven Letterhead. Because you have changed the publication to read-only, Publisher will generate an error message. You then will choose a new file name and save the file, as shown in the steps on the next page.

1

- Click the Save button on the Quick Access Toolbar to display the Save As dialog box. Do not navigate to another location.

- Click the Save button (Save As dialog box) to display the Confirm Save As dialog box (Figure 5–36).

Q&A

What would happen if the file were not read-only?

Clicking the Save button would have saved the edited letter, replacing the custom template.

Figure 5–36

2

- Click the Yes button (Confirm Save As dialog box) to try to save the file. A Save As warning dialog box will be displayed (Figure 5–37).

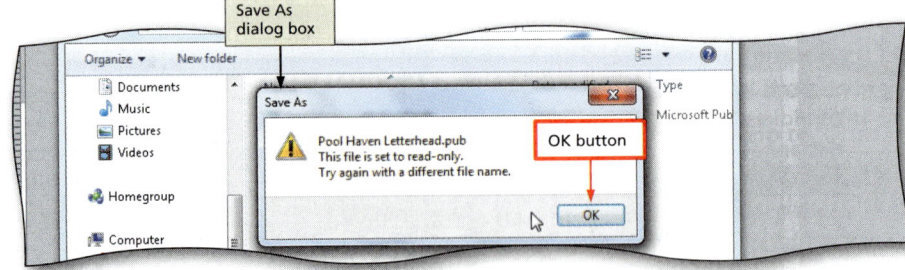

Figure 5–37

3

- Click the OK button to return to the Save As dialog box.

- Click the File name text box, delete the previous file name and then type **Vincent Letter** as the new file name (Figure 5–38).

4

- Click the Save button (Save As dialog box) to save the file with the new file name.

Other Ways

1. Click File tab, click Save As button, change file name, click Save button (Save As dialog box)

2. Press CTRL+S, change file name, click Save button (Save As dialog box)

Figure 5–38

To Print the Letter

The following steps print a hard copy of the Vincent letter.

1 Click the File tab to open the Backstage view and then click the Print tab to display the Print gallery.

2 Verify the printer name in the Printer box will print a hard copy of the publication. If necessary, click the Printer box arrow to display a list of available Printer options and then click the desired printer to change the currently selected printer.

3 Click the Print button in the Print gallery to print the letter on the currently selected printer (Figure 5–39).

Pool Haven

1750 Quincy Street
Springfield, SC 31692

Phone: 803-555-2795
Fax: 803-555-2796
E-mail: info@poolhaven.biz

March 12, 2012

Dear Mr. and Mrs. Vincent:

Thank you for allowing me to come to your home and give you an estimate on your new swimming pool. It was a pleasure to meet you.

As you can see in the literature that I left with you, our pools are constructed with the highest-quality materials, and we have the most experienced installers in the industry. Our customers consistently give us high marks for the quality of our pools and service. Pool Haven's two-year maintenance package provided free of charge with every new pool installation includes opening and closing your pool and water testing throughout the pool season.

Spring is our busiest time of the year. If you decide to proceed with your swimming pool, please let me know as soon as possible. Feel free to call with any further questions you have. I look forward to hearing from you.

Sincerely,

Max Richards

Manager

Great Quality. Reasonable Prices.

Figure 5–39

To Close a Publication without Quitting Publisher

The following step closes the letter without quitting Publisher.

 Click the File tab to open the Backstage view and then click the Close command to close the publication without quitting Publisher and to return to the New template gallery.

Break Point: If you wish to take a break, this is a good place to do so. You can quit Publisher now. To resume at a later time, start Publisher and continue following the steps from this location forward.

Envelopes

Envelopes are manufactured in a variety of sizes and shapes. The most common sizes are #6 personal envelopes, which measure $3\frac{5}{8} \times 6\frac{1}{2}$ inches, and #10 business envelopes, which measure $4\frac{1}{8} \times 9\frac{1}{2}$ inches. You also can customize the page layout to instruct Publisher to print envelopes for invitations, cards, and mailers, or to merge an address list with an envelope template to avoid using labels at all.

Although the majority of businesses outsource the production of their preprinted envelopes, most desktop printers have an envelope-feeding mechanism that works especially well for business envelopes. Check your printer's documentation for any limitations on the size and shape of envelopes. For testing purposes, you can print the envelope on $8\frac{1}{2}\text{-}\times\text{-}11$-inch paper, if necessary.

To Create an Envelope

The following steps use the New template gallery to produce a business-sized envelope for Pool Haven. The envelope automatically uses information from the business information set created earlier in this project.

1
- With the New template gallery still displayed, click Envelopes to display the available templates.

- Scroll down to the More Installed Templates area and then click the Batik preview.

- If necessary, choose the Sapphire color scheme and the Galley font scheme.

- If necessary, click the Business information box arrow and then click Pool Haven to select the set.

- Click the Page size button arrow to display the list of page sizes (Figure 5–40).

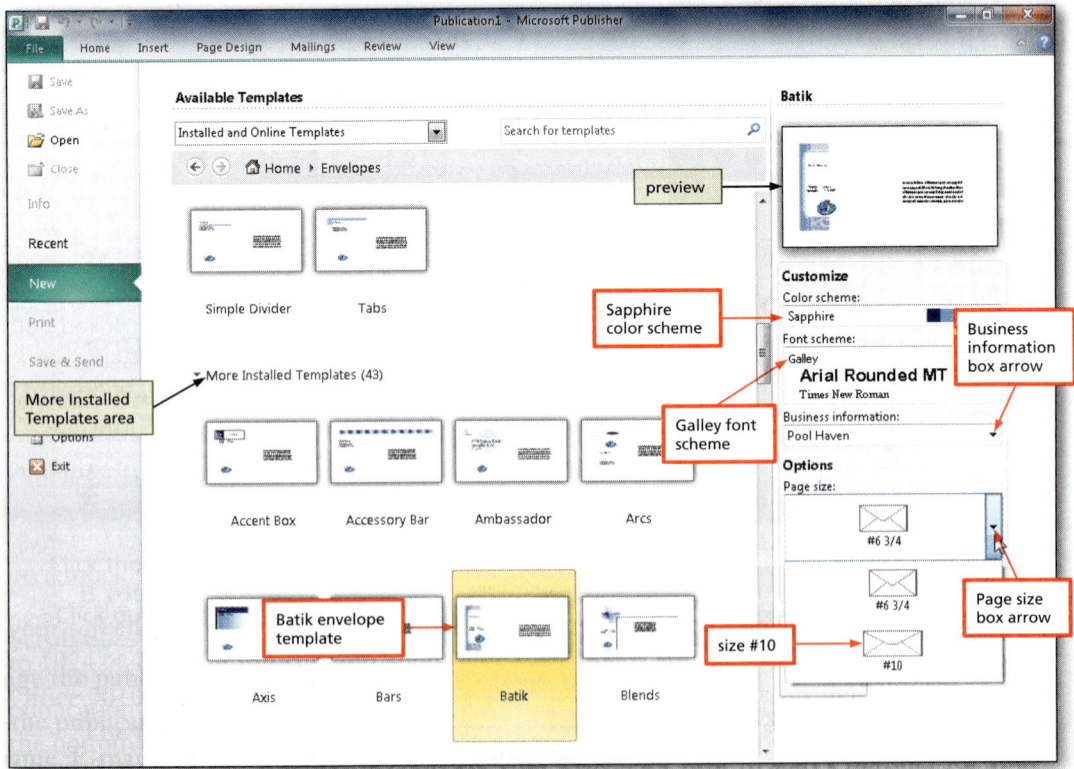

Figure 5–40

Business Cards

Another way companies are reducing publishing costs is by designing their own business cards. A **business card** is a small publication, 3½ × 2 inches, printed on heavy stock paper. It usually contains the name, title, business, and address information for an employee as well as a logo, distinguishing graphic, or color to draw attention to the card. Many employees want their telephone, pager, and fax numbers on their business cards in addition to their e-mail and Web page addresses, so that colleagues and customers can reach them quickly.

Business cards can be saved as files to send to commercial printers or printed by desktop color printers on special perforated paper.

To Create a Business Card

Because the business information set contains information about the Pool Haven company and its manager, using a Publisher business card template is the quickest way to create a business card. Not only does the template set the size and shape of a typical business card, it also presets page and printing options for easy production.

The following steps use the New template gallery to produce a business card for the manager of Pool Haven. The created business card automatically uses information from the business information set edited earlier in this project.

1 With the New template gallery still displayed, click Business Cards to display the templates.

2 Scroll down to the More Installed Templates area and then click the Batik preview.

3 If necessary, choose the Sapphire color scheme, the Galley font scheme, and a Landscape page size.

4 If necessary, click the Business information box arrow and then click Pool Haven to select the set.

5 If necessary, place a check mark in the Include logo check box.

Figure 5–48

6 Click the Create button in the New template gallery to create the business card. Zoom as necessary to display the entire business card in the Publisher workspace (Figure 5–48).

To Edit the Logo

The following steps position and scale the logo from the business information set.

1 Select the logo.

2 Click the Object Position button on the status bar to display the Measurement toolbar.

3 Select the text in the Horizontal Position box and then type **2.14** to replace it. Press the TAB key to advance to the next box.

4 Type **.24** in the Vertical Position box and then press the TAB key.

5 Type **1.17** in the Width box and then press the TAB key.

6 Type **.54** in the Height box and then press the ENTER key (Figure 5–49).

Figure 5–49

To Insert and Edit the Tagline or Motto Field

The following steps insert the Tagline or motto field from the business information set and then position, scale, and fit the text in the text box.

1 Click the scratch area so that no objects are selected in the page layout, and display the Insert tab.

2 Click the Business Information button (Insert tab | Text group) to display the list of business information fields and commands.

3 Scroll as necessary and then click the Tagline or motto field to insert it into the publication.

4 On the Measurement toolbar, select the text in the Horizontal Position box and then type `.61` to replace it. Press the TAB key to advance to the next box.

5 Type `1.46` in the Vertical Position box and then press the TAB key.

6 Type `.91` in the Width box and then press the TAB key.

7 Type `.33` in the Height box and then press the ENTER key.

8 Do not change the default values in the other boxes.

9 Right-click the text in the Tagline or motto text box to display the shortcut menu and then click Best Fit to autofit the text (Figure 5–50).

10 Click the Close button on the Measurement toolbar to close it.

11 Click outside the text box to deselect the text.

Figure 5–50

To Set Publication Properties

Because you also plan to send the business cards to a commercial printer, it is important to set publication properties. The following steps set publication properties.

1 Display the Backstage view and, by default, select the Info tab.

2 Click the Publication Properties button in the right pane of the Info gallery and then click Advanced Properties to display the Publication Properties dialog box. If necessary, click the Summary tab.

3 Type `Business Card` in the Title text box.

4 Type `Max Richards` in the Author text box.

5 Type **Pool Haven** in the Company text box (Figure 5–51).

6 Click the OK button (Publication1 Properties dialog box) to save the settings.

Figure 5–51

To Save the Business Card

The following steps save the business card with the file name, Pool Haven Business Card.

1 With a USB flash drive connected to one of the computer's USB ports, click the Save button in the Backstage view to display the Save As dialog box.

2 Type **Pool Haven Business Card** in the File name text box to change the file name. Do not press the ENTER key.

3 Navigate to the Publisher folder on your USB flash drive so that you can save your file in that location.

4 Click the Save button (Save As dialog box) to save the publication on the selected drive with the entered file name.

To Print the Business Cards

You have the choice of printing multiple business cards per sheet or only one card per sheet. Layout options allow you to set specific margins to match specialized business card paper. The following steps print the business cards.

1

- Display the Backstage view and then click the Print tab to display the Print gallery.

- Verify that the printer name on the Printer Status button will print a hard copy of the publication. If necessary, click the Printer box arrow to display a list of available printer options and then click the desired printer to change the currently selected printer.

- Click the Pages button to display the Pages list (Figure 5–52).

Figure 5–52

2

- If necessary, click 'Multiple copies per sheet' to select the option.

- If necessary, type 10 in the 'Copies of each page' box.

- Click the Layout Options button to display the Layout Options dialog box.

- Make sure your settings match those in Figure 5–53.

Figure 5–53

- Click the Close button (Layout Options dialog box) to close the Layout Options dialog box.

- Click the Print button in the Print gallery to print the business cards on the currently selected printer (Figure 5–54).

Figure 5–54

Plan Ahead

Create files in portable formats.
You might have to distribute your artwork in a variety of formats for customers, print shops, Webmasters, and e-mail attachments. The format you choose depends on how the file will be used, but portability is always a consideration. The publication might need to be used with various operating systems, monitor resolutions, computing environments, and servers.

It is a good idea to discuss with your customer the types of formats he or she might need. It usually is safe to begin work in Publisher and then use the Save As command or Print command to convert the files. PDF is a portable format that can be read by anyone using a free reader, which is available on the Web. The PDF format is platform- and software-independent. Commonly, PDF files are virus free and safe as e-mail attachments.

Creating Portable Files

The final step is to create a portable file of the business card for document exchange between computers. Publisher offers two choices: PDF or XPS. **PDF** stands for **Portable Document Format**, a flexible file format based on the PostScript imaging model that is cross-platform and cross-application. PDF files accurately display and preserve fonts, page layouts, and graphics. The content in a PDF file is not changed easily, but it can be viewed by everyone with a free viewer available on the Web. **XPS** stands for **XML Paper Specification** and is a format that preserves document formatting and enables file sharing. XPS is Microsoft's portable format similar to Adobe's PDF. When the XPS file is viewed online or printed, it retains exactly the format that you intended; however, like PDF files, the data in XPS files cannot be changed easily.

You might want to create a portable file for an outside printing service or to display your publication on the Web. Publisher allows you to set additional options for quality, graphics, and document properties when creating portable files.

To Publish in a Portable Format

The following steps publish the business card in a portable format using high-quality settings and maintaining document properties.

1

- Display the Backstage view and then click Save & Send tab to display the Save & Send gallery.

- Click the Create PDF/XPS Document tab to display the Create a PDF/XPS Document pane (Figure 5–55).

Figure 5–55

2

- Click the Create PDF/XPS button to display the Publish as PDF or XPS dialog box.

- Navigate to the desired save location (in this case, the Publisher folder in the CIS 101 folder [or your class folder] on the USB flash drive) (Figure 5–56).

Figure 5–56

3

- Click the Options button (Publish as PDF or XPS dialog box) to display the Publish Options dialog box.

- If necessary, in the 'Specify how this publication will be printed or distributed.' area, click 'High quality printing' (Publish Options dialog box).

- If necessary, in the 'Include non-printing information' area, click both check boxes to select them.

- Do not change any of the other default values (Figure 5–57).

 Experiment

- Click each choice in the 'Specify how this publication will be printed or distributed.' list to view the descriptions and other settings. When you are done, click 'High quality printing'.

Figure 5–57

4

- Click the OK button (Publish Options dialog box) to close the Publish Options dialog box.

- Click the Publish button (Publish as PDF or XPS dialog box) to create the portable file (Figure 5–58).

Q&A

Why does my display look different?

Your computer may not have the same PDF reader installed. In that case, the file opens with an XPS reader.

5

- Click the Close button on the PDF or XPS title bar to close the display of the portable file.

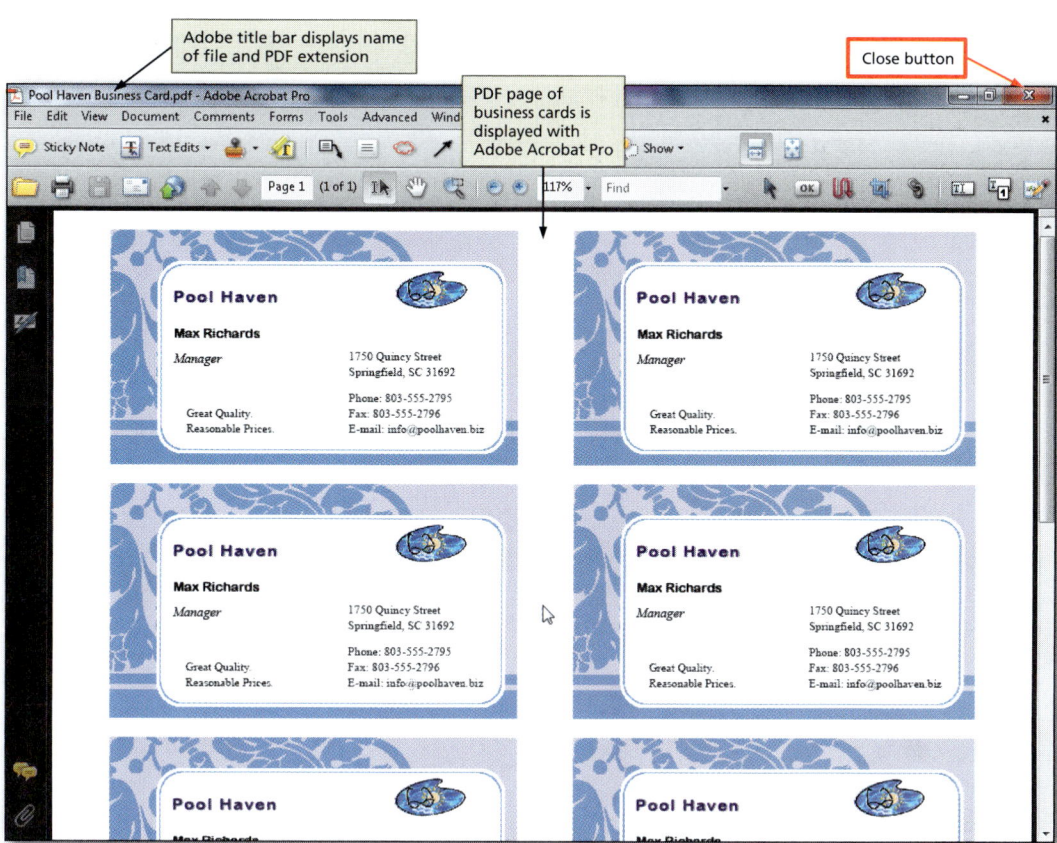

Adobe title bar displays name of file and PDF extension

Close button

PDF page of business cards is displayed with Adobe Acrobat Pro

Figure 5–58

Other Ways

1. Click File tab, in Backstage view, click Save As button, click 'Save as type' box arrow (Save As dialog box), click PDF (*.pdf), click Options button, select options, click OK button (Publish Options dialog box), click Save button (Save As dialog box)

Embedding Fonts

If you plan to send the Publisher file to a professional printing service or to other users, they may or may not have the same fonts available on their computer as you do on yours. Thus, any fonts peculiar to your printer or new font styles that you created may have to be substituted. When the publication is opened, Publisher usually displays a dialog box that informs the user of the substitution. Publisher tries to find a similar font based on the text ornamentation, but your publication will not look exactly as it did. One option is to create a PDF or XPS as you did earlier in the chapter, which would maintain the look of the publication; however, the PDF or XPS user cannot make significant changes to the design. If you want to preserve your font settings and create a fully editable file, you should **embed** or save the fonts with the publication. Optionally, you can embed a **subset** of the font, which means that it will embed only the specific characters you used in the publication.

Most common fonts, such as Times New Roman, do not have to be embedded because most users will already have that font. In general, TrueType fonts can be embedded only if their licensing allows embedding; however, all of the TrueType fonts that are included in Publisher allow licensed embedding.

Embedded fonts increase the file size of your publication, so you may want to limit the number of fonts that you embed. You can choose to embed all fonts, only certain individual fonts, or subsets of certain fonts. Embedding fonts is one of the best ways to ensure that a font is always available.

Table 5–3 on the next page displays some of Publisher's embedding options.

BTW

Pack and Go Wizard
Publisher automatically embeds TrueType fonts by default when you use the Pack and Go Wizard as you did in Chapter 2. If you do not use the Pack and Go Wizard, you have to make choices related to embedding.

Table 5–3 Embedding Options

Type of Embedding	Kinds of Fonts (If Any)	Advantages	Restrictions
Full Font Embedding		The recipient does not need the same font to view or edit the file.	You must own the embedded font by owning your printer or by purchasing the font. Fully embedded fonts create a large file size.
	Print And Preview Fonts	Viewable fonts are embedded in the publication.	The recipient cannot edit the publication.
	Licensed, Installable Fonts	Embedded fonts, licensed as installable, may be installed permanently for use in other publications and programs.	No restrictions exist.
	Licensed, Editable Fonts	Embedded fonts that are licensed as editable are available for use in other publications and programs.	The publication with the editable fonts must remain open in order for the recipient to use the font.
	True Type Fonts	True Type fonts include permissions defined by the original publisher of the font that detail when and how the font may be embedded.	The True Type fonts can be applied to a publication only if the embedded fonts are installed on the local computer.
Subset Font Embedding		The recipient does not have to own the font to view it.	Only the characters that you use in the publication are included in the font family. Subset font embedding creates a file that is larger than one with no embedding but smaller than one with full font embedding.
No Font Embedding		File size does not change.	The recipient needs to have the same fonts installed or accept a substitution.
Save as PDF or XPS		Fonts, layout, and design are maintained.	Recipient has limited editing capabilities.

To Embed Fonts

The following steps embed the fonts with the business card. Because other workers at Pool Haven may want to use this file to create their own business cards, you will embed all of the characters in the heading font, rather than just a subset. You will not embed the common system fonts that most users will have, in this case Times New Roman, in order to reduce the file size slightly.

- With the Pool Haven Business Card still displayed in the workspace, display the Backstage view and, by default, select the Info tab.

- Click the Commercial Print Settings button in the Info gallery to display the list of settings (Figure 5–59).

Q&A

What will users see when they open the file?

A dialog box will verify that some fonts were embedded and allow the user to substitute those if necessary.

Figure 5–59

- Click Manage Embedded Fonts to display the Fonts dialog box.

- Click to place a check mark in the 'Embed TrueType fonts when saving publication' check box (Fonts dialog box).

- If necessary, click to place a check mark in the 'Do not embed common system fonts' check box and the 'Subset fonts when embedding' check box (Figure 5–60).

Q&A

What does the Embed/Don't Embed button do?

If you own the font but do not want others to use it, you can click to select the specific font in the list and then click the Embed/Don't Embed button. In that case, the Embed Font column changes from yes to no, and the Don't Embed button changes to the Embed button. You must select a specific font in the list to enable the button.

Figure 5–60

- Click the OK button (Fonts dialog box) to close the Fonts dialog box.

To Save the File Again

The following step saves the business card file again, this time with the embedded font settings.

1 Click the Save button on the Quick Access Toolbar to overwrite the previously saved file.

To Delete the Business Information Set

The following steps delete the Pool Haven business information set. Deleting the business information set does not delete the information from saved publications.

1

- Display the Insert tab.

- Click the Business Information button (Insert tab | Text group) to display the list of business information fields and commands.

- Click Edit Business Information to display the Business Information dialog box.

- If necessary, click the Select a Business Information set box arrow and then click Pool Haven to select the set (Figure 5–61).

Figure 5–61

2

- Click the Delete button (Business Information dialog box) to delete the business information set (Figure 5–62).

Q&A
Will this delete the fields from the current business card?

No. It will delete only the set. All publications containing that data will remain unchanged.

3

- When Publisher displays a dialog box asking you to confirm the deletion, click the Yes button.

- Click the Close button (Business Information dialog box) to close the Business Information dialog box.

Figure 5–62

To Quit Publisher

This project is complete. The following steps quit Publisher.

1 To quit Publisher, click the Close button on the right side of the title bar.

2 If a Microsoft Office Publisher dialog box is displayed, click the Don't Save button so that any editing changes you have made to the business card are not saved.

Chapter Summary

In this chapter you have learned how to personalize and customize publications with business information sets. You created the business information set with its many components and then used the business information set to create a letterhead. You created a new style and applied it to text boxes in the letterhead, using the Measurement toolbar for exact placement and scaling. You added a text box with an automatic date, and saved it as a read-only file. Finally, you used the business information set to creating a business card and envelope. The items listed below include all the new Publisher skills you have learned in this chapter.

1. Create a Letterhead Template (PUB 269)
2. Create a Business Information Set (PUB 271)
3. Apply a Business Information Set in the New Template Gallery (PUB 274)
4. Change the Business Information Set of an Existing Publication (PUB 275)
5. Insert a Business Information Field (PUB 275)
6. Display the Measurement Toolbar (PUB 276)
7. Position Objects Using the Measurement Toolbar (PUB 277)
8. Sample a Font Color (PUB 279)
9. Create a New Style (PUB 280)
10. Apply the New Style (PUB 281)
11. Create a Formatted Text Box (PUB 283)
12. Insert an Automatic Date (PUB 284)
13. Set the Read-Only Attribute (PUB 286)
14. Open a Publication from the Recent Documents List (PUB 287)
15. Type a Letter (PUB 289)
16. Save the Letter (PUB 289)
17. Create an Envelope (PUB 292)
18. Address the Envelope (PUB 294)
19. Choose Settings and Print the Envelope (PUB 295)
20. Print the Business Cards (PUB 300)
21. Publish in a Portable Format (PUB 303)
22. Embed Fonts (PUB 306)
23. Delete the Business Information Set (PUB 307)

Learn It Online

Test your knowledge of chapter content and key terms.

Instructions: To complete the Learn It Online exercises, start your browser, click the Address bar, and then enter the Web address **scsite.com/pub2010/learn**. When the Publisher 2010 Learn It Online page is displayed, click the link for the exercise you want to complete and then read the instructions.

Chapter Reinforcement TF, MC, and SA
A series of true/false, multiple choice, and short answer questions that test your knowledge of the chapter content.

Flash Cards
An interactive learning environment where you identify chapter key terms associated with displayed definitions.

Practice Test
A series of multiple choice questions that test your knowledge of chapter content and key terms.

Who Wants To Be a Computer Genius?
An interactive game that challenges your knowledge of chapter content in the style of a television quiz show.

Wheel of Terms
An interactive game that challenges your knowledge of chapter key terms in the style of the television show *Wheel of Fortune*.

Crossword Puzzle Challenge
A crossword puzzle that challenges your knowledge of key terms presented in the chapter.

Apply Your Knowledge

Reinforce the skills and apply the concepts you learned in this chapter.

Creating Stationery

Instructions: Start Publisher. Open the publication, Apply 5-1 Chopper Repair Letterhead, from the Data Files for Students. See the inside back cover of this book for instructions on downloading the Data Files for Students, or contact your instructor for more information about accessing the required files.

The publication you open contains the default business information fields. You will create the new business information set, publish the file in a portable format, and create an envelope. The resulting publications are shown in Figure 5–63.

Figure 5–63

Perform the following tasks:

1. Click the Business Information button (Insert tab | Text group) and then click Edit Business Information. If necessary, click the New button (Business Information dialog box).

2. Enter the information from Table 5–4 and insert the logo file. The picture for the logo is available on the Data Files for Students.

3. Click the Save button (Create New Business Information Set dialog box) to save the business information set with the name, Chopper Repair.

4. Click the Update Publication button (Business Information dialog box) to change the fields in the current letterhead.

5. Select the logo and then click the Measurement button (Drawing Tools Format tab | Size group) to display the Measurement toolbar.

   a. Select the text in the Horizontal Position box and then type `6.48` to replace it. Press the TAB key to advance to the next box.

   b. Type `.69` in the Vertical Position box and then press the TAB key.

   c. Type `1.49` in the Width box and then press the TAB key.

   d. Type `.74` in the Height box and then press the ENTER key.

   e. Close the Measurement toolbar.

   f. Click the scratch area to deselect the logo.

6. Scroll to the bottom of the page and zoom to 100%. Click the Business Information button (Insert tab | Text group) to display its list. One at a time, insert the fields: Individual name, Job position or title, and Tagline or motto. Position the fields across the bottom of the letterhead as shown in Figure 5–63.

7. One at a time, apply a style to each of the three text boxes by selecting the text and then clicking the Styles button (Home tab | Styles group). Choose the Heading 4 style.

8. Display the Backstage view and then click Save As. Save the publication using the file name, Apply 5-1 Chopper Repair Letterhead Edited.

9. To publish the letterhead as a PDF in order to send it to a commercial printer, display the Backstage view and then click the Save & Send tab. Click Create PDF/XPS Document to display the Create a PDF/XPS Document pane.

10. Click the Create a PDF/XPS button to open the Publish as PDF or XPS dialog box. Navigate to your storage device and appropriate folder, if necessary.

11. Click the Options button (Publish as PDF or XPS dialog box) to display the Publisher Options dialog box. If necessary, in the 'Specify how this publication will be printed or distributed' area, click 'High quality printing'. If necessary, in the 'Include non-printing information' area, click both check boxes to select them. Do not change any of the other default values.

12. Click the OK button (Publisher Options dialog box) to close the Publisher Options dialog box. Click the Publish button (Publish as PDF or XPS dialog box) to create the portable file. View the PDF file and then close the Adobe Reader window.

Table 5–4 Chopper Repair Business Information Set

Field Name	Company Data
Individual name	Devin Sturgis
Job position or title	Owner
Organization name	Chopper Repair
Address	8400 County Road 71 North Munster, SD 57904
Phone, fax, and e-mail	Phone: 605-555-BIKE Fax: 605-555-2454 E-mail: devin@sturgis.biz
Business Information set name	Chopper Repair
Tagline or motto	We open the road for you!
Logo	Apply 5-1 Motorcycle Logo.png

Continued >

Apply Your Knowledge *continued*

13. Close the letterhead publication without quitting Publisher to display the New template gallery.

14. Choose the Bars envelope template in size #10. Use the default font and color schemes. Click the Create button to display the publication in the Publisher workspace. If necessary, update the publication with the business information set.

15. Print the envelope with appropriate printer settings.

16. Click the Business Information button (Insert tab | Text group) and then click Edit Business Information. Click the Delete button (Business Information dialog box) to delete the Chopper Repair business information set.

17. Save the envelope with the file name, Apply 5-1 Chopper Repair Envelope, and then quit Publisher.

18. Submit the files as specified by your instructor.

Extend Your Knowledge

Extend the skills you learned in this chapter and experiment with new skills. You may need to use Help to complete the assignment.

Adding Styles to the Quick Access Toolbar

Instructions: Start Publisher. Open the publication, Extend 5-1 Insurance Thank You from the Data Files for Students. See the inside back cover of this book for instructions on downloading the Data Files for Students, or contact your instructor for more information about accessing the required files.

You will add the Styles button to the Quick Access Toolbar, apply styles to the publication, and then remove the button from the Quick Access Toolbar.

Perform the following tasks:

1. Use Help to learn more about customizing the Quick Access Toolbar.

2. If necessary, click the Page Number button on the status bar to show the Page Navigation pane.

3. Right-click the Styles button (Home Tab | Styles Group) to display the shortcut menu.

4. Click the Add to Quick Access Toolbar command to add the Styles button to the Quick Access Toolbar.

5. Select the text on Page 1 of the thank you card. Click the Styles button on the Quick Access Toolbar and then choose the Pete Hayes Insurance style.

6. Click the Page 2 and Page 3 icon in the Page Navigation pane to display the inside pages in the Publisher workspace.

7. Select the text on Page 2 (in the upper portion of the page layout). Click the Styles button on the Quick Access Toolbar and then choose the Heading 4 style, if necessary.

8. Select the text on Page 3 (in the lower portion of the page layout). Click the Styles button on the Quick Access Toolbar and then choose the Body Text 5 style.

9. Click the Page 4 icon in the Page Navigation pane to display the back page in the Publisher workspace.

10. Select the text on Page 4 of the thank you card. Click the Styles button on the Quick Access Toolbar and then choose the Pete Hayes Insurance style.

11. Click the Customize Quick Access Toolbar button to display its menu and then click More Commands to display the Publisher Options dialog box and, by default, the Customize the Quick Access Toolbar gallery.

12. Click the Styles button in the Customize Quick Access Toolbar list (Figure 5–64).

13. Click the Remove button (Publisher Options Dialog box) to remove the Styles button from the Quick Access Toolbar. Click the OK button to return to the publication.

Figure 5–64

14. Change the publication properties. Save the revised publication and then submit it in the format specified by your instructor.

15. Quit Publisher.

Make It Right

Analyze a publication and correct all errors and/or improve the design.

Correcting Errors in a Custom Template

Instructions: Start Publisher. Open the publication, Make It Right 5-1 Holiday Letter, from the Data Files for Students. See the inside back cover of this book for instructions on downloading the Data Files for Students, or contact your instructor for more information about accessing the required files.

The publication is a letterhead that is not user friendly, as shown in Figure 5–65. The large text box in the center of the publication is difficult to see. You are to insert text to help the user determine where they are to type. Include an automatic date, and the words, ENTER TEXT HERE, to help guide the user. Change the document properties, including keywords, as specified by your instructor. Save the revised document with the file name, Make It Right 5-1 Holiday Letter Template.

Figure 5–65

Once the modifications are complete, set the read-only attribute so that the user cannot accidentally save the edited file and overwrite the template file. Submit the file in the format specified by your instructor.

In the Lab

Design and/or create a publication using the guidelines, concepts, and skills presented in this chapter. Labs are listed in order of increasing difficulty.

Lab 1: Creating a Letterhead

Problem: Your friend is the volunteer commissioner for the local children's soccer league. Because he is responsible for organizing the teams, ordering equipment, and scheduling games, fields, and officials, he has asked you to create some stationery for his various pieces of correspondence. You prepare the letterhead shown in Figure 5–66. Because this is the only publication he needs, it is not necessary to save the business information set.

From the desk of the commissioner...

Paul Cooper
454 Royal Avenue
Blue Moon, MO 64118
(816) 555-5179

Figure 5–66

Continued >

In the Lab *continued*

Instructions: Perform the following tasks:

1. Start Publisher with a blank publication. Click the Page Size button (Page Design tab | Page Setup group) and then click Page Setup to display the Page Setup dialog box. Change each margin in the Margin guides area to .5 inches, if necessary.

2. At the bottom of the page, insert a graphic relating to soccer. Resize and crop it as necessary. Insert a text box next to the graphic. Change the font size to 20 and then type the name and address as shown in Figure 5–66 on the previous page.

3. Display the Page Design tab and choose the Lagoon color scheme.

4. Click the Shapes button (Insert tab | Illustrations group), and then click Bevel. Drag a bevel shape at the top of the page.

5. Click the Measurement button (Drawing Tools Format tab | Size group) and use the Measurement toolbar to adjust the size of the bevel as follows: .5-inch horizontal and vertical positioning, 7.5 inches wide, and 1.5 inches tall. Close the Measurement toolbar.

6. Click the Shape Fill button arrow (Drawing Tools Format tab | Shape Styles group), point to Gradient, and then click More Gradients in the Gradients gallery. Click the Gradient tab (Fill Effects dialog box). Click the One Color option button. Choose the Accent 2 color. Drag the Dark to Light scroll box all the way to the right. Click the OK button (Fill Effects dialog box).

7. Click the Shape Outline button arrow (Drawing Tools Format tab | Shape Styles group), and choose a red color.

8. Right-click the bevel and then click Add Text on the shortcut menu. Click the Font Color button arrow (Home tab | Font group), and choose a red color. Choose a script font that resembles handwriting and a font size of at least 24. Type `From the desk of the commissioner ...` to complete the text. Press CTRL+E to center the text.

9. Change the publication properties, as specified by your instructor. Save the publication on a USB flash drive using the file name, Lab 5-1 Soccer Letterhead, and then print a copy.

10. Quit Publisher.

In the Lab

Lab 2: Creating an Interactive Fax Cover

Problem: Because the company that you work for sends a large number of faxes, your boss has asked you to create an interactive fax cover that will be put on the company server for all employees to use. He wants to make sure no one modifies the template for fax cover that you create (Figure 5–67).

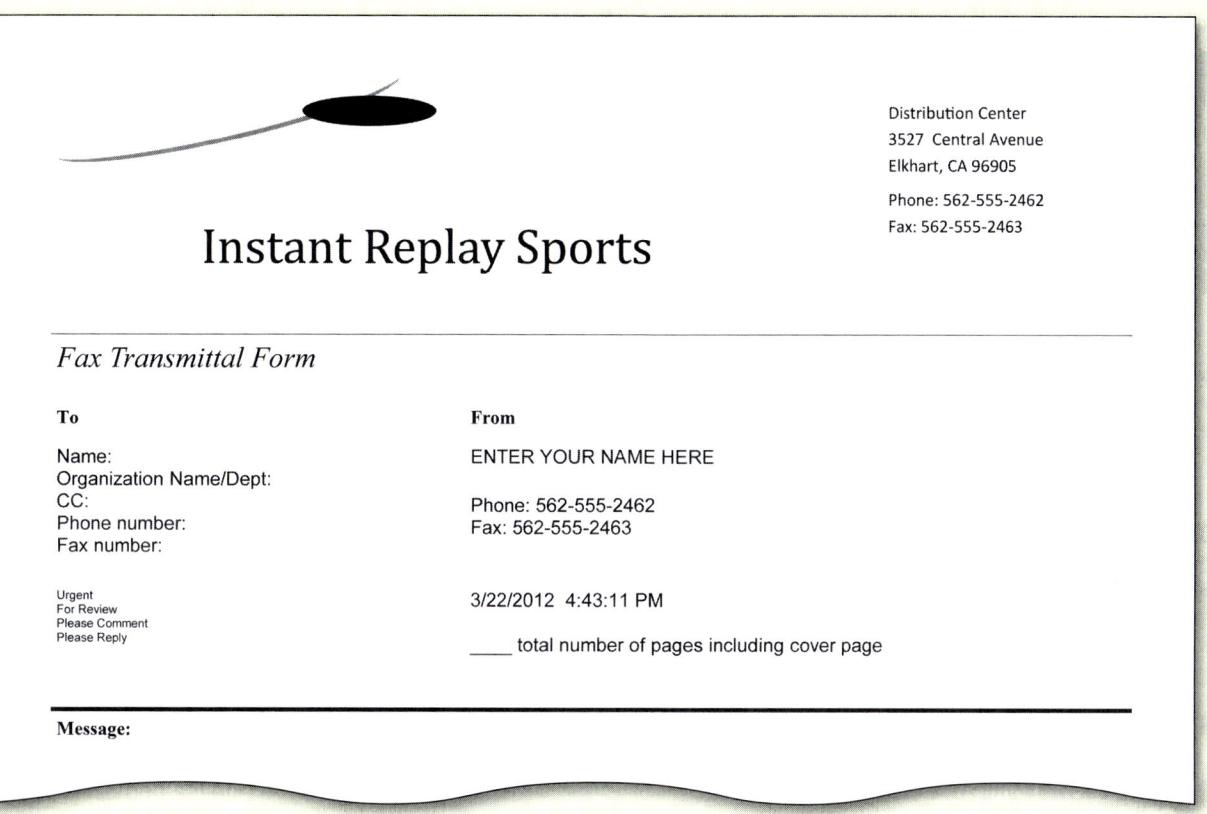

Figure 5–67

Instructions: Perform the following tasks:

1. Start Publisher.

2. Click Business Forms in the New template gallery and then click the Arcs Fax Cover thumbnail. Select the Black and gray color scheme and the Office 3 font scheme. Choose not to include a logo and then click the Create button to create the publication.

3. Display formatting marks.

4. To create the business information set and updated the publication:

   a. Click the Business Information button (Insert tab | Text group) and then click Edit Business Information to display the Create Business Information Set dialog box. (*Hint:* If the Business Information dialog box is displayed instead, click the New button.)

   b. Enter the information from Table 5–5. Leave the other fields blank. If a logo is displayed, click the Remove button (Create New Business Information Set dialog box).

   c. When you are finished entering data, click the Save button (Create New Business Information Set dialog box) and then click the Update Publication button (Business Information dialog box).

Table 5–5 Data for Business Information Set

Field Name	Company Data
Individual name	ENTER YOUR NAME HERE
Organization name:	Instant Replay Sports
Address	Distribution Center 3527 Central Avenue Elkhart, CA 96905
Phone, fax, and e-mail	Phone: 562-555-2462 Fax: 562-555-2463
Business Information set name	Instant Replay Sports

Continued >

5. To enter the date and time:

   a. In the publication, click the text box containing the date, time, and number of pages information to select it.

   b. Click the Date & Time button (Insert tab | Text group) to display the Date and Time dialog box.

   c. Choose a format that includes both the date and time.

   d. Click to place a check mark in the Update automatically check box (Date and Time dialog box).

   e. Click the OK button (Date and Time dialog box) to enter the formatted date and time into the text box.

   f. Press the ENTER key twice and then type, ____ `total pages including cover page` to finish the text.

6. Click the Message text box to display the insertion point. Press the ENTER key twice to position the insertion point below the word, Message.

7. Change the publication properties, as specified by your instructor. Save the publication on a USB flash drive, using the file name, Lab 5-2 Instant Replay Sports Fax Cover.

8. Quit Publisher.

9. To set the read-only attribute:

   a. Click the Start button on the Windows 7 taskbar to display the Start menu.

   b. Type `Replay Sports` as the search text in the 'Search programs and files' text box and watch the search results appear on the Start menu.

   c. Right-click Lab 5-2 Instant Replay Sports Fax Cover in the search results to display the shortcut menu. Click Properties on the shortcut menu to display the Properties dialog box.

   d. On the General tab (Properties dialog box), click to place a check mark in the Read-only check box in the Attributes area.

   e. Click the OK button (Properties dialog box) to close the dialog box and apply the read-only attribute.

10. Submit the publication in the format specified by your instructor.

In the Lab

Lab 3: Evaluating Styles and Special Effects

Problem: You decide to create and print a publication that will display different kinds of styles, line spacing, and special effects so that you can see how your printer generates the styles compared to what you see on the screen.

Instructions: Perform the following tasks:

1. Start Publisher and open a blank publication.
2. Click the Scheme Fonts button (Page Design tab | Schemes group) and then choose the Aspect font scheme.
3. Create six large text boxes on the page. In each text box, type your first name, press the ENTER key, and then type your last name.
4. One at a time, create a new style with the settings shown in Table 5–6 and apply them individually to the text boxes. If the font listed in the table is not available on your computer, choose a similar font.

    a. To choose the font, font size, and font color use the appropriate buttons on the Home tab.

    b. For the effect, select the text and then right-click to display the shortcut menu. Point to Change Text and then click Font.

    c. To change the line spacing, select the text and then right-click to display the shortcut menu. Point to Change Text and then click Paragraph. Replace the text in the Between lines box with the data from the table.

    d. To change the paragraph spacing, select the text and then right-click to display the shortcut menu. Point to Change Text and then click Paragraph. Replace the text in the After paragraphs box with the data from the table.

    e. For the sixth style, choose your own settings, using a different font.

Table 5–6 Style Settings

Style Name	Font	Font Size	Font Color	Effect	Line Spacing	After Paragraph Spacing
A12	Arial	10	green	Superscript	1 sp	12 pt
T36	Times New Roman	36	red	Engrave	1 sp	6 pt
C12	Courier New	12	blue	Emboss	1.19 sp	6 pt
S18	Script MT Bold	18	black	Outline	1.5 sp	9 pt
G24	Garamond	24	purple	All caps	2 sp	12 pt

5. Resize text boxes as necessary to display both lines of your name and to display all text boxes on the same page.
6. Change the publication properties, as specified by your instructor.
7. Save the publication with the file name, Lab 5-3 Style Gallery. Submit it as specified by your instructor.
8. Quit Publisher.

Cases and Places

Apply your creative thinking and problem solving skills to design and implement a solution.

Note: To complete these assignments, you may be required to use the Data Files for Students. See the inside back cover of this book for instructions on downloading the Data Files for Students, or contact your instructor for information about accessing the required files.

1: Stationery for a College

Academic

You work part time in the community relations department at Quanta College. Your supervisor has asked you to create a letterhead to be used for correspondence. Use the Tabs letterhead template to create a letterhead for Quanta College. Choose the Fjord color scheme and the Median font scheme. Create a business information set for Quanta College, using the fields from Table 5–7.

Table 5–7 Quanta College Business Information Set	
Field Name	**Company Data**
Organization name	Quanta College
Address	8006 Howard Avenue P. O. Box 8006 Quanta, AZ 85919
Phone, fax, and e-mail	Phone: 928-555-4700 Fax: 928-555-4705 info@quanta.edu
Business Information set name	Quanta College
Tagline or motto	Where Learning Creates Impact…
Logo	Case 5-1 Logo.png file

Insert the tagline or motto at the bottom of the letterhead. Select the text in the name of the college and then sample the color from the logo and increase the font size. Print a copy of the letterhead and save it on your storage device. Delete the business set when you are finished.

2: Creating a Personal Business Card

Personal

As part of your internship search, you need to create a business card that you can give to potential employers. Start Publisher and choose a Business Card template from the list. Choose a color and font scheme. Edit the business information set to include your personal data. Use your own name and the title of the job you would like to have. Enter the name and address of your school or workplace as the organization. Update the publication. Print the business card using appropriate printer settings. Delete your business information set if you used a laboratory computer.

3: Creating a New Text Style

Professional

The Baker's Dozen donut shop would like you to create a text style that employees can import into all of their current publications. Using a blank page, create a text box with the name of the donut shop as text. Create a new style using the Harlow Solid Italic font or a decorative italic font on your computer. Use a 48-point, bright red font. Add the Engrave font effect. Save the style with the name, Baker's Dozen. Embed all possible fonts and then save the publication for the donut shop to use. Print a copy for your instructor.

6 | Working with Publisher Tables

Objectives

You will have mastered the material in this chapter when you can:

- Apply WordArt shapes and shape outlines
- Change page orientation
- Snap objects to margin guides
- Align relative to margin guides
- Create tables and enter data
- Insert and delete rows and columns in tables
- Apply table formats
- Select table rows, columns, and cells

- Center and align table data
- Merge, split, and divide cells diagonally
- Create a 12-month calendar
- Format tables with borders
- Embed an Excel table in a Publisher publication
- Use Excel tools on the Publisher Ribbon to format a table

6 | Working with Publisher Tables

Introduction

A table is a good way to present a large amount of data in a small, organized space. Tabular data, or data that can be organized into related groups and subgroups, is best presented in rows and columns with appropriate headings. A well-defined, descriptive table will have three general characteristics. First, the data will be meaningful; it will relate closely to the purpose of the publication. The data in a table will support or provide evidence of any analyses or conclusions. Second, a table will be unambiguous — it will have clear labels, titles, headings, legends, or footnotes. The purpose of the table will be evident, and the scale relationships will be well defined. Third, a table should be efficient so that the reader can quickly understand the data and its presentation, in order to draw conclusions and apply the data to a particular situation. An efficient table is formatted appropriately and read quickly.

While many tables are created using Microsoft Excel, Publisher tables are formatted easily and fit well in many kinds of publications. Readers can understand the purpose of a publication table and promptly retrieve the important information. As you also will learn in this chapter, many of Excel's features can be embedded for use in Publisher tables.

Project — Schedule, Calendar, and Business Table

The decision to use a table in a publication is based on a need to organize a large amount of information in an easily recognizable format and to reduce the amount of text necessary to explain the situation. From tables of content to bank rate tables to timetables, you may need to display text, graphics, dates, or color in many different tabular ways. Publisher allows you to create tables from scratch or use tables that already are organized for specific purposes.

In this project, you will create three different publications that incorporate tables for a chain of restaurants called Kyra's Kitchen, as shown in Figure 6–1. A wait staff schedule (Figure 6–1a) will outline employee work hours for a given week. A promotional calendar (Figure 6–1b) will present each month as a table and advertise special dishes. Finally, a letter to the restaurant managers (Figure 6–1c) will contain an embedded table with totals and formatting.

Home   Insert   Page Design   Mailings   Review

Kyra's Kitchen

Staff \ Days	Monday	Tuesday	Wednesday	Thursday	Friday	Saturday
Andhra	11-6	11-6	11-6		4-close	4-close
Blair	4-close	4-close	4-close		4-close	4-close
Chris		4-close	4-close	4-close		
Dixon	11-2		11-2	11-2	4-close	4-close
Ensile	2-8		2-8	4-close	2-8	2-8
Farad	4-close	11-2		11-6	11-2	11-2

Wait Staff Schedule for the Week of January 16

(a) Schedule

(b) Promotional Calendar

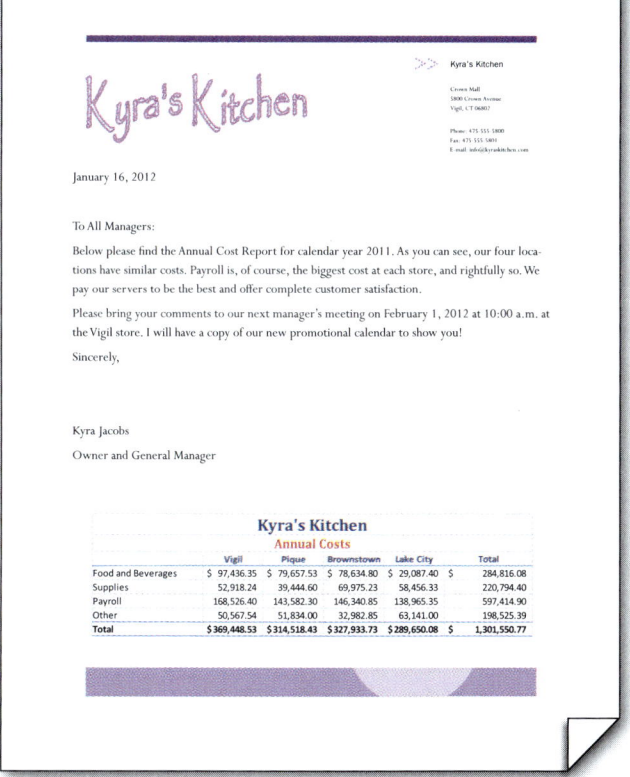

(c) Letter

Figure 6–1

Overview

As you read through this chapter, you will learn how to create the publications shown in Figure 6–1 on the previous page by performing these general tasks:

- Design a reusable, formatted WordArt object to serve as a heading in publications.
- Create a formatted table from scratch.
- Edit and format text, rows, and columns in a table.
- Merge and create diagonals in table cells.
- Design a promotional calendar that uses tables.
- Embed table data from an Excel worksheet into a Publisher publication.

Plan Ahead

> **General Project Guidelines**
>
> When you create Publisher publications, the actions you perform and decisions you make will affect the appearance and characteristics of the finished publication. As you create publications, such as the project shown in Figure 6–1, you should follow these general guidelines:
>
> 1. **Branding a company.** Creating reusable components such as business sets, logos, and a stylistic company name helps create a positive perception of a company and creates identifiable branding. A brand identity should be communicated in multiple ways with frequency and consistency throughout the life of a business.
>
> 2. **Use tables effectively to present data.** Use tables to present numeric and tabular information in an easy to digest format. Work with the customer to design a table that is clear and concise. Make sure the overall heading and the row and column headings employ standard wording and measurements. Format the table for easy reading.
>
> 3. **Create promotional pieces.** To complement the advertising and marketing of a product or service, create promotional pieces that will increase company recognition. Make sure that promotional pieces are useful to customers and not just gimmicky. Remember that calendars impose a date in promotional material.
>
> 4. **Embed and link data appropriately.** When table data is static and unlikely to change, embed the data in the publication. Sales history, past performance, totals, and votes are examples of data that can be taken from the source once, without retyping the figures into a new table. When data will change often, consider linking the data source to the publication. Prices, projections, investments, rates, and scoring are examples of data that will change over time. When the data changes, your publication's data should update automatically.

To Start Publisher

The following steps, which assume Windows 7 is running, start Publisher based on a typical installation. You may need to ask your instructor how to start Publisher for your computer. For a detailed example of the procedure summarized below, refer to the Office 2010 and Windows 7 chapter at the beginning of this book.

1 Click the Start button on the Windows 7 taskbar to display the Start menu.

2 Type `Microsoft Publisher` as the search text in the 'Search programs and files' text box, and watch the search results appear on the Start menu.

3 Click Microsoft Publisher 2010 in the search results on the Start menu to start Publisher and open the Backstage view.

4 If the Publisher window is not maximized, click the Maximize button next to the Close button on its title bar to maximize the window.

To Select a Blank Publication and Adjust Settings

The following steps select an 8.5 × 11" blank print publication, adjust workspace settings, and choose schemes that will apply to a wait staff schedule for Kyra's Kitchen.

1 Click the Blank 8.5 × 11" thumbnail in the New template gallery to create a blank publication in the Publisher window.

2 Collapse the Page Navigation pane.

3 If it is not selected already, click the Special Characters button (Home tab | Paragraph group) to display formatting marks.

4 Display the Page Design tab.

5 Click the More button (Page Design tab | Schemes group) and then click Lilac to choose a color scheme.

6 Click the Scheme Fonts button (Page Design tab | Schemes group) and then click Equity to choose a font scheme.

Creating Reusable Parts

The customer, Kyra's Kitchen, wants several publications including a wait staff schedule, a publicity calendar, and a letter to the managers. Certain objects will repeat in all publications, including the color and font scheme you selected previously, the business information set, and the name of the company in a WordArt object to serve as a recognizable branding of the restaurant.

Branding a company. Sometimes a brand is as simple as golden arches; other times it is a stylistic font that identifies a popular soda, no matter what the language. Developing and marketing a brand takes time and research. When desktop publishers are asked to help with brand recognition, they can suggest reusable colors, fonts, schemes, logos, business information sets, graphics, and other tools to assist the company in creating a customer-friendly, consistent brand.

Plan Ahead

Creating a Business Information Set

Table 6–1 on the next page displays the data for each of the fields in the business information set that you will create in this project. Recall that a business information set stores fields of information about a company. Sets are stored with unique names.

Table 6–1 Data for Business Information Fields	
Fields	**Data**
Individual name	Kyra Jacobs
Job position or title	Owner and General Manager
Organization name	Kyra's Kitchen
Address	Crown Mall 5800 Crown Avenue Vigil, CT 06802
Phone, fax, and e-mail	Phone: 475-555-5800 Fax: 475-555-5801 E-mail: info@kyraskitchen.com
Tagline or motto	For all of your dining and catering needs
Logo	<none>
Business Information set name	Kyra's Kitchen

To Create a Business Information Set

The following steps create a business information set for Kyra's Kitchen, which will be used in multiple publications.

1 Display the Insert tab.

2 Click the Business Information button (Insert tab | Text group) to display the list of business information fields and commands.

3 Click Edit Business Information to display the Create New Business Information Set dialog box. If Publisher displays the Business Information dialog box, click the New button (Business Information dialog box).

4 Enter the data from Table 6–1, pressing the TAB key to advance from one field to the next (Figure 6–2).

5 Click the Save button (Create New Business Information Set dialog box).

6 Click the Update Publication button (Business Information dialog box).

Figure 6–2

To Insert a WordArt Object

The following steps insert a WordArt object to use as a brand.

① Click the WordArt button (Insert tab | Text group) to display the WordArt gallery.

② Click the Fill - Blue, Outline - Blue, Wave preview in the WordArt Transform Styles area of the WordArt gallery to select it.

③ Type **Kyra's Kitchen** (Edit WordArt Text dialog box) to enter the text.

④ Click the Font box arrow (Edit WordArt Text dialog box) and then click Papyrus or a similar font.

⑤ If necessary, click the Size box arrow (Edit WordArt Text dialog box) and then click 36 to choose a 36-point font size.

⑥ Click the OK button (Edit WordArt Text dialog box) to close the dialog box and insert the WordArt object (Figure 6–3).

BTW

WordArt
Design experts recommend using WordArt sparingly. As a rule, use WordArt as decoration rather than to convey information. Use only one WordArt object per publication.

Figure 6–3

To Change the Shape of a WordArt Object

The following steps change the shape of the WordArt object by setting a warp style using the WordArt Tools Format tab. The WordArt Tools Format tab is one of Publisher's tool tabs that is displayed only when needed.

1

• With the WordArt object selected, click the Change WordArt Shape button (WordArt Tools Format tab | WordArt Styles group) to display the WordArt Shape gallery (Figure 6–4).

Experiment

• Point to each style in the WordArt Shape gallery and watch how the WordArt object changes. You may have to scroll the workspace horizontally to see both the gallery and the WordArt object.

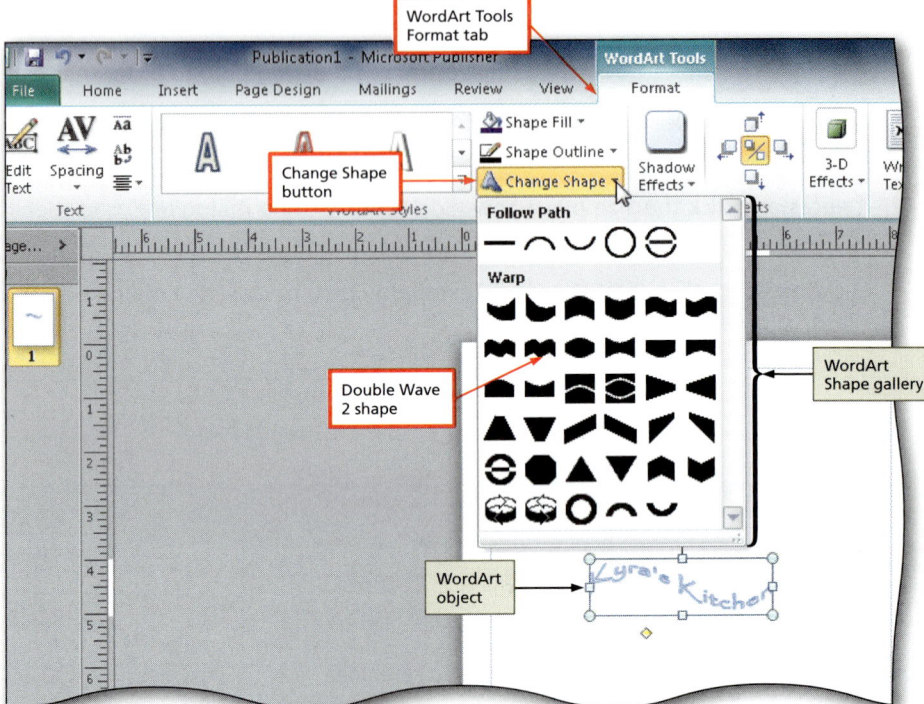

Figure 6–4

2

• Click Double Wave 2 in the Warp area of the WordArt Shape gallery to apply the shape (Figure 6–5).

Q&A

What other kinds of formatting can I apply to WordArt objects?

Using the WordArt Tools Format tab, you can change the character spacing, letter height, patterns, or pictures, and add shadows or 3-D effects.

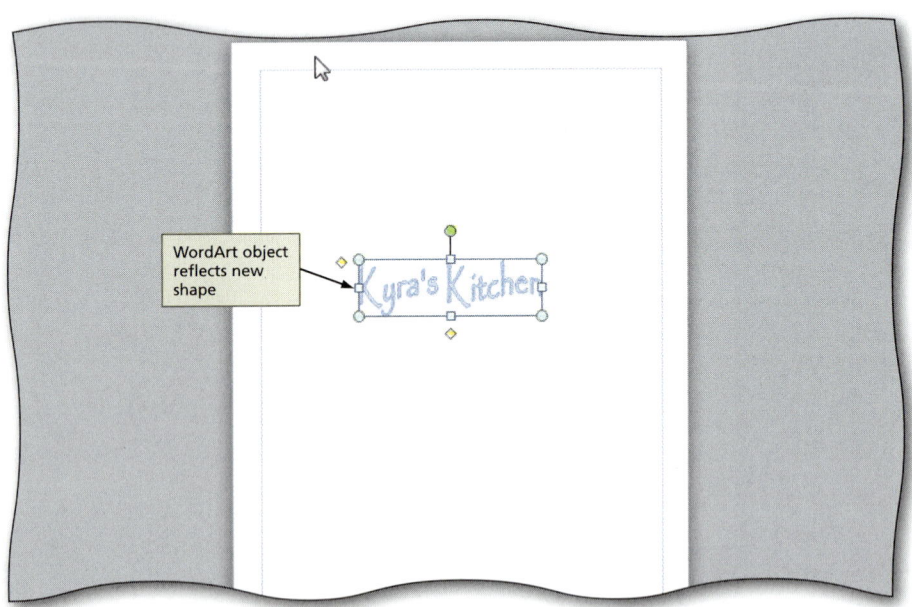

Figure 6–5

Other Ways

1. Click Change WordArt Shape button on Mini toolbar, select shape

To Change the Shape Outline

The following steps change the outline color of the WordArt shape.

1
- With the WordArt object selected, click the Shape Outline button arrow (WordArt Tools Format tab | WordArt Styles group) to display the WordArt Shape Outline gallery (Figure 6–6).

🔍 Experiment
- Point to various colors in the Shape Outline gallery and watch how the WordArt object changes.

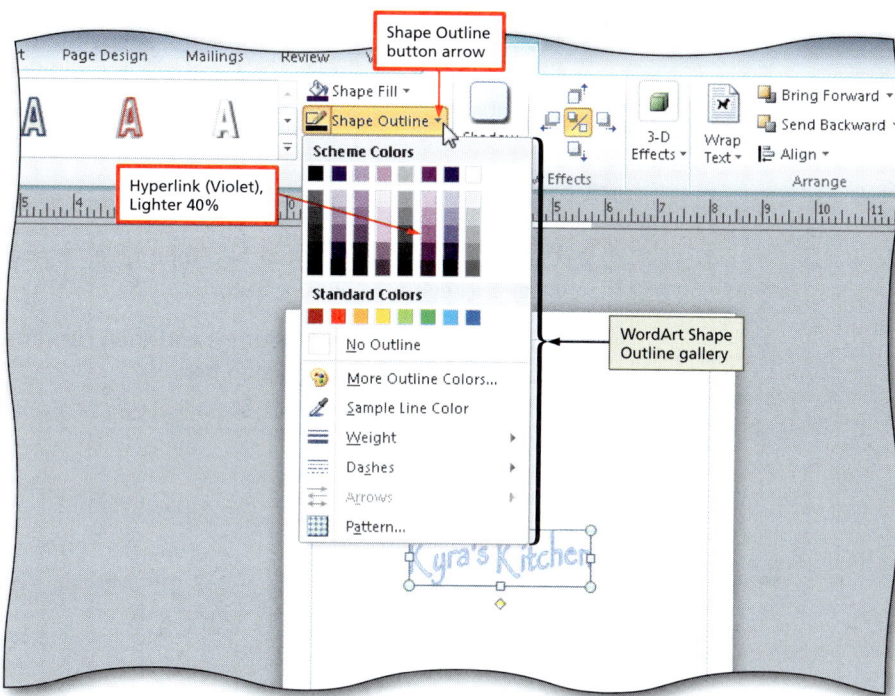

Figure 6–6

2
- Click the Hyperlink (Violet), Lighter 40% color to change the color of the shape outline (Figure 6–7).

Q&A What does the Shape Fill button do?

When you click the Shape Fill button (WordArt Tools Format tab | WordArt Styles group), you can choose to fill the WordArt letters with a color, picture, gradient, texture, or pattern.

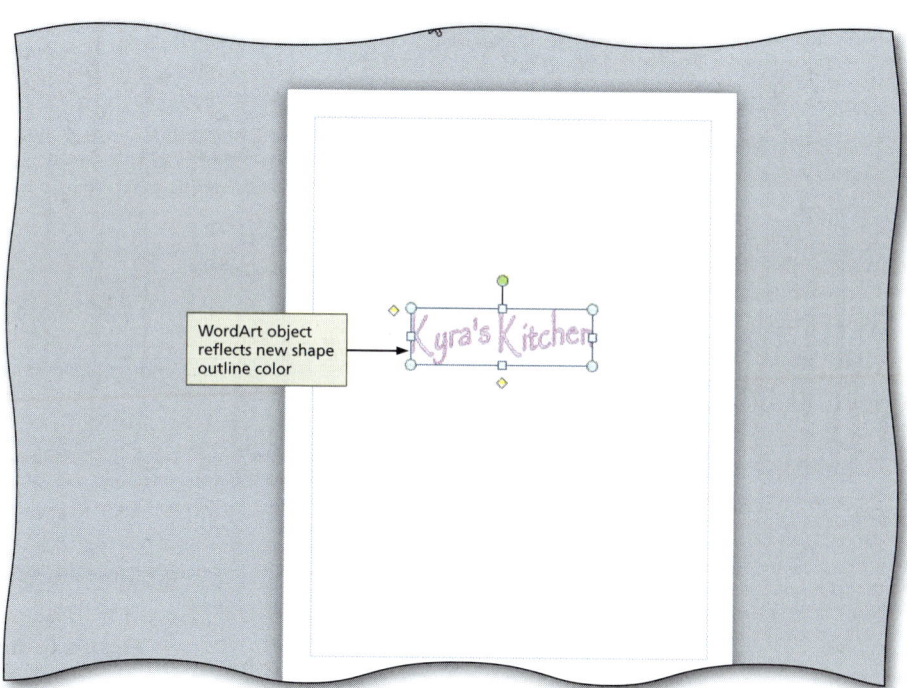

Figure 6–7

Other Ways
1. Click Shape Outline button arrow on Mini toolbar, select color

To Add an Object to the Building Block Library

The following steps add the formatted WordArt object to the Building Block library, so that you can use it in multiple publications.

1 Right-click the WordArt graphic to display the shortcut menu and then click Save as Building Block to display the Create New Building Block dialog box.

2 Type **Kyra's Kitchen Graphic** to replace the text in the Title text box.

3 Press the TAB key to move to the Description text box and then type **WordArt name brand to use in all publications** to insert a description.

4 Click the Keywords text box and then type **kyra kitchen wordart violet** to enter keywords (Figure 6–8).

5 Accept all other default settings and then click the OK button (Create New Building Block dialog box) to close the dialog box.

Figure 6–8

To Change the Page Orientation

When a publication is in **portrait orientation**, the short edge of the paper is the top of the publication. You can instruct Publisher to lay out a publication in **landscape orientation**, so that the long edge of the paper is the top of the publication. The following steps change the page orientation of the publication from portrait to landscape.

1

- Display the Page Design tab.

- Click the Page Orientation button (Page Design tab | Page Setup group) to display the orientation options (Figure 6–9).

Figure 6–9

2

- Click Landscape to change the orientation of the page (Figure 6–10).

Q&A Could I have chosen a template with landscape orientation?

Yes, if you know in advance that you want landscape orientation, choose one of the landscape orientation templates. If you have already created objects, use the Page Orientation button (Page Design tab | Page Setup group).

Figure 6–10

BTW

Placing WordArt Precisely
To place WordArt at a precise location on the page layout, right-click the WordArt object and then click Format WordArt on the shortcut menu. Click the Layout tab (Format WordArt dialog box) and enter the precise location in the 'Position on page' boxes.

To Snap an Object to the Margin Guide

The following step moves the WordArt object to the top of the page and snaps it to the margin. **Snapping** is a magnet-like alignment that occurs between object borders and margin guides.

- Verify that both the Guides and Objects check boxes (Page Design tab | Layout group) contain check marks.

- Drag the WordArt object toward the top margin guide. When a blue snapping line appears even with the top of the WordArt object (Figure 6–11), release the mouse button to snap the object to the margin guide.

Figure 6–11

To Align Relative to Margin Guides

In word processing applications, the right, center, and left alignment tools always refer to the current margins of the page. In desktop publications applications, the alignment tools refer to the text box in which you are working. You still can align items relative to the margin of the page, however, by using the Align button that exists on each of the formatting tabs (Drawing Tools, Text Box Tools, WordArt Tools, and Picture Tools). The following steps align the WordArt object horizontally, relative to the margin guides.

- Select the WordArt object and, if necessary, display the WordArt Tools Format tab.

- Click the Align button (WordArt Tools Format tab | Arrange group) to display the alignment options (Figure 6–12).

Figure 6–12

2
- Click Relative to Margin Guides to change how Publisher aligns the object.
- Click the Align button (WordArt Tools Format tab | Arrange group) again, to display the enabled alignment options (Figure 6–13).

Q&A
My alignment options were enabled already. Did I do something wrong?

No. If your alignment options were enabled, it may be that someone already had turned on the Relative to Margin Guides feature.

Figure 6–13

3
- Click Align Center to center the WordArt object with respect to the margins (Figure 6–14).

Q&A
What do the Distribute commands do?

When you have more than one object selected, the Distribute commands create equal distance between the selected objects, either horizontally or vertically.

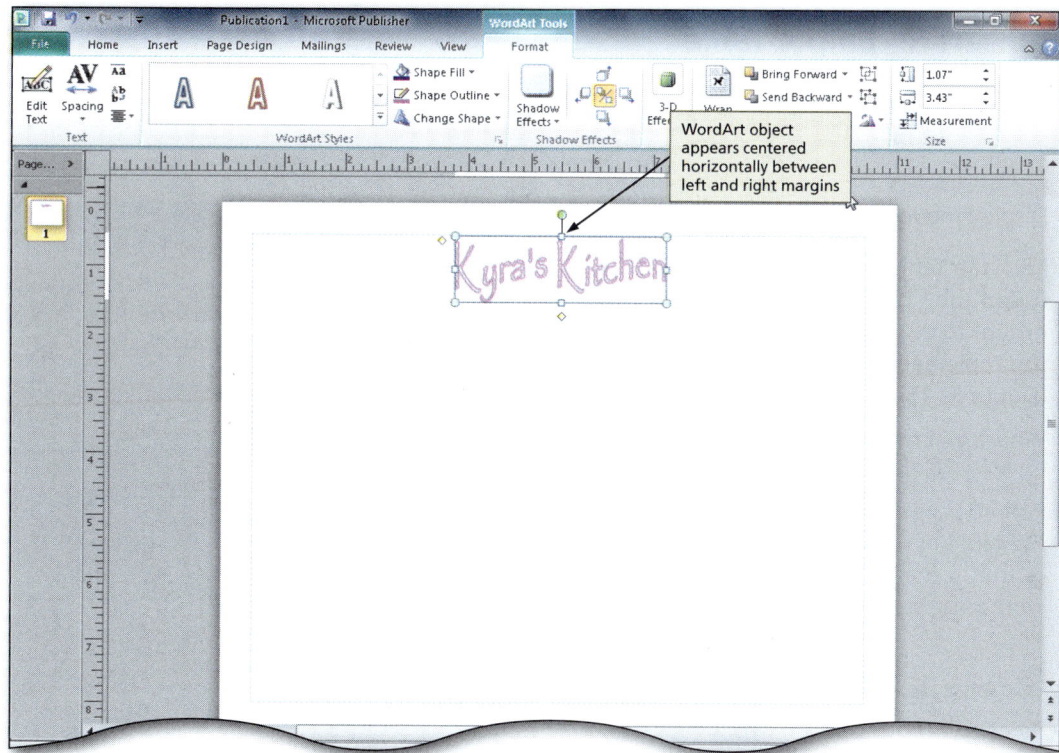

Figure 6–14

Using Tables

The next step in creating the wait staff schedule is to place a table listing the employees, the days of the week, and the hours they work (shown in Figure 6–1a on page PUB 323). A Publisher **table** is a collection of contiguous text boxes that are displayed in rows and columns. The intersection of a row and a column is called a **cell**, and cells are filled with text or graphical data. Within a table, you easily can rearrange rows and columns, change column widths and row heights, and insert diagonal lines. You can format the cells to give the table a professional appearance. You also can edit the inner gridlines and outer border of a table. For these reasons, many Publisher users create tables rather than using large text boxes with tabbed columns. Tables allow you to enter data in columns as you would for a schedule, price list, resume, or table of contents.

Plan Ahead

Use tables effectively to present data. Work with the customer to design a table that is clear and concise. Use recognizable labels for each row and column. Use standard scales and measures. Make sure the reader does not have to spend a lot of time to identify the purpose of the table and grasp the data they are seeking. Use borders, colors, fonts, and alignment to delineate each row and/or column.

The first step in creating a table is to insert an empty table in the publication. When inserting a table, you must specify the total number of rows and columns required, which is called the **dimension** of the table. In Publisher, the first number in a dimension is the number of columns, and the second is the number of rows. For example, in Publisher, a 2 × 1 table (pronounced "two by one") consists of two columns and one row.

To Insert an Empty Table

The following steps insert an empty table with eight columns and seven rows.

1

- Display the Insert tab.

- Click the Table button (Insert tab | Tables group) to display the Table gallery (Figure 6–15).

Q&A

Where will the table be inserted?

Publisher inserts the table in the center of the workspace window.

Experiment

- Point to various cells on the grid to see a preview of various table dimensions in the publication window.

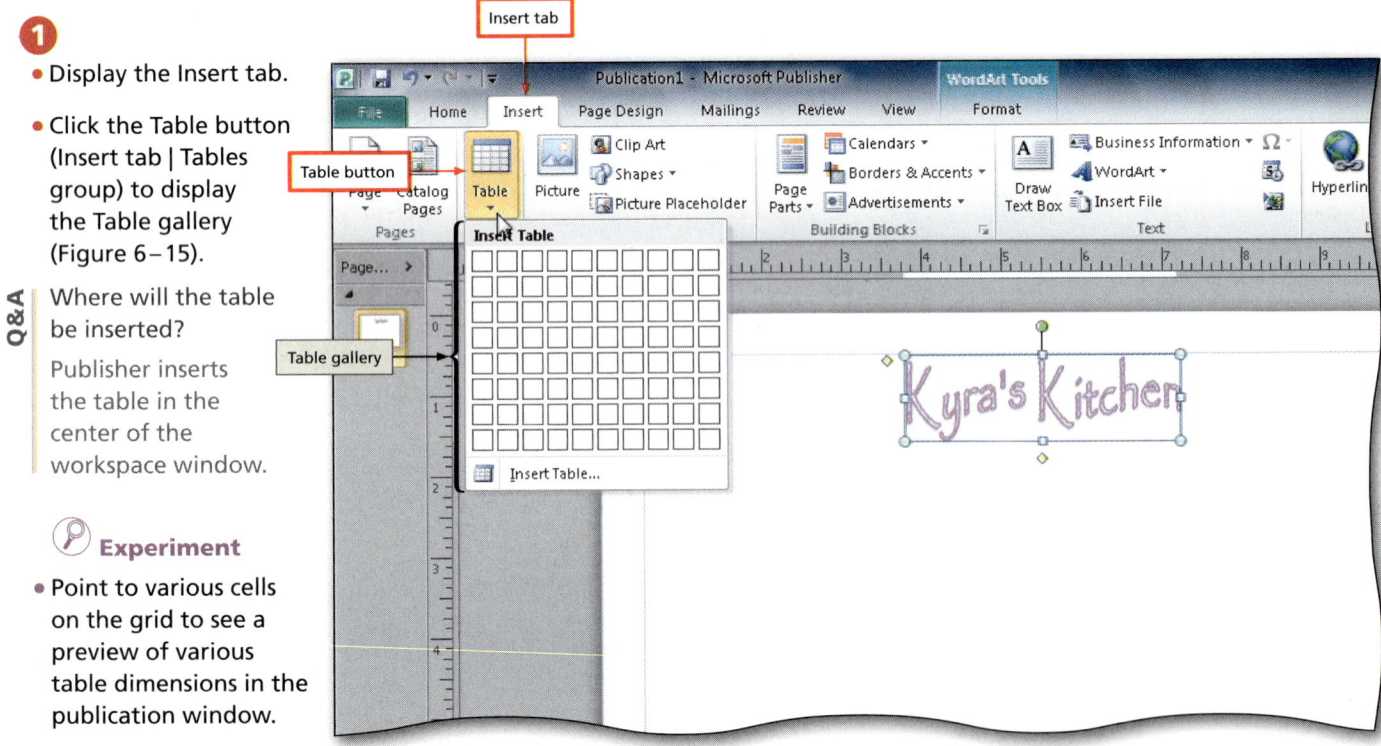

Figure 6–15

2

- Position the mouse pointer on the cell in the eighth column and seventh row of the grid to preview the desired table dimension (Figure 6–16).

Q&A

What if I do not know exactly how many rows I need?

You often do not know the total number of rows that a table will require. Thus, many Publisher users create one row initially and then add more rows as needed.

Figure 6–16

3

- Click the cell in the eighth column and seventh row of the grid to insert an empty 8 × 7 table (Figure 6–17).

Q&A

What are the small circles in the table cells?

Each table cell has an **end-of-cell mark**, which is a formatting mark that assists you with selecting and formatting cells. Recall that formatting marks do not print on a hard copy. The end-of-cell marks currently are left aligned, that is, positioned at the left edge of each cell.

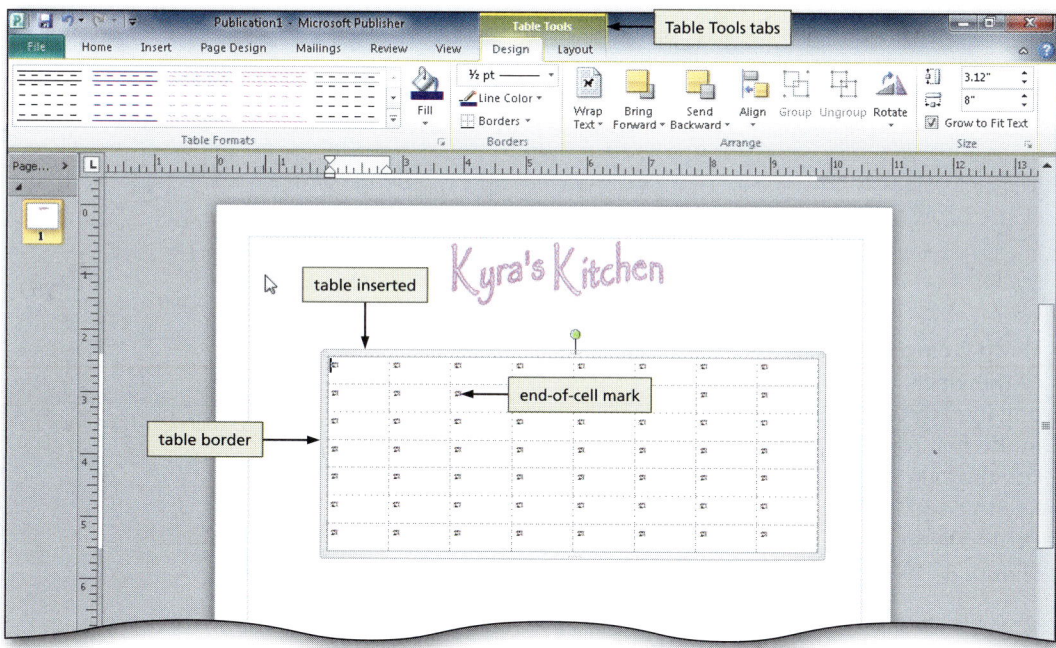

Figure 6–17

Other Ways

1. Click Table button (Insert tab | Tables group), click Insert Table in Table gallery, enter number of columns and rows (Create Table dialog box), click OK button

2. Click Table button (Home tab | Objects group), click desired dimension

To Enter Data in a Table

The next step is to enter data in some of the cells of the empty table. To place data in a cell, you click the cell and then type. To advance rightward from one cell to the next, press the TAB key. When you are at the rightmost cell in a row, press the TAB key to move to the first cell in the next row; do not press the ENTER key. The ENTER key is used to begin a new paragraph within a cell. One way to add new rows to a table is to press the TAB key when the insertion point is positioned in the bottom-right corner cell of the table. The following steps enter data in the first row of the table, beginning with the second column.

1

- Press the F9 key to zoom the table to 100%.

- Click the first row, second column cell to position the insertion point.

- Type **Monday** and then press the TAB key to advance the insertion point to the next cell.

- Type **Tuesday** and then press the TAB key to advance the insertion point to the next cell (Figure 6–18).

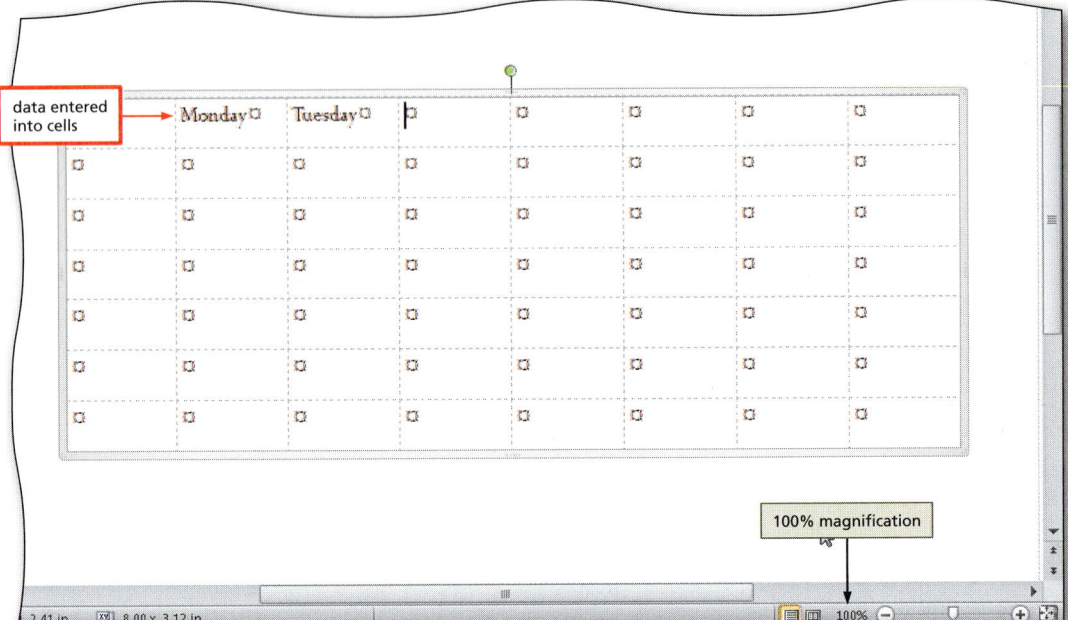

Figure 6–18

Q&A What if I have more data than will fit in a cell?

By default, the data you enter in a cell wordwraps just as text wordwraps between the margins of a text box. You can turn off that feature by clicking to remove the check mark in the Grow to Fit Text check box (Table Tools Design tab | Size group).

2

- Finish typing the days of the week, one in each cell in the first row. Use the TAB key to advance the insertion point (Figure 6–19).

Q&A How do I edit cell contents if I make a mistake?

Click in the cell and then correct the entry.

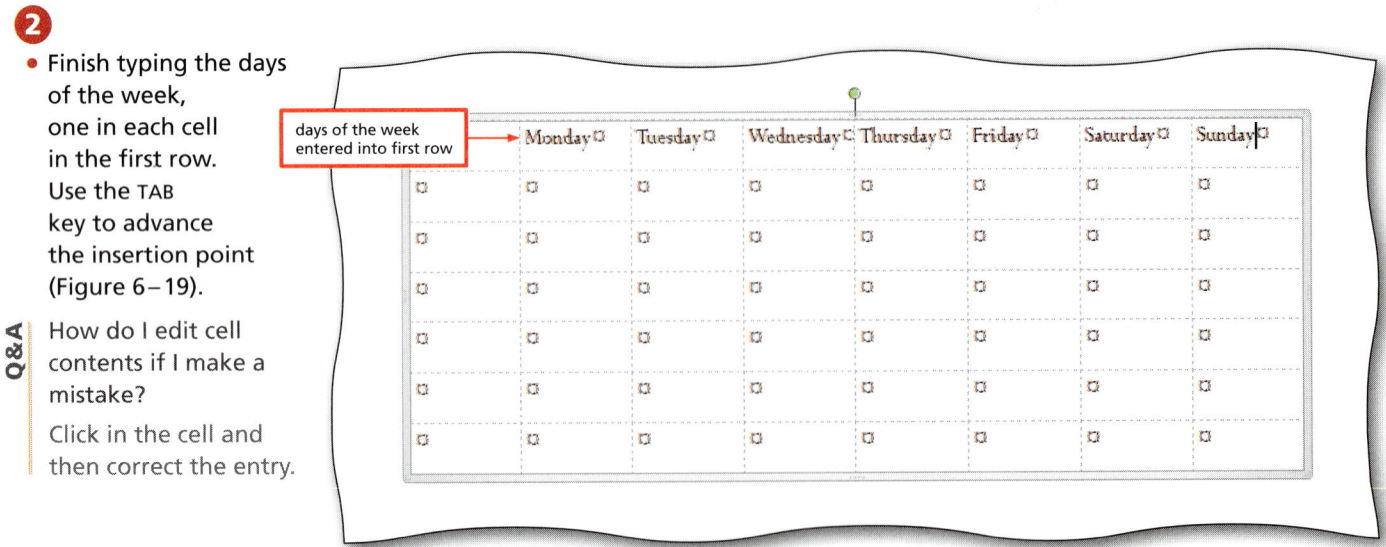

Figure 6–19

To Delete a Column

When working with tables, two new tabs are displayed on the Publisher Ribbon. The Table Tools Layout tab offers buttons and commands that help you in inserting, deleting, merging, and aligning rows, columns, and cells. The Table Tools Design tab provides formatting, borders, and alignment options.

The following steps delete column eight, because the restaurant is closed on Sundays. Deleting a column also deletes any text or graphics in the column cells.

1
- If necessary, position the insertion point in the cell containing the word, Sunday.

- Click Table Tools Layout on the Ribbon to display the Table Tools Layout tab.

- Click the Delete Rows or Columns button (Table Tools Layout tab | Rows & Columns group) to display the options (Figure 6–20).

Q&A
How would I delete just the data in the column?

Drag to select the column and then press the DELETE key. Or, right-click the selection and then click Delete Text on the shortcut menu.

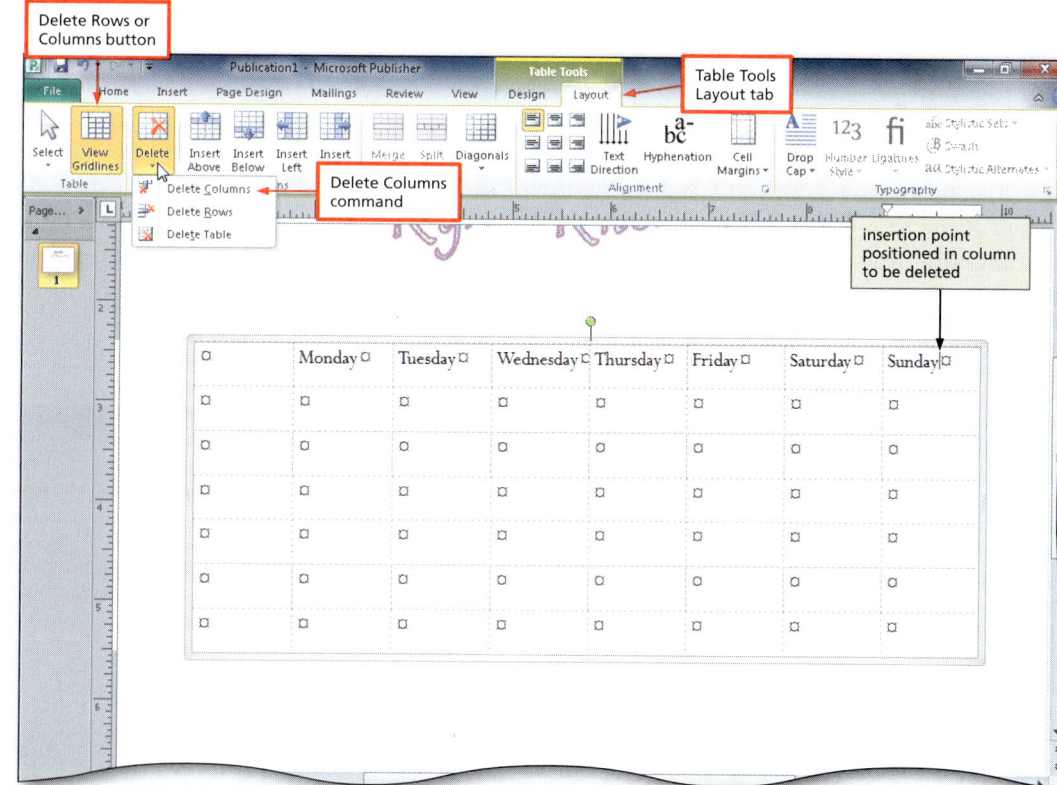

Figure 6–20

2
- Click Delete Columns to delete the current column (Figure 6–21).

Q&A
How would I delete more than one column?

You could delete them one at a time, or, later in this chapter, you will learn how to select multiple cells, rows, and columns. Once they are selected, you use the same button to delete them.

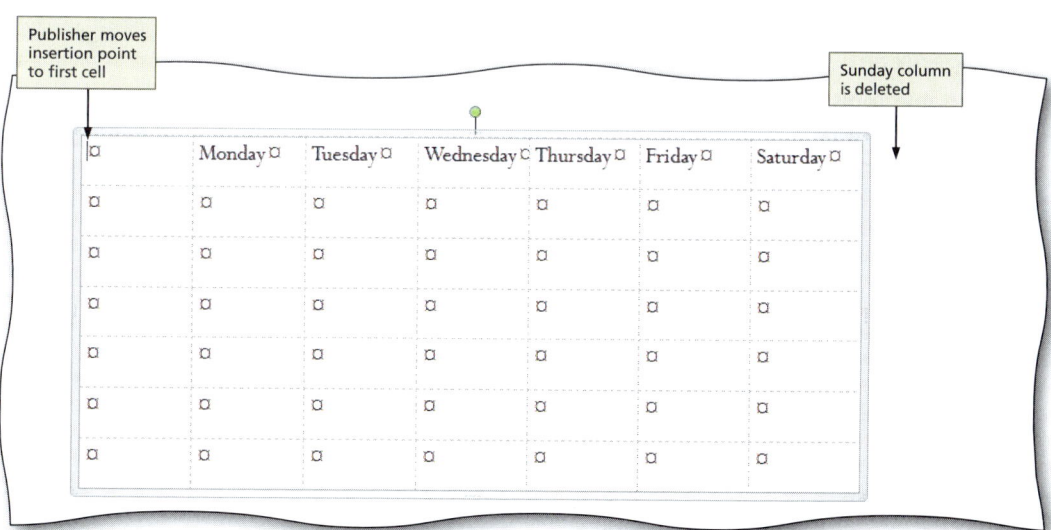

Figure 6–21

Other Ways
1. Right-click cell, point to Delete on shortcut menu, click Delete Columns

TO DELETE A ROW

If you wanted to delete a row in a table rather than a column, you would perform the following steps.

1. Position the insertion point in the row that you want to delete.
2. Click the Delete Rows of Columns button (Table Tools Layout tab | Rows & Columns group) and then click Delete Rows to delete the current row. Or, you could right-click the row, point to Delete on the shortcut menu, and then click Delete Rows.

To Insert a Row

The next step is to insert a row at the top of the table because you want to create a table heading on a row by itself at the top of the table. As discussed earlier, you can insert a row at the end of a table by positioning the insertion point in the bottom-right corner cell and then pressing the TAB key. You cannot use the TAB key to insert a row at the beginning or middle of a table. Instead, you use the Insert Rows Above or Insert Rows Below button. The following step inserts a row in a table.

- Position the mouse pointer somewhere in the first row of the table because you want to insert a row above this row.

- If necessary, display the Table Tools Layout tab.

- Click the Insert Rows Above button (Table Tools Layout tab | Rows & Columns group) to add a new row (Figure 6–22).

🔎 **Experiment**

- On the Table Tools Layout tab, point to each of the buttons in the Rows & Columns group to view the ScreenTips. In addition, look at the pictures on the buttons themselves, which will help you identify each function.

Figure 6–22

Other Ways

1. Right-click row, point to Insert on shortcut menu, click appropriate Insert command

TO INSERT A COLUMN

If you wanted to insert a column in a table rather than a row, you would perform the following steps.

1. Position the insertion point in the column to the left or right of where you want to insert the column.

2. Click the Insert Columns to the Left button (Table Tools Layout tab | Rows & Columns group) to insert a column to the left of the current column, or click the Insert Columns to the Right button (Table Tools Layout tab | Rows & Columns group) to insert a column to the right of the current column. Or, you could right-click the column, point to Insert on the shortcut menu, and click Insert Left or Insert Right on the Insert submenu.

To Apply a Table Format

The next step is to apply a table format to the table. The Table Format gallery (Table Tools Design tab | Table Formats group) allows you to format a table with a variety of colors and shading. The following steps apply a table format to the table in the publication.

1

- Click the table to remove the previous selection.

- Click Table Tools Design on the Ribbon to display the Table Tools Design tab.

- Click the More button in the Table Formats gallery (Table Tools Design tab | Table Formats group) to expand the gallery (Figure 6–23).

Q&A

Why are the table formats black, purple, and gray?

Publisher displays table formats that match the colors in the chosen color scheme, in this case, the Lilac color scheme you chose earlier in the chapter.

Figure 6–23

 Experiment

- Point to various table styles in the Table Formats gallery and watch the format of the table change in the publication window.

2
- Click Table Style 28 in the Table Format gallery to apply the selected style to the table (Figure 6–24).

Q&A

Can I add rows or columns after I have applied a table style?

You may get unpredictable results. Some table styles replicate the pattern correctly when you add a column but do not alternate colors when you add a row. If you add rows or columns, you may need to reapply the table style.

Figure 6–24

Other Ways

1. Click More button (Table Tools Design tab | Table Formats group), click Table AutoFormat, select format, click OK button (Auto Format dialog box)

Selecting Table Contents

When working with tables, you may need to select the contents of cells, rows, columns, or the entire table. Table 6–2 identifies ways to select various items in a table.

Table 6–2 Selecting Items in a Table

Item to Select	Action
Cell	Point to the left edge of the cell and click when the mouse pointer changes to a small solid upward-angled pointing arrow. Or, position the insertion point in the cell, click the Select button (Table Tools Layout tab | Table group), and then click Select Cell on the Select menu. Or, right-click the cell, point to Select on the shortcut menu, click Select Cell.
Column	Point to the border at the top of the column and click when the mouse pointer changes to a small solid downward-pointing arrow. Or, position the insertion point in the column, click the Select button (Table Tools Layout tab | Table group), and then click Select Column on the Select menu. Or, right-click the column, point to Select on the shortcut menu, click Select Column.

Table 6–2 Selecting Items in a Table (continued)

Item to Select	Action
Row	Point left of the row and click when the mouse pointer changes to a right-pointing block arrow. Or, position the insertion point in the row, click the Select button (Table Tools Layout tab | Table group), and then click Select Row on the Select menu. Or, right-click the row, point to Select on shortcut menu, click Select Row.
Multiple cells, rows, or columns adjacent to one another	Drag through cells, rows, or columns.
Multiple cells, rows, or columns not adjacent to one another	Select the first cell, row, or column (as described above) and then hold down the CTRL key while selecting the next cell, row, or column.
Next cell	Press the TAB key.
Previous cell	Press SHIFT+TAB.
Table	Click somewhere in the table, then click the Select button (Table Tools Layout tab | Table group), click Select Table. Or, right-click the table, point to Select on the shortcut menu, click Select Table.

To Select a Row

The following steps select the entire top row of the table.

1

- Point to the left side of the first row to display a right-pointing block arrow (Figure 6–25).

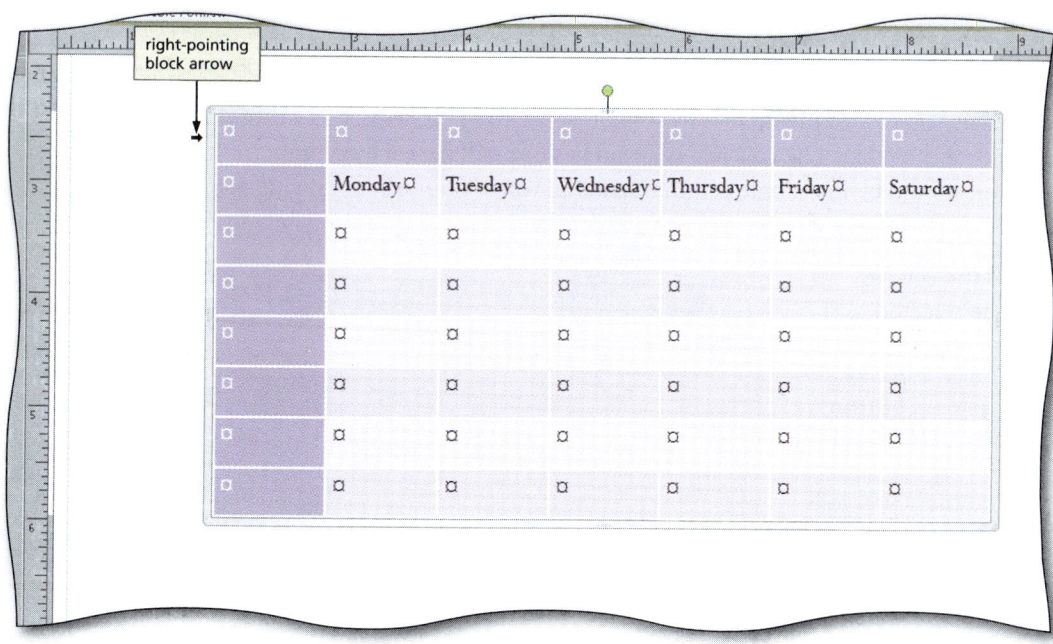

Figure 6–25

I do not see the arrow. What should I do?

Move the mouse pointer slightly to the left or right. The arrow appears when you are approximately 1/8-inch from the edge of the table.

2

- Click to select the row.

- Display the Table Tools Layout tab (Figure 6–26).

Q&A

How do I select multiple, adjacent rows without dragging through them?

Point to the left side of the first row to display the right-pointing block arrow and then drag straight down until all desired rows are selected.

Other Ways

1. Click in row, click Select Table button (Table Tools Layout tab | Table group), click Select Row

2. Right-click row, point to Select on shortcut menu, click Select Row

Figure 6–26

To Merge Cells

The top row of the table is to contain the date of the week as a heading, which should be centered above the columns of the table. The row just selected has one cell for each column, in this case, seven cells. The heading of the table, however, should be in a single cell that spans all rows. Thus, the following step merges the seven cells into a single cell.

1

- With the cells to merge selected (as shown in Figure 6–26), click the Merge Cells button (Table Tools Layout tab | Merge group) to merge the seven cells into one cell.

- Click outside the table to view the merged cell (Figure 6–27).

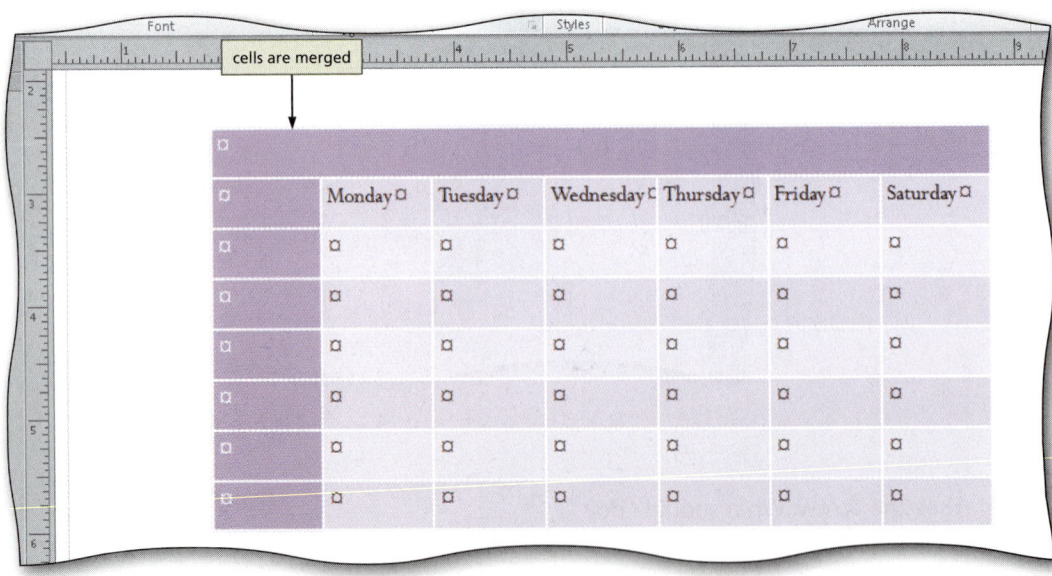

Figure 6–27

TO SPLIT CELLS

Sometimes you want to split a merged cell back into multiple cells. If you wanted to split cells, you would perform the following steps.

1. Position the insertion point in the cell to split.
2. Click the Split Cells button (Table Tools Layout tab | Merge group).

To Enter More Data in a Table

The following steps enter the remaining data in the table.

1 Position the insertion point in the first row and then type `Wait Staff Schedule for the Week of January 16` as the heading.

2 Click the first cell in the third row. Type **Andhra** and then press the TAB key to advance the insertion point to the next cell. Type **11-6** and then press the TAB key to advance the insertion point to the next cell.

3 Continue entering the data in each cell, as shown in Figure 6–28.

Wait Staff Schedule for the Week of January 16						
	Monday	Tuesday	Wednesday	Thursday	Friday	Saturday
Andhra	11-6	11-6	11-6		4-close	4-close
Blair	4-close	4-close	4-close		4-close	4-close
Chris		4-close	4-close	4-close		
Dixon	11-2		11-2	11-2	4-close	4-close
Ensile	2-8		2-8	4-close	2-8	2-8
Farad	4-close	11-2		11-6	11-2	11-2

data is entered into cells

Figure 6–28

To Format Text in the Date Heading

The following steps format the text in the heading row.

1 Triple-click the text in the first row to select it.

2 Display the Home tab.

3 Click the Font Size box arrow (Home tab | Font group) and then click 24 to change the font size.

4 Click the Center button (Home tab | Paragraph group) to center the text.

5 Click outside the table to view the formatting (Figure 6–29).

text is formatted

Figure 6–29

To Align Data in Cells

The next step is to change the alignment of the cell data in the second through seventh columns of the table. In addition to aligning text horizontally in a cell (left, center, or right), you can align it vertically within a cell (top, center, bottom). When the height of the cell is close to the same height as the text, however, differences in vertical alignment are not readily apparent. The following steps center data in cells both horizontally and vertically.

1
● Starting in the second row, select the cells in the second through seventh columns by dragging through them (Figure 6–30).

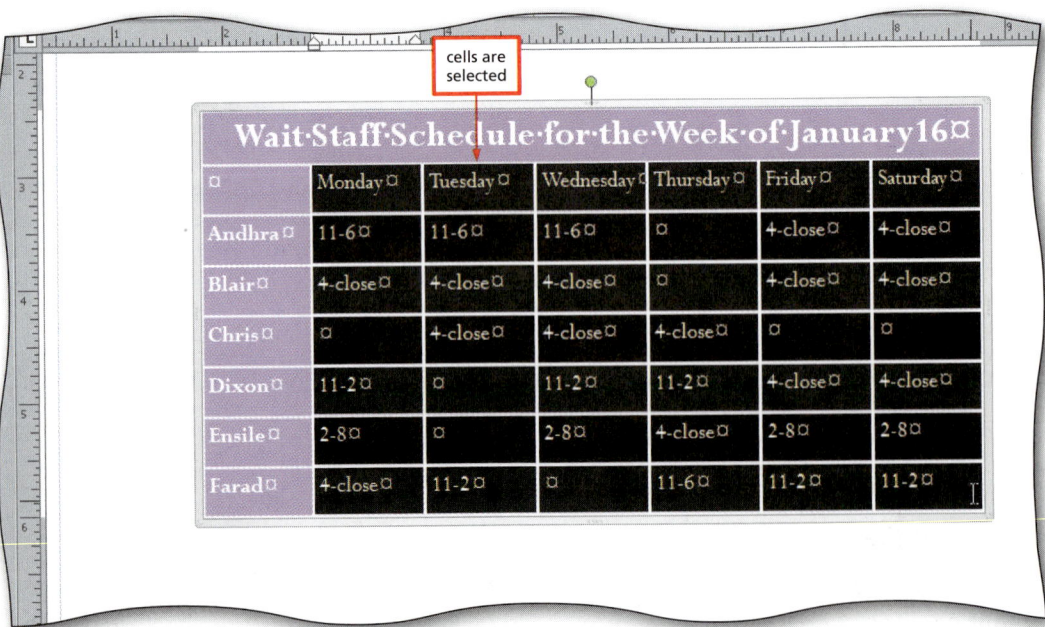

cells are selected

Figure 6–30

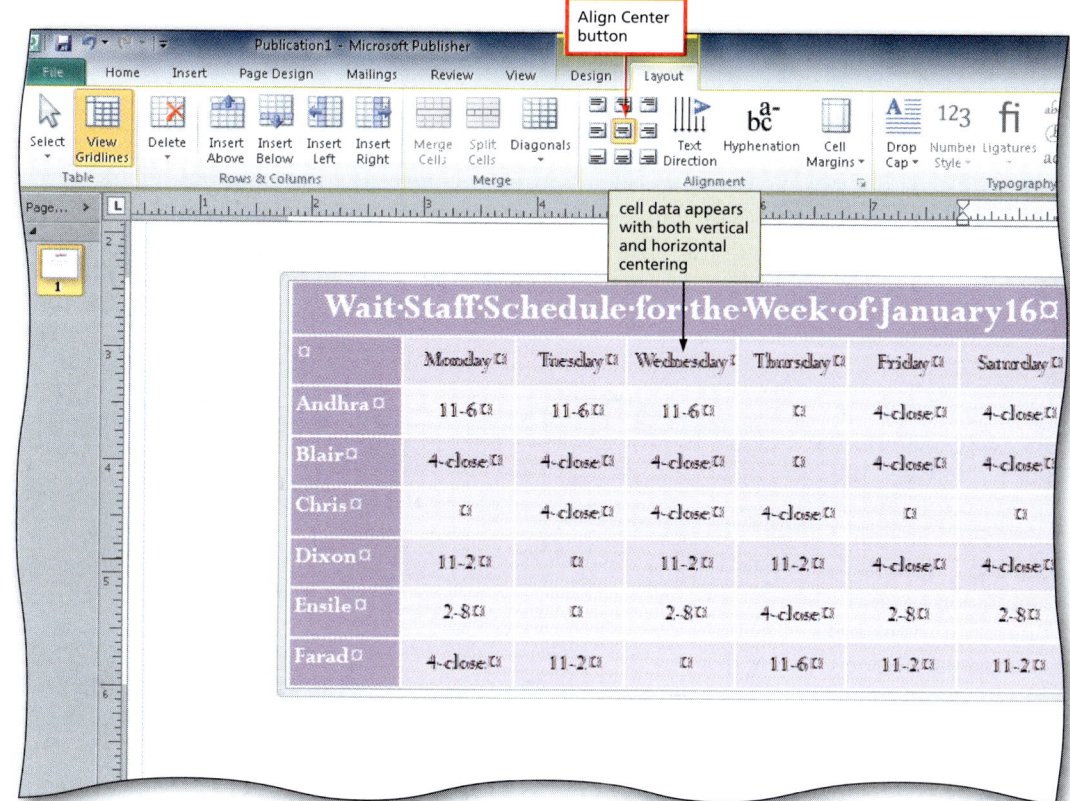

2

- If necessary, display the Table Tools Layout tab.

- Click the Align Center button (Table Tools Layout tab | Alignment group) to center the contents of the selected cells.

- Click in the table to remove the selection (Figure 6–31).

Experiment

- Point to each of the buttons in the Alignment group to view the ScreenTips.

Figure 6–31

To Align the First Column

The following steps align the first column of cell data to the left horizontally and centered vertically.

1 Starting in the second row, drag through the cells in the first column to select them.

2 Click the Align Center Left button (Table Tools Layout tab | Alignment group) to align the contents of the first column.

3 Click in the table to remove the selection (Figure 6–32).

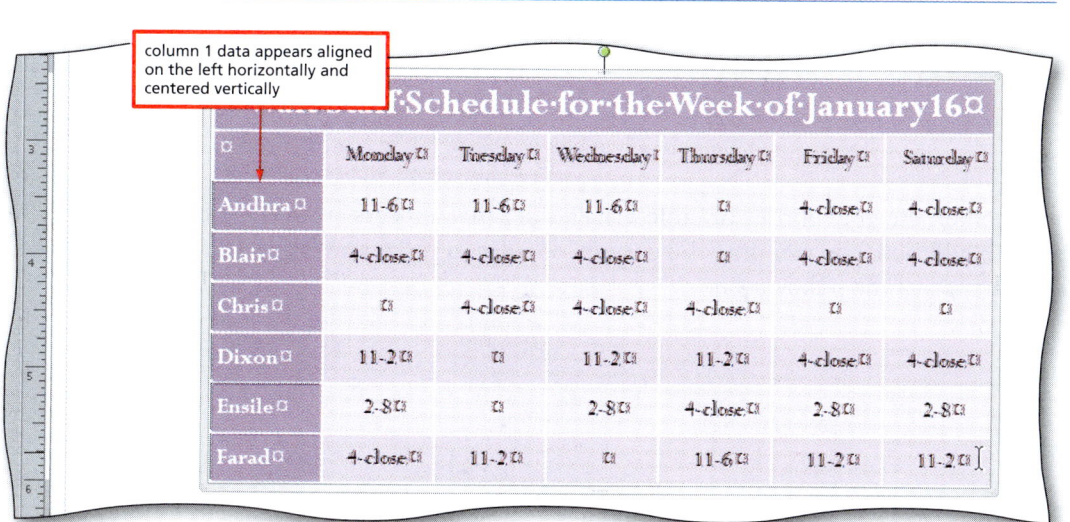

Figure 6–32

To Change Column Width

When you first create a table, all of the columns have the same width and all of the rows have the same height. To change the column width, drag the right border of the column. To change the row height, drag the bottom border of a row. When you drag a border, the current column or row changes size; all of the other columns or rows remain the same, increasing or decreasing the size of the entire table. If you SHIFT+drag a border, the table remains the same size; the rows or columns on either side of the border change size.

The following step resizes the first column.

- With no selection in the table, point to the border between the first two columns until the mouse pointer displays a double-headed arrow and then drag to the left, approximately one-half inch to decrease the column width (Figure 6–33).

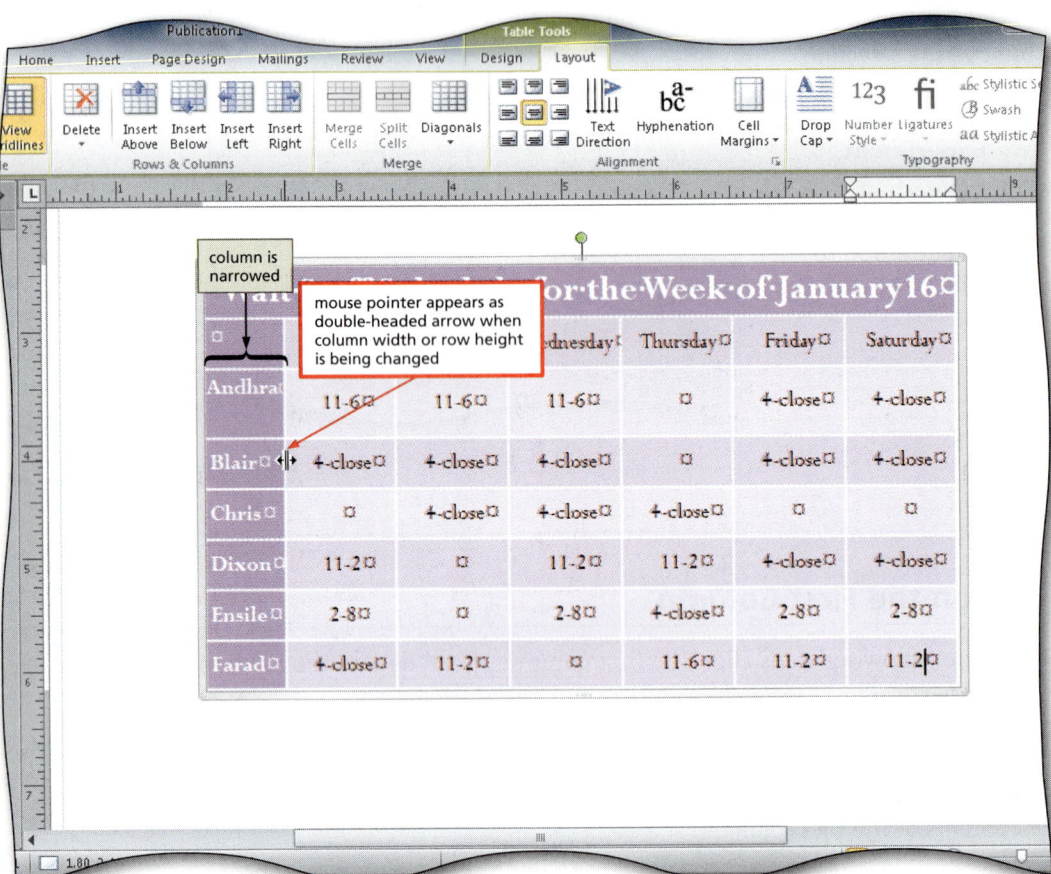

Figure 6–33

To Resize the Table

Just like the picture placeholder, the gray border or table placeholder that appears around the table can be dragged to reposition the table. In addition, you can drag the corners or sides to resize the table. The following steps resize the table to fit the lower portion of the publication.

1

- Zoom to 70% and scroll to display the entire table.

- Point to the lower-right corner of the table border.

- When the mouse pointer changes to a double-headed arrow, drag down and to the right until the table border snaps to the lower-right corner margin guides (Figure 6–34).

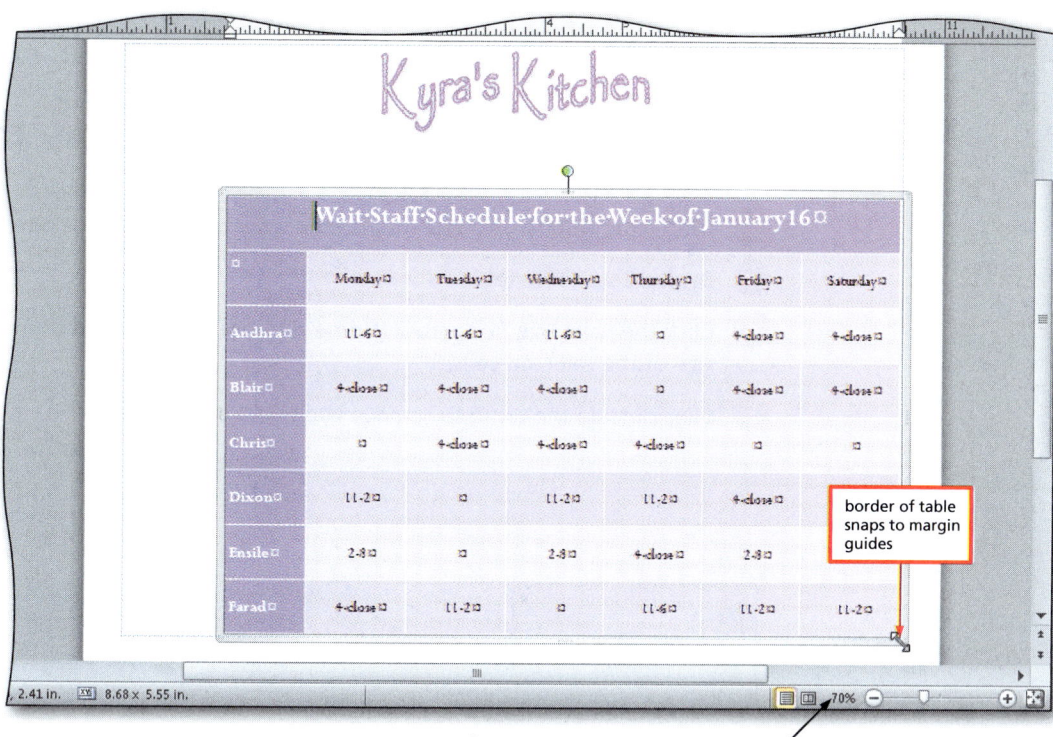

Figure 6–34

2

- Drag the upper-left corner of the table border to a position that snaps to the left margin, just below the WordArt object (Figure 6–35).

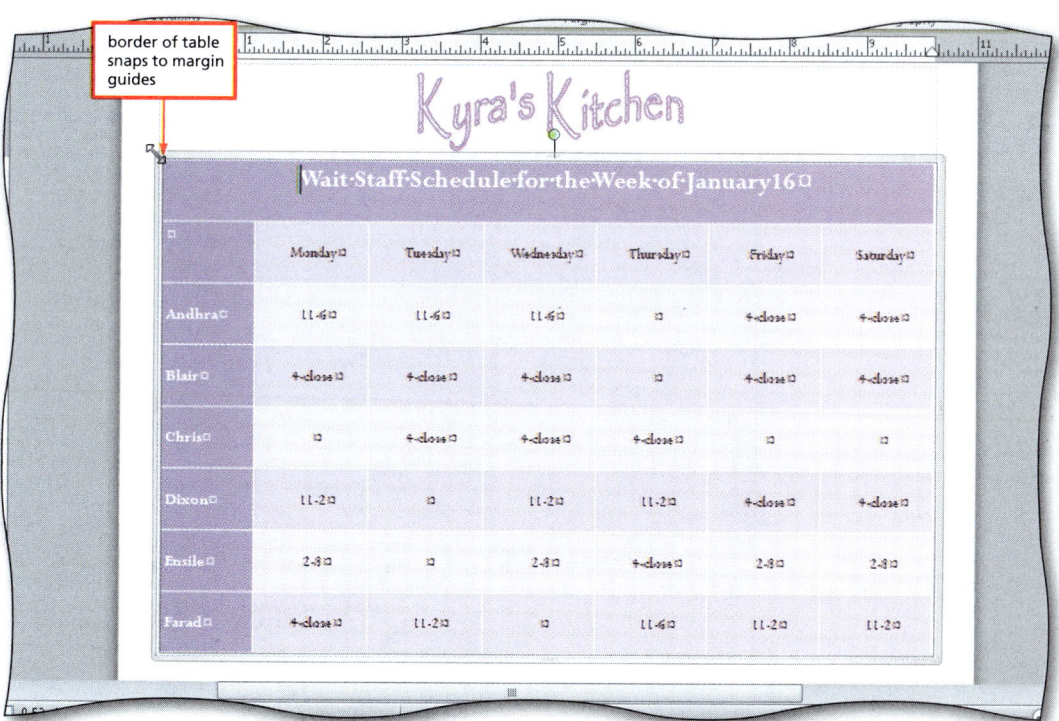

Figure 6–35

Other Ways

1. Right-click table, click Format Table on shortcut menu, enter size of table in Size sheet (Format Table dialog box), click OK button

To Format Multiple Cells

The following steps change the font size of all the cells except the heading cell in the first row.

1 Point to the left of the second row until the mouse pointer changes to a right-pointing block arrow.

2 Drag straight down to select all of the rows except the first one.

3 Display the Home tab.

4 Click the Font Size box arrow (Home tab | Font group) and then click 20 to change the font size of the selected cells.

5 Click outside the table to remove the selection (Figure 6–36).

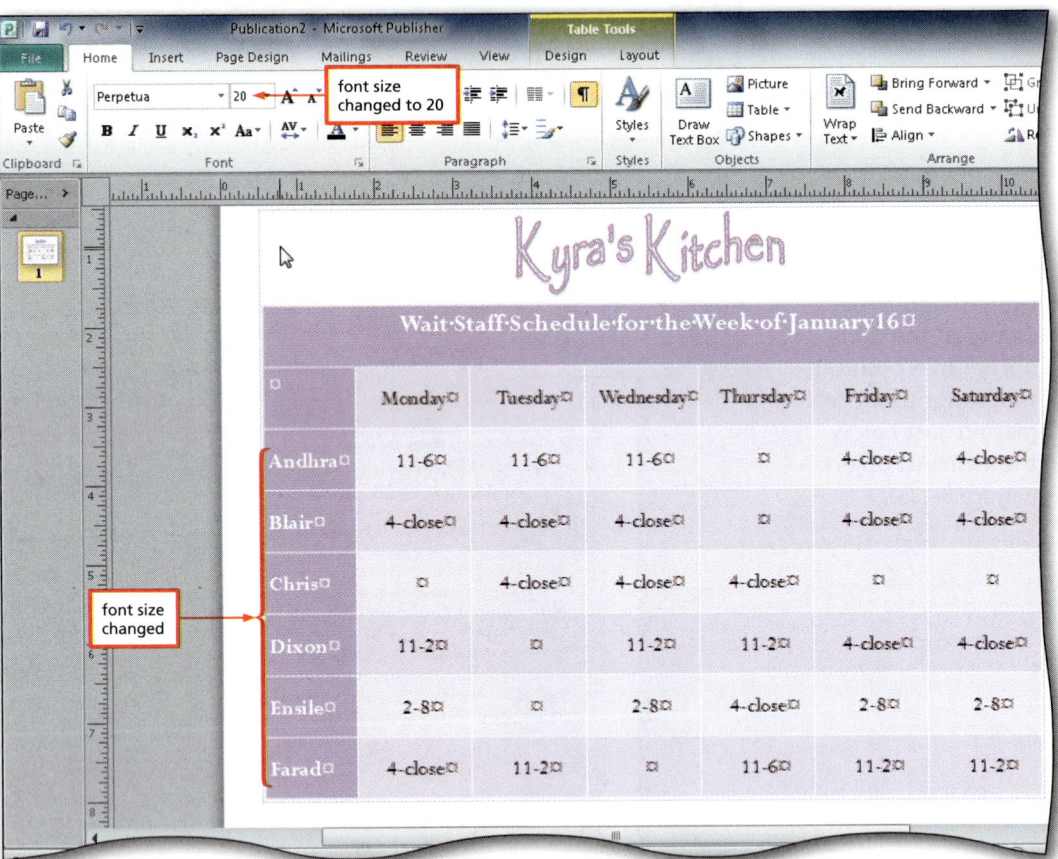

Figure 6–36

To Create a Cell Diagonal

The following steps create a cell diagonal to accommodate a heading for both the staff column and the days of the week row — in the same cell. A **cell diagonal** is a line that splits the cell diagonally, creating two triangular text boxes. Commonly used for split headings or multiple entries per cell, the cell diagonal can be slanted from either corner.

1

- Click the cell in the first column, second row of the table.

- If necessary, display the Table Tools Layout tab.

- Click the Diagonals button (Table Tools Layout tab | Merge group) to display the Diagonals list (Figure 6–37).

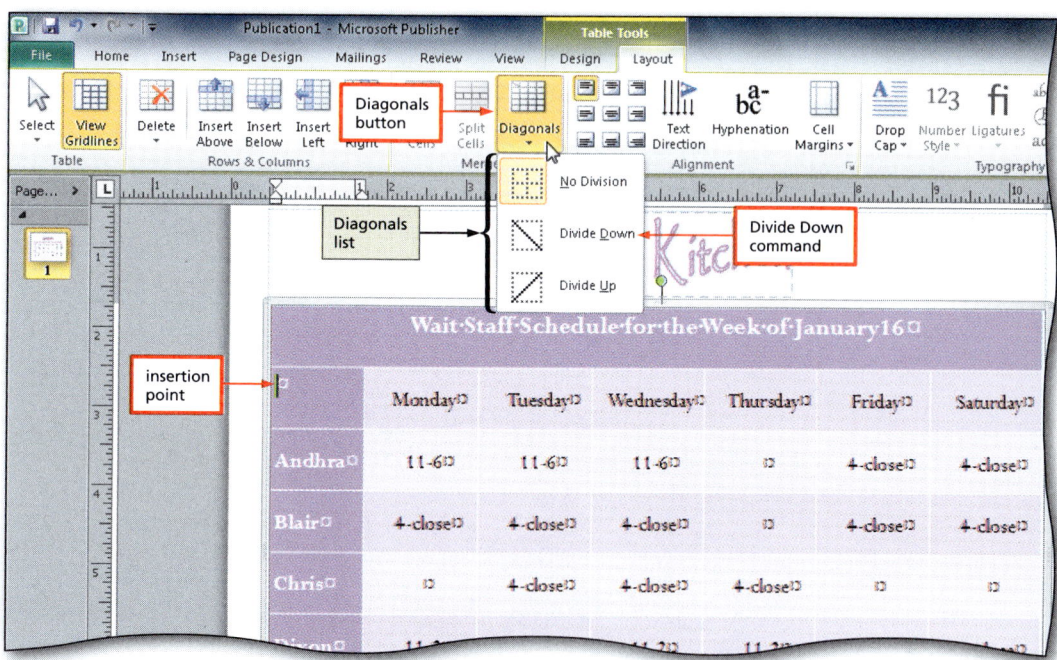

Figure 6–37

2

- Click Divide Down to create a diagonal in the cell.

- Click outside the table to remove the selection (Figure 6–38).

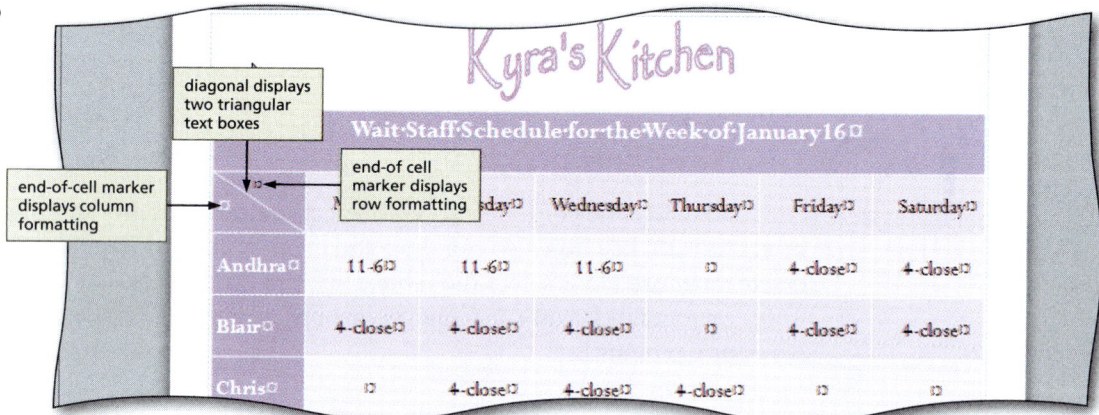

Figure 6–38

To Enter and Format Data in the Diagonal Cell

The following step enters data into both halves of the diagonal cell.

1 Click the left half of the cell with the cell diagonal to position the insertion point.

2 Click the Align Bottom Left button (Table Tools Layout tab | Alignment group) to select the alignment.

3 Display the Home tab.

4 Click the Font Size box arrow (Home tab | Format group) and then click 16 to select a font size of 16.

5 Type `Staff` to complete the column heading.

6 Click the right half of the cell with the cell diagonal to position the insertion point.

7 Change the font size to 16.

8 Display the Table Tools Layout tab.

9 Click the Align Center Right button (Table Tools Layout tab | Alignment group) to set the alignment.

10 Type `Days` to complete the row heading (Figure 6–39).

Figure 6–39

Deleting Table Data

To delete the contents of a cell, select the cell contents and then press the DELETE or BACKSPACE key. You also can drag and drop or cut and paste the contents of cells. To delete an entire table, select the table, click the Delete Rows or Columns button (Table Tools Layout tab | Rows & Columns group), and then click Delete Table on the Delete Rows or Columns list.

To Save the Publication

You have performed many tasks while creating this publication and do not want to risk losing work completed thus far. Accordingly, you should save the document. The following steps save the schedule with the file name, Wait Staff Schedule.

1 With a USB flash drive connected to one of the computer's USB ports, click the Save button on the Quick Access Toolbar to display the Save As dialog box.

2 Type `Wait Staff Schedule` in the File name text box to change the file name. Do not press the ENTER key because you do not want to close the dialog box at this time.

3 Navigate to the desired save location (in this case, the Publisher folder in the CIS 101 folder [or your class folder] on the USB flash drive).

4 Click the Save button (Save As dialog box) to save the publication in the selected folder on the selected drive with the entered file name.

To Print the Schedule

The following steps print a hard copy of the Wait Staff Schedule.

1 Click the File tab to open the Backstage view and then click the Print tab to display the Print gallery.

2 Verify the printer name on the Printer Status button will print a hard copy of the publication. If necessary, click the Printer Status button to display a list of available printer options and then click the desired printer to change the currently selected printer.

3 Click the Print button in the Print gallery to print the schedule on the currently selected printer (Figure 6–40).

Kyra's Kitchen

Wait Staff Schedule for the Week of January 16					
Days / **Staff** — Monday	Tuesday	Wednesday	Thursday	Friday	Saturday
Andhra — 11-6	11-6	11-6		4-close	4-close
Blair — 4-close	4-close	4-close		4-close	4-close
Chris —	4-close	4-close	4-close		
Dixon — 11-2		11-2	11-2	4-close	4-close
Ensile — 2-8		2-8	4-close	2-8	2-8
Farad — 4-close	11-2		11-6	11-2	11-2

Figure 6–40

To Close a Publication without Quitting Publisher

The following step closes the publication without quitting Publisher.

1 Click the File tab to open the Backstage view and then click Close to close the publication without quitting Publisher and to return to the New template gallery.

Calendars

The next series of steps creates a calendar. A **calendar** is a specialized table or set of tables that Publisher can format with any combination of months and year. Calendar cells, like table cells, can be formatted with color, borders, text, and styles. You can create calendars as independent, stand-alone publications, or insert them as building blocks into other publications. Calendars are used for many purposes other than just presenting the date. Information that changes from day to day can be presented as text in a calendar, such as school lunches, practice schedules, homework assignments, appointments, or meetings. Colors and graphics are used in calendars to display holidays, special events, reminders, and even phases of the moon.

Plan Ahead

> **Create promotional pieces.** A **promotional piece** or **promo** is an inclusive term for a publication or article that includes advertising and marketing information for a product or service known to and purchased by customers and clients.
>
> Including calendars in a publication dates the material, because the publication may not be useful after the calendar date has passed. Companies should consider carefully whether to include calendars in publications.

To Create a 12-Month Calendar

The following steps create a 12-month calendar that Kyra's Kitchen will use as a promotional piece.

 1

- Click Calendars in the New template gallery (Backstage view) to display the calendar templates.

- Click the Art Right calendar template to select it.

- Click the Color scheme box arrow in the Customize area and then click Lilac in the list to choose a color scheme.

- Click the Font scheme box arrow and then click Equity in the list to choose a font scheme.

- If necessary, click the Business information box arrow and then click Kyra's Kitchen to select it.

- If necessary, scroll to display the remaining settings (Figure 6–41).

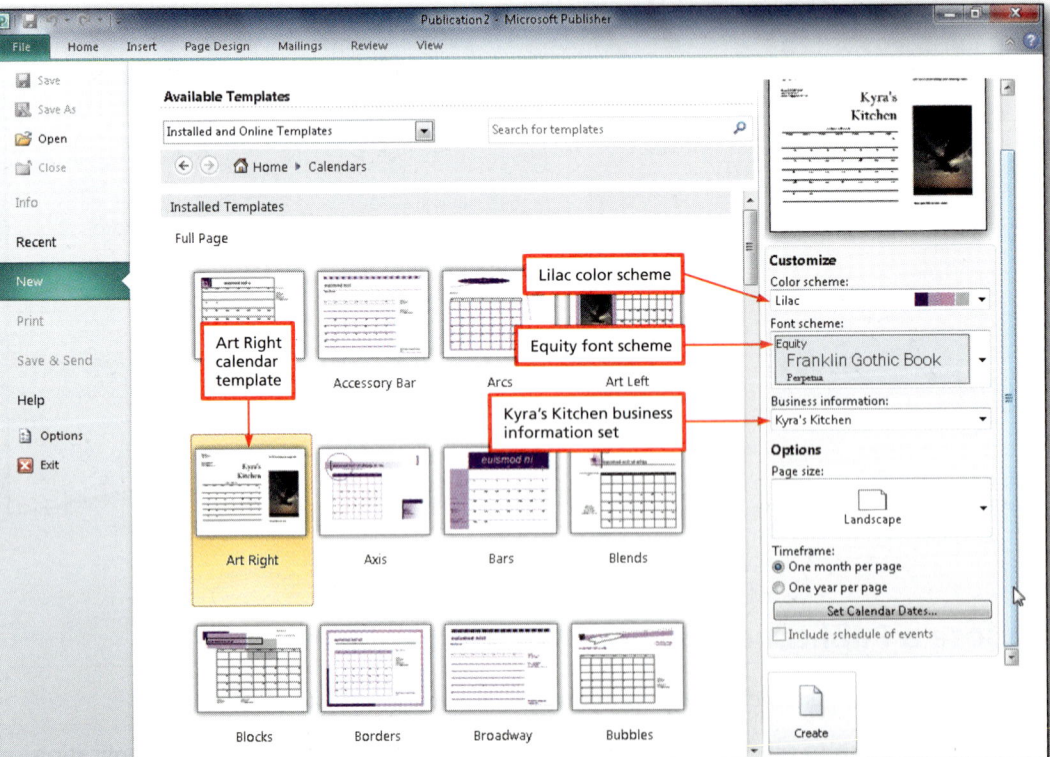

Figure 6–41

2

- If necessary, click the Page size box arrow in the Options area and then click Landscape in the list to choose a landscape orientation.

- If necessary, click the 'One month per page' option button to select it.

- Click the Set Calendar Dates button to display the Set Calendar Dates dialog box (Figure 6–42).

Figure 6–42

3

- Click the box arrow for the Start date month (Set Calendar Dates dialog box) to display the list of months (Figure 6–43).

Figure 6–43

How can I create a one-month calendar?

To create just one month on one page, use the same month and date in both the Start date and End date boxes (Set Calendar Dates dialog box).

4

- Scroll as necessary and click January to select the starting month.

- If necessary, click the up or down arrow on the Start date year box (Set Calendar Dates dialog box) until 2012 is displayed.

- Click the End date box arrow and then click December to choose the ending month.

- If necessary, click the up or down arrow on the End year box until 2012 is displayed (Figure 6–44).

Q&A What kind of object is the year box with the up and down arrows?

Microsoft refers to this as a numerical up and down box. It commonly is used for fixed data in a sequential list from which the user can choose. You also can type into a numerical up and down box.

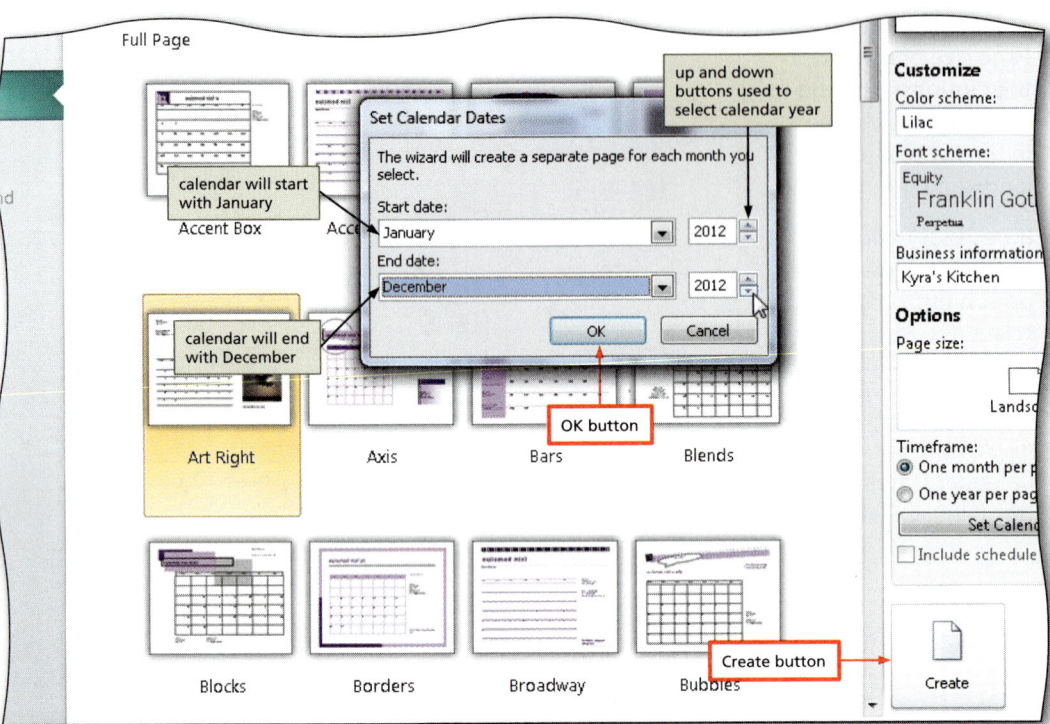

Figure 6–44

5

- Click the OK button (Set Calendar Dates dialog box) to set the dates and close the dialog box.

- Click the Create button (Backstage view | New template gallery) to create the calendar (Figure 6–45).

Q&A Why do so many thumbnails appear in the Page Navigation pane?

Because you selected a yearly calendar, Publisher created 12 pages, one for each month of the year.

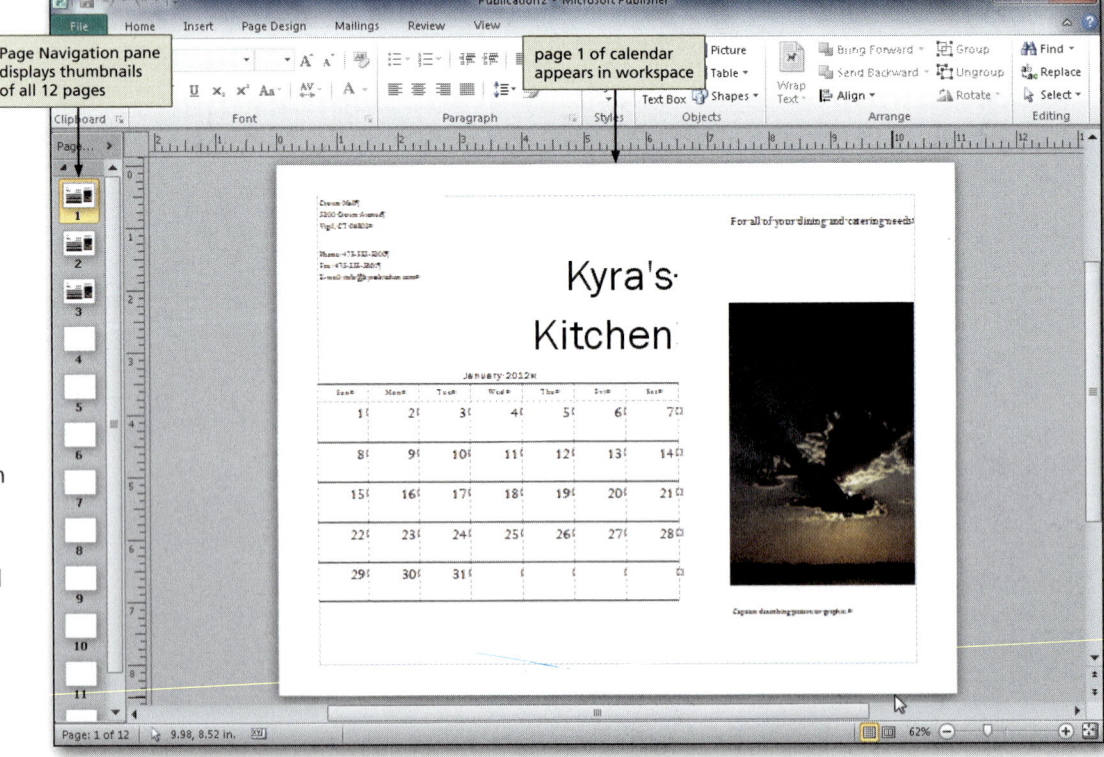

Figure 6–45

Customizing the Calendar

The next steps in customizing the calendar include changing the heading, clip art, and caption on each page. Table 6–3 displays the information for the clip art and captions.

Table 6–3 Data for Kyra's Kitchen Calendar		
Month	**Clip Art Search Term**	**Caption**
January	flapjacks	Try our breakfast flapjacks
February	bagels	Freshly baked bagels
March	brewed	Bottomless cup of coffee
April	fruits	Fresh fruit plate
May	sandwich	Let us cater your next luncheon
June	iced tea	Splashing lemon tea
July	shrimp salad	Shrimp salad
August	diners	Join us for lunch
September	potato salad	Engaging salads
October	halibut	Spiced halibut
November	steak	Steak 'n' fries
December	desserts	A wide range of desserts

To Edit the Clip Art

The following steps edit the clip art image on page 1.

1 Click the graphic on page 1 to select the picture placeholder. Click again to select only the picture.

2 Display the Insert tab.

3 Click the Clip Art button (Insert tab | Illustrations group) to display the Clip Art task pane.

4 Type `flapjacks` in the Search for text box.

5 Click the Results should be box arrow and then click to display a check mark only in the Photographs check box.

6 Click to display a check mark in the Include Office.com content check box.

7 Click the Go button to search for photographs related to the term, flapjacks.

8 Click a clip similar to the one shown in Figure 6–46 on the next page.

Figure 6–46

To Edit More Graphics

The following steps edit the rest of the graphics in the calendar. The search terms are listed in Table 6–3 on the previous page. Choose photographs rather than illustrations, and choose clips with portrait orientation that relate to the caption listed in the table.

1 With the Clip Art task pane still displayed, click the next page in the Page Navigation pane to display the next month.

2 Click the graphic to select the picture placeholder. Click again to select only the picture.

3 Type the search term from Table 6–3 in the Search for box. (In the case of February, you would type **bagels** in the Search for box.)

4 Click the Go button to search for photographs related to the search term.

5 Click a clip with a portrait orientation that will complement the caption listed in Table 6–3.

6 Repeat Steps 1 through 5 to change each of the graphics for the 12-month calendar.

7 Close the Clip Art task pane.

To Edit the Captions

The following steps edit the caption for each of the pictures.

1 Click the first page in the Page Navigation pane.

2 Click the caption below the graphic.

3 Type the new caption from Table 6–3 on page PUB 355.

4 Repeat Steps 1 through 3 for each of the pages in the calendar.

To Edit the Heading

The following steps edit the heading on each page of the calendar.

1 Click the first page in the Page Navigation pane.

2 Right-click the text, Kyra's Kitchen, to display the shortcut menu.

3 Click Delete Object on the shortcut menu to delete the current heading.

4 Click the Page Parts button (Insert tab | Building Blocks group) to display the stored page parts and then click the Kyra's Kitchen WordArt object to insert it into the publication.

5 Drag the border of the graphic until the WordArt object is positioned above the table and aligned on the right with the right side of the calendar table (Figure 6–47).

6 Repeat Steps 1 through 5 for each page of the calendar.

Figure 6–47

Borders

Rather than applying a table style, you can create your own style of table by adding borders, colors, fills, and line styles. A **border** is the line that displays along the edge of a cell, row, column or table. Publisher allows you to add all borders, individual borders, inside or outside borders on multiple cells, or no border at all. It is important to select the cell, row, or column before adding a border.

To Select the Table

The following steps select the table in preparation for adding borders to each cell.

1 Click the first page in the Page Navigation pane.

2 Click the table.

3 Display the Table Tools Layout tab.

4 Click the Select Table button (Table Tools Layout tab | Table group) to display the list.

5 Click Select Table to select the table (Figure 6–48).

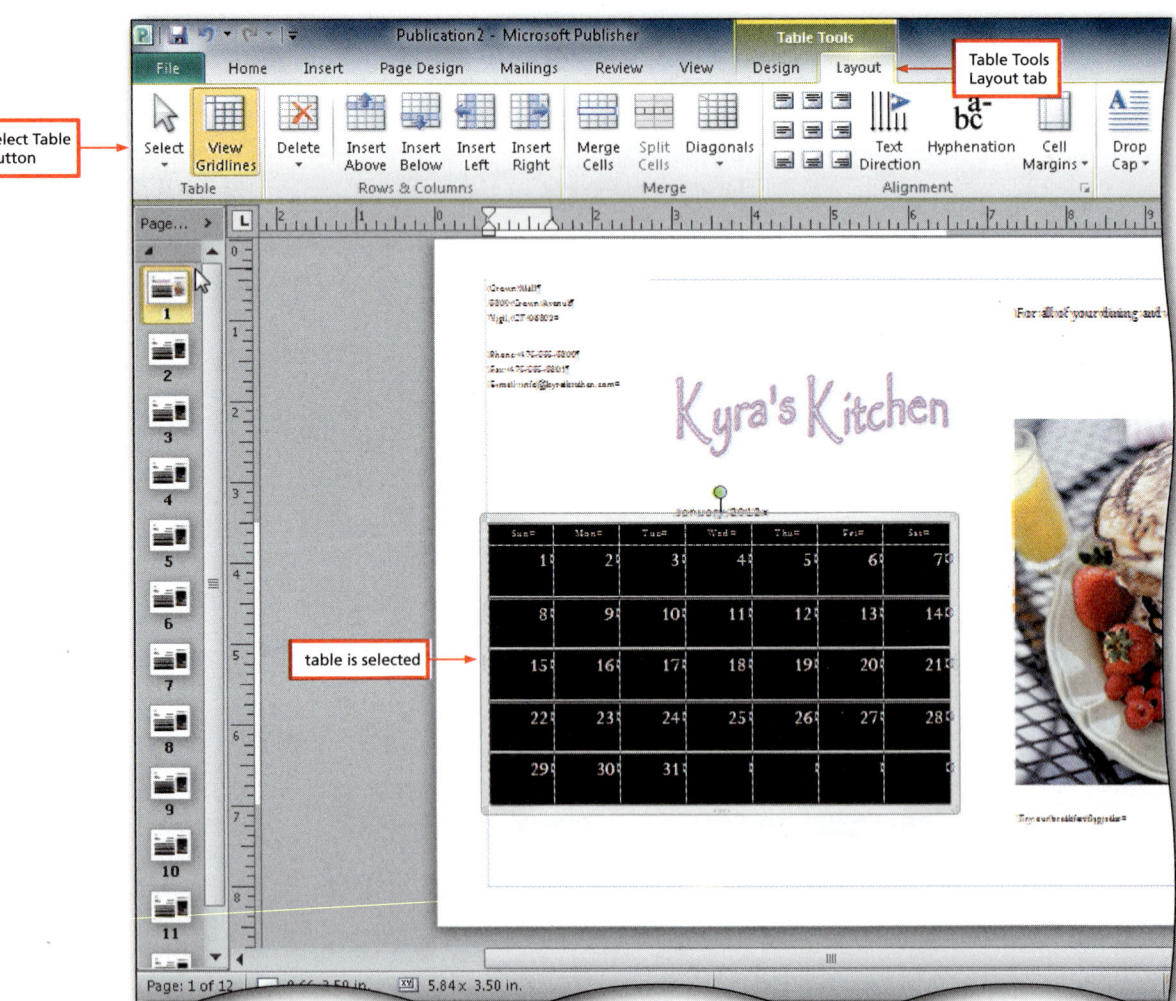

Figure 6–48

To Add Borders to a Table

The following steps add borders to all of the cells in the selected calendar table.

1

- With the table selected, display the Table Tools Design tab.

- Click the Borders button arrow (Table Tools Design tab | Borders group) to display the list of border options (Figure 6–49).

Q&A What are the gray dotted vertical lines in the table?

Publisher displays nonprinting boundaries around each cell so that you can see the cells more clearly.

Figure 6–49

2

- Click All Borders to add borders to all four sides of all cells.

- Click outside the table to see the borders more clearly (Figure 6–50).

Q&A What color are the borders?

Publisher uses the second accent color in your current color scheme as the default color for table borders. You can change the color by clicking the Line Color button (Table Tools Design tab | Borders group).

Figure 6–50

Other Ways
1. Select table, right-click table, click Format Table on shortcut menu, in	Colors and Lines sheet (Format Table dialog box), click all borders button	in Presets area, click OK button

To Add Borders to the Remaining Tables

The following steps add borders to the other tables in the calendar.

1 Click the next page in the Page Navigation pane.

2 Click the table on the page. Click the Select Table button (Table Tools Layout tab | Table group) and then click Select Table.

3 Click the Borders button (Table Tools Design tab | Borders group) to add borders to all four sides of all cells.

4 Repeat Steps 1 through 3 for each month in the calendar.

To Save the Calendar

The following steps save the calendar with the file name, Kyra's Kitchen Calendar.

1 With a USB flash drive connected to one of the computer's USB ports, click the Save button on the Quick Access Toolbar to display the Save As dialog box.

2 Type `Kyra's Kitchen Calendar` in the File name text box to change the file name. Do not press the ENTER key because you do not want to close the dialog box at this time.

3 Navigate to the Publisher folder on your USB flash drive so that you can save your file in that location.

4 Click the Save button (Save As dialog box) to save the publication on the selected drive with the entered file name.

TO PRINT THE CALENDAR

If you wanted to print the calendar, you would perform the following steps.

1. Click the File tab to open the Backstage view and then click the Print tab to display the Print gallery.

2. Verify the printer name on the Printer Status button will print a hard copy of the publication. If necessary, click the Printer Status button to display a list of available printer options and then click the desired printer to change the currently selected printer.

3. Click the Print button in the Print gallery to print the calendar on the currently selected printer. The calendar will print on 12 pages of paper.

To Close the Calendar without Quitting Publisher

The following step closes the calendar without quitting Publisher.

1 Click the File tab to open the Backstage view and then click Close to close the publication without quitting Publisher and to return to the New template gallery.

Using Excel Tables

In Chapter 2, you learned how to edit a story using Microsoft Word from within Publisher. In this chapter, you will learn how to use Microsoft Excel when you create a Publisher table. An advantage of integrating Excel is that you can use Excel tools to enhance your tables with items such as totals, averages, charts, and financial functions.

You have two choices when integrating Excel functionality. You can create an embedded table with some Excel functionality, or you can create a linked, or automatically updated, table from an Excel worksheet, giving you full Excel functionality.

An **embedded** table uses Excel data, but the data becomes part of the Publisher publication and must be edited with Publisher running. Publisher displays Excel tabs on the Ribbon to help you edit an embedded table. A **linked** table is connected permanently to an Excel worksheet. When you edit a linked table, Microsoft Excel starts for full functionality. You can edit a linked table in Excel or Publisher. If you edit in Excel, the table is updated automatically the next time you open the Publisher publication. In either case, the data you use from the Excel file is called the **source** document. Publisher is the **destination** document.

Embed and link data appropriately. Determine the best way to create Excel-enhanced tables. An **Excel-enhanced table** is one that uses Excel tools to enhance Publisher's table formatting capabilities and one that adds table functionality. You can paste, create, or insert an Excel-enhanced table into your Publisher publication. Two types of Excel-enhanced tables are available: embedded and linked.

- If you want to use a table from another document, but you want the data to remain static (unchanging), then create an embedded table.

- If you want to ensure that the most current version of the data appears in the table, then link the table.

When using files or objects created by others, do not use the source document until you are certain it does not contain a virus or other malicious program. Use an antivirus program to verify that any files you use are free of viruses and other potentially harmful programs.

Plan Ahead

The decision on which type of table to use depends on the data. You would embed a table when you want a static or unchanging table that you edit in Publisher. For example, a table from last year's sales probably is not going to change; thus, if you paste it into a Publisher brochure about the company's sales history, it will look the same each time you open the publication.

You would link a table when the data is likely to change, and you want to make sure the publication reflects the current data in the Excel file. For example, suppose you link an Excel worksheet to a Publisher investment statement and update the worksheet quarterly in Excel. With a linked table, any time you open the investment statement in Publisher, the latest update of the worksheet will be displayed as part of the investment statement; in other words, the most current data always will appear in the statement.

The actual process of integrating an Excel table can be performed in one of three ways. You can create an embedded table from scratch, you can paste an embedded or linked table, or you can insert an embedded or linked table from a file.

In this project, you will create a letter and insert an embedded table. You then will format the Excel-enhanced table.

To Create the Letterhead

The following steps create a letterhead that Kyra's Kitchen will use to send a letter and table to the managers.

1 Click Letterhead in the New template gallery (Backstage view) to display the letterhead templates.

2 Click the Arrows template to select it.

3 If necessary, click the Color scheme box arrow in the Customize area and then click Lilac in the list to choose a color scheme.

4 If necessary, click the Font scheme box arrow and then click Equity in the list to choose a font scheme.

5 If necessary, click the Business information box arrow and then click Kyra's Kitchen to select it.

6 If necessary, click to remove the check mark in the Include logo check box.

7 Click the Create button to create the letterhead (Figure 6–51).

letterhead is created using company color and font schemes and company business information set

Figure 6–51

To Insert the Building Block

The following steps insert the Kyra's Kitchen WordArt object into the publication.

1 Display the Insert tab.

2 Click the Page Parts button (Insert tab | Building Blocks group) and then click the Kyra's Kitchen WordArt object to insert it into the publication.

3 Drag the object to the top-left corner of the page (Figure 6–52).

company building block

Figure 6–52

To Type the Letter

The following steps create a text box and enter text for the body of the letter.

1 Click the Draw Text Box button (Insert tab | Text group) and then drag to create a text box below the WordArt object, approximately 7.5 inches wide and 4.5 inches tall.

2 Press the F9 key to zoom to 100%.

3 Type the text shown in Figure 6–53.

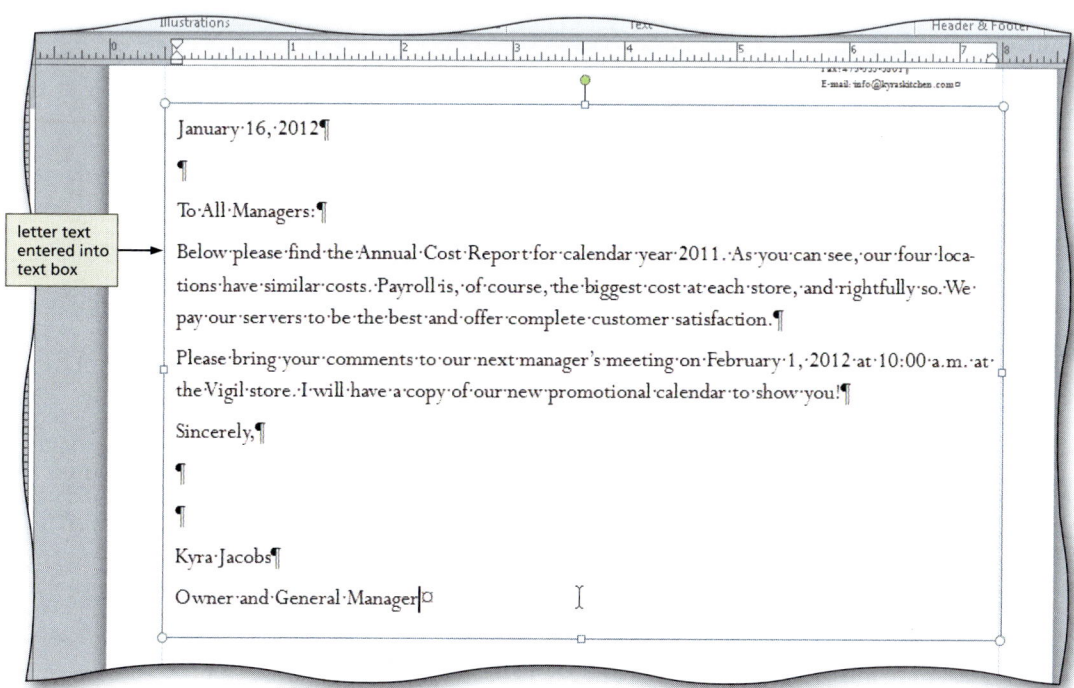

letter text entered into text box

Figure 6–53

To Create an Embedded Table

Embedding means using a copy of a source document in a destination document without establishing a permanent link. Embedded objects can be edited; however, changes do not affect the source document. For example, if a business embedded an Excel worksheet into its Publisher electronic newsletter that contained updatable fields, users viewing the publication in Publisher could enter their personal data into the embedded table and recalculate the totals. Those users would not need access to the original Excel worksheet.

The following steps create an embedded table showing last year's annual costs for the four Kyra's Kitchen locations. You will retrieve the values from an Excel file that is available on the Data Files for Students. See the inside back cover of this book for instructions on downloading the Data Files for Students, or contact your instructor for information about accessing the required files.

1

- Scroll to the right of the page layout to display more of the scratch area in the Publisher workspace.

- Display the Insert tab.

- Click the Insert Object button (Insert tab | Text group) to display the Insert Object dialog box (Figure 6–54).

Q&A Why should I insert the table in the scratch area?

It is easier to work with tables outside of the publication and then move them onto the page layout after editing.

 Experiment

- Scroll through the list of object types to view the different kinds of documents and graphics that you can embed. Click the object types to read a description in the Result area.

Figure 6–54

2

- Click the Create from File option button (Insert Object dialog box) (Figure 6–55).

Q&A What does the Create New option button do?

You would click the Create New option button if you wanted to create an embedded table or other object from scratch.

Figure 6–55

3

- Click the Browse button to display the Browse dialog box.

- Navigate to your USB storage location or the location of the Data Files for Students on your computer.

- Double-click the folder labeled Chapter 06 to display the files in the folder.

- Double-click the Excel file named Annual Costs (Browse dialog box) to select the file and return to the Insert Object dialog box.

- Click the OK button (Insert Object dialog box) to embed the data from the Excel file.

- If necessary, drag the border of the embedded table so it does not overlap the page layout (Figure 6–56).

embedded table appears in publication

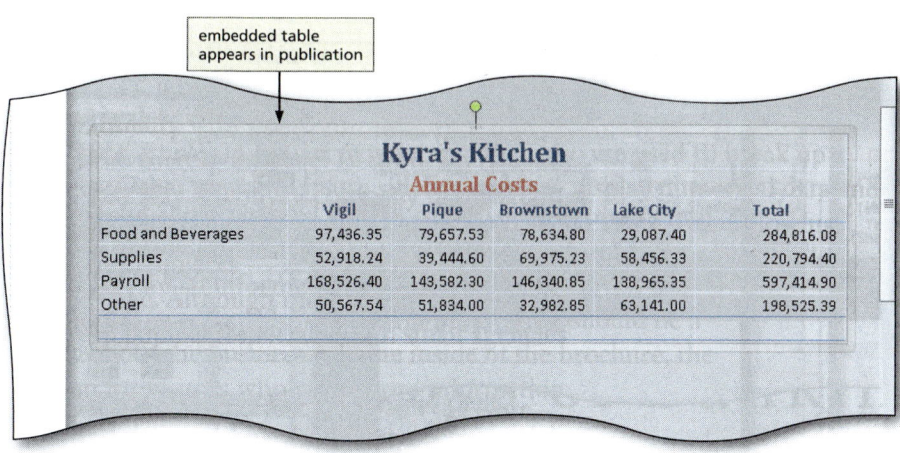

Figure 6–56

TO CREATE AN EMBEDDED TABLE FROM SCRATCH

If you wanted to create an embedded table from scratch, you would perform the following steps.

1. In Publisher, display the Insert tab.
2. Click the Insert Object button (Insert tab | Text group).
3. Click the Create New option button (Insert Object dialog box).
4. In the Object type box (Insert Object dialog box), click Microsoft Office Excel Worksheet, or Microsoft Office Excel 2007 Workbook.
5. Click the OK button (Insert Object dialog box) to insert the table.
6. Double-click the table and insert data into each cell.

TO INSERT A LINKED TABLE

If you wanted to create a linked table, you would perform the following steps.

1. In Publisher, display the Insert tab.
2. Click the Insert Object button (Insert tab | Text group).
3. Click the Create from File option button (Insert Object dialog box) and click to display a check mark in the Link check box.
4. Click the Browse button to display the Browse dialog box.
5. Navigate to your USB storage location or the location of the Data Files for Students on your computer and double-click the desired Excel file.
6. Click the OK button (Insert Object dialog box) to link the data from the Excel file.

TO COPY AND PASTE AN EMBEDDED TABLE

If you wanted to copy and paste from an Excel worksheet to create an embedded table, you would perform the following steps.

1. Start Microsoft Excel 2010.
2. Select the cells to include in the embedded table and press CTRL+C to copy them.
3. Start Microsoft Publisher 2010.
4. Click the Paste button arrow (Home tab | Clipboard group) and then click Paste Special in the gallery.

BTW

Scratch Area
Placing objects in the scratch area is an easy way to move them from one page to the next. Simply drag the object into the blank scratch area of the workspace, click the new page icon in the Page Navigation pane, and then drag the object onto the new page. Publisher allows you to save a publication with objects still in the scratch area of the workspace. Be sure to remove them, however, to avoid confusion before submitting a file to a commercial printer.

5. Click the Paste option button (Paste Special dialog box) and click New Table in the As box.

6. Click the OK button (Paste Special dialog box) to embed the table.

TO COPY AND PASTE A LINKED TABLE

If you wanted to copy and paste from an Excel worksheet to create a linked table, you would perform the following steps.

1. Start Microsoft Excel 2010.

2. Select the cells to include in the embedded table and press CTRL+C to copy them.

3. Start Microsoft Publisher 2010.

4. Click the Paste button arrow (Home tab | Clipboard group) and then click Paste Special in the gallery.

5. Click the Paste Link option button (Paste Special dialog box).

6. Click the OK button (Paste Special dialog box) to link the table.

To Format an Embedded Table

Double-clicking most embedded objects does not start the source application; rather, it activates a subset of the source application commands on a Ribbon that displays in the destination application. The embedded features allow you to edit the object. Editing the object in Publisher does not change any saved files in the source application.

The following steps format the first and last rows of numerical data in the embedded table. The Excel cell references in the following steps represent the intersection of the column (indicated by a capital letter) and the row (indicated by a number). For example, the first cell in column A is cell A1; the third cell in column B is cell B3, and so forth.

1

- Double-click the table to display the Excel tabs on the Publisher Ribbon.

- Drag through cells B4 through F4 to select them (Figure 6–57).

Q&A

What happened to the File tab and the other Publisher tabs?

Publisher displays Excel functionality while you are working on an embedded table. When you click outside the table, the Publisher tabs will reappear.

Figure 6–57

2

- Click the Accounting Number Format button (Excel Home tab | Number group) to apply dollar signs to the cells (Figure 6–58).

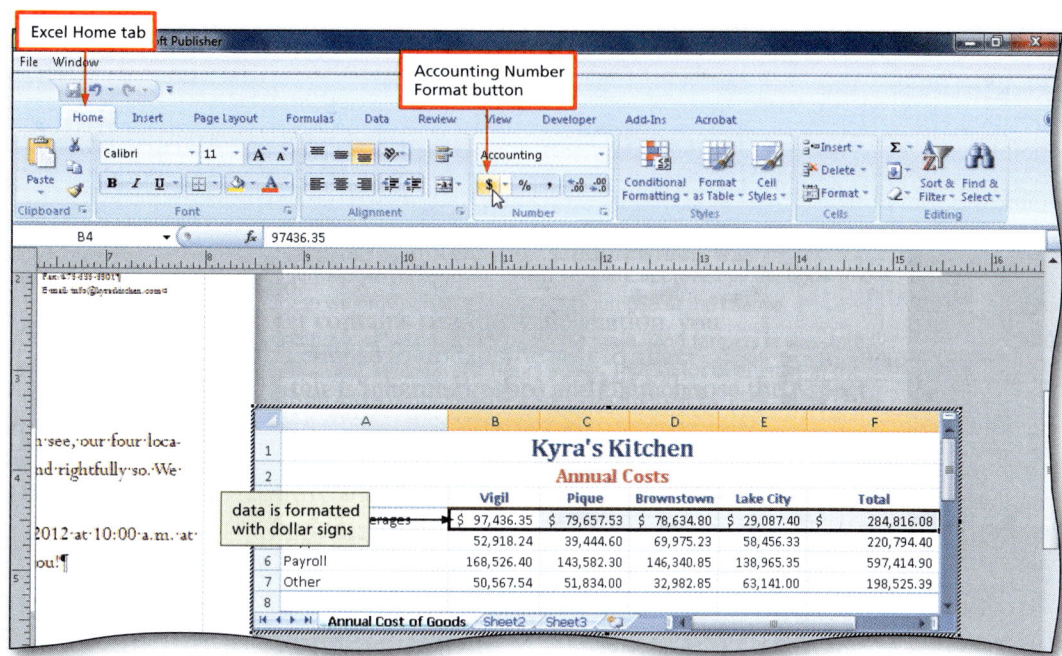

Figure 6–58

To Sum in an Embedded Table

The following steps sum the columns of the embedded table. You will use the Sum button (Excel Home tab | Editing group) to create a total. When you click the Sum button, the values to be summed appear in a **marquee**, or dotted flashing border.

1

- Click cell A8 and type the word **Total** to enter data into the cell (Figure 6–59).

Q&A

Why does the text appear bold?

Text typed into embedded tables retain the formatting of the original worksheet. Cell A8 was bolded in the embedded worksheet.

Q&A

How do you use the text box at the bottom of the ribbon?

The text box is called the formula bar. You may type text, numbers, formulas, and functions in either the formula bar or in the cell; sometimes it is easier to edit in the formula bar.

Figure 6–59

2

- Click cell B8 to position the insertion point.

- Click the Sum button (Excel Home tab | Editing group) to sum the cells and then click the Enter button on the formula bar to display the total (Figure 6–60).

Q&A

What other math operations can I perform?

You can type any formula into the formula bar using real numbers or cell references. You also can click the Microsoft Office Excel Help button on the Ribbon to learn about many mathematical functions that will help you with formulas that are more complex.

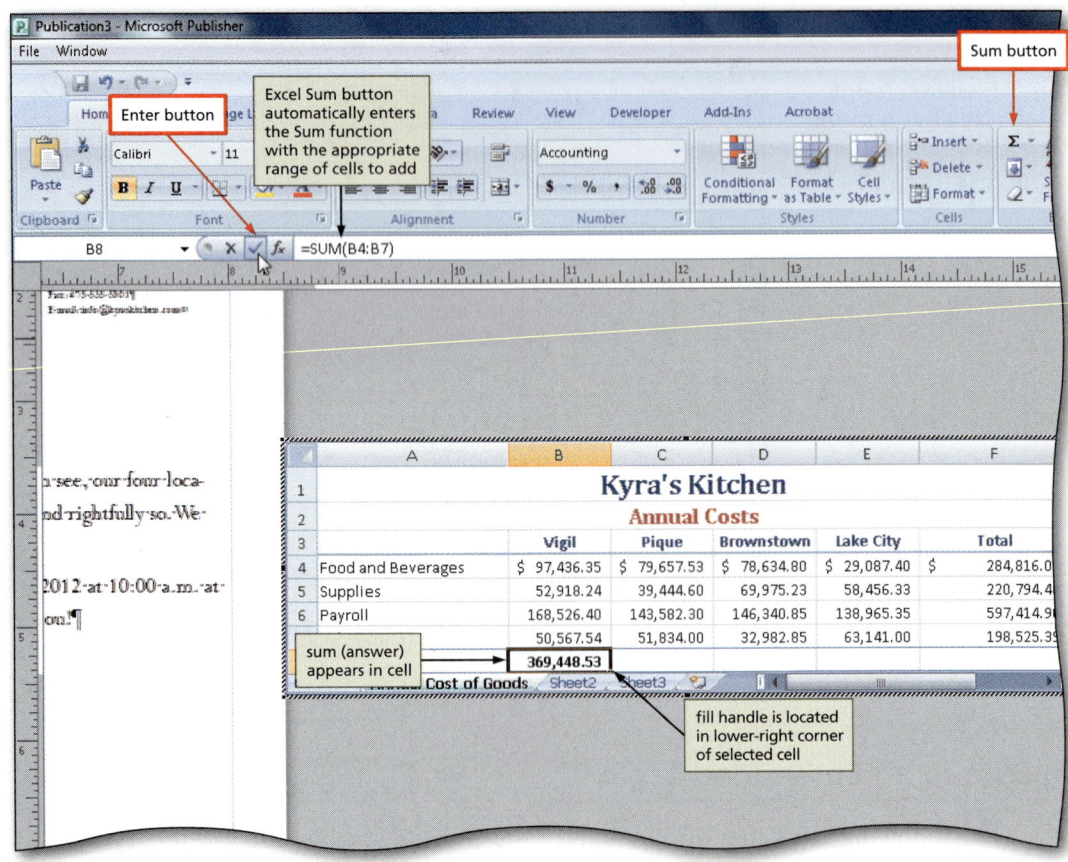

Figure 6–60

3

- Drag the fill handle in the lower right corner of cell B8 across and through cells C8 through F8 to replicate the sum across the columns (Figure 6–61).

Q&A

How does the fill handle replicate the sum?

When you drag to the right, the sum is adjusted to include the same number of cells above the total line in each column. When you drag down, the sum is adjusted to include cells to the left in each row.

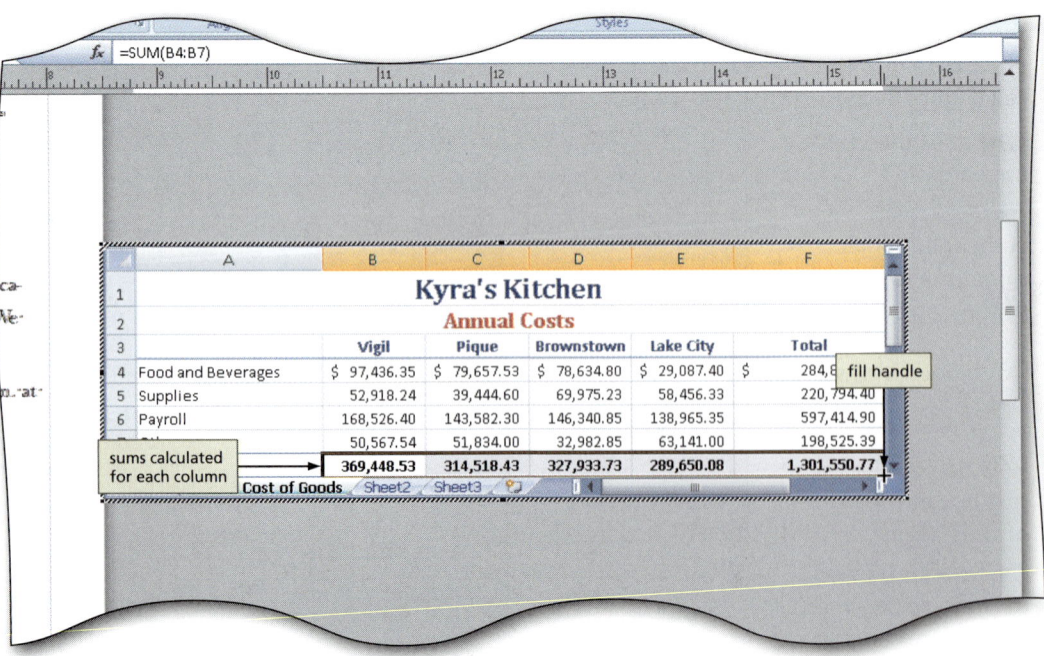

Figure 6–61

To Format the Totals

The following steps format the totals in row 8.

1 If necessary, drag cells B8 through F8 to select the cells.

2 Click the Accounting Number Format button (Excel Home tab | Number group) to apply dollar signs to the cells (Figure 6–62).

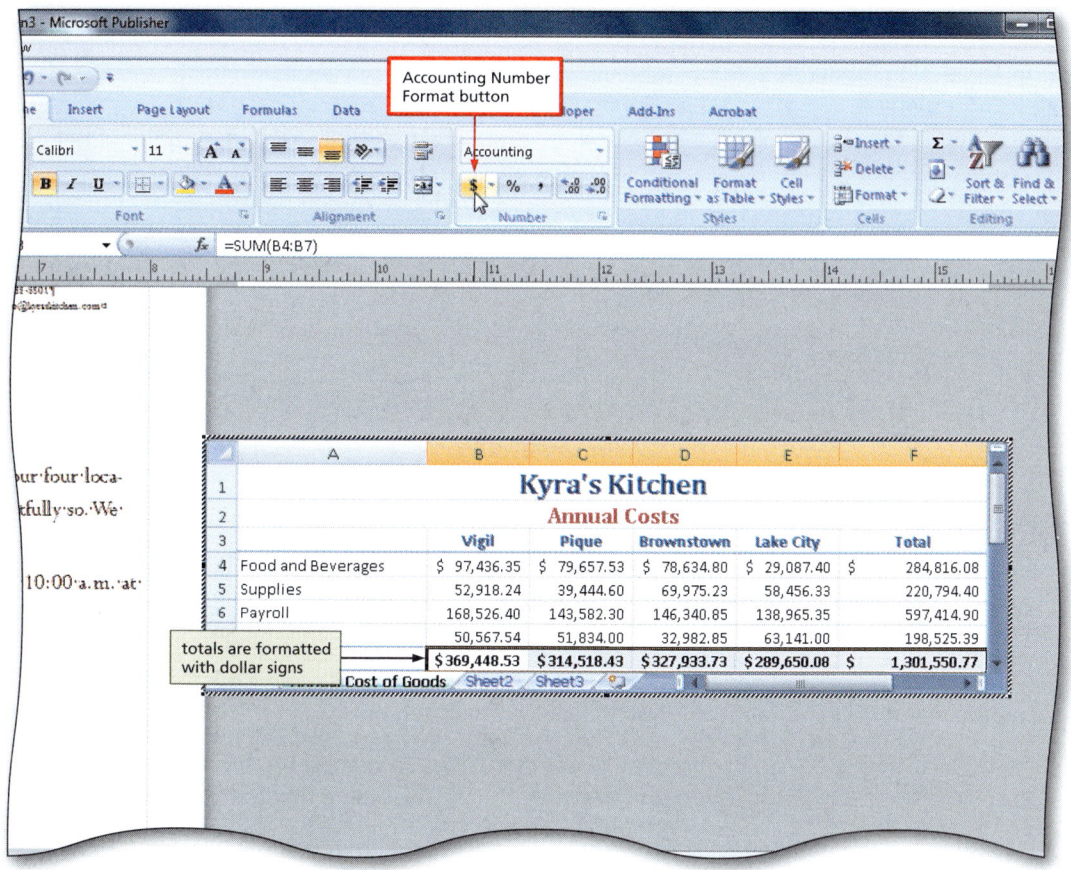

Figure 6–62

To Move and Position the Table

The following steps move and reposition the embedded table.

1 Click outside the table to deselect it.

2 Zoom to 80%.

3 If necessary, click the table to display the table border.

4 Drag the border of the table to position the table in the lower portion of the letter as shown in Figure 6–63 on the next page.

BTW

Using Linked Objects
When you open a publication that contains linked objects, Publisher displays a dialog box asking if you want to update the Publisher publication with data from the linked file. Click the Yes button only if you are certain the linked file is from a trusted source; that is, you should be confident that the source file does not contain a virus or other potentially harmful program before you instruct Publisher to link the source document to the destination document.

Figure 6–63

To Save the Letter

The following steps save the letter and embedded table with the file name, Manager Letter.

1 With a USB flash drive connected to one of the computer's USB ports, click the Save button on the Quick Access Toolbar to display the Save As dialog box.

2 Type **Manager Letter** in the File name text box to change the file name. Do not press the ENTER key because you do not want to close the dialog box at this time.

3 Navigate to the Publisher folder on your USB flash drive so that you can save your file in that location.

4 Click the Save button (Save As dialog box) to save the publication on the selected drive with the entered file name.

To Print the Letter

The following steps print a hard copy of the Manager Letter.

1 Click the File tab to open the Backstage view and then click the Print tab to display the Print gallery.

2 Verify the printer name on the Printer Status button will print a hard copy of the publication. If necessary, click the Printer Status button to display a list of available printer options and then click the desired printer to change the currently selected printer.

3 Click the Print button in the Print gallery to print the schedule on the currently selected printer (Figure 6–64).

Kyra's Kitchen

Crown Mall
5800 Crown Avenue
Vigil, CT 06802

Phone: 475-555-5800
Fax: 475-555-5801
E-mail: info@kyraskitchen.com

January 16, 2012

To All Managers:

Below please find the Annual Cost Report for calendar year 2011. As you can see, our four locations have similar costs. Payroll is, of course, the biggest cost at each store, and rightfully so. We pay our servers to be the best and offer complete customer satisfaction.

Please bring your comments to our next manager's meeting on February 1, 2012 at 10:00 a.m. at the Vigil store. I will have a copy of our new promotional calendar to show you!

Sincerely,

Kyra Jacobs

Owner and General Manager

Kyra's Kitchen
Annual Costs

	Vigil	Pique	Brownstown	Lake City		Total
Food and Beverages	$ 97,436.35	$ 79,657.53	$ 78,634.80	$ 29,087.40	$	284,816.08
Supplies	52,918.24	39,444.60	69,975.23	58,456.33		220,794.40
Payroll	168,526.40	143,582.30	146,340.85	138,965.35		597,414.90
Other	50,567.54	51,834.00	32,982.85	63,141.00		198,525.39
Total	**$369,448.53**	**$314,518.43**	**$327,933.73**	**$289,650.08**	**$**	**1,301,550.77**

Figure 6–64

To Quit Publisher

This project is complete. The following steps quit Publisher.

1 To quit Publisher, click the Close button on the right side of the title bar.

2 If a Microsoft Office Publisher dialog box is displayed, click the Don't Save button so that any editing changes you have made to the business card are not saved.

Chapter Summary

In this chapter, you learned how to use tables to present data in efficient and meaningful ways. First, you formatted a WordArt object to assist in branding a company name. Next, you created and formatted tables and data, including the use of table styles, merging, and cell diagonals. Next, you created a calendar with a bordered table. Finally, you embedded data from Excel into a Publisher publication and used the Excel-enhanced tools to format the table and perform calculations. The items listed below include all the new Publisher skills you have learned in this chapter.

1. Change the Shape of a WordArt Object (PUB 328)
2. Change the Shape Outline (PUB 329)
3. Change the Page Orientation (PUB 330)
4. Snap an Object to the Margin Guide (PUB 332)
5. Align Relative to Margin Guides (PUB 332)
6. Insert an Empty Table (PUB 334)
7. Enter Data in a Table (PUB 336)
8. Delete a Column (PUB 337)
9. Delete a Row (PUB 338)
10. Insert a Row (PUB 338)
11. Insert a Column (PUB 339)
12. Apply a Table Format (PUB 339)
13. Select a Row (PUB 341)
14. Merge Cells (PUB 342)
15. Split Cells (PUB 343)
16. Align Data in Cells (PUB 344)
17. Change Column Width (PUB 346)
18. Resize the Table (PUB 346)
19. Create a Cell Diagonal (PUB 348)
20. Create a 12-Month Calendar (PUB 352)
21. Add Borders to a Table (PUB 359)
22. Create an Embedded Table (PUB 364)
23. Create an Embedded Table from Scratch (PUB 365)
24. Insert a Linked Table (PUB 365)
25. Copy and Paste an Embedded Table (PUB 365)
26. Copy and Paste a Linked Table (PUB 366)
27. Format an Embedded Table (PUB 366)
28. Sum in an Embedded Table (PUB 367)

Learn It Online

Test your knowledge of chapter content and key terms.

Instructions: To complete the Learn It Online exercises, start your browser, click the Address bar, and then enter the Web address **scsite.com/pub2010/learn**. When the Publisher 2010 Learn It Online page is displayed, click the link for the exercise you want to complete and then read the instructions.

Chapter Reinforcement TF, MC, and SA
A series of true/false, multiple choice, and short answer questions that test your knowledge of the chapter content.

Flash Cards
An interactive learning environment where you identify chapter key terms associated with displayed definitions.

Practice Test
A series of multiple choice questions that test your knowledge of chapter content and key terms.

Who Wants To Be a Computer Genius?
An interactive game that challenges your knowledge of chapter content in the style of a television quiz show.

Wheel of Terms
An interactive game that challenges your knowledge of chapter key terms in the style of the television show *Wheel of Fortune*.

Crossword Puzzle Challenge
A crossword puzzle that challenges your knowledge of key terms presented in the chapter.

Apply Your Knowledge

Reinforce the skills and apply the concepts you learned in this chapter.

Formatting a Table

Instructions: Start Publisher. Open the publication, Apply 6-1 Expenses Table Draft, from the Data Files for Students. See the inside back cover of this book for instructions on downloading the Data Files for Students, or contact your instructor for more information about accessing the required files.

The publication you open contains a Publisher table that you are to edit and format. The revised table is shown in Figure 6–65.

Monthly Expenses			
Expense \ Month	January	February	March
Decorations	170.88	129.72	74.73
Postage	65.90	62.90	69.91
Computer Supplies	17.29	18.50	19.12
Paper Supplies	46.57	41.67	48.70
Food/Beverages	122.04	99.88	100.00
Hall Rental	120.00	120.00	120.00
Total	542.68	472.67	432.46

Figure 6–65

Continued >

Apply Your Knowledge *continued*

Perform the following tasks:

1. Select the table and zoom to 100%.

2. Apply Table Style 43 from the Table Formats gallery (Table Tools Design tab | Table Formats group).

3. Insert a row above row 1 and merge the cells in row 1. Change the font size to 24. Type **Monthly Expenses** and then center the text.

4. Select all cells except row 1 and change the font size to 18.

5. Click column 1, row 2, and add a Divide Down cell diagonal. Click the left side and change the font size to 12. Type **Expense** on the left side of the diagonal. Click the right side and change the font size to 12. Click the Font Color button arrow (Home Tab | Font group) and then click Accent 5 (White) to change the color. Click the Bold button (Home Tab | Font group) to bold the text. Type **Month** on the right side of the diagonal.

6. Drag to select the three cells that have the names of the months and then press CTRL+E to center the month headings.

7. Drag to select all of the cells containing numeric data and then use the Align Center Right button (Table Tools Layout tab | Alignment group) to format the numbers.

8. Click the Line Color button (Table Tools Design tab | Borders group) and then click Main (Black).

9. Select row 2 and then add inside vertical borders. Select row 9 and add inside vertical borders.

10. Select rows 3 through 8 and then add inside borders.

11. Select the table and then add outside borders.

12. Change the publication properties, as specified by your instructor.

13. Click File on the Ribbon and then click Save As. Save the publication using the file name, Apply 6-1 Expenses Table Modified.pub.

14. Submit the revised publication as specified by your instructor.

Extend Your Knowledge

Extend the skills you learned in this chapter and experiment with new skills. You may need to use Help to complete the assignment.

Editing Graphics

Instructions: Start Publisher. Open the publication, Extend 6-1 Housing Table, from the Data Files for Students. See the inside back cover of this book for instructions on downloading the Data Files for Students, or contact your instructor for more information about accessing the required files.

You will add a 3-D Column chart to the publication so that it appears as shown in Figure 6–66.

	1-Bedroom Units	2-Bedroom Units
Sublevel	10	11
First Floor	11	12
Second Floor	12	18
Third Floor	15	12
Totals	48	53

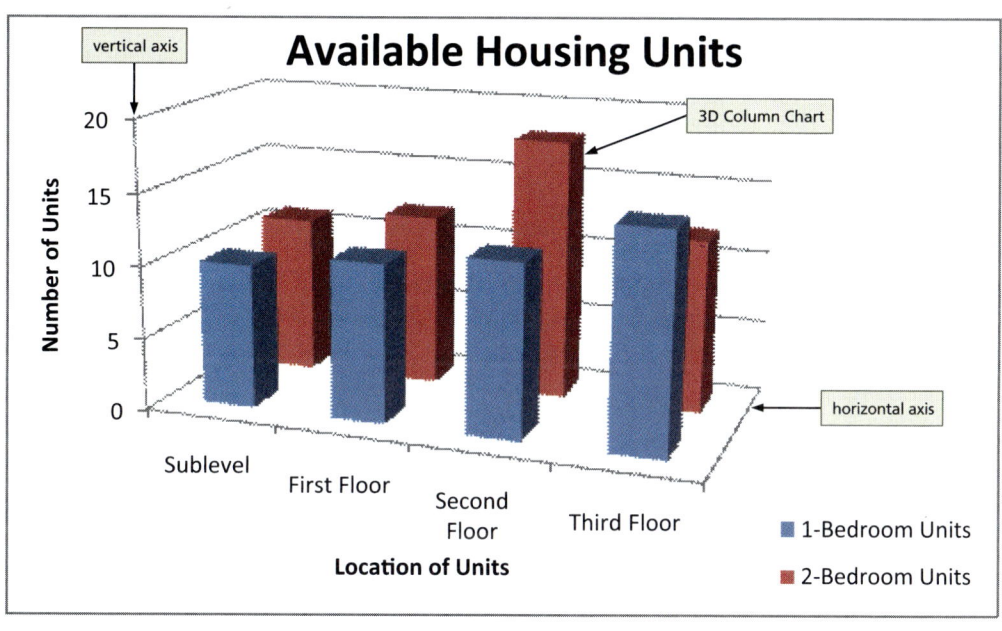

Figure 6–66

Continued >

Perform the following tasks:

1. Use Help to learn more about adding an Excel chart to a Publisher publication.

2. Zoom to 40%. Double-click the table so that the Excel tabs appear on the Publisher Ribbon.

3. Drag the bottom center sizing handle of the table down, until it snaps to the lower margin guide.

4. Drag to select cells A1 through C5. Do not include the totals.

5. Click the Column button (Excel Insert tab | Charts group) to display the column chart types, and then click the 3-D Column preview to add the chart to the publication.

6. Click outside the table to display the Publisher tabs on the Ribbon. Zoom to 120% and scroll to center the chart in the workspace.

7. Double-click the table to enable the Excel tabs on the Publisher Ribbon. Point to each part of the table, labels, and legend to identify the various parts of the chart.

8. Click to select the Depth (Series) Axis labels that appear just to the right of the horizontal axis and then press the DELETE key to delete the labels.

9. Move the chart legend to the lower-right corner of the chart.

10. Use the buttons on the Excel Chart Tools Layout tab to add titles to the chart, the x-axis, and the y-axis. One at a time, triple-click each placeholder text to select it and then replace the titles as shown in Figure 6–66 on the previous page. *Hint:* The y-axis, also called the vertical axis, uses a rotated title.

11. Drag the chart sizing handles to resize the chart to approximately 15 rows high.

12. Click the Plot area and then drag the border down to make more room for the chart title, if necessary.

13. Click outside the chart to deselect it. Click to remove the check mark in the Gridlines check box (Excel View tab | Show/Hide group).

14. Click outside the table to display the Publisher tabs on the Ribbon. Change the publication properties, as specified by your instructor. Save the revised publication with a new file name. Print the publication and then submit it in the format specified by your instructor.

Make It Right

Analyze a publication and correct all errors and/or improve the design.

Correcting Replacement Text and Spelling Errors

Instructions: Start Publisher. Open the publication, Make It Right 6-1 Music Table, from the Data Files for Students. See the inside back cover of this book for instructions on downloading the Data Files for Students, or contact your instructor for more information about accessing the required files.

You decide to improve the embedded table for a guitar store by changing the fonts, formatting it with dollar signs, providing row and column totals, and branding the name of the store with a WordArt object.

Perform the following tasks:

1. Double-click the table to enable the Excel tabs on the Publisher Ribbon.

2. Format row 1 to increase the font size.

3. Click cell F3 and then click the Sum button to display the marquee around the values to include in the addition (Figure 6–67).

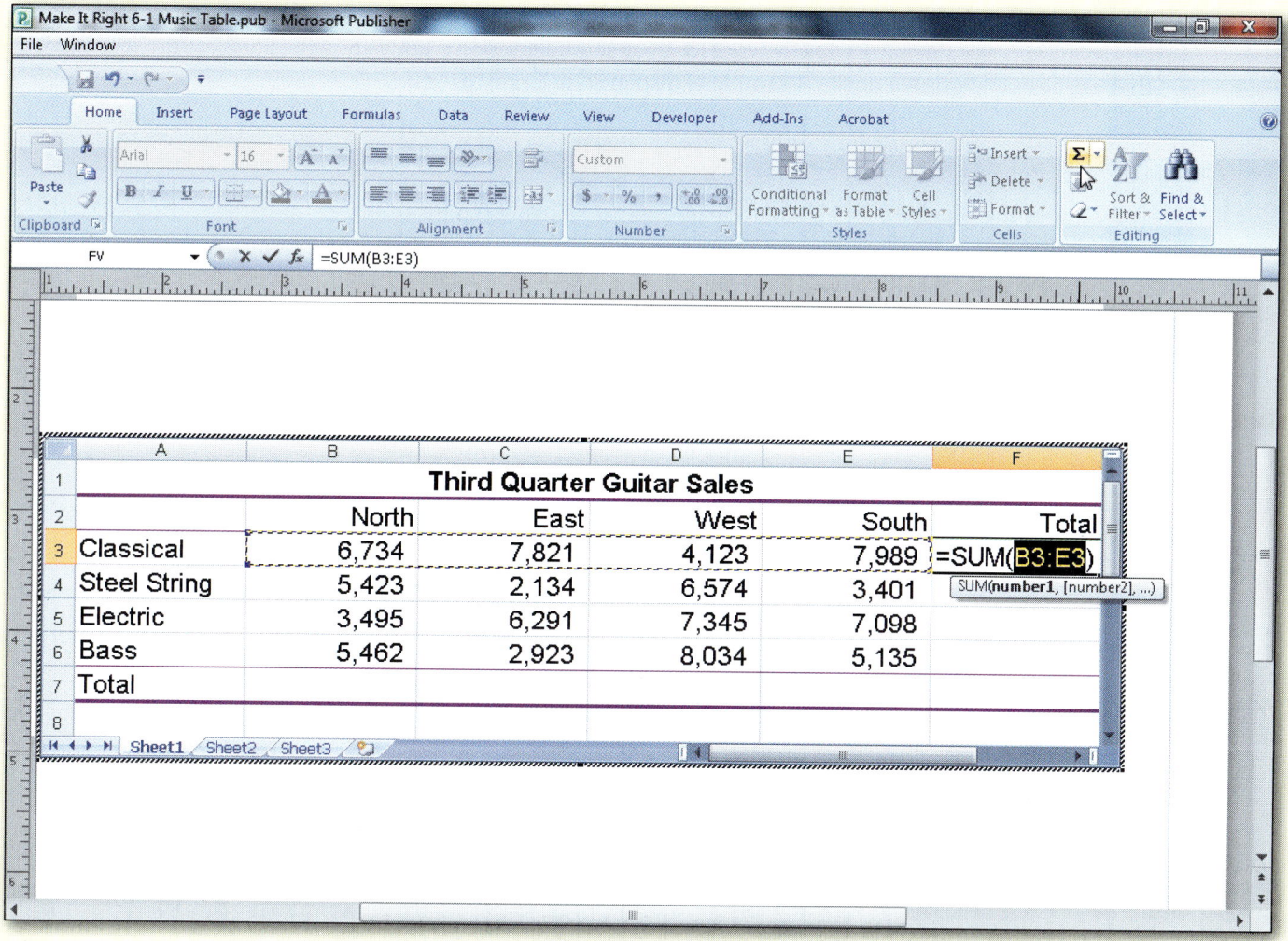

Figure 6–67

4. Click the Enter button on the formula bar to display the total.

5. Drag the fill handle down to create totals for the other rows. Do not include the total row.

6. Repeat Steps 3 through 5 to create totals for each column.

7. Format the first row of numbers (row 3) and the last row of numbers (row 7) with dollar signs. If decimal places are displayed, click the Decrease Decimal button (Excel Home tab | Number group) until only whole dollar amounts are displayed.

8. Click outside the table to display the Publisher tabs on the Ribbon.

9. Add a formatted WordArt object above the table with the name of the company, Guitar Mania.

10. Change the publication properties, as specified by your instructor. Save the revised publication with a new name and then submit it in the format specified by your instructor.

In the Lab

Design and/or create a publication using the guidelines, concepts, and skills presented in this chapter. Labs are listed in order of increasing difficulty.

Lab 1: Creating a Table with Graphics

Problem: As an office automation specialist at the college, you have been asked to create a flyer to send out to prospective dormitory residents. The flyer should contain a table showing some of the features that are available in each dorm. A sample is displayed in Figure 6–68.

Instructions: Perform the following tasks:

1. Start Publisher.
2. Choose the Blank 8.5 × 11" thumbnail to create a blank publication.
3. Click the More button (Page Design tab | Schemes Group) to display the gallery of color schemes. Select the Black and Gray color scheme.
4. If necessary, change the margins to .5 inches and change the page orientation to landscape.
5. Create a 5 × 5 table. Resize the table to fill the page layout within the margins. Click the More button (Table Tools Design tab | Table Formats group) and then click Table Style 35 to format the table.

Figure 6–68

6. Right-click the table border. Click Format Table on the shortcut menu to display the Format Table dialog box. In the Colors and Lines sheet (Format Table dialog box), click the Border Art button. Choose a border similar to the Weaving…Strips border shown in Figure 6–68. Enter 24 in the Weight box and then click the OK button (Format Table dialog box) to return to the table.

7. Enter the names of the dorms in the first column, beginning with the second row. Select the four cells containing the dormitory names. Click the Align Center Left button (Table Tools Layout tab | Alignment group) to align the cells. Increase the font size to 14. If necessary, drag the border between columns one and two approximately one-half inch to the right, so that the dorm names are displayed on single lines.

8. Merge the cells across row one, and insert the heading shown in Figure 6–68. Center the heading and format it bold if necessary. Increase the font size to 36. Drag the border below row one, up to decrease the height of the row as shown in Figure 6–68.

9. Click the cell in column 2, row 2. Use the Clip Art task pane to locate a graphic of television. Resize the graphic to fit in the cell. Use the copy and paste technique to paste copies of the graphic in the cells as shown in Figure 6–68. SHIFT-click each of the three graphics to select them. Click the Align button (Home tab | Arrange group). If Relative to Margins Guides is selected, click to deselect it, then choose the option to align their left edges.

10. Repeat Step 10 for graphics of fans, cafeterias, and handicap accessibility.

11. In column 3, row 5, insert a WordArt object with the text, Air. Use an appropriate WordArt style and shape outline.

12. When all graphics have been aligned on their corresponding left edges, align their top edges with the other graphics in each row.

13. Change the publication properties as specified by your instructor. Save the publication on your storage medium with the file name, Lab 6-1 Dorm Facilities Table. Print a copy.

In the Lab

Lab 2: Creating an Origami Box

Problem: A local youth organization has asked you to create party favors for their annual Blue and Gold Banquet. You would like to include foil-covered chocolates (in blue and gold, of course) at each place setting. Because you are on a tight budget, you decide to try your hand at designing a do-it-yourself gift box to hold the candies. After printing it on heavy card stock paper, you use the ancient art of origami paper folding to create two boxes, one slightly larger than the other for a top and bottom box set (Figure 6–69 on the next page).

Instructions: Perform the following tasks:

1. Start Publisher with a blank publication.

2. Use the Insert Table button (Insert tab | Tables group) to insert a 4 × 4 table. Resize the table to be 6-inches square.

3. Select the table and format it with all borders in black.

4. With the table still selected, click the Diagonals button (Table Tools Layout tab | Merge group) and then click Divide Up.

Continued >

In the Lab *continued*

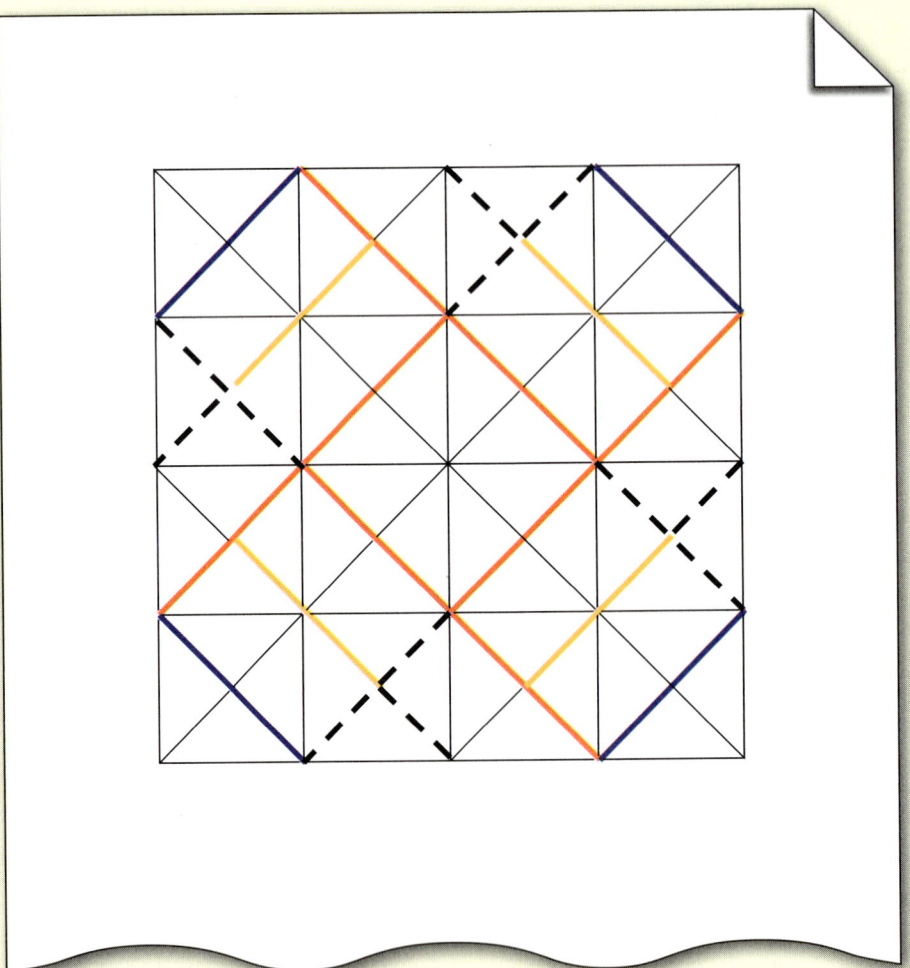

Figure 6–69

5. To insert diagonal lines in the other direction:
   a. Click the Shape button (Insert tab | Illustrations group) and then click the Line shape.
   b. SHIFT+drag to draw a line from the upper-left corner of the table to the lower-right.
   c. Repeat the process to draw six more lines to dissect the table cells the opposite way, creating an X in each cell. *Hint:* Holding down the SHIFT key while drawing the line ensures a straight 45-degree line.

6. If desired, you may draw colored and dotted lines over the other lines in the publication to make your publication match Figure 6–69. Otherwise, skip to Step 9 and use the figure as a reference for folding and trimming.

7. To draw colored lines:
   a. Click the Shapes button (Insert tab | Illustrations group) and then click the Line shape.
   b. In column 1, row 1, drag to draw a short line, as shown in blue in Figure 6–69.
   c. With the line still selected, click the Shape Outline button arrow (Drawing Tools Format tab | Shape Styles group) and then click blue. Click the Shape Outline button arrow again, point to Weight, and then click 3 pt in the list to increase the weight of the line.
   d. Repeat the process for each short colored line in the figure.

8. To create dotted lines:

   a. Click the Shapes button (Insert tab | Illustrations group) and then click the Line shape.

   b. In column 1, row 2, drag to draw a short line as shown dotted in Figure 6–69.

   c. With the line still selected, click the Shape Outline button arrow (Drawing Tools Format tab | Shape Styles group) and then point to Dashes. Choose a dashed line style and weight that is similar to the figure.

   d. Repeat the process for each short dotted line in the figure.

9. Save the publication with the file name, Lab 6-2 Origami Box, on your storage medium. Print the publication and then, using Figure 6–69 as a guide, trim the printout and fold the bottom of the box set as follows:

   a. Cut around the edge of the table and on the dotted lines.

   b. Fold the orange lines first to form a box shell, keeping the tabs on the inside.

   c. Next, fold the blue lines inward, over the top of the previous folds.

   d. Finally, fold the yellow lines, working around from one corner of the box to the next.

10. To create a larger box that will serve as the top or cover, press CTRL+A to select the table and all the lines. Click the Group button (Drawing Tools Format tab | Arrange group) to group the objects. SHIFT+drag a corner sizing handle until the box is approximately one-half inch larger. Print and assemble the top of the box set. *Hint:* you may cheat and use a small piece of tape to hold down the "blue" fold if you like.

In the Lab

Lab 3: Creating a Brand

Problem: Universal Benefits, a statewide insurance company, would like you to create a branding of their name that they can use on all publications. You decide to format their name in WordArt to create a new brand.

Instructions: Prepare the brand shown in Figure 6–70. Insert a WordArt object using the Book Antiqua font or a similar font with a font size of 36. Change the Shape Fill to the Denim texture. Change the Shape Outline to dark blue. Change the WordArt shape to Chevron Down. Click the Shadow Effects button (WordArt Tools Format tab | Shadow Effects group) and choose Shadow Style 14. Click the Shadow Effects button (WordArt Tools Format tab | Shadow Effects group) again and then click Shadow Color. Choose a light blue color. Use the Nudge buttons (WordArt Tools Format tab | Shadow Effects group) to position the shadow slightly above the text and centered. Resize the WordArt object to approximately 3 inches tall and 5 inches wide. Change the document properties, as specified by your instructor. Save the publication with Lab 6-3 Universal Benefits Brand as the file name.

Figure 6–70

Cases and Places

Apply your creative thinking and problem solving skills to design and implement a solution.

Note: To complete these assignments, you may be required to use the Data Files for Students. See the inside back cover of this book for instructions on downloading the Data Files for Students, or contact your instructor for information about accessing the required files.

1: Create a Custom Table

Academic

The office assistant for the Computer Technology department would like to have a publication that instructors could use to submit their book order information. She has asked you to create a publication in landscape orientation that includes a table with six columns and seven rows. Merge the cells in the first row and then type **Bookstore Order Form** in the merged cells. The cells in the last row should be merged and provide a place for the instructor name and course number. The cell in the first column of the second row should display a Divide Down cell diagonal. Type **Course and Section Number** in the left side of the cell diagonal. Type **Book Information** in the right side of the cell diagonal. Across the other columns in row two, include headings for Author, Title, Edition or Date, Publisher, and ISBN. Format the table, cells, and borders appropriately.

2: Create a Linked Table

Personal

You keep a list of stocks in your friend's retirement portfolio. The stocks are stored in an Excel file named, Case 6-2 Stock Portoflio, on the Data Files for Students. The Excel file updates the current stock files from the Web, but you would like to have a Publisher publication that you could print out periodically to provide your friend with the updated totals. Create a blank publication. Use the Insert Object button (Insert tab | Text group) to create a linked table from a file. *Hint:* Click the Link check box (Insert Object dialog box) to link the file. When the table appears in Publisher, double-click it to open the Excel worksheet. Click the Update Current Values button. After the values have updated, close the Excel worksheet. If necessary, click the Save button or the Enable button (Excel dialog box) to exit the Excel worksheet. Save the publication and print a copy of the table.

3: Employee Time Card

Professional

A+ Auto Repair needs a time card. The owner has just hired two extra mechanics and an office manager because business is booming. Using a blank landscape publication, create a time card table with no formatting. Create a text box at the top of the publication containing the text, A+ Auto Repair Time Card. Create a table with eight rows — one for headings and one for each day of the week. The table should have six columns — one for headings, two sets of alternating In: and Out: columns, and a column for totals. After you create the table, insert another row at the bottom to display a grand total. In the new row, format the first four columns with only top borders. Format the rest of the cells in the table with all borders. In column 5, row 9, type the word **Total**. Create a text box at the bottom of the publication for the employees to enter their name, employee number, and date. Print multiple copies for the A+ Auto Repair's employees.

7 Advanced Formatting and Merging Publications with Data

Objectives

You will have mastered the material in this project when you can:

- Edit the master page
- Recolor and compress a graphic to create a watermark
- Explain character spacing techniques
- Track and kern characters
- Use the Measurement toolbar to edit character spacing
- Set a tab stop and enter tabbed text
- Differentiate among tab styles

- Produce a form letter
- Use the Mail Merge Wizard
- Create and edit a data source
- Incorporate grouped field codes
- Select and filter records in a data source
- Insert field codes and preview results
- Print selected copies of merged publications

7 | Advanced Formatting and Merging Publications with Data

Introduction

Whether you want individual letters sent to everyone on a mailing list, personalized envelopes for a mass mailing, an invoice sent to all customers, or a printed set of mailing labels to apply to your brochures, you can use Publisher to maintain your data and make the task of mass mailing and merged document creation easier.

Merged publications, such as form letters, should be timely and professional looking, yet at the same time, personalized. Used regularly in both business and personal correspondence, a **form letter** has the same basic content no matter to whom it is sent; however, items such as name, address, city, state, and zip code change from one form letter to the next. Thus, form letters are personalized to the addressee. An individual is more likely to open and read a personalized letter or e-mail than a standard Dear Sir or Dear Madam message. With word processing and database techniques, it is easy to generate individual, personalized documents for a large group and include features unique to desktop publishing. A **data source** or **data file** is a file that may contain only a list of names and addresses, or it also may include paths to pictures, product part numbers, postal bar codes, customer purchase history, accounts receivable, e-mail addresses, and a variety of additional data to use in merged publications.

Advanced formatting techniques include scaling, tracking and kerning characters; creating aligned tabs; and editing master pages. A **master page** is a background area similar to the header and footer area in traditional word processing software. On the master page, you can include a watermark to be used as both decoration and identification, as well as to provide security solutions to prevent document fraud. Fine tuning publications with advanced formatting makes them stand out from typical template publications and enhances their customized look and feel.

Project — Merging Form Letters and Ticket Numbers

The project in this chapter uses advanced formatting techniques to create a customized form letter and individual tickets with merged fields for each addressee from a Publisher mailing list, as shown in Figure 7–1. The letter, formatted with a graphic watermark (Figure 7–1a), thanks each person who bought tickets to a small venue concert. The ticket (Figure 7–1b) displays concert and seating information.

The letter contains merged fields, including names, addresses, and the number of tickets. The ticket displays a unique ticket number, seat, and row.

(a) Form Letter

(b) Merged Ticket

Figure 7–1

Overview

As you read through this chapter, you will learn how to create the publications shown in Figure 7–1 on the previous page by performing these general tasks:

- Create a watermark on the master page.
- Use character spacing and tabbing techniques.
- Create a data source.
- Compose the main document.
- Use a Microsoft Excel file as a data source.
- Create individualized tickets.
- Preview, save, and print merged publications.

Plan Ahead

General Project Guidelines

When creating a Publisher publication, the actions you perform and decisions you make will affect the appearance and characteristics of the finished publication. As you create form letters and tickets, such as those shown in Figure 7–1 on the previous page, you should follow these general guidelines:

1. **Create watermarks on the master page.** Using the master page for objects on multipage publications, such as headers, footers, watermarks, or other repeating elements, saves time because you have to create the object only once. On single page publications, the master page commonly is used for a watermark that appears behind text and other objects on the page. Make sure the watermark does not interfere with the viewer's ability to read the text in the publication.

2. **Identify the main document for the form letter.** When creating form letters, you either can create the letter from scratch or use a letterhead template. Then, you customize the resulting letter by writing the text and inserting unique field codes. Use text, graphics, formats, and colors that reflect you or your business. Consider unique character spacing. Include a name, postal mailing address, and telephone number. If you have an e-mail address and Web address, include those as well.

3. **Create or specify the data source.** The data source contains the variable, or changing, values for each letter. A data source can be a Publisher recipient list, an Access database table, an Outlook contacts list, or an Excel worksheet. If the necessary and properly organized data already exists in one of these Office programs, you can instruct Publisher to use the existing file as the data source for the mail merge. Otherwise, you can create a new data source.

4. **Compose the main document for the form letter.** A main document contains the constant, or unchanging, text, punctuation, spaces, and graphics. It also includes field codes for the parts of the document that should change, referencing the data in the data source properly. The finished publication should look like a symmetrically framed picture with evenly spaced margins, all balanced below an attractive letterhead. The content of the main document for the form letter should contain proper grammar, correct spelling, logically constructed sentences, flowing paragraphs, and sound ideas. Be sure to proofread it carefully.

5. **Merge the main document with the data source to create the form letters.** Merging is the process of combining the contents of a data source with a main document. You can print the merged letters on the printer or place them in a new publication, which you later can edit. You also have the option of merging all data in a data source or merging just a portion of it.

When necessary, more specific details concerning the above guidelines are presented at appropriate points in the chapter. The chapter also will identify the actions performed and decisions made regarding these guidelines during the creation of the form letters shown in Figure 7–1 as well as related files.

To Start Publisher

The following steps, which assume Windows 7 is running, start Publisher based on a typical installation. You may need to ask your instructor how to start Publisher for your computer. For a detailed example of the procedure summarized below, refer to the Office 2010 and Windows 7 chapter at the beginning of this book.

1 Click the Start button on the Windows 7 taskbar to display the Start menu.

2 Type `Microsoft Publisher` as the search text in the 'Search programs and files' text box, and watch the search results appear on the Start menu.

3 Click Microsoft Publisher 2010 in the search results on the Start menu to start Publisher and open the Backstage view.

4 If the Publisher window is not maximized, click the Maximize button next to the Close button on its title bar to maximize the window.

To Open a Publication

The following steps open the Taxon Letterhead file from the Data Files for Students. See the inside back cover of this book for instructions on downloading the Data Files for Students, or contact your instructor for information about accessing the required files. For a detailed example of the procedure summarized below, refer to the Office 2010 and Windows 7 chapter at the beginning of this book.

1 Click Open in the Backstage view to display the Open Publication dialog box.

2 Navigate to the location of the file to be opened (in this case, the Data Files for Students, in the Publisher folder, and then in the Chapter 07 folder).

3 Double-click Taxon Letterhead to open the selected file and display the opened publication in the Publisher window.

4 If necessary, close the Page Navigation pane and click the Special Characters button (Home tab | Paragraph group) to display special characters (Figure 7–2).

Figure 7–2

Plan Ahead

Create watermarks on the master page.

As a graphic visible in the background on some publications, watermarks may be translucent; other watermarks can be seen on the paper when held up to the light. Other times the paper itself has a watermark when it is manufactured. Watermarks are used as both decoration and identification, as well as to provide security solutions to prevent document fraud. Creating watermarks on the master page makes the elements repeat on each page of the publication. A master page can contain anything that you can put on a publication page, as well as headers, footers, page numbers, the date and time, and layout guides unique to the master page.

BTW

Master Pages

You can create multiple master pages if you want a variety of layouts in a publication that has more than one page. The Add Master Page button (Master Page tab | Master Page group) opens the New Master Page dialog box, allowing you to name the new master page, such as Master Page A, Master Page B, and so on.

Watermarks and Master Pages

A **watermark** is a semitransparent graphic that is visible in the background on a printed page. In Publisher, you create watermarks by placing text or graphics on the master page. When you open the master page, Publisher displays a new tab on the Ribbon (Figure 7–3). While other tabs are available to help you manipulate objects on the master page, when finished, you should click the Close Master Page button (Master Page tab | Close group) to return to the main tabs on the Ribbon.

Figure 7–3

BTW

Master Pages

This textbook uses two master pages. Notice the headers at the top of this page and the top of the next page. On Master Page A, the page number appears first. Master Page B is a mirrored header with the page number appearing last. Master Page B also displays a vertical graphic with the name of the chapter on the right side of each B page.

Each publication starts with one master page. If you have a multipage publication, you can choose to use two different master pages for cases such as facing pages in a book; in that case, you might want different graphics in the background of each page. If you want to display master page objects only on certain pages, the Apply To button (Master Page tab | Master Page group) provides several options. This is useful for cases such as background images on every page except the title page in a longer publication, or for placing a watermark on the inside page of a brochure but not on the front page.

To View the Master Page

In the Taxon letterhead, you will create a watermark that uses a picture of a guitar. The following steps access the master page.

1

- Click View on the Ribbon to display the View tab (Figure 7–4).

Figure 7–4

2

- Click the Master Page button (View tab | Views group) to access the master page (Figure 7–5).

Q&A

Why is the scratch area a different color?

Publisher uses a different color to remind you that you are not in the regular publication window. It helps you to remember to close the master page before continuing with the other objects in the publication.

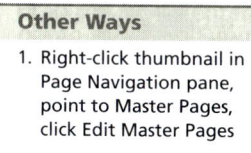

Other Ways

1. Right-click thumbnail in Page Navigation pane, point to Master Pages, click Edit Master Pages

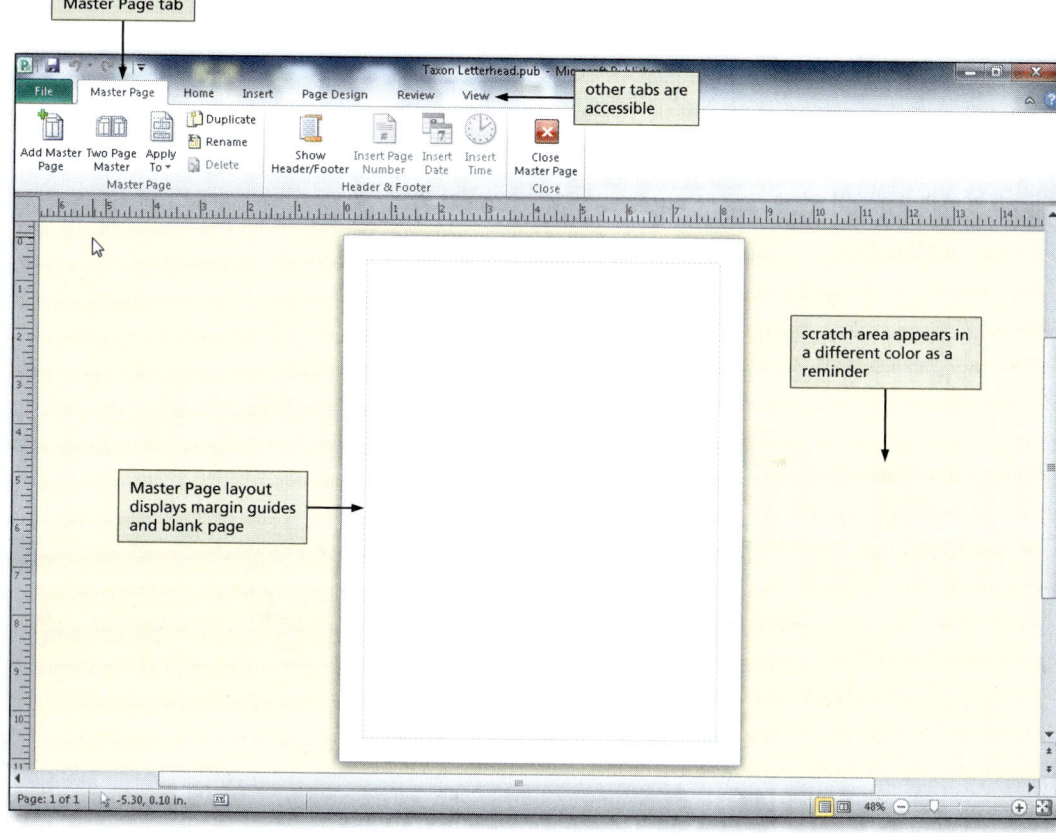

Figure 7–5

Graphic Adjustments

Recall that you inserted graphics or pictures into publications by choosing them from the Clip Art task pane and by importing them from a file. You added a picture style and created a formatted graphic shape. For more advanced graphic techniques, the Adjust group on the Picture Tools Format tab provides ways to edit graphics other than by changing size, position, and style (Figure 7–6 on the next page).

BTW

Recoloring Graphics
You can recolor most pictures inserted into Publisher. This procedure does not apply to pictures that are in Encapsulated PostScript (EPS) format, however. EPS is a graphic file format that is created using the PostScript page description language. EPS graphics are designed to be printed to PostScript compatible printers and cannot be recolored.

Figure 7–6

Brightness is the percentage of black or white added to a main color. The higher the brightness percentage, the more white the image contains. **Contrast** is the saturation or intensity of the color. The higher the contrast percentage, the more intense the color. When you **recolor** a graphic, you make a large-scale color change; the color applies to all parts of the graphic, with the option of leaving the black parts black. It is an easy way to convert a color graphic to a black and white line drawing so that it prints more clearly. The reverse also is true; if you have a black and white graphic, you can convert it to a tint or shade of any one color.

The Change Picture button allows you to change the picture while maintaining the placement and size in the publication. The Reset Picture button discards any changes you have made to the picture.

Compress means to reduce the storage size of your publication by changing the internal size of the picture. When you click the Compress Pictures button, Publisher displays the Compress Pictures dialog box. Table 7–1 describes the compression settings.

Table 7–1 Compress Pictures Settings	
Setting	**Description**
Current combined image size	Displays the current combined size of all pictures in the publication.
Estimated combined image size after compression	Displays the estimated combined size of all pictures in the publication after compression settings.
'Delete cropped areas of pictures' check box	Deletes the pixel information that normally is stored for cropped areas of pictures.
'Remove OLE data' check box	Removes the internal part of a graphic that is used when the graphic is linked or embedded. While the picture itself appears the same, you no longer are able to open that picture by using the software in which it was created originally.
Resample pictures check box	Makes a resized picture smaller by deleting the residual data from the picture's original size. You should avoid making the picture larger after resampling.
'Convert to JPEG where appropriate' check box	Converts the picture to a JPEG file.
Commercial Printing option button	Compresses pictures except JPEG files to 300 pixels per inch (ppi).
Desktop Printing option button	Compresses pictures to 220 ppi and a 95 JPEG quality level.

Table 7–1 Compress Pictures Settings (continued)	
Setting	**Description**
Web option button	Compresses pictures to 96 dots per inch (dpi) and a 75 JPEG quality level.
'Apply to all pictures in the publication' option button	Applies the compression settings to all of the pictures in the publication.
'Apply to selected pictures only' option button	Applies the compression settings to only the selected picture or pictures.

To Insert and Place the Watermark Graphic

The following steps insert the graphic of a guitar that will be used for the watermark. You then will recolor and compress the graphic.

1 Display the Insert tab.

2 Click the Insert Picture from File button (Insert tab | Illustrations group) to display the Insert Picture dialog box.

3 Navigate to the location of the picture (in this case, the Data Files for Students, in the Publisher folder, and then in the Chapter 07 folder). For a detailed example of this procedure, refer to Steps 3a–3c in the To Save a File in a Folder section in the Office 2010 and Windows 7 chapter at the beginning of this book.

4 Double-click the Guitar file to insert it in the middle of the Master Page.

5 Resize the picture to fill the page, within the margin guides. Refer to page PUB 97 for more information about resizing graphics (Figure 7–7).

BTW

Scaling Graphics
Scaling, when it applies to graphics, means changing the vertical or horizontal size of the graphic by a percentage. Scaling can create interesting graphic effects. For example, a square graphic could become a long thin graphic suitable for use as a single border if the scale height were increased to 200% and the scale width were reduced to 50%. Caricature drawings and intentionally distorted photographs routinely use scaling. When used for resizing, scaling is appropriate to make a graphic fit in tight places.

guitar picture fills the page layout on the master page

Figure 7–7

To Recolor the Picture

The following steps recolor the picture.

1

• With the picture selected, click the Recolor button (Picture Tools Format tab | Adjust group) to display the Recolor gallery (Figure 7–8).

Experiment

• Point to each of the thumbnails in the Recolor gallery and watch the picture change on the master page.

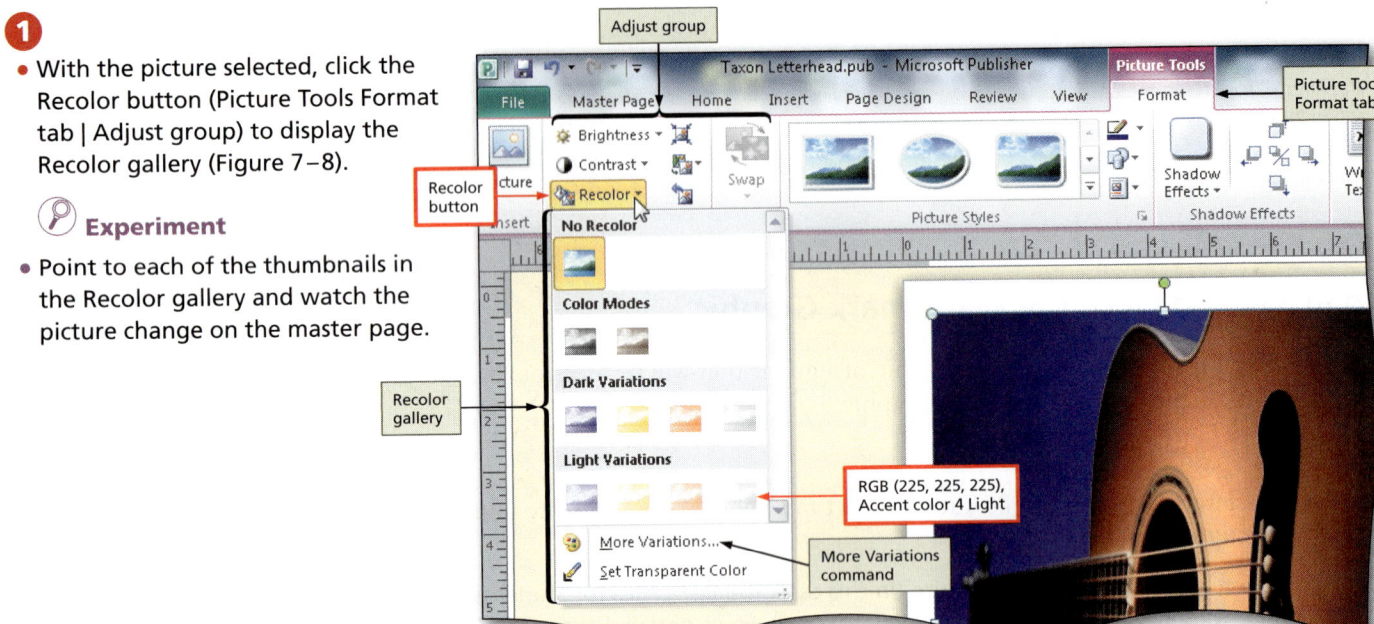

Figure 7–8

2

• Click RGB (225, 225, 225), Accent color 4 Light to change the picture to grayscale (Figure 7–9).

Q&A

What does the More Variations command in the Recolor gallery do?

It displays the Recolor Picture dialog box, which allows you to make further edits to the picture, including leaving the black parts black; this provides interesting effects when you recolor to colors other than black and white.

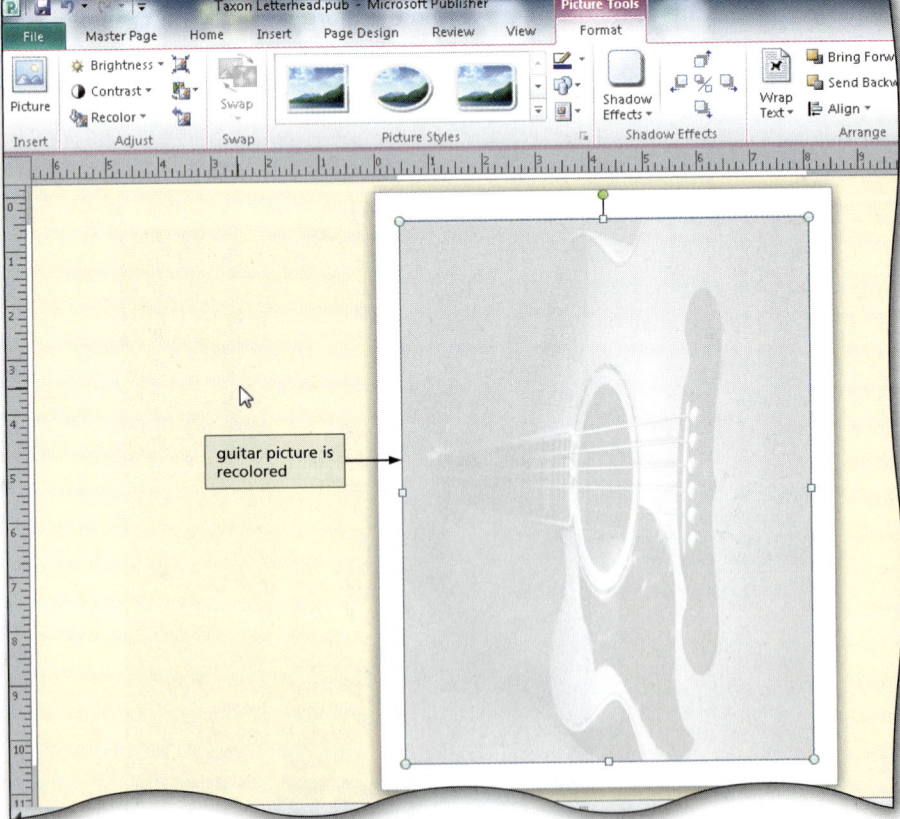

Figure 7–9

To Compress the Picture

The following steps compress the picture to reduce the size of the file when it is saved.

1

- With the picture selected, click the Compress Pictures button (Picture Format Tools tab | Adjust group) to display the Compress Pictures dialog box.

- Click the Desktop Printing option button to compress the picture for desktop printing.

- If necessary, click the 'Apply to all pictures in the publication' option button (Figure 7–10).

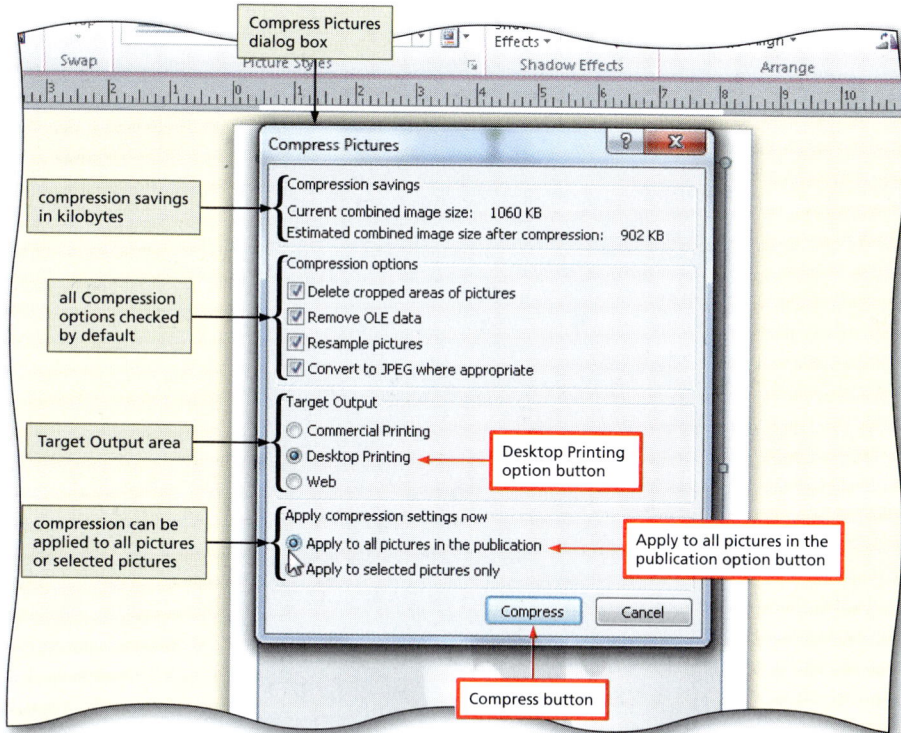

Figure 7–10

2

- Click the Compress button (Compress Pictures dialog box) to begin the compressing process and to display a Microsoft Publisher dialog box (Figure 7–11).

Q&A

How much storage space will I save?

The size of the saved file will vary, but you should save approximately 100 kilobytes.

3

- Click the Yes button (Microsoft Publisher dialog box) to confirm the compression.

Figure 7–11

To Close the Master Page

You are finished with the watermark. The following step closes the master page and returns to the regular page layout and Publisher workspace.

 1

- Display the Master Page tab.

- Click the Close Master Page button (Master Page tab | Close group) to close the master page (Figure 7–12).

Q&A

What else could I add to the master page?

You could add a background effect, headers, footers, or any text or graphics that you want to appear on every page of a multipage publication.

watermark appears in publication layout

Figure 7–12

To Save the Publication

You have performed many tasks while creating this publication and do not want to risk losing work completed thus far. Accordingly, you should save the publication.

The following steps assume you already have created folders for storing your files, for example, a CIS 101 folder (for your class) that contains a Publisher folder (for your assignments). Thus, these steps save the publication in the Publisher folder in the CIS 101 folder on a USB flash drive using the file name, Concert Tickets Form Letter. For a detailed example of the procedure summarized below, refer to the Office 2010 and Windows 7 chapter at the beginning of this book.

1 With a USB flash drive connected to one of the computer's USB ports, click File on the Ribbon to display the Backstage view.

2 Click the Save as command to display the Save As dialog box.

3 Type **Concert Tickets Form Letter** in the File name text box to change the file name. Do not press the ENTER key after typing the file name because you do not want to close the dialog box at this time.

4 Navigate to the desired save location (in this case, the Publisher folder in the CIS 101 folder [or your class folder] on the USB flash drive).

5 Click the Save button (Save As dialog box) to save the publication in the selected folder on the selected drive with the entered file name.

**Plan
Ahead**

Identify the main document for the form letter.
Create a letterhead or use a letterhead template as the basis for the form letter. Be sure it includes all essential letterhead elements. If necessary, adjust the tracking and kerning of text to make the text more legible. Set new and appropriate tabs. Always save the main document before beginning the merge process.

To Insert Letterhead Information

The following steps create and enter text into two text boxes, one at the top of the letterhead and one at the bottom.

- Scroll to the upper portion of the publication, and then zoom to 100%.

- Click the Draw Text Box button (Home tab | Objects group) and then drag to draw a text box, just below the music border graphic, that extends from the left margin to the right margin approximately .75 inches tall.

- Type **Taxon Acoustic Rock Series** to enter the heading.

Figure 7–13

- Right-click the text to display the shortcut menu and then click Best Fit.

- Press CTRL+E to center the text (Figure 7–13).

2

- Scroll to the lower portion of the page layout and draw a text box, just above the decorative graphic, that extends from the left margin to the right margin approximately .5 inches tall.

Figure 7–14

- Type **Ticket hotline phone: 555.816.1973 | 81509 North Oak, Envision, MO, 64118 | www.taxontickets.com** to enter the company information.

3

- Press CTRL+E to center the text (Figure 7–14).

Spacing between Characters

Sometimes you need to fine-tune the spacing between characters on the page. For instance, you may want to spread characters apart for better legibility. Other times, you may want to move characters closer together for space considerations, without changing the font or font size. Or, you may be using a font that employs **proportional spacing** or different widths for different characters. For example, in a proportionally spaced font, the letter i is narrower than the letter m. This book uses a proportionally spaced font, as do most books, newspapers, and magazines.

The opposite of proportional spacing is **monospacing**, where every letter is the same width. Older printers and monitors were limited to monospaced fonts because of the dot matrix used to create the characters. Now, almost all printers, with the exception of line printers, are capable of printing with either proportionally spaced or monospaced fonts. Because most fonts use proportional spacing, the scaling, tracking, and kerning features in Publisher allow you many ways to make very precise character spacing adjustments.

Scaling, the process of shrinking or stretching text, changes the width of individual characters in text boxes. Recall that the WordArt toolbar has a button for scaling; however, scaling also can be applied to any text box by using the Measurement toolbar.

Tracking, or **character spacing**, refers to the adjustment of the general spacing between all selected characters. Tracking text compensates for the spacing irregularities caused when you make text much bigger or much smaller. For example, smaller type is easier to read when it has been tracked loosely. Tracking maintains the original height of the font and overrides adjustments made by justification of the margins. Tracking is available only if you are working on a print publication. It is not available with Web publications.

Kerning, or **track kerning**, is a special form of tracking related to pairs of characters that can appear too close together or too far apart, even with standard tracking. Kerning can create the appearance of even spacing and is used to fit text into a given space or adjust line breaks. For instance, certain uppercase letters such as T, V, W, and Y often are kerned when they are preceded or followed by a lowercase a, e, i, o, or u. With manual kerning, Publisher lets you choose from normal, expanded, and condensed kerning for special effects. Text in smaller point sizes usually does not need to be kerned, unless the font contains many serifs.

You can adjust the spacing between characters using the lower three boxes on the Measurement toolbar boxes as explained in Table 7–2. Some spacing techniques also can be performed using the Ribbon or in dialog boxes.

BTW

Kerning
The term kerning comes from the printing industry where typesetters would shave off portions of the rectangular letter blocks so that letters could fit closer together. The kern is the part of a metal typeface that projects beyond its body.

BTW

Leading
Leading is similar to tracking, except that it applies formatting to the line spacing instead of character spacing. Leading measures the vertical distance between lines of text — ignoring any letters that descend below the line.

Table 7–2 Character Spacing Tools on the Measurement Toolbar		
Box Name	**Specifies**	**Preset Unit of Measurement**
Tracking	General space between characters	Percent
Text Scaling	Width of the characters	Percent
Kerning	Subtle space between paired characters	Point size

To Track Characters

The following steps select the text at the bottom of the page and then track the small text more loosely.

1

- If necessary, click the text in the text box to position the insertion point.

- Press CTRL+A to select all of the text.

- Click the Character Spacing button (Home tab | Font group) to display the Character Spacing gallery (Figure 7–15).

🔍 **Experiment**

- Point to each of the choices in the Character Spacing gallery and watch how the text changes.

Q&A What is the difference between tracking, scaling, and autofitting?

Tracking increases or decreases the spaces between the characters. Scaling changes the width of the characters themselves. Autofitting changes the font size, which is both the width and height of the characters.

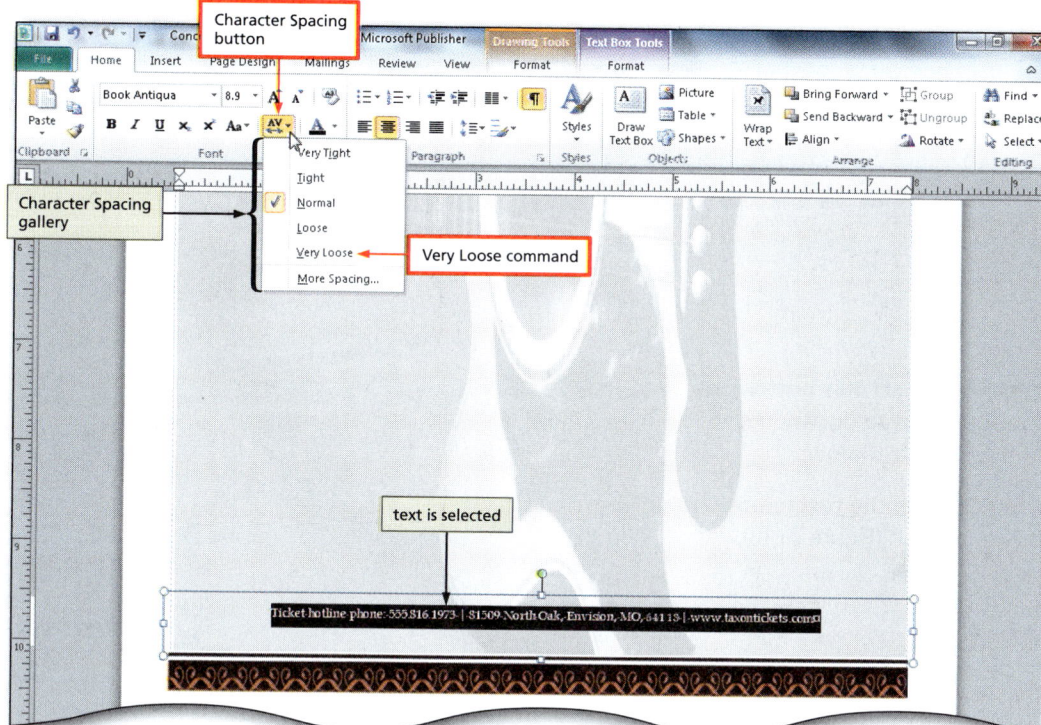

Figure 7–15

2

- Click Very Loose to track the text more loosely (Figure 7–16).

Q&A How is tracking measured?

Tracking is a percentage of how much space is inserted between characters. Tight tracking reduces the percentage. Loose tracking increases the percentage. When you choose Very Loose, the text is tracked 125%.

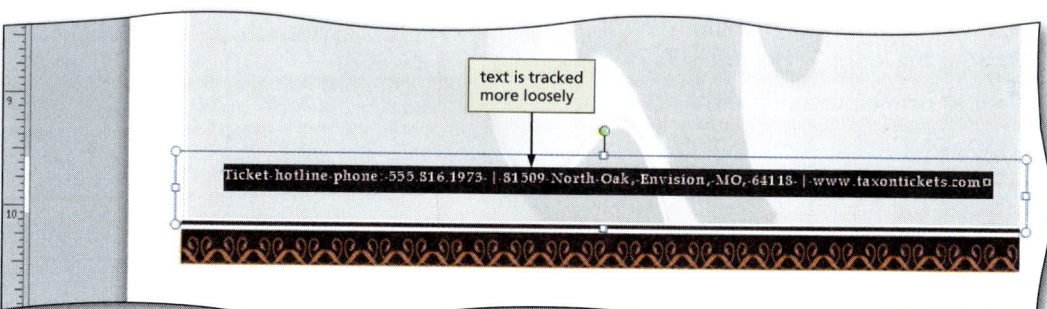

Figure 7–16

Other Ways	
1. Click Object Size button on status bar, enter tracking setting in Tracking box on Measurement toolbar	2. Right-click text, point to Change Text, click Character Spacing, enter tracking setting (Character Spacing dialog box), click OK button

To Kern Character Pairs

The following steps kern the first two letters in the heading so that the spacing adjusts to match the other words more closely.

- Scroll to the upper portion of the page.

- Drag to select the letters Ta in the heading (Figure 7–17).

Figure 7–17

- Click the Object Size button on the status bar to display the Measurement toolbar.

- Drag through the text in the Kerning box to select it (Figure 7–18).

Figure 7–18

- Type **-2.95** and then press the ENTER key to move the letter, a, closer to the letter, T (Figure 7–19).

Q&A

What is the measurement setting?

When you enter a negative number, you are condensing the points between the characters. Recall that a point is approximately equal to 1/72nd of an inch. Therefore, you are moving the characters .24 inches closer together.

Figure 7–19

- Click outside the text box to deselect the text.

- Close the Measurement Toolbar.

Other Ways

1. Right-click selected text, point to Change Text on shortcut menu, click Character Spacing, | enter kerning setting (Character Spacing dialog box), click OK button

To Create a Text Box

The following steps create a text box for the body of the letter.

1 Display the View tab and then click the Whole Page button (View tab | Zoom group) to display the whole page.

2 Display the Home tab and then click the Draw Text Box button (Home tab | Objects group). Draw a text box that fills the area between the other two text boxes, from margin to margin.

3 Change the font size to 12 (Figure 7–20).

Figure 7–20

Working with Tabs and the Ruler

The **ruler** appears above the Publisher workspace and contains buttons, markers, margins, and measurements to help you place tabs, text, and objects. A **tab**, or **tab stop**, is a horizontal location inside a text box designated by a tab stop marker on the Publisher ruler. A **tab stop marker** appears darkened on the ruler as either a straight line, L-shaped marker, or T-shaped marker. A **margin marker** appears as either a gray triangle or gray rectangle on the ruler. Margin markers set and indicate margins on the left and right of a text box. A special **first-line indent marker** allows you to change the left margin for the first line only in a paragraph. The typing area within the text box boundaries appears in light gray on the ruler; the rest of the ruler is a darker gray. Numbers on the ruler represent inches, but inches can be changed to centimeters, picas, pixels, or points. The **tab selector** is located at the left end of the ruler. It displays an icon representing the alignment of the text at the tab stop (Figure 7–21).

Zero Point
You can CTRL+click or CTRL+drag the tab selector to change the publication's **zero point** or **ruler origin**. The zero point is the position of 0 inches on the ruler. It is useful for measuring the width and height of objects on the page without having to add or subtract from a number other than zero. To change the ruler back, double-click the tab selector.

Figure 7–21

Table 7–3 explains the functions of the markers and buttons on the ruler, as well as how to modify them.

Units of Measurement
If you want to change the unit of measurement on the ruler, display the Backstage view and then click Options. Click Advanced and then click the 'Show measurements in units of' box arrow. Choose the preferred unit of measurement and then click the OK button (Publisher Options dialog box).

Table 7–3 Ruler Tools			
Tool Name	**Description**	**How to Change**	**Other Ways**
First-line indent marker	A downward pointing triangle that indicates the position at which paragraphs begin	Drag to desired location	Double-click margin marker, enter location in First line box (Paragraph dialog box)
Left indent marker	An upward pointing triangle that indicates the left position at which text wraps	Drag to desired location	Double-click margin marker, enter location in Left box (Paragraph dialog box)
Move both markers	A small rectangle used to move both the left indent marker and the first-line indent marker at the same time	Drag to desired location	Right-click text box, click Text Box tab (Format Text box dialog box), enter text box margins
Object margins	Gray indicates the area outside the object margin; white indicates the area inside the object margin	Resize object	Right-click text box, click Size tab (Format Text box dialog box), enter height and width
Right indent marker	An upward pointing triangle that indicates the rightmost position at which text wraps to the next line	Drag to desired location	Double-click margin marker, enter location in Right box (Paragraph dialog box)
Tab selector	Displays the current alignment setting: left, right, center, or leader	Click to toggle choice	Double-click tab stop marker, select alignment (Paragraph dialog box)
Tab stop marker	Displays the location of a tab stop	Click to create; drag to move	Double-click ruler, set tab stop location (Paragraph dialog box)

Recall that the Special Characters button (Home tab | Paragraph group) shown in Figure 7–2 on page PUB 387 makes special nonprinting characters visible to help you format text passages, including tab characters (→), end-of-paragraph marks (¶), and end-of-frame marks (¤).

You can drag markers to any place on the ruler within the text box boundaries. You can click and hold a marker to display a dotted line through the publication, which allows you to see in advance where the marker will be set. Markers are paragraph-specific, which means that when you set the tabs and indents, they apply to the current paragraph. Once the tabs and indents are set, however, pressing the ENTER key carries forward the markers to the next paragraph.

With tab stops, you can align text to the left, right, center, or at a decimal character. Publisher also can insert special leading characters before a tab, such as dashes, dots, or lines. Table 7–4 lists the types of tab alignments and their common uses.

Tab Stop Alignment
The tab stop alignment can be changed by clicking the Paragraph Dialog Box Launcher button (Home tab | Paragraph group), by double-clicking an existing marker, or by clicking the tab selector until it displays the type of tab that you want.

Table 7–4 Types of Tab Alignments		
Name	**Action**	**Purpose**
Left tab	Text begins at tab stop and is inserted to the right	Used for most tabbing
Right tab	Text begins at tab stop and is inserted to the left	Used for indexes, programs, and lists
Center tab	Text is centered at the tab stop as it is typed	Used to center a list within a column
Decimal tab	Aligns numbers only, based on a decimal point, independent of the number of digits	Used for aligning currency amounts in a list
Leader tab	Text begins at tab stop and is inserted to the left; space preceding the tab is filled with chosen character	Used for table of contents, printed programs, church bulletins, etc.

BTW

Default Tabs
Default tabs are set every .5 inches in a text box; default tabs do not display markers.

To Set a Tab Stop

The following step uses the horizontal ruler to set, or insert, a tab stop at the 3.5" position in the form letter text box.

1
- With the insertion point located in the main text box of the form letter, press the F9 key to zoom to 100%.

- Click the horizontal ruler at the 3.5" mark to create a left tab stop. Move the mouse pointer to view the tab stop marker (Figure 7–22).

Figure 7–22

Q&A Is the tab always a left-justified tab?

Left-aligned is the default tab setting. If you want to change the tab type, click the tab selector until you see the tab type you want and then click the ruler at the tab stop location.

Other Ways

1. Click Paragraph Dialog Box Launcher button (Home tab | Paragraph group), click Tabs tab (Paragraph dialog box), set tab stop, click OK button

To Enter Tabbed Text

The following steps enter tabbed text.

1
- Press the TAB key to move the insertion point to the tab stop (Figure 7–23).

Q&A How do I delete a tab?

To delete a tab, drag the tab marker from its location in the ruler to the tab selector and drop it there. Or, you can click the Paragraph Dialog Box launcher button (Home tab | Paragraph group) and then click the Tabs tab (Paragraph dialog box). Select the tab stop location and click the Clear button.

Figure 7–23

- Display the Insert tab.

- Click the Date & Time button (Insert tab | Text group) to display the Date and Time dialog box.

- Click the third available format and click the Update automatically check box (Figure 7–24).

Figure 7–24

- Click the OK button (Date and Time dialog box) to insert the current date at the tab stop.

- Press the ENTER key twice to insert a blank line (Figure 7–25).

Q&A Why is my date different?

Publisher inserts the current date; your display should reflect the current date (the date you create this publication).

Figure 7–25

BTW

Tabs vs. Indents
Sometimes it is difficult to determine whether to use tab stops or indents. Use tab stops when you want to indent paragraphs as you go, or when you want a simple column. When the tab stop is positioned for a long passage of text, using the TAB key to indent the first line of each paragraph is inefficient, because you must press it each time you begin a new paragraph. In these cases, it is better to use an indent because it automatically carries forward when you press the ENTER key.

To Save an Existing Publication with the Same File Name

You have made several modifications to the publication since you last saved it. Thus, you should save it again. The following step saves the document again. For an example of the step listed below, refer to the Office 2010 and Windows 7 chapter at the beginning of this book.

1 Click the Save button on the Quick Access Toolbar to overwrite the previously saved file.

Break Point: If you wish to take a break, this is a good place to do so. You can quit Publisher now. To resume at a later time, start Publisher, open the file called Concert Tickets Form Letter, and continue following the steps from this location forward.

Merging Data into Publications

The process of generating an individualized publication for mass mailing involves creating a main publication and a data source. The main publication contains the constant or unchanging text, punctuation, space, and graphics, embedded with variables or changing values from the data source. A data source or database is a file where you store all addresses or other personal information for customers, friends and family, or merchants with whom you do business. The term **database** generically describes a collection of data, organized in a manner that allows easy access, retrieval, and use of that data. **Merging** is the process of combining the contents of a data source with a main publication.

Personalized contact with your customers can result in increased revenue. Addressing customers by name and remembering their preferences is the kind of personal attention that builds customer loyalty. When retail establishments keep close track of customers' interests, customers usually respond by returning and spending more time and money there. When you include content in a mailing that addresses your customers' specific interests, the customers are more likely to pay attention and respond.

Publisher allows users to create data sources internally, which means using Publisher as both the creation and editing tool. Publisher creates a database that can be edited independently by using Microsoft Access; however, you do not need to have Microsoft Access or any database program installed on your system to use a Publisher data source.

If you plan to **import**, or bring in data, from another application, Publisher can accept data from a variety of other formats, as shown in Table 7–5.

BTW

Recipient Lists
You can maintain multiple recipient lists for data sources, such as employees or vendors, if you use different file names.

BTW

Main Publications
When you open a main publication, Publisher attempts to open the associated data source file, too. If the data source is not in exactly the same location (i.e., drive and folder) as when it originally was merged and saved, Publisher displays a dialog box indicating that it cannot find the data source. When this occurs, click the Find Data Source button to display the Open Data Source dialog box, and locate the data source file yourself.

Table 7–5 Data Formats

Data-Creation Program	File Extension
Any text files, such as those generated with WordPad or Notepad where tabs or commas separate the columns, and paragraph marks separate the rows	.txt, .prn, .csv, .tab, and .asc
dBase	.dbf
Microsoft Access (database tables and projects)	.ade, .adp, .mdb .mde, .accdb, and .accde
Microsoft Data links	.udl
Microsoft Excel	.xls and .xlsx
Microsoft FoxPro	.fxd
Microsoft List Builder	.bcm
Microsoft Office Address Lists	.mdb
Microsoft Office List Shortcuts	.ols
Microsoft Outlook (Contacts list)	.pst
Microsoft Word (tables or merge data documents)	.doc, .docx, and .docm
ODBC File DSNs	.dsn
SQL Server and Office Database Connections	.odc
Web pages	.htm, .html, .asp, .mht, .mhtml

Creating a Data Source

A data source is a file that contains the data that changes from one merged publication to the next. As shown in Figure 7–26, a data source often takes the form of a table containing a series of rows and columns. Each row is called a **record**. The first row of a data source is called the **header record** because it identifies the name of each column. Each row below the header row is called a **data record**. Data records contain the text that varies in each copy of the merged publication. The data source for this project contains five data records. In this project, each data record identifies a different person who has purchased tickets for a concert. Thus, the five form letters will be generated from this data source.

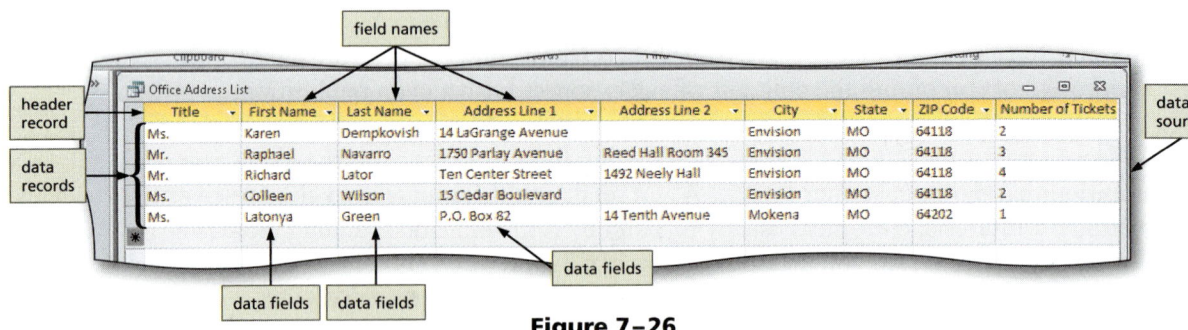

Figure 7–26

Each column in the data sources is called a **data field**. A data field represents a group of similar data. Each data field must be identified uniquely with a name, called a **field name**. For example, First Name is the name of the data field (column) that contains the first names of those who purchased tickets. In this project, the data source contains nine data fields with the following field names: Title, First Name, Last Name, Address Line 1, Address Line 2, City, State, ZIP Code, and Number of Tickets.

In Publisher, data sources sometimes are called **recipient lists** or **address lists**. Publisher allows you to create as many data sources as you like, providing a customizable interface in which to enter the data.

Plan Ahead

Create the data source.

When you create a data source, you will need to determine the fields it should contain. That is, you will need to identify the data that will vary from one merged document to the next. Following are a few important points about fields:

- For each field, you may be required to create a field name. Because data sources often contain the same fields, some programs create a list of commonly used field names that you may use.

- Field names must be unique; that is, no two field names may be the same.

- Fields may be listed in any order in the data source. That is, the order of fields has no effect on the order in which they will print in the main document.

- Organize fields so that they are flexible. For example, break the name into separate fields: title, first name, and last name. This arrangement allows you to customize fields.

To Use the Mail Merge Wizard

The following steps begin the process of creating a data source by using the Mail Merge Wizard. A **wizard** is a tool that guides you through the steps of a process or task by asking a series of questions or presenting options. The Mail Merge Wizard displays a task pane with steps to create the data source and the form letter.

1

- Click Mailings on the Ribbon to display the Mailings tab.

- Click the Mail Merge button arrow (Mailings tab | Start group) to display the list (Figure 7–27).

Figure 7–27

2

- Click Step by Step Mail Merge Wizard to display the Mail Merge task pane.

- Click the 'Type a new list' option button (Mail Merge task pane) to select it (Figure 7–28).

Q&A

Can I use other tabs and Ribbon commands while the Mail Merge task pane is open?

Yes, the task pane will remain open in the workspace while you edit the form letter.

 Experiment

- Drag the border between the Mail Merge task pane and the publication window to change the way Publisher displays task pane examples. Your display may differ.

Figure 7–28

3

- Click the 'Next wizard step' link at the bottom of the task pane to display the New Address List dialog box (Figure 7–29).

Q&A

How can I display the New Address List dialog box without going through the wizard?

You can click the Select Recipients button arrow (Mailings tab | Start group) and then click Type New List.

Figure 7–29

To Customize Data Source Columns

Publisher provides a list of 13 commonly used field names. This project uses 8 of the 13 field names supplied by Publisher: Title, First Name, Last Name, Address Line 1, Address Line 2, City, State, ZIP Code. This project does not use the other five field names supplied by Publisher: Company Name, Country or Region, Home Phone, Work Phone, and E-mail Address. Thus, you will delete those field names and create one new field named, Number of Tickets.

The following steps customize the columns in the New Address List dialog box.

1

- With the New Address List dialog box displayed, click the Customize Columns button (New Address List dialog box) to display the Customize Address List dialog box.

- Click Company Name in the Field Names area to select it (Figure 7–30).

Figure 7–30

2

- Click the Delete button (Customize Address List dialog box) to delete the field. When Publisher displays a dialog box asking if you are sure you want to delete the field, click the Yes button (Microsoft Publisher dialog box) (Figure 7–31).

Q&A What other options do I have for customization?

You can add a new column, rename a column to better describe its contents, or move columns up and down to place the fields in the desired order.

Figure 7–31

3

- Select, delete, and confirm the deletion of the Home Phone, Work Phone, and E-mail Address fields (Figure 7–32).

Q&A Can I delete multiple columns at one time?

No, you must select them and delete them individually.

Figure 7–32

4

- With Country or Region selected, click the Rename button to display the Rename Field dialog box.

- Type **Number of Tickets** in the To text box to name the new field (Figure 7–33).

Figure 7–33

5

- Click the OK button (Rename Field dialog box) to close the dialog box and return to the Customize Address List dialog box.

- If the fields are not in the same order as shown in Figure 7–34, select a field and then click the Move Up button or the Move Down button to correct the order.

 Experiment

- Experiment with moving the fields to different locations by selecting individual fields and then clicking the Move Up button or the Move Down button.

Figure 7–34

6

- Click the OK button (Customize Address List dialog box) to close the dialog box and return to the New Address List dialog box (Figure 7–35).

Q&A

Where is the Number of Tickets column?

You can use the scroll bar in the New Address List dialog box to view the other columns and the new field name.

Figure 7–35

Other Ways

1. Click Select Recipients button arrow (Mailings tab | Start group), click Edit Recipient List, click Customize Columns button (New Address List dialog box), select customizations, click OK button (Customize Address List dialog box)

Entering Data in the Data Source

Table 7–6 displays the customer data for the concertgoers.

Table 7–6 Customer Data								
Title	First Name	Last Name	Address1	Address2	City	State	ZIP Code	Number of Tickets
Ms.	Karen	Dempkovish	14 LaGrange Avenue		Envision	MO	64118	2
Mr.	Raphael	Navarro	1750 Parlay Avenue	Reed Hall Room 345	Envision	MO	64118	3
Mr.	Richard	Lator	Ten Center Street	1492 Neely Hall	Envision	MO	64118	4
Ms.	Colleen	Wilson	15 Cedar Boulevard		Envision	MO	64118	2
Ms.	Latonya	Green	P.O. Box 82	14 Tenth Avenue	Mokena	MO	64202	1

Notice that some customers have no Address Line 2. For those customers, you will leave that field blank. As you enter data, do not press the SPACEBAR at the end of the field. Extra spaces can interfere with the proper display of the merged fields.

To Enter Data in the Data Source File

The following steps enter the first record into the data source file, using the information from Table 7–6.

1
- With the New Address List dialog box still displayed, if necessary, click the box in the first row, below the Title heading.

- Type **Ms.** in the Title box and then press the TAB key.

- Type **Karen** in the First Name box and then press the TAB key.

- Type **Dempkovish** in the Last Name box and then press the TAB key (Figure 7–36).

Q&A What if the data is wider than the entry box?

Publisher will allow up to 256 characters in each entry box and move the text to the left, out of sight, as you type. The non-displayed text will be saved with the rest of the data.

Figure 7–36

2

- Continue to enter data from the first row in Table 7–6. Press the TAB key to advance to each new text box. Press the TAB key twice to leave a field empty. Do not press the TAB key at the end of the row (Figure 7–37).

Q&A

What does the Find button do?

When you click the Find button, Publisher displays the Find Entry dialog box. In this dialog box, you can look for specific pieces of data that have been typed so far in the data source. The Find Entry dialog box lets you search the entire list or specific fields.

Figure 7–37

To Create New Entries in the Data Source

The next step creates new entries or rows in the data source.

1

- Click the New Entry button (New Address List dialog box) to create a new row in the list and then enter the data from the second row of Table 7–6.

- Continue to add data from Table 7–6, clicking the New Entry button (New Address List dialog box) after each row of information in the table is complete. Press the TAB key to move from column to column. Press the TAB key twice to skip an empty field.

- When you complete the last entry, do not click the New Entry button (New Address List dialog box) (Figure 7–38).

Figure 7–38

To Save the Data Source

The following steps save the data source file on a USB flash drive with the name Concert Customer List.

1

- With a USB flash drive connected to one of the computer's USB ports, click the OK button (New Address List dialog box) to display the Save Address List dialog box.

- Type **Concert Customer List** in the File name box. Do not press the ENTER key because you do not want to close the dialog box at this time.

- Navigate to the desired save location (in this case, the Chapter 07 folder in the Publisher folder in the CIS 101 folder [or your class folder] on the USB flash drive). For a detailed example of this procedure, refer to the Office 2010 and Windows 7 chapter at the beginning of this book (Figure 7–39).

Figure 7–39

2

- Click the Save button (Save Address List dialog box) to save the file and to display the Mail Merge Recipients dialog box (Figure 7–40).

Q&A

What kinds of tasks can be performed using the Mail Merge Recipients dialog box?

You can select specific recipients, add new recipients, filter, sort, or create a new list. You will learn more about the Mail Merge Recipients dialog box later in the chapter.

3

- Click the OK button (Mail Merge Recipients dialog box) to close the dialog box.

Figure 7–40

<table>
<tr><td>

Plan Ahead

</td><td>

Compose the body of the form letter.

A main document contains both the constant, or unchanging, text, as well as field codes for merged fields. Be sure the main document for the form letter includes all essential business letter elements. All business letters should contain a date line, inside address, message, and signature block. Many business letters contain additional items such as a special mailing notation(s), an attention line, a salutation, a subject line, a complimentary close, reference initials, and an enclosure notation. It should use proper grammar, correct spelling, logically constructed sentences, flowing paragraphs, and sound ideas. Be sure to proofread it carefully.

</td></tr>
</table>

Inserting Field Codes

A publication designed for merging not only must be connected to its data source, but also must contain form fields, sometimes called field codes, in the publication. A **field code** is placeholder text in the publication that shows Publisher where to insert the information from the data source. Once the publication is merged with the address list, the field codes are replaced with unique information. For example, a form letter may say, Thank you for your business, to every customer, but follow it with the individual customer's name, such as John. In this case, you would type the words, Thank you for your business, insert a comma, and then insert the field code, First Name, from the data source. Publisher would insert the customer's name so that the letter would read, Thank you for your business, John.

You can format, copy, move, or delete a field code just as you would regular text. Field codes need to be spaced and punctuated appropriately. For instance, if you want to display a greeting such as Dear Katie, you need to type the word, Dear, followed by a space before inserting the First Name field code. You then would type a comma after the field code, to complete the greeting.

To insert a field code from the Mail Merge task pane, you either can position your insertion point in the publication and click the field code, or drag the field code from the task pane to the publication, dropping it at the appropriate location.

Publisher allows you to insert field codes from the address list into the main publication one field at a time or in predefined groups. For example, if you wanted to display the amount due from an address list, you would choose that single field from the task pane. To use predefined groups, you would use a **grouped field code**, which is a set of standard fields, such as typical address fields or salutation fields, preformatted and spaced with appropriate words and punctuation. For example, instead of entering the field codes for Title, First Name, Last Name, Company Name, Address Line 1, and so on, you can choose the grouped field, Address Block, that includes all the fields displayed correctly.

To Insert Grouped Field Codes

The following steps insert grouped field codes for the address block and greeting line in the form letter.

1

- Click to ensure that the insertion point is positioned two lines below the date in the publication.

- Zoom to 100%.

- Click the Address block link (Mail Merge task pane) to display the Insert Address Block dialog box.

- If necessary, click each of the enabled check boxes so that they contain check marks.

- If necessary, click the format, Mr. Joshua Randall Jr., in the 'Insert recipient's name in this format' list. If necessary, click the Previous button in the Preview area until the first recipient in your data source is displayed (Figure 7–41).

Figure 7–41

Q&A What is the difference between an Address block and Address fields?

The Address block link will include fields in the current data source. If you choose Address fields, Publisher displays a list of typical address fields that could be matched with different data sources. That way, if you choose to send a form letter to two different address lists, Publisher will try to match the fields consistently. For example, one address source might include a middle initial or company name, while another one might not.

 Experiment

- One at a time, click the formats in the 'Insert recipient's name in this format' list. View the changes in the preview. Click the Next button to view other entries from the address list.

2

- Click the OK button to insert the address block into the form letter.

- Click at the end of the inserted address block to reveal the field code (Figure 7–42).

Q&A What do the chevron symbols represent?

Each field code displays chevrons to let you know that it is not actual text. When you point to a field code, Publisher also displays a smart tag named Merge Field. When you click the Merge Field button, a field code menu displays commands to help you edit or delete the field code.

Figure 7–42

3

• Press the ENTER key twice and then click the Greeting line link (Mail Merge task pane) to display the Insert Greeting Line dialog box.

Experiment

• One at a time, click the box arrows to view the various kinds of greeting formats. Notice how the preview changes with each selection.

• If necessary, choose the various settings shown in Figure 7–43.

Figure 7–43

4

• Click the OK button (Insert Greeting Line dialog box) to insert the Greeting Line field code into the publication.

• Click after the Greeting Line field code and then press the ENTER key twice to move the insertion point in the publication (Figure 7–44).

Figure 7–44

To Insert Individual Field Codes

The following steps insert individual field codes as you type the body of the form letter. You will finish the merge process later in this chapter.

- With the insertion point positioned two lines below the greeting line, type **Thank you for ordering tickets for the Grim Survivors concert on April 28, 2012. Enclosed are your** and then press the SPACEBAR.

- In the task pane, scroll in the list of recipient information to display Number of Tickets. Click Number of Tickets to insert the field code into the publication.

- Press the SPACEBAR to insert a blank space (Figure 7–45).

Figure 7–45

- Type **tickets.** and then press the SPACEBAR again to complete the sentence (Figure 7–46).

Q&A

Why did my line wrap differently?

Subtle differences in the width of the text box can create a big difference in where wordwrap occurs. Your line may wrap at a different location.

Figure 7–46

3

- Type `Your seating is the best available at the time of your purchase.` to complete the paragraph.

- Press the ENTER key twice to insert a blank line (Figure 7–47).

new text

Figure 7–47

4

- Type `Enjoy the concert!` and then press the ENTER key twice.

- Press the TAB key, type `Sincerely,` and then press the ENTER key twice.

- Press the TAB key. Type `Taxon Ticket Desk` and then press the ENTER key twice.

- Type `Enclosure` to finish the letter (Figure 7–48).

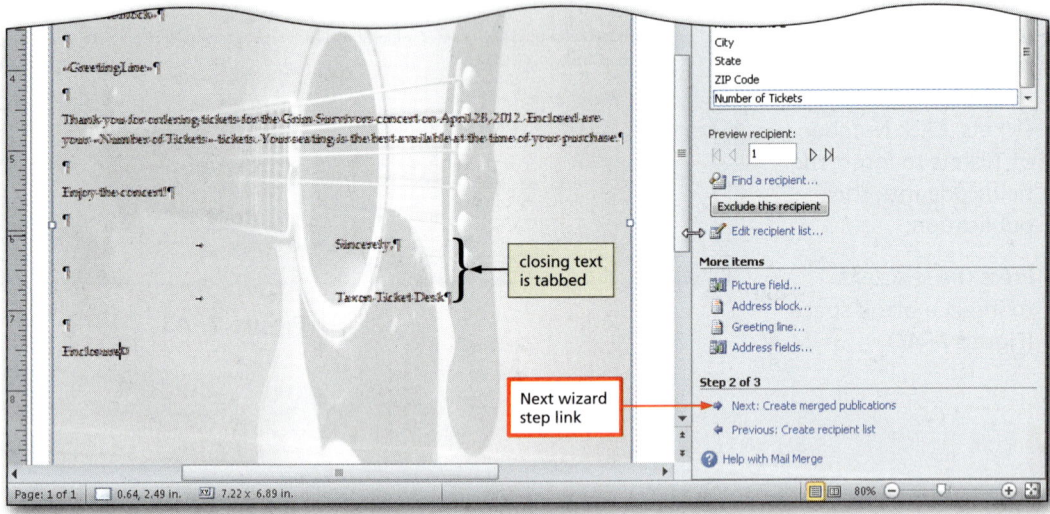

closing text is tabbed

Next wizard step link

Figure 7–48

Other Ways

1. Drag field from Mail Merge task pane into publication

Plan Ahead

Merge the main document with the data source to create the form letters.
Merging is the process of combining the contents of a data source with a main document. You can print the merged letters on the printer or place them in a new document, which you later can edit. You also have the options of merging all data in a data source or merging just a portion of it using a filter or sort.

To Create the Merged Publication

The following step creates the merged publication — a letter to each recipient.

1
- Click the 'Next wizard step' link at the bottom of the Mail Merge task pane to display Step 3 of 3 (Figure 7–49).

Q&A

How do I know if the merge was successful?

You can preview the form letters in the next set of steps, or you can click the Preview Results button (Mailings tab | Preview Results group).

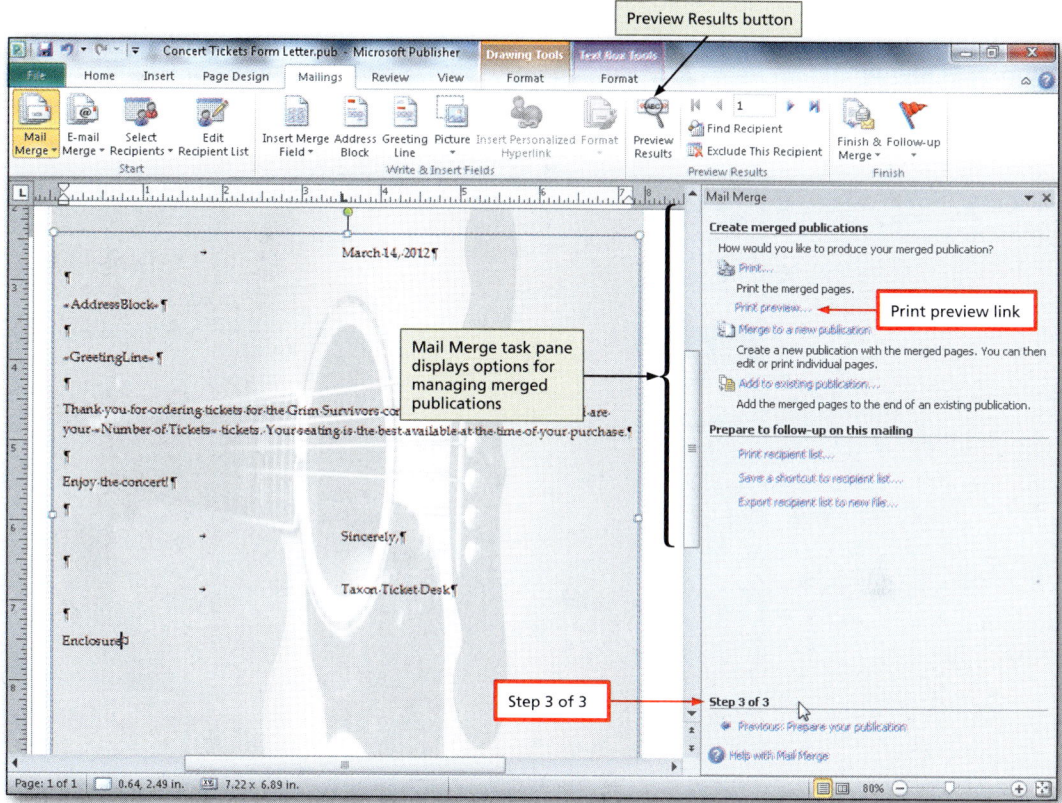

Figure 7–49

Managing Merged Publications

You have several choices in previewing, saving, printing, and exporting merged publications. Table 7–7 describes the merged publication options shown in Figure 7–49.

Table 7–7 Merged Publication Options

Option	Description
Print	Print all pages with merged data, one at a time.
Print Preview	Preview each page of the merged pages.
Merge to a new publication	Create a new publication with the merged pages, which you can edit further or print.
Add to existing publication	Add the merged pages to the end of the existing publication.
Print recipient list	Create a hard copy of the recipient list of the current merge for your records, including filters or sorts.
Save a shortcut to recipient list	Create a shortcut to the address list used in the current merge.
Export recipient list to new file	Create a new file based on the filtered or sorted address list used in the current merge.

To Preview the Form Letters

The following steps preview the form letters.

1
- Click the Print Preview link (Mail Merge task pane) to display the Print gallery in the Backstage view (Figure 7–50).

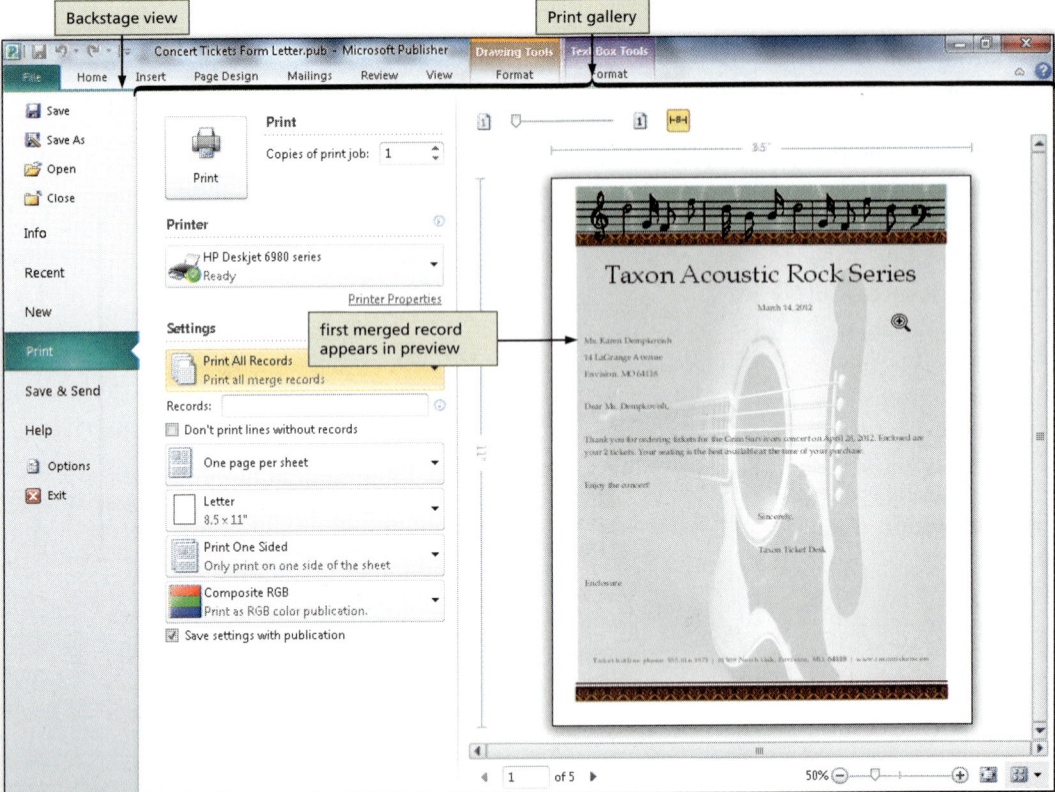

Figure 7–50

2
- Click the Next Sheet button at the bottom of the gallery to display the next letter (Figure 7–51).

 Experiment
- Click the Next Sheet and Previous Sheet buttons to move through the various merged letters.

3
- Click File on the Ribbon to return to the publication layout.

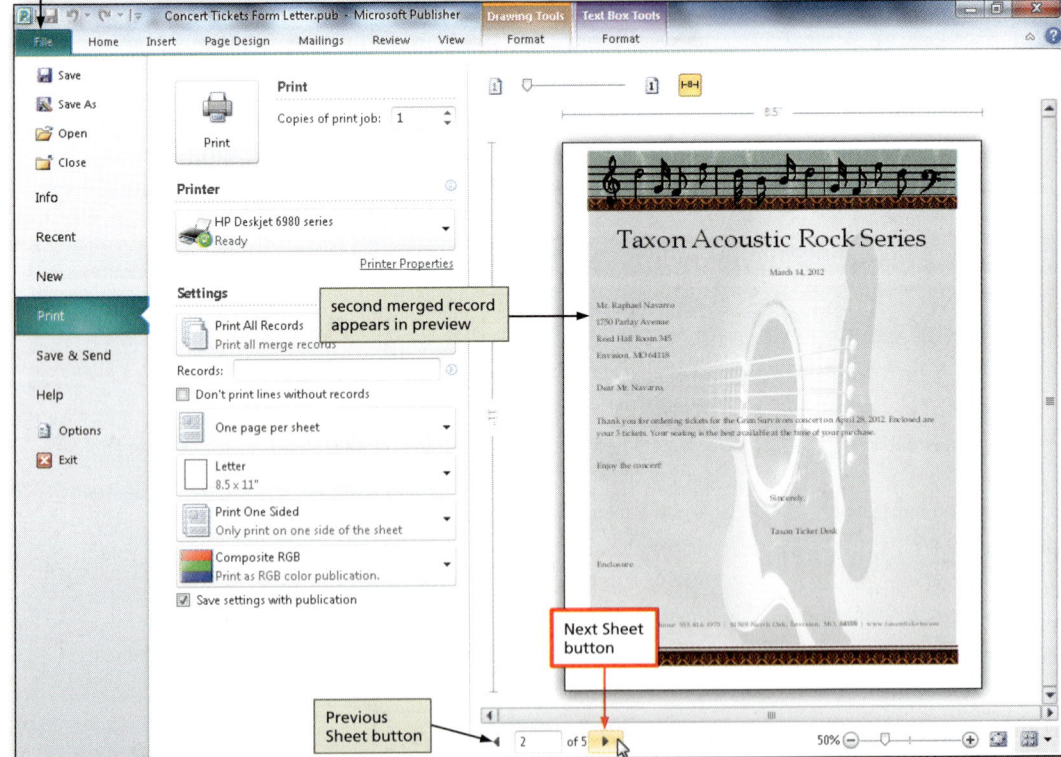

Figure 7–51

Other Ways

1. Click Preview Results button (Mailings tab | Preview Results group), click Next Record button

TO PRINT MERGED PAGES

If you wanted to print the merged publication, you would perform the following steps.

1. Ready the printer. Click the Print link (Mail Merge task pane).
2. When Publisher displays the Backstage view, verify the printer name that appears on the Printer Status button will print a hard copy of the publication. If necessary, click the Printer Status button to display a list of available printer options and then click the desired printer to change the currently selected printer.
3. Click the Print button to print the merged pages.
4. Retrieve the printouts.

To Close the Mail Merge Task Pane

The following step closes the Mail Merge task pane.

1 Click the Close button on the Mail Merge task pane title bar to close the task pane.

To Save Again

The publication is complete. The following step saves the publication again. For an example of the step listed below, refer to the Office 2010 and Windows 7 chapter at the beginning of this book.

1 Click the Save button on the Quick Access Toolbar to overwrite the previously saved file.

To Close the Publication

The next step closes the publication without quitting Publisher.

1 Display the Backstage view and then click the Close command to close the publication without quitting Publisher.

Break Point: If you wish to take a break, this is a good place to do so. You can quit Publisher now. To resume at a later time, start Publisher and continue following the steps from this location forward.

Creating Tickets

A **ticket** is a paper document or voucher to prove that a person has paid for admission or is entitled to a service. Tickets come in all sizes and are used for events, establishments, raffles, exchanges, or even as proof of receipt. Tickets may be numbered and may identify certain seating, dates, times, and charges. Tickets sometimes have a tear-off or ticket stub that is detached once the service is rendered.

The concertgoers will receive tickets along with the form letter. The theater venue has a database of row and seat number that you will merge with the ticket publication to produce a ticket for each seat in the theater, which is stored in a Microsoft Excel worksheet. This time, you will merge and insert field codes manually rather than through the wizard.

To Copy the Data Source File

Publisher recommends that the publication and its data source reside in the same folder location; therefore, the following steps copy the Microsoft Excel worksheet file from the Data Files for Students to your save location (commonly a USB drive). See the inside back cover of this book for instructions on downloading the Data Files for Students, or contact your instructor for information about accessing the required files. If you already have downloaded the Data Files for Students to the same location that you are using to create files in this chapter, you can skip these steps.

1 Click the Start button on the Windows 7 taskbar to display the Start menu.

2 Click Computer to open the Computer window.

3 Navigate to the location of the file to be opened (in this case, the Data Files for Students, to the Publisher folder, and then to the Chapter 07 folder). For a detailed example of this procedure, refer to Steps 3a–3c in the To Save a File in a Folder section in the Office 2010 and Windows 7 chapter at the beginning of this book.

4 In the Chapter 07 folder, right-click the Ticket Number and Seating List file to display its shortcut menu and then click Copy on the shortcut menu to copy the file.

5 Navigate to the desired save location (in this case, the Publisher folder in the CIS 101 folder [or your class folder] on the USB flash drive). Right-click a blank part of the right pane in the Publisher folder to display the folder's shortcut menu and then click Paste on the shortcut menu to paste the file (Figure 7–52).

6 Close the folder window.

Figure 7–52

To Open the Concert Ticket File

The following steps open the Publisher file, Concert Ticket, from the Data Files for Students. See the inside back cover of this book for instructions on downloading the Data Files for Students, or contact your instructor for information about accessing the required files.

1 In the Publisher window, click Open in the Backstage view to display the Open Publication dialog box.

2 Navigate to the location of the file to be opened (in this case, the Data Files for Students, to the Publisher folder, and then to the Chapter 07 folder). For a detailed example of this procedure, refer to the Office 2010 and Windows 7 chapter at the beginning of this book.

3 Double-click Concert Ticket to open the selected file and display the opened publication in the Publisher window (Figure 7–53).

Figure 7–53

The Mailings Tab

The Mailings tab (Figure 7–54) contains buttons and boxes to help you merge publications and data sources manually rather than through the wizard. The Start group connects you with your data source and provides access to creating, editing, and filtering lists. The Write & Insert Fields group allows you to place field codes in your publication. Using the Preview Results group, you can preview the merged publication in the publication window rather than in the Print gallery. Finally, the Finish group provides access to the same merge management tasks that are contained in Step 3 of 3 on the Mail Merge task pane (Figure 7–49 on page PUB 417).

Figure 7–54

To Select Recipients

The following steps select recipients from the Microsoft Excel worksheet that you copied to your save location earlier. The file contains the ticket numbers, seats, and rows for the concert.

- If necessary, click Mailings on the Ribbon to display the Mailings tab.
- Click the Select Recipients button (Mailings tab | Start group) to display its list (Figure 7–55).

Figure 7–55

- Click Use Existing List to open the Select Data Source dialog box.

- Navigate to the location of the file to be opened (in this case, the CIS 101 folder, and then to the Publisher folder) (Figure 7–56).

Experiment

- Click the All Data Sources button to view the many kinds of data source files that can be merged into a Publisher main publication.

Figure 7–56

- Double-click Ticket Number and Seating List to access the file and to display the Select Table dialog box.

- If necessary, click Sheet1$ in the list of tables.

- If necessary, click to display a check mark in the 'First row of data contains column headers' check box (Figure 7–57).

Q&A

Does the Microsoft Excel worksheet contain three tables?

By default, the Select Table dialog box shows references to the first three sheets of any given Excel file and would show named ranges if they existed.

Figure 7–57

• Click the OK button (Select Table
dialog box) to select the table and
display the Mail Merge Recipients
dialog box (Figure 7–58).

Figure 7–58

To Filter Data

Because the concert venue is reserving Row A tickets for members of the band, the following steps filter the
data so that no tickets will be issued for Row A.

1

• Click the Filter link (Mail Merge
Recipients dialog box) to display
the Filter and Sort
dialog box.

• If necessary, click the Filter
Records tab and then click the
Field box arrow to display its list
(Figure 7–59).

Q&A

What is the difference between
filter and sort?

Filtering examines all records
and then displays only those that
meet specific criteria that you
specify. Sorting merely rearranges
the records in a specific order, but
displays them all.

Figure 7–59

2

• Click Row in the list to filter by row.

• Click the Comparison box arrow to display its list (Figure 7–60).

Figure 7–60

3

• Click 'Not equal to' in the Comparison list to filter rows that are not equal to A.

• Press the TAB key to advance to the next box and then type **A** to insert the Compare to value (Figure 7–61).

Q&A

Will the filter delete all the tickets in row A?

No. It changes only which tickets will be used in the merge. The filter and sort links do not change your data source or mail merge permanently.

Figure 7–61

4

- Click the OK button (Filter and Sort dialog box) to accept the filter (Figure 7–62).

Q&A How did the recipient list change?

Compare Figure 7–62 to Figure 7–58 on page PUB 423. Notice the ticket rows now start with row B. Row A has been filtered out.

5

- Click the OK button (Mail Merge Recipients dialog box) to close the dialog box.

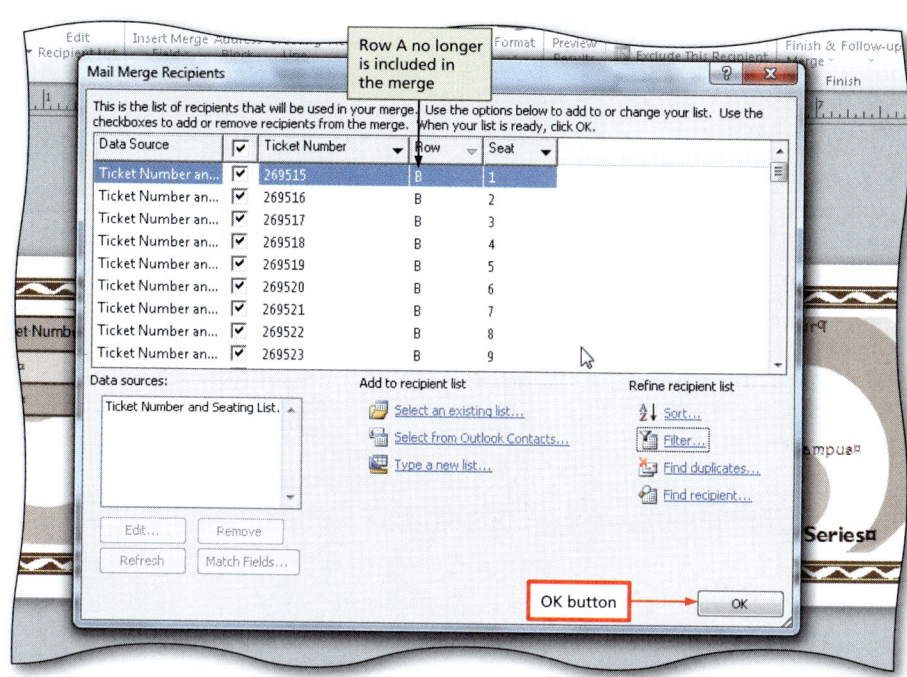

Figure 7–62

Other Ways

1. Click Edit Recipient List link (Mail Merge task pane | Step 2 of 3), click Filter link, enter filter settings

To Insert Merge Field Codes

The following steps use the Ribbon to insert merge field codes.

1

- In the publication, click the empty text box to the right of the first Ticket Number box.

- Click the Insert Merge Field button (Mailings tab | Write & Insert Fields group) to display the list of fields (Figure 7–63).

Q&A Is the empty text box part of a table?

Yes. Both the ticket stub and ticket display as a 3 × 3 table to hold the ticket information.

Figure 7–63

2

- Click Ticket Number in the list to insert the field code (Figure 7–64).

Q&A

Why did the field code wrap to the next line?

The letters in the field code itself are wider than the table cell. When the publication is merged, the ticket numbers will fit on one line.

Figure 7–64

3

- Repeat Steps 1 and 2 to insert the ticket numbers, rows, and seat for both the ticket stub and the ticket (Figure 7–65).

Q&A

How do I format the data in the field codes?

You can format field codes in the same way you format text in other parts of your publication. If the field is an Address Block or Greeting Line, you can edit the text using the Format button (Mailings tab | Write & Insert Fields group).

Figure 7–65

To Preview Results

The following step uses the Ribbon to preview the merged publication in the Publisher workspace.

1

• Click the Preview Results button (Mailings tab | Preview Results group) to display the data in the publication, rather than the fields codes (Figure 7–66).

 Experiment

• Click the Next Record and Previous Record buttons (Mailings tab | Preview Results group) to view other tickets.

Figure 7–66

Other Ways

1. Click Edit Recipient List link (Mail Merge task pane | Step 2 of 3), drag field into publication

To Print a Page of Tickets

The following steps print one page of tickets. If desired, you can insert special ticket paper or a heavy card stock paper in the printer to produce the tickets.

1

• Click the Finish & Merge button (Mailings tab | Finish group) to display its list (Figure 7–67).

Figure 7–67

2

- Click Merge to Printer to open the Print gallery in the Backstage view.

- Verify the printer name that appears on the Printer Status button will print a hard copy of the publication. If necessary, click the Printer Status button to display a list of available printer options and then click the desired printer to change the currently selected printer.

- In the Settings area, click the Print All Records button to display its list (Figure 7–68).

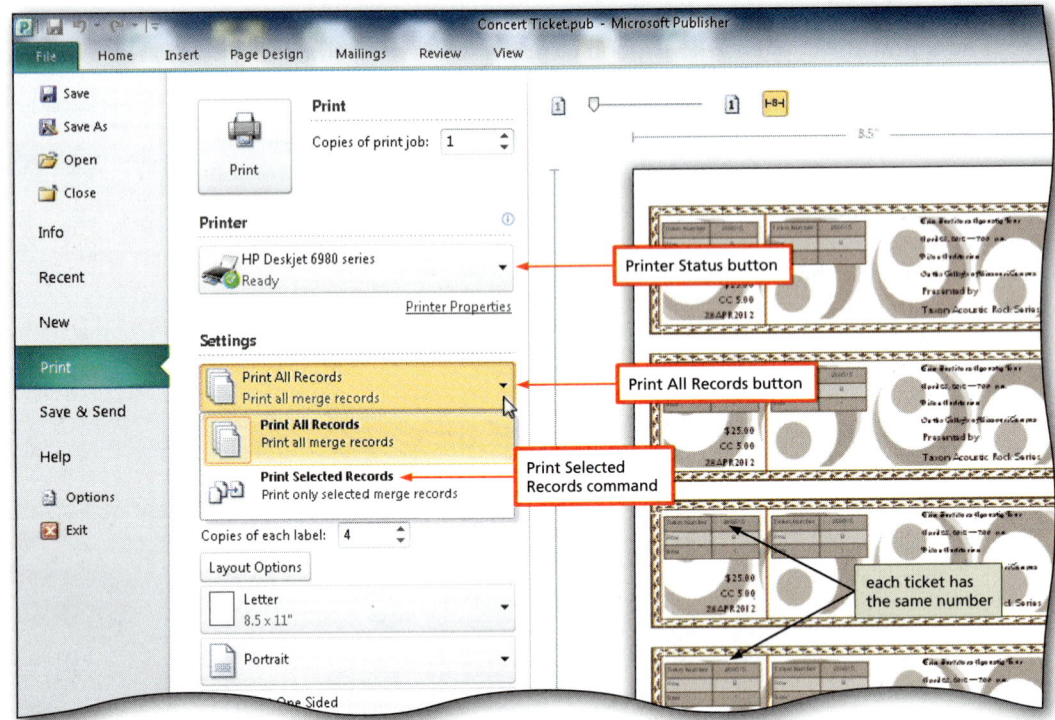

Figure 7–68

Q&A Why do all of the tickets display the same number?

The Merge to Print command creates one record per page. You will change that setting in the next step.

3

- Click Print Selected Records to specify which tickets to print.

- Click the Records text box and then type 1-4 to print the first four tickets.

- Click the 'Multiple copies per sheet' button to display its list (Figure 7–69).

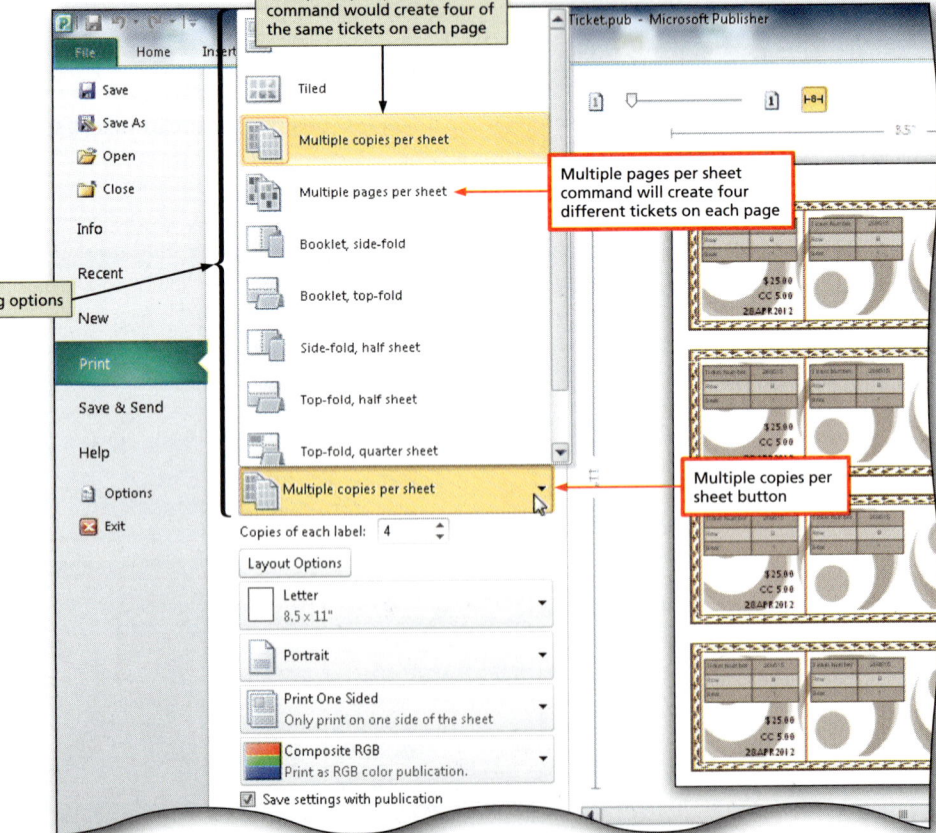

Figure 7–69

4

- Click 'Multiple pages per sheet' to choose the option.

- If necessary, type **1** in the 'Copies of each label' box.

- Verify that other settings match those shown in Figure 7–70.

 Q&A What is the difference between multiple copies per sheet and multiple pages per sheet?

The 'Multiple copies per sheet' command repeats the record data on all the copies on your printed page. The 'Multiple pages per sheet' command does not repeat the data; each ticket on the printed page has a different row, seat, and ticket number.

5

- Click the Print button in the Print gallery to print the publication on the currently selected printer.

- When the printer stops, retrieve the hard copy (Figure 7–71).

Figure 7–70

each ticket has a different number

Figure 7–71

Other Ways

1. Click Edit Recipient List link (Mail Merge task pane | Step 3 of 3), click Print link, enter print settings in Print gallery (Backstage view), click Print button

To Save the Publication with a New Name

The tickets are complete. You should save the file with a new file name before quitting Publisher.

1 With a USB flash drive connected to one of the computer's USB ports, click File on the Ribbon to display the Backstage view.

2 Click the Save as command to display the Save As dialog box.

3 Type `Concert Ticket Merged` in the File name text box to change the file name. Do not press the ENTER key after typing the file name because you do not want to close the dialog box at this time.

4 Navigate to the desired save location (in this case, the Publisher folder in the CIS 101 folder [or your class folder] on the USB flash drive).

5 Click the Save button (Save As dialog box) to save the publication in the selected folder on the selected drive with the entered file name.

To Quit Publisher

This project is complete. The following steps quit Publisher.

1 To quit Publisher, click the Close button on the right side of the title bar.

2 If a Microsoft Office Publisher dialog box is displayed, click the Don't Save button so that any editing changes you have made to the business card are not saved.

Chapter Summary

In this chapter, you have learned how to merge data files with publications. First, you created a form letter with a watermark and special character and tab formatting in the letterhead. Then, you created a Publisher data source, customizing the fields. Next, you merged the form letter with the data source, inserting field codes using the Mail Merge Wizard. Finally, you created a ticket and used a Microsoft Excel data file to merge fields manually using the Ribbon. You printed one page of tickets. The items listed below include all the new Publisher skills you have learned in this chapter.

1. View the Master Page (PUB 388)
2. Recolor the Picture (PUB 392)
3. Compress the Picture (PUB 393)
4. Close the Master Page (PUB 394)
5. Insert Letterhead Information (PUB 395)
6. Track Characters (PUB 397)
7. Kern Character Pairs (PUB 398)
8. Set a Tab Stop (PUB 401)
9. Enter Tabbed Text (PUB 401)
10. Use the Mail Merge Wizard (PUB 404)
11. Customize Data Source Columns (PUB 406)
12. Enter Data in the Data Source File (PUB 409)
13. Create New Entries in the Data Source (PUB 410)
14. Save the Data Source (PUB 411)
15. Insert Grouped Field Codes (PUB 413)
16. Insert Individual Field Codes (PUB 415)
17. Create the Merged Publication (PUB 417)
18. Preview the Form Letters (PUB 418)
19. Select Recipients (PUB 421)
20. Filter Data (PUB 423)
21. Insert Merge Field Codes (PUB 425)
22. Preview Results (PUB 427)
23. Print a Page of Tickets (PUB 427)

Learn It Online

Test your knowledge of chapter content and key terms.

Instructions: To complete the Learn It Online exercises, start your browser, click the Address bar, and then enter the Web address **scsite.com/pub2010/learn**. When the Publisher 2010 Learn It Online page is displayed, click the link for the exercise you want to complete and then read the instructions.

Chapter Reinforcement TF, MC, and SA
A series of true/false, multiple choice, and short answer questions that test your knowledge of the chapter content.

Flash Cards
An interactive learning environment where you identify chapter key terms associated with displayed definitions.

Practice Test
A series of multiple choice questions that test your knowledge of chapter content and key terms.

Who Wants To Be a Computer Genius?
An interactive game that challenges your knowledge of chapter content in the style of a television quiz show.

Wheel of Terms
An interactive game that challenges your knowledge of chapter key terms in the style of the television show *Wheel of Fortune*.

Crossword Puzzle Challenge
A crossword puzzle that challenges your knowledge of key terms presented in the chapter.

Apply Your Knowledge

Reinforce the skills and apply the concepts you learned in this chapter.

Creating Merged Invoices
Instructions: Start Publisher. Copy the data source file, Chapter 07 Recipient List, from the Data Files for Students to your storage location and appropriate folder. See the inside back cover of this book for instructions on downloading the Data Files for Students, or contact your instructor for information about accessing the required files. See page PUB 420 for instructions on copying and pasting the file from one folder to another.

The publication is an invoice that needs to be merged with a data source to produce current billing information. You are to kern characters, set tabs, edit the recipient list, and then merge and print. The first merged invoice is shown in Figure 7–72.

Continued >

Apply Your Knowledge *continued*

Victory Lawn Care
8642 Parkway Ave.
Joshua, MA 02179

Invoice

Invoice Date:	May 3, 2012	Bill To:	
Customer ID:	1331	Mr. Patrick Sheilds	
Due Date:	June 1, 2012	8115 Melbourne Lane	
		Eden, OH 46123	

Description	Amount Due
Mowing	$ 75.00

Terms: 30 days

Figure 7–72

Perform the following tasks:

1. Open the publication, Apply 7-1 Lawn Care Invoice from the Data Files for Students. Save the publication on your storage device, in the same folder as the Chapter 07 Recipient List, with the new name Apply 7-1 Lawn Care Invoice Modified.

2. Drag to select the letters Vi in the company name. Click the Object Size button on the Publisher status bar to display the Measurement toolbar. In the Kerning box, type -2.95 to move the two letters closer together. Close the Measurement toolbar.

3. Click the text box for Invoice Date, Customer ID, and Due Date. Press the F9 key to zoom to 100%. Press CTRL+A to select all of the text. Click the 1.5" mark on the horizontal ruler to set a left tab. In the text box, click after the words, Invoice Date, and then press the TAB key. Type **May 3, 2012** at the tab stop to enter the Invoice Date. Repeat the process for the Due Date and type **June 1, 2012** at the tab stop.

4. Display the Mailings tab. Click the Mail Merge button arrow (Mailings tab | Start group) and then click Step by Step Mail Merge Wizard.

5. In the Mail Merge task pane, if necessary, click the 'Use an existing list' option button and then click the 'Next wizard step' link. When Publisher displays the Select Data Source dialog box, navigate to your storage device and then double-click the file, Chapter 07 Recipient List.

6. In the Mail Merge Recipients dialog box, locate the Data sources box. Select the file name in the box and then click the Edit button (Mail Merge Recipients dialog box) to display the Edit Data Source dialog box.

7. Click the New Entry button (Edit Data Source dialog box) and enter your name and address as new data. Create a fictitious description and dollar amount. Click the OK button. When Publisher asks if you want to update and save the list, click the Yes button. When the Mail Merge Recipients dialog box again is displayed, click the OK button.

8. In the publication, select the placeholder text in the Bill To text box. In the Mail Merge task pane, select the group field code, Address block, and choose an appropriate address style in the Insert Address Block dialog box. Click the OK button (Insert Address Block dialog box) to close the dialog box.

9. In the publication, in the Invoice text box, click to the right of the colon following the words, Customer ID. Press the TAB key to move the insertion point to the tab stop. Insert the Customer ID field from the Mail Merge task pane.

10. Click in the table cell below the word, Description. Insert the Description field from the Mail Merge task pane.

11. Click the table cell below the word, Amount Due. Type $ and then press the SPACEBAR to begin the entry. Insert the Amount Due field from the Mail Merge task pane. Type .00 to finish the entry.

12. Save the publication again, using the same file name, on your storage device.

13. If you wish to print hard copies of the merged publication, do the following:

   a. Click the 'Next wizard step' link (Mail Merge task pane). Click the Print link (Mail Merge task pane) to display the Print gallery in the Backstage view.

   b. Verify the printer name that appears on the Printer Status button will print a hard copy of the publication. If necessary, click the Printer Status button to display a list of available printer options and then click the desired printer to change the currently selected printer.

   c. Change any other settings. If you wish to print only one page, type 1 in the Records box.

   d. Click the Print button in the Backstage View to print the merged pages.

   e. Retrieve the printouts.

14. See your instructor for ways to submit this assignment.

Extend Your Knowledge

Extend the skills you learned in this chapter and experiment with new skills. You may need to use Help to complete the assignment.

Filtering and Sorting a Recipient List

Instructions: Start Publisher. If you have not done so before, copy the data source file, Chapter 07 Recipient List, from the Data Files for Students to your storage location and folder. See the inside back cover of this book for instructions on downloading the Data Files for Students, or contact your instructor for information about accessing the required files. See page PUB 420 for instructions on copying and pasting the file from one folder to another. Open the publication, Extend 7-1 First America Bank Envelope, from the Data Files for Students. In this assignment, you will filter an address list for recipients living in two specific cities. Next, you will sort the list by last name and then by first name to create an alphabetical listing. Finally, you will apply the merged address block to an envelope publication.

Perform the following tasks:

1. Use Help to learn more about printing, exporting, and sorting recipient lists.

2. Save the publication with the name, Extend 7-1 First America Bank Envelope Modified.

3. Access the Mail Merge task pane. Use the list named Chapter 07 Recipient List from your storage location.

4. In the Mail Merge Recipients List dialog box, click the Filter link. Choose to filter the list with City equal to Eden. Click the And box arrow (Filter and Sort dialog box) then click OR to add a second filter with City equal to Gladstone.

5. In the Mail Merge Recipients dialog box, click the Sort link. Sort the list alphabetically first by last name and then by first name, in ascending order (Figure 7–73).

6. In the Mail Merge task pane, click the 'Next wizard step' link and then select the grouped field named Address block. Choose an appropriate address style. When Publisher displays the text box, autofit, resize, and reposition the text box so that it creates an appropriate envelope address.

7. Return to the Mail Merge task pane and proceed to the next wizard step. Click the 'Export recipient list to a new file' link (Mail Merge task pane), and save the filtered list with the file name, Extend 7-1 Eden and Gladstone Residents.

8. Click the 'Print recipient list' link (Mail Merge task pane) and include only the First Name, Last Name, Address, City, State, and Zip Code fields. Submit the copies to your instructor.

Figure 7–73

Make It Right

Analyze a publication and correct all errors and/or improve the design.

Correcting Character and Field Spacing

Instructions: Start Publisher. Open the publication, Make It Right 7-1 Golf Course Label, from the Data Files for Students. See the inside back cover of this book for instructions on downloading the Data Files for Students, or contact your instructor for more information about accessing the required files.

The publication is a large mailing label with tracking and spacing errors, and errors in the formatting of the field codes. The banner at the top also needs to be recolored as shown in Figure 7–74. You are to correct the errors and compress the pictures.

Figure 7–74

Perform the following tasks:

1. Select the text, Tee Time Golf Course. On the Measurement toolbar, track the text more loosely.

2. Kern the letters Te and Ti in Tee Time. Set the kerning to -1.95 using the Measurement toolbar.

3. In the address field codes, insert spaces between each field code. Insert a comma after the field code, City.

4. Select the banner graphic at the top of the label. Use the Picture Tools Format tab and the Adjust group to recolor the graphic. Use a darker variation of the green coloring.

5. Compress all pictures in the publication to reduce the file size.

6. Save the publication with the file name, Make It Right 7-1 Golf Course Label Modified.

7. Send an electronic copy of the file to your instructor via e-mail if your instructor gives you permission to do so.

In the Lab

Design and/or create a publication using the guidelines, concepts, and skills presented in this chapter. Labs are listed in order of increasing difficulty.

Lab 1: Creating a Form Letter

Problem: A university has received an address list of interested students from local high school guidance counselors. The admissions department would like to send out a letter to prospective students (Figure 7–75).

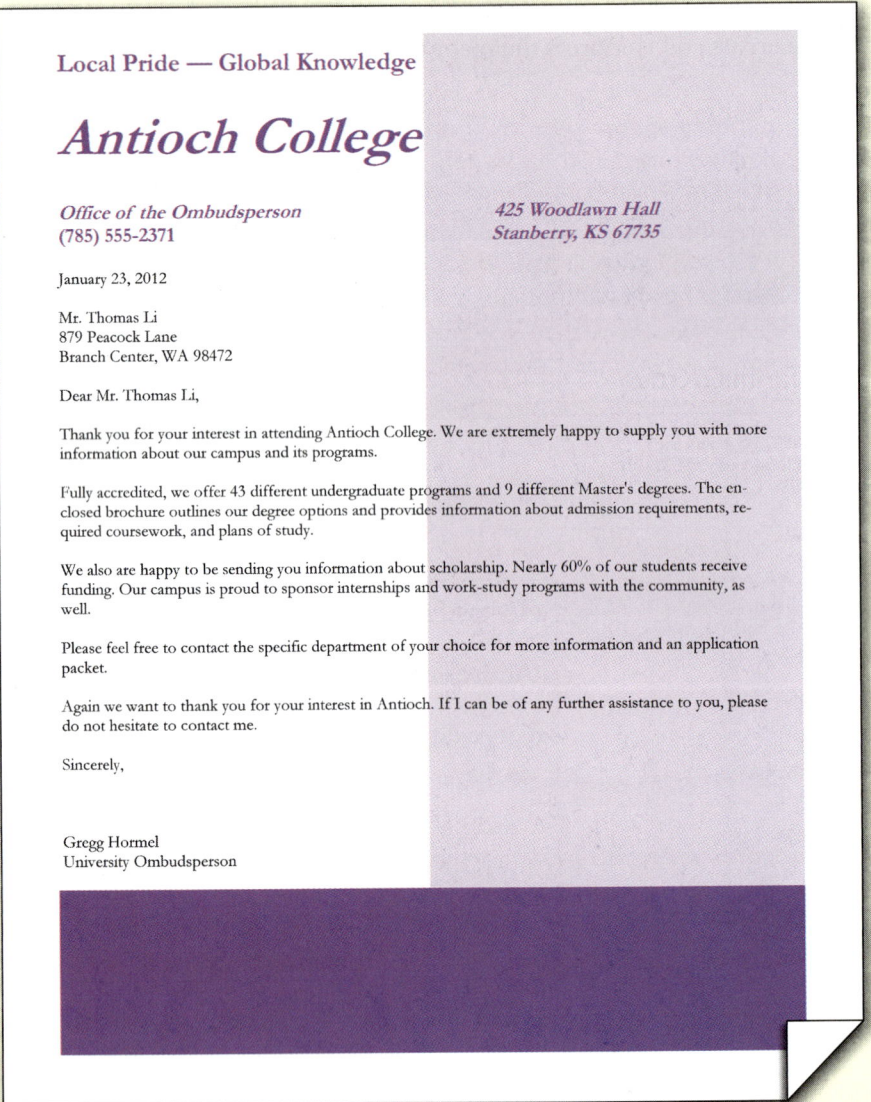

Figure 7–75

Instructions: Perform the following tasks:

1. Start Publisher with a blank 8.5 × 11" page. Use the Page Design tab to choose the Orchid color scheme and the Modern font scheme.

2. At the top of the publication, create three text boxes that begin at the left margin, approximately 6 inches wide and 1 inch tall.

   a. In the first text box, type `Local Pride – Global Knowledge` and then format the text to use a color from the color scheme, bold the text, and use a font size of 18.

b. In the second text box, type `Antioch College` and then format the text to use a color from the color scheme. Bold and italicize the text and use a font size of 36.

c. Position your insertion point in the third text box. Click the tab selector on the left side of the horizontal ruler, until a right tab is displayed. Click the ruler at approximately 5.75 inches to create a tab. Use a font color from the color scheme and then bold and italicize the font. Type `Office of the Ombudsperson` and then press the TAB key. Type `425 Woodlawn Hall` and then press the ENTER key. Type `(785) 555-2371` and then press the TAB key. Type `Stanberry, KS 67735` to complete the text.

3. Create a large rectangle shape on the right size of the letter as shown in Figure 7-75. Fill it with the light purple color from the color scheme. Send it backward, behind the text.

4. Create a large rectangle shape at the bottom of the letter. Fill it with the dark purple color from the color scheme.

5. Access the Step by Step Mail Merge Wizard and click the 'Type a new list' option button.

6. Click the 'Next wizard step' link. When the New Address List dialog box is displayed, click the Customize Columns button (New Address List dialog box) and then delete all columns that do not appear in Table 7–8. When you are finished, click the OK button (Customize Address List dialog box) to return to the New Address List dialog box.

7. Enter the data from Table 7–8. Enter your name as a fifth record to the address list. When Publisher asks you to name the address list, navigate to your storage device and save the file with the name, Lab 7-1 College Recipient List.

Table 7–8 College Recipient List						
Title	**First Name**	**Last Name**	**Address**	**City**	**State**	**Zip Code**
Mr.	Dang	Chou	764 Clay Street	Colby	KS	67701
Ms.	Michelle	Knight	267 Green Way	Scott City	KS	67871
Mr.	Raphael	Garcia	345 Norton Ave.	Goodland	KS	67735
Mr.	Patrick	See	1422 88th St.	Hays	KS	67601

8. Create a large text box to hold the letter. In the text box, insert the current date and then press the ENTER key twice.

9. With the insertion point in the text box, insert the grouped field named Address block from the Mail Merge task pane. Choose an appropriate style. When Publisher inserts the Address block into the publication, click after the field code, and then press the ENTER key twice.

10. Insert the grouped field named Greeting Line from the Mail Merge task pane. Choose an appropriate style. Click after the field code in the publication and then press the ENTER key twice.

11. Click the Insert File button (Insert tab | Text group). Navigate to the Data Files for Students. See the inside back cover of this book for instructions on downloading the Data Files for Students, or contact your instructor for information about accessing the required files. Select the Microsoft Word file named, Lab 7-1 Antioch College Letter, and insert it as the body of the letter. Adjust the font size as necessary to make sure the letter fits on the page.

12. Save the publication using the file name, Lab 7-1 College Form Letter.

13. In the Mail Merge Task pane, click the 'Next wizard step' link. Click the print link.

14. When Publisher displays the Print gallery, navigate to the letter with your name and print one copy. Submit it to your instructor.

In the Lab

Lab 2: Create a Set of Play Tickets

Problem: A local theater company needs tickets that are individualized for seat assignments as shown in Figure 7–76. You will create the ticket and then merge it with an Excel spreadsheet that contains the seat numbers. The spreadsheet is located in the Data Files for Students. See the inside back cover of this book for instructions on downloading the Data Files for Students, or contact your instructor for information about accessing the required files. Copy and paste the file, Lab 7-2 Play Ticket Seat Numbers, to your storage location (see page PUB 420 for copy and paste instructions).

Instructions: Perform the following tasks:

1. Start Publisher. Choose the blank business card template labeled North American Size 3.5 × 2".

2. Select the Redwood color scheme and the Metro font scheme, and then create the publication.

3. In the publication, draw a text box approximately 3 × .5 inches. Position it in the upper center of the card. Change the font size to 26. Type `A KING'S RANSOM` in the text box. Right-justify the text.

4. Draw a text box approximately 2.1 × .4 inches. Position it right-aligned with the previous text box. Change the font size to 18. Type `A play in three acts` in the text box. Right-justify the text.

5. Draw another text box approximately 2.1 × .4 inches. Position it left-aligned with the previous text box. Change the font size to 7. Type `Friday, February 24, 2012 at 7:30 p.m.` and then press the ENTER key. Type `Stellar Auditorium — 303 Main Street` to complete the text.

6. Click the Table button (Insert tab | Tables group) and insert a 6 × 1 table size. Select the table and then display all borders. To resize the table, click the Object Size button on the Publisher status bar to display the Measurement toolbar. Type `2.2` in the Width box. Type `.3` in the Height box. Position the table in the lower right corner of the page layout, within the margin guides.

7. Drag to select all the cells and then set the font size to 6. Type `Section` in the first cell, `Row` in the third cell, and `Seat` in the fifth cell.

8. Insert a graphic using the Clip Art task pane. Search using the keyword, king. Insert a picture similar to the one shown in Figure 7–76. Position the picture in the lower-left corner of the publication.

9. To create the border, click the Shapes button (Insert tab | Illustrations group) and then click Rectangle in the Shapes gallery. Draw a rectangle around all of the objects. Right-click the rectangle and then click Format AutoShape on the shortcut menu. In the Colors and Lines sheet (Format AutoShape dialog box), click the BorderArt button and select a border similar to the one shown in Figure 7–76.

Figure 7–76

10. Access the Mail Merge task pane. Choose to use an existing list. When Publisher displays the Select Data Source dialog box, navigate to your storage device and choose the Lab 7-2 Play Ticket Seat Numbers file. Choose the Sheet1$ table. Do not filter or sort the data.

11. In the publication, click the second cell in the table and then click Section in the list of fields (Mail Merge task pane). Click the fourth cell in the table and then click Row in the list of fields. Click the sixth cell in the table, and then click Seat in the list of fields.

12. Save the publication on your storage device with the name, Lab 7-2 Play Tickets.

13. In the Mail Merge task pane, choose to create the merged publication. Click the Print link (Mail Merge task pane) to display the Print gallery. Select Multiple pages per sheet. Choose to print records 1–8, which will print the first page of tickets. Submit the printout to your instructor.

In the Lab

Lab 3: Using Tab Stops in a Publication

Problem: Your student club is having a bake sale. They have asked you to prepare the sign shown in Figure 7–77.

Instructions: Perform the following tasks: Create a blank publication with one large text box. Center the words, Bake Sale, on the first line of the text box, using a large, bold font. Press the ENTER key and then change the font size to 28 and the justification to left. Press the ENTER key again to move down in the text box. Click the tab selector box until it displays the center tab. Click the ruler at the 3.5" mark to create a center tab. Click the tab selector box until it displays a right tab. Click the ruler at the 6.75" mark to create the right tab. Type the text from Table 7–9. Save the file. Print a copy of the sign.

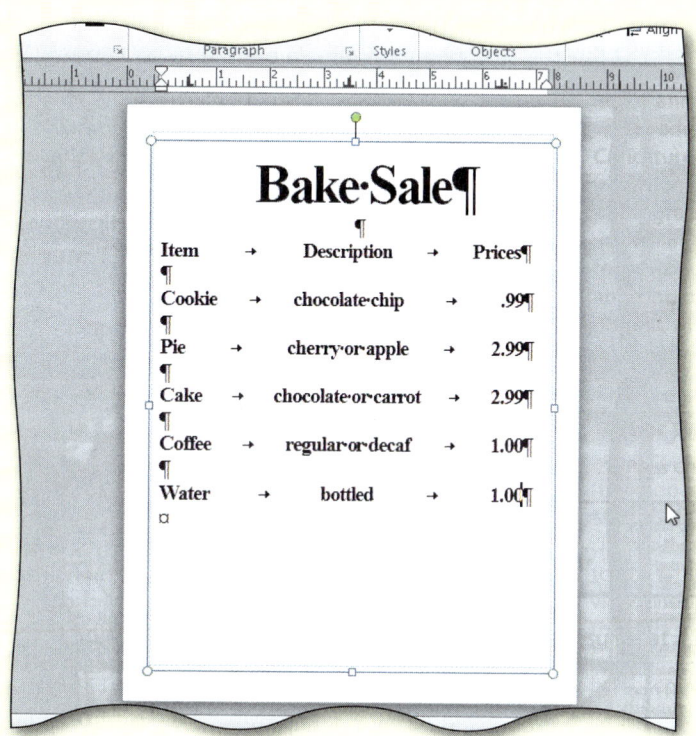

Figure 7–77

Table 7–9 Data for the Bake Sale Sign		
Item	**Description**	**Prices**
Cookie	chocolate chip	.99
Pie	cherry or apple	2.99
Cake	chocolate or carrot	2.99
Coffee	regular or decaf	1.00
Water	bottled	1.00

Cases and Places

Apply your creative thinking and problem solving skills to design and implement a solution.

Note: To complete these assignments, you may be required to use the Data Files for Students. See the inside back cover of this book for instructions on downloading the Data Files for Students, or contact your instructor for information about accessing the required files.

1: Update a Recipient List

Academic

The Department of English wants to update its database of graduate students. Specifically, they want to be able to sort the data by last name, but the database contains the first and last names in the same field. Copy the data source file, Case 7-1 Graduate Students, from the Data Files for Students to your storage location and appropriate folder. Start Publisher with a blank publication. Click the Select Recipients button (Mailings tab | Start group) and navigate to your storage location. Double-click the Case 7-1 Graduate Students file. When the Mail Merge Recipients dialog box appears, select the file in the Data sources box, and then click the Edit button. Use the Customize Columns button (Mail Merge Recipients data base) to create a new column entitled Last Name. Move the new column up below the column entitled, Name. Rename the Name column with the new title, First Name. Edit the data in the fields to split the first name and last name. When prompted save the updated list.

2: Create a Movie Logo

Personal

Create a one-page flyer from scratch, advertising your favorite movie. Design a text-based logo for the title of the movie. Use a font that goes with the theme of the movie. For example, a comedy movie might use the Joker, Jokewood, or Comic Sans fonts; a classic movie might use a serif font; or a horror movie might use the Showcard Gothic or the Chiller font. Use the Measurement toolbar to edit the character spacing. Use a font size of at least 48. Adjust the text scaling of the first letter of each word to give your text logo its own special character. Kern at least one character pair to improve the logo. Change the tracking on all of the characters.

3: Create a Form Letter and Data Source

Professional

You are activities chairperson for a Summer Day Camp. Letters must be sent to parents informing them of the event rules. Create a form letter using the following information: First United Church; 6100 Ridge Road; Allegria, NM, 87501; Telephone: (505) 557-4700; Fax: (505) 557-4701. Create the data source shown in Table 7–10. Customize the columns as necessary. Use the name and address field codes for the first part of the address. Enter the same city, state, and postal code for all letters: Allegria, NM, 87501. The first paragraph of the letter will include the Child Gender field code and should say: Summer Day Camp is scheduled from July 23 through 27 at the church outdoor shelter. Camp will be from 9:00 A.M. to 3:00 P.M. each day. Your <<Child Gender>> should bring the following items, labeled with the child's name, in a backpack: extra socks and shoes, sweatshirt, raincoat, water bottle, insect repellent, mess kit, and sit-upon. The next paragraph should say: If you have any questions, please contact Donna at 557-4700.

Table 7–10 Data for Summer Day Camp Address List

Title	First Name	Last Name	Address Line 1	Address Line 2	Child Gender
Mrs.	Lourdes	Nunez	1567 Katuche		son
Ms.	Juanita	Espinoza	1145 Santa Fe Drive		daughter
Dr.	Melinda	Enderly	1235 Main St.	Suite 102	daughter
Mr.	Michael	Louks	9876 Desert Road	Apt. 107	son

8 | Generating Data-Driven Catalogs

Objectives

You will have mastered the material in this chapter when you can:

- View, rename, and duplicate a master page
- Add a background to a master page
- Insert headers and footers
- Correct and edit publications using AutoCorrect
- Apply alternating master pages
- Create catalog pages

- Use the catalog merge area
- Select a data source
- Format picture fields
- Find and exclude entries
- Preview and merge catalogs
- Work with the Graphics Manager
- Translate text

8 | Generating Data-Driven Catalogs

Introduction

Businesses need quick and efficient ways to market their products and services. **Direct marketing**, also called **direct response advertising**, is a form of advertising that reaches its audience without using traditional advertising media such as newspapers, television, or radio. With direct marketing, companies communicate directly with the consumer using advertising techniques such as fliers, catalogs, promotional letters, and street advertising. Companies can track the success of direct marketing more easily than when using other media. A message in a catalog for example, to call or e-mail, can be tracked as a positive response from the customer.

Businesses of all sizes use direct marketing. A well-executed direct marketing campaign can offer a positive return on investment because the message is not hidden by complicated branding. Direct marketing advertisements should be straight to the point, offering a product, service, or event, and explaining how to obtain that product, service, or event.

As a marketing tool, a catalog helps you compete for preferred status with buyers. Catalogs streamline the buying cycle by providing complete descriptions and easy buying steps, eliminating inefficiencies, omissions, and lost opportunities. Planned and distributed correctly, catalogs reach a wider market than brochures and newsletters, and they reduce redundant forms of contact, such as answering questions over the telephone or running repeated newspaper ads.

As most businesses keep track of their inventory and statistics in electronic databases, it is efficient to use that data to build custom marketing pieces such as catalogs, for print media or for e-commerce applications on the Web. A publication directly populated and updated from a database is considered a **data-driven publication**. Many businesses customize catalogs and use customer profiling to target certain markets. A catalog is a significant investment due to production, printing, and distribution costs. Publishing a catalog can be the largest single marketing cost in an annual budget.

Project — Textbook Catalog

Figure 8–1 displays a catalog describing textbooks from a textbook publishing company. The catalog has pictures of the textbook covers, descriptions of the books, and other pieces of data in which the customer might be interested. The catalog contains 12 pages, printed on both sides of 8.5 × 11-inch paper, and folded.

Publisher's catalog merge differs from its mail merge in two distinctive ways. The catalog merge is designed with graphics or pictures in mind. It is easy to incorporate pictures into the merge process—pictures that change from record to record. Secondly, a catalog merge includes all records in one longer booklet publication, rather than separate pages like letters. Toward that end, Publisher provides a unique merge area that desktop publishers use to design their presentation with fields that change from record to record, and layout that does not.

Figure 8–1

Overview

As you read this chapter, you will learn how to create the catalog shown in Figure 8–1 by performing these general tasks:

- Create alternating master pages for a catalog.

- Insert a background, header, and footer.

- Correct typographical errors and misspellings using the AutoCorrect feature.

- Use catalog pages to create a repeatable merge area.

- Merge a catalog with its data source and insert fields.

- Format, find, and exclude entries or records in the data source.

- Work with the Graphics Manager.

- Translate a sentence in the catalog.

- Preview, merge, and print a catalog.

General Project Guidelines

When creating a Publisher publication, the actions you perform and decisions you make will affect the appearance and characteristics of the finished document. As you create a catalog, such as the one shown in Figure 8–1 on the previous page, you should follow these general guidelines:

1. **Plan your catalog layout.** Organize your layout around your product or service, and focus on how that product or service will help your customer or audience. Use fonts and color to attract your target audience.

2. **Use high-quality graphics.** An eye-catching graphical image should convey the catalog's overall message. It could show a product, service, result, or benefit, or it could visually convey a message that is not expressed easily with words.

3. **Use efficient methods to move through the catalog and merged pages.** Use appropriate Publisher tools to move through the catalog, including the Catalog Tools Format tab and the Graphics Manager.

4. **Translate text that is important to readers of another language.** Use the Translation tool for short passages of text or individual words in your publications. If the entire publication needs to be translated, use a professional translator.

When necessary, more specific details concerning the above guidelines are presented at appropriate points in the chapter. The chapter also will identify the actions performed and decisions made regarding these guidelines during the creation of the catalog shown in Figure 8–1.

To Start Publisher

The following steps, which assume Windows 7 is running, start Publisher based on a typical installation. You may need to ask your instructor how to start Publisher for your computer. For a detailed example of the procedure summarized below, refer to the Office 2010 and Windows 7 chapter at the beginning of this book.

1 Click the Start button on the Windows 7 taskbar to display the Start menu.

2 Type `Microsoft Publisher` as the search text in the 'Search programs and files' text box, and watch the search results appear on the Start menu.

3 Click Microsoft Publisher 2010 in the search results on the Start menu to start Publisher and open the Backstage view and the New Template gallery.

4 If the Publisher window is not maximized, click the Maximize button next to the Close button on its title bar to maximize the window.

Catalogs

A **catalog** is a collection of pictures and descriptive details, representing items for sale or services. Publisher has catalog templates to assist you in designing catalogs, and it provides a catalog merge that quickly and easily populates the catalog. A catalog merge is the process of combining information from a product list data source with a template to create pages that display multiple records per page. You can add the merged pages to an existing publication or create a new publication.

Typically, Publisher catalog templates create eight pages of content with replaceable graphics and text boxes. You can select the page size, font scheme, and color scheme of the catalog, just as you do with other publications. Additionally, with catalogs, you can choose the content layout of specific pages, selecting the number of columns, forms, calendars, featured items, or table of contents for those pages. Alternately, you can create a catalog from scratch, designing your pages one at a time, or by using a blank catalog template, as you will do in this project.

Plan
Ahead

Plan your catalog layout.
Due to the graphical, full-color nature of most catalogs and the high-quality paper that commonly is used, planning is essential to keep a catalog project on schedule and within budget. You must identify resource requirements and formulate strategies that drive business growth. Typically, a business can reuse and repurpose catalog content for other forms of advertisements, such as seasonal promotion publications. Many companies store pictures and data together in database files ready to populate catalogs, brochures, and Web sites. Here are some general rules when you are planning your layout:

- Create your catalog in a common size. It will be less costly at both the printer and the post office.
- Use an even number of pages to avoid blank pages in your catalog. Check ahead of time to find out how many records of data are in the data source.
- Alternate headers and footers as necessary to create outside edge page numbers.
- Create a layout that will attract your audience. A business-to-business catalog (B2B) is different from a business-to-consumer (B2C) catalog. Catalogs for young people will have a different look than a catalog for older people. Make the style of your catalog match the style desires of your audience.
- Repeat layout designs or use alternating pages for consistency. Do not make the customer look for information in two places. For example, keep your prices in approximately the same place in each repeating element.
- Repeat some objects to provide consistency. User headers and footers or a background to create a cohesive unit.
- Keep the name of the product close to any pictures or graphics.
- Limit the fonts to two or three, and use WordArt sparingly.

To Create a Two-Page Spread

The following steps choose a blank catalog template, and set the font and color schemes for the catalog. Because it is a catalog template, Publisher will offer to create multiple pages, using a two-page spread. A **two-page spread**, or simply a **spread**, refers to the way inner pages appear as two adjacent, facing pages in a book, catalog, magazine, or other publication.

- In the New Template gallery, click Catalogs to view the available templates.

- Scroll to the middle portion of the gallery to display the Blank Sizes area.

- Click the 1/2 Letter Booklet 5.5 × 8.5" template to select it.

- In the Customize area, select the Module color scheme and the Office Classic 1 font scheme.

- Click the Create button to display the catalog and the Microsoft Publisher dialog box (Figure 8–2).

Figure 8–2

- Click the Yes button (Microsoft Publisher dialog box) to have Publisher create an even number of pages in the publication.

- If the Page Navigation pane does not appear, click the Page Number button on the status bar.

- If the Page Navigation pane is collapsed, click the Expand Page Navigation Pane button at the top of the Page Navigation.

Q&A Why did Publisher display three icons in the Page Navigation pane?
The front and back of a catalog are single pages. Pages 2 and 3 appear as a two-page spread.

BTW

BTWs
For a complete list of the BTWs found in the margins of this book, visit the Publisher 2010 BTW Web page (scsite.com/pub2010/btw).

Alternating Master Pages

Recall that a master page is background area used to create repeatable elements such as headers, footers, watermarks, and layout guides. You created a watermark in an earlier chapter and placed it on the master page, so that it would appear on every page of your printed publication. In publications that have more than one page, you can create multiple, alternating master pages for a more versatile publication design. For example, in publications that use a spread, it is common to create multiple master pages for verso (left) and recto (right) pages or for the front and back pages.

In Publisher, the default is Normal view. **Normal view** is the view where you perform most of the tasks while creating a publication. **Master Page view** shows you the page or pages that contain the elements that you want to repeat on multiple pages.

Backgrounds

A **background**, or page fill, is a color, gradient, pattern, texture, picture, or tint that fills the entire page. This adds visual interest to the publication or provides contrast when you do not want to use a plain white page. Recall that you added a gradient fill to a shape in an earlier chapter; backgrounds work the same way. Applying a background in Normal view creates the background on that page only. Applying a background in Master Page view creates a background on every page. Publisher has a gallery from which you may choose a background, or you can create your own background.

To Add a Background to a Master Page

The following steps add a background to the master page.

1
- Press CTRL+M to display the master page.

- Display the Page Design tab and then click the Background button (Page Design tab | Page Background group) to display the gallery of backgrounds (Figure 8–3).

 Experiment
- Point to each of the backgrounds and watch the live preview.

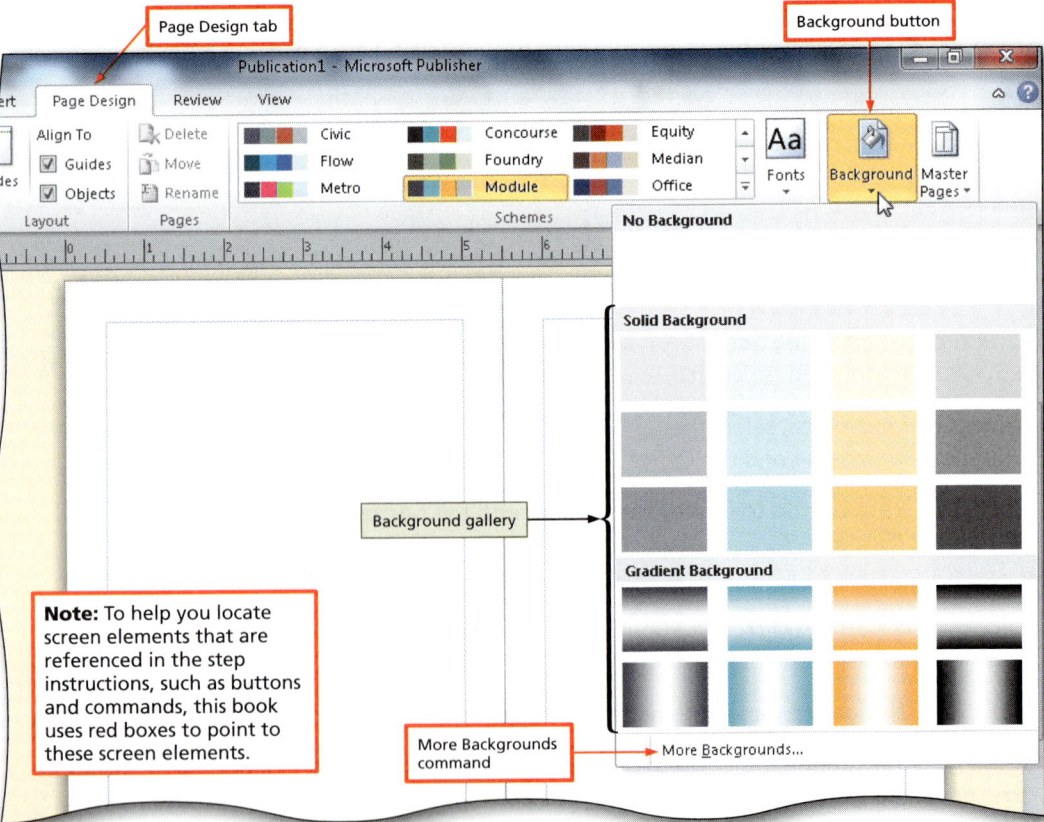

Figure 8–3

2

- Click More Backgrounds to display the Fill Effects dialog box.

- Click the Texture tab (Fill Effects dialog box) to display the available textures.

- Click the Parchment texture to select it (Figure 8–4).

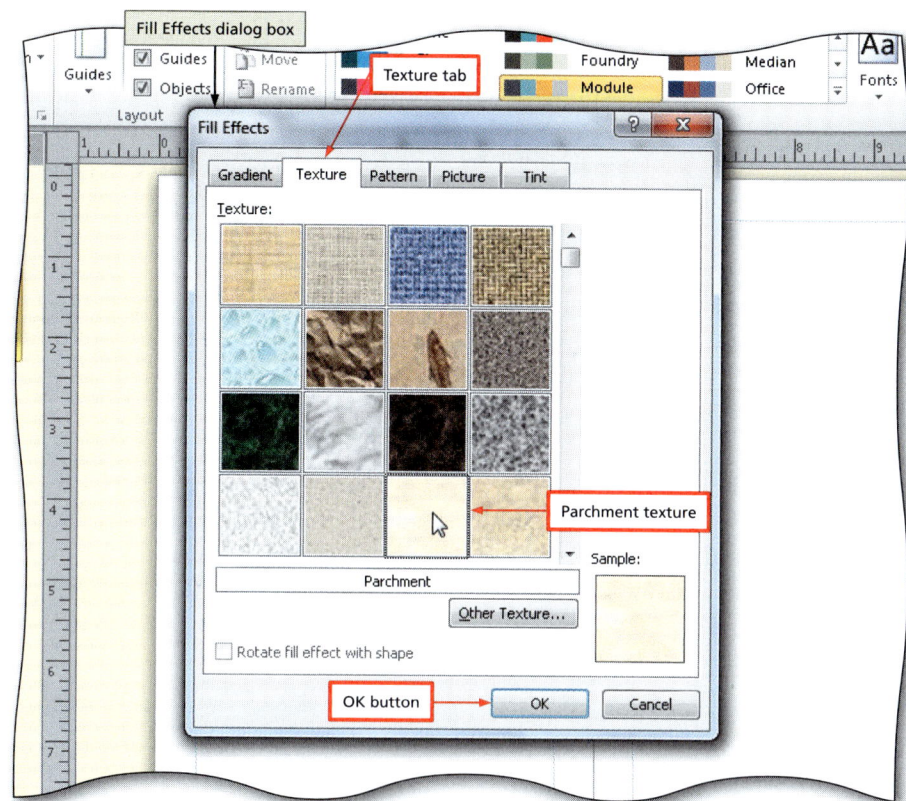

Figure 8–4

3

- Click the OK button (Fill Effects dialog box) to apply the background to the master page (Figure 8–5).

Q&A

Could I have created the background in Normal view?

Yes, but it would have applied to only the current page. Creating the background in Master Page view applies it to all pages.

Figure 8–5

Headers and Footers

A **header** is text and graphics that print at the top of each page in a publication. Similarly, a **footer** is text and graphics that print at the bottom of every page. In Publisher, headers print one-half inch from the top margin of every page, and footers print one-half inch from the bottom margin of every page. In addition to text and graphics, headers and footers can include document information such as the page number, current date, current time, and author's name.

The Show Header/Footer button (Master Page tab | Header & Footer group) toggles between the header and footer areas, displaying a text box in which you can insert text elements. If you want to use a graphic, you must insert the graphic and drag it to the header area.

To Insert a Header

The following steps add a graphic header to the master page. To complete these steps, you will be required to use the Data Files for Students. See the inside back cover of this book for instructions on downloading the Data Files for Students, or contact your instructor for information about accessing the required files.

Later in the chapter, you will add a footer that appears only on the inside pages.

- In Master Page view, display the Insert tab.

- Click the Insert Picture from File button (Insert tab | Illustrations group) to display the Insert Picture dialog box.

- Navigate to the Data Files for Students and the Chapter 08 folder (Figure 8–6).

Q&A Could I use the Show Header/Footer button?

The Show Header/Footer button (Master Page tab | Header & Footer group) creates a text box for you to enter a text header or footer or insert predefined text objects such as date or page number. When inserting a graphic, you simply drag it to the header or footer area.

Figure 8–6

- Double-click the file named, Left Masthead, to insert it into the publication.

- Drag the graphic to the top of the left page (Figure 8–7).

Figure 8–7

- Repeat Steps 1 and 2 to insert the graphic named, Right Masthead, and then drag it to the header area on the right page. Use the pink navigation guides to align the graphic with the previous one (Figure 8–8).

Figure 8–8

Other Ways

1. To enter a text header, click the Show Header/ Footer button (Master Page tab | Header & Footer group), type text

To Duplicate the Master Page

Creating a second master page by duplicating the first will retain the background and headers. The following steps create a second master page.

- Display the Master Page tab.

- Click the Duplicate button (Master Page tab | Master Page group) to display the Duplicate Master Page dialog box.

- With the Description text box selected, type **Inside Pages** to describe the duplicate master page (Figure 8–9).

Q&A

How does Publisher use the description that I entered?

The description appears in a ScreenTip when you point to the master page in the Page Navigation pane. You can change the description by clicking the Rename button (Master Page tab | Master Page group).

Figure 8–9

- Click the OK button (Duplicate Master Page dialog box) to close the dialog box.

Other Ways

1. Right-click thumbnail (Page Navigation pane), click Insert Duplicate Page on shortcut menu, right-click new thumbnail, click Rename on shortcut menu, enter description, click OK button (Rename Master Page dialog box)

To Insert Alternating Footers

The master page for the front and back of the catalog will not display a footer. The inside pages will display a footer with a page number and the company's Web site address.

In many publications that contain facing pages, the page number is located on the outside edges of the pages. In Publisher, you accomplish this task by specifying one type of footer for left pages and another type for right pages. The following steps create alternating footers for the inside pages.

- With master page B selected, click the Show Header/Footer button (Master Page tab | Header & Footer group) and then click the button again to move to the footer area.

- Type **Page** and then press the SPACEBAR.

- Click the Insert Page Number button (Master Page tab | Header & Footer group) to enter the page number placeholder (Figure 8–10).

Q&A Could I have just typed the # symbol?

No. The symbol that Publisher inserts is a field code that automatically is populated with the page number.

Figure 8–10

- Press the TAB key twice.

- Type **www.scsite.com** to enter the Web address (Figure 8–11).

Q&A Were tab stops created automatically?

Yes, the footer text box has a center tab and a right tab because most users place footer information at one of those two locations or at the left margin.

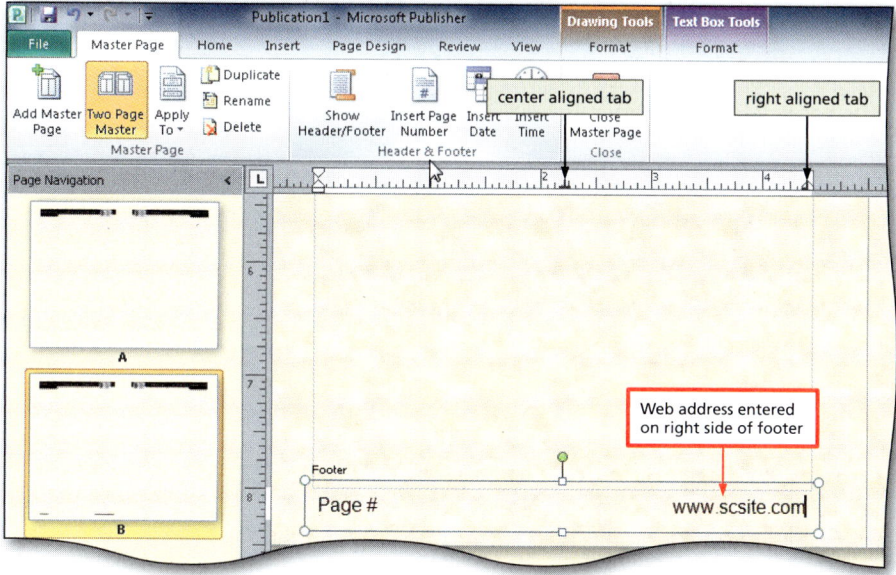

Figure 8–11

- Click the bottom of the right page in the two-page spread to display the footer text box for the alternating footer (Figure 8–12).

Figure 8–12

To AutoCorrect as You Type

As you type, you may make typing, spelling, capitalization, or grammar errors. For this reason, Publisher provides an **AutoCorrect** feature that automatically corrects these kinds of errors as you type them in the publication. For example, if you type ahve, Publisher automatically changes it to the correct spelling, have, when you press the SPACEBAR or type a punctuation mark, such as a period or comma.

The AutoCorrect feature is not limited to misspelled words. Publisher will correct typographical errors such as two capitalized letters at the beginning of a word, a lowercase letter at the beginning of a sentence, and accidental use of the CAPS LOCK key, among others.

Publisher has predefined these typographical errors and many commonly misspelled words, which it automatically corrects for you. The following steps intentionally misspell the word, the, as teh to illustrate the AutoCorrect feature.

1
- In the footer text box, type **teh** to enter the intentional misspelling (Figure 8–13).

Figure 8–13

2
- Press the SPACEBAR and watch Publisher automatically correct the misspelled word (Figure 8–14).

3
- Backspace to remove the word, the, from the footer.

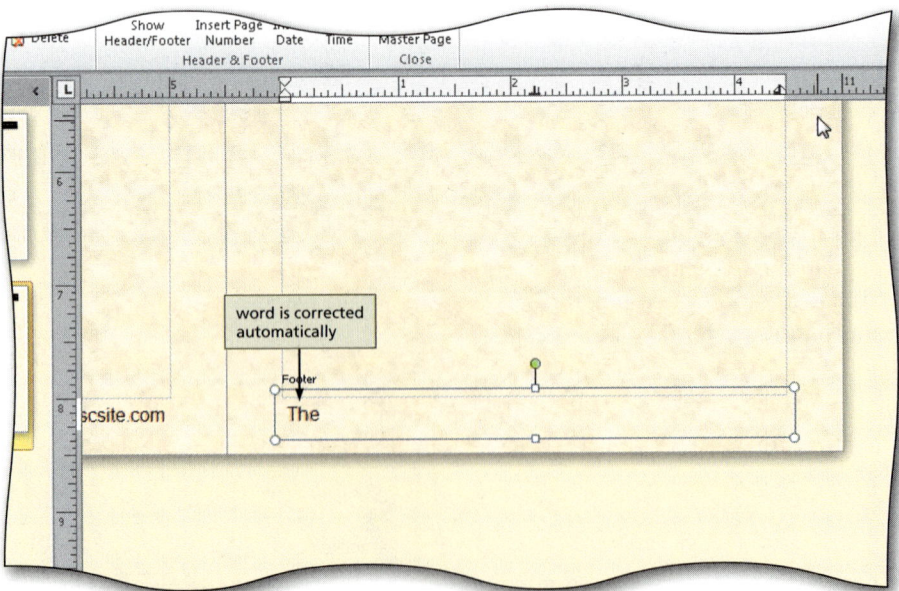

Figure 8–14

To Use the AutoCorrect Options Button

When you position the mouse pointer on text that Publisher automatically corrected, a small blue box appears below the text. If you point to the small blue box, Publisher displays the AutoCorrect Options button. When you click the **AutoCorrect Options button**, Publisher displays a menu that allows you to undo a correction or change how Publisher handles future automatic corrections of this type. The following steps use the AutoCorrect Options button and menu.

- At the left margin of the footer text box, type `www.scsite .com` and watch Publisher automatically capitalize the first letter (Figure 8–15).

Q&A

Why did Publisher insert a capital W on this footer and not the other one?

This footer begins with the Web address. Publisher interprets this as the beginning of a sentence, and capitalizes the first letter.

Figure 8–15

- Move the mouse pointer close to the capital W.

- Point to the small blue box to display the AutoCorrect Options button (Figure 8–16).

Figure 8–16

- Click the AutoCorrect Options button to display the AutoCorrect Options menu (Figure 8–17).

Q&A

How would I remove the AutoCorrect Options button from the screen?

When you move the mouse pointer, the AutoCorrect Options button will disappear from the screen. Or, you can press the ESCAPE key twice.

Figure 8–17

4
- Click Stop Auto-capitalizing First Letters of Sentences to change the setting (Figure 8–18).

letter no longer is capitalized

Footer

scsite.com   www.scsite.com

Figure 8–18

To Complete the Footer

The following steps complete the footer by inserting the word, Page, and a page number placeholder.

1 Press the TAB key twice. Type the word `Page` and then press the SPACEBAR.

2 Click the Insert Page Number button (Master Page tab | Header & Footer group) to enter the page number placeholder (Figure 8–19).

Insert Page Number button

page number field code

Footer

scsite.com   www.scsite.com   Page #

Figure 8–19

To Create an AutoCorrect Entry

In addition to the predefined list of AutoCorrect spelling, capitalization, and grammar errors, you can create your own AutoCorrect entries to add to the list. For example, if you tend to type the word, contact, as contat, you should create an AutoCorrect entry for it. The following steps create an AutoCorrect entry.

• Click File on the Ribbon to open the Backstage view (Figure 8–20).

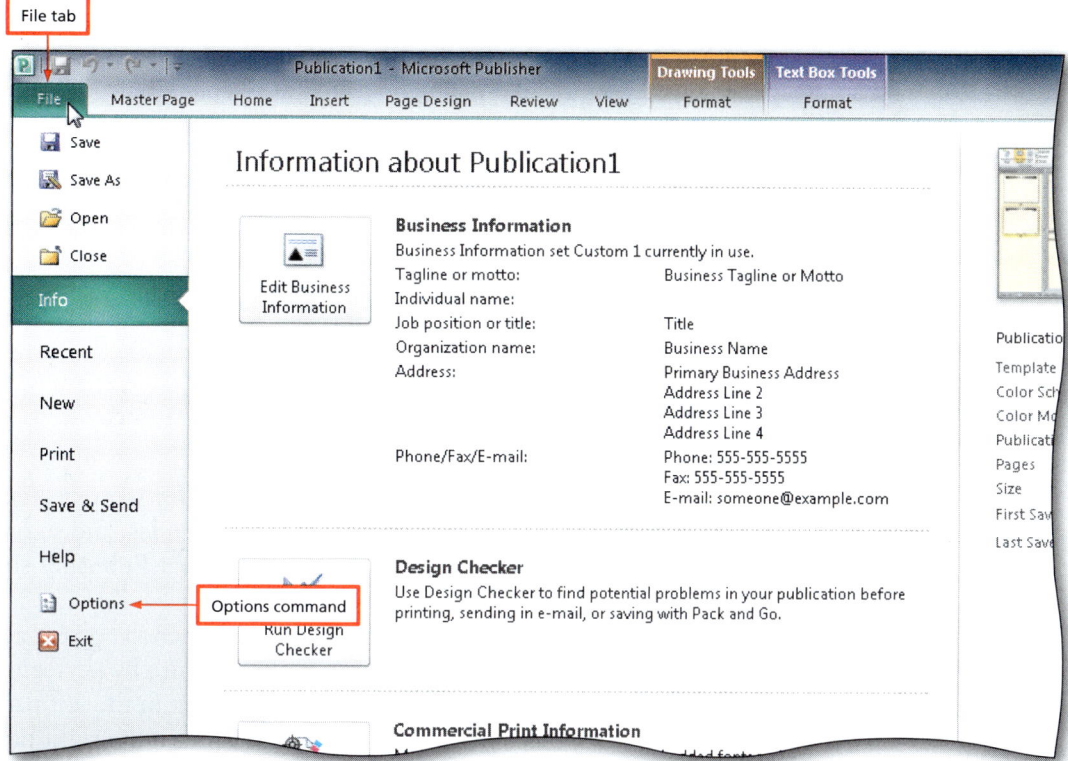

Figure 8–20

❷

• Click Options in the Backstage view to display the Publisher Options dialog box.

• Click Proofing in the left pane (Publisher Options dialog box) to display proofing options in the right pane.

• Click the AutoCorrect Options button in the right pane to display the AutoCorrect dialog box.

• When Publisher displays the AutoCorrect dialog box, type **contat** in the Replace text box.

• Press the TAB key and then type **contact** in the With text box (Figure 8–21).

Figure 8–21

 Experiment

• Scroll to view the list of autocorrected entries.

- Click the Add button (AutoCorrect dialog box) to add the entry alphabetically to the list of words to correct automatically as you type. (If your dialog box displays a Replace button instead, click it and then click the Yes button in the Microsoft Publisher dialog box to replace the previously defined entry.)

- Click the OK button (AutoCorrect dialog box) to close the dialog box.

- Click the OK button (Publisher Options dialog box) to close the dialog box.

The AutoCorrect Dialog Box

In addition to creating AutoCorrect entries for words you commonly misspell or mistype, you can create entries for abbreviations, codes, and so on. For example, you could create an AutoCorrect entry for asap, indicating that Publisher should replace this text with the phrase, as soon as possible.

If, for some reason, you do not want Publisher to correct automatically as you type, you can turn off the 'Replace text as you type' feature by performing the following steps. Click Options in the Backstage view, click Proofing in the left pane (Publisher Options dialog box), click the AutoCorrect Options button in the right pane (Figure 8–21), remove the check mark from the 'Replace text as you type' check box, and then click the OK button in each open dialog box.

The AutoCorrect sheet in the AutoCorrect dialog box (Figure 8–21) contains other check boxes that correct capitalization errors. If you type two capital letters in a row, such as TH, Publisher makes the second letter lowercase, Th. If you begin a sentence with a lowercase letter, Publisher capitalizes the first letter of the sentence. If you type the name of a day in lowercase letters, such as tuesday, Publisher capitalizes the first letter in the name of the day, Tuesday. If you leave the CAPS LOCK key on and begin a new sentence, such as aFTER, Publisher corrects the typing, After, and turns off the CAPS LOCK key for you.

Sometimes, you do not want Publisher to AutoCorrect a particular word or phrase. For example, you may use the code WD. in your publications. Because Publisher automatically capitalizes the first letter of a sentence, the character you enter following the period will be capitalized (in the previous sentence, it would capitalize the letter i in the word, in). To allow the code WD. to be entered into a publication and still leave the AutoCorrect feature turned on, you would set an exception. To set an exception to an AutoCorrect rule, click Options in the Backstage View, click Proofing in the left pane (Publisher Options dialog box), click the AutoCorrect Options button in the right pane, click the Exceptions button (Figure 8–21), click the appropriate tab in the AutoCorrect Exceptions dialog box, type the exception entry in the text box, click the Add button, click the Close button (AutoCorrect Exceptions dialog box), and then click the OK button in each of the remaining dialog boxes.

To Apply Master Pages

The final step in creating the multiple master pages is to apply them appropriately. The following steps apply master page B to all pages in the catalog, and then apply master page A to the first and last pages.

1

- With master page B still selected in the Page Navigation pane, click the Apply To button (Master Page tab | Master Page group) to display its list (Figure 8–22).

Figure 8–22

2

- Click Apply to All Pages to apply master page B with its alternating footers to all pages in the catalog.

- Click the Close Master Page button (Master Page tab | Close group) to return to Normal view (Figure 8–23).

Figure 8–23

3

- If necessary, click Page 1 in the Page Navigation pane to select it.

- Press CTRL+M to return to Master Page view.

- Select master page A.

- Click the Apply To button (Master Page tab | Master Page group) to display its list (Figure 8–24).

Figure 8–24

4

- Click Apply to Current Page to apply master page A, which has no footer, to Page 1 of the catalog.

- Click the Close Master Page button (Master Page tab | Close group) to return to Normal view (Figure 8–25).

Figure 8–25

5

- Click Page 4 in the Page Navigation pane to select it.

- Press CTRL+M to return to Master Page view and select master page A.

- Click the Apply To button (Master Page tab | Master Page group) and then click Apply to Current Page to apply master page A to Page 4.

- Click the Close Master Page button (Master Page tab | Close group) to return to Normal view (Figure 8–26).

Experiment

- Click each of the thumbnails and view the headers and footers.

Other Ways

1. Right-click thumbnail in Page Navigation pane, click Master Pages on shortcut menu, choose desired master page

Figure 8–26

To Save the Publication

You have performed many tasks while creating this catalog and do not want to risk losing work completed thus far. Accordingly, you should save the publication. The following steps assume you already have created folders for storing your files, for example, a CIS 101 folder (for your class) that contains a Publisher folder (for your assignments). Thus, these steps save the publication in the Publisher folder in the CIS 101 folder on a USB flash drive using the file name, Textbook Catalog.

1 With a USB flash drive connected to one of the computer's USB ports, click the Save button on the Quick Access Toolbar to display the Save As dialog box.

2 Type **Textbook Catalog** in the File name text box to change the file name. Do not press the ENTER key after typing the file name because you do not want to close the dialog box at this time.

3 Navigate to the desired save location (in this case, the Publisher folder in the CIS 101 folder [or your class folder] on the USB flash drive).

4 Click the Save button (Save As dialog box) to save the publication in the selected folder on the selected drive with the entered file name.

Creating the Main Publication

You have created master pages that will serve as the background to the catalog. In the next section, you will add graphics to page 1, and text and graphics to pages 2, 3, and 4. Then, you will insert catalog pages, finally merging the data to finish the catalog.

**Plan
Ahead**

Use high-quality graphics

Most catalogs appeal to customers better when they use high-quality, color pictures and graphics. Use a picture or photograph when you want to display a specific person, place, or thing. Use a graphic, such as clip art, when you do not have a photograph or when you are describing a general concept or service. Consult a graphics specialist to help choose high-resolution graphics; however, keep in mind that the images will require more memory and storage space.

To Add Graphics to Page 1

The following steps add two graphics to Page 1, which will serve as the cover of the catalog. To complete these steps, you will be required to use the Data Files for Students. See the inside back cover of this book for instructions on downloading the Data Files for Students, or contact your instructor for information about accessing the required files.

1 Click Page 1 in the Page Navigation pane and then click the Show Whole Page button on the status bar.

2 Display the Insert tab. Click the Insert Picture from File button (Insert tab | Illustrations group) to display the Insert Picture dialog box.

3 Navigate to the Data Files for Students and the Chapter 08 folder.

4 Double-click the file named, Front Cover Graphic, to insert it into the publication. Drag the graphic to the lower-right corner of the page and snap it to the margin guide.

5 Click the Insert Picture from File button (Insert tab | Illustrations group) again and insert the file named, Front Cover Book. Drag the graphic to the upper-left portion of the page and snap it to the margin guide, below the header.

6 SHIFT+drag the lower-right sizing handle of the graphic to a location above the white figures in the previous graphic (Figure 8–27).

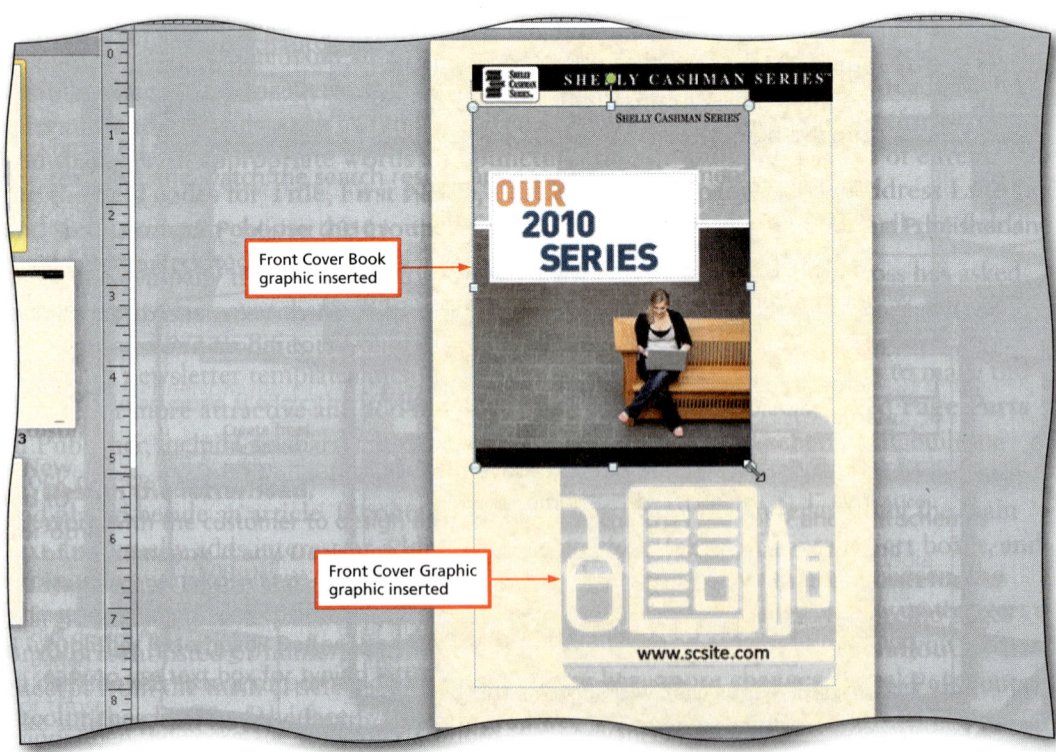

Figure 8–27

To Insert Graphics on Page 2

The following steps add graphics to page 2, which is the inside cover page. To complete these steps, you will be required to use the Data Files for Students. See the inside back cover of this book for instructions on downloading the Data Files for Students, or contact your instructor for information about accessing the required files.

1 Click Page 2 and Page 3 in the Page Navigation pane and then click the Show Whole Page button on the status bar.

2 Display the Insert tab. Click the Insert Picture from File button (Insert tab | Illustrations group) to display the Insert Picture dialog box.

3 Navigate to the Data Files for Students and the Chapter 08 folder, if necessary.

4 Double-click the file named, Cengage Learning, to insert it into the publication. Drag the graphic to the lower-left corner of the page and snap it to the margin.

5 Click the Insert Picture from File button (Insert tab | Illustrations group) again to display the Insert Picture dialog box and navigate to the Data Files for Students and the Chapter 08 folder, if necessary.

6 Double-click the file named, Front Cover Book, to insert it into Page 2 of the publication. Display the Picture Tools Format tab and then click the Crop button (Picture Tools Format tab | Crop group). Crop the graphic to display only the white rectangle with the words, Our 2010 Series.

7 Click the Crop button (Picture Tools Format tab | Crop group) again to hide the crop handles. Drag the cropped graphic to a location in the upper-center of the page (Figure 8–28).

Figure 8–28

To Use an AutoCorrect Entry

As you insert a text box on Page 2 and type, you will use the AutoCorrect entry that you created earlier in the chapter. You also will choose to stop automatically capitalizing the first letter in every line.

- Display the Home tab.

- Click the Draw Text Box button (Home tab | Objects group) and then drag the mouse pointer to draw a text box in the lower half of Page 2, between the two graphics.

- Click the Font Size box arrow (Text Box Tools Format tab | Font group) and then click 16 in the list to set the font size.

- Press CTRL+E to center (Figure 8–29).

Figure 8–29

- Type **For more information** and then press the ENTER key.

- Type **or to order books,** and then press the ENTER key.

- Type **contat** to enter the misspelled word (Figure 8–30).

Figure 8–30

❸

- Press the SPACEBAR to watch Publisher correct the word.

- Type `your` and then press the ENTER key.

- Type `Cengage Learning Representative` and then press the ENTER key.

- Type `at 1-800-354-9706` and then press the ENTER key.

- Type `or visit us on the Web at` and then press the ENTER key.

- Type `cengagelearning.com` to complete the text (Figure 8–31).

Figure 8–31

To Insert Text on Page 3

The following steps add text to page 3. To complete these steps, you will be required to use the Data Files for Students. See the inside back cover of this book for instructions on downloading the Data Files for Students, or contact your instructor for information about accessing the required files.

❶ Display the Insert tab.

❷ Click the Draw Text Box button (Insert tab | Text group) and then drag the mouse pointer to draw a text box that begins at the left margin aligned with the top of the upper graphic on Page 2 and ends at the right margin aligned with the top of the lower graphic on Page 2. Use the layout guides and snapping to position the text box.

❸ Click the Insert File button (Insert tab | Text group) and navigate to the Data Files for Students and the Chapter 08 folder, if necessary.

❹ Double-click the file named Page 3 Text to insert it into the text box.

❺ When the text appears, right-click the text and then click Best Fit on the shortcut menu to autofit the text (Figure 8–32 on the next page).

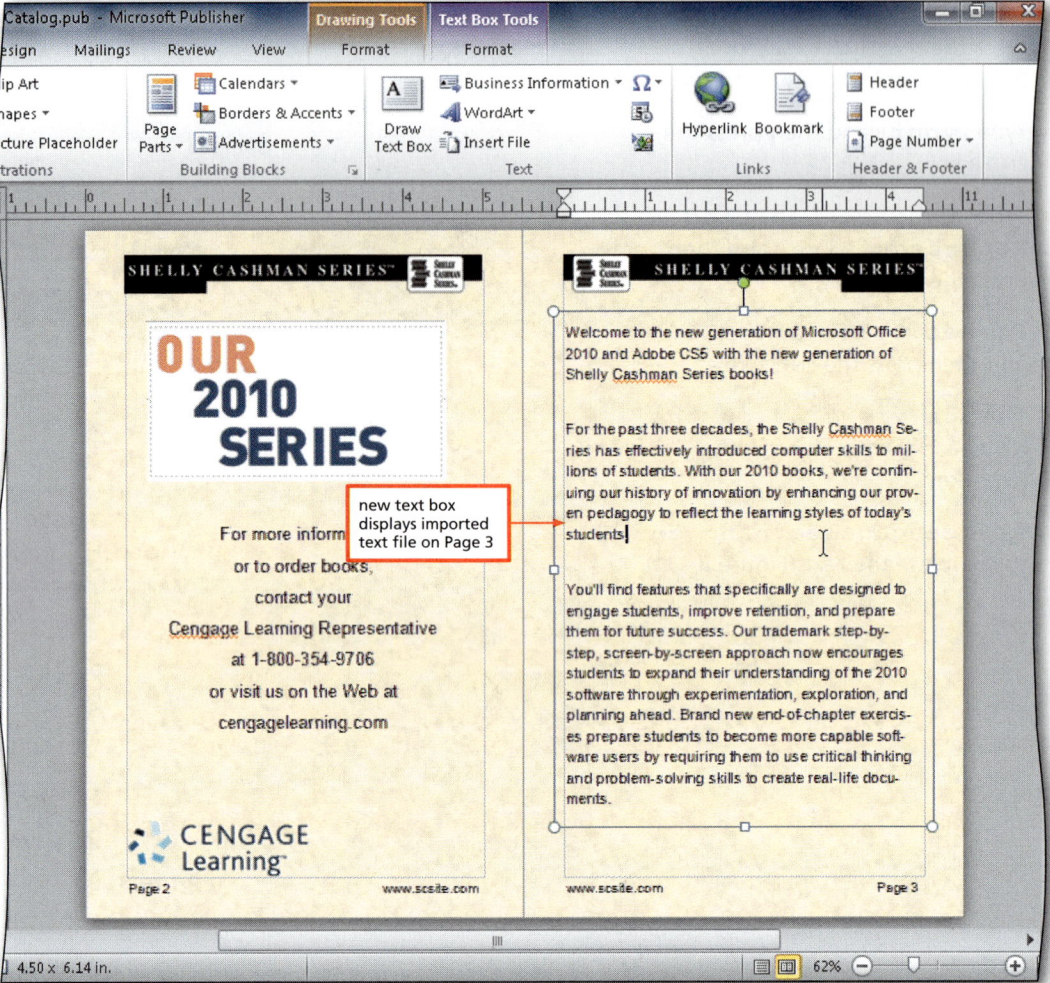

Figure 8–32

To Insert Text on Page 4

The following steps add text to page 4, the back page. To complete these steps, you will be required to use the Data Files for Students. See the inside back cover of this book for instructions on downloading the Data Files for Students, or contact your instructor for information about accessing the required files.

1 Click Page 4 in the Page Navigation pane.

2 Click the Draw Text Box button (Insert tab | Text group) and then drag a text box that begins at the left margin just below the header and ends at the right margin approximately 7 inches from the top of the page. Use the vertical ruler and snapping to help you position the text box.

3 Click the Insert File button (Insert tab | Text group) and navigate to the Data Files for Students and the Chapter 08 folder, if necessary.

4 Double-click the file named Page 4 Text to insert it into the text box.

5 Right-click the text and then click Best Fit on the shortcut menu to autofit the text (Figure 8–33).

Figure 8–33

To Save an Existing Publication with the Same File Name

You have made several modifications to the publication since you last saved it. Thus, you should save it again. The following step saves the publication again.

1 Click the Save button on the Quick Access Toolbar to overwrite the previously saved file.

Break Point: If you wish to take a break, this is a good place to do so. You can quit Publisher now. To resume at a later time, start Publisher, open the file called Textbook Catalog, and continue following the steps from this location forward.

Generating the Catalog Merge

Recall that the merge process requires a main publication and a data source. The main publication contains the constant or unchanging text, punctuation, space, and graphics, embedded with variables or changing values from the data source. The data source is a file with fields of information that will change. Catalog merges include pictures, and all records commonly are merged into a single publication.

The data source for Publisher's catalog merge normally is a table of data that includes information about the product or service, unique product numbers or ID numbers, and paths to pictures you want to use in the catalog. A **path** is the route Publisher must take through your computer's stored files to find the picture file and the file name. For example, if a .jpg picture file named Dog is located on the USB (E:) storage device in a folder named Pictures, the path would be E:\Pictures\Dog.jpg. If the file is located in the same folder as the merged publication, the path is simply the file name; thus, in the previous example, the path would be Dog.jpg.

Generally, for classroom purposes you should keep the main publication and the product list data source in the same folder on the same storage device. If you are using the Data Files for Students, these data sources may be stored in a different location from your saved publications; thus, they should be moved or copied to your storage device.

Plan Ahead

> **Use efficient methods to move through the catalog and merged pages.**
> A file with many graphics and merged pages sometimes refreshes more slowly on the screen. If you move to a new page, or edit the data source, it may take several moments to open. Use the Previous Sheet button and Next Sheet button (Catalog Tools Format tab | Preview Page group) to view each record. Consider using the Graphics Manager to turn off the display of graphics and minimize the Page Navigation pane. Sometimes it is better to edit the database outside of the publication, so that you do not have to wait for the updated screens.

To Copy the Data Source Files

Publisher recommends that the publication and its data source reside in the same folder location; therefore, the following steps copy a folder named Textbook Data Source Files from the Data Files for Students to your save location (commonly a USB drive). See the inside back cover of this book for instructions on downloading the Data Files for Students, or contact your instructor for information about accessing the required files. If you already have downloaded the Data Files for Students to the same location that you are using to create files in this chapter, you can skip these steps.

1 Click the Start button on the Windows 7 taskbar to display the Start menu.

2 Click Computer to open the Computer window.

3 Navigate to the location of the file to be opened (in this case, the Data Files for Students, to the Publisher folder, and then to the Chapter 08 folder). For a detailed example of this procedure, refer to Steps 3a–3c in the To Save a File in a Folder section in the Office 2010 and Windows 7 chapter at the beginning of this book.

4 In the Chapter 08 folder, right-click the Textbook Data Source Files folder to display its shortcut menu and then click Copy on the shortcut menu to copy the file.

5 Navigate to the desired save location (in this case, the Publisher folder in the CIS 101 folder [or your class folder] on the USB flash drive).

6 Right-click a blank part of the right pane in the Publisher folder to display the folder's shortcut menu and then click Paste on the shortcut menu to paste the folder.

7 Close the folder window.

Catalog Pages

Catalog pages contain a unique merge area for positioning field codes for text and pictures. The **merge area**, also called the **repeatable area**, is a box in the publication into which you can insert field codes. The merge area repeats for each record in the file, because catalog merges merge all records to a single publication.

You start the catalog merge by clicking the Catalog Pages button on the Insert tab. If you start from scratch, you must insert catalog pages. Publisher then automatically adds a page or pages to your publication and inserts a catalog merge area. The merge area can be resized and adjusted for multiple records per page. You can format fields or objects added to the merge area using normal formatting techniques.

When the merge is complete, data from the data source will populate each field, and the catalog merge area will repeat to display multiple records.

To Create Catalog Pages

The following steps create catalog pages.

1

- Click the Page 2 and Page 3 thumbnail in the Page Navigation pane and show the whole page if necessary.

- Display the Insert tab and then click the Catalog Pages button (Insert tab | Pages Group) to display catalog pages (Figure 8–34).

Figure 8–34

2

- Drag the lower-right sizing handle of the merge area to the lower-right corner and snap it to the margins.

- If necessary, adjust the merge area so it fits below the header (Figure 8–35).

Q&A How will adjusting the size of the merge area affect my catalog?

Filling the catalog page with the merge area will cause each record to be displayed on its own page in the final version of the catalog.

Figure 8–35

To Apply a Master Page to the Catalog Pages

The following steps apply master page B to the catalog pages, so that they will contain the header and footer with page numbering.

1 Press CTRL+M to view the master page.

2 Select master page B in the Page Navigation pane.

3 Click the Apply To button (Master Page tab | Master Page group) and then click Apply to Current Page in the list.

4 Close the Master Page view.

To Select the Data Source

The following steps select an existing data source. The data source is located in the folder that you copied to your storage location earlier in the chapter on page PUB 466.

1

- With the catalog page still selected, click the Add List button (Catalog Tools Format tab | Start group) to display the commands (Figure 8–36).

Q&A

What if I want to create a new list?

You would choose the Type New List command. A dialog box will be displayed similar to the New Address List dialog box on page PUB 406. You can customize fields and insert data just as you did in Chapter 7.

Figure 8–36

2

- Click Use Existing List to display the Select Data Source dialog box.

- Navigate to your storage location (in this case, the Publisher folder in the CIS 101 folder [or your class folder] on the USB flash drive) and double-click the folder named Textbook Data Source Files (Figure 8–37).

Figure 8–37

3

• Double-click the Textbook Database file to display the Catalog Merge Product List dialog box (Figure 8–38).

4

• Click the OK button (Catalog Merge Product List dialog box) to close the dialog box and connect the data source to the publication.

Figure 8–38

The Catalog Tools Format Tab

When performing a catalog merge, Publisher displays the Catalog Tools Format tab, which contains specialized formatting tools for catalog pages and merging (Figure 8–39). The Layout group contains a gallery of preset page layouts and buttons to change the number of rows and columns and set the order of record placement. The Repeating Areas button (Catalog Tools Format tab | Layout group) allows you to choose to repeat the same layout on all pages, or to specify a custom layout by row or column. The Insert group allows you to insert text and pictures manually from the data source. The Preview Page and Merge groups are similar to those on the Mailings tab that you learned about in Chapter 7.

Figure 8–39

To Insert a Picture Field

The following steps insert the picture from the data source or product list into the catalog merge area. Fields or objects inserted in the catalog merge area will repeat for each record in the data source. Objects outside the area will not repeat. You can resize and reposition objects in the catalog merge area.

1

- Click to select the catalog merge area.

- Click the Picture Field button (Catalog Tools Format tab | Insert group) to view the available commands (Figure 8–40).

Figure 8–40

2

- Click Cover in the list (Figure 8–41).

Figure 8–41

3

- On the status bar, click the Object Size button to display the Measurement toolbar.

- Enter the position and size settings as shown in Figure 8–42.

Q&A

My picture does not appear. Did I do something wrong?

No. To conserve memory resources on your computer, Publisher may not display the pictures until the file is ready to preview or print.

Figure 8–42

4

- Close the Measurement toolbar.

- Click the catalog merge area outside of the Picture box to deselect the Cover field box.

To View Boundaries

To assist you in placing the other fields in the catalog merge area, the following steps turn on the boundaries display.

1 Display the View tab.

2 Click to display a check mark in the Boundaries check box (View tab | Show group).

To Insert Text Fields

The following steps insert the remaining fields from the data source into the publication.

1

• Display the Catalog Tools Format tab.

• If necessary, deselect the Cover picture field.

• Click the Text Field button (Catalog Tools Format tab | Insert group) to view the list of fields (Figure 8–43).

Q&A

Could I use the Cover field and insert the picture from this list?

No. The list contains text fields. If you were to try to insert the text field code named, Cover, Publisher would insert the data from the field itself, not the picture. You would see the words, Front Cover.tif in the merge.

Figure 8–43

2

• Click Title in the list to insert the Title field code into the catalog merge area.

• Drag the boundary of the Title field box to a location below the Cover picture field. Drag the right sizing handle to the right margin to increase the size of the text box.

• Select all of the field code and then change the font size to 24.

• Click outside the Title field box to deselect it (Figure 8–44).

Figure 8–44

3

- Repeat Steps 1 and 2 for each of the other fields. Place them in the catalog merge area as shown in Figure 8–45. Use a font size of 14 for the Authors and Description fields. Use a font size of 12 and right-justification for the Number of Pages field and the ISBN fields.

Figure 8–45

To Save Again

You have made several modifications to the publication since you last saved it. Thus, you should save it again. The following step saves the publication again.

1 Click the Save button on the Quick Access Toolbar to overwrite the previously saved file.

Break Point: If you wish to take a break, this is a good place to do so. You can quit Publisher now. To resume at a later time, start Publisher, open the file called Textbook Catalog, and continue following the steps from this location forward.

To Find Entries

Because the entire merged publication is not searchable via regular means until you merge it to a new file, Publisher provides other methods for finding information in the entries. Publisher looks through the data source for the keyword(s) and then navigates to that page in the catalog publication.

The following steps find an entry based on keywords.

1

- Display the Catalog Tools Format tab, if necessary.

- Click the Find Entry button (Catalog Tools Format tab | Preview Page group) to display the Find Entry dialog box (Figure 8–46).

Figure 8–46

2

- In the Find text box, type `design concepts` to enter the search term.

- Click the This field box arrow to display the list of fields (Figure 8–47).

Figure 8–47

3

- Scroll as necessary and then click Description in the list of fields.

- Click the Find Next button (Find Entry dialog box) to search for the keywords.

- Drag the title bar of the dialog box to reposition the dialog box so that you can view the entry (Figure 8–48).

Q&A What would happen if Publisher could not locate the search term?

In those cases, Publisher would display a dialog box stating it could not find the search text you entered.

4

- Click the Close button (Find Entry dialog box) to close the dialog box.

Figure 8–48

TO EXCLUDE ENTRIES

If you wanted to exclude an entry from your data source, you would perform the following steps. Note that these steps cannot be undone.

1. Navigate to the record that you wish to exclude either by using the Find Entry button (described in the previous steps), or by clicking the Next Catalog Page button or the Previous Catalog Page button (Catalog Tools Format tab | Preview Page group).
2. When the desired record is displayed, if necessary, click the catalog merge area around that entry to select it.
3. Click the Exclude Entry button (Catalog Tools Format tab | Preview Page group) to exclude the record.

To Turn Off Boundaries

The following steps turn off the boundaries so that Publisher will display a more realistic preview.

1 Display the View tab.

2 Click to remove the check mark in the Boundaries check box (View tab | Show group).

To Preview the Merge

The following step previews the merged publication.

1
- Display the Catalog Tools Format tab.

- Click the Preview Results button (Catalog Tools Format tab | Preview Page group) to display the merged pages (Figure 8–49).

Q&A Why does the Catalog Page Number box on the Ribbon say 3?

Publisher is displaying the third full page of merged fields; the box does not take into account the pagination of the catalog, nor the fact that each spread contains two records.

Q&A Why do the page numbers appear incorrectly?

The page numbers will appear correctly in the print preview and on the hard copy.

🔍 **Experiment**
- Click the Next Catalog Page button and the Previous Catalog Page button (Catalog Tools Format tab | Preview Page group) to display other pages of the catalog.

Figure 8–49

The Graphics Manager

The Graphics Manager helps you manage and display all the pictures you have inserted into your publication, such as embedded pictures or linked pictures. An **embedded picture** is one that is copied or placed into the publication without retaining any outside connections. When you save a publication with an embedded picture, Publisher saves the picture, as is, in the publication. A **linked picture** is an image that is displayed in the publication but is stored outside of the publication. In order to view, print, or manipulate the image, you must have access to that external picture file.

You must submit that image as a separate file when you use an outside printing service. You can use the Graphics Manager to check the status of each picture, such as whether a picture is linked or embedded, whether it has been modified, or whether a link to an external picture is missing.

The Graphics Manager also controls display options. You can view all the pictures related to a publication, or you can see only those pictures that are missing or have been modified since the last time you saved the publication. The Graphics Manager can display thumbnails of all graphics in the publication using the Graphics Manager task pane. You can order the pictures in the Graphics Manager task pane, by file name, page number, extension, or size, showing the details about each one.

If you have many pictures in a publication with multiple pages, you can navigate quickly to a particular picture by pointing to it in the Graphics Manager task pane, clicking the box arrow next to the picture, and then clicking Go to this Picture.

BTW

Embedded vs. Linked
If you want to change a picture's status from embedded to linked, or vice versa, the Graphics Manager uses Save As dialog boxes to assist you.

To Work with the Graphics Manager

The following steps display the Graphics Manager task pane and then change the display of the pictures so that quicker editing is possible and fewer system resources are consumed. You also will view information about each of the pictures.

1

- Display the View tab.

- Click to display a check mark in the Graphics Manager check box (View tab | Show group), which will display the Graphics Manager task pane.

- Click the Sort by box arrow (Graphics Manager task pane) to display the list of picture details (Figure 8–50).

Figure 8–50

2

- Click Page number in the list to view the pictures sorted by page number (Figure 8–51).

Figure 8–51

3

- Point to Front Cover Book.tif (Page 1) to display the picture's box arrow.

- Click the box arrow to display actions you can perform related to the picture (Figure 8–52).

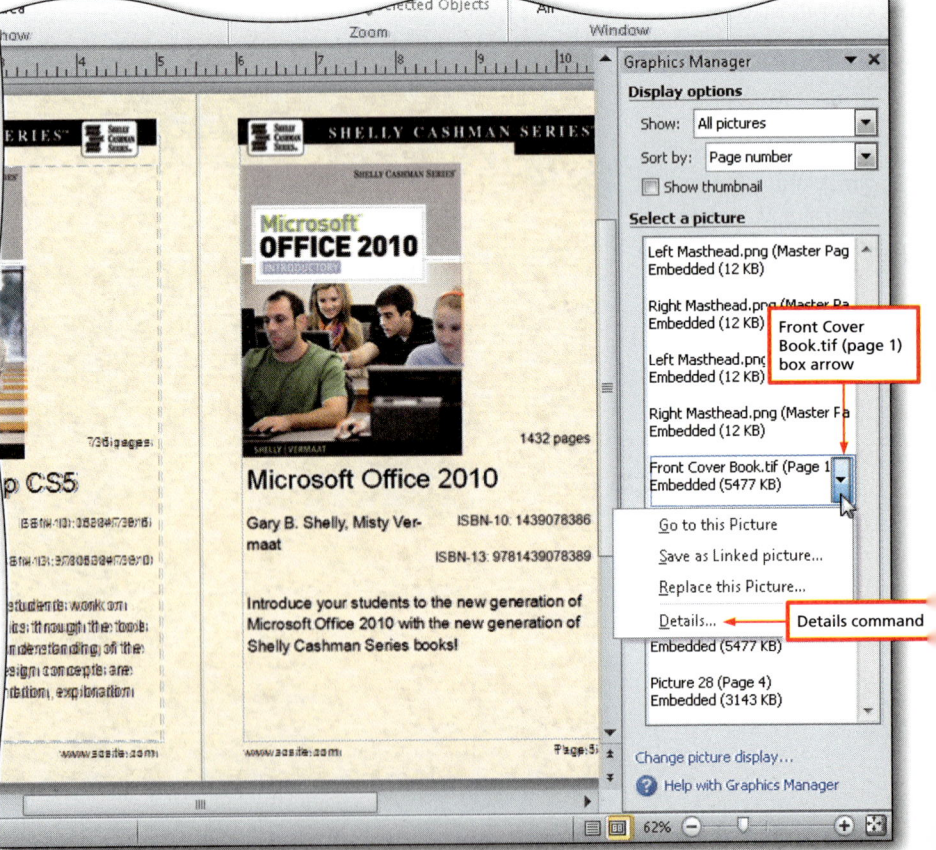

Figure 8–52

4
- Click Details to display the Details dialog box (Figure 8–53).

Figure 8–53

5
- Click the Close button (Details dialog box) to close the dialog box.

- In the lower portion of the Graphics Manager task pane, click the 'Change picture display' link to display the Picture Display dialog box.

- Click the Hide pictures option button to select it (Figure 8–54).

Figure 8–54

6

- Click the OK button (Picture Display dialog box) to hide the pictures in the display (Figure 8–55).

🔎 **Experiment**

- Click each of the thumbnails in the Page Navigation pane to see how quickly the pages are displayed when pictures are hidden.

Figure 8–55

To Redisplay the Pictures and Close the Graphics Manager

The following steps redisplay the pictures throughout the publication and close the Graphics Manager task pane.

1 Click the 'Change picture display' link in the Graphics Manager task pane to display the Picture Display dialog box.

2 Click the 'Fast resize and zoom' option button (Picture Display dialog box) to select it.

3 Click the OK button to close the dialog box.

4 Click the Close button in the Graphics Manger task pane to close it.

BTW

Translation
The Translate command is only available in the following Microsoft Office programs: Word, Outlook, OneNote, PowerPoint, Publisher, Excel, and Visio.

Translating Text

Publisher can translate phrases, paragraphs, and individual words to a different language. Many of the modern languages are installed automatically when you install Publisher. Other languages require installation the first time you use them. To translate text to some languages, such as right-to-left languages, you may need to satisfy certain operating system requirements.

Publisher's translation capability requires Web access. When you click the Translate Selected Text button (Review tab | Language group), the Research task pane appears and accesses a Web-based service, such as World Lingo or Microsoft Translator. In the Research task pane, you can set the language from which and to which you wish to translate. The translated text appears in the task pane.

**Plan
Ahead**

> **Translate text that is important to readers of another language.**
> Use the Translation tool for short passages of text or individual words in your publications. If the entire publication needs to be translated, use a professional translator. While the translator is not a substitute for learning the language and knowing how tone and sentence structure affects the meaning, it may be appropriate for those times when you need to look up short phrases or translate a single word.

To Enter Text

The following steps create a text box at the bottom of the last page in the catalog and then enter a phrase in English.

1 Navigate to Page 6 and display the Home tab.

2 Click the Draw Text Box button (Home tab | Objects group) and then drag the mouse pointer to draw a text box that fills the lower portion of the page, below the previously created text box and filling the area between margins.

3 Press the F9 key to zoom to 100%.

4 Change the font size to 14. Type `Selected titles are available in Spanish.` and then press the ENTER key to move to the next line (Figure 8–56).

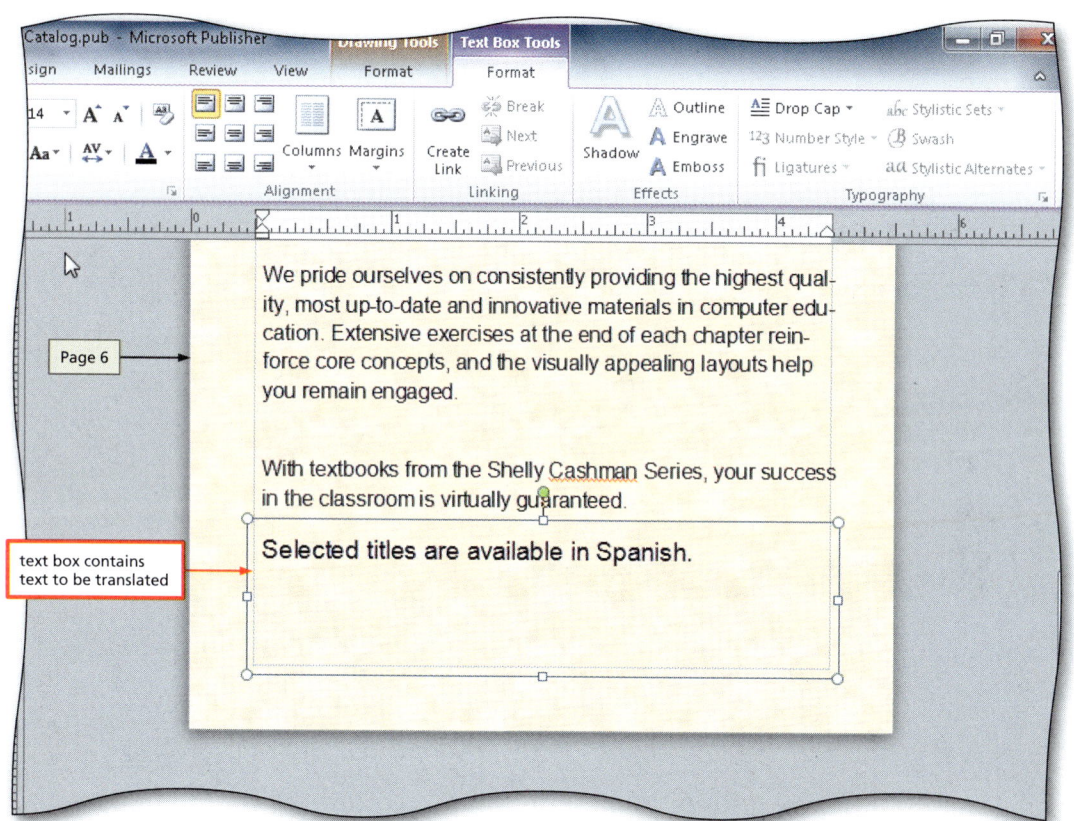

Figure 8–56

To Translate Text and Insert

The following steps translate the text to Spanish. You must have a Web connection to perform these steps.

1
- Drag to select the text you wish to translate.

- Click Review on the Ribbon to display the Review tab.

- Click the Translate Selected Text button (Review tab | Language group) to display the Research task pane (Figure 8–57).

Figure 8–57

2
- In the Translation area of the Research task pane, click the From box arrow to display the list of languages (Figure 8–58).

Figure 8–58

3

• If necessary, click English (U.S.) in the list.

• Click the To box arrow to display the list of languages and then click Spanish (International Sort) to translate the selected text from English to Spanish (Figure 8–59).

Experiment

• Click the To box arrow and then choose other languages and view the translations. When you are finished, click the To box arrow and then click Spanish (International Sort).

Figure 8–59

4

• Drag to select the translated text and then right-click to display the shortcut menu (Figure 8–60).

Q&A

Is it possible to have the translator automatically insert my text?

That depends on your translation service. In Figure 8–60, the translation is performed by World Lingo. If you click the Translation Options link, you can choose a different translation service that may give you the option of automatically inserting the text.

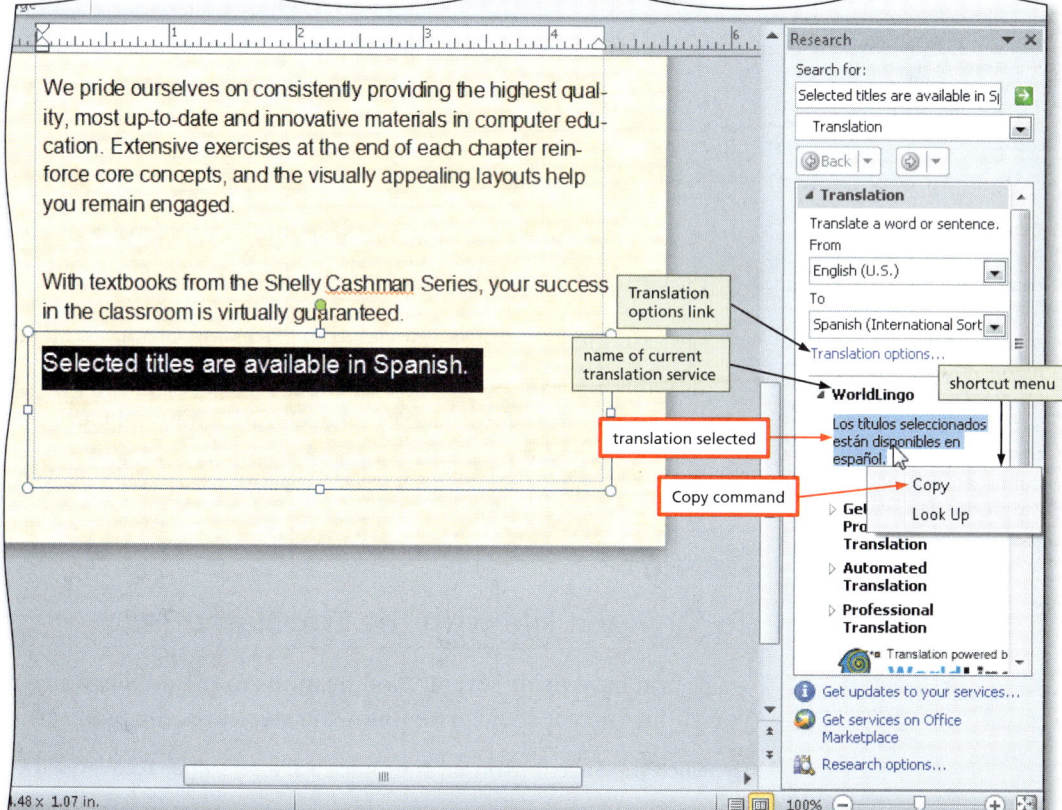

Figure 8–60

5

- Click Copy on the shortcut menu to copy the translation.

- In the publication, click below the selected text to deselect it.

- Right-click below the text and then click Paste on the shortcut menu to paste the translation (Figure 8–61).

6

- Click the Close button in the Research task pane to close the task pane.

Figure 8–61

To Check the Spelling

The following steps check the spelling of the entire publication.

1 Click Page 1 in the Page Navigation pane.

2 Click the Spelling button (Review tab | Proofing Group) to start the spell checking process.

3 As Publisher flags proper names, choose to ignore all. As Publisher flags the Spanish words, choose to ignore them. Correct any legitimate misspellings.

4 Because Publisher checked the master pages for spelling errors, click the Close Master Page button (Master Page tab | Close group) to return to Normal view.

To Save the File with the Translated Text

You have made several modifications to the publication since you last saved it. Thus, you should save it again. The following step saves the publication again.

1 Click the Save button on the Quick Access Toolbar to overwrite the previously saved file.

Merging Catalogs

You have three choices in finalizing the merge. You can merge the pages and create a new document using the Merge to New Publication button (Catalog Tools Format tab | Merge group). In that new document, the merged pages will not need a preview. You will be able to edit the merged text and graphics; all 12 pages will appear in the Page Navigation pane. Another choice is to add the pages to another publication using the Add to Existing Publication button (Catalog Tools Format tab | Merge group). This option is useful when you have created catalog pages independent of any template and want to add them back into another publication. A third option is to print it using the Print button (Catalog Tools Format tab | Merge group), which retains the merged nature of the catalog.

To Merge to a Printer

The following steps print the contents of the Textbook Catalog file.

1

- Click Page 4 in the Page Navigation pane to display the Catalog Tools Format tab, if necessary.

- Click the Show Whole Page button, if necessary (Figure 8–62).

Figure 8–62

2

- Click the Merge to Printer button (Catalog Tools Format tab | Merge group) to display the Print gallery in the Backstage view (Figure 8–63).

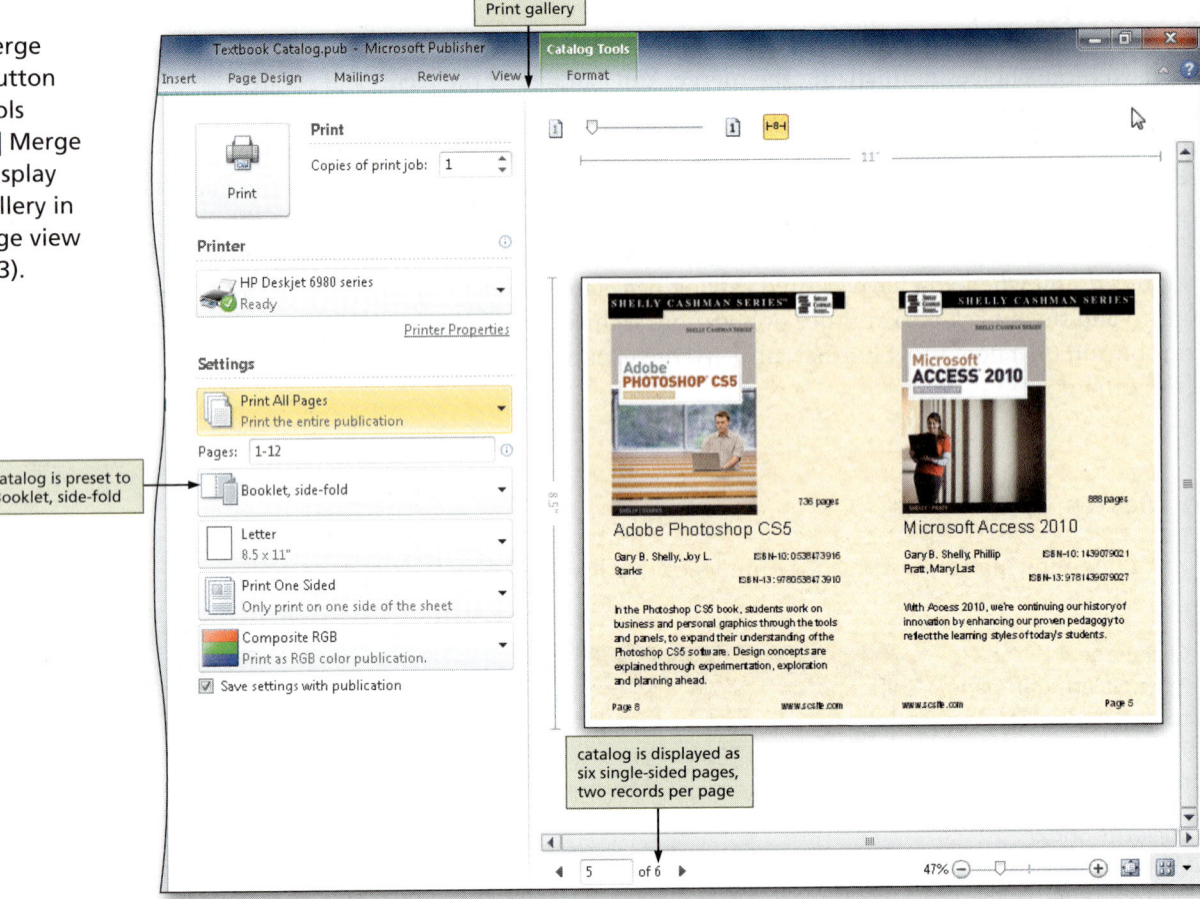

Figure 8–63

3

- Click the Print One Sided button to display your printer's duplex settings (Figure 8–64).

Q&A

How many pages does the catalog contain?

The catalog contains 12 pages. Printed on both sides, the entire catalog can be printed using three pieces of 8.5 × 11" paper. Because you started with a blank catalog template, many of the settings in the Print gallery are preset for you.

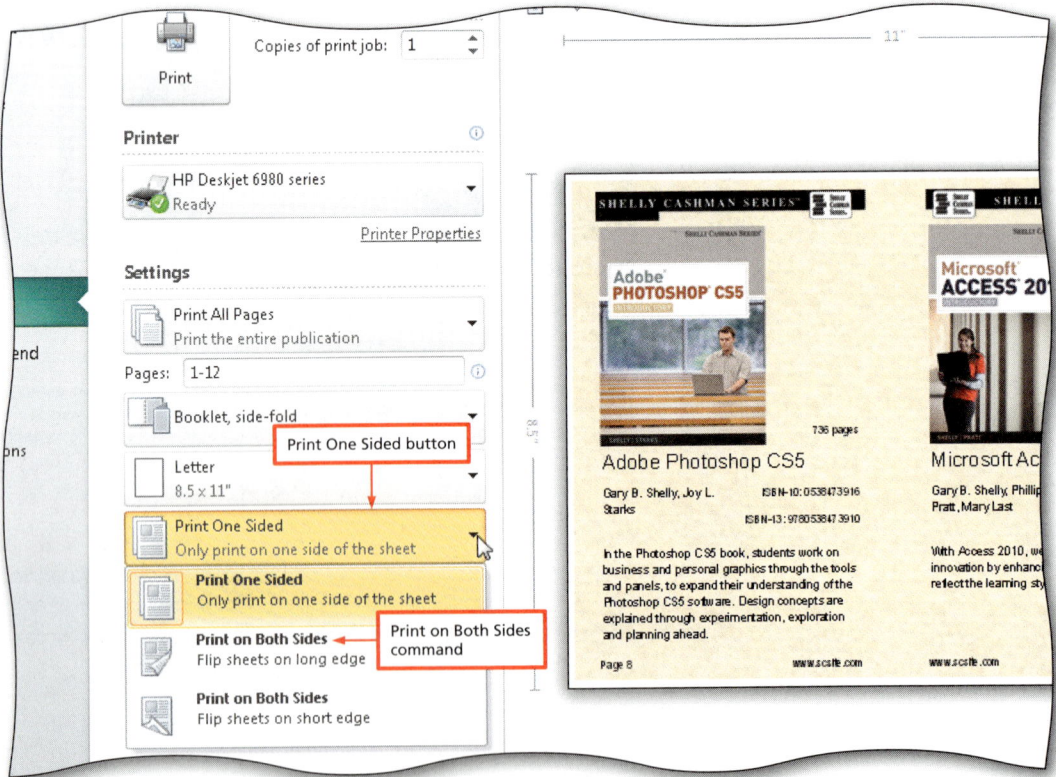

Figure 8–64

4

- If you have the choice, click the Print on Both Sides option. If you do not have the option, choose an appropriate option (Figure 8–65).

What are the new buttons at the bottom of the Print gallery preview area?

If you chose duplex or two-sided printing, you will see a Front button and a Back button, allowing you to preview exactly how the pages will be collated or arranged.

Experiment

- To preview the pages, click the Next Sheet button. Click the Front button. Click the Back button. Click the Previous Sheet button.

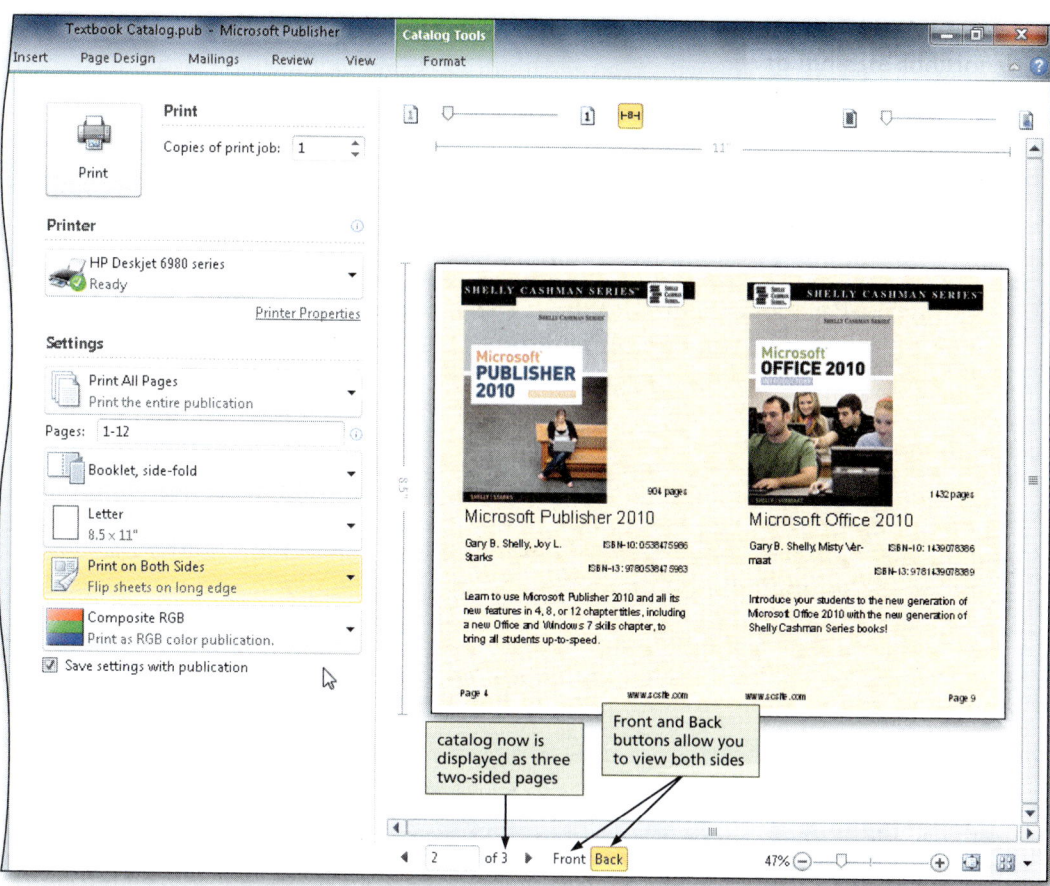

catalog now is displayed as three two-sided pages

Front and Back buttons allow you to view both sides

Figure 8–65

5

- Click the Print button in the Print gallery to print the document on the currently selected printer.

- When the printer stops, retrieve the hard copy shown in Figure 8–1 on page PUB 443.

To Quit Publisher

This project is complete. The following steps quit Publisher.

1 To quit Publisher, click the Close button on the right side of the title bar.

2 If a Microsoft Office Publisher dialog box appears, click the Don't Save button so that any editing changes you have made to the catalog are not saved.

Printer Problems
Older printers may not have enough printer memory to handle the many graphics included in the catalog. Wait a few moments. If your printer does not continue, right-click the printer icon on the status bar and then click your printer name to display its dialog box. Right-click the file name and then click Cancel on the shortcut menu. Try printing the catalog on a different printer.

Chapter Summary

In this chapter, you learned how to create a data-driven catalog. First, you created alternating master pages with headers and footers. You learned about the AutoCorrect features of Publisher. Then, you created catalog pages with a special merge area. Next, you merged the product list data source, inserting field code for both text and graphics, and formatting them. Finally, you created a text box and translated a phrase using the translation feature in Publisher. You merged the catalog and printed it. The items listed below include all the new Publisher skills you have learned in this chapter.

1. Create a Two-Page Spread (PUB 445)
2. View and Rename a Master Page (PUB 446)
3. Add a Background to a Master Page (PUB 446)
4. Insert a Header (PUB 448)
5. Duplicate the Master Page (PUB 450)
6. Insert Alternating Footers (PUB 450)
7. AutoCorrect as You Type (PUB 452)
8. Use the AutoCorrect Options Button (PUB 453)
9. Create an AutoCorrect Entry (PUB 454)
10. Apply Master Pages (PUB 456)
11. Use an AutoCorrect Entry (PUB 462)
12. Create Catalog Pages (PUB 467)
13. Select the Data Source (PUB 469)
14. Insert the Picture Field (PUB 471)
15. Insert Text Fields (PUB 472)
16. Find Entries (PUB 474)
17. Preview the Merge (PUB 476)
18. Work with the Graphics Manager (PUB 477)
19. Translate Text and Insert (PUB 482)
20. To Merge to a Printer (PUB 485)

Learn It Online

Test your knowledge of chapter content and key terms.

Instructions: To complete the Learn It Online exercises, start your browser, click the Address bar, and then enter the Web address `scsite.com/pub2010/learn`. When the Publisher 2010 Learn It Online page is displayed, click the link for the exercise you want to complete and then read the instructions.

Chapter Reinforcement TF, MC, and SA
A series of true/false, multiple choice, and short answer questions that test your knowledge of the chapter content.

Flash Cards
An interactive learning environment where you identify chapter key terms associated with displayed definitions.

Practice Test
A series of multiple choice questions that tests your knowledge of chapter content and key terms.

Who Wants To Be a Computer Genius?
An interactive game that challenges your knowledge of chapter content in the style of a television quiz show.

Wheel of Terms
An interactive game that challenges your knowledge of chapter key terms in the style of the television show *Wheel of Fortune.*

Crossword Puzzle Challenge
A crossword puzzle that challenges your knowledge of key terms presented in the chapter.

Apply Your Knowledge

Reinforce the skills and apply the concepts you learned in this chapter.

Creating a Real Estate Catalog

Instructions: Copy the folder, Apply 8-1 Houses, from the Data Files for Students to your storage location and appropriate folder. See the inside back cover of this book for instructions on downloading the Data Files for Students, or contact your instructor for information about accessing the required files. Start Publisher.

You are to create a catalog of local houses for sale as shown in Figure 8–66. When folded and printed on both sides, the catalog page numbers will appear in the correct order.

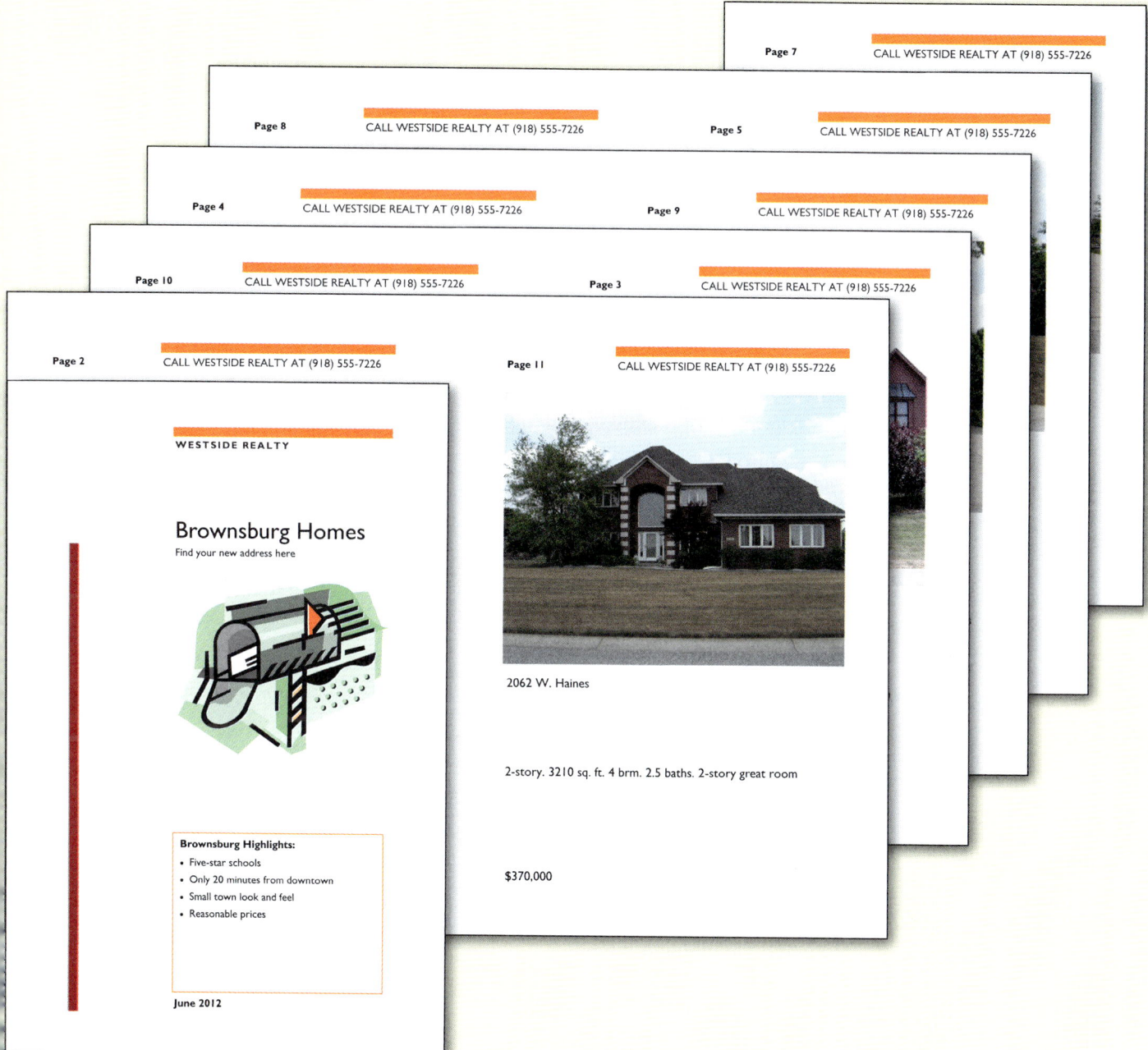

Figure 8–66

Continued >

Apply Your Knowledge *continued*

Perform the following tasks:

1. In the New template gallery, click catalogs and then click the Color Band preview.

2. In the Customize area, select the Aspect color scheme and the Facet font scheme.

3. Click the Create button.

4. In the Page Navigation pane, one at a time, delete pages 2 through 7 by right-clicking the thumbnail and then clicking Delete on the shortcut menu. When Publisher displays a Delete Page dialog box, select Both pages, if necessary, and then click the OK button. If Publisher displays a message about the multipage spread, click the OK button.

5. To edit Page 1:

   a. Select the text in the Business Name text box. Type `Westside Realty` to replace the text.

   b. Click the text in the Catalog Title text box. Type `Brownsburg Homes` to replace the text.

   c. Click the text in the Catalog Subtitle text box. Type `Find your new address here` to replace the text.

   d. Click the text, Sidebar Heading. Type `Brownsburg Highlights:` to replace the text.

   e. Click the bulleted list in the sidebar. Type `Five-star schools` and then press the ENTER key. Type `Only 20 minutes from downtown` and then press the ENTER key. Type `Small town look and feel` and then press the ENTER key. Type `Reasonable prices` to complete the bulleted list.

   f. Click the text in the Date text box. Type `June 2012` to replace the text.

6. Click the Page 2 thumbnail in the Page Navigation pane, and then click the Catalog Pages button (Insert tab | Pages group) to insert catalog pages.

7. Resize the catalog merge area to fill the entire page.

8. To create and then select a data source:

   a. Click the Add List button (Catalog Tools Format tab | Start group) and then click Use Existing List.

   b. Navigate to the location of the copied folder, Apply 8-1 Houses. Double-click the folder, and then double-click the Apply 8-1 Homes.mdb file to display the Catalog Merge Product List dialog box.

   c. Because you will use all 10 records in this database, click the OK button to connect to the database.

9. To insert fields:

   a. Click the Picture Field button (Catalog Tools Format tab | Insert group), and then click Picture in the list.

   b. In the catalog merge area, drag the border of the inserted picture field to the upper-left corner and then resize the picture to fill the upper portion of the catalog merge area.

   c. Click the catalog merge area outside of the picture field to deselect it.

   d. Click the Text Field button (Catalog Tools Format tab | Insert group), and then click Address in the list. Position the address text box below the picture box and resize it to fill the area left to right. Deselect the address text box.

   e. Repeat Step 9d to insert the Description and Price fields.

   f. Format the fields as necessary.

10. To replace other text:

    a. On page 2 of the catalog, select all of the text in the TO ORDER text box at the top of the page. Type `Call Westside Realty at (918) 555-7226` to replace the text.

    b. On page 4 of the catalog, zoom and scroll as necessary to replace the address text with `4700 Chesterfield Drive, Brownsburg, OK 74079` as the address.

    c. Replace the phone/fax/e-mail text by typing `Phone: (918) 555-7226 Fax: (918) 555-7220 E-mail: NewHome@Westside.com` as the new text.

    d. If necessary, change the business name text to Westside Realty.

11. Delete the Organization logo from the bottom of Page 4.

12. Preview the results.

13. Save the file in the same folder as your data source, with the name, Apply 8-1 Brownsburg Homes Catalog.

14. See your instructor for ways to submit this assignment.

Extend Your Knowledge

Extend the skills you learned in this chapter and experiment with new skills. You may need to use Help to complete the assignment.

Using Translation Services

Instructions: Start Publisher. Open the publication, Extend 8-1 Welcome Poster, from the Data Files for Students. See the inside back cover of this book for instructions on downloading the Data Files for Students, or contact your instructor for information about accessing the required files.

In this assignment, you will investigate different translation services and compare the results, creating a final poster as shown in Figure 8–67 on the next page.

1. Use Help to learn more about choosing translation services.

2. Save the publication with the name, Extend 8-1 Welcome Poster Modified.

3. One at a time ALT+click each of the Welcome words to open the Research task pane. Each time, choose a different language from the To box list.

4. For two of the languages, click the Translation options link. In the 'Available language pairs' area, scroll to a pair that translates from English to another language, and then click the translation service box arrow. Choose a different language translation service and compare the translation.

5. If available, click the Insert button in the Research task pane to insert the new translation into the poster.

6. Format each of the text boxes for Best Fit.

7. Save the publication again, and print a copy for your instructor.

Continued >

Extend Your Knowledge *continued*

Figure 8–67

Make It Right

Analyze a publication and correct all errors and/or improve the design.

Correcting Alternating Headers and Footers

Instructions: Start Publisher. Open the publication, Make It Right 8-1 Booklet, from the Data Files for Students. See the inside back cover of this book for instructions on downloading the Data Files for Students, or contact your instructor for more information about accessing the required files.

The publication is an eight-page publication with a header only on the left pages. Your job is to create alternating footers for inside pages of the booklet, and a centered footer for the front and back page as shown in Figure 8–68 on the next page.

Perform the following tasks:

1. Go to Master Page view.

2. Create a footer on the right page, with the word, Page, and the page number right-justified. Align the new footer horizontally, with the footer on the left.

3. Apply the new master page to all pages in the booklet.

4. Close Master Page view.

5. Click Page 8 in the Page Navigation pane. Press CTRL+M to return to Master Page view.

6. Create a second master page. Use a single-page layout. Create a footer with the page number centered at the bottom of the page, and no header. Apply the new master page to the current page of the document. Close Master Page view.

7. Save the document with the file name, Make It Right 8-1 Booklet Modified. See your instructor for ways to submit this assignment.

Continued >

Make It Right *continued*

Figure 8–68

In the Lab

Design and/or create a publication using the guidelines, concepts, and skills presented in this chapter. Labs are listed in order of increasing difficulty.

Lab 1: Creating a Product List

Problem: A travel agency has asked you to create a product list about popular National Parks, which the agency can merge into several different publications.

Instructions: Perform the following tasks:

1. Create a new folder on your storage device and name it, Lab 8–1 National Parks.

2. One at a time go to each of the Web sites listed in the first column of Table 8–1. Right-click the picture in the upper-right corner of the Web site and then click Save Picture As or Save Image As on the shortcut menu. The pictures on the National Park Service Web site are considered to be in the public domain. They may be copied as permitted by applicable law. Save the picture on your storage device inside the folder created in Step 1. Save the file with the name shown in the second column of Table 8–1.

Table 8–1 National Park Service Photos

URL	Picture Name
http://www.nps.gov/acad/index.htm	Acadia.jpg
http://www.nps.gov/grca/index.htm	Grand Canyon.jpg
http://www.nps.gov/yose/index.htm	Yosemite.jpg
http://www.nps.gov/yell/index.htm	Yellowstone.jpg
http://www.nps.gov/romo/index.htm	Rocky Mountain.jpg
http://www.nps.gov/havo/index.htm	Hawaii Volcanoes.jpg

3. Start Publisher with a blank 8.5 × 11" page and the default color and font schemes.

4. Click the Catalog Pages button (Insert tab | Pages group) to display the Catalog Tools Format tab.

5. Click the Add List button (Catalog Tools Format tab | Start group) and then click Type New List to open the New Product List dialog box.

6. Click the Customize Columns button and then rename the columns to match the column headings in Table 8–2. Add new columns as necessary.

Continued >

In the Lab *continued*

Name	Location	Acreage	Picture	Description	Established	URL
Acadia National Park	Bar Harbor, Maine	47,000	Acadia.jpg	Acadia National Park has mountains, national coastline, and plenty of historic sites. Visit the Bass Harbor Head lighthouse, and take a boat cruise to learn about wild sea life.	1901	http://www.nps.gov/acad/
Grand Canyon National Park	Grand Canyon, Arizona	1,218,375	Grand Canyon.jpg	Grand Canyon National Park is one mile deep and is easily accessed by the South Rim. Attend ranger programs, visit the Museum, and you can even hike the mile down to the canyon's bottom. Beware though; it's hard to get back up!	1919	http://www.nps.gov/grca/
Yosemite National Park	Yosemite National Park, California	747,956	Yosemite.jpg	Yosemite National Park is home to giant sequoias, waterfalls, and vast amounts of wilderness. Hike up rock walls, camp, and see plenty of wildlife.	1890	http://www.nps.gov/yose/
Yellowstone National Park	Yellowstone National Park, Wyoming	2,221,776	Yellowstone.jpg	See the most wildlife in one place! Yellowstone boasts bears, wolves, elk, and buffalo. It's also home to the most geothermal activity in the U.S.	1872	http://www.nps.gov/yell/
Rocky Mountain National Park	Estes Park, Colorado	265,800	Rocky Mountain.jpg	If you want to get your Rocky Mountain High, you have to visit Rocky Mountains National Park. Go from 8,000 feet to over 14,000 multiple times within one park. See nature in all its splendor.	1915	http://www.nps.gov/romo/
Hawaii Volcanoes	Hawaii Island, Hawaii	333,000	Hawaii Volcanoes.jpg	Hawaii Volcanoes displays the results of 70 million years of volcanism, migration, and evolution. The park highlights two of the world's most active volcanoes and offers insights on the birth of the Hawaiian Islands.	1916	http://www.nps.gov/havo/

Table 8–2 National Parks Database

7. Click the OK button (Customize Product List dialog box). Enter the fields of data from Table 8–2.

8. When you are finished, click the OK button (New Product List dialog box) to display the Save Address List dialog box. Navigate to the folder you created in Step 1. Name the file, National Parks Database and then click the Save button (Save Address List dialog box).

9. Compare your Catalog Merge Product List dialog box with the one shown in Figure 8–69.

10. Close the publication without saving.

11. If your instructor permits, send the National Park Database.mdb file to your instructor as an e-mail attachment.

Figure 8–69

In the Lab

Lab 2: Create a Cactus Identification Catalog

Instructions: Start Publisher. Download the folder named, Lab 8-2 Cacti, from the Data Files for Students. See the inside back cover of this book for instructions on downloading the Data Files for Students, or contact your instructor for more information about accessing the required files.

The folder contains pictures of various cacti and a data source file with the names and descriptions of the pictures. You are to use a catalog template to design a catalog that will display the pictures and descriptions of the cacti for a park district publication. A sample catalog is displayed in Figure 8–70 on the next page.

Continued >

In the Lab *continued*

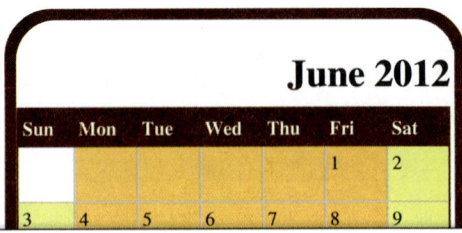

June 2012

Sun	Mon	Tue	Wed	Thu	Fri	Sat
					1	2
3	4	5	6	7	8	9

Page 2   Your guide to identifying the host of the desert

Name:	Barrel
Genus:	Echinocactus grusonii
Size:	up to 10 feet
Food use:	pulp can be used to make

Page 3   Your guide to identifying the host of the desert

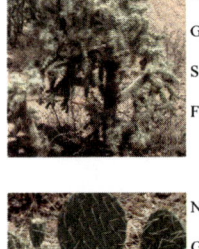

Name:	Silver Cholla
Genus:	Cylindropuntia fulgida
Size:	up to 8 feet
Food use:	some fruit is edible

Name:	Desert Prickly Pear
Genus:	Opuntia engelmannii
Size:	up to 8" in diameter
Food use:	inner fruit can be made into jelly

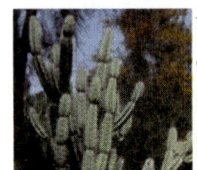

Name:	Cereus
Genus:	Cereus lamprospermus
Size:	up to 30 feet
Food use:	some fruit is edible

Your guide to identifying the host of the desert

Cactus Calling

Inside

Pictures and descriptions of the most popular cacti

Size and genus

Find out which cacti are edible

Calendar of Events

Caleb Park District

Summer 2012

Figure 8–70

1. Start Publisher. Choose to display the catalog templates. Select the Studio template with the default size of 5.5 × 8.5, the Desert color scheme, and the Versatile font scheme.

2. When the publication is displayed in the workspace, delete all but the front and back pages.

3. On page 1:

   a. Select the text in the Catalog Subtitle text box and then type `Your guide to identifying the host of the desert` as the new subtitle.

   b. Select the text in the Catalog Title text box, press CTRL+B to bold the text, and then type `Cactus Calling` to enter the new title.

   c. Right-click the graphic on page 1, point to Change Picture, and then click Change Picture. Navigate to the picture with the file named, Front Cover Cactus, which is located in the folder named Lab 8-2 Cacti on the Data Files for Students. Double-click the file to insert it into the publication and then drag the cropping handles to include the entire picture.

   d. In the center text box, type the following:

      `Inside`
      * `Pictures and descriptions of the most popular cacti`
      * `Size and genus`
      * `Find out which cacti are edible`
      * `Calendar of Events`

   e. In the Business Name text box, type `Caleb Park District` as the name of the business.

   f. In the Date text box, type `Summer 2012` to complete the entries on page 1.

4. On Page 2, insert catalog pages to display the catalog merge area. Move the catalog merge area below the header.

5. Click the Add List button (Catalog Tools Format tab | Start group) and then click Use Existing List.

6. In the Select Data Source dialog box, navigate to the location of the Data Files for Students. In the folder named Lab 8-2 Cacti folder, select the file named, Cactus Address List. When the list is displayed, click the OK button to display the catalog merge area on page 2. Use a 1 × 3 layout so that all six records will fit across the two-page spread.

7. Use the Picture Field button (Catalog Tools Format tab | Insert group) to insert the picture field into the catalog merge area. Position the picture box in the upper-left corner of the catalog merge area.

8. Insert a table inside the catalog merge area that fills the empty space beside the picture, choosing 4 rows and 2 columns, with no formatting.

9. In the first column of the table, enter the following row headings, making certain to type a colon (:) after each heading: Name, Genus, Size, and Food use. Use the Text Field button (Catalog Tools Format tab | Insert group) to enter the corresponding field codes in the second column.

10. On page 4:

    a. Delete the organization logo.

    b. Insert a calendar for June 2012. When the calendar is displayed, select the weekday cells and then use the Fill button (Table Tools Design tab | Table Formats group) to fill the cells with Accent 2 from the color scheme. Fill the weekend cells with the Accent 3 color. Apply other formatting to match Figure 8–70.

Continued >

In the Lab *continued*

    c. Below the calendar, insert a rectangle shape approximately .5 inches square. Fill the rectangle with the Accent 2 color. Create a text box next to the rectangle approximately 3 inches wide and .5 inches tall. Using a font of size 10 or larger, type `Open from 10 a.m. to 7 p.m.` in the text box.

    d. Below the previous rectangle and text box, insert another similar rectangle shape, filled with the Accent 3 color. Create a similar text box. Using a font of size 10 or larger, type `Open from 10 a.m. to 10 p.m.` in the text box.

    e. If necessary, in the Business Name text box, type `Caleb Park District` to replace the text.

    f. In the address text box, type:

        `5200 Park Drive`
        `Tucson, AZ  85719`

    g. In the phone text box, type:

        `Phone: 520-555-4800`
        `Fax: 520-555-4801`

11. Navigate to Page 2. Select the text in the To Order box at the top of the page. Type `Your guide to identifying the host of the desert` to replace the synchronized text.

12. Run the spell checker and design checker, fixing any errors. Preview the results using the Catalog tools Format tab.

13. Save the new publication with the name, Lab 8-2 Cactus Catalog.

14. Submit the merged file in the format specified by your instructor.

In the Lab

Lab 3: Using a Product List to Create a Poster

Problem: Your summer internship involves working as a desktop publisher for a poster design company. They have asked you to create a poster of seashells. Because all the pictures are stored in a folder and referenced via a database, you decide to try using the catalog merge to import the pictures for a single page poster, as shown in Figure 8–71.

Instructions: Perform the following tasks:
Copy the folder named, Lab 8-3 Shells, from the Data Files for Students to your personal storage location. Start Publisher and open a blank publication. Insert catalog pages. For the data source, select the Shells database in the folder. Use the Rows and Columns button (Catalog Tools Format tab | Layout group) to create a layout of 1 × 6. Move the catalog merge area down approximately 1 inch. Resize it to be approximately 1.5 inches tall and fill the area between the margins. If necessary, adjust the size and position of the merge area so that all six of the merged fields fit on the page. Insert a Picture field in the left part of the catalog merge area and resize the picture field to be approximately 1.5 inches tall, filling the catalog merge area vertically. Deselect the picture field. Insert the Name text field on the right. Delete page 1 in the Page Navigation pane. Use WordArt to create an overall heading containing the text, The Shells of Pipina Beach. Insert the Waterdroplets page background. Save the file and submit it as directed by your instructor.

Figure 8–71

Cases and Places

Apply your creative thinking and problem solving skills to design and implement a solution.

Note: To complete these assignments, you may be required to use the Data Files for Students. See the inside back cover of this book for instructions on downloading the Data Files for Students, or contact your instructor for information about accessing the required files.

1: Creating AutoCorrect Entries

Academic

The Department of Communications at your school has asked you to create a series of AutoCorrect entries that will be used as shortcuts for their staff and faculty. Start Publisher, click Options in the Backstage view, and then click Proofing (Publisher Options dialog box). Click the AutoCorrect Options button to display the AutoCorrect dialog box. Enter the AutoCorrect entries from Table 8–3. When you are finished, return to the Backstage view and then open a blank publication. Create a text box and test the entries.

Table 8–3 AutoCorrect Entries	
Replace	**With**
DOC	Department of Communications
CMS	Communications
CMT	Communication Technology
TC	Telecommunications
COAS	College of Arts and Sciences

2: Translate a Menu

Personal

Your friend is having a New Year's Eve party with a French theme and has sent you a copy of the menu she is planning. You do not have a strong background in French, so you decide to use Publisher's translation feature to find out what foods you will be served. Open the file named Case 8-2 French Menu from the Data File for Students. Translate and replace as many of the menu items as you can find in the translation service. Save the file with the file name, Case 8-2 English Menu.

3: Create a Catalog

Professional

Using a digital camera, take pictures of at least eight different locations of interest in your city. Record the locations of the buildings and their significance to the community. Create a new folder on your storage device and store the eight pictures in that folder. Open a catalog template in Publisher, and delete all but the first and last pages. Insert a blank catalog page, and then click the Add List button (Catalog Tools Format tab | Start group). Use the Type New List command to create a new data source. Customize the columns and include fields such as building name, location, description, and picture. In the picture field, enter the names of the digital files. Choose to store the address list in the same folder as the pictures. Use the Catalog Tools Format tab to merge the data from your address list in a 4 × 2 catalog merge area. Save the merged publication in the same folder as the pictures and address list.

9 | Sharing and Distributing Publications

Objectives

You will have mastered the material in this chapter when you can:

- Select and format an e-mail template
- Change the size of an e-mail page
- Set the e-mail page background
- Create a callout
- Insert symbols and special characters
- Use the Research task pane
- Create a cited definition
- Insert a hot spot and a mailto hyperlink
- Choose options for the Design Checker
- Preview an e-mail message using Publisher
- Send an HTML-enabled e-mail message
- Send a publication as an e-mail attachment
- Create and print greeting cards

9 | Sharing and Distributing Publications

Introduction

Publisher makes it easy to share and distribute publications. Sending e-mail messages, attaching publications to e-mail messages, mailing publications using the postal service, and uploading publications to Web sites are among the ways that desktop publishers can market and correspond electronically with customers, business associates, and friends.

E-mail, short for electronic mail, is a popular form of communication used to transmit messages and files via a computer network. For businesses, e-mail can be an efficient and cost-effective way to keep in touch with customers and interested parties. E-mail is used in ways similar to traditional mail. With it, you can send correspondence, business communications, and other types of publications. An e-mail may display traditional correspondence-related text and graphics and may include hyperlinks similar to a Web page, as well as attachments. Many e-mail messages sent from companies or organizations include a way for recipients to unsubscribe from the mailing list. When recipients **unsubscribe**, they remove their names and addresses from the mailing list.

Publications that sometimes are attached to an e-mail message (or more traditionally are mailed using a postal service) include graphics, postcards, and greeting cards, among others.

Project — Distributed Publications

You may find the need to share and distribute Publisher files with others electronically. To ensure that others can read and/or open the files successfully, Publisher presents a variety of formats and tools to assist with sharing documents. In this chapter, you will create and send several publications, including an e-mail message, a postcard, and a greeting card. Figure 9–1a displays an e-mail message sent to a list of participants or members of a sports fan club. Figure 9–1b displays an e-postcard sent to new members as an attachment. Figure 9–1c displays a greeting card to be sent via the postal service. The publications include colorful headings, graphics, and directions for obtaining more information.

When you send an e-mail message, recipients can read it using HTML-enabled e-mail programs such as Gmail, AOL Mail, Yahoo! Mail, or the current versions of Microsoft Outlook and Outlook Express. **HTML-enabled e-mail** allows the sender to include formatted text and other visuals to improve the readability and aesthetics of the message. The majority of Internet users can access HTML-enabled e-mail. Recipients do not need to have Publisher installed to view e-mail messages, because the page you send will be displayed as the body of the e-mail message. Sending a one-page publication by e-mail to a group of customers or friends is an efficient and inexpensive way to deliver a message.

Publisher provides several ways to create an e-mail message. You can use a template or create an e-mail from scratch. Publisher's e-mail templates are preformatted and use placeholder text and graphics that download quickly and are suitable for the body of an e-mail message.

(a) Event E-Mail

(b) Publication Sent as an E-Mail Attachment

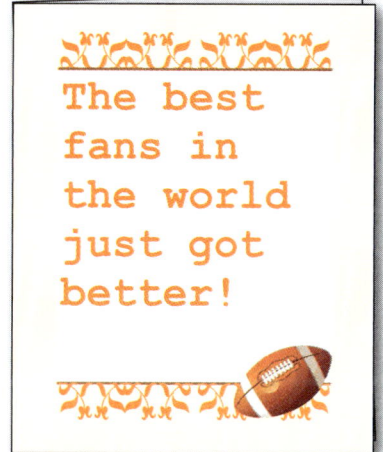

(c) Greeting Card

Figure 9–1

A second way to create an e-mail is to send a single page of another publication. This expands the use of your existing content, although you may need to adjust the width of your publication in order for it to fit in an e-mail message.

Another way is to send an entire publication as an attachment; however, this requires that the recipient have Microsoft Publisher 2002 or a later version installed to view it. When the recipient opens the attached file, Publisher automatically opens and displays the publication. Unless you convert a multipage publication into a single page e-mail message, it must be sent as an e-mail attachment.

Finally, you can create an **e-mail merge** when you want to send a large number of messages that are mostly identical, but you also want to include some unique or personalized information in each message. An e-mail merge, which uses the mail merge techniques that you learned about in Chapter 7, creates content that is personalized for each recipient on a mailing list.

The type of publication you choose depends on the content and the needs of the recipients. Table 9–1 describes specific audiences and the appropriate kinds of e-mail publications.

Table 9–1 Publisher E-Mail Types			
Audience Characteristic	**E-Mail Message**	**E-Mail Merge**	**E-Mail Attachment**
Recipients definitely have Publisher installed			X
Recipients may not have Publisher installed	X	X	
Recipients need to read and print the content in its original format			X
Recipients may not have HTML-enabled e-mail	X	X	
Recipients need personalized messages		X	

Overview

As you read this chapter, you will learn how to create the flyer shown in Figure 9–1 by performing these general tasks:

- Edit an e-mail template.
- Create a callout.
- Insert symbols, special characters, hyperlinks, hot spots, and mailto hyperlinks.
- Check, preview, and send an e-mail message.
- Send a publication as an attachment.
- Create a folded publication.

Plan Ahead

General Project Guidelines

When creating a Publisher publication, the actions you perform and decisions you make will affect the appearance and characteristics of the finished document. As you create publications, such as the ones shown in Figure 9–1, you should follow these general guidelines:

1. **Use the correct format and size for e-mail messages.** Be sure to start with a Publisher e-mail template or resize your publication to fit standard e-mail message sizes. When using a template, choose one that matches the purpose of the e-mail. Use graphics sparingly, keeping in mind the download time.

2. **Correctly format symbols, hyperlinks, and hot spots.** Use the symbol dialog box to create symbols and characters not found on the keyboard. Create and double-check all hyperlinks for purpose and type. A **hyperlink** is usually a colored and underlined text that you click to go to a file, a location in a file, a Web page, or an e-mail address. Create hot spots around graphics as necessary. A **hot spot** is a hyperlink that appears as a graphic, picture, button, or shape.

3. **Preview and check the e-mail message.** There is no substitute for careful proofreading, but also use the e-mail design check and spelling check functionality available in Publisher. Preview the e-mail message in a Web browser, and check all links.

4. **Employ attachments as necessary.** If your publication is not in an e-mail format, or if it cannot be converted to one, attach the publication to the e-mail as a separate file. For large publications and multipage publications, consider compressing the file.

When necessary, more specific details concerning the above guidelines are presented at appropriate points in the chapter. The chapter also will identify the actions performed and decisions made regarding these guidelines during the creation of the publications shown in Figure 9–1.

To Start Publisher

The following steps, which assume Windows 7 is running, start Publisher based on a typical installation. You may need to ask your instructor how to start Publisher for your computer. For a detailed example of the procedure summarized below, refer to the Office 2010 and Windows 7 chapter at the beginning of this book.

1 Click the Start button on the Windows 7 taskbar to display the Start menu.

2 Type `Microsoft Publisher` as the search text in the 'Search programs and files' text box, and watch the search results appear on the Start menu.

3 Click Microsoft Publisher 2010 in the search results on the Start menu to start Publisher and open the Backstage view and the New Template gallery.

4 If the Publisher window is not maximized, click the Maximize button next to the Close button on its title bar to maximize the window.

E-Mail Templates

Each of Publisher's design sets features several e-mail templates, so you can create and send e-mail that is consistent in design with the rest of the business communication and marketing materials that you create using Publisher. Table 9–2 lists the types of e-mail templates and their purpose.

> **Use the correct format and size for e-mail messages.**
> Choose a template carefully, as Publisher will supply many of the necessary elements, such as text, graphics, and links. Decide if you really need the long e-mail format, or change the page length to the short e-mail format. If you use a wallpaper or stationery, keep it simple or a solid color. Use graphics sparingly, keeping in mind the download time.

BTW

E-Mail Templates
E-mail templates contain text boxes, logos, hyperlinks, and graphics. To customize the e-mail message, you replace the placeholder text and graphics with your own content, just as you would in any other template publication.

Plan Ahead

Table 9–2 Types of E-Mail Templates	
Type	**Purpose**
Event/Activity	A notice of a specific upcoming activity or event containing a combination of pictures, dates, times, maps, agenda, and the ability to sign up
Event/Speaker	A notice of a specific upcoming event that includes a speaker and usually contains pictures, dates, times, and a map
Featured Product	A publication that provides information about a company and a specific product or service, including graphics and Web page links for more information
Letter	A more personalized document to correspond with one or more people, including specific information on a single topic
Newsletter	Informs interested clientele about an organization or business with stories, dates, contact information, and upcoming events
Product List	A sales-oriented publication to display products, prices, and special promotions including Web page links for more information

BTW

E-Mail Marketing
Using e-mail for marketing purposes has many benefits, including low cost, immediate communication, interactivity, and the ability to contact multiple customers. It makes it easy to track positive and negative responses, visits to Web pages, and increases in specific product sales. Considerate and thoughtful e-mail marketing can reinforce positive interaction with your business

To Select an E-Mail Template and Choose Settings

The following steps select an e-mail template from the New template gallery and choose settings. For the e-mail message created in this chapter, you will choose an Event/ Activity e-mail template. You do not have to be connected to the Internet or have an e-mail program on your system in order to create the e-mail. You can create and save the e-mail message on a flash drive rather than send it via e-mail.

① Click the E-mail thumbnail in the More Templates area in the New template gallery to display the e-mail templates.

② Scroll as necessary to view the More Installed Templates area and the Event/Activity category.

③ Click the Marquee thumbnail.

④ In the Customize area, choose the Citrus color scheme and the Data font scheme.

⑤ Click the Create button to create the template with the chosen settings.

⑥ Display the View tab. If necessary, click to display a check mark in the Boundaries check box (View tab | Show group).

⑦ Display the Home tab. If necessary, click the Special Characters button (Home tab | Paragraph group) to display paragraph marks and special characters.

⑧ Close the Page Navigation pane (Figure 9–2).

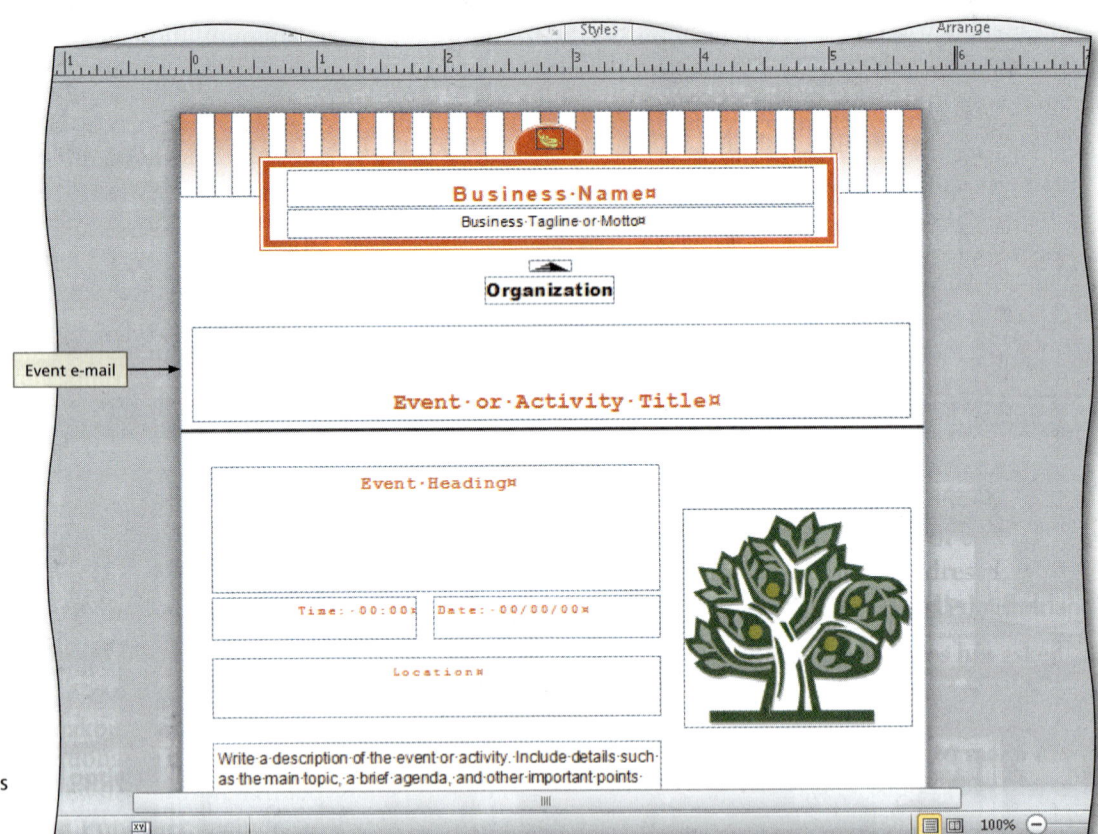

Figure 9–2

To Change the E-Mail Message Page Size

The following steps change the page size of the e-mail message.

1

- Display the Page Design tab.

- Click the Page Size button (Page Design tab | Page Setup group) to display the list of page sizes.

- If necessary, scroll to the bottom of the list (Figure 9–3).

 Could I choose Page Setup to customize the page size?

Yes, you can set the margins and choose various paper sizes and layouts in the Page Setting dialog box. The e-mail sizes include the standard width of 5.818 inches but differing lengths, including a long e-mail (up to 66 inches), a short e-mail (up to 11 inches), or a custom size.

Figure 9–3

2

- Click Short to choose a short page format (Figure 9–4).

Figure 9–4

To Set the E-Mail Background

You can add a background to an e-mail or Web publication by applying a color, gradient, picture, texture, or pattern. A background should not be detailed or busy, because it appears behind the text and graphics. Simple backgrounds will not add significantly to the download time. People include e-mail backgrounds, also called **wallpaper** or **stationery**, to add interest to their e-mail messages, to convey or enhance the message, to grab the reader's attention, or to emulate business letterhead. A background also can make your e-mail message stand out from those who simply use black text on a white background. Publisher especially is useful for those e-mail programs that do not offer wallpaper.

The following steps choose a solid background for the e-mail page.

- Click the Background button (Page Design tab | Page Background group) to display the Background gallery (Figure 9–5).

Experiment

- Point to each of the solid and gradient backgrounds in the gallery and watch the e-mail page change.

Figure 9–5

- Click 10% tint of Accent 1 to apply it to the e-mail page (Figure 9–6).

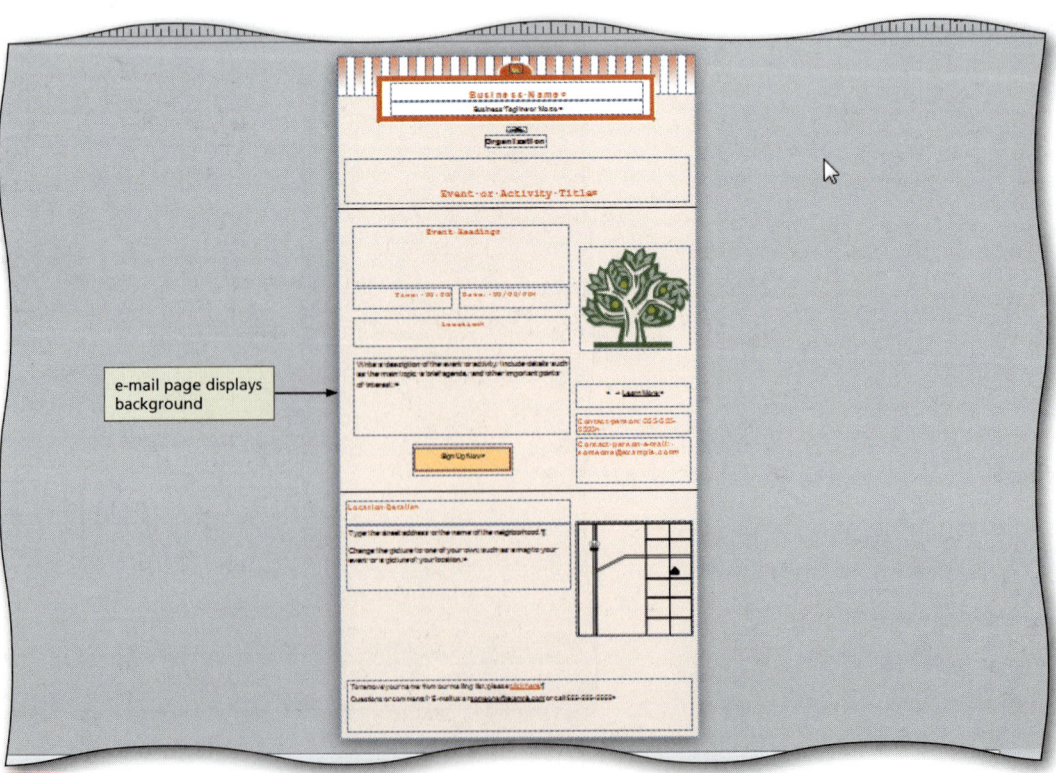

Figure 9–6

To Edit the Headings

The following steps edit the headings, which appear in the upper portion of most event, activity, or announcement e-mails.

1 Select the text in the Business Name text box at the top of the page and press the F9 key to zoom to 100%. Type `ORION FAN ZONE` to replace the text.

2 Select the text in the Business Tagline or Motto text box. Type `Orion fans are the best in the world!` to replace the text.

3 Select the placeholder text in the Event or Activity Title text box. Type `Don't Forget the Tailgate Party` to replace the text.

4 Select the placeholder text in the Event Heading text box. Type `Tailgating with Orion Fan Zone` to replace the text (Figure 9–7).

Figure 9–7

To Edit Text Boxes in the Middle Section

The following steps edit the text boxes in the middle portion of the e-mail message where details about the event or activity usually appear.

1 Scroll down to the middle portion of the page. Select the 00:00 text in the Time text box. Type `Noon` to replace the text.

2 Select the 00/00/00 text in the Date text box. Type `10/20/12` to replace the text.

3 Select the placeholder text in the Location text box. Type `Orion Stadium Parking Lot` to replace the text.

BTW
Background vs. Master Pages
A background is not the same as a master page. When you add a background to an e-mail message, the publication's master page does not change. Avoid changing the master pages in e-mail and Web publications. Special effects applied to master pages do not display correctly when they are viewed in some Web browsers.

BTW
Using Pictures as Backgrounds
If you select a custom picture file for your background texture, make sure it is 20 kilobytes (KB) or smaller. Large picture files will require people who are viewing your e-mail message to wait a long time for the graphic to download. If you select a picture for a background, the picture is repeated (or tiled).

4 Select the placeholder text in the description text box. Type `Let us do the tailgating work for you at the Orion Fan Zone tent located on the northeast corner of the stadium parking lot. This is a perfect option for fans coming via bus, light rail, or those who just don't want to put together their own tailgate party. Our giant tent provides an area for you to come together with other Orion fans before regular season home games and build excitement you can carry with you inside the stadium.` to replace the text (Figure 9–8).

Figure 9–8

To Edit Text Boxes in the Lower Section

The following steps edit text in the lower portion of the e-mail message. Many event e-mail messages list contact information, how to join, how to unsubscribe, and other links in the lower portion of the e-mail message.

1 Select the placeholder text in the Location Details text box and then type `Become a Member` to replace the text.

2 Select both paragraphs of text in the street address text box and then type `As a registered Orion Fan Zone member, you can access the interactive sections of OrionFootball.com so that you can share your thoughts in the Bulletin Board or Chat Room areas, as well as play fun games like Fantasy Forecast.` to replace the text.

3 In the text box at the bottom of the page, select the e-mail address placeholder text and then type `FanZone@OrionFootball.com` to replace the text.

4 Select the placeholder text, or call 555-555-5555, and then type `or call 866-555-FANS` to replace the text (Figure 9–9).

Figure 9–9

To Delete Objects

The following steps delete objects in the e-mail message that will not be used.

1 Select the Organization logo in the upper portion of the page and then press the DELETE key to delete the logo.

2 Select the Contact person phone number text box and then press the DELETE key to delete it.

3 Select the Contact person e-mail text box and then press the DELETE key to delete it.

To Move and Resize Objects

The following steps move the button to a location in the lower portion of the e-mail message and move the title text box closer to the other headings.

1 SHIFT+drag the Sign Up Now button downward to a location just above the last text box on the page.

2 At the top of the page, drag the border of the Don't Forget the Tailgate Party text box up to move the text box closer to the banner heading, but do not overlap their borders. Drag the lower-center sizing handle up until there is little blank space in the text box below the words (Figure 9–10).

text box moved
up and resized

Figure 9–10

To Insert Clip Art

Most of the e-mail templates contain graphics that you can edit to suit your publication. You edit e-mail graphics in the same way that you edit graphics in other publications. You can select a clip art image, insert a graphic from a file, or import a graphic from a scanner or digital camera. The following steps edit the graphic that appears next to the time and date text boxes.

1 Scroll as necessary and then click the graphic that appears next to the time and date text boxes to select it.

2 Display the Insert tab.

3 Click the Clip Art button (Insert tab | Illustrations group). When the Clip Art task pane is displayed, search for clip art related to the word, football.

4 Click a graphic similar to the one shown in Figure 9–11 and then close the Clip Art task pane and deselect the picture.

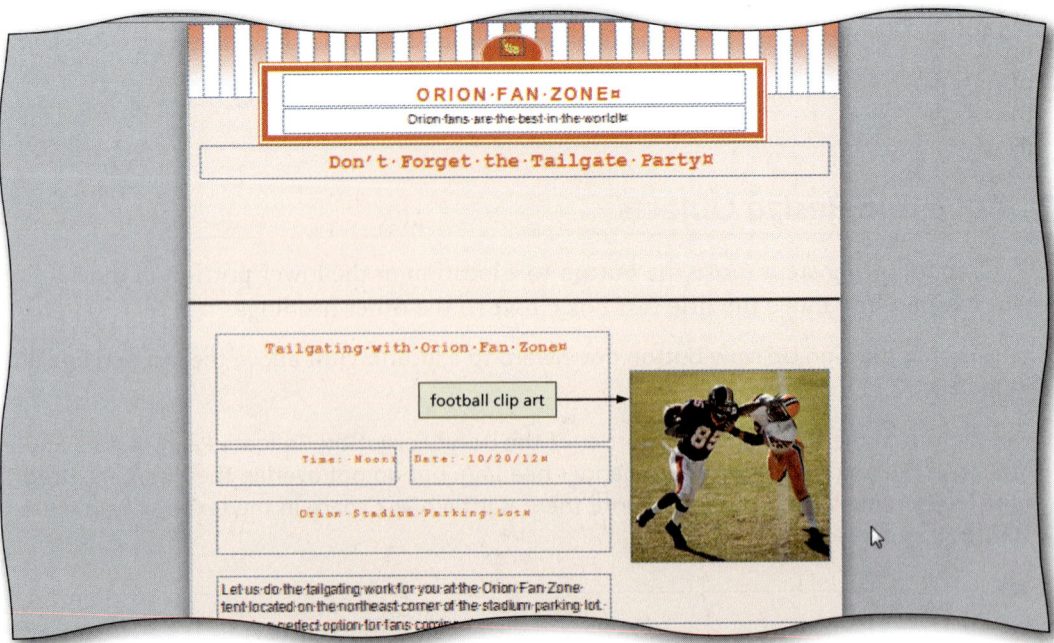

football clip art

Figure 9–11

To Insert a Picture from a File

The following steps edit the graphic that displays a map, using a file from the Data Files for Students. See the inside back cover of this book for instructions on downloading the Data Files for Students, or contact your instructor for information about accessing the required files.

1 Scroll as necessary and then right-click the graphic that displays a map.

2 Point to Change Picture on the shortcut menu and then click Change Picture to display the Insert Picture dialog box.

3 Navigate to the Data Files for Students and the Chapter 09 folder.

4 Double-click the file named Stadium Map to replace the template graphic (shown in Figure 9–12).

5 Deselect the graphic.

To Create a Callout

A **callout** is a combination of text and a graphic used to explain a particular part of an image. The following steps use an arrow and an oval to create a callout that points out the location of the tailgate party.

1

• Click the Shapes button (Insert tab | Illustrations group) and then click the Arrow shape in the gallery.

• In the publication, drag downward to create an arrow approximately 1.5 inches long that ends at (or points to) the northeast corner of the stadium on the map graphic (Figure 9–12).

Figure 9–12

2

- Display the Insert tab.

- Click the Shapes button (Insert tab | Illustrations group) again and then click the Oval shape in the gallery.

- In the publication, drag to create an oval in the blank area at the top of the arrow (Figure 9–13).

Figure 9–13

3

- Right-click the oval and then click Add Text on the shortcut menu.

- Type **Tailgating Tent** to complete the callout (Figure 9–14).

Figure 9–14

Symbols and Special Characters

In Publisher, a **symbol** is a character that is not on your keyboard, such as ½ and ©, or **special characters**, such as an em dash (—) or ellipsis (…). Some special symbols use ASCII characters or Unicode characters. **ASCII** and **Unicode** are coding systems that represent text and symbols in computers, communications equipment, and other devices that use text.

> **Correctly format symbols, hyperlinks, and hot spots.**
> Limit the use of symbols and special characters in e-mails, as some may not display correctly. Make sure you check for terms that may need copyright, trademark, and registration symbols. Double-check all hyperlinks for purpose and type. Create hot spots around graphics as necessary. Use mailto hyperlinks to help the recipient respond via e-mail.

Plan Ahead

To Insert a Symbol from the Symbol Dialog Box

In the e-mail message, a check mark inside a small square box appears before the reminder heading. The check mark is not located on the keyboard; Publisher, however, provides a method of inserting special symbols. The following steps insert a symbol in the e-mail.

1
- Click before the word, Don't, in the third heading.
- Display the Insert tab.
- Click the Insert Symbol button (Insert tab | Text group) to display the Insert Symbol gallery (Figure 9–15).

Q&A
What if the symbol I want to insert already appears in the Insert Symbol gallery?

You can click any symbol shown in the Insert Symbol gallery to insert it in the document.

Figure 9–15

2

- Click More Symbols in the Insert Symbol gallery to display the Symbol dialog box.

- Click the Font box arrow to display the list of available fonts (Figure 9–16).

Q&A

Which font should I choose from the list?

When you are unsure where the special character you need might be located, it is a good idea to choose the (normal text) font and start looking at the top of the list. The check mark symbol used in this chapter is located in the **Wingdings** font set — a group of graphical design symbols.

Figure 9–16

3

- Scroll as necessary in the list and then click Wingdings to display the symbols.

- In the list of symbols, if necessary, scroll to the check mark symbol shown in Figure 9–17 and then click the symbol to select it.

Q&A

Does the symbol have a special name?

Publisher uses the font name and a number, Wingdings 254, to identify the symbol.

Figure 9–17

4
- Click the Insert button (Symbol dialog box) to place the selected symbol in the publication to the left of the insertion point.

- Click the Close button (Symbol dialog box) to close the dialog box.

- Press the SPACEBAR to insert a blank space (Figure 9–18).

Other Ways
1. Press ALT+Unicode number

Figure 9–18

To Insert a Special Character Using the Symbol Dialog Box

In the e-mail message, the name of the sports fan club uses the trademark special character, ™. This special character is not on the keyboard. The following steps insert a trademark special character after the words, Orion Fan Zone, in the heading.

1
- Click after the words, Orion Fan Zone, in the overall heading (shown in Figure 9–18).

- Click the Insert Symbol button (Insert tab | Text group) to display the Insert Symbol gallery.

- Click More Symbols in the Insert Symbol gallery to display the Symbol dialog box.

- Click the Special Characters tab and then click the desired special character (in this case, Trademark) in the list of special characters (Figure 9–19).

Figure 9–19

2

- Click the Insert button (Symbol dialog box) to place the selected special character in the publication.

- Click the Close button (Symbol dialog box) to close the dialog box (Figure 9–20).

Q&A

What is the difference between a symbol and a special character?

The special character list is a subset of symbols that are used often in professional typing tasks.

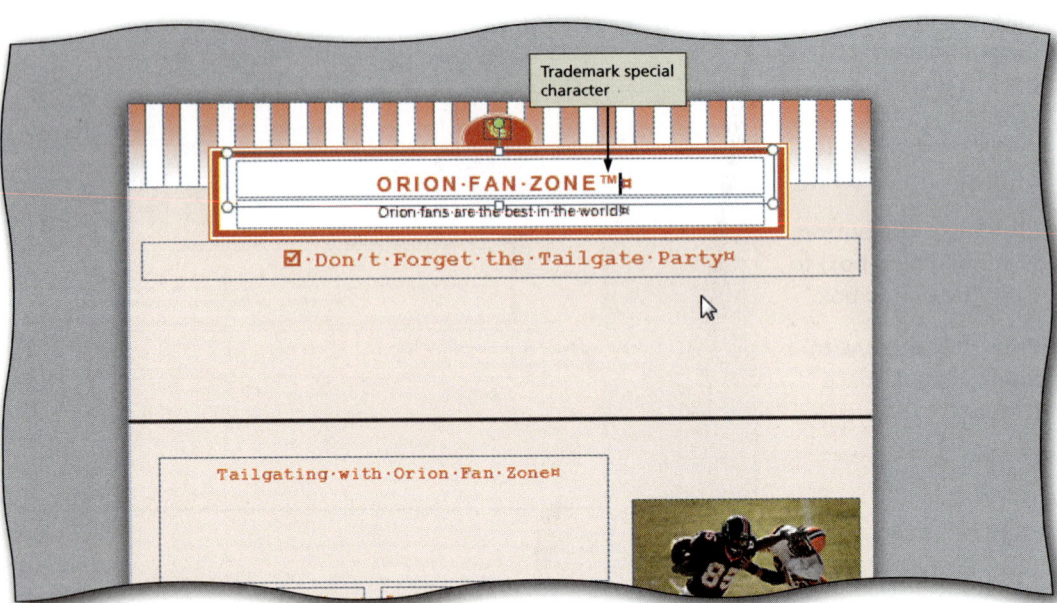

Figure 9–20

3

- Repeat Steps 1 and 2 to add the trademark special character to each occurrence of Orion Fan Zone in the e-mail message.

Other Ways
1. Press ALT+Unicode number

To Insert a Symbol from the Insert Symbol Gallery

In the e-mail message, other check mark symbols should be placed beside the time and beside the date. Once you insert a symbol using the Symbol dialog box, Publisher adds that symbol to the Symbol gallery so that it is more readily available. The following steps use the Symbol gallery to insert more symbols.

1

- Position the insertion point at the desired location, in this case before the word Time in the Time text box.

- Click the Insert Symbol button (Insert tab | Text group) to display the Insert Symbol gallery (Figure 9–21).

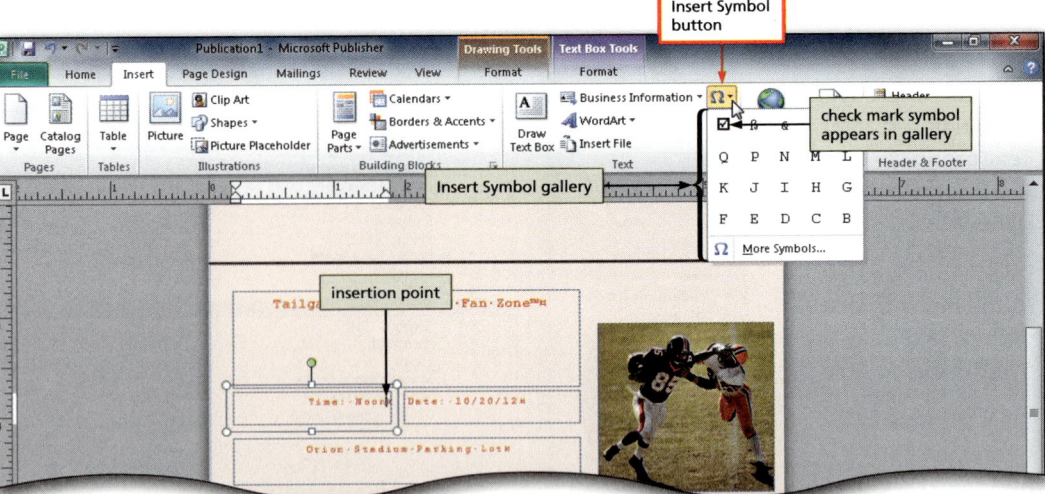

Figure 9–21

2

- Click the check mark symbol in the Insert Symbol gallery to insert the symbol at the location of the insertion point and then press the SPACEBAR (Figure 9–22).

Q&A

Do I need to change the font or font size?

No. The Symbol dialog box inserts the character using the current font and font size at the location of the insertion point.

Figure 9–22

3

- Repeat Steps 1 and 2 to include the check mark symbol and a blank space before the word Date (Figure 9–23).

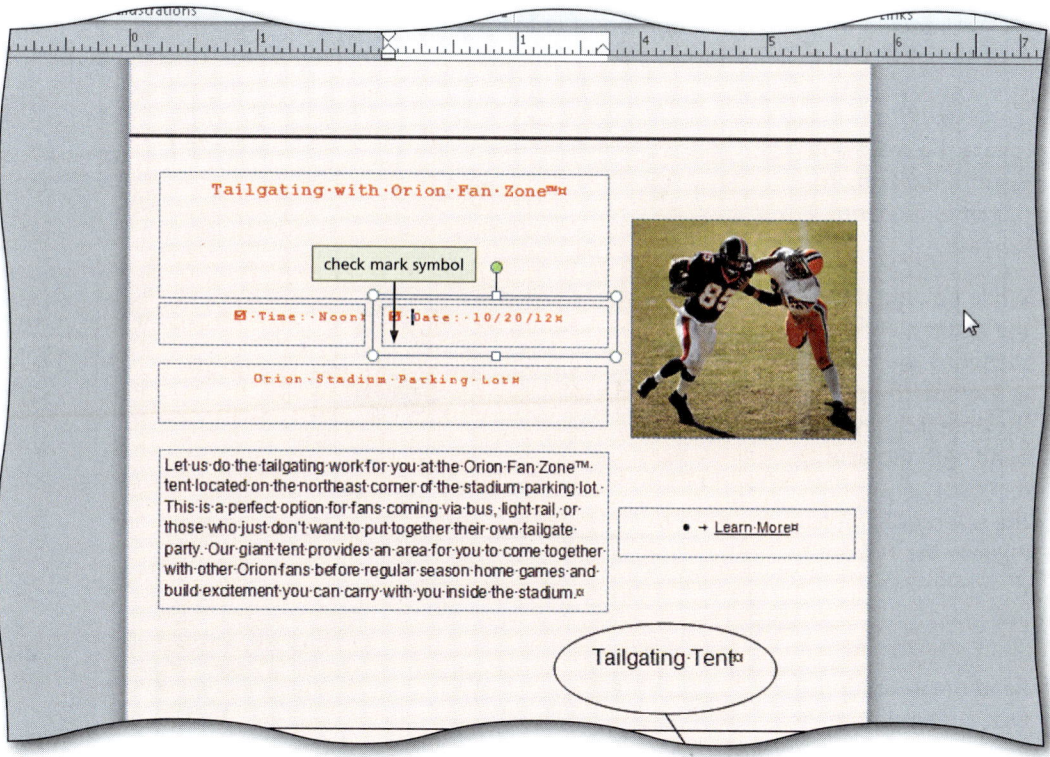

Figure 9–23

To Save the E-Mail Message

You have performed many tasks while creating this e-mail message and do not want to risk losing work completed thus far. Accordingly, you should save the publication.

1 With a USB flash drive connected to one of the computer's USB ports, click the Save button on the Quick Access Toolbar to display the Save As dialog box.

2 Type `Orion Fan Zone E-mail` in the File name text box to change the file name. Do not press the ENTER key after typing the file name because you do not want to close the dialog box at this time.

3 Navigate to the desired save location (in this case, the Publisher folder in the CIS 101 folder [or your class folder] on the USB flash drive).

4 Click the Save button (Save As dialog box) to save the document in the selected folder on the selected drive with the entered file name.

BTW

Research Options
Clicking the Research options link at the bottom of the Research task pane displays the Research Options dialog box, where you can view or modify the list of installed services.

Research Task Pane

From within Publisher, you can search various forms of reference information. Services include a dictionary and, if you are connected to the Web, an encyclopedia, a search engine, and other Web sites that provide information such as stock quotes, news articles, and company profiles.

To Use the Research Task Pane

You decide to include a definition of tailgating in the e-mail message. The following steps use the Research task pane to look up a definition of a term. You must be connected to the Internet to perform these steps.

1
- Locate the word you want to look up, in this case, the word, Tailgate.

- While holding down the ALT key, click the word you want to look up to open the Research task pane and display a dictionary entry for the referenced word. Release the ALT key (Figure 9–24).

🔑 **Experiment**
- Read the definitions that appear in the Research task pane.

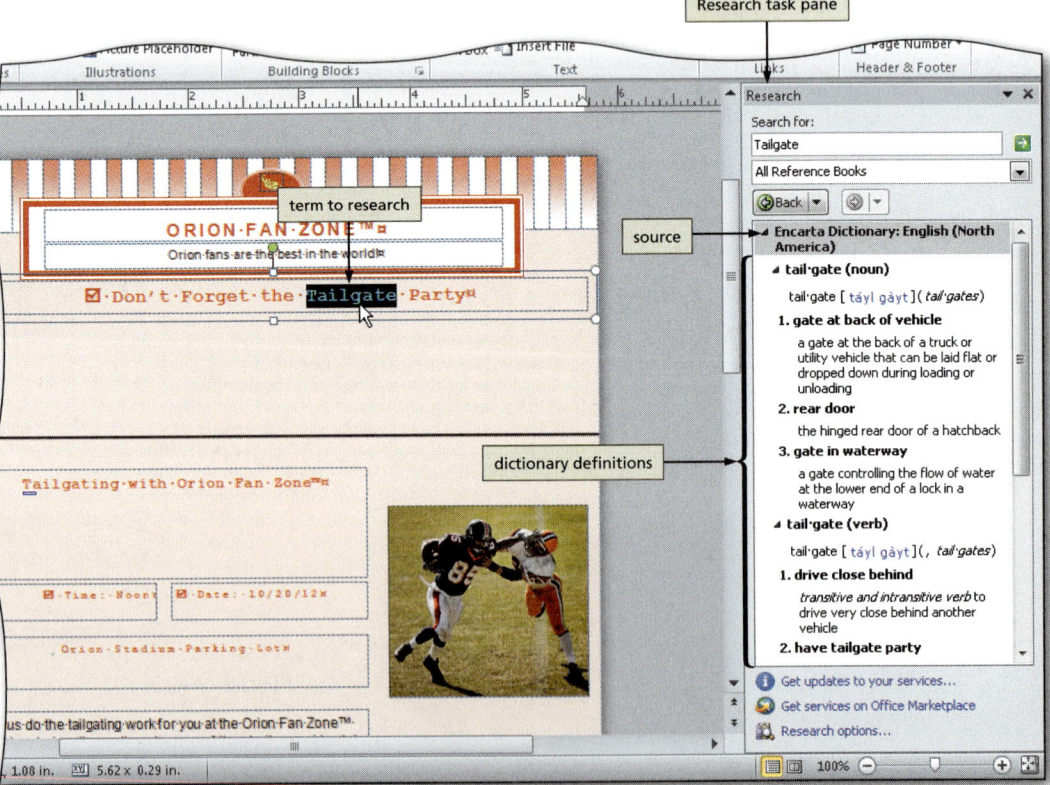

Figure 9–24

2

- Click the All Reference Books box arrow in the Research task pane to display a list of search locations (Figure 9–25).

Figure 9–25

3

- Click All Research Sites in the list to display Web sites with information about the referenced word (Figure 9–26).

Q&A

Can I copy information from the Research task pane into my publication?

Yes, you can use the Copy and Paste commands. When using Publisher to insert material from the Research task pane or any other online reference, however, be careful not to plagiarize.

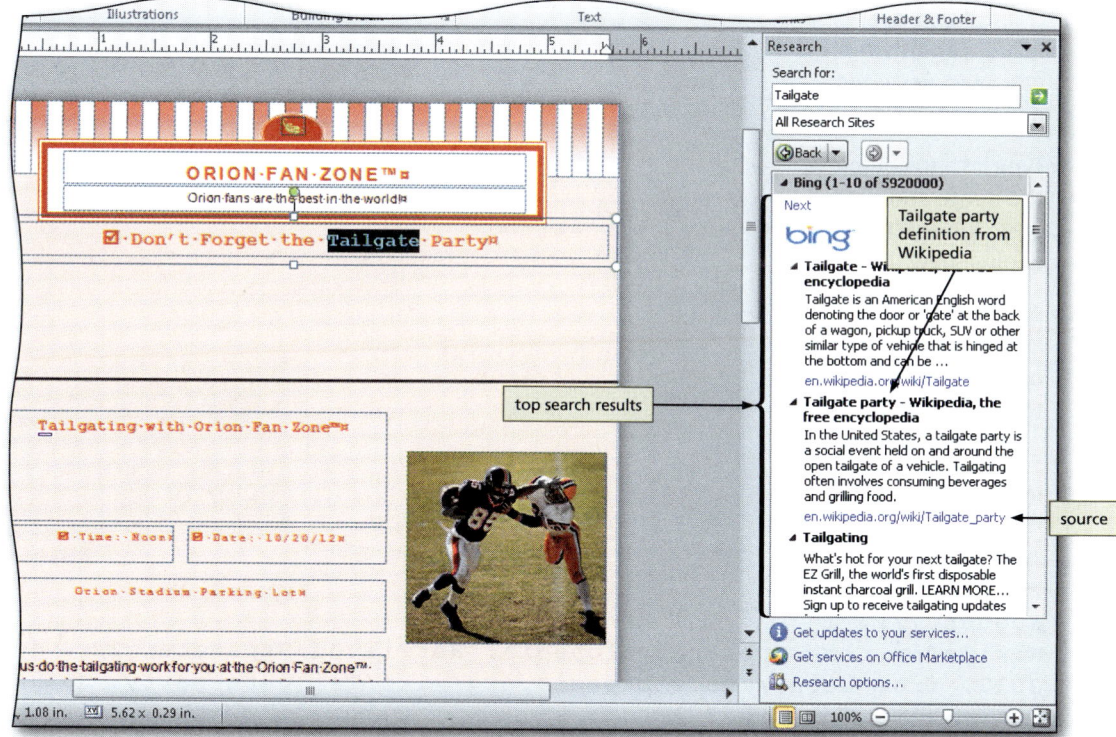

Figure 9–26

To Create a Cited Definition

The following steps copy and paste the definition into a new text box and create a citation.

1

- Click the Draw Text Box button (Insert tab | Text group).

- In the e-mail message, drag to create a 1-inch tall text box below the heading as shown in Figure 9–28. The right and left margins of the text box should align with the heading text box.

- Select the text in the Tailgate party entry of the Research task pane, beginning with the words, a tailgate party.

- Press CTRL+C to copy the definition (Figure 9–27).

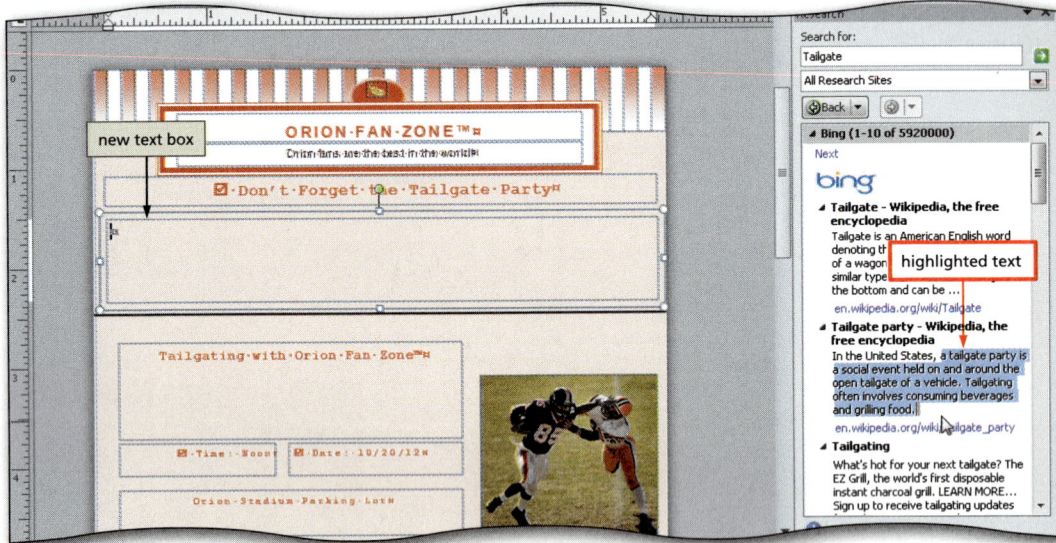

Figure 9–27

2

- In the publication, click in the newly created text box. Type " . . . and then press CTRL+V to paste the definition.

- Type " to complete the quote and then press the ENTER key to begin a new line.

- Right-click the text and then click Best Fit on the shortcut menu to autofit the text.

- Position the insertion point on the new blank line. Type Tailgate Party. (2010, August 17). In Wikipedia, the free encyclopedia. Retrieved September 12, 2012, from http://en.wikipedia.org/wiki/Tailgate_party. to complete the citation (Figure 9–28).

- Click the Close button in the Research task pane.

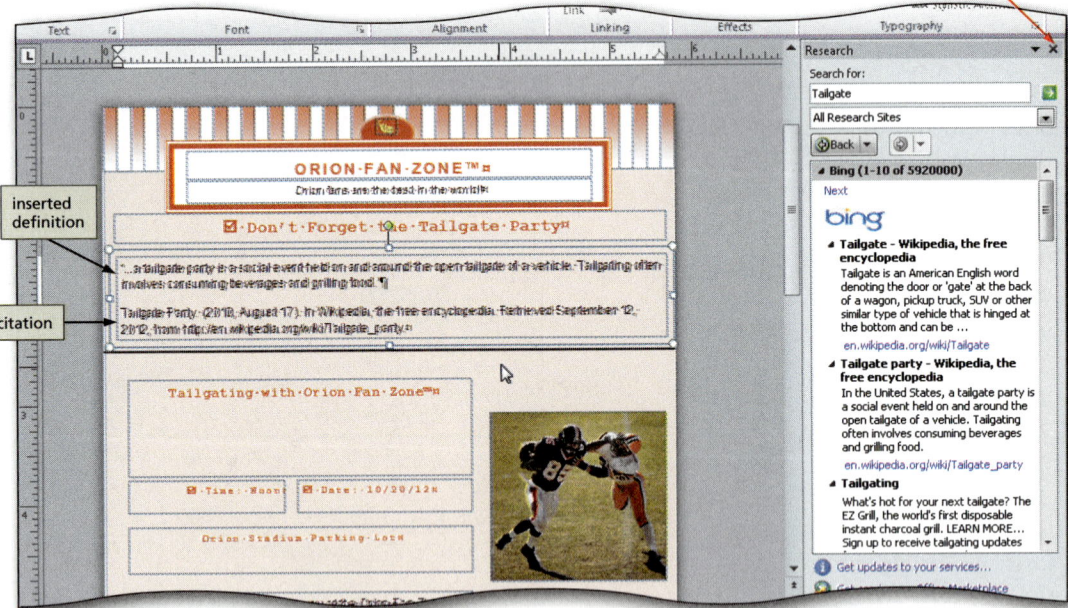

Figure 9–28

Other Ways
1. Click Research button (Review tab | Proofing group), enter term, click Start searching button (Research task pane)

Creating Hyperlinks and Hot Spots

E-mail messages can contain hyperlinks just as Web pages do. A hyperlink is usually colored and underlined text that you click to go to a file, a location in a file, a Web page, or an e-mail address; but, hyperlinks also can be a graphic, picture, button, or shape. When the hyperlink is not text, it is called a hot spot.

BTW

Research Services
When you install Publisher, it selects a series of services (reference books and Web sites) that it searches through when you use the Research task pane. You can view, modify, and update the list of services at any time.

Editing the Hyperlink

In the body of the e-mail letter template, the words, Learn More, should display as a hyperlink to open the fan club's Web page. In the final text box at the bottom of the page, the words, click here, should display as a hyperlink that starts the user's e-mail program and creates a new message.

To Insert a Hyperlink

The following steps insert a hyperlink into the publication.

1

- In the middle of the e-mail message, select the placeholder text, Learn More.

- Press CTRL+K to display the Insert Hyperlink dialog box.

- Type **www .orionfootball .com** in the Address box (Figure 9–29).

2

- Click the OK button (Insert Hyperlink dialog box) to create the hyperlink.

Figure 9–29

To Insert a Hot Spot

The steps on the next page insert a hyperlink for the map graphic that becomes a hot spot when the user views the e-mail message.

- Select the graphic that you wish to use as a hot spot (in this case, the map graphic).

- Press CTRL+K to display the Insert Hyperlink dialog box.

- In the Address box, type `http://www.bing.com/maps` to create the hyperlink hot spot (Figure 9–30).

2

- Click the OK button (Insert Hyperlink dialog box) to create the link.

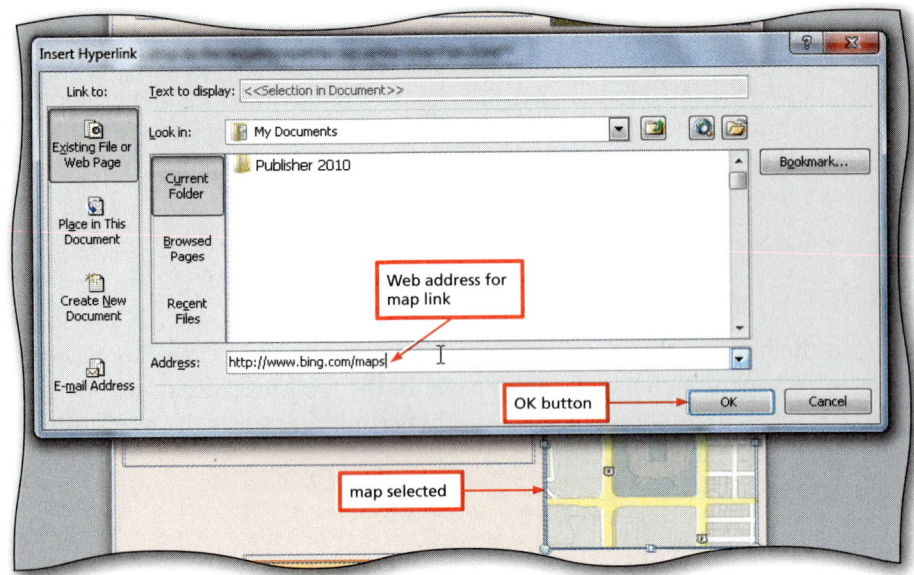

Figure 9–30

To Insert a Mailto Hyperlink

When clicked, a **mailto** hyperlink starts the user's e-mail program. Mailto is part of a **Uniform Resource Identifier (URI)**, a compact sequence of characters that identifies an abstract or physical resource. The general format of a URI is to identify a resource, sometimes called a **scheme,** and then follow it with a colon. Publisher creates the URI for you. The following steps insert a mailto hyperlink.

1

- Select the placeholder text, click here, in the text box at the bottom of the page.

- Press CTRL+K to display the Insert Hyperlink dialog box.

- Click the E-mail Address button in the Link to bar on the left.

- In the E-mail address text box, type `unsubscribe@ orionfootball.com` as the entry.

- In the Subject text box, type `e-mail recipient wishes to unsubscribe` as the entry (Figure 9–31).

Figure 9–31

Q&A Why did Publisher add the word, mailto, to the e-mail address?

Because you clicked the E-mail Address button in the Link to bar, Publisher knows you want to create a mailto hyperlink and automatically creates the prefix for you.

Q&A How will Publisher use the text in the Subject text box?

When the user clicks the mailto link, Publisher will fill in the Subject line of the e-mail message automatically with the entered text. That way, the recipient of the e-mail message will know that the request to unsubscribe came from an e-mail message rather than from the Web site or other mechanism.

2

- Click the OK button (Insert Hyperlink dialog box) to create the mailto hyperlink.

3

- Repeat Steps 1 and 2 to create a mailto hyperlink for the words, Sign Up Now which appears as a button in the lower portion of the e-mail message (Figure 9–32).

Will viewers of the e-mail message see the mailto prefix?

If the user positions the mouse over the link, the mailto prefix, colon, and e-mail address may appear on their status bar.

Figure 9–32

Design Issues in E-Mail

Because e-mail messages are generated electronically and are displayed in the user's e-mail program, you must keep in mind several design issues. As with Web pages, you want to make sure that the spacing, text, fonts, and hyperlinks are displayed correctly. The Design Checker offers some specific checks for e-mail publications that it does not perform with print publications. Table 9–3 displays the checks that Publisher uses to evaluate e-mail publications.

Preview and check the e-mail message.
Check for design issues specific to e-mail messages, including overlapping, hyphenation, fonts, and links. Preview the e-mail publication in a Web browser and check all links. Consider sending the e-mail message to yourself first so that you can see how it will look before sending it to other recipients.

Plan Ahead

Table 9–3 Design Issues	
Object	**Check Performed**
HTML fragment	Looks for any HTML code fragment that is partially off the page
Hyperlink	Looks for instances in which a hyperlink on one Web page links to another page in a publication
Overlapping text	Looks for any object that is on top of a text box
Object	Looks for any object that is partially off a publication page
Object with text	Looks for any object that contains text and has been rotated
Shape with hyperlink	Looks for any shape that has a hyperlink on top of it
Table borders	Looks for instances in which a table has borders that are less than .75 point thick
Text box with zero margins	Looks for any text box that has a margin that is set to zero
Hyphenation	Looks for any hyphens in the text
Cell diagonal	Looks for text that is located in a diagonal table cell
Font	Looks for text that is not formatted in a Web-safe font
Text overflow	Looks for any text box in which the text is too big
Vertical text	Looks for any text box that contains vertically rotated text

You can specify which checks Publisher will use when evaluating e-mails and other types of publications using the Design Checker Objects dialog box.

To Choose Design Checker Options

The following steps display the Design Checker dialog box and select Design Checker options for e-mail publications. Specifically, you will ask publisher to ignore text and shapes that are grouped together. These grouped objects become images in an e-mail and cannot be separated, although hot spots and hyperlinks are maintained.

- Click File on the Ribbon to display the Backstage view.

- If necessary, click the Info tab and then click the Run Design Checker button to display the Design Checker task pane.

- Click the Design Checker Options link (Design Checker task pane) to display the Design Checker Options dialog box (Figure 9–33).

Experiment

- Click the Sort by box arrow and notice the options for sorting design issues.

Figure 9–33

- Click the Checks tab (Design Checker Options dialog box) to view a list of all checks for all types of publications.

- Click the Show box arrow to view the subcategories of checks (Figure 9–34).

Figure 9–34

3
- Click E-mail checks to view the design issues that Publisher looks for in e-mail publications.

- Click to remove the check mark in the 'Object is overlapping text' check box so that Publisher will ignore any overlapping (Figure 9–35).

4
- Click the OK button (Design Checker Options dialog box) to apply the changes.

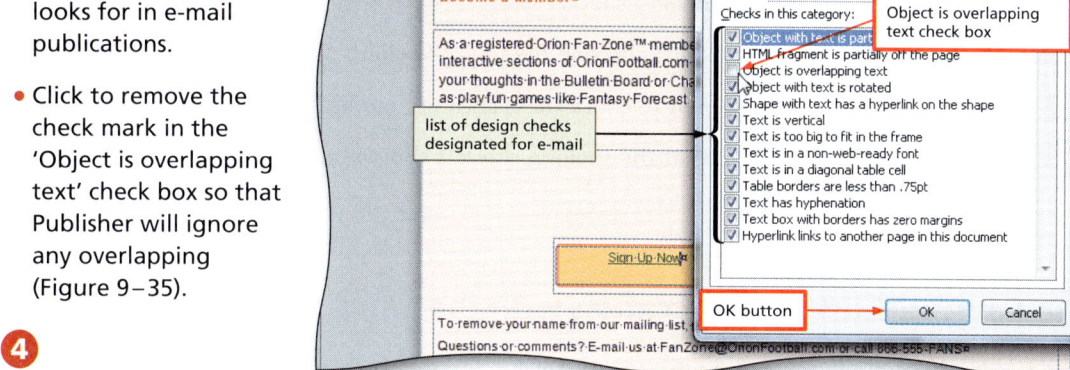

Figure 9–35

To Check for Design Errors

The following steps check the publication for e-mail design errors.

1 With the Design Checker task pane still displayed, click to display a check mark in the 'Run e-mail checks (current page only) check box. Remove any other check marks in the task pane.

2 Correct any problems listed in the task pane. If you have hyphenation errors, click the Hyphenation button (Text Box Tools Format tab | Text group). In the Hyphenation dialog box, clear the 'Automatically hyphenate this story' check box. Delete any hyphens that remain in your text (Figure 9–36).

3 Click the Close Design Checker button to close the Design Checker task pane.

BTW

Hyphenation
If your e-mail publication contains text with hyphenation, some e-mail programs may insert gaps in the e-mail message and it may not appear as you intended. To fix the problem, click the Hyphenation button (Text Box Tools Format tab | Text group). In the Hyphenation dialog box, clear the 'Automatically hyphenate this story' check box. Delete any hyphens that remain in your text.

Figure 9–36

To Check for Spelling Errors

The following steps check the publication for spelling errors.

1 Press the F7 key to start the spelling check.

2 If necessary, correct any problems noted in the Check Spelling dialog box.

3 When Publisher asks if you want to check the rest of the publication, click the Yes button.

4 When Publisher notifies you that the spelling check is complete, click the OK button.

To Save an Existing Publication with the Same File Name

You have made several modifications to the document since you last saved it. Thus, you should save it again. The following step saves the document again. For an example of the step listed below, refer to the Office 2010 and Windows 7 chapter at the beginning of this book.

1 Click the Save button on the Quick Access Toolbar to overwrite the previously saved file.

BTW

E-Mail Service Providers
Many e-mail service providers use a Web browser interface, so setting up an e-mail program is not necessary. Corporate and business communications commonly use the Microsoft Outlook e-mail program, which allows access to e-mail addresses for everyone in the company, along with tools to manage other forms of communication and scheduling.

Sending an E-Mail Message Using Publisher

E-mail messages can be sent to one or more people. Many organizations create a **listserv**, which is a list of interested people with e-mail addresses who want to receive news and information e-mail messages about the organization. A listserv e-mail sends one e-mail message to everyone on the list. Listserv e-mail messages always should contain an unsubscribe link that allows recipients to remove their names from the list to prevent receiving future e-mail messages.

When you choose to send a Publisher e-mail message, Publisher opens special text boxes to allow you to enter the e-mail addresses and subject line. Publisher also displays special buttons for e-mail options (Figure 9–37).

Figure 9–37

Before you send an e-mail message, you should always proofread it and then check it for design errors and spelling errors, as you did in the previous steps. With e-mail publications, you also should preview the publication.

To Preview an E-Mail Message

The following steps describe how to preview an e-mail message to see how it will look on the user's computer.

• Click File on the Ribbon to display the Backstage view.

• Click the Save & Send tab to view the Save & Send gallery.

• Click the E-mail Preview tab (Figure 9–38).

Figure 9–38

• Click the E-mail Preview button in the right pane to preview the e-mail publication in your default browser (Figure 9–39).

Experiment

• Scroll through the e-mail message and try clicking the hyperlinks. The Orion Fan Zone Web site is fictional and will not be displayed, but the click here hyperlink will display an e-mail dialog box if your system is configured with an e-mail program, such as Microsoft Outlook. If you are connected to the Internet, try clicking the hot spot on the graphic of the map to make sure it works properly.

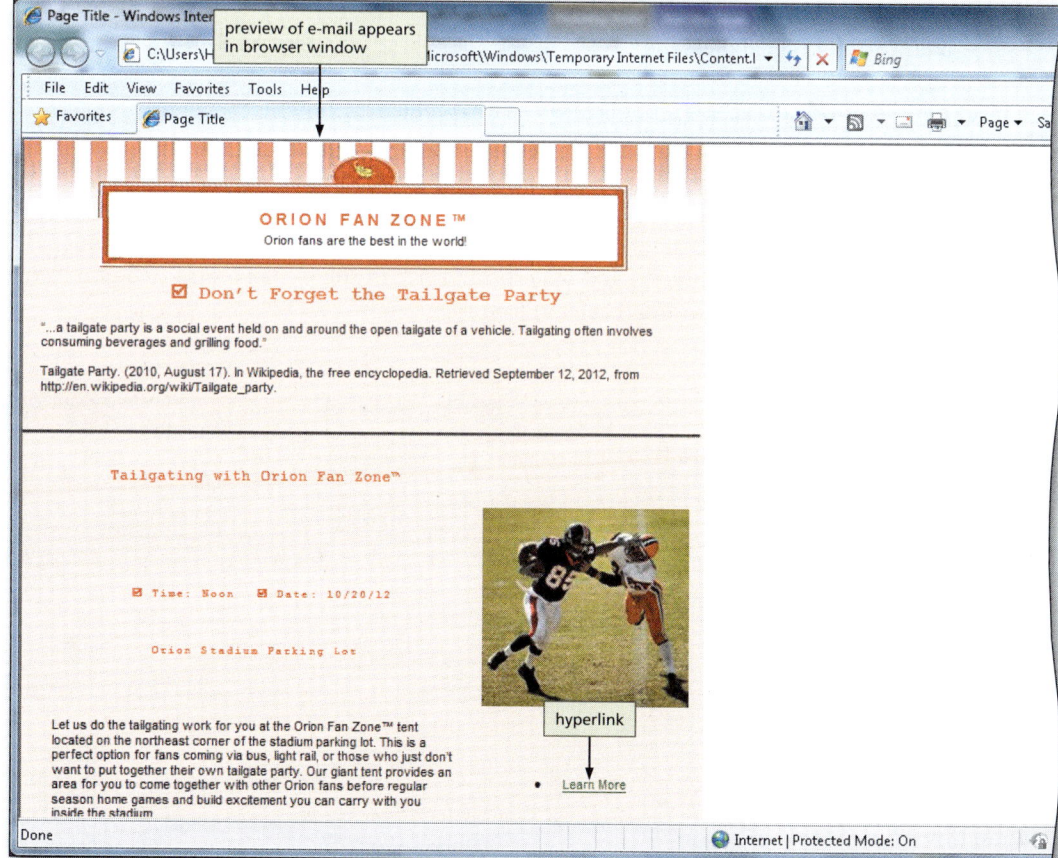

Figure 9–39

• Click the Close button on your browser's title bar.

To Send an E-Mail Message Using Publisher

The following steps send an e-mail message using Publisher's Send E-Mail command. You do not have to send the e-mail message, nor do you have to be connected to the Internet to perform the steps.

- Click File on the Ribbon to display the Backstage view.

- Click the Save & Send tab to view the Save & Send gallery.

- If necessary, click the Send Using E-mail tab (Figure 9–40).

Q&A What is the purpose of the Send as PDF and Send as XPS buttons?

Depending on which button you click, Publisher converts the current document to either the PDF or XPS format and then attaches the PDF or XPS document to the e-mail message.

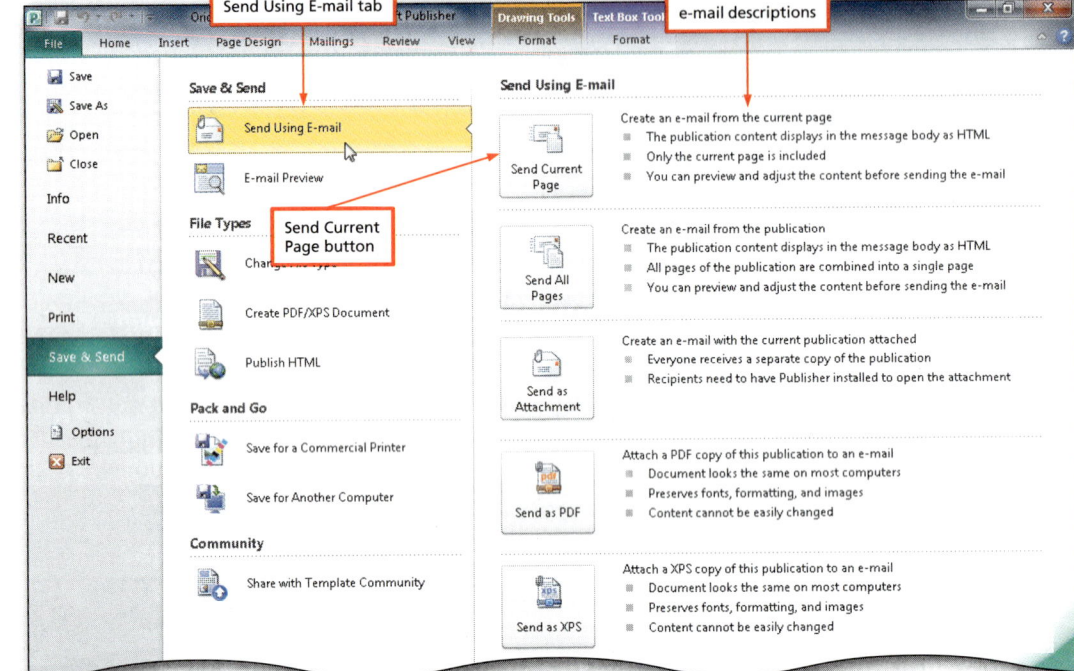

Figure 9–40

Q&A Do most people prefer to receive a publication as an e-mail attachment?

It is not necessarily better to use attachments. For immediate viewing, such as an announcement, letter, or card, it is better to send a single page in the body of an e-mail message. If you do send an attachment, the person receiving your e-mail message must have Publisher installed on his or her computer in order to open and view the publication. Additionally, with a large attachment, you may run the risk of the e-mail message being blocked by firewalls and filters at the receiving end.

- Click the Send Current Page button to display the special boxes and buttons used for e-mailing (Figure 9–41).

Q&A What if my system wants to configure Outlook to send an e-mail message?

If you are not sure how to configure your computer for e-mail, or you do not want to check your e-mail via an e-mail program,

 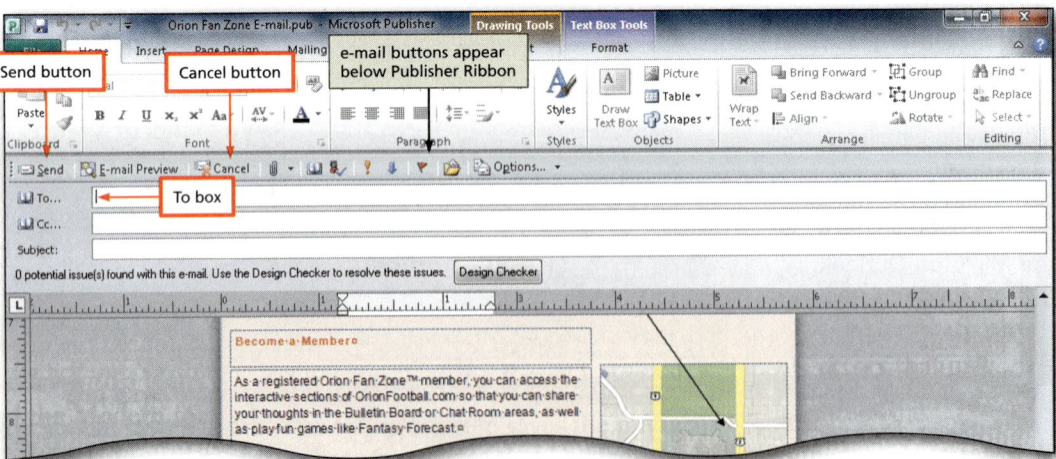

Figure 9–41

click the Cancel button. Configuring your computer with an e-mail program is not complicated, however. Windows 7 asks for your name, your e-mail address, and your password. It then determines the kind of e-mail program and connection you need.

- If you want to send the e-mail message, type your e-mail address in the To box, enter a subject, and then click the Send button. Otherwise, to cancel the request, click the Cancel button.

Q&A

What if I want to send an e-mail message to someone who does not have Publisher installed?

E-mail messages appear in the body of the e-mail and do not require Publisher. If you are sending an attachment and are worried that your recipient may not have Publisher installed on his or her computer, you can send your publication in a different format. Publisher can create PDF files or XPS files, which have free or inexpensive viewers. Once converted, the files then can be attached to an e-mail message.

Sending Print Publications as E-Mail Messages

In general, it is better to start with an e-mail publication template such as the e-mail letter or e-mail newsletter. If, however, you want to send a page of another publication as an e-mail message, you may need to modify the width and margins to ensure that the message will be displayed attractively for e-mail recipients. The typical page size of an e-mail message is 5.818 by 11 inches, which ensures the recipients will not need to scroll horizontally to view the entire width of the message.

To Modify the Paper Size and Margins

If you wanted to change the page design settings of a print publication to create an e-mail publication you would perform the following steps. It is a good idea to send the e-mail publication to yourself first, so that you can view the publication and look for problems.

1. Click the Page Setup Dialog Box Launcher (Page Design tab | Page Setup group) to display the Page Setup dialog box.
2. Click the Layout type box arrow (Page Setup dialog box) and then click E-mail.
3. Enter the new width and height measurements in the Width and Height boxes.
4. Click the OK button.

To Send a Multiple Page Publication as an E-Mail Message

If you wanted to send a multiple-page publication as an e-mail publication you would perform the following steps. These steps may require that you reconfigure your e-mail program. See your instructor for ways to reconfigure. It is a good idea to send the e-mail publication to yourself first, so that you can view the publication and look for problems.

1. Open the publication that contains the page or pages that you want to send as an e-mail message.
2. Display the Backstage view and then click the Save & Send tab.
3. Click the Send Using E-mail tab and then click the Send All Pages button.
4. If necessary, click the No option button (Send All Pages as Message dialog box) and then click the OK button.
5. Edit objects as necessary and then rearrange text and graphics. If Publisher cannot determine where to fit some objects, the Extra Content task pane will display the objects for you to place manually.

BTW

E-Mails from Print Publications
If you already have created specific print publications that you would like to send electronically, you can convert the publication to a single-page e-mail message. For example, if you create a newsletter for customers, you can send it to everyone on your e-mail list, in addition to distributing it on paper.

BTW

Converting from Print Publications
When you convert the publication, Publisher offers the options of sending the current page or all pages. If you choose to send all pages, Publisher combines the contents of all pages into one e-mail page.

To Close the Publication

The following step closes the publication without quitting Publisher.

1 Display the Backstage view.

2 Click the Close button. If Publisher offers to save the publication again, click the Don't Save button.

Postcards

A **postcard** is a rectangular piece of mail intended for writing and sending without an envelope. People use postcards for greetings, announcements, reminders, and business contacts. Most postcards are rectangular, at least 3½ inches high and 5 inches long — some are larger. A common size is 4 inches by 6 inches.

Plan Ahead

> **Employ attachments as necessary.**
> Publications created for print must be attached as a separate file when using e-mail, especially when converting the publication is not possible. Remember that users must have Publisher installed in order to open a publication. If you are unsure, save the publication in the PDF or XPS format and attach it. For large publications and multipage publications, consider compressing the file.

Many times, a postcard is an effective marketing tool used to generate prospective leads at a low cost. Businesses and organizations produce a postcard with a photo, graphic, advertisement, or coupon. Some postcards, such as picture postcards, leave space on one side to write a brief message. People purchase picture postcards to mail to friends or to serve as reminders of their vacation. Sometimes a picture postcard is mailed to attract attention and direct people to Web sites or business locations. A postcard must portray its message or theme clearly in an eye-catching manner, keeping in mind the relevant audience.

Publisher has several postcard templates, including postcards for marketing, calendars, and real estate, as well as many blank templates to create postcards from scratch. In the past, postcards typically have been mailed using a postal service; however, many companies and individuals are sending **e-postcards** electronically as attachments. An **attachment** is an electronic file sent along with an e-mail message; however, the recipient must perform some steps to open the file — it does not display within the body of the e-mail message. Table 9–4 displays some of the best practices for attachments.

Table 9–4 Best Practices for Attachments	
Practice	**Reasoning**
Post or publish large attachments.	It is better to post large files on the Web or on a shared resource, when possible.
Limit your attachments to under 5 megabytes.	Check with your Internet service provider (ISP) to verify the maximum allowable size of attachments.
Send multiple attachments using several e-mail messages.	Some e-mail programs have per-message limits.
Use compressed graphic file formats.	Smaller graphics are more likely to be opened and viewed.
Employ a file compression utility.	File compressing, sometimes called zipping, reduces the file size and keeps files together.
Review your Sent Items folder.	E-mails and attachments take up room in the sender's e-mail as well as the recipient's. Delete older sent items as necessary.

To Open a Postcard File

The following steps open a postcard from the Data File for Students. See the inside back cover of this book for instructions on downloading the Data Files for Students, or contact your instructor for information about accessing the required files. The postcard is a coupon that will be sent electronically as an attachment to new members of the fan club.

1 Click Open in the Backstage view to display the Open Publication dialog box.

2 Navigate to the location of the file to be opened (in this case, the Publisher folder in the Data Files for Students).

3 Click Orion Fan Zone Postcard to select the file to be opened.

4 Click the Open button (Open Publication dialog box) to open the selected file and display the opened publication in the Publisher window (Figure 9–42).

Figure 9–42

To Send a Postcard as an Attachment

The following steps send the postcard as an attachment. You do not have to be connected to the Internet or have an e-mail program installed on your computer in order to perform these steps.

1

- Display the Backstage view.

- If necessary, click the Save & Send tab and then click Send Using E-mail.

- Click the Send as Attachment button to display the Untitled Message (HTML) dialog box.

- In the To box, type **newmembers@ orionfootball .com** to enter the name of the listserv.

- In the Subject box, type **Saturday's tailgating** to enter the subject.

- Click the message area, and then type **Thank you for joining the Orion Fan Zone. Attached is a coupon you may use at next Saturday's tailgate party. We look forward to seeing you!** to enter the message (Figure 9–43).

Figure 9–43

2

- If you want to send the e-mail attachment, replace the e-mail address with your own, and then click the Send button to send the e-mail message along with its attachment and to close the e-mail window. Otherwise, close the Untitled Message (HTML) dialog box without saving.

To Close the Publication

The following steps close the publication without saving and without quitting Publisher.

1 Display the Backstage view.

2 Click the Close button. If Publisher offers to save the publication again, click the Don't Save button.

Greeting Cards

A **greeting card** is a folded card, usually with pictures or illustrations that conveys an expression of friendship, holiday greetings, or other sentiment. Greeting cards can be mailed using a postal service, or they can be sent as e-cards using Web services or e-mail.

In Publisher, the greeting card templates include categories such as birthdays, holidays, special occasions, and thank-yous. The greeting cards can be folded in half or in quarters and may contain a variety of layouts, in addition to the usual color and font schemes. Publisher also contains blank greeting card templates.

Creating a greeting card is no different from creating other publications. You only need to be mindful of how the pages and folds are organized. In the Publisher workspace, Page 1 is the front of the card, Pages 2 and 3 are the inside of the card, and Page 4 is the back of the card. When you print using a standard paper size, all four pages will print on a single side of one piece of paper. The inside of the card will print upside down in comparison to the front and the back; however, folding remedies that. Your other option is to purchase special greeting card paper and direct Publisher to print Pages 1 and 4 on the front and Pages 2 and 3 on the back. These choices are available in the Print gallery in the Backstage view.

To Open a Blank Greeting Card Template

The following steps open a blank greeting card template to be folded in quarters.

1 In the New template gallery, click the Greeting Cards thumbnail.

2 Scroll down to the Blank Sizes area and then click 1/4 Letter Side Fold, 4.25 × 5.5" template.

3 Click the Create button.

4 When Publisher asks if you want to insert the other three pages, click the Yes button.

5 Click the Page Number button on the status bar to view all four pages of the greeting card in the Page Navigation pane (Figure 9–44).

Figure 9–44

To Apply a Background to Each Page

The following steps apply a background to each page of the publication, just as you did with the e-mail message.

1 Display the Page Design tab.

2 Click the Background button (Page Design tab | Page Background group) to display the Background gallery.

3 Click 10% tint of Accent 2 to apply it to Page 1.

4 Click Page 2 and Page 3 in the Page Navigation pane and repeat Steps 2 and 3 to apply the background.

5 Click Page 4 in the Page Navigation pane and repeat Steps 2 and 3 to apply the background.

6 Click Page 1 in the Page Navigation pane to return to page 1 (Figure 9–45).

background applied

Figure 9–45

To Insert a Border

The following steps insert a building block border, which will serve as the top and bottom edge in the greeting card.

1

- Display the Insert tab.

- Click the Borders & Accents button (Insert tab | Building Blocks group) to display the Borders & Accents gallery.

- Scroll to the Emphasis area (Figure 9–46).

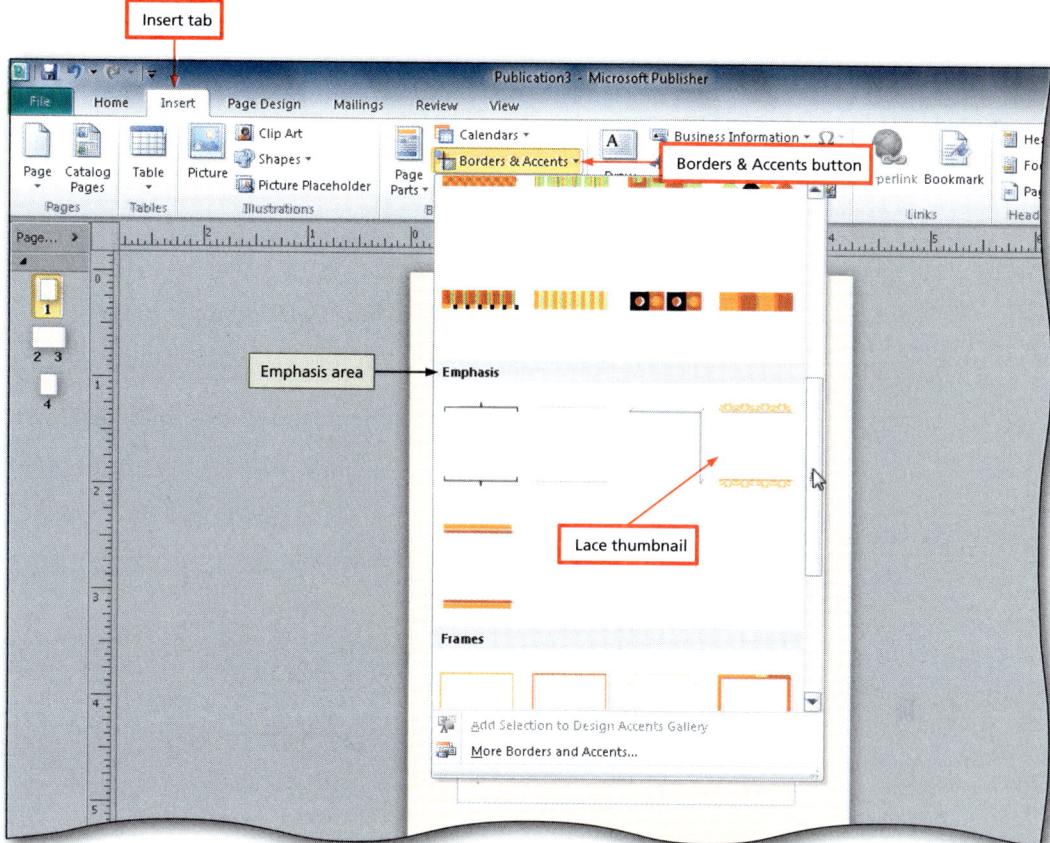

Figure 9–46

2

- Click the Lace border thumbnail to insert it into the publication.

- Resize the Lace border to fill the area between margins (Figure 9–47).

Figure 9–47

To Insert Text on Page 1

The following steps insert text on Page 1 of the greeting card.

1 Select the Lace graphic and then click the white area in the middle of the graphic to select that part of the grouped object. Right-click the Lace graphic and then click Add Text on the shortcut menu.

2 Display the Home tab.

3 Click the Styles button (Home tab | Styles group) and then click Heading 2 in the list.

4 Click the Font Color box arrow (Home tab | Font group) and click Accent 2 (Light Orange).

5 Click the Font Size box arrow (Home tab | Font group) and then click 36 in the list.

6 Type **The best fans in the world just got better!** to complete the text (Figure 9–48).

Figure 9–48

To Insert a Picture on Page 1

The following steps insert a picture on Page 1 of the greeting card.

1 Display the Insert tab.

2 Click the Clip Art button (Insert tab | Illustrations group). When the Clip Art task pane is displayed, search for clip art related to the word, football.

3 Click a graphic similar to the one shown in Figure 9–49. Resize and reposition it as necessary.

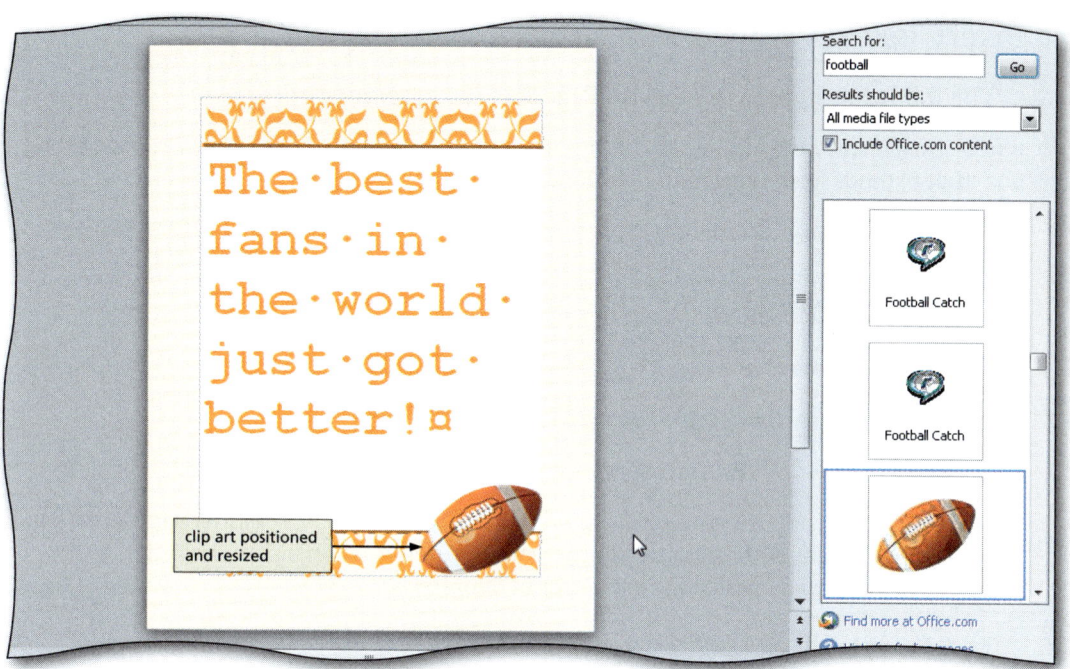

Figure 9–49

To Insert a Picture on Page 2

The following steps insert a picture on Page 2 of the greeting card.

1 Navigate to Page 2.

2 Using the Clip Art task pane, click a graphic similar to the one shown in Figure 9–50.

3 Drag the rotation handle to change the orientation of the photo. Resize and reposition it as necessary.

4 Close the Clip Art task pane.

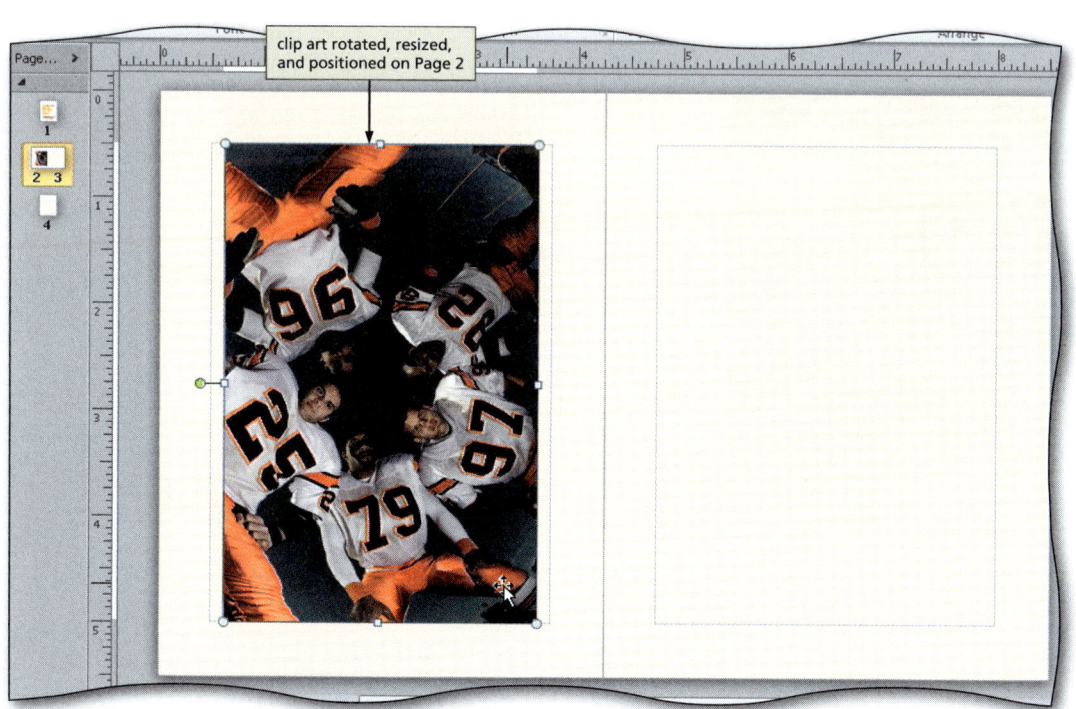

Figure 9–50

To Insert Text on Page 3

The following steps insert text on Page 1 of the greeting card.

1 If necessary, display the Home tab. In the center of the page on Page 3, draw a large text box that extends from margin to margin, approximately 2.5 inches tall.

2 Click the Styles button (Home tab | Styles group) and then click Heading 2 in the list.

3 Click the Font Color box arrow (Home tab | Font group) and click Accent 2 (Light Orange). Click the Font Size box arrow (Home tab | Font group) and then click 20 in the list.

4 Press CTRL+E to center the text.

5 Type `It's because you joined!` and then press the ENTER key.

6 Type `Thank you for` and then press the ENTER key.

7 Type `becoming a member` and then press the ENTER key. If Publisher capitalizes the letter b, point to the letter, click the AutoCorrect Options button below the letter, and then click Stop Auto-capitalizing First Letter of Sentences.

8 Type `of the` and then press the ENTER key.

9 Type `Orion Fan Zone` and then insert the trademark special character using the Symbol dialog box.

10 Type a period (.) to complete the sentence (Figure 9–51).

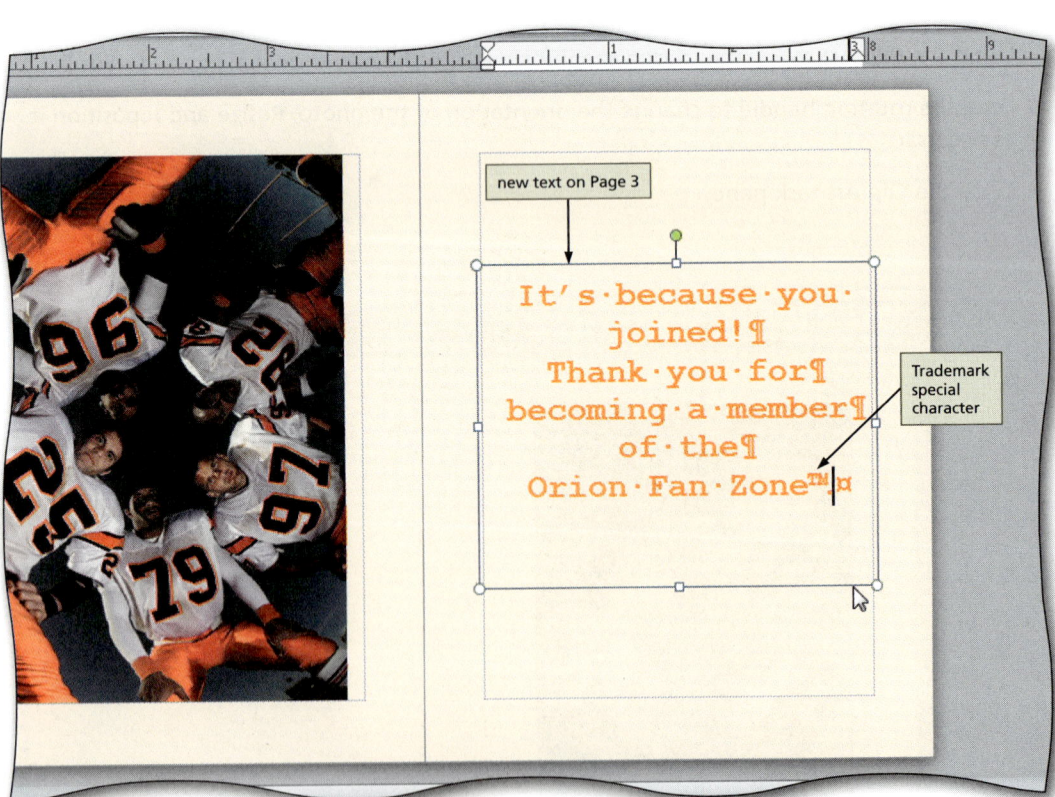

Figure 9–51

To Save the Greeting Card

You have performed many tasks while creating this greeting card and do not want to risk losing the work completed thus far. Accordingly, you should save the publication.

1 With a USB flash drive connected to one of the computer's USB ports, click the Save button on the Quick Access Toolbar to display the Save As dialog box.

2 Type **Orion Greeting Card** in the File name text box to change the file name. Do not press the ENTER key after typing the file name because you do not want to close the dialog box at this time.

3 Navigate to the desired save location (in this case, the Publisher folder in the CIS 101 folder [or your class folder] on the USB flash drive).

4 Click the Save button (Save As dialog box) to save the document in the selected folder on the selected drive with the entered file name.

To Print a Folded Publication

The following steps print the greeting card using a single sheet of 8.5 × 11 inch paper.

1

- Display the Backstage view and then click the Print tab to display the Print gallery.

- If necessary, click the first button in the Settings area and then choose Print All Pages.

- If necessary, type 1-4 in the Pages text box.

- If necessary, click the second button in the Settings area, and then click Side-fold, quarter sheet (Figure 9–52).

Figure 9–52

• Click the Print button to print the publication.

• Retrieve the printout (Figure 9–53).

folded greeting card →

The best fans in the world just got better!

Figure 9–53

To Quit Publisher

The project is now complete. The following step quits Publisher.

1 Click the Close button on the Publisher title bar. If Publisher displays a dialog box, click the Don't Save button.

Chapter Summary

This chapter introduced you to creating an e-mail message by illustrating how to select and format an e-mail template. The chapter then showed how to edit the background, text boxes, and graphics. Next, you learned how to insert a symbol and special character. You created hyperlinks, hot spots, and mailto hyperlinks. After checking the publication for design errors and previewing the e-mail message, you sent the publication as an e-mail message. You also learned how to send a publication as an attachment. Finally, you created a distributed publication for regular mail as you designed and printed a greeting card. The items listed below include all the new Publisher skills you have learned in this chapter.

1. Change the E-Mail Message Page Size (PUB 508)
2. Set the E-Mail Message Background (PUB 510)
3. Create a Callout (PUB 515)
4. Insert a Symbol from the Symbol Dialog Box (PUB 517)
5. Insert a Special Character Using the Symbol Dialog Box (PUB 519)
6. Insert a Symbol from the Symbol Gallery (PUB 520)
7. Use the Research Task Pane (PUB 522)
8. Create a Cited Definition (PUB 524)
9. To Insert a Hyperlink (PUB 525)
10. Insert a Hot Spot (PUB 525)
11. Insert a Mailto Hyperlink (PUB 526)
12. Choose Design Checker Options (PUB 528)
13. Preview an E-Mail Message (PUB 531)
14. Send an E-Mail Message Using Publisher (PUB 532)
15. Modify the Paper Size and Margins (PUB 533)
16. Send a Multipage Publication as an E-Mail Message (PUB 533)
17. Send a Postcard as an Attachment (PUB 535)
18. Insert a Border (PUB 538)
19. Print a Folded Publication (PUB 543)

Learn It Online

Test your knowledge of chapter content and key terms.

Instructions: To complete the Learn It Online exercises, start your browser, click the Address bar, and then enter the Web address **scsite.com/pub2010/learn**. When the Publisher 2010 Learn It Online page is displayed, click the link for the exercise you want to complete and then read the instructions.

Chapter Reinforcement TF, MC, and SA

A series of true/false, multiple choice, and short answer questions that test your knowledge of the chapter content.

Flash Cards

An interactive learning environment where you identify chapter key terms associated with displayed definitions.

Practice Test

A series of multiple choice questions that tests your knowledge of chapter content and key terms.

Who Wants To Be a Computer Genius?

An interactive game that challenges your knowledge of chapter content in the style of a television quiz show.

Wheel of Terms

An interactive game that challenges your knowledge of chapter key terms in the style of the television show *Wheel of Fortune*.

Crossword Puzzle Challenge

A crossword puzzle that challenges your knowledge of key terms presented in the chapter.

Apply Your Knowledge

Reinforce the skills and apply the concepts you learned in this chapter.

Create an Event E-Mail

Instructions: Open the file Apply 9-1 Insurance E-mail from the Chapter 09 folder on the Data Files for Students. See the inside back cover of this book for instructions on downloading the Data Files for Students, or contact your instructor for information about accessing the required files. Start Publisher.

You are to add a page background, insert hyperlinks, and add a symbol to create the e-mail publication shown in Figure 9–54.

Figure 9–54

Perform the following tasks:

1. With a USB flash drive connected to one of the computer's USB ports, click File on the Ribbon to open the Backstage view.

2. Click Save As command to open the Save As dialog box.

3. Type `Apply 9-1 Insurance E-mail Edited` in the File name text box to change the file name. Navigate to the desired save location (in this case, the Publisher folder in the CIS 101 folder [or your class folder] on the USB flash drive).

4. Click the Save button (Save As dialog box) to save the document in the selected folder on the selected drive with the entered file name.

5. Display the Page Design tab.

6. Click the Background button (Page Design tab | Page Background group) to display the Background gallery. Click 30% tint of Accent 3 to apply it to the e-mail page.

7. Position the insertion point after the words, Silas Grant Insurance, in the heading. Click the Insert Symbol button (Insert tab | Text group) and then click More Symbols. In the Verdana font set, insert the registered (®) sign.

8. Repeat Step 7 for the second occurrence of the words, Silas Grant Insurance.

9. Change the expiration date to 06/01/12.

10. Change the e-mail address to sgrant@YourInsurance.biz and then create a mailto hyperlink for the e-mail address. Insert a subject line with the words, Refer a Friend from the Web site.

11. Insert a hyperlink that links the second occurrence of the company name with www.YourInsurance.biz.

12. Create a hot spot for the Facebook graphic that links to www.facebook.com.

13. Create a hot spot for the Twitter graphic that links to www.twitter.com.

14. Check the e-mail publication for design and spelling errors. Preview the e-mail and check the links.

15. Save the e-mail publication again with the same file name.

16. If you have permission, send the publication to your instructor as an e-mail message.

Extend Your Knowledge

Extend the skills you learned in this chapter and experiment with new skills. You may need to use Help to complete the assignment.

Creating Links Using Bookmarks

Instructions: Start Publisher. Open the publication, Extend 9-1 Vehicle Diagnostics E-mail from the Data Files for Students. See the inside back cover of this book for instructions on downloading the Data Files for Students, or contact your instructor for more information about accessing the required files.

You will edit the e-mail message that uses the Long page design by creating links that help the viewer move down the page to inserted bookmarks (Figure 9–55 on the next page).

Continued >

Extend Your Knowledge *continued*

ConnectNow

Communications, security, hands-free calling, navigation, and remote diagnostics

Your Vehicle Diagnostics Report

Dear ConnectNow Customer:

See your diagnostics report below for your vehicle's status

Renew your subscription now!

♦ More details...

In this report:

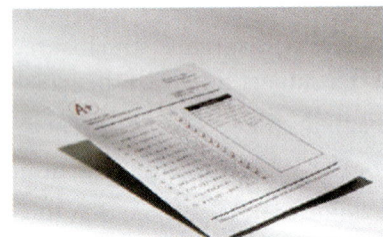

Vehicle Maintenance
Vehicle Diagnostics
Vehicle History
ConnectNow
Dealer Location

To remove your name from our mailing list, please click here.

Questions or comments? E-mail us at info@connectnow.biz or call 216-555-7534

Vehicle Maintenance

Remaining Oil Life: 56%

Mileage: 36,893

No required maintenance due at this time.

Based on oil life and mileage readings, next required maintenance estimated at 50,000 miles.

♦ More details...

Figure 9–55

Perform the following tasks:

1. Use Help to learn more about inserting bookmarks in Publisher.

2. Click the Bookmark button (Insert tab | Links group) to open the Bookmark dialog box.

3. Type `Vehicle Maintenance` in the Bookmark name text box to assign a name to the bookmark and then click the Add button (Bookmark dialog box) to close the dialog box.

4. When Publisher displays the bookmark symbol as an object in the publication, drag the symbol to the correct location in the publication, in this case, beside the Vehicle Maintenance heading as shown in Figure 9–55.

5. Deselect the Bookmark.

6. Repeat Steps 2 through 5 for each of the other headings: Vehicle Diagnostics, Vehicle History, ConnectNow, and Dealer Location.

7. With the bookmarks assigned and positioned, scroll to the top of the page.

8. Select the text, Vehicle Maintenance, and then press CTRL+K to display the Insert Hyperlink dialog box.

9. In the Link to bar (Insert Hyperlink dialog box), click the Place in This Document button. *Hint:* If a plus sign appears beside any of the places listed in the 'Select a place in this document' box, click the plus sign to display the embedded locations. Click Vehicle Maintenance in the 'Select a place in this document' box (Insert Hyperlink dialog box), and then click the OK button to close the dialog box.

10. Repeat Steps 8 and 9 for the other four links at the top of the page: Vehicle Diagnostics, Vehicle History, ConnectNow, and Dealer Location.

11. Save the publication with the name, Extend 9-1 Vehicle Diagnostics E-mail Edited.

12. Check the publication for design errors related to e-mail messages. Save the revised publication and then send it as an e-mail message to your instructor.

13. Quit Publisher.

Make It Right

Analyze a publication and correct all errors and/or improve the design.

Correcting Alternating Headers and Footers

Instructions: Start Publisher. Open the publication, Make It Right 9-1 Sign, from the Data Files for Students. See the inside back cover of this book for instructions on downloading the Data Files for Students, or contact your instructor for more information about accessing the required files.

The publication is a sign from a travel agency. You are to use symbols to correct the punctuation in the Spanish question in the lower part of the sign. The edited sign appears in Figure 9–56 on the next page.

Continued >

Make It Right *continued*

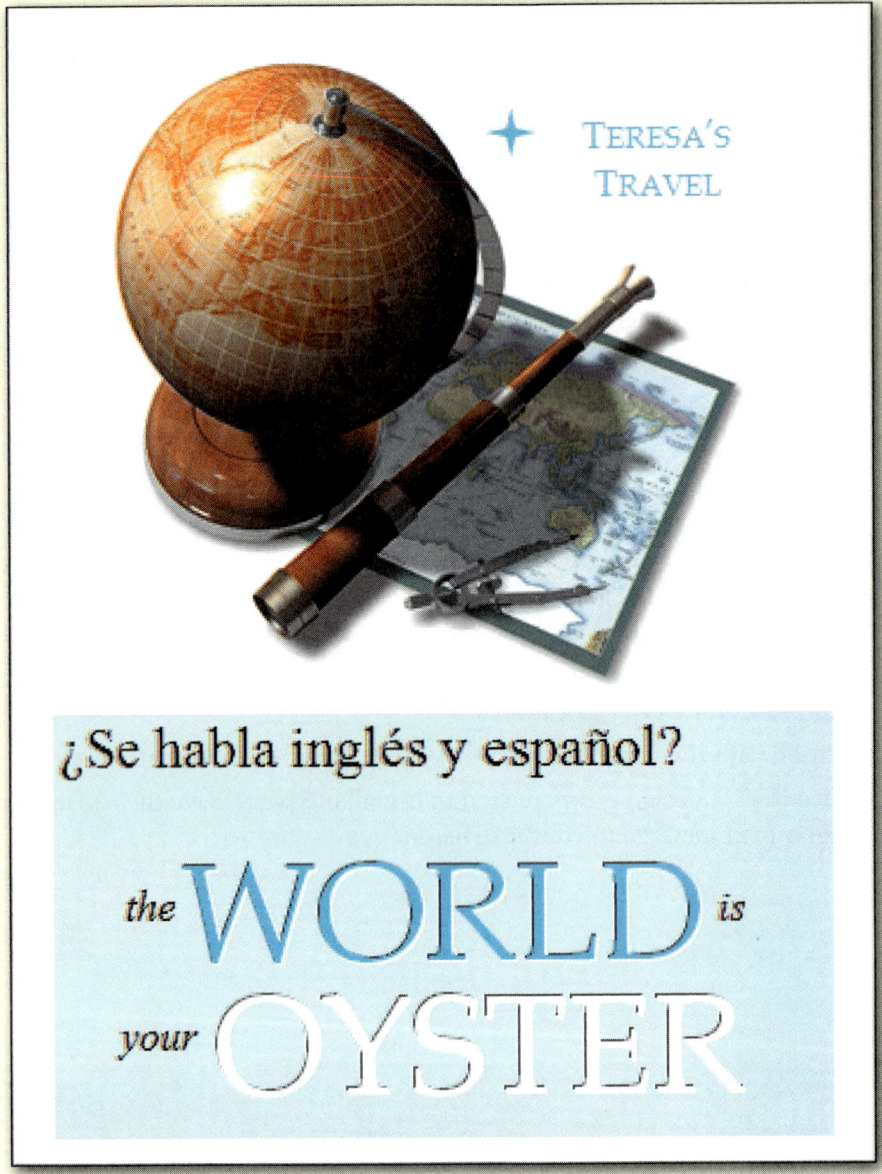

Figure 9–56

Perform the following tasks:

1. Display the Insert tab and position the cursor before the word Se, in the Spanish phrase.

2. Click the Insert Symbol button (Insert tab | Text group) and then click More Symbols to display the Symbol dialog box.

3. Scroll down to locate the inverted question mark and insert it. Close the Symbol dialog box.

4. Select the letter e in the word, ingles.

5. Display the Symbol dialog box again and insert the symbol, é. Close the Symbol dialog box.

6. Select the letter, n, in the word, espanol.

7. Display the Symbol dialog box again and insert the symbol, ñ.

8. Save the document with the file name, Make It Right 9-1 Sign Edited. See your instructor for ways to submit this assignment.

In the Lab

Design and/or create a publication using the guidelines, concepts, and skills presented in this chapter. Labs are listed in order of increasing difficulty.

Lab 1: Creating an E-Mail Featured Product List

Problem: You work for a company that sells music on the Web. Your boss wants you to send an e-mail message to all previous customers advertising the newest songs. You decide to use a Publisher E-mail Featured Product template to design the e-mail message previewed in Figure 9–57.

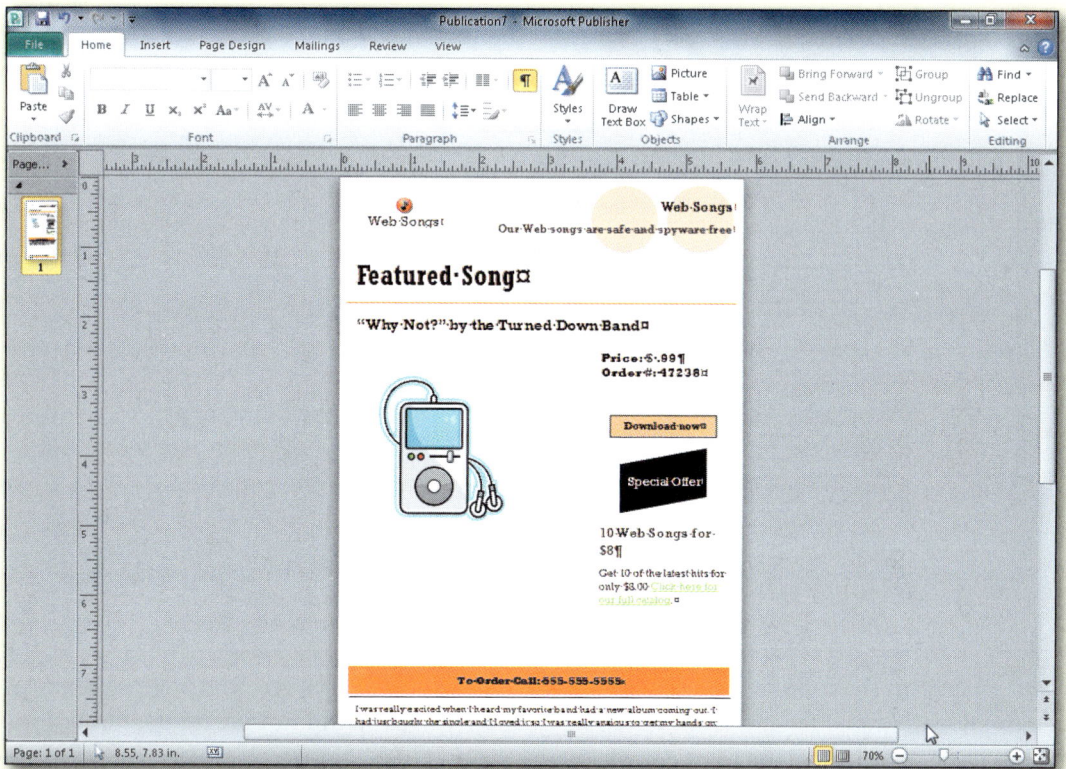

Figure 9–57

Instructions: Perform the following tasks:

1. Start Publisher and choose the Watermark Featured Product E-mail template. Select the Aspect color scheme and the Foundry font scheme. Select a short page size.

2. Add a background to the e-mail message by clicking the Background button (Page Design tab | Page Background group) and then choosing a background.

3. Devise a name for your music company and replace it in the heading. Use the phrase, Our Web songs are safe and spyware free, as the tag line text.

4. Replace the logo graphic with a piece of clip art. Use the keyword, media, in your search. Replace the logo text with the words, Web Songs!.

5. Replace the larger graphic with one picturing an MP3 player.

6. Describe your favorite artist or song in the lower text boxes.

7. Edit the hyperlink at the bottom to reflect your e-mail address.

8. Check the publication for spelling and design errors.

9. Save the publication with the file name Lab 9-1 Web Songs E-mail. Preview the e-mail.

10. If you have permission, send the publication to your instructor as an e-mail message. Include an appropriate subject line in the Subject text box.

In the Lab

Lab 2: Sending a Newsletter as an E-Mail Message

Problem: You created the newsletter shown in Figure 3–1 on page PUB 135. You decide to send the first page of the newsletter as an e-mail. The preview appears in Figure 9–58.

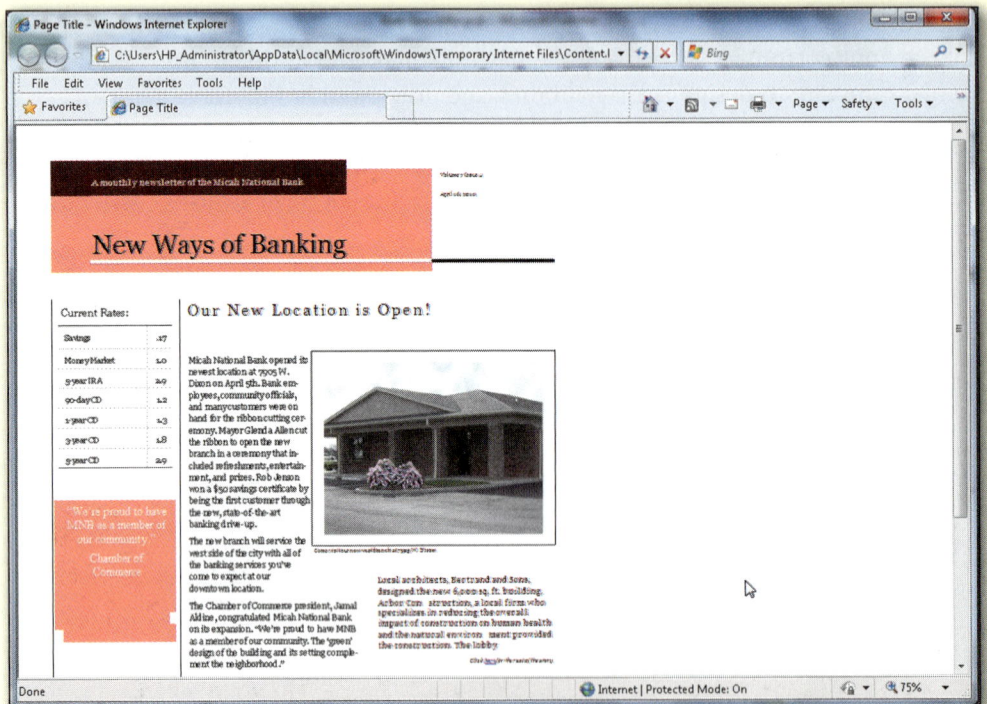

Figure 9–58

Instructions: Perform the following tasks:

1. Open the Bank Newsletter file you created in Chapter 3. (If you did not create the publication in Chapter 3, see your instructor for a copy.)

2. Open the Backstage view and then click the Save & Send tab. If necessary, click the Send Using E-mail tab and then click the Send Current Page button. If Publisher asks to set up an e-mail program such as Outlook, see your instructor for ways to configure the e-mail program.

3. Select the lower-right text box on page 1. Select the text, Continued on page 2, and then type **Click here for the rest of the story.** to replace the text.

4. Select the word, here, in the new text and create a hyperlink to www.mnb.com.

5. In the e-mail portion of the ribbon, click the Design Checker button and correct the errors as follows:

   a. For any non-Web-ready font errors, select the text and change the font to Times New Roman.

   b. For narrow table border errors, select the table, and then click the Cell Margins button (Table Tools Layout tab | Alignment group). Choose a wide margin setting.

   c. For text with hyphenation, click the Hyphenation button (Text Box Tools Format tab | Text group). In the Hyphenation dialog box, clear the 'Automatically hyphenate this story' check box. Delete any hyphens that remain in the text.

   d. For other errors, confirm that the text will be converted to an image in the e-mail letter.

   e. For thin table border errors, point to the error in the Design Checker window, then click the button arrow that appears. Select Fix: Increase Table borders to .75pt to fix the error.

6. Save the publication as Lab 9-2 Newsletter E-mail.

7. Preview the e-mail and then return to the publication and fix any other errors.

8. If you have permission, send the publication to your instructor as an e-mail message. Include an appropriate subject line in the Subject text box.

In the Lab

Lab 3: Creating an E-Mail Poster from Scratch

Problem: The local civic club has asked you to design and then distribute by e-mail a sign that they can use to remind people to vote in the upcoming election. You decide to design an e-mail publication from scratch using a blank e-mail template. Figure 9–59 displays the poster in a browser as a preview.

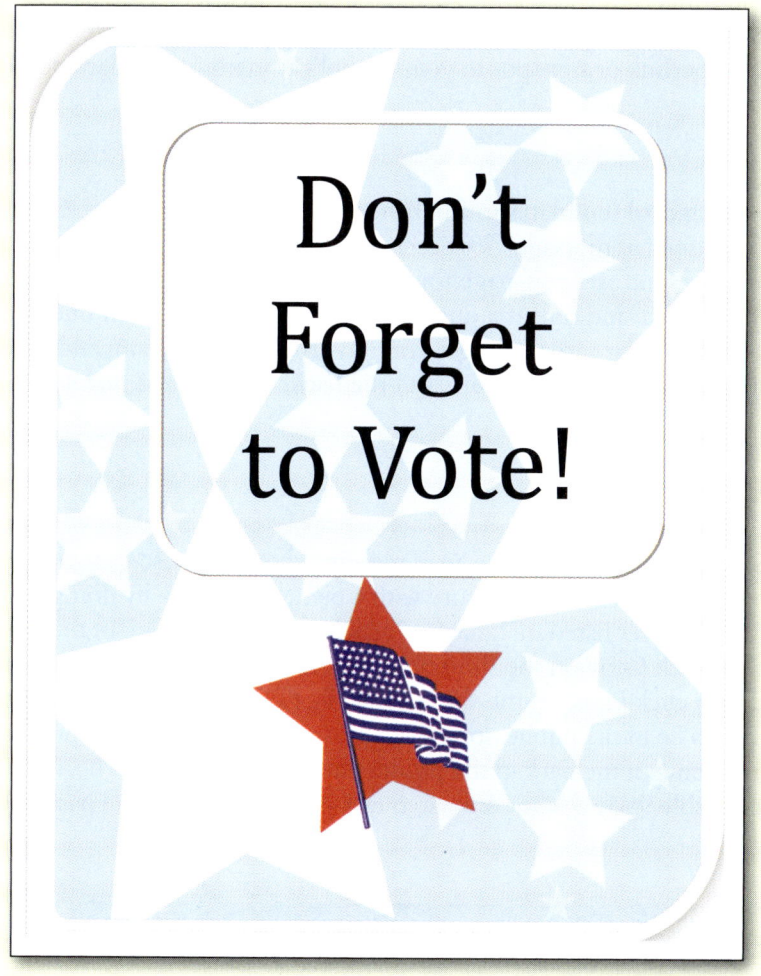

Figure 9–59

Instructions: Perform the following tasks:

Open the Short e-mail template in the Blank Sizes area in the New template gallery. Insert a page background using the file named, Patriotic Background, from Chapter 09 of the Data Files for Students. Create a rounded rectangle shape with a border and shadow, and then insert the text, Don't Forget to Vote! Change the font and font size as necessary. Save the file on your storage device with the name, Lab 9-3 Vote Reminder E-mail. Check the publication for design and spelling errors. Preview the publication and then send it to yourself as an e-mail message.

Cases and Places

Apply your creative thinking and problem solving skills to design and implement a solution.

Note: To complete these assignments, you may be required to use the Data Files for Students. See the inside back cover of this book for instructions on downloading the Data Files for Students, or contact your instructor for information about accessing the required files.

1: Create a Reminder E-Mail

Academic

The local school district wants to send a reminder to the parents of new students who have registered for the school year that begins this fall. The e-mail message should remind parents and students of kindergarten registration, the dates that vaccinations are due, band and sports tryout, and Back to School night. It should contain a link to the academic calendar and the district's Web page. Choose an Event/ Actitivy template and replace the main event with a reminder list of bulleted items. Replace graphics as necessary and create a hyperlink or hot spot to your school's academic calendar and Web site.

2: Create a Greeting Card

Personal

Look through the greeting card templates in Publisher's New template gallery. Choose four different templates with different kinds of messages. For each, choose a different color and font scheme. Create one as a half-page side fold, one as a half-page top fold (you may have to change the page orientation), one as a quarter-page side fold, and one as a quarter-page top fold. Save each one with a descriptive file name. Print and fold the greeting cards. Choose your favorite, open it again, and tailor it to a specifc person, event, gift, or holiday. Include a picture. On the back, create a text box with the words, Custom created by, and then include your name.

3: Create a Catalog

Professional

The National Park Service wants to send an e-mail message about its most famous parks. Open a product list e-mail template. Replace each product picture with a picture of a park by doing the following: one at a time, visit each of the Web sites listed in Table 9–5. Right-click the picture in the upper-right corner of the Web site and then click Copy on the shortcut menu. Return to Publisher, right-click one of the product pictures, and then click Paste on the shortcut menu. (The pictures on the National Park Service Web site are considered to be in the public domain, and, as such, they may be copied as permitted by applicable law.) Use the name of the park in the product headings. Make each heading a hyperlink to the Web addresses listed in Table 9–5. Use the Research task pane to research the park and create a cited description for each park.

Table 9–5 National Park Web Sites
Web Address
http://www.nps.gov/acad/
http://www.nps.gov/grca/
http://www.nps.gov/yose/
http://www.nps.gov/yell/
http://www.nps.gov/romo/
http://www.nps.gov/havo/

10 Editing Large-Scale Publications

Objectives

You will have mastered the material in this project when you can:

- Insert, collapse, expand, and merge sections
- Specify starting page numbers and their associated formats
- Remove page numbers from specific pages
- Apply BorderArt
- Set text box and cell margins
- Change text direction

- Use preset guide patterns
- Link text boxes across pages using the Ribbon
- Duplicate pages
- Find and replace text
- Replace a word using the thesaurus
- Insert page breaks
- Create and use bookmarks

10 | Editing Large-Scale Publications

Introduction

Large-scale publications — those consisting of 10 pages or more — require special techniques in editing, formatting, and printing. Planning and maintaining a consistent style is imperative. Large-scale publications require judicious use of sections, headers, footers, tables of contents, front matter, end matter, appendices, cover pages, graphics, styles, headings, and additional formatting considerations.

Examples of large-scale publications include books, magazines, catalogs, conference agendas, and proceedings, among others.

Project — Creating a Conference Agenda

The project in this chapter creates a 16-page conference agenda. The front and back of the agenda have a black background. The front has white text and a graphic. The inside pages have features such as a map, author statement, table of contents, master pages, linked text boxes, page numbering, columns, and page borders (Figure 10–1).

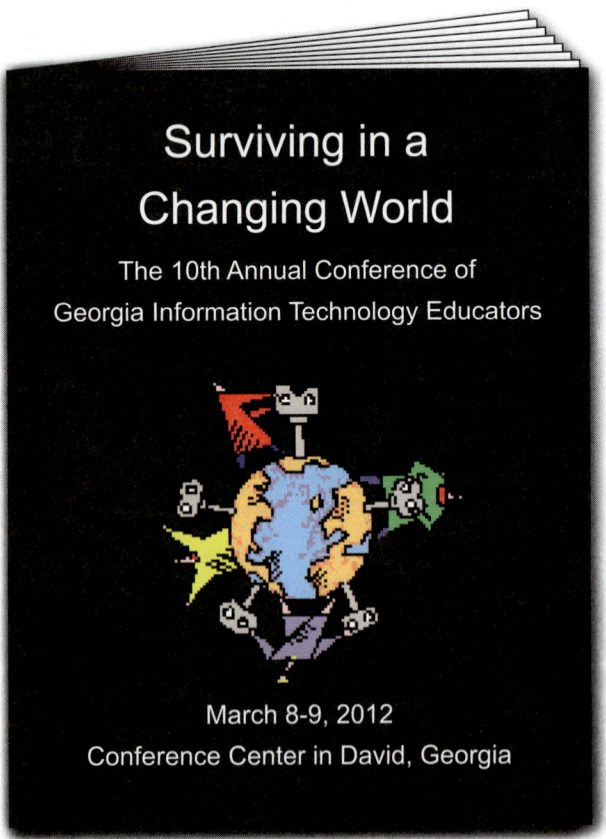

Figure 10–1

Overview

As you read through this chapter, you will learn how to create the publication shown in Figure 10–1 by performing these general tasks:

- Insert and design pages in the publication.
- Apply sections and pagination.
- Create a matching front and back cover.
- Insert BorderArt.
- Create a table of contents and bookmarks.
- Use the thesaurus.
- Find and replace characters.
- Create bookmarks for faster navigation.

Plan Ahead

General Project Guidelines

When creating a Publisher publication, the actions you perform and decisions you make will affect the appearance and characteristics of the finished publication. As you create a large-scale publication, such as the one shown in Figure 10–1, you should follow these general guidelines:

1. Plan your pages. When creating large-scale publications, organize your pages by purpose, including front cover, front matter, content pages, end matter, and back cover. Use sections and appropriate pagination for each section. Reserve the master page for objects such as headers, footers, page borders, page numbers, watermarks, or other repeating elements, making sure they do not interfere with the viewer's ability to read the text in the publication.

2. Use correct pagination. Decide which pages should not have page numbers, such as title pages, cover pages, and sometimes blank pages. If the front matter is more than two or three pages, many large-scale publications number those pages with lowercase Roman numerals. Appendices sometimes use letters of the alphabet to number pages. Decide on starting page numbers for each section.

3. Use BorderArt and backgrounds sensibly. When you use BorderArt, make sure it does not overwhelm the page and is used to enhance the page. Use a graphic that has meaning for the topic and one that will look good in a small, square format. Coordinate with your printing service regarding page backgrounds. If the background is solid color, the publication may print on colored stock rather than knockout colors to white, a process explained later in the chapter.

4. Employ global tools. Publisher has many tools to help you move through the publication globally. Use find and replace to make consistent changes in a large-scale publication. Use bookmarks to help online readers find sections in the publication. Update the table of contents last, after you have made all page break decisions.

When necessary, more specific details concerning the above guidelines are presented at appropriate points in the chapter. The chapter also will identify the actions performed and decisions made regarding these guidelines during the creation of the conference agenda shown in Figure 10–1, as well as related files.

To Start Publisher

The steps on the next page, which assume Windows 7 is running, start Publisher based on a typical installation. You may need to ask your instructor how to start Publisher for your computer. For a detailed example of the procedure summarized below, refer to the Office 2010 and Windows 7 chapter at the beginning of this book.

1 Click the Start button on the Windows 7 taskbar to display the Start menu.

2 Type **Microsoft Publisher** as the search text in the 'Search programs and files' text box, and watch the search results appear on the Start menu.

3 Click Microsoft Publisher 2010 in the search results on the Start menu to start Publisher and open the Backstage view.

4 If the Publisher window is not maximized, click the Maximize button next to the Close button on its title bar to maximize the window.

To Open a Blank Publication and Select a Font Scheme

The following steps open a blank 8.5 × 11 inch publication and select the Office Classic 1 font scheme.

1 In the New template gallery, click the Blank 8.5 × 11" thumbnail to open a blank publication.

2 If necessary, press CTRL+SHIFT+Y to display special characters.

3 Display the Page Design tab.

4 Click the Scheme Fonts button (Page Design tab | Schemes group) and then click Office Classic 1 from the Scheme Fonts gallery.

5 Display the View tab.

6 If necessary, click to place check marks in the Boundaries, Guides, Rulers, Page Navigation, and Scratch Area check boxes (View tab | Show group).

7 If the Page Navigation pane is expanded, click the Collapse Page Navigation Pane button to collapse it (Figure 10–2).

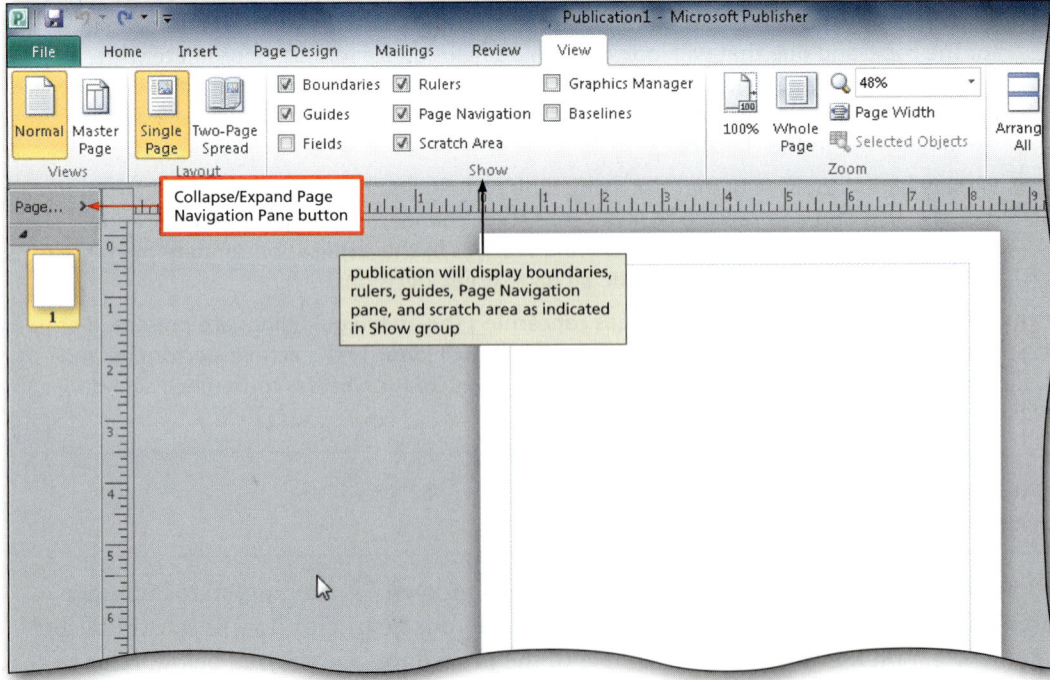

Figure 10–2

Designing the Layout

Recall that a layout is the way pages, component parts, or individual items are arranged in a publication. In the past, you used template layouts for your pages and also created objects on a blank page, thereby designing your own layout. When working with a large-scale publication, you need to plan for the cover, the back, and the inside of the front and back covers, as well as the inner pages, which sometimes are called **content pages** or **body copy**. A publication also may contain sectional elements such as front matter and end matter. **Front matter** is a term that refers to content at the beginning of a book or publication that is neither a cover page nor content page, such as a forward, preface, or table of contents. **End matter** includes appendices, an index, reference pages, glossaries, or other lists. In the conference agenda in this chapter, you will need to decide on the layout of content pages, such as columns, borders, and pagination, among others.

Plan your pages.
Large-scale publications should contain some or all of the following sections:

- Cover page: A cover page needs to contain the complete title and author, along with graphics or colors to encourage the reader to open the publication.

- Inside front cover page: Normally, the inside cover page is blank, but some books use the space for author comments, references, or other noncontent material.

- Front matter: Front matter includes a table of contents, notes from the editor or author, publication data, and other information to guide users through the content.

- Content pages: The content pages contain all of the text and graphics that comprise the book's contents, minus the front matter and end matter.

- End matter: The end matter may contain appendices, an index, reference pages, glossaries, or other lists.

- Inside back cover page: Like the inside front cover page, the inside back cover page normally is blank, but it may contain reference material or additional information about the text or author.

- Back cover page: The back cover page may contain only graphics or color, or it may contain additional information about the content, such as a summary, online content, ISBN numbers, bar codes, and references to other pertinent publications.

Plan Ahead

To Insert More Pages

The following steps insert seven more blank pages into the publication using the shortcut menu.

1 Right-click Page 1 in the Page Navigation pane to display the shortcut menu and then click Insert Page to display the Insert Page dialog box.

2 If necessary, click the 'After current page' option button to select it and then click the OK button (Insert Page dialog box).

3 Repeat Steps 1 and 2 until the publication has a total of eight pages (Figure 10–3 on the next page).

Figure 10–3

To Create Sections

The cover page and back page of the agenda will have a black background. The inside cover page and inside back cover page will be blank. The front matter and content pages will contain different layouts and page numbering. To assist with pagination and organization, Publisher uses **sections**, or dividers, in the Page Navigation pane to separate the pages logically. You can expand or collapse sections to facilitate editing. The following steps create sections for the front and back of the agenda, for the front matter, and for the content section — a total of four sections.

1

• Right-click Page 3 in the Page Navigation pane to display the shortcut menu (Figure 10–4).

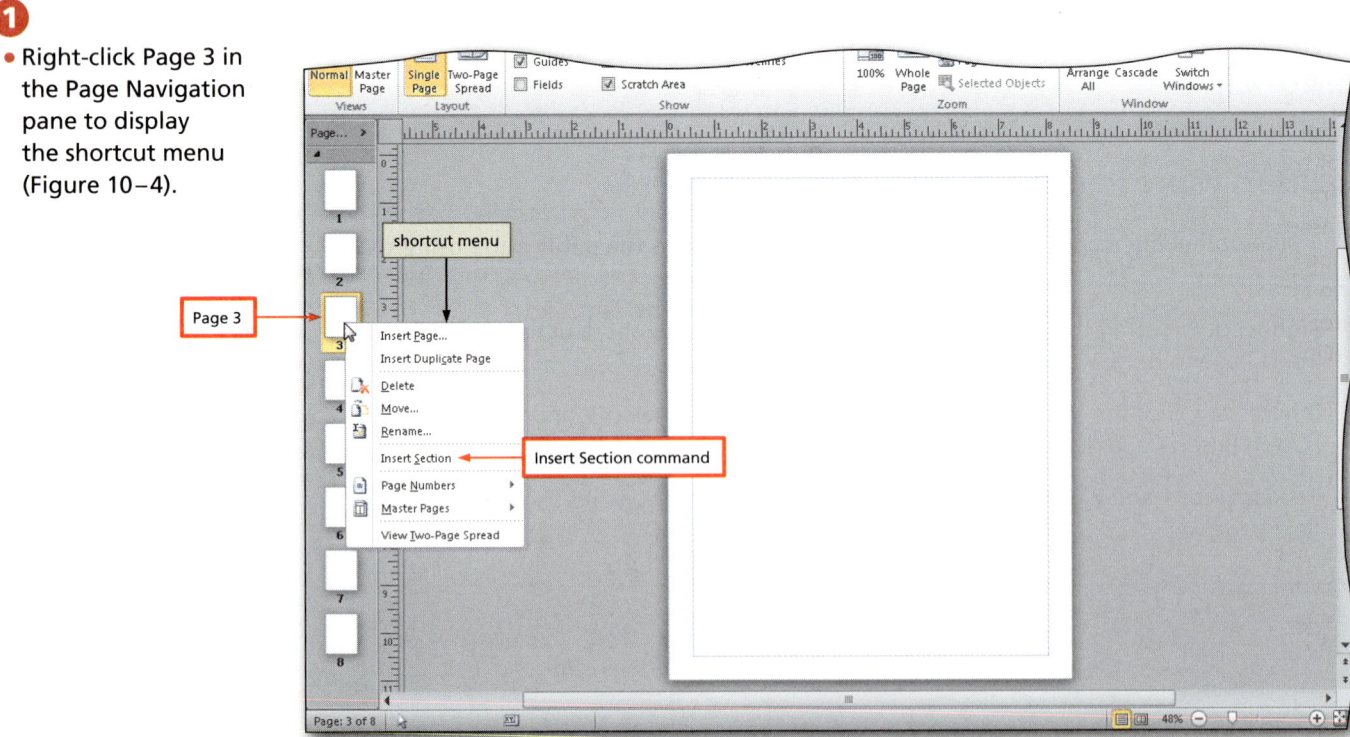

Figure 10–4

2

• Click Insert Section on the shortcut menu to create a section in the Page Navigation pane for the cover page and inside cover page (Figure 10–5).

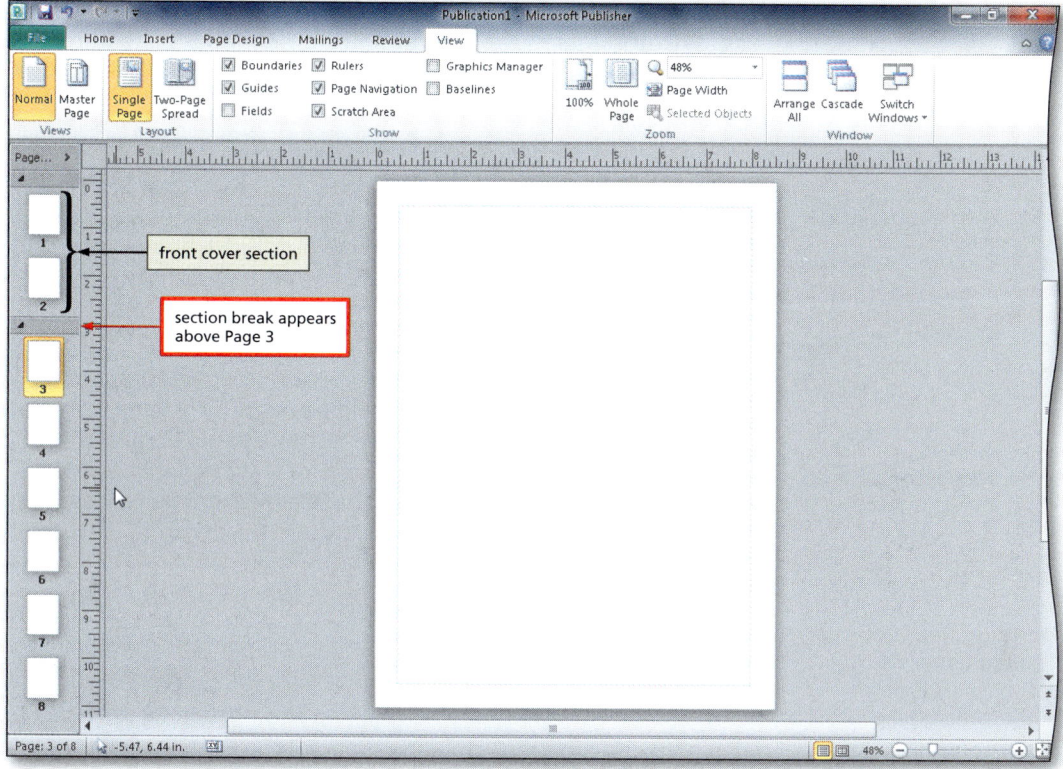

Figure 10–5

3

• Right-click page 6 of the publication and then click Insert Section on the shortcut menu to create a section for the front matter.

• Right-click page 7 of the publication and then click Insert Section on the shortcut menu to insert a section for content pages (Figure 10–6).

Figure 10–6

Pagination

Pagination refers to the way a publication applies page numbers, including the location, whether the cover will be included in the page numbering system, and the number with which you wish to start. When inserting page numbers in a large-scale publication, it is common for the cover, inside cover, inside back cover, and back cover pages not to be numbered. Page numbering, therefore, begins with the third actual page. If the front matter contains many pages, those pages are numbered sequentially using lowercase Roman numerals. In those cases, page number 1 begins after the front matter.

Plan Ahead

> **Use correct pagination.**
> Using the correct pagination helps readers navigate through the sections of a large-scale publication. Decide which pages should not display page numbers, such as title pages, cover pages, and blank pages. Use lowercase Roman numerals for front matter. Use numerals for content pages. Appendices sometimes use pages numbered with letters of the alphabet. Decide on starting page numbers for each section. Be consistent; page numbers that change locations or styles within a publication are disconcerting to readers.

BTW

Deleting Sections
You cannot delete a section, per se; however, you can merge the section with the previous section, effectively removing it. You also can delete all of the pages within a section, which also removes it.

As you learned in a previous chapter, you can use headers and footers to place page numbers using the master page; however, you also can insert page numbers using the Insert tab on the Ribbon. The information ultimately is stored on a master page, but the advantage of using the Ribbon is that you can specify what number you wish to use as a starting page number, an especially useful technique for chapters and sections of books. Additionally, using the Ribbon, you can insert page numbers in text boxes other than the header and footer.

To Insert Page Numbers Using the Ribbon

The following steps insert a page number at the bottom center of each page.

 1
- Display the Insert tab.

- Click the Page Number button (Insert tab | Header & Footer group) to display the list (Figure 10–7).

Figure 10–7

- Click Bottom Center to insert page numbers at the bottom center of each page.

- Zoom to 150% and scroll to the bottom of the page to view the page numbers (Figure 10–8).

page number of selected page is displayed

your selected page may differ

Figure 10–8

To Specify a Starting Page Number

The conference agenda's front matter will appear after the inside cover page. The following steps specify a starting page number, i, that will appear on the third page of the publication.

1

- In the Page Navigation pane, select the third page of the publication.

- Click the Page Number button (Insert tab | Header & Footer group) to display the list (Figure 10–9).

Page Number button

Page 3

Format Page Numbers command

Figure 10–9

2

- Click Format Page Numbers to display the Page Number Format dialog box.

- Click the Number format box arrow to display its list (Figure 10–10).

Experiment

- Scroll through the Number format list and view the different kinds of page numbering formats, including cardinal numbers, Roman numerals, letters, ordinal numbers, or spelled out numbers (i.e., one, two, three).

Figure 10–10

3

- Click 'i, ii, iii, …' in the list.

- Click the 'Start this section with' option button to select it.

- Select the text in the 'Start this section with' box and then type **1** to specify the starting page number (Figure 10–11).

Q&A

Why should I type 1 when I want to start with page i?

The 'Start this section with' box requires an integer. The page number is page 1 of the section; the format on the page number is lowercase Roman numerals. You would type a 1 even if you were asking Publisher to use letters on each page.

Figure 10–11

4
- Click the OK button (Page Number Format dialog box) to apply the page number (Figure 10–12).

🔍 **Experiment**
- Click different pages in the Page Navigation pane to view the page numbers on each page.

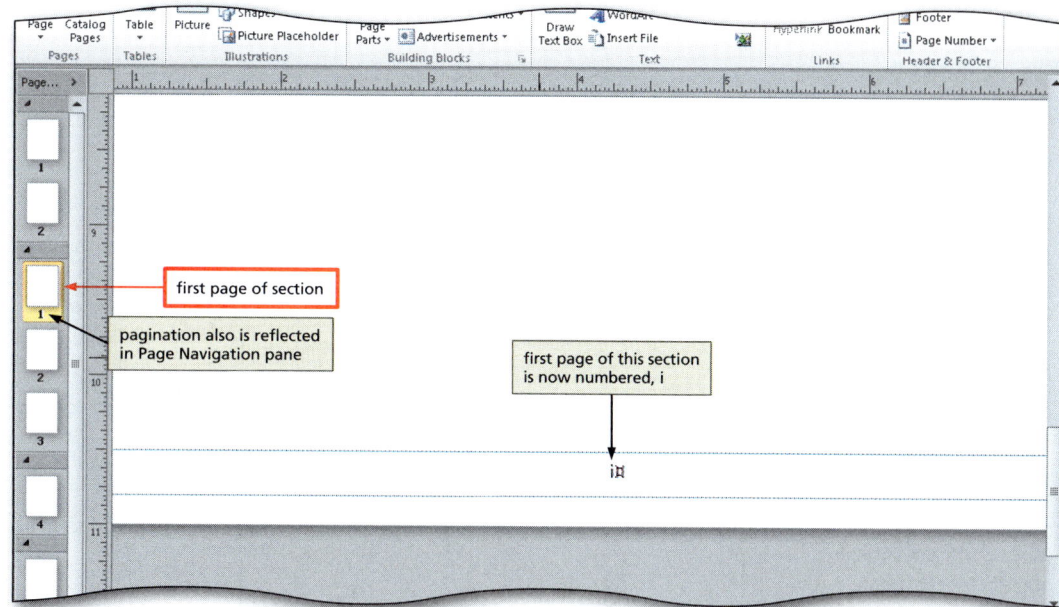

first page of section

pagination also is reflected in Page Navigation pane

first page of this section is now numbered, i

Figure 10–12

To Specify a Starting Page Number Using the Shortcut Menu

The following steps apply the number 1 to the sixth page of the publication.

1
- In the Page Navigation pane, right-click the sixth page of the publication, which appears as the first page in the third section.

- Point to Page Numbers on the shortcut menu to display the Page Numbers submenu (Figure 10–13).

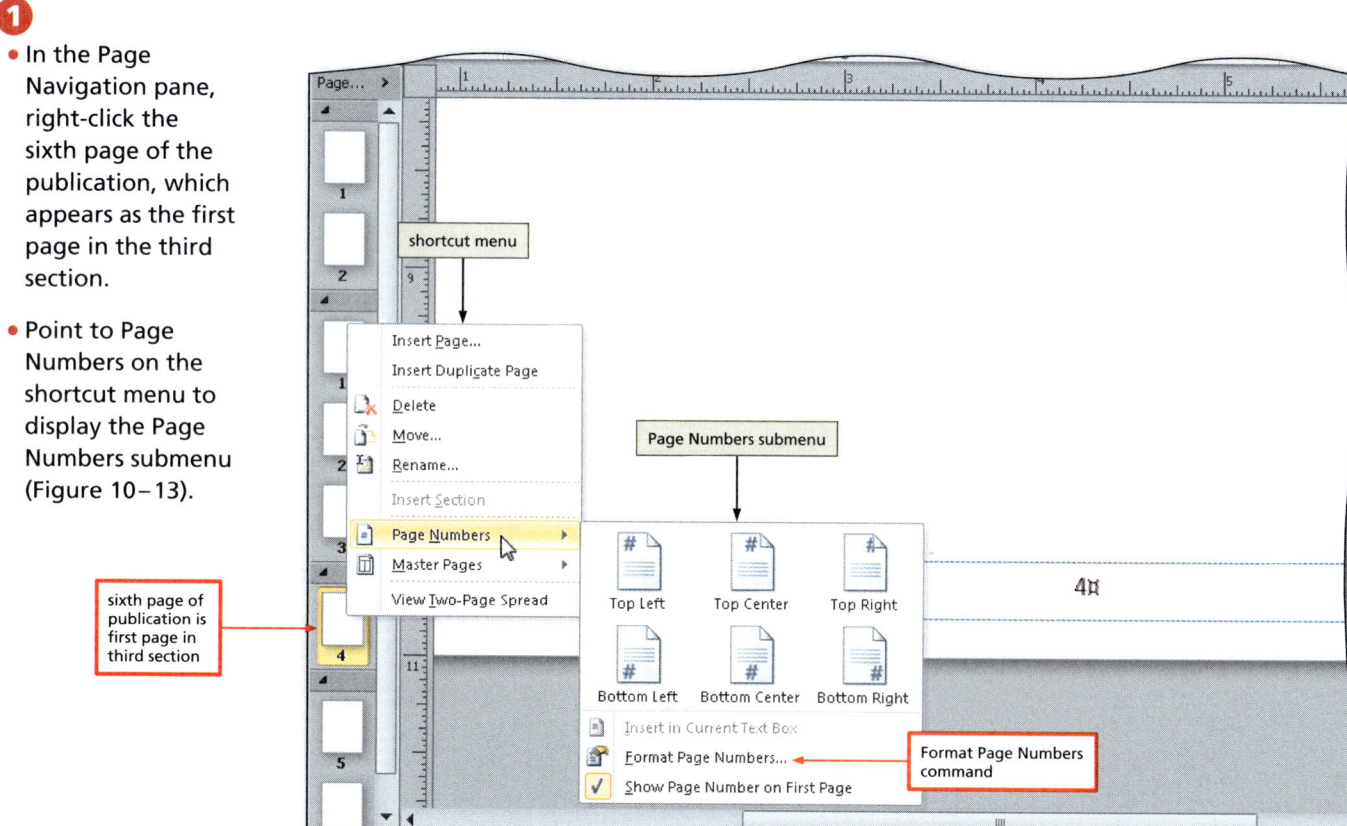

shortcut menu

Page Numbers submenu

sixth page of publication is first page in third section

Format Page Numbers command

Figure 10–13

2

- Click Format Page Numbers to display the Page Number Format dialog box.

- If necessary, click the Number format box arrow to display its list and then scroll as necessary to click 1, 2, 3 in the list.

- Click the 'Start this section with' option button to select it.

- Select the text in the 'Start this section with' box and then type 1 to replace it (Figure 10–14).

Figure 10–14

3

- Click the OK button (Page Number Format dialog box) to apply the page number format to the page (Figure 10–15).

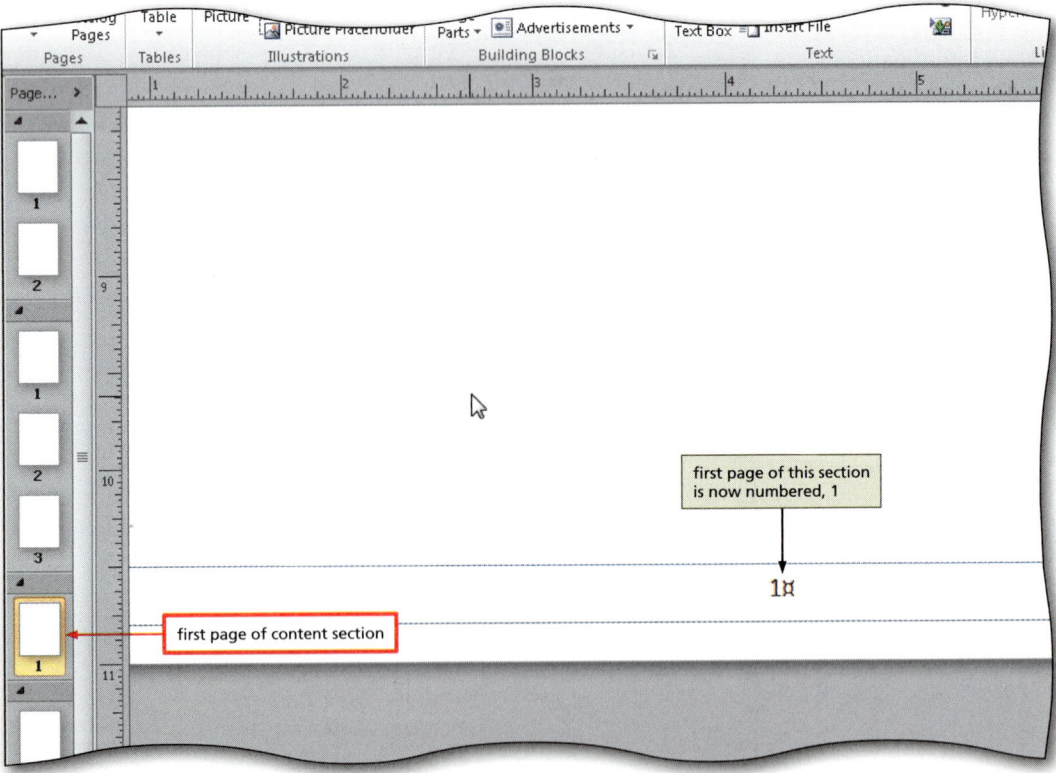

Figure 10–15

To Remove Page Numbering from Specific Pages

The final step in paginating this publication is to remove page numbers from the first and last sections of the publication. Because page numbers and their formats are saved in a master page, the following steps remove page numbering by choosing to apply no master page to the specific pages in the publication.

1
- In the Page Navigation pane, right-click the first page of the publication to display the shortcut menu and then point to Master Pages to display the Master Pages submenu (Figure 10–16).

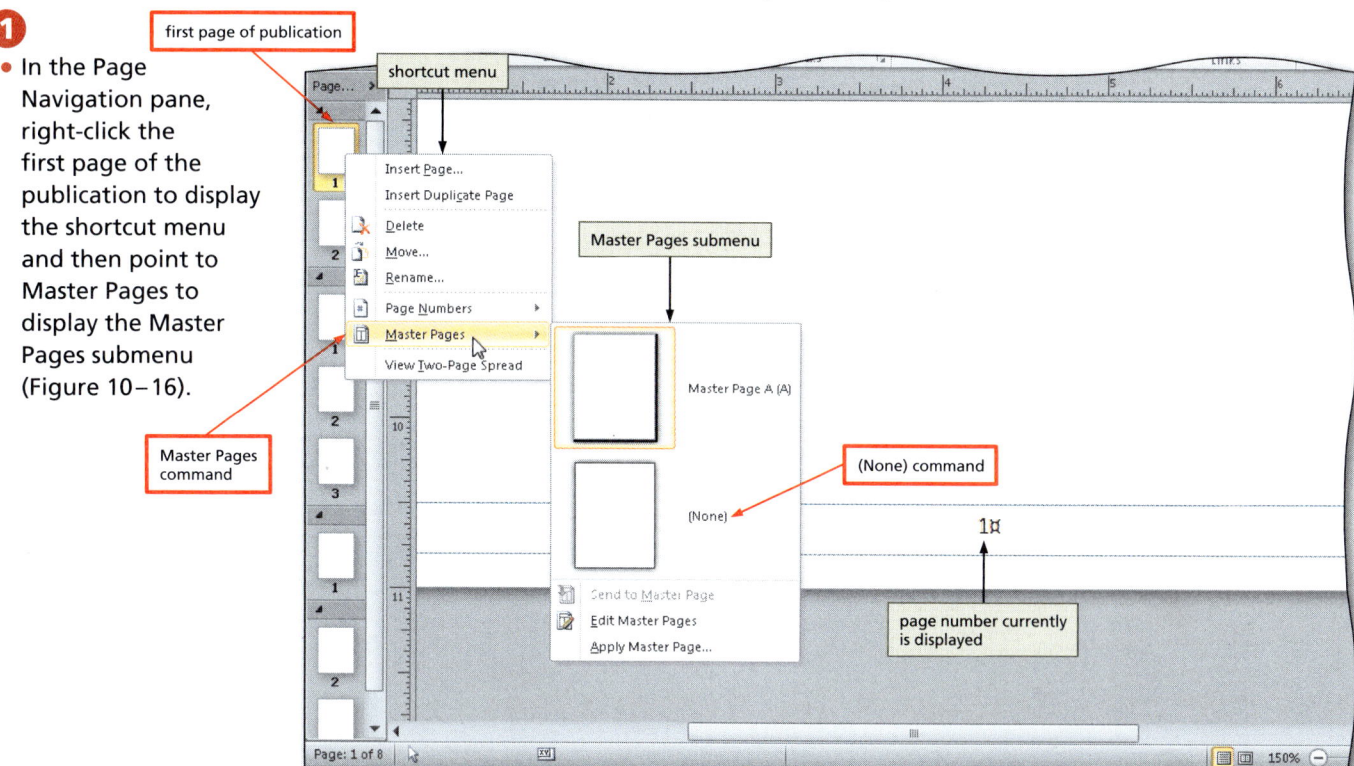

Figure 10–16

2
- Click (None) to remove the master page and thus remove page numbering from the page (Figure 10–17).

3
- Repeat Steps 1 and 2 for the second, seventh, and eighth pages of the publication, so that page numbering will not appear on those pages.

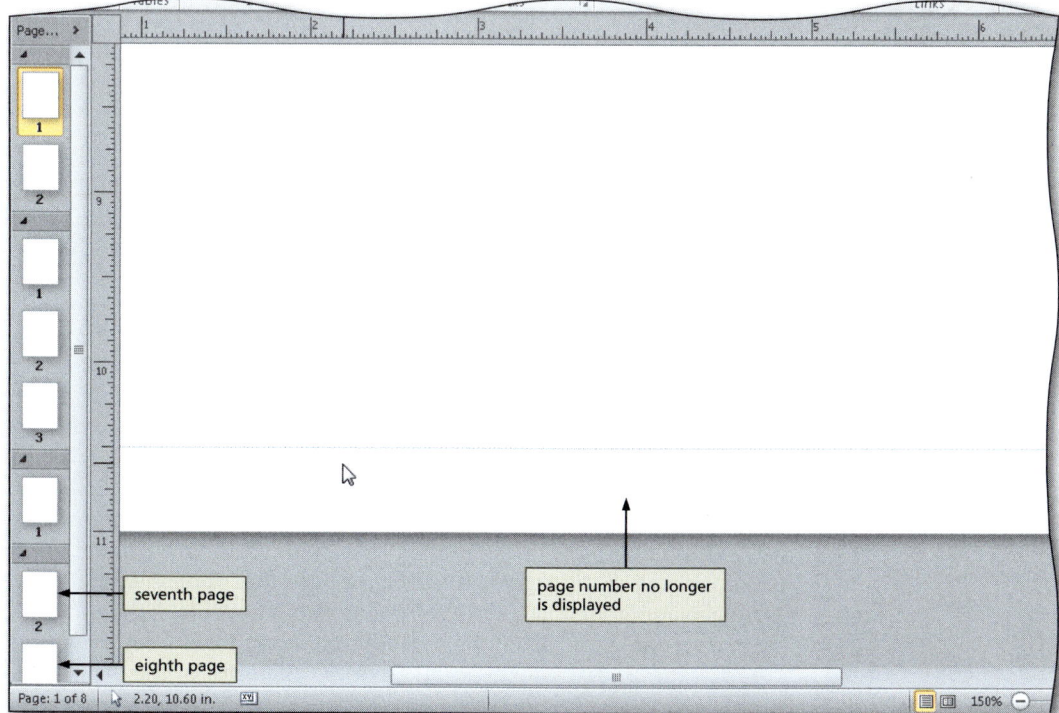

Figure 10–17

BTW

Formatting Page Numbers
You can format page numbers in the same manner as you format any text — with fonts, font sizes, font colors, alignments, and special effects, among others.

To Save the Publication

You have performed many tasks while creating this publication and do not want to risk losing work completed thus far. Accordingly, you should save the publication.

The following steps assume you already have created folders for storing your files, for example, a CIS 101 folder (for your class) that contains a Publisher folder (for your assignments). Thus, these steps save the publication in the Publisher folder in the CIS 101 folder on a USB flash drive using the file name, Conference Agenda. For a detailed example of the procedure summarized below, refer to the Office 2010 and Windows 7 chapter at the beginning of this book.

1 With a USB flash drive connected to one of the computer's USB ports, click File on the Ribbon to display the Backstage view.

2 Click the Save As command to display the Save As dialog box.

3 Type `Conference Agenda` in the File name text box to change the file name. Do not press the ENTER key after typing the file name because you do not want to close the dialog box at this time.

4 Navigate to the desired save location (in this case, the Publisher folder in the CIS 101 folder [or your class folder] on the USB flash drive).

5 Click the Save button (Save As dialog box) to save the publication in the selected folder on the selected drive with the entered file name.

BTW

Custom Borders
When you choose a custom piece of clip art or a picture to use as a border, Publisher will warn you if the picture is not square or is too complex to use as a border.

BorderArt and Backgrounds

BorderArt is a group of customizable graphical borders, such as crosses, hearts, apples, balloons, or decorative shapes, which can be added as an edge or border to a shape, a text box, or the entire page. When applied to the entire page, BorderArt makes the page margins stand out and adds interest to the page.

Alternately, you can incorporate a watermark as you did in previous chapters, or you can create a solid background. Creating a solid color background requires you either to create a shape that fills the entire page or to use a page background filled with a tint or shade effect. In a previous chapter, you used the Fill Effects dialog box to apply gradients and pictures. Shades and tints are applied in the same manner. Recall that a tint is a color created from a base color mixed with a percentage of white. A shade, on the other hand, is a mixture of a base color and black.

Plan Ahead

Use BorderArt and backgrounds sensibly.
For a graphic-based, repeating border, use a graphic that has meaning for the topic and one that will look good in a small, square format around the edges of the page. BorderArt does not have to appear on all four sides of a page. If the BorderArt were going to be used on more than one page, it would be more efficient to place it on a repeating master page. Then, as you add objects and text to your pages, the border will be out of the way, preventing you from editing it by accident. Solid backgrounds deserve special consideration. Consult with your printing service to find out the best way to create the background in a publication. **Knockout** is a printing term that applies when two colors print over the top of one another. Many print services knockout or remove the bottom color so that overprinting does not occur. When the bottom color is white, as in the case of white text on a dark background, the text is knocked out to the color of the paper.

To Duplicate a Master Page

You will create a master page for the BorderArt, but it also will need to have a page number. The following steps duplicate the Publisher-generated master page that holds the page number formatting information.

1 Click the Show Whole Page button on the Publisher status bar.

2 Press CTRL+M to view the master page.

3 Click the Duplicate button (Master Page tab | Master Page group) to display the Duplicate Master Page dialog box.

4 Type **Content Pages** in the Description text box (Figure 10–18).

5 Click the OK button (Duplicate Master Page dialog box) to create the new master page.

BTW

BTWs
For a complete list of the BTWs found in the margins of this book, visit the Publisher 2010 BTW Web page (scsite .com/pub2010/btw).

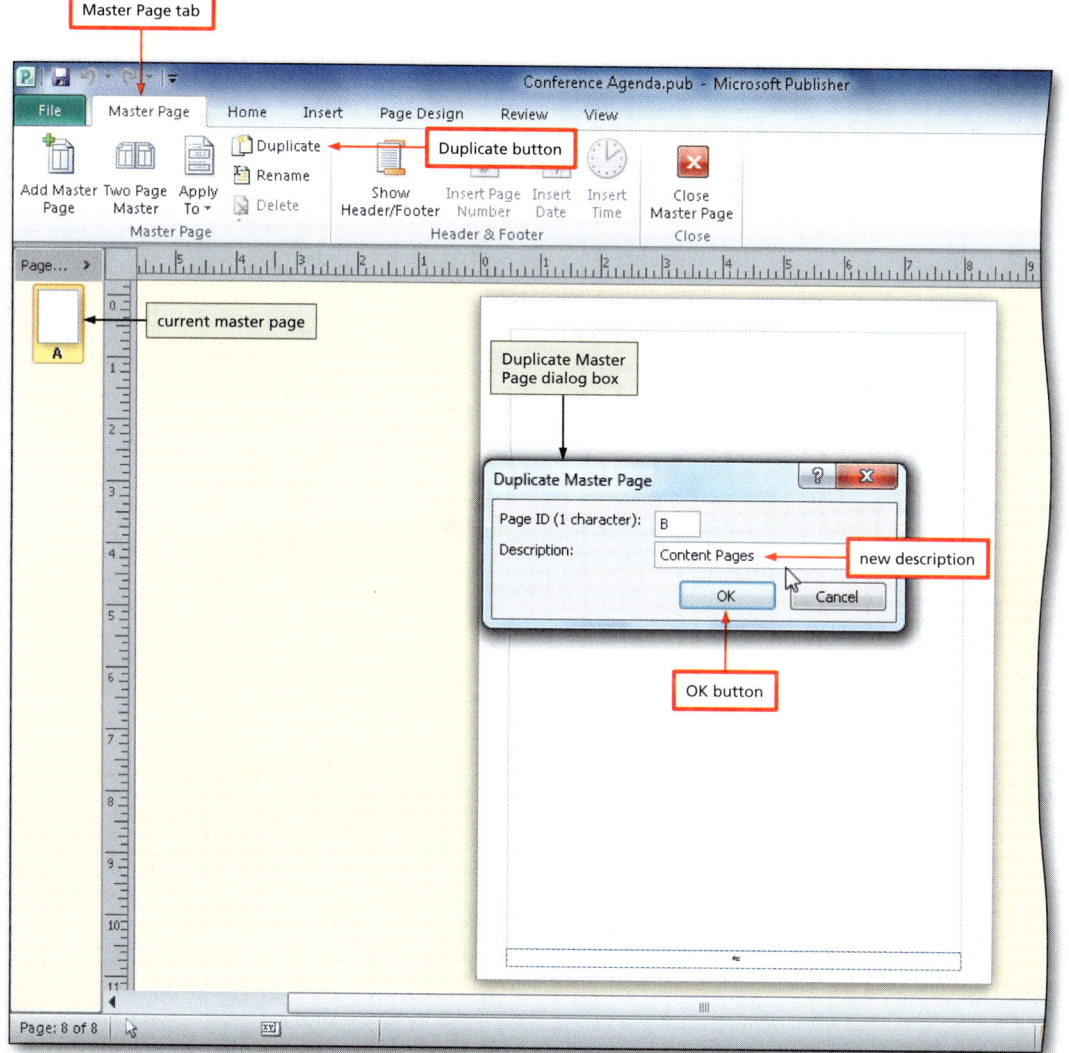

Figure 10–18

To Create BorderArt

The following steps create a rectangle shape on the Content Pages master page and then use BorderArt to create a page border for the content pages of the agenda.

1

- Display the Insert tab.

- Click the Shapes button (Insert tab | Illustrations group) and then click the Rectangle shape.

- Drag to draw a rectangle that fills the page and snaps to the margin guides.

- Right-click the shape to display the shortcut menu (Figure 10–19).

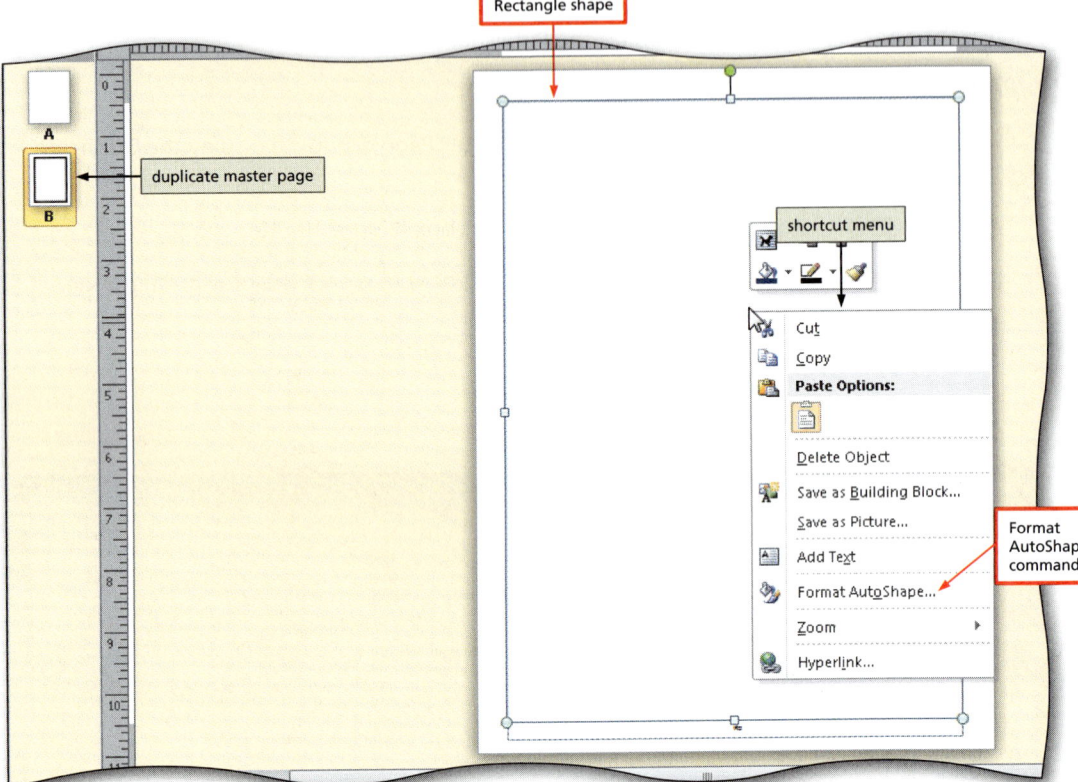

Figure 10–19

2

- Click Format AutoShape on the shortcut menu to display the Format AutoShape dialog box.

- If necessary, click the Colors and Lines tab (Figure 10–20).

Figure 10–20

3

- Click the BorderArt button to display the BorderArt dialog box.

- Scroll as necessary in the Available Borders area and click the Push Pin in Note 2 border to select it.

- If necessary, click the 'Stretch pictures to fit' option button to select it (Figure 10–21).

🔍 **Experiment**

- Scroll to view all of the available borders in the list. Notice some are repeating square elements and others use special corners.

Figure 10–21

4

- Click the OK button (BorderArt dialog box) to return to the Format AutoShape dialog box (Figure 10–22).

Could I further edit the BorderArt to change the color or size?

Yes, the settings in the Format AutoShape dialog box in Figure 10–22 are the default settings; however, you can change the size by changing the point value in the Weight box, or change the color by clicking the Color box arrow and selecting a color.

Figure 10–22

5
- Click the OK button (Format AutoShape dialog box) to apply the border.

- Click outside the shape to deselect it (Figure 10–23).

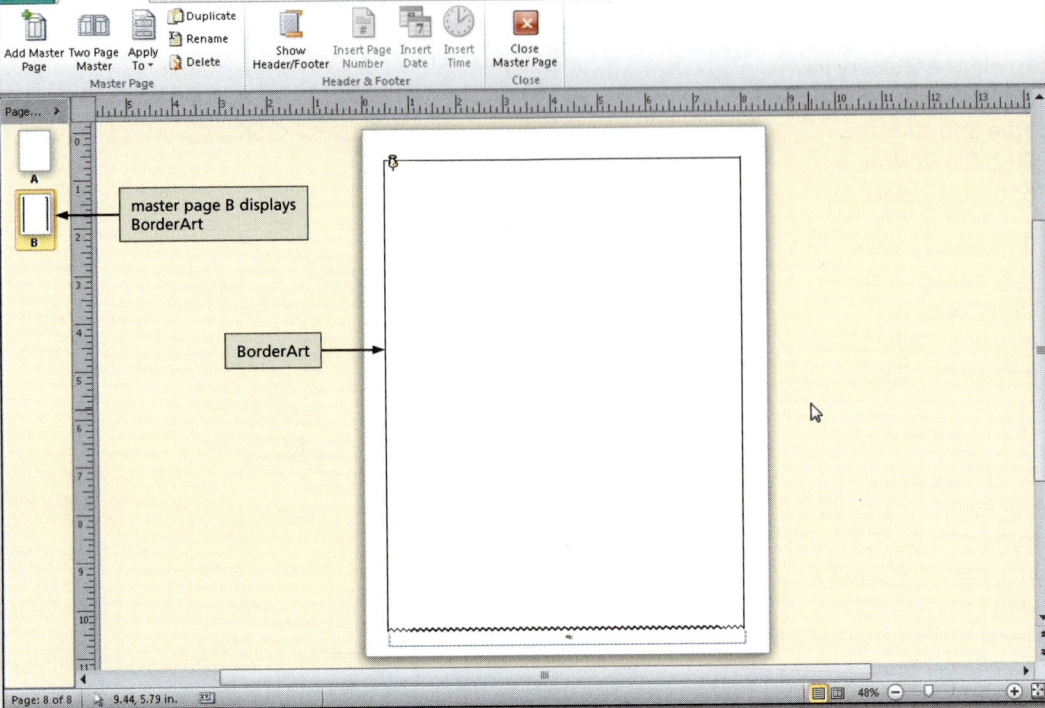

Figure 10–23

Other Ways

1. Select shape, click Format Shape Dialog Box Launcher (Drawing Tools Format tab | Shape Styles group), click BorderArt button (Format AutoShape dialog box), select border, click OK button (BorderArt dialog box), click OK button (Format AutoShape dialog box)

BTW

The Create Custom Button
The Create Custom button (BorderArt dialog box on the previous page) displays the Create Custom Border dialog box in which you can either search for other clip art to use as a border or import a picture from a file.

To Insert Repeating Text

At the bottom of each content page, the conference administrators have asked you to place a message about name badges and cell phones. Because this is a repeating element, the followings steps place the text at the bottom of the Content Pages master page.

1 Zoom to 100% and scroll to the bottom of the master page.

2 Display the Home tab.

3 Click the Draw Text Box button (Home tab | Objects group) and then draw a text box at the bottom of the page, just above the bottom border, that fills the area between margins, approximately .25 inches tall.

4 If necessary, click the Font Size box arrow (Text Box Tools Format tab | Font group) and then click 12 in the list.

5 Press CTRL+E to center the text.

6 Type **Name badges are to be worn during all sessions. Please silence cell phones during sessions.** to complete the text (Figure 10–24).

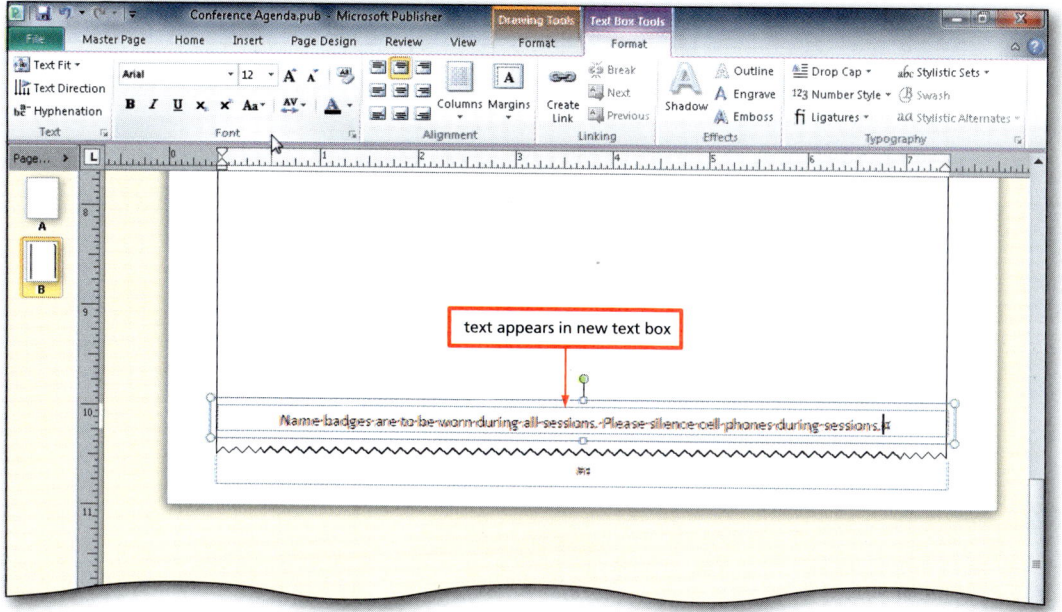

Figure 10–24

To Close the Master Page and Apply It

You are finished with the BorderArt and repeating text. The following steps close the master page and return to Normal view. You then will apply the new master page to the sixth page of the publication.

1. Press CTRL+M to close the master page.

2. Right-click the sixth page in the Page Navigation pane, point to Master Pages on the shortcut menu, and then click Content Pages (B) in the list to apply the master page with the border (Figure 10–25).

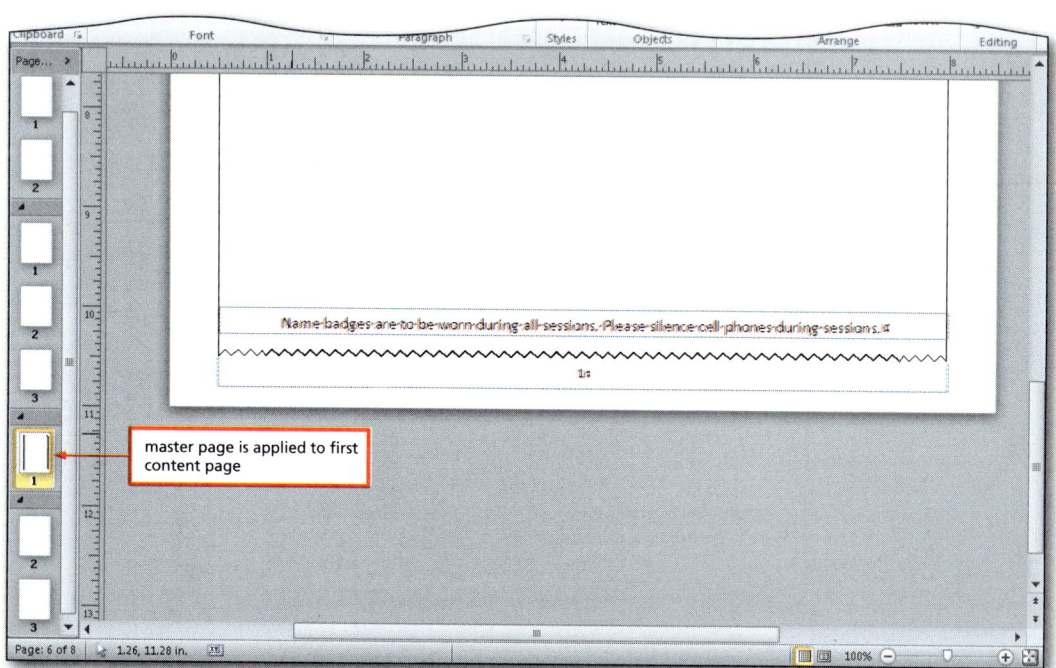

Figure 10–25

To Create a Shade Background

The following steps insert a solid black background on the first and last pages of the agenda. To achieve a solid black, you will use a 0% shade in the Fill Effects dialog box.

- Select the first page of the publication.

- Display the Page Design tab.

- Click the Background button (Page Design tab | Page Background group) to display the Background gallery (Figure 10–26).

Experiment

- Point to each of the backgrounds to watch the page layout change.

Figure 10–26

- Click More Backgrounds to display the Fill Effects dialog box.

- Click the Tint tab and then click 0% Shade in the Tint/Shade area (Figure 10–27).

Figure 10–27

3
- Click the OK button (Fill Effects dialog box) to apply the effect.

- Click the Show Whole Page button on the Publisher status bar (Figure 10–28).

page background is filled with 0% shade

Show Whole Page button

Figure 10–28

4
- Repeat Steps 1 through 3 for the last page of the publication (Figure 10–29).

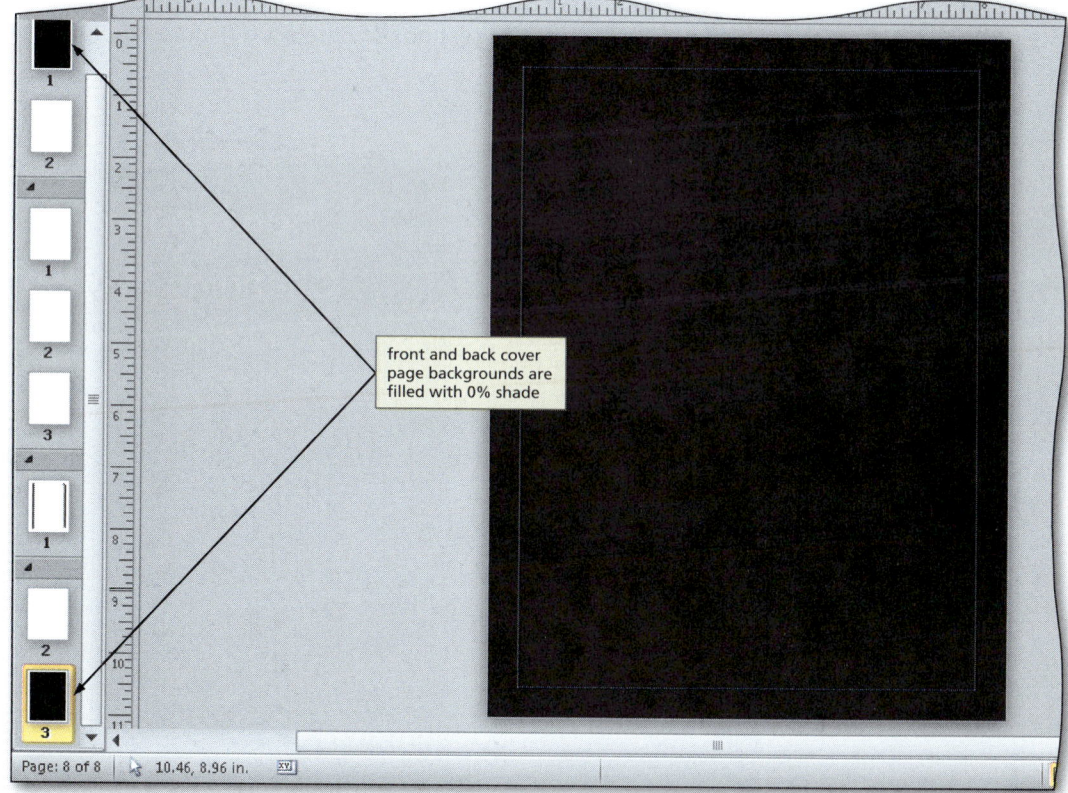

front and back cover page backgrounds are filled with 0% shade

Page: 8 of 8   10.46, 8.96 in.

Figure 10–29

To Enter the Title and Subtitle

The following steps add a title and subtitle to the cover page of the conference agenda. Because the cover is black, you will need to use white text so that it is visible against the black background.

1 Select the first page of the publication in the Page Navigation pane.

2 Display the Home tab.

3 Click the Draw Text Box button (Home tab | Objects group) and then draw a text box beginning at the upper-left margin guide, extending to the right margin guides, approximately 2 inches tall.

4 Click the Font Size box arrow (Text Box Tools Format tab | Font group) and then click 48 in the list.

5 Click the Font Color button arrow (Text Box Tools Format tab | Font group) and then click Accent 5 (White) in the list.

6 Press CTRL+E to center the text.

7 Type `Surviving in a` and then press the ENTER key. Type `Changing World` to complete the title text. Click outside the text box to deselect it.

8 Draw a second text box below the first, from the left margin to the right margin, approximately 1.5 inches tall. Do not overlap the text boxes.

9 Change the font size to 28 and the font color to white.

10 Center the text.

11 Type `The 10th Annual Conference of` and then press the ENTER key. Type `Georgia Information Technology Educators` to complete the subtitle text. Click outside the text box to deselect it (Figure 10–30).

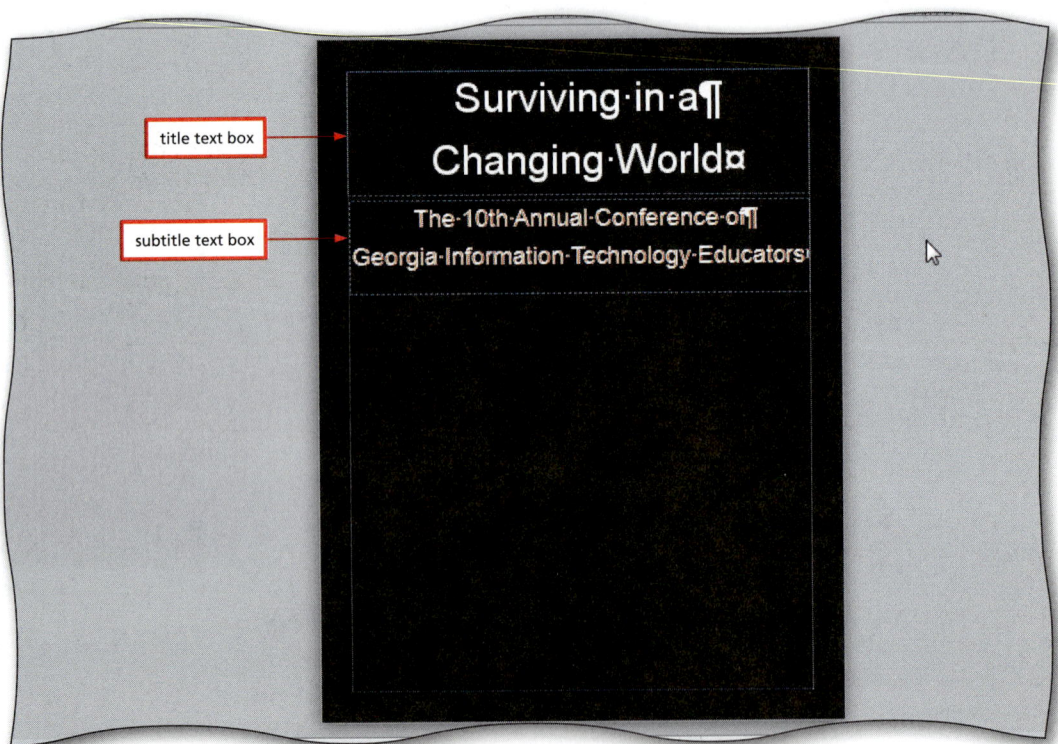

Figure 10–30

To Complete the Cover Page

To complete the cover page, the following steps insert a graphic and a text box with the date and location.

1 Display the Insert tab.

2 Click the Clip Art button (Insert tab | Illustrations group) to display the Clip Art task pane.

3 Search for clip art related to the term, Earth, and insert a graphic similar to the one shown in Figure 10–31.

4 SHIFT+drag a corner sizing handle to resize the graphic to approximately 4 inches square and place it below the subtitle text box. Click outside the graphic to deselect it and close the Clip Art task pane.

5 Display the Home tab. Click the Draw Text Box button (Home tab | Objects group) and then draw a text box beginning at the lower-left margin guide, extending to the right margin guides, approximately 1.5 inches tall.

6 Change the font size to 28 and the font color to white.

7 Center the text.

8 Type **March 8-9, 2012** and then press the ENTER key. Type **Conference Center in David, Georgia** to complete the text. Click outside the text box to deselect it. (Figure 10–31).

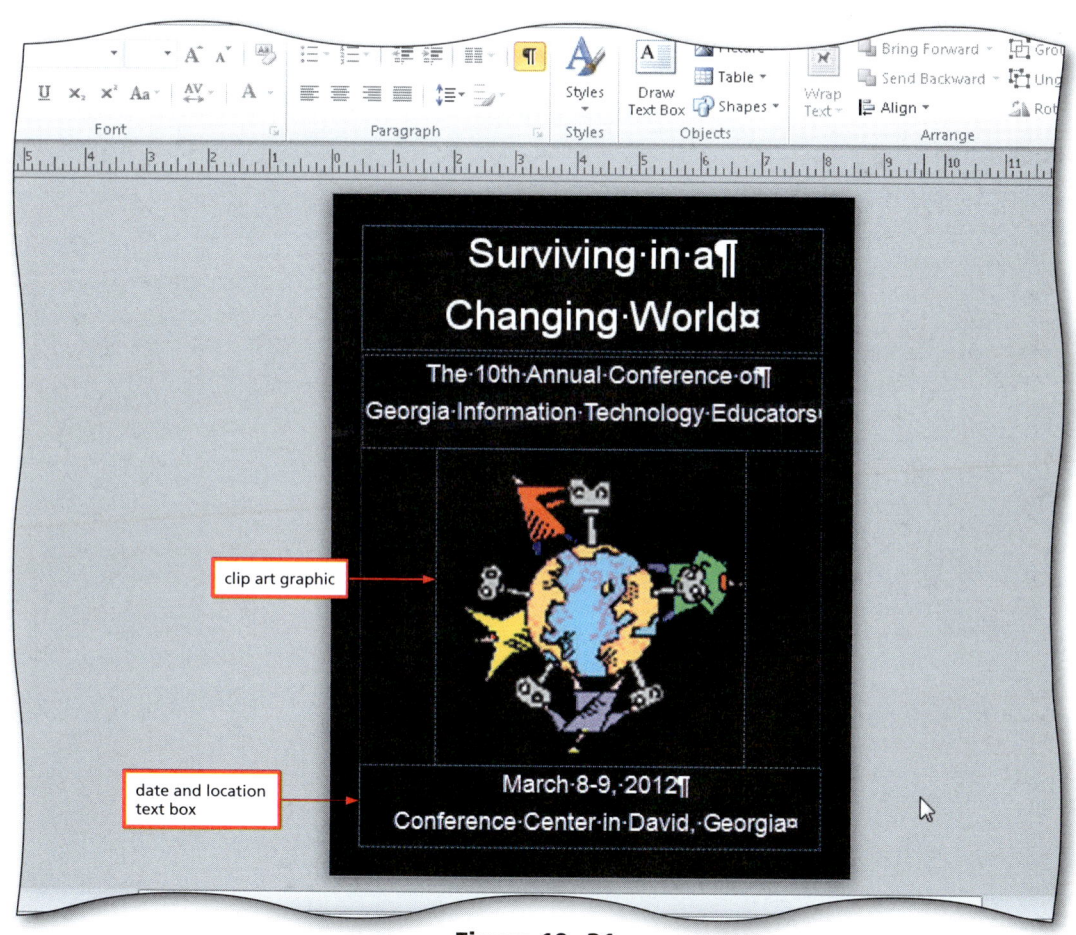

Figure 10–31

To Collapse Sections

The front and back pages of the conference agenda are complete. The following steps collapse those sections in the Page Navigation pane so they do not clutter the screen.

- Select the third page of the publication.

- In the Page Navigation pane, click the Collapse Section button above the first page of the publication to collapse the front cover section (Figure 10–32).

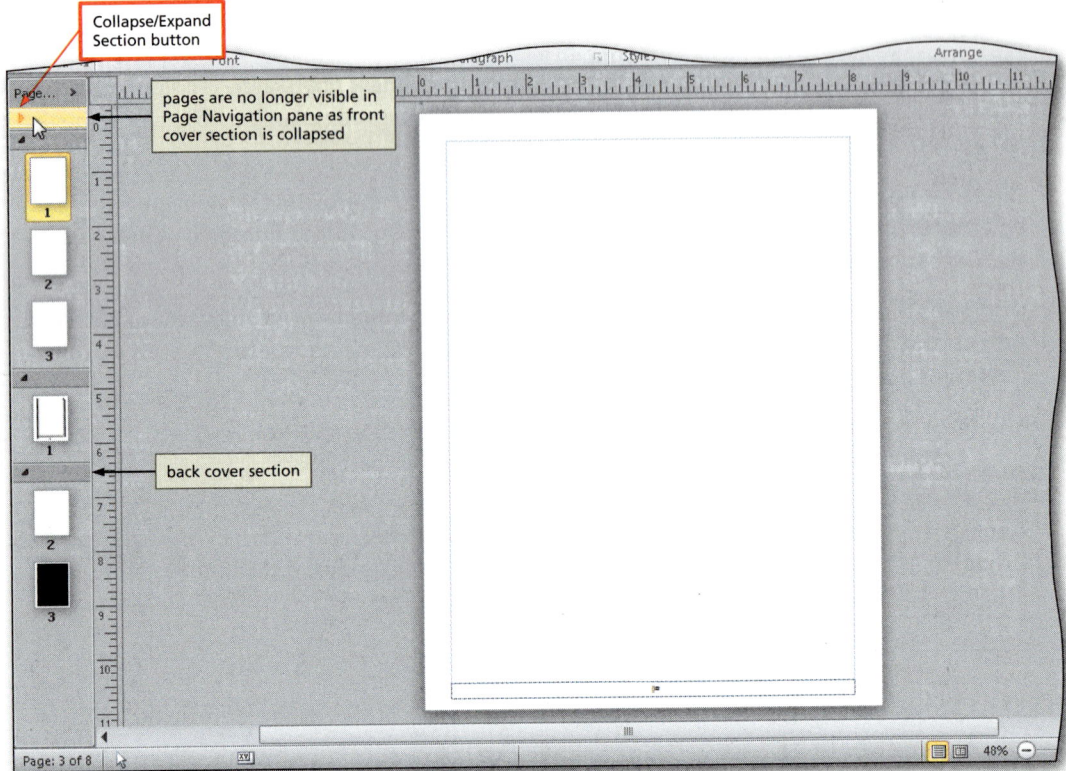

Figure 10–32

- Click the Collapse Section button above the next-to-last page in the Page Navigation pane to collapse the back cover section (Figure 10–33).

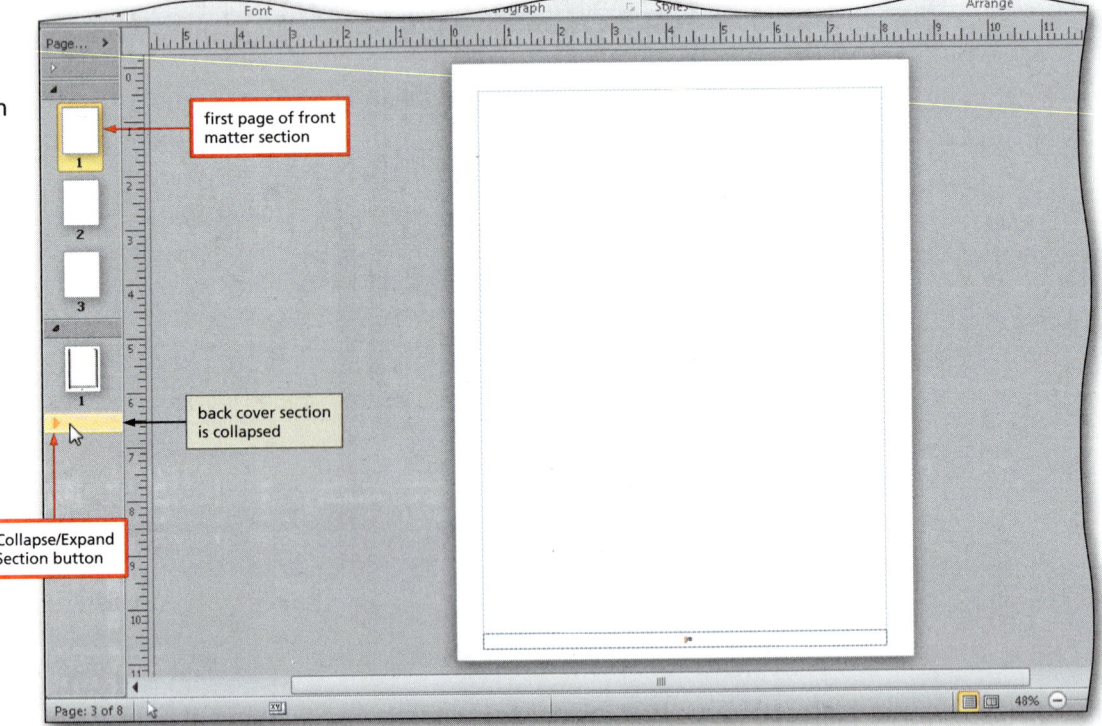

Figure 10–33

To Save an Existing Publication with the Same File Name

You have made several modifications to the publication since you last saved it. Thus, you should save it again. The following step saves the publication again.

1 Click the Save button on the Quick Access Toolbar to overwrite the previously saved file.

Cell and Text Box Margins

Like page margins, you can adjust the margins within table cells and within text boxes. The default margin for a text box and for a cell is approximately 0.04 inches. In some cases, that may place the text too close to the edge or border. After creating a table of contents, you will change the margin in the table of content cells for the conference agenda so that the page numbers are farther away from the margin and its border, thereby improving readability.

To Insert a Table of Contents Building Block

The following steps insert and resize a table of contents on the third page of the front matter.

1 Click the third page of the front matter with the page number iii.

2 Display the Insert tab.

3 Click the Show Building Block Library Dialog Box Launcher (Insert tab | Building Blocks group) to display the Building Block Library dialog box.

4 Click the Page Parts folder (Building Block Library dialog box).

5 Scroll as necessary and then click the All Tables of Contents folder.

6 Double-click the Bars table of contents to insert it in the publication.

7 Click the Object Position button on the status bar to display the Measurement toolbar.

8 Type **1.75** in the Horizontal Position box, **.7** in the Vertical Position box, **5** in the Width box, and **6** in the Height box to resize and position the table (Figure 10–34 on the next page).

9 Close the Measurement toolbar.

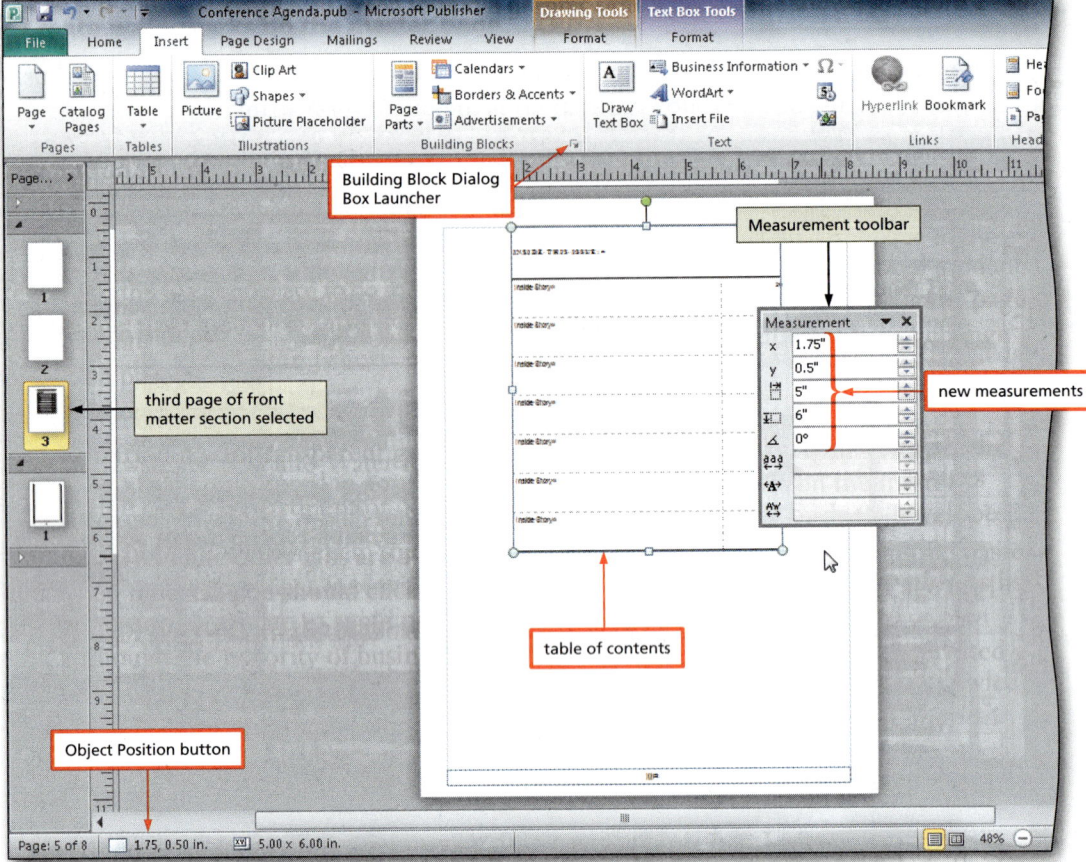

Figure 10–34

To Format the Table of Contents

The table of contents contains a text box for the title and a table below it, grouped together. The following steps select and format the table borders.

1. Click any row in the table of contents to position the insertion point in the table.

2. Display the Table Tools Layout tab.

3. Click the Select button (Table Tools Layout tab | Table group) and then click Select Table in the list.

4. Display the Table Tools Design tab.

5. Click the Line Color button (Table Tools Design tab | Borders group) and then click Main (Black).

6. Click the Borders button arrow (Table Tools Design tab | Borders group) and then click All Borders in the list (Figure 10–35).

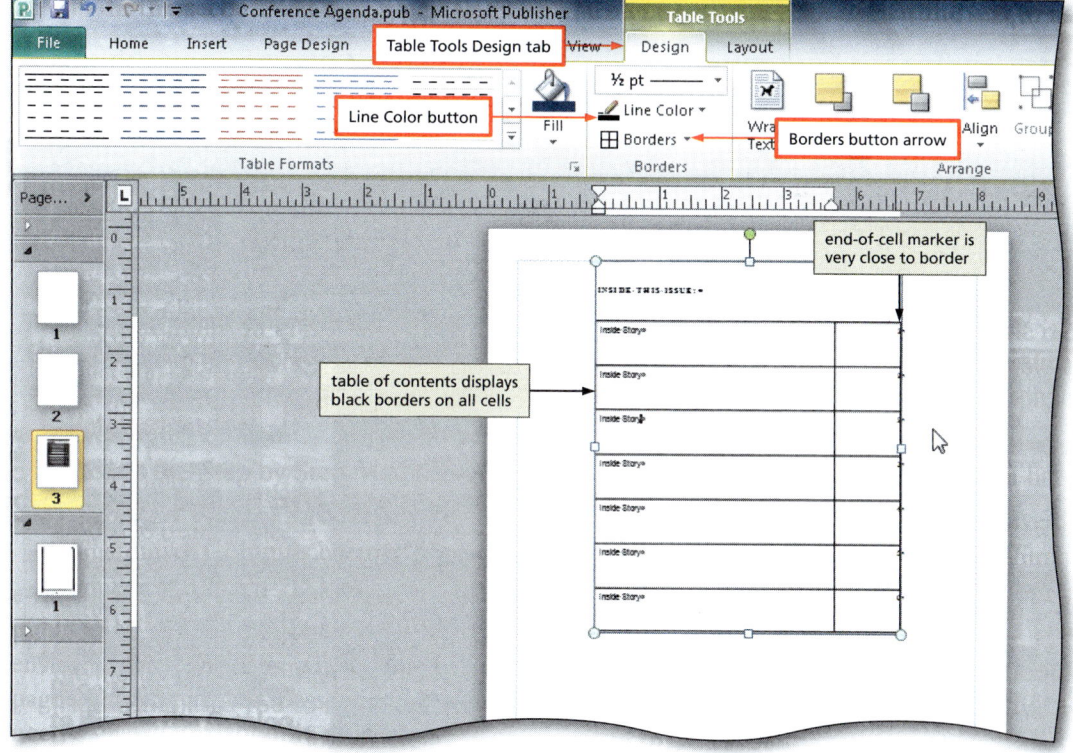

Figure 10–35

To Change Cell Margins

The following steps increase the right margin of the cells in the second column. Because you change the cell margin, the page number will not appear as close to the border.

1
- Drag through the second column of the table to select the cells.

- Display the Table Tools Layout tab.

- Click the Cell Margins button (Table Tools Layout tab | Alignment group) to display the Cell Margins gallery (Figure 10–36).

Experiment
- Point to each of the cell margin choices in the Cell Margins gallery and watch the margins change in the table.

Figure 10–36

2

- Click Custom Margins to display the Format Table dialog box. If necessary, click the Cell Properties tab.

- Select the text in the Right box and then type **.3** to change the right margin (Figure 10–37).

Q&A

Could I use the Numeric Up and Down buttons in the Right box?

Yes, those buttons change the text in the box by .1 inch, each time you click them.

Figure 10–37

3

- Click the OK button (Format Table dialog box) to apply the new margin to the cells.

- Click outside the table to deselect the cells (Figure 10–38).

Q&A

Should I enter new text in the table of contents?

You will update the table of contents later in the chapter, after you complete all pages.

Other Ways

1. Right-click cell, click Format Table on shortcut menu, click Cell Properties tab (Format Table dialog box), enter cell margin, click OK button

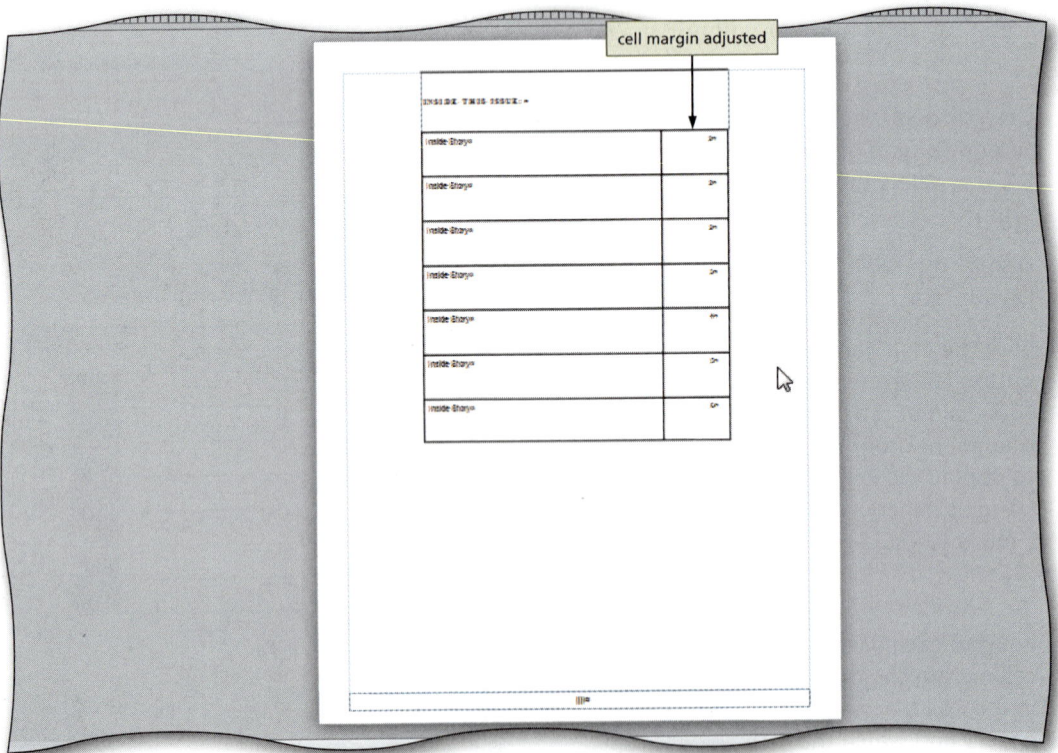

Figure 10–38

TO CHANGE TEXT BOX MARGINS

If you wanted to change the margins of a text box, rather than a cell, you would perform the following steps.

1. Select the text box by clicking its boundary.

2. If necessary, display the Text Box Tools Format tab.

3. Click the Margins button (Text Box Tools Format tab | Alignment group) and then either choose a preset value from the Margins gallery, or click Custom Margins and enter the margin values.

To Insert a Graphic

The following steps insert a graphic on Page ii of the front matter from the Data Files for Students. See the inside back cover of this book for instructions on downloading the Data Files for Students, or contact your instructor for information about accessing the required files.

1 In the Page Navigation pane, select the second page of the front matter section.

2 Display the Insert tab.

3 Click the Insert Picture from File button (Insert tab | Illustrations group) to display the Insert Picture dialog box and navigate to the Data files for Students, in the Publisher folder, in the Chapter10 folder.

4 Double-click the file named, Map, to insert it into the publication.

5 Click the Object Position button on the status bar to display the Measurement toolbar.

6 Type .98 in the Horizontal Position box, .8 in the Vertical Position box, 6.54 in the Width box, and 9.39 in the Height box to resize and position the table (Figure 10–39).

7 Close the Measurement toolbar.

BTW

Q&As
For a complete list of the Q&As found in many of the step-by-step sequences in this book, visit the Publisher 2010 Q&A Web page (scsite .com/pub2010/qa).

Figure 10–39

To Insert a Text File

The following steps insert a text file on Page i of the front matter from the Data Files for Students. See the inside back cover of this book for instructions on downloading the Data Files for Students, or contact your instructor for information about accessing the required files.

1 Select the first page of the front matter section.

2 Display the Home tab.

3 Draw a large text box that fills the page.

4 Display the Insert tab.

5 Click the Insert File button (Insert tab | Text group) to display the Insert Text dialog box and navigate to the Data files for Students, in the Publisher folder, in the Chapter10 folder.

6 Double-click the file named, President's Greeting, to insert it into the publication.

7 Click the Object Position button on the status bar to display the Measurement toolbar.

8 Type `.7` in the Horizontal Position box, `1.15` in the Vertical Position box, `5.75` in the Width box, and `8` in the Height box to resize and position the table (Figure 10–39).

9 Close the Measurement toolbar.

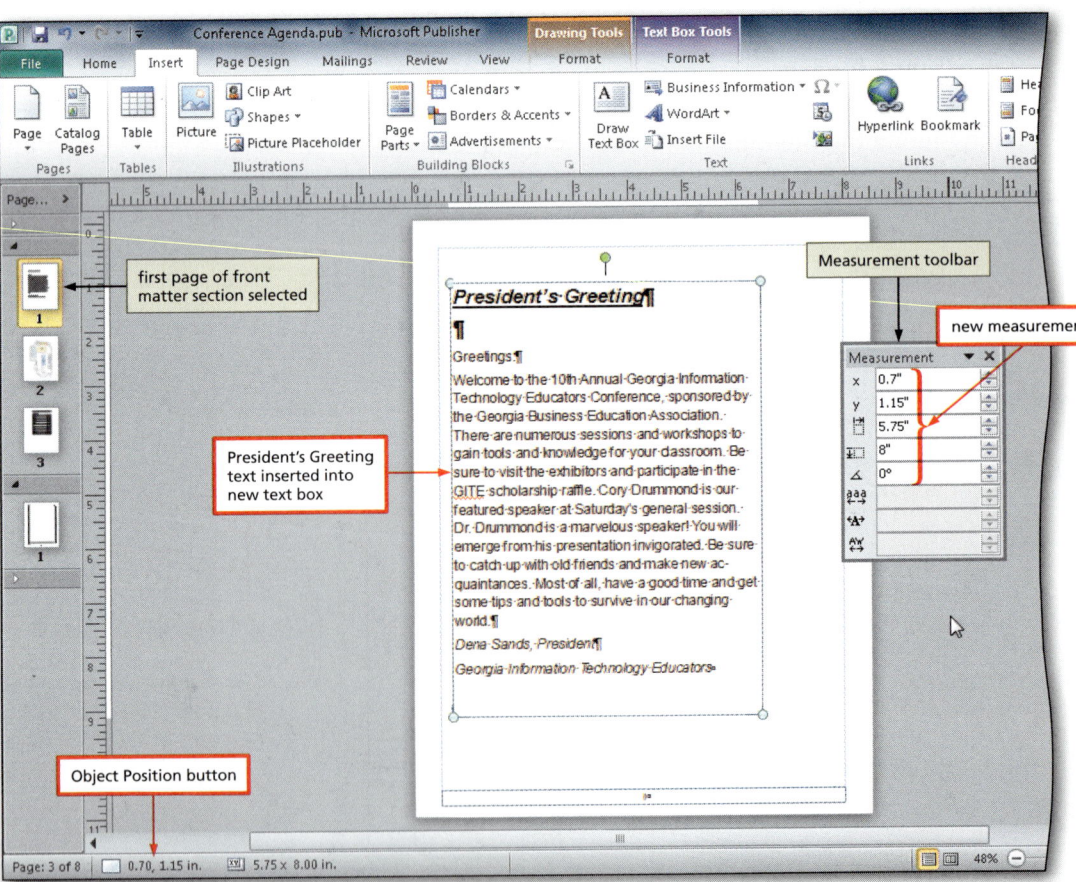

Figure 10–40

To Change the Text Direction

The following steps create a second text box on the first page of the front matter, and change the text direction.

1

• Draw a text box on the right side of the page that extends from the top margin to the bottom margin, approximately 1 inch wide (Figure 10–41).

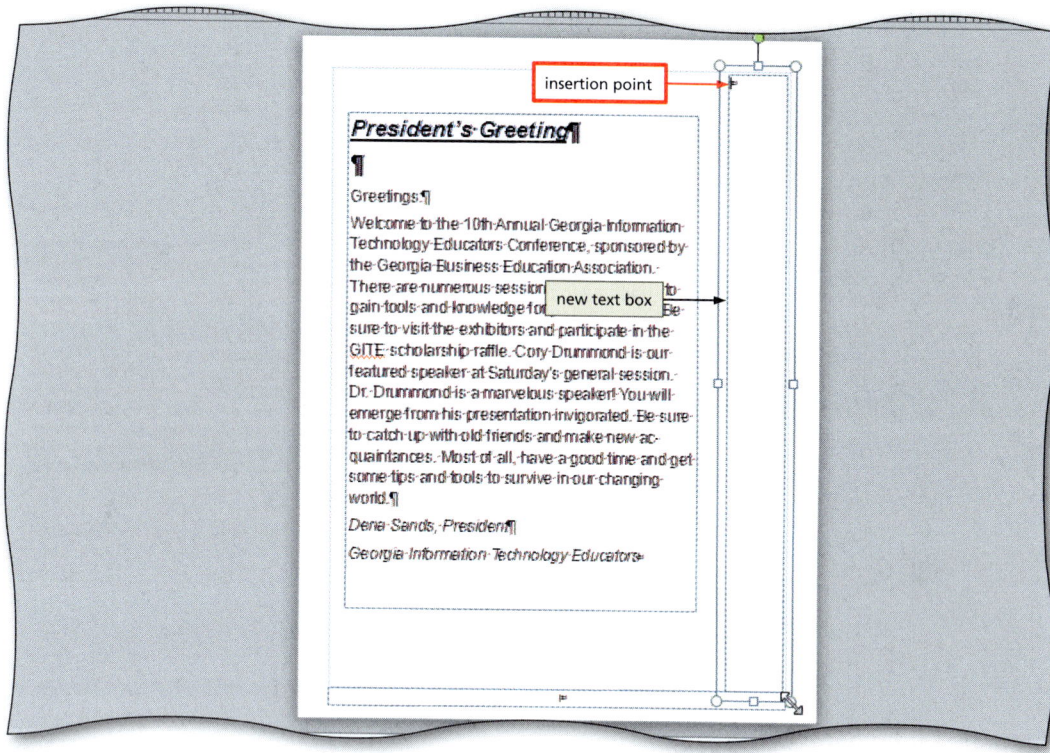

Figure 10–41

2

• Press CTRL+E to center the text.

• Click the Text Direction button (Text Box Tools Format tab | Text group) to change the text direction (Figure 10–42).

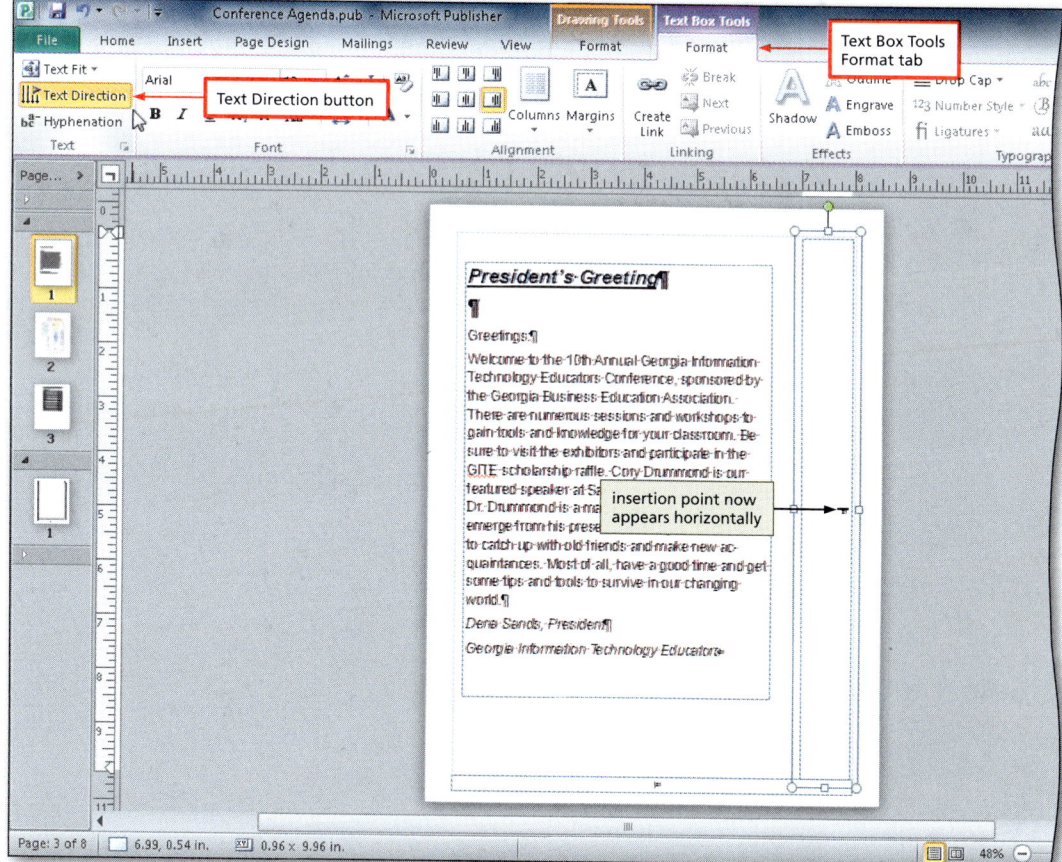

Figure 10–42

3

- Type **Surviving in a Changing World** to enter the text.

- Click the Text Fit button (Text Box Tools Format tab | Text group) and then click Best Fit to autofit the text (Figure 10–43).

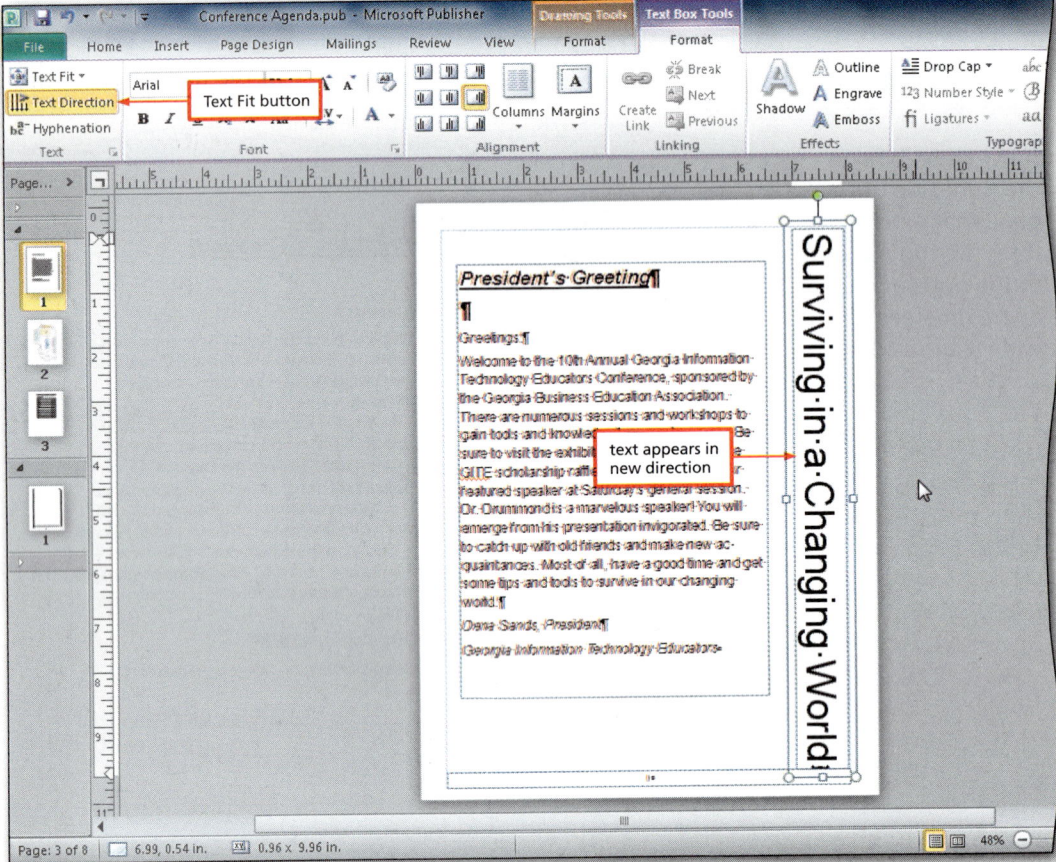

Figure 10–43

Ruler Guide Patterns

Recall that you have used ruler guides — green, dotted, nonprinting lines — by dragging from the rulers to help you align objects and provide visual reference. You also can use built-in ruler guide patterns from a list of page designs. These ruler guides are preset to contain headings, columns, and grids. Along with margin guides that are blue, the ruler guides also provide straight edges and snapping capabilities.

In the conference agenda, you will choose a set of ruler guides in order to display two columns with headings. You will insert two text boxes, link them together, and then duplicate the page several times. Finally, you will link the text boxes across pages and insert the text.

To Select a Guide Pattern

The following steps select a guide pattern from the list of preset patterns.

1

- Select the single page from the content section.

- Display the Page Design tab.

- Click the Guides button (Page Design tab | Layout group) to display the list (Figure 10–44).

Figure 10–44

2

- Click 2 Columns with Heading to select it (Figure 10–45).

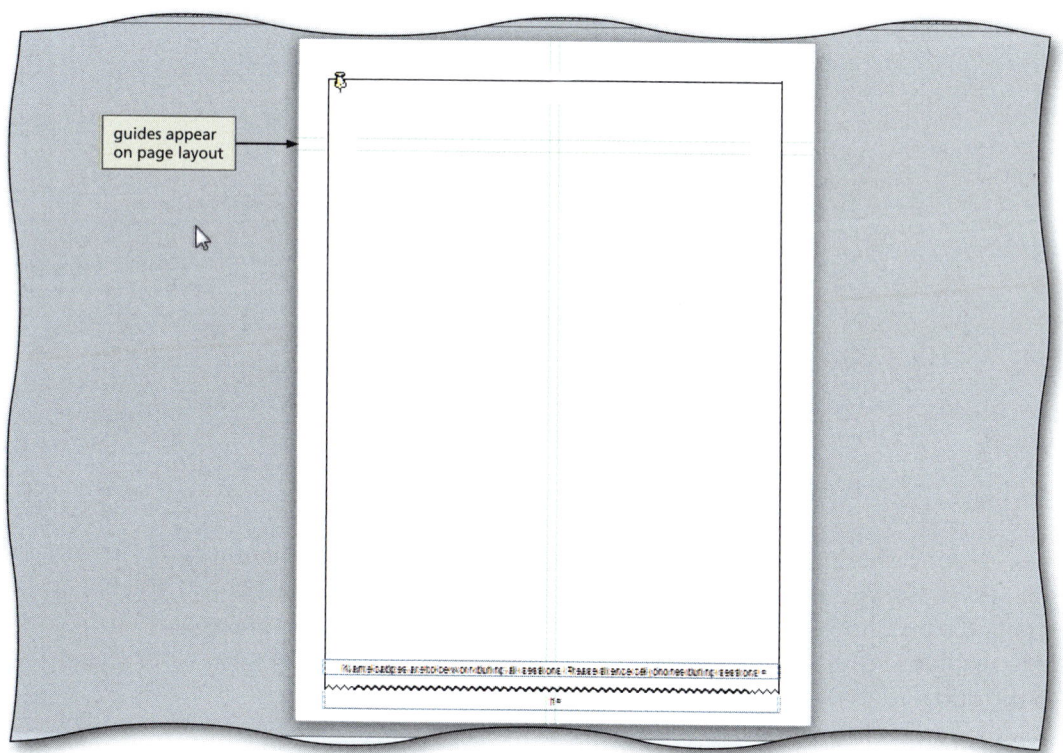

Figure 10–45

To Draw and Copy a Text Box

The following steps draw a text box to create one column of text and then copy it to create a second column the exact same size.

1 Display the Home tab.

2 Draw a text box that fills the left side of the page, 3.67 inches wide and 8.17 inches tall as measured on the status bar. It is important that your text box align with the column guides. Do not include the heading area.

3 CTRL+drag the text box to create a copy on the other side (Figure 10–46).

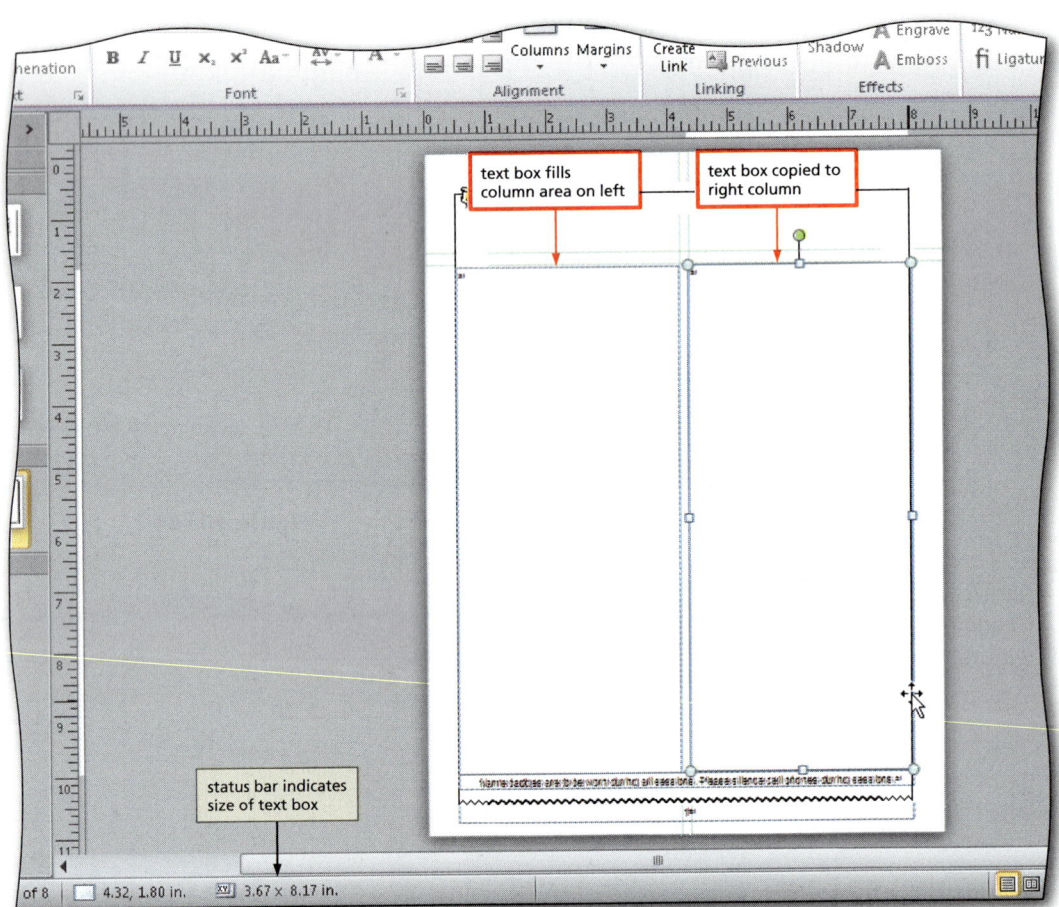

Figure 10–46

To Link Text Boxes Using the Ribbon

In an earlier chapter, you linked a story from one text box to another after inserting text. Recall that you used the Text in Overflow button when the story did not fit in the first text box. If you link text boxes before importing or typing the text, however, the Text Box Tools Format tab contains several tools to help you create, break, and move between linked text boxes. The following steps link the two text boxes, so that text inserted later will flow from one to the other.

1

- Click the text box on the left side of the page.

- Click the Create Link button (Text Box Tools Format tab | Linking group) to start the linking process.

- Move the mouse pointer over the first text box (Figure 10–47).

Create Link button

mouse pointer appears as full bucket over source text box

Figure 10–47

2

- Move the mouse pointer to the second text box and then click it to link the text boxes (Figure 10–48).

 Q&A

Why does my mouse pointer look like a bucket?

Publisher uses the bucket icon to show that the text should flow into the clicked text box. The bucket is upright when you move over the original text box. It tips when you move over any other text box, as if it is pouring in the text.

mouse pointer appears as pouring bucket over destination text box

Figure 10–48

To Duplicate a Page

The following steps duplicate the entire page including all objects — in this case, text boxes, links, master page objects, and guides.

- Right-click the selected page in the Page Navigation pane to display the shortcut menu (Figure 10–49).

Figure 10–49

- Click Insert Duplicate Page on the shortcut menu to create a duplicate (Figure 10–50).

Q&A

Why did the duplication create another section?

The section breaks are attached to the first page in the section. Because this section so far contains only one page, Publisher copied the page and the section break. It also expanded all of the sections in preparation for moving pages or merging sections.

Other Ways

1. Click Insert Blank Page button arrow (Insert tab | Pages group), click Insert Duplicate Page

Figure 10–50

To Merge Sections

The following steps merge the original page and the duplicated page into a single section.

1
- In the Page Navigation pane, right-click the section title bar above the seventh page of the publication to display the section shortcut menu (Figure 10–51).

section break above seventh page

shortcut menu

Merge with Previous Section command

Figure 10–51

2
- Click Merge with Previous Section on the shortcut menu to merge the duplicate page into the same section as the original page (Figure 10–52).

sections merged

Figure 10–52

BTW

Moving Pages across Sections
If you do not want to merge sections, you can move single pages from one section to another by dragging and dropping them in the Page Navigation pane.

To Create More Duplicate Pages

A total of nine content pages will use the same layout; therefore, you need to duplicate the page seven more times. The following steps create more duplicate pages.

1 Right-click the second page of the content section and then click Insert Duplicate Page on the shortcut menu.

2 Repeat Step 1 six times until nine total pages appear in the section.

3 Collapse all sections except the content section (Figure 10–53).

content section contains nine identical pages

Figure 10–53

To Link Text Boxes across Pages

The final step before importing the text file that contains the agenda is to link the text boxes across pages. The following steps link the text boxes.

1 Select the first page of the content section.

2 In the document window, click the second text box (on the right) and display the Text Box Tools Format tab.

3 Click the Create Link button (Text Box Tools Format tab | Linking group) to start the linking process.

4 In the Page Navigation pane, select the next page.

5 Click the first text box (on the left) on the page to link across pages.

6 Beginning on the second page of the content section, repeat Steps 2 through 5 to link each of the pages in the content section. Once you link the eighth page to the ninth page, you are finished linking.

To Import Text

The following steps import a text file for the agenda from the Data Files for Students. See the inside back cover of this book for instructions on downloading the Data Files for Students, or contact your instructor for information about accessing the required files.

1 Select the first page of the content section and click the left text box.

2 Display the Insert tab.

3 Click the Insert File button (Insert tab | Text group) to display the Insert Text dialog box and navigate to the Data Files for Students, in the Publisher folder, in the Chapter10 folder.

4 Double-click the file named, Agenda Text, to insert it into the publication (Figure 10–54).

Figure 10–54

To Save Again

You have made several modifications to the publication since you last saved it. Thus, you should save it again. The following step saves the publication again.

1 Click the Save button on the Quick Access Toolbar to overwrite the previously saved file.

Find and Replace

Many kinds of application software offer you the ability to find or search for specific characters. Most also allow you to search for and then replace text. Publisher's Find and Replace commands use a task pane to help you determine search parameters and how the replacement will be made. For example, you can search for matches that use whole words only or occurrences that match in case. You also can search forward or backward through the publication, as well as searching it in its entirety. In Publisher, you have to find the search string one occurrence at a time. The Replace command offers you choices of replacing one occurrence at a time or replacing all occurrences.

Plan Ahead

Employ global tools.

Publisher tools that help you locate information in large-scale publications are called global tools. Use find and search techniques to make consistent corrections. Replace overused words, or find better terms with synonyms from the built-in thesaurus. Create manual page breaks to make content flow better and keep paragraphs together. Insert bookmarks at logical locations that you may need to locate frequently.

You can search for individual characters, symbols, spaces, formatting marks, or entire words and phrases. Table 10–1 displays some of the wildcard and formatting marks for which you can search. A **wildcard** is a character that may be substituted for any possible characters when searching. Publisher uses the ? (question mark) as a wildcard character.

Table 10–1 Wildcard and Format Searching			
Search Characters	**Searches for**	**Example**	**Finds**
?	wildcard	s?t	sat, sit, subset, stalwart, etc.
^^	caret	^^	next occurrence of ^
^?	question mark	^?	next occurrence of a question mark
^12	page break	^12	next inserted page break
^n	soft return	^n	next occurrence of a soft return
^nnn	search for ASCI character	^233	next occurrence of é
^p	hard return	^pTo	new line that begins with the word To, Today, etc.
^t	tab character	^t^t	two tabs together
^w	white space	^w	next occurrence of any kind of white space, including tabs

To Use the Find Command

Sometimes, you may want to find an occurrence of a certain character or phrase in a long publication. For example, you may want to know if any presentations about green technology will be held at the conference. The following steps use the Find command to locate the word, green.

1

- In the Page Navigation pane, select the first page of the content section.

- Display the Home tab.

- Click the Find button (Home tab | Editing group) to display the Find and Replace task pane (Figure 10–55).

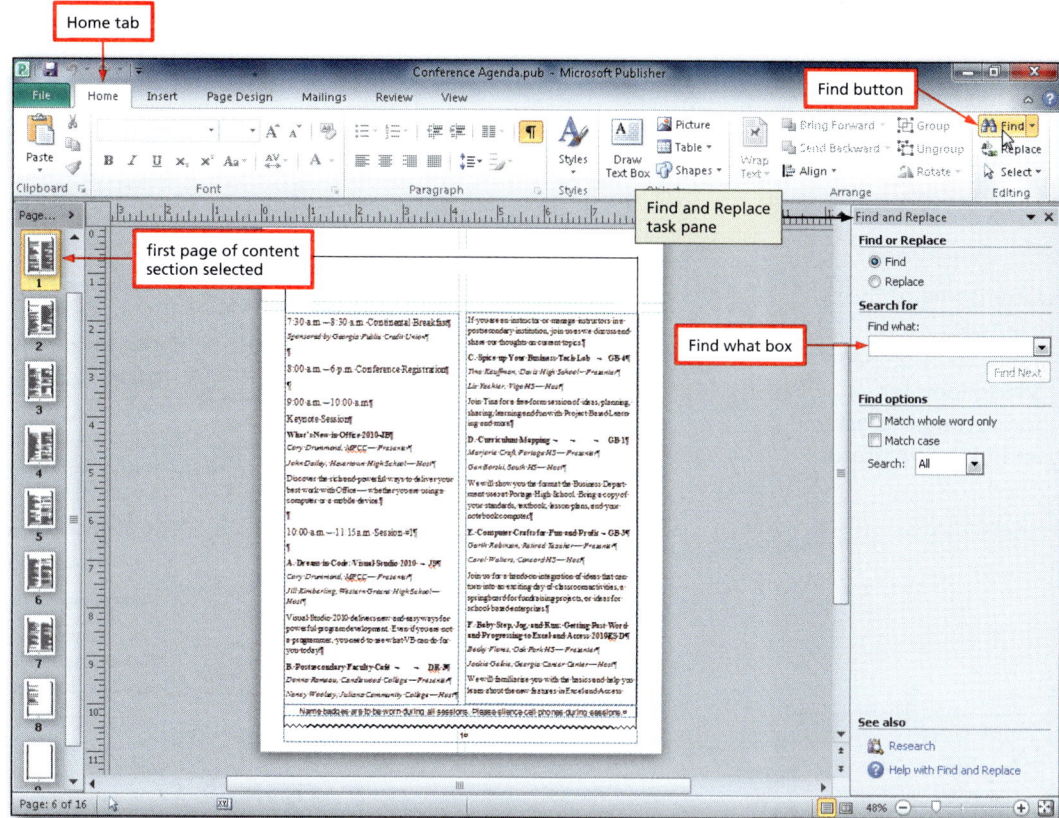

Figure 10–55

2

- In the Find what box, type **green** to enter the search term.

- Click the Find Next button.

- Press the F9 key to zoom to 100% (Figure 10–56).

Q&A

Why did Publisher find the word, Greene?

With none of the check boxes selected in the Find and Replace task pane, Publisher is looking for any sequence of the letters, green. It would find evergreen or greenish, with any combination of lowercase and uppercase letters.

Figure 10–56

3

- Click the Find Next button again to find the next occurrence of the word (Figure 10–57).

Experiment

- Enter some of the examples from Table 10–1 on page 594 to look for formatting characters and to use wildcards.

Other Ways

1. Press CTRL+F, enter characters to find, click Find Next button

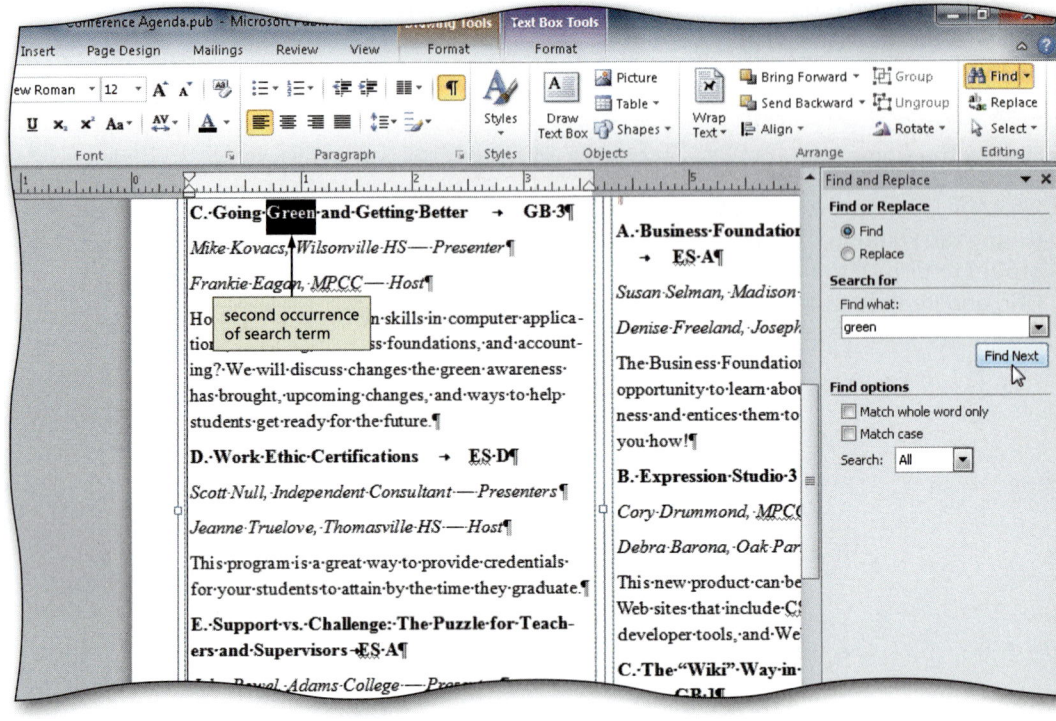

Figure 10–57

To Find Whole Words Only

The following step uses the Find command to locate the whole word, form, rather than any of its versions, such as forms or format.

1

- Select the current text in the Find what box, type **form** to enter the new search term.

- Click to display a check mark in the 'Match whole word only' check box.

- Click the Find Next button (Figure 10–58).

Q&A

Do I need to start at the first page of my publication?

No, Publisher will search from the current location and continue searching all text boxes on all pages.

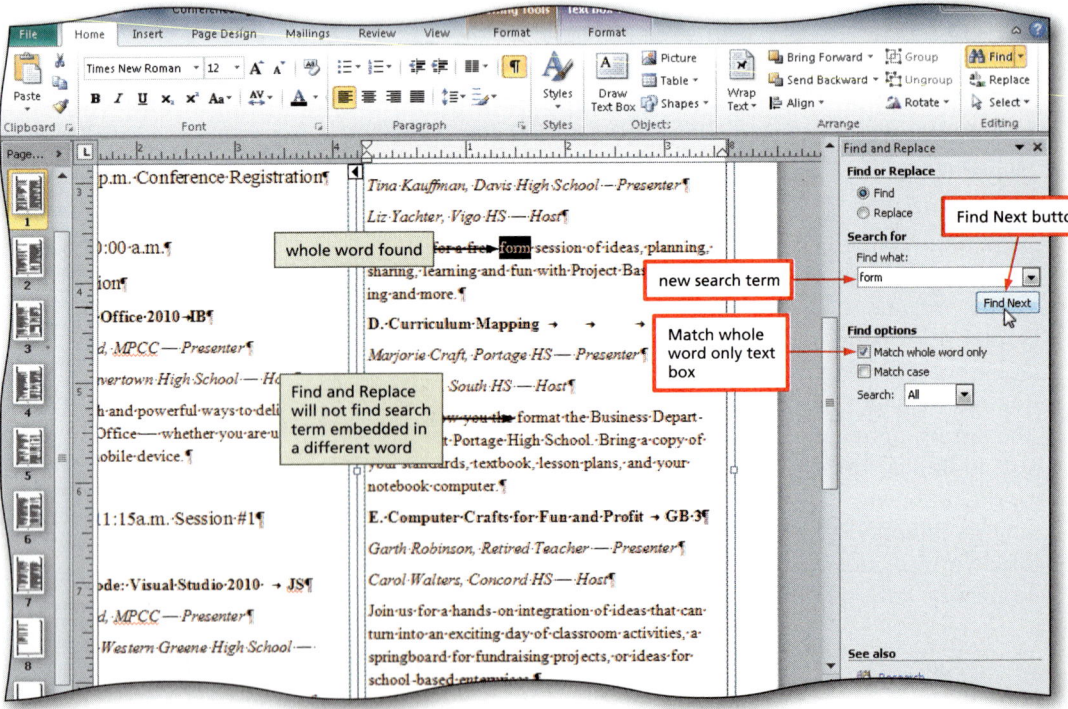

Figure 10–58

To Use the Replace Command

Sometimes, you may want to make changes to a character or set of characters across multiple locations in a publication. For example, some date or place may change and you need to make sure you locate and change all of the occurrences. In the conference agenda, the conference center has informed you that because the JS room is under construction, presentations are being moved to the IB room. The following steps use the Replace command to search for the capital letters JS and replace them with IB.

 1

- In the Find and Replace task pane, click the Replace option button to display the Replace settings.

- Select the current text in the Find what box and then type **JS** to enter the new search term.

- Press the TAB key to move to the Replace with box.

- Type **IB** in the Replace with box to specify the replacement term.

- If necessary, click to place a check mark in the 'Match whole word only' check box.

- Click to place a check mark in the Match case check box.

- Click the Find Next button (Figure 10–59).

Figure 10–59

 2

- Click the Replace button to replace the current selection and to move to the next occurrence (Figure 10–60).

Figure 10–60

● Click the Replace
All button to
replace all of the
other occurrences
(Figure 10–61).

Q&A

Can I use the Replace
All button in all
circumstances?

No. You must be
extremely careful
about specifying exact
text and parameters in
the Find and Replace
task pane. Do not click
the Replace All button
unless you absolutely
are sure that your
search term will not
be misunderstood.

● When Publisher
finishes replacing
the text, click the OK
button (Microsoft
Publisher dialog box)
to close the dialog
box.

● Click the Close button
in the Find and Replace task
pane to close the task
pane.

Figure 10–61

Other Ways

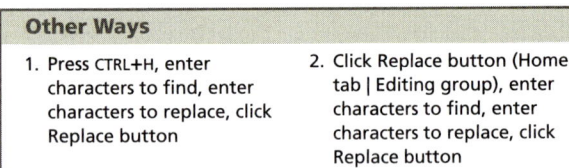

1. Press CTRL+H, enter
   characters to find, enter
   characters to replace, click
   Replace button

2. Click Replace button (Home
   tab | Editing group), enter
   characters to find, enter
   characters to replace, click
   Replace button

Thesaurus

When writing, you may discover that you used the same word in multiple locations or
that a word you used was not quite appropriate. In these instances, you will want to look
up a **synonym**, or a word similar in meaning to the duplicate or inappropriate word.
A **thesaurus** is a book of synonyms. Publisher provides a thesaurus for your convenience.

To Use the Thesaurus

In the conference agenda, you would like to find a synonym for the word, fantastic, in the first paragraph of the front matter. The following steps show how to find a suitable synonym.

• Expand the front matter section in the Page Navigation pane.

• Select the first page of the front matter section.

• Display the Review tab.

• Select the word, fantastic, that appears approximately half-way through the letter. Do not select the spaces on either side of the word.

• Click the Thesaurus button (Review tab | Proofing group) to display the Research task pane (Figure 10–62).

Figure 10–62

• Scroll in the Thesaurus area to display more synonyms.

• Point to the word, marvelous, to display the box arrow and then click the box arrow to display the list of options (Figure 10–63).

Figure 10–63

3

- Click Insert to replace the word, fantastic, in the document with the word, marvelous (Figure 10–64).

Q&A

What if the list of synonyms does not display a suitable word?

The Research task pane displays a complete thesaurus; however, if you do not find a suitable word, you can scroll to the bottom of the list and look up the term in other reference books. You also can look up an **antonym**, which is a word with an opposite meaning.

4

- Click the Close button in the Research task pane to close the task pane.

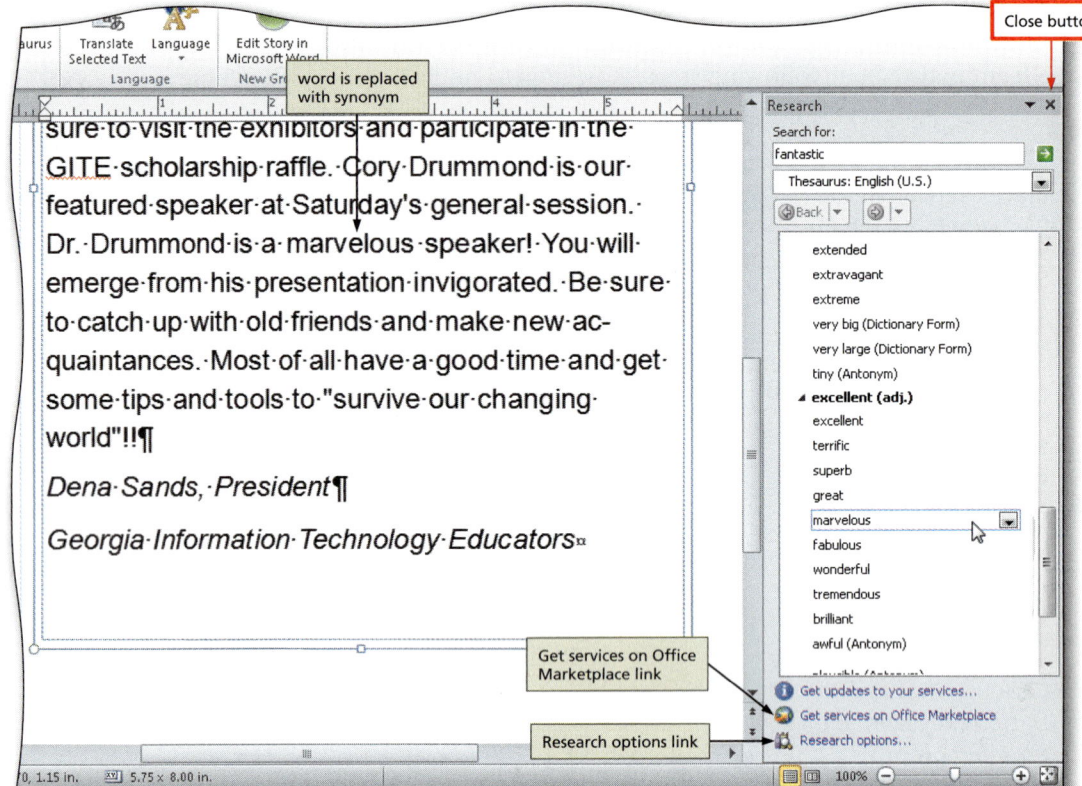

Figure 10–64

Other Ways

1. Right-click word, click Look Up on shortcut menu, choose synonym

2. Press SHIFT+F7, choose synonym

Research Task Pane Options

When you install Publisher, it selects a series of services (reference books and Web sites) through which it searches when you use the Research task pane. You can view, modify, and update the list of services at any time. To ensure you have the most recent updates to the selected services, or if you wish to add other services, click the Get Services on Office Marketplace link at the bottom of the Research task pane (Figure 10–64).

Clicking the Research options link at the bottom of the Research task pane displays the Research Options dialog box, where you can view or modify the list of installed services. You can view information about any installed service by clicking the service in the list and then clicking the Properties button. To activate an installed service, click the check box to its left; likewise, to deactivate a service, remove the check mark. To add a particular Web site to the list, click the Add Services button, enter the Web address in the Address text box, and then click the Add button in the Add Services dialog box. To update or remove services, click the Update/Remove button, select the service in the list, click the Update (or Remove) button in the Update or Remove Services dialog box, and then click the Close button. You also can install parental controls, if minor children use Publisher, through the Parental Control button in the Research Options dialog box.

Page Breaks

It is important to look at large-scale publications with an eye for appropriate page and column breaks. You do not want a heading to display without its subordinate content. In schedules, you may want mornings, afternoons, or days all on the same page. You may decide a column should not break in the middle of a short paragraph.

Publisher does not have the same kinds of widow and orphan controls common to most word processing programs; therefore, you must insert page breaks manually to correct poor wrapping across columns or pages. Manually inserting page breaks is a good idea because it forces you to make careful decisions about the length of pages and to evaluate how text wraps in columns. Authors and editors insert page breaks after making layout decisions and after most editing has taken place.

To View a Two-Page Spread

The following steps view the conference agenda in a two-page spread, which will help you to see where the agenda wraps incorrectly to another page. The View Two-Page Spread command also will group the pages by twos in the Page Navigation pane.

1
- In the Page Navigation pane, right-click the first content page to display the shortcut menu (Figure 10–65).

Figure 10–65

2

- Click View Two-Page Spread on the shortcut menu to change how the publication appears in the document window.

- If necessary, click the Show Whole Page button to view all of the two-page spread (Figure 10–66).

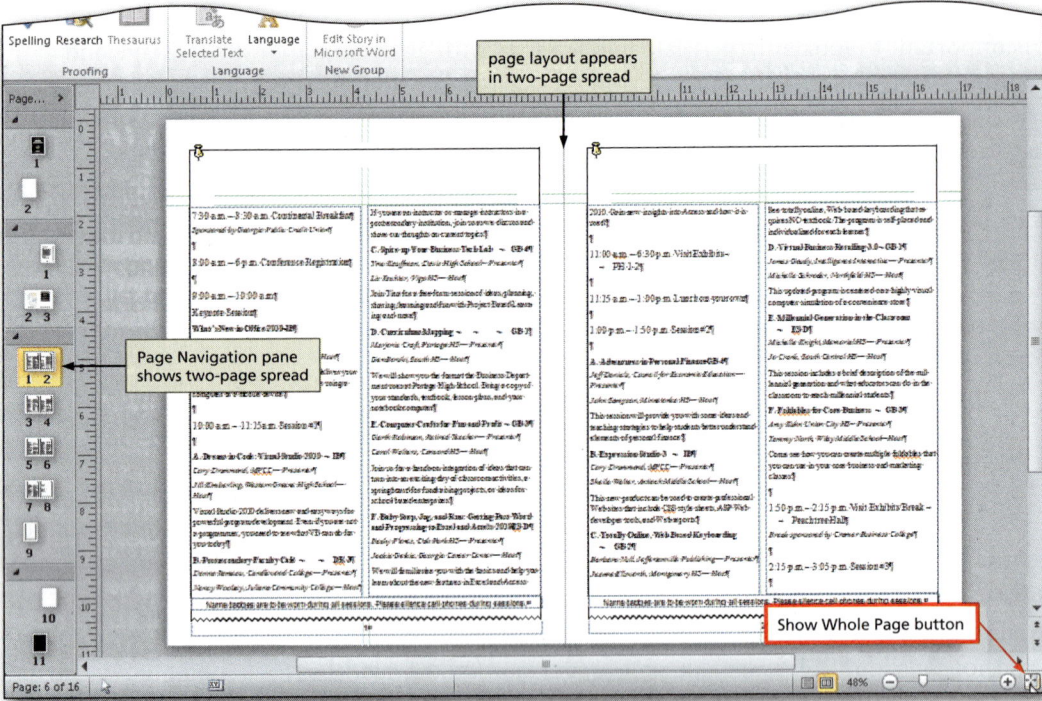

Figure 10–66

To Insert a Page Break

The following steps look for specific places where the natural wrapping of text results in presentation information being split across columns. In those cases, you will insert a page break.

1

- If necessary, select the first and second content pages in the Page Navigation pane.

- Click before the letter B near the bottom of the first column on the left page.

- If your text wraps differently, adjust the size of the text box so that it matches Figure 10–67.

Q&A

Why am I inserting a page break at that location?

The title and presenter of presentation B are at the bottom of the column, while the

Figure 10–67

description is at the top of the next column. Inserting a page break at that location will keep all of the information about presentation B together in the second column.

2

- Press CTRL+ENTER to insert a page break and move all of presentation B's information to the next column (Figure 10–68).

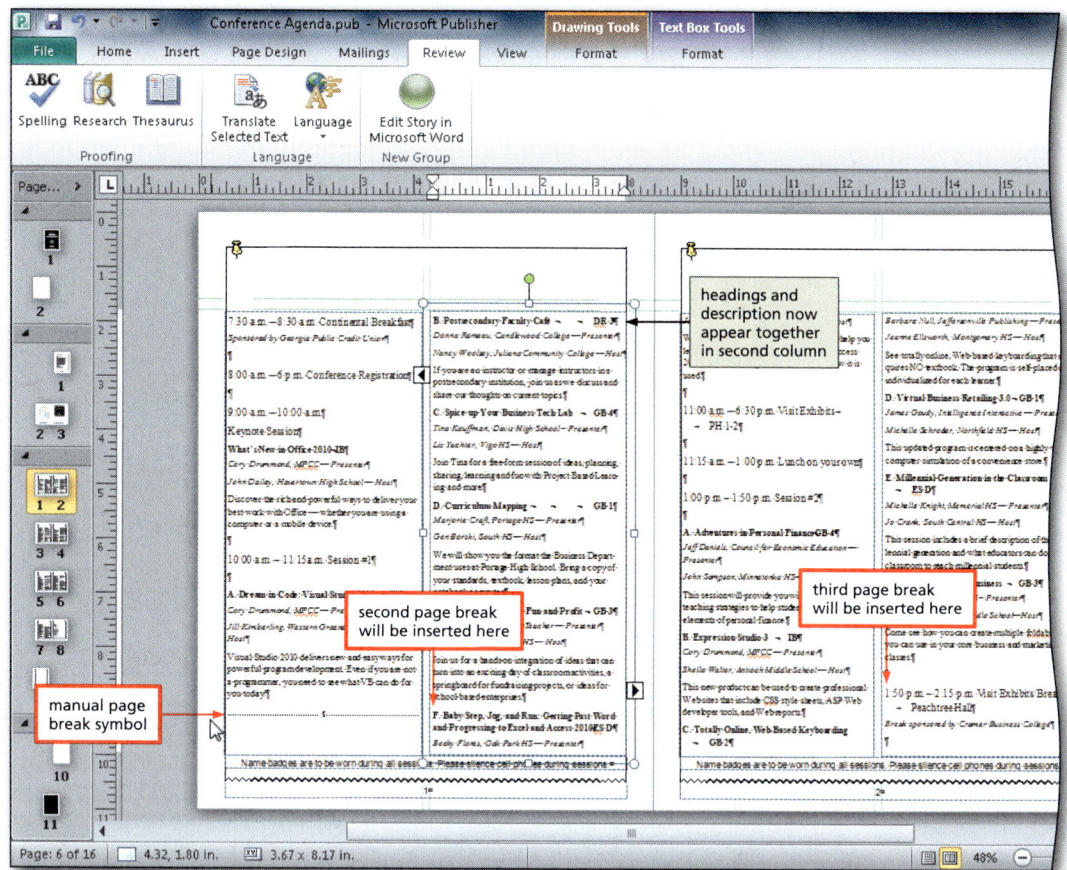

Figure 10–68

To Insert More Page Breaks

The following steps insert additional page breaks to keep sessions and headings together in the same column.

1 Position the insert point before presentation F at the bottom of the second column on the left page. Press CTRL+ENTER to insert a page break (Figure 10–68).

2 Position the insert point before the time 1:50 at the bottom of the second column on the right page. Press CTRL+ENTER to insert a page break. Publisher will move to Page 3 and Page 4 of the content section.

3 Click before the time 3:10 in the second column on the left page and then press CTRL+ENTER to insert a page break.

4 Position the insert point before the time 4:50 at the bottom of the second column on the right page. Press CTRL+ENTER to insert a page break. Publisher will move to Page 5 and Page 6 of the content section.

5 Click before the time 9:15 in the second column on the right page and then press CTRL+ENTER to insert a page break.

6 Select Page 7 and Page 8 of the content section in the Page Navigation pane to display the pages.

7 Click before the time 10:15 in the second column on the left page and then press CTRL+ENTER to insert a page break (Figure 10–69).

8 Insert a final page break after the last line of text on page 8 to move the insertion point to page 9.

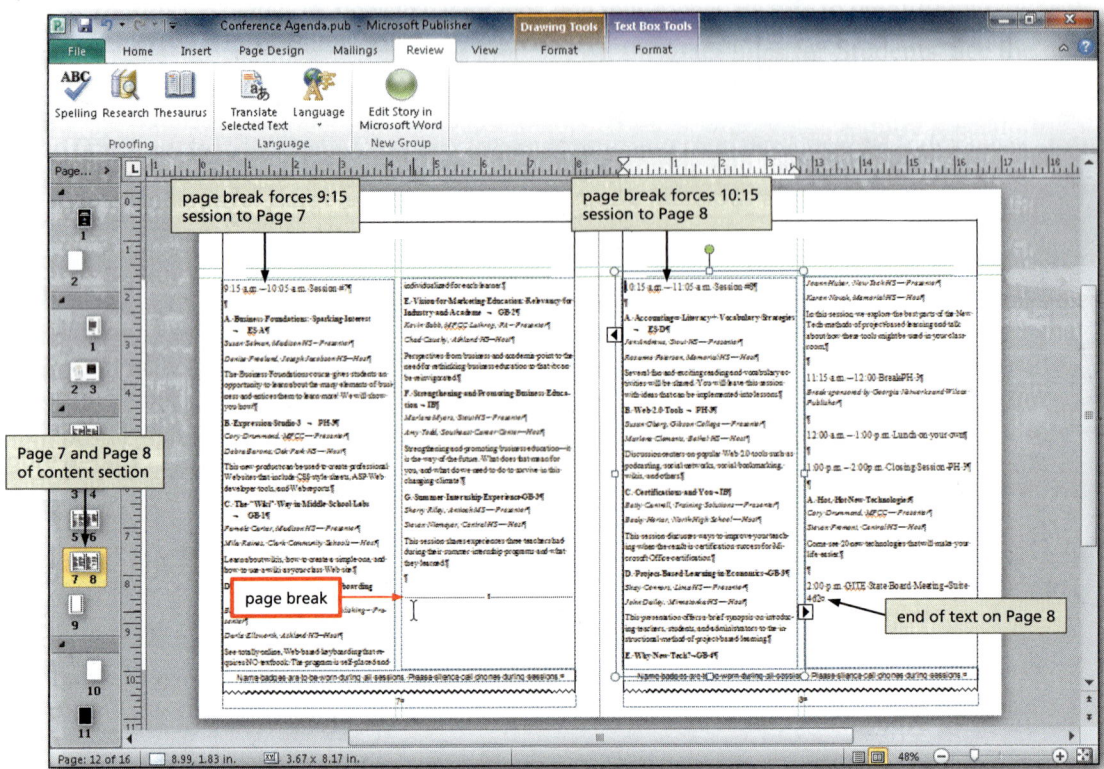

Figure 10–69

To Import Text on Page 9

The following steps import a text file for the sponsors list on the last content page, from the Data Files for Students. See the inside back cover of this book for instructions on downloading the Data Files for Students, or contact your instructor for information about accessing the required files.

1 Click the first text box on page 9.

2 Display the Insert tab.

3 Click the Insert File button (Insert tab | Text group) to display the Insert Text dialog box and navigate to the Data Files for Students, in the Publisher folder, in the Chapter10 folder.

4 Double-click the file named, Sponsors, to insert it into the publication (Figure 10–70).

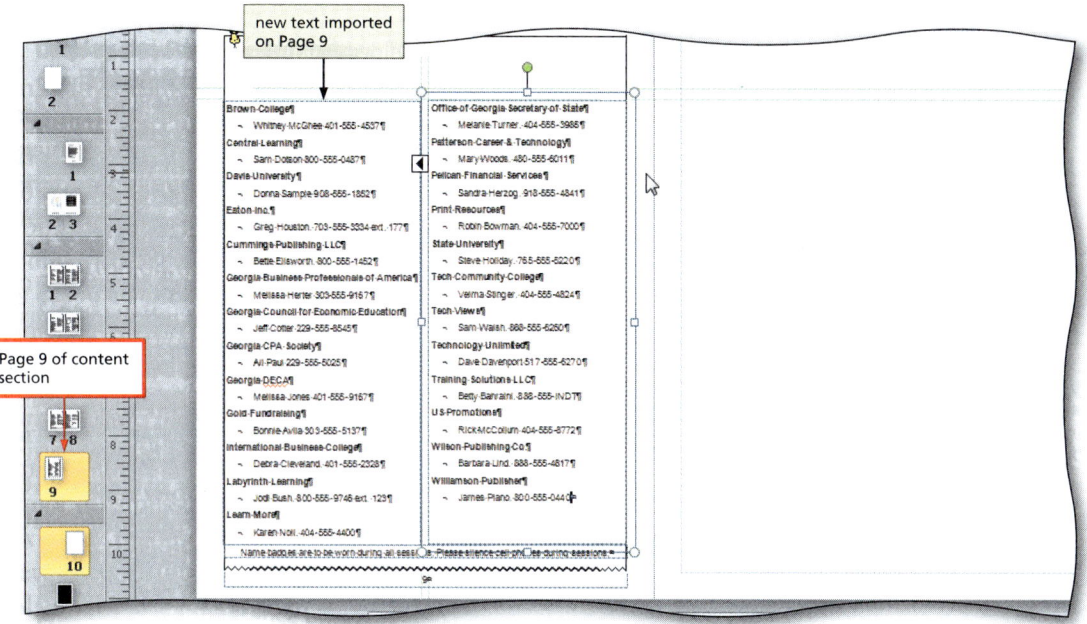

Figure 10–70

To Insert Headings

The following steps insert headings on content pages.

1 Select the first and second content pages in the Page Navigation pane.

2 Display the Home tab.

3 Draw a text box that fills the heading area above the first column on the left page.

4 Change the font size to 20.

5 Click the Align Center button (Text Box Tools tab | Alignment Group) to position the insertion point.

6 Type `Friday March 8, 2012` to insert the text (Figure 10–71).

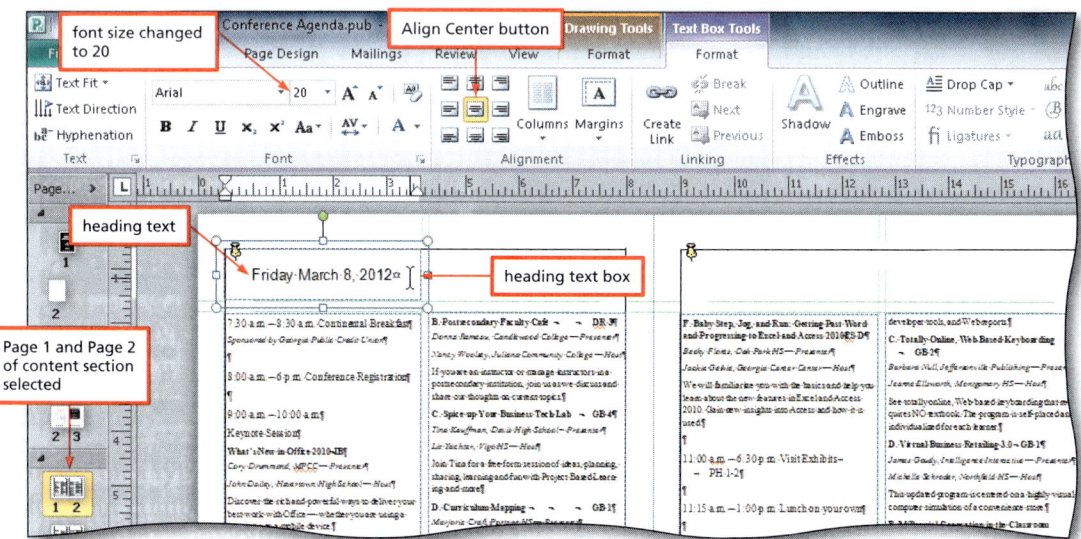

Figure 10–71

To Copy and Paste the Heading

The following steps copy and paste the heading text box to subsequent pages.

1 Click the boundary of the text box to select the text box rather than the text.

2 Press CTRL+C to copy the text box and then deselect it.

3 Press CTRL+V to paste a copy of the text box and then drag its border to position the copy at the top of the first column on the second page.

4 Select the third and fourth content page and paste copies at the upper-left of each page.

5 Select the fifth and sixth content page and paste copies at the upper-left of each page.

6 In the copied text box on the sixth page, triple-click the text to select it and then type `Saturday March 9, 2012` to replace the text.

7 Copy the Saturday heading text box and paste it on the seventh and eighth pages.

8 Select the ninth page and create a similar heading with the words, Support Our Sponsors!

Updating the Table of Contents

Table 10–2 displays the table of contents for the conference agenda, based on the page breaks you inserted earlier.

Table 10–2 Table of Contents	
Item	**Page Number**
President's Greeting	i
Conference Center Map	ii
Keynote Session	1
Friday, March 8, 2012 — Session #1	1
Friday, March 8, 2012 — Session #2	2
Friday, March 8, 2012 — Session #3	3
GITE Regional Meetings	4
Friday, March 8, 2012 — Session #4	4
Friday, March 8, 2012 — Session #5	5
GITE District Coordinator's Meeting	5
Saturday, March 9, 2012 — Session #6	6
Saturday, March 9, 2012 — Session #7	7
Saturday, March 9, 2012 — Session #8	8
Saturday, March 9, 2012 — Closing Session	8
GITE State Board Meeting	8
Sponsors	9

To Update the Table of Contents

The following steps update the table of contents.

1 If necessary, expand the front matter section in the Page Navigation pane.

2 Select the second page (Page 2 and Page 3) of the front matter.

3 In the top text box, triple-click to select the text, change the font size to 20, and then type **Table of Contents** to replace the text.

4 Zoom and scroll as necessary while you enter the information from Table 10–2 to replace the placeholder text in the table.

5 When you fill all cells, click the last cell and press the TAB key to insert a new line in the table. Repeat as necessary to finish the table (Figure 10–72).

Figure 10–72

To Save Again

You have made several modifications to the publication since you last saved it. Thus, you should save it again. The following step saves the publication again.

1 Click the Save button on the Quick Access Toolbar to overwrite the previously saved file.

Break Point: If you wish to take a break, this is a good place to do so. You can quit Publisher now. To resume at a later time, start Publisher, open the file called Conference Agenda, and continue following the steps from this location forward.

Navigating through a Large-Scale Publication

To make it easier to navigate through a large publication, Publisher provides two commands that help both designers and viewers of the publication. The 'Go to page' command allows you to move quickly to a given page number to edit or read the information. A **bookmark** is a physical location in a publication that you name for reference purposes. Used to organize large publications, a named bookmark allows you to display its associated text quickly, instead of scrolling through the publication pages to locate an object or text.

Bookmarks display as small flags in page layout only; they do not print in printed publications. Bookmarks are saved, however, when the publication is saved. They serve as a searchable reference when viewing the publication online and can be referenced as a hyperlink within the Publisher publication and when converting the publication to the PDF format.

To Use the Go To Page Command

The following steps use the 'Go to page' command to move quickly to the first page of the front matter, which is the third page of the publication.

1
- If necessary, display the Home tab.
- Click the Find button arrow (Home tab | Editing group) to display its list (Figure 10–73).

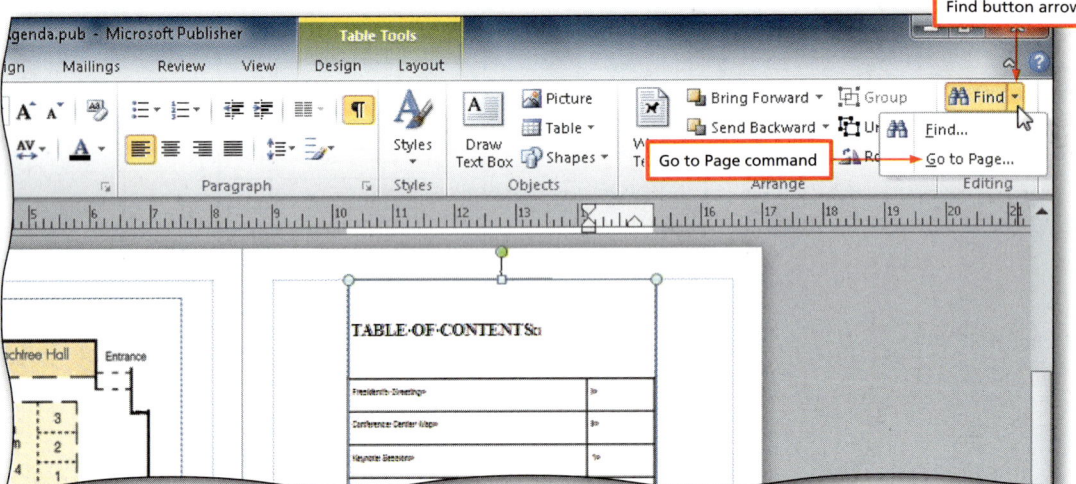

Figure 10–73

2
- Click Go to page to display the Go To Page dialog box.
- Type 3 to replace the text in the 'Go to page' text box (Figure 10–74).

Figure 10–74

3

- Click the OK button to go to the desired page (Figure 10–75).

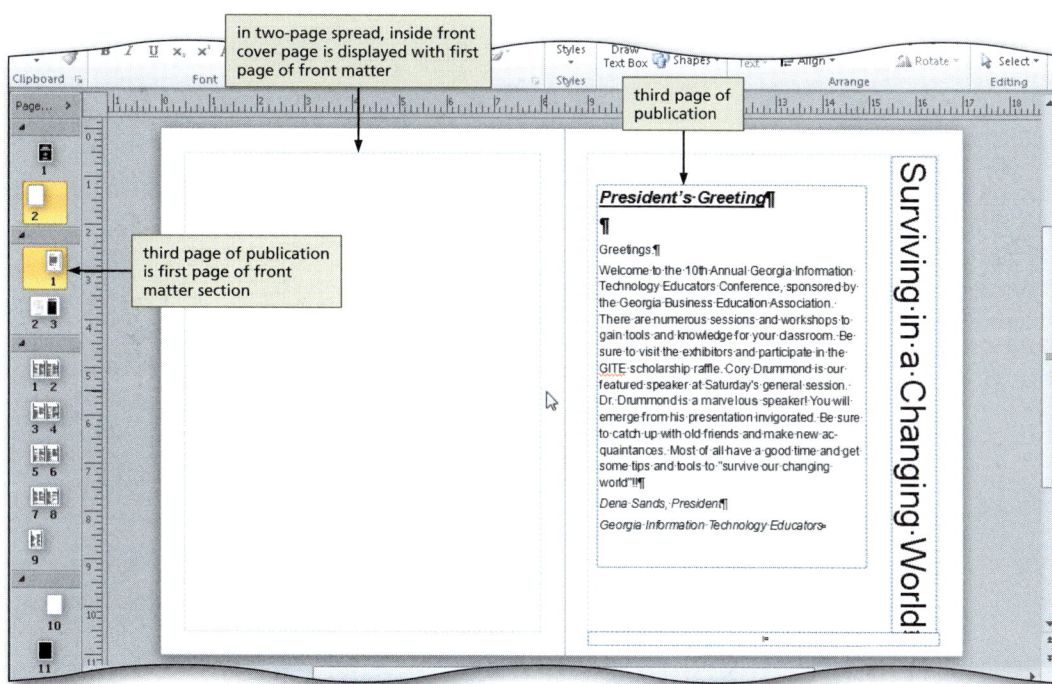

in two-page spread, inside front cover page is displayed with first page of front matter

third page of publication

third page of publication is first page of front matter section

President's Greeting¶

¶

Greetings¶

Welcome to the 10th Annual Georgia Information Technology Educators Conference, sponsored by the Georgia Business Education Association. There are numerous sessions and workshops to gain tools and knowledge for your classroom. Be sure to visit the exhibitors and participate in the GITE scholarship raffle. Cory Drummond is our featured speaker at Saturday's general session. Dr. Drummond is a marvelous speaker! You will emerge from his presentation invigorated. Be sure to catch up with old friends and make new acquaintances. Most of all have a good time and get some tips and tools to "survive our changing world"!¶

Dena Sands, President¶

Georgia Information Technology Educators

Surviving in a Changing World

Figure 10–75

Other Ways

1. Press CTRL+G, enter page number, click OK button (Go To Page dialog box)

To Create a Bookmark

The following steps create a bookmark for the president's greeting so that you can find it more quickly when you edit the publication.

1

- Display the Insert tab.

- Click the Bookmark button (Insert tab | Links group) to display the Bookmark dialog box.

- Type **President's Greeting** in the Bookmark name text box (Figure 10–76).

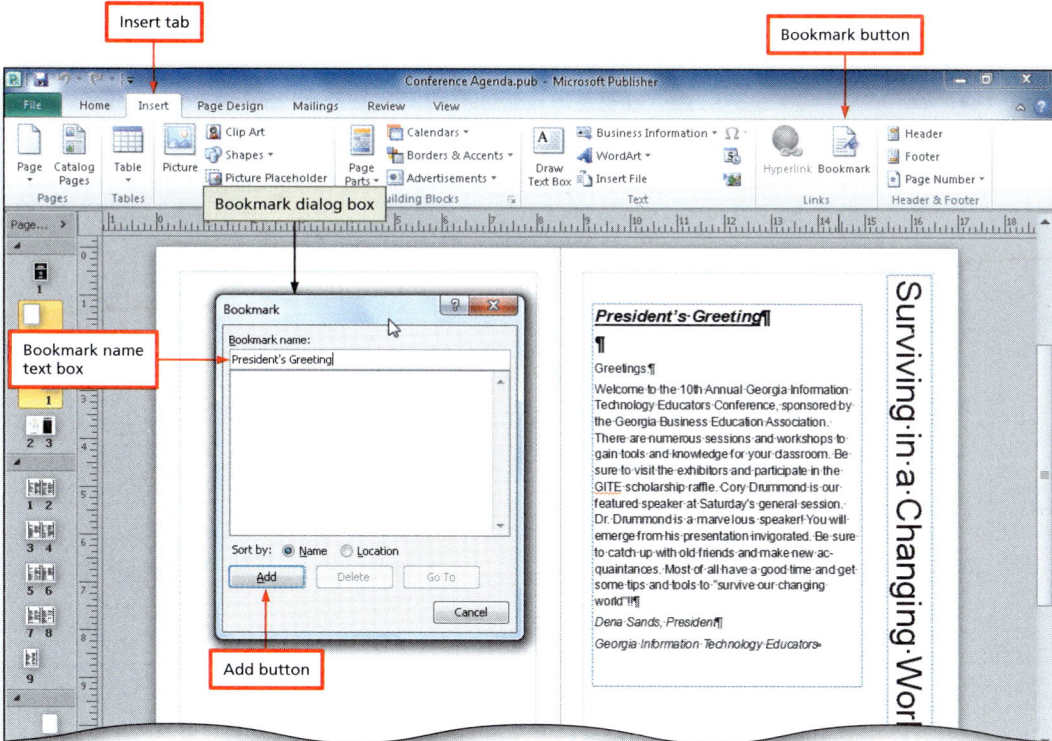

Insert tab

Bookmark button

Conference Agenda.pub - Microsoft Publisher

Bookmark dialog box

Bookmark name text box

Bookmark

Bookmark name:

President's Greeting

Sort by: ● Name ○ Location

Add   Delete   Go To

Cancel

Add button

President's Greeting¶

¶

Greetings¶

Welcome to the 10th Annual Georgia Information Technology Educators Conference, sponsored by the Georgia Business Education Association. There are numerous sessions and workshops to gain tools and knowledge for your classroom. Be sure to visit the exhibitors and participate in the GITE scholarship raffle. Cory Drummond is our featured speaker at Saturday's general session. Dr. Drummond is a marvelous speaker! You will emerge from his presentation invigorated. Be sure to catch up with old friends and make new acquaintances. Most of all have a good time and get some tips and tools to "survive our changing world"!¶

Dena Sands, President¶

Georgia Information Technology Educators

Surviving in a Changing World

Figure 10–76

2
- Click the Add button to insert the bookmark into the publication.

- Drag the bookmark to a location just left of the heading, President's Greeting (Figure 10–77).

Figure 10–77

To Create More Bookmarks

The following steps create additional bookmarks for each portion of the publication that is referenced in the table of contents.

1 Press CTRL+G to display the Go To Page dialog box. Type 4 in the 'Go to page' text box and then press the ENTER key to move to the fourth page of the publication.

2 Click the Bookmark button (Insert tab | Links group) to display the Bookmark dialog box. Type **Conference Center Map** in the Bookmark name text box and then press the ENTER key to insert the bookmark.

3 Drag the bookmark to a location just outside the upper-left corner of the map and then deselect it.

4 Repeat Steps 1 through 3 for each item in the first column of Table 10–2 on page PUB 606. Because the Bookmark dialog box will not accept special characters, use a name for each session, such as Session 1.

To Use Bookmarks to Create Hyperlinks

The following steps create hyperlinks in the table of contents that connect to the bookmarks in the publication.

1

- Navigate to the table of contents page and then drag to select the text, President's Greeting.

- Press CTRL+K to display the Insert Hyperlink dialog box.

- Click the Place in This Document button in the Link to bar.

- Click President's Greeting in the 'Select a place in this document' area to choose the desired bookmark (Figure 10–78).

Q&A

What is the purpose of the Change Title button?

Each page of a publication has an internal bookmark initially named Page Title. You can edit that name by selecting the Page Title in the list and then clicking the Change Title button. That bookmark name also would appear on the title bar of a Web browser should the publication be used on the Web.

Figure 10–78

2

- Click the OK button (Insert Hyperlink dialog box) to create the hyperlink (Figure 10–79).

Figure 10–79

3

- Repeat Steps 1 and 2 for each of the items in the table of contents. Link each item to its corresponding bookmark name in the Insert Hyperlink dialog box (Figure 10–80).

Other Ways

1 Select text, click Insert Hyperlink button (Insert tab | Links group), click Place in This Document button (Insert Hyperlink dialog box), select bookmark, click OK button

Figure 10–80

To Test a Hyperlink

The following step tests one of the hyperlinks to make sure it navigates to the correct location.

1

- In the table of contents, CTRL+click the President's Greeting hyperlink to jump to the bookmark (Figure 10–81).

Q&A

Why did the mouse pointer shape change to a hand?

When positioned over a hyperlink, the mouse pointer changes to a hand as soon as you press the CTRL key.

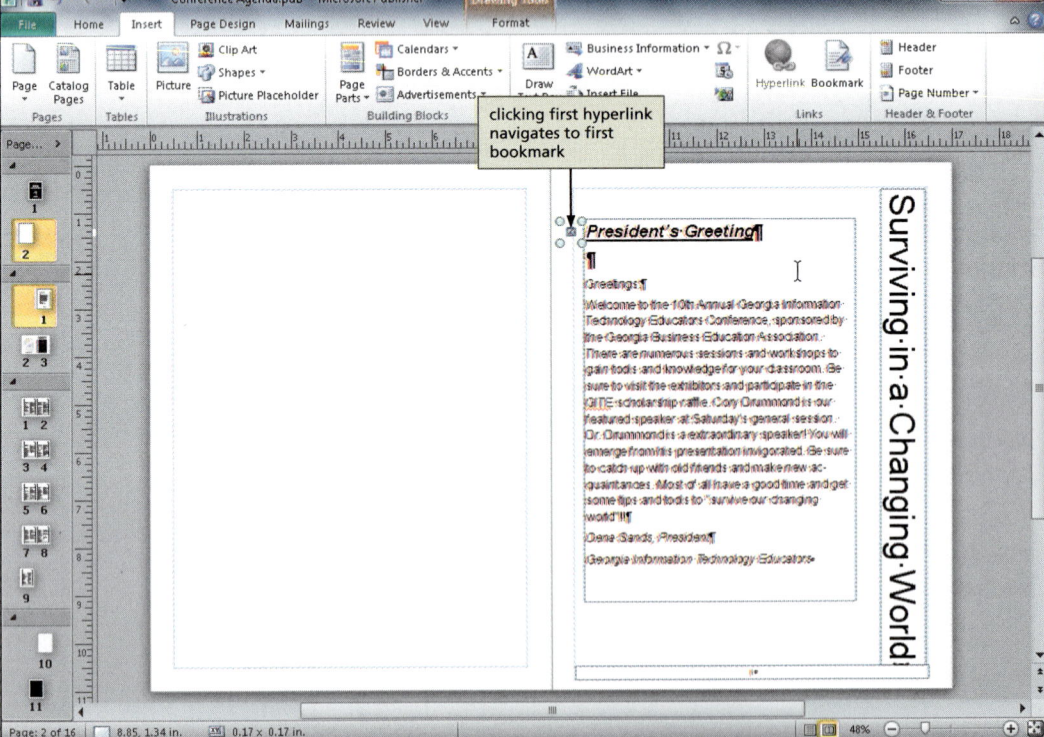

Figure 10–81

To Check the Publication for Spelling and Design Errors

The following steps check the publication for spelling and design errors.

1 Press the F7 key to start checking the spelling. Choose to ignore names and acronyms.

2 When Publisher asks if you want to check the rest of the publication, click the Yes button and finish checking the spelling. If necessary, close the Master Page view.

3 Click File on the Ribbon to display the Backstage view.

4 If necessary, click the Info tab and then click the Run Design Checker button (Backstage view | Info gallery) to display the Design Checker task pane. Ignore any design errors related to too much space at a margin. Ignore the warning about the low-resolution nature of the clip art.

5 Fix any other errors found by the Design Checker.

6 Close the Design Checker task pane.

To Save the Final Version

The publication is complete. The following step saves the publication.

1 Click the Save button on the Quick Access Toolbar to overwrite the previously saved file.

To Save in the PDF Format

To review and test the hyperlinks in a different application, the following steps save the Publisher file in the PDF format.

1 With a USB flash drive connected to one of the computer's USB ports, click File on the Ribbon to display the Backstage view.

2 Click the Save & Send tab and then click Create PDF/XPS Document in the File Types area to display the gallery.

3 Click the Create PDF/XPS Document button in the right pane (Backstage view | Save & Send gallery) to display the Publish as PDF or XPS dialog box.

4 If necessary, type `Conference Agenda` in the File name text box to change the file name. Do not press the ENTER key after typing the file name because you do not want to close the dialog box at this time.

5 Navigate to the desired save location (in this case, the Publisher folder in the CIS 101 folder [or your class folder] on the USB flash drive).

6 If necessary, click the 'Save as type' button arrow and then click PDF (*.pdf) in the list.

7 Click the Publish button (Publish as PDF or XPS dialog box) to save the publication in the selected folder on the selected drive with the entered file name (Figure 10–82 on the next page).

BTW

XPS Files and Readers
If you decide to save your publication as an XPS (XML Paper Specification) file rather than a PDF file, you can read it using a viewer that comes with Windows 7. To start the viewer, click the Start button on the Windows 7 taskbar to display the Start menu. Type `XPS Viewer` as the search text in the 'Search programs and files' text box and then click XPS Viewer search results.

conference agenda is displayed as PDF document

Figure 10–82

To Navigate with Bookmarks in a PDF File

The bookmarks and hyperlinks you created in the Publisher file automatically are created in the PDF file. Recall that PDF files open using an application such as Adobe Reader or Adobe Acrobat. The following steps move to the table of contents in the PDF file and then test one of the hyperlinks.

1

• With the PDF file open, click the Next Page button on the toolbar several times to display the table of contents page (Figure 10–83).

Q&A

My reader does not have a Next Page button. What is the best way to navigate in the PDF file?

Your application may use the RIGHT ARROW key to move down through the document, page by page.

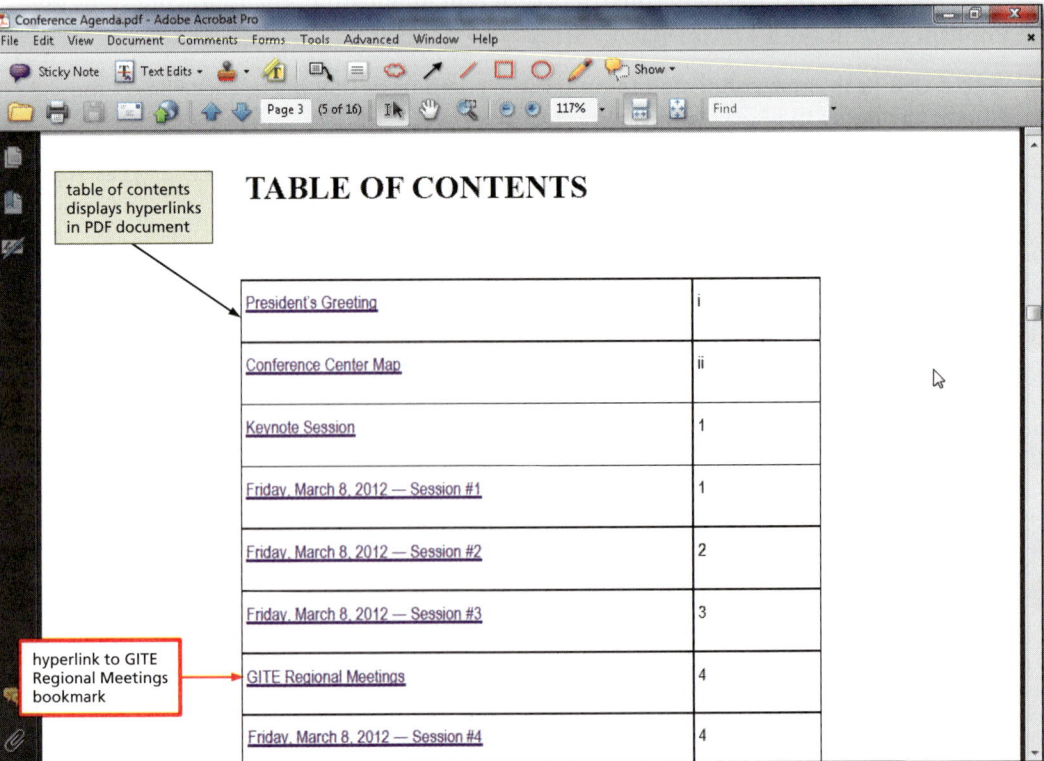

table of contents displays hyperlinks in PDF document

hyperlink to GITE Regional Meetings bookmark

Figure 10–83

2
- Click the GITE Regional Meetings link to display that page in the conference agenda (Figure 10–84).

3
- Click the Close button on the viewer's title bar to close the program.

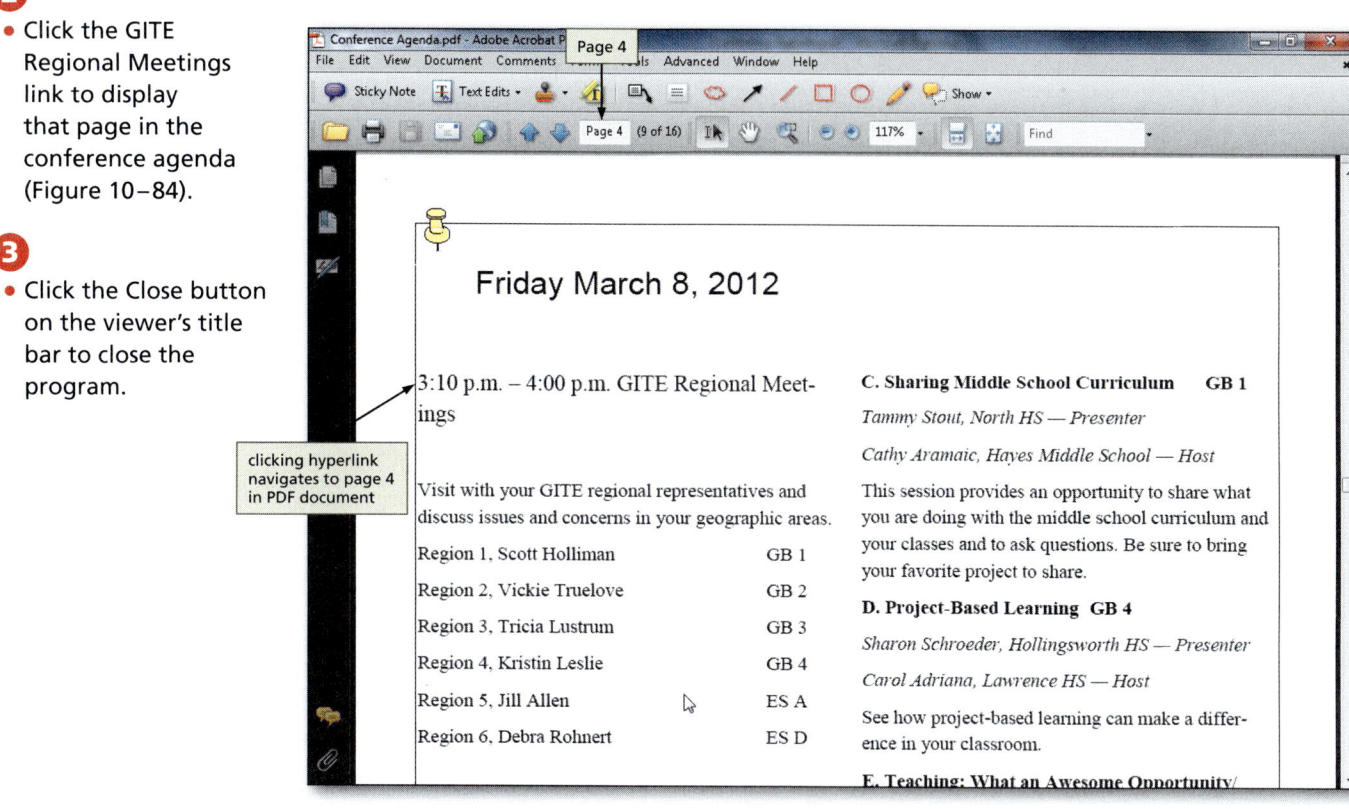

clicking hyperlink navigates to page 4 in PDF document

Figure 10–84

To Quit Publisher

This project is complete. The following steps quit Publisher.

1 To quit Publisher, click the Close button on the right side of the title bar.

2 If a Microsoft Office Publisher dialog box is displayed, click the Don't Save button so that any editing changes you have made to the conference agenda are not saved.

Chapter Summary

In this chapter, you worked with large-scale publications by inserting and duplicating pages, assigning master page designations, and paginating page parts. You learned how to create and work with sections in the Page Navigation pane. Then, you created BorderArt and a shaded page background. After inserting the front matter, you created guides and linked text boxes for the content pages of the agenda. Next, you used global editing tools such as find and replace, the thesaurus, and the 'Go to page' command. Finally, you created bookmarks and hyperlinks to help viewers navigate from the table of contents to the various pages. The items listed below include all the new Publisher skills you have learned in this chapter.

1. Create Sections (PUB 560)
2. Insert Page Numbers Using the Ribbon (PUB 562)
3. Specify a Starting Page Number (PUB 563)
4. Specify a Starting Page Number Using the Shortcut Menu (PUB 565)
5. Remove Page Numbering from Specific Pages (PUB 567)
6. Create BorderArt (PUB 570)
7. Create a Shade Background (PUB 574)
8. Collapse Sections (PUB 578)
9. Change Cell Margins (PUB 581)
10. Change Text Box Margins (PUB 583)
11. Change the Text Direction (PUB 585)
12. Select a Guide Pattern (PUB 586)
13. Link Text Boxes Using the Menu (PUB 588)
14. Duplicate a Page (PUB 590)
15. Merge Sections (PUB 591)
16. Use the Find Command (PUB 594)
17. Find Whole Words Only (PUB 596)
18. Use the Replace Command (PUB 597)
19. Use the Thesaurus (PUB 599)
20. View a Two-Page Spread (PUB 601)
21. Insert a Page Break (PUB 602)
22. Use the Go To Page Command (PUB 608)
23. Create a Bookmark (PUB 609)
24. Use Bookmarks to Create Hyperlinks (PUB 611)
25. Test a Hyperlink (PUB 612)
26. Navigate with Bookmarks in a PDF File (PUB 614)

Learn It Online

Test your knowledge of chapter content and key terms.

Instructions: To complete the Learn It Online exercises, start your browser, click the Address bar, and then enter the Web address `scsite.com/pub2010/learn`. When the Publisher 2010 Learn It Online page is displayed, click the link for the exercise you want to complete and then read the instructions.

Chapter Reinforcement TF, MC, and SA
A series of true/false, multiple choice, and short answer questions that test your knowledge of the chapter content.

Flash Cards
An interactive learning environment where you identify chapter key terms associated with displayed definitions.

Practice Test
A series of multiple choice questions that test your knowledge of chapter content and key terms.

Who Wants To Be a Computer Genius?
An interactive game that challenges your knowledge of chapter content in the style of a television quiz show.

Wheel of Terms
An interactive game that challenges your knowledge of chapter key terms in the style of the television show *Wheel of Fortune*.

Crossword Puzzle Challenge
A crossword puzzle that challenges your knowledge of key terms presented in the chapter.

Apply Your Knowledge

Reinforce the skills and apply the concepts you learned in this chapter.

Paginating a Large-Scale Publication

Instructions: Open the file, Apply 10-1 Book Template, from the Chapter 10 folder on the Data Files for Students. See the inside back cover of this book for instructions on downloading the Data Files for Students, or contact your instructor for information about accessing the required files. Start Publisher.

You are to add sections, page numbering, and a border to the template. Table 10–3 displays the sections to create and the page numbering formats.

Table 10–3 Pagination for Apply 10–1 Book Template Edited		
Publication Pages	**Section**	**Page Numbering**
1 – 2	front cover	none
3 – 6	front matter	i, ii, iii, …
7 – 15	content	1, 2, 3, …
16 – 18	end matter	continuing 1, 2, 3, …
19 – 20	back cover	none

A sample page is shown in Figure 10–85.

Figure 10–85

Continued >

Apply Your Knowledge *continued*

Perform the following tasks:

1. With a USB flash drive connected to one of the computer's USB ports, click File on the Ribbon to open the Backstage view.

2. Click Save As to display the Save As dialog box.

3. Type `Apply 10-1 Book Template Edited` in the File name text box to change the file name. Navigate to the desired save location (in this case, the Publisher folder in the CIS 101 folder [or your class folder] on the USB flash drive).

4. Click the Save button (Save As dialog box) to save the document in the selected folder on the selected drive with the entered file name.

5. If necessary, turn on boundaries, rulers, guides, page navigation, and the scratch area by clicking the appropriate check boxes (View tab | Show group).

6. To create sections:

    a. To create a section for the cover page and inside cover page, right-click Page 3 in the Page Navigation pane and then click Insert Section on the shortcut menu.

    b. To create a section for the four pages of front matter, right-click Page 7 in the Page Navigation pane and then click Insert Section on the shortcut menu.

    c. To create a section for the nine pages of content, right-click Page 16 in the Page Navigation pane and then click Insert Section on the shortcut menu.

    d. To create a section for the three pages of end matter, right-click Page 19 in the Page Navigation pane and then click Insert Section on the shortcut menu.

7. To insert page numbers on every page:

    a. Display the Insert tab.

    b. Click the Page Number button (Insert tab | Header & Footer group) and then click Top Right to insert page numbers.

    c. Zoom to 100% to view the page numbers.

    d. Double-click the page number and format it to be bold and use a font size of 16.

    e. Close Master Page view.

8. To format page numbers for the front matter:

    a. Right-click Page 3 in the Page Navigation pane, point to Page Numbers on the shortcut menu, and then click Format Page Numbers to display the Page Number Format dialog box.

    b. Click the Number format box arrow (Page Number Format dialog box) and then click 'i, ii, iii, …' in the list.

    c. Click the 'Start this section with' option button (Page Number Format dialog box) and then type `1` as the starting page number.

    d. Click the OK button (Page Number Format dialog box) to apply the page number formatting.

9. To format page numbers for the content pages:

    a. Right-click Page 7 in the Page Navigation pane, point to Page Numbers on the shortcut menu, and then click Format Page Numbers to display the Page Number Format dialog box.

    b. Click the Number format box arrow (Page Number Format dialog box) and then click '1, 2, 3, …' in the list.

    c. Click the 'Start this section with' option button (Page Number Format dialog box) and then type `1` as the starting page number.

    d. Click the OK button (Page Number Format dialog box) to apply the page number formatting.

10. To remove page numbers from the front cover section and back cover section:

    a. Right-click the first page in the Page Navigation pane, point to Master Pages on the shortcut menu, and then click None.

    b. Right-click the second page in the Page Navigation pane, point to Master Pages on the shortcut menu, and then click None.

    c. Right-click the next-to-the-last page in the Page Navigation pane, point to Master Pages on the shortcut menu, and then click None.

    d. Right-click the last page in the Page Navigation pane, point to Master Pages on the shortcut menu, and then click None.

11. Press CTRL+M to access Master Page view. If necessary, click the Show Whole Page button on the Publisher status bar.

12. Click the Duplicate button (Master Page tab | Master Page group) and name the page, BorderArt. Click the OK button (Duplicate Master Page dialog box).

13. To create a border for the content pages:

    a. Display the Insert tab. Click the Shapes button (Insert tab | Illustrations group) and then click the Rectangle shape.

    b. Drag the mouse pointer to draw a rectangle that fills the entire page from the upper-left margin to the lower-right margin. Do not include the page number area.

    c. Right-click the rectangle and then click Format AutoShape on the shortcut menu.

    d. Click the BorderArt button (Format AutoShape dialog box) and then scroll as necessary to select the Triangles border.

    e. Click the OK button (BorderArt dialog box) to select the border.

    f. Click the OK button (Format AutoShape dialog box) to apply the border.

14. Press CTRL+M to close the master page.

15. Collapse all sections and then expand the third section that includes the content pages.

16. In the Page Navigation pane, right-click the first page in the content section, point to Master Pages on the shortcut menu, and then click BorderArt (B).

17. Repeat Step 16 for each of the nine pages in the content section.

18. Save the publication again with the same file name.

19. If you have permission, send the publication to your instructor as an e-mail message attachment.

Extend Your Knowledge

Extend the skills you learned in this chapter and experiment with new skills. You may need to use Help to complete the assignment.

Creating a Custom Border

Instructions: Start Publisher. Open the publication, Extend 10-1 Science Lab Handout, from the Data Files for Students. See the inside back cover of this book for instructions on downloading the Data Files for Students, or contact your instructor for more information about accessing the required files.

A fourth-grade teacher would like you to add a customized border around a handout she is planning to give her students. The handout, with the new border, is shown in Figure 10–86 on the next page.

Continued >

Extend Your Knowledge *continued*

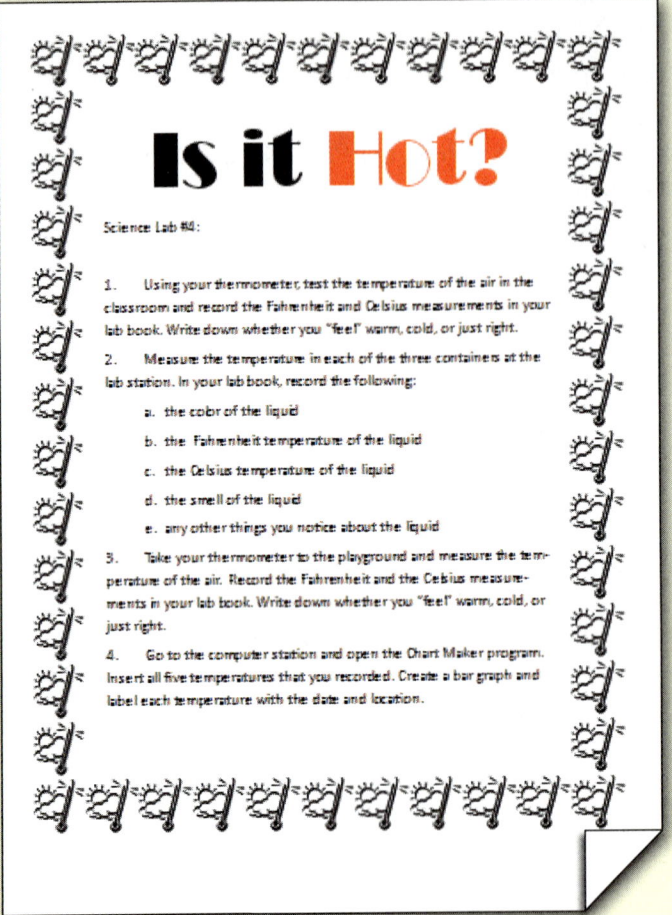

Figure 10–86

Perform the following tasks:

1. Use Help to learn more about customizing BorderArt in Publisher.

2. Change to Master Page view.

3. Insert a rectangle shape that fills the entire page. Right-click the rectangle and then click Format AutoShape on the shortcut menu to display the Format AutoShape dialog box.

4. Click the BorderArt button (Format AutoShape dialog box).

5. To create a custom border, click the Create Custom button (BorderArt dialog box).

6. If necessary, click to display a check mark in the Use Clip Organizer to select the picture check box (Create Custom Border dialog box). Click the Select Picture button.

7. If necessary, click to display a check mark in the Include content from Office.com check box (Insert BorderArt dialog box). Type **thermometer** in the Search text box and then click the Go button.

8. When Publisher displays the thermometer clip art, click a graphic similar to the one shown in Figure 10–86, and then click the OK button (Insert BorderArt dialog box).

9. When Publisher displays the Name Custom Border dialog box, if necessary, select the text in the 'Type a name for your custom border' box, and then type **Thermometer** to replace the text.

10. Click the OK button (Name Custom Border dialog box). If Publisher displays a dialog box saying the graphic is too complex to create a border, return to the Insert BorderArt dialog box and choose a different clip. If Publisher displays a dialog box saying the name, Thermometer, already has been used, type a different name.

11. When you have chosen a clip and named it, click the OK button (BorderArt dialog box) to choose the border.

12. Type **48** in the Weight box (Format AutoShape dialog box) to change the size of the BorderArt and then click the OK button.

13. Close the Master Page view and look at the result. If the border is too large or too small, return to the Format AutoShape dialog box and change the weight.

14. Save the publication with the file name, Extend 10-1 Science Lab Handout Edited.

15. Print a copy for your instructor.

Make It Right

Analyze a publication and correct all errors and/or improve the design.

Updating a Publication Using Search and Replace

Instructions: Start Publisher. Open the publication, Make It Right 10-1 Company Manual Page, from the Data Files for Students. See the inside back cover of this book for instructions on downloading the Data Files for Students, or contact your instructor for more information about accessing the required files.

The publication is a page from a company manual that has incorrect terminology, the wrong page number for its place in a longer publication, and incorrect margins. The author of the manual also has requested that a bookmark be placed on each section of the manual so that the table of contents can be linked. The edited page is shown in Figure 10–87.

QA Documentation Procedures

All documentation related to the management system of the Signature Company or to the execution of individual customer contracts is controlled, ensuring that it is issued to the appropriate personnel, under the correct level of authority. Documents should be revised and reissued as necessary, and all superseded versions should be removed from the point of use.

Such documentation may include:

Specifications, Customer Orders, Plans/Drawings,
QA Manual/Operating Procedures,
National/International Standards and Codes of Practice

The QA manual is maintained by the QA Manager who ensures that the appropriate items, at the correct revision levels, are issued to all who need them within the Signature Company.

National standards and codes of company practice are maintained by support engineers who ensure that documents are available within the Signature Company, and are issued at the correct revision levels. External suppliers of documentation are contacted regularly to ascertain that the documents held remain current.

The distribution of standard documents is controlled and recorded on distribution lists, which also show the current issue status. Distribution lists are reviewed and updated as changes occur in the Signature Company.

All changes to documents are reviewed and approved by the QA Manager who is responsible for the original issue and changes where appropriate. The nature of the change is indicated on the document. Master copies of the revised documents are retained as a record of the changes.

Each customer contract has a file which contains all relevant information. Information is held on the company's computer system for ease of access and manipulation.

23

Figure 10–87

Continued >

Make It Right *continued*

Perform the following tasks:

1. Change the margin of the text box to the Wide setting. *Hint*: See page PUB 583 for more information about changing the margins of a text box.

2. Click the Page Number button (Insert tab | Header & Footer group) and then click Format Page Numbers. Set the Page number to 23, which is the location that this page will appear in a longer document.

3. Press CTRL+H to display the Find and Replace task pane. Select the Match case check box. Change all the occurrences of the term, Company (with matched case), to Signature Company.

4. Change all the occurrences of the term, quality assurance, to QA. Do not select the Match case check box.

5. Highlight the word, obsolete, in the first paragraph. *Hint:* Do not include the spaces around the word in the selection. Click the Thesaurus button (Review tab | Proofing group) and then choose a synonym from the Research task pane.

6. Select the heading at the top of the page and copy it. Click the Bookmark button (Insert tab | Links group) and then paste the name into the Bookmark name text box (Bookmark dialog box). Click the Add button. Drag the bookmark to the upper-left corner of the page.

7. Save the document with the file name, Make It Right 10-1 Manual Page Edited. See your instructor for ways to submit this assignment.

In the Lab

Design and/or create a publication using the guidelines, concepts, and skills presented in this chapter. Labs are listed in order of increasing difficulty.

Lab 1: Formatting Cell Margins, Vertical Text, and Tints

Problem: You have agreed to participate in a countywide expense study for local utilities. You decide to create a table to submit to the survey team. Table 10–4 displays your expenses for the first five months of the year.

Table 10–4 Data for Monthly Expenses					
	Electric	Gas	Refuse	Phone	Internet
January	148.77	166.89	15.00	32.53	55.00
February	137.67	99.44	15.00	27.33	55.00
March	135.34	92.55	15.00	22.86	55.00
April	125.20	60.89	15.00	30.97	55.00
May	158.13	12.06	15.00	26.55	55.00

The final copy of your monthly expenses table appears in Figure 10–88.

Monthly Home Expenses

	Electric	Gas	Refuse	Phone	Internet
January	148.77	166.89	15.00	32.53	55.00
February	137.67	99.44	15.00	27.33	55.00
March	135.34	92.55	15.00	22.86	55.00
April	125.20	60.89	15.00	30.97	55.00
May	158.13	12.06	15.00	26.55	55.00

Figure 10–88

Instructions: Perform the following tasks:

1. Start Publisher with a blank 11 × 8.5–inch landscape publication.

2. Set the font scheme to Office 1 and the color scheme to Office.

3. Create a heading with a vertical text direction:

   a. Create a text box on the left side of the publication, approximately 1 inch wide, which runs from the top to the bottom of the publication.

   b. Set the font size to 36 and change the text direction to vertical text.

   c. Select the text box and display the Home tab.

   d. Click the Rotate button (Home tab | Arrange group) and then click Flip Vertical to rotate the text box.

   e. In the text box, type **Monthly Home Expenses** to create the heading and then deselect the text box.

4. To create the table:

   a. Display the Insert tab.

   b. Click the Insert Table button (Insert tab | Tables group) and create a 6 × 6 table that fills the rest of the page.

   c. Enter the text from Table 10–4.

   d. Select the entire table and then display the Table Tools Layout tab.

   e. Click the Align Center button (Table Tools Layout tab | Alignment group) to center all cells.

   f. Click the Cell Margins button (Table Tools Layout tab | Alignment group) and then click Wide to change the cell margins.

5. To add a tint to the page background:

   a. Display the Page Design tab.

   b. Click the Background button (Page Design tab | Page Background group), then click More Backgrounds to display the Fill Effects dialog box.

   c. Click the Tint tab (Fill Effects dialog box) and then click the Base color box arrow. Click the Accent 2 color.

   d. When Publisher displays the tints and shades of the color you chose, choose the 30% tint and click the OK button (Fill Effects dialog box).

6. Save the publication as Lab 10-1 Monthly Expenses Table.

7. Print the publication and turn it in to your instructor.

In the Lab

Lab 2: Creating a Table of Contents

Note: To complete this assignment, you will be required to use the Data Files for Students. See the inside back cover of this book for instructions on downloading the Data Files for Students, or contact your instructor for information about accessing the required files.

Problem: Northland Middle School is nearly finished with its 2012 yearbook template. The staff would like you to create a table of contents and link it to the sections in the book. In addition to selling print copies, Northland posts its yearbook as a PDF file online. You decide to use Publisher bookmarks to design a table of contents as shown in Figure 10–89.

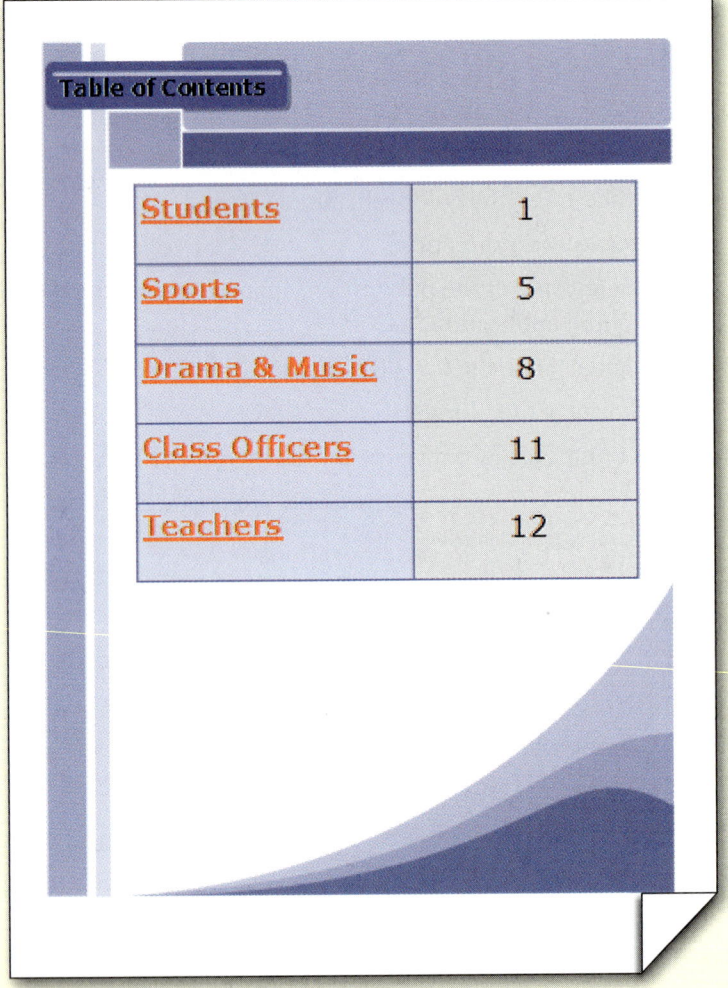

Figure 10–89

Instructions: Perform the following tasks:

1. Start Publisher and open the file named, Lab 10–2 Student Yearbook, from the Data Files for Students.

2. Press CTRL+F to display the Find and Replace task pane. Search for the first occurrence of the word, Students.

3. Display the Insert tab and then use the Bookmark button (Insert tab | Links group) to create a bookmark named, Students. Drag the bookmark to the top of the page.

4. Repeat Steps 2 and 3 for the words, Sports, Drama & Music, Class Officers, and Teachers. At the first occurrence of each term, create a bookmark on that page with the appropriate name.

5. Use the 'Go to page' command to return to the third page of the publication. Fill in the table of contents with the following information: Students on page 1; Sports on page 5; Drama & Music on page 8; Class Officers on page 11, and Teachers on Page 12.

6. One at a time, select the text in the first column. Press CTRL+K to display the Insert Hyperlink dialog box. Click the Place in This Document button (Insert Hyperlink dialog box) and then select the appropriate bookmark.

7. Save the publication with the file name, Lab 10-2 Student Yearbook Edited.

8. CTRL+click each of the links to make sure they work.

9. Save the file in the PDF format and test the links.

10. Submit this assignment as directed by your instructor.

In the Lab

Lab 3: Creating a One-Page Newsletter

Problem: The Young Explorers Club has sent you the text for a one-page newsletter. You decide to design the page with guides, linking text boxes, and page breaks. The completed publication appears in Figure 10–90.

Young Explorers Club

Outing

The Nature Exploration outing is Saturday, September 22, from 10:00 a.m. to 3:00 p.m. at Camp Ottawa.

The following explorers signed up for this event:

Helen   Leila

Jackie   Whitney

Rachel   . Willow

Please drop off your daughter by 8:30 a.m. at the Coal City Grocerland parking lot.

We will return between 4:00 p.m. and 4:15 p.m. Please arrive promptly at 4:00 p.m. at the same parking lot to pick up your daughter.

Thanks!

Fund-Raiser

Our unit will have a craft booth at the Fall Harvest Festival at Camp Ottawa on Saturday, October 20. Profits from all sales will go directly to our unit.

If you would like to donate a craft or staff the booth, call Mary at 555-0909.

Thank You!

We would like to thank each of you for donating to the World Young Explorer Foundation.

Your donation helps Young Explorers around the world.

Family Bowling

Registrations for Family Bowling are due at our next meeting. The event is from 6:00 p.m. to 8:00 p.m. at Lemont Lanes on Friday, December 14.

The fee is $7 per person and includes bowling and family-style buffet. Bumper lanes will be available for children ages seven years old and under.

Next Meeting

At our next meeting, we will be making sit-upons — to sit on at outdoor events when the ground is damp.

Figure 10–90

Continued >

In the Lab *continued*

Instructions: Perform the following tasks:
Start Publisher with a blank 8.5 × 11–inch publication. Set the font scheme to Office 1. Set the color scheme to Civic. Use the 3 Columns with Heading preset guide. Draw a text box in the first column area and then copy and paste it to the other two column areas. Link the text boxes. Insert a text file from the Data Files for Students named Young Explorers Text. Insert Page breaks to keep headings and stories together. Delete any blank lines at the bottom of a column. Insert two appropriate clip art graphics. Resize and position them so that they do not interrupt the column flow. Insert a WordArt heading and format each heading in the text. Save the publication and send it to your instructor as directed.

Cases and Places

Apply your creative thinking and problem solving skills to design and implement a solution.

Note: To complete these assignments, you may be required to use the Data Files for Students. See the inside back cover of this book for instructions on downloading the Data Files for Students, or contact your instructor for information about accessing the required files.

1: Create a Research Paper Template

Academic
Because you often write research papers for your courses, you decide it would be convenient to have a template in which you can type or import text. Start Publisher with a blank 8.5 × 11–inch publication. Set the font scheme to Office 1 and the color scheme to Black & White. Create a large text box that fills the page. Set the margin of the text box to .5 inches. Duplicate the page several times to create a total of seven pages. Go to Page 2 and create a section. Link the text box to the one on Page 3 and then link subsequent pages. Insert page numbering on every page except the title page.

2: Create a Resume

Personal
Now that you have had some desktop publishing experience, you decide to use Publisher to create a new resume highlighting your skills. In the New template gallery, choose a Resume template. Replace the template text with your personal information. Change the direction of the text that contains your name, so that your name runs down the side of the resume. Change the margins on any text box or cell margin that seems too close to the edge. Change the page background. Replace several terms using the thesaurus.

3: Create a Menu with BorderArt

Professional
A local restaurant is designing its new menu. The owners would like you to add borders around each portion of their menu. Open the file named, Case 10-3 Menu Draft, from the Data Files for Students. Navigate to Page 2. Draw a rectangle around each of the six portions of the menu. For each rectangle, add BorderArt that is representative of the group: appetizers, salads, etc. Consider clicking the Create Custom button (BorderArt dialog box) and to search for and possibly incorporate unique clips.

11 | Creating an Interactive Web Site

Objectives

You will have mastered the material in this project when you can:

- Create and format a Web masthead
- Insert a navigation bar
- Add pages to a Web site
- Insert an animated graphic and alternative text
- Set Web page options
- Insert a background sound
- Insert form controls

- Use return data labels
- Set form control properties
- Edit form properties
- Insert a Web hot spot
- Create an HTML code fragment
- Use VBA to create a message box
- Set the security level in Publisher

11 | Creating an Interactive Web Site

Introduction

Interactive Web sites are Web sites that allow visitors to enter information or interact with the Web site. Interactive Web sites often obtain feedback from visitors and allow visitors to navigate and view more features of the Web site. Some Web sites allow for e-commerce so that visitors can buy and sell products. **E-commerce**, short for **electronic commerce**, is a business transaction that occurs over an electronic network such as the Internet. E-commerce has become established in the business world as an inexpensive and efficient way to increase visibility and, therefore, sales. Customers visit, browse, make purchases, and ask for assistance at a Web site, just as they would at a physical location. Using server tools or through direct communication, visitor information may be passed to the server for processing in order to store, confirm, or respond to an inquiry.

An **electronic form** is used on a Web page to request and collect information, comments, or survey data, and to conduct business transactions. An electronic form is a collection of **form controls**, which are the individual buttons, boxes, and hyperlinks that let Web site visitors communicate with Web site owners. Electronic forms must include a submit button; otherwise, Web site visitors cannot return their form data to the Web site owner.

Publisher 2010 no longer includes the capability of creating new Web publications. You can, however, edit existing Web publications. If you open an existing Web publication, the Web tab will appear on the Ribbon. The Web tab provides you with Web publication tools; the tab is not available unless you open a Web publication or a downloaded template. Programs such as Expression Web and Dreamweaver provide more tools specifically for advanced Web site development; however, Publisher's Web capabilities allow for the creation of basic sites with interactive feedback.

The Building Block Library contains many Web-based objects, including mastheads, navigation bars, buttons, and forms — all designed to look good and load quickly on the Web. Additionally, the Code group on the Web tab contains many features to assist in designing forms from scratch. Most desktop publishers use a combination of rapid form development techniques, such as the use of templates, Web controls, or Building Block objects, to tailor their Web site to suit their needs.

When you click a Web form control or any command or button, Publisher follows a prewritten, step-by-step set of instructions to accomplish the task. For example, when you click the Save button on the Quick Access toolbar, Publisher follows a precise set of steps to save your publication. In Publisher, this series of instructions is called a **procedure**. A procedure also is referred to as a **program,** or **code**.

The process of writing a procedure is called **computer programming**. Each Publisher command or button has a corresponding procedure that executes when you click the command or button. **Execute** means that the computer carries out the step-by-step instructions. In a Windows environment, an event causes the instructions associated with a task to be executed. An **event** is an action such as clicking a button, clicking a command, dragging a scroll box, or right-clicking selected text.

Although Publisher has many buttons and commands, it does not include a command or button for every possible task. Thus, Microsoft has included with Publisher a powerful programming language called Visual Basic for Applications. The **Visual Basic for Applications (VBA)** programming language allows you to customize and extend the capabilities of Publisher to suit your own needs.

Project — Creating an Interactive Web Site

To illustrate some of the Web site features of Microsoft Publisher, this chapter presents a series of steps to create an interactive Web site for a county department of health. You will use Publisher to create a form for the Web site that sends data to its owner, as well as other Web objects, including a navigation bar, animated graphics, a background sound, form controls, and HTML code. A **navigation bar** is a set of buttons or hyperlinks that allows visitors to move to any page within the Web site. You can place navigation bars on a page vertically, horizontally, along the top, along the bottom, or down the side. Additionally, navigation bars can be duplicated in multiple places on the page for easy access while scrolling through the page.

You do not need extensive knowledge of HTML. Recall that HTML (Hypertext Markup Language) is a formatting language that programmers use to format documents for display on the Web. Publisher provides user-friendly tools and controls to make it easy for even beginners to design interactive and highly effective Web sites.

Figure 11–1a shows the home page for the site, and Figure 11–1b shows a Web form created for the site. This project also demonstrates the use of a VBA-generated dialog box to remind the designer to upload the most recent copy of the publication to the Web (Figure 11–1c).

(a) **Web Site Home Page**

(b) **Web Site Web Form**

(c) **VBA Dialog Box**

Figure 11–1

Overview

As you read through this chapter, you will learn how to create the Web site publications shown in Figure 11–1 by performing these general tasks:

- Create a Web masthead.
- Use the Web tab on the Ribbon to insert a navigation bar.
- Add a sound, animated graphics, and alternative text to a Web site.
- Add a new Web page to the site.
- Insert form controls and set their properties.
- Create a hot spot and a scrolling marquee.
- Use VBA to create a message box.

Plan Ahead

General Project Guidelines

When creating a Publisher publication, the actions you perform and decisions you make will affect the appearance and characteristics of the finished publication. As you create an interactive Web site, such as the project shown in Figure 11–1, you should follow these general guidelines.

1. **Design navigation in your Web site.** The most important feature of a Web site is its navigation capabilities. Visitors need to be able to find information easily. They expect a navigation bar with links to other pages on your site. Use a logical order to present the pages and to create a navigation bar that is virtually identical on all pages.

2. **Design and create a functional form.** Design a well-thought-out draft of the form, and be sure to include all essential form elements. Sketch the form on paper first to view the overall affect and placement of the objects before creating the elements on the computer screen. Essential elements include the form's title, text, and graphics; data entry fields; and data entry instructions. A form control or data entry field is a placeholder for data that a user enters in the form. If the data entered in the form will be analyzed by a program other than Publisher, create the data entry fields so that the entries are stored in separate fields that can be shared with other programs and, therefore, filtered, sorted, and exported easily.

3. **Test the form.** Be sure that the form works as you intended. Fill in the form as if you were a user. Have others fill in the form and provide feedback to you as to whether the form is organized in a logical manner, is easy to understand and is complete. If any errors or weaknesses in the form are identified, correct them and then test the form again.

4. **Add macros to automate tasks.** In Publisher, a macro consists of VBA code. To add macros, you do not need a computer programming background. To write advanced VBA code, however, you should be familiar with computer programming.

5. **Incorporate security in a document.** Publisher provides several tools that allow you to secure your documents. For example, you can add a digital signature, set the security level, and save with a backup or versions.

When necessary, more specific details concerning the above guidelines are presented at appropriate points in the chapter. The chapter also will identify the actions performed and decisions made regarding these guidelines during the creation of the Web site in this chapter.

To Start Publisher

The following steps, which assume Windows 7 is running, start Publisher based on a typical installation. You may need to ask your instructor how to start Publisher for your computer. For a detailed example of the procedure summarized below, refer to the Office 2010 and Windows 7 chapter at the beginning of this book.

1 Click the Start button on the Windows 7 taskbar to display the Start menu.

2 Type `Microsoft Publisher` as the search text in the 'Search programs and files' text box, and watch the search results appear on the Start menu.

3 Click Microsoft Publisher 2010 in the search results on the Start menu to start Publisher and open the Backstage view and the New Template gallery.

4 If the Publisher window is not maximized, click the Maximize button next to the Close button on its title bar to maximize the window.

To Open a Publication

The following steps open the Blank Web Page file from the Data Files for Students. See the inside back cover of this book for instructions on downloading the Data Files for Students, or contact your instructor for information about accessing the required files. For a detailed example of the procedure summarized below, refer to the Office 2010 and Windows 7 chapter at the beginning of this book.

1 Click Open in the Backstage view to display the Open Publication dialog box.

2 Navigate to the location of the file to be opened (in this case, the Data Files for Students, in the Publisher folder, and then in the Chapter 11 folder).

3 Double-click Blank Web Page to open the selected file and display the opened publication in the Publisher window.

4 If necessary, click the Special Characters button (Home tab | Paragraph group) to display special characters.

5 Display the View tab and then verify that your check box settings (View tab | Show group) match those shown in Figure 11–2.

6 Click the Page Width button (View tab | Zoom area).

7 If necessary, collapse the Page Navigation pane.

Figure 11–2

To Select Color and Font Schemes

The following steps choose a color and font scheme for the Web site.

1 Display the Page Design tab.

2 Click the Scheme Fonts button (Page Design tab | Schemes group) and then click the Urban font scheme in the gallery.

3 Click the More button (Page Design tab | Schemes group) and then click the Office color scheme in the gallery.

Creating a Business Information Set

Table 11–1 displays the data for each of the fields in the business information set that you will create in this project. Recall that Publisher will populate fields automatically from the business information set as you add objects to the Web page.

Table 11–1 Data for Business Information Fields	
Fields	**Data**
Individual name	Josiah Walter
Job or position or title	Director, Department of Health
Organization name	Adams County
Address	355 South Bethesda Haley, TN 38122
Phone, fax, and e-mail	Phone Number: (731) 555-9222 Fax Number: (731) 555-9383 E-Mail: info@adamscountyhealth.org
Tagline or motto	Caring for the community
Business Information set name	Adams County

To Create a Business Information Set

The following steps create a business information set for Adams County.

1 Display the Insert tab. Click the Business Information button (Insert tab | Text group) and then click Edit Business Information.

2 If Publisher displays the Business Information dialog box, click the New button (Business Information dialog box) to display the Create New Business Information Set dialog box.

3 Enter the data from Table 11–1.

4 Click the Save button (Create New Business Information Set dialog box) to save the data. Click the Update Publication button (Business Information dialog box) to return to the blank publication.

Editing the Home Page

A **home page** is the opening page or main document that is displayed when you visit a Web site. Typically, the home page welcomes you and introduces the purpose of the site and the sponsoring business. Home pages commonly provide links to the **secondary pages** or lower-level pages in the site. The home page is the first page that Web site visitors will see, so it should explain the site's purpose, content, and layout.

To Create a Web Masthead

The following steps create a masthead on the home page of the Web site.

1
• Click the Show Building Block Library Dialog Box Launcher (Insert tab | Building Blocks group) to display the Building Block Library (Figure 11–3).

Figure 11–3

2
• Click the Page Parts folder to open it and then scroll to the Mastheads area. If necessary, click the All Mastheads folder.

• Click the Art Boxes masthead to select it (Figure 11–4).

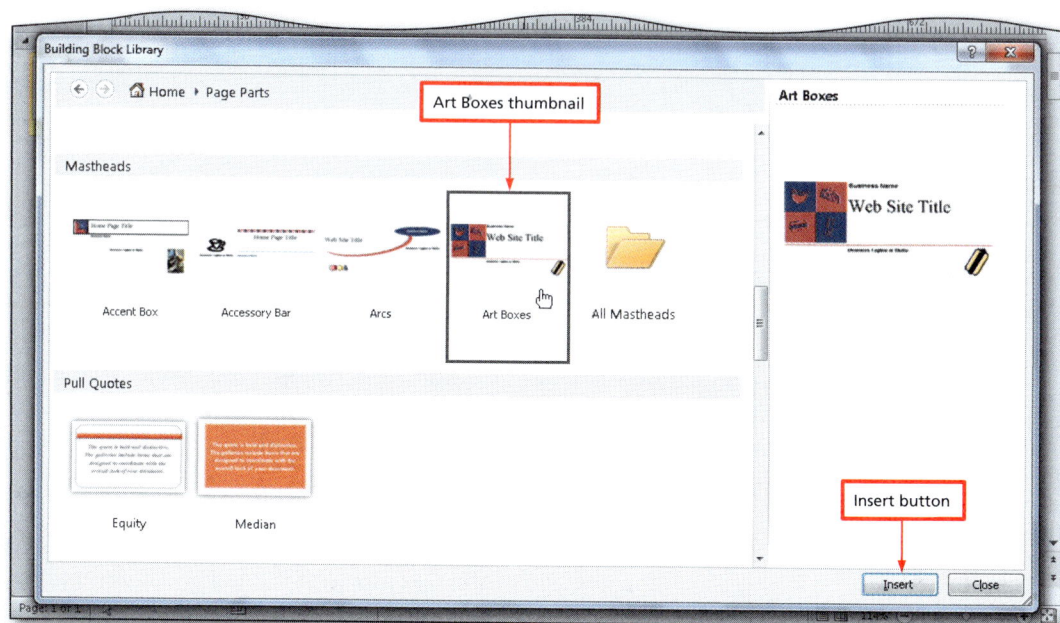

Figure 11–4

3

- Click the Insert button (Building Block Library dialog box) to insert the masthead into the publication.

- Resize the masthead to fill the upper part of the page, approximately 192 pixels tall (Figure 11–5).

Q&A

Why does the ruler show pixels?

When working with Web publications, Publisher automatically changes the unit of measurement to pixels because the publication will be displayed on a monitor rather than be printed. Additionally, there are no margin guides.

Figure 11–5

4

- Click the Web Site Title placeholder text to select it, and then type **Department of Health** to replace the text (Figure 11–6).

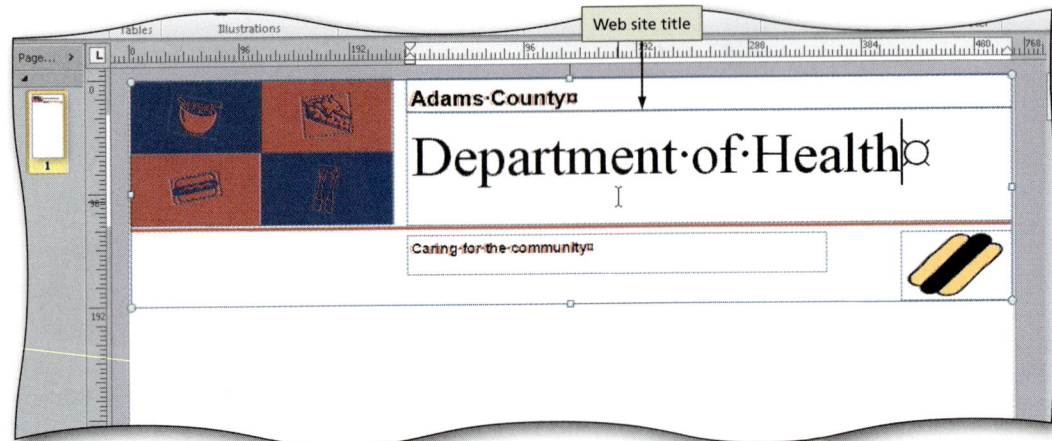

Figure 11–6

BTW

Web Mastheads
The Building Block folder for Web mastheads appears only if the publication is a Web publication. Web templates are not available in the New Template gallery. You can use the Blank Web Page file from the Data Files for Students to start new Web publications.

To Import Text

The following steps import text for Page 1 of the Web site from a Word document included on the Data Files for Students. See the inside back cover of this book for instructions on downloading the Data Files for Students, or contact your instructor for more information about accessing the required files.

1 Zoom to 70% magnification.

2 Below the masthead, draw a text box approximately 500 pixels wide and 500 pixels tall. Align the left side of the text box with the tag line, Caring for the community.

3 Right-click the text box to display the shortcut menu. Point to Change Text on the shortcut menu and then click Text File to display the Insert Text dialog box.

4 Navigate to the Data Files for Students and then double-click the file, Page 1 Story, to insert the text file (Figure 11–7). A Converting message dialog box will appear during the process.

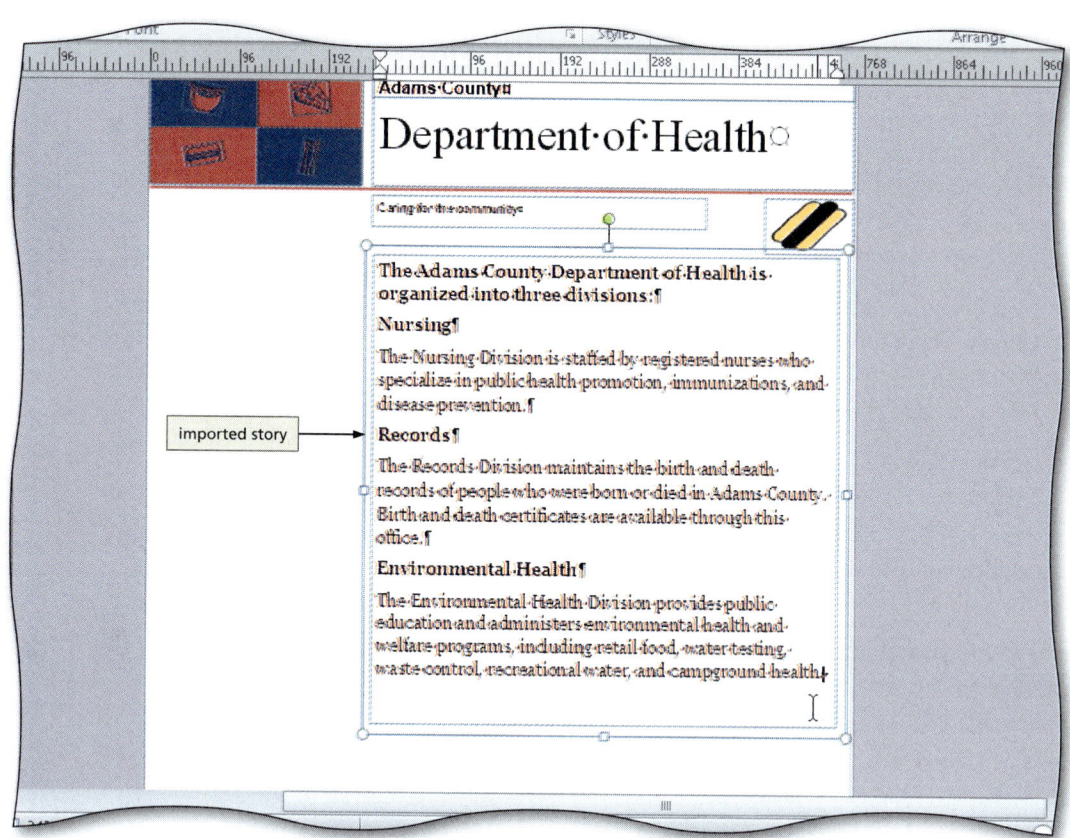

Figure 11–7

To Save a Publication

The following steps assume you already have created folders for storing your files, for example, a CIS 101 folder (for your class) that contains a Publisher folder (for your assignments). Thus, the following steps save the publication in the Publisher folder in the CIS 101 folder on a USB flash drive using the file name, Health Web Publication. For a detailed example of the procedure summarized below, refer to the Office 2010 and Windows 7 chapter at the beginning of this book.

1 With a USB flash drive connected to one of the computer's USB ports, click File on the Ribbon to display the Backstage view.

2 Click Save As to display the Save As dialog box.

3 Type **Health Web Publication** in the File name text box to change the file name. Do not press the ENTER key after typing the file name because you do not want to close the dialog box at this time.

4 Navigate to the desired save location (in this case, the Publisher folder in the CIS 101 folder [or your class folder] on the USB flash drive).

5 Click the Save button (Save As dialog box) to save the publication in the selected folder on the selected drive with the entered file name.

Navigation Bars

Navigation bars include buttons, text, and shapes to help the visitor navigate to other pages in the Web site. Publisher navigation bars are grouped objects and are synchronized across pages. You can change the components in a navigation bar by editing them individually or by using the Navigation Bar Properties dialog box. You can set the **page title**, which is displayed in the browser title bar, using the Navigation Bar Properties dialog box. Because the navigation bar is a synchronized object, new pages in the Web site will contain the linked navigation bar, and changing it on one page of the Web site changes it on all pages.

Plan Ahead

Design navigation in your Web site. Publisher has navigation bars in its Building Block Library. Make sure you edit the bars appropriately, and use terms that are common to most Web sites. For instance, visitors expect links such as Locations, Contact Us, and About.

To Insert a Navigation Bar

The following steps insert a navigation bar.

- Click Web on the Ribbon to display the Web tab.

- Click the Navigation Bar button (Web tab | Web Page Navigation group) to display the Building Block Library dialog box.

- Click the Counter navigation bar thumbnail to select it (Figure 11–8).

Figure 11–8

2

- Click the Insert button (Building Block Library dialog box) to insert the navigation bar into the publication.

- Drag the navigation bar to a location below the left side of the masthead as shown in Figure 11–9.

Q&A Why does only one button appear in the navigation bar?

You have only one page in the Web site so far. As you add other pages, the navigation bar will expand to include more buttons.

Other Ways

1. Click Building Block Library Dialog Box Launcher (Insert tab | Building Blocks group), click Navigation Bars folder (Building Block Library dialog box), select navigation bar, click Insert button

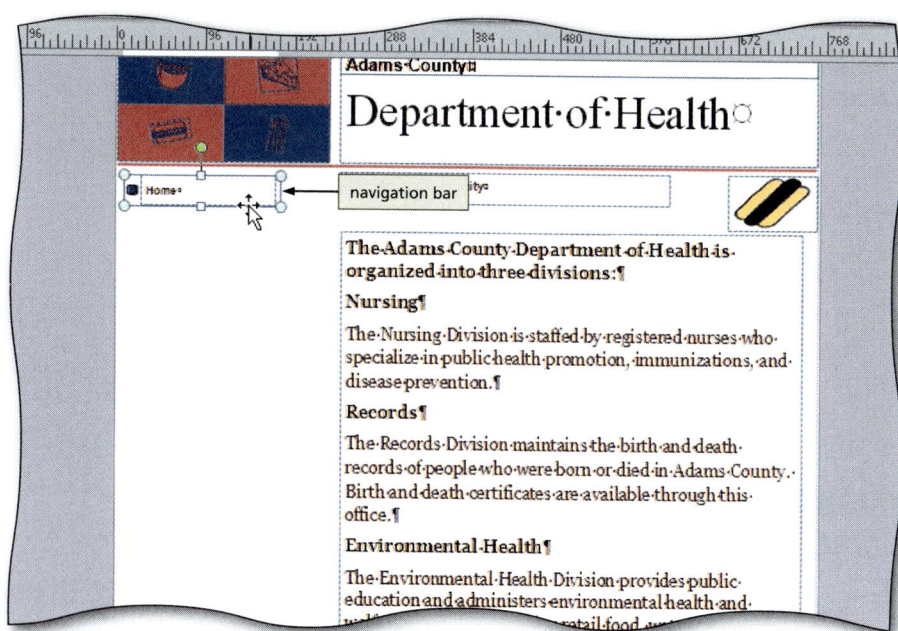

Figure 11–9

To Add Secondary Pages to a Web Site

The following steps add a new page to the Web site. Publisher provides a list of common page types, such as a contact page or about page, from which you may choose. For example, you can add a page about employees, products, or photos, among others. Each of the pages you add will retain the font, color, and navigation bar of the home page.

1

- In the Page Navigation pane, right-click the Page 1 thumbnail to display the shortcut menu (Figure 11–10).

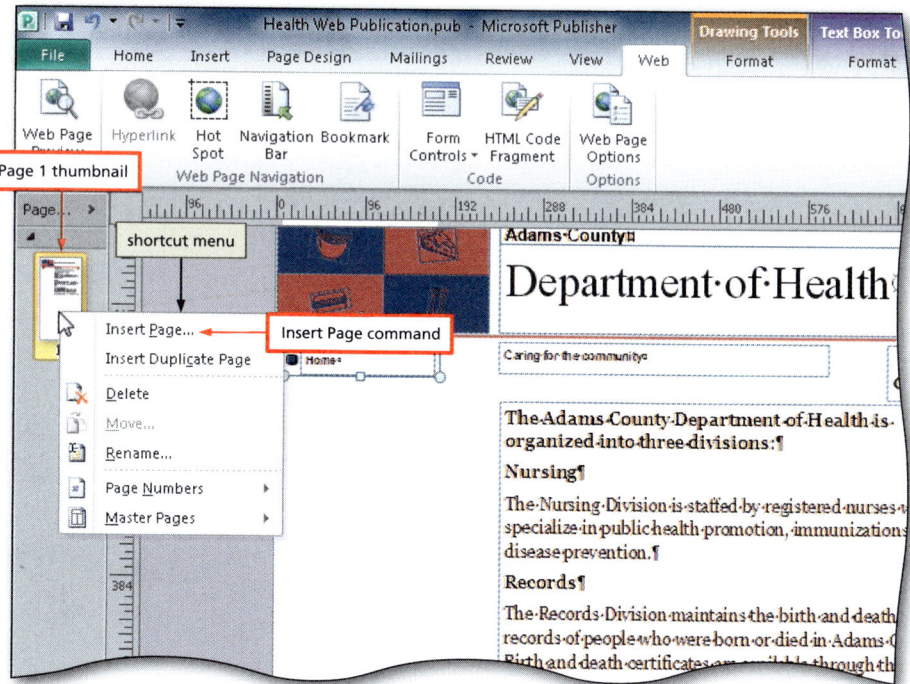

Figure 11–10

2

- Click Insert Page on the shortcut menu to display the Insert Web Page dialog box.

- Click Calendar in the 'Select a page type' list to choose a calendar page (Figure 11–11).

 Experiment

- Click the Calendar with Links command to preview how many pages would be added if you were to choose that command. Click other pages to display different previews. Click Calendar to choose a single calendar page.

Figure 11–11

3

- Click the OK button (Insert Web Page dialog box) to insert the page into the publication (Figure 11–12).

Q&A

How does Publisher choose which month to display in the calendar?

Publisher displays the current month based on your computer's system date. Later in the chapter, you will change the calendar.

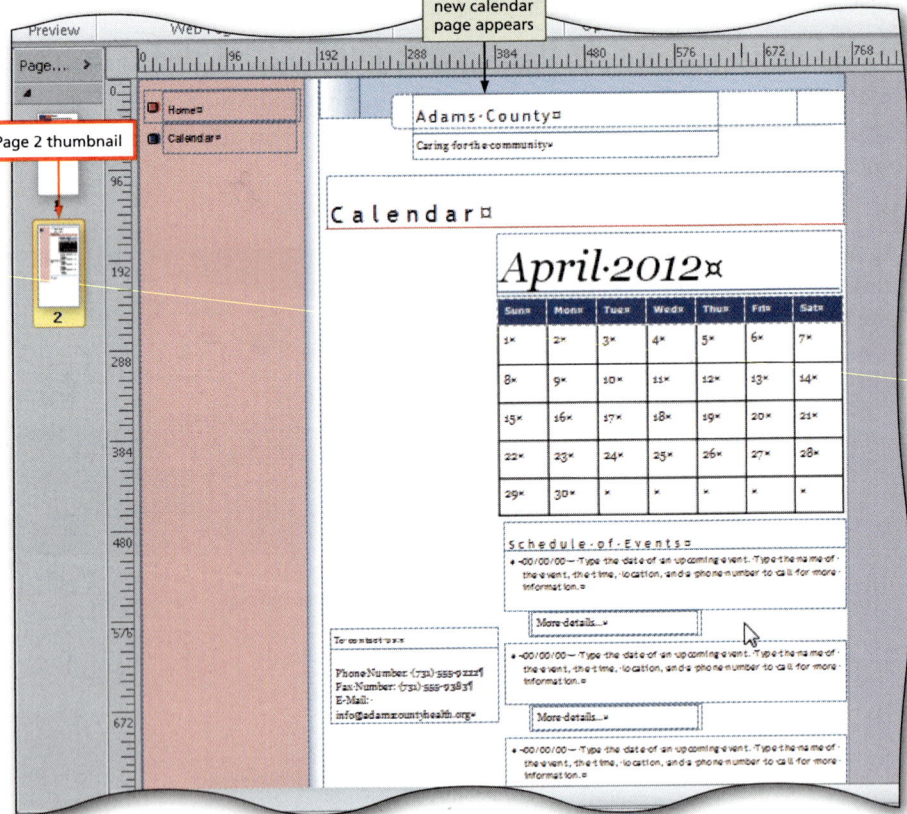

Figure 11–12

Other Ways

1. Click Page button arrow (Insert tab | Pages group), click Insert Page, click desired page type (Insert Web Page dialog box), click OK button

To Add More Pages

The following steps add a contact page and a blank page to the Web site.

1 In the Page Navigation pane, right-click the Page 2 thumbnail to display the shortcut menu and then click Insert Page on the shortcut menu to display the Insert Web Page dialog box.

2 Click Contact Us in the 'Select a page type' list and then click the OK button (Insert Web Page dialog box) to insert a third page into the publication.

3 In the Page Navigation pane, right-click the Page 3 thumbnail to display the shortcut menu and then click Insert Page on the shortcut menu to display the Insert Web Page dialog box.

4 Click Blank in the 'Select a page type' list and then click the OK button (Insert Web Page dialog box) to insert a fourth page into the publication (Figure 11–13).

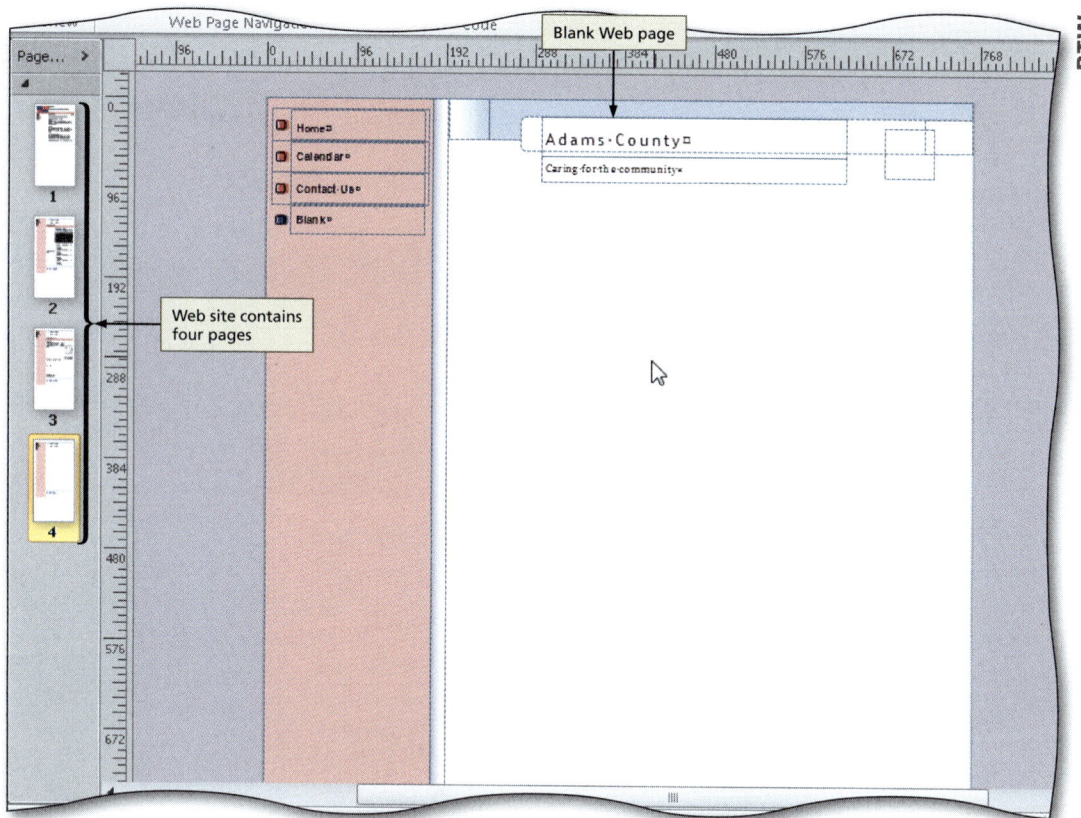

BTW

More Web Page Settings
The More button (Insert Web Page dialog box) displays the Insert Page dialog box, which allows you to specify whether the new page will be added before or after the current pages, how many pages you wish to add, and whether to adjust the navigation bar to include the new page(s).

Figure 11–13

To Edit the Navigation Bar Properties

The following steps edit the navigation bar properties to change the text that appears on the button of the navigation bar and to set the page title that appears in the browser title bar.

1

- Navigate to Page 1 of the publication.

- Right-click the navigation bar to display its shortcut menu (Figure 11–14).

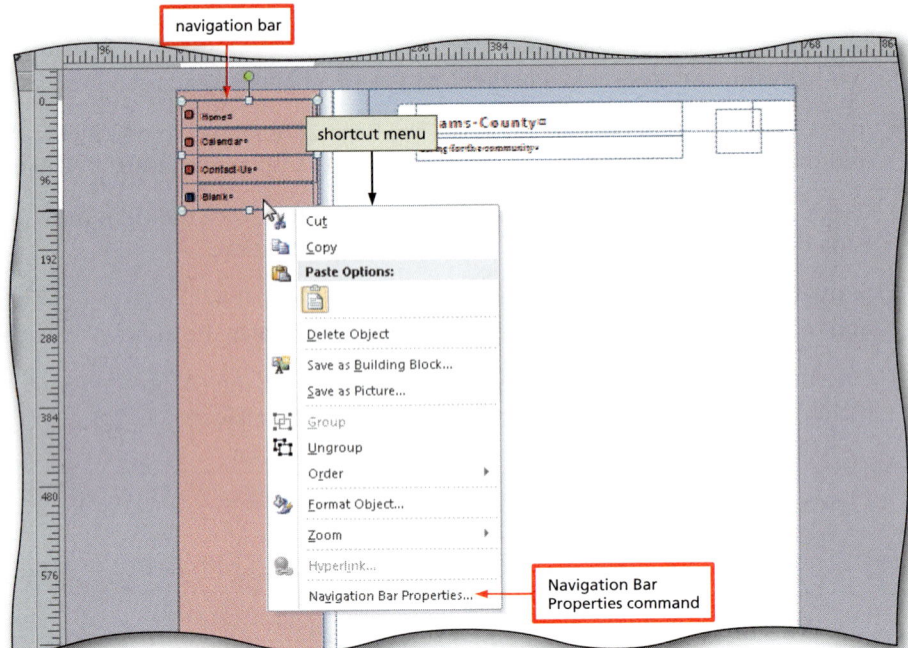

Figure 11–14

2

- Click Navigation Bar Properties on the shortcut menu to display the Navigation Bar Properties dialog box.

- In the Links area, click Calendar to select the link (Figure 11–15).

Figure 11–15

3

- Click the Modify Link button (Navigation Bar Properties dialog box) to display the Modify Link dialog box.

- Select the text in the 'Text to display' text box and then type **Immunization Clinics** to change the navigation bar (Figure 11–16).

 Where will the new text appear on the Web page?

Text entered in the 'Text to display' text box will appear on the navigation bar itself.

Figure 11–16

4

- Click the Change Title button (Modify Link dialog box) to display the Enter Text dialog box.

- Type **Adams County Immunization Clinics** to replace the text (Figure 11–17).

Q&A Where will the title be displayed on the Web page?

The title will appear on the Web browser's title bar when you view the Web page. The title also appears in a ScreenTip when you point to the thumbnail in the Page Navigation pane.

Figure 11–17

5

- Click the OK button (Enter Text dialog box) to set the page title.

- Click the OK button (Modify Link dialog box) to return to the Navigation Bar Properties dialog box.

- In the Links area, select Contact Us and then click the Modify Link button (Navigation Bar Properties dialog box).

- Select the text in the 'Text to display' text box and then type **Location** to change the navigation bar text.

- In the 'Select a place in this document' area, click Page 3. Contact Us to select it (Figure 11–18).

Figure 11–18

6

- Click the Change Title button (Modify Link dialog box) to display the Enter Text dialog box.

- Type **Adams County Health Location** to change the page title (Figure 11–19).

Figure 11–19

7

- Click the OK button (Enter Text dialog box) to set the page title.

- Click the OK button (Modify Link dialog box) to return to the Navigation Bar Properties dialog box.

- In the Links area, select Blank and then click the Modify Link button (Navigation Bar Properties dialog box) to display the Modify Link dialog box.

- Select the text in the 'Text to display' text box and then type **Forms & Publications** to change the navigation bar text.

- In the 'Select a place in this document' area, click Page 4. Blank to select it (Figure 11–20).

Figure 11–20

8

- Click the Change Title button (Modify Link dialog box) to display the Enter Text dialog box.

- If necessary, select the text in the Page title text box and then type **Adams County Forms & Publications** to change the page title (Figure 11–21).

Figure 11–21

9

- Click the OK button (Enter Text dialog box) to name the page.

- Click the OK button (Modify Link dialog box) to complete the modifications.

- Click the OK button (Navigation Bar Properties dialog box) to return to the publication.

- Press the F9 key to zoom the selected navigation bar to 100% magnification (Figure 11–22).

Figure 11–22

10

- Navigate to Page 1 of the publication.

- If your Home page navigation bar did not synchronize the titles, double-click the text in the navigation bar itself and edit the text as necessary.

To Save an Existing Document with the Same File Name

You have made several modifications to the document since you last saved it. Thus, you should save it again. The following step saves the document again. For an example of the step listed below, refer to the Office 2010 and Windows 7 chapter at the beginning of this book.

1 Click the Save button on the Quick Access Toolbar to overwrite the previously saved file.

Web Graphics

When using graphics on Web pages, you must take into consideration visual appeal, download time, resolution, and purpose. Unless the home page is a picture gallery, just a few graphics are sufficient to create visual appeal and catch the visitor's eye. Keep in mind that each image added to a Web page increases the amount of time it takes to download the page. In addition, some people browse the Web with images turned off in order to speed up the process; others turn off graphics to make the page more accessible.

Even though the computer screen is lower in resolution than most printed pages, Web graphics easily can rival the quality of color images printed on paper. **Resolution** refers to the number of horizontal and vertical pixels in a display device or the sharpness and clarity of an image. A high-resolution graphic makes a Web page more visually appealing but increases the download time.

Purpose may be the most important consideration in using Web graphics; they should help convey the Web site's message, not clutter the layout. The graphics should add interest or color, brand a company, draw attention, show relationships, or simplify complex information.

BTW

Graphics
The number and type of graphics you use on your page will be a compromise between what is appealing visually and what makes the best sense for your target audience.

To Ungroup the Masthead

The following steps ungroup the masthead for further editing of the graphics.

1 Display the Home tab.

2 Click the masthead to select it.

3 Click the Ungroup button (Home tab | Arrange group) to ungroup the masthead.

To Replace Graphics

The following steps replace the graphics in the upper-right corner of the masthead.

1 Click the Clip Art button (Insert tab | Illustrations group) to display the Clip Art task pane. Limit the search results to Illustrations.

2 Select the picture of the salad bowl in the upper-left corner of the masthead and zoom to 150%. Search for a clip art of a baby, similar to the one shown in Figure 11–23 and click it to replace the salad bowl.

3 Repeat Step 2 to replace the picture of the piece of pie with a picture of a nurse similar to the one shown in Figure 11–23.

4 Repeat Step 2 to replace the picture of the hot dog on the left side of the masthead with a picture of a stethoscope similar to the one shown in Figure 11–23.

5 Repeat Step 2 to replace the picture of the salt and pepper shakers with a picture of a patient in a wheelchair similar to the one shown in Figure 11–23.

6 Resize the graphics as necessary.

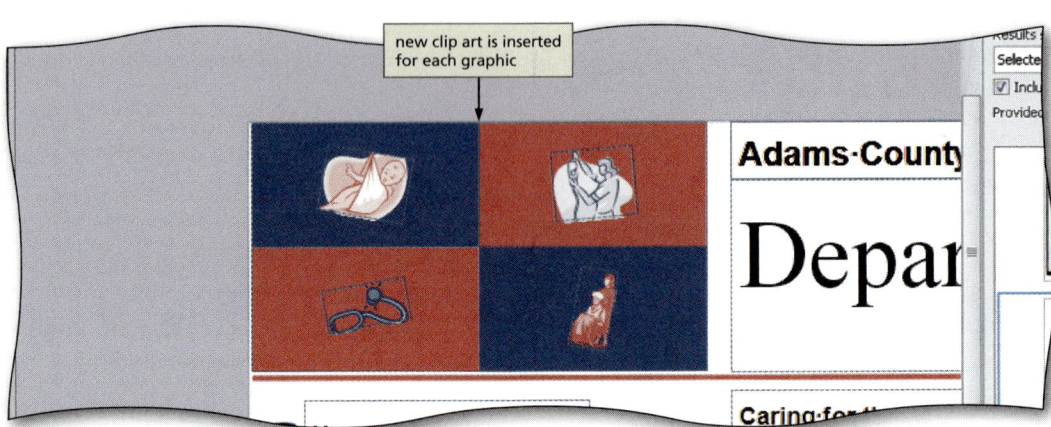

new clip art is inserted for each graphic

Figure 11–23

Animated Graphics

An **animated graphic** is a picture that displays animation when viewed in a Web browser. While too much animation may distract users, a subtle animated graphic may convey the Web site owner's message or style.

To Preview an Animated Graphic

The following steps preview an animated graphic using the Clip Art task pane.

1
- On the right side of the masthead, click the hot dog graphic to select it.
- In the Clip Art task pane, type **heart** in the Search for box.
- Limit the search results to Videos.
- Click the Go button to perform the search (Figure 11–24).

Q&A How do I know if the clip art is animated?

Animated clip art or movies display a star in the lower-right corner of the preview in the Clip Art task pane.

Figure 11–24

2

- Click the button on any thumbnail to display its menu (Figure 11–25).

What are some of the other commands on the button menu?

The Make Available Offline command gives you the opportunity to save the graphic on your computer. The Edit Keywords command displays a dialog box where you can edit searchable keywords in order to find clip art more easily.

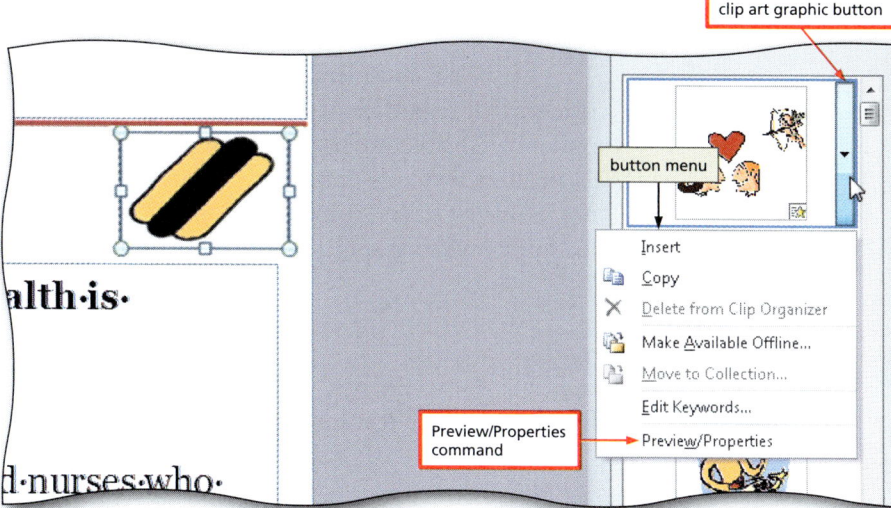

Figure 11–25

3

- Click Preview/Properties on the button menu to display the Preview/Properties dialog box (Figure 11–26).

🔍 **Experiment**

- Click the Next or Previous button several times to view the animation for each of the graphics found in the keyword search.

4

- Click the Close button (Preview/Properties dialog box) to close the preview.

Figure 11–26

To Insert a Graphic

The next step inserts the animated graphic on the home page.

1 In the Clip Art task pane, click a graphic similar to the one shown in Figure 11–26 to insert it into the publication.

2 Move the graphic to a position in the lower-right corner of the masthead. Close the Clip Art task pane.

Alternative Text

A special consideration when using graphics on the Web is accessibility. Screen readers that read Web pages for people with disabilities can provide feedback about pictures, but only if the picture has alternative text. **Alternative text** is descriptive text that appears as an alternative to a graphic image on Web pages. Graphics without alternative text are not usable by screen readers. Web browsers may display alternative text when graphics are loading or when graphics are missing. Screen readers read the alternative text out loud.

To Add Alternative Text

The following steps insert alternative text for the five graphics on the home page.

- Right-click the graphic of the heart and then click Format Picture on the shortcut menu. When Publisher displays the Format Picture dialog box, click the Web tab.

- Type **An animated graphic displays a picture of a beating heart.** in the Alternative text text box (Figure 11–27).

- Click the OK button (Format Picture dialog box) to apply the alternative text.

Figure 11–27

To Add More Alternative Text

The following steps add alternative text to the four pictures on the other side of the masthead.

1 On the other side of the masthead, right-click the photograph of the baby, and then click Format Picture on the shortcut menu. Click the Web tab (Format Picture dialog box).

2 Type **A picture of a baby cradled in a blanket** in the Alternative text text box.

3 Click the OK button (Format Picture dialog box) to assign the alternative text.

4 Repeat Steps 1, 2, and 3, for the picture of the nurse with an IV bottle, the picture of the stethoscope, and the picture of the patient in a wheelchair.

Setting Web Page Options

Publisher's **Web page options** allow you to customize the way the Web page is displayed and how it works on the Web. You can edit the page title, the file name, search engine information, and the background sound. While the page title is the text that will appear in the browser's title bar, the file name is the name of the individual Web page as it is stored on a server.

The search engine information, such as description and keywords, create **meta tags** in Web publications; these tags are HTML specification tags that tell search engines what data to use. The **description** is a sentence or phrase that you create to describe your Web site. The description appears in most search engine results pages. The description should encourage people to click the link to your Web site. The **keywords** are a list of words or phrases that some search engines may use to locate your page. While keywords are used less frequently than they once were, you still should insert them and make sure they accurately reflect the content of the Web page for effective searching.

To Edit Web Page Options

The following steps enter special options for the Web page.

1

- Display the Web tab.

- Click the Web Page Options button (Web tab | Options group) to display the Web Page Options dialog box.

- If necessary, select any text in the Page title text box and then type **Adams County Department of Health Home Page** to replace the text.

- If necessary, select any text in the File name text box and then type **index** to replace the text (Figure 11–28).

Figure 11–28

Q&A

Why is the home page named index?

It is standard practice to name the main page of any Web site or directory, index. Web servers recognize index as the main page and, thus, do not require visitors to type the file name at the end of the URL when navigating to the page.

2

- In the Description text box, type **Welcome to the home page of the Department of Health for Adams County, Tennessee.** to describe the Web site.

- In the Keywords text box, type **adams county department of health immunizations records nursing environmental health** to create the keywords list (Figure 11–29).

Q&A

Do I need to type commas between the keywords?

It is not necessary to type commas after each keyword. The search engines that still use keyword meta tags can accept the data either way.

Figure 11–29

To Insert a Background Sound

When you add a **background sound** to a Web publication, the sound plays when you view the Web page in a browser. Adding sound generates interest, attracts attention, and can add a certain style to your Web site. Disadvantages of adding sound include additional download time and visitors who navigate away from the Web site because they may not want to listen. You should use sound only to enhance the site and do so only in appropriate amounts.

The following steps insert a background sound from the sounds that are provided with an initial installation of Publisher. The location of sound clip art commonly is C:\Program Files\Microsoft Office\CLIPART\PUB60COR. Your instructor may specify a different location for your sound clip art.

1

- With the Web Page Options dialog box still displayed, click the Browse button to display the Background Sound dialog box.

- If necessary, navigate to the location of sound clip art on your system (Figure 11–30).

Q&A

Can I hear the sound before I choose it?

Yes. On most computers, you can right-click a sound file and a shortcut menu will appear that contains a Play command. Check with your instructor about using sound and speakers in lab situations.

Figure 11–30

2

- Scroll as necessary and click the SCHOL_02.MID file or other sound file on your computer (Figure 11–31).

Q&A

I do not see the file extension. Did I do something wrong?

File extensions may be hidden on your computer. If you want to turn them on, click the Start button, click Computer, and then press the ALT key to display the menu. Click Tools on the menu bar, click Folder Options, and then click the View tab. Finally, click to remove the check mark in the 'Hide extensions for known file types' check box.

Q&A

What does the extension MID mean?

MID or MIDI (pronounced middy) stands for Musical Instrument Digital Interface and is the electronic music industry's standard that defines how devices represent sounds electronically. Most computer sound cards support the MID extension.

Figure 11–31

3

- Click the Open button (Background Sound dialog box) to select the sound.

- Click the OK button (Web Page Options dialog box) to return to the publication.

To Save Again

The following step saves the publication again.

1 Click the Save button on the Quick Access Toolbar to overwrite the previously saved file.

Break Point: If you wish to take a break, this is a good place to do so. You can quit Publisher now. To resume at a later time, start Publisher, open the file called Health Web Publication, and continue following the steps from this location forward.

Editing a Calendar Web Page

On Page 2 of the Web site, you will need to edit the text below the calendar. You also will need to change the calendar to the appropriate date and then format it. After editing the page, you will name the page in the Web Site Options dialog box. Table 11–2 displays the text you will enter.

Table 11–2 Page 2 Edits	
Template Text	**New Text (or edits)**
Schedule of Events	Immunization Clinics
First bulleted text box	05/05/12, 10:00 a.m. – 4:00 p.m. at Adams County Department of Health
Second bulleted text box	05/09/12, 6:00 p.m. – 8:00 p.m. at Adams High School
Third bulleted text box	05/19/12, 10:00 a.m. – 4:00 p.m. at Fairfield Mall
Fourth bulleted text box	05/28/12, 6:00 p.m. – 8:00 p.m. at Adams County Department of Health
Each of the More details… boxes	hyperlink to http://www.cdc.gov/vaccines/default.htm

To Edit Objects on Page 2

The following steps edit the objects on Page 2 of the Web site.

1 Navigate to page 2.

2 Individually, select the text in the text boxes listed in Table 11–2 and edit them as directed. Navigate and zoom as necessary.

3 To create the hyperlinks, select the placeholder text, press CTRL+K, and then click the Existing File or Web Page button (Insert Hyperlink dialog box). Type the Web address in the Address box and then click the OK button (Figure 11–32).

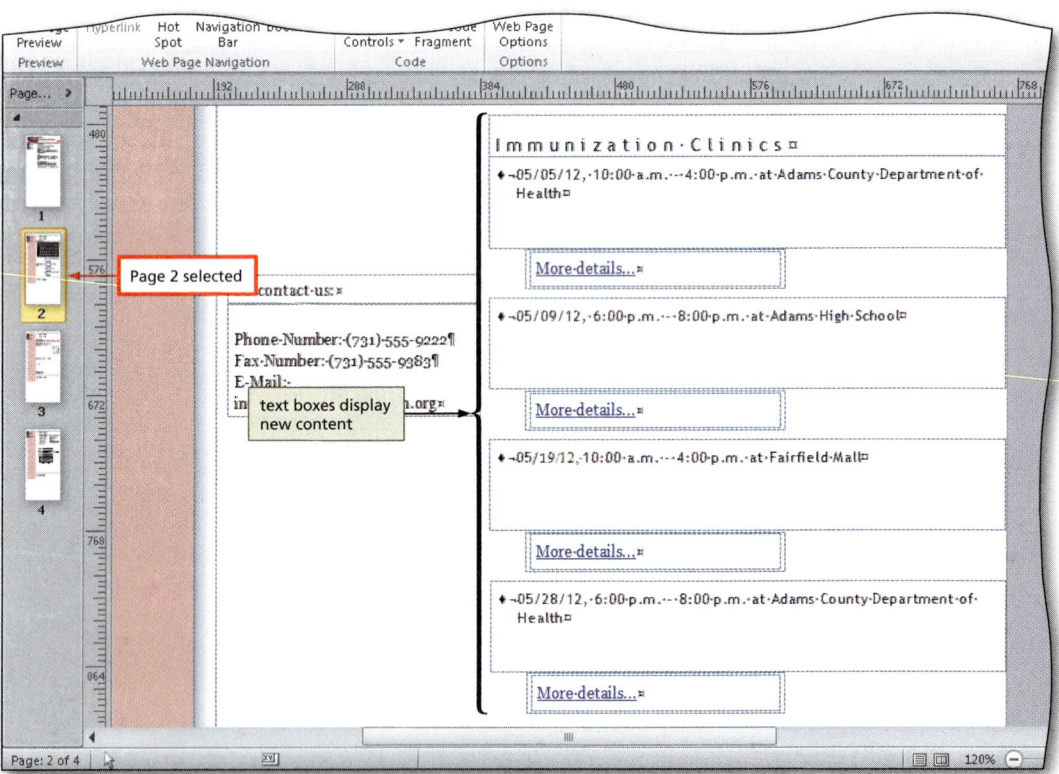

Figure 11–32

To Replace the Calendar

The following steps replace the calendar on Page 2 of the Web site.

1 Click the border of the calendar to select it and then press the DELETE key to delete the calendar.

2 Display the Insert tab. Click the Calendars button (Insert tab | Building Blocks group) and then click More Calendars in the Calendars gallery to display the Building Block Library dialog box.

3 Click the Accent Box calendar and then, on the right side of the dialog box, change the date to May 2012.

4 Click the Insert button (Building Block Library dialog box) to insert the calendar into the publication.

5 Resize the calendar and position it in the same location as the previous calendar (Figure 11–33).

Figure 11–33

To Format the Calendar

The following steps highlight specific dates on the calendar by shading the cell.

1 Select the cell for May 5. Right-click to display the shortcut menu and then click Format Table on the shortcut menu to display the Format Table dialog box.

2 In the Fill area, click the Color box arrow (Format Table dialog box) and then click Yellow in the Standard Colors area.

3 Click the OK button (Format Table dialog box) to apply the color.

4 Repeat Steps 1 through 3 for the cells that display May 9, 19, and 28 (Figure 11–34).

Figure 11–34

Editing a Contact Us Web Page

The next steps make changes on the Location page of the template for the Web site. Table 11–3 displays the template text or object and the new text or required edits. You will name the Web page file using the Web Page Options dialog box.

Table 11–3 Page 3 Edits	
Template Text	**New Text (or edits)**
Contact Us	Location
Heading	Main Office
First paragraph box	Take Highway 55 into Haley. Turn East on Main. Turn right on South Bethesda.
Company or Organization Name	Adams County Department of Health
Type your street address or the name of your neighborhood.	<delete text box>

To Edit Objects on Page 3

The following steps edit the objects on Page 3 of the Web site.

1 Navigate to page 3.

2 Individually, select the text-based objects in Table 11–3 and edit them as directed in the table.

3 To add alternative text to the map, right-click the graphic and then click Format Picture on the shortcut menu. Click the Web tab (Format Picture dialog box) and then enter an appropriate, short description.

4 Click the OK button to apply the alternative text (Figure 11–35).

BTW

Forms
When you create a standard business form, it may be easier to edit one of Publisher's preformatted forms from the Building Block Library or to select a Forms page from the Insert Web Page dialog box (Figure 11–11) than it is to start from scratch. The checkbox form controls on Publisher forms are combinations of small rectangles and text boxes permanently grouped together. The text boxes, tables, and lines in other parts of the forms are preformatted to appear and print correctly.

Figure 11–35

Form Controls

Form controls are the individual boxes and buttons used by Web site visitors to enter data. Each form control has editable properties and values that change its appearance and functionality. The data from a form control is transmitted from the visitor to the site owner via a submit button. Publisher supports six types of form controls.

Determine how the form data will be analyzed. Make sure your form controls are the correct type for each piece of data. Determine the properties for each control, such as its return data type, and then make a list of possible values that it can contain. Arrange data entry fields in logical groups on the form and in an order that users would expect. Data entry instructions should be succinct and easy to understand. Ensure that users can change and enter data only in designated areas of the form.

Plan Ahead

A **check box** is a square box that presents a yes/no choice. It displays a check mark or X when selected. Several check boxes may function as a group of related but independent choices. An **option button** or **radio button** is a round button that presents one choice.

When selected, an option button circle is filled in. When grouped, option buttons function like multiple-choice questions — they are mutually exclusive. The difference between an option button and a check box is that users can select only one option button within a group but any number of check boxes. In Publisher, checkbox form controls and option button form controls both display a label you can edit. Furthermore, you can choose to display either form control as selected or not selected at start up.

A **list box** presents a group of items in a list. Visitors can scroll to select from one or any number of choices in the list box. You determine the available choices and the number that may be selected when you set list box properties.

If you want Web visitors to type information in a text box, you insert a **textbox** form control. Sensitive information, such as credit card information or passwords, can be displayed as asterisks or bullets. Textbox form controls are different from regular text box controls that display text entered during the design process. Textbox form controls appear as white boxes, with an insertion point for data entry by the Web user.

A **text area**, or multiline text box, provides a means of entering information by making available to the visitor a larger text box with multiple blank lines. Most Web sites include regular text boxes as instruction labels next to textbox and text area form controls to assist visitors in entering the correct information.

You must include a **submit button** on every form. This button allows visitors to send you their form data. You can create a **reset button** by using a second submit button form control with different properties. Reset buttons are optional, but they provide a simple way to clear form data and allow the Web visitor to start over. A submit button can display any words in its visible label, such as Send or Clear.

Each form control has a set of **properties** or attributes, such as a return data label, text, width, or other settings. These properties change the appearance and functionality of the form control. To edit the properties of a form control, you double-click the control. One of those properties is a logical **return data label**, also called an **internal data label**. This return data label references and identifies the visitor-supplied information when it is submitted to the Web site owner. For instance, a return data label with the word, Course#, could accompany a user-supplied course number in an e-mail submission. Without a return data label, a random number in the e-mail might be hard to decipher.

Labels

Some Publisher form controls do not include text to prompt the Web user for specific kinds of data entry. In these cases, it is appropriate to use a text box, placed close to the form control, as a label. A **label** is an instructive word or words directing the user to enter suitable data. Because the Web form will collect seven pieces of individual information entered by the user, each one needs a label to instruct and assist the user in filling out the form.

Guides help align labels and form controls so that they are displayed in a professional-looking manner on the Web page. The following steps create guides to help align the labels and form controls.

To Create Guides

1 Navigate to Page 4 and zoom to page width.

2 Drag from the horizontal ruler to create a guide at approximately the 384 pixels measurement on the vertical ruler.

3 Drag from the vertical ruler to create a guide at approximately the 272 pixels measurement on the horizontal ruler.

To Create Text Boxes for Labels

You first will create an instructional text box at the top of the page to serve as a heading. Then you will create text boxes to serve as labels for the form controls. The following steps create those text boxes.

- Starting at the left vertical ruler guide, draw a text box under the masthead approximately 470 pixels wide and 32 pixels tall.

- Type `Please select the forms you would like to receive and fill in the information below:` to complete the text.

- Click outside the text box to deselect it (Figure 11–36).

Figure 11–36

- Beginning at the intersection of the guides, drag downward and to the right to draw another text box approximately 85 pixels wide and 25 pixels high.

- Change the font size to 10.

- Select the border of the text box and then press CTRL+C to copy the text box (Figure 11–37).

Figure 11–37

3

- Deselect the text box.

- Press CTRL+V to paste a copy of the text box. Drag the copy below the original so that it snaps to the guide (Figure 11–38).

copy of text box

Figure 11–38

4

- Repeat Steps 2 and 3 to create a total of seven text boxes that will serve as labels, positioning them as shown in Figure 11–39. If necessary, align the text boxes.

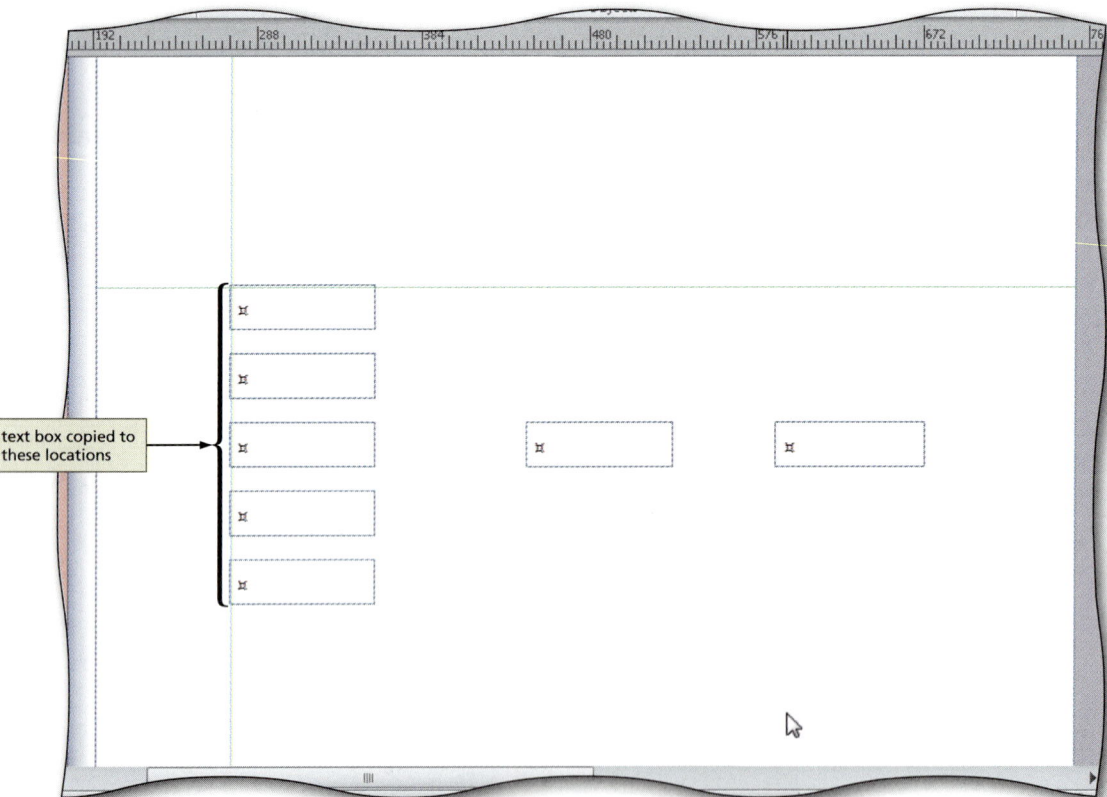

text box copied to these locations

Figure 11–39

To Complete the Labels

The following steps complete the labels by entering text in each of the text boxes.

1 Click inside the first text box and then type **Name:** to enter the text.

2 Click each of the remaining text boxes and type the new label for each, as shown in Figure 11–40.

Figure 11–40

Textbox Form Controls

The Web form contains seven textbox form controls to collect information from customers. These form controls correspond to the seven labels created in the previous steps. By placing textbox form controls close to their labels and by changing the size or width of the controls to approximate the amount of data expected from the user, you can help the user to enter information correctly. Later, you will set properties to provide additional help for users.

Table 11–4 displays the textbox form controls you will use in the Web site.

Table 11–4 Adams County Textbox Form Controls		
Form Control	**Return Data Label**	**Value**
Textbox	name	(none)
Textbox	address	(none)
Textbox	city	(none)
Textbox	state	(none)
Textbox	zip	(none)
Textbox	telephone	(none)
Textbox	email	(none)

To Insert Textbox Form Controls

The following steps insert textbox form controls.

- Display the Web tab.

- Click the Form Controls button (Web tab | Code group) to display the list of form controls (Figure 11–41).

Figure 11–41

- Click Textbox to place a textbox form control in the publication.

- Drag the textbox form control to the right of the Name label.

- Drag a right sizing handle of the textbox form control to create a box that is approximately 250 pixels wide.

- Press CTRL+C to copy the control (Figure 11–42).

Figure 11–42

Q&A

Should I align the textbox form control with the top or bottom of the label?

Align the label and its corresponding textbox form control at their tops. Use the pink layout guides as indicators, or select both objects and use the Align button (Drawing Tools format tab | Arrange group).

3

- Deselect the textbox form control.

- Press CTRL+V six times to create a total of seven textbox form controls, dragging each copy to the right of a label.

- Resize the textbox form controls to approximate the data they will contain from the user. You do not have to be exact.

- Resize, align, and distribute the labels and controls as necessary (Figure 11–43).

each label has a corresponding textbox form control

Figure 11–43

To Edit Textbox Form Control Properties

Recall that each form control has a set of properties or attributes that change the appearance and functionality of the form control, including default text, the number of characters, the capability to hide sensitive information with asterisks, and a return data label.

With a textbox form control, the return data label is an important property. If the data is submitted to a database, the return data label must match the database field name exactly for the data to be stored correctly. If the data is submitted to the Web site owner via e-mail or some other tool, a return data label helps differentiate among the various data fields.

The width of a textbox form control keeps the user from entering too much information. For example, the width of a ZIP code should be less than 10, even if the user enters a dash and the four-digit ZIP code extension. Limiting the user to 10 characters will help assure that he or she is entering the correct data in the correct box. Unless they are set otherwise, a textbox form control allows the user to enter a maximum of 255 characters, no matter how wide the visible box is on the form.

The following steps edit the properties of the textbox form controls by assigning return data labels and setting field widths.

BTW

Return Data Labels

If you plan to use multiple words in your return data labels, do not use spaces. Use an underscore between words, such as return_customer, or use initial caps on each word with no spaces, such as ReturnCustomer. If you are using a previously created database, check with the database administrator for the exact spelling of field names. Some database programs will not accept spaces in field names; consequently, upon submission, Publisher forms that update databases might generate an error if a space were included.

1

- Double-click the textbox form control located to the right of the Name label to display the Text Box Properties dialog box.

- Select the text in the 'Return data with this label' text box and then type **name** to replace the text.

- Do not change the value for the number of allowable characters (Figure 11–44).

Figure 11–44

Q&A

When would I enter a default text value?

You can use the Default text box to include text that might appear inside the form control itself, such as, Please enter your name here. Because you already created labels for each textbox form control, default instruction text is not necessary.

2

- Click the OK button (Text Box Properties dialog box) to set the properties.

3

- Repeat Step 1 and 2 for each of the other textbox form controls. Use the return data labels listed in Table 11–4 on page PUB 657. Allow only two characters for the state textbox form control, only 10 characters for the ZIP code textbox form control, and only 14 characters for the telephone textbox form control.

Other Ways

1. On shortcut menu, click Format Form Properties, enter properties, click OK button (Text Box Properties dialog box)

To Insert a Text Area Form Control

A text area form control allows users to enter multiple lines of text. On the Web, the scroll bar and scroll arrows become active when the text area begins to fill. The Web form will use a text area to allow users to enter additional comments, such as a question or other information.

The following step creates a text area for the form.

BTW

Helping the User
You can help the user enter correct information by assigning the number of characters allowed in a text box and by resizing the text box to be just slightly larger than the allowed number of characters. That way, users will have both a visual and a programmed reminder regarding the appropriate length for data.

BTW

Sensitive Data
The 'Hide sensitive data with asterisks' check box should be selected if the user is entering a password, Social Security number, credit card number, or other sensitive data. This option replaces the information entered by the user with asterisks as he or she types, preventing others from seeing the data. To set a maximum width, you can type numbers directly into the 'Number of characters allowed' box, or use the box arrows to increase or decrease the number.

1
- Click the Form Controls button (Web tab | Code group) and then click Text Area to insert a text area form control.

- Drag the text area form control to a location below the e-mail label and form control, as shown in Figure 11–45.

- Resize the text area to approximately 275 × 75 pixels.

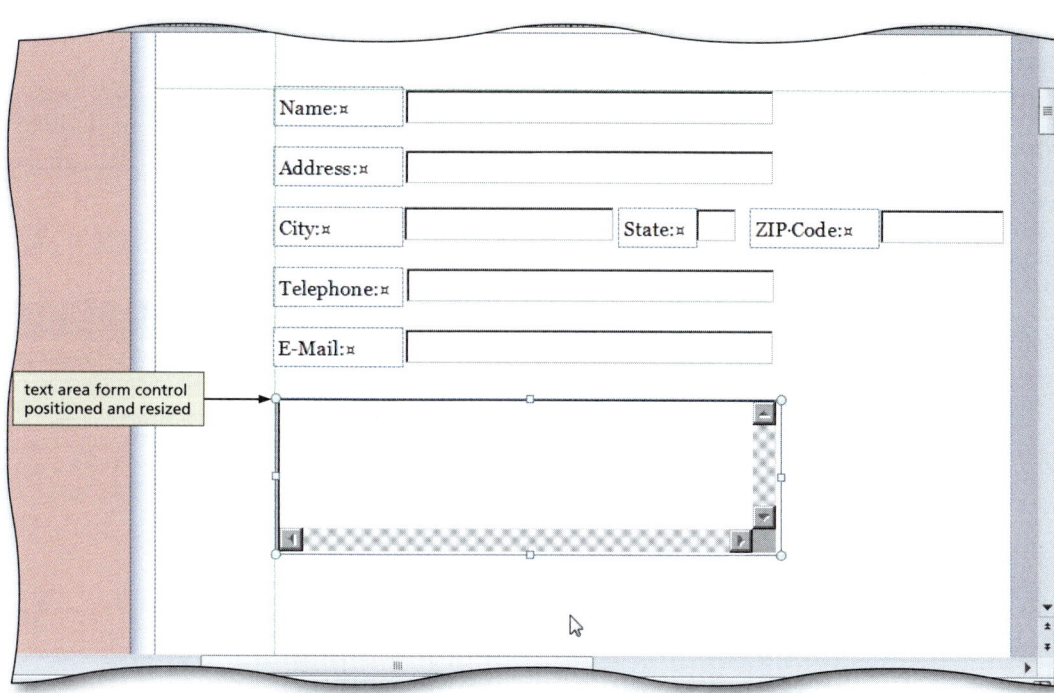

Figure 11–45

To Edit Text Area Form Control Properties

Text Area form control properties include default text and a return data label. The following steps edit the properties to include the text that will appear as the default text.

1
- Double-click the text area form control to display the Text Area Properties dialog box.

- In the Default text text box, type **Enter other comments here.** as the new text.

- Select the text in the 'Return data with this label' text box and then type **comments** to replace the text (Figure 11–46).

2
- Click the OK button (Text Area Properties dialog box) to set the properties.

Figure 11–46

Other Ways

1. On shortcut menu, click Format Form Properties, enter properties, click OK button (Text Area Properties dialog box)

BTW

Checkbox Properties
Text in the Checkbox
value text box will
appear in submitted
data. For example, in
an e-mail message, the
Web site owner would
see the return data label,
incident_report, followed
by the word, Yes. He or
she then would know to
send an incident report
form to the Web site visitor.

Checkbox Form Controls

Publisher provides checkbox form controls to allow users to submit yes and no responses without having to type the words in a text box. Unlike textbox form controls, checkbox form controls come with their own labels. When clicked, the checkbox form control displays a check mark.

Table 11–5 displays the checkbox form controls you will use in the Web site.

Table 11–5 Adams County Checkbox Form Controls		
Form Control	**Return Data Label**	**Value**
Checkbox	immunization_card	Yes
Checkbox	immunization_schedule	Yes
Checkbox	incident_report	Yes
Checkbox	inspection_report	Yes

To Insert Checkbox Form Controls

The following steps create four check boxes for Web site visitors to specify which forms and publications they wish to receive.

- Scroll to a location above the name box.

- Click the Form Controls button (Web tab | Code group) and then click Checkbox to insert a checkbox form control in the publication.

- Drag the checkbox form control so that it snaps to the vertical layout guide at approximately 150 pixels from the top of the page.

- Widen the control to approximately 180 pixels.

- Click to select the text beside the check box.

- Type **Immunization Record Card** to replace the text (Figure 11–47).

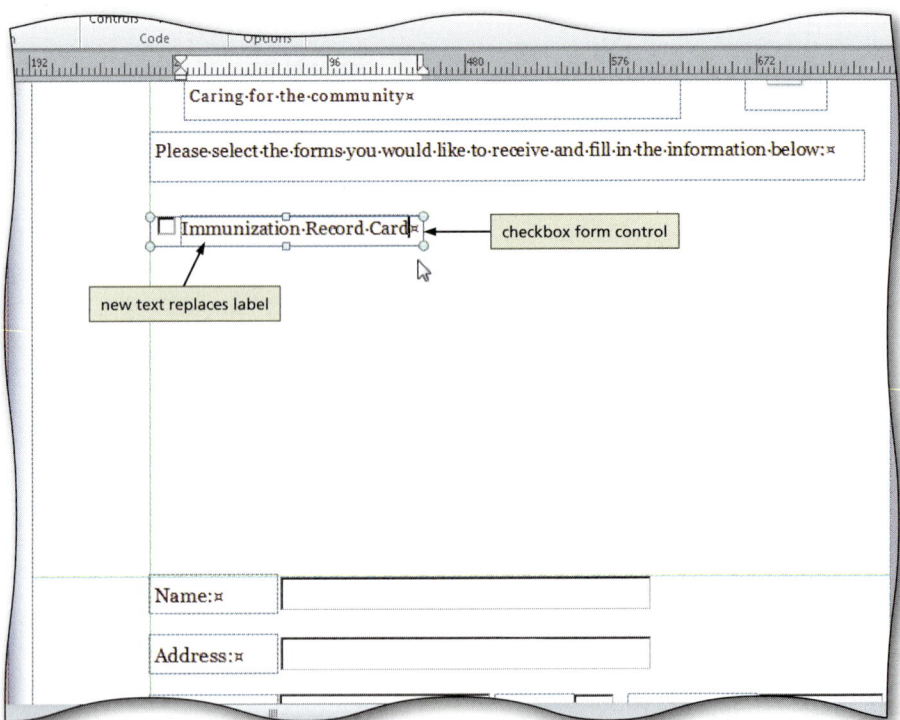

Figure 11–47

2

- Repeat Step 1 to create three additional checkbox form controls with the words Immunization Schedule, Incident Report Form, and Inspection Request.

- Position the checkbox form controls below each other. Align and distribute as necessary (Figure 11–48).

Q&A

Could I use option button form controls for these user decisions?

No, because you want the user to be able to check as many of the forms as they desire. Option button form controls would limit them to only one choice in the group.

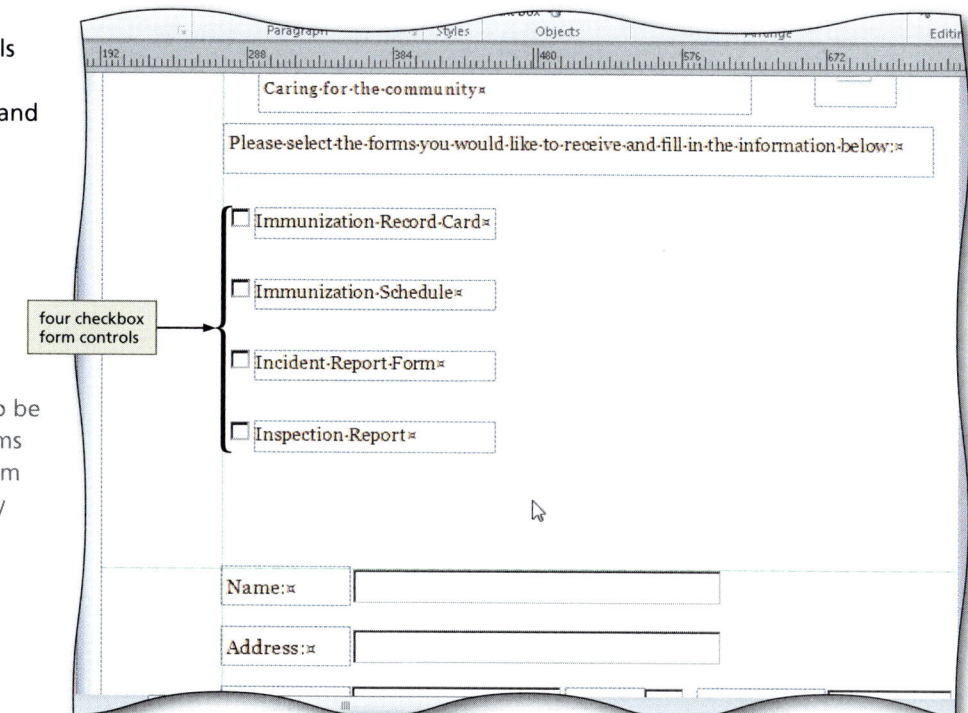

Figure 11–48

To Edit Checkbox Form Control Properties

Checkbox form control properties include the capability to display the check box as selected or not selected, a return data label, and a checkbox value. The checkbox value accompanies the return data label when the form is submitted. By specifying a value such as checked, true, or yes, the Web site owner knows the information is from the checkbox form control and knows whether it contains a check mark.

Checkbox form controls are grouped objects in Publisher, consisting of a check box and a label. Therefore, when editing the properties, you must double-click the box portion of the control rather than its text label to display the Checkbox Properties dialog box.

The following steps edit the checkbox form control properties.

1

- Select the first checkbox form control. Double-click the small check box to display the Checkbox Properties dialog box.

- Select the text in the 'Return data with this label' text box and then type **immunization_card** to replace the text.

- If necessary, type **Yes** in the Checkbox value text box (Checkbox Properties dialog box) to assign the value (Figure 11–49).

Figure 11–49

Q&A

Do I need to use an underscore between words?

If the data from the Web form updates a database, the return data label must match the database field name exactly for the data to be stored correctly. The underscore enhances readability while following the rule that database field names may not contain a space.

Q&A

When would it be appropriate to choose Selected?

The Selected option button is used to display a check mark in the check box when Web site visitors first view the form. You might want to display a selected check box to encourage visitors to inquire about specific options or if it is the owner's practice to include information by default.

2

- Click the OK button to close the dialog box.

3

- Repeat Steps 1 and 2 for the other checkbox form controls. Use the return data labels listed in Table 11–5 on page PUB 662.

- If necessary, enter **Yes** for the checkbox value.

To Insert Option Button Form Controls

Publisher provides option button form controls to allow users to make one choice from a group of options. Like checkbox form controls, option button form controls provide their own labels. When selected, the option button form control displays a filled-in circle or bullet.

Publisher groups multiple option button form controls automatically so that users may select only one. For example, visitors to the Web site can specify that they are residents of the county or nonresidents, but not both.

The following steps create two option buttons that will indicate whether the user is a resident of the county.

1

- Click the Form Controls button (Web tab | Code group) and then click Option Button.

- When the Option Button form control is inserted in the publication, drag it to the right of the first checkbox form control.

- Click the label text and then type **Resident of Adams County** to replace the text.

- Resize the form control as necessary to display all of the text (Figure 11–50).

Figure 11–50

2

- Create another option button form control just below the first one. Use the words **Nonresident** as the label (Figure 11–51).

3

- Align and resize the controls as necessary.

Figure 11–51

To Edit Option Button Form Control Properties

Option button form control properties include the capability to display the option button as selected or not selected, a return data label, and an option button value.

A special consideration with option button form controls is their logical grouping. At times, you may want to use multiple groups of option buttons. For example, a Web site that sells T-shirts might need option button groupings for size, for color, and for neckline. Because option buttons are mutually exclusive, selecting a color could turn off a previously selected size, unless you specify the logical grouping. To group the buttons logically, Publisher requires that you use the same return data label for each member within a group. The option button value identifies the member in the group and accompanies the return data label when the form is submitted. Typically, the option button value is a word that describes the selected option button.

The following steps edit the option button form control properties.

BTW

Check Boxes and Option Buttons
Check boxes and option buttons are grouped objects in Publisher; that is, the physical box or button is grouped with an accompanying text box label. To ungroup or regroup them, select them and then press CTRL+SHIFT+G.

BTW

Return Data Values
The return data value for option buttons is a string, or alphabetic value. Therefore, if your form data is going to populate a database, the database field must be declared as a string. Check boxes can return either strings or numbers, typically 0 for off and 1 for on, when the check box data is transferred to a database.

- Select the first option button form control. Double-click the circular option button to display the Option Button Properties dialog box.

- Select the text in the 'Return data with this label' box, and then type **customer_type** to replace the text.

- Select the text in the 'Option button value' box, and then type **resident** to replace the text (Figure 11–52).

Q&A Why does the 'Return data with this label' box display a box arrow?

You might have multiple groups of option buttons, each group with a different name. The box arrow allows you to choose in which group the button should belong.

Figure 11–52

- Click the OK button (Option Button Properties dialog box) to set the properties.

- Select the Nonresident option button form control. Double-click the circular option button to display the Option Button Properties dialog box.

- Click the 'Return data with this label' box arrow, and then click customer_type in the list.

- Select the text in the 'Option button value' text box and then type **nonresident** to replace the text (Figure 11–53).

Q&A When will the Option button value be used?

Text in the Option button value box will appear in submitted data. For example, in an e-mail, the Web site owner would see the return data label, customer_type, followed by the word, nonresident, and thus know how to reply.

Figure 11–53

- Click the OK button (Option Button Properties dialog box) to set the properties.

To Insert a List Box Form Control

A list box form control offers users one or more specific choices displayed in a boxed area. Designers use a list box rather than grouped option buttons when the choices are related closely, such as a list of quantities; when the list is long, such as a list of states; or when users may make more than one choice from the list. You can customize list boxes with item text, initial selections, and return values that can be updated and reordered easily. List boxes can display multiple choices, or they can be resized to display only one choice. In that case, they are considered drop-down list boxes; users must click a box arrow to display additional choices.

The following step creates a list box with a box arrow to gather information from users regarding how they want information sent to them.

1

- Click the Form Controls button (Web tab | Code group) and then click List Box to create a list box on the page.

- Drag the list box form control to a location below the option button form controls.

- Drag the lower-center sizing handle upward, until the list box form control displays only Item One to create a drop-down list box (Figure 11–54).

Q&A

What is the difference between a list box and a drop-down list box?

Publisher's term, list box, refers to both kinds of choice boxes. The height of the list box you create determines how many choices will display. Typically, a list box displays many of its choices on the screen — as many as will fit within the size of the control. If you resize the control to display only one choice at a time, it becomes a drop-down list box with a box arrow to display the rest of the choices.

Figure 11–54

To Edit List Box Form Control Properties

List box form control properties include the return data label, the ability to choose more than one item in the list, and several appearance options, including the ability to edit the choices, create new choices, and move the choices in the list. The width of the list box form control adjusts to accommodate the longest entry in the list.

Like option buttons, the return data label is the same for all items in the list. When the form is submitted, the Web site owner can determine which item the user chose simply by looking at the item's value. You also can decide if individual items should appear as selected.

The following steps edit the list box form control properties.

Drop-Down List Boxes

If you resize your list box form control to display only one item, the item always will be the original Item One from your list, even if you rearrange the items. If you no longer want the item to appear first, delete it and add another one. Then click the Move Up button (List Box Properties dialog box) to position the new item at the top.

1

- Double-click the list box to display the List Box Properties dialog box.

- Select the text in the 'Return data with this label' text box and then type `contact_method` to replace the text.

- In the Appearance area, select Item One (Figure 11–55).

Figure 11–55

2

- Click the Modify button to display the Add/Modify List Box Item dialog box.

- In the Item text box, type `How do you wish to be contacted?` to replace the text (Figure 11–56).

Q&A Why am I including directions or instructions in the list of contact methods?

Using instructions as the first item in the list will cause the instructions to display on the Web page, even if a person does not click the box arrow. The Web site owner will be able to determine if the visitor answered the question or left it at the default value.

Figure 11–56

3

- Click the OK button (Add/Modify List Box Item dialog box) to apply the settings.

- In the Appearance area, select Item Two and then click the Modify button to display the Add/Modify List Box Item dialog box.

- In the Item text box, type `via e-mail` to replace the text (Figure 11–57).

Q&A When will the Item value be used?

Text in the Item value text box will appear in the submitted data. For example, in an e-mail message, the Web site owner would see the return data label, contact_type, followed by the words, on the Radio, and thus know his or her radio marketing has been effective.

Figure 11–57

4

- Click the OK button (Add/Modify List Box Item dialog box) to apply the settings.

- Edit the third item to create a choice labeled, via U.S. mail.

- Click the Add button (List Box Properties Dialog box) to create a fourth item labeled, via telephone (Figure 11–58).

What are the other tools in the List Box Properties dialog box?

The 'User can select more than one item' check box allows users to CTRL+click to select multiple items in a list box that displays multiple items. The Move Up and Move Down buttons allow you to rearrange items in the list.

Figure 11–58

5

- Click the OK button (List Box Properties dialog box) to set the properties.

- Reposition the control as necessary (Figure 11–59).

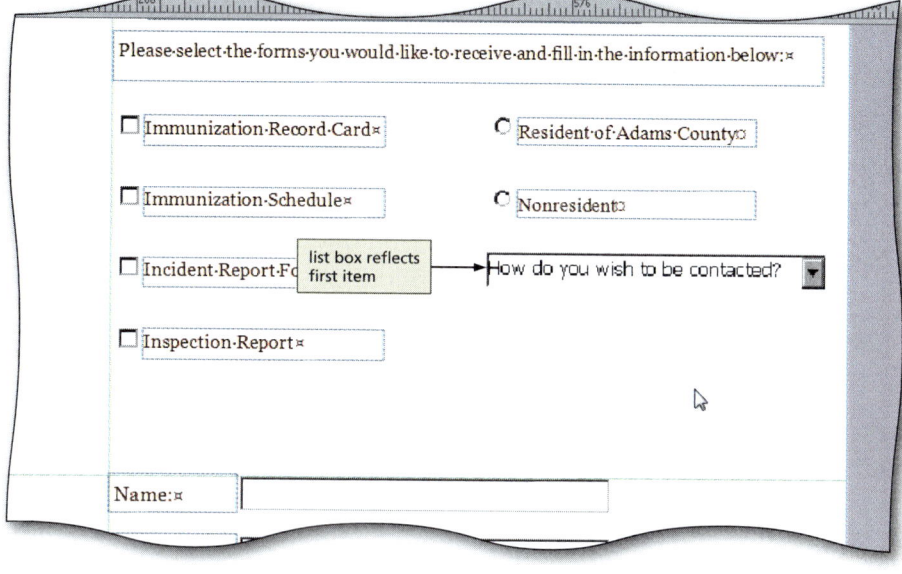

Figure 11–59

Other Ways

1. On shortcut menu, click Format Form Properties, enter properties, click OK button (List Box Properties dialog box)

To Insert Submit Form Controls

A submit form control creates a Submit button, which the user clicks to submit data from all controls on the form. Three kinds of submission are available: saving the data in a file on the Web server, sending the data via e-mail, and using a program provided by an Internet service provider (ISP).

Adams County Department of Health wants the data from the Web form sent via e-mail, and wants a second button labeled Reset, which will allow users to clear previous entries. The submit button form control is a special kind of command button used to issue commands in a graphical user interface. You can tailor the button by changing its caption and its type or purpose. The two available types of command buttons in Publisher are Submit and Reset. The following steps create these two buttons.

1

- Scroll to a location below the comments box.

- Click the Form Controls button (Web tab | Code group) and then click Submit to display the Command Button Properties dialog box.

- If necessary, click the Submit option button to select it (Figure 11–60).

Q&A Can I add a picture to the button?

Yes. If you click the Image check box (Command Button Properties dialog box), you can browse to select a picture file that becomes a clickable button when the Web page is displayed in a browser. You cannot combine words and pictures on a button unless the picture file already contains the words. Pictures or graphics with plain backgrounds and distinctive shapes work best. You may need to resize the graphic once it is inserted into the publication.

Figure 11–60

2

- Click the OK button to place the control on the page.

- Drag to reposition the Submit button to a location below the comments area, as shown in Figure 11–61.

Q&A Can I change the words on the button?

Yes. If you remove the check mark in the 'Button text is same as button type' check box (Command Button Properties dialog box), you can type new text in the Button text text box.

Figure 11–61

- Click the Form Controls button (Web tab | Code group) and then click Submit to display the Command Button Properties dialog box.

- Click the Reset option button to select it (Figure 11–62).

Figure 11–62

4

- Click the OK button (Command Button Properties dialog box) to place the control on the page.

- Drag to reposition the Reset button to the right of the Submit button, as shown in Figure 11–63.

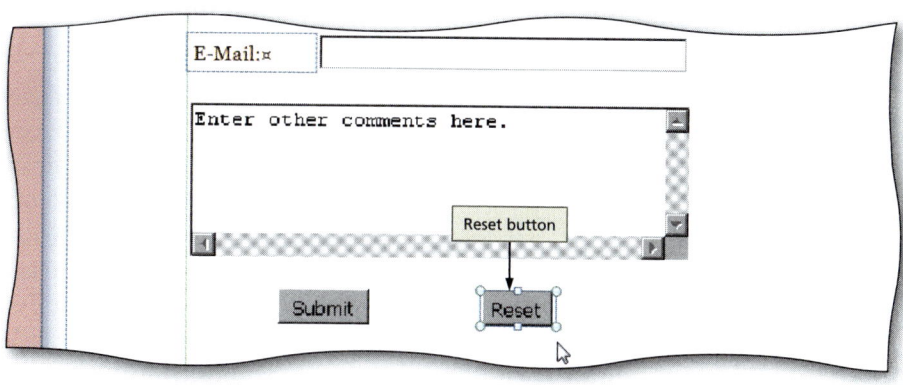

Figure 11–63

To Edit Form Properties

Form properties include specifying the data retrieval method and entering data retrieval information. The following steps edit form properties.

1

- Double-click the submit button form control to display the Command Button Properties dialog box.

- Click the Form Properties button to display the Form Properties dialog box (Figure 11–64).

 Experiment

- Click each of the option buttons to view what type of data is needed for each of the retrieval methods.

Figure 11–64

2

- Select the 'Send data to me in e-mail' option button to display the settings.

- Select the text in the 'Send data to this e-mail address' box, and then type **info@adamscountydoh .org** to replace the text (Figure 11–65).

3

- Click the OK button (Form Properties dialog box) to set the form properties.

- Click the OK button (Command Button Properties dialog box) to return to the publication.

Figure 11–65

Other Ways

1. In any properties dialog box, click Form Properties button, choose data retrieval method (Form Properties Dialog box), enter settings, click OK button

BTW

The Reset Command Button
The Reset command button in Publisher automatically restores all fields back to their original or default values. Publisher clears the text boxes and text areas or restores their default text. Check boxes and option buttons are reset, and list boxes display their default settings. If a choice originally was set to be displayed as selected, it will appear selected again when the user clicks the Reset button, no matter what choices were made originally.

Web Hot Spots

To facilitate user interaction, Web pages also may contain hot spots. Recall that a hot spot is a location other than text that contains a hyperlink, typically a graphic, picture, or other identifiable area. Users may click the hot spot in the same way they click other hyperlinks.

When viewing a Web page with a browser, the mouse pointer changes to a hand when positioned on a hot spot. The change in the mouse pointer icon is called a **mouse-over event**. Events are an integral part of the object-oriented concepts used in Web technology. Even the click of a hyperlink or button is considered an event.

To Insert a Web Hot Spot

The following steps create a hot spot for the masthead at the top of the page. Users of the form will be able to click the masthead to send an e-mail to the company.

1
- Navigate to Page 1.
- Scroll to the top of the page layout and zoom to page width.
- Click the Hot Spot button (Web tab | Web Page Navigation group) and then drag a rectangle that includes the entire masthead.
- When Publisher displays the Insert Hyperlink dialog box, click the E-mail Address button in the Link to bar.
- Type `info@ adamscounty .org` in the E-Mail address text box.
- Press the TAB key and then type `E-mail from the Web Site Masthead` in the Subject text box (Figure 11–66).

2
- Click the OK button to close the dialog box.

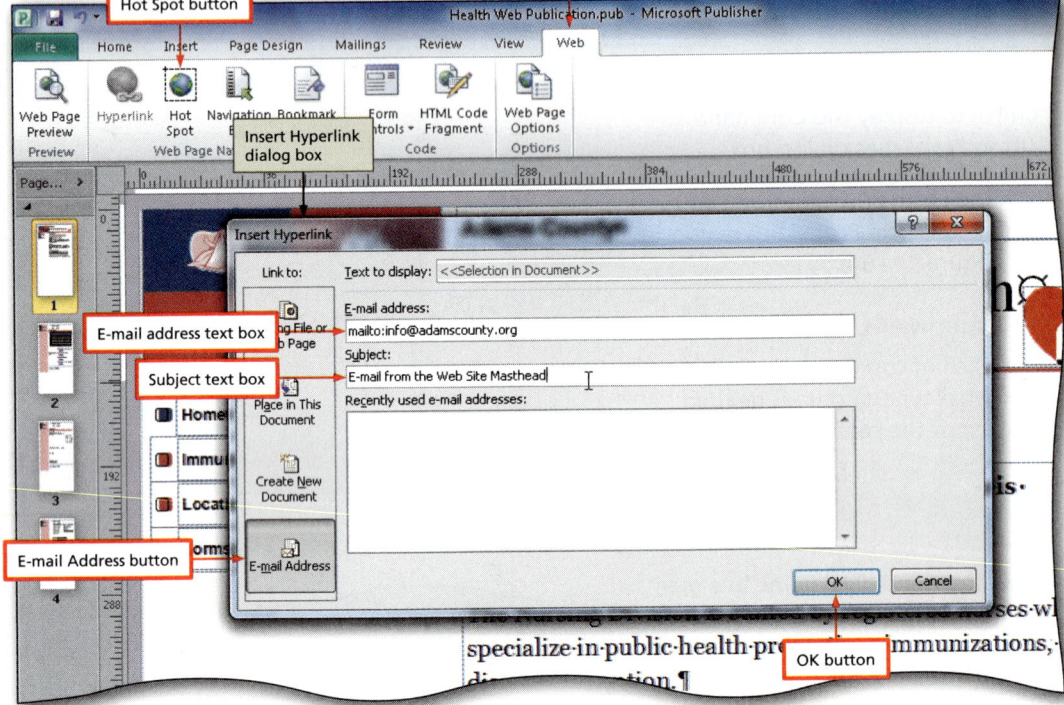

Figure 11–66

Other Ways

1. Select desired graphic, click Insert Hyperlink button (Web tab | Web Page Navigation group), select settings, click OK button (Insert Hyperlink dialog box)

2. Select desired graphic, press CTRL+K, select settings, click OK button (Insert Hyperlink dialog box)

HTML Code Fragments

An **HTML code fragment** is code that you add to your Web page to create features such as a counter, a scrolling marquee, or advanced data collection objects. Publisher does not supply HTML code fragments. You must have the correct HTML code to insert into the HTML code fragment object.

Creating a Scrolling Marquee

The Adams County Department of Health wants a scrolling message to remind visitors of the telephone number, but it wants to limit the number of scrolls so that the message does not become annoying. The following steps insert an HTML code fragment to create a scrolling marquee. A **scrolling marquee** is an animation technique that displays text that scrolls across the screen.

HTML code fragments appear as code in a frame on the Web page. The result of the HTML code appears when you preview or publish your Web page, as shown in the next steps. The text will scroll from the right side of the screen to the left, displaying in the width of the HTML Code Fragment box.

Table 11–6 lists the HTML code lines and their purposes.

Table 11–6 HTML Code	
HTML Code	**Purpose**
`<font size="5" face="courier" color=red>`	Opens font tag and sets face and color
`<marquee behavior=scroll loop=3>`	Opens marquee tag and sets behavior
`For more information, call Adams County Department of Health at (731) 555-9222...`	Sets text
`</marquee></font>`	Closes settings

To Insert an HTML Code Fragment

The following steps insert an HTML code fragment to display a scrolling marquee across the top of the home page, just below the masthead.

1
- Click the HTML Code Fragment button (Web tab | Code group) to display the Edit HTML Code Fragment dialog box.

- Enter the HTML code that is displayed in the first column of Table 11–6, making certain you press the ENTER key at the end of each line (Figure 11–67).

Q&A Can I copy HTML code from the Web?

Yes. Many Web sites offer free code fragments for a variety of purposes. Make sure you understand what actions the code performs, and ensure that it is from a trusted source. Also make sure that the code has no copyright restrictions.

Figure 11–67

2

- Click the OK button to close the dialog box. If Publisher displays a dialog box containing a message about HTML tags, click the No button.

- Drag the HTML Code Fragment object to a location just below the Department of Health heading.

- Resize the HTML Code Fragment object to fill the area below the heading as shown in Figure 11–68.

Q&A

What if I make a mistake while typing the HTML code?

Errors in HTML code fragments may cause performance or security problems for your Web site. Publisher does not verify HTML code fragments for accuracy or security. You can always double-click the control and fix your errors.

Figure 11–68

BTW

Server Settings
In order for the submit button to work properly on the Web, your Internet service provider (ISP) must support Microsoft FrontPage version 3.0 or later server extensions. If you are unsure whether your ISP supports the extensions, contact your ISP or ask your instructor for more information about your school's Web hosting policy and servers.

To Save the Publication with Completed Form Controls

Now that the form is complete, it is a good time to save the publication again. The following step saves the publication.

1 With a USB flash drive connected to one of the computer's USB ports, click the Save button on the Quick Access Toolbar to save the publication again with the same name.

Plan Ahead

Test the form. Be sure that the form works as you intended. Fill in the form as if you were a user. Have others fill in the form to be sure it is organized in a logical manner and is easy to understand and complete. Correct any errors or weaknesses in the form and test the form again. Finally, publish the form on the Web.

To Preview and Test a Web Site

In the following steps, you will preview the Web site. You will view the animation, listen to the background sound if your system has speakers, test the navigation bar, view all the pages, enter data into the Web form, check the scrolling marquee, and test the hot spot and Reset button.

1

- Click the Web Page Preview button (Web tab | Preview group) to display the Web site in a browser.

- If necessary, maximize the browser window (Figure 11–69).

Q&A

Why does my marquee display incorrectly?

If you do not see the scrolling text or if it appears incorrectly, there are several possible reasons. You may have made errors in typing the HTML code, or the HTML code fragment might overlap another object. Additionally, different browsers interpret HTML in different ways, with potentially varying results.

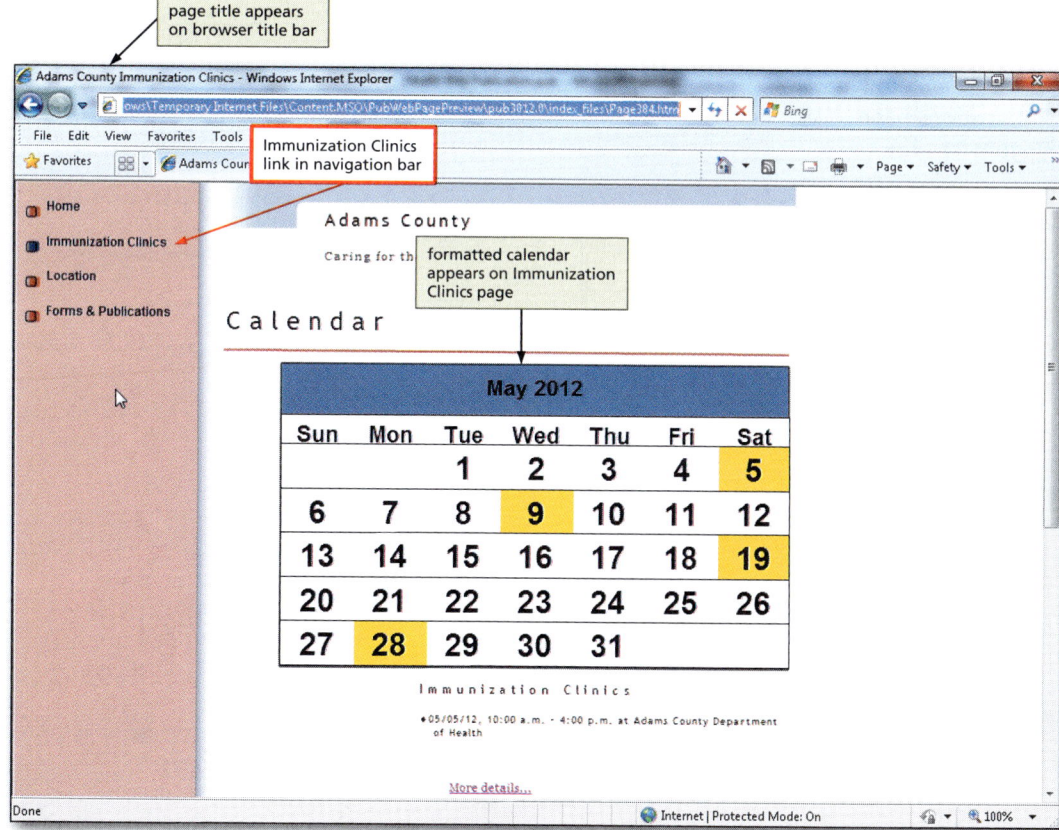

Figure 11–69

Experiment

- Point to the masthead to see the mouse pointer change to a hand over the hot spot.

2

- Click Immunization Clinics in the navigation bar to display the Immunization Clinics page (Figure 11–70).

Experiment

- Scroll as necessary to view the page.

Figure 11–70

3

- Click Location in the navigation bar to display the Location page (Figure 11–71).

🔍 **Experiment**

- Scroll as necessary to view the page.

page title appears on browser title bar

Locations link

Figure 11–71

4

- Click Forms & Publications in the navigation bar to display the Forms & Publications page (Figure 11–72).

Forms & Publications link

page title appears on browser title bar

Figure 11–72

5

- Click a check box, select an option, and click the list box arrow (Figure 11–73).

Q&A Will the Submit button work?

It is possible to enter text, make choices, and click the Reset button in the Web page preview; however, the Submit button will not work until the Web page is uploaded to an appropriate server.

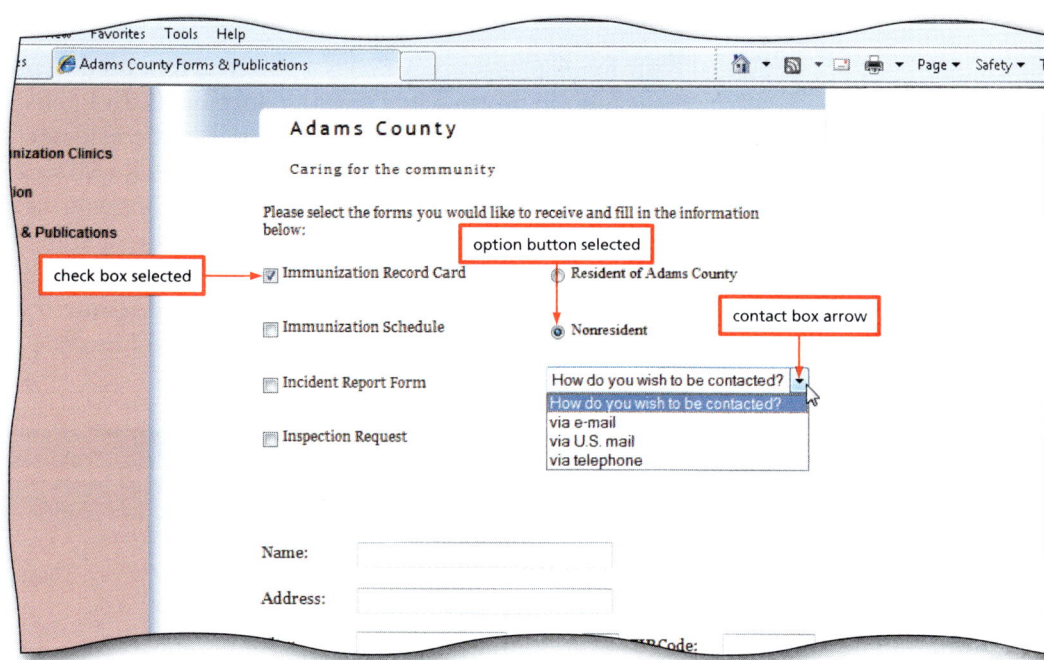

Figure 11–73

6

- Click the Reset button to reset all of the form controls (Figure 11–74).

Experiment

- Enter your name and address in the appropriate boxes. Type a comment in the text area form control. When you are finished, click the Reset button.

7

- Click the Close button on the browser title bar to close the window.

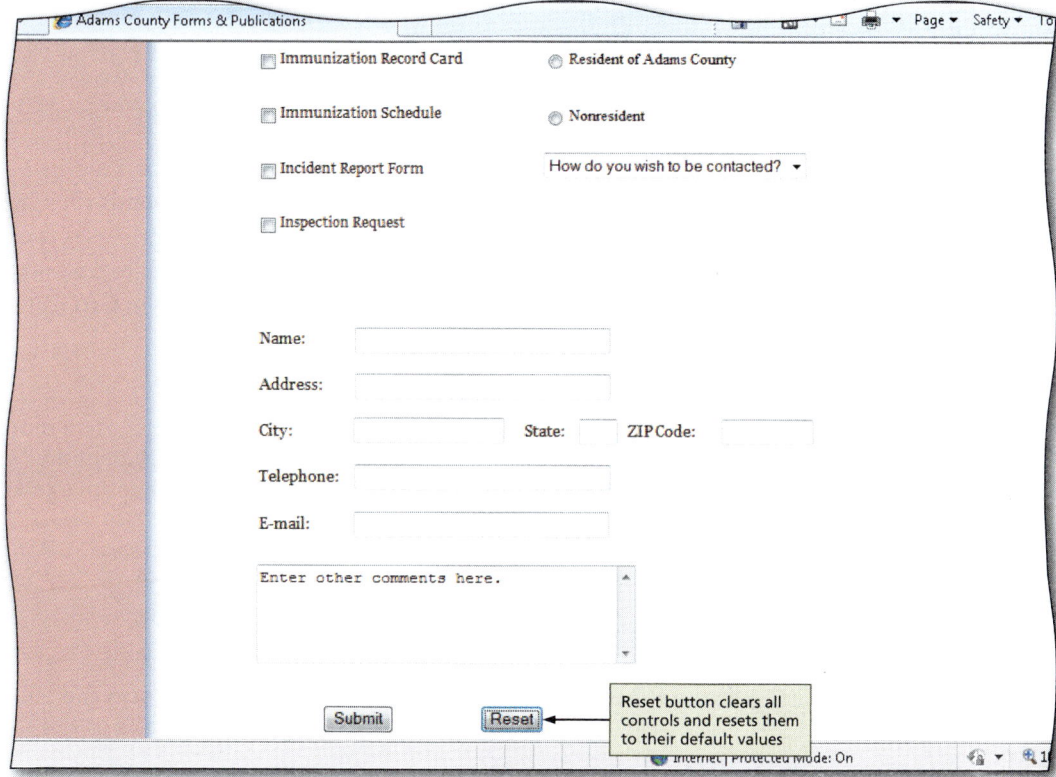

Figure 11–74

Visual Basic for Applications

Visual Basic for Applications (VBA) is a powerful tool used to program how Publisher and other applications perform while creating documents. In Publisher, VBA provides you with the ability to run macros, write procedures, and create new menus and buttons.

A **macro** is a procedure made up of VBA code. Recall that a procedure is a precise, step-by-step series of instructions. In some applications, you can create new macros by recording keystrokes of common tasks that you wish to automate. In Publisher, you can run macros recorded elsewhere or program the macros yourself.

Publisher has seven prenamed macros, called **document events**, which execute automatically when a certain event occurs. Table 11–7 lists the name and function of these document events.

BTW

Other Macros
You can modify the procedure or event associated with any command on Publisher's Ribbon, and you can create custom tabs, groups, and shortcut menus using VBA. VBA is an extensive programming language with a detailed Help library. To find out more about functions you can use in document events, type `document events` in the 'Type a question for help' box on the right of the Microsoft Visual Basic menu bar.

Table 11–7 Document Events	
Macro Name	**Runs**
BeforeClose	Immediately before any open publication closes.
ShapesAdded	When one or more new shapes are added to a publication. This event occurs whether shapes are added manually or via program code.
Undo	When a user undoes the last action performed.
Redo	When reversing the last action that was undone.
Open	When you open a publication containing the macro.
ShapesRemoved	When a shape is deleted from a publication.
WizardAfterChange	After the user chooses an option in the wizard pane that changes any of the following settings in the publication: page layout (page size, fold type, orientation, label product), print setup (paper size or print tiling), adding or deleting objects, adding or deleting pages, or object or page formatting (size, position, fill, border, background, default text, text formatting).

The name you use for an automatic macro depends on when you want certain actions to occur. In this project, when a Publisher user closes the Health Web Publication, you want a message box to appear, reminding the user to upload the appropriate files to the Web. Thus, you will see how to create a BeforeClose macro using the Visual Basic Editor.

Plan Ahead | **Add macros to automate tasks.** A macro is a shortcut to a more complicated task. Using VBA, a powerful programming language included with Publisher, you can customize and extend the capabilities of Publisher. Add macros for repetitive tasks or to automate procedures and format results.

To Display the Developer Tab

The following steps edit the Ribbon settings to display the Developer tab on the Ribbon.

1

- Display the Backstage view and then click the Options button to display the Publisher Options dialog box.

- Click Customize Ribbon in the left pane.

- In the Main Tabs list, click to display a check mark in the Developer check box (Figure 11–75).

Figure 11–75

2

- Click the OK button (Publisher Options dialog box) to accept the setting change.

- Click Developer on the Ribbon to display the Developer tab (Figure 11–76).

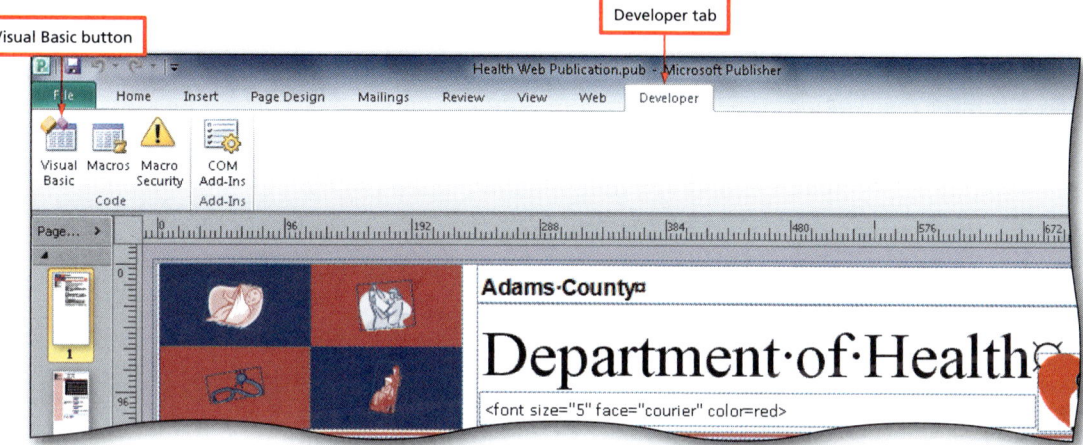

Figure 11–76

Using the Visual Basic Editor

The **Visual Basic Editor** is a full-screen editor that allows you to enter a procedure by typing lines of VBA code as if you were using word processing software. VBA displays a **code window** in which you may choose document events and type code.

Because the code window is similar to a text box or word processor window, at the end of a line, you press the ENTER key or use the down arrow key to move to the next line. If you make a mistake in a code statement, you can use the ARROW keys and the DELETE or BACKSPACE keys to correct it. You also can move the insertion point to lines requiring corrections.

To Open the VBA Code Window

The following step opens the VBA coding window. The document event will apply only to the current publication. Other publications will not have access to the macro created in this publication.

- Click the Visual Basic button (Developer tab | Code group) to open the Microsoft Visual Basic window.

- If necessary, double-click the Microsoft Visual Basic title bar to maximize the window.

- If the Project window does not appear, click View on the menu bar and then click Project Explorer.

- In the Project window, if a plus sign appears next to Project (Health Web Publication.pub), click the plus sign.

- If a plus sign appears next to Microsoft Office Publisher Objects, click the plus sign.

Figure 11–77

- Double-click ThisDocument to open the code window (Figure 11–77).

Other Ways

1. Press ALT+F11

Entering Code Statements and Comments

The BeforeClose event in the Health Web Publication includes a code statement that calls a function called MsgBox. A **function** is a keyword, already programmed in VBA, which activates a procedure. The **MsgBox function** displays a message in a dialog box and then waits for the user to click a button. In its simplest forms, the code statement includes the function keyword, MsgBox, and the text that will appear in the message box enclosed in quotation marks. VBA programmers use a message box to display copyright information about a publication, remind users to save publications in a certain location, or let Web users know their submission was complete.

Adding comments before and within a procedure helps you remember the purpose of the macro and its code statements later. **Comments** begin with the keyword, Rem, or an apostrophe (') and are displayed in green in the code window. Comments have no effect on the execution of a procedure; they simply provide information about the procedure, such as its name and description.

To Program a BeforeClose Event

The following steps insert a comment and code statement in the BeforeClose event. VBA provides beginning and ending code statements for document event procedures. To enhance readability, it is common practice to indent comments and code within these statements.

1

- In the Project window, click the Object box arrow and then click Document in the list to choose the object.

- Click the Procedure box arrow and then click BeforeClose in the list to choose the procedure to code (Figure 11–78).

Q&A Why did Publisher create two procedures?

The beginning and ending code statements for the BeforeClose and Open procedures appear in the code window. Publisher automatically displays the Open procedure, but it will have no effect on this publication.

Figure 11–78

2

- Press the TAB key. Type **'When the publication closes, a reminder message box will be displayed.** and then press the ENTER key to enter the comment line.

- Type **MsgBox "Remember to upload this file to the Web site."** to complete the code (Figure 11–79).

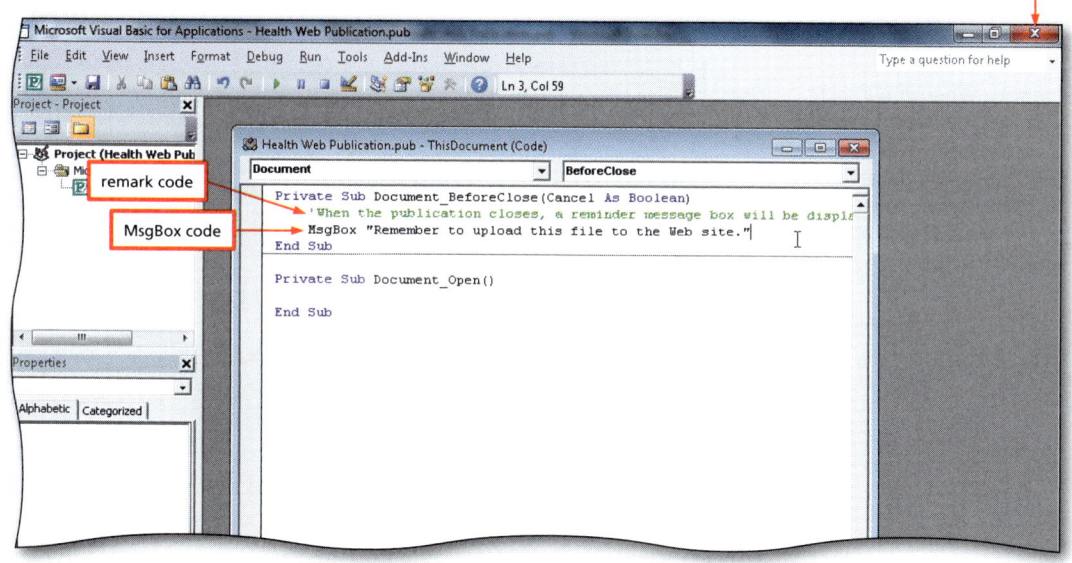

Figure 11–79

Q&A Why did I press the TAB key?

Pressing the TAB key indents the lines of code. The TAB key has no effect on how the code executes; it merely aids in readability.

3

- Click the Close button on the Microsoft Visual Basic for Applications title bar to close the VBA code window.

Security Levels

A **computer virus** is a potentially damaging computer program designed to affect, or infect, your computer negatively by altering the way it works without your knowledge or permission. Currently, more than one million known computer viruses exist, and new viruses are discovered each day. The increased use of networks, the Internet, and e-mail has accelerated the spread of computer viruses.

<table>
<tr><td>**Plan
Ahead**</td><td>**Incorporate security in a document.** Digital signatures and security levels are two ways that Publisher helps you secure your documents. Be sure to notify all parties who open your document or publish your Web pages that you have implemented security features.</td></tr>
</table>

To combat this problem, most computer users run antivirus programs that search for viruses and destroy them before they ever have a chance to infect the computer. Macros are a known carrier of viruses because of the ease with which a person can write code for a macro. For this reason, you can reduce the chance your computer will be infected with a macro virus by setting a **security level** in Publisher. Security levels allow you to enable or disable macros. An **enabled macro** is a macro that Publisher will execute, and a **disabled macro** is a macro that is unavailable to Publisher.

Table 11–8 summarizes the four available security levels in Publisher.

Digital Signatures
Several companies provide authenticated, certified digital signatures via the Web. Digital signatures are encrypted code attached to electronic communications to verify the sender's identity. When you attach a digital signature to a macro project, Publisher will display the digital signature when the user of the file is asked to enable macros.

Table 11–8 Publisher Security Levels	
Security Level	**Condition**
Very High	Publisher will execute only macros installed in trusted locations. All other signed and unsigned macros are disabled when the publication is opened.
High	Publisher will execute only macros that are digitally signed. All other macros are disabled when the publication is opened.
Medium	Upon opening a publication that contains macros from an unknown source, Publisher displays a dialog box asking if you wish to enable the macros.
Low	Publisher turns off macro virus protection. The publication is opened with all macros enabled, including those from unknown sources.

Setting Security Levels in Publisher

If Publisher security is set to very high or high and you attach a macro to a publication, Publisher will disable the macro when you open the publication. Because you will create a macro with VBA code in this project, you should ensure that your security level is set to medium. Thus, each time you open this Publisher publication or any other document that contains a macro from an unknown source, Publisher displays a dialog box warning that a macro is attached and allows you to enable or disable the macros. If you are confident of the source (author) of the publication and macros, you should click the Enable button in the dialog box. If you are uncertain about the reliability of the source of the publication and macros, you should click the Disable button.

To Set a Security Level in Publisher

The following steps set Publisher's security level.

 1

- Click the Macro Security button (Developer tab | Code group) to display the Trust Center dialog box.

- If necessary, click Macro Settings in the left pane to display the macro options.

- If necessary, click the 'Disable all macros with notification' option button (Figure 11–80).

 2

- Click the OK button (Trust Center dialog box) to apply the settings.

Figure 11–80

Completing the Web Site

To complete the Web site, the final tasks are to check for spelling and design errors, save the publication as both a Publisher publication and as a Web file, and then test the macro.

Checking for Spelling and Design Errors

Recall that Publisher's Design Checker scans the publication for overlapping errors and large graphics that may prevent the page from loading quickly on the Web.

The following steps check for spelling errors, run the Design Checker, and save the publication with the same file name.

To Check the Publication and Save Again

1 Click the Spelling button (Review tab | Proofing group). If Publisher flags any words that are misspelled, fix them.

2 When Publisher asks to check the entire publication, click the Yes button.

3 When Publisher displays a dialog box saying that the spelling check is complete, click the OK button, and then fix any other errors.

4 Display the Backstage view and then click the Run Design Checker button. If the Design Checker identifies any errors, fix them.

5 Close the Design Checker task pane.

6 With a USB flash drive connected to one of the computer's USB ports, click the Save button on the Quick Access Toolbar to save the publication again with the same name.

To Save the Web Site Files

The following steps create Web files to upload to a server.

1 With a USB flash drive connected to one of the computer's USB ports, display the Backstage view and then click the Save & Send tab.

2 Click the Publish HTML tab and then click the Publish HTML button to display the Publish to the Web dialog box.

3 If necessary, type **index.htm** in the File name text box (Figure 11–81).

4 If necessary, navigate to the desired save location (in this case, the Publisher folder in the CIS 101 folder [or your class folder] on the USB flash drive). Click the Save button (Publish to the Web dialog box).

Figure 11–81

Testing the Web Site

After you have published to the Web, you should test your electronic form to make sure it functions as you intended and returns the form data to you. To receive results, change the e-mail address to your own in the Form Properties dialog box (Figure 11–65 on page PUB 671).

TO CHECK FORM CONTROLS FOR ACCURACY

If you wanted to check the form for accuracy, you would perform the following steps.

1. See your instructor for ways to upload your Web files to a server.
2. Use a browser to locate your Web site on the Web.
3. Enter information into several of the text boxes and click one of the option buttons.
4. Click the Reset button.
5. Complete the electronic form. As you use the form, make sure the controls work as you intended.
6. Click the Submit button.
7. Verify that you received the data you entered. If you did not, contact your Internet service provider and ask about their ability to support Microsoft FrontPage server extensions, version 3.0 or above.
8. Check the data to make sure you understand the format in which the responses were returned to you.

To Hide the Developer Tab

The following steps hide the Developer tab so it no longer appears on the Ribbon.

1 Display the Backstage view and then click the Options button to display the Publisher Options dialog box.

2 Click Customize Ribbon in the left pane. In the Main Tabs list, click to remove the check mark in the Developer check box.

3 Click the OK button (Publisher Options dialog box) to accept the setting change.

Testing the Macro and Quitting Publisher

To test the automatic macro, you activate the event that causes the macro to execute. For example, the BeforeClose macro runs whenever you close the Publisher publication. The following steps show the reminder message box that appears when the user quits Publisher.

To Test the Macro and Quit Publisher

- Click the Close button on the Publisher title bar to display the message box created by the macro (Figure 11–82).

- Click the OK button to close the message box. If Publisher asks you to save the publication again, click the Save button.

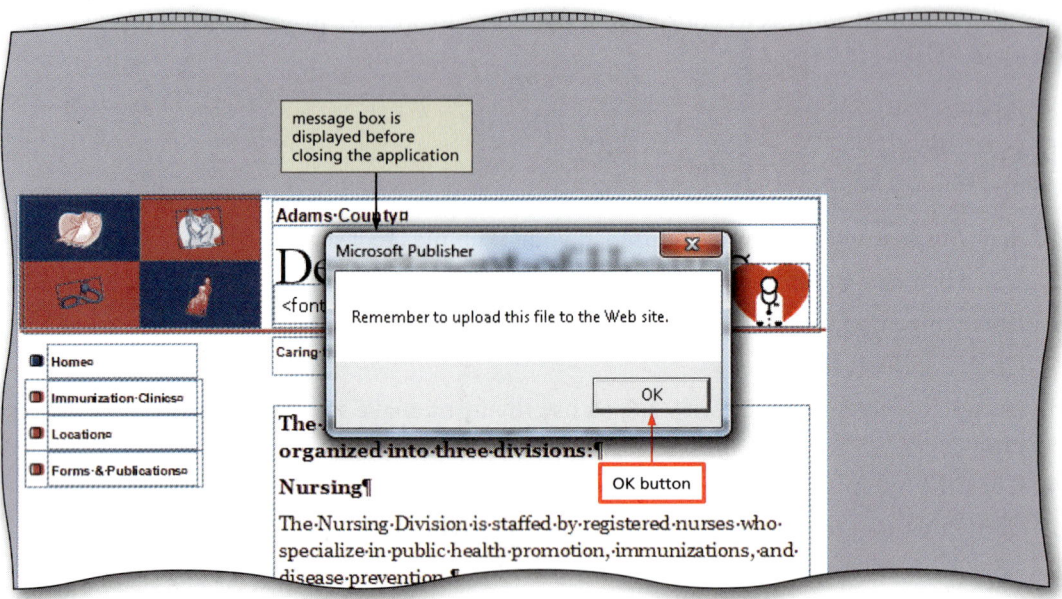

Figure 11–82

Chapter Summary

Chapter 11 introduced you to Web pages and Web forms in Publisher. First, you added a masthead, a story, a navigation bar, an animated graphic, and alternative text to a blank Web page. Then, you created additional pages and set Web page options. You inserted, edited and set properties for form controls. You learned that each form control should have a unique name and a return value for submission purposes. Then, a hot spot and scrolling marquee were added. Finally, you used Visual Basic for Applications to program a message box. The items listed below include all the new Publisher skills you have learned in this chapter.

1. Create a Web Masthead (PUB 633)
2. Insert a Navigation Bar (PUB 636)
3. Add Secondary Pages to a Web Site (PUB 637)
4. Edit the Navigation Bar Properties (PUB 639)
5. Preview an Animated Graphic (PUB 644)
6. Add Alternative Text (PUB 646)
7. Edit Web Page Options (PUB 647)
8. Insert a Background Sound (PUB 648)
9. Create Text Boxes for Labels (PUB 655)
10. Insert Textbox Form Controls (PUB 658)
11. Edit Textbox Form Control Properties (PUB 659)
12. Insert a Text Area Form Control (PUB 660)
13. Edit Text Area Form Control Properties (PUB 661)
14. Insert Checkbox Form Controls (PUB 662)
15. Edit Checkbox Form Control Properties (PUB 663)
16. Insert Option Button Form Controls (PUB 664)
17. Edit Option Button Form Control Properties (PUB 665)
18. Insert a List Box Form Control (PUB 667)
19. Edit List Box Form Control Properties (PUB 667)
20. Insert Submit Form Controls (PUB 669)
21. Edit Form Properties (PUB 671)
22. Insert a Web Hot Spot (PUB 672)
23. Insert an HTML Code Fragment (PUB 673)
24. Preview and Test a Web Site (PUB 674)
25. Display the Developer Tab (PUB 678)
26. Open the VBA Code Window (PUB 680)
27. Program a BeforeClose Event (PUB 681)
28. Set a Security Level in Publisher (PUB 683)
29. Check Form Controls for Accuracy (PUB 685)
30. Test the Macro and Quit Publisher (PUB 686)

Learn It Online

Test your knowledge of chapter content and key terms.

Instructions: To complete the Learn It Online exercises, start your browser, click the Address bar, and then enter the Web address `scsite.com/pub2010/learn`. When the Publisher 2010 Learn It Online page is displayed, click the link for the exercise you want to complete and then read the instructions.

Chapter Reinforcement TF, MC, and SA
A series of true/false, multiple choice, and short answer questions that test your knowledge of the chapter content.

Flash Cards
An interactive learning environment where you identify chapter key terms associated with displayed definitions.

Practice Test
A series of multiple choice questions that tests your knowledge of chapter content and key terms.

Who Wants To Be a Computer Genius?
An interactive game that challenges your knowledge of chapter content in the style of a television quiz show.

Wheel of Terms
An interactive game that challenges your knowledge of chapter key terms in the style of the television show *Wheel of Fortune*.

Crossword Puzzle Challenge
A crossword puzzle that challenges your knowledge of key terms presented in the chapter.

Apply Your Knowledge

Reinforce the skills and apply the concepts you learned in this chapter.

Working with Form Controls
Instructions: Start Publisher. Open the publication, Apply 11-1 Hobby Store Web Page, from the Data Files for Students. See the inside back cover of this book for instructions on downloading the Data Files for Students, or contact your instructor for more information about accessing the required files. The publication is a Web page order form for a hobby store. You are to insert a masthead, a graphic with a picture hyperlink and alternative text, and form controls as described below to create an electronic form. The completed form is shown in Figure 11–83.

Perform the following tasks:
1. Open the Building Block Library and click the Page Parts folder. Open the All Mastheads folder. Insert the Bars Masthead at the top of the publication and resize it to fill the top of the page. Edit each text box in the masthead individually to match Figure 11–83.

2. Ungroup the masthead. Delete the graphic. Use the Clip Art task pane to insert a new animated graphic similar to the one in Figure 11–83. Insert another graphic of your choice lower on the page.

3. Right-click the graphic and then click Format Picture. On the Web tab, insert alternative text describing the picture. Do the same for the graphic in the lower portion of the page.

4. Create a hot spot around the Got a Question text box so that users who click the area can send an e-mail to `webmaster@yourhobby.biz`. Type `E-mail from the Web order form` as the subject of the e-mail.

5. Double-click the Credit Card # textbox form control. When the Text Box Properties dialog box is displayed, click the 'Hide sensitive text with asterisks (***)' check box. Do the same for the Exp. date textbox form control.

Continued >

Apply Your Knowledge *continued*

Figure 11–83

6. Use the Form Controls button (Web tab | Code group) to insert a Submit button and a Reset button at the bottom of the page. Double-click the Submit button and then click the Form Properties button. Have the data sent to the same e-mail address and use the same subject line as the hot spot created in Step 4.

7. Align any controls that seem out of alignment.

8. Run the Design Checker and check the spelling. Fix any errors.

9. Test the Web page by previewing it and clicking all links.

10. Change the publication properties as specified by your instructor.

11. On your storage device, create a folder named Hobby Store Web Site.

12. Save the publication in the new folder with the file name, Apply 11-1 Hobby Store Web Page Edited.

13. Use the Publish HTML button (File tab | Save & Send tab | Publish HTML tab) and save the resulting files in the new folder.

14. Submit the publication in the format specified by your instructor.

Extend Your Knowledge

Extend the skills you learned in this chapter and experiment with new skills. You may need to use Help to complete the assignment.

Editing Graphics

Instructions: Start Publisher. Open the publication, Extend 11-1 Photo Gallery Web Site, from the Data Files for Students. See the inside back cover of this book for instructions on downloading the Data Files for Students, or contact your instructor for more information about accessing the required files. The file contains a home page photo gallery with eight additional pages containing full-size images.

You will edit the Web site shown in Figure 11–84 so that it displays compressed, thumbnail pictures for each photo. The first thumbnail is displayed for you.

Perform the following tasks:

1. Use Help to learn more about thumbnail images and reducing download times.

2. Browse the pages in the publication to become familiar with the page names, layout, and photographs.

3. For each photo:

   a. Navigate to the page and copy the photo. Paste the photo into the scratch area.

   b. Navigate back to page 1. Resize the photo to create a thumbnail image that fits in the area below its caption.

   c. Compress the photo for the Web.

   d. Create a hyperlink or hot spot to link the thumbnail to the appropriate Web page in the site.

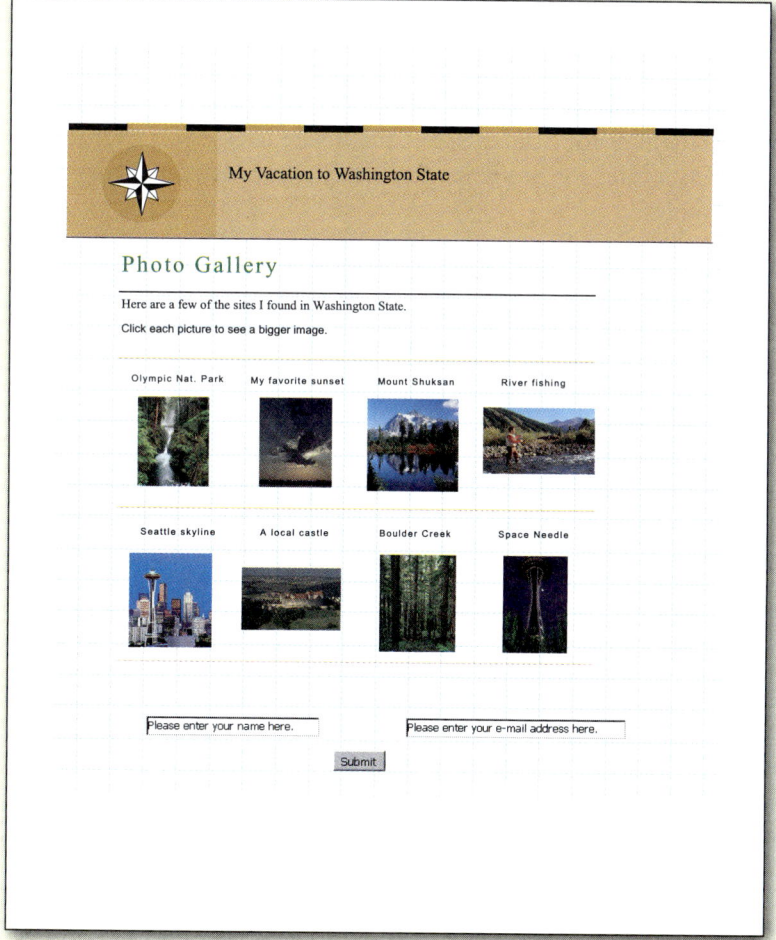

Figure 11–84

Continued >

Extend Your Knowledge *continued*

4. Navigate to page 2. Click the Picture Placeholder button (Insert tab | Illustrations group) and drag an empty picture placeholder to the left of the photo. Search for a clip art image of a back button and insert it into the empty picture placeholder.

5. Press CTRL+K to create a hyperlink back to page 1.

6. Below the back button, create a label that says Return to Photo Gallery.

7. Select both the back button and the label. Copy and paste them on pages 3 through 9.

8. Navigate to page 1. Below the photo gallery, create a Web form to collect the visitor's name and e-mail address. Include a Submit button.

9. Below the Web form, create a scrolling marquee that reads: Thank you for visiting my Web site!

10. Change the publication properties, as specified by your instructor.

11. On your storage device, create a folder named Photo Gallery Web Site. Save the publication in the new folder with the file name, Extend 11-1 Photo Gallery Web Site Modified.

12. Test the Web page by previewing it and clicking each photo.

13. Save the publication as an HTML file and store the resulting files in the new folder.

14. Submit the publication in the format specified by your instructor.

Make It Right

Analyze a publication and correct all errors and/or improve the design.

Correcting Page Titles and File Names

Instructions: Start Publisher. Open the publication, Make It Right 11–1 Financial Services Web Site, from the Data Files for Students. See the inside back cover of this book for instructions on downloading the Data Files for Students, or contact your instructor for more information about accessing the required files.

The publication shown in Figure 11–85 is a prototype Web site for a financial services company. The navigation bar needs to be updated to reflect the three products offered by the company. The pages need to be titled and named. The headings on page 1 need to be linked to the appropriate pages, as well. The company will update the content at a later time.

Perform the following tasks:

1. Edit the navigation bar text boxes to read as follows: Home, Personal, Small Business, and Corporate.

2. Navigate to page 2. Edit the Web page options so that the page title is Personal and the page name is personal.

3. Navigate to page 3. Edit the Web page options so that the page title is Small Business and the page name is small_business.

4. Navigate to page 4. Edit the Web page options so that the page title is Corporate and the page name is corporate.

5. Navigate to page 1. Edit the Web page options so that the page title is Financial Services Corporation and the page name is index. Include appropriate keywords and a description.

6. Create hot spots surrounding each column in the main story. Link the hot spots to the appropriate pages for Personal, Small Business, and Corporate.

7. Preview the publication and check all of the links. Modify the file as necessary to ensure that every link works and every page title is displayed correctly in the browser's title bar.

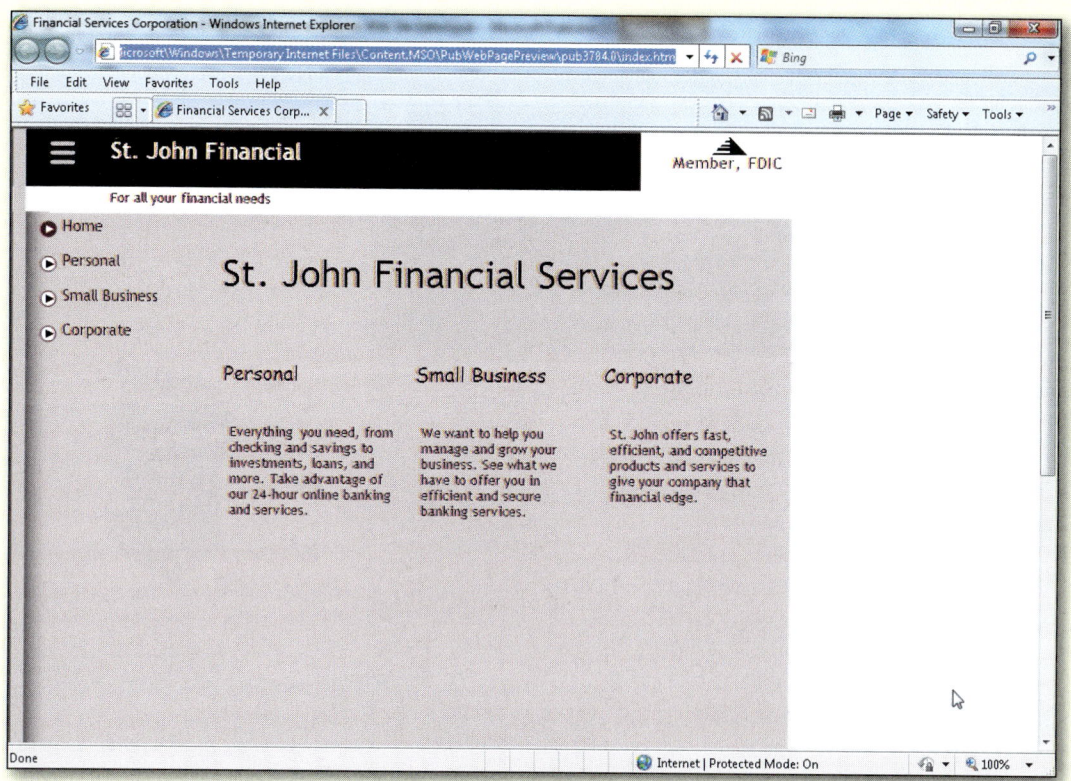

Figure 11–85

8. On your storage device, create a folder named Financial Services Web Site.

9. Save the publication in the new folder with the file name, Make it Right 11-1 Financial Services Web Site Edited.

10. Use the Publish HTML button (File tab | Save & Send tab | Publish HTML tab) and save the resulting files in the new folder.

11. Submit the publication in the format specified by your instructor.

In the Lab

Design and/or create a publication using the guidelines, concepts, and skills presented in this chapter. Labs are listed in order of increasing difficulty.

Lab 1: Creating a Web Order Form

Problem: The Textbook Connection is a bookstore located on a local college campus. They would like a Web order form for students to order textbooks online, as shown in Figure 11–86. Data should be collected about the student, including name, address, telephone number, and credit card information. Also include option buttons for delivery or pick-up and a text area where students can list their course numbers or the names of the books they wish to purchase.

Instructions: Perform the following tasks:

1. Start Publisher and then open the file, Blank Web Page, from the Data Files for Students. See the inside back cover of this book for instructions on downloading the Data Files for Students, or contact your instructor for more information about accessing the required files.

2. Choose the Waterfall color scheme and the Civic font scheme.

Continued >

In the Lab *continued*

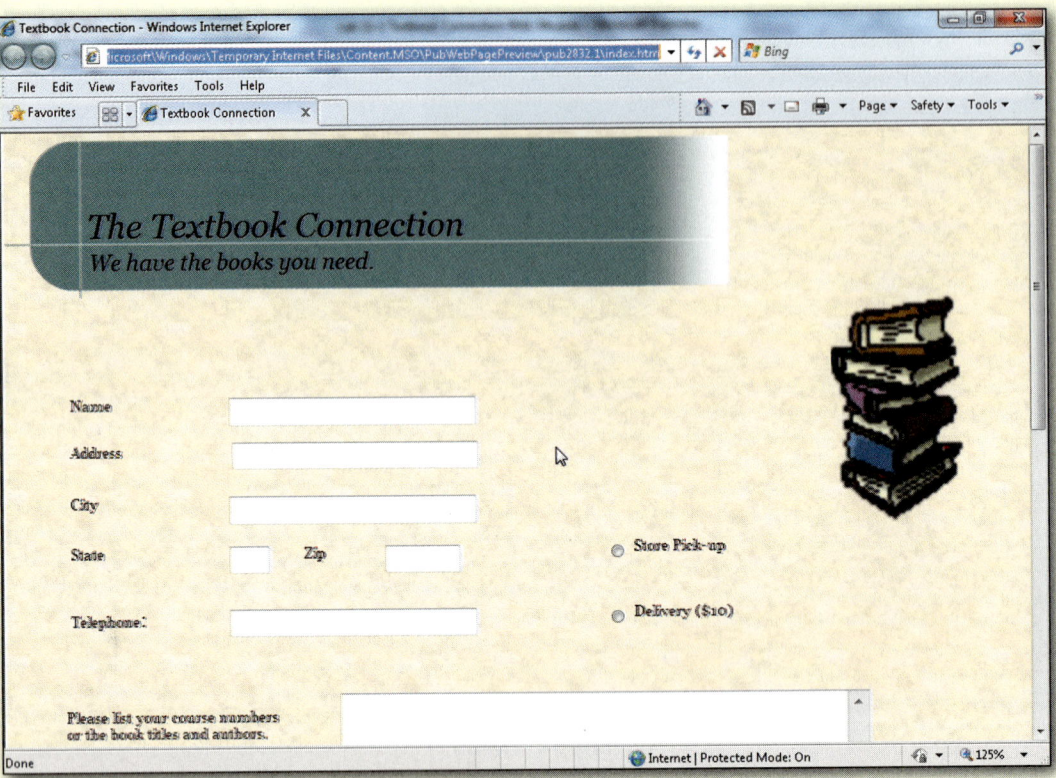

Figure 11–86

3. Click the Background button (Page Design tab | Page Background group) and then click More Backgrounds in the gallery. Click the Texture tab (Fill Effects dialog box) and insert the Parchment background.

4. Use the Building Block Library and the Page Parts folder to choose the Crisscross masthead. In the masthead, click the text in the Web Site Title text box and then type `The Textbook Connection` to replace the text.

5. Select the text in the Business Name text box and then type `We have the books you need.` to replace the text. Delete the Business Tagline or Motto text box.

6. Ungroup the masthead. Right-click the logo and then click Delete Object on the shortcut menu. Search for a clip art image using the search term, book. Limit the search to Videos. Choose a graphic similar to the one shown in Figure 11–86.

7. In the upper half of the Web page, create text box labels for Name, Address, City, State, Zip, and Telephone. Position them as shown in Figure 11–86. Create a textbox form control to accompany each of the labels. Resize the form controls and place them appropriately. Double-click each form control and set the return data label to be the same as the accompanying label. Align and distribute the controls as necessary.

8. To the right of the form controls and labels, create two option button form controls. Change the label text on the first option button to read Store Pick-up. Change the label text on the second option button to Delivery ($10). Double-click each option button and set the return data label to the word, service. Set the option button value to be the same as the accompanying label. Align and distribute the controls as necessary.

9. Below the previously inserted form controls, create a text box containing the following text: Please list your course numbers or the book titles and authors. Position and resize the text box as necessary. Create a text area form control. Move it to the location shown in Figure 11–86 and

resize as necessary. Double-click the text area form control and then set the return data label to read: book_information.

10. Below the previously inserted form controls, create a text box containing the following text: Method of Payment. Create another text box containing the following text: This credit card information may be sent to an unsecured site and may be visible to others.

11. Next, create five option buttons with the following labels: Check, Bill Me, American Express, Visa, and MasterCard. Double-click each option button and set the return data label to the word, payment. Set the option button value to be the same as the accompanying label. Align and distribute the controls as necessary.

12. Create two more text boxes containing the following: Credit Card #: and Exp. date:. Create accompanying textbox form controls. Double-click each control and enter return data labels that match the labels. Choose to hide sensitive data. Move, resize, align, and distribute the controls as necessary.

13. Finally, create a Submit button that sends data to your e-mail address, and a Reset button to clear the form.

14. Check the publication for spelling and design errors. Preview the publication using the Web Page Preview button (Web tab | Preview group).

15. Save the publication with the file name, Lab 11-1 Textbook Connection Web Site, in a new folder. Print a copy for your instructor. Publish the file to the Web.

In the Lab

Lab 2: Creating a Web Page with Picture Hyperlinks and HTML Code Fragments

Problem: Your friend has asked you to make a family home page for him, as shown in Figure 11–87. He wants to include pictures of his wife and children, a background sound, and a scrolling marquee at the top. He has friends and coworkers who routinely use screen readers, so he also has asked you to include alternative text.

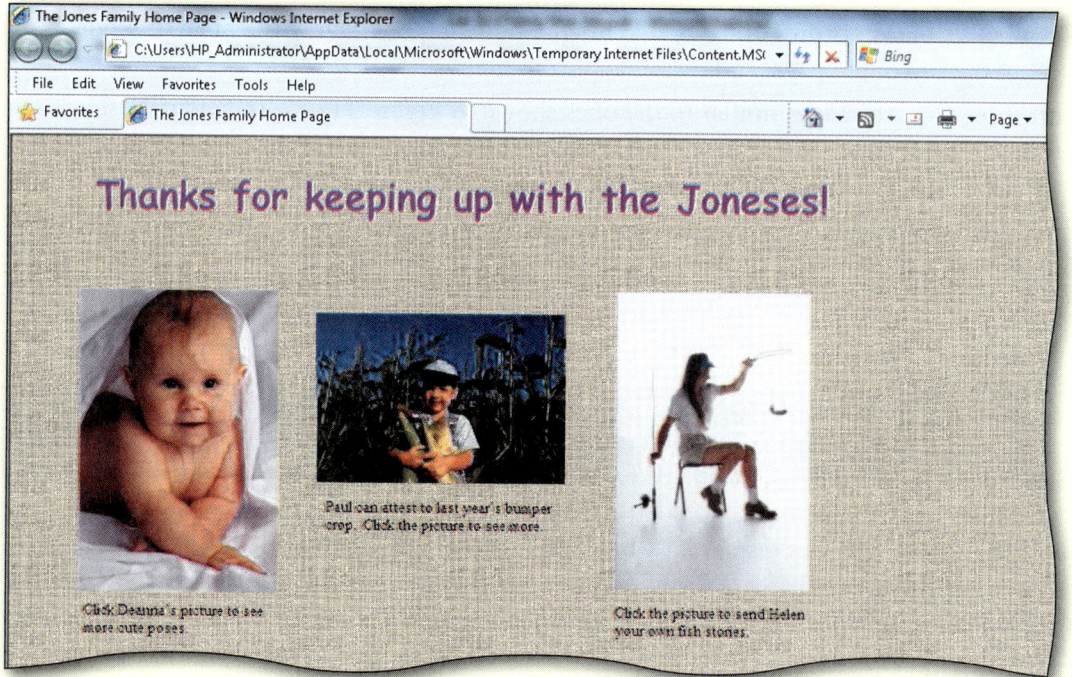

Figure 11–87

Continued >

In the Lab *continued*

The hyperlink information, alternative text, and caption are displayed in Table 11–9.

Table 11–9 Data for Picture Hyperlinks and Alternative Text			
Picture	Hyperlink Information	Alternative Text	Caption
baby	http://www.jonesfamily.com/~deanna	This is a picture of baby Deanna. Click here to see more.	Click Deanna's picture to see more cute poses.
corn	http://www.jonesfamily.com/~paul	This is a picture of 5-year-old Paul in the cornfield. Click here to see more.	Paul can attest to last year's bumper crop. Click the picture to see more.
fish	helen@jonesfamily.com	This is a picture of Helen holding a fish. Click here to send her an e-mail.	Click the picture to send Helen your own fish stories.

Instructions: Perform the following tasks:

1. Start Publisher. Open the file, Blank Web Page, from the Data Files for Students. See the inside back cover of this book for instructions on downloading the Data Files for Students, or contact your instructor for more information about accessing the required files.

2. Choose an appropriate color scheme, font scheme and background.

3. Click the Web Page Options button (Web tab | Options group) to display the dialog box. Type **The Jones Family Home Page** in the Page title text box. Type **index** in the File name box. Type **This is the home page of the Jones family.** in the Description text box. Type **Deanna Paul Helen Fred Jones Des Moines Iowa** in the Keywords text box.

4. Click the Browse button and then select the SWEST_01.MID sound file or other suitable sound on your system. Click the OK button (Web Page Options dialog box) to apply the settings.

5. Click the HTML Code Fragment button (Web tab | Code group). When the Edit HTML Code Fragment dialog box opens, type the following code:

```
<font face="Comic Sans MS, Arial, Helvetica">
<p align="left"><b>
<font color="#9933CC" size="6">
<marquee>Thanks for keeping up with the Joneses!
</marquee></font></b></p>
```

6. Click the OK button (Edit HTML Code Fragment dialog box). Drag the HTML Code Fragment object to the top of the page, and resize it appropriately.

7. Insert three clip art images similar to the ones shown in Figure 11–87. Individually, select each picture and press CTRL+K to create a picture hyperlink. Enter the information from Table 11–9. Enter alternative text and a caption for each picture from Table 11–9.

8. Check the publication for spelling and design errors. Preview the publication using the Web Page Preview button (Web tab | Preview group).

9. Save the publication and the Web site.

In the Lab

Lab 3: Adding VBA Procedures to a Publication

Problem: The Pizza'n Movies restaurant would like to add a copyright notice to its Web site publication. The owner now has asked you to insert a copyright message box each time the publication is opened, as shown in Figure 11–88a. The message box should display the information icon that is represented in VBA by the code, vbInformation. The title bar of the message should contain the name of the business. Table 11–10 lists the code and its purpose to create a copyright message box.

(a) Copyright Message Box

(b) Warning Message Box

Figure 11–88

The owner also wants to warn any employees who edit the publication of accidental deletions (Figure 11–88b). Table 11–11 lists the code and its purpose to create a warning message box that will be displayed when an object in the publication is deleted.

Table 11–10 VBA Code for a Copyright Message Box	
VBA Code	**Purpose**
'When the publication opens, a copyright message box will be displayed.	Comment
MsgBox "This publication is copyrighted by Pizza 'n Movies.", vbInformation, "Pizza 'n Movies"	Function to display message box prompt, icon, title bar caption

Table 11–11 VBA Code for a Warning Message Box	
VBA Code	**Purpose**
'When a user deletes an object in the publication, a confirmation message box will be displayed.	Comment
Dim intResponse As Integer	Declares a storage location for the user's response
intResponse = MsgBox("Do you really want to delete this object?", vbYesNo)	Function to display message box prompt and two command buttons
If intResponse = vbNo Then Publisher.ActiveDocument.Undo	Tests to see if the user clicked the No button and then calls the Undo button procedure

Instructions: Perform the following tasks:

Start Publisher and open the Lab 11-3 Pizza 'n Movies Web Site file on the Data Files for Students. See the inside back cover of this book for instructions on downloading the Data Files for Students, or contact your instructor for information about accessing the required files. Press ALT+F11 to open the Visual Basic Editor window. If necessary, click the plus sign next to Project (Lab 11-3 Pizza 'n Movies Web Site.pub) and then click the plus sign next to Microsoft Publisher Objects. Double-click ThisDocument. Click the Object box arrow and then click Document in the list. Click the Procedure box arrow and then click Open.

Continued >

STUDENT ASSIGNMENTS

In the Lab *continued*

Enter the code from Table 11–10, pressing the TAB key at the beginning of each line. Click the Procedure box arrow and then click ShapesRemoved. Enter the code from Table 11–11, pressing the TAB key at the beginning of each line.

Display the Developer tab. Click the Macro Security button (Developer tab | Code group) to display the Trust Center dialog box. If necessary, click Macro Settings in the left pane to display the macro options. If necessary, click the 'Disable all macros with notification' option button. Click the OK button (Trust Center dialog box) to apply the settings. Save the publication and then test the two macro events by quitting Publisher and reopening the publication. When the Microsoft Office Publisher dialog box appears warning you of possible macro viruses, click the Enable button. When Publisher displays the information dialog box, click the OK button. Delete an object in the publication. When Publisher displays the message box, click the No button. Hide the Developer tab when you are finished.

Cases and Places

Apply your creative thinking and problem solving skills to design and implement a solution.

Note: To complete these assignments, you may be required to use the Data Files for Students. See the inside back cover of this book for instructions on downloading the Data Files for Students, or contact your instructor for information about accessing the required files.

1: Create a Message Box

Academic

Several student workers are editing the Department of Music's latest musical program publication. The chair of the department would like you to write VBA code reminding students to upload the latest copy of the program to the server. A message box should display when the publication closes. Open the file Case 11-1 Jazz Ensemble Program and add the VBA code to create the message box.

2: Track Visitors to a Web Site

Personal

You decide to use Publisher to create form controls to collect information about people who have visited your Web site. Create a Web page using the Blank Web Page file from the Data Files for Students. Choose an appropriate Web masthead; a scrolling marquee that reads, Welcome to My Home Page; and an animated graphic with alternative text. Include textbox form controls for the visitor's name and e-mail address. Make sure to set the return data labels for the text boxes. Include a Submit button that sends data to you in an e-mail and a Reset button.

3: Collect Feedback at a Web site

Professional

Craig Poff is the city planner for Albany. A new city-growth plan has been announced, and pro- and anti-plan groups have flooded his office with responses. Craig wants an online form that people can fill out and submit with their views on specific topics. Specifically, Craig wants sets of grouped option buttons that users can select so that once a user makes a choice on one topic, the others are closed, thus giving a clear-cut response. Use the Blank Web Page file from the Data Files for students and insert an appropriate Web masthead. Create a set named Schools that includes options to use existing schools, expand existing schools, or build new schools. Create a set named Economics that includes options to build new strip malls, build individual businesses, or build no new buildings. Create a set named Parks that includes options to build new parks, expand existing parks, or have no expansion of parks. Make sure to use appropriate data return labels. Include a Submit button.

NOTES

NOTES

NOTES

NOTES

Appendix A

Project Planning Guidelines

Using Project Planning Guidelines

The process of communicating specific information to others is a learned, rational skill. Computers and software, especially Microsoft Office 2010, can help you develop ideas and present detailed information to a particular audience.

Using Microsoft Office 2010, you can create projects such as Word documents, PowerPoint presentations, Excel spreadsheets, and Access databases. Productivity software such as Microsoft Office 2010 minimizes much of the laborious work of drafting and revising projects. Some communicators handwrite ideas in notebooks, others compose directly on the computer, and others have developed unique strategies that work for their own particular thinking and writing styles.

No matter what method you use to plan a project, follow specific guidelines to arrive at a final product that presents information correctly and effectively (Figure A–1). Use some aspects of these guidelines every time you undertake a project, and others as needed in specific instances. For example, in determining content for a project, you may decide that a chart communicates trends more effectively than a paragraph of text. If so, you would create this graphical element and insert it in an Excel spreadsheet, a Word document, or a PowerPoint slide.

Determine the Project's Purpose

Begin by clearly defining why you are undertaking this assignment. For example, you may want to track monetary donations collected for your club's fund-raising drive. Alternatively, you may be urging students to vote for a particular candidate in the next election. Once you clearly understand the purpose of your task, begin to draft ideas of how best to communicate this information.

Analyze Your Audience

Learn about the people who will read, analyze, or view your work. Where are they employed? What are their educational backgrounds? What are their expectations? What questions do they have?

PROJECT PLANNING GUIDELINES

1. DETERMINE THE PROJECT'S PURPOSE
Why are you undertaking the project?

2. ANALYZE YOUR AUDIENCE
Who are the people who will use your work?

3. GATHER POSSIBLE CONTENT
What information exists, and in what forms?

4. DETERMINE WHAT CONTENT TO PRESENT TO YOUR AUDIENCE
What information will best communicate the project's purpose to your audience?

Figure A–1

Design experts suggest drawing a mental picture of these people or finding photos of people who fit this profile so that you can develop a project with the audience in mind.

By knowing your audience members, you can tailor a project to meet their interests and needs. You will not present them with information they already possess, and you will not omit the information they need to know.

Example: Your assignment is to raise the profile of your college's nursing program in the community. How much do they know about your college and the nursing curriculum? What are the admission requirements? How many of the applicants admitted complete the program? What percent pass the state board exams?

Gather Possible Content

Rarely are you in a position to develop all the material for a project. Typically, you would begin by gathering existing information that may reside in spreadsheets or databases. Web sites, pamphlets, magazine and newspaper articles, and books could provide insights of how others have approached your topic. Personal interviews often provide perspectives not available by any other means. Consider video and audio clips as potential sources for material that might complement or support the factual data you uncover.

Determine What Content to Present to Your Audience

Experienced designers recommend writing three or four major ideas you want an audience member to remember after reading or viewing your project. It also is helpful to envision your project's endpoint, the key fact you wish to emphasize. All project elements should lead to this ending point.

As you make content decisions, you also need to think about other factors. Presentation of the project content is an important consideration. For example, will your brochure be printed on thick, colored paper or posted on the Web? Will your PowerPoint presentation be viewed in a classroom with excellent lighting and a bright projector, or will it be viewed on a notebook computer monitor? Determine relevant time factors, such as the length of time to develop the project, how long readers will spend reviewing your project, or the amount of time allocated for your speaking engagement. Your project will need to accommodate all of these constraints.

Decide whether a graph, photo, or artistic element can express or emphasize a particular concept. The right hemisphere of the brain processes images by attaching an emotion to them, so audience members are more apt to recall these graphics long term rather than just reading text.

As you select content, be mindful of the order in which you plan to present information. Readers and audience members generally remember the first and last pieces of information they see and hear, so you should place the most important information at the top or bottom of the page.

Summary

When creating a project, it is beneficial to follow some basic guidelines from the outset. By taking some time at the beginning of the process to determine the project's purpose, analyze the audience, gather possible content, and determine what content to present to the audience, you can produce a project that is informative, relevant, and effective.

Appendix B

Publishing Office 2010 Web Pages Online

With Office 2010 programs, you use the Save As command in the Backstage view to save a Web page to a Web site, network location, or FTP site. **File Transfer Protocol (FTP)** is an Internet standard that allows computers to exchange files with other computers on the Internet.

You should contact your network system administrator or technical support staff at your Internet access provider to determine if their Web server supports Web folders, FTP, or both, and to obtain necessary permissions to access the Web server.

Using an Office Program to Publish Office 2010 Web Pages

When publishing online, someone first must assign the necessary permissions for you to publish the Web page. If you are granted access to publish online, you must obtain the Web address of the Web server, a user name, and possibly a password that allows you to connect to the Web server. The steps in this appendix assume that you have access to an online location to which you can publish a Web page.

To Connect to an Online Location

To publish a Web page online, you first must connect to the online location. To connect to an online location using Windows 7, you would perform the following steps.

1. Click the Start button on the Windows 7 taskbar to display the Start menu.
2. Click Computer in the right pane of the Start menu to open the Computer window.
3. Click the 'Map network drive' button on the toolbar to display the Map Network Drive dialog box. (If the 'Map network drive' button is not visible on the toolbar, click the 'Display additional commands' button on the toolbar and then click 'Map network drive' in the list to display the Map Network Drive dialog box.)
4. Click the 'Connect to a Web site that you can use to store your documents and pictures' link (Map Network Drive dialog box) to start the Add Network Location wizard.
5. Click the Next button (Add Network Location dialog box).
6. Click 'Choose a custom network location' and then click the Next button.
7. Type the Internet or network address specified by your network or system administrator in the text box and then click the Next button.
8. Click 'Log on anonymously' to deselect the check box, type your user name in the User name text box, and then click the Next button.
9. If necessary, enter the name you want to assign to this online location and then click the Next button.

10. Click to deselect the Open this network location when I click Finish check box, and then click the Finish button.

11. Click the Cancel button to close the Map Network Drive dialog box.

12. Close the Computer window.

To Save a Web Page to an Online Location

The online location now can be accessed easily from Windows programs, including Microsoft Office programs. After creating a Microsoft Office file you wish to save as a Web page, you must save the file to the online location to which you connected in the previous steps. To save a Microsoft Word document as a Web page, for example, and publish it to the online location, you would perform the following steps.

1. Click File on the Ribbon to display the Backstage view and then click Save As in the Backstage view to display the Save As dialog box.

2. Type the Web page file name in the File name text box (Save As dialog box). Do not press the ENTER key because you do not want to close the dialog box at this time.

3. Click the 'Save as type' box arrow and then click Web Page to select the Web Page format.

4. If necessary, scroll to display the name of the online location in the navigation pane.

5. Double-click the online location name in the navigation pane to select that location as the new save location and display its contents in the right pane.

6. If a dialog box appears prompting you for a user name and password, type the user name and password in the respective text boxes and then click the Log On button.

7. Click the Save button (Save As dialog box).

The Web page now has been published online. To view the Web page using a Web browser, contact your network or system administrator for the Web address you should use to connect to the Web page.

Index

A

Add Gallery to Quick Access
Toolbar command, PUB 252
adding
See also inserting
alternative text, PUB 646
AutoCorrect entry, PUB 454–456
backgrounds to master pages,
PUB 446–447
borders to tables, PUB 358–360
to Building Block Library,
PUB 234–235
buttons to Ribbon, PUB 157–158
graphics to publications,
PUB 460–461
navigation bars to Web sites,
PUB 635–636
objects to Building Block Library,
PUB 330
pages to newsletters, PUB 142–143
pages to Web sites, PUB 637–639
shadow effects, PUB 245
styles, PUB 237
Address bar, **OFF 22**
address lists
described, **PUB 404**
vs. product lists, PUB 444
Adjust group, Picture Tools Format
tab, PUB 389–390
Adobe InDesign, PUB 205
Advance properties, **PUB 38**,
PUB 39
advertisements, **PUB 181**
and attention getters, PUB 32
inserting and formatting coupons,
PUB 182–183
advertising, direct response,
PUB 442
Aero interface, Windows 7, OFF 2–4
aligning
data in table cells, PUB 344–345
objects, PUB 35, PUB 332–333
textbox form controls,
PUB 658–659
alignment, tab stop, PUB 400–401,
PUB 401
alternative text, **PUB 646**
animated GIFs, cropping, PUB 220
animated graphics
described, **PUB 644**
previewing, PUB 644–645
application software, **OFF 2**

ASCII, **PUB 517**
attachments, e-mail, **PUB 534**
best practices for (table), PUB 534
planning, PUB 506
sending publications as, PUB 505,
PUB 532
attention getters, **PUB 32–33**
audience, analyzing, APP 1–2
audio clips
See also sounds
described, **PUB 96**
AutoComplete boxes, PUB 679
AutoCorrect
creating entry, PUB 454–456
dialog box, using, PUB 456–459
Options button, PUB 453
using entries, PUB 462–463
as you type, **PUB 452**
autofit (text), **PUB 24–25**, PUB 278,
PUB 397
autoflow, **PUB 149–150**
automatic date, inserting,
PUB 283–284
automatic saving, PUB 72
automatically updated properties,
PUB 38
AutoPlay window, OFF 21
AutoShapes, PUB 225

B

background sounds, inserting,
PUB 648–649
backgrounds, **PUB 446**
adding to master pages,
PUB 446–447
creating shade, PUB 574–575
greeting card, PUB 538
vs. master pages, PUB 511
Backstage view, PUB 6, **OFF 32**
closing, PUB 38
closing files using, OFF 36
creating new publications from,
OFF 35
opening files from, OFF 33–34
opening recent files using,
OFF 36–37
Basic interface, Windows 7,
OFF 2–4
BeforeClose events, PUB 680,
PUB 681
blank publications, **PUB 205**
body copy, **PUB 559**

bold, making text, PUB 83
bookmarks, **PUB 607**
creating, PUB 609–610
navigating PDF files using,
PUB 614–615
using to create hyperlinks,
PUB 611–612
BorderArt, **PUB 226**, **PUB 568**
creating, PUB 569–571
editing, PUB 571–572
planning, PUB 568
using, PUB 557
borders, **PUB 358**
See also BorderArt
adding to tables, PUB 358–360
blue selection, PUB 15
customizing, PUB 568, PUB 572
greeting cards, PUB 538–539
planning, PUB 568
setting picture, PUB 30
boundaries
around objects, PUB 239
turning off, PUB 476
viewing catalog, PUB 472
branding companies, PUB 325
breakouts, **PUB 172**
brightness, **PUB 213**, **PUB 390**
broadsheet, **PUB 204**
brochures
creating trifold, PUB 70–72
features of, PUB 73
types and content of, PUB 68–70
bucket icon, PUB 589
Building Block Library, **PUB 32–33**
adding objects to, PUB 330
adding to, PUB 234–235
deleting content from, PUB 251
building blocks, **PUB 32**
creating Web mastheads,
PUB 633–634
inserting, PUB 250–251,
PUB 362–363
inserting table of contents,
PUB 579–580
preformatted forms, PUB 653
sharing, PUB 357
using Building Block Library,
PUB 32–33
Bullet Styles gallery, **PUB 20–21**
bulleted lists, **PUB 19–21**
business cards, **PUB 297**
creating, PUB 297–300
printing, PUB 300–302

business information fields,
    inserting, PUB 275–276
business information sets,
    PUB 266
  creating, PUB 270–275, PUB 326,
    PUB 632
  deleting, PUB 307–308
buttons
  See also specific button
  adding to Ribbon, PUB 157–158
  mouse, OFF 2

C

Calendar with Links command,
    PUB 638
calendars, **PUB 352**
  creating, PUB 352–354
  customizing, PUB 355–360
  editing calendar Web pages,
    PUB 649–652
  saving, printing, PUB 360
callouts, creating, **PUB 515–516**
capitalization, automatic, PUB 453,
    PUB 462–463
Caption gallery, using, PUB 104–105
captions, **PUB 102**
  deleting, PUB 103
  editing, PUB 103–105, PUB 168
  editing picture, PUB 356–357
  setting picture, PUB 30
catalog pages, **PUB 467**
Catalog Tools Format tab,
    PUB 470
catalogs, **PUB 444**
  Catalog Tools Format tab,
    PUB 470
  creating, PUB 459–465
  creating pages, PUB 467–468
  inserting picture fields,
    PUB 471–472
  as marketing tool, PUB 442
  merging, PUB 465–466,
    PUB 485–487
  planning, PUB 444
cell, table, **PUB 334**
  aligning data in, PUB 344–345
  deleting data, PUB 350
  formatting, PUB 348–349
  merging, PUB 341
  selecting contents, PUB 340–341
  splitting, PUB 342
cell diagonal, **PUB 348–350**
centering text, **PUB 45**
Change button, PUB 190

changing
  business information sets in
    publications, PUB 275–276
  font colors, PUB 36–37
  line spacing, PUB 241
  page orientation, PUB 330–331
  publication properties, PUB 38–39
  screen resolution, OFF 30–31
  text orientation, PUB 585–586
  WordArt shapes, outlines,
    PUB 327–329
character spacing, **PUB 396**
character typography, PUB 81
characters
  formatting, PUB 80–83
  inserting special, PUB 517–521
  ligatures, enabling, PUB 85–86
  spacing between, PUB 396–399
  subsetting, **PUB 118**
  swashes, using, PUB 87
  tracking, PUB 397
check boxes
  described, **PUB 653**
  and option buttons, PUB 665
"Check spelling as you type" feature,
    PUB 47
checkbox form controls, inserting,
    PUB 662–664
chevron symbols, PUB 413
citations, creating, PUB 524
Clear Crop command, PUB 216
clip art, **PUB 94**
  animated, PUB 644
  drop caps, PUB 85
  editing, PUB 355–356
  inserting, PUB 184, PUB 514–515
  replacing graphic with, PUB 169
  resizing, PUB 170
  using, PUB 94–97, PUB 166
Clip Art Task pane, PUB 94–96
Clip Organizer, PUB 94
Clipboard, Windows and Office,
    PUB 74
clips, **PUB 27**
closing
  Backstage view, PUB 38
  files using Backstage view,
    OFF 36
  master pages, PUB 394
  publications, PUB 247, PUB 296
CMYK colors, PUB 114, PUB 390
code, **PUB 628**
  entering statements, comments,
    PUB 680–681
  HTML code fragments, **PUB 672**

collapsing
  folders, OFF 23–24
  sections, PUB 578
color palette, PUB 208
color schemes, PUB 6, **PUB 9–11,**
    PUB 269
  applying customized, PUB 249
  deleting, PUB 252
  in tables, PUB 339
colors, PUB 390
  border, PUB 358–360
  changing BorderArt, PUB 571
  changing font, PUB 36–37
  choosing color model, PUB 115
  custom color schemes,
    PUB 208–210
  intensity values of, PUB 37
  More Colors command, PUB 221
  printing considerations,
    PUB 114–115
  recoloring pictures, PUB 220
  Sample Line color command,
    PUB 231
  sampling font, **PUB 279**
  scheme, PUB 222
  selecting for shape outline,
    PUB 230–231
  traps, PUB 229
  Web site schemes, PUB 632
columns
  creating, PUB 238
  creating in text boxes, PUB 239–242
  newspaper formats, PUB 204
columns, table
  aligning, resizing, PUB 345–346
  deleting, PUB 337
  inserting, PUB 339
  selecting contents, PUB 340–341
Command bar, **OFF 22**
commands, **OFF 10**
  See also specific command
  computer shut down, OFF 6
  selecting using keyboard, OFF 16
comments
  entering code, **PUB 680–681**
  inserting, PUB 38
common dialog boxes, **OFF 8**
compressing
  described, **PUB 390**
  pictures, settings, PUB 390–391,
    PUB 393
computer programming, **PUB 628**
computer viruses, **PUB 682**
computers, logging on to,
    OFF 6–7

connecting to online location, APP 3–4

connects described, **PUB 146**

conserving ink, toner, PUB 111

Contact Us Web page, editing, PUB 652–653

'Content for page' list, PUB 141

content pages, **PUB 559**

continued notices, formatting with, **PUB 152–155**

contrast, **PUB 213**, **PUB 390**

controls. *See* form controls

converting
  publications to e-mail messages, PUB 533
  publications to other file formats, PUB 302

copy, cut, paste, delete methods (table), PUB 74

Copy and Paste commands, PUB 523

copy fitting text, **PUB 24–25**

copying
  applied formatting, PUB 92
  copy, cut, paste, delete methods (table), PUB 74
  data source files, PUB 420, PUB 466
  headings, PUB 606
  HTML code from the Web, PUB 673
  master pages, PUB 450, PUB 569
  pages, PUB 590
  and pasting, PUB 74–78
  and pasting embedded or linked tables, PUB 365–366
  Research Task pane information, PUB 523
  text boxes, PUB 588

correcting typing errors, PUB 18–19, OFF 19

coupons
  described, **PUB 182**
  inserting and formatting, PUB 182–183

cover pages, PUB 577

Create Custom button, PUB 572

Create New Business Information Set dialog box, PUB 272, PUB 273

Create New Page Size command, PUB 207

creating
  alternating master pages, PUB 446
  AutoCorrect entry, PUB 454–456

bookmarks, PUB 609–610

BorderArt, PUB 569–571

bulleted lists, PUB 19–21

business cards, PUB 300–302

business information sets, PUB 270–275, PUB 326, PUB 632

calendars, PUB 352–354

callouts, PUB 515–516

catalogs, PUB 459–465, PUB 467–468

citations, PUB 524

color schemes, PUB 209–210

columns, PUB 239–242

custom font schemes, PUB 210–212

custom-sized publications, PUB 204–208

data sources, PUB 404–408

e-mail messages, PUB 504–506

embedded tables, PUB 364–365

envelopes, PUB 292–294

flyers, PUB 5–13

folders, OFF 20–21

folders within folders, OFF 23

gradient fill effects, PUB 227–229

greeting cards, PUB 536–543

hyperlinks, PUB 650

letterhead, PUB 269–270, PUB 395

page sections, PUB 560–561

publications from Backstage view, OFF 35

reusable parts, PUB 325

scrolling marquee, PUB 673

shade backgrounds, PUB 574–575

squares, PUB 226

styles, PUB 280–281

templates, PUB 189–190

text boxes, PUB 77, PUB 239

tickets, PUB 419–427

trifold brochures, PUB 70–72

two-page spread, PUB 445

watermarks on master pages, PUB 388

Web mastheads, PUB 633–634

Web pages from publications, PUB 47–51

cropping
  graphics, PUB 215–219
  vs. resizing, PUB 215

cropping handles, PUB 97

cursive fonts, PUB 83

custom font schemes, **PUB 210–212**

customizing, **PUB 157**
  borders, PUB 572
  calendars, PUB 355–360

color schemes, PUB 208–210

data source columns, PUB 406–408

font schemes, PUB 210–212

Quick Access Toolbar, OFF 18

Ribbon, OFF 36, PUB 157–158

templates, PUB 9–13

Windows 7 desktop, OFF 7

cutting, copying, pasting, deleting methods (table), PUB 74

D

data
  aligning in table cells, PUB 344–345
  deleting table, PUB 350
  entering in tables, PUB 336
  filtering, PUB 423–425
  formatting in field codes, PUB 426
  hiding sensitive (on forms), PUB 660
  linking, PUB 361
  merging into publications, PUB 403–418
  using tables to present, PUB 334

data fields, **PUB 404**

data files, **PUB 384**

data records, **PUB 404**

data sources, **PUB 384**, PUB 386
  copying, PUB 420
  creating, PUB 404–408
  customizing columns, PUB 406–408
  excluding entries, PUB 476
  product lists vs. address lists, PUB 444
  recipient lists for, PUB 403
  saving, PUB 411
  selecting, PUB 469–470

databases, **PUB 403**

data-driven publications, **PUB 442**

date, using an automatic, PUB 283–284

Date & Time button, PUB 402

deleting
  See also removing
  business information sets, PUB 274, PUB 307–308
  captions, PUB 103
  color schemes, PUB 210
  copy, cut, paste, delete methods (table), PUB 74
  customizations, PUB 251–254
  data from business information sets, PUB 273
  data source columns, PUB 407

e-mail message objects, PUB 513
font schemes, PUB 212
graphics, PUB 225
objects, PUB 26–27, PUB 73–74
page sections, PUB 562
pages from newsletters, PUB 142–143
table columns, rows, PUB 337–338
table data, PUB 350
tabs, PUB 401
tear-offs, PUB 44
wrap points, PUB 219
deleting files, OFF 42
Design Checker, PUB 106
running, PUB 108–109, PUB 613
using, PUB 528–529, PUB 683–684
designing
e-mail messages, PUB 527–529
graphics use on Web pages, PUB 643
large-scale publications, PUB 559–561
letterhead, PUB 268
newsletters, PUB 138–139
Web site navigation, PUB 636
with WordArt, PUB 327
desktop, Windows 7
described, OFF 7
shortcuts on, OFF 22
desktop publishing (DTP), **PUB 134**
Developer tab on Ribbon
displaying, PUB 678–679
hiding, PUB 685
Dialog Box Launcher, **OFF 14**
dialog boxes
AutoCorrect, PUB 456–459
common, **OFF 8**
digital printing, PUB 114
digital signatures, PUB 682
dimension (of tables), **PUB 334**
direct marketing, **PUB 442**
direct response advertising, **PUB 442**
disabled macros, **PUB 682**
displaying
See also viewing
Developer tab on Ribbon, PUB 678–679
different tabs on Ribbon, OFF 16
drop caps, PUB 84–85
formatting marks, **PUB 79**, PUB 139, PUB 160
Measurement toolbar, PUB 276–277
Mini toolbar, PUB 36

nonprinting characters, PUB 400
object boundaries, PUB 14–15
Page Navigation pane, PUB 13
Ribbon, OFF 16–17
rulers, PUB 399
text in stylistic sets, PUB 84
Distribute commands, WordArt, PUB 333
distributing publications, PUB 504
document events, **PUB 678**
documents
See also publications
incorporating security in, PUB 682
Don't Save button, OFF 31
drag-and-drop editing
described, **PUB 185**
turning on, off, PUB 186
dragging
to copy, PUB 180
mouse operations, OFF 4
selecting adjacent objects by, PUB 171–172
windows to resize, OFF 44
drawing text boxes, PUB 44–45, PUB 236, PUB 588
drop caps, creating, PUB 84–85
drop-down list boxes, PUB 667
duplicating
See also copying
graphics, **PUB 180**

E

e-commerce, **PUB 628**
editing, **PUB 17**
BorderArt, PUB 571–572
calendar Web pages, PUB 649–652
captions, PUB 103–105, PUB 168
checkbox form control properties, PUB 663–664
clip art, PUB 355–356
Contact Us Web page, PUB 652–653
drag-and-drop, **PUB 185**
form properties, PUB 671
graphics, PUB 213, PUB 356
hyperlinks, PUB 525
list box form control properties, PUB 667–669
mastheads, PUB 143–145
navigation bar properties, PUB 639–642
objects in embedded tables, PUB 366–367

option button form control properties, PUB 665–666
photographs, PUB 220
picture captions, PUB 356–357
sidebars, PUB 173–175
stories in Microsoft Word, PUB 159–166
table cell contents, PUB 336
tear-off boxes, PUB 22
text area form controls, PUB 661
text boxes, PUB 73, PUB 183
textbox form controls, PUB 659
Web page options, PUB 637–638
wrap points, PUB 217–219
effects, font, **PUB 88**
electronic commerce, **PUB 628**
electronic forms
See also forms
described, **PUB 628**
e-mail, **PUB 504**
attachments, creating files in portable formats, PUB 302
marketing, PUB 507, PUB 508
messages. See e-mail messages
sending publications using, PUB 504–506
service providers, PUB 530
templates, PUB 507–516
e-mail merges, **PUB 506**
e-mail messages
creating with templates, PUB 507–513
design issues, Design Checker, PUB 527–529
e-postcards, PUB 534–536
inserting clip art, pictures, PUB 514–515
previewing, PUB 531
sending, using Publisher, PUB 530–533
spell-checking, PUB 530
ways of creating, PUB 504–506
embedded font sets, PUB 114
embedded tables, **PUB 361**
formatting, PUB 366–367
inserting, PUB 364–365
summing in, PUB 367–369
embedded vs. linked pictures, PUB 477
embedding fonts, PUB 305–307
Embed/Don't Embed button, PUB 307
enabled macros, **PUB 682**
Encapsulated PostScript (EPS) files, PUB 118

Encapsulated PostScript (EPS) format, PUB 389
end matter, **PUB 559**
end-of-cell mark, PUB 335
Enhanced ScreenTips, **OFF 14**
envelopes
  creating, addressing, printing, PUB 292–296
  described, **PUB 292**
e-postcards
  described, **PUB 534**
  sending at attachments, PUB 535–536
errors
  See also mistakes
  checking e-mail design, PUB 529
  checking publications for, PUB 106–109, PUB 246
  correcting typing, PUB 18–19, OFF 19
  correcting with AutoCorrect, PUB 452–454
  spelling. *See* spell-checking
events, **PUB 628**
  See also specific event
  document, **PUB 678**
Excel
  embedded tables, inserting, PUB 364–365
  -enhanced tables, **PUB 361**
  tables, using, PUB 361–370
excluding data source entries, PUB 476
execute, **PUB 628**
expanding folders, OFF 23–24
eyedropper (mouse pointer), PUB 279

F

Favorites area, **OFF 23**
field codes, **PUB 412**
  formatting data in, PUB 426
  inserting, PUB 412–416
  inserting merge, PUB 425–426
  and repeatable areas, PUB 467
field names, **PUB 404**
fields
  in business information sets, **PUB 270**
  end of field marker, PUB 79
file extensions and data formats, PUB 403
file management, **OFF 40**
file name, **OFF 19**

File tab, OFF 34
File Transfer Protocol (FTP), **APP 3**
file types, OFF 27
files, **OFF 7**
  closing, OFF 36
  creating in portable formats, PUB 302
  data, **PUB 384**
  importing text, PUB 147–148
  making read-only, PUB 286–287
  moving, renaming, deleting, OFF 40–42
  naming, OFF 25–26
  opening from Backstage view, OFF 33–34
  opening from Windows Explorer, OFF 38–39
  opening recent, using Backstage view, OFF 36–37
  PostScript, using, PUB 118
  saving and organizing, OFF 19–27
  saving in folders, OFF 25–27, OFF 36
Fill command, PUB 216
fill handles, replicating sum using, PUB 368
filling shapes with pictures, PUB 233
fills, **PUB 226**
filtering data, PUB 423–425
Find and Replace commands, PUB 594–598
Find Entry dialog box, PUB 410
first-line indent markers, **PUB 399**, PUB 400
Fit command, PUB 216
flags, **PUB 46**
flipping
  described, **PUB 213**
  graphics, PUB 181
  objects, PUB 213–214
flyer, **PUB 2**
  creating, PUB 5–13
  project, PUB 2–4
  as Web publications, PUB 48
folded publications, printing, PUB 543–544
folder windows, **OFF 22–23**
folders, **OFF 10**
  creating, OFF 20–21, OFF 23
  deleting, OFF 42
  expanding, scrolling through contents, collapsing, OFF 23–24
Microsoft Office, OFF 11
saving files in, OFF 25–27, OFF 36

Font Color gallery, PUB 279
font schemes, PUB 5, **PUB 9–11**, PUB 269
  applying customized, PUB 249
  custom, PUB 210–212
  deleting, PUB 253
  selecting, PUB 558
  for Web sites, PUB 632
font size
  changing, PUB 244
  increasing, PUB 24, PUB 90
  setting, PUB 241
fonts, **PUB 9–11**
  categories of, PUB 9
  changing color, PUB 36–37
  effects, applying, **PUB 88–89**
  embedded sets, PUB 114
  embedding, PUB 305–307
  OpenType, **PUB 83**
  TrueType, **PUB 211**
footers, **PUB 448**
  accessing, PUB 166
  inserting, PUB 450–451
form controls, **PUB 628**, PUB 662–664
  See also specific type
  checking for accuracy, PUB 685
  textbox, PUB 657–660
  types, using, PUB 653–654
form letters, **PUB 384**
  composing body of, PUB 412
  identifying main document for, PUB 395
  previewing, PUB 418
format, **PUB 23**
Format AutoShape dialog box, PUB 571
format described, **PUB 16**
Format Painter
  button, using, PUB 91–92
  formatting attributes, PUB 282
formats
  applying table, PUB 339–340
  data, and file extensions, PUB 403
  newspaper, PUB 204
  portable, creating files in, PUB 302–305
  searching for, PUB 594
formatting
  calendars, PUB 651–652
  characters, PUB 80–83
  data in field codes, PUB 426
  e-mail messages, PUB 507
  embedded tables, PUB 366–367
  fonts, PUB 23–24

multiple table cells, PUB 348
page numbers, PUB 566, PUB 568
symbols, PUB 517
Tables of Content, PUB 580–581
text, PUB 152–155, PUB 343–344
using Format Painter, PUB 91–92
formatting marks, displaying,
    PUB 79, PUB 139, PUB 160
forms, PUB 630
  controls. *See* form controls
  editing properties, PUB 671
  hiding sensitive data on, PUB 660
  using, PUB 93
  using preformatted, PUB 653
formula bar (Excel), PUB 367
Free Rotate command, PUB 215
front matter, **PUB 559**
functions, **PUB 680**

G

galleries
  See also specific gallery
  described, **OFF 14**, **PUB 20**
Go to Page command, PUB 608–609
gradient fill effects, PUB 227–229,
    PUB 243
Gradient gallery, PUB 227
gradients, **PUB 226**
grammar, checking with
    AutoCorrect, PUB 452–454
graphics, **PUB 27**
  adding alternative text, PUB 646
  adding to pages, PUB 460–461
  adjustments, PUB 389–393
  animated, **PUB 644**
  contrast, brightness, PUB 213
  cropping, PUB 215–219
  deleting, PUB 225
  editing, PUB 213
  fitting, PUB 216–217
  flipping, PUB 181
  Format Options button, PUB 250
  inserting, PUB 583
  printers, troubleshooting, PUB 487
  recoloring, PUB 220–222,
    PUB 389, PUB 390
  replacing using Clip Art Task pane,
    PUB 94–97
  replacing Web, PUB 643–644
  replacing with clip art, PUB 169
  resizing, PUB 97, PUB 99
  saving as pictures, PUB 224
  scaling, PUB 213, PUB 391
  ungrouping, PUB 222

using, PUB 27–30
watermarks. *See* watermarks
Web, PUB 643–644
wrapping text around, PUB 170
Graphics Manager, working with,
    PUB 477–480
greeting cards
  creating from template, modifying,
    PUB 536–543
  described, **PUB 536**
grouped field codes
  described, **PUB 412**
  inserting, PUB 413–414
grouped objects, **PUB 93**
grouping, **PUB 222**
  form controls, PUB 654
  objects, PUB 222–223
groups on Ribbon, **OFF 14**
guidelines, project planning, APP 1–2
guides
  creating, PUB 654
  margin, PUB 332
  ruler, PUB 586–587
gutters, **PUB 204**

H

handles, **PUB 34**
header records, **PUB 404**
headers, **PUB 448**
  accessing, PUB 166
  inserting, PUB 448–449
headings, PUB 173
  copying and pasting, PUB 606
  creating text, PUB 238
  e-mail publications, PUB 511
  inserting, PUB 605
headlines, PUB 2, **PUB 146**
health, minimizing wrist injuries,
    OFF 4
Help, obtaining, OFF 42–50
hiding
  Developer tab on Ribbon, PUB 685
  formatting marks, PUB 79
  object boundaries, PUB 14
  Page Navigation pane, PUB 13
  sensitive data on forms, PUB 660
home pages
  described, **PUB 632**
  naming "index," PUB 647
Home tab, **OFF 14**, OFF 17
hot spots, **PUB 506**
  formatting, PUB 517
  inserting, PUB 525–526
  Web, inserting, PUB 672

HTML (Hypertext Markup
    Language), PUB 629
HTML code fragments
  described, **PUB 672**
  inserting, PUB 673–674
HTML-enabled e-mail, **PUB 504**
hyphenation in e-mail, PUB 530
hyperlinks, **PUB 506**
  creating, PUB 650
  editing, inserting, PUB 525–527
  formatting, PUB 517
  testing, PUB 612
  using bookmarks to create,
    PUB 611–612
Hypertext Markup Language
    (HTML), **PUB 48**
hyphenation
  checking, PUB 187–188
  described, **PUB 187**
hyphenation zone, **PUB 187**

I

icons
  See also specific icon
  keyboard code, OFF 15
  user, **OFF 5**
importing, **PUB 145**, **PUB 403**
  styles, PUB 282
  text files, PUB 147–148,
    PUB 155–156, PUB 593,
    PUB 634–635
  text from other programs, PUB 146
indent markers, PUB 400
indents vs. tabs, PUB 402
in-house, **PUB 69**
ink, conserving, PUB 111
Insert Symbols gallery, PUB 517–519
inserting
  See also adding
  background sounds, PUB 648–649
  building blocks, PUB 362–363
  business information fields,
    PUB 275–276
  checkbox form controls,
    PUB 662–664
  clip art, PUB 184, PUB 514–515
  comments, PUB 38
  current date and/or time,
    PUB 283–284
  customized building block,
    PUB 250–251
  embedded tables, PUB 364–365
  field codes, PUB 412–416
  footers, PUB 450–451

graphics, PUB 583
graphics on Web pages, PUB 645
grouped field codes, PUB 413–414
headers, PUB 448–449
headings, PUB 605
hot spots, PUB 525–526
HTML code fragments,
   PUB 673–674
hyperlinks, PUB 525–527
linked tables, PUB 365–366
mailto hyperlinks, PUB 526–527
merge field codes, PUB 425–426
page breaks, PUB 602–604
page numbers, PUB 166,
   PUB 562–563
page sections, PUB 560–561
pages in newsletters, PUB 142–143
patterns, PUB 179–180
photographs into picture
   placeholders, PUB 28–30
picture fields, PUB 471–472
pictures in shapes, PUB 233
pull quotes, PUB 175–177
repeating text, PUB 572–573
shapes, PUB 225–226, PUB 570
submit form controls,
   PUB 669–671
symbols and special characters,
   PUB 517–521
Table of Contents building blocks,
   PUB 579–580
table rows, columns, PUB 338–339
tables, PUB 334–335
text area form controls,
   PUB 660–661
text files, PUB 584
text in pull quotes, PUB 177–178
textbox form controls,
   PUB 658–659
titles, subtitles, PUB 576
watermark graphics, PUB 391
Web hot spots, PUB 672
WordArt objects, PUB 243–244,
   PUB 327
wrap points, PUB 219
insertion point, OFF 19
interactive Web sites, **PUB 628**
interactivity, customizing letterhead
   for, PUB 280–281
internal data labels, **PUB 654**
italicizing text, PUB 81

J

jump lines, **PUB 152**

K

kerning, **PUB 396**, PUB 398,
   PUB 399
keyboard, selecting commands
   using, OFF 16
keyboard shortcuts, **OFF 4–5**
KeyTips, **OFF 15–16**
keywords, **PUB 38**, PUB 648
knockouts, **PUB 568**

L

labels
   creating for list boxes,
      PUB 655–656
   described, **PUB 654**
landscape orientation, **PUB 170**,
   PUB 330–331
languages, translating text into,
   PUB 480–484
layouts
   designing large-scale publication,
      PUB 559–561
   and master pages, PUB 388
leader tab, **PUB 399**
leading, PUB 396
left-aligned tab, PUB 401
left-clicking, OFF 4
letterhead, **PUB 269**
   creating, PUB 269–270, PUB 362,
      PUB 395
   customizing for interactivity,
      PUB 282–285
   designing, PUB 268
   saving, PUB 285
   setting read-only attribute,
      PUB 286–287
   using custom template,
      PUB 287–288
letters
   e-mail template, PUB 507
   printing, PUB 291, PUB 370–371
   saving, PUB 289–290
Libraries area, **OFF 23**
libraries, **OFF 23**
ligatures, enabling, **PUB 85–86**
line spacing, **PUB 241**
linked objects, using, PUB 369
linked tables, **PUB 361**
   copying and pasting, PUB 366
   inserting, PUB 365–366
linked text boxes, **PUB 145**
linked vs. embedded pictures,
   PUB 477

linking
   text boxes, PUB 588–589
   text boxes across pages,
      PUB 592–593
links
   Help, OFF 47
   navigation bars. *See* navigation bars
list boxes, **PUB 654**, PUB 667
lists, creating bulleted, PUB 19–21
listserv, **PUB 530**
live preview, **OFF 14**, **PUB 20**
logging on, **OFF 5**
logos
   described, **PUB 271**
   editing, PUB 298

M

macros, **PUB 678**
   disabled, enabled, **PUB 682**
   testing, PUB 685–686
Mail Merge task pane, PUB 405,
   PUB 412, PUB 419
Mail Merge Wizard, using,
   PUB 404–406
mailing lists, unsubscribing from,
   PUB 504
Mailing tab, using, PUB 421
mailto (hyperlink), **PUB 526–527**
Make Available Offline command,
   PUB 645
managing merged publications,
   PUB 417–419
margin guides, PUB 332
margin markers, **PUB 399**
margins
   page, PUB 533
   within table cells, PUB 579,
      PUB 581–582
   within text boxes, PUB 583
marketing, e-mail, PUB 507,
   PUB 508
Master Page view, **PUB 446**
master pages, **PUB 384**
   applying, PUB 456–459, PUB 573
   vs. backgrounds, PUB 511
   closing, PUB 394
   creating alternating, PUB 446
   creating watermarks on, PUB 386,
      PUB 388
   duplicating, PUB 450, PUB 569
   watermarks and, PUB 388–389
masthead, **PUB 143**
   creating Web, PUB 633–634
   editing, PUB 143–145

math operations in Excel, PUB 368
maximizing windows, **OFF 12**
Measurement toolbar, using, PUB 276–278
memory, printer, PUB 109
menus, **OFF 10**
See also specific menu
shortcut. *See* shortcut menus
merge areas, inserting, PUB 467–468
merge field codes, inserting, PUB 425–426
Merge to Print command, PUB 428
merging, PUB 386, **PUB 403**, PUB 416
catalog merges, PUB 465–466
catalogs, PUB 485–487
data into publications, PUB 403–418
e-mail. *See* e-mail merges
page sections, PUB 591
table cells, PUB 341
message boxes, VBA, PUB 680
metadata, **PUB 38**
MHTML (Mime Hypertext Markup Language), **PUB 48**
Microsoft Access 2010, **OFF 8**, OFF 9
Microsoft Communicator, **OFF 8**, OFF 9
Microsoft Excel 2010, **OFF 8**, OFF 9
Microsoft InfoPath 2010, **OFF 8**, OFF 9
Microsoft Office 2010, **OFF 7**
common features of, OFF 32–40
programs, suites, OFF 8–9
publishing Web pages online, APP 3–4
Microsoft Office folder, OFF 11
Microsoft Office Help, OFF 42–50
Microsoft OneNote 2010, **OFF 8**, OFF 9
Microsoft Outlook 2010, **OFF 8**, OFF 9
Microsoft PowerPoint 2010, **OFF 8**, OFF 9
Microsoft Publisher 2010
See also Publisher
described, **OFF 8**, OFF 9
Microsoft SharePoint Workspace 2010, **OFF 8**, OFF 9
Microsoft Web Apps, **OFF 8**
Microsoft Word, editing stories in, PUB 159–166
Microsoft Word 2010, **OFF 8**, OFF 9

Microsoft XPS Document Writer, PUB 42
MIDI (Musical Instrument Digital Interface), PUB 649
Mini toolbar, **OFF 15**, PUB 167
displaying, PUB 36
formatting fonts using, PUB 23
minimized window, **OFF 27**
minimizing the Ribbon, OFF 16–17
mistakes
See also errors
spell-checking, PUB 46–47
undoing, PUB 27
monitors
color settings, PUB 208
screen resolution, PUB 5, OFF 29–31
monospacing, **PUB 396**
More Business Information command, PUB 272
More Colors command, PUB 210, PUB 221
More Columns command, PUB 240
More Variations command, Recolor gallery, PUB 392
mouse, right and left buttons, OFF 2
move described, **PUB 34**
moving
files, OFF 41
pages across sections, PUB 592
tables, PUB 369–370
text, PUB 75–76, PUB 185–186
windows, OFF 43–44
MsgBox function, **PUB 680**
My Templates button, PUB 189

N

names, user, **OFF 5**
naming
files, OFF 25–26
folders, OFF 20–21
navigating, **OFF 27**
Building Block Library, PUB 32
PDF files with bookmarks, PUB 614–615
through large-scale publications, PUB 607–612
navigation bars, **PUB 629**
adding to Web sites, PUB 635–636
editing properties, PUB 639–642
navigation pane
described, **OFF 22**
in dialog boxes, OFF 27

New Address List dialog box, PUB 406
New Style command, PUB 237
New template gallery, PUB 6–8
newsletters, **PUB 134**
benefits, advantages of (table), PUB 137
design choices, PUB 138–139
designing (project), PUB 134–136
e-mail template, PUB 507
moving pages, changing number of pages, PUB 142–143
printing, PUB 191
revising, PUB 184–190
using graphics in, PUB 166–172
newspaper formats, PUB 204
nonbreaking hyphens, **PUB 187**
nonprinting characters, displaying, PUB 400
Normal style, **PUB 278**
Normal view, **PUB 446**
numerical up and down box, PUB 354

O

objects
See also specific object
adding to Building Block Library, PUB 330
boundaries, displaying and hiding, PUB 14
creating borderless, PUB 231
deleting, PUB 26–27, PUB 73–74, PUB 93–94
deleting from e-mail, PUB 513
editing, PUB 366–367
flipping, PUB 213–214
formatting using Format Painter, PUB 92
grouped, **PUB 93**
linked, using, PUB 369
moving, PUB 34
placing and scaling precisely, PUB 276
positioning using Measurement toolbar, PUB 277–278
reshaping WordArt, PUB 328–329
resizing, aligning, PUB 35
rotating, PUB 213–214
selecting, PUB 14
selecting adjacent, by dragging, PUB 171–172
selecting multiple, PUB 223

shape fills, PUB 226–235
snapping to margin guides,
   PUB 332–333
Office 2010. *See* Microsoft Office
   2010
Office Clipboard, PUB 74
Office Help, OFF 44–49
Office Online Templates, PUB 8
Office.com, PUB 96
Office.com community, PUB 357
opening
   files from Backstage view,
      OFF 33–34
   files from Windows Explorer,
      OFF 38–39
   Page Navigation pane, PUB 72
   publications, PUB 387, PUB 631
   recent files using Backstage view,
      OFF 36–37
   VBA coding window, PUB 680
OpenType, **PUB 83**
operating system, **OFF 2**
Option button form controls,
   PUB 663–665
option buttons
   check boxes and, PUB 665
   described, **PUB 653**
organizing files, OFF 19–27
orientation, page, PUB 330–331
Outlook, PUB 532
overflow area, **PUB 150**

P

Pack and Go Wizard, PUB 116–117,
   PUB 305
page breaks
   described, PUB 601
   inserting, PUB 602–604
Page Navigation pane, OFF 13,
   PUB 354
   collapsing, PUB 206
   hiding, displaying, **PUB 13**
   opening, PUB 72
page numbering
   continued notices, jump lines,
      PUB 152–155
   inserting page numbers,
      PUB 166
page numbers
   formatting, PUB 568
   inserting, PUB 451, PUB 562–563
   removing, PUB 567
   specifying starting, PUB 563–566
   using correct, PUB 557

Page Parts
   described, **PUB 172**
   using, PUB 172–181
page sections
   merging, PUB 591
   moving pages across, PUB 592
page setup, **PUB 206**
page size, **PUB 70**
page titles, **PUB 636**
pages
   adding to Web sites, PUB 637–639
   borders, PUB 569–571
   catalog, **PUB 467**
   changing e-mail size, background,
      PUB 508–510
   changing orientation, PUB 330–331
   content, **PUB 559**
   continuing stories across,
      PUB 149–150
   copying, PUB 590
   deleting customized, PUB 254
   home, **PUB 632**
   linking text boxes across,
      PUB 592–593
   master. *See* master pages
   moving across sections, PUB 592
   moving in newsletters, PUB 142
   navigating to specific,
      PUB 608–609
   opening customized, PUB 248
   Page Parts, using, PUB 172–181
   printing merged, PUB 419
   recto and verso, **PUB 172**
   secondary, **PUB 632**
   setting Page Options,
      PUB 140–141
   Web. *See* Web pages
Pane Navigation pane, PUB 560
panes
   See also specific pane
   described, **OFF 10**
paper considerations, PUB 113–114
paragraph mark (¶), PUB 79
paragraphs, entering text,
   PUB 78–80
passwords, **OFF 5**
pasting, copying and, PUB 74–78,
   PUB 606
paths
   corresponding drives and folders
      (table), OFF 20
   described, **OFF 20**, **PUB 466**
patterns, **PUB 179**, **PUB 226**
   inserting, PUB 179–180
   ruler guide, PUB 586–587

PDF (Portable Document Format)
   described, **PUB 303**
   saving publications in,
      PUB 613–614
PDF files
   converting publications to,
      PUB 302
   navigating with bookmarks in,
      PUB 614–615
photographs, **PUB 96**
   editing, PUB 220
   inserting into picture placeholders,
      PUB 28–30
picture fields, inserting,
   PUB 471–472
picture fills, **PUB 226**
picture placeholders
   inserting photos into, PUB 28–30
   using, PUB 101
picture styles
   applying, PUB 30–31
   described, **PUB 30**
pictures, **PUB 28**
   adding to form controls,
      PUB 670–671
   compressing, PUB 393
   editing captions, PUB 356–357
   embedded vs. linked, PUB 477
   filling shapes with, PUB 233
   flipping, PUB 213–214
   inserting, PUB 213
   inserting in greeting cards,
      PUB 540–541
   recoloring, PUB 220, PUB 392
   saving graphics as, PUB 224
   using as backgrounds, PUB 511
   and wrap points, PUB 217–219
pixels and points, **PUB 232**
placeholder text, **PUB 17–18**
planning
   attachments, e-mail, PUB 534
   BorderArt, PUB 568
   borders, PUB 568
   brochures, PUB 68
   catalogs, PUB 444
   creation of styles, PUB 278
   distribution of publications,
      PUB 40
   e-mail, PUB 506
   Excel table use, PUB 361
   forms, PUB 653
   global tools usage, PUB 594
   interactive Web sites, PUB 630
   large-scale publications, PUB 559
   layout and elements, PUB 212

newsletter layout, printing, PUB 138
newsletters, PUB 136
pagination, PUB 562
for printing, PUB 106, PUB 113
projects, PUB 4, PUB 204, PUB 205, APP 1–2
publications, PUB 2, PUB 268, PUB 324, PUB 386
research, PUB 146
tables, PUB 334
use of graphics, PUB 28
words for text, PUB 16
PNG (Portable Network Graphics) format, **PUB 224**
points, and pixels, **PUB 232**, PUB 398
portable files and formats, creating, PUB 302–305
portrait orientation, **PUB 170**
portrait orientation (page), **PUB 330–331**
positioning
  objects using Measurement toolbar, PUB 277–278
  shapes, PUB 230
  tables, PUB 369–370
  WordArt precisely, PUB 331
postcards, **PUB 534**
PostScript, PUB 389
PostScript files, using, PUB 118
PostScript fonts, PUB 83
PPD (PostScript printer driver), PUB 118
Preview Results group, Mailings tab, PUB 421
previewing
  animated graphics, PUB 644–645
  e-mail messages, PUB 527, PUB 531
  form letters, PUB 418
  live preview described, **OFF 14**, **PUB 20**
  merged publications, PUB 417, PUB 476
  multiple pages, PUB 41
  pages before printing, PUB 110–111
  Web publications, PUB 50–51
  Web sites, PUB 674–677
Previous Locations button, **OFF 22**
Print gallery, PUB 110
printers, merging catalogs to, PUB 485–487

printing
  business cards, PUB 300–302
  calendars, PUB 360
  considerations, options, PUB 113
  folded publications, PUB 543–544
  letters, PUB 291, PUB 370–371
  merged pages, PUB 419
  merged publications, PUB 417
  newsletters, PUB 191
  previewing pages before, PUB 110–111
  printer memory, PUB 109
  publications, PUB 40–42, PUB 246
  publications with settings, PUB 111–112
  recipient lists, PUB 417
  tables, PUB 351
  tickets, PUB 427–428
  traps, PUB 229
procedures
  described, **PUB 628**
  macros, PUB 678
process-color printing, PUB 114
product lists
  vs. address lists, PUB 444
  e-mail template, PUB 507
programs, **PUB 628**
  See also specific program
  Help, obtaining, OFF 49
  maximizing window, OFF 11–12
  Microsoft Office 2010, OFF 8–9, OFF 32–40
  quitting with publication open, OFF 31–32
  starting and using, OFF 9–11
  starting from Windows Explorer, OFF 38–39
  switching between, OFF 24–25
project planning guidelines, APP 1–2
projects
  business cards and stationery, PUB 266–267
  conference agenda, PUB 556–557
  designing newsletter, PUB 134–136
  distributed publications, PUB 504–506
  interactive Web site, PUB 628–629
  merging form letters and ticket numbers, PUB 384–385
  newspaper advertisement, PUB 202–203
  planning, PUB 204, PUB 205
  schedule, calendar, business table, PUB 322–324

spring break brochure, PUB 66–69
textbook catalog, PUB 442–445
promos, **PUB 352**
promotional pieces, **PUB 352**
proofreading
  described, **PUB 184**
  newsletters, PUB 185
properties, **PUB 17**
  See also specific property
  creating templates with changes, PUB 189–190
  form control, **PUB 654**
proportional spacing, **PUB 396**
.pub files, OFF 27
publication properties, **PUB 38**
  automatically collected, PUB 39
  changing, PUB 38–39
publication properties, setting, PUB 299–300
publication window, **OFF 12**
publications
  See also text
  adding graphics to, PUB 460–461
  blank, **PUB 205**
  business information sets, using, PUB 270–275
  callouts, creating, PUB 515–516
  checking for errors, PUB 106–109, PUB 246, PUB 613
  closing, OFF 32, PUB 247
  closing without saving, PUB 296
  creating catalog, PUB 459–465
  creating custom-sized, PUB 204–208
  creating from Backstage view, OFF 35
  customized sizes, schemes, building blocks, PUB 247–250
  data-driven, **PUB 442**
  deletions, additions, modifications, PUB 43–46
  e-mail. See e-mail
  embedding fonts, PUB 305–307
  footers, PUB 448
  headers, PUB 448–449
  inserting pictures, PUB 213
  layouts for large-scale, PUB 559
  managing merged, PUB 417–419
  and master pages, PUB 388–389
  merging data into, PUB 403–418
  navigating large-scale, PUB 607–612
  opening, PUB 43, PUB 387, PUB 631

packaging for publishing service, PUB 116–117
printing, PUB 40–42, PUB 246
printing folded, PUB 543–544
printing with settings, PUB 111–112
saving, PUB 27, PUB 72–73, PUB 350, PUB 394, PUB 402
saving frequently, OFF 19
saving in XPS format, PUB 613–614
saving with same file name, OFF 39–40
searching merge entries, PUB 474–475
sending print, as e-mail messages, PUB 533
sending using e-mail, PUB 504–506
sharing and distributing, PUB 504
spell-checking, PUB 46–47, PUB 107–108
tables. *See* tables
tickets. *See* tickets
using Excel-enhanced tables, PUB 361–370
viewing, OFF 12
volume, issue numbers, PUB 144
Web, **PUB 47**
Publisher
See also specific component or task
e-mail. *See* e-mail
Help, obtaining, OFF 44–50
importing text from other programs, PUB 146–148
opening publications from, PUB 43
overview, starting, OFF 9–12
quitting, OFF 32, PUB 42, PUB 51, PUB 118, PUB 308, PUB 371, PUB 430, PUB 685–686
security, PUB 630, PUB 682–683
starting, PUB 4–5, PUB 43, PUB 69, PUB 204, PUB 324–325
workspace, PUB 13
Publisher 2010, new features, PUB 28
Publisher window
components, OFF 12–19
switching to, OFF 24–25
Publisher's Review tab, PUB 106
publishing
business cards in portable format, PUB 303–305
desktop, **PUB 134**
Office 2010 Web pages online, APP 3–4

services, packaging publications for, PUB 116–117
publishing HTML, **PUB 48**
publishing to the Web, **PUB 48**
pull quotes, **PUB 172**
choosing text for, PUB 178
inserting, PUB 175–177
inserting text in, PUB 177–178
vs. sidebars, PUB 176
pullouts, **PUB 172**
pushpin (cropping mouse pointer), PUB 217

Q

QuarkXpress, PUB 205
Quick Access Toolbar, **OFF 15**
customizing, OFF 18
saving work, PUB 145
Quick Print button, OFF 18
quitting
Office programs, OFF 40
Publisher, OFF 31–32, PUB 42, PUB 51, PUB 118, PUB 308, PUB 371, PUB 430, PUB 685–686

R

radio buttons, **PUB 653**
read-only files, PUB 286–287
recipient lists
described, **PUB 404**
printing, PUB 417
Recent Documents list, **PUB 287**, PUB 288
recoloring, **PUB 220**, **PUB 390**
graphics, PUB 220–222, PUB 389
pictures, PUB 392
records, **PUB 404**
recto (page), **PUB 172**
Recycle Bin, **OFF 7**
Refresh button, **OFF 22**
removing
See also deleting
bold formatting, PUB 83
buttons from Quick Access Toolbar, OFF 18
character formatting, PUB 81
page numbers, PUB 567
Ribbon customization, PUB 162
renaming files, OFF 40–41
repeatable areas, **PUB 467**
repeating text, inserting, PUB 572–573

Replace, and Find commands, PUB 594–598
replacing
graphic using shortcut menu, PUB 166–168
graphic with clip art, PUB 169
placeholder text, PUB 17–18
text, PUB 18–19, PUB 77–78
Research Task pane, using, PUB 522–524, PUB 600
reset buttons, **PUB 654**
resize described, **PUB 34**
resizing
clip art, PUB 170
vs. cropping, PUB 215
e-mail pages, PUB 508–510
graphics, PUB 97, PUB 99
objects, **PUB 34–35**
scaling and, PUB 213
tables, PUB 346–347
windows, OFF 43–44
resolution, **PUB 643**
Restart command, **OFF 6**
Restore Down button, OFF 12
restoring Ribbon, OFF 16–17
return data labels, **PUB 654**, PUB 659
reusable parts
See also business information sets
creating, PUB 325
revising newsletters, PUB 184–190
Ribbon
components, OFF 14–15
customizing, OFF 36, PUB 157–158
displaying Developer tab on, PUB 678–679
formatting fonts using, PUB 23
inserting page numbers using, PUB 562–563
linking text boxes using, PUB 588–589
minimizing, displaying, restoring, OFF 16–17
and screen resolution, OFF 29, PUB 5, PUB 72, PUB 139
settings, PUB 14
right-clicking, OFF 4
rotating
described, **PUB 213**
objects, PUB 213–214
rows, table
deleting, PUB 338
inserting, PUB 338
selecting contents, PUB 341

ruler guide patterns, PUB 586–587
ruler origin, **PUB 400**
rulers, **PUB 399**
  in Print gallery, PUB 110
  working with, PUB 399–402

S

Sample Line color command,
    PUB 231
sampling, **PUB 279**
  colors, PUB 231
  font colors, PUB 279
Save As command, APP 4
Save for Another Computer button,
    PUB 116
saving
  automatically, PUB 72
  business cards, PUB 300
  business information sets, PUB 274
  calendars, PUB 360
  data sources, PUB 411
  envelopes, PUB 294
  files in folders, OFF 25–27, OFF 36
  graphics as pictures, PUB 224
  greeting cards, PUB 543
  letterhead, PUB 285
  letters, PUB 291
  online, OFF 20
  and organizing files, OFF 19–27
  pictures to Building Block Library,
      PUB 234–235
  print publications as Web
      publications, PUB 48–49
  publications, PUB 27, PUB 235,
      PUB 350, PUB 394
  publications in PDF format,
      PUB 613–614
  publications with same file name,
      OFF 39–40, PUB 246, PUB 402
  to USB flash drives, OFF 20–22,
      PUB 459
  Web pages to online location,
      APP 3–4
scaling
  described, **PUB 213**, **PUB 396**
  graphics, PUB 213, PUB 391
scheme colors, PUB 222
schemes
  custom color, PUB 208–210
  custom font, PUB 210–212
  font, PUB 558
scratch area
  described, **PUB 34**
  using, PUB 365, PUB 389

screen resolution, **OFF 29**
  changing, OFF 30–31
  and Ribbon, PUB 5, PUB 72,
      PUB 139
ScreenTips
  descriptions in, PUB 450
  turning on, PUB 28
script fonts, PUB 83
scroll bar, scroll arrows, scroll box,
    OFF 4
scrolling marquee, inserting,
    PUB 673
scrolling through folders, OFF 23–24
search box, **OFF 22**
Search box, starting programs using,
    OFF 32–33
searching
  for Help topics, OFF 45–47
  merge entries, PUB 474–475
  for templates, PUB 70–71
  wildcard and format (table),
      PUB 594
secondary pages, **PUB 632**
section breaks, PUB 590
sections, **PUB 560**
  collapsing, PUB 578
  creating, PUB 560–561
  deleting, PUB 562
security
  incorporating in documents,
      PUB 630
  levels, setting, **PUB 682–683**
Select Table dialog box, PUB 422
selecting
  adjacent objects by dragging,
      PUB 171–172
  data sources, PUB 469–470
  and entering text, PUB 16–19
  multiple objects, PUB 223
  objects generally, **PUB 14**
  sentences, PUB 177, PUB 185
  table contents, PUB 340–342
  templates, PUB 7–8
Send E-Mail command, PUB 532
separating pages, PUB 560–561
services, modifying Research Task
    pane, PUB 600
shade backgrounds, creating,
    PUB 574–575
shades
  described, **PUB 226**
  using, PUB 568
shading styles, PUB 228–229
Shadow Color command, PUB 245
shadow effects, adding, PUB 245

Shape Fill button, WordArt,
    PUB 329
shape fills, **PUB 226**
shape outlines
  changing, PUB 232
  selecting color for, **PUB 230–231**
Shape Styles gallery, PUB 226
shapes, PUB 225
  BorderArt, PUB 226
  changing WordArt object's,
      PUB 328
  filling with pictures, PUB 233
  inserting, PUB 225–226, PUB 570
  positioning, PUB 230
  setting picture, PUB 30
sharing publications, PUB 504
shortcut keys, **OFF 4–5**
shortcut menus, **OFF 18**
  formatting text using, PUB 23
  replacing graphic using,
      PUB 166–168
  specifying starting page numbers
      using, PUB 563–566
shortcuts
  described, **OFF 22**
  macros, **PUB 678**
Show Header/Footer button,
    PUB 448
Show/Hide ¶ button, PUB 160
Shut down command, **OFF 6**
sidebars
  described, **PUB 172**, PUB 176
  editing, PUB 173–175
Single Page view, **OFF 12**
size, page, **PUB 70**
sizing
  fonts, PUB 24, PUB 241
  pages, PUB 206–208
Sleep command, **OFF 6**
sliders, **OFF 31**
smart tag button, **PUB 18**
smart tags
  business information field,
      PUB 276
  described, **PUB 144**
snap (align)
  described, **PUB 45**
  objects to margin guides,
      PUB 332–333
software
  See also specific type
  application, **OFF 2**
sorting vs. filtering, PUB 423
sounds, inserting background,
    PUB 648–649

source documents, **PUB 361**
spacing
  between characters, PUB 396–399
  line. *See* line spacing
Spanish, translating text into,
    PUB 482–484
special characters
  described, **PUB 517**
  inserting, PUB 517–521
Special Characters button,
    PUB 400
spell-checking, PUB 188
  with AutoCorrect, PUB 452–454
  e-mail messages, PUB 530
  foreign language text, PUB 484
  publications, PUB 46–47,
    PUB 107–108, PUB 613
  Web sites, PUB 683–684
  WordArt, PUB 242
splitting table cells, PUB 342
spot colors, PUB 114, PUB 390
spread, **PUB 445**
spring break brochure (project),
    PUB 66–69
squares, creating, PUB 226
Start button, **OFF 10**
Start menu, starting programs using,
    OFF 10
starting
  programs, OFF 9–11
  programs using Search box,
    OFF 32–33
  Publisher, PUB 4–5, OFF 9–12,
    PUB 43, PUB 69, PUB 324–325
  Windows 7, OFF 5–7
statements, entering code,
    PUB 680–681
stationery, **PUB 510**
status bar, **OFF 13**
stories, **PUB 145**
  continuing across pages,
    PUB 149–150
  editing in Microsoft Word,
    PUB 159–166
styles
  adding, PUB 237
  applying, PUB 236–237
  applying new, PUB 281–282
  bullet, PUB 21
  creating new, PUB 278–281
  picture, **PUB 30**
  shading, PUB 228–229
  stylistic sets and alternates,
    PUB 83–85
submit buttons, **PUB 654**

submit form controls
  inserting, PUB 669–671
  server settings, PUB 674
subscripts, PUB 88
subsetting, **PUB 118**
subtitles, entering, PUB 576
suites, **OFF 8**
summing in embedded tables,
    PUB 367–369
superscripts, PUB 88
swashes, using, **PUB 87**
switching between programs,
    OFF 24–25
SWOP (Standard for Web Offset
    Printing), **PUB 118**
Symbol dialog box, PUB 517–520
symbols
  described, **PUB 517**
  inserting, PUB 517–521
synchronized, **PUB 22**
synonyms, looking up, **PUB 598–600**

T

tab selectors, **PUB 399**, PUB 400
tab stop markers, **PUB 399**,
    PUB 400, PUB 451
tab stops
  described, **PUB 399**
  setting, PUB 401
table of contents, **PUB 172**
Table Tools Layout tab, Ribbon,
    PUB 337
tables, **PUB 334**
  adding borders to, PUB 358–360
  adjusting margins within, PUB 579,
    PUB 581–582
  applying formats, PUB 339–340
  color schemes, PUB 339
  embedded. *See* embedded tables
  entering data in, PUB 336
  Excel, using, PUB 361–370
  inserting, entering data into,
    PUB 334–336
  linked. *See* linked tables
  merging cells, PUB 341
  moving, positioning, PUB 369–370
  resizing, PUB 346–347
  selecting contents, PUB 340–342
  splitting cells, PUB 342
  working with, PUB 322
tables of content
  building blocks, inserting,
    PUB 579–580
  updating, PUB 606–607

tabs, **PUB 399**
  deleting, PUB 401
  vs. indents, PUB 402
  leader, **PUB 399**
  on Ribbon, **OFF 14**
  tool tabs, **PUB 17**
  working with, PUB 399–402
tags (file property), PUB 189
task pane, **OFF 14**
tasks, automating with macros,
    PUB 678
tear-offs, **PUB 22**
  deleting, PUB 44
  entering text, PUB 22
Tear-offs gallery, PUB 11
templates, **PUB 5**
  business card, PUB 297
  creating, PUB 189–190
  creating e-mail using, PUB 504
  creating flyers from, PUB 5–8
  creating letterhead, PUB 269–270
  customizing, PUB 9–13
  e-mail, PUB 507–516
  envelope, PUB 292
  greeting card, PUB 537
  with landscape orientation,
    PUB 331
  newsletter, choosing, PUB 138–139
  vs. read-only files, PUB 286
  searching for, PUB 70–71
  storing, PUB 189
  using custom letterhead,
    PUB 287–288
testing
  form controls, PUB 685
  forms, PUB 630
  hyperlinks, PUB 612
  macros, PUB 685–686
  Web sites, PUB 674–677, PUB 685
text
  alternative, **PUB 645**
  autofitting, PUB 24–25
  bold, PUB 83
  centering, PUB 45
  changing direction of,
    PUB 585–586
  copy, cut, paste, delete methods
    (table), PUB 74
  copying and pasting, PUB 75–76
  displaying in stylistic sets, PUB 84
  dropping and dragging,
    PUB 185–186
  entering in publications,
    OFF 35–36
  entering tabbed, PUB 401–402

formatting, PUB 343–344
formatting with continued notices, PUB 152–155
hyphenation, PUB 187–188
importing from other programs, PUB 146
inserting repeating, PUB 572–573
italicizing, PUB 81
ligatures, enabling, PUB 85–86
moving, PUB 185–186
in overflow area, PUB 150
placeholder, **PUB 17**
replacing, PUB 18–19
selecting and entering, PUB 16–19
spacing between characters, PUB 396–399
story, **PUB 145**
translating, PUB 480–484
typing paragraphs, PUB 78–80
underlining, PUB 82
wordwrapping, PUB 79–80, PUB 151
wrapping around graphics, PUB 170
text area
described, **PUB 654**
form controls, PUB 660–661
Text Box Tools Format tab, PUB 236
text boxes, OFF 6, **PUB 17**
changing margins, PUB 583
copying, PUB 588
creating, PUB 77, PUB 239
creating columns in, PUB 240–242
creating for labels, PUB 655–656
drawing, PUB 44–45, PUB 236, PUB 588
editing, PUB 73, PUB 183
editing e-mail, PUB 511–512
linking, PUB 588–589
linking across pages, PUB 592–593
'Type words to search for,' OFF 45–47
text files
importing, PUB 147–148, PUB 155–156, PUB 593, PUB 604–605
inserting, PUB 584
Text in Overflow button, **PUB 151**
textbox form controls, **PUB 654**, PUB 657–660
texture fills, **PUB 226**
thesaurus, PUB 106, **PUB 598–600**
thumbnails, **PUB 6**

tickets, **PUB 419**
creating, PUB 419–427
printing, PUB 427–428
time, inserting current, PUB 283–284
tints, **PUB 226**, PUB 568
titles
entering, PUB 576
(Web) page, **PUB 636**, PUB 641
toggling
between current page view and Whole Page view, PUB 162
described, **PUB 162**
toner, conserving, PUB 111
tool tabs, **OFF 14**, **PUB 17**
tools
Crop, PUB 215
ruler, PUB 400
totaling in embedded tables, PUB 367–369
track kerning, **PUB 396**
tracking
characters, PUB 397
described, **PUB 396**
trademark special character, PUB 519
translating text, PUB 480–484
Transparency sliders, PUB 228
traps (color), **PUB 229**
troubleshooting printing of graphics, PUB 487
TrueType fonts, PUB 83, **PUB 211**, PUB 305
T-shirts, creating designs, PUB 113
two-page spread, PUB 445
Type New List command, PUB 469
typing errors, correcting, PUB 18–19
typography, character, PUB 81

U

underlining text, **PUB 82**
undoing
actions, PUB 27
drag-and-drop edits, PUB 186
moves, PUB 177
wrap point edits, PUB 218
ungrouping
described, **PUB 222**
graphics, PUB 222
Unicode, **PUB 517**
Uniform Resource Identifier (URI), **PUB 526**
unsubscribe, **PUB 504**
Update Scheme from Publication Styles command, PUB 253

updating
business information sets, PUB 271
publications with data from linked files, PUB 369
USB flash drives, PUB 117
expanding, OFF 26
saving files on, OFF 36, PUB 459
saving to, OFF 20–22, OFF 27
user accounts, **OFF 5**
user icons, **OFF 5**, OFF 6
user names, **OFF 5**

V

VBA (Visual Basic for Applications), PUB 282, **PUB 629**, PUB 678
verso (page), **PUB 172**
video, **PUB 96**
viewing
See also displaying
catalog boundaries, PUB 472
master pages, PUB 388–389
publications, OFF 12
two-page spreads, PUB 601–602
views
See also specific view
toggling between current, and Whole Page, PUB 162
visitor counters for Web sites, PUB 673
Visual Basic Editor, PUB 679–681
Visual Basic for Applications (VBA), PUB 282, **PUB 629**, PUB 678
visual layout guides, **PUB 34**

W

wallpaper, **PUB 510**
watermarks, **PUB 388**
creating on master pages, PUB 386, PUB 388
inserting, placing, PUB 391
wavy underlines, PUB 46–47
Web graphics, PUB 643–644
Web hot spots, inserting, PUB 672
Web mastheads, creating, PUB 633–634
Web pages
adding to Web sites, PUB 637
creating from publications, PUB 47–51
editing calendar, PUB 649–652
editing Contact Us, PUB 652–653
form controls. *See* form controls

publishing Office 2010 online,
  APP 3–4
setting options, PUB 647–649
Web publications
 described, **PUB 47**
 previewing, PUB 50–51
Web sites
 adding pages to, PUB 637
 background sounds, inserting,
  PUB 648–649
 checking for spelling, design errors,
  PUB 683–684
 color and font schemes for, PUB 632
 interactive, **PUB 628**
 navigation bars, adding,
  PUB 635–636
 previewing, PUB 674–677
 testing, PUB 674–677, PUB 685
 visitor counters, PUB 673
Weight gallery, PUB 232
Welcome screen, **OFF 5**
Whole Page view, PUB 162
wildcard and format searching
  (table), PUB 594
windows
 folder, OFF 22–23
 maximizing program, OFF 11–12

minimized, **OFF 27**
minimizing, OFF 27–28
moving, OFF 43–44
Publisher, OFF 12–19,
  OFF 24–25
resizing, OFF 44
VBA coding, PUB 680
Windows 7, **OFF 2**
 Basic and Aero, OFF 2–4
 desktop, customizing, OFF 7
 starting, OFF 5–7
Windows Clipboard, PUB 74
Windows Explorer, OFF 28
 creating blank documents from,
  OFF 37–38
 starting programs, opening files
  from, OFF 38–39
Windows Help and Support,
  OFF 49–50
Wingdings, PUB 518
wizards, **PUB 404**
Word. *See* Microsoft Word
WordArt, PUB 242
 objects, inserting, PUB 243–244,
  PUB 327
 placing precisely, PUB 331
 reshaping objects, PUB 328–329

WordArt Shape gallery, PUB 328
wordwrap
 in table cells, PUB 336
 in text boxes, PUB 415
 text, PUB 79–80, PUB 151
World Lingo translation service,
  PUB 483
wrap points, editing, **PUB 217–219**
Write & Insert Fields group,
  Mailings tab, PUB 421

X

XML Paper Specification,
  PUB 303
XPS (XML Paper Specification)
 described, **PUB 303**
 files, creating, PUB 42
 saving publications in, PUB 613–614

Z

zero point, **PUB 400**
zooming
 for editing, PUB 16
 zoom methods (table), PUB 14

Quick Reference Summary

Microsoft Publisher 2010 Quick Reference Summary

Task	Page Number	Mouse	Ribbon	Shortcut Menu	Keyboard Shortcut
Align Data in Cells	PUB 344		Align Center button (Table Tools Layout tab | Alignment group)		
Align Relative to Margin Guides	PUB 332		Align button (WordArt Tools Format tab | Arrange group)		
Alternative Text, Add to Graphic	PUB 646		Format Shape Dialog Box Launcher (Picture Tools Format tab | Picture Styles group), type text in Alternative text text box	Format Picture, Alternative text text box (Format Picture dialog box)	
Animated Graphic, Preview	PUB 644	Preview/Properties (Clip Art task pane | thumbnail button menu)			
AutoCorrect as You Type	PUB 453	AutoCorrect Options button			
AutoCorrect Entry, Create	PUB 455		File tab | Options, Proofing (Publisher Options dialog box), AutoCorrect Options button		
Autofit Text	PUB 25		Format Text Box Dialog Box Launcher (Text Box Tools Format tab | Text group), Text Box tab (Format Text Box dialog box), Best Fit	Best Fit	
Background	PUB 446		Background button (Page Design tab | Page Background group)		
Background Sound	PUB 648		Web Page Options button (Web tab | Options group), Browse button		
Blank Publication, Select	PUB 205		Blank 8 × 11" (File tab | New tab)		
Bold	PUB 83	Bold button on Mini toolbar	Bold button (Home tab | Font group) or Font Dialog Box Launcher (Home tab | Font group), Font tab (Font dialog box), Font style box arrow	Change Text, Font, Font style box (Font dialog box), Bold	CTRL+B
Bookmark, Create	PUB 609		Bookmark button (Insert tab | Links group)		

Microsoft Publisher 2010 Quick Reference Summary (continued)

Task	Page Number	Mouse	Ribbon	Shortcut Menu	Keyboard Shortcut
Bookmark Hyperlink	PUB 611		Insert Hyperlink button (Insert tab | Links group), Place in This Document button (Insert Hyperlink dialog box)		CTRL+K
Bookmarks, Navigate with	PUB 614	Click bookmark			
BorderArt	PUB 570		Format Shape Dialog Box Launcher (Drawing Tools Format tab | Shape Styles group), BorderArt button (Format AutoShape dialog box)	Format AutoShape, Colors and Lines tab (Format AutoShape dialog box), BorderArt button	
Borders, Table	PUB 359	Borders button on Mini toolbar	Borders button arrow (Table Tools Design tab | Borders group)	Format Table, Colors and Lines tab (Format Table dialog box)	
Boundaries, Display	PUB 15	Point to area	Boundaries check box (View tab | Show group)		
Boundaries, Turn On	PUB 239		Boundaries check box (View tab | Show group)		
Building Block, Add to Library	PUB 234		Page Parts button (Insert tab | Building Blocks group)	Select text, Save as Building Block	
Building Block, Delete	PUB 251		Show Building Block Library Dialog Box Launcher (Insert tab | Building Blocks group), click folder, right-click object, Delete		
Building Block, Insert	PUB 32		Show Building Block Library Dialog Box Launcher (Insert tab | Building Blocks group)		
Bullets, Create	PUB 20	Bullets button on Mini toolbar	Bullets button (Home tab | Paragraph group)		
Business Cards, Print	PUB 300		File tab | Print tab, Pages button, 'Multiple copies per sheet'		CTRL+P
Business Information Field, Insert	PUB 275		Business Information button (Insert tab | Text group) or Building Blocks Dialog Box Launcher, click Business Information folder (Building Block Library dialog box), select object, Insert button		
Business Information Set, Create	PUB 271	Smart tag button, Edit Business Information, enter data, Update Publication button (Business Information dialog box)	Business Information button (Insert tab | Text group)		
Business Information Set, Delete	PUB 307		Business Information button (Insert tab | Text group), Edit Business Information, select set, Delete button (Business Information dialog box)		
Calendar, Create	PUB 352		Calendars (File tab | New tab) or Calendars button (Insert tab | Building Blocks group)		

Microsoft Publisher 2010 Quick Reference Summary *(continued)*

Task	Page Number	Mouse	Ribbon	Shortcut Menu	Keyboard Shortcut
Captions Gallery	PUB 104		Caption button (Picture Tools Format tab | Picture Styles group)		
Catalog Pages, Create	PUB 467		Catalog Pages button (Insert tab | Pages group)		
Cell Diagonal, Create	PUB 348		Diagonals button (Table Tools Layout tab | Merge group)		
Cell Margins, Change	PUB 581		Cell Margins button (Table Tools Layout tab | Alignment group), Custom Margins	Format Table, Cell Properties tab (Format Table dialog box)	
Center Text	PUB 45	Center button on Mini toolbar	Center button (Home tab | Paragraph group) or Paragraph Dialog Box Launcher (Home tab | Paragraph group) Indents and Spacing tab, Alignment box arrow (Paragraph dialog box)		CTRL+E
Check Spelling as You Type	PUB 47			Right-click flagged word, click correct word on shortcut menu	
Check Spelling, Entire Publication	PUB 107		Spelling button (Review tab | Proofing group)	Right-click flagged text | Spelling	F7
Checkbox Form Control, Insert	PUB 662		Form Controls button (Web tab | Code group), Checkbox		
Checkbox Form Control Properties	PUB 663		Double-click control		
Clip Art, Insert	PUB 94		Clip Art button (Insert tab | Illustrations group)		
Clip Art Task Pane, Close	PUB 102	Close button on task pane title bar	Clip Art button (Insert tab | Illustrations group)		
Close Publication without Quitting Publisher	PUB 247		Close (File tab)		CTRL+F4
Collapse Sections	PUB 578		Collapse Section button (Page Navigation pane)		
Color Model, Choose	PUB 115		Commercial Print Settings button (File tab | Info tab)		
Color Scheme, Change	PUB 209		More button (Page Design tab | Schemes group)		
Color Scheme, Create New	PUB 209		More button (Page Design tab | Schemes group)		
Color Scheme, Delete Customized	PUB 252		More button (Page Design tab | Schemes group), right-click color scheme, Delete Scheme		
Column, Delete	PUB 337		Delete Rows or Columns button (Table Tools Layout tab | Rows & Columns group)	Delete, Delete Columns	
Column, Insert	PUB 339		Insert Columns to the Left (or Insert Columns to the Right) button (Table Tools Layout tab | Rows & Columns group)	Insert, Insert Left or Insert Right	
Column Width, Change	PUB 346	Drag column border			

Microsoft Publisher 2010 Quick Reference Summary *(continued)*

Task	Page Number	Mouse	Ribbon	Shortcut Menu	Keyboard Shortcut
Columns, Set	PUB 240		Columns button (Home tab | Paragraph group)	Format Text box, Text Box tab (Format Text dialog box), Columns button	
Compress Picture	PUB 393		Compress Pictures button (Picture Tools Format tab | Adjust group), Desktop Printing option button (Compress Pictures dialog box)		
Continue a Story across Pages	PUB 149		Click Yes or No button (Microsoft Publisher dialog box) until desired location is reached		
Continue a Story across Pages, Manually	PUB 151	Text in Overflow button on selected text box	Create Link button (Text Box Tools Format tab | Linking group), navigate to desired text box, click text box		
Continued Notice, Insert	PUB 152		Format Text Box Dialog Box Launcher (Text Box Tools Format tab | Text group), Text Box tab (Format Text Box dialog box), Include "Continued on page…" check box	Format Text Box, Text Box tab (Format Text Box dialog box), Include "Continued on page …" check box	
Copy Text	PUB 75		Copy button (Home tab | Clipboard group)	Copy	CTRL+C
Coupon, Insert	PUB 182		Advertisements button (Insert tab | Building Blocks group) or Building Blocks Dialog Box Launcher (Insert tab | Building Blocks group), Advertisements folder (Building Block Library dialog box)		
Crop	PUB 216	Crop button on Mini toolbar	Crop button (Picture Tools Format tab | Crop group)	Format Picture, Picture tab (Format Picture dialog box)	
Custom Page Size	PUB 206		Page Size button (Page Design tab | Page Setup group), Create New Page Size		
Customize Ribbon	PUB 157		Customize Ribbon button (File tab | Options)	Customize the Ribbon	
Customize Ribbon, Remove	PUB 162		Customize Ribbon button (File tab | Options), Reset button (Publisher Options dialog box)	Customize the Ribbon, Reset button (Publisher Options dialog box)	
Cut Text	PUB 74		Cut button (Home tab | Clipboard group)	Cut	CTRL+X
Data Source, Create New Entries	PUB 410	New Entry button (New Address List dialog box)			
Data Source, Save	PUB 411	Save button (Save Address List dialog box)			

Microsoft Publisher 2010 Quick Reference Summary *(continued)*

Task	Page Number	Mouse	Ribbon	Shortcut Menu	Keyboard Shortcut
Data Source, Select	PUB 469		Add List button (Catalog Tools Format tab | Start group), Use Existing List		
Date and Time, Insert	PUB 401		Date & Time button (Insert tab | Text group)		
Delete Text	PUB 74		Cut button (Home tab | Clipboard group)	Delete Text	CTRL+X or DELETE or BACKSPACE
Design Checker, Run	PUB 108		Run Design Checker button (File tab | Info tab)		
Developer Tab, Display	PUB 678		Customize Ribbon button (File tab | Options), Developer check box (Publisher Options dialog box)		
Drag and Drop Text	PUB 185	Drag selected text to new location, then release mouse button			
Drop Cap	PUB 84		Drop Cap button (Text Box Tools Format tab | Typography group)		
Duplicate Page	PUB 590		Insert Blank Page button arrow (Insert tab | Pages group)	Insert Duplicate Page	
E-Mail Message, Preview	PUB 531		E-mail Preview button (File tab | Save & Send tab | E-mail Preview tab)		
E-Mail, Change Page Size	PUB 508		Page Size button (Page Design tab | Page Setup group)		
E-Mail, Insert a Border	PUB 538		Borders & Accents button (Insert tab | Building Blocks group)		
E-Mail, Modify Paper Size and Margins	PUB 533		Page Setup Dialog Box Launcher (Page Design tab | Page Setup group), Layout type box arrow (Page Setup dialog box), E-mail		
E-Mail, Send Multiple Page Publication	PUB 533		Send All Pages button (File tab | Save & Send tab | Send Using E-mail tab)		
E-Mail, Send Using Publisher	PUB 532		Send Current Page button (File tab | Save & Send tab | Send Using E-mail tab)		
Embedded Table, Copy and Paste	PUB 365		Paste button arrow (Home tab | Clipboard group), Paste Special, Paste option button (Paste Special dialog box)		
Embedded Table, Create	PUB 364		Insert Object button (Insert tab | Text group), Create from File option button (Insert Object dialog box)		
Embedded Table, Format	PUB 366		Use Ribbon in active program to select and apply formats		
Embedded Table, Sum	PUB 367		Sum button (Excel Home tab | Editing group)		
Envelope, Create	PUB 292		Envelopes (File tab | New tab)		

Microsoft Publisher 2010 Quick Reference Summary *(continued)*

Task	Page Number	Mouse	Ribbon	Shortcut Menu	Keyboard Shortcut
Exclude Entries	PUB 476		Exclude Entry button (Catalog Tools Format tab | Preview Page group)		
Filter Data	PUB 423		Filter link (Mail Merge Recipients dialog box), Filter Records tab (Filter and Sort dialog box)		
Find Entries	PUB 474		Find Entry button (Catalog Tools Format tab | Preview Page group)		
Find Text	PUB 594		Find button (Home tab | Editing group)		CTRL+F
Font, Change	PUB 23	Font box arrow on Mini toolbar	Font box arrow (Home tab | Font group)	Change Text, Font, Font box arrow (Font dialog box)	
Font Color, Change	PUB 36	Font Color button arrow on Mini toolbar	Font Color button (Home tab | Font group)		
Font Effect, Apply	PUB 89		Font Dialog Box Launcher (Home tab | Font group)	Change Text, Font, changes setting (Font dialog box)	CTRL+SHIFT+F
Font Scheme, Change	PUB 211		Scheme Fonts box arrow (File tab | New tab) or Fonts button (Page Design tab | Schemes group)		
Font Scheme, Create New	PUB 211		Scheme Fonts button (Page Design tab | Schemes group)		
Font Scheme, Delete Customized	PUB 253		Scheme Fonts button (Page Design tab | Schemes group), right-click font scheme, Delete Scheme		
Font Size, Change	PUB 283	Font Size button on Mini toolbar	Font Size box (Home tab | Font group)	Change Text, Font, Font Size box arrow (Font dialog box)	
Font Size, Decrease	PUB 24	Decrease Font Size button on Mini toolbar	Decrease Font Size button (Home tab | Font group) or Font Size box arrow (Home tab | Font group) or Font Dialog Box Launcher (Home tab | Font group), Size box arrow (Font dialog box)		CTRL+SHIFT+<
Font Size, Increase	PUB 24	Increase Font Size button on Mini toolbar	Increase Font Size button (Home tab | Font group) or Font Size box arrow (Home tab | Font group) or Font Dialog Box Launcher (Home tab | Font group), Size box arrow (Font dialog box)		CTRL+SHIFT+>
Fonts, Embed	PUB 306		Commercial Print Settings button (File tab | Info tab)		
Footers, Alternating	PUB 450		With master page selected, Show Header/Footer button (Master Page tab | Header & Footer group)		

Microsoft Publisher 2010 Quick Reference Summary *(continued)*

Task	Page Number	Mouse	Ribbon	Shortcut Menu	Keyboard Shortcut
Form Properties, Edit	PUB 671		Double-click form control, Form Properties button (Properties dialog box)	Format Form Properties, Form Properties button (Properties dialog box)	
Format Painter	PUB 91	Format Painter button on Mini toolbar	Format Painter button (Home tab | Clipboard group)		CTRL+SHIFT+C, then CTRL+SHIFT+V
Formatting Marks, Display	PUB 79		Special Characters button (Home tab | Paragraph group)		CTRL+SHIFT+Y
Go To Page	PUB 608		Find button arrow (Home tab | Editing group), Go to Page		CTRL+G
Gradient Fill Effect	PUB 227	Shape Fill button on Mini toolbar	Shape Fill button arrow (Drawing Tools Format tab | Shape Styles group) or Format Shape Dialog Box Launcher (Drawing Tools Format tab | Shape Styles group), Colors and Lines tab (Format AutoShape dialog box)	Format AutoShape, Colors and Lines tab (Format AutoShape dialog box), Fill Effects button	
Graphic, Crop	PUB 216	Crop button on Mini toolbar	Crop button arrow (Picture Tools Format tab | Crop group)	Format Picture, Picture tab (Format Picture dialog box), Crop from area	
Graphic, Duplicate	PUB 180				CTRL+drag or CTRL+SHIFT+drag
Graphic, Flip	PUB 181		Rotate button (Drawing Tools Format tab | Arrange group), Flip Horizontal button or Flip Vertical button (Rotate gallery)		
Graphic, Resize	PUB 97				SHIFT+drag sizing handle
Graphics Manager	PUB 477		Graphics Manager check box (View tab | Show group)		
Group Selected Objects	PUB 223		Group button (Picture Tools Format tab | Arrange group)	Group	CTRL+SHIFT+G
Grouped Field Codes, Insert	PUB 413	Click link (Mail Merge task pane)			
Guide Pattern	PUB 586		Guides button (Page Design tab | Layout group)		
Hot Spot, Insert	PUB 525		Select graphic or object, Insert Hyperlink button (Insert tab | Links group)	Hyperlink	CTRL+K
HTML Code Fragment	PUB 673		HTML Code Fragment button (Web tab | Web Page Navigation group)		
Hyperlink, Insert	PUB 525		Insert Hyperlink button (Web tab | Web Page Navigation group) or Insert Hyperlink button (Insert tab | Links group)		CTRL+K

Microsoft Publisher 2010 Quick Reference Summary (continued)

Task	Page Number	Mouse	Ribbon	Shortcut Menu	Keyboard Shortcut
Hyperlink, Test	PUB 612				CTRL+click hyperlink
Hyphenation, Check	PUB 187		Hyphenation button (Text Box Tools Format tab | Text group), Manual button (Hyphenation dialog box)		CTRL+SHIFT+H
Import a File	PUB 147		Insert File button (Insert tab | Test group)	Change Text, Text File	
Individual Field Codes, Insert	PUB 415	Select field in Mail Merge task pane or drag field from Mail Merge task pane into publication			
Italicize	PUB 81	Italic button on Mini toolbar	Italic button (Home tab | Font group) or Font Dialog Box Launcher (Home tab | Font group), Font style box arrow (Font dialog box)	Change Text, Font, Font style box (Font dialog box), Italic	CTRL+I
Kern Character Pairs	PUB 398	Kerning box on Measurement toolbar	Character Spacing button (Home tab | Font group), More Spacing command	Change Text, Character Spacing, Kerning box (Character Spacing dialog box)	
Ligature, Enable	PUB 86		Ligatures button (Text Box Tools Format tab | Typography group) or Symbol button (Insert tab | Text group)		
Line Spacing, Change	PUB 241		Line Spacing button (Home tab | Paragraph group) or Paragraph Dialog Box Launcher (Home tab | Paragraph group)	Change Text, Paragraph, Indents and Spacing tab, Line spacing area (Paragraph dialog box)	
Link Text Boxes	PUB 588		Create Link button (Text Box Tools Format tab | Linking group), click second box		
Linked Table, Copy and Paste	PUB 366		Paste button arrow (Home tab | Clipboard group) Paste Special, Paste Link option button (Paste Special dialog box)		
Linked Table, Insert	PUB 365		Insert Object button (Insert tab | Text group), Create from File option button, Link check box (Insert Object dialog box)		
List Box Form Control, Insert	PUB 667		Form Controls button (Web tab | Code group), List Box		
List Box Properties Form Control Properties	PUB 667		Double-click control	Format Form Properties	
Mail Merge Wizard	PUB 404		Mail Merge button arrow (Mailings tab | Start group)		

Microsoft Publisher 2010 Quick Reference Summary *(continued)*

Task	Page Number	Mouse	Ribbon	Shortcut Menu	Keyboard Shortcut
Mailto Hyperlink, Create	PUB 526		Hyperlink button (Insert tab | Links group), E-mail Address button (Link to bar)		CTRL+K, E-mail Address button (Link to bar)
Master Page, Close	PUB 394		Close Master Page button (Master Page tab | Close group)		
Master Page, Duplicate	PUB 450		Duplicate button (Master Page tab | Master Page group)	Right-click thumbnail (Page Navigation pane), Insert Duplicate Page	
Master Page, View	PUB 388		Master Page button (View tab | Views group)		
Master Pages, Apply	PUB 456		Apply To button (Master Page tab | Master Page group)	Right-click thumbnail (Page Navigation pane), Master Pages, click desired master page	
Measurement Toolbar, Display	PUB 276	Object Position button or Object Size button on status bar	Measurement button (Drawing Tools Format tab | Size group)		
Measurement Toolbar, Position Objects with	PUB 277	Position boxes on Measurement toolbar		Format	
Merge Field Codes, Insert	PUB 425		Insert Merge Field button (Mailings tab | Write & Insert Fields group)		
Merge Sections	PUB 591			Merge with Previous Section	
Merge Table Cells	PUB 342		Merge Cells button (Table Tools Layout tab | Merge group)		
Merge to Printer	PUB 485		Merge to Printer button (Catalog Tools Format tab | Merge group)		
Merge, Preview	PUB 476		Preview Results button (Catalog Tools Format tab | Preview Page group)		
Merged Publication, Create	PUB 417		'Next wizard step' link (Mail Merge task pane)		
Navigation Bar Properties	PUB 639			Navigation Bar Properties	
Navigation Bar, Insert	PUB 636		Navigation Bar button (Web tab | Web Page Navigation group) or Building Block Library Dialog Box Launcher (Insert tab | Building Blocks group), Navigation Bars folder (Building Block Library dialog box)		
Object, Align	PUB 35	Drag boundary until visual layout guides appear	Align button (Drawing Tools Format tab | Arrange group)		

Microsoft Publisher 2010 Quick Reference Summary *(continued)*

Task	Page Number	Mouse	Ribbon	Shortcut Menu	Keyboard Shortcut
Object, Delete	PUB 26		Cut button (Home tab | Clipboard group)	Delete Object	DELETE or BACKSPACE or CTRL+X
Object, Move	PUB 34	Drag boundary or Position boxes on Measurement toolbar			Select object, press RIGHT, LEFT, UP, or DOWN ARROW
Object, Resize	PUB 35	Object Size box on status bar or SHIFT+drag corner sizing handle		Format Picture, Size tab (Format Picture dialog box), Size and Rotate area	
Open a Publication	PUB 43		Open button (File tab)		CTRL+O
Option Button Form Control Properties	PUB 665		Double-click control	Format Form Properties	
Option Button Form Control, Insert	PUB 664		Form Controls button (Web tab | Code group), Option Button		
Pack and Go Wizard	PUB 116		Save for a Commercial Printer button (File tab | Save & Send tab)		
Page Break, Insert	PUB 602				CTRL+ENTER
Page Navigation Pane, Collapse	PUB 13	Collapse Page Navigation Pane button in Page Navigation pane			
Page Navigation Pane, Expand	PUB 12	Expand Page Navigation Pane button in Page Navigation pane			
Page Navigation Pane, Hide	PUB 13	Page Number button on status bar	Page Navigation check box (View tab | Show group)		
Page Numbering, Remove	PUB 567			Right-click page icon (Page Navigation pane), Master Pages, (None)	
Page Numbers, Insert	PUB 562		Page Number button (Insert tab | Header & Footer group)		
Page Options, Set	PUB 140		Options button (Page Design tab | Template group)		
Page Orientation, Change	PUB 330		Page Orientation button (Page Design tab | Page Setup group)		
Pages, Add	PUB 143		Blank Page button (Insert tab | Pages Group)	Right-click page icon (Page Navigation pane), Insert Page	
Pages, Delete	PUB 143			Right-click page icon (Page Navigation pane), Delete	
Paste Text	PUB 75		Paste button (Home tab | Clipboard group)	Paste	CTRL+V

Microsoft Publisher 2010 Quick Reference Summary *(continued)*

Task	Page Number	Mouse	Ribbon	Shortcut Menu	Keyboard Shortcut
Pattern, Insert	PUB 179		Show Building Block Library Dialog Box Launcher (Insert tab | Building Blocks group), Insert button (Building Block Library dialog box)		
Photograph, Insert	PUB 28	Click placeholder icon	Insert Picture from File button (Insert tab | Illustrations group)	Change Picture | Change Picture	
Picture Field, Insert	PUB 471		Picture Field button (Catalog Tools Format tab | Insert group)		
Picture Styles, Apply	PUB 31		More button (Picture Tools Format tab | Picture Styles group)		
Placeholder Text, Replace	PUB 17	Select text then type			
Portable Format, Publish	PUB 303		Create PDF/XPS Document (File tab | Save & Send tab) or Save As button (File tab 'Save as type' box arrow (Save As dialog box)		
Preview Form Letters	PUB 418		Print Preview link (Mail Merge task pane) or Preview Results button (Mailings tab | Preview Results group)		
Preview Multiple Pages	PUB 110		View Multiple Sheets button (File tab | Print tab)		
Preview Results	PUB 427		Preview Results button (Mailings tab | Preview Results group)		
Preview Web Publication in Browser	PUB 50	Double-click Web file name			
Print	PUB 41		Print button (File tab | Print tab)		CTRL+P
Print Merged Pages	PUB 419	Print link (Mail Merge task pane), Print button (Print tab)			
Print, on Both Sides	PUB 112		Print One Sided button (File tab | Print tab)		CTRL+P
Print, on Special Paper	PUB 111		Printer Properties link (File tab | Print tab)		CTRL+P
Publication Options, Choose	PUB 9		Color scheme or Font scheme button (File tab | New Tab)		
Publication Properties, Change	PUB 38		Publication Properties button (File tab | Info tab)		
Pull-Quote, Insert	PUB 175		Page Parts button (Insert tab | Building Blocks group) or Show Building Block Library Dialog Box Launcher (Insert tab | Building Blocks group), Page Parts folder		
Quit	PUB 42	Close button on title bar	Exit button (File tab)		CTRL+F4
Read-Only Attribute, Set	PUB 286			Right-click file in folder window, Properties, General tab (Properties dialog box), Read-only check box	

Microsoft Publisher 2010 Quick Reference Summary *(continued)*

Task	Page Number	Mouse	Ribbon	Shortcut Menu	Keyboard Shortcut
Recolor Picture	PUB 220		Recolor button (Picture Tools Format tab | Adjust group)	Format Picture	
Replace Text	PUB 597		Replace button (Home tab | Editing group)		CTRL+H
Research Services, Update	PUB 522	Get Services on Office Marketplace link (Research task pane)			
Research Services, View or Modify	PUB 522	Research options link (Research task pane)			
Research Task Pane	PUB 522		Research button (Review tab | Proofing group)		ALT+click word
Row, Delete	PUB 338		Delete Rows or Columns button (Table Tools Layout tab | Rows & Columns group)	Delete, Delete Rows	
Row, Insert	PUB 338		Insert Rows Above (or Below) button (Table Tools Layout tab | Rows & Columns group)	Insert, Insert Above or Insert Below	
Sample a Font Color	PUB 279	Font Color button arrow on Mini toolbar	Font Color button arrow (Text Box Tools Format tab | Font group)		
Save as Web Publication	PUB 48		Publish HTML button (File tab | Save & Send tab | Publisher HTML tab)		
Save Graphic as a Picture	PUB 224			Save as Picture	
Save New Publication	PUB 27	Save button on Quick Access Toolbar	Save button (File tab)		CTRL+S
Save Publication, New File Name	PUB 48		Save As button (File tab)		
Save Publication, Same File Name	PUB 40	Save button on Quick Access Toolbar	Save button (File tab)		CTRL+S
Section, Insert	PUB 560			Insert Section	
Security Level, Set	PUB 683		Macro Security button (Developer tab | Code group)		
Select Cell	PUB 340	Triple-click cell	Select button (Table Tools Layout tab | Table group), Select Cell	Select, Select Cell	
Select Column	PUB 340	Point to top border of column and click	Select button (Table Tools Layout tab | Table group), Select Column	Select, Select Column	
Select Next Cell	PUB 341				TAB
Select Objects	PUB 15	Click object border	Select button (Home tab | Editing group)		
Select Objects, Adjacent	PUB 171	Drag around objects			
Select Paragraph	PUB 185	Triple-click			Click at beginning of paragraph, SHIFT+click at end
Select Previous Cell	PUB 341				SHIFT+TAB
Select Recipients	PUB 421		Select Recipients button (Mailings tab | Start group)		

Microsoft Publisher 2010 Quick Reference Summary *(continued)*

Task	Page Number	Mouse	Ribbon	Shortcut Menu	Keyboard Shortcut
Select Row	PUB 341	Point to edge of row and click	Select button (Table Tools Layout tab | Table group), Select Row	Select, Select Row	
Select Table	PUB 341		Select button (Table Tools Layout tab | Table group), Select Table	Select, Select Table	
Select Text, All	PUB 19	Drag through text			CTRL+A
Select Text, Sentence	PUB 177	Drag through text			Click at beginning of sentence, SHIFT+click at end
Send as Attachment	PUB 535		Send As Attachment button (File tab | Save & Send tab | Send Using E-mail tab)		
Set Page Options	PUB 140		Options button (Page Design tab | Template group), Columns box arrow (Page Content dialog box)		
Shadow Effect, Add	PUB 245		Shadow Effects button (WordArt Tools Format tab | Shadow Effects group)		
Shape Outline	PUB 230	Shape Outline button on Mini toolbar	Shape Outline button arrow (Drawing Tools Format tab | Shape Styles group) or Format Shape Dialog Box Launcher (Drawing Tools Format tab | Shape Styles group), Colors and Lines tab (Format AutoShape dialog box)	Format AutoShape, Colors and Lines tab (Format AutoShape dialog box)	
Shape Outline, WordArt	PUB 329	Shape Outline button arrow on Mini toolbar	Shape Outline button arrow (WordArt Tools Format tab | WordArt Styles group)		
Shape, Fill with Picture	PUB 233	Shape Fill button arrow on Mini toolbar	Shape Fill button arrow (Drawing Tools Format tab | Shape Styles group), Picture, Insert button (Select Picture dialog box)	Format AutoShape, Colors and Lines tab (Format AutoShape dialog box), Fill Effects button	
Shape, Insert	PUB 225		Shapes button (Insert tab | Illustrations group)		
Snap Object to Margin Guide	PUB 332	Drag object until blue snapping line is displayed			
Split Table Cells	PUB 343		Split Cells button (Table Tools Layout tab | Merge group)		
Start Publisher	PUB 4	Start button on Windows 7 taskbar or double-click Publisher icon in folder window			

Microsoft Publisher 2010 Quick Reference Summary *(continued)*

Task	Page Number	Mouse	Ribbon	Shortcut Menu	Keyboard Shortcut
Starting Page Number, Specify	PUB 563		Page Number button (Insert tab | Header & Footer group), Format Page Numbers, Number format box arrow (Page Number Format dialog box)	Page Numbers, Format Page Numbers	
Style, Apply	PUB 236		Styles button (Home tab | Styles group)		
Style, Apply New	PUB 281		Styles button (Home tab | Styles group)		
Style, Create New	PUB 280		Styles button (Home tab | Styles group), New Style		
Stylistic Set	PUB 84		Stylistic Sets button (Text Box Tools Format tab | Typography group)		
Submit Form Control Properties	PUB 670		Double-click control	Format Form Properties	
Submit Form Control, Insert	PUB 669		Form Controls button (Web tab | Code group), Submit		
Symbol, Insert	PUB 517		Insert Symbol button (Insert tab | Text group)		ALT+Unicode number
Tab Stop, Set	PUB 401	Click horizontal ruler	Paragraph Dialog Box Launcher button (Home tab | Paragraph group), Tabs tab (Paragraph dialog box)		
Tabbed Text, Enter	PUB 401				TAB
Table Format, Apply	PUB 339		More button (Table Tools Design tab | Table Formats group)		
Table, Insert	PUB 334		Table button (Insert tab | Tables group) or Table button (Home tab | Objects group)		
Table, Resize	PUB 346	Drag corner table border		Format Table, Size tab, size boxes (Format Table dialog box)	
Tear-Offs, Edit	PUB 22	Select tear-off text, type new text			
Template, Create	PUB 189		Save As button (File tab), 'Save as type' button arrow (Save As dialog box)		
Template, Search for	PUB 70		Type search text in 'Search for templates' box (File tab | New tab)		
Template, Select	PUB 7		Click template icon (File tab | New tab)		
Text Area Form Control Properties, Edit	PUB 661		Double-click control	Format Form Properties	
Text Area Form Control, Insert	PUB 660		Form Controls button (Web tab | Code group), Text Area		
Text Box Margins, Change	PUB 583		Margins button (Text Box Tools Format tab | Alignment group)	Format Text Box, Text Box tab (Format Text Box dialog box)	

Publisher Quick Reference

Microsoft Publisher 2010 Quick Reference Summary *(continued)*

Task	Page Number	Mouse	Ribbon	Shortcut Menu	Keyboard Shortcut
Text Box, Draw	PUB 44		Draw Text Box button (Insert tab | Text group) or Draw Text Box button (Home tab | Objects group)		
Text Direction, Change	PUB 585		Text Direction button (Text Box Tools Format tab | Text group)		
Text Field, Insert	PUB 472		Text Field button (Catalog Tools Format tab | Insert group)		
Thesaurus	PUB 599		Thesaurus button (Review tab | Proofing group)	Look Up	SHIFT+F7
Track Characters	PUB 397	Tracking box on Measurement toolbar	Character Spacing button (Home tab | Font group)	Change Text, Character Spacing	
Translate Text	PUB 482		Translate Selected Text button (Review tab | Language group)		ALT+click
Two-Page Spread, Create	PUB 445		File tab | New tab, click desired template (New template gallery)		
Two-Page Spread, View	PUB 601	Two-Page Spread button on status bar	Two-Page Spread button (View tab | Layout group)	View Two-Page Spread	
Underline	PUB 82	Underline button on Mini toolbar	Underline button (Home tab | Font group) or Font Dialog Box Launcher (Home tab | Font group), Font tab (Font dialog box), Underline box arrow	Change Text, Font, Underline box arrow (Font dialog box)	CTRL+U
Undo	PUB 22	Undo button on Quick Access Toolbar			CTRL+Z
VBA Code Window, Open	PUB 680		Visual Basic button (Developer tab | Code group)		ALT+F11
Web Hot Spot, Insert	PUB 672		Hot Spot button (Web tab | Web Page Navigation group) or Insert Hyperlink button (Web tab | Web Page Navigation group)		CTRL+K
Web Masthead, Create	PUB 633		Show Building Block Library Dialog Box Launcher (Insert tab | Building Blocks group), Page Parts folder, All Mastheads folder		
Web Page Options	PUB 647		Web Page Options button (Web tab | Options group)		
Web Site, Insert Secondary Pages	PUB 637		Page button arrow (Insert tab | Pages group), Insert Page, select page type (Insert Web Page dialog box)	Insert Page, select page type (Insert Web Page dialog box)	
Web Site, Preview	PUB 674		Web Page Preview button (Web tab | Preview group)		
WordArt Object, Change Shape	PUB 328	Change WordArt Shape button on Mini toolbar	Change WordArt Shape button (WordArt Tools Format tab | WordArt Styles group)		
WordArt Object, Insert	PUB 243		WordArt button (Insert tab | Text group)		

Microsoft Publisher 2010 Quick Reference Summary *(continued)*

Task	Page Number	Mouse	Ribbon	Shortcut Menu	Keyboard Shortcut
Wrap Points, Edit	PUB 217	Wrap Text button on Mini toolbar	Wrap Text button (Picture Tools Format tab | Arrange group)		
Zoom	PUB 14	Zoom slider or Zoom In or Zoom Out button on status bar; or CTRL+spin mouse wheel	Zoom box arrow (View tab | Zoom group)	Zoom	
Zoom Objects	PUB 16		Selected Objects button (View tab | Zoom group)	Zoom, Objects	F9
Zoom Page Width	PUB 14		Page Width button (View tab | Zoom group)	Zoom, Page Width	
Zoom Whole Page	PUB 14	Show Whole Page button on status bar	Whole Page button (View tab | Zoom group)	Zoom, Whole Page	CTRL+SHIFT+L